THE CONCISE OXFORD

African American Literature

THE CONCISE OXFORD COMPANION TO

African American Literature

EDITORS

William L. Andrews

Frances Smith Foster

Trudier Harris

OXFORD
UNIVERSITY PRESS

2001

OXFORD
UNIVERSITY PRESS

Oxford New York
Athens Auckland Bangkok Bogotá Bombay Buenos Aires
Calcutta Cape Town Dar es Salaam Delhi Florence Hong Kong
Istanbul Karachi Kuala Lumpur Madras Madrid Melbourne
Mexico City Nairobi Paris Singapore Taipei Tokyo Toronto

and associated companies in
Berlin Ibadan

Published by Oxford University Press, Inc.,
198 Madison Avenue, New York, New York 10016–4314

Oxford is a registered trademark of Oxford University Press

Library of Congress Cataloging-in-Publication Data is available

ISBN 0-19-513883-X

1 3 5 7 9 8 6 4 2
Printed in the United States of America
on acid–free paper

Contents

Introduction

Pulitzer Prize-winning author Alice Walker once said that if she were stranded on a desert island and had only one book to read, she would be content with a copy of Zora Neale Hurston's *Their Eyes Were Watching God* (1937). Hurston's novel tells the story of an early twentieth-century black woman of the South, Janie Crawford, and the people she encounters in her lifelong quest for self-determination and fulfillment. With her third husband, a guitar-playing bluesman named Tea Cake (who is just as sweet as his name), Janie achieves her goal. Tea Cake stands beside Janie in her efforts to define freedom and responsibility and to trade materialism for the more spiritual things in life. The compelling drama through which Hurston's novel, completed in only six weeks, brings Janie, her lovers, her friends, and an entire African American community into imperishable vitality is one of the treasures of African American literature.

Walker's discovery of Hurston greatly influenced her life and her literary career. Like Walker, through the doorway opened by a novel such as *Their Eyes Were Watching God,* countless readers have discovered the ever-expanding library of African American literature, founded in the examples of Phillis Wheatley, a young enslaved poet in eighteenth-century Massachusetts, and such outspoken fugitive slaves as William and Ellen Craft and Frederick Douglass in the nineteenth century, and extending forward to figures such as dramatists May Miller and Willis Richardson, poets Countee Cullen and Langston Hughes, and novelists Nella Larsen and Richard Wright in the early twentieth century. Hurston has pointed readers into the richness of the 1950s, when James Baldwin and Lorraine Hansberry gave us, respectively, Gabriel Grimes in *Go Tell It On the Mountain* (1953) and Mama Lena Younger in *A Raisin in the Sun* (1959). In contemporary times readers encounter Randall Kenan, a North Carolina author, who tells of a sixteen-year-old boy who tries to escape his homosexuality by using ancient incantations that he hopes will transform him into a bird. They read Toni Morrison's evocation of a baby ghost in *Beloved* (1987) who haunts a family in Ohio and J. California Cooper's tale of a character in *Family* (1991) whose attempted suicide leaves her in an immortal limbo state watching over her family through hundreds of years. Whether in the realistic realms of a Hurston, Baldwin, or Hansberry or in the fantastic worlds that Kenan, Morrison, and Cooper create or in the many nuanced dimensions in between, African American literature enthralls readers from Maine to California, Minnesota to Florida, Spain to South Africa, Italy to Germany, Canada to Jamaica, Japan and Korea. In its national and international reach, African American literature has attained an unprecedented level of popularity, critical notice, and scholarly inquiry. Since 1970 Rita Dove, Toni Morrison, Gloria Naylor, and Alice Walker have joined Gwendolyn Brooks and Ralph Ellison as winners of prestigious honors such as the Pulitzer Prize, the National and American Book Awards, and, in Morrison's case, the Nobel Prize for Literature. As the readership of African American writing expands and waxes increasingly multiethnic, it is rare to find a library (particularly in schools and universities) that does not collect, or a general-purpose bookstore that does not market, literary work by African Americans. In the academy, the reading and study of African American literature are no longer relegated to what once was called Black Studies. African American writers play increasingly prominent roles in newly reconstituted American literature and American Studies, as well as women's studies and ethnic studies, curricula. In the late twentieth century, research in African American literature and the publication of reference books, especially detailed bibliographies of both primary and secondary writing and biographical dictionaries, have given readers and students of African American literature much valuable information.

The richness of African American literature and the expanding worldwide attention to it stimulated the conception and eventual publication of *The Oxford Companion to African American Literature* in 1997, edited by William L. Andrews, Frances Smith Foster, and Trudier Harris. *The Oxford Companion to African American Literature* is a comprehensive reference volume devoted to the texts and the historical and cultural contexts of African American literature. A big book for a big subject, the *Companion* can answer a wide range of questions on everything from Afrocentricity to *Zami*, the autobiography of the poet Audre Lorde. What you can't do with the 850-page *Companion*, however, is put it in a backpack or a book bag. Thus in an effort to reach an ever-widening audience with a more streamlined, portable reference resource, the editors of the original *Companion* have created this abbreviated *Concise Companion to African American Literature.* The *Concise Companion* has the same purpose and plan and follows the same scholarly standards of the first *Companion.* The *Concise Companion* is simply more tightly focused on the essential elements of any great literature, its most notable authors and their greatest works.

The *Concise Companion to African American Literature* highlights the writers and the writing that have made African American literature valuable and distinctive for more than 250 years. Aware of the dismissal of so much black American writing for so many years because it did not conform to prevailing aesthetic or critical assumptions, our understanding of literature is not restricted to the traditional belletristic genres of poetry, fiction, and drama. In the *Concise Companion to African American Literature,* you will find articles on writers who distinguished themselves as slave narrators, essayists, autobiographers, historians, journalists, and orators as well as those who are chiefly remembered for their novels, their verse, or their contributions to the theater. In addition to the comments on texts that appear in the biographical articles, the *Concise Companion to African American Literature* provides more than 150 articles that describe and appraise the texts that we as editors consider to be major works in the African American literary tradition. The largest genre of works in this category is fiction; plot outlines of more than eighty African American novels may be found in this volume. An equal number of entries is allotted to key texts of poetry, drama, autobiography, essay collections, and children's and young adult literature. In order to recognize the importance of hybrid and experimental texts in African American literature, past and present, the *Concise Companion* contains a wealth of articles on unforgettable and yet hard-to-classify texts such as *David Walker's Appeal, Incidents in the Life of a Slave Girl, The Souls of Black Folk,* and *The Autobiography of Malcolm X.* To provide readers with a firm overview of the length and breadth of African American literary history, the five-part, 10,000-word essay on Literary History that is a hallmark of *The Oxford Companion to African American Literature* appears in full in the *Concise Companion.*

Biographies of writers comprise the largest single category of articles in this volume, from little known figures such as Octavia V. Rogers Albert to celebrated authors such as August Wilson. More than 242 writers receive individual biographical treatment in the *Concise Companion to African American Literature.* Biographical articles vary in length, from 200 words for less prominent authors such as William Johnson to more than 2,000 words for centrally important writers such as James Baldwin and

Toni Morrison. Many factors influence the lengths of biographical articles, among them the amount of information available on a given writer's life, the editors' estimate of the extent and importance of each writer's contribution to African American literature, and the space we could allot to biographies within the scaled-down framework of the *Concise Companion.* Although there are fewer biographies in the *Concise Companion* than in the *Companion,* the *Concise Companion*'s biographies have several enhanced features. First, the most significant literary work that contemporary writers have published and the prizes and awards they have won since the appearance of the original *Companion* are listed in the biographical entries in the *Concise Companion.* Second, the most significant critical and scholarly work on individual African American writers that has been published since the original *Companion* is included in the bibliographies that append the biographies in the *Concise Companion.* Thus the *Concise Companion* keeps the story of the writers and the scholarship on the writers as current as is possible for today's readers.

In addition to biographies of writers, the *Concise Companion to African American Literature* also includes compact biographical treatments and cultural assessments of a considerable number of persons—musicians, sports figures, political leaders, activists, and artists—whose presence in and/or influence on African American literature is of such a magnitude as to be noteworthy. Thus John Coltrane, Marcus Garvey, John Brown, Jackie Robinson, Harriet Beecher Stowe, and Harriet Tubman, to mention just a few figures who have achieved virtually iconic status in African American literature, are profiled in such a way as to lead the reader to literary texts significantly influenced by the person under consideration.

HOW TO USE THIS BOOK

Embarking upon the adventure of this volume, you will quickly discover that African American literature is much more than the protest tradition so frequently associated with Richard Wright or Ann Petry. Have you wondered who the detective novelist is whom President Bill Clinton identified as one of his favorite writers? Look up Walter Mosley and find out what he wrote. Are you curious about the science fiction of MacArthur Prize-winning Octavia Butler and the "Dean of Science Fiction," Samuel Delany? They are both in the *Concise Companion* along with a separate article on Butler's celebrated novel *Kindred* (1979). In these pages the children's fiction of Arna Bontemps, Walter Dean Myers, Alice Childress, and Virginia Hamilton is discussed, as well as the courageous stories of escape and endurance epitomized in narratives such as Margaret Walker's *Jubilee* (1966) and Alex Haley's *Roots* (1976). If you elect a regional approach to the literature, you can meet Raymond Andrews, Tina McElroy Ansa, and Brenda Marie Osbey on southern soil; Elizabeth Keckley, Mary Church Terrell, Ralph Ellison, and Claude Brown in urban territory; and Al Young, Joyce Carol Thomas, and Ishmael Reed in the West. If your interests run to modernist or contemporary stylistic experimenters, key figures such as Jean Toomer, Carlene Hatcher Polite, Xam Wilson Cartier, and Trey Ellis are all here. If poetry is where you begin, be sure to read the articles on Phillis Wheatley, Paul Laurence Dunbar, Gwendolyn Brooks, Rita Dove, and Yusef Komunyakaa. Notice that major volumes of poetry by Wheatley—*Poems on Various Subjects, Religious and Moral* (1773); by Dunbar—*Majors and Minors* (1895) and *Lyrics of Lowly Life* (1896); by Brooks—*A Street in Bronzeville* (1945), for instance; and by Dove—*Thomas and Beulah* (1986)—receive separate treatments in the *Concise Companion.* You can also find and trace the development of African American poetry in the article on Literary History. If drama strikes your fancy, you can look up individual dramatists, such as August Wilson. Find out how many Pulitzer

Prizes he has received; learn how close he is to reaching his goal of writing a play for every decade of African American life in the twentieth century.

Although there are many ways to plunge into the *Concise Companion to African American Literature* and come up with treasure, for those who want to be more systematic in their search, there are two ways to begin. If you have a name or a title, you can search for it by consulting the index in the back of the *Concise Companion.* Or you can head directly into the book itself because its contents are alphabetized.

The index to the *Concise Companion to African American Literature* serves as a comprehensive guide to its subject matter. In addition to providing the page number on which every individual entry in the *Concise Companion* appears, the index also lists additional pages on which many authors, titles, or topics are discussed. For instance, the citation of Frederick Douglass in the index refers not only to the biographical article devoted to Douglass but also to the pages (in several other entries) in which Douglass is mentioned. The index also cites persons, such as Ralph Waldo Emerson, Rosa Parks, Sidney Poitier, and Carl Van Vechten; titles, such as Gunnar Myrdal's *An American Dilemma* (1944) and Alice Walker's *Meridian* (1976); and events and organizations, such as the Harlem Renaissance and the Student Nonviolent Coordinating Committee (SNCC), that are referred to in the *Concise Companion* but do not receive an individual entry. To discover whether a person, title, or a topic is treated in the *Concise Companion* the first place to look is in the index to this volume.

The quickest way to find out if a particular writer or text appears in the *Concise Companion to African American Literature* is to look for a name or title in the book itself.

To find an author's name, look it up according to her or his last name (e.g., Chesnutt, Charles Waddell). You will find that biographies in the *Concise Companion* include the subject's birth and (if known or applicable) death dates, followed by a sentence fragment that briefly identifies her or him. Biographical entries are listed according to how an author signs his or her work, i.e., Iceberg Slim (not Beck, Robert) or Malcolm X (not Little, Malcolm). The given names of these writers and others such as Paulette Williams or Chloe Anthony Wofford are entered as blind entries in this *Companion* with a directive to the name (*see* Ntosake Shange, *see* Toni Morrison) under which the biography of the writer is discussed. To find a literary work in this volume, look up the first important word of its title (e.g., *House behind the Cedars, The*). The titles of entries on literary works are either italicized or put within quotation marks, unlike the titles of biographical entries, which are capitalized.

The *Concise Companion to African American Literature* is extensively cross-referenced to help a reader follow an initial inquiry into a useful related area. An asterisk (*) before a name or title in this volume indicates that a separate article has been devoted to that item in the *Concise Companion.* Occasionally cross-references are given in parentheses within an article. At the end of many articles in this volume are additional cross-references that point the reader to further entries relevant to the reader's interests. Thus the article on Zora Neale Hurston contains internal cross-references that point to additional articles on works by Hurston, such as *Their Eyes Were Watching God,* and to articles on important African American literary figures in Hurston's life who are themselves the subjects of biographical entries in the *Concise Companion.*

Bibliographies are appended to most articles in the *Concise Companion.* The longer the article, the more titles are offered as recommendations for further reading. Titles in these bibliographies are listed chronologically to help the reader follow the development of important scholarship on a given topic. The principal purpose of these bibliographies is to direct the reader of the *Concise Companion* to nonspecialized texts, particularly biographies and critical studies, that will open up, rather than narrow down, the reader's perspective on the writer or literary work at hand.

All the entries in *The Concise Companion to African American Literature* are signed by their authors, who are listed, along with their institutional affiliation (if any) and the title(s) of their article(s), in the list of contributors that follows this introduction to the *Concise Companion.* Our basic request of each contributor, regardless of the subject or scope of her or his article, was to provide readers of this *Companion* with the most reliable, complete, and readable treatment of the topic possible, given the limits of space and the need for succinctness that a one-volume reference book demanded of us all. The interpretive emphases and critical judgments that appear in the *Companion*'s articles reflect the diverse points of view of their authors. As editors who wish neither to beat a drum nor grind an ax for or against any writer or subject in this volume, we have tried to ensure that the critical posture of the *Concise Companion to African American Literature* is historically informed, thoughtfully researched, and fair-minded. The variety of terms available to apply to persons of African descent—Black, black, and African American, for instance—appear in this volume according to the individual tastes and purposes of the contributors. We have selected African American (deliberately unhyphenated) for the title of this volume because we believe this term to be an accurate descriptor of the intersecting ethnic and national literary traditions that form the purview of this volume. We also see African American as the best alternative to the "hyphenated American" designations and politicized naming agendas of the past.

The Concise Companion to African American Literature represents an effort to update the original *Companion to African American Literature* while at the same time distilling the former volume's contents to its biographical and textual essentials. The editors of the *Concise Companion* have not commissioned any new articles on writers or works that were not represented in the original *Companion,* believing that such an undertaking should be left to what we hope will be a second and expanded edition of the entire *Companion to African American Literature.*

ACKNOWLEDGMENTS

The editors of the *Concise Companion* wish to thank the Trade Paperbacks Department of Oxford University Press, particularly Elda Rotor, for proposing this project and for their suggestions and support in the completion of it.

William L. Andrews
Frances Smith Foster
Trudier Harris

Contributors

Christina Accomando, *Assistant Professor, Humboldt State University, California*
Attaway, William; "We Shall Overcome"

Opal Palmer Adisa, *Associate Professor of Ethnic Studies, California College of Arts and Crafts, Oakland*
Davenport, Doris

Sandra Carlton Alexander, *Professor of English, North Carolina Agricultural and Technical State University, Greensboro*

Elizabeth Ammons, *Harriet H. Fay Professor of American Literature, Tufts University, Medford, Massachusetts*
Cooper, Anna Julia; Voice from the South, A

Larry R. Andrews, *Dean, Honors College; Associate Professor of English, Kent State University, Ohio*
Murphy, Beatrice M.

William L. Andrews, *E. Maynard Adams Professor of English, University of North Carolina at Chapel Hill*
Brown, William Wells; Chesnutt, Charles Waddell; Douglass, Frederick; Elaw, Zilpha; Folks from Dixie; Fulton, David Bryant; Green, J.D.; Johnson, William; Lyrics of Lowly Life; Majors and Minors; McGirt, James Ephraim; My Bondage and My Freedom; Narrative of the Life of Frederick Douglass; Pickens, William; Purvis, William; Purvis, Robert; Russwurm, John Browne; Steward Theophilus Gould; Terry, Lucy; Turner, Nat; Wife of His Youth, The

Gary Ashwill, *Department of English, Duke University, Durham, North Carolina*
Clotel; Lee, Spike; L'Ouverture, Toussaint; Redding, J. Saunders; Woodson, Carter G.

Allan D. Austin, *Professor of English and African American Studies, Springfield College, Massachusetts*
Blake; Delany, Martin R.; Henry Blake

Michael Awkward, *Professor of English, University of Pennsylvania, Philadelphia*
Baker, Houston A., Jr.

Marva O. Banks, *Associate Professor of English and Modern Languages, Albany State College, Georgia*
Heard, Nathan C.

Margarita Barcelo, *Assistant Professor of English, Metropolitan State College of Denver, Denver, Colorado*
Walrond, Eric

Philip Barnard, *Associate Professor of English, University of Kansas, Lawrence*
Cenelles, Les; Sejour, Victor

Deborah H. Barnes, *Associate Professor of English, Gettysburg College, Pennsylvania*
Schomburg, Arthur A.; Tubman, Harriet

Anthony Gerard Barthelemy, *Associate Professor of English, University of Miami, Coral Gables, Florida*
Escape, The; Ward, Theodore

Freda R. Beaty, *Assistant Professor of English, Stephen F. Austin State University, Boone, North Carolina*
Andrews, Raymond

Elizabeth Ann Beaulieu, *Department of English, Appalachian State University, Boone, North Carolina*
Tolson, Melvin B.

Herman Beavers, *Associate Professor of English, University of Pennsylvania, Philadelphia*
Autobiography of an Ex-Colored Man, The; Johnson, James Weldon; Up from Slavery; Washington, Booker T.

Joseph Benson, *Professor of English, North Carolina Agricultural and Technical State University, Greensboro*
Sister Outsider

Roger A. Berger, *Everett, Washington*
Cleaver, Eldridge; Haley, Alex Kunta Kinte; Soul on Ice

Germain J. Bienvenu, *Academic Center for Athletes, Louisiana State University at Baton Rouge*
Lanusse, Armand

Susan L. Blake, *Professor of English, Lafayette College, Easton, Pennsylvania*
Poinsettia Jackson

Karen R. Bloom, *Assistant Professor of English, Susquehanna University, Selinsgrove, Pennsylvania*
Boyd, Melba; Lester, Julius

Mary Anne Stewart Boelcskevy, *Department of English and American Literature and Language, Harvard University, Cambridge, Massachusetts*
Hernton, Calvin C.; Waniek, Marilyn Nelson

Brad S. Born, *Assistant Professor of English, Bethel College, North Newton, Kansas*
Banneker, Benjamin; "Heroic Slave, The"; Northrup, Solomon

Melanie Boyd, *Institute for Women's Studies, Emory University, Atlanta, Georgia*
Poston, Ted

Melba Joyce Boyd, *Associate Professor of Africana Studies, Wayne State University, Detroit, Michigan*
Aunt Chloe Fleet; Iola Leroy; "Two Offers, The"

Joanne M. Braxton, *Frances and Edwin L. Cummings Professor of American Studies and English, The College of William and Mary, Williamsburg, Virginia*
Dunbar, Paul Laurence

Marcela Breton, *Danbury, Connecticut*
Davis, Miles

Margaret Bernice Smith Bristow, *Associate Professor of English, Hampton University, Virginia*
Hamilton, Virginia; M.C. Higgins, the Great

Mary Hughes Brookhart, *Independent Scholar, Chapel Hill, North Carolina*
Allen, Samuel W.

E. Barnsley Brown, *Lecturer Department of English, University of North Carolina at Chapel Hill*
Gibson, Patricia Joann

Phiefer L. Browne, *Assistant Professor of English, Fisk University, Nashville, Tennessee*
Austin, Doris Jean; Brown, Linda; Beatrice, Golden, Marita

Elizabeth Brown-Guillory, *Professor of English, University of Houston, Texas*
Childress, Alice; Hero Ain't Nothin' but a Sandwich, A; Like One of the Family; Mildred Johnson

Dickson D. Bruce, Jr., *Professor of History, University of California, Irvine*
Corrothers, James D.; Literary History *article on* Reconstruction Era

Jennifer Burton, *Harvard University, Cambridge, Massachusetts*
Atkins, Russell; Redmond, Eugene

Marilyn D. Button, *Associate Professor of English, Lincoln University, Pennsylvania*
Cornish, Samuel

Keith E. Byerman, *Professor of English and Women's Studies, Indiana State University, Terre Haute*
Major, Clarence

Rudolph P. Byrd, *Associate Professor of American Studies, Graduate Institute of Liberal Arts, Emory University, Atlanta, Georgia*
Cane; Toomer, Jean

Mary C. Carruth, *Assistant Professor of English, Xavier University of Louisiana, New Orleans*
Dusk of Dawn; Grimke, Angelina Weld

Sharon Carson, *Assistant Professor of English, Philosophy, and Religious Studies, University of North Dakota, Grand Forks*
Baker, Josephine; Danner, Margaret Esse; Manchild in the Promised Land; Payne, Daniel A.

Warren J. Carson, *Associate Professor of English, University of South Carolina, Spartanburg*
Brown, Ceci

Steven R. Carter, *Professor of English, Salem State College, Massachusetts*
Collins, Kathleen; King, Woodie, Jr.; Shine, Ted; Wolfe, George

Deborah G. Chay, *Assistant Professor of English, Dartmouth College, Hanover, New Hampshire*
hooks, bell

Miriam M. Chirico, *Department of English, Emory University, Atlanta, Georgia*
Young, Al

Keith Clark, *Assistant Professor of English, George Mason University, Fairfax, Virginia*
Amen Corner, The; Another Country; Braxton, Joanne M.; Gabriel Grimes; Giovanni's Room; Go Tell It on the Mountain; John Grimes; Rufus Scott

Geneva Cobb-Moore, *Associate Professor of English and Women's Studies, University of Wisconsin-Whitewater*
Forten, Charlotte

Alisha R. Coleman, *Plainsboro, New Jersey*
Franklin, Aretha; Herron, Carolivia

Michael Collins, *Department of English and Comparative Literature, Columbia University, New York*
Plumpp, Sterling; Spellman, A.B.

Wayne F. Cooper, *Vinalhaven, Maine*
Home to Harlem

Angelo Costanzo, *Emeritus Professor of English, Shippensburg University of Pennsylvania*
Equiano, Olaudah; Gronniosaw, James Albert Ukawsaw

Valerie Mathews Crawford, *Instructor, Georgia Perimeter College, Atlanta*
Goines, Donald

Daryl Cumber Dance, *Professor of English, University of Richmond, Virginia*
Moore, Opal

Rita B. Dandridge, *Professor of English, Norfolk State University, Norfolk, Virginia*
Meriwether, Louise; Shockley, Ann Allen; Southerland, Ellease

Adenike Marie Davidson, *Assistant Professor of English, University of Central Florida, Orlando*
Black No More; Lutie Johnson; Schuyler, George S.; Street, The

Thadious M. Davis, *Gertrude Conaway Vanderbilt Professor of English, Vanderbilt University, Nashville, Tennessee*
Larsen, Nella

Miriam DeCosta-Willis, *Professor of African American Studies, University of Maryland, Baltimore County*
Wells-Barnett, Ida B.

Kim Jenice Dillon, *Assistant Professor of English, Miami University, Oxford, Ohio*
Bonner, Marita; Shearer, John; Troupe, Quincy Thomas, Jr.

Bobby Donaldson, *Department of History, Emory University, Atlanta, Georgia*
Gayle, Addison, Jr.

C.K. Doreski, *Department of Rhetoric and Humanities, Boston University, Massachusetts*
Cornish, Sam

David F. Dorsey, Jr., *Professor of English and African/African American Studies, Clark Atlanta University, Atlanta, Georgia*
Evans, Mari

David L. Dudley, *Assistant Professor of English, Georgia Southern University, Statesboro*
Brown, Claude; Thomas, Piri

Gerald Early, *Merle Kling Professor of Modern Letters, Washington University, St. Louis, Missouri*
Ali, Muhammad; Crouch, Stanley; Cullen, Countee; Johnson, Jack; Louis, Joe; Robinson, Jackie; Robinson, Sugar Ray

Paula Gallant Eckard, *Senior Lecturer in English, University of North Carolina at Charlotte*
Aun' Peggy; Conjure Woman, The; Moody, Anne; Terrell, Mary Church; Uncle Julius McAdoo

Gregory Eiselein, *Associate Professor of English, Kansas State University, Manhattan*
Garnet, Henry Highland; Langston, John Mercer; Nell, William C.; Walker, David

Arlene A. Elder, *Professor of English and Comparative Literature, University of Cincinnati, Ohio*
Griggs, Sutton E.; Imperium in Imperio; Quest of the Silver Fleece, The

Marilyn Elkins, *Professor of English, California State University, Los Angeles*
Fences; Piano Lesson, The; Wilson, August

Elizabeth Sanders Delwiche Engelhardt, *Institute for Women's Studies, Emory University, Atlanta, Georgia*
Johnson, Fenton; Neal, Larry; West, Cornel

Klaus Ensslen, *Associate Professor of American Literature, Amerika-Institut, University of Munich, Germany*
Bradley, David; Chaneysville Incident, The

Hazel Arnett Ervin, *Associate Professor of English, Morehouse College, Atlanta, Georgia*
Petry, Ann; Tituba of Salem Village

M. Giulia Fabi, *Department of English, University of Bologna, Italy*
Johnson, Amelia E.

SallyAnn H. Ferguson, *Associate Professor of English, University of North Carolina at Greensboro*
Blacker the Berry, The; Dress; Johnson, Helene; Niggerati Manor; Porter, Dorothy; Thurman, Wallace

Robert Fikes, Jr., *Librarian, San Diego State University, California*
Haskins, James; Motley, Willard

Michael W. Fitzgerald, *Associate Professor of History, St. Olaf College, Northfield, Minnesota*
Fortune, T. Thomas

Robert E. Fleming, *Professor of English, University of New Mexico, Albuquerque*
Kelley, William Melvin

P. Gabrielle Foreman, *Assistant Professor of English and Comparative Literary Studies; Occiental College, Los Angeles, California*
Burton, Anne Louise; Frado; Our Nig; Wilson, Harriet E.

Frances Smith Foster, *Charles Howard Candler Professor of English and Women's Studies, Emory University, Atlanta, Georgia*
Boyd, Candy; Detter, Thomas P.; Easy Rawlins; Hansen, Joyce; Harper, Frances Ellen Watkins; Helga Crane; Kindred; Mosley, Walter; Myers, Walter Dean; Passing (the novel); Quicksand; Rivers, Conrad Kent

Virginia C. Fowler, *Associate Professor of English, Virginia Polytechnic Institute and State University, Blacksburg*
Giovanni, Nikki

Robert Elliot Fox, *Associate Professor of English, Southern Illinois University at Carbondale*
Brothers and Keepers; Flight to Canada; Last Days of Louisiana Red, The; Mumbo Jumbo; Papa LaBas; Philadelphia Fire; Raven Quickskill; Reed, Ishmael; Yellow Back Radio Broke-Down

Karla Y.E. Frye, *Assistant Professor of English, University of Alabama, Tuscaloosa*
Elder, Lonne, III; Sounder

Jan Furman, *Associate Professor of English at the University of Michigan, Flint*
Albert, Octavia V. Rogers

Floyd Gaffney, *Professor Emeritus of Theatre, University of California, San Diego*
Day of Absence; Ward, Douglas Turner

Deborah Garfield, *Assistant Professor of English, University of California, Los Angeles*
Delaney, Lucy A.; Matthews, Victoria Earle

Donald B. Gibson, *Professor of English, Princeton University, New Jersey*
Bigger Thomas; Black Boy; Mary Dalton; Native Son; Uncle Tom's Children; Wright, Richard

Glenda E. Gill, *Associate Professor of Drama, Department of Humanities, Michigan Technological University, Houghton*
Millican, Arthenia J. Bates

William A. Gleason, *Assistant Professor of English, Princeton University, New Jersey*
House behind the Cedars, The; Marrow of Tradition, The; Rena Walden

Kenneth W. Goings, *Professor of History, University of Memphis, Tennessee*
Still, William; Still, William Grant

Amy S. Gottfried, *Assistant Professor of Rhetoric, College of General Studies, Boston University, Massachusetts*
Corregidora; Eva Medina Canada; Eva's Man; Jones, Gayl; Ursa Corregidora

Sandra Y. Govan, *Professor of English; Coordinator, Ronald E. McNair Postbaccalaureate Achievement Program, University of North Carolina at Charlotte*
Barnes, Steven; Bennett, Gwendolyn; Delany, Samuel R.; McKnight, Reginald; Neely, Barbara

Nathan L. Grant, *Assistant Professor of African American Studies, State University of New York at Buffalo*
Bass, Kingsley, Jr.; Bullins, Ed; Caldwell, Ben; Clara's Ole Man; Goin' a Buffalo; In New England Winter; Nugent, Richard Bruce

Michael E. Greene, *Professor of English, North Carolina Agricultural and Technical State University, Greensboro*
Cobb, Charles E., Jr.; Marvin X

Farah Jasmine Griffin, *Associate Professor of English, University of Pennsylvania, Philadelphia, Pennsylvania*
Holiday, Billie; Rainey, Ma; Smith, Bessie; West, Dorothy

Johanna L. Grimes-Williams, *Associate Professor of English, Tennessee State University, Nashville*
Lewis, Theophilus

John C. Gruesser, *Associate Professor of English, Kean College of New Jersey, Union*
Bruce, John E.

Beverly Guy-Shetfall, *Anna J. Cooper Professor of English and Women's Studies; Director, Women's Research and Resource Center, Spelman College, Atlanta, Georgia*
Sapphire

Michelle Habell-Pallan, *Assistant Professor of American Ethnic Studies, University of Washington, Seattle*
Mackey, Nathaniel

James C. Hall, *Associate Professor of African-American Studies and English, University of Illinois, Chicago*
Brown, Frank London; Coltrane, John; Parker, Charlie

Stephen Gilroy Hall, *Department of History, Ohio State University, Columbus*
Williams, George Washington

Trudier Harris, *J. Carlyle Sitterson Professor of English, University of North Carolina at Chapel Hill*
Baldwin, James; Dumas, Henry; Fire Next Time, The; Jeffers, Lance; Komunyakaa, Yusef; Mammy; Notes of a Native Son; Sula Peace

Violet J. Harris, *Associate Professor of Curriculum and Instruction (Literacy), University of Illinois, Champaign*
Walter, Mildred Pitts

James V. Hatch, *Professor of Theatre, Graduate Program, The City University of New York*
Dodson, Owen

Heather Hathaway, *Assistant Professor of English, Marquette University, Milwaukee, Wisconsin*
McKay, Claude

Kathleen A. Hauke, *Independent Scholar, Arlington, Virginia*
Fields, Julia

Chanta M. Haywood, *Assistant Professor of African Ameican Literature, Florida State University, Tallahassee*
Greenfield, Eloise

Elanna N. Haywood, *Takoma Park, Maryland*
Miller, E. Ethelbert

James L. Hill, *Professor of English; Dean of the School of Arts and Sciences, Albany State College, Georgia*
Foxes of Harrow, The; Woman Called Fancy, A; Yerby, Frank

Maureen Honey, *Professor of English, University of Nebraska at Lincoln*
Johnson, Georgia Douglas

Helen R. Houston, *Professor of English, Tennessee State University, Nashville*
Franklin, J.E.; Ottley, Roi; Richardson, Willis; This Child's Gonna Live; Wright, Sarah Elizabeth

Sheila Hassell Hughes, *Assistant Professor of English, University of Dayton, Dayton, Ohio*
Fair, Ronald L.; Murray, Pauli; River Niger, The; Walker, Joseph A.

Elwanda L. Ingram, *Professor of English, Winston-Salem State University, North Carolina*
Holman, John

Cassandra Jackson, *Department of English, Emory University, Atlanta, Georgia*
Davis, Ossie

Gregory S. Jackson, *Assistant Professor of English, University of Arizona, Tucson*
Dunham, Katherine

Charles L. James, *Professor of English Literature; Coordinator of Black Studies Program, Swarthmore College, Pennsylvania*
Black Thunder; Bontemps, Arna; God Sends Sunday; Popo and Fifina

Carol S. Taylor Johnson, *Adjunct Professor of Educational and Professional Studies, West Virginia Graduate College, Charleston*
High John the Conqueror

Dianne Johnson, *Associate Professor of English, University of South Carolina, Columbia*
Brownies' Book, The; Tate, Eleanora

Lonnell E. Johnson, *Associate Professor of English, Otterbein College, Westerville, Ohio*
Henderson, George Wylie

Ronna C. Johnson, *Lecturer in American Studies and Women's Studies, Tufts University, Medford, Massachusetts*
His Own Where; Jordan, June; Polite, Carlene Hatcher

Joyce A. Joyce, *Professor and Chair of African American Studies, Temple University*
Don't Cry, Scream; Madhubuti, Haki R.

Allison Kimmich, *Director of Pre-College Programs, Barnard College, New York, New York*
Forbes, Calvin

Debra Walker King, *Associate Professor of English, University of Florida, Gainesville*
Brownfield Copeland; Celie; Color Purple, The; In Search of Our Mothers' Gardens; Possessing Secret of Joy; Shug Avery; Temple of My Familiar, The; Third Life of Grange Copeland, The; Walker, Alice

Lovalerie King, *Assistant Professor of English, University of Massachusetts, Boston*
Cooper, J. California; De Veaux, Alexis; Funnyhouse of a Negro; Kennedy, Adrienne

Lynda Koolish, *Associate Professor of English, San Diego State University, California*
Cuney-Hare, Maud; Miller, May

Karen Ruth Kornweibel, *University of Texas at Austin*
Brown, Lloyd; Iron City

Beverly Threatt Kulii, *Lecturer in English, North Carolina Agricultural and Technical State University, Greensboro*
Brer Rabbit; Lorde, Audre

Vera M. Kutzinski, *Professor of English, African-American Studies and American Studies, Yale University, New Haven, Connecticut*
Wright, Jay

Henry C. Lacey, *Associate Professor of English; Vice-President of Academic Affairs, Dillard University, New Orleans, Louisiana*
Baraka, Amiri; Dutchman; Home: Social Essays; Preface to a Twenty-Volume Suicide Note; System of Dante's Hell, The

John Lang, *Professor of English, Emory and Henry College, Emory, Virginia*
Autobiography of Miss Jane Pittman, The; Dixon, Melvin; Gaines, Ernest J.; McCluskey, John A., Jr.

Candis LaPrade, *Associate Professor of English, Longwood College, Farmville, Virginia*
Lee, Jarena

Robert Lee, *Reader in American Literature, University of Kent at Canterbury, England*
Ai

Charles Leonard, *The California Institute of the Arts, Valencia, California*
Gordone, Charles; No Place to Be Somebody

Keith D. Leonard, *Assistant Professor of English, American University, Washington, D.C.*
Harper, Michael S.

Neal A. Lester, *Professor of English, Arizona State University, Tempe, Arizona*
Ceremonies in Dark Old Men

Emily M. Lewis, *Educational Researcher, Technology Based Learning and Research, Arizona State University, Tempe*
"I Have a Dream"; King, Martin Luther, Jr.; "Letter from Birmingham Jail"

Saundra Liggins, *Department of English and American Studies, University of California, San Diego*
Mathis, Sharon Bell; Zeely

Kathryne V. Lindberg, *Associate Professor of American Literature; Adjunct in Africana Studies, Wayne State University, Detroit, Michigan*
Joans, Ted; Kaufman, Bob

Francoise Lionnet, *Professor of French, UCLA*
Angelou, Maya; I Know Why the Caged Bird Sings

Jeff Loeb, *Senior Teacher, The Pembroke Hill School, Kansas City, Missouri*
Beckham, Barry

Richard A. Long, *Atticus Haygood Professor of Interdisciplinary Studies, Emory University, Atlanta, Georgia*
Burroughs, Margaret Taylor Goss; Fuller, Hoyt; Locke, Alain; New Negro, The

Eric Lott, *Professor of English, University of Virginia, Charlottesville*
Stepin Fetchit

Mason I. Lowance, Jr., *Professor of English, University of Massachusetts—Amherst*
Bibb, Henry

Barbara Lowe, *Graduate Instructor in English, University of Mississippi, Oxford*
Jackson, Jesse; Steptoe, John

John Lowe, *Professor of English, Louisiana State University at Baton Rouge*
Lane, Pinkie Gordon; Osbey, Brenda Marie

Donnarae MacCann, *Visiting Assistant Professor, African American World Studies Program, University of Iowa, Iowa City*
McKissack, Patricia C.; Newsome, Effie Lee

Wanda Macon, *Assistant Professor of English, Jackson State University, Jackson, Mississippi*
Cotillion, The; Fuller, Charles H., Jr.; Greenlee, Sam; Killens, John O.; McMillan, Terry; Soldier's Play, A; Spook Who Sat by the Door, The

Naomi Long Madgett, *Professor Emerita of English, Eastern Michigan University, Ypsilanti*
Randall, Dudley; White, Paulette Childress

Yolanda M. Manora, *Emory University, Atlanta, Georgia*
Jackson, Elaine

Jennifer Margulis, *Department of English, Emory University, Atlanta, Georgia*
Kincaid, Jamaica; McElroy, Colleen; Rahman, Aishah

Carol Marsh-Lockett, *Associate Professor of English, Georgia State University, Atlanta*
Ansa, Tina McElroy; Cleage, Pearl

Daniel J. Martin, *Department of English, University of Kansas, Lawrence*
Early, Gerald

Theodore O. Mason, Jr., *Associate Professor of English, Kenyon College, Gambier, Ohio*
Rampersad, Arnold; Robeson, Paul

Vivian M. May, *Independent Scholar, New York City*
Flowers, A. R.

Barbara McCaskill, *Assistant Professor of English, University of Georgia, Athens*
Hemings, Sally; Spencer, Anne

Jacquelyn Y. McClendon, *Associate Professor of English, The College of William and Mary, Williamsburg, Virginia*
Comedy: American Style; Fauset, Jessie Redmon; There Is Confusion

John McCluskey, Jr., *Professor and Chair of Afro-American Studies, Indiana University at Bloomington*
Fisher, Rudolph; Walls of Jericho, The

Robert E. McGlone, *Assistant Professor of History, University of Hawai'i at Manoa*
Brown, John

Adam Meyer, *Associate Professor of English, Fisk University, Nashville, Tennessee*
Blyden, Edward Wilmot

Mildred R. Mickle, *Department of English, University of North Carolina at Chapel Hill*
Butler, Octavia E.; Dessa Rose (the novel and the character); Rufel, Miss; Williams, Sherley Anne

James A. Miller, *Professor of English, George Washington University, Washington, DC*
Bennett, Hal; Forrest, Leon

Keith D. Miller, *Associate Professor of English, Arizona State University, Tempe*
"I Have a Dream"; King, Martin Luther, Jr.; "Letter from Birmingham Jail"

Keith Bernard Mitchell, *Department of Comparative Literature, University of North Carolina at Chapel Hill*
Brown Girl, Brownstones; Chosen Place, the Timeless People, The; Marshall, Paule; Selina Boyce

Marilyn Sanders Mobley, *Department of English, George Mason University, Fairfax, Virginia*
Bluest Eye, The; Milkman Dead; Morrison, Toni; Pecola Breedlove; Pilate Dead

Jocelyn K. Moody, *Associate Professor of English at the University of Washington, Seattle*
Clifton, Lucille; Everett Anderson; Taylor, Susie King

William R. Nash, *Assistant Professor of American Literature, Middlebury College, Vermont*
Johnson, Charles R.; Man Who Cried I Am, The; Middle Passage (the novel); Rutherford Calhoun; Williams, John A.

Dana D. Nelson, *Professor of English, University of Kentucky, Lexington*
Craft, William and Ellen

Terri Hume Oliver, *Teaching Fellow in English, Harvard University, Cambridge, Massachusetts*
Iceberg Slim

Ted Olson, *Graduate Instructor in English, University of Mississippi, University*
John Henry; Moses

Sondra O'Neale, *Independent Scholar, Los Angeles, California*
Hammon, Jupiter

Nell Irvin Painter, *Edwards Professor of American History, Princeton University, New Jersey*
Truth, Sojourner

Sandra Pouchet Paquet, *Associate Professor of Caribbean and African American Literature; Director, Caribbean Writers Summer Institute, University of Miami, Coral Gables, Florida*
Prince, Mary

Tracy J. Patterson, *Berkeley, California*
Jackson, Angela

James Robert Payne, *Professor of English, New Mexico State University, Las Cruces*
Colter, Cyrus; Cotter Joseph Seamon, Jr.; Cotter, Joseph Seamon, Sr.

Jennifer H. Poulos, *Department of English, Emory University, Atlanta, Georgia*
Thomas, Lorenzo

Cassie Premo, *Independent Scholar, Columbia, South Carolina*
Knight, Etheridge

Arnold Rampersad, *Sara Hart Kimball Professor in the Humanities, Stanford University, Palo Alto, California*
Big Sea, The; Biography; Du Bois, W.E.B.; Hughes, Langston; Madam Alberta K. Johnson; Montage of a Dream Deferred; "Negro Speaks of Rivers, The"; Simple; Souls of Black Folk, The; Weary Blues, The

Ralph Reckley, Sr., *Professor of English, Speech and the Humanities, Morgan State University, Baltimore, Maryland*
Bledsoe, Dr.; Ellison, Ralph; Invisible Man; Mary Rambo; Norton, Mr.; Ras the Destroyer; Rinehart; Shadow and Act; Todd Clifton; Trueblood

Margaret Ann Reid, *Associate Professor of English, Morgan State University, Baltimore, Maryland*
Amini, Johari; Turpin, Waters

Ann Reuman, *Department of English, Tufts University, Medford, Massachusetts*
Cables to Rage; Cancer Journals, The

James W. Richardson, Jr., *Department of English, Morehouse College, Atlanta, Georgia*
Derricote, Toi; Toure, Askia M.

Marilyn Richardson, *Watertown, Massachusetts*
Stewart, Maria W.

Janet M. Roberts, *Department of American and African American Studies, University of California, San Diego*
Thompson, Era Bell

Lawrence R. Rodgers, *Associate Professor of English, Kansas State University, Manhattan*
Downing, Henry F.; Miller, Kelly; Sport of the Gods, The; Talented Tenth, The; Webb, Frank J.

Ruby V. Rodney, *Professor of English, Winston-Salem State University, North Carolina*
Mayfield, Julian

Daniel J. Royer, *Assistant Professor of English and Composition Studies, Grand Valley State University, Allendale, Michigan*
Voice of the Negro, The

John Saillant, *Assistant Professor of English, Western Michigan University*
Allen, Richard

Maggie Sale, *San Francisco, California*
Dove, Rita; Scottsboro Boys; Thomas and Beulah

Wilfred D. Samuels, *Associate Professor of English and Ethnic Studies; Director, African American Studies Program; Coordinator, Ethnic Studies Program, University of Utah, Salt Lake City*
Wideman, John Edgar

Scott A. Sandage, *Assistant Professor of History, Carnegie-Mellon University, Pittsburgh, Pennsylvania*
Anderson, Marian; Lincoln, Abraham

Mark A. Sanders, *Associate Professor of English, Emory University, Atlanta, Georgia*
Hayden, Robert; Hill, Leslie Pinckney; Himes, Chester; "Runagate Runagate"

Elizabeth Schultz, *Professor of English; Chancellor's Club Teaching Professor, University of Kansas, Lawrence*
Parks, Gordon

Robin G. Schulze, *Associate Professor of English, Pennsylvania State University, State College*
Braithwaite, William Stanley

Meryl Schwartz, *Assistant Professor of English, Lakeland Community College, Kirkland, Ohio*
Kelley, Emma Dunham

Daniel M. Scott III, *Assistant Professor of English, Rhode Island College, Providence*
Barrax, Gerald W.; Pharr, Robert Deane

J.D. Scrimgeour, *Assistant Professor of English, DePauw University, Greencastle, Indiana*
Autobiography of Malcolm X, The; Malcolm X

John Sekora, *Professor of English; Dean, School of Graduate Studies, North Carolina Central University, Durham*
Literary History, *article on* Antislavery Era; Slavery

Caroline Senter, *Department of Literature, University of California, San Diego*
Van Dyke, Henry

Barry Shank, *Associate Professor of American Studies, The Ohio State University, Columbus*
Murray, Albert

Joan R. Sherman, *Professor Emerita, Rutgers University, New Brunswick, New Jersey*
Bell, James Madison; Campbell, James Edwin; Horton, George Moses; Vashon, George B.; Whitfield, James Monroe; Whitman, Albery Allson

John C. Shields, *Professor of English, Illinois State University, Normal*
Literary History, *article on* Colonial and Early National Eras; Poems on Various Subjects, Religious and Moral; Smith, Venture; Wheatley, Phillis

Ann Allen Shockley, *Associate Professor of Library Science, Fisk University, Nashville, Tennessee*
Gomez, Jewelle

Jonathan Silverman, *University of Texas at Austin*
"Atlanta Exposition Address"

Deborah Ayer Sitter, *Lecturer in English, Emory University, Atlanta, Georgia*
Sanchez, Sonia; We a BaddDDD People

Joseph T. Skerrett, Jr., *Professor of English, University of Massachusetts at Amherst*
God's Trombones; "Lift Every Voice and Sing"

Valerie Smith, *Professor of English, University of California, Los Angeles*
Lee, Andrea; Literary History, *article on* Late Twentieth Century

Virginia Whatley Smith, *Associate Professor of English, University of Alabama, Birmingham*
Cain, George; Demby, William; Oliver, Diane; Peterson, Louis

Stephen F. Soitos, *Lecturer in English, University of California, Los Angeles*
Micheaux, Oscar

Maia Angelique Sorrells, *College of Notre Dame, Belmont, California*
Caines, Jeannette Franklin

Ann Folwell Stanford, *Associate Professor of English and Associate Dean, School for New Learning, DePaul University, Chicago, Illinois*
Bambara, Toni Cade; Minnie Ransom; Salt Eaters, The

Sandra K. Stanley, *Associate Professor of English, California State University, Northridge*
Coleman, Wanda

Albert E. Stone, *Professor Emeritus of American Studies and English, University of Iowa, Iowa City*
Confessions of Nat Turner, The

Australia Tarver, *Associate Professor of English, Texas Christian University, Fort Worth*
Chase-Riboud, Barbara; Edwards, Junius; Ellis, Trey

Claudia Tate, *Professor of English, Princeton University, New Jersey*
Contending Forces; Hopkins, Pauline E.; Hunter, Kristin; Tillman, Katherine Davis Chapman

Betty Taylor-Thompson, *Professor of English, Texas Southern University, Houston*
Baby Suggs; Beloved; Eva Peace; for colored girls; Hannah Peace; Jadine Childs; Jazz (the novel); Paul D; Sethe Suggs; Shadrack; Shange; Ntozake; Song of Solomon; Son Green; Tar Baby

Lorenzo Thomas, *Associate Professor of English, University of Houston-Downtown, Texas*
Zu-Bolton, Ahmos II

John Edgar Tidwell, *Associate Professor of English, University of Kansas, Lawrence*
Brown, Sterling A.; Davis, Frank Marshall; Slim Greer

Mary Titus, *Associate Professor of English, St. Olaf College, Northfield, Minnesota*
Dunbar-Nelson, Alice Moore

Charles P. Toombs, *Associate Professor and Chair of Africana Studies, San Diego State University, California*
Henson, Josiah; Salaam, Kalamu ya; Thomas, Joyce Carol

Patricia A. Turner, *Associate Professor of African-American and African Studies and American Studies, University of California, Davis*
Sambo; Shine; Stackolee; Uncle Tom

R. Goldman Vander, *Curriculum in Comparative Literature, University of North Carolina at Chapel Hill*
Aubert, Alvin

Marsha C. Vick, *Independent Scholar, Durham, North Carolina*
Cartier, Xam Wilson; Rodgers, Carolyn M.; Sanders, Dori

Wendy Wagner, *Adjunct Instructor in English, Pace University, New York*
Stowe, Harriet Beecher

Gayle Wald, *Assistant Professor of English, George Washington University, Washington, D.C.*
White, Walter

Robbie Jean Walker, *Professor of English; Interim Dean of the School of Liberal Arts, Auburn University at Montgomery, Alabama*
Williams, Samm-Art

Cheryl A. Wall, *Professor of English, Rutgers University, New Brunswick, New Jersey*
Dust Tracks on a Road; Hurston, Zora Neale; Janie Crawford; Jonah's Gourd Vine; Mule Bone; Nanny; Tea Cake; Their Eyes Were Watching God

Jon Wallace, *Professor of English, Graceland College, Lamoni, Iowa*
Elbow Room; McPherson, James Alan

Wendy W. Walters, *Assistant Professor, Emerson College, Boston, Massachusetts*
Coffin Ed Johnson; Cotton Comes to Harlem; Grave Digger Jones; If He Hollers Let Him Go

Jerry W. Ward, Jr., *Lawrence Durgin Professor of Literature, Tougaloo College, Mississippi*
Dent, Tom; For My People; Jubilee; Walker, Margaret

Anne Bradford Warner, *Associate Professor of English, Spelman College, Atlanta, Georgia*
Keckley, Elizabeth

Kenneth W. Warren, *Associate Professor of English, University of Chicago, Illinois*
David Walker's Appeal; Gates, Henry Louis, Jr.

Nagueyalti Warren, *Assistant Dean; Adjunct Associate Professor of African American Studies, Emory University, Atlanta, Georgia*
Aunt Jemima; Fabio, Sarah Webster; Graham, Shirley; Guy, Rosa; Roll of Thunder, Hear My Cry; Taylor, Mildred D.

Kimberly Weaver, *Atlanta, Georgia*
Harris, E. Lynn

George F. Wedge, *Associate Professor Emeritus of English, University of Kansas, Lawrence*
Madgett, Naomi Long

Joe Weixlmann, *Professor of English, Indiana State University, Terre Haute*
Wright, Charles S.

Craig H. Werner, *Professor of Afro-American Studies, University of Wisconsin-Madison*
Literary History, *article on* Early Twentieth Century

Elizabeth J. West, *Assistant Professor of English, Morehouse College, Atlanta, Georgia*
Crummell, Alexander

Craig Howard White, *Associate Professor of Literature and Humanities, University of Houston-Clear Lake, Texas*
Federal Writers' Project; Messenger, The

Margaret B. Wilkerson, *Professor of African American Studies; Director, Center for Theater Arts, University of California, Berkeley*
Beneatha Younger; Hansberry, Lorraine; Mama Lena Younger; Raisin in the Sun, A; Walter Lee Younger

Michelle J. Wilkinson, *Institute of the Liberal Arts, Emory University, Atlanta, Georgia*
Cortez, Jayne

Derek A. Williams, *Appalachian State University, Boone, North Carolina*
Milner, Ron

Kenny Jackson Williams, *Professor of English, Duke University, Durham, North Carolina*
Annie Allen; Brawley, Benjamin; Bronzeville Boys and Girls; Brooks, Gwendolyn; In the Mecca; Maud Martha; Plato, Ann; Street in Bronzeville, A

Kim D. Hester Williams, *Assistant Professor of English, Sonoma State University, California*
Graham, Lorenz

Patricia Robinson Williams, *Professor of British Romantic Literature and Linguistics, Texas Southern University, Houston*
Folks from Dixie; Garvey, Marcus; Lyrics of Lowly Life; Majors and Minors

Roland L. Williams, Jr., *Assistant Professor of American Literature, Temple University, Philadelphia, Pennsylvania*
All God's Dangers; Cobb, Ned; Hammon, Briton

Charles E. Wilson, Jr., *Associate Professor of English, Old Dominion University, Norfolk, Virginia*
Pennington, James W.C.

Jean Fagan Yellin, *Distinguished Professor of English, Pace University, New York*
Incidents in the Life of a Slave Girl; Jacobs, Harriet A.

Kristine A. Yohe, *Assistant Professor of English, Northern Kentucky University, Highland Heights, Kentucky*
Kenan, Randall; Mama Day; Naylor, Gloria; Women of Brewster Place, The

THE CONCISE OXFORD COMPANION TO
African American Literature

AI (b. 1947), poet. Born in Tucson, Arizona, the poet AI, pseudonym of Florence Anthony, looks to a complex American multicultural ancestry—a Japanese father and a mother part black, Choctaw, and Irish. Raised also in Las Vegas and San Francisco, she majored in Japanese at the University of Arizona and immersed herself in Buddhism. Currently based in Tempe, she has received awards from the Guggenheim Foundation, the National Endowment for the Arts, and various universities; she has also been a frequent reader-performer of her work.

So eclectic, not to say peaceable, an upbringing makes a striking contrast with the kind of poetry that has won her ongoing attention. Her particular forte has been to adapt Robert Browning's dramatic monologue to her own purposes, poems whose different voices speak of fracture, violence, revenge, sexual hunger, as if to emphasize the human disorder both beneath (and often enough at the surface of) society.

Cruelty (1973) offers a run of soliloquies dealing with, among other things, suicide, abortion, female masturbation, hanging, child-beating, and the unpredictability of desire. AI's style of poetic utterance has from the outset rarely been other than tough-edged, in the words of an early critic, "as if she made her poem(s) with a knife." Little wonder that the title poem in *Cruelty* begins with an image of a dead wildcat. In *Killing Floor* (1978), a poem like "The Kid" assumes the voice of a boy-murderer, a natural-born killer, who methodically and pathologically destroys his entire family only to emerge sweet-faced and apparently unperturbed.

Sin (1986) attempts yet more complex personae—ruminations, for the most part, of men of power, Joe McCarthy to the Kennedy brothers. In "The Testament of J. Robert Oppenheimer" the note is transcendental, millennial, that of the Manhattan Project leader eventually troubled by the possibilities of nuclear mass-destruction. In "The Good Shepherd," however, the voice, more locally but no less chillingly, belongs to the anonymous mass-murderer of Atlanta's black youth. "Saturn . . . devours its children," says the killer. *Fate: New Poems* (1991) offers a further gallery, equally dark, a speaking dead that includes General George Custer, Mary Jo Kopechne (now the bitter, retrospective party-girl), Elvis Presley, Lenny Bruce, and President Lyndon Johnson.

AI opens her fifth collection, *Greed* (1993), with "Riot Act, April 29, 1992," a poem spoken as if by an unnamed black rioter taken into police custody in South Central Los Angeles, who ruefully construes the looting and fires in the aftermath of Rodney King's beating as "the day the wealth finally trickled down." A similar bittersweet note runs through "Self Defense." Washington, D.C.'s mayor Marion Barry, sentenced for crack possession after an FBI setup, is forced to conclude, "That is how you hold the nigger down." In "Hoover, Edgar J.," law enforcement as paranoia has its say, the meanness at once racist, homophobic, class-loaded. The diatribe ends boastingly and bullyingly: "J. Edgar Hoover rules." Other monologue-poems equally offer markers for the times—whether in the voice of Jack Ruby, or of a witness to the Marcos regime in Manila, or of a street girl contemplating Mike Tyson and the Desiree Washington rape.

As always this amounts to a slightly stylized ventriloquy, creating an effect of distance, things seen at one remove. All has not by any means been praise; critics have on occasion thought the poetry monotone, close to mannerism, too determinedly dour or black-humored. But AI is not to be denied her own kind of verse Gothic, an America, a world, seen as though through disembodied witness and nothing if not at one with her slightly maverick status in contemporary African American poetry. AI won the National Book Award in 1999.

• Paula Giddings, ed., *When and Where I Enter: The Impact of Black Women on Race and Sex in America,* 1984. Cheryl A. Wall, ed., *Changing Our Own Words: Essays on Criticism, Theory, and Writing by Black Women,* 1989. Sandi Russell, *Render Me My Song: African-American Women Writers from Slavery to the Present,* 1990. Claudia Ingram, "Writing the Crises: The Deployment of Abjection in Ai's Dramatic Monologues," *Literature-Interpretation-Theory,* 8:2 (October 1997): 173–191. Karen L. Kilcup, "Dialogues of the Self: Toward a Theory of (Re) Reading Ai," *Journal of Gender Studies,* 7:1 (1998): 5–20.

—A. Robert Lee

ALBERT, OCTAVIA V. ROGERS (1824–c. 1890), biographer of former slaves, educator, and community leader. Octavia Victoria Rogers Albert is best known for her volume of collected slave narratives, *The House of Bondage, or Charlotte Brooks and Other Slaves* (1890). The collection assembles the brief narratives (as told to Albert) of seven former slaves whose earnest testimonies, Albert believed, exposed the brutality of slaveholding in general and the hypocrisy of Christian slaveholding in particular. But more importantly, the narratives demonstrated, according to Albert, the narrators' spiritual courage and strong Christian faith.

Albert was born a slave on 12 December 1824 in Oglethorpe, Georgia, but neither slavery nor its far-reaching effects stifled her achievements. After the Civil War, she attended Atlanta University and became a teacher, interviewer, and researcher. Asserting that the complete story of slavery had not been told, she invited former slaves into her home, taught some to read and write, sang hymns and read scriptures to others, and encouraged them all to recount their histories, which she recorded.

In her comments, which weave a sympathetic and outraged voice throughout the narratives, Albert decries the inhumanity of slavery and continually raises the alarm over slaveholders who professed Christian ideals of compassion and brotherhood; they would carry the sin of slavery upon their souls. But as much as Albert yearned to set straight the record of the past, she also looked with optimism toward the future of the freed people. If they saved their earnings, bought homes, educated their children, built up character, obeyed the laws of the country, served God, and protested injustices, their status would improve.

Albert was married to the Reverend A. E. P. Albert. She met him in 1873 during her first teaching assignment in Montezuma, Georgia, where he was teaching at the same school. They were married the following year on 21 October 1874 and moved to Houma, Louisiana (where Albert conducted her interviews with former slaves). In 1877, her husband was ordained a minister in the Methodist Episcopal Church, and in 1878, Albert, who was a member of the African Methodist Episcopal Church, converted to her husband's denomination. She was baptized by her husband.

Albert's husband and their only child, Laura T. F. Albert, published *The House of Bondage* a few months after the author's death as a serial story in the *Southwestern Christian Advocate*. Its popularity encouraged publication in book form as a memorial to the author.

• Octavia V. Rogers Albert, *The House of Bondage*, 1893; rpt. 1988. Frances Smith Foster, *Written by Herself*, 1993.

—Jan Furman

ALEXANDER, MARGARET WALKER. *See* Walker, Margaret.

ALFRADO. *See* Frado.

ALI, MUHAMMAD (b. 1942), prizefighter. Despite the considerable achievements of such important African American athletes as Jesse Owens, Joe *Louis, Wilma Rudolph, Jim Brown, and Jackie *Robinson, the young brash prizefighter from Louisville, Kentucky, may very well have eclipsed their significance. He surely eclipsed their fame as, at the height of his career in the early and middle 1970s, Muhammad Ali was, without question, the most famous African American in history and among the five most recognized faces on the planet.

Born Cassius Marcellus Clay, Jr., in 1942 (named after both his father and the famous Kentucky abolitionist), the gregarious, handsome, and extraordinarily gifted boxer garnered world attention by winning a gold medal in the 1960 Olympics. He further stunned the sports world by beating the heavily favored Sonny Liston to win the heavyweight title in 1964, and shocked white America by announcing right after that fight that he had joined the militant, antiwhite Nation of Islam, the Black Muslims, whose most well-known figure was the fiery orator *Malcolm X. He also announced that he was changing his name to Muhammad Ali. When he opposed being drafted during the Vietnam War on religious grounds and was subsequently convicted of violating the Selective Service Act in 1967, he was denied a license to fight anywhere in the United States. He was, at this time, among white America, probably the most hated black public figure since heavyweight boxing champion Jack *Johnson. After an exile of three and a half years, Ali returned triumphantly to boxing in 1970, even though he lost his title to Joe Frazier in 1971. He eventually won back his title in 1974, and after losing it once in 1978 regained it again later that year.

Ali exercised an extraordinary influence on African American culture in the 1960s, doing much to keep the Nation of Islam popular in the black community after the assassination of Malcolm X in 1965. He figured in the writings of such important 1960s black literary figures as Amiri *Baraka, Eldridge *Cleaver, Malcolm X, and Larry *Neal, not to mention numerous black journalists and poets. He came to symbolize black manhood and masculinity, unbowed and uncompromising, adversarial and combative, a virtually one-person definition of African American self-determination in the middle and late 1960s. But his boyish bragging and his poetic predictions of doom for his opponents made him an important public prefigure for the performance art of rap. Ali's autobiography, *The Greatest: My Own Story*, was coauthored with Richard Durham and published in 1975. Toni *Morrison served as the book's editor.

—Gerald Early

ALLEN, RICHARD (1760–1831), Philadelphia preacher, church founder, and social leader. Born a slave in the household of a prominent Philadelphian, Richard Allen was sold to a Delaware farmer who allowed him and his brother to work as day laborers to purchase their freedom. In Delaware, Allen also encountered exhorters of the Methodist Society, then still affiliated with the Church of England. The antislavery position of the Methodists attracted him, while their inspiration led him to teach himself to read and write and to feel a spiritual awakening, described at the outset of his autobiography, *The Life, Experience and Gospel Labors of the Rt. Rev. Richard Allen* (1833; rpt. 1960). His 1786 return to Philadelphia introduced him to Absalom Jones, an African American preacher some years his senior, and to African Americans who were hungry for social and religious leadership in their home city. The Methodist emphasis on inner faith and weekly meetings of the faithful nourished Allen's compatriots in times that were frequently trying. Still, at Saint George's Church, an institution African American Philadelphians had supported with their labor and donations, the lay exhorter Allen found himself and his fellow African American worshipers segregated and ultimately ousted from their seats during a service. In response, in 1787, Allen and Jones formed the Free African Society, a benevolent association that evolved into the Bethel Church. In 1799 Allen was ordained by famed Methodist bishop Francis Asbury. During the War of 1812, Allen helped organize twenty-five hundred African Americans who constructed bulwarks to safeguard Philadelphia. African Methodist Episcopal (AME) congregations multiplied until in 1816 their religious leaders established a separate denomination. Allen became the first AME bishop. As this branch of African American religion grew under his care, he also worked as a master shoemaker, organized schools for African American children, denounced both slavery and colonizationist schemes to expatriate African Americans, and aided the first African American newspaper, *Freedom's Journal*. To Allen fell the task of preaching execution sermons for African American Philadelphians condemned by the state.

Allen's sermons, addresses, devotional pieces, and autobiography constitute an important chapter in American writing. Charity, the first of Christian virtues, wrote Allen, should orient white Americans to the bodily and spiritual needs of African Americans, including the need for freedom. With Jones, he recounted African Americans' charitable services during the raging yellow fever of 1793—aiding the sick, caring for orphans, burying the dead—and bitterly noted that not only had whites lied about a supposed African immunity to the disease, but also scorned and insulted their African American benefactors once the epidemic ebbed. Faith and the experience of racial inequities led Allen to an African American reconstruction of Christianity premised upon the conviction that since the gospel addresses the needs of the oppressed, a gospel that serves oppressors is merely a human creation, not a divine one. The expression of this religious reconstruction in his writings and in African American institutions was the genius of Allen's life.

• Charles H. Wesley, *Richard Allen: Apostle of Freedom*, 2d ed., 1969. Carol V. R. George, *Segregated Sabbaths: Richard Allen and the Emergence of Independent Black Churches, 1760–1840*, 1973.

—John Saillant

ALLEN, SAMUEL W. (b. 1917), poet, educator, translator, and lawyer. Born in Columbus, Ohio, Samuel Allen (also known as Paul Vesey) studied creative writing under James Weldon *Johnson at Fisk where he graduated *magna cum laude* in 1938. He received his JD from Harvard in 1941. Until 1968 when he formally left law for literature, he was active in both fields.

He was drafted into the U.S. Armed Services in 1942 and served as an officer, though under the constraints of the segregated system, until 1946. From 1946 to 1947 he was deputy assistant district attorney in New York City. The following year he studied humanities at the New School for Social Research. In 1948 he went to Paris on the GI Bill, and after studying French, studied at the Sorbonne. He was employed variously with the U.S. Armed Forces from 1951 to 1955, as historian, claims officer, and civilian attorney in Wiesbaden, Germany, and in France. After a brief private law practice in Brooklyn, Allen taught law at Texas Southern University from 1958 to 1960. During the Kennedy and Johnson administrations, he served in Washington, D.C., as assistant general counsel in the U.S. Information Agency from 1961 to 1964, and as chief counsel in the U.S. Community Relations Service from 1965 to 1968.

Aided by Richard *Wright in Paris, Allen first published poetry in 1949 in *Présence Africaine*. Upon leaving France to film **Native Son*, Wright asked Allen to take over his role of editing the journal's English materials. Thus Allen became acquainted with that journal's circle of writers and thinkers with whom he shared an enduring commitment to African culture. Allen's interest in francophone African poetry prompted his translating Sartre's *Orphée noir* for *Présence Africaine*. In the early 1950s, more than a decade ahead of American receptivity for such ideas, Allen tried in vain to interest American editors in the writers and ideas represented by *Présence Africaine* (Ellen Conroy Kennedy, *The Negritude Poets*, 1975; 1989). Among other works Allen published in *Présence Africaine* was the influential and frequently reprinted "Negritude and Its Relevance to the American Negro Writer" (1959), which he delivered that same year at the New York Black Writers' Conference. Georg Dickenberger early pointed out that Allen's own poetry reflects the dual consciousness of Africa and America and called him "the first of a new generation" ("Paul Vesey," *Black Orpheus*, Oct. 1958). In 1956 in Germany, Allen's first book of poetry appeared under the pen name Paul Vesey, the name by which many already knew his poetry. The book, *Elfenbein Zähne* (*Ivory Tusks*), consists of twenty poems that appear in both English and German and an afterword by Janheinz Jahn, one of the foremost European Africanists of his day. Many of these poems still rank among his finest. Ezekiel Mphahlele, celebrated South African novelist and critic, quotes Allen as having once said of "The Staircase," "Upon it . . . I would rest my case . . . and that of the Negro in this land" (*Voices in the Whirlwind*, 1972).

After being published mostly in Europe where he was living from 1948 to the mid-1950s, Allen's poetry was not widely known in the United States until the 1960s when his poems began appearing in anthologies by Arna *Bontemps (1963) and Langston *Hughes (1964). In 1962 he coedited, introduced, and contributed to *Pan-Africanism Reconsidered*. In 1968 his second book of poetry, *Ivory Tusks and Other Poems*, was published, though in a limited edition. Even though it shares the title and the title poem with Allen's first book, most of the poems are new.

Since 1968, except for pro bono work for many good causes, Allen's career has been entirely literary. He was Avalon Professor of Humanities from 1968 to 1970 at Tuskegee Institute and visiting professor at Wesleyan University the following year. He taught African and African American literature at Boston University from 1971 until retiring in 1981. Over a two-year period he conducted a writers' workshop on a volunteer basis at Massachusetts Correctional Institute in Norfolk. Eugene *Redmond has called Allen's 1971 essay, "The African Heritage" in *Black World*, a "brilliant and cogent" statement of black artistic expression rooted in Africa (*Drumvoices*, 1976). In 1973 Allen edited *Poems from Africa*, a collection illustrated by Romare Beardon and introduced by Allen, who also translated some of the poems. In 1975 his third book of poetry, *Paul Vesey's Ledger*, appeared as the last of Paul Breman's Heritage series. Written in the three years after Allen stopped practicing law, these poems are intense responses to the suffering, courage, and vitality of both famous and nameless African Americans. The stance is often ironic with the tone varying from elegiac to angry and prophetic. Allen has continued writing, giving readings throughout the United States and abroad, and conducting workshops. He had an NEA Creative Writing Fellowship in Poetry (1979–1980) and residence grants from the Wurlitzer Foundation in Taos and the Rockefeller Foundation Conference and Study Center in Bellagio, Italy. His poetry has been included in over two hundred anthologies, and his work has been translated into French and Italian as well as German.

Every Round and Other Poems (1987) makes available most of Allen's previously published poems as well as excellent new ones. One can trace reworkings of earlier poems and subjects as in "Nat Turner or Let Him Come." More importantly, one can experience the depth and impressive scope; the humor, the outrage, and the humanity; and the consistency of a vision rooted in his African American heritage and experience. One of the poets included in Woodie *King, Jr.'s *The Forerunners: Black Poets in America* (1975), poets whom Addison *Gayle, Jr., terms the literary godparents of those emerging in the 1960s, Samuel Allen has stayed relevant. Although Allen is known and respected among scholars, his poetry calls out for a wider audience and the extensive critical attention it has yet to receive.

• Ruth L. Brittin, "Samuel W. Allen," in *DLB*, vol. 41, *Afro-American Poets since 1955*, eds. Trudier Harris and Thadious M. Davis, 1985, pp. 8–17. Edward A. Scott, "Bardic Memory and Witness in the Poetry of Samuel Allen," in *The Furious Flowering of African American Poetry*, ed. Joanne V. Gabbin, 1999, pp. 47–59.

—Mary Hughes Brookhart

ALLEN, SARAH A. *See* Hopkins, Pauline E.

All God's Dangers, which won a National Book Award in 1974, is a collaboration between an illiterate tenant farmer and a Harvard graduate student. In 1969, the student, Theodore Rosengarten, met the farmer, Ned *Cobb, while researching an Alabama sharecroppers' union. In explaining why he joined the union, the eighty-four-year-old Cobb (named Nate Shaw in *All God's Dangers* for "protection and privacy") told eight hours' worth of stories that "built upon one another so that the sequence expressed the sense of a man 'becoming.'"

Beginning his story in the late nineteenth century, Nate Shaw gives an account of his lineage that reveals "the way of life that [he] was born and raised to." He makes it apparent that his upbringing suffered from social customs gathered from "slavery time days," which turned his "daddy" and others in his family into sharecroppers with a poor sense of worth. The local culture, Shaw indicates, consisted of a racial hierarchy that placed "colored farmers" under the authority of "white landlords." His relatives and neighbors should have received freedom from bondage at the end of the Civil War, when his father was fifteen, but "what they got wasn't what they wanted, it wasn't freedom, really." As in slavery, they found themselves expected "to do whatever the white man directed em to do" without saying a word about "their heart's desire."

While his father resigns himself "to take what come and live for today" and thus simply manages to eke out a living, Shaw, inspired by his grandmother, looks for more out of life. He imagines that skill and diligence can help him to rise in the world "like a boy climbin a tree." By 1931, known throughout his region for his work ethic, he says, "I was doin as well as any poor colored man could do in this country." He has a wife and ten children at the time, lives in a "pretty good old house," and owns two mules as well as two cars. Undoubtedly, he seems set for continued success.

But as boys slip and fall from trees, Shaw takes a step that causes him to lose prestige and much more. One December day in 1932, after joining the Sharecroppers Union, full of pride and emboldened by the union's teachings yet virtually alone, Shaw opposes the efforts of four deputy sheriffs to confiscate a neighbor's property for the benefit of a white landlord. A violent struggle follows; it leaves Shaw wounded and under arrest. He is convicted of a felony in court and sentenced to twelve years in prison.

Shaw serves his time stoically. When he is set free, he returns to a home in disrepair. His wife dying, his children scattered, he has paid a dear price for his act of defiance. Still, he maintains his old outlook. He resumes working on the farm and looking for ways to prosper with dignity. Regardless of others' opinions, Shaw thinks that he has done good for his people by taking his stand and suffering the consequences.

All God's Dangers reflects a literary convention that emerged in the eighteenth century and continues to evolve. Works in this tradition regret that time and again American society has denied African Americans a fair chance to succeed. Looking back to the slave narratives and forward to prominent texts such as **Up from Slavery* (1901), **Black Boy* (1945), and *The *Autobiography of Malcolm X* (1965), *All God's Dangers* exemplifies African American life stories, contending that anyone in an evenhanded society can realize honor and well-being through a commitment to ingenuity and enterprise.

• William Nichols, "This Old 'ism'," *The American Scholar* 44 (Spring 1975): 310–314. Albert E. Stone, "Two Recreate One," in *Autobiographical Occasions and Original Acts: Versions of American Identity from Henry Adams to Nate Shaw*, 1982, pp. 231–264.

—Roland L. Williams, Jr.

Amen Corner, The. James *Baldwin's *The Amen Corner* did not reach Broadway until 1965, twelve years after its completion. A morality play echoing his novel **Go Tell It on the Mountain* (1953), *The Amen Corner* has a laborious history. Although the play failed to generate professional interest, writer Owen *Dodson directed a student production at Howard University in 1955. It opened at the Ethel Barrymore Theatre a decade later on 15 April 1965 under Lloyd Richards's direction.

The drama critiques the church's role in African Americans' lives. Center stage are Sister Margaret, the pastor of a Pentecostal church; Luke, her estranged husband; David, their son; Odessa, Margaret's sister; and church members. Described by the author as a "tyrannical matriarch," Margaret applies a harsh, Calvinistic doctrine to her family and parishioners. However, she fails to heed her opening sermon, "Set thine house in order." Instead, she journeys to Philadelphia to resuscitate a "wicked" church, ignoring threats at home: the "Elders" of her congregation raise questions about her financial and domestic matters; the jazz-playing Luke returns to make amends before dying; and David questions the righteous path that his mother imposes. We also learn that Margaret left Luke after the death of their baby, which Margaret took as a sign from God concerning her marriage to an incontrovertible "sinner." Margaret appears in limbo when Luke dies, David flees, and the church deposes her. However, she finds redemption after acknowledging her rigid Christianity: "It ain't all in the singing and the shouting. It ain't all in the reading of the Bible."

The Amen Corner reflects many of Baldwin's own religious experiences; thus, he deftly incorporates gospel music and sermons and preaching. Like dramas such as T. S. Eliot's *Murder in the Cathedral* and Arthur Miller's *The Crucible*, Baldwin's play foregrounds the powerful role of religion and problematizes "good" and "evil." One of the few African American dramas about the church, *The Amen Corner* is still widely performed.

• Therman B. O'Daniel, ed., *James Baldwin: A Critical Evaluation*, 1977. C. W. E. Bigsby, *The Second Black Renaissance: Essays in Black Literature*, 1980.

—Keith Clark

American Hunger. *See Black Boy.*

AMINI, JOHARI (b. 1935), poet, essayist, short story writer, and chiropractor. Johari Amini, born Jewel Christine McLawler to William and Alma (Bazel) McLawler on 13 January 1935 in Philadelphia, Pennsylvania, changed her name after her consciousness-raising by Haki R. *Madhubuti (then Don L. Lee), whom she met as a thirty-two-year-old freshman at Wilson Junior College. Johari is Swahili for "Jewel," and Amini is Swahili for "honesty and fidelity." Amini believes that the meaning of a name becomes an inherent part of the person carrying that name, and she wanted names that would reflect her personality and her values of honesty and fidelity—values that she lived by and that she wanted her writings to convey.

Amini's meeting Madhubuti was the beginning of a long literary and political association, which is demonstrated in her poetic style as well as in her social criticism. She was a staff member of the Institute of Positive Education, and she was assistant, then associate, editor of Third World Press and *Black Books Bulletin*, institutions that Madhubuti founded. Amini's sociopolitical consciousness-raising is quite evident in her poetry, essays, book and movie reviews, and monographs on health. Her writings exhibit the essence of African American womanhood and the survival of African Americans. Gwendolyn *Brooks praises the poet for understanding the "rubble and mire of society" and then conveying that understanding to others (*Let's Go Somewhere*, 1970). Amini feels that her personal and professional responsibility is fulfilled when she is advising her people through her writings. This concern for her people is her reason for returning to college to become a chiropractor. For Amini, being a chiropractor as well as a writer is a necessary asset for helping African Americans.

The concerns of Amini the poet are the concerns of Amini the woman. These are expressed in a poetic essay entitled "Letter to a Blackwoman's Daughter, Written to Marcia," presumably Amini's daughter Marciana. The letter cautions the daughter about the imperative to define one's blackness, to claim and to affirm one's identity. Doing so is a vital part of a person's survival. Amini has declared in several forums that she is an African American first, then a writer.

Amini and the 1960s poets felt compelled to affirm their blackness as they rejected America's racist society. To demonstrate their defiance and to make their protest more effective, the poets rejected the traditional themes, forms, and language of American poetry. They demanded that their voices be heard, so they used features attributed to the vernacular of African Americans—multiple negation, zero copula, the invariant "be," zero possessives, clipped verb endings, slang vocabulary, unorthodox spelling and capitalization, zero punctuation, and abbreviated words. The rhythmic cadence of the poetry was not the iambic pentameter or other such metrical patterns but free verse with words scattered randomly across the printed page. These nontraditional rhetorical strategies demanded attention in order to convey the urgent message of protest against the inequality and injustices in America. Although Amini uses these nontraditional linguistic strategies, she adamantly cautions that students be taught formal English so that they will be able to function in contemporary society. (She has taught composition and African American literature in colleges in Chicago.) While Amini does not view her linguistic strategies as a part of her political stance, she agrees that the political stance manifested in her writing is who she is; her words reflect the very essence of her being an African American woman in today's society.

Amini's poetry collections are *Images in Black* (1967), *Black Essence* (1968), *A Folk Fable* (1969), *Let's Go Somewhere* (1970), and *A Hip Tale in Earth Style* (1972). Her poems and short stories are included in many journals and anthologies. Her essays in *An African Frame of Reference* (1972) theorize that one's values predetermine one's behavior. Amini's training as a psychologist gives her added insight as to how the larger society imposes its values on African Americans to their psychological detriment. Her interest in the whole person motivated her to write *A Commonsense Approach to Eating* (1975). It is obvious in her writings that Amini's touchstone is African Americans' survival. She emphasizes that survival will come only as people know their identity, which is an absolute priority for survival. Perhaps now that she is a practicing chiropractor in Atlanta, Georgia, Amini will again spew bullet words, for her poetry and essays—even her short stories—provide insightful knowledge that African Americans need.

• Sonia Sanchez, review of *Black Essence, Negro Digest* 18 (Apr. 1969): 91–92. Gwendolyn Brooks, introduction to *Let's Go Somewhere*, 1970. Sarah Webster Fabio, review of *Let's Go Somewhere, Black World* 20 (Dec. 1970): 68, 98. Eugene Redmond, *Drumvoices: The Mission of Afro-American Poetry*, 1976. Fahamisha Patricia Brown, "Johari M. Amini," in *DLB*, vol. 41, *Afro-American Poets since 1955*, eds. Trudier Harrris and Thadious M. Davis, 1985.

—Margaret Ann Reid

ANDERSON, MARIAN (1897–1993), recitalist, opera singer, and diplomat. Marian Anderson's 1939 concert at the Lincoln Memorial, in Washington, D.C., marked the symbolic beginning of the civil rights movement. Born to a poor family in Philadelphia, Anderson came to public attention in 1924 as the winner of a New York Philharmonic voice competition. Because the color line impeded American bookings, the contralto studied and performed in Europe for several years. In 1935, the impresario Sol Hurok brought Anderson back for a successful New York concert. Thereafter, she toured the United States as an acclaimed soloist and sang at the White House in 1936. In 1939, the Daughters of the American Revolution (DAR) refused to allow the singer to perform at Constitution Hall, stating explicitly that their auditorium was available to "white artists only." First Lady Eleanor Roosevelt publicly resigned from the DAR in protest. African American leaders from Howard University and from the NAACP arranged for Anderson to sing instead at the Lincoln Memorial on Easter Sunday. Broadcast over national radio and attended by 75,000 people, the recital was a symbolic triumph that inspired a generation of African American activists and artists. Never a political activist, Marian Anderson nonetheless continued to overturn racial barriers. In 1955, thirty-one years after her New York debut, she became the first African American to sing a role at the Metropolitan Opera. In 1957, she toured India and Asia as a singer and cultural ambassador for the U.S. Department of State; later, President Dwight D. Eisenhower appointed her an alternate representative to the Human Rights Committee of the United Nations. Anderson performed at the inaugurations of Presidents Eisenhower and John F. Kennedy, and in 1963 she returned to the Lincoln Memorial to sing at the March on Washington for Jobs and Freedom. She received the Presidential Medal of Freedom in 1963 and gave her farewell concert in 1965.

• Marian Anderson, *My Lord, What a Morning: An Autobiography*, 1956; rpt. 1984. Allan Keiler, *Marian Anderson: A Singer's Journey*, 1997.

—Scott A. Sandage

ANDREWS, RAYMOND (1934–1991), novelist, essayist, and winner of first James *Baldwin Prize. Raymond Andrews was born near Madison, Georgia, in Morgan County, the fourth of ten children born to sharecropping parents George and Viola Andrews. He helped with the farm work and absorbed the ambience of rural living that was to color his later writings. Andrews left home at fifteen and worked at a variety of jobs while beginning to write. He eventually took a position in New York City with an airline, a job that enabled him to travel extensively in the United States and Europe.

Raymond Andrews's first published piece was an article on baseball, which appeared in *Sports Illustrated* in 1975. In 1976, *Ataraxia*, a small journal edited by Phillip Lee Williams and Linda Williams, excerpted a section from the novel *Appalachee Red*, which was published in its entirety by Dial Press (1978). *Appalachee Red*, winner of the first James Baldwin Prize, was followed by *Rosiebelle Lee Wildcat Tennesee* (1980) and *Baby Sweet's* (1983), completing the trilogy about life in the fictional Muskhogean County, Georgia. After Dial Press was closed by its parent group, Doubleday Press, Andrews's books were out of print until 1987, when they were picked up and reprinted by the Brown Thrasher imprint of the University of Georgia Press. Andrews subsequently went to Peachtree Press to publish his next two books, *The Last Radio Baby: A Memoir* (1991) and *Jessie and Jesus and Cousin Clare* (1991). Peachtree Press plans to publish *Once Upon a Time in Atlanta*, also a memoir, written about the years after Andrews left Madison and moved to Atlanta. Andrews also left manuscripts for two additional novels; their publishing future is unknown.

Andrews's unique style owes a great deal to the cadences of rural southern speech; he noted in the preface to the 1987 edition of *Appalachee Red* that his "American roots (like those of most Afro-Americans) are southern rural." He reported that his earliest favorite writers were Erskine Caldwell, William Faulkner, Sinclair Lewis, and John Steinbeck. Indeed, Andrews remarked that the character Pirate in Steinbeck's *Tortilla Flat* made him realize that the creation of a character was possible.

Andrews primarily drew from a rich lode of oral tradition that he absorbed from his family and community. There are echoes of the southern folk preacher, the streetwise badman who inhabits bars and liquor houses, the folk wisdom of elderly black women who pass on their knowledge to the younger African American girls, and the rhythms of jazz and blues music. Andrews wrote from his own culture, and his broader experiences in the places outside Georgia only helped him to focus more clearly on the culture from which he sprang.

His work, like the man himself, is ribald, often obscene, but never vulgar. It is gently ironic, not confrontational, and not intended to be political. Andrews has said that he intended to include all that life includes—sadness, boredom, sex, happiness, violence, and joy—without trying to proselytize and without attempting to change the essential truth of the way life was at a particular time. In fact he took issue with writers who he felt attempted to show only the oppressor and the oppressed. While some of the characters in Andrews's books might be seen as victims, the intent is to show the humanity of all the inhabitants of a community, not to point to the degradation of one race by another.

Appalachee Red (originally titled *Red, White, and Blue*) explores the way of life of rural blacks in the fictional north Georgia county of Muskhogean, an area much resembling Morgan County, Georgia, Andrews's home. The novel spans nearly thirty years in the history of a small town and in the lives of its denizens, both black and white. The tale is at times comic, at times violent, but is always imbued with Andrews's characteristic knack for storytelling. Upon being queried about the lack of a political statement in the book, Andrews responded that he was not interested in preaching, that he was telling a story.

Andrews, himself the product of mixed marriages and relationships, recognized the conflicts and tensions that existed between races, and recognized the possibility that one race might seem to have the upper hand at certain times, but he chose to focus instead on the inherent humanity in all people, and thus on their similarities rather than their differences. Consequently, in *Appalachee Red*, as in the two other books in the Muskhogean trilogy, blacks and whites and Native Americans mingle, marry, and do business together, sometimes with felicitous results, sometimes with disastrous results.

Men and women also find their own voices through Andrews's exuberant prose; indeed, Andrews remarked that *Appalachee Red* was not about Red, but about Baby Sweet, the woman whom he saves from the clutches of an evil white policeman named Boots. Andrews further commented that *Baby Sweet's*, named for the brothel that Baby Sweet opens on the premises of her house after the mysterious departure of Red, is in fact about Lea; Lea is the product of a racially mixed relationship and has chosen to work for the brothel in order to provide services for the black men of the community.

Andrews's female characters are neither oppressors nor oppressed. They are not marginalized females, dependent only on a man's largesse. The difficulties of being a black woman involved with a white man are, in Andrews's novels, fodder for his utter delight with humanity. Many of the strongest, most memorable characters in the novels are women. The characters, both men and women, are not drawn as mere cardboard figures to be revered for their nobility or pitied for their victimization. Everyone, particularly the women, is given her own sense of power within the context of the situation.

Andrews's characters are quintessentially human—people making decisions as best they can, based on their individual conditions. These are real people, living their lives with no apologies, following the dictates of their hearts. If they from time to time appear to make bad choices, the reader must remember that they are given choices, not simply forced into situations for the purpose of a political agenda.

The Last Radio Baby, Andrews's memoir, is a charming look at the vagaries of growing up in a large, talented family with little money. Eventually the family produced artists (including Benny Andrews, who illustrated all the books for his brother), writers, architects, and poets. The successes of Raymond Andrews and his parents, brothers, and sisters point out the importance to him of community.

Andrews died tragically by his own hand on 25 November 1991. His collected letters and assorted family memorabilia are available in a special collection at Emory University, Atlanta, Georgia. Andrews's novels and memoirs are a valuable addition to the world of contemporary African American literature; they provide a fresh, apolitical look at the world of the rural South and are notable for their vivacity of language and fascinating characterization.

• Melville Herskovitz, T*he Myth of the Negro Past*, 1941. Addison Gayle, Jr., ed., *Black Expression*, 1969. Ladell Payne, *Black Novelists and the Southern Literary Tradition*, 1981. Robert B. Stepto, *From Behind the Veil*, 1979. Peter Bruck and Wolfgang Karrer, *The Afro-American Novel since 1960*, 1982. Charles East, ed., *The New Writers of the South*, 1987. Jeffrey J. Folks, "'Trouble' in Muskhogean County: The Social History of a Southern Community in the Fiction of Raymond Andrews," *Southern Literary Journal* 30:2 (Spring 1998): 66–75.

—Freda R. Beaty

ANGELOU, MAYA (b. 1928), autobiographer, poet, playwright, director, producer, performance artist, educator, and winner of the Horatio Alger Award. A prolific author, with a successful career as a singer, actress, and dancer, Maya Angelou became one of America's most famous poets when she stood before the nation to deliver her poem "On the Pulse of Morning" at President Bill Clinton's inauguration on 20 January 1993. At sixty-four years old, she was the first black woman to be asked to compose such a piece, and the second poet to be so recognized after the pairing of Robert Frost and John F. Kennedy in 1961. Born Marguerite Johnson in St. Louis, but raised in Arkansas, Angelou was a natural choice for the forty-second president and fellow Arkansan. The poem reflects a theme that is common to all of Angelou's published works, namely that human beings are more alike than different, and that a message of hope and inclusion is a most inspiring dream and ideal, something to be savored at such a moment of political change. She writes of the triumph of the human spirit over hardship and adversity. Her voice speaks of healing and reconciliation, and she is a willing symbol for the American nation on the eve of the twenty-first century.

The great-granddaughter of a slave-born Arkansas woman, Angelou has had a rich and varied life, and her serial autobiography intertwines in a harmonious way her individual experiences with the collective social history of African Americans. As she recounts in the first volume of her serial autobiography, **I Know Why the Caged Bird Sings* (1970), Angelou spent her first three years in California. Her father, Bailey Johnson, was a navy cook and her mother, Vivian Baxter, a glamorous and dynamic woman, was a sometime nightclub performer and owner of a large rooming house in San Francisco in the 1940s. When Angelou's parents divorced in the early 1930s, her father sent her and her brother Bailey by train, with name tags on their wrists, to live with his mother, Momma Henderson, who ran the only black-owned general store in Stamps, Arkansas. Angelou writes eloquently of the customs and harsh circumstances of life in the segregated pre-civil rights South, and of the dignity and mutual support that rural blacks extended to one another during the Depression. After Stamps came time in St. Louis with her mother's family, the discovery of urban greed and alienation, and her rape at age eight, a trauma that left her mute for several years. Upon her return to the South, she buried herself in the cocoon of her grandmother's store and in her imagination, and read widely. Books became her lifeline and prepared the terrain for her artistic and literary career. She moved back to California as a teenager, graduated from high school, and gave birth to her only child, Guy Johnson, himself a poet. In the 1960s, Angelou was active in the civil rights movement in the United States and abroad, and became briefly involved with African activist Vusumzi Make. She has been married and divorced.

By the time she was in her early twenties, Angelou had worked at a variety of odd jobs, as a waitress, a cook, and a streetcar conductor, flirting briefly with prostitution and drug addiction. She then worked as a stage performer, establishing a reputation among the avant-garde of the early 1950s, and appearing in *Porgy and Bess* on a twenty-two–nation tour sponsored by the U.S. State Department in 1954–1955. She studied dance with Martha Graham. Off-Broadway, she acted in Jean Genet's *The Blacks* in 1960. She worked as an associate editor for the *Arab Observer* in Cairo, Egypt, in 1961–1962 and as a writer for the Ghanaian *Times* and the Ghanaian Broadcasting Corporation in 1964–1966. She appeared in *Mother Courage* at the University of Ghana in 1964 and made her Broadway debut in *Look Away* in 1973. She directed her own play, *And Still I Rise*, in California in 1976. In 1977, she had a part in the television adaptation of Alex *Haley's **Roots* and received an Emmy Award nomination for best supporting actress. She has lectured on campuses, been a guest on many talk shows, and continues to be an extremely popular speaker. She is currently the Reynolds Professor of American Studies at Wake Forest University in North Carolina.

Her autobiographical fictions include *Gather Together in My Name* (1974) and *Singin' and Swingin' and Gettin' Merry Like Christmas* (1976), which received moderate critical praise; and *The Heart of a Woman* (1981) and *All God's Children Need Traveling Shoes* (1986), which were acclaimed as important works covering exciting periods in African American and African history, the civil rights marches, and the era of decolonization. These narratives survey the difficulties and personal triumphs of a remarkable woman with a keen understanding of the power of language to affect change, and of the role of "image making" in the self-representation of groups who have been historically oppressed. In her interview with Claudia Tate, Angelou acknowledged her debt to the black women writers who were her predecessors, Frances Ellen Watkins *Harper and Zora Neale *Hurston in particular, and to her friend James *Baldwin who encouraged her to write after hearing her childhood stories. Angelou's personal experiences typify the changes that have occurred in America in the course of her lifetime. She consciously strives to be the kind of writer who brings people and traditions together and who appeals to the nobler sentiments of her readers. She is a humanist and a protean personality who has, against all odds, made her own life into the great American success story. Her works have a profound resonance with a long tradition that begins with the eighteenth- and nineteenth-century slave narratives. Her style captures the cadences and aspirations of African American women whose strength she celebrates. She has been instrumental in helping refocus attention on black women's voices.

• Claudia Tate, *Black Women Writers at Work*, 1983, pp. 1–38. Selwyn Cudjoe, "Maya Angelou and the Autobiographical Statement," in *Black Women Writers (1950–1980): A Critical Evaluation,* ed. Mari Evans, 1984, pp. 6–24. Lynn Z. Bloom, "Maya Angelou," in *DLB*, vol. 38, *Afro-American Writers after 1955: Dramatists and Prose Writers*, eds. Thadious M. Davis and Trudier Harris, 1985, pp. 3–12. Françoise Lionnet, "Con Artists and Storytellers: Maya Angelou's Problematic Sense of Audience," in *Autobiographical Voices: Race, Gender, Self Portraiture*, 1989, pp. 130–166. Mary Jane Lupton, *Maya Angelou: A Critical Companion*, 1998.

—Françoise Lionnet

Annie Allen. The second book of poems by Gwendolyn *Brooks, *Annie Allen* (1949) won the Eunice Tietjens Prize offered by *Poetry Magazine* and the 1950 Pulitzer Prize for poetry.

The collection is dominated by a long narrative poem, "The Anniad." Somewhat more complex than some of her earlier poems, "The Anniad" is an exercise in various poetic techniques, employing a diction associated more often with the epic form. The protagonist is not "heroic" in the usual sense of the term, but her ability to survive is just as "heroic" as any figure from classical literature.

The poem charts the changes in a young woman as she moves from her youthful dreams to the reality of married life in the ghetto. We see Annie Allen grow from childhood to womanhood in an atmosphere conditioned by poverty, racial discrimination, parental expectations, and unhappiness. Like Maud Martha, a later Brooks heroine, Annie Allen does not completely give in or give up. In fact, in some respects, Annie Allen is a mirror image of the later **Maud Martha* (1953); however, the latter is a prose narrative with poetic overtones, the former is poetry with prose overtones.

The action of "The Anniad" is simple. In order to get away from home, Annie wants to get married. There then follows a courtship, marriage, and separation because of war. When her husband returns, the marriage is weakened by Annie's expectations and his infidelity. They separate and temporarily reconcile. Eventually he deserts Annie for good.

Annie Allen is another one of Brooks's very ordinary, totally undistinguished characters. She is a product of an urban ghetto, the daughter of Andrew and Maxie Allen. Her parents are typical of those in the generation that actually believed the American dream could be realized, that people would be rewarded for hard work and goodness. Much of Annie's early life is devoted to trying to please her mother, who insists that Annie learn to count her blessings and be grateful for what she has, rather than spend energy longing for what she does not. On one level, of course, this is a realistic approach to life; however, it also represses dreams, hopes, and aspirations. If the external Annie is a nonadventurous, passive soul, the internalization of the character reveals one with an active imagination and ever-present dreams.

The simplicity of the narrative thread belies the complexity of form and interpretation. The poem records the numerous repressive forces that operate upon Annie and, in a measure, imprison her. There are, for example, the limitations that result from interracial discrimination and those that result from a sometimes intraracial prejudice relating to skin color. Like many other such women in similar predicaments, Annie longs to escape but does not really have the courage to do so.

The other poems in the volume are also marked by experimentation and unusual imagery. They differ from Brooks's earlier poetry primarily because she shifts from the reality of locale and the exactness of the surroundings to the reality of the mind. Although set in Chicago, *Annie Allen* is not really a collection of regional poems. Moreover, the volume reveals quite clearly what were to become the dominant themes in Brooks's poetry: the roles of women in an unfriendly urban environment and the moral issues that lead to distinctions between right and wrong.

• Maria K. Mootry and Gary Smith, eds., *A Life Distilled: Gwendolyn Brooks, Her Poetry and Fiction*, 1987.

—Kenny Jackson Williams

Another Country. Immensely complex because of its size and scope, *Another Country* is James *Baldwin's most ambitious novel. This novel of ideas covers myriad issues and themes, all related to the transcending power of love. Through interlocking events and episodes, *Another Country* critiques a "moral" and "democratic" America that fosters prejudice based on race, class, and sexuality. The author began writing it in the mid-1950s, completing it in Istanbul; Dial Press published the novel in 1962, and it became a best-seller.

Baldwin creates characters of various racial, sexual, and social backgrounds to illustrate how personal, cultural, and national identities intersect. We first encounter *Rufus Scott, a black jazz musician and one of the novel's many artists. He mentally and physically abuses his lover Leona, a white Southerner who goes insane. Psychically and physically debilitated by a virulent self-hatred, Rufus portends America's fate if it continues to prevent people from connecting irrespective of differences. Baldwin uses Rufus's suicide as an ironic narrative device, for he permeates the novel and illuminates the characters' wrenching attempts to come together. The phrase Rufus hears in a wailing saxophone, "Do you love me," reverberates throughout the text.

The rest of the book concerns Ida, Rufus's sister and an aspiring singer; Vivaldo, Ida's lover, Rufus's best friend, and an aspiring novelist; Eric, a white actor from the South and Rufus's erstwhile lover who has fled to France; Yves, Eric's current lover; and Cass Silenski and her novelist husband Richard, both Vivaldo's friends. Purposely resisting a discernible plot, Baldwin's postmodernist text traverses spatial, temporal, and personal boundaries: the transatlantic setting includes Greenwich Village, Harlem, Alabama, and France; time vacillates between past and present; and characters who would be labeled straight or gay, black or white, male or female, rich or poor all commingle, albeit painfully. Redemption occurs only when one exorcises his or her demons, often rooted in the aforementioned oppositions. Baldwin's characters must divest themselves of "safe" distinctions—for instance, Vivaldo must atone for failing Rufus through a sexual union with Eric, the novel's unifying figure. Especially cogent is how Baldwin resists facile categories of "good" and "bad" characters: blacks and whites can alternatively be victims and victimizers. Apropos of his religious background, Baldwin posits that only through pain, suffering, and acceptance can one enter another country—a metaphoric utopia that eliminates artificial, socially constructed distinctions. The novel ends with Ida-Vivaldo and Eric-Yves tentatively reconciling.

Another Country remains both manifesto and cultural history, a document of the turbulent 1960s. The novel created controversy both critically and popularly: Robert Bone called it "a failure on the grand scale," while citizens complained to J. Edgar Hoover about its "pornographic" content, which resulted in an FBI inquiry. But other critics such as Langston *Hughes recognized the novel's "power," the basis of which Baldwin himself elucidates: " . . . *Another Country* was harder and more challenging than anything I'd ever attempted, and I didn't cheat in it" (Fred L. Standley and Louis H. Pratt, eds., *Conversations with James Baldwin*, 1989). Indeed, Baldwin's multicultural epic disrupts and challenges American racial and sexual discourse. As its continuing popularity attests, *Another Country* assiduously explores the conundrum of the self and its potential for love.

• Robert A. Bone, *The Negro Novel in America*, 1965. Louis H. Pratt, James Baldwin, 1978.

—Keith Clark

ANSA, TINA McELROY (b. 1949), fiction writer, essayist, and journalist. Tina McElroy Ansa was born in Macon, Georgia, and educated at Mount DeSales, a Catholic school in Macon, and at Spelman College in Atlanta. Early in her career, she worked primarily as a journalist. She freelanced and worked for the *Atlanta Constitution* and for the *Charlotte Observer* (N.C.). She has also conducted writing workshops in Georgia at Brunswick College, Emory University, and Spelman College.

Ansa's best-known work is her fiction. She may be considered a southern writer, for her fiction clearly draws on the physical landscape, specifically the middle Georgia setting, and the mores and folkways that shape the psyche of the American South. Unlike much of southern fiction, however, her tales are devoid of the subtextual exploration of the undercurrent of dysfunction and perversion that exists in the South. That is not to say that her fictive worlds are without dysfunction or moral conflict. Her fiction, however, confronts such problems openly in the worlds of the texts. Her novels and short fiction reflect the positive impact of her having grown up in a middle-class family in the racially segregated South. The South portrayed in her fiction consists of a supportive, closely bonded, and self-sufficient African American community that renders itself impervious to the horrors of southern racism. More specifically, her fiction explores some of the dynamics of the African American female experience.

Ansa's two major works are her novels *Baby of the Family* (1989) and *Ugly Ways* (1993). Both make use of traditional folk beliefs and the conventions of the ghost story. Ansa's fiction avoids self-conscious polemic and the predictability of protest fiction. The soundly middle-class McPhersons of *Baby of the Family* and the Lovejoys of *Ugly Ways* enjoy affluent existences and are relatively unharassed by racism and overt, brutal sexism. The dilemmas faced by these families stem from internal family issues rather than external forces.

Upon its publication, *Baby of the Family* was named a Notable Book of the Year in 1989 and 1990 by the *New York Times Book Review*. The novel won the 1989 Georgia Authors Series Award and was cited by the American Library Association as a best book for young adults in 1990. Set in the fictive town of Mulberry, the novel depicts the coming of age of Lena

McPherson who, like Ansa herself, was born in the late 1940s with a caul, an indicator, according to folk belief, that a child is endowed for life with psychic powers. Unfortunately, her mother, Nellie, discounts folk tradition and inadvertently subjects Lena to a childhood of frustration and fearful experiences. What thus becomes Lena's affliction, however, is countered by the affluence and strong emotional support of the McPherson household. Buffered by the family's love, Lena escapes being overwhelmed by her difference from her peers. Simultaneously, because of her connection to the supernatural, Lena acquires information about African American traditions and roots necessary for her spiritual coming of age. The novel, therefore, suggests that the ideal existence for African Americans is one that embraces traditional American success while respecting African American traditions.

Also set in the fictive middle-Georgia town of Mulberry, *Ugly Ways* portrays southern African American women confronting problems of life in the 1990s. Since its publication the novel has been widely reviewed and has been at the top of the African American Best Sellers/Blackboard list and on best-sellers lists compiled by the *Quarterly Black Review of Books* and the *African American Literary Review*. In the novel, Ansa subverts the image of the African American family dominated and sustained by the strong African American matriarch. In this novel, the three successful Lovejoy sisters, Betty, Emily, and Annie Ruth, who have gathered in Mulberry for the funeral of Mudear, their mother, confront the neuroses that prevent them from fully enjoying life. The barrier to their sound emotional health has been Mudear's emotional absenteeism, psychologically abusive behavior, and her refusal to care for them physically. The story is told from each sister's point of view with Mudear's recalcitrant spirit furnishing commentary and supplying her own story throughout the narrative. Situated, then, in an African American context, *Ugly Ways* is a cautionary tale that suggests the need for reasonable alternatives to the traditional roles assigned to mothers.

In 1996, Ansa published a third novel, *The Hand I Fan With*, which depicts an adult Lena as a successful businesswoman engaged in a steamy affair with a ghost she has conjured up. This novel has been well received as all of Ansa's fiction. Her works are widely read and taught and bear the hallmarks of enduring American classics.

—Carol P. Marsh-Lockett

ATKINS, RUSSELL (b. 1926), poet, composer, theorist, editor, and leading innovator in experimental artistic movements of the 1940s through the 1970s. Born 25 February 1926 in Cleveland, Ohio, Russell Atkins began studying piano at age seven with his mother. From childhood, he exhibited talent in painting, drawing, music, and writing. By age thirteen he had won several poetry contests. Atkins published his first poem in 1944 in his high school yearbook. With the support of prominent literary figures, Atkins published his poetry in journals and newspapers, including *Experiment* (1947–1951) and the *New York Times* (1951).

Atkins continued his studies of music, performance, and the visual arts through Cleveland College, Cleveland Music School Settlement, Cleveland Institute of Music, Karamu Theatre, and Cleveland School of Art. Musical training is a key to Atkins's poetic style since musical structures are central in his writing.

In 1950 Atkins cofounded what is probably the oldest black-owned literary magazine, *Free Lance*, a publication of avant-garde writing that contributed to the development of New American poetry. He created a style of concrete poetry in which visual presentation of words on the page predominates. He experimented stylistically with the extreme use of the apostrophe, embedding of words within words, and use of continuous words. In the mid-1950s he began utilizing an abstract technique he called "phenomenalism," which juxtaposed unfamiliar and familiar elements. Atkins advocated using the imagination "to exploit range, to create a body of effect, event, colors, characteristics, moods, verbal stresses pushed to a maximum." He did not try to make his work comprehensible to casual readers but strove for dense complexity of meaning.

Atkins experimented with "poems in play forms," publishing two plays in 1954, *The Abortionist* and *The Corpse*. Like his poetry, his plays radically challenged conventions of both form and content.

In its 1955–1956 issue, *Free Lance* published Atkins's influential article, "A Psychovisual Perspective for 'Musical' Composition." Using Gestalt theory of pattern formation, Atkins argues for the brain and not the ear as the focus of composition.

In 1960 Atkins published his first collection of poetry, *A Podium Presentation*. Subsequent volumes include *Phenomena* (1961), *Objects* (1963), *Objects 2* (1964), *Heretofore* (1968), *The Nail, to Be Set to Music* (1970), *Maleficium* (1971), *Here in The* (1976), and *Whichever* (1978).

• Eugene Redmond, *Drumvoices: The Mission of Afro-American Poetry, A Critical History*, 1976. Ronald Henry High, "Russell Atkins," in *DLB*, vol. 41, *Afro-American Poets since 1955*, eds. Trudier Harris and Thadious M. Davis, 1985, pp. 24–32.

—Jennifer Burton

"Atlanta Compromise Speech." *See* "Atlanta Exposition Address."

"Atlanta Exposition Address." The turning point of Booker T. *Washington's tenure as African American leader was his address to the Cotton States and International Exposition at Atlanta in 1895. Before the address, referred to as "The Atlanta Compromise Address" or "The Atlanta Exposition Address," Washington was the head of the Tuskegee Institute in Atlanta;

afterward, he was the acknowledged leader of the African American people.

Washington's address essentially ratified the status quo in southern race relations, which had been on a decline since Reconstruction. In the speech he called for African Americans to work for their salvation through economic advancement, and for southern whites to help them on this path. "To those of my race who depend on bettering their condition in a foreign land, or who underestimate the importance of cultivating friendly relations with the Southern white man who is their next neighbor, I would say cast down your bucket where you are, cast it down in making friends, in every manly way, of the people of all races by whom we are surrounded." He also downplayed the quest for civil equality in the South, reassuring his white audience: "In all things that are purely social we can be as separate as the fingers, yet one as the hand in all things essential to mutual progress." Economic advancement was more important to African Americans in the South than civil rights, Washington maintained. Once black people had made a success in the world of work, they could expect ultimately to be respected by whites as fellow citizens.

The African American response to the "Atlanta Exposition Address" was initially supportive. But in *The *Souls of Black Folk* (1903) W. E. B. *Du Bois took exception to what he saw as Washington's abandonment of the historic obligation of African American leadership to demand fair play and justice for their people. Washington's doctrine "has tended to make the whites, North and South, shift the burden of the Negro problem to the Negro's shoulders and stand aside as critical and rather pessimistic spectators; when in fact the burden belongs to the nation." Growing opposition to the ideas articulated in the "Atlanta Exposition Address" led to the founding of the NAACP in 1909.

To his supporters, Washington was making the best of limited oportunities for African Americans in the South. To his detractors, Washington was abetting the continuous subjugation of African Americans by letting whites believe that African Americans were content to wait for the rights guaranteed by the Constitution. As the twentieth century progressed, Du Bois's view prevailed, but for a period of twenty years and more, the views espoused by Washington in the Atlanta Exposition speech generally received widespread approval from African Americans and whites alike.

• August Meier, *Negro Thought in America, 1880–1915*, 1963. Emma Lou Thornbrough, ed., *Booker T. Washington*, 1969.

—Jonathan Silverman

ATTAWAY, WILLIAM (1911–1986), novelist, composer, and scriptwriter. William Attaway was born 19 November 1911, in Greenville, Mississippi, to Florence Parry Attaway, a teacher, and William Alexander Attaway, a physician and founder of the National Negro Insurance Association. When he was five, his family moved to Chicago, taking part in the Great Migration that he later chronicled as a novelist. The family moved to protect the children from the corrosive racial attitudes of the South.

Attaway's early interest in literature was sparked by Langston *Hughes's poetry and by his sister who encouraged him to write for her theater groups. He attended the University of Illinois until his father's death, when Attaway left school and traveled west. He lived as a vagabond for two years, working a variety of jobs and writing. In 1933 he returned to Chicago and resumed his schooling, graduating in 1936. Attaway's play *Carnival* (1935) was produced at the University of Illinois, and in 1936 his short story, "The Tale of the Blackamoor," was published in *Challenge*.

Attaway was involved with the Federal Writers' Project in 1935 and befriended Richard *Wright, whom he once invited to speak to the university literary society. Attaway reported that as Wright read "Big Boy Leaves Home," an unflinching look at the racism and violence that forces one young African American to leave the South, audience members fled, finally leaving only Wright and himself in the room. Attaway understood that the issues he would address in his own fiction might disturb readers, but the event did not dissuade him from providing blunt depictions of racism and struggle.

After graduation, Attaway lived in New York City and held several jobs including labor organizer. While working as an actor, Attaway completed his first novel, written in the tradition of naturalist and proletarian novels of the period. *Let Me Breathe Thunder* (1939) follows two young white migrant farmworkers, Step and Ed, who travel by rail in the west at the end of the Depression. They befriend a nine-year-old Mexican youth, Hi Boy, whose optimism serves as a contrast to Step's cynicism. While many critics emphasized Attaway's focus on whites, some noted the marginalized status of those characters and the strength of the novel's African American characters.

Blood on the Forge (1941), called by critic Robert Bone the most perceptive novel about the Great Migration, centers on three African American half brothers who escape a lynch mob in 1919 and leave Kentucky for the steel mills of Pennsylvania. Like other literature of the migration, this novel questions the notion of the North as the promised land. While the brothers escape the violence of the South, they soon encounter the violence of northern industrial capitalism. The three are ultimately devastated: Big Mat is killed, Chinatown blinded, and Melody spiritually injured. Many critics compared the novel to Wright's **Native Son*, especially linking Big Mat with Wright's *Bigger Thomas. Attaway's use of language that expresses a sense of the folk idiom has been compared to Zora Neale *Hurston's use of African American oral tradition. Ralph *Ellison praised the book's examination of transition and conflict but critiqued its omission of characters not destroyed by the transition north, saying that Attaway understood the destruction of folk culture but missed its regeneration in other forms.

While well received by critics, Attaway's books sold poorly, and he wrote no more novels. Although he published the short story "Death of a Rag Doll" in 1947, he turned his creative focus to composing and arranging music (he was especially interested in West Indian music and collaborated with his friend Harry Belafonte). He published two music-oriented books: *Calypso Song Book* (1957) and *Hear America Singing* (1967). Attaway also explored other media, writing scripts for radio, television, and film. In 1966, he wrote the script for *One Hundred Years of Laughter*, a television special on African American humor. He wrote a screenplay adaptation of *The Man*, Irving Wallace's novel about the first African American president. Attaway's version, foregrounding racial conflict and emphasizing African American voices, was ultimately rejected by the producers.

Attaway had some involvement in the civil rights movement, including the 1965 voting rights march to Selma, Alabama. He lived in Barbados for eleven years, with his wife and two children. His last years were spent in California, where he worked on the script for *The Atlanta Child Murders* (1985). He died in Los Angeles in 1986.

As one of the first African American novelists to focus on the subject, Attaway is primarily known for his contribution to the literature of the Great Migration. He vividly portrayed the causes and often devastating consequences of that exodus. While refusing to sentimentalize, he wrote with compassion and rich detail about working-class characters of different races and their various, usually tragic, struggles.

• Ralph Ellison, "Transition," *Negro Quarterly* 1 (Spring 1942): 87–92. Edward Margolies, "Migration: William Attaway and *Blood on the Forge*," in *Native Sons: A Critical Study of Twentieth-Century Negro American Authors*, 1968, pp. 47–64. Richard Yarborough, afterword in *Blood on the Forge*, 1941; rpt. 1987. Samuel Garren, "'He Had passion': William Attaway's Screenplay Drafts of Irving Wallace's *The Man*," *CLA Journal* 37 (Mar. 1994): 245–260.

—Christina Accomando

AUBERT, ALVIN (b. 1930), poet, educator, editor, short story writer, and dramatist. Born 12 March 1930 in Lutcher, Louisiana, Alvin Bernard Aubert's presence in African American literature is marked by his creative, editorial, and scholarly contributions to the discipline. As a poet his works often reflect upon childhood and adolescence in Louisiana, and through these observations comment on the ubiquitous states of human existence. As the founding editor of *Obsidian*, he has provided a journal with a nurturing environment for the publication of African American literature and theoretical discourse.

Aubert earned a bachelor's degree in English literature with a minor in French from Southern University in Baton Rouge in 1959. As an undergraduate he was encouraged by Blyden Jackson, chair of the English department, to consider graduate studies and a career in teaching. He received a Woodrow Wilson Fellowship for graduate studies to the University of Michigan at Ann Arbor where he completed a master's degree in English literature the following year.

His first teaching position was in the English department at Southern where he coordinated and taught one of the first courses on African American literature offered by the university. Citing his own lack of knowledge as a student, he sought to increase others' awareness of African American literature by reading texts from the Harlem Renaissance to the present. Additional graduate work at the University of Illinois, on sixteenth- and seventeenth-century authors Shakespeare and Milton, illuminated the importance of allusions and their ability to enrich a particular text by referring to myths, the Bible, and earlier literatures. Applying these studies on language to African American literature, he began to recognize the means through which expressive language was capable of eloquently describing everyday activities. Aubert's career continued with his teaching African American literature and creative writing at both the State University of New York in Fredonia (1970–1979) and later at Wayne State University (1979–1992). He founded *Obsidian: Black Literature in Review* in 1975, which functioned as a catalyst for aspiring writers to publish. He remained the journal's editor until it ceased publication in 1982. In 1986 the journal was reissued as *Obsidian II* and is published under the auspices of the English department at North Carolina State University.

Considering the African American poet's relationship to the community, Aubert has at times debated the poet's success or failure in effectively communicating to others. Given the inconclusive nature of the dilemma, he resigned himself to a philosophy that the reader should be educated in language. This "education" was not formal but rather an individual's sensitivity to language and its unlimited potential for conveying and re-creating experiences and sentiments. Aubert rejected notions of artistic compromise and regarded the poet as belonging and committed to poetry.

It was this type of sensibility that provoked criticism from colleagues who often regarded his works as dispassionate and allusive. While others writing during the 1960s and 1970s produced politically and socially charged poems reflecting the times, his poetry remained centered on personal experiences. Therefore his writing contrasted with that of others by reminding readers that, when closely viewed, individual members of the African American community celebrated unique experiences.

Since 1966, Aubert's poetry has been included in numerous journals and anthologies. Over the years his poetry has experienced an evolution of themes and self-awareness. His first collection, *Against the Blues* (1972), primarily focused on childhood in Louisiana while *Feeling Through* (1975), experimenting with techniques, reflected on military experiences, knowledge of African American writings, and adolescence. With *South Louisiana: New and Selected Poems* (1985), he again referenced African American art and literature although the overall collection reflected a diverse range of experiences. This collection along with *If Winter Come: Collected Poems 1967–1992* (1994) included several previously published poems and new poems suggesting Aubert's arrival at a crossroads in life. *If Winter Come* ranges from childhood experiences ("My Dog Ringo/The Dolphin") and relationships ("Woman in Me"), to African Americans ("Like Miles Said," "James *Baldwin, 1924–1987") and the poet's work ("Here Now"). His last collection, *Harlem Wrestler* (1995), incorporates these familiar themes and continues with reflections on national holidays ("Dear Columbus/11-11-93," "MLK Day 1992"), retirement ("Legacies"), self-awareness ("And No Harm's Done to the Tree"), and maturing romance ("Lovely Lady").

Besides poetry, Aubert's creative works have included short stories and plays. His fiction has appeared in literary journals and an anthology. His first play, *Home from Harlem* (1986), was an adaptation of Paul Laurence *Dunbar's *The *Sport of the Gods*. In the mid-1990s Aubert was revising his second play and writing a first novel. Maintaining his tradition, both stories are set in Louisiana.

• James Schokoff, "Aubert's Poems Have Depth," *Buffalo Courier Express*, 8 June 1973, 22. Herbert Woodward Martin, "Alvin Aubert: South Louisiana: New and Selected Poems," *Black American Literature Forum* 21.3 (Fall 1987): 343–348. Jerry W. Ward, Jr., "Alvin Aubert: Literature, History, Ethnicity," *Xavier Review* 7.2 (1987): 1–12. Tom Dent, "Alvin Aubert: South Louisiana: New and Selected Poems," *Black American Literature Forum* 22.1 (Spring 1988): 127–129.

—R. Goldman Vander

AUN' PEGGY, a powerful conjure woman whose magic and spells lie at the heart of *Uncle Julius McAdoo's tales in *The *Conjure Woman* (1899) by Charles Waddell *Chesnutt. Aun' Peggy's abilities, deeply rooted in African American folk knowledge and traditions, add mystery, strength, and purpose to Uncle Julius's stories. Feared and respected by white and black, Aun' Peggy lives as a free woman outside of Patesville (Fayetteville, N.C.). She is a shrewd, independent businesswoman who insists on payment for her services. Working with roots, snakeskins, and "yuther conjuh-fixins," she gives people rheumatism and fits, causes them to waste away, and turns them into animals. Only Uncle Jube (in "The Gray Wolf's Ha'nt") is a more powerful conjurer. Aun' Peggy's spells or "goophers" are used for a variety of purposes, often to resist white control. In "Sis' Becky's Pickaninny" she reunites a slave mother and child by turning the child into a bird. In "Mars Jeems's Nightmare" she turns a cruel plantation owner into a slave so that he might experience firsthand the difficult lives his slaves lead. Some of Aun' Peggy's conjuring is not for the benefit of the African American community. In "The Goophered Grapevine" she casts a deadly spell for Mars Dugal to keep slaves away from his scuppernongs. Thus, Aun' Peggy is a complex character whose power and presence are pivotal in *The Conjure Woman*. She also serves as a literary foremother to such modern-day conjure women as those depicted in Gloria *Naylor's **Mama Day* (1988).

• Sylvia Render, introduction to *The Short Fiction of Charles W. Chesnutt*, 1974. William L. Andrews, *The Literary Career of Charles Chesnutt*, 1980.

—Paula Gallant Eckard

AUNT CHLOE FLEET is the unifying character for six poems in Frances Ellen Watkins *Harper's *Sketches of Southern Life* (1872): "Aunt Chloe," "The Deliverance," "Aunt Chloe's Politics," "Learning to Read," "Church Building," and "The Reunion." This poetry emulates the slave narrative, a literary form that characterized much of the literature written by and about African Americans during the nineteenth century. It is distinctive because Harper invented a dialect technique that used aural association and syntax rather than phonetics to create an authentic black voice. This innovation is seen in literature by African American writers of subsequent generations, a technique that effectively captures the dialect without reducing folk characters to stereotypes or caricatures.

Aunt Chloe's voice represents the agony of all slave women when the slave mistress sells Aunt Chloe's children in order to defray a debt. The dramatic style of the narrative also includes other characters who warn and console Chloe, demonstrating the strength of the slave community as a social and political network. The work's broader setting is the Civil War and Reconstruction, and the poems reflect the perspective of the black woman as Aunt Chloe interprets those events and struggles for freedom, literacy, and self-determination.

The theme of the poetry is a spiritual message that conveys a deep belief in Jesus as the spirit of salvation, rebirth, and justice. Aunt Chloe's voice exhibits wit, tenacity, and strong political views. Recited before black and white audiences, and sometimes before exclusively black female audiences, the book was widely circulated as Harper traveled and promoted black liberation and women's rights throughout the country.

• Frances Smith Foster, ed., *A Brighter Coming Day: A Frances Ellen Watkins Harper Reader*, 1990. Melba Joyce Boyd, *Discarded Legacy: Politics and Poetics in the Life of Frances E. W. Harper 1825–1911*, 1994.

—Melba Joyce Boyd

AUNT JEMIMA, trademark, stereotype, cultural icon to many whites, and racist caricature to many African Americans. For Chris Rutt and Charles Underwood, Aunt Jemima was the perfect symbol for their experiment with the first packaged pancake mix. These white entrepreneurs attended a vaudeville show in 1889, featuring black-faced comedians in a New Orleans–style cakewalk tune entitled "Aunt Jemima." Emblazoned on the posters announcing the act grinned the familiar image of mammy. Rutt appropriated the name and image, for who could better sell processed foods to American housewives than mammy, ready to save them from kitchen drudgery? Barbara Christian's *Black Women Novelists* (1980) analyzes how Jemima kept particular images about white women intact. African American writers used the stereotype subversively, as described by Trudier Harris in *From Mammies to Militants* (1982).

Jemima, the offshoot of irascible mammy, was sweet, jolly, even-tempered, and polite. Jemima, Hebrew for "dove," was Job's youngest daughter, symbolizing innocence, gentleness, and peace. But the name belies its meaning. The caricature connotes not naïveté but stupidity, not peace but docility. Jemima was an obese, darkly pigmented, broad-bosomed, handkerchief-headed, gingham-dressed, elderly servant content in her subjugation.

African American resentment regarding Aunt Jemima stemmed not from a rejection of the maternal or domestic image she presented, but from unabashed attempts to create, with this single image, a monolithic African American woman and market her to the world. By 1900, more than 200,000 Jemima dolls, 150,000 Jemima cookie jars, and numerous memorabilia in the form of black-faced buttons and toothpick holders had been sold.

R. T. Davis brought to life the caricature when he purchased the trademark in 1890. He found a three hundred pound model in the person of Nancy Green, a former slave born in Kentucky, who possessed perfectly even white teeth, a stark contrast to her dark complexion. Green signed a lifetime contract with Aunt Jemima. The highlight of her career was her 1893 appearance at the Chicago World's Fair where her pancake-flipping antics and tales of slavery concretized a negative stereotype of African American women. Ironically, the controversial image transformed her life to one of affluence. Green died a celebrity, lauded as the Pancake Queen.

Anna Robinson promoted Jemima's image from 1933 to 1950, and Edith Wilson, a show personality, transformed her to modern, with a stylish hairdo and pearl earrings. This version adorns the pancake box today, but for many African Americans the light brown skin and updated clothes do little to repair the disfigured image of the past.

• Purd Wright, "The Life of Aunt Jemima, The Most Famous Colored Woman in the World," in *Brands, Trademarks and Good Will: The Story of the Quaker Oats Company*, ed. Arthur F. Marquette, 1967, pp. 137–158. Nagueyalti Warren, "From Uncle Tom to Cliff Huxtable, Aunt Jemima to Aunt Nell: Images of Blacks in Film and the Television Industry," in *Images of Blacks in American Culture*, ed. Jessie Carney Smith, 1988, pp. 51–117.

—Nagueyalti Warren

AUSTIN, DORIS JEAN (c. 1949–1994), novelist and essayist. Doris Jean Austin is the author of one novel, *After the Garden* (1987), and a frequent contributor to such periodicals as *Essence* and the *New York Times Book Review*. In *Essence*, she has published articles such as "The Men in My Life," "Fighting Off the Fears," and "Holistic Healing: Mind: Taming the Demons" (all 1992).

Austin was born in Mobile, Alabama, where she lived until she was six, when her family moved to Jersey City, New Jersey. That city serves as the locale for her fictional creation. She has been a MacDowell Colony fellow and a recipient of the DeWitt Wallace/Reader's Digest Award for Literary Excellence. That recognition came with the publication of *After the Garden*.

Episodic in structure, *After the Garden* takes place over a twenty-three year period, from 1939 to 1962. It presents a self-contained African American world little impacted by the turbulent historical events of the period, although they are mentioned from time to time, and little impacted by white racism. It presents a rich and varied African American world in the middle-class community of Astor Place, the working-class community of Kearney Avenue, the school, the neighborhood bar, and the church.

Growing up in a three-generational household, Austin experienced firsthand the value of strong kinship ties. The novel reflects that. Beginning on the day that heroine Elzina James begins menstruation, the novel is an extended coming-of-age story. Elzina must resolve allegiances to Rosalie Tompkins, the puritanical and strong-willed grandmother who raised her, and her husband Jesse, whom her grandmother despises because of his lower-class background.

The novel is one of the narratives in African American literature that dramatizes the class conflicts and disparate value systems found within the African American community. Rosalie Tompkins, whose life revolves around the church and raising her granddaughter, has only two wishes before she dies: to return to the red clay of her native, beloved Alabama and to see Elzina enrolled at Tuskegee Institute. Her wishes are thwarted when Elzina, at fifteen, loses her virginity to the high-school heartthrob Jesse, of the free-spirited, hard-partying James clan, marries him, and has a son, Charles. The young couple resides in Rosalie's house and the grandmother-granddaughter relationship remains unchanged by Elzina's marriage and presumed adult status. Jesse chafes under Rosalie's thinly veiled contempt for him and resentment over the thwarted plans for her granddaughter. His unemployment and Elzina's refusal to ask her grandmother for money for him to finance a gas station exacerbate the tensions in the marriage. At the height of a quarrel Jesse tells Elzina: "'We ain't got no business married. . . . At least I know my black ass ain't got no business married to no Tompkins! I ain't nothing but a po' ol' field nigger, that's me!'" Jesse becomes an accomplice in an armed robbery and receives a harsh sentence. Although Rosalie dies midway through the novel, she lives on in the values instilled in her granddaughter, whose life revolves around being a model single mother and the proprietor of a well-run, profitable boardinghouse.

Truselle James, Elzina's mother-in-law, the matriarch of the James clan, provides a contrast to Rosalie. Whereas Rosalie's house is like "a musty old museum," Truselle's house, the headquarters of her large extended family, is permeated by the smell of barbecue and the laughter of her grandchildren. The sexlessness of Rosalie, suggested by her long, flat breasts (which remind Elzina of soft, empty leather purses) contrasts with the fecundity of Truselle, who, as a kind of earth mother, has ten children by an assortment of men. The large-hearted Truselle nurtures the troubled members, not only of her own family, but also Orelia Jeter, the mother of Jesse's illegitimate daughter, and even Elzina following her complete nervous collapse brought about by her husband's tragic death from a freak hunting accident. The novel ends on a note of female intergenerational harmony. Just as Truselle as surrogate mother has been instrumental to Elzina's recovery, a recovered Elzina assumes a healing role of surrogate motherhood to Jesse's illegitimate, orphaned daughter.

Well-known African American critic Robert G. O'Meally reviewed the novel in the *New York Times* and praised, above all else, Austin's "courageous confrontation of character"; he deemed it "most impressive." While Austin was not prolific, she certainly struck a note in African American literary creativity and popular magazine writing that warrants further study. *Streetlights: Illuminating Tales of the Urban Black Experience*, which Austin edited with Martin Simmons, was published posthumously in 1996.

• Blyden Jackson, *A History of Afro-American Literature*, 1989. Valerie Smith, *African American Writers*, 1991. Frank N. Magill, *Masterpieces of African-American Literature*, 1992.

—Phiefer L. Browne

Autobiography of an Ex-Colored Man, The. Originally published anonymously in 1912, James Weldon *Johnson's novel *The Autobiography of an Ex-Colored Man* advances the narrative of the "tragic mulatto" who passes for white beyond the constraints imposed by the form as it was practiced in nineteenth-century American literature. Though in some ways conforming to the conventional novel of passing in suggesting that a mixed racial heritage makes a person incapable of functioning in either the black or the white world, Johnson's novel turns this notion on its head by invoking double consciousness, as his narrator makes clear:

> It is this, too, which makes the colored people of this country, in reality, a mystery to the whites. It is a difficult thing for a white man to learn what a colored man really thinks; because, generally, with the latter an additional and different light must be brought to bear on what he thinks. . . . This gives to every colored man, in proportion to his intellectuality, a sort of dual personality. . . .

As this passage demonstrates, Johnson's novel is the first to give voice in fictional form to "the Veil," W. E. B. *Du Bois's construction of African American racial consciousness.

The novel's plot deals with the product of a clandestine love affair between a white Southerner and a fair-skinned African American woman. Compelled to relocate to the North, the unnamed narrator of the story is reared in a small town in Connecticut, where he displays a prodigious talent as a pianist. Learning from his teacher that he is not white, he decides to attend Atlanta University, a black school in the South. But after his funds are stolen, he takes a job in a cigar factory, where he mingles with blacks of different classes and hues while gaining exposure to African American culture. When the factory closes, the narrator moves to New York City and joins a bohemian world in which he works as a ragtime piano player. Attachment to a white patron enables the narrator to make a tour of Europe, where he decides to devote his talent to the development of vernacular African American music into classical musical forms. Returning to the roots of African American musical traditions in the South, the narrator is so shocked by a lynching that he rejects his new vocation and spurns identification with "a people that could with impunity be treated worse than animals." Cutting himself off from his cultural heritage, he returns to New York to pass for white, become a successful businessman, and marry and raise a family on the white side of the color line. Only at the end of the novel does he acknowledge the tragedy of having sold what he calls his "birthright" for "a mess of pottage."

Though reviewers hailed the novel as a sociological study, especially after Johnson acknowledged his authorship in 1927, the greater importance of the book lies in its rejection of didacticism and overt propaganda in favor of a psychological realism that revealed the complex conflicting negotiations informing an African American's quest for identity as an artist, a person of color, and a modern American male.

• Robert B. Stepto, *From Behind the Veil: A Study of Afro-American Narrative*, 1979. Bernard W. Bell, *The Afro-American Novel and Its Tradition*, 1987.

—Herman Beavers

Autobiography of Malcolm X, The. Published posthumously, *The Autobiography of Malcolm X* (1965) was written with the assistance of Alex Haley, and, in all published editions, is accompanied by a long epilogue of Haley's that offers his perspective on Malcolm X and the making of the work. Extremely well received by both whites and African Americans, the work helped give voice to the emerging Black Power movement, offered a spectacular example of dedication and accomplishment, and presented an indictment of racism in the United States. The *Autobiography* covers Malcolm's life from his childhood in East Lansing, Michigan, through his time as a street hustler, prison inmate, Nation of Islam minister, and, finally, his last year as an independent Muslim minister and black nationalist.

As is common with the genre, especially for African Americans, the *Autobiography* is at once a sociological document and an assertion of individuality. Malcolm X vacillates between presenting his life as representative and as exemplary. His account of his criminal past, in which he sold drugs and prostituted women, displays the degrading effects of racism upon African Americans. His account of his transformation in prison, in which he read extensively and adopted the Nation of Islam's strict moral code, presents a story of remarkable dedication and will.

Like much of the literature of the turbulent 1960s, the text also contains the rhetoric of protest. By utilizing personal experience to argue for a major restructuring of American society, the work echoes a mode of African American literature descended from the slave narratives. The later chapters blend accounts of Malcolm's years as a minister with excerpts from his speeches condemning white America. As the text concentrates less on the incidents of Malcolm's life, the drama focuses on the development of Malcolm's philosophy from the strict "all whites are devils" beliefs of the Nation of Islam to a less rigid, more humanist approach to race.

Because Malcolm's life changed rapidly as he composed the *Autobiography*, and because he was assassinated before he read and revised the final draft that Haley had sent him, the book, like the life, seems incomplete. The *Autobiography* captures a mind in flux. Opinions contradict each other in the text, especially those on the Nation, the organization that he credits with saving his life, but that he split from rancorously while he was fashioning his life story. Such contradictions generally enhance the text, for they present an attractive protean self, one willing to learn and change when confronted with new knowledge. The extraordinary blend of so many autobiographical modes, and so many "Malcolms," deeply enriches both the text and its subject.

Through its immediate and enduring popularity, the *Autobiography* is primarily responsible for what biographer Peter Goldman calls the "beatification" of Malcolm X, making him an icon for black pride, achievement, and protest. Without his life story, Malcolm X might have been forgotten. The *Autobiography* guarantees his permanence on the American cultural landscape and arguably stands as the most stunning accomplishment of a remarkable life.

• Peter Goldman, *The Death and Life of Malcolm X*, 2d ed., 1979. David Gallen, *Malcolm X as They Knew Him*, 1992.

—J. D. Scrimgeour

Autobiography of Miss Jane Pittman, The (1971). Widely praised as Ernest J. Gaines's best book, this historical novel builds upon fugitive slave narratives as well as the oral tradition. The first-person narrator, some 110 years old, is one of the most memorable characters in all African American fiction. Set in rural Louisiana, the novel is divided into four parts—The War Years, Reconstruction, The Plantation, and The Quarters—that progress from the 1860s to the 1960s. It is the immediacy and authenticity of Miss Jane's voice, the book's greatest literary achievement, that enable the author to unify the text's panoramic sweep and its highly episodic structure. Jane is both an effectively realized individual and a representative figure, a spokesperson for the African American experience from slavery times to the era of the civil rights movement. Gaines's "Introduction" presents her story as the outcome of a series of interviews by the novel's ostensible editor not only with Jane but with other members of her community, and Gaines thereby stresses both the centrality of the oral tradition in African American culture and the interdependence of the individual and the group. The popular oral history methodology of the time of the novel's composition recognized that people like Miss Jane had been excluded from traditional histories. Gaines thus perceived his book as filling a void in the historical record, as embodying what he termed "folk autobiography."

The opening chapter, in which Jane abandons her slave name, Ticey, and refuses—despite a beating—to relinquish her new name, testifies to Gaines's concern with identity, a major theme in African American literature generally and in the autobiography as a genre. This episode also demonstrates qualities in Jane's character that persist throughout the book, helping to establish her heroic stature: determination, personal integrity, self-assertion, endurance. Much of the novel focuses on the violence with which such attempts at African American self-determination are met by whites: the massacre of the newly emancipated slaves in book 1; the assassination of Ned (whom Jane adopts after his mother is killed in the massacre) in book 2; and the murder of Jimmy Aaron, a civil rights worker, at the end of book 4, an act that fails, however, to prevent Jane from joining the protest march with which the novel closes. The deaths of Ned and Jimmy highlight the book's pervasive religious elements, for both characters are depicted as Christlike figures, men whose blood is shed to redeem their people. In book 3, significantly, Gaines portrays the white Tee Bob in similar terms when Tee Bob commits suicide because southern mores preclude his marrying a Creole. Gaines thus reveals the destructive consequences of racism for the entire South, indeed for all of American society. Written in the years immediately following the civil rights era, Miss Jane's narrative, more than any other single book, helped Americans understand the personal experiences and emotions, as well as the historical events, that had produced the revolution in U.S. race relations during the 1960s.

• Keith E. Byerman, *Fingering the Jagged Grain: Tradition and Form in Recent Black Fiction*, 1985. John F. Callahan, *In the African-American Grain: The Pursuit of Voice in Twentieth-Century Black Fiction*, 1988.

—John Lang

B

BABY SUGGS. Baby Suggs Holy is the mother-in-law of *Sethe Suggs, the protagonist of Toni *Morrison's **Beloved* (1987). The novel begins with Sethe's escape to Baby Suggs, who lives in Ohio. Halle, Sethe's husband and Baby Suggs's son, has succeeded in buying his mother's freedom by working extra on Sundays. Baby Suggs becomes a holy figure and preaches self-love to her people in an open area near her home. Sethe arrives mutilated, bruised, and worn out, and Baby Suggs tenderly ministers to her daughter-in-law and her baby, healing Sethe's body.

After Sethe's arrival, Stamp Paid (the ferryman who brings the former slaves to Ohio) brings them huge buckets of blackberries, and the women decide to have a feast and share the pies with the other colored people in the area. The people, however, resent their generosity and feel that Baby Suggs is showing off; therefore, they fail to warn them of the arrival of schoolteacher, Sethe's owner, who plans to return Sethe and her children to slavery. When Sethe sees schoolteacher, she kills Beloved rather than see her returned to slavery. This incident causes the complete disillusionment of Baby Suggs, and she no longer preaches. She takes to the "keeping room" where she contemplates colors until the end of her life.

Baby Suggs's experiences as a female slave included the loss of most of her children and the additional responsibility of servicing her masters sexually. In rendering the story of the life and death of Baby Suggs, Morrison reminds the reader that Baby Suggs's life has been destroyed by slavery even though she attained physical freedom.

• Brian Finney, "Temporal Defamiliarization in Toni Morrison's Beloved," *Obsidian II* 18 (Spring 1990): 59–77. Wilfred D. Samuels and Clenora Hudson-Weems, *Toni Morrison*, 1990. Trudier Harris, *Fiction and Folklore: The Novels of Toni Morrison*, 1991. Kristin Boudreau, "Pain and the Unmaking of Self in Toni Morrison's Beloved," *Contemporary Literature* 36.3 (Fall 1995): 447–465. Danielle Taylor-Guthrie, "Who Are the Beloved? Old and New Testaments, Old and New Communities of Faith," *Religion and Literature* 27.1 (Spring 1995): 119–129.

—Betty Taylor-Thompson

BAKER, HOUSTON A., JR. (b. 1943), critic, poet, editor, and president of the Modern Language Association (1992). In an October 1985 *Pennsylvania Gazette* profile, Houston A. Baker, Jr., speaks of his intellectual journey from graduate studies in late-Victorian literature to the then relatively uncharted field of African American literature as "a great awakening and a conversion experience rolled into one." Baker's blues journey home has resulted in the field's richest, most consistently probing body of work, and has established him as one of a handful of preeminent scholars of American literature to have emerged in the wake of the civil rights movement struggles of the 1960s.

Born in Louisville, Kentucky, Baker matriculated at Howard University, where he was elected to Phi Beta Kappa, and then earned a PhD in English at the University of California at Los Angeles in 1968. After brief stints at Yale University, the site of his conversion, and the University of Virginia, Baker moved to the University of Pennsylvania in 1974, where he has been, since 1982, a chaired professor in the humanities and, since 1986, director of the Center for the Study of Black Literature and Culture.

In his first book, *Long Black Song* (1972), which examines the resonances of folkloric tropes and images in the works of such figures as Frederick *Douglass, W. E. B. *Du Bois, and Richard *Wright, Baker pursues issues that have dominated his work. Baker's critical project constitutes a search for strategies that help expose the richness, sophistication, and distinctiveness of African American expressivity. Moving from New Critical analyses in *Singers of Daybreak* (1974); to formulations of an African American "anthropology of art" in *The Journey Back* (1980); to the poststructuralist interrogations of history, generational differences between African American critics, and literary form of his most influential study, *Blues, Ideology, and Afro-American Literature* (1984); to encounters with women's texts, feminism, and phenomenology in *Workings of the Spirit* (1991), Baker has sought to identify the constitutive sounds and meanings of blackness. In *Afro-American Poetics* (1988), he argues that "only by paying special attention to the sociology, psychology, and entrancing sounding of race does a critic of Afro-American culture arrive at an inclusive perspective."

For Baker, an informed interdisciplinarity yields an acute understanding of the complexities of the act of African American cultural production. In *The Journey Back* (1980), Baker concludes that **Narrative of the Life of Frederick Douglass* reflects not "the authentic voice of black American slavery" or of blackness more generally, but, rather, "the voice of a self transformed" by Douglass's engagement with "the linguistic codes, literary conventions, and audience expectations of a literate population." Sounding blackness, then, means self-consciously rendering how an articulation of an African American cultural inheritance is influenced by a variety of discursive and historical contexts. His sophisticated analyses of cultural production have been highly influential, and have placed Baker at the center of American academic debates in the 1980s and 1990s about such important topics as race, culture, and class.

• Michael Berube, "Power Surge: Houston Baker's Vernacular Spectacular," *Voice Literary Supplement* 109 (Oct. 1992): 15–17. Houston A. Baker, Jr., *Black Studies, Rap, and the Academy*, 1993.

—Michael Awkward

BAKER, JOSEPHINE (1906–1975), dancer, theater performer, writer, and civil rights activist. Although she spent most of her adult life living in France and touring the world, Josephine Baker was born in St. Louis, Missouri. After a difficult childhood, she left home at thirteen, starting her dance career with a vaudeville troupe called the Dixie Steppers. In the early 1920s, she worked in African American theater productions in New York such as *Shuffle Along* and *Chocolate Dandies.* In 1925 Baker left for Paris to begin her long international career with companies like Revue Nègre, Folies Bergères, and, later, the Ziegfeld Follies.

As her career evolved, Baker increasingly focused on political concerns. During World War II Baker toured North Africa while providing information to French and British intelligence. Later she used her considerable fame to advance civil rights issues during her frequent visits to the United States. In 1951 the NAACP honored her political work by declaring an official Baker Day in Harlem. Baker is also remembered for her advocacy of racial reconciliation: she adopted children of varied races and nationalities and worked throughout her life to promote racial and national cooperation.

Baker's autobiography *Josephine* (1976; trans. to English in 1977), posthumously compiled and coauthored by her estranged husband Jo Bouillon, consists of sections authored by Baker herself intermixed with commentary by Bouillon, numerous friends, professional associates, and several of her adult children. The result is a book at moments autobiographical, but strongly biographical. Her life story is essentially framed by Bouillon's editing, leaving inevitable questions as to the narrative structure that may have emerged in an autobiography completed by Baker herself. Four other volumes, all written in French, also carry some autobiographical interest because of Baker's collaborative involvement: *Les Mémoires de Joséphine Baker* (1927) and *Voyages et aventures de Joséphine Baker* (1931), both authored by Marcel Sauvage; *Joséphine Baker: Une Vie de toutes les coueurs* (1935), by André Rivollet; and *La Guerre secrète de Joséphine Baker* (1948), by Jacques Abtey. Baker also helped plan a novel dealing with racial themes, which was eventually authored by Giuseppe (Pepito) Abatino and Félix del la Camara, entitled *Mon Sang dans tes veines* (*My Blood in Your Veins*, 1931).

• Phyllis Rose, Jazz Cleopatra: *Josephine Baker in Her Time*, 1989.

—Sharon Carson

BALDWIN, JAMES (1924–1987), novelist, essayist, playwright, scriptwriter, director, poet, filmmaker, college professor, lecturer, and expatriate. Easily recognized as one of the leading African American authors, James Baldwin has contributed to a variety of genres in American literary creativity. He has especially used novels and essays to focus on his favorite themes: the failure of the promise of American democracy, questions of racial and sexual identity, the failures of the Christian church, difficult family relationships, and the political and social worlds that shaped the American "Negro" and then despised him for that shaping. Frequently employing a third person plural voice in his essays, Baldwin exhorts the exploiters and the exploited to save the country from its own destructive tendencies. An activist who put his body on the line with his politics, Baldwin was intimidatingly articulate in "telling it like it is" in interviews as well as on paper. A small man whose voice was one of the largest America had ever heard, Baldwin was intent upon pricking the consciences of all Americans in an era—particularly the 1960s—when a liberal climate was especially receptive to that pricking. Pushed slightly into the literary background with the wide publishing of works by African American women writers and the scholarly focus on their works after 1980, Baldwin published fewer book-length works but never lost sight of his ultimate objectives: to write well and to be a good man.

James Arthur Baldwin was born in Harlem, New York, on 2 August 1924. His mother, Emma Berdis Jones, gave birth to James while she was single. When Baldwin was a toddler, Jones married David Baldwin, an itinerant preacher from Louisiana, who would prove to be the bane of young Jimmy's existence. Not only did his stepfather assert that James was ugly and bore the mark of the devil, but he refused to recognize James's native intelligence or his sanctioning by white teachers. This painful autobiographical material would provide the substance of Baldwin's first novel, **Go Tell It on the Mountain* (1953). *John Grimes, the protagonist in that novel, is a precocious child applauded by white teachers and principals, but whose father cannot abide the fact that this "imposter," this illegitimate son, is infinitely more obedient and "holy" than his legitimate son. John also wrestles with homosexual leanings, which the young Baldwin, by contrast, was able to resolve fairly early in life—he had homosexual as well as heterosexual relationships. Homosexuality would serve as the theme for Baldwin's second novel, **Giovanni's Room* (1956), in which a white American slumming in Paris becomes sexually involved with a young Italian. David, the American, contemplates his sexual identity and its negative consequences on the evening that Giovanni, convicted for killing an older man who wanted sexual favors from him, is executed for that crime.

Baldwin grew up as the caretaker for his eight younger siblings. As he cradled babies in his arms, he read avidly, borrowing initially from the two Harlem public libraries and later from the Forty-second Street New York Public Library. One of the works that would prove significant for his later critical development was Harriet Beecher *Stowe's *Uncle Tom's Cabin* (1852). Baldwin asserts that he had read the book so many times by the fifth grade that his mother moved it to a shelf beyond his diminutive reach. Later, Baldwin would criticize the novel for its dependence upon the protest literature tradition. The young Jimmy's writing talent was also discovered early, and his teachers requested special assignments from him on several occasions. At Frederick Douglass Junior High School (P.S. 139), he edited the school newspaper, the *Douglass Pilot*, to which he contributed a short story and several editorials and sketches. Baldwin had the priviledge of studying with Harlem Renaissance poet Countee *Cullen, who not only taught but served as adviser to the literary club.

The best that can be said of Baldwin's teenage years is that they were uneasy. As he recounts in *The *Fire Next Time* (1962), he found himself the target of the police as well as unscrupulous neighbors. Their physical and potential sexual exploitation of him led him to embrace the church at the age of fourteen when he encountered a black woman evangelist, Mother Horn, who asked "Whose little boy are you?" The question so evoked a sense of belonging in Baldwin that he simply replied, "Why, yours," and joined her church. From that time until he was seventeen, Baldwin was a "young minister" in the Pentecostal Church. Heavy doses of Bible reading and abstinence from even simple pleasures like going to the movies led Baldwin to believe he had made a mistake. Church folks were trying to keep him out of the theater, he asserted later, when all along he had been performing in one. The implication that performance was an important (and problematic) feature of church membership would surface in several of Baldwin's works, including especially his play *The *Amen Corner* (1955).

At De Witt Clinton High School, Baldwin published "The Woman at the Well," "Mississippi Legend," and "Incident in London," all stories reflecting a religious influence, in the school newspaper, the *Magpie*. He also served—with Richard Avedon, with whom he would later collaborate on *Nothing Personal*—as editor-in-chief of the newspaper. Upon graduation in 1942, he worked briefly on the construction of a railroad depot in New Jersey, a job from which Baldwin was repeatedly fired. A couple of years later, in 1944, he moved to Greenwich Village, where he began exploring his writing potential more seriously. It was here that he began a novel he first called "Crying Holy," then "In My Father's House," before it would be published as *Go Tell It on the Mountain*. Acquaintance with Richard *Wright led to Wright recommending Baldwin for a Eugene Saxton Fellowship, which he received in 1945. A book review in the *Nation* in 1946 officially launched Baldwin's professional career.

After repeated disastrous racial and personal encounters, Baldwin was convinced that he should leave the country for his own sanity. He bought a one-way ticket to France and sailed on 11 November 1948, shortly after he received a Rosenwald Fellowship. Before his departure, he also terminated wedding plans and threw the engagement rings into the Hudson River. That was the last occasion on which Baldwin seriously considered a heterosexual liaison. His intimate relationships would become decidedly homosexual, although his preference was for bisexuality in his partners.

France might have provided the psychological space that Baldwin needed, but it was not without its racial tensions. Baldwin was acutely aware of the plight of Algerians in France, and he was aware of how white Americans acted toward him and other black Americans on their visits abroad. In **Notes of a Native Son* (1955) he commented on the difficulties presented when "black" (Africans) met "brown" (African Americans) on foreign soil. Tensions were also created when he inadvertently received a bed sheet from a helpful friend who did not mention he had taken it from the hotel at which he resided. Arrested and left to stumble around a jail cell without his shoe strings or belt, Baldwin compared the systemic control of black lives in Paris with that of blacks in America. He concluded that his adopted country was no less racist than his native one. Yet Baldwin would remain in France—except for sojourns in other European locales, in Africa, and periodic returns to the United States for civil rights movement activism (1957, 1960), lecturing, and teaching engagements—until his death in 1987. During returns to the United States in the 1950s and early 1960s, Baldwin marched or conversed with civil rights activists such as Martin Luther *King, Jr., Stokely Carmichael, and *Malcolm X, and he joined Lorraine *Hansberry and others in an infamous meeting with Attorney General Robert Kennedy in 1963.

His early years in Paris enabled Baldwin to interact with such luminaries as Richard Wright, although their relationship would be strained later. It was in part because Baldwin moved to France that black artist Beauford Delaney moved there. He held a special role as a father figure to Baldwin, but his increasing delusions and onset of insanity in later years caused Baldwin much distress before Delaney was finally institutionalized. From France, however, Baldwin continued his creative output, producing essays and plays in addition to novels. Along with *Go Tell It on the Mountain*, *Notes of a Native Son* and *Giovanni's Room* made Baldwin's first decade out of the country a particularly creative period.

Baldwin also spent time in Switzerland. Indeed, he completed *Go Tell It on the Mountain* in the Swiss village home of Lucien Happersberger, who by 1952 had become Baldwin's primary intimate partner. Another stint out of Paris took Baldwin to Istanbul in the

1960s. Biographer David Leeming, who worked as secretary to Baldwin during the period in Istanbul, paints Baldwin during these years as an indefatigable party-goer, with an almost infinite capacity to consume liquor and to get himself into compromising sexual situations. He describes Baldwin as suicidal on many occasions, with well-meaning friends intervening just in the nick of time to prevent some disastrous consequence. Yet for all his personal and psychological lapses, Baldwin remained strikingly productive, with novels, essays, and other creative works pouring from his typewriter.

Out of New York and America physically, but never spiritually or imaginatively, Baldwin returned to his home territory to complete several creative works. **Another Country* (1962) uses New York, Paris, and Alabama as settings for a variety of characters trying to resolve issues of sexual and racial identities. *Tell Me How Long the Train's Been Gone* (1968), *If Beale Street Could Talk* (1974), and *Just above My Head* (1979) all take Baldwin symbolically and physically back to New York, as characters encounter blatant racism, destructively insensitive police and legal systems, and systemic as well as individual obstacles to personal fulfillment.

In the early 1980s, Baldwin traveled to Atlanta, Georgia, to interview persons intimately affected by the Atlanta child murders that took place in 1980 and 1981. He produced his penultimate collection of essays, *The Evidence of Things Not Seen* (1985), about those murders. Not as powerful in conception or execution as his earlier collections of essays, the volume nonetheless reveals a Baldwin eternally committed to racial justice in a country that professes to be democratic and that has sufficient resources for each citizen to reap the fruits of that designation. Baldwin's final collection of essays, *The Price of the Ticket* (1985), includes previously published as well as new material.

The late 1970s to mid-1980s found Baldwin constantly on planes between Paris and New York, as he accepted various lecturing and teaching commitments in the United States, including an arrangement as a spring semester visiting professor at the University of Massachusetts at Amherst. He also accepted teaching appointments at Bowling Green State University and the University of California at Berkeley. As his career moved to a new level, Baldwin easily met the challenges until his very body failed him. He died of cancer in Saint-Paul-de-Vence shortly after midnight on 1 December 1987.

• Fern Marja Eckman, *The Furious Passage of James Baldwin*, 1966. Stanley Macebuh, *James Baldwin: A Critical Study*, 1973. W. J. Weatherby, *Squaring Off: Mailer vs. Baldwin*, 1977. Louis H. Pratt, James Baldwin, 1978. Carolyn Wedin Sylvander, *James Baldwin*, 1980. John W. Roberts, "James Baldwin," in *DLB*, vol. 33, *Afro-American Fiction Writers after 1955*, eds. Thadious M. Davis and Trudier Harris, 1984, pp. 3–16. Trudier Harris, *Black Women in the Fiction of James Baldwin*, 1985. Horace A. Porter, *Stealing the Fire: The Art and Protest of James Baldwin*, 1989. Fred L. Standley and Louis H. Pratt, *Conversations with James Baldwin*, 1989. Quincy Troupe, ed., *James Baldwin: The Legacy*, 1989. Randall Kenan, *James Baldwin: American Writer*, 1994. David Leeming, *James Baldwin: A Biography*, 1994. Trudier Harris, *New Essays on Baldwin's* Go Tell It on the Mountain, 1996. Marcellus Blount, ed., *Representing Black Men* (1996). E. Patrick Johnson, "Feeling the Spirit in the Dark: Expanding Notions of the Sacred in the African-American Gay Community," *Callaloo* 21:2 (Spring 1998): 399–416. David R. Anderson, "The Co-Opted Voice: Politics, History, and Self-Expression in James Baldwin's 'Journey to Atlanta,'" *College Language Association Journal* 42.3 (March 1999): 273–289.

—Trudier Harris

BAMBARA, TONI CADE (1939–1995), novelist, short fiction writer, essayist, filmmaker, lecturer, and educator. Well known for her collections of short stories and her novel, *The *Salt Eaters* (1980), Toni Cade Bambara always insisted that social commitment is inseparable from the production of art. Bambara's early years as a social worker and commitment as a community organizer influenced her work from its earliest beginnings.

Born Toni Cade in 1939 in New York City to Helen Brent Henderson Cade, she and her brother, Walter, grew up in New York, New Jersey, and the South. Bambara's mother, whom she credited as one of her major influences, gave her room to think, dream, and write for herself. Other influences were rooted in the urban environment in which Bambara grew up. She noted especially visiting the Apollo Theater with her father; listening to the music of the 1940s and 1950s; and hearing the trade unionists, Pan-Africanists, Rastas, and others from the Speaker's Corner with her mother. She also cited her editor and friend, Toni *Morrison, as an important influence. Writing as Toni Cade between 1959 and 1970, she changed her name to Bambara when she discovered it as a signature in a sketchbook found in a trunk of her grandmother's things. She had one daughter, Karma.

Bambara's first short story, "Sweet Town," was published in *Vendome Magazine* in 1959, the same year she graduated with a BA in theater arts from Queens College and won the John Golden Award for Fiction, as well as the Pauper Press Award in Journalism from the *Long Island Star*. From 1959 to 1961, Bambara worked as a family and youth caseworker at the New York Department of Welfare and embarked on an MA in American literature from City College of New York. In 1960, her second published short story, "Mississippi Ham Rider," appeared in the *Massachusetts Review*.

In 1961, Bambara worked for a year as Director of Recreation in the psychiatric division of Metro Hospital in New York City. From 1962 to 1965, she worked as Program Director of the Colony Settlement House. Completing her MA in 1965, Bambara taught in City College's SEEK (Search for Education, Elevation, Knowledge) program for four years, working with its black theater group as well as with publications sponsored by SEEK (*Obsidian*, *Onyx*, and the *Paper*). During these years, Bambara's short stories and articles began appearing in such magazines and journals as *Essence*, *Redbook*, *Negro Digest*, *Prairie Schooner*, the *New York Times*, the *Washington Post*, **Phylon*, *Ms.*, *Black World*, and the *Liberator*.

Bambara taught as a writer in residence at Spelman College (1978–1979), the Neighborhood Arts Center (1975–1979), and Stephens College (1976). She also became the founding member of the Southern Collective of African American Writers, as well as working with the Pomoja Writers Guild and several other organizations. Joining the faculty of Livingston College (at Rutgers University) as an assistant professor in 1969, Bambara was active in black student organizations and arts groups for five years, winning a service award from Livingston's black community before leaving in 1974. In 1975, Bambara became a visiting professor in Afro-American Studies at Emory University and in 1977, at Atlanta University where she was also an instructor in the School of Social Work until 1979.

Bambara refused to separate the struggle for civil rights from a commitment to women's struggle for freedom. In 1970, she published *The Black Woman*, an anthology that made connections between civil rights and the women's movement and included fiction, nonfiction, and poetry by well-known writers such as Nikki *Giovanni, Alice *Walker, Paule *Marshall, and Bambara herself, as well as work by her students from the SEEK program. An important book, it was the first to highlight, as issues of justice, African American women's lives. Like much 1970s feminist criticism, it focused on images of women and the connection of those images to women's oppression, but the book was singular because it was firmly rooted in the diverse experience of black women, both celebrating that experience and critiquing popular stereotypes.

A second edited anthology appeared in 1971, *Tales and Stories for Black Folks*. Bambara had meant the book for an audience of high school and college students, but it proved to have broader appeal. The book included a section with stories by Langston *Hughes, Ernest J. *Gaines, Pearl Crayton, Alice Walker, and, as before, the work of students.

Bambara's most famous collection of short stories (most of them written between 1950 and 1970), *Gorilla, My Love*, was published in 1972 and has been reprinted many times. The book contains fifteen stories and "A Sort of Preface" that humorously disclaims any biographical content in the narratives. Set in the rural South as well as the North, most of the stories look at relationships. A major theme centers on the way black women could (and must) participate in supporting and nurturing each other, and healing each other's inner wounds. The book was enthusiastically reviewed as an example of portraits of black life that focused on black love and created memorable characters.

In 1973, Bambara visited Cuba where she met with women's organizations and women workers and was inspired to think further about the connection between writing and social activism, as well as about possibilities for women in the United States. Another important event was her visit to Vietnam in 1975 as a guest of the Women's Union, a visit that moved her more deeply into community organizing.

Influenced by her foreign travel, Bambara's second collection was named after one of its short stories set in southeast Asia. The stories in *The Sea Birds Are Still Alive* (1977) stress the need for people to pull together and organize, as well as to keep their spiritual connections, themes that became increasingly important to Bambara's writing. Reviewers were mixed in their assessment of the collection.

In 1978, Bambara began work on her first novel, *The Salt Eaters*, published in 1980. A novel that one critic has noted is sometimes left unfinished because of its complexity, *The Salt Eaters* focuses on the relationships among such issues as social activism, individual mental and physical health, community well-being, and personal and collective history, as well as the many roots and branches of a spirituality necessary to hold together what Bambara considers to be the primarily dissipated and fractured energies of 1970s social change movements. As with most of her writing, Bambara tends to avoid linear plot, structuring her work in what one critic characterizes as concentric circles. With a dizzying array of characters and settings, the novel employs nearly seamless shifts of time and place to trace the journey of the main character, *Velma Henry—and in fact her entire community—toward healing and wholeness. The novel, considered by its editors at Random House as somewhat experimental, was well received for the most part, but some reviewers criticized the fast pace and numerous characters. Accolades were given for the rich and idiomatic language and Bambara's fine ear for dialogue, as well as for the import and complexity of the story's message. The novel was issued in paperback in 1981, published in 1982 in the United Kingdom, and reprinted by Vintage in 1992. *The Salt Eaters* won the American Book Award and the Langston Hughes Society Award in 1981, as well as awards from Medallion (1986) and the Zora Neale *Hurston Society (1986). In 1981, Bambara received a National Endowment for the Arts Literature Grant.

In essays and interviews, Bambara maintained that underlying all of her writing is the concern that the best traditions of her people be nurtured and called forth to build a strong interior life that is always at the service of social change. With almost missionary fervor, Bambara sought, in her writing and other work, to articulate ways the political, artistic, and metaphysical join together.

Bambara served as general editor for the African American Life Series of Wayne State University Press and judge for the National Book Awards (fiction), as well as sitting on numerous advisory boards from film to literature to community organizations. She was honored with citations of merit from Detroit (1989) and Atlanta (1989), as well as numerous arts and service awards. Her essays and stories have been widely anthologized and reprinted, both in the United States and abroad in Swedish, Dutch, German, Japanese, Norwegian, French, and Spanish presses.

Returning to her original interest in the performing arts in the 1980s, Bambara spent time in filmmaking. In 1986, she worked as writer and narrator for Louis Massiah's *The Bombing of Osage Avenue*, for which she won the Best Documentary Academy Award, the American Book Award, and awards from the Pennsylvania Association of Broadcasters and Black Hall of Fame. She narrated, performed, edited, and wrote for documentary films such as the United Hands Community Land Trust's *More than Property*, Frances Negron's series on Puerto Rico, Nadine Patterson's documentary on Anna Russell Jones, John Akumfrah's *Seven Songs of Malcolm*, and documentaries on John *Coltrane and Cecil B. Moore. Bambara was the coordinating writer for Massiah's film, *W. E. B. Du Bois—A Biography in Four Voices*. Her last novel, *Those Bones Are Not My Child*, about the child murders in Atlanta in 1980, was published posthumously in 1999, as was *Deep Sightings and Rescue Missions: Fiction, Essays, and Conversations* (1996).

Widely anthologized, Bambara's is one of the earliest voices in contemporary African American literature to call intentionally into tension the questions of race and gender. Bambara's work yields fresh significance as scholars apply different methodologies and theoretical lenses to the work, and as general readers continue simply to enjoy it.

• Beverly Guy-Sheftall, "Commitment: Toni Cade Bambara Speaks," in *Sturdy Black Bridges: Visions of Black Women in Literature*, eds. Roseann P. Bell, Bettye J. Parker, and Beverly Guy-Sheftall, 1979, pp. 230–249. Nancy D. Hargrove, "Youth in Toni Cade Bambara's *Gorilla, My Love*," *The Southern Quarterly* 22.1 (1983): 81–99. Eleanor W. Traylor, "Music as Theme: The Jazz Mode in the Works of Toni Cade Bambara," in *Black Women Writers (1950–1980)*, ed. Mari Evans, 1984, pp. 58–70. Alice Deck, "Toni Cade Bambara," in *DLB*, vol. 38, *Afro-American Writers after 1955: Dramatists and Prose Writers*, eds. Thadious M. Davis and Trudier Harris, 1985, pp. 12–22. Keith Byerman, "Healing Arts: Folklore and the Female Self in Toni Cade Bambara's *The Salt Eaters*," *Postscript* (1988): 37–43. Elliott Butler-Evans, *Race, Gender, and Desire: Narrative Strategies in the Fiction of Toni Cade Bambara, Toni Morrison, and Alice Walker*, 1989. Martha M. Vertreace, "A Bibliography of Writings about Toni Cade Bambara," in *American Women Writing Fiction: Memory, Identity, Family, Space*, ed. Mickey Pearlman, 1989, pp. 168–171. Lois F. Lyles, "Time, Motion, Sound and Fury in *The Sea Birds Are Still Alive*," *CLA Journal* 36:2 (1992): 134–144. Derek Alwes, "The Burden of Liberty: Choice in Toni Morrison's *Jazz* and Toni Cade Bambara's *The Salt Eaters*," *African American Review* 30:3 (Fall 1996): 353–365. Mary Comfort, "Liberating Figures in Toni Cade Bambara's *Gorilla, My Love*," *Studies in American Humor* 3:5 (1998): 76–96.

—Ann Folwell Stanford

BANNEKER, BENJAMIN (1731–1806), farmer, mathematician, astronomer, and writer. Benjamin Banneker was born 9 November 1731 in Baltimore County, Maryland, the first child of free African American parents Mary Banneker and Robert, a former slave whose freedom she had purchased and who took her surname upon marriage. Growing up on their tobacco farm, Benjamin received little formal schooling, learning to read and write from his grandmother and attending for several seasons an interracial school where he first developed his lifelong interest in mathematics. Following his parents' deaths and three sisters' departures from home, Banneker remained on the farm, working the crops and cultivating his intellect in relative seclusion.

In 1771, he befriended George Ellicott, a Quaker neighbor whose family had developed a large complex of mills on the adjoining property. With astronomical texts and instruments borrowed from Ellicott, he trained himself to calculate ephemerides, tables establishing the positioning of the sun, moon, and stars for each day of the year. When in 1791 George's cousin Andrew was appointed by President George Washington to conduct the survey of the new Federal Territory (today's District of Columbia), he selected Banneker as his field assistant. After this surveying Banneker returned home to complete an ephemeris for 1792, which failed to find a publisher. Banneker then sought George Ellicott's assistance. Through abolitionist contacts the Ellicotts soon had the material placed with three prospective printers, who were still reviewing it when in August 1791 Banneker sent a manuscript copy of his ephemeris with an accompanying letter to Thomas Jefferson, entreating him to dispel prejudice and exhorting him to fulfill the ideology of the American Revolution and his own Declaration of Independence by granting liberty and unalienable rights to people "of my complexion." While the significance of Banneker's letter and Jefferson's noncommittal response is clear, less evident is Banneker's motivation for writing. Silvio A. Bedini, author of the only full-length biography, *The Life of Benjamin Banneker* (1972), finds Banneker's manifesto uncharacteristic of his quiet temperament, suggesting that he wrote it—perhaps with the encouragement of abolitionist publishers—to draw a response from Jefferson that could in turn be printed to boost the almanac's distribution and extend its message, which indeed occurred.

Published yearly from 1792 through 1797, the Banneker almanacs were widely distributed, appearing in at least twenty-nine separate editions. Featuring Banneker's astronomical tables, the almanacs also included short verse, essays, proverbs, and general practical information selected by the printer, as was customary with the genre. While not responsible for the literary materials in his almanacs, he did become interested in writing during this period and composed short "Dream" narratives as well as verse. Having retired in 1792 from active farming, he spent his remaining years recording in his journal various observations of nature, mathematical puzzles, as well as yearly ephemerides, even after the almanacs' publication ceased. He died at age seventy-five on 9 October 1806. Although his scientific achievements are especially noteworthy, Banneker's correspondence with Jefferson and his success in the popular almanac genre make him an important contributor to early African American literature.

• Silvio A. Bedini, "Banneker, Benjamin," in *DANB*, eds. Rayford W. Logan and Michael R. Winston, 1982, pp. 22–25. Sidney Kaplan and Emma Nogrady Kaplan, "Benjamin Banneker," in *The Black Presence in the Era of the American Revolution*, rev. ed., 1989, pp. 132–151.

—Brad S. Born

BARAKA, AMIRI (b. 1934), poet, playwright, essayist, activist, lecturer, novelist, editor, anthologist, and director. One of the most influential and prolific African American writers of the twentieth century, Amiri Baraka first came to the attention of readers and critics as LeRoi Jones. He was born Everett LeRoy Jones on 7 October 1934 in Newark, New Jersey. His solidly middle-class upbringing figures prominently in his creative work and must be considered one of the major distinguishing features in any comparative treatment of Baraka and other seminal African American literary artists. The son of postal employee Coyt LeRoy Jones and social worker Anna Lois (Russ) Jones, Baraka articulates the angst of the African American middle class with unsurpassed effect in works from every phase of his artistic development. This concern is most apparent in such relatively early works as the Beat-inspired **Preface to a Twenty-Volume Suicide Note* (1961), the theatrical triumph **Dutchman* (1964), the barometric essays collected in **Home: Social Essays* (1966), and *The *System of Dante's Hell* (1965), Baraka's only attempt at the novel. Although completed at a relatively early point in the artist's development, these works evidence the writer's protracted struggle with the issues of racial identity and artistic responsibility, the two concerns that have remained his most dominant themes over the years.

Baraka attended the public schools of Newark, New Jersey, Rutgers University, and Howard University. On leaving Howard University, he enlisted in the U.S. Air Force. Upon his discharge, he settled in New York City, studied comparative literature at Columbia University, and began to cultivate strong relationships with a number of avant garde artists on the Lower East Side of New York City. In association with his first wife, Hettie (Cohen) Jones, whom he married in 1958, Baraka edited the journal *Yugen*, which was dedicated to the publication of works by struggling East Village writers. Around this time, he also served as coeditor of *Floating Bear*, an underground literary newsletter. Moreover, he and Diane di Prima cofounded the American Theater for Poets in 1961. This experimental dramatic troupe, too, was primarily concerned with presenting the works of lesser-known local writers.

Generally recognized as a "mover and shaker" on the Lower East Side art scene, Baraka quickly earned the respect of artists of all mediums, particularly the writers of the so-called Beatnik movement. His emergence as a personality and leader among this group is reflected in a 1964 feature article entitled "King of the East Village," which appeared in the *New York Herald Tribune*. His stature was further enhanced with the publication of his first collection of poems, *Preface to a Twenty-Volume Suicide Note*, and two early dramatic works, *The Baptism* and *The Toilet* (both jointly published in 1967, but performed in 1964 and 1961, respectively).

Although it appeared well past the zenith of the Beat movement, *Preface* is most representative of the literature produced by the more characteristic Beat writers. Reflecting scorn for convention, pretence, and materialism, the poems share also the brooding, self-deprecating tone of these artists. While the two plays of this period are strikingly different in mode of presentation—*The Baptism*, a highly experimental, absurdist effort, and *The Toilet*, a markedly naturalistic work—they too evidence notable Beat tendencies. In both plays, homosexual characters figure prominently as symbols of openness and tolerance, direly needed qualities in the convention-bound, excessively prohibitive straight world.

Despite the clarity of Baraka's Beat-inspired criticism of society, however, the works from this period of the writer's development reflect, paradoxically, a growing unease with the very culture from which they emerge. This is most profoundly felt in the works of *Preface*, which posit a poignant dissatisfaction with the essentially apolitical protestations of the Beats. These poems are most notable in their expressions of concern with the poetic process and with questions of audience and artistic engagement. The author's employment of the racial theme in a number of the poems is indicative of his attempts to effect a reconciliation of his art with his emerging political activism. Examination of Baraka's essays from this period, works that later found their way into *Home: Social Essays*, reveals the depth of his thought on these issues at the time.

The various essays of *Home: Social Essays*, originally published in a number of liberal and leftist journals, present a record of Baraka's artistic transformation from black Beat poet to "Father of the Black Arts movement." Becoming increasingly involved in political and artistic pursuits that took him beyond the confines of the Lower East Side, he shows in these essays an intense disaffection for liberalism, the gradualism of the civil rights movement, all manifestations of cultural shame, and assimilationist behavior by African Americans.

Despite his growing attraction to direct political action and racial concerns (as evidenced in his membership in such Harlem-based groups as the militant "On Guard for Freedom Committee" in 1961), Baraka was still very much involved with the Beat coterie during the writing of many of the aforementioned essays. His poems continued to appear in publications edited and supported by this group. Moreover, his first published fictional efforts appeared during this period in these same journals. Of particular significance was the appearance of *The System of Dante's Hell* (1965), Baraka's only novel. The author's final triumph, however, as denizen of the Lower East Side, was the explosive drama *Dutchman* (1964). Along with the poems of *The Dead Lecturer* (1964), these works reflect the tremendous psychological tension experienced by the artist during this phase of his development. Informed by an increasingly African American frame of reference, they represent, to a great extent, the artist's attempts to rationalize his new posture.

The poems of *The Dead Lecturer* represent Baraka's farewell to the closed, apolitical circle of Beat peers. Marked by an ever-increasing preoccupation with racial concerns, these lyrics evince the artist's crystallization of his commitment to revolutionary action and his disavowal of what he perceives to be the apolitical decadence of former compatriots. In withering attacks on his "friends," the poet shows impatience with the life of reflection and dead-end intellectualism. Manifesting his sense of guilt for not being more actively involved in the rapidly expanding black liberation movement, he frequently invokes the prodigal theme in the poems of *The Dead Lecturer* and the essays of *Home*.

The poems and essays of these early works are also characterized by Baraka's commitment to the articulation of a Black Aesthetic. Poems such as "Black Dada Nihilismus," "Crow Jane," and "Rhythm and Blues 1 (for Robert Williams in Exile)" must be viewed as the lyrical equivalents to such essays as "LeRoi Jones Talking," "A Dark Bag," and "The Revolutionary Theater."

The dramatic works *Dutchman* and *The Slave* (1964) should be seen as highly representative of this transitional period in Baraka's artistic development. Poets and marginal men, the heroes of both works give voice to many of the sentiments expressed in the poetry and prose of this period. Both Clay of *Dutchman* and Walker Vessels of *The Slave* are shown wrestling with the demons of self-denial that Baraka himself was attempting to eradicate between the years 1961 and 1965. C. W. E. Bigsby offers, in *The Second Black Renaissance: Essays in Black Literature* (1980), some of the most perceptive critical commentary available on these two works. Writing of *Dutchman*, he notes, "[It] remains one of the best plays ever written by a black author and one of the most impressive works of recent American theater. . . . At its heart is a consideration of the artistic process, a debate over the legitimacy of sublimating social anguish into aesthetic form." In his treatment of *The Slave*, he refers to the drama as "a personal act of exorcism," a description that could serve as well in discussion of most of the works of this phase of Baraka's artistic and personal development.

Baraka's espousal of a thoroughly political, race-conscious art was given dramatic emphasis by the continued shifting of his base of activities from the Lower East Side to Harlem. His involvement with the Black Arts Repertory Theater/School, located in Harlem, provided him with a base and a vehicle to test the aesthetic theories of the emerging cultural nationalist. Formally opened in early 1965, the Black Arts Repertory Theater/School was of critical importance in the development of the Black Arts movement of the later 1960s and early 1970s. Describing its programmatic thrust and strict adherence to the ideas put forth by Baraka, Larry *Neal noted, "the Black Arts Theater took its programs into the streets of Harlem. For three months, the theater presented plays, concerts, and poetry readings to the people of the community. Plays that shattered the illusions of the American body politic, and awakened Black people to the meaning of their lives" ("The Black Arts Movement," *Drama Review*, Summer 1968). Although short-lived, the Black Arts Repertory Theater/School's influence was widespread. Groups fashioned in its image sprang up throughout the country, and Baraka, its chief architect, was generally recognized as a seminal influence and leader.

Following the demise of the Black Arts Repertory Theater/School, Baraka returned to his hometown of Newark, New Jersey, to continue the work begun in Harlem. In doing so, he established Spirit House and its troupe of actors, called the Spirit House Movers. He also exercised his political acumen by organizing and leading the Black Community Development and Defense Organization, which proved to be an effective force in advancing the cause of Newark's African American community.

It was during this period that the writer changed his name. Having become a proponent of the Kawaida faith, a hybridization of orthodox Islam and traditional African practices, he became Ameer Baraka ("blessed Prince"). Taking on the role of priest in his growing commune, he added the title Imamu ("spiritual Leader") and changed "Ameer" to "Amiri," with no change in its regal connotation. He later dropped the title Imamu.

The poems, plays, and essays of the committed cultural nationalist are characterized by a markedly hortatory or didactic manner. Directed to an African American audience, they were intended to "raise the consciousness" of a divided and debased people. Baraka exerted tremendous influence on a generation of young African American writers during this period.

Haki *Madhubuti (formerly Don L. Lee), Nikki *Giovanni, and Sonia *Sanchez are only a few of the younger writers who attracted the attention of readers and listeners as disciples of Baraka.

The poems of *Black Magic: Collected Poetry, 1961–1967* (1969), *It's Nation Time* (1970), and *In Our Terribleness* (1970) are typical of the verse produced by cultural nationalist, poet/priest Baraka. Black Magic contains a number of poems that reflect the self-accusatory, brooding tone of the Beat and post-Beat periods. However, the latter works more frequently evidence the assured exhortations of the committed revolutionary. Moreover, these efforts are marked by an increase in the use of the language of the streets and black oral modes. In poems such as "Black Art," Baraka also continues the formulation of prescriptive artistic manifestos begun in the essays of *Home*. Like the play, the poem must be put to revolutionary use.

The dramatic works produced in this phase of Baraka's development show an extremely conscious employment of what is, perhaps, best described as the allegorical-didactic technique of medieval drama. Such an approach was logical for the playwright desirous of reaching, and teaching, a largely unlettered audience, hence, such plays as *Experimental Death Unit #1*, *Madheart*, and *Great Goodness of Life*, all published in *Four Black Revolutionary Plays* (1969). It should be noted, however, that Baraka, the avant garde dramatist, is also in evidence here. In addition to the stylized devices of medieval drama, the plays abound with expressionistic techniques. Moreover, Baraka produces what is arguably his most innovative and challenging drama, *Slave Ship: An Historical Pageant* (1967), a moving example of "environmental" or "living" theater, during this phase of his development.

During the early 1970s, Baraka played key roles in the organization of such major African American political conferences as the Pan African Congress of African Peoples in Atlanta (1972) and the National Black Political Convention in Gary, Indiana (1974). Around this same time, he made another dramatic ideological shift by announcing his formal adoption of a Marxist-Leninist perspective. Rejecting a narrowly prescribed cultural nationalism, he notes, in one of his earliest statements from this period ("The Congress of Afrikan People: A Position Paper," **Black Scholar*, Jan./Feb. 1975), "Nationalism is backward when it says we cannot utilize the revolutionary experience of the world . . . the theories and experience of men like Marx, Engels, Lenin, Stalin, Mao Tse-Tung . . . Fidel Castro . . . to utilize all this revolutionary experience and revolutionary theory, by integrating it with the concrete practice of the black liberation movement." With publication of such work as *Hard Facts* (1975), *Poetry for the Advanced* (1979), and *Daggers and Javelins* (1984), Baraka has continued his efforts to reconcile the more positive or useful aspects of cultural nationalism with the scientific accuracy of Marxism. As with his earlier works, the critical reception has been mixed.

Baraka continued his productivity with a series of works in the 1990s. He published *Eulogies* (1996), *Funk love: New Poems, 1984–1995* (1996), and *The Autobiography of LeRoi Jones/Amiri Baraka* (1997). Scholarly interest in his poetry and essays continued as well. Paul Vangelisti edited *Transbluesency: The Selected Poems of Amiri Baraka/LeRoi Jones (1961–1995)* (1995), and two of Baraka's most well known works, *Black Music* and *Home: Social Essays*, were reissued in 1998.

Amiri Baraka's example is in many ways emblematic of the collective experience of African Americans since the momentous decade of the 1960s. His spiritual and artistic journey reflects, in microcosm and, to be sure, in the extreme, the movement from doubt to self-assurance, from self-contempt to self-acceptance. Moreover, in his more recent disavowal of the confining dictums of cultural nationalism, we see a suggestion of the larger African American community's movement toward greater openness to diversity and cross-cultural collaboration. Baraka's greatest contribution, however, lies in his tremendous influence on the direction of post-1960s African American writing. In encouraging a generation of writers to use, confidently and unapologetically, their own rich African American cultural heritage as well as experimental modes of presentation, he proved himself a key facilitator in the maturation of a good number of innovative young artists. By freeing these aspiring writers from all vestiges of cultural shame and the lock-step realistic/naturalistic mode, he contributed immeasurably to African American literature specifically and American literature in general.

[*See also* Literary History, article on Late Twentieth Century.]

• Donald B. Gibson, ed., *Modern Black Poets: A Collection of Critical Essays*, 1973. Theodore Hudson, *From LeRoi Jones to Amiri Baraka: The Literary Works*, 1973. Kimberly Benston, *Baraka: The Renegade and the Mask*, 1976. Werner Sollors, *Amiri Baraka/LeRoi Jones: The Quest for a "Populist Modernism,"* 1978. Lloyd Brown, *Amiri Baraka*, 1980. William C. Fisher, "Amiri Baraka," in *American Writers*, supplement 2, part 1, ed. A. Walton Litz, 1981, pp. 29–63. Henry C. Lacey, *To Raise, Destroy, and Create: The Poetry, Drama, and Fiction of Imamu Amiri Baraka (LeRoi Jones)*, 1981. William J. Harris, *The Poetry and Poetics of Amiri Baraka: The Jazz Aesthetic*, 1985. Robert Elliot Fox, *Conscientious Sorcerers: The Black Post Modernist Fiction of LeRoi Jones/Amiri Baraka, Ishmael Reed, and Samuel R. Delany*, 1987. George Piggford, "Looking into Black Skulls: Amiri Baraka's Dutchman and the Psychology of Race," *Modern Drama* 40:1 (Spring 1997): 74–85. Saba Siddiqui, "Women in Amiri Baraka's Plays," in *New Waves in American Literature*, ed., Desai A. Mutalik, et al. (1999), pp. 38–44.

—Henry C. Lacey

BARNES, STEVEN (b. 1952), novelist, short story writer, television script writer, screenplay writer, lecturer, creative consultant, and martial arts authority. A

Los Angeles native and later resident of Vancouver, Washington, Steven Emory Barnes is the third African American author after 1960 to have chosen science fiction and fantasy writing as his primary profession. Barnes established himself through the 1980s as a determined and disciplined writer, one who had followed a cherished childhood dream to become a commercially successful professional writer.

The youngest child of Emory F. Barnes and Eva Mae (Reeves) Barnes, Steven Barnes grew up in Los Angeles. He attended Los Angeles High, Los Angeles City College, and Pepperdine University, Malibu, California (1978–1980). At Pepperdine he majored in communication arts but withdrew from school before completing a degree, frustrated because he thought no one on the faculty could teach him about building a career as a professional writer. It was not until Barnes made contact with established science fiction writer Ray Bradbury, who sent the novice writer two encouraging letters after reading some of his stories, and with film director, producer, and scriptwriter John Landis, who also encouraged him, that Barnes began to feel he could be successful. Recognizing that more guidance from working writers could help him learn his craft, in 1979 Barnes sought out well-established science fiction author Larry Niven at the Burbank Science Fiction and Fantasy Club and began a literary apprenticeship with him.

From the early 1980s to the mid-1990s the mentoring arrangement between Niven and Barnes proved very productive, resulting in five coauthored novels. As a team the two wrote the progressively linked *Dream Park* novels, a combination of action-suspense and thriller–science fiction set in a near-future, highly technological, Disneyesque theme park. *Dream Park* (1981), *The Barsoom Project* (1989), and *The California Voodoo Game* (1991) comprise the trilogy. Barnes and Niven also collaborated on *The Descent of Anansi* (1982) and *Achilles' Choice* (1991). In 1987 and in 1995, Barnes joined forces with both Niven and Jerry Pournelle to produce *The Legacy of Heorot* (1987) and *Beowulf's Children* (1995).

Working independently, Barnes wrote *The Kundalini Equation* (1986), a novel based upon East Indian myths, and three other books featuring the larger-than-life martial arts expert and zero-gravity "nullboxer" Aubry Knight. Knight became Barnes's black mythic champion, his response to a childhood diet of comic books and fantasy tales without positive images of African Americans performing heroic acts. While young, Barnes began creating his own dark-hued imitation Conan stories to help establish a context for his life. Believing myths are vitally important to all cultures, he went on to fashion the heroic Aubry Knight, who represents an outgrowth of Barnes's understanding of the popular, and profitable, fantastic hero. Giving more flesh to the type, Barnes drew Aubry as a man capable of growth; his Knight must learn what it is to become human, to become a man and not just a fighter. The shattered, vicious, and seemingly dystopian universe Knight inhabits reflects Barnes's fascination with anger and violence, his insight into what he deemed as "the dark side" of human nature or the "dark side of the force." Yet after Aubry Knight has been through hell and back in *Streetlethal* (1983) and *Gorgon Child* (1989), when he reappears in *FireDance* (1993) the world has become more stable, and he has evolved to become a more balanced, mature man. Growth, balance, the unity of mind, body, and spirit, the sometimes thin line between feeling and action—these are all undercurrents in Barnes's independent novels.

Between 1981 and 1996, Barnes published thirteen novels, including a five-part graphic novel called *Fusion for Eclipse Comics* (1987). Although he has not written many, his short stories have been well received. "The Locusts," the first collaboration between Nivens and Barnes, appeared in *Analog* (June 1979) and was nominated for a Hugo, one of two prestigious awards given in science fiction. His stories have been included in Roger Zelazny's *Warriors of Mist and Dream* (1995) anthology and Robert Adam's two *Horseclans* anthologies (1987 and 1988); he has also been published in Isaac Asimov's *Science Fiction Magazine*. In addition, Barnes occasionally writes for television, adapting stories or composing scripts for popular programs such as *The Twilight Zone*, *Real Ghostbusters*, *Baywatch*, and *The Outer Limits*. Barnes has also written several essays for martial arts publications and served as a columnist for *Black Belt Magazine* from 1986 to 1989.

Maintaining that he has no interest in writing either the traditional realistic American novel or the "great American black novel," Steven Barnes declared that his interest has been and remains fantasy fiction. "I once tried to stop writing for two years, just to see if there was something else I could do with myself . . . and there wasn't. I couldn't stop writing. Science fiction gives me the widest areas to play in." The three most important aspects of Steven Barnes's life are creating the science fiction and suspense tales that allow him to develop his own mythos, the martial arts, and his family and friends.

• "Barnes, Stephen Emory," in *CA*, vol. 105, 1982, p. 50. Francis Hamit, "The Self-Evolution of Steven Barnes," *Players* 14.9 (Feb. 1988): 36–40.

—Sandra Y. Govan

BARRAX, GERALD W. (b. 1933), poet and educator. Bridging the poetic radicalism and experimentalism of the 1960s to the lyrical and confessional modes of the 1980s, the poetry of Gerald William Barrax draws on the life of the poet as well as the state of African American experience for its intimate power. Whether relating the details of his life with wife and children or questioning the roles of African American leaders, Barrax's poetry continually invokes anxieties concerning responsibility and participation in contemporary American life.

Born in Attala, Alabama, on 21 June 1933, Barrax spent his early years in the rural South. Once his family moved to Pittsburgh in 1944, Barrax completed his primary and secondary education, worked in the post office, and completed a bachelor's degree at Duquesne University. Upon receipt of a master's degree in English from the University of Pittsburgh in 1969, Barrax moved to North Carolina, where he studied and joined the faculty of North Carolina State University in Raleigh. During this period Barrax lived some of the material that has become crucial concerns of his poetry: the experience of family, of work, of race and racism, and of transcendence. This transcendence—through social participation, through home and family, through an inquisition of doubt and faith—is the most characteristic element of his work.

One can discern three distinct periods within Barrax's work: the first, a period defined loosely by an encounter with existentialism, the Black Arts movement, and experiment with form; the second by the exploration of a distinctly personal, anecdotal, confessional poetic voice; and the third by an elaboration of this confessional tone into a sustained lyricism that addresses both personal and collective anxieties.

Divided into three sections ("Forecast," "Drought," and "Another Kind of Rain"), Barrax's first collection of poetry, *Another Kind of Rain* (1970), describes the search for and the attainment of renewal. One of the text's dominant themes is the father-son relationship, a relationship that has particular resonance in the poet's life (Barrax is separated from his first wife and three sons) and, more generally, in African American experience at large. In poems such as "Efficiency Apartment," "First Carolina Rain," and "Earthlog: Final Entry" the poet explores the disconnection and the painful and joyous connection that persists between himself and his sons. Technically, the poems range from confessional lyrics to free verse poems filled with "street talk" and typographical dynamism. *Another Kind of Rain* also establishes Barrax's wide-ranging eclecticism (alluding variously to Homer, William Shakespeare, Alfred Lord Tennyson, William Butler Yeats, T. S. Eliot, e. e. cummings) that, paired with his intimate tone and confessional subjects, results in an eclectic and allusive document of the persistence of universal themes in contemporary experience.

The unproblematic perspective of the "I" in *Another Kind of Rain* becomes the poet's subject in Barrax's second collection, *An Audience of One* (1980). An exploration of the subjectivity of the poet who moves from one marriage into another, from one family to another, *An Audience of One* plays out a poetic dialogue between objectivity (the preponderant image of the camera in "The Only Way My Dumb Flesh Knows") and subjective possibilities that a new family and new beginnings bring ("I Travel with Her," "Shani"). It is a pivotal work in its movement from poetic duality in his early poems (they were either personal or public, intimate or political) to a fulfillment of the public within the personal, the political within the intimate detail of everyday life. *The Deaths of Animals and Lesser Gods* (1984) extends this renovation of self, family, and community through faith. The transcendent possibilities of belief and of the belief in belief become Barrax's central subject. He asserts the need for certainty, peace, and clarity, which far from separating humanity from the divine actually brings it closer to participation in others and ourselves: "God is love as long as one of us lives."

Barrax's *Leaning Against the Sun* (1992) consolidates the impulses of his decades-long process. After two wives and five children, Barrax celebrates the renewing ritual of domestic tranquility and the identity-building value of attempting to understand God, man, and community. Formally, Barrax returns in some of these poems ("Epigraphs," "Cello Poem") to rhyme and meter. Alluding to his poetic antecedents (Walt Whitman, Denise Levertov, Emily Dickinson), Barrax's meditations on freedom, faith, and manhood gain a rhythmic, musical depth. Transcendence is found in simple tasks and simple moments treasured simply.

Ultimately, Gerald W. Barrax's work offers a vein of allusion, electicism, and inclusiveness to the tradition of African American poetry. An eclectic nexus of tendencies and themes in African American poetry, Barrax's poetry enacts the contradictory and complex discourses motivating the tradition-bound and tradition-breaking impulses of contemporary African American poetry. He continued this tradition in 1998 with the publication of *From a Person Sitting in Darkness: New and Selected Poems.*

• Lorenzo Thomas, review of *The Deaths of Animals and Lesser Gods, Black American Literature Forum* 19 (Fall 1985): 132–133. Lenard D. Moore, "On Hearing Gerald W. Barrax," *Black American Literature Forum* 21 (Fall 1987): 241–242. Dennis Sampson, review of *Leaning Against the Sun, Hudson Review* 45 (Winter 1993): 670–671. Lenard D. Moore, review of *Leaning Against the Sun, African American Review* 28 (Summer 1994): 311–315. Special section of *Callaloo* 20:2 (Spring 1997) is devoted to Barrax.

—Daniel M. Scott III

"Bars Fight." *See* Terry, Lucy.

BASS, KINGSLEY, JR., is the pseudonym of Black Theater movement playwright Ed *Bullins for the publication of *We Righteous Bombers* in the anthology *New Plays from the Black Theatre* (1969) and the play's production at the New Lafayette Theatre in Harlem in May of 1969.

New Plays from the Black Theatre lists Kingsley B. Bass, Jr., as "a 24-year-old Black man murdered by Detroit police during the uprising," but in a panel discussion of *We Righteous Bombers* at the New Lafayette

Theatre (11 May 1969), playwright *Marvin X reported that Bullins in fact wrote the play and used the pseudonym "to suggest the type of play that a brother killed in the Detroit Revolution would have written." Bass, who never existed, seemed able to achieve for himself a fine, if ironic, honor: a small notice by Larry *Neal printed below prefatory notes to the panel discussion (which also contributed to the confusion over the play's authorship) announced Bass's winning the Harriet Webster Updike Award for literary excellence.

We Righteous Bombers is modeled almost strictly after Albert Camus's *Les Justes* (1946; trans., *The Just Assassins*, 1958). Both plays ask whether the decision to commit murder to end the suffering of humanity is an enterprise that can ultimately be legitimated. *Bombers*, however, whose racialized conflict is more deeply visceral and whose concomitant intensity of hatred and fear is further enhanced by elements of expressionistic theater (Bullins constructs time achronologically and uses music and still projections throughout the play), seems even more horrific a presentation of this question than its predecessor. Additionally, the proximity of the play to present-day America and its racial dilemmas lends significantly to the consternation of its audience. Jack B. Moore's suggestion that the play reveals "the realities of hate and fear and desire that the everyday life of black and white behavior only masks" invites speculation of Bullins's motivation to use a pseudonym: the authorial masking and the confusion surrounding it become a metaphor for the play's ability to unmask society and render the apocalypse beneath.

The post-production panel discussion itself produced an array of reactions regarding the importance of the play as a revolutionary work—specifically, its accurate depiction of revolutionary spirit and its psychological impact on a public in search of bold revolutionary characterizations of African Americans. Robert Macbeth, director of the New Lafayette, defended *Bombers* and expected that new plays would naturally evolve from its questions and flaws. Dissenting were Askia M. *Touré and Ernie Mkalimoto, who stated that the only proper image of the African American revolutionary, that of keeper of myth and folklore and designer of a new world history, was cheapened by characterizations of weakness among the play's revolutionaries. Larry Neal and Amiri *Baraka (LeRoi Jones) philosophized that there is a reciprocity between art and activism. Baraka, in his final appeal to the audience, made the claim for a clarity of statement over the "mysticism of art," suggesting that without clarity, such mysticism can plainly deceive, overwhelming artist and audience in more ways than one can ever know.

• Larry Neal, "Lafayette Theatre Reaction to *Bombers*," *Black Theatre* 4 (1969): 16–25. Larry Neal, "Toward a Relevant Black Theatre," *Black Theatre* (1969): 14–15. Jack B. Moore, "The (In)humanity of Assassination: Plays by Albert Camus and Kingsley B. Bass, Jr.," *MELUS* 8.3 (Fall 1981): 45–56.

—Nathan L. Grant

BAUMFREE, ISABELLA. *See* Truth, Sojourner.

BECK, ROBERT. *See* Iceberg Slim.

BECKHAM, BARRY (b. 1944), novelist and publisher. Barry Beckham began his first novel, *My Main Mother* (1969), while he was a senior at Brown University, completing it while living in New York City. He returned to Brown in 1970 as a visiting lecturer in English and, after being appointed to a professorship, remained there for seventeen years, several as director of the graduate creative writing program. In 1972, his second novel, *Runner Mack*, was nominated for the National Book Award, and his play *Garvey Lives!* was produced in Providence. In 1974, he was commissioned to write a biography of New York playground basketball legend Earl Manigault. The book was published in 1981 as a "novelized biography," *Double Dunk*. In 1987, Beckham moved to Washington, D.C., teaching at Hampton University for two years. Partly because of difficulties with publishers over another of his projects, *The Black Student's Guide to Colleges* (1982), he has since dedicated himself to "developing a major black-oriented book company," Beckham House Publishers. At present, Beckham is working on his autobiography, a novel responding to his perceived "need for a description of a passionate black love relationship," and a collaborative autobiography with Jackie Robinson's daughter Sharon.

My Main Mother has a rural setting based on one of Beckham's childhood homes, Woodbury, New Jersey, where his was the only black family in the area. The novel depicts a distraught and highly fragmented narrator who, while sitting in a junked car awaiting the arrival of the police, tells in one night (Scheherazade-like) how and why he killed his mother, whose vain self-indulgence had led her to abandon him by running away with a man to New York to become a singer. While representations of alienating family life suggest the lineage of Richard *Wright, the novel also reflects a gothic tradition that Beckham attributes to the influence of both his writing teacher, novelist John Hawkes, and Franz Kafka.

Runner Mack, Beckham's most accomplished work, is the story of naive Henry Adams, who moves from Mississippi to a northern city dreaming of playing professional baseball, only to be frustrated in his ambitions, first by having to go to work in a factory and later by being drafted into the army. While fighting in the fraudulently conceived "Alaska War," a veiled satire of Vietnam, Henry meets Black Power advocate Runner Mack (based on a New York acquaintance of Beckham's), becomes a revolutionary himself, and eventually participates in an abortive attempt to bomb the White House. The novel's structure is a pastiche of the classic African American ascent narrative, each event representing an aspect of white exploitation of African Americans from slavery to the present, notably through professional sports, military service, and the migration north to work in industry. The factory scenes suggest the surreal, hallucinatory Liberty Paint episode in Ralph *Ellison's **Invisible Man* (1952), while the broad characterizations and conscious employment of African American slave narrative and autobiographical traditions prefigure Ishmael *Reed's **Flight to Canada* (1976).

• Joe Weixlmann, "The Dream Turned 'Daymare': Barry Beckham's *Runner Mack*," *MELUS* 8.4 (Winter 1981): 93–103. Wiley Lee Umphlett, "The Black Man as Fictional Athlete: *Runner Mack*, the Sporting Myth, and the Failure of the American Dream," *Modern Fiction Studies* 33.1 (Spring 1987): 73–83.

—Jeff Loeb

BELL, JAMES MADISON (1826–1902), poet. The "Bard of the Maumee," Ohio's first native African American poet, was born in Gallipolis where he spent his first sixteen years. From 1842 to 1853, Bell worked as a plasterer in Cincinnati and there married Louisiana Sanderlin with whom he had several children. He plied the plasterer's trade in Canada West, Ontario (1854–1860); there he became a friend of John *Brown's, raised funds for Brown's 1859 raid, and later dedicated *The Day and the War* to "The Hero, Saint and Martyr of Harpers Ferry." For the next thirty years, until he settled in Toledo in 1890, Bell pursued the trades of plasterer and poet-lecturer in San Francisco (1860–1865) and many other cities north and south. He championed abolitionism and black educational and legal rights, served as a prominent lay worker for the African Methodist Episcopal (AME) Church, and briefly worked in Republican Party politics. In 1901, at the insistence of Bishop Benjamin Arnett, Bell published his life's poetry in *Poetical Works*.

Bell specialized in long verse-orations (each of 750 to 950 lines) that recounted the history of slavery, the Civil War, emancipation, and Reconstruction: *A Poem* (1862); *A Poem Entitled the Day and the War* (1864); *An Anniversary Poem Entitled the Progress of Liberty* (1866); and *A Poem Entitled the Triumph of Liberty* (1870). These poems require the spirited dramatic recitals Bell offered on his tours, where, William Wells *Brown observed, his "soul-stirring appeals" inspired "enthusiasm of admiration" in his listeners. On the printed page the orations' abstractions, clichés, and monotonously regular iambic tetrameter and rhymes smother both emotional force and intellectual conviction. Occasionally specific references to historical persons and events or variations in stanza length add distinctiveness to Bell's poetic declamations on liberty and racial justice. Collected with the long poems in *Poetical Works* are a dozen conventional shorter poems, most on racial themes, and a daring, vigorous satire of President Andrew Johnson, "Modern Moses, or 'My Policy' Man" (c. 1867). In every age, writes Bell, "an assassin's blow" has raised to power someone "Whose acts unseemly and unwise, / Have caused the people to despise / And curse the hours of his reign, / And brand him with the mark of Cain." Worse than Cain is Johnson, "My liege of graceless dignity," our Judas, Satan's minion, a false *Moses. Exposing Johnson's political treacheries, dissipations, and vulgarities in 377 lines, Bell combines shrewd humor and irony, concrete topicality, and uninhibited personal emotion for his most inventive and readable work. As poet and public speaker, Bell was one of the nineteenth century's most dedicated propagandists for African American freedom and civil rights.

• Benjamin W. Arnett, "Biographical Sketch," in *Poetical Works*, by James Madison Bell, 1901, pp. 3–14. Joan R. Sherman, *Invisible Poets: Afro-Americans of the Nineteenth Century*, 2d ed., 1989.

—Joan R. Sherman

Beloved. Toni *Morrison's fifth novel, *Beloved* (1987), won a Pulitzer Prize in 1988 and is an accurate portrayal of the black slave woman's experience. Beginning in pre–Civil War Kentucky, *Beloved* is the story of *Sethe Suggs and her family. Nineteen years old and pregnant with her fourth child, Sethe wants nothing more than to free her family from slavery. The Suggses had been owned by Mr. Garner, a "humane slave master," but when he dies his brother schoolteacher comes to run the plantation. The Suggses escape but schoolteacher finds them in Ohio, and when Sethe sees him approaching she tries to kill her children—to prevent their return to slavery—but only succeeds in killing her young daughter, Beloved. Realizing Sethe's intentions, schoolteacher leaves and Sethe serves a short jail sentence, nursing her newly born daughter, Denver. She then supports her family as a cook.

Beloved returns to haunt her mother's house. As a baby ghost she turns over tables and makes fingerprints in cakes, ultimately driving her two brothers away. When *Paul D, a former slave from the same plantation, arrives at Sethe's house, he vanquishes the baby ghost by yelling and striking at the air, but she eventually returns as a twenty-year-old spirit in human form with a demanding infantile personality. Because of Sethe's guilt and the "rememory" of tortured slavery, Beloved is able to take over Sethe's mind, body, and heart, following her everywhere, questioning her endlessly, and causing Sethe's mental and physical deterioration. Beloved in turn grows fat to the point of appearing pregnant. Denver, who has isolated herself since she learned that her mother killed Beloved, decides that she must take action when Sethe quits her job and becomes increasingly unable to resist Beloved's outrageous demands for attention and food.

Their resources depleted, Denver symbolically steps off her porch to ask the neighbors for help. They initially respond by mysteriously providing food, and later, when they hear tales of Beloved beating Sethe, they descend upon Sethe's house to perform a rite of exorcism. Humming, singing, and praying, they force Beloved to flee. Morrison hints that Beloved's human form disintegrates. Freedom from the ghost does not bring immediate health for Sethe, although it and the act of seeking assistance serve to reincorporate Denver into the community. Sethe languishes in an effort to will herself to death until Paul D returns to inspire her with a budding desire to live.

Morrison based the novel on the story of Margaret Garner, a slave who in circumstances similar to Sethe's killed one child and tried to kill her three others. The novel is important for depicting the concern slave mothers had for their children and their determination to win freedom for themselves and their offspring. It was critically acclaimed for its poetic language, intricate plot, and understanding portrayal of the forces that would cause Sethe to kill her child. *Beloved* acknowledges the horror of slavery and portrays the horrendous treatment and torturous memories of the slaves' past while documenting the effect of this history on future generations of African Americans.

• Brian Finney, "Temporal Defamiliarization in Toni Morrison's Beloved," *Obsidian II* 18 (Spring 1990): 59–77. Trudier Harris, *Fiction and Folklore: The Novels of Toni Morrison*, 1991. Sunny Falling-rain, "A Literary Patchwork Crazy Quilt: Toni Morrison's *Beloved*," *Uncoverings* 15 (1994): 110–140. Deborah Guth, "'Wonder What God Had in Mind': Beloved's Dialogue with Christianity," *Journal of Narrative Technique* 24.2 (Spring 1994): 83–97. Caroline Rody, "Toni Morrison's *Beloved*: History, 'Rememory,' and a Clamor for a Kiss," *American Literary History* 7.1 (Spring 1995): 92–119.

—Betty Taylor-Thompson

BENEATHA YOUNGER, a character in the 1959 play *A *Raisin in the Sun*, is a mild parody of the author of the play, Lorraine *Hansberry at age twenty, and has no precedent on the American stage. The daughter of *Mama Lena Younger and the sister of *Walter Lee Younger, Beneatha represents the young women of the so-called silent generation of the 1950s on the verge of new and unprecedented freedom. Refusing to labor under typical racial and gender roles, she dares to "seek her identity" or "express" herself by studying guitar, learning horseback riding, and engaging in other activities considered frivolous in a traditional, black, working-class household. Her knowledge of America's rich history and revolutionary present challenge the Tarzan myths of the period. By rejecting a rich, middle-class suitor, she questions prevailing expectations that women should be satisfied as housewives or sex objects. In the original script, Beneatha chooses to wear her hair natural—in an Afro, the first ever on the American stage; however, the material was cut from the first production and later restored in 1987. Beneatha anticipates the next generation of African American women intellectuals.

Beneatha evokes critical character traits of the play's main characters, Lena and Walter Lee. Her atheistic views reveal the complex authoritarian and traditional values held by her mother. Beneatha's plans to study medicine elicit her brother's sexist comment that she should be satisfied with nursing. In the last act, Beneatha's disavowal of her brother's demeaning plans rouses Mama to deliver the most eloquent speech in the play as she reminds Beneatha that her brother deserves her love especially when he is suffering the most. Beneatha remains an unusually provocative depiction of the independent African American woman.

• Doris E. Abramson, *Negro Playwrights in the American Theatre, 1925–1959*, 1969, pp. 165–266. Amiri Baraka, "*A Raisin in the Sun*'s Enduring Passion," in *A Raisin in the Sun and The Sign in Sidney Brustein's Window*, ed. Robert Nemiroff, 1987, pp. 9–20.

—Margaret B. Wilkerson

BENNETT, GWENDOLYN (1902–1981), poet, short-story writer, artist, illustrator, journalist, teacher, and participant in the Harlem Renaissance. Although she never collected her published poetry into a volume nor produced a collection of short stories, Gwendolyn Bennett was recognized as a versatile artist and significant figure in the Harlem Renaissance.

Torn between her ambition to work as a graphic artist and her desire to become a proficient writer using the medium of either poetry or prose, Bennett maintained the profile of an arts activist in New York City's African American arts community for over twenty years. However, the five-year period spanning 1923 to 1928 proved to be the most productive for her as a creative writer. It was within this brief span that James Weldon *Johnson recognized Bennett as a lyric poet of some power.

Born in Giddings, Texas, Bennett led a nomadic childhood before her father, Joshua Robbin Bennett, finally settled his family into comfortable surroundings in Brooklyn, New York. Bennett completed her secondary education at Girls' High, where she had been active in both the literary society and the school's art program. Graduating in 1921, Bennett came of age just as the Harlem Renaissance was beginning to flower. Attempting to remain loyal to both of her dreams, Bennett began college classes at Columbia University in the Department of Fine Arts but she subsequently transferred to and graduated from Pratt Institute in 1924. While studying painting and graphic design at Pratt, Bennett also began seeking artistic outlets in the two major journals accepting work from African American artists—the NAACP's the *Crisis* and the Urban League's *Opportunity*.

Bennett's banner years were 1923 to 1925. The *Crisis* carried a cover she illustrated and her poem "Heritage" was published by *Opportunity* in 1923. In 1924 her commemorative poem "To Usward" was chosen as the dedication poem to honor the publication of a Jessie Redmon *Fauset novel at the showcase Civic Club dinner for Harlem's writers sponsored by Charles S. Johnson of the Urban League. Both "Heritage," with its allusions to "lithe Negro girls" dancing around "heathen fires," and "To Usward," which celebrated the spirit of youth on the march, anticipated and invoked African and African American images, motifs, themes, or cultural icons that became central to much of the literature of the Harlem Renaissance.

In this same period Bennett began a warm, supportive, and sustained association with a cadre of younger writers and artists known in Harlem circles. Belonging to this group were Langston *Hughes, Countee *Cullen, Eric *Walrond, Helene *Johnson, Wallace *Thurman, Richard Bruce *Nugent, Aaron and Alta Douglass, Rudolph *Fisher, and later the irrepressible Zora Neale *Hurston. These young artists supported and encouraged each other and were, in turn, encouraged to pursue their aspirations by older, more established scholars and writers such as Charles S. Johnson, Alain *Locke, W. E. B. *Du Bois, Jessie Fauset, and James Weldon Johnson. In a 1979 interview Bennett noted that it was "fun to be alive and to be part of this. . . ." There was, she observed, "nothing like this particular life in which you saw the same group of people over and over again. You were always glad to see them. You always had an exciting time when you were with them."

The supportive energy Bennett drew from her contact with her peers helped sustain her whether she was in Harlem or not. She kept her connections alive when she went to teach art at Howard University in 1924. She also maintained contact while studying art in Paris from 1925 to 1926. From France she wrote to Hughes and Cullen giving them the news; each wrote back, giving her news of the opportunities available to Negro artists and urging her to write for publication. Returning to Harlem in 1926, Bennett joined with Hughes, Thurman, Nugent, and a few others to form the editorial board of *Fire!!*, a quarterly journal created to serve the younger African American artists. Bennett's "Wedding Day" first appeared in *Fire!!*. Despite her return to Howard (1927–1928), Bennett relied upon her network contacts as news sources to inform her "Ebony Flute," a literary chitchat and arts news column which she produced for *Opportunity* for almost two years.

The Great Depression of the 1930s effectively altered the arts landscape through which Gwendolyn Bennett moved. The new era's change of tone caused a shift in her own artistic sensibility from exuberant and often whimsical personal poetry toward the cause of public advocacy for the arts and artists in the community.

•James Weldon Johnson, ed., *The Book of American Negro Poetry*, 1922; enlarged, 1931. Gloria Hull, "Black Women Poets from Wheatley to Walker," *Negro American Literature Forum* 9 (Fall 1975): 91–96. Walter C. Daniel and Sandra Y. Govan, "Gwendolyn Bennett," in *DLB*, vol. 51, *Afro-American Writers from the Harlem Renaissance to 1940*, ed. Trudier Harris, 1987, pp. 3–10.

—Sandra Y. Govan

BENNETT, HAL (b. 1930), novelist and short fiction writer. Born in Buckingham, Virginia, on 21 April 1930, George Harold Bennett was raised and educated in Newark, New Jersey. He sold his first short story when he was fifteen, became a feature writer for the *Newark Herald News* at the age of sixteen, and edited his high school yearbook. During the Korean War he served a tour of duty in the U.S. Air Force, where he wrote for the Public Information Division and edited a newsletter for U.S. airmen. After his discharge, he continued to pursue his career as a writer, serving as fiction editor for several African American newspapers between 1953 and 1955 and attempting to launch his own newspaper in Westbury, Long Island. After that venture failed, he moved to Mexico, where he attended Mexico City College and became a fellow of the Centro Mexicano de Escritores. During this period he completed most of his first novel, *A Wilderness of Vines*, a manuscript that won him a fiction fellowship from the Bread Loaf Writer's Conference in 1966. Several years later, in 1970, Bennett was selected most promising writer of the year by *Playboy* magazine for his short story "Dotson Gerber Resurrected." He received the PEN/Faulkner Award in 1973.

Between 1966 and 1976, Hal Bennett published five novels; his collection of short fiction, *Insanity Runs in Our Family*, was published in 1977. Bennett's experiences in both Buckingham, Virginia, and Newark, New Jersey, provide the backdrop for his fictional settings of Burnside, Virginia, and Cousinville, New Jersey—the terrain between which many of his characters shuttle back and forth, vainly seeking a salvation that somehow always manages to elude them. Somewhat like William Faulkner's Yoknapatawpha County, Bennett's Burnside and Cousinville are self-contained fictional universes. His novels and short stories are linked by characters who restlessly move north and south—often reappearing in other novels and stories—and by recurring themes and preoccupations. In a broad sense, Bennett's novels recount the saga of African Americans who—like other dreamers, seekers, and outcasts—seek a new life through migration from the South to the North, from the country to the city. In Bennett's case, however, this story is filtered through an iconoclastic, satiric, and absurdist sensibility.

Set in 1939, *A Wilderness of Vines* (1966) introduces the racial pathology of the pre–World War II black community of Burnside, Virginia, a community in which the worship of hierarchies based on color has become elevated to the status of a religion. It also introduces Bennett's recurring stylistic and thematic concerns: his inversion of traditional Christian symbols and images; his preoccupation with sex, salvation, and insanity; his perspective on the corrosive legacy of America's racial history. In many respects, the community of Burnside emerges as a corruption of the garden of Eden—and as a microcosm of the American insanity forged by centuries of racism and sexual hypocrisy. The novel concludes with an act of brutal violence and the exodus north of the key characters, followed by prostitutes, the insane, the downhearted, and the defeated. Bennett's subsequent novels explore the lives and experiences of those characters who have participated in the exodus. *The Black Wine* (1968) spans the years between 1953 and 1960 and is concerned with the lives and fates of those who traveled north to Cousinville. Like *A Wilderness of Vines, The Black Wine* concludes on a note of explosive violence and with ambiguous proclamations of faith. *Lord of Dark Places* (1970) introduces the character of Joe Market, an outrageous, southern-born, black phallic hero, and offers a sustained and profane assault on the racial and sexual mythologies that have haunted American life. The novel begins in 1951 in Burnside and ends in June 1968, shortly after the assassination of Robert Kennedy, with Joe's execution in New Jersey. *Wait until the Evening* (1974) begins in 1944 and ends in 1970, with the central character, Kevin Brittain, plotting the murder of his father in Burnside. *Seventh Heaven* (1976)—the sardonic title conferred upon a seedy housing project in Cousinville—begins in the wake of the urban riots of the 1960s and ends with the Watergate scandal. Like so many of Bennett's characters, Bill Kelsey travels from the South to the North only to be engulfed in the larger madness of American life. Taken together, Bennett's novels constitute an extended saga of post–World War II African American life and a disturbing and satirical vision of the underside of American society.

Bennett's irreverence, iconoclasm, and gift for satire are reminiscent of George S. *Schuyler and Wallace *Thurman, and his sense of the absurd parallels that of Chester *Himes. His novels and his short fiction offer a highly idiosyncratic and often outrageous vision of the possibilities of American life.

• Ronald Walcott, "The Novels of Hal Bennett," part 1, *Black World* 23.8 (June 1974): 36–48, 89–97. Ronald Walcott, "The Novels of Hal Bennett," part 2, *Black World* 23.9 (July 1974): 78–96. Bernard W. Bell, *The Afro-American Novel and Its Tradition*, 1987, pp. 324–329.

—James A. Miller

BIBB, HENRY (1815–1854), fugitive slave narrator and journalist. Henry Bibb is best known through his *Narrative of the Life and Adventures of Henry Bibb, An American Slave*, which was first published by Bibb himself in 1849. While Frederick *Douglass gained credibility through his assertion of authorship and by way of the introductions composed for his narrative by William Lloyd Garrison and Wendell Phillips, Bibb enjoyed no such reception and was forced to subvene the publication of his own story. The narrative is rich in detail, including an account of Bibb's use of "conjuring" to avoid punishment for running away, and the use of "charms" to court his slave wife. Bibb also gives eloquent testimony to the conditions and the culture of slavery in Kentucky and the South. John Blassingame describes it as "one of the most reliable of the slave autobiographies," and it firmly established Bibb, together with Douglass and Josiah *Henson, as one of the leading antebellum slave narrators.

Bibb was born on 10 May 1815, one of seven children. His mother was a resourceful woman named Mildred Jackson, and his father was Kentucky state senator James Bibb. He was owned by Willard Gatewood on whose plantation he served an early life of misery. His siblings were sold away to other plantations, and in his frustration and anger he attempted escape and suffered horrible punishments. He was sold to six different owners, ultimately escaping to Detroit where he became active in the antislavery movement and abolitionist lecture circuit. Outraged by the passage of the Compromise of 1850 and its Fugitive Slave Act, Bibb is said to have remarked, "If there is no alternative but to go back to slavery, or to die contending for liberty, then death is far preferable," a clear echo of Patrick Henry. As he was an escaped slave, he emigrated to Canada, an action appropriated by Harriet Beecher *Stowe in the character of George Harris, who rejects America for Canada. In Canada Bibb became a journalist and founded Canada's first Black abolitionist newspaper, *The Voice of the Fugitive*. Bibb devoted much of the decade preceding the Civil War to activities supporting the removal of American slaves to Canada, collaborating with the Underground Railroad. He viewed Canada as a safety zone for escaped Negroes and purchased a two thousand–acre tract of land near Windsor, Ontario, to become a center for Negro culture. He organized the North American Convention of Colored People, a group that opposed the colonization of African Americans back to Africa. He died young, at age thirty-nine, in 1854. His *Narrative* provides a superb picture of life on the plantation even as it censures slavery as inhuman oppression.

• Roger W. Hite, "Voice of a Fugitive: Henry Bibb and Antebellum Black Separatism," *Journal of Black Studies* 4.3 (Mar. 1974): 269–284. John Blassingame, *The Slave Community: Plantation Life in the Antebellum South*, 1979. Charles Davis and Henry Louis Gates, Jr., *The Slave's Narrative*, 1985. William L. Andrews, *To Tell a Free Story: The First Century of Afro-American Autobiography*, 1986. Charles Heglar, ed., *Narrative of the Life and Adventures of Henry Bibb*, 2000.

—Mason I. Lowance, Jr.

BIGGER THOMAS, the chief character of Richard *Wright's 1940 best-selling novel **Native Son*, is unlike any protagonist ever to have appeared in African American literature. Before Bigger Thomas, black heroes and heroines were generally virtuous, polite, upright, intelligent, sensitive, and knowledgeable. Bigger Thomas is crude, barely literate, unclean, untrustworthy, and a murderer. But Wright emphasizes that Bigger's character is in part the result of a crippling environment. Bigger seems driven by a fear of whites that was the legacy of slavery. Every act he performs has its roots in dread. He fights his friend Gus to conceal his own fear of robbing a white man. He inadvertently suffocates *Mary Dalton because he is terrified of being discovered in a white woman's bedroom. He incinerates Mary because he fears white accusations of rape and murder. He brutally murders Bessie because he fears capture. The ending of the novel finds him having rid himself of fear of whites by discovering through self-examination something of his own identity, by accepting who he is in all its terribleness: "What I killed for I am. . . . Tell Mister. . . . Tell Jan hello. . . ." The conclusion of the novel finds Bigger arriving at a personal and psychological resolution of his situation, not a political or social one.

—Donald B. Gibson

Big Sea, The. Langston *Hughes's first volume of autobiography (1940) covers the years of his life from his birth in 1902 to the spring of 1931. Fundamentally episodic, *The Big Sea* is a succession of brief chapters, written in deceptively simple prose, that recount various adventures through which Hughes had passed during his formative years in Kansas, Illinois, and Ohio; his extended stays with his father in Mexico; his unhappy year at Columbia University; his discovery of Harlem and his visit to Africa and Europe; a year among the black bourgeoisie in Washington, D.C.; and, at great length, his experiences, good and bad, as a star of the Harlem Renaissance.

The book opens with Hughes's decision in 1923, as he set sail as a messboy on a freighter to Africa, to throw overboard all of the many books he had brought on board. It ends with the collapse of his relationship with the wealthy patron who had pampered then dumped him under baffling, hurtful circumstances in 1930. Both episodes were deeply significant. The first had to do with his intimate search for literary and racial identity; the second transformed him into a radical. Yet both are related with such a constant appeal to humor that they epitomize the spirit of the book, which appears to reflect the same triumph of laughter and art over adverse circumstances that marks the African American art form most admired by Hughes: the blues.

Central to the structure of the book is Hughes's depiction of his father. Cold and materialistic, his father disliked not only poetry but other black Americans, who seemed to him passive and unreliable. In response, Hughes casually, sometimes humorously, inscribed a portrait of his father as almost satanic, a figure who tempts his son with wealth if he would betray blacks and poetry. Thus Hughes quietly underscores what he wishes to be seen as the bedrock of his integrity: his twinned devotions to African Americans, on the one hand, and to writing, on the other.

Although Hughes points out that most black Harlemites had no idea a renaissance was going on, much of the book is devoted to the Harlem Renaissance. This section remains the most detailed firsthand account of the era in existence. Another feature of the book is its silence about Hughes's radicalism. Written as World War II was gathering force and as Hughes began to shift toward the political center, the book avoids almost all references to Hughes's leftist ties. Indeed, the story ends precisely when the avoidance of such references would have been almost impossible.

Although Hughes had high hopes for the book, its reception was disappointing, especially compared to that of Richard Wright's **Native Son* the same year. Many reviewers saw the charm of the book without recognizing its depth; Ralph *Ellison, for one, questioned the appropriateness of its tone to a black American's autobiography. However, it is admired both for its extended commentary on the Harlem Renaissance and as a self-portrait by one of the most beloved and deceptively complex of African American artists.

• Arnold Rampersad, *The Life of Langston Hughes*, vol. 1, *1902–1941*: I, *Too, Sing America*, 1986.

—Arnold Rampersad

Black Boy. Richard *Wright's 1945 autobiography *Black Boy* covers his life from four years of age to the moment of his departure from the South (Memphis, Tennessee, where he had earlier migrated from Mississippi) to the North (Chicago) at nineteen. Its subject and title place it in the tradition of African American autobiography, beginning with the nineteenth-century slave narrative, a genre in which the autobiographer describes the particularities of his own life in order to speak of the situation and condition of the race in general. While presenting the details of one life, *Black Boy* is intended to reveal the horrors, cruelties, and privations undergone by the masses of African Americans living in the South (and in the United States as a whole) during the first decades of the twentieth century.

Originally Wright's *Black Boy* was the first section of a much longer work titled *American Hunger* and divided into two parts: "Southern Night," detailing Wright's early life in the South, and "The Horror and the Glory," treating his life in Chicago and describing racism northern style. After Harper & Brothers received the manuscript from Wright, they submitted it to the Book-of-the-Month Club for consideration as a monthly selection. The club agreed to accept it on condition that its first section alone, later titled by Wright *Black Boy*, be published. The complete text of the second section of *American Hunger* was first published in 1977 by Harper & Row. The entire work, composed of both sections, as Wright originally wrote it, was published for the first time in 1992 by the Library of America.

One of the primary themes of Wright's autobiographical narrative involves the influence of racism on the personal interrelations not only among the individuals of the oppressed group but within the family itself. The first episode of the narrative, in which Wright at four years of age innocently burns down the family home, has no racial implications per se, but the response of his mother does. As punishment Wright is so severely beaten with a tree limb that he lapses into semi-consciousness and requires the attention of a physician. The mother's response is in direct correlation to the family's economic circumstance. They are poor because they are black, and the harshness of his punishment reflects the degree of the family's economic loss. On another occasion, when Wright is badly cut behind the ear by a broken bottle in a fight between black and white boys, his mother, instead of extending the comfort and sympathy ordinarily expected of a parent toward a wounded child, beats him to warn him of the dangers of fighting whites.

Black Boy's historical significance lies in its recapitulation of the thrust of black autobiography in its use of the form as a means of righting social wrong. Other African American writers have used literature to perform this function, but none before Wright had been as outspoken. In episode after episode Wright describes through his own experience of racial repression that was undergone by millions of his brothers and sisters. At the same time, he relates the story of his own growth.

• Michel Fabre, *The Unfinished Quest of Richard Wright*, 1973.

—Donald B. Gibson

Black No More. George *Schuyler's first novel, originally published in 1931 by the Macaulay Company and reissued in 1989 by Northeastern University Press, *Black No More* is generally considered the first full-length satire by an African American. In *Black No More*, Schuyler fictionalizes the political ideas that he was best known for: outrage at the notion that race makes difference and at America's social stratification based on race. While society searched for a solution to the "race problem," Schuyler, in this anti-utopian novel, uses satire and science fiction to reveal that race was not the problem.

His satire is aimed specifically at myths of racial purity and white supremacy and presents ways in which the perpetuation of racism serves economic purposes. Greed is the primary motivation of his characters. He caricatures organizations such as the NAACP, the KKK, and the Urban League, presenting their leaders as hustlers in different shades.

In the preface, Schuyler dedicates *Black No More* to all of the "pure Caucasians" of the world, setting up any such readers for a shock. We are then introduced to Max Disher, a brown trickster, and his sidekick, Bunny Brown, and the racist environment in which they live. Max is rejected by a racist white woman, Helen, who is entertained by black cabaret performers but is repulsed at the idea of dancing with a black man. This rejection sends Max to Dr. Crookman, inventor of Black-No-More, Inc., where all traces of blackness are removed and Max becomes Matt. The rest of the novel traces Max's adventures as a Caucasian: he marries the same Helen that previously rejected him, and with Bunny, infiltrates the major racist organization of the country, extorts millions of dollars, and finally flees to Europe. The reader is also privy to the effects of the runaway success of Black-No-More, Inc., on American society. As the black population is changed to white, black race leaders are put out of the "leadership" business; as America loses its cheap black labor, an increasingly violent labor situation erupts; and lying-in hospitals are created to secretly change newborns to white. In an attempt to decipher a "proper" race hierarchy, scientists discover that over half of the Caucasian population has "tainted" blood, including those who most advocated racial purity. Just as America goes wild with frenzy, Dr. Crookman brings order by revealing that the "newly" white are actually two to three shades lighter than the "real" Caucasians. Suddenly white is no longer right and everyone panics while sales increase for skin-darkening lotions. "Normality" is returned at the end of the novel with black being beautiful. Schuyler makes clear that there are advantages to possessing white skin in a society that worships this, but human nature does not change purely because of skin color.

—Adenike Marie Davidson

Black Thunder. Arna Bontemps's novel *Black Thunder: Gabriel's Revolt: Virginia 1800* was published in 1936. This conflation of history and imagination is based on an actual slave rebellion reported in contemporary newspapers and recorded in the *Calendar of Virginia State Papers* (vol. 9, 1890). The chronicle begins in the great house of old Moseley Sheppard whose dependence on old Ben Woodfolk, his faithful house servant, has developed over the years into veiled companionship. Old Bundy, Ben's work-worn counterpart, once a field-hand on the neighboring plantation but now reduced to scavenging throughout the neighborhood, intrudes on Ben's peace to beg for rum and surreptitiously to invite him to join the slave Gabriel's scheme for insurrection. It is old Bundy's misfortune to be observed with his jug of rum by Thomas Prosser, his merciless master, who uses the excuse to beat him to death.

Bundy's murder adds fresh resolve to Gabriel's plans and subverts the comfort of reluctant individuals like old Ben. Indeed, Gabriel had chosen the occasion of Bundy's funeral to elaborate his strategy to amass some eleven hundred men and one woman to take the city of Richmond in their first step toward freedom. The remarkable funeral seems to emerge from a collective preliterate tradition whose origins are African and whose inspiration to freedom arises from the natural world. Under these conditions, old Ben swears allegiance to the conspiracy in the presence of the principal plotters, at first with apprehension and then with deep trepidation.

Gabriel, the strapping six-foot two-inch coachman for Thomas Prosser, had earned the respect of slaves and "free" blacks throughout Henrico County, Virginia, about a year earlier by winning a titan's battle with Ditcher, the brutal driver of slaves from another plantation. Gabriel wins fealty for his resoluteness and a generosity of spirit, which appeals to persons as diverse as Mingo, the literate freeman, and the tempestuous Juba, Gabriel's woman; he finds personal inspiration in the proclamation of General Toussaint *L'Ouverture, the Haitian liberator, who still lived, and in biblical text read aloud by Mingo.

At the appointed hour of insurrection, a relentless, unprecedented downpour transforms Henrico County into a flood plain; Gabriel's insurgents find it impossible to execute their grand design and are forced to pull back in favor of a more propitious time. The delay, however, is sufficient to uncover the treachery of Pharoah, who immediately snatches the opportunity to turn informant. Out of loyalty to Moseley Sheppard, old Ben confesses his role and names leaders.

Across the nation amazement accompanies alarm, for it is inconceivable that illiterate chattel are capable of conceiving such a scheme on their own. Every literate white person who is not native to the region is suspect, as Scotsman John Callender, friend of Thomas Jefferson, rudely learns. Frenchman M. Creuzot, printer, is particularly imperiled and flees north for his safety. Before long all the major figures in the conspiracy, including Gabriel, are captured and hung. Pharoah, meanwhile, literally loses his mind, but perfidious old Ben endures, however uneasily.

Richard *Wright generously noted in his 1936 review that *Black Thunder* broke new ground in African American fiction by addressing concerns not previously touched upon in African American novels. Most critics readily concur that given its myriad voices and many points of view, the controlling idea of the novel is its universal determination toward freedom, a principle that warrants their generous attention to its political purpose. Others, however, noting its contribution to the vernacular tradition, cite meaningful distinctions between literacy and orality as racial and cultural markers.

• Mary Kemp Davis, "From Death Unto Life: The Rhetorical Function of Funeral Rites in Arna Bontemps' *Black Thunder*," *Journal of Ritual Studies* 1 (Jan. 1987): 85–101. Daniel Reagan, "Voices of Silence: The Representation of Orality in Arna Bontemps' *Black Thunder*," *Studies in American Fiction* 19 (Spring 1991): 71–83. Arnold Rampersad, introduction to the 1992 ed., and Arna Bontemps, introduction to the 1968 ed., *Black Thunder: Gabriel's Revolt: Virginia 1800*, 1992.

—Charles L. James

Blacker the Berry, The. Wallace *Thurman's first novel, *The Blacker the Berry: A Novel of Negro Life* (1929) takes its title from an old folk saying, "the blacker the berry, the sweeter the juice." It is an autobiographical satire whose neurotic, dark-skinned protagonist, Emma Lou Morgan, internalizes biases against dark-complexioned people after a midwestern upbringing by colorstruck relatives mimicking racist societal values. Like Thurman, Emma Lou goes to the University of Southern California and then to Harlem. Unlike Thurman, who was primarily drawn to the artistic renaissance blooming there, Emma Lou hopes Harlem will enable her to escape finally the harsh intraracial prejudice that is exacerbated by her sex and egocentrism.

Among the mundane settings of Harlem tenement buildings, employment agencies, public dance halls, rent parties, cabarets, and movie houses, Emma Lou has numerous opportunities to overcome her obsession with color and class consciousness. She is, indeed, discriminated against by both blacks and whites, but not to the degree that she believes. In a crowded one-room apartment filled with liquor-gorging intellectuals resembling Langston *Hughes (Tony Crews), Zora Neale *Hurston (Cora Thurston), and Richard Bruce *Nugent (Paul), Truman (Thurman himself) explains intraracial discrimination by examining the parasitic nature of humankind. He argues that "people have to feel superior to something . . . [other than] domestic animals or steel machines. . . . It is much more pleasing to pick some individual or group . . . on the same plane." Thus, he suggests that mulattoes who ostracize darker-skinned African Americans merely follow a hierarchy of discrimination set by materially powerful white people. Truman's anatomy of racism, however, is ignored by Emma Lou.

The Blacker the Berry received reviews that, while mixed, praised Thurman for his ironic depiction of original settings, characters, and themes then considered off limits for African American literary examination. Many others also criticized him for emphasizing the seamier side of Harlem life. But Thurman was never pleased with *Blacker*, and his caricature of the female protagonist shows why. Emma Lou behaves unlike traditional African American females who tend to revise rather than accept the values of both African American and white men. After she is repeatedly degraded by light-skinned Alva, Emma Lou's spiritual liberation begins only when she acknowledges the Thurmanian and Emersonian ideal that salvation rests with the individual, first expressed by white Campbell Kitchen (Carl Van Vechten). In other words, Thurman becomes trapped in the alien body of Emma Lou and does not have the creative imagination to break her racial fixation by summoning up a female perspective. Instead, Emma Lou trades an obsession with skin color for one that is viewed by a patriarchal society as being even more perverse. When she catches Alva embracing the homosexual Bobbie, Emma Lou finally gathers the strength to leave him. Herein lies an example of the dominant literary problem exhibited by the Harlem Renaissance old guard and avant garde alike. Their art is consumed by the paradox in creating liberated African American male and female voices while mouthing the ethics of the American patriarchy.

• Hugh Gloster, *Negro Voices in American Fiction*, 1948. Bernard W. Bell, *The Afro-American Novel and Its Traditions*, 1987.

—SallyAnn H. Ferguson

BLACUS, HENRICO. *See* Henry Blake.

Blake. Martin R. *Delany's *Blake, or the Huts of America: A Tale of the Mississippi Valley, the Southern United States, and Cuba* is an awkward, brave, and complex novel. Twenty-six chapters from a promised eighty appeared in the *Anglo-African Magazine* (Jan.–July 1859); and, after revisions, the complete tale appeared in the *Weekly Anglo-African Newspaper* (New York City, Nov. 1861–June 1862). Installments appeared on the front pages; the *American Baptist* said *Blake* was "beautifully written"; both Anglo-African introductions encouraged blacks to read it. In part, however, because issues including the last six chapters have been lost, today *Blake*'s realistic portrayal of white carelessness and oppression of black people across the African diaspora is more impressive than its romantic dream of deliverance.

Out of print until 1970 and still lacking an unmodernized critical edition, *Blake* has received complaints about its untrained author's shortcomings: awkward, complex plots and sentences, lack of narrative bridges, inadequate descriptions of action, and a too often passively observant hero. Others have enthusiastically praised *Blake*'s informative range of midcentury sociopolitical conditions, characters, attitudes, and boldly black-nationalist, Pan-African perspective. Fewer have recognized its fifty black-originated or adopted songs and poems, or its varied vernaculars and folklore pointed out in Delany's footnotes and in conversations that are *Blake*'s major story-telling vehicle.

Its plot is complicated. Part 1's first chapter introduces international characters involved in the illegal slave trade. On a Mississippi plantation the novel's unadulterated black hero, Henry (who uses several surnames), finds his slave wife has been sold away to Cuba. He complains about false Christians, confronts his master, and considers running away, but decides instead to organize a slave rebellion conspiracy. He travels through twelve southern states and Indian Territory creating cadres of comrades—male and female—ready to strike upon his signal. He returns to lead his son and wife's parents north to Canada. Part 1 ends with Henry going to New York City and thence to Cuba.

In Part 2, the hero, who now calls himself *Henry Blake, organizes Cuba, rescues his wife, enlists the mulatto elite, works on a slave ship to and from Africa, attempts to turn Africans against the trade, returns to Cuba, and arranges sales of the cargo to coconspirators in his antiwhite revolution.

Blake enlarges Emerson's call for an American epic (1842) and answers African American calls for literature by their own (1844–1854) as it touches all shores known to African Americans. Negatively, *Blake* borrows the doomed tones of Byronic romances and his own *Condition of the Colored People* (1852) and revives two historical heroes dead long before 1850 (Blake from Haiti's General Charles Belair, and Plácido [Gabriel Valdés] from Cuba). Positively, its hero bravely struggles before rescuing his wife as in the *Odyssey*; he is like a *Moses and a looked-for savior from the Bible and black folklore, while occasional footnotes ground hopeful scenes in Delany's personal experiences.

Blake's black hero and its emphasis admit no white abolitionists or underground railroad agents, revising tales of light-skinned heroes and white allies in slave narratives and by contemporary mulatto storytellers Frederick *Douglass, William Wells *Brown, George B. *Vashon, and Frank J. *Webb. Its Afrocentricity counters Euro-centered tales of slave rebels by such whites as Edgar Allan Poe, Richard Hildreth, Harriet Beecher *Stowe, Herman Melville, and J. B. Jones.

• Martin R. Delany, *Blake, or the Huts of America*, ed. Floyd J. Miller, 1970. Kristin Herzog, *Women, Ethnics and Exotics: Images of Power in Mid-Nineteenth Century American Fiction*, 1983. Bernard W. Bell, *The Afro-American Novel and Its Tradition*, 1987. Paul Gilroy, *The Black Atlantic: Modernity and Double Consciousness*, 1993. Eric J. Sundquist, *To Wake the Nations: Race in the Making of American Literature*, 1993.

—Allan D. Austin

BLEDSOE, DR. Dr. Bledsoe, the president of the college from which Ralph *Ellison's narrator is expelled in **Invisible Man* (1952), is pivotal to the novel's structure, for it is Bledsoe who ejects the narrator out of his idyllic setting into the harsh world of reality. It is also Bledsoe who gives the narrator the false sense of security in the letters of recommendation, intended literally to keep the narrator running. In addition to his structural function in the novel, Bledsoe represents the type of leadership that Ellison believed to be detrimental to the development of Blacks. Ellison maintains in **Shadow and Act* (1964) that when he started writing *Invisible Man* he was displeased with the leadership in the Black community: "It seemed to me that [Black leaders] acknowledged no final responsibility to the Negro community for their acts and implicit in their roles were constant acts of betrayal. This made for a sad, chronic division between their values and the values of those they were supposed to represent." Bledsoe typifies the negative qualities of Black leadership. He is a dishonest, Machiavellian schemer. Not only does he have the narrator and the physician at the Golden Day shipped out of his area because they threaten his stability, but he also informs the narrator that he has "played the nigger" to acquire the power and the prestige of his position. He affirms: " . . . I'll have every Negro in the county hanging on a tree limb by morning if it means staying where I am." Such ruthlessness makes Bledsoe a threat to the stability of the community, for it is obvious that he is willing to sacrifice that community in order to maintain power.

It seems too that Bledsoe has alienated himself from the people he serves. In discussing the narrator's punishment with Mr. *Norton, he says to the trustee, "You can't be soft with these people. We mustn't pamper them." The Blacks he serves have become "these people," not "my people," and his use of "we" clearly indicates that he associates himself not with Blacks but with the white power structure. Bledsoe is only concerned with his personal interests. Through his character, Ellison seems to attack much of what is negative in Black leadership.

—Ralph Reckley, Sr.

Bluest Eye, The. The first novel by Nobel Laureate Toni *Morrison, *The Bluest Eye* was published in 1970 and was heralded for its sensitive treatment of African American female identity. It is the tragic story of a young African American girl, *Pecola Breedlove, whose loneliness and desire for love and attention is manifested in her desire to have blue eyes. The novel opens with an epigraph from a Dick and Jane primer that presents an ideal family with a house, mother, father, children, cat, dog, and friend. The story that shapes the novel is narrated through the eyes and voice of Claudia McTeer, whose narrative shifts the reader's attention to a very different world from that of the primer. Before she commits the taboo of telling the community the secret of Pecola's demise, however, she connects her own childhood desire to dismember white dolls, and her transference of that hatred to white girls, with her desire to understand why white girls were loved and African American girls were not.

Claudia then proceeds to tell not only a story of Pecola's painful childhood with an indifferent mother and an alcoholic father, and the trauma of rape by her father that results in her pregnancy and plunge into insanity, but also the story of the community's role in Pecola's tragic fate. The novel both deconstructs the image of the white community as the site of normalcy and perfection and illustrates the realities of life in a poverty-stricken African American community whose socioeconomic status is complicated by the politics of race, especially internalized racism. Pecola's mother, Pauline Breedlove, works as a domestic and escapes from her own feelings of ugliness and low self-worth in the home of her white employer. Pauline's education about female beauty comes from her avid moviegoing but ends abruptly when she loses a tooth and convinces herself she will never look like Jean Harlow. She turns to the church and religion out of resignation to her feelings of unattractiveness and contempt for her husband, Cholly. Her contempt for Cholly colors her relationship with Pecola as well. In one pivotal scene, when Pecola comes to visit her at work and accidentally spills a freshly baked blueberry pie on the floor, Pauline humiliates Pecola by slapping and scolding her while consoling the daughter of her white employer. Cholly Breedlove's attempt to construct an acceptable image of himself as a black man is complicated by memories of a racial incident that alters his ability to love his wife and daughter in appropriate ways. His drunkenness, routine fights with Pauline, and incestuous relationship with Pecola form the context out of which Pecola's own self-loathing develops. The story unravels the community's propensity to scapegoat Pecola, to measure its identity by devaluing and eventually destroying her humanity, to engage in intraracial politics by valuing the skin color and hair texture of some African American girls but not others, and to be seduced by fraudulent characters like Soaphead Church, the bootleg preacher who, out of sympathy, tricks Pecola into thinking he has given her blue eyes.

Published in the midst of the period of pride in blackness associated with the late 1960s and early 1970s, *The Bluest Eye* ultimately calls into question the aesthetics of beauty that, in the words of the novel, "originated in envy, thrived in insecurity, and ended in disillusion." Moreover, though Morrison's first novel was surpassed in critical recognition by the acclaim given to her later novels, it nevertheless marked the beginning of what would be the most significant period of literary production of books by African American women about African American female identity.

• Michael Awkward, *Inspiriting Influences: Tradition, Revision, and Afro-American Women's Novels,* 1989. Trudier Harris, *Fiction and Folklore: The Novels of Toni Morrison,* 1991.

—Marilyn Sanders Mobley

BLYDEN, EDWARD WILMOT (1832–1912), essayist, journalist, educator, statesman, and politician. Little remembered today, Edward Wilmot Blyden was the most important African thinker of the nineteenth century, leading one of the most varied careers of any Black man in that era. Born in Saint Thomas, Blyden came to America in 1850 to attend Rutgers Theological College but was rejected because of his race. He subsequently emigrated to Liberia, grew enamored of African life, and became a staunch supporter of his new homeland. Feeling called upon to undermine misconceptions about "the dark continent" and to encourage Blacks throughout the diaspora to repatriate, Blyden spent the remainder of his life serving this cause in several capacities. As a journalist, Blyden edited the *Liberia Herald* and founded and edited the *Negro* and the *West African Reporter,* two of the first Pan-African journals. As an educator, he served as principal of Alexander High School, Monrovia; Liberia's educational commissioner to Britain and America; professor of classics at, and president of, Liberia College; and director of Mohammedan education in Sierra Leone. As a politician, Blyden was variously Liberian secretary of state, government agent to the interior in Sierra Leone, Liberian ambassador to the Court of Saint James, Liberian minister of interior, unsuccessful candidate for Liberia's presidency, agent of native affairs in Lagos, and Liberian minister plenipotentiary and envoy extraordinary to London and Paris.

Despite these impressive credentials, Blyden remains most significant for his intellectual achievements, writing voluminously on a wide variety of topics. His most famous volume, *Christianity, Islam and the Negro Race* (1887), expounded his belief that the effects of Christianity had been largely detrimental to Africans, while the effects of Islam had been largely salutary. Blyden believed in the popular notion that each race had its own qualities, an idea usually invoked to the disparagement of Africans but which he saw instead as a way of extolling the virtues of "the African personality." One of the first and strongest believers in African nationalism, Blyden felt that the political dominance the European-minded coastal Liberians were then enjoying would eventually, and rightfully, give way to a form of government created by the true, uncorrupted Africans of the interior. Blyden also championed Pan-Africanism, believing that the whole continent needed to work together to protect itself from being divided up by the European powers.

Whether writing as historian (*The Negro in Ancient History,* 1869; *West Africa before Europe,* 1905), pedagogue (*The West African University,* 1872), traveler (*From West Africa to Palestine,* 1873), or sociologist (*African Life and Customs,* 1908), Blyden was always insightful. He invariably emphasized the achievements and potential of Africans and their descendants, to which end he became his own best example. Although not always liked—witness his defeat in the Liberian presidential race and his near-lynching in 1871, both of which he blamed on "traitorous" mulattoes—Blyden was always admired for his intellect. His influence, whether acknowledged or not, can be seen in such later figures as Marcus *Garvey, Aimé Césaire, Léopold Senghor, Kwame Nkrumah, George Padmore, *Malcolm X, and Amiri *Baraka.

• Hollis R. Lynch, *Edward Wilmot Blyden: Pan-Negro Patriot,* 1967. Richard West, *Back to Africa,* 1970.

—Adam Meyer

BONNER, MARITA (1899–1971), essayist, playwright, and short fiction writer. Born 16 June 1899 in Boston, Marita Bonner graduated from Radcliffe in 1922 and taught high school in West Virginia and Washington, D.C. She married William Almy Occomy in 1930. While living in Washington, she was a member of the "S" Street Salon, a group of writers who met usually at the home of Georgia Douglas *Johnson. Encouraged and influenced by writers such as Johnson, May *Miller, Langston *Hughes, Jean *Toomer, Alain *Locke, Countee *Cullen, and other major figures of the Harlem Renaissance, Occomy began to publish works that embodied her concern for the deplorable conditions facing African American men and women living in an America characterized by racial, class, and gender inequities.

Occomy published two essays that Elizabeth Brown-Guillory describes as those "that captured the spirit of the Black Renaissance." "On Being Young—A Woman—and Colored," which won first place in the *Crisis* literary contest of 1925, elucidates the particular situation of African American women whose worth in American mainstream society is doubly devalued and describes segregation's practice of forcing African Americans from diverse backgrounds together—"in a bundle"—as embroilment "in the seaweed of a Black Ghetto." "The Young Blood Hungers" (1928) is militant and apocalyptic in tone as it warns of ensuing violence resulting from poor race relations. The concerns raised in these essays persist in her plays and short stories.

Occomy published three plays. *The Pot Maker: A Play to Be Read* (1927) is an exploration of infidelity. *The Purple Flower* (1928) promotes a revolutionary response to racism, which Margaret Wilkerson describes as "perhaps the most provocative play" written by an African American woman prior to 1950. *Exit, an Illusion: A One-Act Play* (1929) examines the complications of mixed ancestry. Experimental in structure, featuring second-person narration and plot development reliant on a central metaphor, these plays assert moral dilemmas that challenge the characters to prove their worth. Apparently written to be read, the plays were not produced in Occomy's lifetime.

Published mostly in *Opportunity* and the *Crisis,* Occomy's short stories encompass a diverse range of subjects and themes. Class differentiation among African Americans is explored in her first published short story, "The Hands" (1925), and "The Prison-Bound" (1926) addresses issues of class and gender, and notions of "beauty." "Nothing New" (1926) is her first published story of life in Chicago's Black Belt, a setting that predominates her later work, and communicates the tensions and entanglements of racial intermixture. "Drab Rambles" (1927) illustrates how both a female and a male protagonist deal with gender-specific confrontations in their respective struggles against economic hardship and racism.

After 1930, Frye Street—a fictitious "ethnic intersection" where African American residents must coexist with Chinese, Russian, and various other European immigrants—dominates the majority of Occomy's stories. Appearing mostly in *Opportunity,* many of the stories were published in separate parts. Notable works include the trilogy "The Triple Triad on

Black Notes" (1933) and the two-part story "Tin Can" (1934), which won the 1933 literary prize. The various stories thematize issues of colorism, marital betrayal, family strife, and poverty. "A Sealed Pod" (1936), an unflattering image of peas not touching despite their closeness, metaphorizes Frye Street while it chronicles the murder of a young woman by her lover. Three stories published in 1939, "The Makin's," "The Whipping," and "Hongry Fire," differently depict the corrosive effects of the urban environment on children. "Patch Quilt" (1940), set in the rural South, resists the contemporary tendency to romanticize the southern small town, portraying the environment as confining rather than pastoral. Occomy's last published short story, "One True Love" (1941), again illustrates the double bind of the African American woman's position described in "On Being Young—A Woman—and Colored."

Marita Bonner Occomy died in 1971 from injuries sustained in a fire in her Chicago apartment. Publishing for only sixteen years, her literary contribution to African American literature is significant. Her characterization of urban environments as destructive and corrupting prefigures, even perhaps influenced, Richard *Wright's portrayal of the urban in *Native Son* (1940). Her ability to traverse genres and treat a myriad of themes demonstrates not only the versatility of her talents but also the diversity of African American culture and experience during the interwar era.

• Diane Isaacs, "Bonner, Marita/Marita Odetta," in *The Harlem Renaissance: A Historical Dictionary for the Era,* ed. Bruce Kellner, 1984, p. 45. Margaret Wilkerson, introduction to *Nine Plays by Black Women,* 1986. Joyce Flynn, introduction to *Frye Street and Environs: The Collected Works of Marita Bonner,* eds. Joyce Flynn and Joyce Occomy Stricklin, 1987. Joyce Flynn, "Marita Bonner Occomy," in *DLB,* vol. 51, Afro-*American Writers from the Harlem Renaissance to 1949,* ed. Trudier Harris, 1987, pp. 222–228. Nellie McKay, "What Were They Saying? Black Women Playwrights of the Harlem Renaissance," in *The Harlem Renaissance Re-Examined,* ed. Victor Kramer, 1987, pp. 129–147. Elizabeth Brown-Guillory, ed., *Wines in the Wilderness: Plays by African American Women from the Harlem Renaissance to the Present,* 1990.

—Kim Jenice Dillon

BONTEMPS, ARNA (1902–1973), novelist, poet, and librarian. Born in Alexandria, Louisiana, the first child of a Roman Catholic bricklayer and a Methodist schoolteacher, Arna Wendell Bontemps grew up in California and graduated from Pacific Union College. After college he accepted a teaching position in Harlem at the height of the Harlem Renaissance, and in 1926 and 1927 won first prizes on three separate occasions in contests with other "New Negro" poets. The same years marked his marriage to Alberta Johnson and the start of a family of six children.

Bontemps's first effort at a novel (*Chariot in the Cloud,* 1929), a *bildungsroman* set in southern California, never found a publisher, but by mid-1931, as his teaching position in New York City ended, Harcourt accepted **God Sends Sunday* (1931), his novel about the rise and notoriety of Little Augie. This tiny black jockey of the 1890s, whose period of great luck went sour, was inspired by Bontemps's favorite uncle, Buddy.

While teaching at Oakwood Junior College, Bontemps began the first of several collaborations with Langston *Hughes, **Popo and Fifina: Children of Haiti* (1932), a colorful travel book for juveniles that portrays two black children who migrate with their parents from an inland farm to a busy fishing village. The success of this new genre encouraged him to make juvenile fiction an ongoing part of his repertoire.

Residence in the Deep South proved fruitful for his career, for in quick succession he published his best-known short story, "A Summer Tragedy" (1932), the compelling narrative of a simple yet dignified couple worn weary by a lifetime of sharecropping on a southern plantation; wrote a dozen other tales of the South that were compiled years later under the title *The Old South* (1973); completed yet another profitable juvenile book, *You Can't Pet a Possum* (1934), for its time a charming rural Alabama story about an eight-year-old named Shine Boy and his yellow hound, Butch; initiated contact with composer and musician W. C. Handy to ghostwrite Handy's autobiography; and, in a visit to Fisk University in Nashville, "discovered" its rich and seemingly forgotten repository of narratives by former slaves.

Late in 1932 Bontemps started writing **Black Thunder: Gabriel's Revolt: Virginia 1800* (1936), his singular and inspired representation of an actual slave insurrection that failed because of weather and treachery. This work establishes the concept of freedom as the principal motif of his ensuing works and evokes questions regarding differences between writing and orality as racial and cultural markers. But because he was forced out of Oakwood at the end of the 1934 school year, the novel was completed in the cramped space of his father's California home, where the family had retreated.

Ironic relief arrived a year later from the Adventists in the form of a principalship at their Shiloh Academy on Chicago's battered South Side. The venture was bright with promise because the city and the university had attracted a young and savvy coterie of social radicals including Richard *Wright, Margaret *Walker, and Jack Conroy. Favorable critical reception of *Black Thunder* assured Bontemps's celebrity among the group, and his application to the Julian Rosenwald Fund to research and write a third novel met with success. In *Sad-Faced Boy* (1937), he relates the travels to Harlem of three quaint Alabama boys who in time nostalgically discover the charm of their own birthplace. In 1938 he secured an appointment as editorial supervisor to the Federal Writers' Project of the Illinois WPA. He sailed for the Caribbean in the fall of 1938 and put the finishing touches on *Drums at Dusk* (1939), his historical portrayal of the celebrated eighteenth-century black revolution on the island of Santo Domingo.

With great relief he completed *Father of the Blues* (1941), the "autobiography" commissioned by the ever-testy W. C. Handy; he edited his first compilation, *Golden Slippers: An Anthology of Negro Poetry for Young Readers* (1941); he then published a humorous American tall tale for children coauthored with his WPA colleague Jack Conroy titled *The Fast Sooner Hound* (1942); he was awarded two additional Rosenwald grants to pursue a degree and to write a book on "the Negro in Illinois"; and in 1943 he completed a master's degree in library science at the University of Chicago, clearing the way to his appointment as librarian at Fisk University.

In 1946 the controversial musical based on his first novel reached Broadway as *St. Louis Woman* for a short but successful run. Arguably his most distinguished work of the decade was *The Story of the Negro* (1948), a race history since Egyptian civilization that won him the Jane Addams Children's Book Award for 1956. Then, with Langston Hughes, he edited *The Poetry of the Negro* (1949), a comprehensive collection of poems by blacks and tributary poems by nonblacks.

An assortment of histories and biographies, largely written with youths in mind, emerged from Fisk throughout the 1950s and the succeeding civil rights years. Bontemps and Hughes's collaboration produced two anthologies during this period, *The Book of Negro Folklore* (1959) and *American Negro Poetry* (1963).

After Hughes's death in 1967, Bontemps compiled *Hold Fast to Dreams* (1969), a montage of poems by black and white writers. But compilations of a more personal sort rounded off his long career. They include *The Harlem Renaissance Remembered* (1972), featuring an introductory reflection by Bontemps and twelve critical essays on literary figures from the era; *Personals* (1963), a collection of his own poems reissued in 1973 as a third edition with a prefatory personal history; and *The Old South: "A Summer Tragedy" and Other Stories of the Thirties* (1973), which opens with the personal essay "Why I Returned," places most of his short fiction under a single cover.

Retirement from Fisk in 1966 brought recognition in the form of two honorary degrees and distinguished professorial appointments at the University of Illinois (Chicago Circle), Yale University, and back at Fisk as writer in residence. Following his death in 1973, early estimates of his career from Sterling A. *Brown and Aaron Douglas noted that he deserves to be known much better than he has been. Aptly, the Yale appointment included the title of Curator of the James Weldon Johnson Collection at the Beinecke Library, for prevalent views have come to regard him as a chronicler and keeper of black cultural heritage. It is worth noting that the vast and unique body of extant correspondence with his friend Langston Hughes is housed in this archive. Bontemps's most distinctive works are ringing affirmations of the human passion for freedom and the desire for social justice inherent in us all. Arnold *Rampersad called him the conscience of his era and it could be fairly added that his tendency to fuse history and imagination represents his personal legacy to a collective memory.

• Charles H. Nichols, ed., *Arna Bontemps–Langston Hughes Letters, 1925–1967,* 1988. Kirkland C. Jones, *Renaissance Man from Louisiana: A Biography of Arna Wendell Bontemps,* 1992. Charles L. James, "Arna W. Bontemps' Creole Heritage," *Syracuse University Library Associates Courier* 30 (1995): 91–115. Daniel Reagan, "Achieving Perspective: Arna Bontemps and the Shaping Force of Harlem Culture," in *Essays in Arts and Sciences,* 25 (1996): 69–78.

—Charles L. James

BOYD, CANDY (b. 1946), born Marguerite Dawson, educator, activist, and novelist. Educating people about their positive potential has long been Candy Boyd's priority. As a high school student, she tried to stop blockbusting in her native Chicago by convincing three of her friends, an African American, a Jew, and a Protestant, to join her in personal visits to more than two hundred white families. She withdrew from college to work as an organizer for the Southern Christian Leadership Conference. When she finally earned her bachelor's degree from Northeastern Illinois State University, she became, in her own words, a "militant teacher." She worked with Operation PUSH, organized neighborhood beautification projects, and used her Saturdays to take students on excursions to parks, theaters, and other neighborhoods.

When Boyd moved to Berkeley, California, and began teaching in a more diversely multicultural setting, her frustration with literary stereotypes and negative depictions of African Americans was exacerbated by her discovery that Asians, Latinos, and many Euro-Americans suffered similar literary treatment. She decided to write books for children that were honest, interesting, and inspiring. Though she had earned a PhD in education from the University of California and had been teaching for several years, Boyd prepared for this task by taking courses in writing for children and by reading every children's book in the Berkeley Public Library.

Named Professor of the Year at St. Mary's College in 1992, Candy Boyd is renowned for training teachers and creating organizations that encourage and develop reading among young people. In her books, schools are sites for learning and developing responsibility outside the family. Her characters encounter bullies, liars, and other misdirected classmates and teachers. They also build relationships with adults and children who inspire and guide them.

Candy Boyd's books explore complex and perplexing questions about the world and the emotions engendered as youngsters experience it. Her plots generally focus upon family relations complicated by external forces. In *Charlie Pippin* (1987), Charlie's father's experiences in Vietnam hinder family communication. In *Circle of Gold* (1984), the death of Mattie Benson's father requires her mother to work two jobs to support the family. Death and grieving nearly defeat twelve-year-old Toni Douglas in Boyd's second book, *Breadsticks and Blessing Places* (1985; republished as *Forever Friends* in 1986). Toni Douglas wants to please her family by being accepted into King Academy but her frustration with math, her need to babysit her brother, and her desire to socialize with her friends were already interfering when her friend Susan is killed in an automobile accident. First rejected by publishers because of its "relentless" focus on death, *Breadsticks and Blessing Places* was later selected for the Children's Book of the Year List.

Boyd's characters are not merely survivors; they are intriguingly typical, basically competent young people who have (or who create) supportive families and friends to help them face crises and move toward more hopeful futures. The protagonists are generally from working- or middle-class homes and their dilemmas are realistic. Joey Davis in *Chevrolet Saturdays* (1993) was the best science student in his fourth grade class whose testing for the gifted classes was postponed because of budget cuts. Mrs. Hamlin, his fifth grade teacher, however, is an inexperienced and unhappy individual without particular interest or competence in science and with a decided preference for those already certified as high achievers. Misinterpreting Joey's preoccupation with his mother's remarriage and his father's pending move to Chicago as evidence of low intelligence, Mrs. Hamlin recommends Joey be placed in a class for slow learners. Unlike admission to the gifted classes, this transfer threatens to occur without further ado. When his stepfather takes a strong part in challenging the teacher's recommendation, when Joey learns to balance his afterschool job at the neighborhood pharmacy with more positive classroom behavior, and when he atones for the family dog's injury by judiciously nursing him back to health, things begin to work out.

Candy Boyd's novels have received awards from the Children's Book Council, the American Library Association, and the International Reading Association. *Circle of Gold* was designated a Coretta Scott King Honor Book. Like Walter Dean *Myers, Sharon Bell *Mathis, Mildred D. *Taylor, John *Steptoe, and other contemporary African American writers, Boyd's emphasis upon positive development and the strengths of the African American communities does not ignore or downplay the problems and challenges of racism and prejudice. Instead she uses lively, realistic, and compelling characters to illustrate the message that "you make it. It's going to be hard and tough and it's not fair . . . but you make it."

• Barbara Rollock, *Black Authors and Illustrators of Children's Books*, 1988. Sonia Benson, "Candy Dawson Boyd," in *CA*, vol. 138, ed. Donna Dendorf, 1993, pp. 52–55. Sonia Benson, "Candy Dawson Boyd," in *Something about the Author*, vol. 72, ed. Diane Telgen, 1993, pp. 14–19.

—Frances Smith Foster

BOYD, MELBA (b. 1950), poet, educator, editor, essayist, and biographer. Melba Joyce Boyd was born on 2 April 1950 to John Percy Boyd and Dorothy Winn, since divorced, in Detroit, Michigan. She is married with two children. Boyd received her BA in English from Wayne State University in 1971 and an MA in English from the same institution in 1972. She served as a teacher at Cass Technical High School (1972–1973), an instructor at Wayne County Community College (1972–1982), and assistant editor of the *Broadside* (1972–1977; 1980–1982). In 1979, Boyd received her doctorate in English from the University of Michigan at Ann Arbor. She taught at the University of Iowa (1982–1988) and Ohio State University (1988–1989) before becoming the director of Afro-American Studies at the University of Michigan at Flint in 1989. She is currently on the faculty at Wayne State University. Among other awards, she received a Faculty Research Grant from the University of Michigan in 1990 and was Senior Fulbright Lecturer in Germany (1982–1983).

Boyd began publishing poetry after graduating from college. Her earliest work appeared in *The Broadside Annual* and African American periodicals such as the *Black Scholar* and *First World*, and explored the intersection of personal and African American political experience. In 1978 Boyd's first volume of poetry, *Cat Eyes and Dead Wood*, was published with accompanying illustrations by Michele G. Russell. Later volumes, such as [*thirteen frozen flamingoes*] (1988) and *Song for Maya* (1989), also incorporate illustrations. After 1983 Boyd drew on her German experience to write poetry. *Song for Maya* and *thirteen frozen flamingoes* are both published by German presses. The former is written in both German and English, with English on one side of the page and German on the other, while the latter includes occasional German phrases. Boyd has been anthologized in two collections of African American literature, *Black Sister: Poetry by Black American Women, 1746–1980* (1981) and *Sturdy Black Bridges: Visions of Black Women in Literature* (1979). The poet's essay on her poem *Song for Maya*, an exploration of the difficulties being multiracial poses for individuals and for American society, appears in *Missions in Conflict: Essays on U.S.–Mexican Relations and Chicano Culture*, edited by Renate von Bardeleben (1986). Her biography of Frances Ellen Watkins *Harper, *Discarded Legacy: Politics and Poetics in the Life of Frances E. W. Harper*, was published by Wayne State University Press in 1994.

Stylistically, Boyd's poetry has remained consistent. Her earliest published work, such as "silver lace (for herb)" (1978), introduces her characteristic short, powerful lines, concern with individual words, and manipulation of punctuation to create form and meaning. Boyd uses the language and imagery of contemporary culture, creating startling, Sextonesque phrases such as "cultural insurancemen," and often evokes female sexuality through sensory moments. Less frequently she draws on musical patterns and rhyme: "save the bones/for willie jones," for example, or the sibilance of "bussstop." While still concerned with the personal and political issues of race, class, and gender, Boyd's work has gradually become less dependent on the poet's individual experience to communicate meaning and more concerned with others' experience.

• Theresa Gunnels Rush, Carol Fairbanks Myers, and Esther Spring Arata, *Black American Writers Past and Present: A Biographical and Bibliographical Dictionary*, vol. 1, 1975. "Melba Joyce Boyd" in *WWABA*, ed. Shirelle Phelps, 1994, pp. 142–143.

—Karen R. Bloom

BRADLEY, DAVID (b. 1950), author and professor of creative writing. Born and raised in Bedford, Pennsylvania, David Bradley's horizon was shaped by a rural world near the soft-coal region of western Pennsylvania and by his father, a church historian and eloquent preacher, who frequently took his son on trips to the South. After high school Bradley was named Benjamin Franklin National Achievement and Presidential Scholar. In 1972, he graduated summa cum laude from the University of Pennsylvania and was awarded a Thouron Scholarship for the University of London, where he received his MA in 1974, and established a lasting interest in nineteenth-century American history, resulting in the writing of four versions of his second novel when he returned to America.

In 1975, with the publication of his first novel, *South Street*, Bradley showed a keen interest in depicting everyday life and in the use of vernacular language. The book is centered on a black bar, a black church, and a hotel lobby on Philadelphia's South Street. In an ironic black urban version of the Western genre, Bradley has the black poet Adlai Stevenson Brown temporarily live and work amidst the unstable conditions of the black ghetto. Brown functions as a catalyst for the fantasies of hustlers, drinkers, whores, and preachers, whose sexual and material power games, articulated in vividly idiomatic speech and couched in ebullient or caustic humor, add up to a virtuoso dramatization of a vibrant, though depressed, city milieu.

Bradley's second novel, *The *Chaneysville Incident* (1981), won the PEN/Faulkner Award in 1982 and was quickly recognized as a major text of African American fiction. Its protagonist, John Washington, a history professor in Philadelphia, in the process of exploring his family and group history finds himself confronted with his father's dying friend Old Jack (an embodiment of the black oral tradition); with the life plans of his father Moses and his ancestor C. K. Washington (who both tried to exert covert influence on the white power structure); and with his white girl friend, Judith, a psychologist, who eventually helps John to make meaningful a partially buried and fragmented history through an imaginative complementation of the data from several incidents near Chaneysville, especially the voluntary suicide of a group of fugitive slaves when threatened with reenslavement.

After shorter spells as an editor and a professor of English, David Bradley settled at Temple University in Philadelphia as professor of creative writing in 1977. He has published a variety of essays, book reviews, and interviews in prestigious periodicals, magazines, and newspapers treating topics such as black education and literature, the exemplary lives and self-concepts of black athletes, and the status and reception of *Malcolm X. Bradley worked on a *Malcolm X* film script for Warner Brothers between 1984 and 1988 but gave up hope when faced with the systematic evisceration of Malcolm's figure by Hollywood. With Shelley Fisher Fishkin, Bradley edited the three-volume *Encyclopedia of Civil Rights in America* in 1998.

Some rumors about Bradley's working on a detective novel notwithstanding, the author in a 1992 interview claimed to be at work on a nonfiction book about the founding documents and the continuing tradition of racism in America.

• Valerie Smith, "David Bradley," in *DLB*, vol. 33, *Afro-American Fiction Writers after 1955*, eds. Thadious M. Davis and Trudier Harris, 1983, pp. 28–32. David Bradley, "The Business of Writing: An Interview with David Bradley," interview by Susan L. Blake and James A. Miller, *Callaloo* 7 (1984): 19–39. Michael G. Cooke, *Afro-American Literature in the Twentieth Century*, 1984. David Bradley, "An Interview with David Bradley," interview by Kay Bonetti, *Missouri Review* 15 (1992): 69–88.

—Klaus Ensslen

BRAGG, LINDA BROWN. *See* Brown, Linda Beatrice.

BRAITHWAITE, WILLIAM STANLEY (1878–1962), poet, editor, publisher, anthologist, and influential critic who strived to reanimate and draw attention to American verse in the early twentieth century. Born and raised in Boston, William Stanley Braithwaite began life in a prosperous, cultured home but, on the death of his father, was forced to quit school at the age of twelve to help support his family. Lacking formal instruction, Braithwaite rigorously educated himself. He eventually found work as a typesetter in a Boston printing firm. Setting poems by John Keats and William Wordsworth, Braithwaite developed a love of lyric poetry that inspired his own writing. He began to publish poems and reviews in the Boston *Journal* and *Transcript* and eventually produced his first book of poetry, *Lyrics of Life and Love*, in 1904, followed by *The*

House of Falling Leaves (1908). In 1906, Braithwaite started his critical career in earnest with a regular feature in the Boston *Transcript*. From the pages of the *Transcript* and other prestigious newspapers and journals, Braithwaite championed Robert Frost, Edwin Arlington Robinson, and Amy Lowell, and brought serious critical attention to the works of African American poets such as Paul Laurence *Dunbar, James Weldon *Johnson, Georgia Douglas *Johnson, Countee *Cullen, who dedicated *Caroling Dusk: An Anthology of Verse by Negro Poets* (1927) to Braithwaite, and Claude *McKay, whose poem "The Harlem Dancer" remained a favorite of Braithwaite's throughout his career. In 1912, Braithwaite, sensing the American public's increasing appetite for verse, set out to produce a Boston-based magazine of American poetry entitled *Poetry Journal*. After his effort proved ill-fated, primarily because of the almost concurrent appearance of Harriet Monroe's *Poetry: A Magazine of Verse*, Braithwaite turned his attention in 1913 to his *Anthology of Magazine Verse*, an annual collection, inclusion in which soon became a coveted mark of poetic success. Harriet Monroe herself dubbed Braithwaite "Sir Oracle" in grudging reference to his power to determine literary careers.

Throughout his years compiling the *Anthology*, Braithwaite remained committed to the notion that verse should be an expression of spiritual truth and eternal beauty beyond what he conceived of as the limits of merely political or racial concerns. Consistently wary of poetry that he considered polemical or didactic, Braithwaite favored traditional, formal, lyric voices in African American verse over harsher cries, and remained suspicious of African American dialect poetry, like Dunbar's, that, despite its power, he saw as perpetuating the image of the African American as uneducated and poetically unsophisticated. Despite his muted and somewhat romantic editorial preferences, Braithwaite introduced the general poetry-reading public to a wide range of African American voices they might otherwise never have heard.

After weathering the depression with his wife and seven children, Braithwaite accepted a teaching position in 1935 at Atlanta University, where he spent the next ten years as a professor of creative literature. In 1946, he moved to Harlem and spent the remainder of his career compiling his *Selected Poems* (1948) and writing a book on the Brontës before his death in 1962.

• Phillip Butcher, "William Stanley Braithwaite's Southern Exposure: Rescue and Revelation," *Southern Literary Journal* 3.2 (1971): 49–61. Phillip Butcher, ed., *The William Stanley Braithwaite Reader*, 1972. Kenny J. Williams, "An Invisible Partnership and an Unlikely Relationship: William Stanley Braithwaite and Harriet Monroe," *Callaloo* 10.3 (Summer 1987): 516–550.

—Robin G. Schulze

BRAWLEY, BENJAMIN (1882–1939), educator, historian, and critic. As was customary for many black intellectuals during his day, Benjamin Brawley received two college degrees—one from a black institution and one from a predominantly white school. As a graduate of Morehouse College in Atlanta, he was very much influenced by the city's black elite and notion of a "talented tenth." As a graduate of the University of Chicago, he placed a great deal of emphasis upon the life of the mind. After receiving an MA degree from Harvard University, Brawley spent the remainder of his life as a college teacher, historian, and literary critic. Positions at Shaw University and Morehouse College ultimately led to his appointment at Howard University, where he served as the head of the English department.

Brawley was a prolific writer. His essays appeared in the leading journals of his day, and such books as *A Social History of the American Negro* (1921), *Early Negro American Writers* (1935), *Paul Laurence Dunbar: Poet of His People* (1936), and *The Negro Genius* (1937) as well as the many editions of *The Negro in Literature and Art in the United States* give a sense of both the range and the limitations of his scholarship.

Brawley's literary criticism has created tensions within some black communities. Just before his death, he was subjected to a great deal of censure for being too bourgeois. Among some of the younger critics, "Brawleyism" came to signify a type of genteel spirit in life and scholarship that some members of the Harlem Renaissance found objectionable. He, however, found them to be offensive because he thought the renaissance writers emphasized the underclass too much. As a result he took the writers of the Harlem Renaissance to task because he felt they stressed the unusual and the exotic. In his opinion their association with the latter represented "one of the most brazen examples of salesmanship in the United States." He was intent upon defining African American life in terms of its success stories, its heroes, and its similarities to the dominant American culture.

As a critic Brawley searched for a means to relate African American literature to mainstream American and British literature. Yet he found much that was objectionable in modern literature. Like William Stanley *Braithwaite, whose work he admired, Brawley thought free verse lacked meaning and significance because it did not have an identifiable traditional form. He also felt that verse should not generally deal with overt protest. This stance excluded a great deal of the poetry of the Harlem Renaissance. However, it must be said in Brawley's defense that he exhibited impeccable taste in writing and was an excellent stylist. Even though later scholarship has revealed material unavailable to him when he was writing, his studies of African American literature remain perceptive and comprehensive.

• Saunders Redding, "Benjamin Griffith Brawley," in *DANB*, eds. Rayford W. Logan and Michael R. Winston, 1982, pp. 60–61. Steven J. Leslie, "Benjamin Brawley," in *Encyclopedia of*

African American Culture and History, eds. Jack Saltzman, David Lionel Smith, and Cornel West, 1996, pp. 427–428.

—Kenny Jackson Williams

BRAXTON, JOANNE M. (b. 1950), poet and critic. A distinguished writer and teacher, Joanne M. Braxton has published important poetry and criticism while maintaining the significance of historical and communal ties.

Joanne Margaret Braxton was born in Lakeland, Maryland, on 25 May 1950 to Mary Ellen Weems Braxton and Harry McHenry Braxton, Sr. The second of four children, she graduated from Northwestern Senior High School in Hyattsville, Maryland. Braxton found her poetic voice as an undergraduate at Sarah Lawrence College; after graduating, she entered Yale University, where she earned her PhD in American Studies in 1984. Braxton wrote her dissertation on black women's autobiography under the tutelage of scholars Charles Davis and John Blassingame.

Braxton has enjoyed a fruitful publishing career. *Sometimes I Think of Maryland* (1977), a volume of poetry, reflects the centrality of folkloric and familial traditions; Gwendolyn *Brooks hailed it for its economy, courage, and genuine expression of youthful energy. Braxton's critical study, *Black Women Writing Autobiography: A Tradition within a Tradition* (1989), is a pioneering contribution to African American feminist scholarship, presenting trenchant analyses of historical and contemporary figures such as Harriet A. *Jacobs and Maya *Angelou. In addition, Braxton is the editor of *Wild Women in the Whirlwind: Afra-American Culture and the Contemporary Literary Renaissance* (with Andree Nicola McLaughlin, 1990) and *The Collected Poetry of Paul Laurence *Dunbar* (1993). Braxton has also been a Danforth Fellow, a Roothbert Fellow, a Mellon Fellow, an American Council of Learned Societies Fellow, and a member of the Michigan Society of Fellows.

A devoted teacher as well as writer, Braxton has taught at Yale and the University of Michigan. A member of the English and American Studies departments at the College of William and Mary since 1980, she has held the Frances L. and Edwin L. Cummings chair since 1989. A renowned professor, Braxton earned the prestigious "Outstanding Virginia Faculty Award" in 1992. Braxton views herself as a cultural critic and literary historian and encourages students to participate in "reclamation," unearthing stories that have not been told. As she states in the introduction to *Wild Women,* "the current flowering of Black women's writing must be viewed as part of a cultural continuum and an evolving consciousness, a consciousness that will continue to evolve and unfold."

An exemplary scholar and teacher, Braxton has been praised widely and has worked to find her own critical voice and to empower her students so that they might find theirs. Joanne Braxton continues her scholarly and artistic pursuits, researching slave music and preparing more volumes poetry. Her latest volume of poetry, *My Magic Pours Secret Libations,* was published in 1996.

• Edward T. Washington, "Joanne M. Braxton," in *DLB,* vol. 41, *Afro-American Poets since 1955,* eds. Trudier Harris and Thadious M. Davis, 1985, pp. 42–47. Hilary Holladay, "Joanne Braxton Named Outstanding Professor," *William and Mary Alumni Gazette* 60.2 (Sept. 1992): 9.

—Keith Clark

BRENT, LINDA. *See* Jacobs, Harriet A.

BRER RABBIT is the archetypal hero-trickster character from African American oral literature. While Brer Rabbit got much exposure in Joel Chandler Harris's *Uncle Remus: His Songs and His Sayings* (1881), folklorists and literature scholars are well aware of the rich cycle of tales that circulate around this tricky and cunning figure. These tales thrived especially during the pre- and post-slave era up until the mid-1900s. Resembling the two major tricksters of Africa (Anansi, the Ashanti spider, and Ijapa, the Yoruba turtle), "Buh" Rabbit has always seemed to be the most helpless and most afraid of all the animals in the kingdom.

Brer Rabbit is constantly at odds with the likes of Brer Bear, Brer Wolf, and Sly Brer Fox. This trio, singularly or collectively, attempts to humiliate, outsmart, and sometimes even kill Brer Rabbit. In contrast, Brer Rabbit tries to nullify the plans of his stronger archenemies by using his superior intelligence and his quick thinking. He usually gets the better of the bigger and stronger animals.

Since the Brer Rabbit cycle of tales flourished during the time of slavery and almost always involved the weak in a neverending contest with the strong, scholars view these tales as slave expressions of subversive sentiments against the institution of slavery. It was much too dangerous for slaves to reveal to slave owners the harsh realities and cruelties of slavery. But slaves could vent some of their frustrations and hostilities against their masters by participating in the performance of the Brer Rabbit tales.

As time progressed, criticism of slavery became less indirect in Brer Rabbit literature. African American oral literature gave birth to the "John and Ole Boss Tales." In this group of tales, John (sometimes known as George, Sam, Jack, Efan, or Rastus) now becomes the human analogue to Brer Rabbit. John is always in conflict with Ole Master ("Massa" or "Marse") and, like Brer Rabbit, attempts to outwit Ole Boss. Most stories show John winning over the master, but there are a sizable number of tales where "Whitey" outsmarts John.

Although the Brer Rabbit tradition and the John and Ole Boss cycle of tales are not as strong as they once were, it does seem that the "Bad Nigger" oral tales became the substitute for these earlier stories. As long as there is an environment of disparity in America, the underclass will need Brer Rabbit tales to help cope with or mask its displeasure with the inequities of the system.

• Joel Chandler Harris, *Uncle Remus: His Songs and His Sayings,* 1881. Roger D. Abrahams, ed., *Afro-American Folktales: Stories from Black Traditions in the New World,* 1985.

—Elon A. Kulii and Beverly Threatt Kulii

Bronzeville Boys and Girls. Often overlooked in analyses of the career of Gwendolyn *Brooks are her works for children. As a result of her own childhood filled with books, she is committed not only to the importance of reading for young people but also to the notion that there must be some material for them. *Bronzeville Boys and Girls* (1956) is the first in a series of works designed specifically for younger readers. The thirty-four poems in the collection are simple and extremely brief. Most of them rely heavily on the traditional rhyme scheme of abcb often coupled with very short lines. As a result the poetic voice seems to suggest not only poems for a child but poems in the voice of a child. When she turns to poetry for children, there is a strain of romantic idealism as she suggests the beauty of uncrowded nature.

Like the earlier *A Street in Bronzeville* (1945), this collection is also set in Chicago, but it could take place in any crowded urban area, and the characters who are black Chicagoans could be of any race or ethnic group. Race and locale are less important than the fact that the young characters are in the process of self-discovery. Some poems express happiness as does the opening poem "Maxie and Birdie," which records two youngsters having a "tiny tea-party" with "pink cakes." Others are sad as they recount the experiences of children like Lyle, who looks at a tree lovingly because the tree can stay where it is whereas Lyle has "waved goodbye to seven homes." There is Otto who did not get the Christmas present he wanted but is mature enough to hide his feelings from his father. Then there is the contemplative Rudolph, who "is tired of the city" and who explains overcrowding by observing "these buildings are too close to me." These are just a few of the children who populate *Bronzeville Boys and Girls.*

The sense of belonging and a feeling for one's neighborhood inform the poems in this collection. Rather than viewing impoverished or deteriorating surroundings with loathing, Brooks suggests that one can find the beauty in family and home no matter how unpleasant a locale may be.

• Maria K. Mootry and Gary Smith, eds., *A Life Distilled: Gwendolyn Brooks, Her Poetry and Fiction,* 1987.

—Kenny Jackson Williams

BROOKS, GWENDOLYN (b. 1917), poet, novelist, and children's writer. Although she was born on 7 June 1917 in Topeka, Kansas—the first child of David and Keziah Brooks—Gwendolyn Brooks is "a Chicagoan." The family moved to Chicago shortly after her birth, and despite her extensive travels and periods in some of the major universities of the country, she has remained associated with the city's South Side. What her strong family unit lacked in material wealth was made bearable by the wealth of human capital that resulted from warm interpersonal relationships. When she writes about families that—despite their daily adversities—are not dysfunctional, Gwendolyn Brooks writes from an intimate knowledge reinforced by her own life.

Brooks attended Hyde Park High School, the leading white high school in the city, but transferred to the all-black Wendell Phillips, then to the integrated Englewood High School. In 1936 she graduated from Wilson Junior College. These four schools gave her a perspective on racial dynamics in the city that continues to influence her work.

Her profound interest in poetry informed much of her early life. "Eventide," her first poem, was published in *American Childhood Magazine* in 1930. A few years later she met James Weldon *Johnson and Langston *Hughes, who urged her to read modern poetry—especially the work of Ezra Pound, T. S. Eliot, and e. e. cummings—and who emphasized the need to write as much and as frequently as she possibly could. By 1934 Brooks had become an adjunct member of the staff of the *Chicago Defender* and had published almost one hundred of her poems in a weekly poetry column.

In 1938 she married Henry Blakely and moved to a kitchenette apartment on Chicago's South Side. Between the birth of her first child, Henry, Jr., in 1940 and the birth of Nora in 1951, she became associated with the group of writers involved in Harriet Monroe's still-extant *Poetry: A Magazine of Verse.* From this group she received further encouragement, and by 1943 she had won the Midwestern Writer's Conference Poetry Award.

In 1945 her first book of poetry, *A *Street in Bronzeville* (published by Harper and Row), brought her instant critical acclaim. She was selected one of *Mademoiselle* magazine's "Ten Young Women of the Year," she won her first Guggenheim Fellowship, and she became a fellow of the American Academy of Arts and Letters. Her second book of poems, **Annie Allen* (1949), won *Poetry* magazine's Eunice Tietjens Prize. In 1950 Gwendolyn Brooks became the first African American to win a Pulitzer Prize. From that time to the present, she has been the recipient of a number of awards, fellowships, and honorary degrees usually designated as Doctor of Humane Letters.

President John Kennedy invited her to read at a Library of Congress poetry festival in 1962. In 1985 she was appointed poetry consultant to the Library of Congress. Just as receiving a Pulitzer Prize for poetry marked a milestone in her career, so also did her selection by the National Endowment for the Humanities as the 1994 Jefferson Lecturer, the highest award in the humanities given by the federal government.

Her first teaching job was a poetry workshop at Columbia College (Chicago) in 1963. She went on to teach creative writing at a number of institutions including Northeastern Illinois University, Elmhurst College, Columbia University, Clay College of New York, and the University of Wisconsin.

A turning point in her career came in 1967 when she attended the Fisk University Second Black Writers' Conference and decided to become more involved in the Black Arts movement. She became one of the most visible articulators of "the black aesthetic." Her "awakening" led to a shift away from a major publishing house to smaller black ones. While some critics found an angrier tone in her work, elements of protest had always been present in her writing and her awareness of social issues did not result in diatribes at the expense of her clear commitment to aesthetic principles. Consequently, becoming the leader of one phase of the Black Arts movement in Chicago did not drastically alter her poetry, but there were some subtle changes that become more noticeable when one examines her total canon to date.

The ambiguity of her role as a black poet can be illustrated by her participation in two events in Chicago. In 1967 Brooks, who wrote the commemorative ode for the "Chicago Picasso," attended the unveiling ceremony along with social and business dignitaries. The poem was well received even though such lines as "Art hurts. Art urges voyages . . ." made some uncomfortable. Less than two weeks later there was the dedication of the mural known as "The Wall of Respect" at 43rd and Langley streets, in the heart of the black neighborhood. The social and business elites of Chicago were not present, but for this event Gwendolyn Brooks wrote "The Wall." In a measure these two poems illustrate the dichotomy of a divided city, but they also exemplify Brooks's ability both to bridge those divisions and to utilize nonstrident protest.

Gwendolyn Brooks has been a prolific writer. In addition to individual poems, essays, and reviews that have appeared in numerous publications, she has issued a number of books in rapid succession, including **Maud Martha* (1953), **Bronzeville Boys and Girls* (1956), and **In the Mecca* (1968). Her poetry moves from traditional forms including ballads, sonnets, variations of the Chaucerian and Spenserian stanzas as well as the rhythm of the blues to the most unrestricted free verse. In short, the popular forms of English poetry appear in her work; yet there is a strong sense of experimentation as she juxtaposes lyric, narrative, and dramatic poetic forms. In her lyrics there is an affirmation of life that rises above the stench of urban kitchenette buildings. In her narrative poetry the stories are simple but usually transcend the restrictions of place; in her dramatic poetry, the characters are often memorable not because of any heroism on their part but merely because they are trying to survive from day to day.

Brooks's poetry is marked by some unforgettable characters who are drawn from the underclass of the nation's black neighborhoods. Like many urban writers, Brooks has recorded the impact of city life. But unlike the most committed naturalists, she does not hold the city completely responsible for what happens to people. The city is simply an existing force with which people must cope.

While they are generally insignificant in the great urban universe, her characters gain importance—at least to themselves—in their tiny worlds, whether it be Annie Allen trying on a hat in a milliner's shop or De-Witt Williams "on his way to Lincoln Cemetery" or Satin-Legs Smith trying to decide what outlandish outfit to wear on Sundays. Just as there is not a strong naturalistic sense of victimization, neither are there great plans for an unpromised future nor is there some great divine spirit that will rescue them. Brooks is content to describe a moment in the lives of very ordinary people whose only goal is to exist from day to day and perhaps have a nice funeral when they die. Sometimes these ordinary people seem to have a control that is out of keeping with their own insignificance.

Although her poetic voice is objective, there is a strong sense that she—as an observer—is never far from her action. On one level, of course, Brooks is a protest poet; yet her protest evolves through suggestion rather than through a bludgeon. She sets forth the facts without embellishment or interpretation, but the simplicity of the facts makes it impossible for readers to come away unconvinced—despite whatever discomfort they may feel—whether she is writing about suburban ladies who go into the ghetto to give occasional aid or a black mother who has had an abortion.

Trying to determine clear lines of influence from the work of earlier writers to later ones is always a risky business; however, knowing some identifiable poetic traditions can aid in understanding the work of Gwendolyn Brooks. On one level there is the English metaphysical tradition perhaps best exemplified by John Donne. From nineteenth-century American poetry one can detect elements of Walt Whitman, Emily Dickinson, and Paul Laurence *Dunbar. From twentieth-century American poetry there are many strains, most notably the compact style of T. S. Eliot, the frequent use of the lower-case for titles in the manner of e. e. cummings, and the racial consciousness of the Harlem Renaissance, especially as found in the work of Countee *Cullen and Langston Hughes; but, of perhaps greater importance, she seems to be a direct descendant of the urban commitment and attitude of the "Chicago School" of writing. For Brooks, setting goes beyond the Midwest with a focus on Chicago and concentrates on a small neglected corner of the city. Consequently, in the final analysis, she is not a carbon copy of any of the Chicago writers.

She was appointed poet laureate of Illinois in 1968 and has been perhaps more active than many laureates.

She has done much to bring poetry to the people through accessibility and public readings. In fact, she is one of our most visible American poets. Not only is she extremely active in the poetry workshop movement, but her classes and contests for young people are attempts to help inner-city children see "the poetry" in their lives. She has taught audiences that poetry is not some formal activity closed to all but the most perceptive. Rather, it is an art form within the reach and understanding of everybody—including the lowliest among us. In 1994, Gwendolyn Brooks received the National Book Foundation Medal for Distinguished Contribution to American Letters and was named by the National Endowment for the Humanities as its Jefferson Lecturer.

• Gwendolyn Brooks, *Report from Part One,* 1972. Maria K. Mootry and Gary Smith, eds., *A Life Distilled: Gwendolyn Brooks, Her Poetry and Fiction,* 1987. George E. Kent, *A Life of Gwendolyn Brooks,* 1990. Stephen Caldwell Wright, ed., *On Gwendolyn Brooks: Reliant Contemplations,* 1996.

—Kenny Jackson Williams

Brothers and Keepers (1984) is one of John Edgar *Wideman's two major works of nonfiction; the other is *Fatheralong* (1994). Of Wideman's numerous books, it is *Brothers and Keepers* for which he is probably best known to the general reading public. Described by Wideman as a personal essay about his younger brother Robby and himself, it deals with the first of two tragic events in the author's life: Robby's imprisonment for his involvement in a crime, which Wideman previously had given fictional treatment in his novel *Hiding Place* (1981). (The second tragedy, the conviction and imprisonment for murder of Wideman's youngest son, is dealt with somewhat obliquely in Wideman's novel **Philadelphia Fire,* 1990, and in "Father Stories," the final piece in *Fatheralong.*)

One question Wideman wrestles with in the book—and that the reader must wrestle with also—is how can two brothers raised in the same environment (the black neighborhood of Homewood in Pittsburgh, Pennsylvania, locale of the majority of Wideman's fiction) end up having such radically different lives: one a Rhodes Scholar, college professor, and acclaimed author, the other a drug addict with dreams of being a big-time dealer who now is serving a life sentence? This stark polarity—the middle-class professional versus the "gangsta"—is something Wideman attempts to explore and deconstruct in his narrative. It isn't that he fails to recognize that he and his brother are different; rather, since they shared the same family upbringing, the important thing for Wideman is, given the similarities between Robby and himself, what has created the gulf between them? For all his brotherly concern, Wideman cannot absolve Robby from responsibility for the choices he and many other young black men like him have made, yet he is eloquent in evoking the forces in our society that have conspired to distort and limit those choices.

Reviewers as divergent as Christopher Lehmann-Haupt and Ishmael *Reed have found the book's undoubted strengths to be the gripping quality of the story it tells and the skillful interplay between the two quite distinct voices of Wideman and his younger brother.

Wideman has reiterated in several interviews that all of his books are about family—its intricacies, agonies, and strengths. And the troubles and triumphs of a particular family—Wideman's own, rendered in fact and in fiction—are clearly related to the problems and promises of that extended family called the community, the nation. In a time of much rhetorical obeisance to "family values," a book like *Brothers and Keepers* reminds us that the stresses of the nuclear family and those of the national family are mutually interlocked, and that being your brother's keeper in the traditional sense may be one way to avoid his being "caged" by keepers of quite another sort.

Brothers and Keepers is part of the long tradition of tale-telling, self-discovery, and social arraignment that constitutes African American autobiography. Like Nathan McCall's *Makes Me Wanna Holler* (1994) and Brent Staples's *Parallel Time* (1994), Wideman's book continues the story of flight begun in the slave narratives into a present still tormented by the unresolved legacies of "race," where even those black Americans who can be said to have "made it" nevertheless see themselves as fugitives.

—Robert Elliot Fox

BROWN, CECIL (b. 1943), novelist and short story and script writer. Cecil Brown has not been a prolific writer; indeed, the bulk of his literary reputation rests on his first novel, *The Life and Loves of Mr. Jiveass Nigger,* published in 1969. Yet to dismiss Brown as a minor writer based on the lack of prolificacy is to diminish the tremendous impact that his starkly ironic and penetratingly satiric narrative voice has made on the development of contemporary African American letters. Brown's influence has grown tremendously in the quarter century since his literary debut, and the discomfiting hilarity that is his trademark is now far more the rule than the exception in African American literature, particularly among African American male writers.

Cecil Brown was born 3 July 1943 in Bolton, North Carolina, in the southeastern section of the state, to tobacco sharecropper parents. He began his college education at North Carolina A & T State University in Greensboro but later transferred to Columbia University, where he was awarded a BA in English in 1966. He earned an MA degree from the University of Chicago in 1967 before embarking upon the dual career of writer and teacher at the collegiate level. He later earned a PhD in folklore from the University of California at Berkeley.

After a few short articles placed in reputable journals like the *Kenyon Review* and *Negro Digest,* Brown's

The Life and Loves of Mr. Jiveass Nigger appeared in 1969 to mixed, though often exuberant, reviews. Most critics point to the novel's central character, George Washington, as the archetypal figure of the prodigal son who wanders far from home (to Copenhagen in this case), wastes himself in riotous living, meets with adversity and misfortune, and resolves to return home where things are infinitely better than he had earlier supposed. Brown infuses new life into a predictable plot with an insistence on the importance of myth and storytelling, and with a narrative voice that bridges Ralph *Ellison's comic elegance of the 1940s and 1950s with the comic bawdiness and perverseness of writers like Ishmael *Reed, Clarence *Major, Charles R. *Johnson, and Percival Everett of subsequent decades.

Brown continued the development of both theme and technique in subsequent works, most notably in a short story, "The Time Is Now" (1981), in his second novel, *Days Without Weather* (1982), and in his autobiography, *Coming Up Down Home* (1993). Here the homecoming of the prodigal son is more in the spiritual sense of recognizing, embracing, and understanding one's roots. The tone is customarily comic and sardonic.

Dating back to the early years of his career, Cecil Brown has been involved in writing screenplays and stage plays, including some work with the comic actor Richard Pryor. These endeavors, while sustaining him between publishing projects, also demonstrate Brown's appreciation of the comic aspects of African American life and his knowledge that within the comedy one also finds irony, complexity, beauty, and strength.

• Jean M. Bright, "Cecil Brown," in *DLB*, vol. 33, [*Afro-American Fiction Writers after 1955*], eds. Trudier Harris and Thadious M. Davis, 1984, pp. 32–35. Randall Kenan, "Coming Up Down Home: A Memoir of Southern Childhood," *New York Times Book Review*, 22 Aug. 1993, 13.

—Warren J. Carson

BROWN, CLAUDE (b. 1937), autobiographer, writer, and social commentator. Claude Brown was born in New York City on 23 February 1937 to Henry Lee and Ossie Brock Brown, South Carolinians who had come north in 1935 looking for economic opportunities unavailable in the South. Growing up in Harlem involved Claude Brown in crime and violence early in his life. By the time he was ten, he had joined the stealing division of a notorious street gang and had a history of truancy and expulsion from school. At eleven, Brown was sent to the Wiltwyck school for delinquent boys, where he came under the supervision of Dr. Ernest Papanek, whose positive influence in his life Brown would later acknowledge.

Back on the streets after two years at Wiltwyck, at age thirteen Brown was shot during an attempted robbery. A year later, he was sent to the Warwick school for boys, where he completed three terms before his final release in July 1953. From this point on, Brown gradually freed himself from the destructive street life of the Harlem ghetto. He began high school when he was sixteen and graduated in 1957. During these years, Brown held various odd jobs in New York and played jazz in Greenwich Village.

Claude Brown continued his education at Howard University, finishing a degree in government and business in 1965, the same year that Macmillan published his autobiography, **Manchild in the Promised Land*. The work originated from a piece Brown had written for *Dissent* magazine. Encouraged to expand the work into a full-length narrative, Brown produced a 1,537-page manuscript that became, after extensive editing, a hugely successful best-seller. Critics praised the vivid realism of *Manchild* and favorably compared Brown to James *Baldwin, Ralph *Ellison, and Richard *Wright. Like them, Brown was hailed as a powerful, relentless chronicler of the brutal reality of African American life in northern urban cities. Additionally, *Manchild in the Promised Land* was held up as an American success story, the narrative of one who beat the odds of his childhood and saved his own life.

The publication of his autobiography made Claude Brown a new authoritative voice in the African American community. He published a second book, *The Children of Ham,* in 1976. Much less well received than *Manchild,* this book records the stories of thirteen Harlem residents, focusing on their struggles against poverty, crime, and drugs.

Brown has largely dropped from public view since the publication of his books, but his work reveals his continuing concern for the problems facing people in the inner city. For example, his 1987 documentary "Manchild Revisited: A Commentary by Claude Brown" addresses urban crime. In it, Brown supports capital punishment; voluntarism in black neighborhoods to fight crime; more prosecutors, judges, and prisons; and the decriminalization of drugs. Although nothing Brown has done since publishing *Manchild in the Promised Land* has created the sensation that book did, Brown remains a thoughtful, sometimes controversial commentator on African American social issues.

• "Brown, Claude," in *CA*, vols. 73–76, ed. Frances Carol Locher, 1978, pp. 88–189.

—David L. Dudley

BROWN, FRANK LONDON (1927–1962), novelist, activist, and important figure among Chicago-based urban realists. Born in Kansas City, Frank London Brown moved to Chicago at age twelve. Educated at Roosevelt University and the University of Chicago, Brown worked numerous jobs to support his literary ambitions. Most significant of these was his work as an organizer and program officer for the United Packinghouse Workers of America and other labor unions. Brown was profoundly impacted by the musical culture of African American Chicago, most significantly jazz, but also gospel and blues. A devotee of bebop, Brown published a seminal interview with Thelonious

Monk in *Downbeat* and pioneered in the reading of fiction to jazz accompaniment. Many critics have also noted the importance of a trip Brown made as a journalist to cover the Emmett Till murder case. At the time of his death, he was an accomplished writer on the Chicago scene and a regular contributor to *Negro Digest* and various literary magazines. He was also a candidate for a PhD from the University of Chicago's Committee on Social Thought and was director of the Union Research Center.

His reputation is largely based upon his 1959 novel, *Trumbull Park,* an account of the struggles facing African American families attempting to integrate a Chicago housing development. However, his short fiction and especially his 1969 posthumous novel, *The Myth Maker*, deserve greater attention. *Trumbull Park* was typical of social realist fiction in the style of Theodore Dreiser and Upton Sinclair, while *The Myth Maker* demonstrates an interest in Fyodor Dostoyevsky and the existentialist novel. Both texts are clearly influenced by the work of Richard *Wright. Their great accomplishment is the detailed description of the "everyday" of urban African American experience, excellent attention to vernacular speech and dialect, and a philosophically sophisticated account of the rise of despair in the ghetto and the continuing deprecatory impact of institutionalized racism. Both novels are occasionally limited by deficient character and plot development. *Trumbull Park* has received a moderate amount of critical attention and *The Myth Maker* none. Brown's occasional short stories also reveal attention to language and a strong commitment to realism as a mode of expression and investigation. His most popular story, "McDougal" (Abraham Chapman, *Black Voices,* 1968) is noteworthy for its sympathetic treatment of a white trumpet player attempting to succeed as a jazz musician within the very environment of Chicago's 58th Street that Brown had long chronicled.

In addition to the accomplishment of his two novels, Brown's reputation should also be enhanced by his exploration of the possibility of an artistic life irreducibly connected to a life of social action. His participation in leftist political activity and counter-cultural artistic movements at the height of McCarthyism and the Cold War is suggestive of a courageous intellect. His succumbing to leukemia in March of 1962 just prior to the dawning of the Black Arts movement in Chicago is one of the major tragedies of contemporary African American literature.

•Sterling Stuckey, "Frank London Brown—A Remembrance," in *Black Voices,* ed. Abraham Chapman, 1968, pp. 669–676. Maryemma Graham, "Bearing Witness in Black Chicago: A View of Selected Fiction by Richard Wright, Frank London Brown, and Ronald Fair," *CLA Journal* 33 (March 1990): 280–297. Charles Tita, "Frank London Brown," in *Contemporary African American Novelists,* ed. Emmanuel S. Nelson, 1999, pp. 58–63.

—James C. Hall

BROWN, JOHN (1800–1859), also known as Osawatomie Brown, white abolitionist and leader of the Harpers Ferry raid. African American essayists, historians, novelists, playwrights, and poets have found in John Brown both a symbol of sacrifice and a touchstone of commitment to the cause of black freedom. A devoutly religious radical abolitionist descended from six generations of Connecticut farmers, John Brown organized and led the 16–18 October 1859 raid on Harpers Ferry, Virginia (now West Virginia), that ended in seventeen deaths and his own capture and execution on 2 December. His failed attempt to destroy American slavery by force and his eloquent courtroom defense of the rights of slaves made him a hero to African Americans. Frederick *Douglass said of his friend: "I could live for the slave, but he could die for him." W. E. B. *Du Bois's 1909 biography of Brown was an avowed "tribute to the [white] man who of all Americans has perhaps come nearest to touching the souls of black folk."

For some African American writers Brown transcends race and time. In 1974 Lerone Bennett, Jr., claimed that Brown was "of no color . . . of no race or age" and that his example helped African Americans understand the "limitations and possibilities" of their own lives. In Michael S. *Harper's 1972 poetic eulogy, "History as Cap'n Brown," Brown cries, "Come to the crusade . . . not Negroes, brothers." At the height of the Black Power movement, when radicals dismissed Abraham *Lincoln as a reluctant emancipator and white supremacist, they used Brown as an archetype of self-sacrifice against which white liberals might be judged. "If you are for me and my problems," *Malcolm X said in 1965, "then you have to be willing to do as old John Brown did."

Other African American writers celebrate John Brown as a clarion call echoing through the "long black song" of their people's quest for freedom. To promote pride in black heroes, William Blackwell Branch wrote the play *In Splendid Error* (1953) to justify Frederick Douglass's decision not to go with Brown to Harpers Ferry. Yet Branch honors Brown's passion even as he constructs a heroic Douglass whose "cold wisdom" and sense of duty to his people instruct him not to die with Brown. In the 1960s, as Stephen Butterfield has written, alienated young African American radicals sought to kindle the "sacred fire" of John Brown's memory without permitting it to "burn the black out of their souls."

Through the years, African American writers have seen Brown variously as a symbol of humanity and brotherhood, a martyr to the cause of emancipation, a voice for forcible resistance, a prophet of racial strife, God's instrument to ignite a war to end slavery, and a sign of white America's eventual redemption.

• W. E. Burghardt Du Bois, *John Brown,* 1909; rpt. 1962. Benjamin Quarles, ed., *Blacks on John Brown,* 1972. Daniel C. Littlefield, "Blacks, John Brown, and a Theory of Manhood," in *His Soul Goes Marching On,* ed. Paul Finkelman, 1995.

—Robert E. McGlone

BROWN, LINDA BEATRICE (b. 1939), poet, novelist, and professor. Linda Beatrice Brown was a rising young poet of the 1960s and 1970s whose mentor was the poet Gwendolyn *Brooks. She has one published volume of poetry, *A Love Song to Black Men* (1974). In 1984 she published a novel, *Rainbow Roun Mah Shoulder* (under the name Linda Brown Bragg). This work is in the tradition of Zora Neale *Hurston's **Their Eyes Were Watching God* (1937) in its southern African American heroine, skillful use of southern African American speech patterns, and depiction of the interrelatedness of God, nature, and the supernatural in the African American folk community. Some of her first poems appeared in the well-known anthology edited by Rosey Pool entitled *Beyond the Blues* (1960), and her work later appeared in publishing outlets such as the *Black Scholar, Encore, Ebony,* and *Writer's Choice.*

Brown was born in Akron, Ohio, on 14 March 1939 to Raymond and Edith Player Brown. She attended college at the historic all-black, all-female Bennett College in Greensboro, North Carolina, where she had opportunities to hear poetry readings by Langston *Hughes and Sterling A. *Brown. While a junior in college she published her first poem, "Precocious Curiosity," in *Beyond the Blues;* she earned her bachelor's degree in 1961. She furthered her education by obtaining a masters degree in 1962 from Case Western Reserve University, where she was a Woodrow Wilson Teaching Fellow. That was also the year she married Harold Bragg. She spent the next two years on a teaching fellowship at Kent State University. Her son Christopher was born in 1967 and her daughter Willa in 1969. For sixteen years (1970–1986), Brown taught at the University of North Carolina at Greensboro. She also earned a PhD from Union Graduate School in Cincinnati, Ohio, in 1980.

Brown recognizes a variety of influences on her poetry. The English Romantics, the focus of her graduate studies, were an influence on her early poetry. She says later influences were Robert Frost because of his "simplicity, his use of conversational feeling, and his quiet serenity"; Brooks because of "her clean use of language, her unconventional metaphor"; and Haki R. *Madhubuti (Don L. Lee) because of his "rhythmic quality."

A Brown poem may have a conversational or musical rhythm. A line of speech ringing in her head may be the inspiration for a poem with natural, conversational rhythm. A background saturated with music (she took voice lessons for several years) accounts for the musical rhythm of some of her poetry. Her poem "High on Sounds," for instance, has the rhythm of African American music.

Brown writes primarily for an African American audience, and some facet of the African American experience is usually the inspiration for or subject of her poetry. She views her poetry as an instrument for African American survival. She feels the African American poet has the responsibility to make political statements but should also have the freedom to write on any subject. Brown feels no conflict between being political as well as artistic in her poetry.

Like other African American female writers, Brown often writes about the African American male-female relationship. In "Don't Honey Me," she asserts that the African American female has traditionally been independent because of the African American male's preoccupation with survival. In "The Race" the relay race is a metaphor for the African American woman running interference for the survival of African Americans.

Brown depicts the strength of the African American woman in *Rainbow Roun Mah Shoulder* (1984; she returned to using the name Brown when the novel was reissued in 1989). This episodic novel, which takes place from 1915 to 1954, mainly in North Carolina, traces the life and loves of Rebecca Florice. As a young woman Florice leaves her husband and home in New Orleans to obey an inner calling to become a spiritual healer. Florice is a multifaceted character who becomes a pillar of strength to those around her, healing them physically with prayer and a laying on of hands. But she is plagued by tragic relationships with men. When a married minister breaks off an affair of several years' duration with her, she tries to commit suicide. What sustains her are her vocation and her long-term friendship to Ronnie, her goddaughter. The novel ends with Florice's death, but her spirit lives on in Ronnie, the inheritor of her spiritual gifts. A recurring metaphor of butterflies and moths suggests Florice's transformation into a deeply spiritual person and her inner beauty and strength. The National Endowment for the Arts selected the novel "as one of a few titles to represent new American writing in international book exhibits."

Brown's 1994 novel, *Crossing Over Jordan* (published under the name Linda Beatrice Brown), traces the lives of four generations of African American women from the post–Civil War era to the mid-twenty-first century. From Georgia McCloud, born a slave, to her great-granddaughter, Hermine, we see the lonely lives of African American women marred by abuse and sustained by religion. The greater part of the novel shows the mellowing of the mother-daughter relationship in the growing mutual respect of Georgia's granddaughter Story and Story's daughter Hermine, who becomes involved in the tumultuous recent past.

Brown, married to artist Vandorn Hinnant, resides in Greensboro, North Carolina. She is on the faculty at Guilford College, where she teaches African American literature and creative writing.

• Linda Beatrice Brown, interview by Virginia W. Smith and Brian J. Benson, *CLA Journal* 20.1 (Sept. 1976): 75–87. Mary Brookhart, "Linda Beatrice Brown," *Black Women in America,* vol. 1, ed. Darlene Clark Hine, 1993, pp. 179–180. Eric Weil,

"Inner Lights and Inner Lives: The Gospel According to Linda Beatrice Brown," *North Carolina Literary Review* 1:1 (Summer 1992): 106–114.

—Phiefer L. Browne

BROWN, LLOYD (b. 1913), novelist, short fiction writer, journalist, and editor of *New Masses* and *Masses and Mainstream.* Lloyd Louis Brown grew up in an African American home for the elderly. His short story "God's Chosen People" (1948) is based on this experience. Brown had little formal education beyond elementary school; he was self-taught. In 1929, Brown joined the Young Communist Youth League.

A trade union organizer for many years, Brown was incarcerated for seven months in 1941 on conspiracy charges. His prison experience and friendship with the inmate Willie Jones became the basis for his novel **Iron City* (1951), which exposes the Jim Crow nature of the prison system and suggests communism as the answer to the American racial question.

The stories "Jericho, USA" (1946) and "Battle in Canaan" (1947), which center on African American troops being trained for World War II, depict Jim Crow in the army and, like his other fiction, are rich with the folk traditions of Brown's people. Brown spent three and a half years in the army air force during the war.

Brown was an editor of the communist journals *New Masses* and *Masses and Mainstream* (1946–1954), to which he contributed short stories, editorials, articles, and book reviews. He often reviewed works by African American writers. He always reviewed on political grounds, criticizing anticommunist ideas and negative characteristics of African Americans. In his editorials and articles Brown discusses many subjects: racism, civil rights, white chauvinism, censorship, McCarthyism, and the Smith Act.

Perhaps Brown's most important essay is "Which Way for the Negro Writer?" (1951). Brown contradicts his contemporaries who argue for universality and distance from African American subject matter, by asserting that African American writers need to work toward their own people and move with them to universality. He denies that there is a contradiction between universal themes and African American subject matter or forms, claiming that the problem with African American literature is that it has not been close enough to the African American people and culture.

Brown wrote an unpublished novel, *Year of Jubilee,* a chapter of which appeared in *Masses and Mainstream* in 1953 as "Cousin Oscar," but did not publish the novel because literary critics advised against it.

In 1953, for personal not philosophical reasons, Lloyd Brown left the Communist Party. Unlike many other African American authors, Brown did not denounce communism or the Communist Party. He worked for many years with Paul *Robeson, collaborating on Robeson's *Freedom* articles and autobiography *Here I Stand.* In 1996, Brown published *The Young Paul Robeson.* Although his ideas were disseminated widely in the communist journals, his work is largely ignored today

• Jabari Onaje Simama, "Black Writers Experience Communism," PhD diss., Emory University, 1978.

—Karen Ruth Kornweibel

BROWN, STERLING A. (1901–1989), poet, critic, and anthologist. Sterling Allen Brown was born on 1 May 1901 into what some have called the "smug" or even "affected" respectability of Washington's African American middle class. He grew up in the Washington world of racial segregation, which engendered a contradiction between full citizenship and marginalized existence. The son of a distinguished pastor and theologian, Brown graduated with honors from the prestigious Dunbar High School in 1918. That fall, he entered Williams College on a scholarship set aside for minority students. By the time he left in 1922, he had performed spectacularly: election to Phi Beta Kappa in his junior year, the Graves Prize for his essay "The Comic Spirit in Shakespeare and Molière," the only student awarded "Final Honors" in English, and cum laude graduation with an AB degree.

At Harvard University from 1922 to 1923, Brown took an MA degree in English. In retrospect, he always talked about his fortuitous discovery of Louis Untermeyer's *Modern American Poetry* (1921). This anthology, more than any other single work he read, radically altered his view of art by introducing him to the New American Poetry of Edwin Arlington Robinson, Robert Frost, Carl Sandburg, Vachel Lindsay, and other experimenters in melding vernacular language, democratic values, and "the extraordinary in ordinary life." When he left, however, he left knowing what the illustrator of *Southern Road* (1932) would later observe about him: "Harvard only gave you the way to *put it down,* not how to feel about things."

The sensitivity to the philosophical and poetic potential in African American folk life, lore, and language was developed in Brown during a series of teaching assignments in Negro colleges, including Virginia Seminary and College (1923–1926), Lincoln University in Missouri (1926–1928), and Fisk University (1928–1929). In each of these locations, he set about absorbing the cultural and aesthetic influences that would define the folk-based metaphysic of his art. On numerous "folklore collecting trips" into "jook-joints," barbershops, and isolated farms, Brown absorbed the wit and wisdom of Mrs. Bibby, Calvin "Big Boy" Davis, *Slim Greer, and many more actual persons who are refashioned into the many memorable folk characters of his poetry.

The poetry collected into *Southern Road* challenges James Weldon *Johnson's dictum that the poetic and philosophical range of Black speech and dialect is limited to pathos and humor. Although the minstrel and plantation traditions had heavily burdened African

American speech with the yoke of racial stereotypes, Brown, along with Langston *Hughes and Zora Neale *Hurston, admirably demonstrated the aesthetic potential of that speech when it is centered in careful study of the folk themselves. Brown came to this conclusion, as he said in a 1942 speech, when he discovered the way folklore became a lens through which to view African American vernacular language. Taking the approach of a creative writer to folklore, he said: "I was first attracted by certain qualities that I thought the speech of the people had, and I wanted to get for my own writing a flavor, a color, a pungency of speech. Then later, I came to something more important—I wanted to get an understanding of people, to acquire an accuracy in the portrayal of their lives."

Brown found support for his vision of "folk" in the work of Benjamin A. Botkin, whose term "folk-say" suggested a profound shift in folklore studies that Brown knew and approved of. Folklore, as Botkin pointed out, was something more than collecting, verifying, indexing, and annotating sources; it was people talking, doing, and describing themselves. To underscore this new emphasis, Botkin published a series of regional miscellanies under the name *Folk-Say* beginning in 1929. Brown contributed eighteen poems and two essays to editions two through four of *Folk-Say.*

The success of Brown's "theory" of folklore is revealed in its implementation. Brown's poetry received its motivation from a need to reveal the humanity that lies below the surface racial stereotypes only skim. There he found qualities erased by racial stereotype: "tonic shrewdness, the ability to take it, and the double-edged humor built up of irony and shrewd observation." Structurally, he made use of, as he said, "the clipped line, the blues form, and the refrain poem." Those folk forms were complemented by his astute experiments with traditional forms, such as the sonnet, villanelle, and ballad. Brown's frequent allusions to Black folk heroes such as *John Henry, *Stackolee, and Casey Jones also raised ordinary experience to mythic proportions.

Recently, literary historians have acknowledged the persistence of Brown's folk-based aesthetic in his critical and editorial work, too. But despite its coherence, his approach has received little study. Beginning in 1931–1932, when he returned to Harvard for doctoral study, Brown focused his critical writing on examinations of representational issues. The result was "Plays of the Irish Character: A Study in Reinterpretation" (an unpublished 1932 course thesis), "Negro Character as Seen by White Authors" (1933), *The Negro in American Fiction* (1937), and *Negro Poetry and Drama* (1937). The connecting link in Brown's editorial and research work for the Federal Writers' Project, the Carnegie-Myrdal Study, and *The Negro Caravan* (1941), the most comprehensive literary anthology of Black writing of its time, is also his folk-based aesthetic. Collectively, this work points to Brown's need to demonstrate the diversity as well as the complexity of African American life. Against the conclusion of Gunnar Myrdal's *An American Dilemma* (1944) that Black life was a "distorted development, or a pathological condition, of the general American condition," Brown presented evidence that African American folk humor functioned as a strategy for exerting control in an often hostile world. Or when the specious argument was made accusing African Americans of having contributed very little to American literature, Brown, with coeditors Arthur P. Davis and Ulysses Lee, presented *The Negro Caravan* as irrefutable proof of Black literary achievement.

Brown also attempted to correct the myopic lens used to view African Americans by writing a number of prose sketches that were to be collected and published as "A Negro Looks at the South." These pieces included "Out of Their Mouths," "Words on a Bus," "The Muted South," and several more. The shared reference to speech tells us much about Brown's view of language as a vehicle for determining cultural authenticity. That Brown admits to viewing these pieces as poems reveals more about his aesthetic, too. Each dialogue or conversation was a unit of speech and thus needed, as he said, "counterpoint, cadence, rhyming, timing, etc. for impact and truth." Therefore, if cuts had to be made, whole units of dialogue should be cut, not cuts within the unit.

The careful reconsideration of Black speech as a viable medium of artistic expression became for Brown the predominant means for reclaiming the humanity of African Americans. This pursuit, of course, had social implications. Brown and others shared the view that "art is a handmaiden to social policy." Although a staunch believer in the promises of the Constitution, Brown was aware that such provisions as the infamous "three-fifths compromise" began a lengthy list of stumbling blocks to achieving life, liberty, and the pursuit of happiness. The American dream meant for Brown the addition of two-fifths more, making a whole number. The root word in "integration" is "integer," which means "whole or complete." As literary historians and cultural critics reexamine the value of the vernacular in their respective pursuits, Brown's daring efforts to make Black folk speech claim a rightful place for him and his people will be properly acknowledged.

• Sterling A. Brown, "A Son's Return: 'Oh, Didn't He Ramble,'" in *Chant of Saints: A Gathering of Afro-American Literature, Art, and Scholarship,* eds. Michael S. Harper and Robert B. Stepto, 1979, pp. 3–22. Robert G. O'Meally, "An Annotated Bibliography of the Works of Sterling A. Brown," in *The Collected Poems of Sterling A. Brown,* ed. Michael S. Harper, 1980. Kimberly W. Benston, "Sterling Brown's After-Song," *Callaloo* 14, 15; 5.1, 5.2 (1982): 33–42. Joanne V. Gabbin, *Sterling A. Brown: Building the Black Aesthetic Tradition,* 1985. Robert B. Stepto, "Sterling A. Brown: Outsider in the Harlem Renaissance?" in *The Harlem Renaissance: Revaluations,* eds. Amritjit Singh et al., 1989, pp. 73–81. Mark A. Sanders, "Distilled Metaphysics: The Dynamics of Voice and Vision in the Poetry of Sterling A.

Brown," PhD diss., Brown University, 1992. John Edgar Tidwell, "Recasting Negro Life History: Sterling A. Brown and the Federal Writers' Project," *Langston Hughes Review* 12.2 (Summer/Winter 1995): 77–82. John Edgar Tidwell, "'The Summer of '46': Sterling A. Brown among the Minnesotans," *Black Heartland* 1.1 (1996): 27–41.

—John Edgar Tidwell

BROWN, WILLIAM WELLS (1814–1884), antislavery lecturer, slave narrator, novelist, dramatist, and historian. William Wells Brown is generally regarded as the first African American to achieve distinction as a writer of belles lettres. A famous antislavery lecturer and fugitive slave narrator in the 1840s, Brown turned to a variety of genres, including poetry, fiction, travel writing, and history, to help him dramatize his case against slavery while promoting sympathetic and heroic images of African Americans in both the United States and England.

William Wells Brown was born sometime in 1814 on a plantation near Lexington, Kentucky, the son of a white man and a slave woman. Light-complexioned and quick-witted, Brown spent his first twenty years mainly in St. Louis, Missouri, and its vicinity, working as a house servant, a fieldhand, a tavernkeeper's assistant, a printer's helper, an assistant in a medical office, and finally a handyman for James Walker, a Missouri slave trader with whom Brown claimed to have made three trips on the Mississippi River between St. Louis and the New Orleans slave market. Before he escaped from slavery on New Year's Day, 1834, this unusually well-traveled slave had seen and experienced slavery from almost every perspective, an education that he would put to good use throughout his literary career.

After seizing his freedom, Brown (who received his middle and last name from an Ohio Quaker who helped him get to Canada) worked for nine years as a steamboatman on Lake Erie and a conductor for the Underground Railroad in Buffalo, New York. In 1843, the fugitive slave became a lecturing agent for the Western New York Anti-Slavery Society. Moving to Boston in 1847, he wrote the first and still the most famous version of his autobiography, *Narrative of William W. Brown, a Fugitive Slave, Written by Himself,* which went through four American and five British editions before 1850, earning its author international fame. Brown's *Narrative* was exceeded in popularity and sales only by the **Narrative of the Life of Frederick Douglass, an American Slave,* which appeared in 1845. In 1849, Brown went abroad to attend an international peace conference in Paris and to lend his voice to the antislavery crusade in England. In addition to his demanding speaking schedule, he found time to try his hand at a new form of first-person narrative, which he entitled *Three Years in Europe, or Places I Have Seen and People I Have Met* (1852). This was the first travel book authored by an African American; it was favorably received by the British press in general as well as by the American antislavery press. A year later **Clotel, or The President's Daughter,* generally regarded as the first full-length African American novel, was published.

After returning to the United States in 1854, Brown continued his pioneering literary work, publishing *The *Escape, or A Leap for Freedom* (1858), the first drama by an African American. During the 1860s he brought out three more versions of *Clotel: Miralda, or The Beautiful Quadroon* (1860–1861), *Clotelle: A Tale of the Southern States* (1864), and *Clotelle, or The Colored Heroine* (1867). Brown also wrote two volumes of African American history in the 1860s, *The Black Man: His Antecedents, His Genius, and His Achievements* (1863) and *The Negro in the American Rebellion* (1867). The latter is the first military history of the African American in the United States. Brown's final autobiography, *My Southern Home, or The South and Its People* (1880), returned again to the scene of his years in slavery, not to retrace his own steps from bondage to freedom but rather to characterize from an intimate perspective the power struggles between blacks and whites in the South both before and after the Civil War. William Wells Brown died in Chelsea, Massachusetts, on 6 November 1884.

In the modest, understated plain style of Brown's autobiographies, it is often the ordinary, the representative, and the nonheroic—even the antiheroic—that come to the fore. Brown's willingness to focus on these aspects of his experience reveals a striking brand of realism in his first-person writing. Like many of his African American literary contemporaries during the 1850s, Brown felt obliged to create characters that epitomized the ideals of aspiring men and women of color in order to educate an American readership that saw mostly the defamation of African American character in newspapers, magazines, and books. Thus the real and the ideal maintain an uncertain balance in Brown's writing. Nevertheless the tension between them and the problematic ways Brown tried to resolve them tell us much about the conflicting aesthetic and ideological agendas underlying early African American literature.

• William Edward Farrison, *William Wells Brown,* 1969. Sidonie Smith, *Where I'm Bound: Patterns of Slavery and Freedom in Black American Autobiography,* 1974. William L. Andrews, *To Tell a Free Story: The First Century of Afro-American Autobiography,* 1760–1865, 1986. Blyden Jackson, *A History of Afro-American Literature,* vol. 1, *The Long Beginning, 1746–1895,* 1989. John Ernest, *Resistance and Reformation in Nineteenth-Century African-American Literature,* 1995.

—William L. Andrews

BROWNFIELD COPELAND. The brownish autumn color of a dying Georgia cotton field was the inspiration for Brownfield Copeland's naming. This character, presented in Alice *Walker's novel *The *Third Life of Grange Copeland* (1970), is the son of

Grange and Margaret Copeland. His life, like his name, symbolizes the decay, death, and violence that often trails behind human resignation to hopelessness.

When Brownfield is fifteen, his father abandons him and his mother commits suicide. The young boy sets out on a journey that leads him to a life of sex and irresponsibility in the juke joint world of his father's lover, Josie, and her daughter, Lorene. After years of scandalous living, Brownfield meets and marries Mem, Josie's niece. Their relationship is a good one, at first. But because of Brownfield's inability to break out of an agricultural system that supports the virtual enslavement of tenant farmers, their relationship sours. Brownfield grows enraged and brutal toward his wife and eventually kills her. Unlike his father, who acknowledges his wrongs and attempts to make amends, Brownfield refuses to accept responsibility for anything he does and pays for that refusal with his life.

Brownfield is a vindictive, cruel, and abusive man. There is no doubt that he is a poor representation of African American manhood. But contrary to the negative criticism the novel has received, Walker's artistic treatment of this character is revealing. Without overstating her argument, Walker presents the condition of a soul entrapped by racism and self-defeat that is both horrifying and painfully realistic.

—Debra Walker King

Brown Girl, Brownstones. Paule *Marshall's first novel, *Brown Girl, Brownstones,* published in 1953, is considered a first in many respects in the development of the African American novel. It is one of few novels up until that time written by an African American author that thoughtfully and accurately concerns itself with the interior life of a young African American female protagonist. It is also one of the first African American novels to accurately portray the complexities of African American mother-daughter relationships, and it portends the kinds of feminist writing that contemporary African American women writers would come to produce.

The novel is a *bildungsroman,* that is, a novel of development. It is perhaps the first in which a young African American girl and her coming-of-age take center stage. It is also one of the first to deal with cross-cultural conflict of two different groups of people of African descent. The protagonist, *Selina Boyce, is the daughter of first-generation Barbadian immigrant parents, Deighton and Silla, who have come to America in search of the ever elusive American dream. In the novel, Silla Boyce represents the new breed of West Indian immigrants, hell-bent to conquer America, "this man country." She is determined to acquire her piece of the American dream and initially works as a cleaning woman for the uptown whites so that one day she, too, will be able to own property, or "buy house" as she and her other West Indian neighbors refer to it. Her husband, Deighton, on the other hand, has his heart and mind set on eventually returning to Barbados once they have acquired enough money. Selina, as a young girl, is torn between two worlds: that of her mother, who is strong, determined, and mean enough to do anything short of murder to own property, and that of her father, who simply does not have the fortitude to be successful and who dreams of returning to Barbados.

The possibility for Deighton's return home presents itself in the novel when a deceased sister wills him a small piece of property in Barbados. Silla is determined to stay in America, for she feels that there is nothing in Barbados for her or her family. She is obsessed with owning a brownstone and goes so far as to forge Deighton's signature on legal documents so that she can get the money for the property she covets. She does so, but at a very high price. Deighton, overwhelmed and mournful of his lost dreams, spends all of the money in one frivolous spree to spite his wife. He is subsequently deported, turned in by Silla as being an illegal alien. Fraught with despair, he dies within a few miles of the coast of Barbados, though it is ambiguous whether he is pushed off the ship or commits suicide. This leaves Silla alone with her newly acquired brownstone as well as her guilt, and Selina with the task of coming to terms with strong, ambivalent feelings toward her mother and her own West Indian American heritage.

• Trudier Harris, "No Outlet for the Blues: Silla Boyce's Plight in *Brown Girl, Brownstones,*" *Callaloo* 17–19 (1983): 57–67. Vanessa D. Dickerson, "The Property of Being in Paule Marshall's *Brown Girl, Brownstones,*" *Obsidian II* 6 (1991): 1–13.

—Keith Bernard Mitchell

Brownies' Book, The. From January 1920 through December 1921, W. E. B. *Du Bois and Augustus Granville Dill published *The Brownies' Book,* a young people's magazine dedicated especially to African American children from six to sixteen years of age. Although this was an independent publishing effort, the magazine functioned as the youth counterpart to the *Crisis,* NAACP's magazine. Novelist Jessie Redmon *Fauset served as the associate editor and contributed regularly. (Other frequent contributors were Langston *Hughes and Nella *Larsen.) At a cost of fifteen cents a copy or one dollar and fifty cents per year, its circulation was approximately five thousand per month.

Among the objectives of *The Brownies' Book* were "to make colored children realize that being 'colored' is a normal, beautiful thing" and "to make them familiar with the history and achievements of the Negro race" (*Crisis,* Oct. 1919). With only one exception, all of the drawings in the magazine were by black artists. Depicting black children from various classes and geographical regions, the magazine spoke powerfully to the social, psychological, spiritual, intellectual, and aesthetic needs and sensibilities of a range of people. To a large degree, its publication marks the genesis of what is now called African American children's literature.

• Violet Harris, "*The Brownies' Book:* Challenge to the Selective Tradition in Children's Literature," PhD diss., University of Georgia, 1986. Dianne Johnson, *Telling Tales: The Pedagogy and Promise of African American Literature for Youth,* 1990.

—Dianne Johnson-Feelings

BRUCE, JOHN E. (1856–1924), columnist, editor, essayist, historian, novelist, and orator. Born a slave in Maryland, John Edward Bruce grew up in Washington, D.C. Developing an interest in journalism, he worked as a general helper in the office of the Washington correspondent for the *New York Times* in 1874. By the time Bruce was twenty he was writing for newspapers, using the pen name "Rising Sun," and in 1879 he started his own paper, the *Argus,* in Washington, D.C. In 1884 Bruce began writing under the name "Bruce Grit" in the *Cleveland Gazette* and the *New York Age,* eventually becoming one of the most widely read and influential African American journalists of his era. In his writings and speeches, Bruce decried mixed-race marriages, denounced Euro-American imperialism, aggressively promoted race pride and solidarity, championed self-help, and advocated the study of black history to combat the anti-Negro rhetoric of the post-Reconstruction period.

Bruce served as a conduit linking people of African descent separated by age and geography. A prolific letter writer and a member of several African American organizations, including the Prince Hall Masons, the American Negro Academy, and the Negro Society for Historical Research, which he founded with Arthur A. *Schomburg in 1911, Bruce knew key nineteenth-century figures such as Alexander *Crummell and Edward Wilmot *Blyden, met and corresponded with Africans who had studied in or visited the United States, and wrote for African periodicals and Duse Mohammed Ali's London-based *African Times* and *Orient Review.* He was one of Marcus *Garvey's most important contacts when the Jamaican first came to America in 1916, introducing him to prominent people in New York, including W. E. B. *Du Bois. Bruce held the title of Duke of Uganda in the Universal Negro Improvement Association (UNIA), wrote a weekly column for Garvey's *Negro World* beginning in 1918, became an important liaison between the UNIA and African organizations, and was given a hero's funeral at Harlem's Liberty Hall in a ceremony attended by more than five thousand people, at which Garvey spoke.

Ralph L. Crowder has suggested that Bruce represents a significant nationalist force in African American society at the turn of the century that was independent of the movements associated with Du Bois and Booker T. *Washington. Crowder attributes Bruce's obscurity today to his refusal to court white recognition or approval. Bruce wrote *Biographical Sketches of Eminent Negro Men and Women in Europe and the United States* (1910) and *The Awakening of Hezekiah Jones* (1916), a novel about the political astuteness of African Americans that has received almost no critical attention, as well as several pamphlets about African American history and politics. He also wrote an early detective novel containing scenes set in Africa entitled *The Black Sleuth,* which appeared serially from 1907 to 1909 (John E. Bruce Papers, Schomburg Center for Research in Black Culture, New York). Nearly fifty years after Bruce's death, some of his newspaper pieces and speeches were published in *The Selected Writings of John Edward Bruce* (1971), which helped to generate some short-lived critical interest in the author.

• Peter Gilbert, "The Life and Thought of John Edward Bruce," in *The Selected Writings of John Edward Bruce: Militant Black Nationalist,* ed. Peter Gilbert, 1971, pp. 1–9. Ralph L. Crowder, "John Edward Bruce: Pioneer Black Nationalist," *Afro-Americans in New York Life and History* 2 (July 1978): 47–66. Ernest Kaiser, "Bruce, John Edward (Bruce Grit)," in *DANB,* eds. Rayford W. Logan and Michael R. Winston, 1982, pp. 76–77.

—John C. Gruesser

BULLINS, ED (b. 1935), born Edward Artie, African American playwright and pioneering artist of the Black Theater movement of the 1960s and 1970s. In the typical Ed Bullins play, characters move through a gritty existence toward little that can be called self-realization or existential triumph. Indeed, these traditional outcomes have little to do with the world Bullins conceives, which is a world created by the "natural"—not naturalistic, as Bullins cautions—style of his drama.

Much of the tension and energy of Bullins's plays comes from his memory of the tough North Philadelphia neighborhood where he was raised. As a youth he developed an early association with street life, whose bootleg whiskey, gang violence, and sudden deaths—Bullins himself was nearly fatally stabbed but miraculously recovered—have strong reverberations in much of his work. In 1952 Bullins dropped out of high school to join the Navy; this experience also commands attention in his plays, as recurrent characters Cliff Dawson and his half-brother Steve Benson are former Navy men.

Bullins moved to Los Angeles in 1958 after having returned from the Navy to a still dangerous Philadelphia. "I went to Los Angeles because it was the farthest I could go," he says. At Los Angeles City College Bullins took courses and began writing in 1961; he also founded a campus literary magazine, the *Citadel.* Restlessness, however, caused him to travel around the country to learn more about how African Americans lived. He returned to California in 1964, this time to San Francisco, and there he began writing plays. The one-act play *How Do You Do?* was his first, and Bullins's own pleasure with it convinced him to remain with theater. But because many critics thought his work obscene, he could not find a producer. He staged his own plays in almost any available space, and finally his small company took their talents to coffeehouses and pubs in the San Francisco area.

The plays of LeRoi Jones (later Amiri *Baraka), notably **Dutchman* and *The Slave,* perhaps saved a despairing Bullins from giving up playwriting entirely. Jones's plays, using elements of Absurdist theater to portray the irony of African American life, greatly influenced Bullins and also fueled a revolutionary spirit among other African American artists in the San Francisco area. Bullins joined them to form Black Arts West, a militant cultural and political organization; he later became the cultural director of the Black House Theater in nearby Oakland. Among the participants in Black House were Bobby Seale, Eldridge *Cleaver, and Huey Newton—three actors who, as revolutionaries, would shortly enter the national consciousness as leaders of the Black Panther Party, of which Bullins became minister of culture.

Bullins's commitment to art over ideology was in early evidence when the Black House experienced a schism between members who wanted to use theater for revolutionary propaganda and those who saw theater's potential for cultural change. While writing agitprop plays to satisfy the revolutionary wing, he also developed his own theatrical ventures but soon found that the radicalized cultural atmosphere of the African American West Coast would not support his efforts. Bullins left Black House in 1967, was thus unconnected to any production support, and was preparing to leave the United States. Robert Macbeth, who directed the New Lafayette Theatre in Harlem, had read a copy of Bullins's **Goin' a Buffalo* (1968), a circumstance that forestalled Bullins's departure. Upon deciding to produce Bullins's *In the Wine Time,* Macbeth brought Bullins to New York to aid in the running of the theater, whose reputation thereafter was founded principally on Bullins's own work.

Bullins's most ambitious dramaturgical project has been his Twentieth-Century Cycle, a proposed series of twenty plays on the African American experience that deals not with race relations but primarily with the everyday lives of African Americans. Though both *Clara's Ole Man* (1965) and *Goin' a Buffalo* are considered noncycle plays, they nevertheless exhibit the characteristic of detailed African American life to be found in the five plays common to the Cycle; additionally, Bullins's intimation about the placement of *Goin' a Buffalo* in a 1972 *New York Times* interview with Clayton Riley suggests its later admission to this group, which canonically lists *In the Wine Time* (1968), **In New England Winter* (1971), *The Duplex* (1970), *The Fabulous Miss Marie* (1971), and *Home Boy* (1976).

The "natural" style of Bullins's plays is evident in his choice of having his characters reveal themselves to one another and to the audience, but disclosing only what they wish. Bullins never imposes his own view upon the action, an approach apparently consistent with the demands of a Black Aesthetic, the code for an African American naturalness and heightening of sensibility. Music is a very important part of a Bullins play, particularly the Cycle plays; the popular jazz and rhythm-and-blues recordings of the time in which the plays are set ensure a fidelity to everyday African American life not found in more stylized productions. The music that is part of *In the Wine Time,* for example, comes from a radio, which has its own role written into the script; art here imitates life or, perhaps more accurately, merges with it.

The idea of naturalness also informs one of his most expressive contributions to drama. In the essay "A Short Statement on Street Theatre," Bullins prescribes the "short, sharp, incisive" play that "subliminally broadcasts blackness"; to masses of African Americans, the immediacy of the skit or short political farce is designed to convey great communicative power. "Each individual in the crowd," writes Bullins, "should have his sense of reality confronted, his consciousness assaulted." Similarly, the stage plays, as portrayals of African American life startling in their immediacy, seek to challenge the audience with elements of violence, alcoholism, and infidelity—components of a determinism that is finally a species of naturalism. It represents not only life as Bullins knew it but also depicts the psychosocial anger of African American culture, a culture in opposition to prevailing Euro-American mores and structures of power.

Though by 1977 Bullins had written more than fifty plays, his efforts to be staged on Broadway were forever to be thwarted. His closest and most heroic attempt was *The Taking of Miss Janie* (1975), whose story of an interracial relationship that culminates in a rape explores the conflict between blackness and white liberalism. It won the prestigious New York Drama Critics Circle Award and was called the best American play of the year. Other awards include three Obie awards for outstanding drama, one National Endowment for the Arts grant, four Rockefeller Playwright grants, the distinguished Vernon Rice Award (for *Clara's Ole Man*), and a Creative Artists Public Service Program award. In 1972 Bullins headed the playwright's workshop at the New York Shakespeare Festival, and when the New Lafayette was in danger of closing in 1973, Bullins became a playwright in residence at the American Place Theater.

Bullins's notable attempts in other genres include a collection of his early short stories, *The Hungered One* (1971), and a novel, *The Reluctant Rapist* (1973), in which the character Steve Benson, a veteran of several Bullins plays and widely regarded as Bullins's alter ego, embodies the twin senses of disillusionment and bewilderment that mark so many of the plays. As guest editor of a special African American theater issue of *Drama Review* (Summer 1968), Bullins featured not only his own work but also that of Jones, Ben *Caldwell, Ron *Milner, and others; Larry *Neal's "The Black Aesthetic," the landmark essay of the period, also appeared in this number.

Known in both theatrical and political circles for the incisive race consciousness with which he fashioned his work, Bullins made news in 1977 by having collaborated with white composer Mildred Kayden on the musicals *Storyville* and *Sepia Star.* This did not, however, lead to a departure from established philosophy. The tragic accidental death of his son Edward, Jr., in 1978 led to Bullins's return to the West Coast and the establishment of the Bullins Memorial Theatre, whose *Black Theatre Newsletter* not only featured news of productions of plays by other prominent African American playwrights but also listed some forty-four Bullins plays available for production.

Despite an apparent reluctance to acknowledge the influcncc of playwrights other than Baraka earlier in his career, Bullins later confessed to a broader eclecticism; he sees the dramaturgy of Eugene O'Neill and Samuel Beckett as having been additional significant influences and also notes that African American novelist Chester *Himes and Iranian poet Idris Shah have had their own profound effect on his work. These writers lcnd elements of suspense and lyrical renditions of the absurd to later plays by Bullins, notably *A Teacup Full of Roses* (1989) and *Dr. Geechee and the Blood Junkies* (1991), both antidrug plays. *Salaam, Huey Newton, Salaam* (1990), a play on the life of the celebrated Black Panther activist, was published in the collection *Best Short Plays of 1990.* After a tempestuous thirty-year odyssey through art, culture, and politics that began on the West Coast, Bullins seemed to have come full circle; with playwright Jonal Woodward, he headed the Bullins/Woodward Theater Workshop in San Francisco, which stages plays, teaches playwriting seminars, and holds theater workshops. By September 1995, however, Bullins left the workshop to accept a professorship in theater at Northeastern University. *Boy x Man* (1995), the latest addition to the Twentieth-Century Cycle, was staged in October 1995 in Greensboro, North Carolina.

The complex themes of revolution that characterized the African American stage of the 1960s and 1970s are easily measured and shaped by the work of Bullins; the efficacy of the rueful defiance he brought to this stage is reflected in his complete domination of Off-Broadway theater for more than a decade. Bullins's natural style and codification of the period's African American dramaturgical techniques are a historical and logical development of the techniques of the Free Southern Theater, which sought to use drama as a means of organizing African Americans in the South. The rawness of the Bullins plays, however, makes them seem to some to be a leap through tradition. If the critical response to the plays appears uneven—if their perceived greatness is mixed with an interpretation of African American anger deemed to be antiwhite by some, and even anti-American by others—then the debate, which Bullins's work perforce extends, as to the synergy of art and a consciousness of insurrection and its possible consequences must continue.

• Ed Bullins, ed., *Drama Review* 12 (1967–1968). Ed Bullins, interviewed by Marvin X, *New Plays from the Black Theater,* ed. Ed Bullins, 1969. Ed Bullins, introduction to *The Theme Is Blackness,* 1972. Clayton Riley, "Bullins: 'It's Not the Play I Wrote,'" *New York Times,* 19 Mar. 1972, 1. Jervis Anderson, "Profiles—Dramatist," *New Yorker,* 16 June 1973, 40–79. Richard Scharine, "Ed Bullins Was Steve Benson (But Who Is He Now?)," *Black American Literature Forum* 13 (Fall 1979): 103–109. Genevieve Fabre, *Drumbeats, Masks and Metaphor,* 1983. John L. DiGaetani, *In Search of a Postmodern Theater,* 1991. Nathan L. Grant, "The Frustrated Project of Soul in the Drama of Ed Bullins," in *Language, Rhythm, and Sound: Black Popular Cultures into the Twenty-First Century,* ed. Joseph Adjaye and Adrianne R. Andrews, 1997, pp. 90–102. Samuel A. Hay, *Ed. Bullins: A Literary Biography,* 1997.

—Nathan L. Grant

BURROUGHS, MARGARET TAYLOR GOSS (b. 1917), poet, visual artist, educator, and arts organizer. Margaret Burroughs was born in St. Rose, Louisiana, near New Orleans, but was brought at the age of five by her parents, Alexander and Octavia Pierre Taylor, to Chicago where she grew up, was educated, and where her distinctive career has unfolded. She attended the public schools of Chicago, including the Chicago Teacher's College. In 1946, she received a BA in education and in 1948, an MA in education from the Art Institute of Chicago. From 1940 to 1968 she was a teacher in the Chicago public schools and subsequently a professor of humanities at Kennedy-King College in Chicago (1969–1979).

Burroughs has a national reputation as a visual artist and as an arts organizer. Her long exhibition record as a painter and printmaker began in 1949 and has included exhibitions throughout the United States and abroad. A retrospective of her work was held in Chicago in 1984. As an organizer she has been associated with the founding and conduct of a number of arts organizations. It was her founding in 1961 of the DuSable Museum of African-American History, however, that placed her among the outstanding institution builders of her generation. She served as a director of the museum until her appointment as a Commissioner of the Chicago Park District in 1985.

Burroughs has also had a commitment to progressive politics, as exemplified by her contributions to such publications as *Freedomways,* founded by, among others, W. E. B. *Du Bois and Paul *Robeson, both of whom were special heroes to her. She has felt a special affinity to the Mexican muralists and both studied and collaborated with artists in Mexico.

Burroughs began her writing career by doing articles and reviews for the Associated Negro Press, founded and directed by Claude Barnett. Her work as an educator led her into writing for children. Her works in this category include *Jasper, the Drummin' Boy* (1947) and the anthology *Did You Feed My Cow?* (1956), both of which underwent subsequent editions.

Burroughs has made a distinctive contribution as a poet and as an editor of poets. The bulk of her poems are published in the volumes *What Shall I Tell My Children Who Are Black?* (1968) and *Africa, My Africa*

(1970). Her most notable work as an editor was her collaboration with Dudley *Randall in the production of the commemorative volume *For Malcolm* (1967). The forty-three poets represented include established poets such as Gwendolyn *Brooks, Margaret *Walker, and Robert *Hayden; as well as a younger group associated with the Black Arts movement, such as Sonia *Sanchez, Amiri *Baraka, Larry *Neal, and Mari *Evans. Burroughs's own poem on *Malcolm X was also included. In this poem, "Brother Freedom," Burroughs places Malcolm in a pantheon with Toussaint *L'Ouverture, Joseph Cinque, Nat *Turner, and other heroes of black consciousness. Burroughs also contributed to the rediscovery of the poet Frank Marshall *Davis by editing *Jazz Interlude* (1987).

Burroughs's own poems exult in African and African American culture, taking imagery primarily from the urban milieu of Chicago in which she has spent her life. Her connection to Africa has been solidified by annual trips to the continent beginning in the late 1960s and continuing to the 1990s. As an early and often lonely pioneer of black consciousness, Burroughs welcomed in her poetry the apparent explosion in the ranks of those subscribing to her vision, particularly among the young. Her welcome, however, was tempered by a critical stance informed by her own progressive politics. In the poem "Only in This Way," for example, she downplays "wayout hairdos" in favor of blacks "knowing and accepting" themselves.

The influence of Margaret Burroughs has been felt in a variety of organizations with which she has been associated, as well as by those who have participated in programs of the DuSable Museum. As an essayist, poet, and writer for children, her literary endeavors have interfaced directly with other aspects of her creative and social agendas.

• Eugene Feldman, *The Birth and the Building of the DuSable Museum*, 1981.

—Richard A. Long

BURTON, ANNIE LOUISE (1860–?), autobiographer. Slave narratives are usually recognized and treated as an antebellum genre. Yet a significant group of ex-slaves who were children at the close of the Civil War also published their autobiographies. Annie Burton is one of the few such authors who, instead of dictating her story to someone else, wrote her own narrative. For some readers, Burton's *Memories of Childhood's Slavery Days* (1909) may seem to be a disjointed and nostalgic tale of what she calls the "Great Sunny South." She breaks the narrative into eight sections: two autobiographical sketches, "a vision," a piece she authored for her graduating essay, a radically progressive essay by the black minister Dr. P. Thomas Stanford entitled "The Race Question in America," her own short "historical composition," and her "favorite poems" and "favorite hymns." The first section is a wistful sketch of her childhood in Clayton, Alabama, which then transforms into a chronicle of her economic life as an adult. She calls the second, in which she describes her mother, who ran away before the war and then came back to claim her children, a sequel; both are primarily accounts of travel, work, worth, and compensation.

Burton's pining memories of plantation days seem to align her prose with Thomas Nelson Page's revisionist "happy darky" novels, while her representation of her later economic ventures invokes the revisionist re-historicizing of white violence offered by Booker T. *Washington. Yet Burton uses nostalgia as a cover and then disrupts the expectations her readers might have. While she seems to echo both the postbellum revision of slavery and Washington's vision of "industrial education" and economics, by including Stanford's piece, she challenges Washington's paradigmatic postbellum narrative **Up from Slavery* (1901). Like Harriet E. *Wilson, for example, Annie Burton evokes the idealized plantation mansion in order to critique her place in the hierarchy it symbolizes.

• William L. Andrews, "The Representation of Slavery and the Rise of Afro-American Literary Realism (1865–1920)," in *Slavery and the Literary Imagination*, eds. Deborah McDowell and Arnold Rampersad, 1989, pp. 62–80.

—P. Gabrielle Foreman

BUTLER, OCTAVIA E. (b. 1947), short fiction writer, novelist, and science fiction writer. Hugo and Nebula award–winning author, and a MacArthur Fellow, Octavia E. Butler was born on 22 June 1947 in Pasadena, California. Butler has helped to enrich the ever-expanding genre of speculative fiction by adding to it a previously excluded experience: the African American female's. She makes a way out of no way by drawing on her experiences growing up in one of America's most culturally diverse states. In struggling against the odds of racism and sexism, breaking into and publishing prolifically in America and abroad in the predominantly white and male dominated science fiction genre, Butler has made a substantial contribution to African American culture and literature.

Butler's emphasis on slavery and its cultural implications (the mixing of races and cultures) predominates from her science fiction to her critically acclaimed and only mainstream novel to date, **Kindred* (1979). In viewing her works we see that all of her characters try to free themselves from some system of bondage. This leitmotif of bondage situates her firmly in the African American literary tradition, which is infused with the racial memories of slavery. However, Butler not only appropriates slavery, she attempts to move beyond it.

In her first work, *Patternmaster* (1976), she devises a plot based on genetic evolution and vassalage, and this provides the framework for each successive novel. Several subthemes from slavery, like survival of the fittest, patterns of control and organization, sexual propagation or biological order, and allusions to African traditions, develop. In *Patternmaster* these subthemes situate themselves in a tier of societies based on the refinement, or lack thereof, of telepathic ability, and this pattern develops through an intricate process of breeding to evolve to a state of linked minds governed by the strongest telepath. With this pattern of mental prowess, Butler inadvertently suggests how it is ironic that the human mind can evolve and unify, and yet still rely on a slave system to maintain order.

In *Mind of My Mind* (1977) the slave state is shown in its protagonist, Mary, who breaks free of the bonds of poverty and racial oppression to establish the pattern of minds that will culminate in *Patternmaster. Survivor* (1978) picks up the strain of race stratification and enslavement by outlining an African Asian girl's experiences dealing with humans, fighting addiction to an alien drink, "meklah," and joining the alien Garkohns, a race of furry aliens whose planet humans have colonized in an attempt to escape the Clayark invasion on earth. Butler published the historical novel *Kindred* next, and its subject matter positions it chronologically into a segment of *Wild Seed* (1980), because it explores the maintenance of the slave plantation. The encounters with systems of bondage in both works also illuminate the ethical issues of propagation, biological order, and cultural and racial interbreeding that are associated with slavery, by having their protagonists decide just how much they are willing to do to survive and make sure that their future generation succeeds.

Wild Seed continues the motif of slavery and propagation by going to the ancestral African beginning of the pattern and relating how it was conceived and instigated by Doro, a Nubian *ogbanje* (a spirit who cannot die and who manifests itself by continually being born into bodies that die). Butler plays with a societal order based not on race, but on a genetic capacity for telepathic power. The protagonist, a female African shapeshifter called Anyanwu, makes the Middle Passage and works to undercut Doro's need to kill. By the appropriation of the Middle Passage, an *ogbanje,* and an African shapeshifter and healer, Butler recreates her former works' tension, which comes from having to decide how to free oneself from racial-biological or mental-telepathic slavery. Either, she suggests, is a slave state of mind that will destroy.

The next wave of fiction develops a paradigm of biological enslavement due to alien intervention and drug addiction. In *Clay's Ark* (1984); the Xenogenesis Trilogy, *Dawn* (1987), *Adulthood Rites* (1988), and *Imago* (1989); and *Parable of the Sower* (1993), the slave state is also located in the biological realm. These stories focus on humans who, through alien integration or drug abuse, are reprogrammed along a biological drive to reproduce or destroy at all costs. The price becomes cultural deconstruction and genetic mutation into something beyond human. However, what is interesting about the trilogy is how societal structure is determined not just by genetic mutation but also by the need to interact with one's environment on mutually beneficial terms that help both survive. *Parable of the Sower* moves to economic and spiritual enslavement caused by drug addiction. In this story Butler creates a multicultural society or family united by acceptance of a spiritual worldview of change, "earthseed," to combat the spiritual deterioration and cultural chaos hinted at in *Clay's Ark.*

In 1998, Butler continued the narrative of Lauren Olamina from *Parable of the Sower* with the publication of *Parable of the Talents,* the second novel in her Parable series. Slavery and enslavement remain key issues as Lauren and her followers try to adhere to their Earthseed philosophy in a hostile religious environment. Their opponents conquer them physically and put them in concentration camps; to further punish what they perceive as wayward Americans, they take away all the children of Earthseed believers, including Lauren's weeks-old daughter, in an effort to train the children away from Earthseed.

Like her novels, the pattern of slavery and multicultural generation resulting from a slave state derives from Butler's earlier short stories: "Crossover" (1971), "Near of Kin" (1979), and "The Evening and the Morning and the Night" (1987). Two, "Speech Sounds" (1983) and "Bloodchild" (1984), won Hugo Awards. The tie between Butler's short stories and her fiction comes from her daring to explore taboo and untouched material, for in them she travels the realms of incest, chemical poisoning and the genetic mutations that result, and the tension of bonds between men and women. And she did this well before it became fashionable to do so. Butler's works, whether viewed as science fiction or not, develop the slave state to arrive at an evolution of the mind.

• Veronica Mixon, "Futurist Woman: Octavia Butler," *Essence,* Apr. 1979, 12, 15. Frances Smith Foster, "Octavia Butler's Black Female Future Fiction," *Extrapolation* 23.1 (1982): 37–48. Sandra Y. Govan, "Connections, Links, and Extended Networks: Patterns in Octavia Butler's Science Fiction," *Black American Literature Forum* 18.2 (Spring 1984): 82–87. Ruth Salvaggio, "Octavia Butler and the Black Science-Fiction Heroine," *Black American Literature Forum* 18.2 (Spring 1984): 78–81. Joe Weixlmann, "An Octavia E. Butler Bibliography," *Black American Literature Forum* 18.2 (Spring 1984): 88–89. Thelma J. Shinn, "The Wise Witches: Black Women Mentors in the Fiction of Octavia E. Butler," in *Conjuring: Black Women, Fiction, and Literary Tradition,* eds. Marjorie Pryse and Hortense J. Spillers, 1985, pp. 203–215. Octavia E. Butler, "*Black Scholar* Interview with Octavia Butler: Black Women and the Science Fiction Genre," interview by Frances M. Beal, *Black Scholar* 17.2 (Mar.–Apr. 1986): 14–18. Sandra Y. Govan, "Homage to Tradition: Octavia Butler Renovates the Historical Novel," *MELUS* 13.1–2 (Spring–Summer 1986): 79–96. Octavia E. Butler, "An Interview with Octavia E. Butler," interview by Randall Kenan, *Callaloo* 14.2 (1991): 495–504. Rebecca J. Holden, "The High Costs of Cyborg Survival: Octavia Butler's Xenogenesis Trilogy," *Foundation: the International Review of Science Fiction* 72 (Spring 1998): 49–56; this issue contains other articles on Butler. Jim Miller, "Post-Apocalyptic Hoping: Octavia Butler's Dystopian/Utopian Vision," *Science Fiction Studies* 25:2 (75) (July 1998): 336–360.

—Mildred R. Mickle

C

Cables to Rage, published in London in 1970 by Paul Breman Limited, was the second volume of poetry written by African American poet, essayist, and activist Audre *Lorde. While this collection was only republished once (1972) under the same title, more than two-thirds of the pieces in the early volume were later selected for inclusion in *Chosen Poems: Old and New* (1982) and *Undersong: Chosen Poems Old and New, Revised* (1992).

Although Lorde's poetry was published in several British and European anthologies as well as in African American literary magazines during the 1960s, it was not until she received a grant from the National Endowment for the Arts in 1968 that she was able to devote herself full-time to her writing. Her experience as a poet in residence at Tougaloo College in Mississippi (her first trip to the Deep South, her first workshop situation with young African American students, her first time away from her children) and the circumstances that followed her stay there (Martin Luther *King, Jr.'s assassination, Robert Kennedy's death, a close friend's accident) made her see the shortness of life and the necessity for immediate action. The pieces in her second volume of poetry reflect this urgency and the function, for Lorde, of art to protest if not change destructive social patterns.

Rooted in her anger at the racism and sexism that have marked the history of the United States, the poems in *Cables to Rage* introduced themes that carried through much of Lorde's work: violence, hunger, cloaks of lies, dishonest silences, struggle for voice, faith in the capacity to love, growth through dreams, desperate hope and defiance amid dying and loss, and painful birthing. Recurrent in these poems are images of shedding and of fiery renewal: obsolete or false coverings (snakeskin, cocoon, weeds, dead poems) must be stripped and discarded so that the new can grow. While many African American poets of her time focused on black nationalism and urban realism, Lorde placed relationships amid global concerns and gave voice to what many had rejected, hidden, or ignored. "Martha," for instance, Lorde's first overtly lesbian poem to be published and the longest piece in the volume, was strategically centered in *Cables to Rage.* A writer who saw herself in relational dialogue with the rest of the world, Lorde explained that her work owed much to her ancestors, to the love and support of women, and to African and African American artists, and she insisted in her poetry and prose that without community, coalition across differences, and freedom from all oppression, there is no true liberation at all.

• Claudia Tate, ed., *Black Women Writers at Work,* 1983, pp. 100–116. Audre Lorde, "My Words Will Be There," in *Black Women Writers, 1950–1980,* ed. Mari Evans, 1984, pp. 261–268.

—Ann E. Reuman

CAIN, GEORGE (b. 1943), novelist. Little information exists about George Cain other than from his autobiographical novel *Blueschild Baby.* He speaks through his alter ego, and in effect, Cain utilizes the trope of the *doppleganger* or "double" popularized by German writers and by African American historian W. E. B. *Du Bois in his theory of double consciousness.

Born during October or November 1943, Cain grew up in Harlem and showed academic promise as an adolescent. He entered Iona College (New Rochelle, N.Y.) on a basketball scholarship but left to travel in California, Mexico, and Texas. Upon returning to New York in 1966, Cain started *Blueschild Baby* and spent four years completing the project. In the interim, he married and moved to Bedford Stuyvesant in Brooklyn with his wife, Jo Lynne, and daughter, Nataya, to whom he dedicates the work.

Blueschild Baby is a blues refrain of suffering delineating the hero's addiction to heroin. Originally published in 1970, its popularity resurged in the mid-1990s because of recognition by African American scholars of Cain's prescient message. Drug addiction still ravages the African American community, though its cause is crack cocaine. The reader is introduced on the first page of the novel to the hero, Georgie Cain, in the throes of withdrawal—alternate dreamfulness and wakefulness, a runny nose, and a queasy stomach that signal he needs a fix. Georgie the parolee shows fear of the police because a drug infraction would return him to prison for another two years.

Blueschild Baby, however, is also an autobiographical novel of emancipation similar to the slave narrative, but the white master this time is "horse," the street name for heroin. In its progression from Georgie's enslavement to freedom from drugs, the novel incorporates archetypal devices attendant to quests—the hero's journey to salvation, his death-rebirth experience, and his redemption by triumphing over evil. The work also parallels **Native Son* with its viewpoint limited to the hero's perspective as he struggles against naturalistic forces threatening to expose or kill him during Georgie's drug adventures on the streets of Harlem, Brooklyn, or New Jersey.

Temporal shifts reflect Georgie's sane or disoriented thinking according to his drug intake. Past and present oscillate as do Georgie's physical or psychological movements when he returns to his Harlem childhood, New Jersey home, or private school experiences. Black Harlem would seem to be the archetypal site that had fostered Georgie's drug problem, but that is the ironic twist to Georgie's journey to self-knowledge. He actually begins to use drugs recreationally while attending Brey Academy, a white private school where he is one of two African American students. Hashish relieves the pressures of feeling economically displaced or scholastically and athletically mandated to be a basketball hero. Hard drugs inevitably become Georgie's coping device to handle these racial adjustments. At the end, a black woman, Nandy, is Georgie's salvation. *Blueschild Baby* is a gripping narrative of emancipation from drugs.

• Houston A. Baker, Jr., "From the Inferno to the American Dream: George Cain's *Blueschild Baby,*" in *Singers of Daybreak,* 1974, pp. 81–89. Edith Blicksilver, "George Cain" in *DLB,* vol. 33, *Afro-American Fiction Writers after 1955,* eds. Thadious M. Davis and Trudier Harris, 1984, pp. 41–43. Gerald Early, foreword to *Blueschild Baby,* 1987.

—Virginia Whatley Smith

CAINES, JEANNETTE FRANKLIN (b. 1937), writer. The works of Jeannette Franklin Caines are generally concerned with parent-child communication and other social and political issues. Jeannette Caines often presents these topics in the voice of a child. *Abby* (1973) explores the dynamics of adoption and the complex issues surrounding the expansion of the family, while her second book, *Daddy* (1977), deals with divorce and the necessity of maintaining healthy relationships between the child and both parents. *Chilly Stomach* (1986) concerns the difficulties of defining and confronting sexual abuse. Often Caines's books end without a resolution to the problem. This encourages thought and discussion and facilitates effective communication and problem solving between parents and children.

Caines was born in New York in 1937 and has dedicated much of her life to improving the quality of children's and young adult literature. In addition to receiving the National Black Child Development Institute's Certificate of Merit and Appreciation, she has been a member of the Coalition of One Hundred Black Women, the Council for Adoptable Children, and the Negro Business and Professional Women of Nassau County. Her academic concentration in psychology and child development and her professional and entrepreneurial success lend her credibility and effectiveness as an author of children's literature.

• Barbara T. Rollock, "Caines, Jeannette Franklin," in *Black Authors and Illustrators of Children's Books,* 1988, p. 22. "Caines, Jeannette Franklin," in *Authors of Books for Young People,* eds. Martha E. Ward et al., 1990, p. 105.

—Maia Angelique Sorrells

CALDWELL, BEN (b. 1937), dramatist of the Black Arts movement of the 1960s, known particularly for the sardonic style he employed in examining the lives of African Americans. Born in Harlem, Ben Caldwell had an early engagement with the arts. Having come of age in the 1960s, he was one of many sensitive and creative young African Americans to have been influenced by the work of Amiri *Baraka (then LeRoi Jones), who read Caldwell's plays and encouraged him.

During 1965 and 1966 Caldwell lived in Newark, New Jersey, with Baraka and several other artists; he refers to this time as his "Newark Period," in which he wrote *Hypnotism* (1969) and his most critically acclaimed work, *The Militant Preacher* (1967), which later appeared in *A Black Quartet: Four New Plays* under the title *Prayer Meeting, or The First Militant Minister* (produced, 1969; published, 1970). The remaining plays are by other outstanding Black Arts playwrights: Baraka, Ron *Milner, and Ed *Bullins.

Caldwell's plays uniquely satirize not only the racism and the naïveté of whites, but also those African Americans who seek either to emulate whites, be unduly materialistic, or anchor themselves to stereotypes. Some of these works also employ revolutionary rhetoric common to the period, but as Stanley *Crouch suggests, Caldwell's movement to agitprop from a deftly crafted concatenation of satirical moments renders the whole formulaic, clinical, and trite.

Many of his works are very short one-act plays; four of these, appearing in a special issue of *Drama Review* (vol. 12, 1967–1968), occupy only eleven pages. Caldwell's great power, however, is his ability to communicate racial issues with both mordancy and a superb economy of dramaturgy. The revolutionary spirit compromised through materialism is the theme of *Riot Sale, or Dollar Psyche Fake Out,* as a weapon that shoots currency makes rioting African Americans stop to gather the money and run to nearby stores; *Top Secret, or A Few Million after B.C.* focuses on a secret meeting between the President and select members of his cabinet to discover a method of imposing birth control on African Americans. The method: convincing African Americans, many of whom wish to emulate whites anyway, that having more than two children is uncivilized.

One of his more mature efforts in this vein is *The King of Soul, or The Devil and Otis Redding* (1969), in which the theme of materialism is further complicated by both the history of the exploitation of talented entertainers such as Redding and by the inclusion of Redding and the Faustian bargain he makes—though never understands. This kind of pithy acidity helped earn Caldwell a Guggenheim Fellowship in 1970.

After 1970, Caldwell wrote essays and poetry in addition to drama. As late as 1982, the Henry Street Settlement's New Federal Theater had staged *The World of Ben Caldwell,* a series of sketches that attempted to reveal the absurdity of the American dream. In one of these comic sketches, actor Morgan Freeman portrayed risqué stand-up comedian Richard Pryor; actors Reginald Vel Johnson and Garrett Morris alternated portrayals of actor-comedian Bill Cosby. Mel Gussow, reporting in the *New York Times,* wrote that Caldwell showed such deftness and caustic cleverness in these sketches that he might well consider writing material for Pryor.

Since 1968 Caldwell has run the Third World Cultural Center in New York's South Bronx, where plays, poetry readings, and various other artistic activities are staged. By the early 1980s, Caldwell's interests had turned increasingly to the visual arts; in 1983 in New York's Kenkeleba Gallery he participated in an exhibit that connected the media of painting and jazz with such artists as Camille Billops, Norman Lewis, Faith Ringgold, and Romare Bearden. In 1991, however, a fire swept through his Harlem apartment, destroying more than forty years' worth of manuscripts, paintings, and memorabilia. Undaunted, Caldwell is returning to writing the acerbically witty monologues and sketches that won him notoriety in the late 1970s and early 1980s; his most frequent writing of these has been for African American humorist and political activist Dick Gregory.

Though his particular brand of satire is far less in evidence in today's African American theater, Caldwell's central themes represent his unalloyed gift to this period of revolutionary drama. The short skit or one-act play whose most compact and devastating message with respect to the spirit of African American revolution was the exposure of African American self-hatred and self-deception is a gift considered by some to have been given with the left hand. But while some may decry it as antirevolutionary, it appears nevertheless to have an important and inexorable progressive aspect: while enumerating the evils of the adversary, it courts reflection on the foibles of the insurgent.

• Charles D. Peavy, "Satire and Contemporary Black Drama," *Satire Newsletter* 7 (Fall 1969): 40–49. Ronald V. Ladwing, "The Black Comedy of Ben Caldwell," *Players* 51.3 (1976): 88–91. Stanley Crouch, "Satireprop," *Village Voice,* 27 Apr. 1982, 104. Mel Gussow, "Federal Office 'World of Ben Caldwell,'" *New York Times,* 10 April 1982, 13.

—Nathan L. Grant

CAMPBELL, JAMES EDWIN (1867–1895), journalist and poet. The son of Lethia (Stark) and James Campbell was born in Pomeroy, Ohio, and graduated from Pomeroy High School in 1884. He taught school in Ohio and participated in Republican politics there. In West Virginia (1890–1894) Campbell served as principal of Langston School (Point Pleasant) and of the newly opened Collegiate Institute (Charleston), an agricultural and mechanical arts school for African American youths. He married Mary Champ, a teacher, in 1891. Moving to Chicago, Campbell joined the staff of the *Times-Herald* and contributed articles and poems to several periodicals. His promising career was tragically cut short when he died of pneumonia in Pomeroy at age twenty-eight.

Campbell published two poetry collections: *Driftings and Gleanings* (1887) and *Echoes from the Cabin and Elsewhere* (1895); the latter contains what some have judged to be the finest group of dialect poems of the nineteenth century. Campbell's peers and leading critics during and after his lifetime praised his poems in the Gullah dialect for their originality; hard realism; aptness of phrasing, rhymes, and rhythms; and truth to the spirit, philosophy, and humor of antebellum plantation folk. Jean Wagner (*Black Poets of the United States,* 1973) notes that Campbell's "racial consciousness," "satirical spirit," and religious skepticism foreshadow the poetry of the Harlem Renaissance.

Campbell captures "the joy and pathos" of cabin life without lapsing into minstrelsy or surrendering race pride. He varies verse forms, moods, and speech patterns to suit individualized subjects, and leavens pungent satire with sympathetic appreciation for folkways. A few poems emulate traditional animal fables, such as "Ol' Doc' Hyar," in which wily Doctor Hare loses a patient but not his fee: "'Not wut fokses does, but fur wut dee know / Does de folkses git paid'—an' Hyar larfed low." Other dialect lyrics include work songs, lullabies, or vivid portrayals of activities such as horse trading, good eating, backsliding from church, and superstitions. In standard English, Campbell's poems celebrate wine, women, song, and the beauties of nature; his "The Pariah's Love" (300 lines) recounts an interracial love affair. These serious, metrically varied verses are aesthetically superior to most of the century's African American poetry, but his dialect poetry dedicated to "the Negro of the old regime" remains his most notable work.

• Carter G. Woodson, "James Edwin Campbell, a Forgotten Man of Letters," *Negro History Bulletin* 2 (Nov. 1938): 11. Frank R. Levstick, "James Edwin Campbell," in DANB, eds. Rayford W. Logan and Michael R. Winston, 1982, pp. 32–36. Joan R. Sherman, *Invisible Poets: Afro-Americans of the Nineteenth Century,* 2d ed., 1989.

—Joan R. Sherman

Cancer Journals, The. *The Cancer Journals,* published in 1980 by Spinsters Ink, was the first major prose work of African American poet and essayist Audre *Lorde as well as one of the first books to make visible the viewpoint of a lesbian of color. In this collection, Lorde challenged traditional Western notions of illness and advocated women's ability, responsibility, and right to make decisions about their health.

A three-part piece developed from journal entries and essays written between 1977 and 1979, *The Cancer Journals* chronicles Lorde's experiences with her mastectomy and its aftermath. The first section of the book, "The Transformation of Silence into Language and Action," is a short address that was delivered by Lorde on a lesbians and literature panel of the Modern Language Association in 1977, soon after she had recovered from surgery that discovered a benign breast tumor. The second chapter, subtitled "A Black Lesbian Feminist Experience," frankly describes the emotions experienced by one without role models through the course of diagnosis, surgery, and recovery. Central to this section is Lorde's recognition of her fierce desire to survive, to be a warrior rather than a victim, and her acknowledgment of the network of women whose love sustained her. The last chapter, entitled "Breast Cancer: Power vs. Prosthesis," traces the development of Lorde's decision not to wear a prosthesis, a cosmetic device that she felt placed profit and denial of difference over health and well-being.

In each of the sections of the book, Lorde sought the strength that could be found at the core of the experience of cancer. Balancing her "wants" with her "haves," she used this crisis to change patterns in her life. Rather than ignoring pain and fear, she acknowledged, examined, and used them to better understand mortality as a source of power. This tendency to face and metabolize pain Lorde saw as a particularly African characteristic. Death, she realized, had to be integrated with her life, loving, and work; consciousness of limitations and shared mourning of her loss increased her appreciation of living. Underlining the possibilities of self-healing, specifically the need to love her altered body, Lorde further stressed the importance of accepting difference as a resource rather than perceiving it as a threat. Perhaps most crucially, Lorde realized through the experience of cancer the necessity of visibility and voice. Seeing silence as a tool for separation and powerlessness, she understood the important function of her writing not only to free herself of the burden of the experience but also to share her experiences so that others might learn. Survival, she wrote, is only part of the task; the other part is teaching.

In 1981, *The Cancer Journals* won the American Library Association Gay Caucus Book of the Year Award. In 1982, Lorde published *Zami: A New Spelling of My Name,* a "biomythography" that she claimed was a "lifeline" through her cancer experience. Six years after her mastectomy, Lorde was diagnosed with liver cancer, the meaning of which she explored in the title essay of *A Burst of Light* (1988). That *The Cancer Journals, Zami,* and *A Burst of Light,* the three works that perhaps most directly reveal Lorde's deeply felt vulnerabilities and affirmations, were all published by small feminist presses and neglected by mainstream publishing firms attests to the work still to be done. Before she died, Lorde in an African naming ceremony took the name Gambda Adisa, meaning Warrior: She Who Makes Her Meaning Known.

• Claudia Tate, ed., *Black Women Writers at Work,* 1983. Audre Lorde, "My Words Will Be There," in *Black Women Writers, 1950–1980,* ed. Mari Evans, 1984, pp. 261–268.

—Ann E. Reuman

Cane. A classic of the New Negro movement or Harlem Renaissance, Jean *Toomer's *Cane* (1923) captures the spirit of experimentalism at the core of American modernism. A seminal work of sketches, poetry, and drama, *Cane*'s ancestry is as complex as that of its author who was physically white but racially mixed and who defined himself not as an African American but as an American. Hybridity and innovation are the defining features of the artist as well as the classic he produced. *Cane* bears the influence of Gertrude Stein's *Three Lives* (1909), James Weldon *Johnson's *The *Autobiography of an Ex-Colored Man* (1912), Sherwood Anderson's *Winesburg, Ohio* (1919), and slave narratives. It exercised a shaping influence upon the poetry of Langston *Hughes and Sterling A. *Brown, and Zora Neale *Hurston's **Their Eyes Were Watching God* (1937).

Conceived in Sparta, Georgia, where, during the summer of 1921 Toomer was acting principal of the Sparta Agricultural and Industrial Institute, *Cane* is a record of Toomer's discovery of his southern heritage, an homage to a folk culture that he believed was doomed to extinction because of the migration of African Americans from the South to the North, and a meditation upon the forces that he believed accounted for the spiritual fragmentation of the modern era. Published in 1923 by Horace Liveright, several of the sketches and poems of *Cane* had first appeared in the *Crisis, Double Dealer, Liberator, Modern Review, Broom,* and *Little Review.* When he submitted the manuscript to Liveright, Toomer had only written the sketches, poems, and drama that comprise the first and third sections, and which are set in the fictional community of Sempter, Georgia. Impressed by the poetic treatment of African American folklife but desirous of a lengthier manuscript, Liveright suggested that Toomer enlarge the work. Subsequently, the stories and poems that have Chicago and Washington, D.C., as their setting were added to what is now the middle section of *Cane.*

Although praised by reviewers, *Cane* sold less than five hundred copies when it was first published. Many readers were unprepared for the daring treatment of black sexuality, miscegenation, and slavery. The ambiguous nature of *Cane*'s form also alienated many readers. The lyricism, the calculated mixture of poetry and prose, the experimental narrative strategies, and shifting point of view defy conventional definitions of the novel. These elements remain the basis for an ongoing scholarly debate regarding *Cane*'s formal identity.

While scholars are divided on questions of genre and meaning, there is widespread agreement regarding *Cane*'s central place in the African American literary tradition. Retrieved from obscurity in 1969 with the publication of a new edition, *Cane*'s influence is clearly discernible in the writings of such contemporary African American writers as Ernest J. *Gaines, Alice *Walker, Michael S. *Harper, Charles R. *Johnson, and Gloria *Naylor. These and other writers admire *Cane* for the challenge it poses to conventional definitions of the novel, its nuanced representation of African American history and culture, and its deeply philosophical approach to questions of identity.

• Nellie Y. McKay, *Jean Toomer, Artist: A Study of His Literary Life and Work, 1894–1936,* 1984. Rudolph P. Byrd, *Jean Toomer's Years with Gurdjieff: Portrait of an Artist, 1923–1936,* 1990.

—Rudolph P. Byrd

CARTIÉR, XAM WILSON (b. 1949), novelist. Xam Wilson Cartiér, the Missouri-born author, pianist, artist, and dancer, moved to San Francisco in young adulthood to pursue her artistic gifts. Having gained recognition in the early 1980s as the author of successful television scripts and stage dramas, she published her first novel, *Be-Bop, Re-Bop,* in 1987. The story of an unnamed African American woman who is searching for identity, this first-person narrative also provides a broad view of the African American experience—its highs and lows, its past and present, its male and female perspectives, and its rural and urban environments. The narrator, who has been greatly influenced by her father and his love of jazz, reflects on her father's experiences in the 1930s and 1940s, examines her own youth in the 1950s, and recalls her relationships with her mother and her former husband. Cartiér demonstrates the power of the bebop style of jazz to help the narrator alleviate her hardships, recall personal and collective ancestral roots, and improvise her actions and reactions as she begins to overcome her sense of alienation and construct a new life with her young daughter.

With a similar emphasis on the power and emotion of jazz, Cartiér's second novel, *Muse-Echo Blues* (1991), follows the fantasies of Kat, a 1990s African American pianist who has composer's block. While coping with this difficulty and others involving relationships with men, Kat muses about the jazz scene of the 1930s and 1940s. She finds herself transported into the lives of two foresisters: Kitty, who loved a drug-addicted saxophone player named Chicago; and Lena, a jazz singer who had abandoned her son, this same Chicago, years before. Kat finds strength and artistic inspiration in the sorrowful but affirming legacy of these African American women who teach her to transform their jazz sensibility into the creation of her own music.

Like other African American postmodern novelists, Cartiér exposes the perversity of American racism while illuminating and affirming both the speech and dialect and the music that many African Americans use to express reality. She thematizes language and the telling of one's own story by using jazz-influenced African American speech as an aesthetic device to unite collective memory and recollections with current realities. She incorporates African American music in the storytelling process and the content of her fiction, which produces the kind of tension that exists between the music-making and statement in the polyrhythmic creations of jazz musicians. Both novels manifest characteristics akin to the Jazz Aesthetic: musical rhythm and "scat" syntax in the speech patterns, the feel of improvisation in the italicized fantasies and the temporal variations on the major themes, and spontaneity in the witty, riff-like comments on narrative events. Cartiér's successful fusion of jazz language and rhythms with narrative is a major innovation in the African American novel, comparable to those of Langston *Hughes, Bob *Kaufman, and other creators of African American jazz poetry.

• Valerie Smith, "Dancing to Daddy's Favorite Jam," *New York Times,* 13 December 1987, 7:12. Rayfield Allen Waller, "'Sheets of Sound': A Woman's Bop Prosody," *Black American Literature Forum* 24.4 (Winter 1990): 791–802.

—Marsha C. Vick

CELIE is the protagonist of Alice *Walker's novel *The *Color Purple* (1982). Her story is a testimony against death and dying—not the death of the corporal being, but one more intensely painful than that. Celie's battle is against a spiritual death that begins with her silent acceptance of abuse and disrespect. At fourteen, she is raped by a man she believes to be her natural father. Later, she is beaten by her husband, who also brings his lover to live in their home. Celie is so oppressed by the men in her life that by the time she matures, only a remnant of her spirit, enshrined within the letters she writes, remains.

Some readers find Celie's story incomprehensible. They simply cannot fathom how an African American woman could live as passively as Celie does. The reason for the character's docility is easy to explain: it is all she knows. She is so conditioned by abuse that she even advises Harpo, her stepson, to abuse his wife, Sofia.

Celie's salvation is found within the refuge of female love and support. There she gains confidence and self-respect. Her most notable female influence is her husband's lover, *Shug Avery, a woman who nurses Celie's dying spirit and transforms it. Shug becomes Celie's lover, teaching her the beauty of her own body, the wonders of true love, and the value of a positive self-image. Empowered by this new knowledge, Celie breaks through the chains of male domination to celebrate the beauty, the power, and the joy that has always been hers to claim.

• Linda Abbandoonato, "Rewriting the Heroine's Story in *The Color Purple,*" in *Alice Walker: Critical Perspectives Past and Present,* eds. Henry Louis Gates and K. A. Appiah, 1988, pp. 296–308. Daniel W. Ross, "Celie in the Looking Glass: The Desire for Selfhood in *The Color Purple,*" *Modern Fiction Studies* 34.1 (1988): 69–84.

—Debra Walker King

Cenelles, Les. *Les Cenelles,* published in 1845 in New Orleans, was the first anthology of poetry by Americans of color. The title's use of the word "cenelles," meaning holly or hawthorne berries, suggests that the volume contains the collected fruit of the Creole community that produced it. Edited by poet and educator Armand *Lanusse (1812–1867), the collection features the work of seventeen New Orleans poets who, like Lanusse, were well-to-do "free people of color" *(gens de couleur libres)*, a group with a unique cultural life distinct from that of whites on the one hand and slaves on the other. Contributors range from prosperous merchants such as cigar maker Nicol Riquet and mason Auguste Populus to such locally well-known figures as Lanusse, who worked to found black educational institutions; Joanni Questy, a widely read journalist for the militant newspaper *La tribune de la Nouvelle Orléans;* and Victor *Séjour, whose highly successful playwriting career in Paris made him antebellum Louisiana's most distinguished writer.

Lanusse explains in the introduction that the collection is intended to defend his community and race, preserving for future readers its high level of cultural-educational achievement. Culture serves here as a means of refuting and struggling against rationales for a racially divided society.

In content and form, the eighty-four poems in *Les Cenelles* are modeled on French romanticism. They are self-consciously elegant, conventional poetic statements (conventionality here is an index of sophistication) ranging from the facetious to the elegiac and tragic. Principle themes are love, both disappointed and fulfilled; disillusionment and the contemplation of death (five poems concern suicide); and the vicissitudes and dignity of the poetic vocation. Considering its general emphasis on disappointment and disillusionment, the collection is not, as some commentators suggest, primarily a group of light, sentimental love poems. Love in romantic poetry is a surrogate for higher aspirations that for this racially defined community remain frustrated and unfulfilled. When love appears in positive terms, it is cultural refinement and elevation rather than simple passion that is being affirmed.

Les Cenelles reflects the Creole community's experience of imposed limitations and thwarted ambitions in antebellum America. It also manifests the community's deep cultural orientation toward France. Faced with separatism and eager to develop an elite cultural space of their own, Lanusse and his cocontributors look to Parisian models in order to celebrate one aspect of their heritage and to contest another. Both thematically and in its linguistic and cultural distance from the rest of antebellum culture, this first anthology of African American poetry bespeaks its authors' social alienation as well as their attempts to overcome it through culture.

• Edward Maceo Coleman, ed., *Creole Voices*, 1945 (contains rpt. of *Les Cenelles*). Rodolphe Lucien Desdunes, *Nos Hommes et Notre Histoire*, 1911; republished as *Our People and Our History*, tr. Dorothea Olga McCants, 1973.

—Philip Barnard

Ceremonies in Dark Old Men. Lonne *Elder III's *Ceremonies in Dark Old Men* (1969) is a dramatization of rituals—of survival, of friendship, of deception and manipulation, of self-deception, of black male friendship, of shifting intrafamilial allegiances, and of black manhood. As Elder presents the ineffectual lives of a Harlem family entrapped by rituals of economic and spiritual dependence, he urges African Americans and African American communities to become aware of and to break free of "ceremonies" that assuredly lead to personal loss and tragedy. Echoing Douglas Turner *Ward's warning to black Americans whose "happiness" and survival are predicated upon white America's relationship to black America in *Happy Ending* (1966), *Ceremonies* challenges the myth that the social, political, and economic plight of black America rests in white people's hands. Through layers of ritual, Elder demonstrates the futility, corruption, and internal disruptions that result from efforts to undermine a capitalist system that seeks to determine and define African Americans' worth and selfhood.

That the play is specifically concerned with black male rituals is at the heart of Elder's barbershop setting, where two old men claim a territorial space that removes them temporarily from a world that has deemed them powerless and insignificant. The checkerboard ritual reaffirms not only their friendship, manifested in playful dares and insults, but it also symbolizes the lack of control Russell Parker especially feels in a world where he is for whatever reasons unable to find satisfactory employment options. In the hours that Parker's daughter Adele is away working to support the family, Parker can reign supreme despite the fact that the barbershop is not providing an income for him and he is subsequently forced to rely on Adele for his survival. Parker and his friend Jenkins's efforts to manipulate and deceive each other in this game represent the larger game of the "business" deal Parker reluctantly becomes part of despite his initial misgivings.

While Jenkins and Parker are content to hide their activities from Adele, Parker's sons, Theodore and Bobby, are convinced that the only way to assume their black manhood is to become economically empowered "by any means necessary." That they end up profiting from stealing, scheming, bootlegging, and hiding from the law, capitalizing on racism, and compromising their moral values becomes problematic only when parental roles are reversed and breakdowns occur in familial and personal trust. No longer are honesty and fairness acceptable as each participant in this game becomes trapped by personal greed and selfishness. With Bobby's death and with internal trusts violated, rituals of deception and self-deception become an initiation rite for Adele and Theodore. That Parker is still trapped in the fantasies of his own alleged past manhood when others' efforts were devoted to making his life more pleasant renders the play's ending all the more tragic as he is unable or unwilling to accept the reality of his younger son's "business-related" death.

Unsurprisingly, the play's chauvinistic presentation of black women is characteristic of many "revolutionary" plays of the 1960s wherein black manhood is synonymous with race consciousness. As a champion of political and social awareness, Elder, like Amiri *Baraka, Ben *Caldwell, Ron *Milner, and Ed *Bullins, relegates black women to positions of relative insignificance. Indeed, the younger black males adopt the attitudinal and behavioral rituals of the older men who see women as objects for their own personal satisfaction. Parker truly believes that his deceased wife enjoyed working herself to death to make him happy. Even Adele is direction-less when she is unable to fill her nurturing role for the males in her family. Only through violence, alleged sexual prowess, and economic autonomy can black males in this play validate themselves in a world that makes them otherwise powerless.

Ceremonies is Elder's challenge to black Americans to free themselves of the psychological chains that bind and limit their possibilities for attaining fulfilled selfhood personally and collectively. Only through an abandonment of selfish ideals, Elder demonstrates, can an African American community become whole and autonomous.

• Lance Jeffers, "Bullins, Baraka, and Elder: The Dawn of Grandeur in Black Drama," *CLA Journal* 16 (Sept. 1972): 32–48. Chester J. Fontenot, "Mythic Patterns in *River Niger* and *Ceremonies in Dark Old Men,*" *MELUS* 7 (Spring 1980): 41–49.

—Neal A. Lester

Chaneysville Incident, The. In David *Bradley's *The Chaneysville Incident* (1981), the protagonist John Washington, professor of history in Philadelphia, when called to the deathbed of Jack Crawley, his father's closest friend, finds himself involuntarily plunged into confronting his family and group history. Nearby Chaneysville, a station of the pre-emancipation Underground Railroad for fugitive slaves in western Pennsylvania, becomes the symbolic stage. John's personal ambivalence and distrust toward white America have increasingly led to emotional paralysis and sardonic detachment, affecting both his scholarship and his love for Judith, a white psychologist. Jack Crawley's stories rekindle John's interest in the life, death, and legacy of his father Moses (especially the library spiked with clues for reconstructing black history). John learns about his father's covert control of local white politicians (via a "moonshine" dossier), and about a concrete Chaneysville incident where Moses (with Jack's help) prevented the lynching of their friend Josh White and afterward eliminated the gangleaders. John uncovers a subversive black counterhistory in the plan of his forebear C. K. Washington to undermine the South's economy by leading as many slaves as possible to freedom. According to local legend, C. K. and thirteen slaves committed collective suicide at Chaneysville. (Bradley's mother discovered their unmarked graves in 1969.)

John's efforts to understand this first Chaneysville incident (ritually emulated by his father's suicide at the slaves' gravesite) remain abortive despite intensive research and an impressive card catalog. When Judith (descendant of Virginia slaveholders) joins John and questions his motives, the factual gaps of the Chaneysville riddle can be imaginatively bridged to restore a suppressed and fragmented history. The slaves, C. K., and his wife chose death to avoid being recaptured, and a white miller respectfully buried them. John and Judith repeat the act of mutual empathy, and by ritually burning the card catalog at the end reopen the emotional and cultural space for their relationship.

History and storytelling (or fictionalization) are seen as converging or germane enterprises in Bradley's novel (recalling new historiographic theory as initiated by Hayden White). His text dramatizes an impressive array of documented and invented history, of vernacular and formal dis-course (bridging oral and literary conventions). It combines modes of white mainstream narrative (the self-reflexive Jamesian narrator John, Faulknerian rhetoric and ritualizations of landscape and hunting, essayistic digressions) with specifically African American forms of narrative: the dialogical use of voices; African cultural concepts (death as a continuum of the living and their ancestors, embodied in the voices in the wind heard by John, and in suicide as going home); the creative resumption and reinvention of the earlier slave narrative; and novels by Ishmael *Reed, Charles R. *Johnson, and Toni *Morrison. Without slurring over the antagonistic nature in America of unjust white power versus black marginalization and resistance, the novel proffers a utopian outlook for a possible convergence of black and white self-concepts via a therapeutic acceptance of the other's past and perspective. Bradley's novel is an eloquent example in a growing number of narrative texts by African American authors engaged in an intensive reassessment and reappropriation of their historical past.

• Martin J. Gliserman, "David Bradley's *The Chaneysville Incident:* The Belly of the Text," *American Imago* 43.2 (1986): 97–120. Klaus Ensslen; "Fictionalizing History: David Bradley's *The Chaneysville Incident,*" *Callaloo* 11.2 (1988): 280–296. Klaus Ensslen, "The Renaissance of the Slave Narrative in Recent Critical and Fictional Discourse," in *Slavery in the Americas,* ed. W. Binder, 1993, pp. 601–626. Matthew Wilson, "The African-American Historian: David Bradley's *The Chaneysville Incident,*" *African American Review* 20.1 (1995): 97–107.

—Klaus Ensslen

CHASE-RIBOUD, BARBARA (b. 1936), sculptor, poet, novelist, essayist, and literary and visual pluralist. As a visual artist and writer Barbara Dewayne

Chase-Riboud (D'ashnash Tosi) blends African worlds with European, Asian, and Muslim worlds. Embracing differences is central to her idea of coupling or combining opposites. Chase-Riboud was born in Philadelphia to parents who encouraged her talents in the arts. With their support, her interest in the visual arts grew. She received a BFA from Temple University (1957). In the same year she was awarded a John Hay Whitney Fellowship to study art in Rome. Returning to the United States, Chase-Riboud completed an MFA at Yale (1960). From 1957 to 1977 Chase-Riboud exhibited widely in Europe, the Middle East, Africa, and the United States. Although she is not an expatriate, Chase-Riboud lives with her second husband, Sergio Tosi, in Paris and Rome.

Her world travels with her first husband (photojournalist Marc Riboud) during the 1960s inspired Chase-Riboud's initial efforts as a writer. *From Memphis to Peking* (1974) is her collection of poetry based on the motif of traveling spiritually, physically, and sensually to Egypt (Memphis) and the People's Republic of China, where she was the first woman visitor since the 1949 revolution. With her publication of *Sally Hemings* (1979) and *Echo of Lions* (1989), Chase-Riboud can be included in the African American neo–slave narrative tradition, which extends from Margaret *Walker's **Jubilee* (1966) to J. California *Cooper's *Family* (1991). Although Chase-Riboud is not the first African American novelist to treat the alleged Jefferson-Sally *Hemings affair (see William Wells *Brown, **Clotel*, 1853), her novel reignited the controversy over the authenticity of the relationship. At the heart of Sally Hemings is the interrelationship among love, politics, and slavery. Chase-Riboud suggests that Jefferson's abandonment of antislavery sentiments is due to his relationship with Hemings, his wife's half sister, whom he keeps in bondage because setting her free would mean she would have to leave Virginia. *Valide: A Novel of the Harem* (1986) depicts slavery in the Ottoman Empire during the late eighteenth century. Chase-Riboud uncovers the little known world of the harem through the protagonist, a Martinican woman who is captured and sold to Sultan Abdulhamid I. The woman rises through the ranks of the harem to become valide when her son becomes sultan. Although still a slave, as valide, she holds the highest position for women in the empire. The novel portrays harem women as living lives of boredom and self-indulgence, engaging in murder or manipulation in the competition to be chosen by the sultan. *Portrait of a Nude Woman As Cleopatra* (1987), Chase-Riboud's second collection of poems, connects her visual and literary talents. Observing a Rembrandt sketch with the same title, Chase-Riboud was inspired to write a narrative dialogue between Mark Antony and Cleopatra framed by Plutarch's story. In *Echo of Lions* (1989) Chase-Riboud presents the story of Joseph Cinque and fifty-three men who, as slave captives, murder most of the slave ship's crew and attempt to sail back to Africa. The Africans land off the coast of Long Island and are jailed but John Quincy Adams successfully defends them.

In all of her literary works, Chase-Riboud gives a voice to those silenced by history. Pursuing this theme, she achieves a synthesis of human experience, bringing the past and present, the African and European worlds together. Chase-Riboud published *Barbara Chase-Riboud: The Monument Drawings* in 1997.

• Charitey Simmons, "Thomas Jefferson: Intimate History, Public Debate," *Chicago Tribune*, 3 July 1979, 2, 4. Theresa Leininger, "Barbara Chase-Riboud," in *Notable Black American Women*, ed. Jessie Carney Smith, 1992, pp. 177–181.

—Australia Tarver

CHESNUTT, CHARLES WADDELL (1858–1932), short story writer and novelist. Charles W. Chesnutt was the most influential African American writer of fiction during the late nineteenth and early twentieth centuries. From 1899 to 1905, during which time he published two collections of short stories and three novels, Chesnutt skillfully enlisted the white-controlled publishing industry in the service of his social message. More successfully than any of his predecessors in African American fiction, Chesnutt gained a hearing from a significant portion of the national reading audience that was both engaged and disturbed by his analyses and indictments of racism.

Born in Cleveland, Ohio, in 1858, the son of free African American émigrés from the South, Charles Chesnutt grew up in Fayetteville, North Carolina, during the turbulent Reconstruction era. By his late teens he had distinguished himself sufficiently as a teacher to be appointed assistant principal of the local normal school for persons of color. But his marriage in 1878 and his impatience with the restrictions of his life in the South fueled his ambitions to find better opportunities in the North where he might pursue a literary career. In 1884, Chesnutt moved to Cleveland, where he settled his family, passed the Ohio state bar, and launched a business career as a legal stenographer.

In August 1887, the *Atlantic Monthly* printed Chesnutt's "The Goophered Grapevine," his first important work of fiction. Set in North Carolina and featuring an ex-slave raconteur who spins wonderful tales about antebellum southern life, "The Goophered Grapevine" was singular in its presentation of the lore of "conjuration," African American hoodoo beliefs and practices, to a white reading public largely ignorant of black folk culture. In this story, Chesnutt also introduced a new kind of African American storytelling protagonist, *Uncle Julius McAdoo, who shrewdly adapts his recollections of the past to secure his economic advantage in the present, sometimes at the expense of his white employer. In March 1899, The **Conjure Woman*, a collection of "conjure stories" based on the model established in "The Goophered Grapevine," made its debut under the prestigious imprint of Boston's Houghton

Mifflin publishing house. The most memorable stories in the collection, such as "The Goophered Grapevine" and "Po' Sandy," portray slavery as a crucible that placed black people under almost unbearable psychological pressures, eliciting from them tenacity of purpose, firmness of character, and imaginative ingenuity in order to preserve themselves, their families, and their community.

In the fall of 1899, Houghton Mifflin published a second Chesnutt short story collection, *The *Wife of His Youth and Other Stories of the Color Line*. The majority of the stories in *The Wife of His Youth* explore the moral conflicts and psychological strains experienced by those who lived closest to the color line in Chesnutt's day, namely, mixed-race persons like himself. After reading *The Wife of His Youth,* some critics, like the noted white novelist William Dean Howells, wrote admiringly about Chesnutt's realistic portrayals of life along the color line. But other reviewers were put off by his unapologetic inquiries into topics considered too delicate or volatile for short fiction, such as segregation, mob violence, miscegenation, and white racism.

Around the same time, Chesnutt closed his prosperous court-reporting business in Cleveland to pursue his lifelong dream—a career as a full-time author. In the next six years he published three novels of purpose, *The *House Behind the Cedars* (1900), *The *Marrow of Tradition* (1901), and *The Colonel's Dream* (1905), which surveyed racial problems in the postwar South and tested out a number of possible social, economic, and political solutions. *The House Behind the Cedars,* a novel of passing, was generally well received, and *The Marrow of Tradition* was reviewed extensively throughout the country as a disturbing but timely study of a contemporary southern town in the throes of a white supremacist revolution. Yet by the time Chesnutt began writing *The Colonel's Dream,* the story of a failed attempt to revive a southern town blighted by exploitation and racism, the author knew that his brand of fiction would not sell well enough to sustain his experimental literary career. Although he continued writing and speaking on various social and political issues after *The Colonel's Dream,* Chesnutt was able to publish only a handful of short stories in the last twenty-five years of his life. Among African American readers, however, admiration for his achievement never waned. In 1928, the NAACP awarded him its Spingarn Medal for his "pioneer work as a literary artist depicting the life and struggles of Americans of Negro descent, and for his long and useful career as scholar, worker, and freeman of one of America's greatest cities."

In 1931 in "Post-Bellum—Pre-Harlem," an essay in literary autobiography, Chesnutt accepted the fact that writing fashions had passed him by, but he took pride in pointing out how far African American literature and the attitude of the white literary world toward it had come since the days when he first broke into print. Although he was too modest to do so, Chesnutt might have claimed an important role in preparing the American public for the advent of the New Negro author of the 1920s. In a basic sense, the new movement followed his precedent in unmasking the false poses and images of its era in order to refocus attention on the real racial issues facing America. Today, historians of African American writing point out that Charles Chesnutt deserves credit for almost single-handedly inaugurating a truly African American literary tradition in the short story. He was the first writer to make the broad range of African American experience his artistic province and to consider practically every issue and problem endemic to the American color line worthy of literary attention. Because he developed literary modes appropriate to his materials, Chesnutt also left to his successors a rich formal legacy that underlies major trends in twentieth-century black fiction, from the ironies of James Weldon *Johnson's classic African American fiction of manners to the magical realism of Charles R. *Johnson's contemporary neo–slave narratives.

[*See also* Aun' Peggy; Rena Walden.]

• Helen M. Chesnutt, *Charles Waddell Chesnutt: Pioneer of the Color Line,* 1952. Sylvia Lyons Render, ed., *The Short Fiction of Charles W. Chesnutt,* 1974. Frances Richardson Keller, *An American Crusade: The Life of Charles Waddell Chesnutt,* 1978. William L. Andrews, *The Literary Career of Charles W. Chesnutt,* 1980. Richard H. Brodhead, ed., *The Journals of Charles W. Chesnutt,* 1993. Eric J. Sundquist, *To Wake the Nations: Race in the Making of American Literature,* 1993. Ernestine Pickens, *Charles W. Chesnutt and the Progressive Movement,* 1994. Joseph R. McElrath and Robert C. Letiz, eds. *"To Be an Author": Letters of Charles W. Chesnutt, 1889–1905,* 1997. Henry B. Wonham, *Charles W. Chesnutt: A Study of the Short Fiction,* 1998.

—William L. Andrews

CHILDRESS, ALICE (1916–1994), actress, director, playwright, novelist, columnist, essayist, lecturer, and theater consultant. Alice Childress established herself as a cultural critic and champion for the masses of poor people in America. Her writings reflect her commitment to the underclass whose lives are often portrayed inaccurately in American literature. Her works explore the debilitating effects of racism, sexism, and classism on people of color as they struggle daily to maintain their dignity. She portrays African Americans who triumph largely because of familial and community support. Childress's works censure American government for its exploitation of the poor in the name of capitalism. Her writings clearly speak against a government that would rather support African Americans as charity cases than allow them to succeed or fail on their own. Her integrity as a writer is evidenced by her refusal to recreate versions of long-held negative stereotypes of African Americans, even though this has cost her financial security.

Alice Childress was born on 12 October 1916 in Charleston, South Carolina. At the tender age of five, she boarded a train bound for Harlem where she grew up under the nurturing hand of her grandmother, Eliza Campbell. Her grandmother's yen for the arts motivated her to expose Childress to museums, libraries, art galleries, theaters, and concert halls. Childress credits her grandmother for teaching her the art of storytelling. Her grandmother also made a point of exposing Childress to Wednesday night testimonials at Salem Church in Harlem. At these testimonials poor people told of their troubles, which Childress stored up for future writing.

Childress attended Public School 81, The Julia Ward Howe Junior High School, and then Wadleigh High School for three years, before dropping out when both her grandmother and mother died in the late 1930s. A voracious reader with a curious intellect, Childress discovered the public library as a child and read two or more books a day. Always very independent and capable, Childress held down a host of jobs during the 1940s to support herself and her daughter Jean, an only child from her first marriage. She worked as an assistant machinist, photo retoucher, domestic worker, salesperson, and insurance agent, all jobs that kept her in close proximity to working-class people like those characterized in her works. Her characters in fiction and drama included domestic workers, washerwomen, seamstresses, and the unemployed, as well as dancers, artists, and teachers.

Childress married professional musician and music instructor Nathan Woodard on 17 July 1957. A reticent and very private person, Childress disclosed little about her life after 1957, except that her only child died on Mother's Day in 1990. Childress resided in Long Island, New York, with Woodard at the time of her death on 14 August 1994. She was at work on her memoirs and a sixth novel.

Childress began her writing career in the early 1940s shortly after she chose acting as a career. In 1943 Childress began an eleven-year association with the American Negro Theater (ANT), an organization that served as a home for countless African American playwrights, actors, and producers, such as Sidney Poitier, Ossie *Davis, Ruby Dee, and Frank Silvera. Childress involved herself in every aspect of the theater as was the tradition upheld by anyone connected with ANT. Childress is recognized as one of the founders of ANT, which institutionalized theater in the African American community. As a result of her commitment to ANT, in the 1950s Childress was instrumental in getting advanced, guaranteed pay for union Off-Broadway contracts in New York.

Childress's first play, *Florence* (1949), was prompted by a challenge from longtime friend Sidney Poitier who insisted that a strong play could not be written overnight. Poitier lost his bet because *Florence,* written overnight, is a well-crafted play that levels an indictment against presumptuous whites who think they know more about African Americans than African Americans know about themselves. *Florence* is also about the need for African Americans to reject stereotyped roles. On another level, *Florence* pays tribute to African American parents who encourage their children to reach their fullest potential by any means necessary. Her first play reveals Childress's superb skill at characterization, dialogue, and conflict.

Following the ANT production of *Florence,* Childress went on to write a host of plays and children's books, including *Just a Little Simple* (1950), *Gold through the Trees* (1952), *Trouble in Mind* (1955), *Wedding Band: A Love/Hate Story in Black and White* (1966), *The World on a Hill* (1968), *String* (1969), *The Freedom Drum,* retitled *Young Martin Luther King* (1969), *Wine in the Wilderness* (1969), *Mojo: A Black Love Story* (1970), *When the Rattlesnake Sounds* (1975), *Let's Hear It for the Queen* (1976), *Sea Island Song,* retitled *Gullah* (1984), and *Moms* (1987). Alice Childress's plays incorporate the liturgy of the African American church, traditional music, African mythology, folklore, and fantasy. She has experimented by writing sociopolitical, romantic, biographical, historical, and feminist plays.

Childress's *Trouble in Mind* garnered for her the Obie Award for the best Off-Broadway play of the 1954–1955 season. When the media praised her for being the first African American woman to win this award, Childress insisted that she would feel proud when she was the one hundredth poor woman of color to be recognized for her talent. She felt that to be the "first" only pointed out that African Americans have been denied opportunities. *Trouble in Mind* attacks the stereotyping of African Americans. *Wedding Band,* which was broadcast nationally on ABC television but which was banned from an Atlanta, Georgia, theater in 1966, explores the explosiveness of interracial love in a Jim Crow South Carolina. *Wine in the Wilderness,* perhaps Childress's best-known play, was presented on National Educational Television (NET) in 1969. The play pokes fun at bourgeois affectation. Childress levels an indictment against middle-class African Americans who scream brotherhood, togetherness, and Black Power, but who have no love or empathy for poor, uneducated, and unrefined African Americans. Tommorrow Marie, the heroine, teaches these vapid bourgeois the ugliness of their own superciliousness. Childress's *Sea Island Song* (1979) was commissioned by the South Carolina Arts Commission, which officially designated the time of the play's run as Alice Childress Week in Columbia and Charleston.

Childress's writings have garnered for her several awards, including writer in residence at the MacDowell Colony; featured author on a BBC panel discussion on "The Negro in the American Theater"; winner of a Rockefeller grant administered through the New Dramatists and an award from the John Golden Fund for Playwrights; and a Harvard appointment to the Radcliffe Institute for Independent Study (now Mary Ingraham Bunting Institute) from which she received a graduate medal.

While Alice Childress was principally a playwright, she was also a skilled novelist. Her first novel, **Like One of the Family: Conversations from a Domestic's Life* (1956), demonstrates Childress's quick wit as the heroine, a domestic, teaches her white employers to see their own inhumanity. *A *Hero Ain't Nothin' But a Sandwich* (1973) was made into a movie with Childress as author of the screenplay. This novel explores the necessity of African Americans' taking responsibility for nurturing their young sons. *A Short Walk* (1979) provides historical and cultural insights into the African American experience from the Harlem Renaissance to the civil rights movement of the 1960s. *Rainbow Jordan* (1981) explores the ramifications of growing up Black and female under the guidance of a host of women from the community. While her mother abandons her, Rainbow's surrogate mothers nurture and usher her into adulthood. Childress's most recent novel, *Those Other People* (1989), addresses issues of homophobia, racism, sexism, and classism. Childress's incisive language and skillfull manipulation of multiple narrators place her with writers such as William Faulkner and Ernest J. *Gaines. Her novels, like her plays, portray poor people who struggle to survive in a capitalist America. She incorporates African American history in her novels to instruct young African Americans about the heroic lives that have paved a way for them to succeed.

Possessing great discipline, power, substance, wit, and integrity, Alice Childress stands out as a writer who was always a step ahead of her contemporaries. She deliberately chose not to write about what was in vogue, but instead wrote about controversial and delicate matters and had the audacity to reject a Broadway option because the producer wanted her to distort her vision of African Americans. Alice Childress's brilliance, her intense and microscopic penetration into life, and her deft handling of language match such great twentieth-century dramatists as Anton Chekhov, August Strindberg, Jean Anouilh, Sean O'Casey, Noel Coward, Tennessee Williams, Wole Soyinka, and Sholem Aleichem, a playwright that Childress singled out as one of her favorite writers. Peopling her works with characters who are challenging, innovative, and multidimensional, Childress became a frontrunner in the development of African American theater and a novelist of significant merit. Alice Childress's major contribution to African American life and culture was her balanced portrayal of Black men and women working together to heal their wounds and survive whole in a fragmented world. The men and women in her works do not give up on each other; often the strong and spirited women reach out to save their men from disaster. Childress passionately created dignified images of African Americans, particularly America's dispossessed and disinherited.

[*See also* Mildred Johnson.]

• Alice Childress, "Knowing the Human Condition," in *Black American Literature and Humanism,* ed. R. Baxter Miller, 1981, pp. 8–11. Trudier Harris, "Alice Childress," in *DLB,* vol. 38, *Afro-American Writers after 1955: Dramatists and Prose Writers,* eds. Thadious Davis and Trudier Harris, 1985, pp. 66–79. Elizabeth Brown-Guillory, "Alice Childress: A Pioneering Spirit," *SAGE* 4 (Spring 1987): 104–109. Elizabeth Brown-Guillory, *Their Place on the Stage: Black Women Playwrights in America,* 1988. Elizabeth Brown-Guillory, ed., *Wines in the Wilderness: Plays by African American Women from the Harlem Renaissance to the Present,* 1990. *Drama Criticism,* vol. 4, ed. Lawrence Trudeau, 1992, pp. 64–94. Alma Jean Billingslea-Brown, "The 'Blight of Legalized Limitation' in Alice Childress' *Wedding Band,*" in *Law and Literature Perspectives,* ed. Bruce L. Rockwood and Roberta Kevelson, 1996, pp. 39–51. Beth Turner, "Simplifyin': Langston Hughes and Alice Childress Re/member Jesse B. Stemple," *Langston Hughes Review* 15:1 (Spring 1997): 37–48.

—Elizabeth Brown-Guillory

Chosen Place, the Timeless People, The. Paule *Marshall's second novel, *The Chosen Place, the Timeless People* (1969) is thematically the culmination of almost all her concerns as a novelist. Written on the cusp of both the feminist and Pan-African movements, it concerns itself not only with personal as well as public revolution in terms of both revolt and coming full circle to self-actualization, but also ageism, Western hegemony, and nuclear proliferation. According to Marshall, it is her best-loved novel, and this is due in large part to the stunning delineation of the heroine, Merle Kimbona.

The novel concerns itself with Bourne Island, a tiny imaginary landscape set in the Caribbean. It is an island replete with contradictions that become part of a special development project instigated by the American-based Philadelphia Research Institute and carried out by one of its numerous divisions, the Center for Applied Social Research, in the hopes that it will bring this "backward" island into the twentieth century. Almost ironically, the island itself is nearly equally divided geographically. Half of it, Bournehills, wallows in poverty, while the other half, New Bristol, has taken advantage of corrupt modernization schemes and equally corrupt politics to bring itself into the modern era. It is the hope of these twentieth-century missionaries to bring profound political, social, and economic change to the island.

The protagonist of the novel, Merle Kimbona, is the link between these two disparate worlds, the past and the future. She is known and loved by both those who call for progress and those who fear for the destruction of a particular culture that that progress will more than likely obliterate. Merle is the thematic conduit through which these two opposing forces might eventually come together in the poverty stricken Bournehills. In fact, Merle is described in the novel as somehow being Bournehills itself. She represents a division that is not only a part of her own personal history but also the history of the island itself.

The Chosen Place, the Timeless People is perhaps Marshall's most political novel. In the narrative she weaves mini history lessons in the hopes that she as a writer might initiate a kind of healing in the psychological rift borne by blacks of the diaspora that has been brought about by the broken and divided history of African peoples located throughout the world. The heroic, ancestral figure of Cuffee Ned, the larger-than-life leader of a slave revolt, is one of the historical figures that Merle, as well as Paule Marshall as author, feels will help the people of Bourne Island, and black people in general, to reconstitute their historically and psychologically fragmented sense of self. She feels that by following his spiritual lead, there is nothing that can prevent the people, the "li'l fella," from rising out of the muck and mire of political, social, economic, and historical oppression. To accomplish this, the people, like Merle herself, must come to terms with their fragmented past before they will be able to forge a viable future.

• Joseph T. Skerrett, Jr., "Paule Marshall and the Crisis of the Middle Years: *The Chosen Place, the Timeless People,*" in *Callaloo* 17–19 (1983): 69–73. Hortense J. Spillers, "*Chosen Place, Timeless People:* Some Figurations on the New World," in *Conjuring: Black Women, Fiction, and Literary Tradition,* 1985, pp. 151–175.

—Keith Bernard Mitchell

CLARK, AL C. *See* Goines, Donald.

CLAY, CASSIUS MARCELLUS, JR. *See* Ali, Muhammad.

CLEAGE, PEARL (b. 1948), poet, playwright, prose writer, performance artist, and editor of *Catalyst* magazine. Pearl Cleage was born in Detroit, Michigan, and was educated at Howard University, Spelman College, and Atlanta University. Early in her life her family encouraged an African American view of the world. Her father, Jaramogi Abebe Azaman (Albert Cleage), founded and developed Black Christian Nationalism. She also came under the direct influence of the political and intellectual ferment of the 1960s and 1970s.

Cleage's writing is highly polemical. A strong political spirit and commitment to the liberation of African Americans, particularly African American women, infuse her work. While she ultimately advocates the healthy solidarity of the African American community, she also broaches the taboo topics of sexism and violence against women in the African American community. She refuses to subordinate discussions of gender to race and sometimes makes the link between the two. Her writings, therefore, both invite political discussion and inspire literary analysis.

Her first books, *We Don't Need No Music* (1971), *The Brass Bed and Other Stories* (1990), and *Mad at Miles: The Blackwoman's Guide to Truth* (1991), have received little or no critical attention. However, *Deals with the Devil and Other Reasons to Riot* (1993) has received substantially more public attention and popular acclaim. While this work blends personal experience and observation with a celebration of the African American female perspective and experience, the greatest confluence of Cleage's craft and vision is found in her dramas. These works advocate the necessity of African American women empowering themselves as individuals, surmounting the differences of class, personal experience, and philosophy, and forming supportive networks as models of survival for the African American community.

Cleage's plays are frequently performed and are beginning to appear in print. *Hospice* (1983) earned five Audelco Recognition Awards for achievement Off Broadway. This one-act play portrays an exchange between Alice Anderson, a forty-seven-year-old cancer patient, and her thirty-year-old daughter, Jenny, who is about to give birth. In keeping with the theme of the need for strong relationships between women, the play explores the complicated mother-daughter relationship and mandates healing where ruptures exist. *Chain* (1992) and *Late Bus to Mecca* (1992) similarly explore the condition of African American women. In *Chain* Cleage depicts the impact of drugs on the African American community through the story of Rosa Jackson, a sixteen-year-old addict whose empowerment is sabotaged by her drug-addicted boyfriend and the desperation of her parents. *Late Bus to Mecca* dramatizes the value of African American sisterhood. The play depicts an encounter between Ava Gardner Johnson and a nameless African American woman who is too physically and psychologically battered to speak. Although a prostitute, the resourceful and self-assured Ava is able to offer love and support to another African American woman and affirm the viability of her own philosophy. *Flyin' West* (1994) portrays black participation in frontier development resulting from the 1860 Homestead Act and dramatizes intraracial and gender dynamics in that experience. Cleage published a novel, *What Looks Like Crazy on an Ordinary Day,* in 1997, and had a new play, *Blues for an Alabama Sky,* produced by the Alliance Theatre in Atlanta. The play was published in 1999; her collection, *Flyin' West and Other Plays,* was also published that year.

Cleage's art is womanist in spirit and effort. Her work stands as a testament to the union of artistic vision, political and cultural sensibility, and analytic intellect.

• Freda Scott Giles, "The Motion of Herstory: Three Plays by Pearl Cleage," *African American Review* 31:4 (Winter 1997): 709–712.

—Carol P. Marsh-Lockett

CLEAVER, ELDRIDGE (b. 1935), essayist, sociocultural theorist, and minister. Born in Wabbaseka, Arkansas, Leroy Eldridge Cleaver moved west to Los Angeles in 1946, where his family lived in an impoverished African American/Chicano neighborhood. In 1953 and 1957 Cleaver was convicted for narcotics possession and assault and spent almost thirteen years in the California penitentiary system. While in prison he affiliated with the Black Muslims and became an ardent follower of *Malcolm X.

After his 1966 parole Cleaver worked for *Ramparts* magazine and met several radical and countercultural activists, among them Huey Newton and Bobby Seale, cofounders of the Oakland-based Black Panther Party, of which he soon became the minister of information. On 6 April 1968 Cleaver was wounded and arrested after a violent encounter between the Black Panthers and the Oakland police.

In February 1968 Cleaver published **Soul on Ice*, an enormously popular and influential collection of essays and letters on American culture, race and gender relations, and his own prison life. *Soul on Ice* gained Cleaver instant national recognition as the potential intellectual and political heir to Malcolm X. During 1968 Cleaver became involved in several political controversies, including an invitation to lecture at the University of California at Berkeley and his own legal struggle to remain free. Ordered back to prison, Cleaver fled the country on 27 November 1968 and spent the next seven years in Cuba, Algeria, and France. He continued to publish radical essays in *Black Panther, Ramparts,* and the *Black Scholar.*

During his exile he became increasingly disenchanted with the Third World and authoritarian communism and returned in 1975 as a political conservative to prison in the United States, totally rejected by his former associates. He also began a religious odyssey that took him through evangelical Christianity to the Mormon Church, some of which is chronicled in *Soul on Fire* (1978), a conversion autobiography.

• Robert Scheer, ed., *Eldridge Cleaver: Post-Prison Writings and Speeches,* 1969. Kathleen Rout, *Eldridge Cleaver,* 1991.

—Roger A. Berger

CLIFTON, LUCILLE (b. 1936), poet, juvenile fiction writer, autobiographer, and educator. Lucille Sayles Clifton was born in Depew, New York, to Samuel L. and Thelma Moore Sayles. Her father worked for the New York steel mills; her mother was a launderer, homemaker, and avocational poet. Although neither parent was formally educated, they provided their large family with an appreciation and an abundance of books, especially those by African Americans. At age sixteen, Lucille entered college early, matriculating as a drama major at Howard University in Washington, D.C. Her Howard associates included such intellectuals as Sterling A. *Brown, A. B. *Spellman, Chloe Wofford (now Toni *Morrison), who later edited her writings for Random House, and Fred Clifton, whom she married in 1958.

After transferring to Fredonia State Teachers College in 1955, Clifton worked as an actor and began to cultivate in poetry the minimalist characteristics that would become her professional signature. Like other prominent Black Aesthetic poets consciously breaking with Eurocentric conventions, including Sonia *Sanchez and her Howard colleague, LeRoi Jones (Amiri *Baraka), Clifton developed such stylistic features as concise, untitled free verse lyrics of mostly iambic trimeter lines, occasional slant rhymes, anaphora and other forms of repetition, puns and allusions, lowercase letters, sparse punctuation, and a lean lexicon of rudimentary but evocative words.

Poet Robert *Hayden entered her poems into competition for the 1969 YW-YMHA Poetry Center Discovery Award. She won the award and with it the publication of her first volume of poems, *Good Times.* Frequently inspired by her own family, especially her six young children, Clifton's early poems are celebrations of African American ancestry, heritage, and culture. Her early publications praise African Americans for their historic resistance to oppression and their survival of economic and political racism. Acclaimed by the *New York Times* as one of the best books of 1969, *Good Times* launched Clifton's prolific writing career.

In 1970 Clifton published two picture verse books for children, *The Black BC's* and *Some of the Days of Everett Anderson.* *Everett Anderson, a small boy living in the inner city, became the protagonist of eight of the fourteen works of juvenile fiction she published between 1970 and 1984. One in this series, *Everett Anderson's Goodbye,* received the Coretta Scott King Award in 1984. Another of her children's books, *Sonora Beautiful* (1981), represents a thematic departure for Clifton in that it features a white girl as the main character. Like her poetry, Clifton's short fiction extols the human capacity for love, rejuvenation, and transcendence over weakness and malevolence even as it exposes the myth of the American dream.

Clifton's prose maintains a familial and cultural tradition of storytelling. Adapting a genealogy prepared by her father, *Generations: A Memoir* (1976) constitutes a matrilineal neo–slave narrative; it traces the Sale/Sayles family from its Dahomeian ancestor who became known as Caroline Sale Donald (1823–1910) after her abduction in 1830 from West Africa to New Orleans, Louisiana. Most of the biographical sketches in *Generations* are written from a first-person perspective in which various family members are represented as narrating their own stories. In them, Clifton further honors African American oral and oratorical traditions with her use of black vernacular.

In 1987 Clifton reprinted her complete published poems in *Good Woman: Poems and a Memoir,* which, in addition to *Generations,* contains *Good Times, Good News about the Earth* (1972), *An Ordinary Woman* (1974), and *Two-Headed Woman* (1980), a Pulitzer Prize nominee and winner of the Juniper Prize. The themes of these exceptional poems reflect both Clifton's ethnic pride and her womanist principles, and integrate her race and gender consciousness. Casting her persona as at once plain and extraordinary, Clifton challenges pejorative Western myths that define women and people of color as predatory and malevolent or vulnerable and impotent. Her poems attest to her political sagacity and her lyrical mysticism. Poem sequences throughout her works espouse Clifton's belief in divine grace by revising the characterization of such biblical figures as the Old Testament prophets, Jesus, and the Virgin Mary, and in *An Ordinary Woman* she shows herself in conflict and consort with Kali, the Hindu goddess of war and creativity.

Good Woman also narrates a personal and collective history as it addresses the poet's enduring process of self-discovery as poet, woman, mother, daughter, sibling, spouse, and friend. Some of its most complex and effective poems mourn Thelma Sayles's epilepsy, mental illness, and premature death when Clifton was twenty-three. A persistent witness to America's failed promises to former slaves, Native Americans, and other victims of its tyranny, Clifton is nonetheless witty and sanguine as she probes the impact of history on the present. She testifies to the pain of oppression manifested in her parents' tormented marriage, in racism that undermines progressive movements for social change, in disregard for the planet Earth as a living and sentient being.

In 1987 Clifton published *Next: New Poems,* most of which are constructed as "sorrow songs" or requiems. Some lament personal losses—the deaths by disease of the poet's mother at age forty-four on 13 February 1959; of her husband at age forty-nine on 10 November 1984; and of a Barbadian friend, "Joanne C.," who died at age twenty-one on 30 November 1982. Other poems grieve for political figures or tragedies, including an elegy sequence for the American Indian chief, Crazy Horse, and a trilogy mourning the massacres at Gettysburg, Nagasaki, and Jonestown. The persona also testifies to the crime and tragedy of child molestation, a theme developed in poem sequences featuring the mythical African shape-shifter in both *Next* and *The Book of Light* (1993). In the tradition of Langston *Hughes, Gwendolyn *Brooks, and Etheridge *Knight, Clifton's heroic meditations in *The Book of Light* offer pithy and grievous contemplations of diverse epistemological and metaphysical questions.

Clifton served as Poet Laureate of Maryland from 1979 to 1982. Her achievements also include fellowships and honorary degrees from Fisk University, George Washington University, Trinity College, and other institutions; two grants from the National Endowment of the Arts; and an Emmy Award from the American Academy of Television Arts and Sciences. Clifton is Distinguished Professor of Humanities at St. Mary's College in Maryland and had a position at Columbia University from 1995 to 1999.

• Andrea Benton Rushing, "Lucille Clifton: A Changing Voice for Changing Times," in *Coming to Light: American Women Poets in the Twentieth Century,* eds. Diane Wood Middlebrook and Marilyn Yalom, 1985, pp. 214–222. Lucille Clifton, *Quilting,* 1991. Shirley M. Jordan, ed., *Broken Silences: Interviews with Black and White Women Writers,* 1993. Alicia Ostriker, "Kin and Kin: The Poetry of Lucille Clifton," in *Literary Influence and African American Writers,* ed. Tracy Mishkin, 1996, pp. 301–23.

—Joycelyn K. Moody

Clotel. The first known full-length African American novel, *Clotel,* by William Wells *Brown, was originally published in London as *Clotel, or The President's Daughter: A Narrative of Slave Life in the United States* (1853). It first appeared in the United States as *Miralda, or The Beautiful Quadroon: A Romance of American Slavery Founded on Fact* (serialized in the *Weekly Anglo-African* during the winter of 1860–1861), then in book form, substantially revised, as *Clotelle: A Tale of the Southern States* (1864) and *Clotelle, or The Colored Heroine: A Tale of the Southern States* (1867).

Based on persistent rumors about Thomas Jefferson's relations with a slave mistress, *Clotel* begins with the auction of Jefferson's mistress (Currer) and her two daughters by Jefferson (Clotel and Althesa). Currer and Althesa both die in the course of the narrative, Althesa in particularly tragic circumstances: she has married her owner and raised two daughters as free white women. When she and her husband die, their daughters are sold into slavery by their father's creditors.

Clotel's owner in Virginia falls in love with her, fathers a child by her, and, despite vague promises of marriage, sells her. She escapes from a slave dealer and returns to Virginia disguised as a white man to free her daughter, Mary, still a house slave. Unfortunately, Clotel returns in the midst of Nat *Turner's insurrection (1831). The unusually vigilant authorities detect her imposture, seize her, and transfer her to prison in Washington, D.C. When Clotel bolts from her captors, they pursue and trap her on a bridge over the Potomac, and she leaps to her death in the river. Mary ultimately escapes to England, where she marries George Green, another fugitive and a veteran of Turner's rebellion.

Clotel, like other examples of early African American fiction, retains some features of slave narratives. Brown, himself a fugitive slave, bases many of the novel's details, anecdotes, and characters on incidents and figures in his own life. Like slave narratives, the novel emphasizes its basis in fact in order to buttress its authority as an indictment of slavery. *Clotel,* however, outstrips most slave narratives in its use of a variety of genres and voices, from anecdotes, vignettes of slave life, newspaper accounts, and folklore to songs, poems, and abolitionist rhetoric.

Clotel also bears a strong resemblance to white abolitionist fiction, especially its predecessor, Harriet Beecher *Stowe's *Uncle Tom's Cabin* (1852), though Brown's ironic tone sets it somewhat apart from such works. Like Stowe's Little Eva, *Clotel*'s Georgiana Peck is a virtuous white woman responsibie, just before her own tragic death, for freeing the slaves on her father's plantation. The novel follows abolitionist propaganda in emphasizing slavery's destruction of the family and its corrosive effect on sexual mores, black and white, and contains an important development of the "tragic mulatto" theme. Most daringly, *Clotel* attacks not only the hypocrisy of slaveowning and slavery-condoning Christians but also the similar hypocrisy of such republican icons as Jefferson, suggesting that the existence of slavery fatally compromised the very ideals of the republic.

• Robert A. Bone, *The Negro Novel in America,* rev. ed. 1965. William E. Farrison, *William Wells Brown: Author and Reformer,* 1969. Bernard W. Bell, *The Afro-American Novel and Its Tradition,* 1987. William L. Andrews, "The Novelization of Voice in Early African American Narrative," *PMLA* 105.1 (Jan. 1990): 23–34.

—Gary Ashwill

COBB, CHARLES E., JR. (b. 1943), poet, essayist, and journalist. Charles E. Cobb, Jr., was born in Washington, D.C., in 1943. The son of a Methodist minister, he lived in several eastern states before enrolling in the African American program at Howard University in 1961. He left in 1962 to work for five years with the Student Nonviolent Coordinating Committee (SNCC) in several southern states, and was involved in the tense struggle for voting rights in Mississippi.

Cobb's first volume of poetry, *In the Furrows of the World* (1967), illustrated with his own photographs, grew out of his civil rights work and his 1967 visit to Vietnam. The poems were written in lyrical free verse with little capitalization or punctuation, and expressed concern, anger, and hope. Some of the poems, like "Nation," spoke with quiet eloquence of a time when African Americans would have a proud sense of self and nationhood.

After his SNCC years, Cobb worked with the Center for Black Education in Washington from 1968 to 1969, and then served on the board of directors of Drum and Spear Press from 1969 to 1974. In 1969 he also made an extended visit to Tanzania, where he came to recognize the need for an intensive examination of the link between African Americans and their African heritage. Cobb published another volume of poetry, *Everywhere Is Yours,* in 1971. The eight poems in that volume continued the theme of hope in the face of oppression. One particularly moving poem in the volume, "Koyekwisa Ya Libala," was an account of an African wedding and included several passages of wisdom from the ancient priest, incorporated into the marriage chant. In another poem, "To Vietnam," Cobb implied a parallel between Vietnamese nationalism and the fight against American racism. Cobb also discussed his African experience in *African Notebook: Views on Returning Home* in 1971. He advocated an intensive examination of the link between African Americans and their African heritage, but he also advised against the American tendency to romanticize Africa because of ignorance. His concern with the lesson Africa could teach was also reflected in another poem, "Nation No. 3," from *Everywhere Is Yours,* where he spoke of standing "son to Mother Africa" and claiming all its experience as his own.

Cobb's more recent work as an essayist and journalist has reflected his interest in social, environmental, and political issues. He served as foreign affairs reporter for the Public Broadcasting System from 1976 to 1979, and wrote and produced numerous documentaries from 1979 to 1985. He also wrote freelance articles for several journals, and joined the staff of *National Geographic* in 1985. His credits for *National Geographic* include articles on such places as Grenada, Zimbabwe, and the Outer Banks of North Carolina. Although Cobb has turned his focus away from poetry, his writing has matured, and the vitality and concern with people, their rights and possibilities, that energized his earliest work has continued.

• James Forman, *The Making of Black Revolutionaries,* 1972, pp. 297–299. Charles E. Cobb, Jr., interview by Howell Raines, *My Soul Is Rested,* 1977, pp. 244–248. Clara Williams, "Charles E. Cobb, Jr.," in *DLB,* vol. 41, *Afro-American Poets since 1955,* eds. Trudier Harris and Thadious M. Davis, 1985, pp. 60–64. "Cobb, Charles E., Jr.," in *CA,* vol. 142, ed. James G. Lesniak, 1994, pp. 77–78.

—Michael E. Greene

COBB, NED (1885–1973), autobiographer. Born in Alabama, Ned Cobb was a tenant farmer and social activist who spent twelve years in a penitentiary for staging a protest that turned violent. Though an illiterate man, Cobb had a talent for storytelling that enabled him in his eighties to relate the story of his life to Theodore Rosengarten, a Harvard graduate student, who recorded the older man's account and eventually had it published under the title **All God's Dangers: The Life of Nate Shaw* (1974). The book contains a long, episodic narrative that portrays Shaw (Cobb's pseudonym) as a thoughtful and industrious person whose prison sentence resulted from a clear refusal to tolerate social inequality.

In *All God's Dangers,* Shaw appears in contrast to his father, Hayes Shaw, a former slave turned sharecropper, who has grown accustomed to "take what come and live for today." While Nate Shaw observes that the social order confines "poor colored farmers" to an outrageous second-class citizenship and thereby strips them of ambition, from his youth he plans on "climbin up in the world like a boy climbin a tree." By learning as much as he can about farming his crop and diligently applying the knowledge that he gains, Shaw manages to make a decent enough living to raise ten children in "a pretty good old house." His fortune changes, however, beginning in December 1932, when he takes a stand for equality by defying four deputy sheriffs sent to seize a neighbor's property in order to compensate a white landlord. A bloody confrontation lands Shaw in jail for over a decade and decimates his family.

All God's Dangers compares favorably to slave narratives written by Olaudah *Equiano, Frederick *Douglass, and Harriet A. *Jacobs, all of whom represent learning as a source of freedom. Shaw's personal narrative belongs to an "as-told-to" tradition of African American autobiographies transcribed by an amanuensis, which includes *The *Confessions of Nat Turner* (1831) as well as *The *Autobiography of Malcolm X* (1965). Since Shaw lived from the Reconstruction era of the late nineteeth century through the civil rights movement of the mid-twentieth, his story serves as a valuable chronicle of the manner in which African Americans in rural communities struggled for equality during the period of legal segregation in the United States.

—Roland L. Williams, Jr.

COFFIN ED JOHNSON makes up half of Chester *Himes's two-man African American detective team. Coffin Ed and his partner *Grave Digger Jones almost always act in tandem, and rarely is one seen without the other throughout Himes's nine-book series of detective novels. Like his partner, Coffin Ed is a middle-class workingman who lives in Astoria, Long Island. Each day he and Grave Digger drive together to Harlem, their regular beat as detectives. Leaving behind their stable, yet rarely mentioned, family lives with wives and children, they step daily into the chaotic pandemonium of Himes's Harlem.

Violence is a relentless part of the two detectives' jobs, indeed of the whole urban environment as created by Himes. Coffin Ed, in fact, suffers a brutal brush with the daily violence of his job: in *For Love of Imabelle* (1957), Himes's first Harlem crime novel, a villain throws acid in Coffin Ed's face. This vicious attack scars the detective both physically and emotionally for the rest of the series. Coffin Ed's acid-scarred face is often described in grotesque and frightening terms and comes to represent the potential terror he himself could unleash. As a result of this incident, Ed is known to be very quick to the trigger and subject to extremely violent rages when interrogating suspected criminals. This is one of the few characteristics that distinguishes him from his partner, Grave Digger. Grave Digger often acts as the restraining voice or hand when Ed seems close to the edge of excessive force.

• Robert E. Skinner, *Two Guns from Harlem: The Detective Fiction of Chester Himes*, 1989.

—Wendy W. Walters

COLEMAN, WANDA (b. 1946), poet, short fiction writer, and performer. Identifying herself as an "L. A. poet," Wanda Coleman not only grew up in Los Angeles, California, but also uses that city as her primary urban setting for the raw, imagistically graphic, and politically charged poetry and short stories that she writes. Desiring to "rehumanize the dehumanized," Coleman focuses upon the lives of the "down and out"; thus she populates her texts with working-class individuals struggling against daily indignities and social outcasts struggling simply to survive. The primary voice represented in her poems is that of the African American woman whose head is bloodied but unbowed, who is just as tough as the harsh city in which she lives.

Born Wanda Evans in Watts to George and Lewana Evans, Coleman found herself drawn to poetry as a young child, and, encouraged by her parents to write, she published several poems by the time she was fifteen. During the 1960s, she became a political activist and, influenced by Ron Karenga's Afrocentric "US" movement, wrote, as she put it, "for the cause." Later, resisting the rhetoric of political movements, Coleman conceived of her cultural role as that of the artist, not of the political activist or social scientist who felt compelled to be "Wanda the Explainer." Nevertheless, significantly shaped by the civil rights movement, she continued to write of the disenfranchised and dispossessed, and the themes of racism, sexism, poverty, and marginalization would continue to permeate her work.

Although she resists being defined by any one tradition, Coleman acknowledges that her writing has been influenced by the blues tradition and the music of the African American church as well as the prosody of such poets as Ezra Pound, Edgar Allan Poe, and Charles Olson. Moreover, attesting to the hybrid influences of a multicultural Los Angeles, Coleman's work has also been affected by a wide range of cultural images and sounds—from the visceral works of Los Angeles poets such as Charles Bukowski, to the Latino/a influence of the Southwest, to the rhythmic sounds of Black English vernacular. Despite the demands of her life—raising three children, often juggling more than one job—Coleman has found the time to write and perform her works. Since the late 1970s, Coleman has had eight books published: *Art in the Court of the Blue Fag* (1977), *Mad Dog Black Lady* (1979), *Images* (1983), *A War of Eyes and Other Stories* (1988), *Dicksboro Hotel and Other Travels* (1989), *African Sleeping Sickness: Stories and Poems* (1990), *Heavy Daughter Blues: Poems and Stories* (1991), and *Hand Dance* (1993).

Coleman has received recognition for her work: an Emmy for her writing (1976), a National Endowment for the Arts grant (1981–1982), and a Guggenheim Fellowship for poetry (1984). Coleman won the 1999 Lenore Marshall Poetry Prize from the Academy of American Poets for *Bathwater Wine* (1998). In 1999, she published her first novel, *Mambo Hips and Make Believe.* Distinguishing herself from other African American writers from the South and the East, Coleman sees herself as a distinctly West Coast writer. Despite her ambivalent relationship with Los Angeles, she remains dedicated to depicting the varied lives in the city, giving voice to the dispossessed, making visible the invisible, putting a human face onto anonymous statistics.

• Tony Magistrale, "Doing Battle with the Wolf: A Critical Introduction to Wanda Coleman's Poetry," *Black American Literature Forum* 23 (Fall 1989): 539–554. Wanda Coleman, "Sweet Mama Wanda Tells Fortunes: An Interview with Wanda Coleman," interview by Tony Magistrale and Patricia Ferreira, *Black American Literature Forum* 24 (Fall 1990): 491–507. Kathleen K. O'Mara, "Wanda Coleman," in *DLB*, vol. 130, *American Short Story Writers since World War II*, ed. Patrick Meanor, 1993, pp. 82–88.

—Sandra K. Stanley

COLLINS, KATHLEEN (1941–1988), playwright, scriptwriter, filmmaker, director, novelist, short story writer, and educator. Born Kathleen Conwell in Jersey City, she was the daughter of Frank and Loretta Conwell. Her father, who had worked as a mortician, became the principal of a high school now named after him and the first black New Jersey state legislator. In 1963, after receiving her BA in philosophy and religion from Skidmore College, Collins worked on black southern voter registration for the Student Nonviolent Coordinating Committee. In 1966 she earned an MA in French literature and cinema through the Middlebury program at Paris's Sorbonne. Joining the editorial and production staff at a New York City Public Broadcasting Service station, Collins worked as a film editor and began writing stories. In 1974, soon after ending her marriage to Douglas Collins, she became a professor of film history and screenwriting at the City College of New York. Adapting Henry H. Roth's fiction for the screen in *The Cruz Brothers and Mrs. Malloy* (1980), Collins became the first African American woman to write, direct, and produce a full-length feature film. Her film won first prize at the Sinking Creek Film Festival.

Collins's second feature, *Losing Ground* (1982), directed, coproduced, and based on an original screenplay by her, won Portugal's Figueroa de Foz Film Festival and garnered international acclaim. (Her screenplay, which differs in some significant ways from the film, is included in *Screenplays of the African American Experience,* 1991, edited by Phyllis Rauch Klotman.) A philosophical comedy that probes painful and deadly serious experiences, *Losing Ground* begins with a discussion of existentialism's roots in the futile attempt to explain away the chaos of war and ends with a symbolic act of violence that provides a release from order. It centers on a philosophy professor's efforts to escape the confinements of academic living, marriage to an abstract painter who denies her respect and private space, and her own cold and orderly mind by moving from the analytical study of ecstasy to the experience itself.

While making films, Collins produced equally remarkable drama. *In the Midnight Hour* (1981) portrayed a black middle-class family at the outset of the civil rights movement. *The Brothers* (1982) was named one of the twelve outstanding plays of the season by the Theatre Communications Group and published in Margaret B. Wilkerson's *Nine Plays by Black Women* (1986). It delineates the impact of racism and sexism on a black middle-class family from 1948 to 1968 as articulated by six intelligent, witty, and strikingly different women. The brothers themselves, though never seen, are vibrant presences through the women's remarks and mimicry.

In 1983 Collins reencountered Alfred Prettyman whom she had known twenty years earlier and four years later they were married. One week after their marriage, she learned that she had cancer. At the time of her death, she had completed a new screenplay, *Conversations with Julie,* her sixth stage play, *Waiting for Jane,* and a final draft of her novel, *Lollie: A Suburban Tale.* As more of her work appears, her already fine reputation as filmmaker and playwright will surely rise and be further enhanced by a new reputation in fiction.

• Note: Much of the published information on Kathleen Collins is unreliable, particularly because another writer has the same name and several sources have blended information about the two writers.

• Bernard L. Peterson, Jr., "Kathleen Collins," in *Contemporary Black American Playwrights and Their Plays,* 1988, pp. 116–118. Phyllis Rauch Klotman, "Kathleen Collins: Biographical Sketch," in *Screenplays of the African American Experience,* 1991, p. 123. Seret Scott, "Kathleen Conwell Collins Prettyman," in *The Encyclopedia of African American Culture and History,* forthcoming.

—Steven R. Carter

Color. Harper and Brothers published *Color,* Countee *Cullen's first volume of verse, in 1925. At the time it was considered a signal event in the New Negro Renaissance as Cullen, who was well known because most of these poems had been published previously in impressive literary magazines, was so highly regarded by both blacks and whites. Critics received the book more enthusiastically than any subsequent Cullen work. At twenty-two, Cullen seemed a major literary star in the making, a full-blown lyric poet of considerable power and possibilities, more skilled in versification, more educated, and more fully developed as a poetic talent than any of his contemporaries and certainly any of his predecessors. Although ambivalent about seeing himself as a racial poet, about one-third of *Color* deals with African American themes and some of these works—"Heritage," "Incident," "Yet Do I Marvel," and "The Shroud of Color"—are among the most famous and best-remembered poems not only of Cullen's entire canon but also of African American poetry as a genre. Clearly several of these racial poems established Cullen's main themes of alienation from the white West, quest for a theological purpose for black suffering, a hatred of segregation and racism, which played upon pity and irony, and the conflict between a Christian present and a pagan past. Most of the poems employ the forms of the sonnet, rhymed couplets, and ballad stanzas, and most were composed while Cullen was an undergraduate at New York University.

• Darwin Turner, *In a Minor Chord: Three Afro-American Writers and Their Search for Identity,* 1971. Alan Shucard, *Countee Cullen,* 1984. Gerald Early, ed., *My Soul's High Song: The Collected Writings of Countee Cullen, Voice of the Harlem Renaissance,* 1991.

—Gerald Early

Color Purple, The. *The Color Purple* (1982) is Alice *Walker's most magnificent and controversial literary achievement. The novel outraged African American male critics as well as a few female critics who argued that Walker's story did not reveal an accurate picture of African American life. One California mother was so insulted by the novel's content that she attempted to ban it from public school libraries. Others claimed that the novel was flawed because it defined a woman's identity in relationship to her sexual experiences. Even the language of the novel's protagonist has been found lacking. Regardless of its initial reception, accolades for Walker's piercing story of an abused, African American woman have included the Pulitzer Prize (1983), the National Book Award (1983), and an Academy Award nomination. It has attracted the appreciation of the masses and ignited passions within both popular culture and academic thought.

The Color Purple is the first African American, woman-authored, epistolary novel. It embodies Walker's womanist views without being reduced to a mere platform for ideological rhetoric. In this novel, Walker's writing reveals the transformative power of female bonding and female love. It offers frank portrayals of bisexual, lesbian, and heterosexual relationships amidst situations that penetrate the core of female spiritual and emotional development.

The novel opens with a demand for silence that leaves a fourteen-year-old girl named *Celie with no way to express her pain and confusion except in the letters she writes to God. Celie is raped repeatedly by her stepfather, Alphonso, and has two children by him—children he gives away without her consent. Later, she is forced into a loveless marriage, leaving her sister Nettie alone with Alphonso. Nettie escapes his sexual advances by moving in with Celie and her husband, Mr. Albert. This arrangement is no better than the previous one and Nettie is again forced to leave. She ultimately ends up in Africa where she writes to Celie of her experiences.

For Celie, marriage is nothing more than a shift within the quicksands of abuse and male domination. Albert beats her because she is not *Shug Avery, the woman he loves but does not have the courage to marry. Surprisingly, Celie and Shug develop an intimate relationship. More than anyone, Shug's influential presence and acceptance give Celie the strength she needs to redefine herself, take charge of her life, and leave Albert. Shug and Celie move to Memphis where Celie begins a career designing and selling unisex pants. After her stepfather's death, she returns to her family home. Nettie also returns with Celie's two children. The novel ends with a reconciliation of Celie and Albert's friendship.

Both *The Color Purple* and the subsequent film directed by Steven Spielberg (1985) have opened the minds of millions to the plight of African American women in crisis. If knowledge and personal insight is empowering, then *The Color Purple* offers those who acknowledge its truths a wealth of strength. And for women like Celie, it is a starting point for change and healing.

• Calvin C. Hernton, "Who's Afraid of Alice Walker," in *The Sexual Mountain and Black Women Writers: Adventures in Sex, Literature and Real Life,* 1987, pp. 1–36. Henry Louis Gates, Jr., "Color Me Zora: Alice Walker's (Re) Writing of the Speakerly Text," in *The Signifying Monkey,* 1988, pp. 239–258.

—Debra Walker King

COLTER, CYRUS (b. 1910), novelist, lawyer, U.S. Army captain, and professor. After careers in government service, law, the Army, and academia, Cyrus Colter began writing at fifty. Colter placed his first short story, "A Chance Meeting," in Threshold in 1960. He went on to place stories in such little magazines as *New Letters, Chicago Review,* and *Prairie Schooner.* Fourteen of his stories are collected in his first book, *The Beach Umbrella* (1970). In 1990 Colter published a second collection of short fiction, *The Amoralists and Other Tales.*

Colter's first novel, *The Rivers of Eros* (1972) relates the efforts of Clotilda Pilgrim to raise her grandchildren to lives of respectability. When Clotilda discovers that her sixteen-year-old granddaughter is involved with a married man, the grandmother becomes obsessed with the idea that the girl is repeating her grandmother's own youthful mistakes. Clotilda eventually kills the girl in order to stop what she perceives as a pattern of transgression. Other memorable characters include Clotilda's roomer Ambrose Hammer, who is researching a "History of the Negro Race," and the granddaughter's lover, who in contrast with the hopeful Hammer, is cynical about the prospects of blacks in America. *Rivers* is significant for its portrayal of a range of black society, as well as for its representation of place, its Chicago setting.

The Hippodrome (1973), a more experimental novel, opens with Jackson Yeager, a writer on Christian topics, in flight, carrying his wife's head in a bag. She had been involved with a white man, who was left mutilated by Yeager. Yeager finds refuge with Bea, who runs the Hippodrome, where blacks perform a sexual theater for whites. Yeager is required to perform yet cannot bring himself to do so. He flees and is joined by Darlene, who has also escaped from the Hippodrome, which Yeager comes to think of as perhaps a fantasy. Critics noting Yeager's sense of being subject to chance, of discrepancies between appearance and reality, and his feelings of the absurdity of life suggest the novel's existentialist French connection.

With *Night Studies* (1980) Colter returned to what some have regarded as his own realist-naturalist ground. In the first book of this four-part work, we are introduced to the three main characters: John Calvin Knight, leader of the Black Peoples Congress; Griselda Graves, a seemingly white young woman unaware of her black racial heritage, who appears irresistibly drawn to the Black Peoples Congress political organization; and Mary Dee Adkins, a young black woman of wealthy background. When she learns that marriage to her white lover is not a possibility because of his family's opposition, Mary Dee, too, plunges into the black political movement.

Following an assassination attempt, John Knight is hospitalized. Under medication and through semiconscious reveries Knight envisions scenes of the Middle Passage, slavery, and Reconstruction. This panorama of African American history comprises Book Two. Following a climactic scene at the end of Book Three, in which Knight vainly attempts to promulgate his moderate position at an unruly meeting of the Black Peoples Congress, Book Four concludes with Knight's retreat from political activity to solitary study—"night studies"—of black history. Critics have acknowledged Colter's effective presentation of a wide range of black and white voices in *Night Studies,* as well as the novel's compelling suggestion of the influence of the African American past on present America.

In his complexly structured narrative of *A Chocolate Soldier* (1988) Colter continues his exploration of black social history through the central character, Rollo "Cager" Lee. A questionably reliable theological student manqué narrates this work, in contrast with an anonymous third-person narrator used in Colter's previous novels. As Reginald Gibbons has noted, in reformulating in *A Chocolate Soldier* the question "Why were we slaves?"—the essential question that haunted Knight in *Night Studies*—Colter raises issues of black history as well as issues about the novel itself.

In his late work *City of Light* (1993) Colter presents Paul Kessey, a fair-skinned, wealthy Princeton graduate who founds in Paris the Coterie, a group whose aim is to establish an African homeland for disaffected blacks of the diaspora. In addition to important political and class themes, *City of Night* is noteworthy for its psychological study of Kessey, who has obsessively focused his love on two unattainable women, his dead mother and his mistress, who is happily married to someone else. Overall, Colter's life and work exemplify the worth of growth, experiment, and change.

• Robert M. Farnsworth, "Conversation with Cyrus Colter," *New Letters* 39 (Spring 1973): 16–39. John O'Brien, *Interviews with Black Writers,* 1973, pp. 17–33. Robert M. Bender, "The Fiction of Cyrus Colter," *New Letters* 48 (Fall 1981): 92–103. Helen R. Houston, "Cyrus Colter," in *DLB*, vol. 33, *Afro-American Fiction Writers After 1955,* eds. Thadious M. Davis and Trudier Harris, 1984, pp. 48–52. Gilton Gregory Cross et al., "Fought for It and Paid Taxes Too: Four Interviews with Cyrus Colter," *Callaloo* 14 (Fall 1991): 855–897. Reginald Gibbons, "Colter's Novelistic Contradictions," *Callaloo* 14 (Fall 1991): 898–905.

—James Robert Payne

COLTRANE, JOHN (1926–1967), saxophonist, composer, and iconic figure. John Coltrane's immersion in modern jazz took place in bands led by Eddie Vinson, Dizzy Gillespie, and Johnny Hodges. In 1955 he joined the Miles *Davis quintet and was soon identified as one of the most talented tenor saxophonists of the era. The story of Coltrane becoming a major African American cultural icon really began, however, in 1957. In that year he underwent a spiritual "conversion" concomitant with his overcoming a drug addiction. A brief but salient collaboration with Thelonius Monk followed and Coltrane was on his way to becoming one of the major innovators in jazz. Associated with the radical improvisatory style called "Free Jazz" (or pejoratively "anti-jazz"), Coltrane's own contribution was sometimes referred to as "sheets of sound," a lightning fast style of improvisation, with great attention given to melodic freedom. His mid-1960s recordings were increasingly complex and dense, often reflecting an interest in Eastern and African music, and were marked by radical experimentation in instrumentation. Coltrane died at age forty of a liver ailment.

Coltrane had a major impact on literary artists who came of age in the 1960s. Kimberly Benston has suggested that the "Coltrane poem" exists as a distinct genre within contemporary African American literature. Coltrane's premature death has generated a most compelling body of elegies. There is no question that at some level many artists were affected by his creativity and genius, but the evidence suggests that Coltrane's spirituality as much as his musicianship created disciples. Coltrane's monumental 1964 work *A Love Supreme* became a kind of musical scripture to many poets, novelists, and playwrights. His commitment to experimentation, his cross-cultural interests, in addition to his search for a life contrary to the sterility of the mainstream, made Coltrane a hero to a generation whose hopes were nurtured by the energy of the Black Arts movement.

• Art Lange and Nathaniel Mackey, *Moment's Notice: Jazz in Poetry and Prose,* 1993. Eric Nisenson, *Ascension: John Coltrane and His Quest,* 1993.

—James C. Hall

Confessions of Nat Turner, The. Page for page, no antebellum slave narrative had a swifter impact on the American public than *The Confessions of Nat Turner* (1831). Published by its Virginian author, a white lawyer and slaveholder named Thomas R. Gray, and printed by Lucas & Deaver, Baltimore, the book followed quickly upon the capture and execution, 5 November 1831, of Nat *Turner. Quickly copyrighted, as many as forty or fifty thousand copies were printed. Public curiosity and horror at news of the bloodiest of nineteenth-century American slave revolts led Gray to compile *The Confessions* speedily and successfully. Historians and critics allege that the book has become a rarity, although many university and some public libraries possess copies. A second edition appeared in 1881 and many reprints followed in this century, especially during the 1960s after the publication of William Styron's controversial novel *The Confessions of Nat Turner* (1967).

Part dictation, part paraphrase of Turner, and part editorial commentary by Gray, the narrative must be read with caution. Nevertheless, Gray is a prime source of information and ideology associated with Nat Turner's life and the revolt and one white Southerner's immediate response. Gray's horrified condemnation of the slave's messianic attack upon slavery is mixed with mystery and finally with awe. Turner's reported words encourage these responses. The prophet role adopted by Turner and enthusiastically embraced by northern abolitionists and later by African Americans and their allies, emerges in passages of succinct power such as the following: "Ques. Do you not find yourself mistaken now? Ans. Was not Christ crucified." Another is Gray's summary:

> He is a complete fanatic, or plays his part most admirably. The calm, deliberate composure with which he spoke of his late deeds and intentions, the expression of his fiend-like face when excited by enthusiasm, still bearing the stains of the blood of helpless innocence about him; clothed with rags and covered with chains; yet daring to raise his manacled hands to heaven, with a spirit soaring above the attributes of man; I looked on him and my blood curdled in my veins.

In the 1830s, these passages played persuasively upon diverse readers' imaginations disturbed also by historic events: in the North, the spread of the antislavery movement, the appearance of William Lloyd Garrison's *Liberator*, John Browne *Russwurm's freedom's *Journal*, and David *Walker's *Appeal*. In Virginia and across the South, as the slave population grew, Nat Turner helped provoke a historic debate on abolition in the Virginia legislature (1831–1832) and the strengthening of Black Codes, and reawakened anxious memories of the conspiracies of Gabriel Prosser (1800) and Denmark Vesey (1822). American authors have long been inspired by *The Confessions,* notably Harriet Beecher *Stowe, Arna *Bontemps, Robert *Hayden, Herbert Aptheker, Daniel Panger, Vincent Harding, and Sherley Anne *Williams.

• Herbert Aptheker, *Nat Turner's Slave Rebellion,* 1966. Albert E. Stone, *The Return of Nat Turner,* 1992.

—Albert E. Stone

Conjure Woman, The. A collection of seven short stories by Charles Waddell *Chesnutt published in 1899, *The Conjure Woman* focuses on plantation and slave life in eastern North Carolina. Written in the local color tradition, the work reveals Chesnutt's mastery of the dialect story and the plantation tradition popular in the late nineteeth century. Unlike the fiction of such white writers as Thomas Nelson Page and Joel Chandler Harris, Chesnutt's stories do not sentimentalize plantation life in the Old South. Instead, *The Conjure Woman* reveals the destructive and dehumanizing force of slavery.

Set in Patesville (Fayetteville), North Carolina, the stories contain both a frame narrator and a folk narrator. John, a midwestern businessman transplanted to the South, takes up grape cultivation as a living and hires *Uncle Julius McAdoo, an aged ex-slave, as his coachman. John's narration provides the outer framework for the stories, while Uncle Julius's tales about slave life, conjuring, and superstitions create a complex inner structure.

As a newcomer to the South, John's favorable descriptions of the countryside, the agricultural potential of the area, and the pleasing manners and customs of its people render an idyllic portrait of the New South. In certain respects, *The Conjure Woman* can be viewed as part of the reconciliation movement in southern literature that developed after the Civil War to appeal to both northern and southern readers. Uncle Julius enhances this conciliatory effort to a small degree, as one of his purposes is to instruct John, his wife Annie, and the reader about southern life and culture. On the surface, he seems simple and naive, but he successfully uses his wily storytelling gifts to outwit his employer. Moreover, the stories Julius tells subtly undercut the wholesome picture of the New South that John describes in his frame narration.

A masterful trickster, Julius tells stories that reveal the inglorious past of the plantation South. His stories center on the conjuring activities of *Aun' Peggy, a freewoman who earns her living through working spells and magic. In most of the stories, Julius describes the plight of slaves whose only real defense against the inhumanity of slavery lies in Aun' Peggy's conjure spells. In "Mars Jeems Nightmare," she turns a plantation owner into a slave, and he learns firsthand of his overseer's cruelty. In "Po' Sandy," "Sis Becky's Pickaninny," and "Hot Foot Hannibal," slaves turn to Aun' Peggy's magic to help keep their loved ones close, sometimes to no avail. In "The Goophered Grapevine" Aun' Peggy's conjuring serves less sympathetic purposes when she casts a spell on Mars Dugal's grapevines to keep the slaves from stealing the scuppernongs. Henry, an aged slave, falls victim to her conjuring and finds that his life mysteriously and tragically parallels the growing process of the vines.

In "The Conjurer's Revenge" and "The Gray Wolf's Ha'nt," Uncle Julius shifts the focus from Aun' Peggy to free black conjure men, whose spells are used for spite and revenge against plantation slaves. In "The Conjurer's Revenge" a slave is transformed into a mule for stealing from the conjurer, while in "The Gray Wolf's Ha'nt" another slave suffers a conjurer's evil and vengeful retaliation for the death of the conjurer's son.

While stories in *The Conjure Woman* do not tackle the social and racial problems explored in Chesnutt's *The *Wife of His Youth and Other Stories of the Color Line* (1899), Uncle Julius's tales are emotionally moving and contain deeply troubling messages about slavery. Most important, they reveal the essential humanity of slave characters with great empathy and understanding.

• William L. Andrews, *The Literary Career of Charles W. Chesnutt*, 1980. Eric J. Sundquist, "Charles Chesnutt's Cakewalk," in *To Wake the Nations*, 1993, pp. 271–454.

—Paula Gallant Eckard

Contending Forces. The first of four novels written by Pauline E. *Hopkins, *Contending Forces: A Romance Illustrative of Negro Life North and South* was published by the Colored Co-operative Publishing Company of Boston in 1900. The novel is Hopkins's manifesto on the value of fiction to social activism in black America at the turn of the century. By relying on the stock devices of sentimental melodrama, the novel refutes stereotypes about degraded mulattoes and licentious black women, celebrates the work ethic among upwardly mobile African Americans of the post-Reconstruction period, and provides a historically accurate depiction of the racist oppression that they endured. Like Frances Ellen Watkins *Harper's **Iola Leroy* (1892), *Contending Forces* recalls a tragic antebellum story as the basis of another about emancipatory optimism.

In 1780 Charles Montfort moves his family from Bermuda to North Carolina to operate a cotton plantation. Almost immediately a rival planter, Anson Pollock, suspects that Montfort's beautiful wife, Grace, is partly black. He murders Montfort, claims Grace as his concubine, and makes slaves out of her sons, Charles and Jesse. Grace commits suicide to escape Pollock. He sells Charles to an Englishman, who frees him and takes him to England. Jesse eventually escapes to New England, where he becomes a progenitor of the Smith family—the widow Ma Smith and her children, Will and Dora—of the novel's main plot.

The postbellum story is set in Boston. Will is a Harvard philosophy student (reminiscent of W. E. B. *Du Bois), and Dora assists her mother in running a comfortable boarding house. Two tenants, Sappho Clark, a beautiful white mulatta with a secret southern past, and John Langley, who is engaged to Dora, share the Smith household. Will falls in love with Sappho and asks her to marry him, but John blackmails her in an attempt to make her his mistress. She abandons Will in order to escape John. In a letter left for Will, Sappho reveals John's immoral intentions and her past suffering as a victim of interracial rape. Will shares this information with Dora who breaks her engagement with John. Frustrated by his unsuccessful attempt to find Sappho, Will goes abroad to pursue his studies. Dora eventually marries Dr. Arthur Lewis, the head of a Louisiana industrial school for Negroes, while John dies seeking his fortune in mining for gold. Will returns to the United States and marries Sappho.

Early scholars of African American literature regarded the writings of Hopkins and her black female contemporaries as unworthy of literary merit. This critical viewpoint prevailed until the 1980s when scholars reclaimed the artistic complexity and political interventionary agendas of Hopkins's writings. The novel unites racial activism and woman-centered concerns as well as redefines a virtuous black womanhood on the bases of the moral integrity of female character and the nobility of her labor rather than on the legacy of sexual violation or the elitism of class privilege.

• Hazel V. Carby, *Reconstructing Womanhood: The Emergence of the Afro-American Woman Novelist*, 1987. Richard Yarborough, introduction to *Contending Forces*, 1988. Claudia Tate, *Domestic Allegories of Black Political Desire*, 1992.

—Claudia Tate

COOPER, ANNA JULIA (1858–1964), educator, scholar, writer, feminist, and activist. Anna Julia Haywood Cooper was born in Raleigh, North Carolina, the daughter of a slave, Hannah Stanley Haywood, and her white master, George Washington Haywood, with whom neither she nor her mother maintained any ties. At age nine she received a scholarship to attend the St. Augustine's Normal School and Collegiate Institute for newly freed slaves, and in 1877 she married an instructor at the school, a Bahamian-born Greek teacher named George Cooper. Left a widow in 1879, she never remarried. She enrolled in 1881 at Oberlin College, where educator and activist Mary Church (later *Terrell) also studied, and elected to take the "Gentleman's Course," rather than the program designed for women. She received her bachelor's degree in 1884, and after teaching for a year at Wilberforce University and then returning briefly to teach at St. Augustine's, she went back to Oberlin to earn her master's degree in mathematics in 1887.

Cooper was recruited that same year to teach math and science and later Latin at the Washington Colored High School in Washington, D.C., also known as the M Street School and, later, the Paul Laurence Dunbar High School. In 1902 she became the principal of this elite public school, which during its history educated many African American leaders. In 1906, however, she was forced to resign in what was known as the "M Street School Controversy"; Cooper was attacked for lax disciplinary policies and for including among the boarders in her house a male teacher, John Love, to whom she was known to be close, although the exact character of their relationship remains unclear. In the opinion of current scholars, Cooper was dismissed because of the racism and sexism of white critics, who, among other things, objected to her refusal to embrace vocational training for all African American youth. She moved to Lincoln University in Jefferson City, Missouri, where she taught until a new superintendent in 1910 recalled her to the M Street School. While she was in Missouri, Cooper declined a marriage proposal from Love.

Although she worked full-time, in the 1910s Cooper studied for her PhD at Columbia University and in the summers at the Sorbonne. She wrote her dissertation on French attitudes toward slavery and was awarded the doctorate from the University of Paris in 1925 at the age of sixty-seven, making her, according to current knowledge, the fourth African American woman to receive the PhD. She continued to teach following her retirement from the M Street School in 1930, serving from 1930 to 1940 as president of Frelinghuysen University, a night school for working people. When necessary, she held classes in her home at 201 T Street NW, and she stayed on as the registrar of this institution until 1950.

Committed to the struggle for both race and gender equality, Cooper was an active, vocal participant in the Woman's Era at the turn of the century. She helped found the Colored Women's League of Washington, D.C., in 1892. She was one of a very small number of African American women asked to speak at the World's Congress of Representative Women at the Chicago World's Fair in 1893, an event she and others criticized for its racism. She was one of the few women invited to talk at the first Pan-African Conference in London in 1900, organized by, among others, W. E. B. *Du Bois. She participated in the founding of the Colored Women's YWCA in 1905 and established the first chapter of the Camp Fire Girls in 1912. Also during these years of full-time employment and active feminist and racial organizational work, Cooper adopted and raised a relative's five orphaned grandchildren.

Anna Julia Cooper's most famous writing is her only booklength work, the major feminist text, *A *Voice from the South* (1892). Cooper's book mingles and manipulates Victorian ideologies of true womanhood and turn-of-the-century racial uplift rhetoric to advocate racial justice and equal rights for African American women. Cooper also wrote *Legislative Measures Concerning Slavery in the United States* (1942) and *Equality of Races and the Democratic Movement* (1945), and she is the editor of the two-volume *Life and Writings of the Grimké Family* (1951).

Committed throughout her life to an activist belief in the power of education to change lives individually and collectively, Cooper is today grouped with other well-known social and political leaders at the turn of the century, such as W. E. B. Du Bois, Ida B. *Wells-Barnett, Mary Church Terrell, and Fannie Barrier Williams. She died in her sleep in Washington, D.C., on 27 February 1964.

• Hazel Carby, *Reconstructing Womanhood: The Emergence of the Afro-American Woman Novelist,* 1987. Mary Helen Washington, introduction to *A Voice from the South,* 1988. David W. H. Pellow, "Anna 'Annie' J. Cooper," in *Notable Black American Women,* ed. Jessie Carney Smith, 1992, pp. 218–224. Debra Calhoun and Glenda Elizabeth, "Anna J. Cooper," in *African American Women: A Biographical Dictionary,* ed. Dorothy C. Salem, 1993, pp. 124–126. Elizabeth Alexander, "'We Must Be about Our Father's Business': Anna Julia Cooper and the In-Corporation of the Nineteenth-Century African-American Woman Intellectual," in Sherry-Lee Linkon, ed. *In Her Own Voice: Nineteenth-Century American Women Essayists,* 1997, pp. 61–80. Charles Lemert and Esme Bhan, eds., *The Voice of Anna Julia Cooper,* 1998.

—Elizabeth Ammons

COOPER, J. CALIFORNIA (b. 19?), short fiction writer, playwright, and novelist. Joan California Cooper's birthdate is conspicuously absent from available written material about her life and work. She was born in Berkeley, California, to Maxine Rosemary and Joseph C. Cooper, and she has a daughter, Paris Williams.

Cooper's success as a writer must be attributed solely to natural gifts. She began composing plays and performing them before family and friends when she was a very young child. Indeed, the first glimpse by the public-at-large of Cooper's work was through her plays; she had written at least seventeen by the mid-1990s, including: *Everytime It Rains; System, Suckers, and Success; How Now; The Unintended; The Mother; Ahhh; Strangers;* and *Loners. Strangers* earned the 1978 Black Playwright of the Year award and was performed at the San Francisco Palace of Fine Arts. *Loners,* anthologized in Eileen Ostrow's Center Stage (1981), is the story of Cool, a somewhat egotistical man of thirty-seven who realizes too late that his inability to commit to the shy but strong Emma results in his own loneliness. Emma tires of Cool's callous neglect and decides to marry someone who is not so self-centered that he fails to notice her quiet strength. Cooper's plays have been performed before live audiences, as well as on radio and public television. She is a prolific writer, who, like Emily Dickinson, took up writing to satisfy a private, personal need; much of her early work was long hidden from public view until her plays began to receive attention.

Cooper is better known for her short stories, whose narrators witness and relate tale after tale with a folksy, homespun wisdom in conversation with the reading audience that brings to mind the relationship between Alice *Childress's urban domestic workers, *Mildred Johnson and Marge, in **Like One of the Family* (1956). Cooper has published five short story collections: *A Piece of Mine* (1984); *Homemade Love* (1986), which won the 1989 American Book Award; *Some Soul to Keep* (1987); *The Matter Is Life* (1991); and *Some Love, Some Pain, Sometime* (1995).

Like Alice *Walker, whose company published Cooper's first collection of short stories, Cooper acts in spiritual communion with certain characters who relate their experiences; as medium, Cooper retells the stories in writing. Her primary characters are usually women who have been victimized in some way by the men in their lives. Cooper's profound messages come packaged in what appear to be simple and straightforward stories; this method is reminiscent of one often employed by Frances Ellen Watkins *Harper. Her writing shares Harper's didacticism, but Cooper's reliance on the Ten Commandments for many of her themes is not as conducive to invoking Christian piety. One story from the collection *A Piece of Mine*, entitled "One Hundred Dollars and Nothing!," retells the rise and fall of a boastful but unenterprising man who marries a well-to-do, enterprising woman named Mary. The husband, Charles, feels he has done the nappy-headed, bow-legged Mary a favor by marrying her, and he is fond of telling Mary that, with one hundred dollars and nothing, he could outperform her anyday. Mary endures years of abuse by Charles, and she eventually dies; but, prior to her death, she is able to set into motion events that will leave Charles with one hundred dollars and nothing more. She punishes Charles from the grave. The female protagonists in *A Piece of Mine* survive, through spiritual (and often physical) transcendence, all manner of abuse and neglect. They emerge with a greater realization of their inner strength, self-actualized.

Homemade Love consists of thirteen short stories about girls who, despite warning and example, fall into the same traps as their parents. "Without Love" is the story of the parallel lives of two friends. Totsy, neglected by her alcohol-abusing mother, is sexually active at eleven and becomes an unwed teenage mother. Her friend Geneva narrates the story of Totsy's early reliance on sex without love and the impact such an attitude has on Totsy's inability to mature and become self-actualized. Geneva, by contrast, combines sex with love and marriage, works hard to achieve a middle-class lifestyle, and grows old and content with her husband by her side as her best friend. Totsy is finally forced by the circumstances of old age and declining health to rely on the son she has never nurtured. *Homemade Love* simply suggests that homemade love is what nurtures the mind, body, and soul.

Cooper has also written two novels, *Family* (1991) and *In Search of Satisfaction* (1994). *Family* is narrated by Clora, the freed spirit of an enslaved woman who committed suicide. Clora follows the experiences of and watches over her favorite child, Always. Because the narrator exists in spirit only, she is superomniscient, able to enter into and disclose other characters' states of mind. *In Search of Satisfaction* echoes the simple message heard in much of Cooper's other work: happiness comes from within. In a note to that novel, Cooper uses the analogy of the three little pigs to make the point that each of us is responsible for laying the proper foundation for our own personal satisfaction. Cooper published *The Wake of the Wind* in 1998.

The American Library Association's Literary Lion Award (1988) and the James Baldwin Writing Award (1988) are only two of the many prizes presented to Cooper for her writing. Cooper is a person who carefully guards those matters that she considers private. She resides in rural Texas.

• J. California Cooper, interview by Lynn Gray, *FM Five* (Nov.–Dec. 1985): 1, 12. Alice Walker, "J. California Cooper," in *Contemporary Literary Criticism*, vol. 56, ed. Roger Matuz, 1989, pp. 69–72. Barbara J. Marshall, "Kitchen Table Talk: J. California Cooper's Use of Nommo—Female Bonding and Transcendence," in *Language and Literature in the African American Imagination*, 1992, pp. 91–102. Rebecca Carroll, "J. California Cooper," in *I Know What the Red Clay Looks Like*, ed. Carol Alisha Blackshire-Belay, 1994, pp. 63–80. Kristine A. Yohe, "J. California Cooper," in *The Oxford Companion to Women's Writing in the United States*, eds. Cathy N. Davidson and Linda Wagner-Martin, 1995, p. 218. Madelyn Jablon, "Woman Storytelling: The Voice of the Vernacular," in *Ethnicity and the American Short Story*, ed. Julia Brown, 1997, pp. 47–62.

—Lovalerie King

CORNISH, SAM (b. 1935), poet, essayist, editor of children's literature, photographer, educator, and figure in the Black Arts movement. Born into urban poverty in Baltimore, Maryland, on 22 December 1935, Samuel James Cornish was the youngest of the two sons of Herman and Sarah Cornish. From his older brother Herman he learned early the lessons of the street, which he later would incorporate into a street-tough observancy in his poetry.

Cornish served in the U.S. Army Medical Corps (1958–1960), then returned to Baltimore, where he published two poetry collections—*In This Corner: Sam Cornish and Verses* (1961) and *People Beneath the Window* (1964). While working at the Enoch Pratt Free Library, he became part of Baltimore's political and literary underground, self-publishing a sixteen-page pamphlet entitled *Generations and Other Poems* (1964). A subsequent edition of *Generations* (1966) appeared when Cornish was editing *Chicory,* a literary magazine by children and young adults in the Community Action Target Area of Baltimore. Lucian W. Dixon and Cornish edited a selection from the magazine entitled *Chicory: Young Voices from the Black Ghetto* (1969). In 1968 Cornish won the Humanities Institute of Coppin State College Poetry Prize for his "influence on the Coppin poets" and a grant from the National Endowment for the Arts. Soon poets as diverse as Maxine Kumin, Clarence *Major, and Eugene *Redmond would acknowledge Cornish's significance.

By 1970 Cornish was represented in the LeRoi Jones (Amiri *Baraka) and Larry *Neal anthology *Black Fire* (1968) as well as in the Clarence Major collection *New Black Poetry* (1969). He reconsidered his early poems of black historicized kinship, restructuring them into the Beacon Press's *Generations* (1971). After a brief stay in Boston, Cornish returned to Baltimore to work in secondary school and college writing programs. While there, Cornish published *Sometimes* (1973) with Cambridge's Pym-Randall Press. Teaching poetry in the schools led to several children's books: *Your Hand in Mine* (1970), *Grandmother's Pictures* (1974), and *My Daddy's People* (1976).

Returning to Boston in the mid-1970s, Cornish worked with the Educational Development Corporation and attended Goddard College in Vermont. He appeared in a host of new anthologies, from George Plimpton and Peter Ardery's *American Literary Anthology* (1970) and Harry Smith's *Smith Poets* (1971), to Ted Wilentz and Tom Weatherly's *Natural Process* (1972) and Arnold Adoff's *One Hundred Years of Black Poetry* (1972). *Sam's World* (1978) continued the historical and genealogical project of *Generations.*

Since the 1980s Cornish has divided his time between bookselling and teaching creative writing and literature at Emerson College in Boston. *Songs of Jubilee: New and Selected Poems, 1969–1983* (1986) recasts earlier work into sequences of a historical and biographical nature. His autobiographical narrative, *1935: A Memoir* (1990), blends poetry and prose into a montage of twentieth-century history. The poems of *Folks Like Me* (1993) offer political and cultural portraits of African Americans from the depression to the early 1960s. Current projects include the next volume of his autobiography, *1955,* and a critical study of Langston *Hughes.

• Jon Woodson, "Sam Cornish," in *DLB,* vol. 41, *Afro-American Poets since 1955,* eds. Trudier Harris and Thadious M. Davis, 1985, pp. 64–69. C. K. Doreski, "Kinship and History in Sam Cornish's *Generations,*" *Contemporary Literature* 33 (Winter 1992): 665–687.

—C. K. Doreski

CORNISH, SAMUEL (1795–1858), evangelist, educator, social activist, journalist, and editor of America's first African American newspaper. Samuel E. Cornish's many antebellum social, religious, and political involvements aimed at ameliorating the condition of African Americans in the United States. Born in Sussex County, Delaware, Cornish was ordained in the New York Presbytery as an evangelist (1822) and served various churches intermittently until 1847. During his thirty-year public career, he was associated with over eighteen organizations for racial uplift, including four New York City newspapers: *Freedom's Journal,* the *Rights of All,* the *Weekly Advocate,* and the *Colored American.* In March 1827 he started *Freedom's Journal,* the first African American newspaper, to counter racist propaganda and provide a forum of communication among African Americans. After about six months Cornish left the journal in the hands of his coeditor, John Browne *Russwurm, but resumed editorial responsibilities in March 1828 when Russwurm emigrated to Liberia, changing the paper's name in May 1829 to the *Rights of All.* Cornish's editorial policy, which continued until the paper's death on 29 October 1829, reflects his dislike of the colonization movement.

Cornish is credited with editing the *Weekly Advocate* from January 1837 until 4 March 1837, when its name was changed to the *Colored American.* He continued as editor until 18 April 1838, advocating nonpartisan responsible journalism and optimism regarding the future of African Americans. Cornish's other involvements included the African Free Schools, the Negro Convention movement, the American Anti-Slavery Society, and the American Missionary Society.

Cornish's life was saddened by the death of his wife Jane Livingston in 1844, the emigration of his son William to Liberia, the death of his oldest daughter, Sarah, in 1846, and the mental derangement of his daughter Jane in 1851. Cornish nevertheless remained active in public life until his death in 1858.

• I. Garland Penn, *The Afro-American Press and Its Editors,* 1891; rpt. 1969. Frankie Hutton, *The Early Black Press in America, 1827–1860,* 1993.

—Marilyn D. Button

Corregidora. In 1975, while still a graduate student at Brown University, Gayl *Jones published *Corregidora,* her first novel. A work that combines stark, deliberately raw language with poetry and dreamlike lyricism, it is narrated by *Ursa Corregidora, a Kentucky blues singer who weaves her own story of thwarted desire and artistic strivings with that of her family. As Brazilian slaves and prostitutes, her great-grandmother and grandmother are repeatedly raped by their master, Old Corregidora, who fathers Ursa's grandmother as well as her mother, until Great Gram commits an undisclosed act of violence that makes him murderously obsessed with her. She flees to Kentucky, returning only to retrieve her now pregnant daughter. Like her mother, Ursa has heard this story since birth and has been frequently instructed to raise a child who will in turn bear witness to Corregidora's atrocities; thus does Great Gram try to empower her family, changing her daughters' identity from chattel to bearers of vengeance. But when Ursa is pregnant, her jealous husband (Mutt Thomas) pushes her down a flight of stairs and she loses the baby. Her injuries require a hysterectomy, and Ursa's resulting distress at being unable to "make generations" also affects her capacity for sexual pleasure.

After turning away from Cat Lawson, a friend whose lesbianism disconcerts her, Ursa marries again, only to have the marriage end when her husband accuses her of frigidity. Alternately yearning for and despising Mutt, a man marked by his own family scars of slavery and possessiveness, Ursa spends the next twenty years singing and writing songs, and grappling with her family's fraught histories of sexual desire and violent abuse. Mutt's reappearance catalyzes an uneasy reunion for Ursa, merging undercurrents of violence with the possibility of healing. Performing fellatio, Ursa finally realizes what Great Gram did to Corregidora (she bit his penis just before orgasm), and thus recognizes the victim's own capacity for violence. Ursa also recognizes the combination of pain and pleasure, power and vulnerability, that constitutes what Jones has called "the blues relationship" between men and women. In acknowledging her own blues relationship with Mutt, Ursa sees how desire survives, however maimed and thwarted, even after a history of abuse. Yet the novel's ambiguous close finds Ursa still searching for a song and identity of her own to replace the angry refrain of vengeance her mothers have taught her.

Critical perspectives about *Corregidora* focus on its use of African American oral traditions: the frequent call-and-response pattern of Jones's dialogue, the spiraling refrains of the blues, the improvisations of jazz, the echoes of black dialects, the emphasis on performance as part of black folklore. Additionally, Jones's depiction of a female African American singer relates to themes in contemporary black women's writing about the search for a voice and the defiance of a rigid, imposed, and usually sexual identity. Perhaps equally important, *Corregidora*'s portrayal of the complexities between mothers and daughters meshes with Jones's treatment of the double-edged sword of memory for African Americans, who need to remember their history without being imprisoned by it.

• Keith Byerman, *Fingering the Jagged Grain: Tradition and Form in Recent Black Fiction,* 1985. Missy Dehn Kubitschek, *Claiming the Heritage: African-American Women Novelists and History,* 1991. Sally Robinson, *Engendering the Subject: Gender and Self-Representation in Contemporary Women's Fiction,* 1991.

—Amy S. Gottfried

CORROTHERS, JAMES D. (1869–1917), writer and minister. Born in Michigan, James D. Corrothers was raised in the predominantly white community of South Haven by his paternal grandfather, a man of Cherokee and Scotch-Irish ancestry. He moved to Muskegon at age fourteen, supporting himself and his grandfather. Shortly thereafter he moved to Indiana, then to Springfield, Ohio, working as a laborer. There, in his teens, he began his literary career, publishing a poem, "The Deserted School House," in the local newspaper.

Corrothers's literary career received a boost when, at eighteen, he relocated to Chicago. Working in a white barber shop, he met journalist-reformer Henry Demarest Lloyd and showed him some poems. Lloyd arranged for their publication in the Chicago *Tribune,* getting Corrothers a custodial job in the *Tribune* offices. Corrothers was soon asked to do an article on Chicago's African American elite. He was chagrined when the story appeared, rewritten by a white reporter in a way that stereotyped its subjects; he was equally chagrined when the paper's editor refused to pay him for his efforts.

Corrothers returned to day labor and even did some boxing, but remained dedicated to writing. In 1890 he appeared before Thomas Fortune's National Afro-American League, reading his poem "The Psalm of the Race," a work protesting American discrimination but predicting a brighter future.

Beginning in 1890, Corrothers furthered his education. An aunt in Chicago helped him enter Northwestern University, where, with additional support from Lloyd and temperance activist Frances Willard, he studied from 1890 to 1893. He also spent a brief period at Bennett College, in North Carolina.

Leaving Northwestern, Corrothers did freelance reporting for Chicago dailies. Influenced by humorist Finley Peter Dunne, Hoosier poet James Whitcomb Riley, and dialect poet Paul Laurence *Dunbar, he also began writing dialect poetry and sketches for the Chicago *Journal,* focusing on working-class African American urban life. These pieces brought him his first popularity; nevertheless, within a year, aware that racism limited his opportunities in journalism, he entered the African Methodist Episcopal (AME) ministry, subsequently taking posts in Bath, New York, and in Red Bank and Hackensack, New Jersey. Forced by scandal from the AME Church in 1902, he soon reentered the field as a Baptist. In the last two years of his life, he became a Presbyterian, pastoring a church in Westchester, Pennsylvania.

Corrothers's ministerial career did not exclude further literary work. He continued to find success in dialect. His sentimental "'Way in de Woods, an' Nobody Dar" appeared in one of America's leading magazines, *Century,* in 1899, quickly followed there by other dialect pieces. He also collected and published his newspaper sketches in book form as *The Black Cat Club* (1902).

The Black Cat Club was, and has remained, Corrothers's most noted work, its urban setting marking him as an innovator within the dialect tradition. Corrothers also integrated authentic folk materials into his sketches, although his "dialect" came more from literary than from folk sources. The book's real strength was its satire, including a thinly veiled attack on Booker T. *Washington and even on the uncritical vogue for dialect within African American letters. Corrothers was ambivalent about dialect and later said he regretted having written the book; he was no less ambivalent about the African American working classes, whose lives the book portrayed. Still, along with his earlier work, *The Black Cat Club* gave him a national audience, one he continued to cultivate through such poems as the self-reflective "Me 'N' Dunbar" (1903) and "An Awful Problem Solved" (1903), which turned the form toward protest.

Corrothers also worked increasingly in standard English, writing sentimental pieces and protest verse. Among the more important was "The Snapping of the Bow" (1901), condemning racism but expressing the belief that, ultimately, "the race might rise." Toward the end of his career, reflecting a less sanguine perspective, Corrothers wrote "At the Closed Gate of Justice" (1913), protesting the apparently intractable character of American racial injustice.

Also toward the end of his career, Corrothers returned to prose. Most notable was a two-part story, "A Man They Didn't Know" (1913–1914), predicting a war pitting the United States against dark-skinned Japanese and Mexican enemies, one in which he portrayed African American loyalty as an uncertain but crucial factor. He also published his autobiography, *In Spite of the Handicap* (1916), seeking to justify his career and his views of American racial problems.

Corrothers was one of the most widely published African American writers of the late nineteenth and early twentieth centuries. As a result, he did much to bring visibility to African American letters.

• Kevin K. Gaines, *Uplifting the Race: Black Leadership, Politics, and Culture in the Twentieth Century,* 1966. Richard Yarborough, "James D. Corrothers," in *DLB,* vol. 50, *Afro-American Writers before the Harlem Renaissance,* ed. Trudier Harris, 1986, pp. 52–62. Dickson D. Bruce, Jr., *Black American Writing from the Nadir: The Evolution of a Literary Tradition, 1877–1915,* 1989. Dickson D. Bruce, Jr., "James Corrothers Reads a Book; or, The Lives of Sandy Jenkins," *African American Review* 26 (Winter 1992): 665–673. Kevin Gaines, "Assimilationist Minstrelsy As Racial Uplift Ideology: James D. Corrothers's Literary Quest for Black Leadership," *American Quarterly* 45 (Sept. 1993): 341–369.

—Dickson D. Bruce, Jr.

CORTEZ, JAYNE (b. 1936), literary and performance poet, significant figure in the development of jazz-poetry readings and recordings, director, and publisher. Jayne Cortez's significance as an African American poet resonates beyond the printed page. The immense reputation Cortez has garnered worldwide comes from her performances combining live music, especially jazz, with powerfully spoken poetry. The strength of her performance, however, does not detract from her achievement as a literary figure. For example, Cortez received the Before Columbus Foundation American Book Award for excellence in literature in 1980 and the New York Foundation for the Arts award for poetry in 1987. In addition, Cortez was twice honored with a National Endowment of the Arts fellowship. Cortez's commitment to African American artistic expression is many faceted and consistent. She has been heralded for meshing surrealist images with raw, jarring descriptive detail. Her tone is serious and sometimes sarcastic but always full of pleasure and pain and politics. Among others, she cites Langston *Hughes, Aimé Césaire, Léon Damas, Nicolás Guillén, and Sterling A. *Brown as literary inspirations for her work.

Born in Fort Huachuca, Arizona, on 10 May 1936, Jayne Cortez resides in New York City. In 1954 Cortez married jazz musician Ornette Coleman and gave birth to their son, Denardo, in 1956. Cortez studied drama in Los Angeles and cofounded the Watts Repertory Theatre Company in 1964, where she remained artistic director until 1970. This was her formal initiation into the world of performance: directing, acting, and reciting poetry to live audiences. By 1972 Cortez had moved to New York City and published two volumes of poetry—*Pisstained Stairs and the Monkey Man's Wares* (1969) and *Festivals and Funerals* (1971)—before founding her own publishing company, Bola Press. ("Bola" is a Yoruba word meaning successful.) From 1977 to 1983 Cortez was a writer in residence and a literature professor at Livingston College of Rutgers University.

Cortez's first volume, *Pisstained Stairs and the Monkey Man's Wares,* focuses mainly on music and the musician's significance to the black community. Love and the blues, drugs and the drudgery of ghetto life abound in this work. The much cited "How Long Has Trane Been Gone" is an example of the elegiac style of poetics popular in Cortez's work. The move toward political poetics surfaces in the title poem of Cortez's second volume, *Festivals and Funerals.* This collection confirms Cortez's desire to integrate African and American cultural signs into her poetry. Still, the need to actively pledge her allegiances does not deny Cortez a moment to self-reflect as in "I Would Like to Be Serene," where she reminds us that the geographies of the heart map a politics of love.

New York and Nigeria, Satchmo and Orisha coexist in Cortez's third volume of poetry, *Scarifications* (1973). The poems are full of the gritty and raw word concoctions that began in *Pisstained Stairs,* but they are more irreverent and less imitable. As the title suggests, *Scarifications* is littered with scabs and bumps, blood and tears, spit and sweat. Thus, the body and the city intersect with traditional and modern African emblems to create a surreal sensory extravaganza.

In *Mouth on Paper* (1977) Cortez stresses the significance of reading aloud by writing poems that come alive upon vocalization. The power of chanting becomes resoundingly obvious in this volume where repetition and rhythm birth orality and musicality. The title, *Mouth on Paper,* best describes Cortez's aesthetic expectations. In *Firespitter* (1982), Cortez continues the balancing act between the art on the page and art of the stage. The politics of gender are also significant in *Firespitter* as two of its most noted poems deal with violence against women: "If the Drum Is a Woman" and "Rape." These pieces exemplify not only Cortez's ability to do praise songs for our artists and political leaders but also her strength at depicting the unknown and unsung survivors of racial and sexual oppression. The uncompromising tone of these poems makes clear Cortez's position: the war against women must be fought and won. It was also in 1982 that Cortez published *There It Is,* her third album of poetry.

In 1984 Cortez published *Coagulations: New and Selected Poems.* One of the new poems, "Everything Is Wonderful," epitomizes Cortez's brand of sarcasm by enumerating exceptions to the title pronouncement. This poem and many others have been reprinted in anthologies and journals worldwide. Cortez's latest volume is entitled *Poetic Magnetic* (1991); recent collections featuring her work include *The Jazz Poetry Anthology* (1991) and *Every Shut Eye Ain't Asleep: An Anthology of Poetry by African Americans since 1945* (1994), edited by Yusef *Komunyakaa and Michael S. *Harper, respectively. In 1996, she published *Somewhere in Advance of Nowhere.*

In addition to publishing the majority of her books through Bola Press, Cortez has used the company for her sound recordings. After her first recording, *Celebrations and Solitudes* (1975), Bola Press issued all other accompanied readings: *Unsubmissive Blues* (1980), *There It Is* (1982), and *Maintain Control* (1986). [Her son Denardo Coleman and the band "The Firespitters" are the regular musicians on these recordings, and Ornette Coleman was a guest artist on *Maintain Control.*] Cortez's latest recording is *Everywhere Drums.*

Jayne Cortez's involvement in the Black Arts movement and her successful development of a jazz-poetry mediating between the likes of Amiri *Baraka and The Last Poets has earned her a definitive place in the African American literary tradition. Furthermore, her surrealist aesthetics and womanist ideology make Cortez's work acutely unique in its attempt to liberate black voices through artistic activism. Moving from the period of the Black Arts jazz-poetry of the 1960s and 1970s into the current cultural renaissance of music and letters in the 1980s and 1990s, Jayne Cortez's life suggests the performance art of a womanist-warrior-poet.

• D. H. Melhem, *Heroism in the New Black Poetry: Introductions and Interviews,* 1990. D.H. Melhem, "A *MELUS* Profile and Interview: Jayne Cortez," *MELUS* 21:1 (Spring 1996): 71–79. Kimberly N. Brown, "Of Poststructuralist Fallout, Scarification, and Blood Poems," in *Other Sisterhoods: Literary Theory and U.S. Women of Color,* ed. Sandra Kumamoto Stanley, 1998, pp. 63–85.

—Michelle J. Wilkinson

Cotillion, The. *The Cotillion, or One Good Bull Is Half the Herd* (1971), represents John O. *Killens's presentation of assimilation, classism, and self-hatred set in the 1970s. The book explores African American family traditions and the political and social ramifications that influence these customs.

In *The Cotillion,* Killens steps into a community of African Americans and explores their dark sides. This satirical novel attacks the classism and assimilation that dominated many African American communities. Killens's character Lumumba represents that breed of African Americans who attempt to redefine themselves by separating themselves from their Eurocentric standards. In contrast to Lumumba's ideology, there exists a community of women that symbolizes the vise-grip Eurocentricism has on the African American.

Although most criticism of *The Cotillion* dealt with the theme of Afrocentricity versus Eurocentricity, the text also has a strong commentary on African American adolescence. Yoruba is coming of age and experiencing an identity crisis concerning her blackness and sexuality: to be an African queen for her new love, Lumumba, or a girl with "bourgeois inconsistencies." She is a product of middle-class blacks who place higher value on how society perceives the adolescent from this upwardly mobile environment than on self-worth. Killens allows Yoruba's sexual awareness to become a part of her maturation as a woman and an individual. Killens demonstrates the impact of socialization on the sexual attitudes of middle-class blacks. He further implies that societal expectations and myths about African American women cause adolescents to think that only whores enjoy sex. As with Yoruba, most adolescents have been taught to fear sexual desires that involve sexual intercourse. Killens also asserts through Yoruba that coming of age for many adolescents is synonymous with becoming aware of their sexual identities which is in direct conflict with the views and values of their hypocritical communities.

Killens explores the impact of socialization on sexual attitudes of middle-class blacks. Societal expectations and myths about African American women cause Yoruba's mother in the text to think that only whores enjoy sex. He creates a character who society considers bourgeois and sexually repressed but who does not conform to such expectations. Creating such characters as Lumumba and Yoruba reaffirms Killens's goal of writing literature that revolves around social protest and cultural affirmation.

Killens creates a subplot in the text that further demonstrates his satirical examination of the inner workings of so-called middle-class African Americans. Through Yoruba and Lumumba, the reader must examine the conventions of Mrs. Youngblood, whose blood is "old" and sterile because she has accepted the conventions of white America as her own. Through these characters, Killens allows readers to examine the mirroring of characters with conventions and vice-versa. Killens gives readers Yoruba, who confronts the repressive beliefs brought on by racism and classism and accepts the love and affection of her male counterpart, as a model.

• Wanda C. Macon, "Adolescent Characters' Sexual Behavior in Selected Fiction of Six Twentieth Century African American Authors," PhD diss., Ohio State University, 1992, pp. 59–65 and 101–110.

—Wanda Macon

COTTER, JOSEPH SEAMON, JR. (1895–1919), poet, journalist, and forerunner of the African American cultural renaissance of the 1920s. Born in Louisville, Kentucky, son of the poet Joseph Seamon *Cotter, Sr., Joseph Seamon Cotter, Jr., in his brief life established himself as an accomplished and innovative voice amid the lively post–World War I American poetry scene. Avoiding the dialect poetic style of his father and of the family friend Paul Laurence *Dunbar, the younger Cotter experimented widely with modern free verse and traditional forms before his untimely death from tuberculosis at age twenty-three. Cotter's best-known work is his collection *The Band of Gideon* (1918), which was followed by the sonnet series "Out of the Shadows" (1920) and "Poems" (1921), the latter two published posthumously in the *A.M.E. Zion Quarterly Review.*

After graduation from Louisville Central High School in 1911, Cotter enrolled at Fisk University, where he worked on the *Fisk Herald,* a monthly published by the university literary societies. Apart from his precociously early reading in the family library, the work on the *Fisk Herald* represents the earliest documented sign of Cotter's literary predilections. During his second year at Fisk, Cotter had to return home to Louisville due to the onset of tuberculosis.

Upon his return home, Cotter accepted a position as an editor and writer for the Louisville newspaper the *Leader,* and he began to establish his brief yet brilliant career as poet. Grief over his sister's death inspired the early tribute "To Florence"; it remains one of his most moving poems. Precluded from military service in World War I because of his deteriorating physical condition but stimulated by his own interest and by the war service of a close friend, Cotter produced a number of poems, including "Sonnet to Negro Soldiers" and "O, Little David, Play on Your Harp," which place him among the best Great War poets.

Other notable poems of the *Gideon* collection include the title poem, which recalls the style of the traditional southern black preacher and seems to encode protest regarding the treatment of black World War I veterans. Among the best modernist free verse pieces are "The Mulatto to His Critics" and the provocative "Is It Because I Am Black," which dramatically interrogates those who would dismiss or patronize the African American narrator.

Outstanding among the poems appearing in the final *A.M.E. Zion* series is "Rain Music," which anticipates the rhythm, theme, and style of works of Langston *Hughes and other Harlem Renaissance poetic innovators. Also first published in the *Zion Quarterly* and, until recently, overlooked is Cotter's impressive nineteen-sonnet sequence "Out of the Shadows," which concludes with a moving evocation of a child dreamt of to fulfill the love celebrated in the sonnets. Cotter's posthumous publications also include the one-act World War I play "On the Fields of France," which appeared in the *Crisis* in 1920. With his lively experimentation in free verse and traditional forms, his use of natural idiom, and his sense of the brilliant potential of African American verbal expression, Joseph Seamon Cotter, Jr., clearly prefigures the 1920s African American cultural renaissance.

• Eugene B. Redmond, *Drumvoices: The Mission of Afro-American Poetry,* 1976, pp. 155–169. James Robert Payne, "Joseph Seamon Cotter, Jr.: Toward a Reconsideration," in *Joseph Seamon Cotter, Jr.: Complete Poems,* ed. James Robert Payne, 1990, pp. 1–22.

—James Robert Payne

COTTER, JOSEPH SEAMON, SR. (1861–1949), poet, fictionist, educator, and community leader. Born near Bardstown, Kentucky, Joseph Seamon Cotter had to leave school at age eight to work at a variety of jobs because of family financial exigencies. Cotter had been a precocious child, learning to read at the age of three from a mother who had the gifts, as Cotter wrote later, of "a poet, storyteller, a maker of plays." When Cotter was twenty-two the prominent Louisville educator William T. Peyton encouraged the promising young man to return to school. After some remediation and two night school sessions, Cotter was able to begin his teaching career. His first Louisville position was at the Western Colored School, where he began in 1889. He went on to a career of more than fifty years as teacher and administrator with the Louisville public schools. In 1891 Cotter married his fellow educator Maria F. Cox, with whom he had three children, including the important poet in his own right Joseph Seamon *Cotter, Jr.

Although known in his own time as a prominent educator and African American civic leader, as well as for his prolific authorship in varied genres, today Cotter is remembered primarily for his poetry. In his first collection, *A Rhyming* (1895), we see the young Cotter experimenting with varied poetic forms, including the traditional ballad and the Italian sonnet. Cotter's second book, *Links of Friendship* (1898), is another eclectic collection in varied forms that includes a poem on "The Negro's Loyalty" during the Spanish American War, a loyalty unswerving despite "the mob that puts me to the rack." The clear reference to lynchers who ravaged black America in Cotter's day belies the poet's reputation for silence about such painful American issues. A dialect piece in *Links* resulted from a visit by Paul Laurence *Dunbar to the Cotter family in 1894. The visit instigated several poetic exchanges between Dunbar and Cotter.

Cotter went on to publish three more collections of poetry, including the *Collected Poems of Joseph S. Cotter, Sr.* (1938) and the *Sequel to "The Pied Piper of Hamelin" and Other Poems* (1939), whose title poem, a response to Robert Browning's poem "The Pied Piper," is regarded as among Cotter's finest. Overall, as A. Russell Brooks has noted, *Sequel* may well be Cotter's most successful book.

Cotter's blank verse four-act play *Caleb, the Degenerate* (1903), which reflects views of Booker T. *Washington, is essentially closet drama, mainly of historical interest, as is the case with his other plays. Cotter's short story collection *Negro Tales* (1912) has received little attention; several of the stories may merit reappraisal. His pamphlet on the *Twenty-fifth Anniversary of the Founding of Colored Parkland or "Little Africa"* (1934) recalls Cotter's leadership in the formation of the Parkland African American community of Louisville in 1891. Cotter's final work, the miscellany *Negroes and Others at Work and Play* (1947), appeared two years before his death. Overall, it may be said that Joseph Seamon Cotter, Sr., provided a sustaining voice during one of the most difficult eras of African American history, and he was a man who backed his words with action in building the African American community.

• Ann Allen Shockley, "Joseph S. Cotter, Sr.: Biographical Sketch of a Black Louisville Bard," *CLA Journal* 18 (Mar. 1975): 327–340. A. Russell Brooks, "Joseph Seamon Cotter, Sr.," in *DLB*, vol. 50, *Afro-American Writers before the Harlem Renaissance,* eds. Trudier Harris and Thadious M. Davis, 1986, pp. 62–70.

—James Robert Payne

Cotton Comes to Harlem, Chester *Himes's sixth detective novel in a series of nine, all written after the author had left the United States for France, was first published in French by Plon under the title *Retour en Afrique* (1964) and later in the United States by G.P. Putnam's Sons as *Cotton Comes to Harlem* (1965). Considered by many critics to be Himes's best detective novel, *Cotton Comes to Harlem* was also produced as a Hollywood film by Samuel Goldwyn, Jr., in 1970, directed by Ossie *Davis.

The book opens with a scene of a rally in Harlem conducted by Reverend Deke O'Malley, ex-con and leader of a phony back to Africa movement. While in the process of amassing $87,000 from eighty-seven Harlem families, O'Malley's own operation is robbed by white gunmen. As in all of Himes's detective novels, images of pandemonium and absurd violence are vividly, and often comically, described. Himes's two detectives, *Coffin Ed Johnson and *Grave Digger Jones, pursue the missing $87,000, which winds up hidden in a bale of cotton. The thief, a white Southerner named Colonel Robert L. Calhoun, is promoting his own crooked repatriation scheme of sorts, a back-to-the-Southland crusade whereby urban African Americans would "return" to the South as paid agricultural laborers.

When Coffin Ed and Grave Digger finally apprehend Calhoun, they demand that he give them $87,000 from his own bank account to repay the eighty-seven Harlem families their hard-earned money. In the final comic irony of the novel, the original $87,000 turns up in the hands of junkman Uncle Bud, who uses it to move to Africa and buy five hundred cattle to exchange for one hundred wives, setting himself up as a latter-day Solomon. The comical juxtaposition of Calhoun's absurd back-to-the-Southland movement and O'Malley's corrupt back to Africa movement represents Himes's satirical commentary on repatriation in the modern era.

• Gilbert H. Muller, *Chester Himes*, 1989. Robert E. Skinner, *Two Guns from Harlem: The Detective Fiction of Chester Himes*, 1989.

—Wendy W. Walters

CRAFT, WILLIAM (c. 1826–1900) and **ELLEN** (1826–1891), escaped slaves, antislavery activists, and educators. William Craft authored *Running a Thousand Miles for Freedom* (1860), which chronicled his escape with his wife Ellen from Georgia to Boston in 1848, and their subsequent move to London after the passage of the Fugitive Slave Act (1850).

The Crafts were heralded for the brazen method of their escape. The fair-skinned Ellen disguised herself as an invalid white man, and William posed as "his" servant. They simply, and quite publicly, rode the train from Macon, Georgia, to Philadelphia, where they revealed themselves to a local abolitionist.

As Blyden Jackson has observed (*History of Afro-American Literature,* 1989), the Craft story was convincing and therefore useful for abolitionism. The narrative focuses mainly on the journey from Georgia to Philadelphia, and then from Boston to London, cultivating dramatic tension from its unsensational narrative style. Craft expertly presents memorable characters (such as the white gentleman who befriends the disguised Ellen and vouches for "his" ownership of William, allowing them to continue their journey) and memorable scenes (such as innkeepers realizing too late that they had mistakenly assumed Ellen was "white" when they let her a room). The narrative focus on tricking unsuspecting whites cultivates what William L. Andrews (*To Tell a Free*

Story, 1986) describes as "interstitiality," as the Crafts "temporarily confuse the lines separating sexual, racial and social classification."

Ellen's triple play on race, gender, and class passing has engaged recent critical interest. In its advertisement of successful passing, the Craft narrative initiates a tradition of literary explorations of passing, such as James Weldon *Johnson's The **Autobiography of an Ex-Colored Man* (1912), Nella *Larsen's **Passing* (1929), and George S. *Schuyler's **Black No More* (1931). William Craft's narrative is also significant, as Valerie Smith notes (*Self-Discovery and Authority in Afro-American Narrative,* 1987), because unlike most slave narratives by men, it presents the escape as a joint endeavor.

• Dorothy Sterling, *Black Foremothers,* 1979. Mary Ellen Doyle, "Slave Narratives As Rhetorical Art," in *The Art of the Slave Narrative,* eds. John Sekora and Darwin Turner, 1982, pp. 83–95. R. J. M. Blackett, *Beating against the Barriers,* 1986. Barbara McCaskill, "A Stamp on the Envelope Upside Down Means Love," in *Multicultural Literature and Literacies: Making Space for Difference,* eds. Suzanne Miller and Barbara McCaskill, 1993, pp. 77–102. Lindon Barrett, "Hand-Writing: Legibility and the White Body in *Running a Thousand Miles for Freedom, American Literature* 69 (June 1997): 315–36. R.J.M. Blackett, ed., *Running a Thousand Miles for Freedom,* 1999.

—Dana D. Nelson

CROUCH, STANLEY (b. 1945), jazz and cultural critic. Stanley Crouch was born in Los Angeles. His father was a heroin addict and his mother a hard-working domestic who taught him to read before he entered school. Although Crouch attended both East Los Angeles Junior College and Southwest Junior College, he never earned a degree. In effect, he is an autodidact and his work reflects the strengths and weaknesses of the untrained intellectual. During the 1960s, Crouch became enamored of black nationalism and the theater. He was well known in black nationalist circles and was an actor, director, and playwright. He also was a drummer leading his own jazz combo during these days, recording an album with Impulse Records called *Ain't No Ambulances for No Niggahs Tonight.* In the 1970s, Crouch, deeply influenced by the works of Ralph *Ellison and Albert *Murray, began to distance himself from the black nationalists. In 1975 he moved to New York and began to write for the *Village Voice*, an association that ended in 1988 when he punched out another *Voice* writer in an argument over rap music. Many of his *Voice* pieces were collected in his first book, *Notes of a Hanging Judge,* published in 1990. Crouch has subsequently won both the Whiting Writer's Prize and the MacArthur Fellowship. In 1996 he was finishing a long-awaited biography of jazz saxophonist Charlie *Parker, as well as a novel entitled "First Snow in Kokomo." Acerbic and withering in his critical attacks, Crouch is often characterized as a conservative or even a race traitor. He is placed with black thinkers critical of the civil rights movement in *Challenging the Civil Rights Establishment: Profiles of a New Black Vanguard* (1993) by Joseph G. Conti and Brad Stetson. Crouch sees himself in the tradition of Ellison and Murray, understanding black American life as rich and complex, not necessarily warped by white racism and completely disconnected from an African past. Moreover, he sees himself in the tradition of an H. L. Mencken or George S. *Schuyler as a satiric denouncer of all forms of cant, quackery, and nonsense. Crouch continues his iconoclastic writing on race and social values in *The All-American Skin Game* (1995) and *Always in Pursuit* (1993).

—Gerald Early

CRUMMELL, ALEXANDER (1819–1898), scholar, educator, lecturer, essayist, and Episcopal minister. Born in New York City to Charity and Boston Crummell, Alexander grew up in a family that placed great emphasis on freedom, independence, and education. Although his parents had not experienced the privilege of a formal education, they placed Alexander in the Mulberry Street School and hired additional private tutors for him. When Crummell decided to enter the priesthood, he applied for entry into the theological seminary of the Episcopal Church. According to Crummell's own account in his 1894 retirement address, "Shades and Lights," the admissions board denied his application because its policy was to exclude blacks from positions in the church hierarchy. Crummell was then forced to study privately with sympathetic clergy. These early studies shaped the stoic and methodical style that remained evident throughout his long career as writer and orator. Although he was ordained an Episcopal priest in 1844, it was not until 1847 that Crummell's dream of a formal education became reality. While in England raising funds for his New York mission, the Church of the Messiah, Crummell found English philanthropists who offered financial assistance for his education at Queen's College. When he received his AB degree in theology in 1853, Crummell found himself among a small number of formally accredited black scholars. It was not until after emancipation that African Americans entered into academia in significant numbers.

His studies completed, Crummell sailed for Liberia, where he spent nearly twenty years as missionary, educator, and statesman. After returning to the United States in 1873, he assumed the rectorship of St. Mary's Episcopal Church in Washington, D.C. Leaders such as Crummell now turned their attention to the question of how blacks would improve their lot in the hostile post-Reconstruction environment. As a public speaker and writer Crummell countered charges of black racial inferiority. In 1897, three years after his retirement from the ministry, Crummell spearheaded the establishment of the American Negro Academy, the first African American scholarly society in the United States. By the time of his death in 1898 Crummell had become the august statesman among black scholars and professionals. In his 1914 publication, *The Negro in American History,* black activist John Cromwell remembered Crummell as "easily the ripest literary scholar, the writer of the most graceful and faultless English and the most brilliant conversationalist the race has produced in this country."

As a writer Crummell was best known for his occasional sermons and his sociopolitical tracts. Traces of Crummell's activism are evident as early as 1840, when he participated in the New York Negro Convention Movement focusing on voting rights for blacks. While active as a young man in the antislavery movement and local political campaigns, Crummell's first collection of sermons and essays, *The Future of Africa,* was not published until 1862 during his Liberian residency. In his early years Crummell had renounced the idea of the removal of African Americans to Africa but altered his position during his stay in England. As a resident of Liberia, Crummell envisioned its future as an autonomous black nation. Consequently, Crummell campaigned actively for the colonization movement. *The Future of Africa* can be viewed as Crummell's treatise on what would later be called black nationalism. In this collection of ten essays Crummell traced the progress of Liberia, often echoing the nationalist propaganda of colonial American writers. Not unlike Cotton Mather's vision of America as a fulfillment of biblical prophecy, Crummell foresaw in Liberia the fulfillment of God's prophecy for the civilization of blacks. Just as Benjamin Franklin had encouraged industrious and hardworking men to seek their fortunes in America, Crummell in his essay "The Relations and Duties of Free Colored Men in America to Africa" recommended that those black men seeking their fortunes in Africa should be men with "high souls and lofty resolves," "men of force and energy," and most importantly, men with "strong moral proclivities." In "The Negro Race Not under a Curse," Crummell denounced the popular theological notion that blacks had been doomed by God's curse upon the descendants of Ham. In "Hope for Africa," he spoke of the "divine providence," which he deemed the promise of the "regeneration of Africa and her children."

In 1882 Crummell published *The Greatness of Christ*—a collection of sermons more religious in scope and ruminative in style than his earlier more political tract, *The Future of Africa.* With a vision akin to that of the transcendentalists and romantics, Crummell merged his logical rhetorical style with his spiritual vision. In his sermon "Joseph," Crummell examined man's metaphysical relationship with nature and God, suggesting that "the natural is the sign and symbol of the spiritual; for all things go by doubles in God's system." Similarly, in the sermon "The Greatness of Christ," he drew parallels between occurrences in nature and those in human development. Unfailingly, Crummell guided his contemplations of the abstract back to real-world considerations. In "Joseph," Crummell juxtaposed the condition of the biblical Joseph and that of African Americans. In "The Destined Superiority of the Negro" he constructed a biblical typology that served as political rhetoric. In Crummell's estimation African Americans were a prototype of the emancipated Hebrews who eventually emerged out of Egypt stronger than the nation that had dominated them.

In his 1891 treatise, *Africa and America,* Crummell returned to more immediate and worldly themes. These essays and addresses illustrate the pressing concerns of African Americans in post-Reconstruction America—the abuse of black women in the South at the hands of the white male ruling class, the prevailing presence of racial discrimination in the postwar era, and the problem of labor and education for the emancipated African Americans (verifying the existence of a discourse among black leaders long before the Booker T. *Washington–W. E. B. *Du Bois debate on classical versus industrial education for blacks).

Collectively, the writings of Alexander Crummell not only reveal the political, social, and spiritual concerns of a nineteenth-century African American but they also represent part of the framework from which modern-day African American political rhetoric has developed. Crummell's practice of countering racism and discrimination through the application of historical and scientific information would be adopted by turn-of-the-century African American scholars who followed his example of turning scholarship into a weapon for political and social activism.

• Alfred A. Moss, Jr., *The American Negro Academy*, 1981. Wilson Jeremiah Moses, *Black Messiahs and Uncle Tom,* 1982. Alfred A. Moss, Jr., "Alexander Crummell: Black Nationalist and Apostle of Western Civilization," in *Black Leaders of the Nineteenth Century,* eds. Leon Litwack and August Meier, 1988, pp. 237–251. Wilson Jeremiah Moses, *Alexander Crummell: A Study of Civilization and Discontent,* 1989. J. R. Oldfield, *Alexander Crummell and the Creation of an African-American Church in Liberia,* 1990.

—Elizabeth J. West

CULLEN, COUNTEE (1903–1946), poet, anthologist, novelist, translator, children's writer, and playwright. Countee Cullen is something of a mysterious figure. He was born 30 March 1903, but it has been difficult for scholars to place exactly where he was born, with whom he spent the very earliest years of his childhood, and where he spent them. New York City and Baltimore have been given as birthplaces. Cullen himself, on his college transcript at New York University, lists Louisville, Kentucky, as his place of birth. A few years later, when he had achieved considerable literary fame during the era known as the New Negro or Harlem Renaissance, he was to assert that his birthplace was New York City, which he continued to claim for the rest of his life. Cullen's second wife, Ida, and some of his closest friends, including Langston *Hughes and Harold Jackman, said that Cullen was born in Louisville. As James

Weldon *Johnson wrote of Cullen in *The Book of American Negro Poetry* (rev. ed., 1931): "There is not much to say about these earlier years of Cullen—unless he himself should say it." And Cullen—revealing a temperament that was not exactly secretive but private, less a matter of modesty than a tendency toward being encoded and tactful—never in his life said anything more clarifying.

Sometime before 1918, Cullen was adopted by the Reverend Frederick A. and Carolyn Belle (Mitchell) Cullen. It is impossible to state with certainty how old Cullen was when he was adopted or how long he knew the Cullens before he was adopted. Apparently he went by the name of Countee Porter until 1918. By 1921 he became Countee P. Cullen and eventually just Countee Cullen. According to Harold Jackman, Cullen's adoption was never "official." That is to say it was never consummated through proper state-agency channels. Indeed, it is difficult to know if Cullen was ever legally an orphan at any stage in his childhood.

Frederick Cullen was a pioneer black activist minister. He established his Salem Methodist Episcopal Church in a storefront mission upon his arrival in New York City in 1902, and in 1924 moved the Church to the site of a former white church in Harlem where he could boast of a membership of more than twenty-five hundred. Countee Cullen himself stated in *Caroling Dusk* (1927) that he was "reared in the conservative atmosphere of a Methodist parsonage," and it is clear that his foster father was a particularly strong influence. The two men were very close, often traveling abroad together. But as Cullen evidences a decided unease in his poetry over his strong and conservative Christian training and the attraction of his pagan inclinations, his feelings about his father may have been somewhat ambivalent. On the one hand, Frederick Cullen was a puritanical Christian patriarch, and Cullen was never remotely that in his life. On the other hand, it has been suggested that Frederick Cullen was also something of an effeminate man. (He was dressed in girl's clothing by his poverty-stricken mother well beyond the acceptable boyhood age for such transvestism.) That Cullen was homosexual or of a decidedly ambiguous sexual nature may also be attributable to his foster father's contrary influence as both fire-breathing Christian and latent homosexual.

Cullen was an outstanding student at DeWitt Clinton High School (1918–1921). He edited the school's newspaper, assisted in editing the literary magazine, *Magpie,* and began to write poetry that achieved notice. While in high school Cullen won his first contest, a citywide competition, with the poem "I Have a Rendezvous with Life," a nonracial poem inspired by Alan Seeger's "I Have a Rendezvous with Death." At New York University (1921–1925), he wrote most of the poems for his first three volumes: **Color* (1925), *Copper Sun* (1927), and *The Ballad of the Brown Girl* (1927). If any event signaled the coming of the Harlem Renaissance, it was the precocious success of this rather shy black boy who, more than any other black literary figure of his generation, was being touted and bred to become a major crossover literary figure. Here was a black man with considerable academic training who could, in effect, write "white" verse—ballads, sonnets, quatrains, and the like—much in the manner of Keats and the British Romantics (albeit, on more than one occasion, tinged with racial concerns) with genuine skill and compelling power. He was certainly not the first Negro to attempt to write such verse but he was first to do so with such extensive education and with such a complete understanding of himself as a poet. Only two other black American poets before Cullen could be taken so seriously as self-consciously considered and proficient poets: Phillis *Wheatley and Paul Laurence *Dunbar. If the aim of the Harlem Renaissance was, in part, the reinvention of the native-born Negro as a being who can be assimilated while decidedly retaining something called "a racial self-consciousness," then Cullen fit the bill. If "I Have a Rendezvous with Life" was the opening salvo in the making of Cullen's literary reputation, then the 1924 publication of "Shroud of Color" in H. L. Mencken's *American Mercury* confirmed the advent of the black boy wonder as one of the most exciting American poets on the scene. After graduating Phi Beta Kappa from NYU, Cullen earned a master's degree in English and French from Harvard (1925–1927). Between high school and his graduation from Harvard, Cullen was the most popular black poet and virtually the most popular black literary figure in America. One of Cullen's poems and his popular column in *Opportunity* inspired A'Leila Walker—heiress of Madame C. J. Walker's hair-care products fortune and owner of a salon where the black and white literati gathered in the late 1920s—to name her salon "The Dark Tower."

Cullen won more major literary prizes than any other black writer of the 1920s: first prize in the Witter Bynner Poetry contest in 1925, *Poetry* magazine's John Reed Memorial Prize, the Amy Spingarn Award of the *Crisis* magazine, second prize in *Opportunity* magazine's first poetry contest, and second prize in the poetry contest of *Palms.* In addition, he was the second black to win a Guggenheim Fellowship.

Cullen was also at the center of one of the major social events of the Harlem Renaissance: On 9 April 1928 he married Yolande Du Bois, only child of W. E. B. *Du Bois, in one of the most lavish weddings in black New York history. This wedding was to symbolize the union of the grand black intellectual patriarch and the new breed of younger Negroes who were responsible for much of the excitement of the Renaissance. It was an apt meshing of personalities as Cullen and Du Bois were both conservative by nature and ardent traditionalists. That the marriage turned out so disastrously and ended so quickly (they divorced in 1930) probably adversely affected Cullen, who remarried in 1940. In 1929, Cullen published *The Black Christ and Other Poems* to less than his accustomed glowing reviews. He was bitterly disappointed that *The Black Christ,* his longest and in many respects most complicated poem, was considered by most critics and reviewers to be his weakest and least distinguished.

From the 1930s until his death, Cullen wrote a great deal less, partly hampered by his job as a French teacher at Frederick Douglass Junior High. (His most famous student was James *Baldwin.) But he wrote noteworthy, even significant work in a number of genres. His novel *One Way to Heaven,* published in 1934, rates as one of the better black satires and is one of the three important fictional retrospectives of the Harlem Renaissance, the others being Wallace *Thurman's *Infants of the Spring* and George S. *Schuyler's **Black No More.* Cullen's *The Medea* is the first major translation of a classical work by a twentieth-century black American writer. Cullen's contributions to children's literature, *The Lost Zoo* and *Christopher Cat,* are among the more clever and engaging books of children's verse, written at a time when there was not much published in this area by black writers. He also completed perhaps some of his best, certainly some of his more darkly complex, sonnets. He was also working on a musical with Arna *Bontemps called *St. Louis Woman* (based on Bontemps's novel *God Sends Sunday*) at the time of his death from high blood pressure and uremic poisoning on 9 January 1946.

For many years after his death, Cullen's reputation was eclipsed by that of other Harlem Renaissance writers, particularly Langston Hughes and Zora Neale *Hurston, and his work had gone out of print. In the last few years, however, there has been a resurgence of interest in Cullen's life and work and his writings are being reissued.

• Blanche E. Ferguson, *Countee Cullen and the Negro Renaissance,* 1966. Margaret Perry, *A Bio-Bibliography of Countee P. Cullen, 1903–1946,* 1966. Arna Bontemps, ed., *The Harlem Renaissance Remembered,* 1972. Arthur P. Davis, *From the Dark Tower: Afro-American Writers, 1900 to 1960,* 1974. Alan R. Shucard, *Countee Cullen,* 1984. Gerald Early, ed., *My Soul's High Song: The Collected Writings of Countee Cullen, Voice of the Harlem Renaissance,* 1991.

—Gerald Early

CUNEY-HARE, MAUD (1874–1936), concert pianist, music lecturer, folklorist, and historian. Maud Cuney-Hare is remembered for her literary accomplishments as a gifted playwright, biographer, and music columnist for the *Crisis.* Born in Galveston, Texas, on 16 February 1874, to teacher and soprano Adelina Dowdie and Norris Wright Cuney, an important Texas political figure who was the (defeated) Republican candidate for the 1875 Galveston mayoral race, Maud Cuney-Hare was educated in Texas and became musical director at the Deaf, Dumb and Blind Institute in Austin, Texas. She held other church and college teaching positions before returning to Boston and devoting her life to performance, scholarship, and literary pursuits. She championed the 24 May 1917 Cambridge, Massachusetts, restaging of Angelina Weld *Grimké's *Rachel* (1916), which, according to critic Robert Fehrenbach was "the first time a play written by an Afro-American that dealt with the real problems facing American Blacks in contemporary, white, racist society was performed by entirely Black companies." The biography she wrote about her father, *Norris Wright Cuney: Tribune of the Black People* (1913), suggests that he was instrumental in encouraging self-respect, courage, and resistance in his daughter, themes that emerge in her play, *Antar of Araby.* The biography reveals that while she was a student at the New England Conservatory of Music in Boston, the executive committee of the conservatory wrote Norris Cuney a letter, asking that he find another place for his daughter to live, explaining, "We have a large number of pupils who are affected by race prejudices, and the Home must be conducted so as to insure the comfort and satisfaction of the largest number possible." Not only was her father's response heated and unequivocal but the incident galvanized students at nearby Harvard as well; W. E. B. *Du Bois (at one time engaged to Maud Cuney, before her marriage to William Hare in 1906) has written of how he was one of a group of Harvard students who "rushed to her defense when the New England Conservatory of Music tried to 'Jim Crow' her in the dormitory." Cuney-Hare edited an anthology of nature poems, *The Message of the Trees: An Anthology of Leaves and Branches* (1918). A collector of folk songs and dances, she traveled to Cuba, the Virgin Islands, Haiti, Puerto Rico, and Mexico documenting the African sources for much European and world music, among these, the Moorish origins of the Spanish fandango in Spain and the Afro-Cuban sources of the Haitian Méringüe. "History and Song in the Virgin Islands," a 1993 essay she wrote for the *Crisis,* includes a riveting account of the 1848 slave insurrection of Saint Croix, when more than five thousand slaves "stormed the fort and demanded freedom," later burning the town down. Cuney-Hare documents the song "Queen Mary," named for "an intrepid woman slave [who] was the Joan of Arc of the rebellion." Her play *Antar of Araby* (1929) borrows from foreign legend to recount a story of a man, enslaved by his own father, whose dark skin and inferior social status are impediments to the fulfillment of his talents, his happiness, and his marriage to the woman he loves. Clearly influenced by Shakespeare's diction and themes, the drama pivots on Prince Shedad's belated recognition of Antar's worth. King Zoheir eventually blesses Antar with the words, "God protect thee, thou black in face and fair in deeds." In warrior service to the king, Antar discovers the royal lineage of his own mother, thus entitling him by rank to compete for his beloved Abla, the Arab chieftain's daughter; the power of the play, however, lies in the fact that his new social status is of little concern to Abla, who declares her unwavering love for Antar while he is still a slave. Maud Cuney-Hare died of cancer 13 February 1936, one month after the publication of her last major work, *Negro Musicians and Their Music.* The study notes African sources for African American music, with a particularly interesting section on spirituals as hymns of consolation and coded means of communication; it includes a carefully researched appendix of African musical instruments. Maud Cuney-Hare has left an important legacy; she was instrumental in establishing and documenting a musical and theatrical arts movement in Black America.

—Lynda Koolish

D

DANNER, MARGARET ESSE (1915–1984), poet and community activist. Born in Pryorsburg, Kentucky, Margaret Esse Danner spent her later youth in Chicago, where she also attended college at Loyola University and Northwestern University. Although she had been writing in the 1940s, and in 1945 had received an award at the poetry workshop of the Midwestern Writers Conference, her work began to receive widespread attention in the early 1950s, when she was awarded the John Hay Whitney Fellowship for "Far From Africa: Four Poems." This work was published in *Poetry* magazine in 1951, and Danner went on to become the first African American to work as an editor for the same magazine in 1956. She was poet in residence at Wayne State University in 1961 and later at Virginia Union State University. In the early 1960s Danner joined other activists in Detroit to start Boone House for the Arts. She made a long-anticipated trip to Africa in 1966, where she presented her work at the World Exposition of Negro Arts in Dakar, Senegal. During the 1970s, Danner worked as poet in residence at LeMoyne-Owen College in Memphis, Tennessee. In 1973 she and many other noted African American women poets read their work at the Phillis Wheatley Poetry Festival. Danner worked collaboratively with Dudley *Randall to publish *Poem Counterpoem* (1966). Danner's other published collections are *To Flower* (1962); *Impressions of African Art Forms* (1968, including poems originally published in the 1950s); *Iron Lace* (1968); *The Down of a Thistle: Selected Poems, Prose Poems, and Songs* (1976).

When Danner wrote a short preface to her poetry for Addison *Gayle, Jr.'s interpretive anthology *The Forerunners: Black Poets in America* (1975), she placed her work in the long historical trajectory of African experience and influence: "I have lived long enough to see black poets applying a degree of honesty that augurs well for the salvation of the individuality of one's artistic endeavor." In her black contemporaries Danner found "the same aesthetic excellence that created the Benin Bronze and the Pyramids is still active today. . . . As for my poetry: I believe that my dharma is to prove that the Force for Good takes precedence over the force for evil in mankind. To the extent that my poetry adheres to this purpose it will endure."

Gayle, an important spokesman for the Black Aesthetic, considered Danner a key transitional, or "bridge," writer in African American literature, claiming her as one representative example of post-renaissance (e.g., Harlem; Chicago) African American artists who were shifting away from literature of "reaction" or "service." Instead Gayle and other Black Aesthetic critics saw in Danner an emerging Africa-based voice of "Blackness," citing especially her extensive use of complex metaphor, imagery, and symbolism based in African history and aesthetic tradition. Gayle called Danner a "literary godparent" to later, more nationalistic and/or Afrocentric poets. Interestingly, and in some contrast to this assessment, her work is listed among the "lyric" (as opposed to "social") poets in other treatments of African American literary history.

Danner's work is not only notable for its creative appropriation of African and Caribbean experience (e.g., "And through the Caribbean Sea"), but also for its pervasive, often ironic, inclusion of political metaphor. She uses, for example, metaphoric images of "prison" in her work to emphasize the artistic containment of African American writers/artists by the aesthetic expectations of white culture. Her poetry also expresses moments of ironic critique of Black Nationalist racial politics (e.g., "The Rhetoric of Langston Hughes," or "A Grandson in Hoticeberg") but balances this critique with intricately developed metaphoric, often "essentialist," celebrations of African history and Pan-African identity. Poems here often emphasize the displacement that occurs in translating African tradition to Western culture (e.g., "Etta Moten's Attic," and "Dance of the Abakweta"). Much of her work also directly confronts white racism, along with what she suggests is the spirit-defying political aesthetic of Western literary tradition (e.g., "Garnishing the Aviary," "The Visit of the Professor of Aesthetics," and "Best Loved of Africa").

In Danner's 1966 poetic dialogue with Dudley Randall (*Poem Counterpoem*), the complexity of artistic, political, and spiritual content in her work is very much evident. She was at that time a Baha'i, and in one poetic response to Randall's poem "Ballad of Birmingham," she writes, in "Passive Resistance," of the deep challenge of nonviolent political postures, suggesting in the possible irony of her work that the tactic may be spiritually and morally suspect. This is just one example of the way much of her work is situated within the political and aesthetic debates of the 1960s yet speaks to issues of continued importance.

• Addison Gayle, Jr., ed., *The Black Aesthetic,* 1971. Don L. Lee, "Toward a Definition: Black Poetry of the Sixties (After Leroi Jones)," in *The Black Aesthetic,* ed. Addison Gayle, Jr., 1971, pp. 222–233. Dudley Randall, *The Black Poets,* 1971.

—Sharon Carson

DAVENPORT, DORIS (b. 1949), performance poet, writer, educator, and Georgia Council for the Arts/Individual Artist Award recipient. Born in Gainesville, Georgia, Doris Davenport was the oldest of seven children of working-class parents. The poetry Davenport writes is honest, unapologetic, satirical, and almost always woman-centered. Refusing to be restricted by a singular definition, Davenport embraces multiple identities and refers to herself as an Appalachian, southern, African American, lesbian-feminist, two-headed woman, daughter of Chango and Oya (gods from the west African Yoruba pantheon religion). As Davenport says, "Poetry has a function like air; it is necessary."

Exposing ills inherent in our society and ridiculing contradictions is Davenport's agenda, the thread that runs through her poetry. Influenced primarily by the African American communities in northeast Georgia, Davenport counts as her literary mentors Zora Neale *Hurston, Langston *Hughes, Toni *Morrison, and Nikki *Giovanni. Her first two poetry collections, *It's Like This* (1980) and *Eat Thunder & Drink Rain* (1983) are very personal and mostly explore relationships.

In *It's Like This,* davenport establishes her feminist focus in the poem "Vision I: Genesis for Wimmin of Color." She examines the U.S. social-racial landscape that attempts to obliterate African American women. As an insurgent poet, Davenport makes readers see that which is often overlooked. She knows African American "wimmin's" reality is much more than the popular stereotype.

In *Eat Thunder & Drink Rain,* no one is exempt from Davenport's critical eye. The poems have as themes love and breaking up, as in "I Despise Mushy Sentimental Lovesick Lesbian Poetry Worse Than I Do Backgammon But (for SM)," to "All The Way Live," and "Isa Said," which are reminiscent of Langston Hughes's blues poems. Many of the poems explore lesbian relationships, but even here Davenport challenges the fallacies, as in "Dogmatic Dykes." This poem deftly engages lesbians who don traditional patriarchal roles. As with other poems, Davenport doesn't merely condemn, she asks questions, such as "when will the real wimmin / appear?" forcing accusers and readers to move ahead.

An iconoclastic visionary, Doris Davenport celebrates the oral tradition. Her words leap off the page and caress or grate the reader's ear. Her use of African American vernacular recalls Ntozake *Shange's poetry, but hers is a friendlier voice, southern, slow-paced, intimate. This quality is most striking in "Miz Anna—On Death" from *Voodoo Chile* (1991).

Her work recalls Audre *Lorde, the African American lesbian poet. Although Lorde's cerebral, interior style differs from Davenport's, they share a philosophical outlook: the intersection of personal and political voices. The poem "interlude" from Davenport's latest volume aptly encapsulates her poetic intent and situates her firmly among the griots of our time. This succinct poem has an urgent tone that engages readers in dialogue. Her poetic is clearly informed by call and response, a motif still evident in African American churches, theater, and music traditions.

Voodoo Chile and *Chango's Daughter,* an autobiography in progress, connect Davenport to her African religious roots, which have been distorted in this society. Similar to the revolutionary stance of the 1960s, when African Americans claimed the word "black" to identify themselves and reinvested it with positive attributes, Davenport restores African American ethos to a place of honor by claiming voodoo and Chango.

A critic and scholar, Davenport has a PhD in literature from the University of Southern California (1985), an MA in English from the State University of New York, Buffalo (1971), and a BA in English from Paine College, Augusta, Georgia (1969). She has taught at several colleges, including the University of North Carolina at Charlotte, the University of Oklahoma, and Bowling Green State. She has reviewed many literary texts and has written numerous articles on pedagogy, African American "wimmin" poetry, and lesbian themes. Her poems have been published in several journals, including *Azalea, Matrix, Feminary, Callaloo, Black American Literature Forum,* and *Catalyst.*

As of mid-1996, Doris Davenport resides in Sautee, Georgia, where she is a freelance writer and performance poet very much in demand.

—Opal Palmer Adisa

David Walker's Appeal. First published in pamphlet form in Boston, Massachusetts, in September of 1829, *David Walker's Appeal,* the full title of which is *David Walker's Appeal. In Four Articles; Together with a Preamble to the Coloured Citizens of the World, but in Particular, and Very Expressly, to Those of the United States of America,* was a bold attack on American slavery. The initial printing may have totaled only a few hundred copies, but before its author's death in 1830, the pamphlet had gone through three editions and had been circulated not only among abolitionists in the North but among blacks in the South as well. The *Appeal* coupled an unsparing critique of the United States's hypocrisy in sanctioning chattel slavery with an incendiary call to blacks, both slave and free, to resist slavery, actively and, if need be, violently.

Owing to the fact that his mother was a free woman, David *Walker (1785–1830), was born legally free in Wilmington, North Carolina. After traveling extensively through the South as a young man, during which time he confirmed to himself the pervasive misery of blacks under slavery, Walker came to Boston, where he established a clothing store in 1827 and became active in abolitionist circles, working as the Boston agent for the New York abolitionist weeklies, *Freedom's Journal* and *Rights of All.* Walker's experience in the South, his involvement with abolitionism, and his considerable reading contributed to his authoring of his *Appeal.*

The *Appeal* consists of a preamble and four articles. In each of the articles Walker argued that the "wretchedness" of black populations is a "consequence," respectively, of: slavery in the United States, which he charged, was more degrading than any form of slavery the world had seen; ignorance, or the denial of education to blacks; religion, specifically the teachings and actions of Christian preachers; and colonization, in particular the arguments by Henry Clay in favor of removing blacks from the United States. A scathing jeremiad in its tone, the *Appeal* repeatedly warned whites of the retribution to come should they persist in the enslavement and degradation of blacks. At the same time, it chastised blacks for their complicity in their own bondage via a willingness to content themselves with meager material satisfaction and smatterings of learning. Throughout, Walker crafted his critique with an eye to refuting claims of innate black inferiority, taking on directly Thomas Jefferson's *Notes on the State of Virginia* (1787). The *Appeal* also took the nation to task by contrasting the words of the Declaration of Independence with whites' treatment of enslaved African Americans.

Although the *Appeal* was widely denounced, Walker's efforts at broad distribution through the mails and clandestine couriers successfully placed his pamphlet in southern cities in Georgia, Virginia, Louisiana, and North Carolina. In many of these states, response to the pamphlet between 1829 and 1831 took the form of legislation that outlawed the teaching of slaves to read and write, prohibited the public assembly of free blacks, and criminalized the dissemination of antislavery materials. Although scholars have not been able to link the *Appeal* conclusively to the Nat *Turner insurrection of 1831, its prominence in radical abolitionism is unquestionable. Among black abolitionists the *Appeal* remained influential. In 1848, the *Appeal* was republished with Henry Highland *Garnet's *An Address to the Slaves of the United States.*

• Herbert Aptheker, "One Continual Cry": *David Walker's Appeal to the Colored Citizens of the World (1829–1830), Its Setting and Its Meaning,* 1965. Vincent Harding, *There Is a River: The Black Struggle for Freedom in America,* 1981. Wilson Jeremiah Moses, *Black Messiahs and Uncle Toms: Social and Literary Manipulations of a Religious Myth,* 1982. James Turner, introduction to *David Walker's Appeal,* 1993.

—Kenneth W. Warren

DAVIS, FRANK MARSHALL (1905–1987), poet, journalist, and autobiographer. During the Depression and World War II, Frank Marshall Davis was arguably one of the most distinctive poetic voices confronting W. E. B *Du Bois's profound metaphor of African American double consciousness. Complementing a career that produced four collections of poetry was one as a foremost journalist, from 1930 to 1955. Through the "objective" view of a newspaperman and the "subjective" vision of a poet, Davis struggled valiantly to harmonize Du Bois's dilemma of the color line.

Frank Marshall Davis was born on 31 December 1905 in Arkansas City, Kansas, "... a yawn town fifty miles south of Wichita, five miles north of Oklahoma, and east and west of nowhere worth remembering" (*Livin' the Blues*). His mention of interracial schools suggested a harmonious small-town life; the reality, however, barely concealed deeper racial tensions. Housing, jobs, movie theaters, and all facets of life were tacitly divided by the color line. Retrospectively, he describes his life in "Ark City" as suspended uncertainly in limbo, between the worlds of Euro- and African Americans.

At Kansas State College, Davis nurtured his twin passions of journalism and poetry from 1923 to 1926 and again from 1929 to 1930. His successful careers as newsman and poet rendered unimportant the fact that he never received a baccalaureate degree. For over thirty years he served as editor, managing editor, executive editor, feature writer, editorial writer, correspondent, sports reporter, theater and music critic, contributing editor, and fiction writer for the Chicago *Evening Bulletin,* Chicago *Whip,* Gary (Ind.) *American,* Atlanta *World,* Chicago *Star,* the Associated Negro Press, *Negro Digest,* and the Honolulu *Record.* In a rather difficult period for publishing African American poetry, he brought out *Black Man's Verse* (1935), *I Am the American Negro* (1937), *Through Sepia Eyes* (1938), and *47th Street: Poems* (1948). These two modes of self-expression effectively placed him in a unique position to observe African American cultural development and to advocate social change.

Davis's various news writings generally challenged such persistent lies as the position that African Americans had no cultural past and therefore had contributed very little to American cultural development. In this case, Davis made "Rating the Records" and "Things Theatrical," two of his weekly features for the Associated Negro Press, collectively imply a composite history of African American music. The social consequences of this strategy were enormous. The columns demonstrated West African roots of African American music; provided, in their promotion of racially integrated bands, a model for American society to aspire to; and demonstrated African Americans' contributions to American cultural distinctiveness.

Davis found poetry to be a complementary mode of self-expression. Esteemed critics like Harriet Monroe, Stephen Vincent Benét, Alain *Locke, and Sterling A. *Brown perceived much to celebrate in Davis's poetry. In *Black Man's Verse* (1935), they saw "authentic inspiration," technical innovation, wonderfully realistic portraiture, and vivid images. Davis's verse is characterized by robust statements of urban themes, a fierce social consciousness, a strong declamatory voice, and an almost rabid racial pride. Technically, he found free verse to be the best form to "contain" his thought since, like jazz and improvisation, it represented a rebellion against conventional or standardized forms of poetry. Davis's poem "Lynching," for instance, offers "stage" directions for performing the poem to the accompaniment of orchestral music. But the experiment with music, mood, and language did not consistently win critical approval. Other Davis poems sometimes invited disagreement about whether they achieved epic sweep or simple oratory.

By moving to Hawaii in 1948, Davis removed himself from the vortex of civil rights and labor activity on the mainland. The larger significance of his relocation was that it took him away from his best chance for a sustained literary career. In 1973 Davis rose from the depths of historical anonymity when Dudley *Randall, Stephen Henderson, and Margaret Taylor Goss *Burroughs brought him to the attention of the younger, Black Arts poets. From that time until his death in 1987, Davis enjoyed a brief celebrity. His older poems were reprinted; he also wrote, in addition to new poems, three autobiographical narratives, including *Livin' the Blues* (1992), "That Incredible Waikiki Jungle," and *Sex Rebel: Black* (1968).

The recovery of Davis's life and work has profound significance for redrawing traditional boundaries of African American literary history and cultural criticism. Guided by Alain Locke's designation of "newer Negro," Davis assists us in extending the usual geographical site and era for the so-called Harlem Renaissance. At the same time, his discovery by the 1960s Black Arts movement causes us to reconsider the conflicted relationship of younger writers to their literary ancestors. Finally, as we seek to understand more fully the age of the Depression and World War II, cultural critics will find Davis's wide-ranging news writing to be indispensable.

• W. E. B. Du Bois, *The Souls of Black Folk,* 1903. Alain Locke, "Deep River: Deeper Sea: Retrospective Review of the Literature of the Negro for 1935," *Opportunity* 14 (1936): 6–10. Harriet Monroe, review of *Black Man's Verse, Poetry: A Magazine of Verse,* 48.5 (1936): 293–295. Jean Wagner, *Black Poets of the United States,* 1973. Frank Marshall Davis, "Mystery Man: An Interview with Frank Marshall Davis," interview by Dudley Randall, *Black World* 23.3 (1974): 37–48. Frank Marshall Davis, *Livin' the Blues: Memoirs of a Black Journalist and Poet,* ed. John Edgar Tidwell, 1992. Langston Hughes, "Chicago's South Side Comes Alive," review of *47th Street: Poems,* Associated Negro Press News Release, 18 Aug. 1948, 4–5. Special Issue on Frank Marshall Davis, *Langston Hughes Review* 14 (Spring-Fall 1996).

—John Edgar Tidwell

DAVIS, MILES (1926–1991), jazz trumpeter and bandleader. Miles Davis's musical legacy is a haunting muted tone on ballads, the selection of complementary sidemen, and a visionary genius that placed him at the forefront of jazz's epochal stages including bop, cool, hard bop, third stream, and fusion. His accomplishments include the groundbreaking nonet sessions known as the *Birth of the Cool* (1949); the modal *Kind of Blue* (1959); the collaborations with arranger Gil Evans in *Porgy and Bess* (1958) and *Sketches of Spain* (1960); and the use of electronic instrumentation and improvisation on the best-selling *Bitches Brew* (1969). Davis also scored the Louis Malle film *Ascenseur Pour L'Echafaud* (1957).

Davis's arresting trumpet style, lyrical and elliptical, and his complicated public persona made him a living legend. His good looks and sartorial elegance, his taste for Ferraris and beautiful women, his boxing avocation, and his abhorrence of nostalgia and sentimentality projected a quintessentially hip image. The sobriquet "Prince of Darkness" identified the contradictory aspects of his personality, an exquisite musical sensibility and a brooding, volatile temperament. Davis was fascinated and repelled by a mixture of hauteur, mystery, and aloofness. He turned his back on audiences and failed to introduce sidemen. This refusal to ingratiate himself to a largely white public was a pointed criticism of African American entertainers who mugged and clowned and made Davis an early representative of black nationalism. In 1959 Davis was beaten by a white policeman enraged at seeing him with a white woman. The incident received international attention and became emblematic of American racism. That same year Davis was interviewed by Alex *Haley for *Playboy,* inaugurating the magazine's famous feature, and confirming Davis as an outspoken critic of racism. Davis's persistent ability to refashion himself fired the public imagination and made him a compelling figure throughout his forty-year career.

• Jack Chambers, *Milestones: The Music and Times of Miles Davis,* 1989. Miles Davis with Quincy Troupe, *Miles: The Autobiography,* 1989.

—Marcela Breton

DAVIS, OSSIE (b. 1917), playwright, actor, film director, and author of young adult fiction. Born in Cogsdell, Georgia, Ossie Davis grew up in nearby Waycross. He studied at Howard University for three years, then traveled to New York to pursue a career in the theater. With the encouragement of Alain *Locke, Davis obtained a position with the Rose McClendon Players of Harlem, while writing in his spare time. The following year, he joined the U.S. Army, serving in the Medical Corps and in Special Services. While stationed in Liberia, he wrote and produced *Goldbrickers of 1944,* a musical variety show. Discharged in 1945, Davis returned to New York and gained the lead role in the play *Jeb,* which propelled his stage career. Also starring in the play was Davis's future wife, Ruby Dee, with whom he would continue to costar in plays and later in film. Among Davis's stage, film, and television credits are *The Joe Louis Story* (1953), *The Fugitive* (1966), *Do the Right Thing* (1989), and *Kings on the Hill* (1993). Davis is recognized as a political activist dedicated to the civil rights movement, and he acted as master of ceremonies for the March on Washington (1963).

Davis is best known as the creator of *Purlie Victorious* (1961), a three-act comedy which was later adapted as the feature film, *Gone Are the Days* (1963), and as the musical *Purlie* (1970). This satirical depiction of traditional southern racial relations tells the story of a black preacher who successfully vies to procure five hundred dollars from a white plantation owner to contribute to initiating an integrated church in a black community. Its mordant yet humorous representations of southern life make it clear that the issues of the play expand beyond the borders of its fictional setting, Cocthipee County. The play probes the racism of the Jim Crow South and the nation, and also explores issues of African American unity, pride, leadership, and community power. Among Davis's other plays are *Alice in Wonder* (1952), later expanded into *The Big Deal* (1953), which is stirred by political aggression against militant blacks during the McCarthy era and tells the story of a black television performer who is caught between his personal beliefs and the loss of his career when he is asked to testify against his brother-in-law; *Montgomery Footprints* (1956), which focuses on the civil rights movement; *Curtain Call* (1963), based on the life of black Shakespearean actor, Ira Aldridge; *Escape to Freedom* (1978); a children's play derived from the childhood of Frederick *Douglass; *Langston Hughes: A Play* (1982); which tells the story of the poet and playwright; and *Bingo* (1985); a musical based on William Brashler's book *Bingo Long's Traveling All Stars and Motor Kings* (1985), about a black baseball team in the 1930s. Other plays by Davis include *The Mayor of Harlem* (1949), *Point Blank* (1949), *Clay's Rebellion* (1951), *What Can You Say, Mississippi?* (1955), *Alexis Is Fallen* (1974), and *They Seek a City* (1974).

Davis is also the author of several screenplays such as *Cotton Comes to Harlem* (1969), coauthored with Arnold Perl and directed by Davis, which is based on the novel of the same title by Chester *Himes; *Black Girl* (1972), also coscripted and directed by Davis; *Count Down at Kusini* (1976), about a liberation movement in a fictional African country; and *Teacher, Teacher* (1963), a television film in which Davis also starred, winning an Emmy Award for his performance.

Davis's first novel, *Just Like Martin* (1992), intended for young adult audiences, focuses on the height of the civil rights movement as seen through the eyes of a young black boy living in Alabama.

Davis has used the stage not only as a center of entertainment but also as a space for political and social critique and as a historical commemorative rich with the struggles of the African American community. His children's works also follow in this tradition and chronicle important moments in the history of African Americans with an instructional aim in mind. In 1998, together with his wife Ruby Dee, he published *With Ossie and Ruby: In This Life Together.*

• Lewis Funke, *The Curtain Rises: The Story of Ossie Davis,* 1971. Bernard L. Peterson, Jr., "Davis, Ossie," in *Contemporary Black American Playwrights and Their Plays: A Biographical Directory and Dramatic Index,* 1988, pp. 130–133.

—Cassandra Jackson

Day of Absence. Douglas Turner *Ward's *Day of Absence* (1965) is set in any small town in the Deep South. The action begins on a quiet street where Clem and Luke, two country crackers, are seated on a sparse stage talking, when they suddenly realize that something is wrong. It finally occurs to them that none of the town's black people have been seen since the previous evening. When this fact becomes general knowledge, the establishment comes to the brink of chaos. Without its black labor force, the town is paralyzed because of its dependence on this sector of the community.

The only blacks who can be found are lying in the hospital—in comas. In a final effort to retrieve the missing black population, Mayor Henry R. E. Lee makes a personal appeal on television. He begs and pleads and threatens black absentees. When no immediate response is forthcoming, a white mob confronts him and bedlam races through the entire community.

The final scene opens with Clem and Luke in their favorite spots the following morning when Rastus, a slow-moving, servile type enters upon the stage. When questioned concerning his whereabouts on "yestiddy," he appears not to remember. Ward offers no definitive answer.

Despite the serious message about the underlying economic importance and potential power of black people to this country, *Day of Absence* invites an audience to share in the experiences of these white townpeople through the devices of storytelling and slapstick dialogue. The text is interwoven with seemingly unrelated and fragmented actions, which move from farcical humor through sociopolitical propaganda to melodramatic insights that dramatize the subtext of what would be possible if black people just disappeared for one day.

The play received mixed reviews from the New York critics. Martin Gottfried of *Women's Wear Daily* summarily dismissed the play as "childish, dull and silly." On the other hand, Howard Taubman, drama critic, for the *New York Times*, felt that "the most serious trouble with *Day of Absence* is Mr. Ward's failure to sustain a strong dramatic line. He is full of invention . . . and his satirical thrusts often find their mark despite the loose structure of the piece." There was criticism by some blacks who felt that Ward should have chosen another comic form for propaganda rather than drawing what they considered to be a negative image of black stereotypes. In spite of this mixed criticism, *Day of Absence* ran for 504 performances, and Ward was honored with two Obie awards—one for his performance as mayor and one for writing the play.

A crucial component in the development of the African American theater during the 1960s was the necessity to cultivate sympathetic audiences who could share African American experiences from slavery through the civil rights era and beyond. Ward chose to accomplish this through the biting edge of humor. The external elements of colloquial and topical language, together with movement and gesture of farcical expansion, are funny to the core; yet just below the surface one can experience vicariously the hurt, suffering, and humiliation associated with this form and style of drama.

• Fred Beauford, "The Negro Ensemble Company: Five Years against the Wall," *Black Creation* 3 (Winter 1972): 16–18. Trudier Harris, *From Mammies to Militants: Domestics in Black American Literature,* 1982, pp. 143–154.

—Floyd Gaffney

DELANEY, LUCY A. (c. 1830–c. 1890s), ex-slave, writer, and political and religious leader. Born to slaves, Lucy Delaney cherished her St. Louis childhood. Like Frederick *Douglass and Harriet A. *Jacobs, however, she soon witnessed the breach between its "joyful freedom" and slavery's later realities. When owner Major Taylor Berry, who had arranged for the family's emancipation, was killed in a duel, and his widow died, the family remained enslaved. With Lucy's father sold South, mother Polly fiercely urged her two daughters' escape. While Nancy fled to Canada and Polly to Chicago, the latter returned to bondage to protect Lucy. Polly successfully petitioned the St. Louis courts for her own liberation, and later for Lucy's in 1844. Visiting Nancy in Toronto, Lucy wed Frederick Turner, soon to be killed in a steamboat explosion; her second marriage to Zachariah Delaney in St. Louis endured at least forty-two years. When their four children died young, Delaney tempered her mourning with a liberationist's salvo: they "were born free and died free!" Lucy finally located her father outside Vicksburg, Mississippi.

Delaney's autobiography, *From the Darkness Cometh the Light* (c. 1891), concentrates less on the escape, literacy, and achievement of freedom that punctuate earlier slave narratives than on the liberating feats of slave-motherhood. Delaney joins the celebrants of African American maternalism—Jacobs, Sojourner *Truth, Annie Louise *Burton, Toni *Morrison, and others. Written to "invoke [my mother's] spirit," it commences with Polly Crocket's "free" birth and her kidnapping into slavery. Despite her "commonplace virtues," Polly releases motherhood from its ties to "pure womanhood['s]" fragility, realigning nurture with liberation. Hardly feminine genuflection, Polly's triumph in male-dominated courts is matched by her daughter's refusal to be whipped. Darkness culminates in Delaney's perpetuating her dead mother's legacy of freedom in her election to numerous civic posts, including the presidency of the "Female Union"—the first society for African American women—and of the Daughters of Zion.

• William L. Andrews, introduction to *From the Darkness Cometh the Light or Struggles for Freedom* (c. 1891), in *Six Women's Slave Narratives,* 1988, pp. 9–64. Rosalie Murphy Baum, "Delaney, Lucy A.," in *African American Women: A Biographical Dictionary,* ed. Dorothy Salem, 1993, pp. 150–151.

—Deborah Garfield

DELANY, MARTIN R. (1812–1885), political activist, early Afrocentric ideologue, explorer, lecturer, newspaper editor and correspondent, U.S. Army major, and author of several tracts and a novel. Martin Robison Delany's haphazard education began clandestinely before his family's escape from slave-state Virginia in 1822. By 1832, in Pittsburgh, Delany, always proudly black and Africa-respecting, had joined the local African Education, Antislavery, Temperance, Philanthropic, Moral Reform, and Young Men's Bible societies. Further, he cofounded the Theban Literary Society—named after the Egyptian city.

By 1836 he began studying medicine, insisting upon civil rights, and preaching professional training for African Americans rather than barbering or manual labor suggestive of servant or second-class status. When black suffrage was rescinded in Pennsylvania in 1838, Delany, alone, passed through slave territory to then independent Texas to test its potential as a home for free blacks (1839–1840), his first adventure in emigration and exploration. Disappointed, but with scenes and dialogues he would use later in **Blake,* his only novel, he returned to Pittsburgh.

In 1843 Delany married (eventually there were seven children named after American and foreign blacks he admired) and launched the *Mystery,* a weekly newspaper that promoted civil rights, provoked blacks and whites by its challenges to old-fashioned understandings of race, and defended black writing and called for more.

When Frederick *Douglass began his own newspaper in December 1847, he asked Delany to join him. For eighteen months Delany worked for the *North Star* traveling, lecturing, and providing informative letters and editorials. By the summer of 1849 Delany's writing began to include apocalyptic undercurrents in prose and verse about the sins of whites and an imminent revolution in the religious and political thinking of blacks in the United States and Cuba. These black-nationalist, Pan-African thoughts reappeared in *Blake.*

Following the imposition of the Fugitive Slave Act (1850), Delany considered emigration to Canada, studied medicine at Harvard, practiced in Pittsburgh, taught school, was denied a patent because he was not recognized as a citizen, and published his first book: *The Condition, Elevation, Emigration, and Destiny of the Colored People of the United States, Politically Considered* (1852)—a prickly, unsentimental, and independent portrayal of African American conditions, with praise of productive blacks, criticism of disappointing white allies, and an argument for the need to seek another country.

In 1853 Delany wrote a defense of black Freemasonry and three letters criticizing Harriet Beecher *Stowe's *Uncle Tom's Cabin* for its treatment of pureblacks, its colonizationist conclusion, its slave languages, and for the author's having thought she could tell the story of his people. He may have felt some chagrin at not having published his novel first.

In 1854 Delany organized a National Emigration Convention and gave a black nationalist address arguing that almost anyplace was better than the United States. He moved to Canada in 1856, met with John *Brown in 1858, and he wrote. In 1859 the new black-owned and edited *Anglo-African Magazine* published four short pieces and part of *Blake*. The *Anglo-African* pushed it, moving installments to its front page, but few printed responses have been found.

In May 1859 Delany visited Africa, again seeking a land where his people might become part of the ruling element. In 1861, after seven weeks in Liberia, seven months in Nigeria, and an equal time in Great Britain seeking help for his African emigration plans, Delany returned to Canada. His *Official Report of the Niger Valley Exploring Party* offered corroboration that, as he wrote, "I have outgrown, long since, the boundaries of North America." From November 1861 through May 1862, *Blake* appeared in the *Weekly Anglo-African* newspaper. Ten footnotes reflecting Delany's African adventures were appended. Again, few contemporary responses are known; one reader promised a dramatization.

The remainder of Delany's literary life is closely tied to his political responses to America's Civil War and Reconstruction failures. In 1863 and 1864 he recruited troops; in February 1865 he became a major in the U.S. Army. From 1865 through July 1868 he was a Freedman's Bureau officer; then he was in and out of several positions between lectures, politicking, and job-seeking in South Carolina, where hopes for black advances rose and fell: in the Bureau of Agriculture (1870); in real estate (1871); in a customs office (1872–1873); in political campaigning (1874); in a newspaper editor's chair (1875); as a trial justice and would-be Liberian emigrationist (1875–1879); and, back North, an occasional lecturer (1880–1883) and a private Central American trade agent (1884).

Delany wrote newspaper articles, letters, and pamphlets on capital, land, labor, citizenship, and home ownership, but his two most interesting essays were attempts to assert the once and future contributions of black people to the world. In "The International Policy of the World towards the African Race" (1867), he argued that Europeans had suppressed the facts about the historical precedence of black philosophy, religion, and civilization. In his *Origin of Races and Color* (1879, 1880) Delany cited the Bible and classical writers in defense of his race and then offered original speculations on relations between Ethiopian bloodlines, religion, and civilization. A voice crying in the wilderness then, his theme has been taken up again today.

Delany may have written much more, but on the night President Lincoln was shot in April 1865, his stored papers were lost in a fire at Wilberforce University. Though hit with numerous bitter disappointments, only an occasional victory, and much neglect, one young man called the elderly Delany in 1882 the "blackest, jolliest, and most brilliant Negro I have ever seen or known." One eulogist even recalled Delany's "romance" (*Blake*) in 1885.

An energetic, unpolished lecturer and writer, Delany's unguided literary steps were clumsy. But his persistent interest in all things black, positive and negative, past and present, far and near, repay critical attention. Further, *Blake*'s affinities of tone, attitude, characterization, and speech with Sutton E. *Griggs's **Imperium in Imperio* (1899), W. E. B. *Du Bois's *Dark Princess* (1928), Zora Neale *Hurston's *Moses, Man of the Mountain* (1939), and Arna *Bontemps's **Black Thunder* (1936), without any known direct influence, signal the existence of an African American literary river.

• Frank A. Rollin, *Life and Public Services of Martin R. Delany,* 1868; rpt. 1883. Howard H. Bell, *Search for a Place: Black Separatism and Africa,* 1860, 1969. Dorothy Sterling, *The Making of an Afro-American: Martin Robison Delany 1812–1885,* 1971. Victor Ullman, Martin R. Delany: *The Beginnings of Black Nationalism,* 1971. Floyd J. Miller, *The Search for a Black Nationality: Black Colonization and Emigration, 1787–1863,* 1975. Nell Irvin Painter, "Martin R. Delany: Elitism and Black Nationalism," in *Black Leaders of the Nineteenth Century*, eds. Leon Litwack and August Meier, 1988, pp. 148–171. Robert S. Levine, *Martin Delany, Frederick Douglass, and the Politics of Representative Identity,* 1997. Robert Reid-Pharr, "Violent Ambiguity: Martin Delany, Bourgeois Sadomasochism, and the Production of a Black National Masculinity" in Marcellus Blount and George P. Cunningham, eds. *Representing Black Men,* 1996, pp. 73–94.

—Allan D. Austin

DELANY, SAMUEL R. (b. 1942), novelist, short story writer, poet, critic, editor, essayist, educator, director, former folk singer, lecturer, script writer for comic books, and winner of the Hugo and Nebula awards for science fiction, the Pilgrim Award for excellence in science fiction criticism (1985), and the Bill Whitehead Memorial Award for Lifetime Excellence in Gay and Lesbian Literature (1993). Delany has written criticism using the aliases K. Leslie Steiner and S. L. Kermit.

Samuel R. Delany was the first highly visible and extraordinarily successful African American author to adopt the "marginal" subgenre of science fiction and make it his special province, both as a creator and a critic. A Harlem native, "Chip" Delany was the only son of Samuel R. Delany, Sr., and Margaret Carey Boyd Delany, owners of Levy and Delany, a Harlem funeral parlor. His background provided the gifted young Delany with rich and varied experiences despite strained relations with his father, problems at school largely caused by an undiagnosed dyslexia, various experiments with sexuality, and psychiatric counseling sessions. At home he studied both the violin and the guitar; he read a variety of books including classical mythology, the works of diverse African American authors, and science fiction and fantasy stories. His summers were spent in racially integrated upstate New York youth camps, and he kept a journal from childhood. From 1947 to 1956, Delany attended Manhattan's private and progressive Dalton Elementary school, where he interacted with white upper-class children and adopted the "liberal-Jewish world view," to which, as he noted in a 1986 *Science Fiction and Criticism* interview, he still subscribes. In 1956 he enrolled in the public Bronx High School of Science (BHSS), where he excelled in math and science. At BHSS he met Jewish poet and child prodigy Marilyn Hacker; they married in 1961, separated in 1975, and divorced in 1980. In 1960, and from 1962 to 1963, he attended New York's City College. Delany's recollections of the pleasures, stresses, textures, and tensions of his childhood were metaphorically summarized for authors Michael Peplow and Robert Bravard (*Samuel R. Delany: A Primary and Secondary Bibliography, 1962–1979,* 1980) as "a virtually ballistic trip through a socio-psychological barrier of astonishingly restrained violence."

Called variously a child prodigy, a boy wonder, and the wunderkind of science fiction, Delany began to write when he was quite young. As a child, he had been introduced to the genre by parents, campmates, schoolmates, or friends discussing Jules Verne, Ray Bradbury, and Robert Heinlein tales. Subsequently, he came to appreciate the works of Theodore Sturgeon, Alfred Bester, and Arthur C. Clarke. As a preteen he had penned sword-and-sorcery fantasies in his journals; as an adolescent he wrote several unpublished novels; and at nineteen, he published his first novel, *The Jewels of Aptor* (1962).

Since his debut as a published writer Delany has written eighteen novels; three short story collections, *Driftglass, Distant Stars,* and *Driftglass/Starshards;* and two memoirs, including the extended autobiographical essay *Heavenly Breakfast* (1979), focused largely on his experiences in a San Francisco commune in 1967–1968, and *The Motion of Light in Water* (1988), a fuller autobiographical statement treating his life in New York and his development as an artist and writer from 1957 to 1965. In addition, he produced five collections of critical essays focused on science fiction, and in 1994, published *Silent Interviews,* a collection of written interviews that had appeared in a variety of journals; the subtitle, *On Language, Race, Sex, Science Fiction and Some Comics,* indicates the breadth of Delany's interests as a fiction writer, essayist, and critic.

Delany's early novels, from *Jewels* and his *The Fall of the Towers* trilogy (1963–1965), through *The Ballad of Beta-2* (1965), *Babel 17* (1966), and *The Einstein Intersection* (1967, originally to be called *A Fabulous, Formless Darkness*) to *Nova* (1968) can be characterized as "space opera." That is, while creating his original tales in far more "literary language" than was typical, and weaving into his plots heroic artists/outcasts as protagonists who were frequently black and/or female, the stories also adopted many of the conventions associated with formulaic science fiction. The settings were exotic, the action occurred in the distant future, and the accent fell on technology: spaceships, computers, aliens, intergalactic battle. His later novels, beginning with *The Tides of Lust* (1973, also published as *Equinox*), *Dhalgren* (1975), *Triton* (1976), and *Stars in My Pocket Like Grains of Sand* (1984), were more complex, more challenging, more anthropologically grounded with a more sophisticated narrative structure, a more theoretical underpinning, and a much greater allusive poetic density. Yet from his early science fiction to that of his later period, the essential topography of Delany's tales remained consistent. Issues of race, gender, freedom, desire, language, mythology, sexuality, semiotics, signs, slavery, psychology, and power persisted in his fictions. Also at issue in virtually all of his stories is his fascination with both literary and linguistic theory and historical linguistics.

The 1980s saw Delany devote most of his energy to the even more marginal form connected to science fiction called fantasy fiction or sword and sorcery. *The Return to Neveryon* series (1979–1987) consists of four volumes—*Tales of Neveryon* (1979), *Neveryona: Or the Tale of Signs and Cities* (1983), *Flight from Neveryon* (1985), and *The Bridge of Lost Desire* (1987)—interconnected "prehistorical" tales. As densely allusive and metaphorically postmodern as his later science fiction novels, the tales tell the stories of developments in a prehistoric empire with a preindustrial society. As central to each tale as the issues previously cited are Delany's depictions of political intrigue and the movement of a society from a barter to a cash economy. Already stylistically sophisticated, the intricacies of the Neveryon series are further complicated by Delany's deft blending of fiction and fact through the appended fictive critical voices of S. L. Kermit and K. Leslie Stein. Additionally, "The Tale of Plagues and Carnivals," in *Flight from Neveryon,* juxtaposes against the plot line entries from Delany's journals regarding the spread of AIDS in New York City.

Almost from the inception of his career Delany has been considered by various reviewers to be one of the most "artistic," "accomplished," "interesting," "gifted," "intelligent," "challenging," and "literate" writers in science fiction. Although often erroneously associated with science fiction's mid-1960s New Wave group, a primarily English phenomenon whose authors published in the journal *New Worlds,* and whose stories were largely set in the near future, Delany has insisted that he belongs more appropriately to its American counterpart, that group of writers associated with Harlan Ellison and the series of *Dangerous Visions* (1967) anthologies he edited. In 1999, Delany published *Bread & Wine: An Erotic Tale of New York.*

In "Toto, We're Back," a 1986 interview first published in the *Cottonwood Review* and subsequently reprinted in *Silent Interviews,* Delany addressed the issue of labeling and marginality he has confronted as an African American writer of science fiction. "The constant and insistent experience I have had as a black man, as a gay man, as a science fiction writer in racist, sexist, homophobic America, with its carefully maintained tradition of high art and low, colors and contours every sentence I write." Delany's bold insistence on his multiple identities helped create for science fiction a broader audience and helped to generate additional African American contributors to the field.

• George Slusser, *The Delany Intersection: Samuel R. Delany Considered As a Writer of Semi-Precious Words,* 1977. Samuel R. Delany, *The Jewel-Hinged Jaw: Notes on the Language of Science Fiction,* 1978. Peter S. Alterman, "Samuel R. Delany," in *DLB,* vol. 8, *Twentieth-Century American Science Fiction Writers,* eds. David Cowart and Thomas L. Wymer, 1981, pp. 119–128. E. F. Bleider, ed., *Science Fiction Writers: Critical Studies of the Major Authors from the Early Nineteenth Century to the Present Day,* 1982. Jane Branham Weedman, Samuel R. Delany, 1982. Sandra Y. Govan, "Samuel R. Delany," in *DLB,* vol. 33, *Afro-American Fiction Writers after 1955,* eds. Thadious M. Davis and Trudier Harris, 1984, pp. 52–59. Robert Elliot Fox, *Conscientious Sorcerers: The Black Postmodernist Fiction of LeRoi Jones/Amiri Baraka, Ishmael Reed, and Samuel R. Delany,* 1987. Samuel R. Delany, "Black to the Future: Interviews with Samuel R. Delany, Greg Tate, and Tricia Rose," interview by Mark Derry, *South Atlantic Quarterly* 92.4 (Fall 1993): 775–778. Sylvia Kelso, "'Across Never': Postmodern Theory and Narrative Praxis in Samuel R. Delany's Neveryon Cycle," *Science Fiction Studies* 24:2 (72) (July 1997): 289–301. Michael Bronski, "Samuel Delany: Ghosts of Times Square," *Publishers Weekly* 246: 28 (July 12, 1999): 68–69.

—Sandra Y. Govan

DEMBY, WILLIAM (b. 1922), journalist, actor, film adapter, and expatriate novelist. W. E. B. *Du Bois argued in *The *Souls of Black Folk* (1903) that African Americans possessed a unique "double consciousness" because of their "twin rooted" heritage of being both African and American. For William Demby, this dichotomy of racial and national oppositions became an asset rather than a handicap. Born 25 December 1922 in Pittsburgh, Pennsylvania, Demby spent his formative years in a middle-class, multiethnic neighborhood where its three African American families resided harmoniously with first-generation immigrants. Individualism prevailed concomitantly with nationalism so that people felt proudly ethnic, but still American, recalls Demby. He never felt divided because of nationalistic practices of discriminating against blacks.

Demby's parents, however, experienced the color problem that Du Bois predicted would be facing the twentieth century. William Demby and Gertrude Hendricks had been aspiring architectural and medical students to Philadelphia's colleges, but were denied entrance. They lived during the race riots and lynchings of blacks punctuating America after World War I. When they married in this period and moved from Mead to Pittsburgh where William and his siblings were born, the senior Demby redirected his goals. He first worked in a munitions factory and then joined Hopewell Natural Gas Company as a file clerk, which enabled him to support his family comfortably.

Pittsburgh's diverse community inspired young William's fledgling creative impulses to blend the real and fantastic like Romantic writers. Ghosts of Indians seemed to dwell in the woods near the thirteen-year-old's home. Ordinary transaction sheets that he processed as an after-school file clerk at Hopewell Gas Company seemed filled with Romantic characters. By the time Demby completed high school with friends and classmates who were ethnically Irish, Polish, or Italian; religiously Catholic or Protestant; or politically Socialist, Republican, or Democratic, he had become conscious of both ethnic pride and ethnic hate. His father owned one of the few radios in the neighborhood, and Demby heard the fearsome messages of fascist dictators Adolf Hitler and Benito Mussolini and the awesome prizefight between Joe *Louis and Max Schmeling in 1936 that diminished notions of Aryan superiority. This multiplicity of cultures sparked exciting musings, recalls Demby, practically forcing him to become a writer.

Demby's family's move south after his graduation from Langley High School in 1941 greatly influenced his worldview. The predominantly black world of Clarksburg, West Virginia, enthralled Demby. A socialist, writer, and jazz musician in high school, he further pursued these musical and philosophical interests at West Virginia State College. Demby took writing classes from poet-novelist Margaret *Walker and pursued his first love, jazz, to the extent that it became academically detrimental. With World War II in progress, Demby frequently skipped classes to play at the Cotton Club in South Carolina. His absenteeisms eventually compelled Demby to join the army in 1942 and he spent the bulk of his two-year tour in Italy. Following his discharge, Demby earned a BA in liberal arts in 1944 at Fisk University, Nashville, Tennessee.

Europe, nonetheless, beckoned Demby to return. When he migrated to Italy in 1947, Demby began a fifty-year, self-imposed exile that was broken only by periodic trips to America for temporary employment or vacations. He initially went to Rome to study painting because jazz had begun to change from swing to bebop. Demby quickly became involved with Rome's artists, including Roberto Rossellini for whom he adapted two films. His present-day position of film adapter of Italian films into English stems from this early period.

Affiliating with Rome's artistic members eventually inspired Demby to become a writer. But unlike expatriate Richard *Wright, Demby never felt compelled to avow allegiance to any movement or political group. Instead, Demby incorporated the dualistic symbolism of his bicultural heritage as a structuring trope in his writings where fact and fiction collide or merge. A prominent feature of Demby's three novels, for instance, is his integration of his alter ego or fictional writer persona in his works. In *Beetlecreek* (1950), Demby's first novel, he posits a fictional community reminiscent of Clarksburg, West Virginia. Primarily about a rite-of-passage experience of a black Pittsburgh youth and his meeting with an elderly, reclusive, white male resident of Beetlecreek, the story employs the motifs of simultaneity and destiny that cause the paths of Johnny Johnson and Bill Trapp to intersect in tragedy. This bleak, naturalistic novel earned Demby international acclaim and representation by Mondodavi, one of Italy's prestigious publishing houses.

With *The Catacombs* (1965) and *Love Story Black* (1978), Demby's alter ego is less camouflaged in the characterizations of William Demby and Professor Edwards, the respective fictional writers of each work. A motto of the real Demby is that "The novel to be born will be written." *The Catacombs* is about the act of writing over a two-year period at which time the writer's kernel idea literally is born and becomes self-controlling. Doris, the persona Demby invents, assumes an autonomous life in the real world surrounding the Roman catacombs. *Love Story Black* repeats the fact and fantasy dualism when Edwards becomes involved in the fantasies of an eighty-year-old virgin, ex-vaudeville performer while writing her life story.

In the 1950s and 1960s, Demby also produced a series of journalistic tracts—"The Geisha Girls of Pontocho," "They Surely Can't Stop Us Now," "A Walk in Tuscany," and "Blueblood Cats of Rome"—whose subjects reflect Demby's global consciousness. His belief in individualism among diverse groups at a global level was evident by his interracial marriage to Italian poet-writer Lucia Drudia with whom he shared an "artistic marriage." Their son, James, is an Italian composer. In the late 1990s, Demby was working on his next novel about Tillman, a cook from his old army outfit. To William Demby the author, the real world and the fantastic have no boundaries.

• Edward Margolies, "The Expatriate As Novelist: William Demby," in *Native Sons: A Critical Study of Twentieth-Century Black American Authors,* 1968, pp. 173–189. Robert Bone, "William Demby's Dance of Life," *Tri-Quarterly* 15 (Spring 1969): 127–141. Robert Bone, introduction to *The Catacombs,* 1965; rpt. 1969. John O'Brien, ed., *Interviews with Black Writers,* 1973, pp. 34–53. Roger Whitlow, *Black American Literature: A Critical History,* 1973, pp. 122–125. Margaret Perry, "William Demby," in *DLB,* vol. 33, *Afro-American Fiction Writers after 1955,* eds. Thadious M. Davis and Trudier Harris, 1984, pp. 59–64.

—Virginia Whatley Smith

DENT, TOM (1932–1998), poet, essayist, oral historian, dramatist, cultural activist, and noted figure in the Black Arts movement. Thomas Covington Dent, who prefers to be known as Tom Dent, was born on 20 March 1932 in New Orleans, Louisiana, the son of Dr. Albert Dent, president of Dillard University, and Jessie Covington Dent, a concert pianist. During his formative years in New Orleans, Dent wrestled with the sense of African American identity and the sense of place that seems to be the legacy of southern writers. Thus, it is not surprising that issues of political and cultural history are so germinal in his mature works.

After completing his early education in New Orleans, Dent earned his BA in political science from Morehouse College in 1952. Some of his earliest writing appeared in the campus newspaper, the *Maroon Tiger,* for which he served as editor during his senior year. After doing graduate work at Syracuse University, he served in the U.S. Army (1957–1959) and then moved to New York, where he worked for the New York *Age,* a black weekly, and for the NAACP Legal Defense Fund. He became a member of On Guard for Freedom, a cultural nationalist group. In 1962 he moved to the Lower East Side and founded the Umbra Workshop with Calvin C. *Hernton and David Henderson. This group chose Dent to be the editor of its poetry journal *Umbra,* which lasted for two issues (1963 and 1964) before the group dissolved.

What might be considered the first phase of Dent's literary career is marked by his concern with escaping from the restrictions of his black middle-class origins and acquiring a clear understanding of the issues of liberation, black nationalism, and cultural identity that occupied African American intellectuals in the late 1950s and early 1960s. It was Dent's idea that Umbra should be a collective of writers and artists who were exploring craft and discovering their voices and visions. It was within the group, as Dent revealed in an essay ("Lower East Side," *African American Review,* Winter 1993), that he discovered more respect for diversity and possibilities for rendering his vision of what history might mean. However much Dent profited from his discussions with such writers as Hernton, Henderson, Lorenzo *Thomas, Ishmael *Reed, Askia M. *Touré, and Norman Pritchard, his deepest concerns were focused on how the African American imagination fuses politics, aesthetics, and history. In 1964 some of his earliest poems appeared in the anthologies *New Negro Poets, U.S.A.* and *Schwartzer Orpheus.*

Dent returned to New Orleans in 1965, convinced of his need to rediscover his southern past and of his ability to use the insights and ideas he had gained in New York. He began working for Free Southern Theater (FST) as an associate director, a position that initiated an intense period of writing, civil rights activity, and work in building cultural groups. In 1967 Dent wrote his most famous play, *Ritual Murder,* one of the most eloquent examinations of black-on-black crime in African American theater. Aware of the need to help young writers develop a cultural base in New Orleans, Dent served as director of the FST Writers' Workshop or BLKARTSOUTH (1968–1973), becoming the mentor of Kalamu ya *Salaam and other writers whose work appeared in *New Black Voices* (1972). He saw this group and the Congo Square Writers Union, which he founded in 1973, as outgrowths of his Umbra experiences. While he continued to write reviews and articles for such magazines as *Freedomways, Southern Exposure,* and *Black World,* Dent also cofounded the journals *Nkombo* (1969) and *Callaloo* (1975). His first book of poems *Magnolia Street* was published in 1976. By the time his second poetry volume *Blue Lights and River Songs* (1982) appeared, Dent was very deeply involved in the work of the Southern Black Cultural Alliance (founded in 1974), a federation of community theater groups, had begun to tape oral histories about jazz in New Orleans and with key figures in the civil rights movement, and had begun work on an autobiography with Andrew Young. In the early 1990s Dent worked as executive director of the New Orleans Jazz and Heritage Foundation before he resigned to work on *Southern Journey,* an oral history of the civil rights movement and the contemporary South. That memoir was published in 1997 as *Southern Journey: A Return to the Civil Rights Movement.*

Dent is quite representative of African American writers who despite the quality of their work seem best known for their influence on other writers and their contributions in building cultural institutions. Once his work is given critical attention, the value of the unity he has sought between literature and history may be valorized.

• Tom Dent, Gilbert Moses, and Richard Schechner, eds., *The Free Southern Theater by the Free Southern Theater,* 1969. Lorenzo Thomas, "The Shadow World: New York's Umbra Workshop and Origins of the Black Arts Movement," *Callaloo* 4 (1978): 53–76. Lorenzo Thomas, "Tom Dent," in *DLB,* vol. 38, *African American Writers after 1955: Dramatists and Prose Writers,* eds. Thadious M. Davis and Trudier Harris, 1985, pp. 86–92. Michel Oren, "The Umbra Poets' Workshop, 1962–1965: Some Socio-Literary Puzzles," in *Studies in Black American Literature,* vol. 2, eds. Joe Weixlmann and Chester J. Fontenot, 1986, pp. 177–223. Jerry W. Ward, Jr., "Thomas C. Dent: A Preliminary Bibliography," *Obsidian II* 4 (Winter 1989): 103–112. Kim Lacy Rogers, *Righteous Lives: Narratives of the New Orleans Civil Rights Movement,* 1993.

—Jerry W. Ward, Jr.

DERRICOTTE, TOI (b. 1941), poet and educator. In Toi Derricotte's poetry, the taboo, the restricted, and the repressed figure prominently; they are often the catalysts that prompt her to write, to confess the painful. Often stylistically compared to so-called confessional poets like Sylvia Plath and Anne Sexton, Derricotte, in opting for candor over decorum, wants her "work to be a wedge into the world, as what is real and not what people want to hear." This self-dubbed "white-appearing Black person," reared as a Catholic in a black, working-class Detroit community, complicates the myth of monolithic blackness with poems that speak into consciousness obscure, unconventional black bodies. And in an academy whose poststructuralist theories often either depersonalize bodies with esoteric discourse or overemphasize them with hyperbolic identity politics, Toi Derricotte's poems brave the charged, murky depths of much current poetry, stamping the language with her own complex, quirky vision—a vision both concrete and abstract, both quotidian and phantasmagoric.

Toi Derricotte was born on 12 April 1941, the daughter of Antonia Baquet, a Creole from Louisiana, and Benjamin Sweeney Webster, a Kentucky native, and later half-sister to Benjamin, Jr. At around ten or eleven years old, Derricotte began a secret journal that included, among other things, the disintegration of her parents' marriage and the death of her grandmother on whom she was very emotionally dependent. During her years at Detroit's Girls Catholic Central, Derricotte recounts a religious education that she felt was steeped in images of death and punishment, a Catholicism that, according to the poet, morbidly paraded "the crucifixion, saints, martyrs in the Old Testament and the prayers of the Mass." Coupled with these images were Derricotte's surreal reminiscences of childhood visits to her paternal grandparents' home, the bottom part of which served as a funeral parlor where bodies were prepared for viewing. Often she would stay overnight at her grandparents', where, unafraid, she would "pray over the bodies . . . especially . . . disturbed when young people died, children, babies."

Her first attempt at sharing her poems with others came when, at fifteen, she visited a cousin, a medical school student who was then taking an embryology class. Encouraged by a trip they took to the Chicago Museum to see fetuses and embryos at various stages of development, Derricotte, who was careful not to show her poems to her parents who never "even alluded to babies before birth . . . [or] talked to [her] about sex," anxiously showed them to this cousin who pronounced them "sick, morbid." Faced with this unexpected rebuff, Derricotte remembers being faced with several choices: "I could have said something is wrong with me and stopped writing, or I could have continued to write, but written about the things I knew would be acceptable, or I could go back underground." For Derricotte, the choice was obvious: rather than risk ostracism for openly writing about the forbidden, she opted "to go back underground."

In 1959 Derricotte graduated from Girls Catholic Central and enrolled that autumn in Wayne State University as a special education major. In 1962, her junior year at Wayne State, she gave birth to a son in a home for unwed mothers. This act of rebellion was but a presage of things to come, as Derricotte, after graduating in 1965, left Detroit for the East Coast. Her move to New York City in 1967 was a momentous one, for it was here among white, mostly female intellectuals that Derricotte's poetic voice resurfaced. Unlike the African American poets of the Black Arts movement, many of whom heeded Amiri *Baraka's call for an artistic expression that was decidedly black nationalist, proletarian, and accessible, Derricotte wrote, instead, deeply personal, troubling, often difficult poems that talked more of black families haunted by gender oppression and familial strife than of Black Power and racial solidarity.

Having "paid her dues" as a student in numerous workshops where she endured the canon's litany of dead and near-dead white male poets like Matthew Arnold, Ezra Pound, T. S. Eliot, and Robert Lowell, often as the only black student, Derricotte first published in a "major" magazine, the *New York Quarterly,* in the fall of 1972. Her literary reputation and publications flourished, culminating in her first book, *The Empress of the Death House,* published in 1978 by Lotus Press. Derricotte's second book, *Natural Birth,* was published in 1983 by The Crossing Press. Her third book, *Captivity,* first published in 1989 by University of Pittsburgh Press, has enjoyed second (1991) and third (1993) printings. In 1996, Norton Publishing Company accepted for publication Derricotte's *The Black Notebooks,* a book she began in 1974 when her family became one of the first black families to move into Upper Montclair, New Jersey.

• Calvin C. Hernton, "Black Women Poets: The Oral Tradition," in *The Sexual Mountain and Black Women Writers,* 1987, pp. 119–155. Charles H. Rowell, "Beyond Our Lives: An Interview with Toi Derricotte," *Callaloo* 14.3 (Summer 1991): 654–664.

—James W. Richardson, Jr.

Dessa Rose. Sherley Anne *Williams's *Dessa Rose* (1986) is a historical novel that fits into the neo–slave narrative tradition. In other words it tries to revise the eighteenth- and nineteenth-century slave narratives that were written as a part of the antislavery movement, in part by adding an African American woman's narrative as a valid representation of slavery. This novel consists of three primary sections that are framed by a prologue and an epilogue. In the three larger sections, Williams provides differing viewpoints on *Dessa Rose herself. She begins with "The Darky," which presents a white male's, Adam Nehemiah's, perceptions of the protagonist as he attempts to record the story of her rebellion on a slave coffle. Perhaps this section alludes to William Styron's flawed historical fiction *The Confessions of Nat Turner* (1967). The next section, "The Wench," incorporates Dessa's interactions with a white mistress and circumstantial abolitionist, Miss *Rufel, and consequently deconstructs their roles as slave and mistress. Lastly, "The Negress" provides Dessa's viewpoint on her experiences meeting Miss Rufel and the runaway slaves in their impromptu Underground Railroad. In this section the characters engage in a mock minstrel show that travels through the South and ironically enough sells the troupe into slavery to economically liberate these former slaves. *Dessa Rose* seeks not only to reconstruct the Black woman's voice, which has been traditionally silenced, but it also attempts to create a possible and positive fiction of a slave who successfully leads a rebellion and who has truly escaped slavery.

The central critical issues surrounding *Dessa Rose* are those of the creation of text and of history. Creation adopts several meanings, because critics view it as the function of revising the historical text of the slave narrative, the function of the mother who creates the text of/for the child, the re-creation of a slave rebellion, and the modeling of two female slave rebels: Dessa, a black slave, and Rufel, a white woman, who is equally enslaved to her role as mistress. Williams revises Styron's *The Confessions of Nat Turner,* a neo–slave narrative that has received much criticism for what many felt to be an inaccurate portrayal of Nat Turner. The issues of the mother's role and of reconstructing the slave narrative to include the female rebel slave's story address feminist theory in that they revise what woman is and state that Dessa as slave and Rufel as mistress are more than roles assigned by society. Williams, then, creates her own rebellion both by deconstructing the roles of female slave and white mistress, by having these two become friends and work together in a minstrel parody of the slave auction to gain economic freedom, and by formally revising the slave narrative genre of the past as well as William Styron's neo–slave narrative on Nat *Turner.

• Mary Kemp Davis, "Everybody Knows Her Name: The Recovery of the Past in Sherley Anne Williams's *Dessa Rose,*" *Callaloo* 40.1 (1989): 544–558. Mae G. Henderson, "(W)riting *The Work* and Working the Rites," *Black American Literature Forum* 23.4 (Winter 1989): 631–660. Anne E. Goldman, "'I Made the Ink': (Literary) Production and Reproduction in *Dessa Rose* and *Beloved,*" *Feminist Studies* 16.2 (Summer 1990): 313–330. Marta E. Sanchez, "The Estrangement Effect in Sherley Anne Williams' *Dessa Rose,*" *Genders* 15 (Winter 1992): 21–36.

—Mildred R. Mickle

DESSA ROSE. As the protagonist and narrator of Sherley Anne *Williams's critically acclaimed neo–slave narrative and historical novel, **Dessa Rose* (1986), Dessa revises the trope of the "slave woman." In her interactions with Nemi, a white male amanuensis who attempts to record her life story, and Miss *Rufel, a white mistress of a half-finished plantation, she controls the narrative by giving them limited information on herself and by serving as omniscient narrator of the entire novel. Her control of the narrative best refutes the notion of slave woman, because although she is physically constrained by jail and the aftereffects of childbirth, she stresses that what matters most is that she owns her own mind. Unlike Nemi and Miss Rufel,

Dessa has few misconceptions about the world she inhabits.

In refuting the concept of slave woman, Dessa fulfills her most important function: she stands as a heroine and a positive and possible fiction. Dessa speaks in and offers the perspective of a successful African American female insurrectionist to the literary realm, where traditionally African American women have been silenced. Yet what marks her most is that this former slave woman character narrates her story to her children and ensures that it is passed down. Dessa's acquired literacy represents the act of making history and, as such, contributes to the evergrowing body of African American texts.

• Mary Kemp Davis, "Everybody Knows Her Name: The Recovery of the Past in Sherley Anne Williams's *Dessa Rose,*" *Callaloo* 40.1 (1989): 544–558.

—Mildred R. Mickle

DETTER, THOMAS P. (c. 1826–?), journalist, short story writer, minister, and politician. While details of Thomas Detter's early life are sketchy, it appears he was born in Maryland and educated in Washington, D.C., public schools. According to his father's will, he was to have been apprenticed as a shoemaker until his twenty-first birthday. Detter emigrated to San Francisco, California, in 1852, one of many African Americans lured by the economic prospects of gold and silver mining and the greater freedom of the western frontier. He quickly established himself as a community leader, becoming the Sacramento County delegate to the first Colored Citizens of the State of California Convention; serving on the State Executive Committee of that and other civil rights organizations; and campaigning in California, Nevada, Washington, and the Idaho Territory for public education, voting rights, and the admission of testimony by African Americans in court cases. Along with poet James Monroe *Whitfield, Detter was one of the first African Americans to serve on a jury in Nevada. By 1864, Thomas Detter was known as "one of the old wheelhorses" of the western civil rights movement.

In 1871, when he published *Nellie Brown, or The Jealous Wife with Other Sketches,* Thomas Detter was about forty years old and living in the isolated frontier settlement of Elko, Nevada. Detter was not, however, an unknown writer; his reputation as a correspondent for the *San Francisco Elevator* and the *Pacific Appeal* had been established for more than a decade. Detter wrote commentaries on national and local social and political issues. He was an outspoken abolitionist and a fervent supporter of Reconstruction. His newspaper columns often included eulogies for local community leaders and writers, as well as for national figures such as Charles Sumner and Jeremiah B. Sanderson. Perhaps his most unusual contributions were the essays he published about the status and prospects of new gold or silver mines and his descriptions of towns that cropped up in response to the expansion of railroads. Detter traveled extensively throughout the Pacific Northwest, living in various mining camps and frontier settlements, plying his trade as a barber, selling his patented cough syrups and hair restoratives, and writing articles designed to encourage African Americans to relocate to these newly established towns and territories. His newspaper reports generally focused on the grand natural beauty and the economic opportunities of the expanding territories while emphasizing the abundant rewards that African Americans of courage, persistence, and optimism could achieve.

Detter's only known separately published volume, *Nellie Brown, or The Jealous Wife with Other Sketches,* includes fiction and essays set in antebellum Virginia and Maryland, Louisiana and Cuba, Idaho and California. Published in San Francisco and distributed throughout the western United States, *Nellie Brown* is among our earliest examples of the African American literary tradition on the western frontier. The title story, "Nellie Brown, or The Jealous Wife" is a novella about the misadventures that occur when greed inspires gossip and emotions overcome logic. It is one of the early examples of "divorce fiction" that was developing in nineteenth-century American literature and as such represents a singular innovation in the African American literary tradition. "The Octoroon Slave of Cuba" is an unusual alternative to the tragic mulatto themes of such works as William Wells *Brown's **Clotel* and Frank J. *Webb's *The Garies and Their Friends.* "Uncle Joe" is an adaptation of the African American trickster tale that resembles the later work of Charles Waddell *Chesnutt. Detter's essays are candidly opinionated but insightful and useful. Whether he was evaluating the impact of the "Central Pacific Railroad," predicting the future prospects of "Idaho City," or relating the painful folly of racial discrimination during "My Trip to Baltimore," Detter wrote to inspire and to inform his readers. Like his contemporaries Frances Ellen Watkins *Harper, Frederick *Douglass, Martin R. *Delany, and others, Thomas Detter was an activist writer, an innovator in African American fiction, and a pioneer of the African American press.

• Elmer E. Rusco, "Good Time Coming?" *Black Nevadans in the Nineteenth Century,* 1975. Frances Smith Foster, introduction to *Nellie Brown, or The Jealous Wife with Other Sketches,* 1996.

—Frances Smith Foster

DE VEAUX, ALEXIS (b. 1948), poet, playwright, novelist, short fiction writer, editor, lecturer, performer, educator, activist, and prize-winning essayist and author of children's stories. Born 24 September 1948 in New York City to Richard Hill and Mae De Veaux, Alexis De Veaux received a BA from Empire State College in 1976. She earned both an MA (1989) and a PhD (1992) at the State University of New York at Buffalo.

An internationally recognized author, De Veaux has published her work in English, Spanish, Japanese, Serbo-Croatian, and Dutch. She has lectured and performed across the United States, as well as abroad in Kenya (1985 NGO Forum, Nairobi), Holland (Melkweg International Women's Festival, Amsterdam), Cuba (UNEAC Writers Union, Havana), and Japan (Tokyo Joshi Women's University, Tokyo; Black Studies Association, Osaka). Her published works include six books (*Na-Ni,* 1973; *Spirits in the Street,* 1973; *Don't Explain: A Song of Billie Holiday,* 1980; *Blue Heat: Poems and Drawings,* 1985; *An Enchanted Hair Tale,* 1987; and *The Woolu Hat,* 1995) and five short stories ("Remember Him A Outlaw," 1972; "The Riddles of Egypt Brownstone," 1980, rpt. 1990; "All Shut Eyes Ain't Closed, All Goodbyes Ain't Gone," 1983; "Adventures of the Dread Sisters," 1991; and "The Ethical Vegetarian," 1995). In addition De Veaux has published dozens of articles and essays on various subjects, including "Jayne Cortez, Revolutionary Mouth on Paper" (*Essence,* 1978) and "SisterLove" (*Afrekete: An Anthology of Black Lesbian Writing,* 1995). One of her plays, "The Tapestry" (1986), is included in the anthology *Nine Plays by Black Women Playwrights.* Others have been produced Off-Broadway and in regional theaters across the country, and one play, "Circles" (1972), was produced at KCET-TV, California (1976).

New York City is the setting for a number of De Veaux's works, but the cultural mood is an amalgam of African rhythm and everyday Western urban drama. Readers experience her stories through a lens induced by the author's lived experience as an urban African American woman. The novel *Spirits in the Street* is a young Harlemite insider's poetic reminiscence expressing a range of emotions from outrage over Vietnam- and Nixon-era events to a joyous embracing of that part of the self which is of African origin. Centered on Harlem's 114th Street, the novel recalls school desegregation, police brutality, outrage over the incarceration of Angela Davis, and city streets filled with peddlers, hookers, and hustlers. *Na-Ni,* De Veaux's award-winning, illustrated children's story, presents a child's eye view of evil forces at work within the African American community and is set within the block of 133rd Street between Lenox and Seventh avenues. *Don't Explain* is a straightforward if somewhat unusual biography of singer Billie *Holiday. Lady Day's Harlem-centered life comes packaged like a jazzy blues love song expressing the singer's passions, frustrations, pain, and joy as if experienced firsthand by its author.

An artist-activist, De Veaux's life exemplifies a progression from a concern with the development of a positive personal identity to the expression of a global vision of peaceful coexistence and freedom from the tyranny of oppression in its various manifestations. Her activism is a practical application of the theories embodied in her creative and expository writing and is demonstrative of a life that extends far beyond the confines of the welfare years of her own youth echoed in *Na-Ni.* De Veaux's involvement in projects like "Motherlands: From Manhattan to Managua to Africa, Hand to Hand," a video documentary (1986), underscores her commitment to assume a part of the responsibility for healing a worldwide human community suffering from centuries of cultural conflict.

The author is the recipient of numerous awards, including the Art Books for Children Award (Brooklyn Museum, 1974 and 1975), Coretta Scott King Awards (1981 and 1988), a National Endowment for the Arts Fellowship (1981), a Creative Artists Public Service Grant (New York, 1981), Unity in Media Awards (1982 and 1983), the Fannie Lou Hamer Award for Excellence in the Arts (1984), a PBS research and script development grant (PBS 1989), and the Lorraine Hansberry Award for Excellence in African American Children's Literature (1991).

De Veaux served as contributing editor and editor at large for *Essence* from 1978 to 1990. She was a cofounder of the Flamboyant Ladies Theater Company (1977–1984) and the founder of the Gap Tooth Girlfriends Writing Workshop (1980–1984). She has served as master artist for the New Haven, Connecticut, board of education (1974–1975), and she has taught writing and women's studies at several colleges and universities. De Veaux is an assistant professor of women's studies in the Department of American Studies at the State University of New York at Buffalo.

• Claudia Tate, "Alexis De Veaux," in *Black Women Writers at Work,* ed. Claudia Tate, 1983, pp. 49–59. Priscilla R. Ramsey, "Alexis De Veaux," in *DLB,* vol. 38, *Afro-American Writers after 1955: Dramatists and Prose Writers,* eds. Thadious M. Davis and Trudier Harris, 1985, pp. 92–97. Jewelle L. Gomez, "Alexis De Veaux," in *Contemporary Lesbian Writers of the United States: A Bio-bibliographical Critical Sourcebook,* eds. Sandra Pollack and Denise D. Knight, 1993, pp. 174–180.

—Lovalerie King

DIXON, MELVIN (1950–1992), novelist, poet, educator, scholar, and translator. Born in Connecticut, Melvin Dixon earned his BA at Wesleyan University (1971) and his MA and PhD at Brown University (1973, 1975). His first book, *Change of Territory* (1983), a collection of free-verse poems, reflects his interest in his family's southern roots and his experiences—including a visit to Africa—while he was living in Paris in the mid-1970s. For Dixon, a change of territory affords new perspectives and new or enlarged identities, themes mirrored in the book's four-part structure. The opening poem, "Hungry Travel," focuses on his parents' departure for Connecticut from North Carolina's Blue Ridge Mountains. Other poems expand the poet's concept of kin to include literary influences such as Jean *Toomer, Richard *Wright, Zora Neale *Hurston, Ralph *Ellison, and Robert *Hayden. The long poem "Bobo Baoulé," which comprises part 3, emphasizes racial ancestry as it recounts the enslavement of a young African, then leaps forward in time to one of his descendants, who has returned to Africa with the Peace Corps. The book's closing poem, "Hemispheres," with its imagery of roundness, also highlights this pattern of departure and return, in this case the poet's homecoming—though the poem anticipates further travel as well, ongoing journeys of external and internal exploration.

Dixon's first novel, *Trouble the Water* (1989), winner of the Nilon Award for Excellence in Minority Fiction, also employs the journey motif as it examines the burden of the past that haunts its protagonist, Jordan Henry, who returns to his childhood home. Set primarily in rural North Carolina along the Pee Dee River, the book traces Jordan's efforts to free himself from his grandmother's expectation—which led him to flee to the North at age thirteen—that he will avenge his seventeen-year-old mother's death in childbirth by killing his father. Dixon's complex interweaving of past and present, his skillful handling of a varied cast of characters that includes the Haitian conjure woman Mam'Zilie, his poetic evocation of the forces of nature, and his powerful use of water as an archetypal symbol—all make this first novel far more than yet another example of the southern gothic tradition. Although the climactic confrontation between Jordan and his father is somewhat contrived and the resolution of the conflict occurs too quickly and easily, Dixon effectively addresses moral issues that transcend the particulars of Jordan Henry's life.

Dixon's second novel, *Vanishing Rooms* (1991), is set in New York City's Greenwich Village. The book has frequently been compared to James *Baldwin's **Giovanni's Room* (1956), for not only do both books deal with homosexuality but Dixon has acknowledged the profound influence Baldwin's writing had on his own. Unlike Baldwin, however, Dixon focuses on an interracial gay relationship, one shattered in the opening chapter by the brutal murder of his African American protagonist's white lover. Dixon's use of three first-person narrators—Jesse, the protagonist, a dancer; Ruella, another member of the dance company and the person to whom Jesse turns when Metro is killed; and fifteen-year-old Lonny, one of the four white teenagers responsible for the murder—demonstrates Dixon's mastery of style, tone, characterization, and narrative technique. This use of multiple narrators is also meant to suggest, Dixon has noted, the social and political dimensions of racism and homophobia, problems that cannot be solved on an individual basis. Among Dixon's major achievements here is his sensitive portrait of Lonny, who unexpectedly evokes the reader's sympathy and understanding despite the violence he has helped to provoke. While Jesse must confront the racism that undermined his relationship with Metro, Lonny comes to recognize that he himself might easily have been the victim of his friends' savagery. The novel's graphic scenes of sexual violence, including Metro's murder and the gang rape of the imprisoned Lonny, are deeply disturbing, but they testify to the horrifying consequences of racism and homophobia. In Dixon's highly imagistic prose the voices of people like Jesse and Lonny are heard for almost the first time in American literature.

In addition to his poetry and fiction, Dixon published a volume of literary criticism, *Ride Out the Wilderness: Geography and Identity in Afro-American Literature* (1987). He also translated from French both Geneviève Fabre's *Drumbeats, Masks, and Metaphor: Contemporary Afro-American Theatre* (1983) and *The Collected Poetry of Léopold Sédar Senghor* (1991), whose work Dixon came to admire during his year in Senegal as a Fulbright lecturer (1985–1986). Dixon's promising career was cut short by his death from AIDS. The final section of his posthumous collection of poems, *Love's Instruments* (1995), speaks powerfully about the effects of the AIDS epidemic on his generation.

• Wilfrid R. Koponen, "Melvin Dixon," in *Contemporary Gay American Novelists,* ed. Emmanuel S. Nelson, 1993, pp. 110–115. Hermine D. Pinson, "Geography and Identity in Melvin Dixon's Change of Territory," *MELUS* 21:1 (Spring 1996): 99–111. Maurice Wallace, "The Autochoreography of an Ex-Snow Queen: Dance, Desire, and the Black Masculine in Melvin Dixon's *Vanishing Rooms,*" in *Novel Gazing: Queer Readings in Fiction,* ed. Eve Kosofsky Sedgwick, 1997, pp. 379–400.

—John Lang

DODSON, OWEN (1914–1983), poet, novelist, and playwright. For the major portion of his life, fate favored Owen Vincent Dodson. Born the ninth child of a poor Brooklyn family, he attended excellent schools: Bates College in Lewiston, Maine, for his BA (1932–1936) and the Yale School of Drama, where he earned his MFA in playwriting (1936–1939). He taught theater and literature in the best African American universities—Atlanta, Hampton, and Howard—and won major writing grants: General Education Board (1937); Rosenwald Fellowship (1943); Guggenheim Fellowship (1953); Rockefeller (1968). In recognition of his contribution to the theater, President Lyndon Johnson invited Dodson to the White House for celebration of Shakespeare's quadricentennial birthday.

In August of 1946, he saw the publication of his first volume of poetry, *Powerful Long Ladder,* which established his national reputation. M. L. Rosenthal wrote in the *New York Herald Tribune Weekly Book Review,* "The positive achievements of *Powerful Long Ladder* are its vividness, its solid strength in picturing pain and disgust without losing the joy of life which marks the best artist. . . ." Several poems in the volume have become standards. Dodson's use of metaphor and conceit, which sometimes jarred readers, nonetheless added "to our stock of available reality."

Poetry remained the seminal source for his first full-length drama, *Divine Comedy* (1938), a tale concerning the charismatic preacher Father Divine. Recipient of the Maxwell Anderson Verse Award (1942), the play became the first quality verse drama by an African American. His second verse play, *Garden of Time* (1939), reinterpreted the Medea story. Twenty-seven of his thirty-seven plays and operas have been produced—two at the Kennedy Center.

In February 1951 Farrar, Straus and Giroux released *Boy at the Window,* Dodson's first and best novel. The *Washington Post* critic caught the novel's essence, "Eloquent Writing: Child's Eye View of the Adult World." The autobiographical story concerned a sensitive nine-year-old growing up in a working-class neighborhood of Brooklyn in the 1920s. The heart of the novel is the death of his beloved mother, a death the boy feels he should have been able to prevent by his religious conversion. The prose, rich in imagery and metaphor, captures the intimate thoughts and voice of a child: the language is clearly the style of a poet.

In 1952 Dodson received a Guggenheim Fellowship to write a sequel, *Come Home Early, Child,* which did not find a publisher until 1977. Breaking into two sections, the latter half surrealistic, the novel may be seen as a harbinger of later surreal scenes in the novels of Ishmael *Reed, Clarence *Major, and Toni *Morrison.

It was not until his retirement from the theater department at Howard University that he was able to return to poetry, publishing in *The Harlem Book of the Dead* (1978). Camille Billops, a visual artist, had contracted the Harlem photographer James Van Der Zee to issue a series of his funeral photographs. Dodson agreed to write poems as captions for the photos.

He considered *The Confession Stone: Song Cycle* (1970) a series of monologues spoken by the Holy Family concerning the life of Jesus, to be his masterpiece. The simplicity of the language portrays the humanity of the Holy Family. His final collection of poems, "Life on the Streets," has never been published; however, in May of 1982 the New York Public Theatre staged the work as poetry in performance.

Except for an authorized biography, *Sorrow Is the Only Faithful One* (1993), very little critical study has been written about Dodson's poetry or plays. The reasons for this neglect are complex: First, he was an academic, and the prejudice of "those who can, do; those who can't, teach" obscured Dodson's creative reputation. Second, he was master of several crafts: theater, narrative, and poetry, making him difficult to label in a culture where image and label are vital for reputation. Third, although Dodson was in touch with his time, the time was not in touch with him. He was too young to be included in the illustrious Harlem Renaissance and too much of a humanist to please the publishers of the angry, militant black writers in the 1960s. Finally, racism did take its toll: considered a "black writer," he had to find his publication almost solely within that designation.

• Bernard L. Peterson, Jr., "The Legendary Owen Dodson," *Crisis* 86 (Nov. 1979): 373–378. James Hatch, Douglas A. M. Ward, and Joe Weixlmann, "The Rungs of a Powerful Long Ladder: An Owen Dodson Bibliography," *Black American Literature Forum* 14 (Summer 1980): 60–68. James V. Hatch, *Sorrow Is the Only Faithful One: The Life of Owen Dodson,* 1993. *Callaloo,* 20 (1997).

—James V. Hatch

DOMINI, RAY. *See* Lorde, Audre.

Don't Cry, Scream. Published in 1969 by Haki R. *Madhubuti's Third World Press, *Don't Cry, Scream* is his third collection of poetry and begins with an introduction by Gwendolyn *Brooks. Brooks addresses the most important contribution that Madhubuti makes to African American literary history: Madhubuti's poetry demonstrates his intense goal of enlightening Black people about the psychological, economical, political, and historical forces that stifle their well-being.

David Lloren's thorough profile of Haki Madhubuti, which appeared in the March 1969 issue of *Ebony,* followed the publication of *Don't Cry, Scream* and was a major influence in bringing Madhubuti's work to the attention of a wide audience. Haki Madhubuti begins this third collection of poetry with a preface entitled "Black Poetics / for the many to come." His spelling of "blackpoetry" and "blackpeople" as one word suggests that Blackness and humanity are inseparable or inextricable. For him, then, as a Black writer, the Blackness of his poetry is an inextricable aspect of his subject matter and of the ways in which he shapes his ideas. The first poem in the collection, entitled "Gwendolyn Brooks," poetically captures the exchange of knowledge that took place when he and some of the other poets from OBAC (Organization of Black American Culture) met Brooks and ends with the idea of how the stereotyping of Gwendolyn Brooks as a "negro poet" completely fails to capture her greatness. In two related poems, "History of the Poet As a Whore (to all negro poets who deal in whi-te paronomasia)" and "a poem for negro intellectuals (if there bes such a thing)," he refers to Black poets who shun their commitment to the Black community as paper prostitutes and describes the "blk/man" and "blk/woman" actions needed to change the lives of "a people deathliving / in / abstract realities."

Like the "negro intellectual" and the poet as whore, the Black man described in what perhaps remains one of Madhubuti's most well known poems, "But He Was Cool or: he even stopped for green lights," is Black in appearance or form but has no substance or commitment. The strength of Madhubuti's dedication to Blackness in *Don't Cry, Scream* lies in his use of Black music as poetic reference, in his use of revolutionary jazz musicians as cultural heroes ("Don't Cry, Scream" and "blackmusic / a / beginning"), and in the poems that explore the evil associated with the assassinations of Dr. Martin Luther *King, Jr., and *Malcolm X ("Assassination" and "Malcolm Spoke / who listened?"). The most sustained poem in the collection, "Nigerian Unity / or little niggers killing little niggers (for brothers Christopher Okigbo & Wole Soyinka)," examines how the West's fight for gold in Africa and its commodification of Blackness underlay the Biafran Civil War in which the Yoruba fought the Igbo. Both Nigerian writers, Christopher Okigbo was an Igbo who joined the seceded Biafrans and was killed early in the war, and Wole Soyinka, a Yoruba who was opposed to the war, was arrested and jailed for the duration of the war for allegedly collaborating with the rebel Igbos. In this poem Madhubuti makes the connection between the commodification of Blacks in Africa and in the West and suggests how this commodification causes Blacks to fight each other.

The poems entitled "Black Sketches" and "blackwoman" capture the essence of Madhubuti's style, which separated him and his peers of the late 1960s from the mainstream tradition in white poetry. These concise sketches, because they are so short, highlight the use of slashes to emphasize rhythm, nonacademic or nonstandard English, and Black street language, including the dozens and signifying, that characterize much of the poetry of the young Black writers of the 1960s. To date literary criticism has not yielded substantial analyses of Madhubuti, who has published seven collections of poetry in addition to *Don't Cry, Scream.*

• Paula Giddings, "From a Black Perspective: The Poetry of Don L. Lee," in *Amistad 2,* eds. John A. Williams and Charles Harris, 1971, pp. 299–318. Catherine Daniels Hurst, "Haki R. Madhubuti (Don L. Lee)," in *DLB,* vol. 41, *Afro-American Poets since 1955,* eds. Trudier Harris and Thadious M. Davis, 1985, pp. 222–232.

—Joyce A. Joyce

DOUGLASS, FREDERICK (1818–1895), orator, journalist, editor, and autobiographer. Frederick Douglass, author of the most influential African American text of his era, rose through the ranks of the antislavery movement in the 1840s and 1850s to become the most electrifying speaker and commanding writer produced by black America in the nineteenth century. From the outbreak of the Civil War until his death, Douglass was generally recognized as the premier African American leader and spokesman for his people. Douglass's writing was devoted primarily to the creation of a heroic image of himself that would inspire in African Americans the belief that color need not be a permanent bar to their achievement of the American dream, while reminding whites of their obligation as Americans to support free and equal access to that dream for Americans of all races.

The man who became internationally famous as Frederick Douglass was born on Maryland's Eastern Shore in February 1818, the son of Harriet Bailey, a slave, and an unknown white man. Although he recalls witnessing as a child the bloody whipping of his Aunt Hester by his master, Douglass says in his autobiographies that his early experience of slavery was characterized less by overt cruelty than by deprivations of food, clothing, and emotional contact with his mother and grandmother. Sent to Baltimore in 1826 by his master's son-in-law, Thomas Auld, Frederick spent five years as a servant in the home of Thomas Auld's brother, Hugh. At first, Hugh's wife Sophia treated the slave boy with unusual kindness, giving reading lessons to Frederick until her husband forbade them. Rather than accept Hugh Auld's dictates, Frederick took his first rebellious steps toward freedom by teaching himself to read and write.

In 1833 a quarrel between the Auld brothers brought Frederick back to his home in Saint Michaels, Maryland. Tensions between the recalcitrant black youth and his owner convinced Thomas Auld to hire Frederick out as a farm worker under the supervision of Edward Covey, a local slave breaker. After six months of unstinting labor, merciless whippings, and repeated humiliations, the desperate sixteen-year-old slave fought back, resisting one of Covey's attempted beatings and intimidating his tormentor sufficiently to prevent future attacks. Douglass's dramatic account of his struggle with Covey would become the heroic turning point of his future autobiographies and one of the most celebrated scenes in all of antebellum African American literature.

In the spring of 1836, after a failed attempt to escape from slavery, Frederick was sent back to Baltimore to learn the caulking trade. With the aid of his future spouse, Anna Murray, and masquerading as a free black merchant sailor, he boarded a northbound train out of Baltimore on 3 September 1838 and arrived in New York City the next day. Before a month had passed Frederick and Anna were reunited, married, and living in New Bedford, Connecticut, as Mr. and Mrs. Frederick Douglass, the new last name recommended by a friend in New Bedford's thriving African American community. Less than three years later Douglass joined the radical Garrisonian wing of the abolitionist movement as a full-time lecturer.

After years of honing his rhetorical skills on the antislavery platform, Douglass put his life's story into print in 1845. The result, **Narrative of the Life of Frederick Douglass, an American Slave, Written by Himself,* sold more than thirty thousand copies in the first five years of its existence. After a triumphal twenty-one-month lecture tour in England, Ireland, and Scotland, Douglass returned to the United States in the spring of 1847, resolved, against the advice of many of his Garrisonian associates, to launch his own newspaper, the *North Star.* Authoring most of the articles and editorials himself, Douglass kept the *North Star* and its successors, *Frederick Douglass's Paper* and *Frederick*

Douglass's Monthly, in print from 1847 to 1863. One of the literary highlights of the newspaper was a novella, "The *Heroic Slave," which Douglass wrote in March 1853. Based on an actual slave mutiny, "The Heroic Slave" is regarded as the first work of long fiction in African American literature.

A rupture of the close relationship between Douglass and Garrison occasioned a period of reflection and reassessment that culminated in Douglass's second autobiography, **My Bondage and My Freedom* (1855). Although he had befriended and advised John *Brown in the late 1850s, Douglass declined Brown's invitation to participate in the Harpers Ferry raid but was forced to flee his Rochester, New York, home for Canada in October 1859 after he was publicly linked to Brown. Applauding the election of Abraham *Lincoln and welcoming the Civil War as a final means of ending slavery, Douglass lobbied the new president in favor of African American recruitment for the Union Army. When the war ended, Douglass pleaded with President Andrew Johnson for a national voting rights act that would give African Americans the franchise in all the states. Douglass's loyalty to the Republican Party, whose candidates he supported throughout his later years, won him appointment to the highest political offices that any African American from the North had ever won: federal marshal and recorder of deeds for the District of Columbia, president of the Freedman's Bureau Bank, consul to Haiti, and chargé d'affaires for the Dominican Republic.

The income Douglass earned from these positions, coupled with the fees he received for his popular lectures, most notably one entitled "Self-Made Men," and his investments in real estate, allowed Douglass and his family to live in comfort in Uniontown, just outside Washington, D.C., during the last two decades of his life. His final memoir, *Life and Times of Frederick Douglass,* first published in 1881 and expanded in 1892, did not excite the admiration of reviewers or sell widely, as had his first two autobiographies. But the *Life and Times* maintained Douglass's conviction that his had been a "life of victory, if not complete, at least assured." *Life and Times* shows Douglass dedicated to the ideal of building a racially integrated America in which skin color would cease to determine an individual's social value and economic options. In the last months of his life Douglass decried the increasing incidence of lynching in the South and disputed the notion that by disenfranchising the African American man a more peaceful social climate would prevail throughout the nation. Yet Douglass never forsook his long-standing belief that the U.S. Constitution, if strictly and equally enforced, remained the best safeguard for African American civil and human rights.

In the history of African American literature, Douglass's importance and influence are virtually immeasurable. His *Narrative* and *My Bondage and My Freedom* gave the world the most compelling and sophisticated renditions of an African American selfhood seen in literature up to that time. Douglass's artistry invested this model of selfhood with a moral and political authority that subsequent aspirants to the role of African American culture hero—from the conservative Booker T. *Washington to the radical W. E. B. *Du Bois—would seek to appropriate for their own autobiographical self-portraits. In twentieth-century African American literature, from Paul Laurence *Dunbar's brooding poetic tribute "Douglass" (1903) to the idealistic characterization of Ned Douglass in Ernest J. *Gaines's novel, *The *Autobiography of Miss Jane Pittman* (1971), the criterion for an African American male heroism that uses words as a weapon in the struggle for self- and communal liberation remains the example set by Frederick Douglass.

• Benjamin Quarles, *Frederick Douglass,* 1948. Philip S. Foner, ed., *The Life and Writings of Frederick Douglass,* 1950–1975. John W. Blassingame, ed., *The Frederick Douglass Papers,* 1979–. Dickson J. Preston, *Young Frederick Douglass,* 1980. Waldo E. Martin, *The Mind of Frederick Douglass,* 1984. William L. Andrews, *To Tell a Free Story: The First Century of Afro-American Autobiography, 1760–1865,* 1986. William S. McFeely, *Frederick Douglass,* 1990. Eric Sundquist, ed., *Frederick Douglass: New Literary and Historical Essays,* 1990. William L. Andrews, ed., *Critical Essays on Frederick Douglass,* 1991. John Ernest, *Resistance and Reformation in Nineteenth-Century African-American Literature,* 1995. Robert S. Levine, Martin Delany, *Frederick Douglass, and the Politics of Representative Identity,* 1997.

—William L. Andrews

DOVE, RITA (b. 1952), poet, novelist, short story writer, dramatist, essayist, educator, and U.S. poet laureate. Highly prolific and greatly appreciated poet Rita Dove was born on 28 August 1952 in Akron, Ohio, the daughter of Elvira Dove and Ray Dove, a chemist. She attended Miami University in Ohio, graduating summa cum laude in 1973. A Fulbright scholarship sent her during 1974–1975 to the University of Tübingen in West Germany. She received an MFA in creative writing from the Iowa Writers Workshop at the University of Iowa in 1977. In Iowa she met her German husband, Fred Viebahn, a novelist with whom she has one child, a daughter named Aviva. That year she published the first of three chapbooks, *Ten Poems.* The following year she received the first of two literary awards from the National Endowment for the Arts (she received the second in 1989), and in 1980 at age twenty-seven she published both her second chapbook, *The Only Dark Spot in the Sky,* and her first book of poetry with a major press, *The Yellow House on the Corner* (1980).

Coming of age a decade after the peak of the Black Arts movement, Dove writes poetry remarkably different from that of the previous generation, which was loose and improvisational in style, with urgent and inspired lyrics. Indeed, Dove has been called the most disciplined and technically accomplished poet since

Gwendolyn *Brooks. Although her poems often focus on African American people, past and present, she finds many things of interest in them, not just their circumstances as racial subjects. She also extends her vision to include people of many backgrounds in order to investigate the complexities of perspective. In *The Yellow House on the Corner,* for example, she tells the story of how one enslaved woman thwarts the escape of a group of slaves when she helps the driver regain his horse. Rather than polarizing their positions, as the previous generation would have done, she illustrates their connection in the woman's recognition that she may be related to the driver. Her recognition and its result well represent one of the most profound horrors of slavery.

In 1981 Dove joined the faculty at the Arizona State University, Tempe. In 1982 she spent a year as a writer in residence at the Tuskegee Institute, publishing her third and final chapbook, *Mandolin* (1982). Her next volume, *Museum* (1983), was (as every subsequent volume would be) published by a major publishing house. Two years later she tried her hand at short stories, publishing the collection *Fifth Sunday* (1985). During her tenure at Arizona State Dove participated in the national literary scene in innumerable ways: as a literary advisory panel member of the National Endowment for the Arts (1984–1986); as the chair of the poetry grants panel for the National Endowment for the Arts in 1985; and on the board of directors of the Associate Writing Programs (1985–1988), including serving as their president in 1986–1987. In 1987 she also began her long association as associate editor and commissioner, respectively, of two central institutions of African American culture, *Callaloo,* a journal of criticism and the arts known for publishing contemporary poetry, and the Schomberg Center for Research in Black Culture. Her literary efforts were recognized with many honors, including a fellowship from the Guggenheim Foundation (1983–1984) and the Lavan Younger Poets Award from the Academy of American Poets (1986). Her work during this period culminated in **Thomas and Beulah* (1986), for which she won the 1987 Pulitzer Prize for poetry.

Loosely based on the lives of Dove's maternal grandparents, *Thomas and Beulah* is divided into two sequences, the first about Thomas and the second about Beulah. Although its subjects live together for decades, the poem sequences reveal lives that barely intersect, with the two more often moving in their own directions. More personal than Dove's previous work, this volume illustrates her ability to bring vitality and insight to the ordinary and everyday.

In 1988 Dove had a Bellagio residency sponsored by the Rockefeller Foundation, but she spent most of the year as a Mellon fellow at the National Humanities Center in North Carolina. That year and the year following she received honorary doctorates from Miami University and Knox College, respectively. In 1989 she published another volume of poems, *Grace Notes,* and accepted a faculty position at the University of Virginia, where she spent the next three years at the Center for Advanced Studies. In 1993 the University of Virginia promoted her to an endowed chair as the Commonwealth Professor of English. While writing she also remained active in national poetry competitions. In 1991 alone, she served as a judge for the Walt Whitman Award of the Academy of American Poets; the Pulitzer Prize in poetry; the National Book Award poetry panel; and the Literary Lion of the New York Public Library. That same year she also was inducted into the Ohio Women's Hall of Fame. Not content to stick to poetry, Dove extended her writing talents, publishing her first novel, *Through the Ivory Tower* (1992), and her first play, *The Darker Face of the Earth* (1994).

Through the Ivory Gate traces the life of a talented young African American woman, Virginia King, who becomes an artist in residence at a primary school in the town where she grew up—Akron, Ohio. Alternating between present moments and flashbacks, the story links Virginia's current life to powerful, sometimes painful recollections of her girlhood. The novel presents a series of shorter stories that through accretion build a sense of the richness of this woman's life and her connections not only to the friends and family around her, but to place, culture, and region.

1993 was a particularly big year for Rita Dove. Her list of accomplishments and awards extended even further, again illustrating her appeal to both African Americans and all Americans more generally. She published another volume of poetry, *Selected Poems,* received the Great American Artist Award from the NAACP, and became the youngest and first African American poet laureate. Dove read at the White House and spoke at the two-hundredth-anniversary celebration of the U.S. Capitol. Accolades in 1994 include the Renaissance Forum Award for Leadership in the Literary Arts from the Folger Shakespeare Library; the Golden Plate Award from the American Academy of Achievement; the Carl Sandburg Award from the International Platform Association; and additional honorary doctorates from Tuskegee; University of Miami; Washington University; Case Western University; University of Akron; and in 1995 from Arizona State University; Boston College; and Dartmouth College. Recent publications include *Mother Love* (1995), *The Poet's World* (1995), and *On the Bus with Rosa Parks* (1999).

• Robert McDowell, "The Assembling Vision of Rita Dove," *Callaloo* 9.1 (Winter 1986): 61–70. Arnold Rampersad, "The Poems of Rita Dove," *Callaloo* 9.1 (Winter 1986): 52–60. Ekaterini Georgoudaki, "Rita Dove: Crossing Boundaries," *Callaloo* 14.2 (Spring 1991): 419–433. Susan M. Trosky, ed., *CA,* New Revision Series, vol. 42, 1994, pp. 127–128. Helen Vendler, "Rita Dove: Identity Markers," *Callaloo* 17.2 (Summer 1994): 381–398. *Callaloo,* 19 (1966).

—Maggie Sale

DOWNING, HENRY F. (1846–1928), sailor, novelist, playwright, and historian. Born in New York City into a family of successful free African Americans who ran an oyster business, Henry Downing was the nephew of the esteemed politician George Thomas Downing. Henry Downing served two terms in the U.S. Navy (1864–1865 and 1872–1875). Following the Civil War, he traveled around the world, a journey punctuated by a three-year residence in Liberia, where his cousin Hilary Johnson later served as president (1884–1892). After returning to New York, he became politically active in the Democratic Party. For his strong support, President Cleveland appointed Downing consul to Loanda, Angola, a West African colony of Portugal, where he served less than a year before resigning in 1888. After returning to New York for several years, he emigrated to London in 1895, where he remained for twenty-two years. There he began a productive, if undistinguished, career as a writer. With at least six unpublished plays already written, he had five plays published (and likely performed) in 1913 alone. Melodramatic fare expressing minimal interest in race issues, these include *The Arabian Lioness, or The Sacred Jar; Human Nature, or The Traduced Wife; Lord Eldred's Other Daughter; The Shuttlecock, or Israel in Russia;* and *Placing Paul's Play,* coauthored with his second wife, Margarita Doyle. The reception of these plays remains unknown. Shortly before leaving London for New York, he published a novel, *The American Cavalryman: A Liberian Romance* (1917), whose plot follows a relationship founded on mistaken racial identity in order to glorify the possibilities of American blacks settling in Liberia. His final drama, *The Racial Tangle* (1920), which also centered on race-based romantic intrigue, was made into the silent film *Thirty Years Later* (1928) by Oscar *Micheaux. Downing's last works were *Liberia and Her People* (1925) and *A Short History of Liberia* (n.d.), both of which were philosophically compatible with Marcus *Garvey's back to Africa movement.

• Clarence G. Contee, Sr., "Downing, Henry F[rancis]," in *DANB,* eds. Rayford W. Logan and Michael R. Winston, 1982, pp. 188–189. Bernard Bell, *The Afro-American Novel and Its Tradition,* 1987, p. 78. Bernard L. Peterson, Jr., "Downing, Henry F. (Francis)," in *Early Black American Playwrights and Dramatic Writers: A Biographic Directory and Catalog of Plays, Films, and Broadcasting Scripts,* 1990, pp. 62–63.

—Lawrence R. Rodgers

DU BOIS, SHIRLEY GRAHAM. See Graham, Shirley.

DU BOIS, W. E. B. (1868–1963), essayist, novelist, journalist, critic, and perhaps the preeminent African American scholar-intellectual. William Edward Burghardt Du Bois was born in Great Barrington, Massachusetts, in 1868. He was born into a small community of blacks who had settled in the region since at least the Revolutionary War, in which an ancestor had fought. His mother, Mary Sylvina Burghardt, married a restless young visitor to the region, Alfred Du Bois, who disappeared soon after the birth of his son. Du Bois grew up a thorough New Englander, as he recalled, a member of the Congregational Church and a star student in the local schools, where he was encouraged to excel.

In 1885 he left Great Barrington for Nashville, Tennessee, to enter Fisk University. The racism of the South appalled him: "No one but a Negro going into the South without previous experience of color caste can have any conception of its barbarism." Nevertheless he enjoyed life at Fisk, from which he was graduated in 1888. He then enrolled at Harvard, where he completed another bachelor's degree in 1890 before going on to graduate school there in history.

At Harvard his professors included William James, George Santayana, and the historian A. B. Hart. He then spent two years at the University of Berlin studying history and sociology and coming close to earning a second doctorate. Du Bois enjoyed his stay in Europe, which greatly expanded his notions about the possibilities of culture and civilization. Then, in 1894, he dropped back, as he himself put it, into "nigger-hating America."

Despite his education, most jobs were closed to him. In the next few years Du Bois taught unhappily at black Wilberforce University in Ohio, carried out a complex project in empirical sociology in a black section of Philadelphia for the University of Pennsylvania, and then, in 1897, settled in to teach economics, history, and sociology at Atlanta University.

His doctoral thesis, *The Suppression of the African Slave-Trade to the United States 1638–1870,* was published in 1896 as the first volume of the Harvard Historical Studies, to be followed in 1899 by his acclaimed study in empirical sociology, *The Philadelphia Negro.* However, in 1903, as Du Bois became more disenchanted with race relations in the South and increasingly saw social science as relatively powerless to change social conditions, he moved away from strict scholarship to publish a landmark collection of prose pieces, *The *Souls of Black Folk.*

This volume, which expressly attacked Booker T. *Washington, the most powerful black American of the age, brought Du Bois to controversial prominence among blacks. Brilliantly written and extraordinarily rich and complex as a portrait of black life, it also became a sort of Bible for younger black intellectuals and artists in America.

Du Bois's growing dissatisfaction with scholarship in general led him while at Atlanta to ventures in journalism as editor of two magazines, the *Moon* and the *Horizon,* between 1905 and 1909. He also published a biography, *John Brown* (1909), about the martyr of Harpers Ferry, that underscored his growing interest in radical action. Finally, in 1910, he gave up his professorship in Atlanta to move to New York as director of publicity of the new NAACP and as founder and editor of its magazine, the *Crisis.*

Du Bois quickly made the journal a trumpet against all forms of racism, as well as a reliable vehicle for writers young and old. Aiming consciously to stimulate artistic activity among younger blacks, he wrote of a coming renaissance. In 1911 he himself published a novel, *The Quest of the Silver Fleece,* about blacks and cotton in the South, that suggested the influence of Frank Norris. In 1915, reflecting a deepening knowledge of Africa, came *The Negro,* his Pan-Africanist account of the history of blacks in Africa and around the world. In 1920 he published his second collection of fugitive pieces, this time including some verse, *Darkwater: Voices from within the Veil.* This volume showed him starkly alienated and embittered, especially as compared to the self-portrait in *The Souls of Black Folk,* with which the new volume invited comparison.

Between 1919 and 1926, Jessie Redmon *Fauset served as literary editor of the *Crisis* and helped to attract early work by Countee *Cullen, Langston *Hughes, and other young writers of the Harlem Renaissance. In 1926, however, in a *Crisis* symposium called "The Negro in Art," Du Bois attacked many of the younger writers for failing to recognize their political responsibilities. "All art is propaganda," he insisted, in a reversal of an earlier position, "and ever must be, despite the wailing of the purists." To illustrate his point, he contributed a novel, *Dark Princess* (1928), about a black American man, the beautiful Indian princess with whom he falls in love, and a plot among representatives of the darker nations of the world to rid themselves forever of white domination.

In 1934, with the *Crisis* circulation greatly reduced and the Renaissance exhausted by the Great Depression, Du Bois resigned from the NAACP after years of tension with other leaders. He returned to Atlanta University to teach there. The next year he published *Black Reconstruction in America,* a massive treatise built largely on secondary material, about the post–Civil War period in the South. The work was highly colored by Du Bois's renewed interest in Marxism, to which he had been drawn earlier, and by his sometimes overwhelming dramatic sense. In 1940 his autobiography **Dusk of Dawn: An Essay Toward an Autobiography of a Race Concept* explored the relationship between his life and the evolution of theories of race in America and elsewhere.

In 1944 Du Bois rejoined the NAACP in New York as director of special research. Before long, however, he was again in conflict with the Association leaders over his growing interest in Communism and what he saw as their conservatism. In 1948 the Association fired him, this time for good. He joined forces with Paul *Robeson and others in the Council of African Affairs, an anticolonialist organization, but also associated himself openly with other elements of the international Left. In 1950 he ran unsuccessfully for the U.S. Senate on the Labor Party ticket. In 1951 he was indicted by a grand jury and arrested for operating as the unregistered agent of a foreign power because of his involvement with a group called the Peace Information Center, of which he was chairman. After the trial judge threw out the case, Du Bois wrote about his experiencesin *In Battle for Peace: The Story of My Eighty-Third Birthday* (1952).

In the 1950s he consolidated his links to Communism. He was prominent in the outcry against the execution of the Rosenbergs and took part in their funeral service. The government retaliated by seizing his passport and holding it for several years. Still Du Bois continued to write. In his last years he published *The Black Flame,* a trilogy of novels: *The Ordeal of Mansart* (1957), *Mansart Builds a School* (1959), and *Worlds of Color* (1961). These novels offered an encyclopedic account of modern African American and world history seen from a radical perspective, mainly through the experiences of a stalwart though intellectually mediocre African American educator, Manuel Mansart. The trilogy was ignored by virtually all American critics and reviewers, black or white.

In 1959, after much travel following the restoration of his passport, he emigrated to Ghana. He did so at the invitation of its president, Kwame Nkrumah, to begin work on an *Encyclopedia Africana,* in which Du Bois had taken an almost lifelong interest. At the same time, he publicly applied for membership in the U.S. Communist Party. In Africa, he renounced his U.S. citizenship and became a citizen of Ghana. He died in Accra in August 1963.

Merely as the author of five novels and enough poems for a slender volume, Du Bois deserves a place in African American literary history. However, his impact on black literature went well beyond his efforts as a poet or writer of fiction. *The Souls of Black Folk* revolutionized African American self-perception by locating the black personality and character in the context of history, sociology, religion, music, and art as it had never been located before. Du Bois's concept of double consciousness and his image of black Americans as living behind a veil in America, which he developed in harmony with astute critical analyses of history and sociology, opened up the representational world for black artists responding to the crisis in which African Americans have been forced to live.

His many brilliant essays, backed by a rare command of black history and social complexity, were a resource on which generations of black intellectuals and artists drew. The grand tribute given Du Bois by Arthur Spingarn of the NAACP when Du Bois resigned from the organization in 1934 is hardly off the mark: "He created, what never existed before, a Negro intelligentsia, and many who have never read a word of his writings are his spiritual disciples and descendants."

[*See also* Graham, Shirley.]

• Francis L. Broderick *W. E. B. Du Bois: Negro Leader in a Time of Crisis,* 1959. Elliott Rudwick, *W. E. B. Du Bois: Propagandist of the Negro Protest,* 1968. Shirley Graham Du Bois, *His Day Is*

Marching On: A Memoir of W. E. B. Du Bois, 1971. Herbert Aptheker, ed., *Annotated Bibliography of the Published Writings of W. E. B. Du Bois,* 1973. William L. Andrews, ed., *Critical Essays on W. E. B. Du Bois,* 1985. Herbert Aptheker, ed., *The Complete Published Works of W. E. B. Du Bois,* 35 vols., 1973–1985. Nathan I. Huggins, ed. *W. E. B. Du Bois: Writings,* 1990. Arnold Rampersad, *The Art and Imagination of W. E. B. Du Bois,* 1990. David Levering Lewis, *W. E. B. Du Bois: Biography of a Race, 1868–1919,* 1993. Shamoon Zamir, *Dark Voices: W.E.B. Du Bois and American Thought, 1888–1903,* 1996.

—Arnold Rampersad

DUMAS, HENRY (1934–1968) poet, short fiction writer, and mythologizer. The literary legacy of Henry Dumas is one that has been kept alive almost single-handedly by fellow poet Eugene *Redmond. Dumas inspires interest not only for his unique vision of black people in the diaspora, but because of the tragedy of his own life. Mistakenly shot down by a New York City Transit policeman on 23 May 1968, when he was a mere thirty-three, his life is emblematic of the precarious position of black men in America and the painful situation of a talented young man dying so young. Observers can only speculate, sadly, about what he might have accomplished if he had somehow escaped the fate assigned to him. In many ways Dumas has become a cultural icon in African American literary circles.

Henry Dumas was born on 20 July 1934 in Sweet Home, Arkansas, where he spent his early years and was saturated with the religious and folk traditions of that soil. He claimed Moms Mabley and gospel music as particular influences upon him. At the age of ten, he was taken to Harlem, where he attended public schools and graduated from Commerce High School in 1953. He enrolled in City College that year but left to join the Air Force. Stationed at Lackland Air Force Base in San Antonio, Texas, he maintained his interest in religion by teaching Sunday school while there. Dumas also spent a year on the Arabian Peninsula, where he developed an interest in the Arabic language, mythology, and culture.

Dumas married Loretta Ponton on 24 September 1955, while he was still in the military. He fathered two sons before he came to his untimely death. The first son, David, was born in 1958, after Dumas had completed his tour of duty and enrolled at Rutgers University. His second son, Michael, was born in 1962, three years before Dumas terminated his part-time attendance at Rutgers; he did not complete his degree. Though he had compelling duties as a husband, father, and IBM worker (1963–1964), Dumas was nonetheless active in civil rights and humanitarian activities, including transporting food and clothing to protesters living in Mississippi and Tennessee.

In 1967 Dumas went to Southern Illinois University as a teacher, counselor, and director of language workshops in its Experiment in Higher Education program. It was here that he met Eugene Redmond, a fellow teacher in that program. Over the course of the ten months Dumas lived in East St. Louis, he and Redmond forged the collaborative relationship that would prove so fruitful to Dumas's posthumous career. He and Redmond read their poetry at common gatherings; Redmond especially remembers Dumas reading "Our King Is Dead," his elegy for Martin Luther *King, Jr. Dumas also frequented the offices of the *East St. Louis Monitor,* which Redmond edited and which featured an obituary on Dumas on 6 June 1968.

Dumas's first collection of short fiction is entitled *"Arks of Bones" and Other Stories* (edited by Redmond in 1974), which includes nine stories and in which his largely mythic vision of African American existence is apparent. In *"Ark of Bones,"* for example, Dumas depicts an ark that lands in a river in Arkansas, to which a young African American boy, Headeye, is called to assume his priestly role on the ship. The ship contains bones, bones of black people who died in the Middle Passage or who have otherwise lost their lives in a repressive, racist world. The only living inhabitants on the ark are the eternal caretakers of the bones; Headeye has been selected to become one of these and is initiated into the role he must play. Like *Velma Henry in Toni Cade *Bambara's *The *Salt Eaters* or the general pattern in which African Americans, especially preachers, are chosen by forces beyond this world for duties in this world, Headeye finally accepts the fact that he hears voices that other people do not hear, that he has one foot in the realm of the empirical and one foot in the realm of the extranatural. Instances of otherworldly phenomena permeating the natural environment also occur in other stories in the collection.

Redmond's commitment to making Dumas's work readily available to scholarly communities continued in the publication of *Goodbye, Sweetwater* (1988) and *Knees of a Natural Man: The Selected Poetry of Henry Dumas* (1989). The first volume contains eight of the stories that first appeared in *"Ark of Bones,"* along with excerpts from Dumas's unfinished novel, *Jonoah and the Green Stone* (1976), stories from *Rope of Wind* (1979), and three selections from "Goodbye Sweetwater." One of the stories in the final section is "Rain God," which develops the African American folk belief that, when it is raining and the sun is shining, the devil is beating his wife. Three young black boys literally witness this phenomenon as they are on their way home one rainy-sunny day. The second volume contains previously published as well as unpublished poems, including several poems with the title "Kef" and an accompanying number, and "Saba," with the same pattern. Some of the poems in *Knees* had appeared in *Play Ebony: Play Ivory* (1974), a collection of Dumas's poetry, which Redmond edited singly in 1974 and which he had coedited in 1970. Dumas's poetry is inspired by African American music, particularly blues and jazz (he studied with Sun Ra), and he develops themes consistent with the Black Aesthetic of the 1960s. His poetry also focuses, in keeping with his fiction, on themes of nature and the natural world.

Readers coming to Dumas's works are most struck by his extraordinary vision, his unusual ways of looking at the world, at the experiences of African Americans, and at the intersections of natural and supernatural phenomena. Redmond had done yeoman work in encouraging interest in Dumas's fictional and poetic creations. It remains to be seen whether the planted seeds will indeed sprout into a critical industry.

• Eugene B. Redmond, introduction to *"Ark of Bones" and Other Stories,* 1974. Carolyn A. Mitchell, "Henry Dumas," in *DLB,* vol. 41, *Afro-American Poets since 1955,* eds. Trudier Harris and Thadious M. Davis, 1985, pp. 89–99. Eugene B. Redmond, "The Ancient and Recent Voices within Henry Dumas," introduction to *Goodbye Sweetwater,* 1988. Eugene B. Redmond, "Poet Henry Dumas: Distance Runner, Stabilizer, Distiller," introduction to *Knees of a Natural Man: The Selected Poetry of Henry Dumas,* 1989. Dana A. Williams, "Making the Bones Live Again: A Look at the 'Bones People' in August Wilson's Joe Turner's Come and Gone and Henry Dumas' *"Ark of Bones,"' College Language Association Journal* 42: 3 (March 1999): 309–19.

—Trudier Harris

DUNBAR, PAUL LAURENCE (1872–1906), poet, fiction writer, essayist, songwriter, linguistic innovator, and prophet. Paul Laurence Dunbar published in such mainstream journals as *Century, Lipincott's Monthly,* the *Atlantic Monthly,* and the *Saturday Evening Post.* A gifted poet and a precursor to the Harlem Renaissance, Dunbar was read by both blacks and whites in turn-of-the-century America.

Dunbar, the son of two former slaves, was born in Dayton, Ohio, and attended the public schools of that city. He was taught to read by his mother, Matilda Murphy Dunbar, and he absorbed her homespun wisdom as well as the stories told to him by his father, Joshua Dunbar, who had escaped from enslavement in Kentucky and served in the Massachusetts 55th Regiment during the Civil War. Thus, while Paul Laurence Dunbar himself was never enslaved, he was one of the last of a generation to have ongoing contact with those who had been. Dunbar was steeped in the oral tradition during his formative years and he would go on to become a powerful interpreter of the African American folk experience in literature and song; he would also champion the cause of civil rights and higher education for African Americans in essays and poetry that were militant by the standards of his day.

During his years at Dayton's Central High, Dunbar was the school's only student of color, but it was his scholarly performance that distinguished him. He served as editor in chief of the school paper, president of the literary society, and class poet. His poetry grew more sophisticated with his repeated readings of John Keats, William Wordsworth, Samuel Taylor Coleridge, and Robert Burns; later he would add American poets John Greenleaf Whittier, Henry Wadsworth Longfellow, and James Whitcomb Riley to his list of favorites as he searched ardently for his own poetic voice. But it was his reading of Irwin Russell and other writers in the plantation tradition that led him into difficulty as he searched for an authentic poetic diction that would incorporate the voices of his parents and the stories they told.

After graduating from high school in 1891, racial discrimination forced Dunbar to accept a job as an elevator operator in a Dayton hotel. He wrote on the job during slack hours. He became well known as the "elevator boy poet" after James Newton Mathews invited him to read his poetry at the annual meeting of the Western Association of Writers, held in Dayton in 1892.

In 1893 Dunbar published his first volume of poetry, *Oak and Ivy,* on the press of the Church of the Brethren. That same year he also attended the World's Columbian Exposition, where he sold copies of his book and gained the patronage of Frederick *Douglass and other influential African Americans.

In 1895 Dunbar initiated a correspondence with Alice Ruth Moore, a fair-skinned black Creole teacher and writer originally from New Orleans. Three years later he married Alice in secret and over the objections of her friends and family. During the years of their marriage, Dunbar began to suffer from tuberculosis and the alcohol prescribed for it. The Dunbars separated permanently in 1902 but remained friends, and Alice continued to be known as "the widow of Paul Laurence Dunbar" even after her 1916 marriage to publisher Robert J. Nelson. The Dunbars had no children.

Dunbar published eleven volumes of poetry including *Oak and Ivy* (1893), **Majors and Minors* (1895), **Lyrics of Lowly Life* (1896), *Lyrics of the Hearthside* (1899), *Poems of Cabin and Field* (1899), *Candle-Lightin' Time* (1901), *Lyrics of Love and Laughter* (1903), *When Malindy Sings* (1903), *Li'l Gal* (1904), *Howdy, Honey, Howdy* (1905), and *Lyrics of Sunshine and Shadow* (1905). Dunbar's so-called *Complete Poems* were published posthumously in 1913. The most complete edition of Dunbar's poetry, *The Collected Poetry of Paul Laurence Dunbar,* containing a selection of sixty poems not published in 1913, did not appear until 1994. Dunbar's published fiction includes *The Uncalled* (1898), **Folks from Dixie* (1898), *The Strength of Gideon and Other Stories* (1900), *The Fanatics* (1901), and *The *Sport of the Gods* (1902), but he remains best known for his poetry.

Much of the controversy surrounding Paul Laurence Dunbar concerns his dialect poetry, wherein some scholars, such as the late Charles T. Davis, felt that Dunbar showed the greatest glimmers of genius. Sterling A. *Brown, writing in *Negro Poetry and Drama* in 1937, asserted that Dunbar was the first American poet to "handle Negro folk life with any degree of fullness" but he also found Dunbar guilty of cruelly "misreading" black history. This points to the basic flaw in Paul Laurence Dunbar's attempts to represent authentic

African American folk language in verse. He was not able to transcend completely the racist plantation tradition made popular by Joel Chandler Harris, Thomas Nelson Page, Irwin Russell, and other white writers who made use of African American folk materials and who showed the "old time Negro" as if he were satisfied serving the master on the antebellum plantation.

While Dunbar sought an appropriate literary form for the representation of African American vernacular expression, he was also deeply ambivalent about his undertaking in this area. He recognized that many of his experiments yielded imperfect results and he was concerned that prominent white critics such as William Dean Howells praised his work for the wrong reasons, setting a tone that other Dunbar critics would follow for years as they virtually ignored his standard English verse and his published experiments with Irish, German, and Western regional dialects.

Some African American critics saw a concession to racism evident in Dunbar's black dialect poetry, and while it is unlikely that any perceived concession was intentional, it can certainly be argued that dialect poems like "Parted" and "Corn Song" were more derivative of the plantation school than they were original productions of African American genius. Yet, during his lifetime, Dunbar's work was praised by Frederick Douglass, Booker T. *Washington, and W. E. B. *Du Bois, among others.

Negative treatment of Dunbar's poetry by black critics including scholar-poet James Weldon *Johnson did not surface fully until the New Negro movement of the 1920s. On the other hand, poets Countee *Cullen and Langston *Hughes publicly admired and emulated Dunbar. A considered reading of poems like "We Wear the Mask," "When Malindy Sings," "Frederick Douglass," "The Colored Soldiers," or "The Haunted Oak" affirms Dunbar's loyalty to the black race and his pride in its achievements, as well as his righteous anger over racial injustice.

In the second half of the twentieth century Paul Laurence Dunbar was rediscovered. In 1972 centenary conferences marking the hundredth anniversary of Dunbar's birth were held at the University of Dayton and the University of California at Irvine, with prominent black poets and writers in attendance. At the Irvine conference, poet Nikki *Giovanni suggested that Dunbar's "message is clear and available . . . if we invest in Dunbar the integrity we hope others will give us."

A new edition of Dunbar's poems subsequently put long out-of-print Dunbar poems back on the classroom shelf, making it possible for teachers to acquaint a new generation of poets and scholars with Dunbar's work.

[*See also* Dunbar-Nelson, Alice Moore.]

• Addison Gayle, Jr., *Oak and Ivy: A Biography of Paul Laurence Dunbar,* 1971. Jay Martin, ed., *A Singer in the Dawn: Reinterpretations of Paul Laurence Dunbar,* 1975. Jay Martin and Gossie Hudson, eds., *Paul Laurence Dunbar Reader,* 1975. Peter Revell, Paul Laurence Dunbar, 1979. Marcellus Blount, "The Preacherly Text: African American Poetry and Vernacular Performance," *PMLA* 107 (May 1992): 582–593. Joanne M. Braxton, ed., *The Collected Poetry of Paul Laurence Dunbar,* 1993.

—Joanne M. Braxton

DUNBAR-NELSON, ALICE MOORE (1875–1935), short fiction writer, poet, diarist, journalist, and public speaker. Born in New Orleans, of mixed African American, Native American, and European American background, Alice Moore graduated from Straight College with a teaching degree in 1892. She published her first book, *Violets and Other Tales,* in 1895, a multigenre collection, including short stories, poetry, and essays. The volume anticipates much of Dunbar-Nelson's later work, reflecting her interest in a range of literary forms, attraction to romantic themes and language, attention to class differences, and ambivalence about women's roles. Notable, too, is a characteristic absence of racial designation, perhaps a consequence of Dunbar-Nelson's complex and occasionally conflicting attitudes toward the intersecting lines of class and color shaping her Creole heritage.

After a courtship begun in correspondence, Moore married the poet Paul Laurence *Dunbar in 1898. The marriage, complicated by Dunbar's extensive travel and poor health, ended in 1902, and Dunbar-Nelson resumed her teaching career. Although she twice married, finding happiness with her third husband, journalist Robert Nelson, she retained the Dunbar name.

In 1899, Dunbar-Nelson published her finest literary work, *The Goodness of St. Rocque and Other Stories.* The collection of short fiction richly reflects New Orleans Creole culture, connecting Dunbar-Nelson to the late-nineteenth-century local color tradition. These stories are complicated by recurring imagery of disguise and entrapment that often suggests meanings masked by the romantic narrative. It is notable that in later short fiction uncollected or unpublished in her lifetime Dunbar-Nelson far more explicitly confronted questions of gender and race. Much of this later work is included in the three-volume *Works of Alice Dunbar-Nelson* (1988) edited by Gloria T. Hull.

Although fiction was Dunbar-Nelson's best medium, during the Harlem Renaissance period she was known primarily as a poet. Traditional in form, her poetry treats primarily romantic themes with elevated, poetic language. Between 1917 and 1928, her poems appeared in the *Crisis* and *Opportunity,* and were included in several anthologies, notably James Weldon **Johnson's Book of American Negro Poetry* (1931).

In 1921 and from 1926 to 1931, Alice Dunbar-Nelson kept a personal diary. Edited by Gloria T. Hull, *Give Us Each Day: The Diary of Alice Dunbar-Nelson* (1984) details Dunbar-Nelson's professional labors, travels, friendships, and recurring financial difficulties and refers to her lesbian relationships.

In addition to her work as an educator, Alice Dunbar-Nelson brought her skills and energy as speaker, writer, and organizer to movements for social change. She was active in the Women's Club movement, worked for suffrage, helped found the Industrial School for Colored Girls in Delaware, and in 1922 was a leader in the fight for passage of the Dyer Anti-Lynching Bill. Her work as a public speaker and interest in oratory provided the foundation for two edited volumes, *Masterpieces of Negro Eloquence* (1914) and *The Dunbar Speaker and Entertainer* (1920). Toward the end of her career, Dunbar-Nelson turned from teaching to journalism and public speaking. From 1926 to 1930, she wrote regular newspaper columns in which she forthrightly commented on issues her fiction addressed only indirectly. From 1928 to 1931 she did extensive public speaking as executive secretary of the American Friends Inter-Racial Peace Committee.

Alice Dunbar-Nelson remains significant for the range of her written work, the complex, muted voice of her short fiction, and the rare, invaluable record her diary provides of the public and private life of an early twentieth-century African American woman writer.

• Gloria T. Hull, *Color, Sex, and Poetry: Three Women Writers of the Harlem Renaissance*, 1987. Violet Harrington Bryan, "Race and Gender in the Early Works of Alice Dunbar-Nelson," in *Louisiana Women Writers: New Essays and a Comprehensive Bibliography*, 1992, pp. 121–138.

—Mary Titus

DUNHAM, KATHERINE (b. 1909 or 1910), choreographer, dancer, anthropologist, and writer. Characterized for much of her professional life as a woman with a double identity, as Broadway's grande dame of American dance and as a pioneering dance anthropologist of world renown, Katherine Dunham has influenced generations with her wide array of talent. Born in Glen Ellyn, Illinois, she attended the University of Chicago, where she studied anthropology and first began to pursue the study of dance with professional aspirations. During the Great Depression Dunham opened a series of dance schools, all of which closed prematurely for financial reasons but not before they earned Dunham the attention and company of such noted individuals as Arna *Bontemps, Langston *Hughes, Horace Mann, Sterling North, Charles Sebree, and Charles White. As the recipient of a 1935 Julius Rosenwald Foundation Fellowship for the study of anthropology and dance traditions in the Caribbean, Dunham united her work in anthropology with her innovations in modern dance. She used her anthropological fieldwork to synthesize and transform indigenous Caribbean dance movements into theatrical dance forms; this study, subsequently backed by a Rockefeller Foundation Fellowship, culminated in a master's degree in anthropology from the University of Chicago and a doctoral degree in anthropology from Northwestern University.

In 1944 Dunham founded the Katherine Dunham School of Dance in New York, which immediately became the cradle of African American dance until it closed in 1955. Renowned for her technique and the ethnological studies on which she based her performance choreography, her company was the first all-Black dance company to tour the world in the late 1940s and early 1950s.

Dunham's versatility as a performance artist and dancer brought her fame on the Broadway stage and in such films as *The Emperor Jones* (1939), the musical *Cabin in the Sky* (1940), *Carnival of Rhythm* (1942), and *Stormy Weather* (1943). Although Katherine Dunham continued to appear in films throughout the 1940s, her chosen medium was the concert stage, upon which she would make social, artistic, and intellectual statements. As a performer she was vividly flamboyant, popularly remembered for her sudden bursts of energy to produce acrobatic executions. But Dunham's work was not purely aesthetic; she used her creative output to contest the social injustices of her time. During the 1930s and 1940s, she used choreography and dramatic presentation to protest Jim Crow practices in transportation, education, and public accommodations. In 1951 she created Southland, a dramatic ballet inspired by the murder of Emmet Till, to depict and condemn southern lynching and all such practices of race hatred.

In 1972, Dunham directed *Treemonisha,* a ragtime opera by Scott Joplin, at the Wolf Trap Farm for the Performing Arts in Virginia.

Dunham has authored numerous scholarly articles, magazine essays, and several books, including *Journey to Accompong* (1946), an account of her experiences as an anthropologist among the Marrons, a people living in isolated mountain regions of Jamaica; *A Touch of Innocence* (1959), a third-person autobiography of her childhood; *Island Possessed* (1969); *Kassamance, a Fantasy* (1974); and *Dances of Haiti* (1983), the authoritative study on the subject. Katherine Dunham's legacy has been made public by her 1992 donation of a substantial portion of her costume collection, paintings, African and Caribbean folk and contemporary art, her vast collection of musical instruments from around the world, and her papers and films to the Missouri Historical Society in St. Louis.

• Ruth Beckford, *Katherine Dunham,* 1979. Darlene Donloe, *Katherine Dunham,* 1993. Constance Valis Hill, "Katherine Dunham's Southland: Protest in the Face of Repression," *Dance Research Journal* 26.2 (Fall 1994): 1–10.

—Gregory S. Jackson

Dusk of Dawn. Published in 1940, *Dusk of Dawn: An Essay Toward an Autobiography of a Race Concept* is the second of four works by W. E. B. Du Bois that are considered autobiographical. A generic mix of autobiography and sociological commentary, *Dusk of Dawn* seeks to reclaim the social and historical identities of early twentieth-century African Americans rather than to narrate and create the life of a singular self. As Du Bois cautions in his preface, *Dusk of Dawn* is "the autobiography of a concept of race," and not "mere autobiography." That is, Du Bois subordinates his personal chronicle to the collective sociopolitical goal of exposing America's history of racism.

Comprising nine chapters, the work may be divided into three sections. The first four chapters relate personal data about the author. Like other African American life-writers, Du Bois shapes the story of his growing manhood around his attainment of education. He chronicles his life from his New England childhood in Great Barrington, Massachusetts, to his attendance at Fisk University where he embraced his African American identity, to his graduation from Harvard University, and, finally, to his study and travel in Germany. Marking the transition between Du Bois's personal autobiography and his sociological analysis is his explanation of his ideological disagreements with his literary and historical forefather Booker T. *Washington, whose promotion of the industrial education of African Americans and of white patronage differed from Du Bois's vision of the "Talented Tenth" of African Americans who would become the leaders of their own community. The second section of *Dusk of Dawn* treats the history of the concept of race in America and its effect on both African Americans and whites. Du Bois presents race as a social construct and not as a biological certainty. Refuting the scientific definition of race, he suggests that what unifies nonwhites is not a common genetics but the social heritage of slavery and discrimination. The last section of *Dusk of Dawn,* consisting of the book's last two chapters, recollects public and controversial moments in the author's life, such as his founding of the *Crisis* and his resignation from the NAACP, and includes his commentary on current national and international trends.

Dusk of Dawn illuminates Du Bois's stance on key political issues: he promotes voluntary self-segregation as an advancement for African Americans; he clarifies that although he accepts Marx's economic analysis of society, he is not a communist; and he sees the rise of Hitler as symptomatic of the racism entrenched in Western civilization. Although *Dusk of Dawn* may be placed within the autobiographical tradition established by such writers as Booker T. Washington and James Weldon *Johnson and by the nineteenth-century slave narrators, it departs from its predecessors in its surrender of personal history to sociopolitical analysis. It portrays Du Bois as a man in search of community in a world, an American, and an African American culture based on divisions caused primarily by racial or class differences.

• Arnold Rampersad, *The Art and Imagination of W. E. B. Du Bois,* 1976. W. E. B. Du Bois, *Dusk of Dawn,* 1940; rpt 1984. William L. Andrews, ed., *Critical Essays on W. E. B. Du Bois,* 1985. Anthony Appiah, "The Uncompleted Argument: Du Bois and the Illusion of Race," in *"Race," Writing, and Difference,* ed. Henry Louis Gates, Jr., 1986, pp. 21–37.

—Mary C. Carruth

Dust Tracks on a Road. Zora Neale *Hurston's 1942 memoir is a book she did not want to write, and many of her admirers have wished she had not written it. Its factual information is often unreliable, its politics are contradictory, and it barely discusses Hurston's literary career, which is ostensibly the reason she wrote it. From the beginning it defies readers' expectations of autobiography. Only in the third chapter does Hurston begin the story of her own life, and she introduces it with a warning: "This is all hear-say. Maybe some of the details of my birth as told me might be a little inaccurate, but it is pretty well established that I really did get born." Hurston, who regularly took ten years off her age, had reason to practice this deception, but *Dust Tracks* is less than forthcoming about many facts of her life.

The book won the 1942 Anisfield-Wolf Book Award, sponsored by *Saturday Review* magazine, for its contribution to race relations. The prize says more about the state of race relations than about the clarity of Hurston's views. Some of the contradictions are deliberate, as in the chapter "My People, My People," a riff on the paradoxes of race in America. But other contradictions in the book derived from the publisher's last-minute insistence on extensive revisions, notably the deletion of the chapter "Seeing the World As It Is," which included an extended critique of U.S. imperialism in Asia. After the United States entered World War II, editors deemed Hurston's foreign policy views unpatriotic. Without these opinions, the book's politics seemed reactionary to many readers. Editors insisted on other changes as well. Some of the folklore Hurston recorded was too sexually explicit, and some of her personal opinions libelous. *Dust Tracks* was by far Hurston's most heavily edited book, and few of the changes were for the better.

And yet, passages in *Dust Tracks* are as engaging as any Hurston wrote. Recollections of her childhood are vividly evoked: Hurston chronicles adventures with her imaginary playmate; the "lying sessions" on Joe Clarke's Eatonville store porch, where "God, Devil, *Brer Rabbit, Brer Fox, Sis Cat . . . and all the wood folk walked and talked like natural men"; and the death of her mother. Equally vibrant are the descriptions of her field work, particularly her friendship with Big Sweet, a woman she met in a sawmill camp in Polk County, Florida, who became her protector and guide, and her interviews with Cudjo Lewis, reputed to be the sole survivor of the last known slave ship to dock on U.S. shores. In other chapters she describes the drama of revival meetings, recounts her friendships with novelist Fannie Hurst and singer-actress Ethel Waters, and offers guarded reflections on romantic love.

Recent editions restore the deleted sections of *Dust Tracks,* although it is impossible to reconstruct from surviving manuscripts the exact text Hurston intended. *Dust Tracks* may be best appreciated as a "lying session," which invites readers to listen to Hurston improvise on various topics.

• Nellie McKay, "Race, Gender, and Cultural Context in Zora Neale Hurston's *Dust Tracks on a Road*," in *Life/Lines: Theorizing Women's Autobiography*, eds. Bella Brodzki and Celeste Schenck, 1988, pp. 175–188. Claudine Raynaud, "'Rubbing a Paragraph with a Soft Cloth?' Muted Voices and Editorial Constraints in *Dust Tracks on a Road*," in *De/Colonizing the Subject: The Politics of Gender in Women's Autobiography*, eds. Sidonie Smith and Julia Watson, 1992, pp. 34–64.

—Cheryl A. Wall

Dutchman. Amiri *Baraka's (Le Roi Jones's) most widely known dramatic work, *Dutchman* was first presented at the Cherry Lane Theater in New York City in March 1964. This explosive examination of race relations in America, easily the most talked about play of the year, brought its writer the *Village Voice*'s Obie Award in recognition of the play being the most outstanding Off-Broadway production of the year. This highly controversial play was given film treatment in 1967.

Because of its lean, parable-like quality, *Dutchman* has frequently been compared to the work of Edward Albee, perhaps the leading American dramatist of the period. Several critics have emphasized the similarities between *Dutchman* and Albee's *The Zoo Story* in particular. A masterful example of the writer's handling of fundamental dramatic conventions, *Dutchman* moves, like the train of its setting, with powerful bursts of energy and periodic lulls. Marked by a number of dramatic reversals and rapidly accelerating tension, this play is also characterized by an effective synthesis of realistic and naturalistic tendencies, as well as the suggestion of such mythical influences as the Flying Dutchman, Adam and Eve, and Lilith.

Dutchman must be seen as a highly provocative theatrical handling of the thematic concerns treated in the poems of *The Dead Lecturer* (1964), the volume of guilt-ridden, self-conscious lyrics produced toward the close of Baraka's Beat period. Evidencing the strong influence of Howard University sociologist E. Franklin Frazier, author of *Black Bourgeoisie* (1957), *Dutchman* is a sharply focused indictment of those African Americans who desire to assimilate into mainstream American society. In doing so, these individuals deny all vestiges of the racial past and make every effort to distance themselves from the reality of black existence in America. Given symbolic treatment in the character Clay, such individuals seek validation in the acceptance of white America, as symbolized by the character Lula. As his name implies, Clay is the black American who allows himself to be molded into the image of white, middle-class society. His tragic end, however, at the hands of Lula, evidences the suicidal nature of his longings.

An equally important focal point of *Dutchman* is that of the proper orientation of the black artist, a matter of preeminent concern in the poetry of *The Dead Lecturer* and various essays written by Baraka during this period. In search of a legitimate and thoroughly engaged black art, Baraka frequently derides what he perceives as the derivative and evasive creative efforts of black writers, himself included. In "The Myth of a Negro Literature," for example, he urges the black writer to write unapologetically, from "the point of view of the black man in this country: as its victim and its chronicler." Referring to himself as the "great would-be poet" of "some kind of bastard literature," Clay places himself clearly in the rear guard of the movement toward a black sociopolitical consciousness as well as artistic authenticity.

Despite the numerous works that followed *Dutchman*, it remains Baraka's best-known and most critically acclaimed effort. Unequaled in its taut handling of the most pervasive and persistent of national issues, *Dutchman* secured Baraka's reputation as an important American dramatist.

• C. W. E. Bigsby, "Black Drama: The Public Voice," in *The Second Black Renaissance: Essays in Black Literature*, 1980.

—Henry C. Lacey

E

EARLY, GERALD (b. 1952), essayist, cultural critic, editor, educator, and poet. Born in Philadelphia, Gerald Early earned degrees from University of Pennsylvania (BA 1974) and Cornell University (MA 1980, PhD 1982). He is the Merle Kling Professor of Modern Letters and the director of African and Afro-American Studies at Washington University in St. Louis. His first essay collection, *Tuxedo Junction: Essays on American Culture* (1989), treats cultural topics such as politics, Miss America, boxing, and jazz. The relevance of popular culture for Early comes from its connection to the marginalized in American society and from the enormous creative involvement of African Americans in it. Through popular culture, musicians, sports figures, and writers have at once asserted and subverted the language and symbolism of mainstream culture. Early notes how the appropriation of white discourse cast two of his literary forebears, Frederick *Douglass and Zora Neale *Hurston, into the double role of criticizing dominant culture while inevitably being part of it. The contrast between Early's youth in a working-class, mainly African American neighborhood and his adult life among many middle-class whites informs his concern with double consciousness and identity. He organizes a larger exploration of the double role of African Americans in his editing of *Lure and Loathing: Essays on Race, Identity, and the Ambivalence of Assimilation* (1993).

In editing the two-volume collection *Speech and Power: The African-American Essay and Its Cultural Content from Polemics to Pulpit* (1992–1993), Early asserts that one cannot adequately appreciate African American literature without an ample understanding of the essay in the hands of the African American. He also notes the impact of H. L. Mencken's essays on African American writers, including Richard *Wright and Langston *Hughes. Although conscious of the general influence of the African American autobiographical tradition (especially the work of Douglass) and the sermonic tradition found in James *Baldwin and Martin Luther *King, Jr., Early himself wanted to write essays after reading Amiri *Baraka's **Home: Social Essays* (1966).

In *The Culture of Bruising: Essays on Prizefighting, Literature, and Modern American Culture* (1994), as in *Tuxedo Junction,* he writes less about baseball, boxing, or music and more about the surrounding symbols, personalities, and narratives from which he then draws meaning or provokes thought. As an essayist, he sets himself apart from rigidly academic criticism and theory and relies on a variety of unconventional references including personal experience, which he uses to verify or enrich his observations about cultural issues. The final essays of *The Culture of Bruising* turn more toward the personal, and he continues this autobiographical work in *Daughters: On Family and Fatherhood* (1995), where stories from his life illuminate familiar concerns such as class divisions within race, racial prejudice, and assimilation

In addition to the works mentioned above, Early has edited *My Soul's High Song: The Collected Writings of Countee *Cullen, Voice of the Harlem Renaissance* (1991) and has published *One Nation under a Groove: Motown and American Culture* (1995) and *How the War in the Streets Is Won: Poems on the Quest of Love and Faith* (1995). His work has appeared in the annual anthology *Best American Essays,* and he received the National Book Critics Circle Award in 1994 for *The Culture of Bruising.*

—Daniel J. Martin

EASY RAWLINS. Ezekiel (Easy) Rawlins, the protagonist in Walter *Mosley's detective novels, was a World War II veteran who had earned a high school diploma in night school, migrated to South Central Los Angeles, and was "threatenin' on some college" when he lost his job at Champion Aircraft. Needing to make the mortgage payment on his home, he accepted a job searching for a missing blonde. Several deaths later, Easy had solved the mystery, gained ten thousand dollars, rescued a sexually abused Mexican boy, and begun a career as a private investigator.

Unlike *Grave Digger Jones, *Coffin Ed Johnson, Aaron Gunner, Mari MacAllister, Joe Cinque, Tamara Hayle, and other African American crime fighters, Easy Rawlins is not an errant police officer struggling to maintain order in the midst of chaos. Rawlins is an ordinary working man with many loyal friends and a good reputation in his community. His forays into detective work, however, are generally marked by a certain amateurism that earns him bruises and beatings and fails to win him any permanent allies in the precincts. During the first four novels, Easy marries, divorces, and adopts two children, making him if not the only, at least one of a few, private investigators whose family life is integral to the plots. Rawlins's sidekick is his best friend, Raymond Alexander or "Mouse," a five-foot-six-inch psychotic whose readiness to kill Easy for an imagined slight is only slightly offset by his willingness to die to save Easy's life.

—Frances Smith Foster

EDWARDS, JUNIUS (b. 1929), novelist and short story writer. Junius Edwards's presentation of the soldier in his novel *If We Must Die* (1961) and short stories "Liars Don't Qualify" (1961) and "Duel with the Clock" (1967) is a part of an African American continuum from Frank *Yerby and John O. *Killens to George Davis and John A. *Williams. Like these writers, Edwards's works depict the impact of racial, psychological, and personal problems on the African American soldier. In "Duel with the Clock" a soldier seeks escape from army duty through drugs. In "Liars Don't Qualify" Edwards confronts the hypocrisy of the town that denies returning soldiers the same freedoms they had fought to preserve. This story is also the foundation for *If We Must Die,* a novel of multifaceted irony. Its simplicity of language and character does not belie the dehumanization of African Americans; the entrenched dominance of the southern white power structure during the 1950s; and the violence that affects the life of any African American perceived as a threat to this structure. The self-esteem of the main character, a returning Korean War veteran, is contrasted with the white voter registrar, who refuses to allow the veteran to register on the grounds that he lied about being a member of the Army Reserve. The veteran is later beaten and threatened with castration. Because Edwards was born in Alexandria, Louisiana, and in his twenties during the Korean War, his novel may have resulted from observation or experience. He studied in Chicago and at the University of Oslo and won the Writer's Digest Short Story Contest (1958) and a Eugene Saxton Fellowship (1959). He continues to publish in such anthologies as *Calling the Wind* (1993), which Clarence *Major edited.

—Australia Tarver

ELAW, ZILPHA (c. 1790–?), preacher and spiritual autobiographer. Zilpha Elaw was born around 1790 to free parents who brought her up in the vicinity of Philadelphia, Pennsylvania. In her midteens, while working as a domestic servant, she began to have religious visions. She was converted to Christianity and joined a Methodist society in an outlying region of Philadelphia in 1808. Two years later she married Joseph Elaw, a fuller, and moved with him to Burlington, New Jersey, where their daughter was born in 1812.

During a camp meeting in 1819, Zilpha Elaw became convinced that she had been called to preach the gospel. Her *Memoirs* state that the ministers of the Methodist Society of Burlington endorsed her aspirations and that she enjoyed initial success in her local ministry despite her husband's opposition. In 1823, Joseph Elaw died, forcing his widow to find employment as a domestic. A few years thereafter Elaw opened a school for African American children in Burlington but closed it two years later because of a growing uneasiness about having neglected her ministry. In the spring of 1828, Elaw undertook a solitary preaching mission to the slaveholding states of Maryland and Virginia. Returning home in 1830, she labored as an itinerant self-supported preacher in the Middle Atlantic and northeastern states for the next decade. In the summer of 1840, Elaw went to England, where she preached for five years and wrote *Memoirs of the Life, Religious Experience, and Ministerial Travels and Labours of Mrs. Zilpha Elaw, an American Female of Colour,* a 172-page spiritual autobiography and ministerial narrative published in London in 1845. Although the end of Elaw's *Memoirs* suggests that she planned soon to return to the United States, nothing is known about her after 1845. Elaw's *Memoirs* testify vividly to her dauntless independence, her boldly visionary sense of mission, and her radical spiritual individualism.

• William L. Andrews, ed., *Sisters of the Spirit: Three Black Women's Autobiographies of the Nineteenth Century,* 1986. Joanne M. Braxton, *Black Women Writing Autobiography,* 1989.

—William L. Andrews

Elbow Room. James Alan *McPherson's 1977 collection of twelve short stories, *Elbow Room,* won the Pulitzer Prize for literature in 1978. In his second collection of short stories, McPherson explores the search for, or in some cases the resistance to, psychological elbow room in twentieth-century America. For Virginia Valentine of "Elbow Room," the ideal is "a self as big as the world." For others, like the intrusive narrator of the same story, the goal is to discover fresh dimensions of stories and of selfhood. For still others, like the narrator of "Story of a Scar," the point is to resist growth and human intimacy.

McPherson's handling of the latter narrator illustrates what critics have widely praised as one of his greatest achievements: the ability to universalize the experience of African Americans. The narrator of "Story of a Scar" is black, but his need to translate a scarred woman's story into self-confirming terms and thus remain ignorant of his own inadequacies is a human, not a racial trait. The same point may be made of Virginia's desire to broaden her sense of self. She confronts racism at every turn, but her ideal transcends color.

Critics have also admired McPherson's objectivity and craft. Whether they be black or white, cruel or kind, McPherson's characters are multidimensional and emphatically alive, especially in their speech, for *Elbow Room* is rich with compelling voices that ring in the ear long after the reading is over. McPherson's narrative voice is equally engaging. Like a poet, he is as interested in modulating a sentence as he is in telling a tale. As a consequence, his stories convey a satisfying sense of order and narrative control even though many of them describe suffering and struggle.

Two secondary themes in *Elbow Room* are the power of storytelling (for good and ill) and language.

Both themes are central in "The Story of a Dead Man" and "Elbow Room." Each is told by a first-person narrator whose conflicts with other characters, and whose dubious assessment of them, is of primary interest.

So is their language. In "The Story of a Dead Man," for example, a law-abiding narrator uses the vocabulary of the white, educated middle class to resist the appeal (to him as well as to others) of a jive-talking and probably criminal cousin. By pitting his polished vocabulary and syntax against his cousin's crude and occasionally obscene vernacular, the narrator protects himself against self-discovery.

Although critics are not unanimous on the issue, most find an optimism in *Elbow Room* that distinguishes it from the bleakness of McPherson's first book, *Hue and Cry* (1969). In addition to claiming that McPherson is mainly concerned with black, not universal, issues, William Domnarski believes that misery and despair prevail in *Elbow Room* as they did in *Hue and Cry* ("The Voices of Misery and Despair," *Arizona Quarterly,* 1986). Edith Blicksilver and Jon Wallace argue otherwise, seeing in *Elbow Room* evidence of McPherson's belief in the possibility of justice, openness, and change.

• Edith Blicksilver, "The Image of Women in Selected Stories by James Alan McPherson," *CLA Journal* 22.4 (1979): 390–401. Jon Wallace, *The Politics of Style in Fiction by Berger, McGuane and McPherson,* 1992.

—Jon Wallace

ELDER, LONNE, III (1931–1996), dramatist and screenwriter. As an artist, Lonne Elder III expressed a commitment to conveying the "truth" about African American life in his works. Toward that end, Elder drew much of his material from his own life's experiences. His most celebrated drama, **Ceremonies in Dark Old Men,* is the playwright's attempt to reflect the reality of black experience in the twentieth century. Similarly, Elder's screenplays **Sounder* and *Melinda* are infused with the writer's commitment to realistic, humanistic portrayals of African Americans. Elder, who worked as a political activist, actor, waiter, dock worker, and card dealer, brought that diversity and political commitment to his work as an artist.

Elder was born in Americus, Georgia, in 1931, but moved as an infant with his family to New Jersey. After the death of his father and, soon afterward, his mother, Elder was taken in by an aunt and uncle in Jersey City, New Jersey, where he remained until completing high school. As an adolescent and teenager Elder followed his uncle, who was a numbers runner, through their neighborhood in Jersey City, collecting betting slips. Upon graduating from high school, Elder attended New Jersey State Teachers College, quitting before completing the second semester. He was soon drafted into the Army and stationed at Fort Campbell, Kentucky. It was during this time that Elder, who had held an avid interest in reading and writing since he was a child, came into contact with one of his most influential mentors, scholar and poet Robert *Hayden, who was a professor at nearby Fisk University in Nashville, Tennessee. Hayden encouraged Elder's writing and urged him to read as much as possible, giving close attention to form. Elder referred to his time with Hayden as providing a more valuable education than college. Upon leaving the Army in 1953, Elder moved to Harlem to pursue his writing career in earnest. He performed a number of odd jobs, including acting, in order to support his writing, and became active with the Harlem Writer's Guild, where his writing was further encouraged by John O. *Killens. For three years during this period (1953–1956), Elder shared an apartment with dramatist Douglas Turner *Ward. This relationship strongly influenced Elder's decision to focus his energies on writing for the theater. During the late 1950s, Elder continued to learn the crafts of writing, acting, and producing for the stage and worked in summer stock and with a mobile acting company. In 1959, at the request of the playwright, Elder made his acting debut as Bobo in Lorraine *Hansberry's *A *Raisin in the Sun* at the Ethel Barrymore Theatre in New York City.

Elder's first play, *A Hysterical Turtle in a Rabbit's Race,* which remains unpublished, was written in 1961. The play reveals his concern with the forthright, realistic portrayal of the black family and contains themes that would emerge in Elder's later works, particularly the celebrated *Ceremonies.*

Between 1963 and 1969, Elder spent his time writing and producing plays, with the earliest version of *Ceremonies* read and staged at Wagner College, New York, in 1965. This powerful work garnered numerous grants and fellowships for the playwright, who then studied drama and filmmaking at Yale University from 1965 to 1967. In 1967 Elder was commissioned by the New York City Mobilization for Youth to write a play. That work, *Charades on East Fourth Street,* was performed at Expo '67 in Montréal, Canada. From 1967 to 1969 he worked as a scriptwriter for the ABC series *N.Y.P.D.* and with the Negro Ensemble Company as coordinator of the directors/playwrights' unit, and acted in Ward's **Day of Absence.* Ward played the main character, Russell B. Parker, in *Ceremonies* when it was produced at the St. Mark's Playhouse by the Negro Ensemble Company in 1969. Later that year, the play moved to the Pocket Theatre. In 1975 Elder adapted the play for television for ABC.

The works he wrote for both stage and screen reflect Elder's fusion of the lessons of his experience with a commitment to the activist role of the artist. His adaptation in 1972 of the children's book *Sounder* into a screenplay that resulted in a critically acclaimed family film is a testament to this creative vision. Of that production, Elder said that he wanted to create a film that marked a departure from the blaxploitation films of the 1970s. Ironically, just such a film, written by Elder, was released just prior to *Sounder* to mostly negative reviews. Despite its blaxploitation tendencies and Elder's ultimate disappointment in its overall message, that film, *Melinda,* also shows his concern with reflecting realistic, truthful aspects of African American lives. Elder attempted to convey the many struggles imposed on the lives of African Americans and the equally diverse ways in which they respond to and overcome adversity. His works portray the survival techniques African Americans employ in response to various forms of oppression. Although he analyzed the larger actions of the "oppressors" and emphasized the importance of including the "oppressor's" point of view, Elder revealed the effects of those actions on a microcosmic level, in the personal lives and communities of his African American characters. Hence, as in *Ceremonies,* Elder relied on the rituals and traditions of African Americans to transmit larger ideas that reflect the complexity of their lives and communities. As with *Sounder,* Elder infused the play with subtle and overt challenges to the notion that African Americans must succumb to the pressures of living in a racist, sexist society. Instead, Elder suggested, they must determine from within their daily lives the values by which to live and survive intact.

Elder also wrote scripts for the series *McCloud* (1970–1971) and the movies *The Terrible Veil* (1963) and *A Woman Called Moses* (1978), all for NBC. Other screenplays include *Part Two, Sounder* (1976) for ABC and the adaptation of *Bustin' Loose* in 1981 for Universal Pictures.

Just as the imprint of studying, association with, and tutelage of several African American writers and actors can be seen in Elder's work, so his vision as a dramatist and screenwriter influenced the works of a younger generation of dramatists, screenwriters, and contemporary filmmakers, particularly John Singleton and Spike *Lee.

• Liz Gant, "An Interview with Lonne Elder III," *Black World* 22 (Apr. 1973): 38–48. Rochelle Reed, "Lonne Elder III on *Sounder,*" *Dialogue on Film* 2 (May 1973): 2–12. Wilsonia E. D. Cherry, "Lonne Elder III," in *DLB,* vol. 38, *Afro-American Writers after 1955,* eds. Thadious M. Davis and Trudier Harris, 1985, pp. 97–103. "Lonne Elder III," in *Black Literature Criticism,* vol. 1, ed. James P. Draper, 1992, pp. 661–671.

—Karla Y. E. Frye

EL-HAJJ MALIK EL-SHABAZZ. *See* Malcolm X.

ELLIS, TREY (b. 1962), novelist, journalist, essayist, and proponent of the New Black Aesthetic. Trey Ellis's novels, *Platitudes* (1988) and *Home Repairs* (1993), are testimonials to a declaration of artistic independence from earlier generations of African American writers from the Harlem Renaissance to the Black Arts movement. As part of a generation of youth of middle-class parents, Ellis feels that the artistic traditions that he sees as having identified African Americans in the past—themes involving southern poverty, slavery, rural isolation and deprivation, and militant or radical responses to racism—can be fused with our materialistic and technological culture and should be parodied and satirized. Ellis sees his own development as exemplary, being a part of both the African American and white worlds. In fact he labels himself and others like him as cultural hybrids, being influenced by numerous aspects of African American and Western values.

Ellis was born to parents who were college professors. He attended private high schools in New Haven, Connecticut, before graduating from Phillips Academy, in Andover, Massachusetts. He completed a BA in creative writing at Stanford and has traveled to Italy and Africa. Ellis lives in California.

Both of Ellis's novels have autobiographical strains. The central male characters come from middle-class families, have attended Ivy League schools, and are often the only African Americans in class or in social gatherings. Both characters are urbane easterners who fit very well into the diverse, fast-paced lifestyle of New York. When Ellis wrote *Platitudes* he was working as a translator in Italy, but his talent for recall of the physical and cultural qualities of New York City is remarkable. *Platitudes* is a story about a writer's appeal for help in developing his story about a middle-class youth; it is answered by an established female writer who writes her own version of the story set in the South, in her eyes, a more "valid" reflection of the African American experience. The parody of both writers' versions of the story and of the attention given to female writers like Alice *Walker points to the "platitudes" of Ellis's novel. Ellis's New Black Aesthetic is provocative but ignores some issues for critics such as Martin Favor, Eric Lott, and Tera Hunter. Ellis's call for cultural fluidity and improvisation to inspire and agitate the reader is not as successful in *Home Repairs.* Written in the form of a diary, the novel presents the development of a youth from age sixteen to his early thirties. The diary of the protagonist becomes a tool for emotional release and self-education. Like *Platitudes, Home Repairs* is filled with the images of popular culture: songs, brand names, films. However, images of Hugh Heffner and his playboy world seem to overtake the novel. The protagonist's journey to manhood becomes a one-dimensional preoccupation with sex, sexual fantasies, and conquests. The value of Ellis's new aesthetic is that he represents the next generation of writers to whom audiences look for direction. So far, *Platitudes* exemplifies this new direction best. In 1999, Ellis published his novel *Right Here, Right Now.*

• "Trey Ellis" in *Contemporary Literary Criticism,* vol. 55, ed. Roger Matuz, 1988, pp. 50–54. Trey Ellis, "The New Black Aesthetic," *Callaloo* 12 (Winter 1989): 233–243. Tera Hunter, "'It's a Man's Man's Man's World': Specters of the Old Re-Newed in Afro-American Culture and Criticism," *Callaloo* 12 (Winter

1989): 247–249. Eric Lott, "Response to Trey Ellis's 'The New Black Aesthetic,'" *Callaloo* 12 (Winter 1989): 244–246. Martin Favor, "Ain't Nothin' Like the Real Thing, Baby," *Callaloo* 16 (Summer 1993): 694–705.

—Australia Tarver

ELLISON, RALPH (1914–1994), sculptor, amateur photographer, electrician, collegiate actor, huntsman, editor, essayist, short story writer, and novelist. Ralph Ellison is recognized nationally and internationally as one of America's most prominent literary personalities. Best known as a novelist, he was also a scholar who taught at many of America's most prestigious colleges and universities and a literary and social critic who prodded America to recognize the humanity of its minorities. And like Nick Aaron Ford, Alain *Locke, Hugh M. Gloster, and other Black scholar-critics before him, he was not afraid to chide Black literary artists for not living up to their creative potential. An Uncle Tom to some, a literary father figure to others, Ralph Ellison has secured his niche in the canon of African American and American letters.

Named after another literary giant, Ralph Waldo Emerson, Ralph Waldo Ellison was born in Oklahoma City, Oklahoma, on 1 March 1914. His father, Lewis Alfred Ellison, originally from Abbeyville, South Carolina, was a soldier who had served in Cuba, the Philippine Islands, and China before marrying Ida Millsap of White Oak, Georgia, and migrating to Oklahoma, where he became a construction worker and later a small-scale entrepreneur. Ralph Ellison's great-grandparents were slaves, but Ellison insists that they were strong Black people who, during Reconstruction, held their own against southern whites.

An upwardly mobile couple, Lewis and Ida moved to Oklahoma because it was still considered the American frontier, and the Ellisons felt that it would provide better opportunities than the South for self-realization. Still, Oklahoma was not free of prejudice and racism, and Ellison's childhood was, to some extent, circumscribed, but not overly repressive. His father died when he was three years old, so his mother worked as a domestic, a custodian, and sometimes as a cook to support her two sons, Ralph and Herbert.

Growing up in the Southwest did not destroy Ellison's self-image or his will to dream. Desiring to break free of the restrictions of race, Ellison and his childhood friends decided to be Renaissance men, a concept that seems to have acted as a grounding force throughout his life. His activities in high school, his various interests in college—music, literature, sculpture, theater—and his vocation and various avocations as an adult indicate that the concept helped him realize his full potential.

Ellison was educated in a segregated school system in Oklahoma, graduating from Douglas High School in 1931. He excelled in music at Douglas High, but like W. E. B. *Du Bois of Great Barrington, Massachusetts, who was given a scholarship to attend Fisk University because the good people of Massachusetts did not want him to integrate their school system, Ellison was given a scholarship to attend Tuskegee Institute (in Alabama) so he would not attend a white college or university in Oklahoma. He was not financially able to attend Tuskegee immediately upon graduation, however, and he matriculated in 1933, after hitching a ride to Alabama on a freight train.

In *Going to the Territory* (1986), his second book of essays, Ellison describes the South as restrictive because of "the signs and symbols that marked the dividing lines of segregation." He insists, too, that a great deal of his education at Tuskegee was away "from the use of the imagination, away from the attitudes of aggression and courage.... There were things you didn't do because the world outside was not about to accommodate you." Ellison was also baffled by the political alliances Tuskegee made with whites, especially the school's relationship with Dr. Robert E. Park, a professor at the University of Chicago's School of Sociology. Ellison observed that it was with the help of Dr. Park, whom many considered the power behind Booker T. *Washington, that Tuskegee gained a national reputation. Yet this same sociologist along with Ernest Burgess wrote *Introduction to the Science of Sociology* (1924), a textbook often used at Tuskegee, in which he disparages the Black man's intellect by affirming that "the Negro is by natural disposition neither an intellectual nor an idealist.... He is primarily an artist, loving life for its own sake. His metier is expression rather than action. He is, so to speak, the lady among the races."

Despite his misgivings, Ellison found Tuskegee to be a progressive institution. There he met Morteza Sprague, the head of the English department and to whom he later dedicated his first book of essays, **Shadow and Act* (1964). Ellison went to Tuskegee to study music because William L. Dawson, an accomplished composer and choir director, headed the department. True to his Renaissance man ideal, Ellison studied sculpting under the direction of Eva Hamlin, an art instructor who was later responsible for his meeting and studying with August Savage, a Black sculptor in New York.

Though Ellison made no serious formal attempt to study literature at Tuskegee, it was while working in the library there that he began to explore literature, examining T. S. Eliot's *The Waste Land* (1922). Ellison found the poem intriguing because, as he explains in *Shadow and Act,* he was able to relate his musical experience to it: "Somehow its rhythms were often closer to those of jazz than were those of the Negro poets." It was the fascination with the poem's musicality that really got Ellison interested in writing. As he confesses in *Going to the Territory,* "Somehow in my uninstructed reading of Eliot and Pound, I had recognized a relationship between modern poetry and jazz music. . . . Indeed, such reading and wondering prepared me not simply to meet [Richard] Wright but to seek him out."

In 1936, at the end of his junior year, Ellison left Tuskegee to find summer employment in New York, hoping to earn enough money to return to his studies in the fall. Though he did not earn enough to get back to Tuskegee, he met Arna *Bontemps and Langston *Hughes, and they helped him to meet Richard *Wright, who first encouraged him to write. At the time, Wright was the editor of the *New Challenge*, and for the first issue he persuaded Ellison to review Waters *Turpin's *These Low Grounds.* Ellison then wrote a short story, "Hymie Bull," for the magazine, and his writing career was begun.

The summer Ellison came to New York, the Great Depression had sapped America's economic and industrial growth. The Harlem Renaissance, which depended heavily on white philanthropy for its existence, ran out of steam with the crash of 1929, because many of its patrons were not able to continue their financial support of the movement. Fortunately, the New York *Federal Writers' Project was established by the WPA, and Ellison and other writers were able to continue their careers. It was during this time that he worked in the Black community gathering and recording folk material that became an integral aspect of **Invisible Man* (1952).

Ellison's early writings reflect Richard Wright's creative imagination, but as Ellison continued to hone his craft, his writings demonstrated "the richness and complexity" of his own vision. Mark Busby maintains that Ellison's style was unique because of the way he combined such diverse elements as realism, surrealism, folklore, and myth in *Invisible Man.* Ellison has written short stories, but he is most recognized for this novel, *Shadow and Act, Going to the Territory,* and several sections of an unpublished novel. *Invisible Man* is the story of the nameless narrator, a Black man who learns to assert himself. *Shadow and Act* has been described as autobiographical, but it only reveals the young Ellison, the Ellison who, to a great extent, is still under the influence of Wright's vision and feels it necessary to defend himself. *Going to the Territory* reveals a mature Ellison—the literary statesman, the ambassador of good will between the races, the philosopher who believes not so much in the integration of the races as he does in a culturally pluralistic society.

Ellison died on 16 April 1994, leaving unpublished his second novel, which he had begun around 1958. A fire at his summer home in Plainsfield, Massachusetts, destroyed much of the manuscript, forcing him to reconstruct much of what he had already done. At least eight excerpts of the novel have been published, and Ellison appeared on public television and on college campuses reading sections of the work and assuring his audience that the novel was forthcoming. James Alan *McPherson, writing in *Speaking for You* (ed. Kimberly W. Benston, 1987), says of this unpublished work that, though Ellison had written more than enough material for a novel, he was "worried about how the work [would] hold up as a total structure." McPherson maintains that Ellison achieved a unique style, one that combined elements from minstrelsy and the preaching of Black Baptist ministers, yet had the timing of Count Basie. And of the author's intent McPherson affirms, "Ellison was trying to solve the central problem of American literature. He was trying to find forms invested with enough familiarity to reinvent a much broader and much more diverse world for those who take their provisional identities from groups." In early 1996 it was announced that Ellison had also left behind six unpublished short stories, all probably predating *Invisible Man.* Two were immediately printed in the *New Yorker* (Apr. 29/May 6 issue), and all six were scheduled to be published by Random House in late 1996, together with his previously published stories. In 1996, John F. Callahan edited *Flying Home and Other Stories.* Callahan also edited segments of Ellison's long-awaited second novel and published it as *Juneteenth* (1999).

An author's standing in a literary tradition rests on how well he or she perceives that tradition and how much he or she contributes to or changes it. Ellison insists that he was following the great writers of the world and claims as his literary ancestors such giants as T. S. Eliot, Henry James, Ernest Hemingway, Mark Twain, Herman Melville, Fyodor Dostoevsky, and William Faulkner. And since his greatest work, *Invisible Man,* is episodic, he could have added to his literary ancestors Miguel de Cervantes, Alain-Rene Lesage, Thomas Nash, Daniel Defoe, and Henry Fielding. In his use of African American folk material he was following Charles Waddell *Chesnutt and Zora Neale *Hurston. Though Ellison does not claim Richard Wright as a literary ancestor, he did embrace Wright's vision of naturalistic determinism; however, Ellison found that Wright's vision was too narrow to represent the Black experience in America. He believed that Wright's writing, in many instances, only perpetuated in the larger community stereotypical images that the Black writer should attempt to deflate. In *Shadow and Act,* Ellison maintained that too many books written by Black authors were aimed at a white audience, the danger in this being that Black writers then tended to limit themselves to their audience's assumptions about what Black people were like or should be like. Because of this dynamic, the Black writer is reduced to pleading the humanity of his own race, which Ellison saw as the equivalent of questioning whether Blacks were fully human, an indulgence in a false issue that Blacks could ill afford. Believing that a naturalistic/deterministic mode could not define the Black experience, Ellison created a style that embraces the strength, the courage, the endurance, and the promise as well as the uniqueness of the Black experience in America.

In breaking away from the traditional literary path of Black writers, Ellison became a liberator, freeing Black literature from American literary colonialism and bringing it to national and international independence. Ellison's liberating spirit is evident in such writers as McPherson, Ernest J. *Gaines, Leon *Forrest, and Clarence *Major, and in the surrealism of Ishmael *Reed, the folk tradition of Toni *Morrison, the historical tradition exhibited by Gloria *Naylor, and the spirituality of Toni Cade *Bambara. These writers have developed alternative modes of expression or, as Ellison would say, they have realized new literary possibilities. They write not only about the Black experience in America but also about the American experience. While writing in the tradition of the great writers, Ellison blazed a literary trail for younger writers to follow. His innovative style was probably the first step in helping Black writers to break the literary constraints of the sociological tradition in African American letters. And, according to Mark Busby, Ellison has also had a "profound effect" on mainstream writers.

Ralph Ellison, more so than any other Black writer, brought change to the African American (and also to the American) literary canon because he refused to accept prescribed formulas for depicting the Black American. He brought a fierce reality to his vision that neither Blacks nor Caucasians were quite ready to accept. But his truth was/is so eminent, so palpable that neither race could deny it. Ellison will be remembered in literature and in life for making Blacks visible in a society where they had been invisible.

[*See also* Bledsoe, Dr.; Mary Rambo; Norton, Mr.; Ras the Destroyer; Rinehart; Todd Clifton; Trueblood.]

• Robert A. Bone, *The Negro Novel in America,* rev. ed., 1965. Therman B. O'Daniel, "The Image of Man As Protrayed by Ralph Ellison," *CLA Journal* 10 (June 1967): 277–284. Addison Gayle, Jr., ed., *The Black Aesthetic,* 1972. John Hersey, ed., *Ralph Ellison: A Collection of Critical Essays,* 1974. Robert G. O'Meally, *The Craft of Ralph Ellison,* 1980. John F. Callahan, "Chaos, Complexity, and Possibility: The Historical Frequencies of Ralph Waldo Ellison," in *Speaking for You: The Vision of Ralph Ellison,* ed. Kimberly W. Benston, 1987, pp. 125–143. James Alan McPherson, "Invisible Man," in *Speaking for You: The Vision of Ralph Ellison,* ed. Kimberly W. Benston, 1987, pp. 15–29. Jack Bishop, *Ralph Ellison,* 1988. Kerry McSweeney, *Invisible Man: Race and Identity,* 1988. Alan Nadel, *Invisible Critics: Ralph Ellison and the American Canon,* 1988. Mark Busby, *Ralph Ellison,* 1991. Ralph Ellison, *The Collected Essays of Ralph Ellison,* ed. John F. Callahan, 1995. Maureen F. Curtin, "Materializing Invisibility as X-Ray Technology: Skin Matters in Ralph Ellison's Invisible Man," *Literature, Interpretation, Theory* 9:4 (April 1999): 281–311. Julia Eichelberger, *Ideology and the Individual in Novels by Ralph Ellison, Toni Morrison, Saul Bellow, and Eudora Welty,* 1999.

—Ralph Reckley, Sr.

EL MUHAJIR. *See* Marvin X.

EQUIANO, OLAUDAH (1745–1797), slave and spiritual autobiographer, creator of the slave narrative genre, and abolitionist leader. Olaudah Equiano (later also known as Gustavus Vassa) was eleven years of age when he was kidnapped in the African country that is now known as Nigeria. As he was taken to the slave ship on the coast, he witnessed the corrupting influences of European intrusions upon the African societies. Sent to Barbados and then to Virginia, he escaped a sentence to plantation slavery when he was purchased by a British captain who changed the youth's name to Gustavus Vassa and placed him in service aboard ship. Equiano spent the next ten years of his captivity on several vessels engaged in commerce and sometimes in naval warfare.

After his daily slave duties, the industrious and thrifty Equiano worked at various private enterprises that eventually enabled him to save enough funds to purchase himself out of bondage. On 10 July 1766, he became a freeman, but continued working aboard ships. In the ensuing years, Equiano traveled to many countries in Europe, the Middle East, the Caribbean, and North, Central, and South America. He even journeyed on a scientific expedition to the Arctic regions.

When he served as a young slave on various ships, Equiano formed close relationships with the sailors, who taught him how to read and introduced him to Christianity. They fired up a lifelong desire for learning that he especially pursued whenever he visited friends in England. The religious spark ignited by the sailors led in later years to a lengthy and intense spiritual conversion experience, after which Equiano chose the Methodist faith. Eventually he settled in England, where in 1792 Equiano married the Englishwoman Susanna Cullen; they had two daughters.

In the 1780s, when the British Parliament debated whether to end the slave trade, Equiano became an active participant in the antislavery movement. In order to sway the minds of those involved in the controversy, he undertook the writing of a two-volume autobiography describing his life of bondage and freedom and giving his eyewitness account of the sufferings and injustices endured by thousands of enslaved men and women. The result was *The Interesting Narrative of the Life of Olaudah Equiano, or Gustavus Vassa, the African,* which appeared in England in 1789, and in 1791 in the United States. From 1789 to 1794 the *Narrative* ran through eight editions in Great Britain. Translations were made into Dutch in 1790, German in 1792, and Russian in 1794. Nineteen editions were produced in the United States and Europe by the mid-nineteenth century.

In his lengthy account, Equiano mixes his personal remembrances of African societies, slave experiences, and a freeman's life in the West with the facts and ideas he derived from his wide range of reading in works of history, geography, religion, politics, and commerce. He is at his best when re-creating the opposing feelings of awe and fear that grip him when he comes into contact with both the marvels and terrors of the Western world. A vital part of Equiano's narrative is the winning of his freedom. He becomes a new man as he is reborn into a society where he now can operate on a free plane of existence. His physical and spiritual liberations enable him to complete himself as a person who can assume new and commanding roles in life. These roles include his taking charge of a vessel during a storm at sea, serving as a parson when required, and even acting as an overseer of slaves. In his mature years, the proudest roles are those of abolitionist leader and autobiographer. Thus readers of the *Interesting Narrative* come to see Equiano as an intelligent, clever, and complex man.

Equiano's slave narrative displays one of the first attempts by an African writer to enter the literary world of Western culture. Equiano followed the spiritual autobiographical tradition of St. Augustine and John Bunyan, but added to it a new dimension consisting of social protest. His new type of personal story influenced how black narrative literature was written throughout the antislavery era. Thus Equiano's autobiography became the prototype of the slave narratives that appeared after his great work. Looking over the whole range of African American literature, one can see the structure and elements of the slave narrative genre in such important works as Frederick *Douglass's **Narrative of the Life of Frederick Douglass* (1845), Harriet Beecher *Stowe's *Uncle Tom's Cabin* (1852), Harriet A. *Jacobs's **Incidents in the Life of a Slave Girl* (1861), Richard *Wright's **Black Boy* (1945), Ralph *Ellison's **Invisible Man* (1952), and Toni *Morrison's **Beloved* (1987).

• William L. Andrews, *To Tell a Free Story: The First Century of Afro-American Autobiography, 1760–1865,* 1986. Angelo Costanzo, *Surprizing Narrative: Olaudah Equiano and the Beginnings of Black Autobiography,* 1987. Keith A. Sandiford, *Measuring the Moment: Strategies of Protest in Eighteenth-Century Afro-English Writing,* 1988. Paul Edwards, introduction to *The Life of Olaudah Equiano,* 1989. *The Interesting Narrative of the Life of Olaudah Equiano,* ed. Vincent Carretta, 1995.

—Angelo Costanzo

Escape, The. Although erroneously thought to be the first play written by an African American, William Wells *Brown's closet drama *The Escape, or A Leap for Freedom* was the first dramatic work by an African American to be published. Issued as an octavo pamphlet of fifty-two pages by Robert F. Wallcut of Boston in 1858, the publication of *The Escape* attests to its popularity and confirms the play's value as antislavery propaganda. Brown claims in the author's preface to have written the play for his "own amusement and not with the remotest thought that it would ever be seen by the public eye." However after his friends arranged for him to read it "before a Literary Society," public readings soon followed with great success. Encomiums published in the 1858 octavo suggest that at least some viewed the work not only as propaganda but also as serious drama. Typical of the praise lavished on the play is the excerpt from the *Auburn* (N.Y.) *Daily Advertiser* quoted in the octavo: "MR. BROWN'S Drama is, in itself, a masterly refutation of all apologies for slavery, and abounds in wit, satire, philosophy, argument and facts, all ingeniously interwoven into one of the most interesting dramatic compositions of modern times." In addition to the acclaim provided by the publisher, positive notice of *The Escape* also appears in William Lloyd Garrison's the *Liberator* (10 Sept. 1858; 8 Oct. 1858) and the *National Anti-Slavery Standard* (25 Dec. 1858).

Less than riveting as drama, *The Escape* has real value as antislavery propaganda and genuine potential to stir an audience when read by an orator of even moderate skill. Its flowery and elevated diction, however, deny the characters speech that approximates dialogue between real people. Although much of the play's soaring rhetoric sounds stilted and false, "the main features in the Drama are true," Brown affirms, and his audience no doubt concurred.

The Escape dramatizes the struggle of Melinda and her husband to reach freedom in Canada. A comely mulatto woman, Melinda endures the unremitting sexual harassment of her master, Dr. Gaines. Prefiguring Dr. Flint in Harriet A. *Jacobs's 1861 **Incidents in the Life of a Slave Girl,* Gaines torments Melinda even as he promises privileges, money, and freedom if she would abandon her husband and enter into a liaison with her master. In addition to the abuse of Dr. Gaines, Melinda suffers the harsh and jealous maltreatment of her mistress, Mrs. Gaines. After predictable trials and tribulations the slave couple finally escape to freedom in Canada.

Readers familiar with Brown's 1853 novel **Clotel* will recognize themes common to the novel and the play, most notably the sexual abuse of black women in slavery, the development of a class of phenotypically white women to use as sex slaves, the systematic and intentional intellectual degradation and deprivation of slaves, and the accompanying pathologies that deform the personality of the slave and slave holder. Yet, even as it focuses on these themes, *The Escape* celebrates the love of a couple willing to endure any hardship to remain true to each other.

• William Edward Farrison, *William Wells Brown: Author and Reformer,* 1969.

—Anthony Gerard Barthelemy

EVA MEDINA CANADA narrates Gayl *Jones's **Eva's Man* (1976). Simultaneously drawn to and repelled by men, she has experienced a series of abusive sexual encounters from an early age, beginning with her unwilling submission to a little boy's probing with a dirty Popsicle stick. Her mother's lover tries to molest her, her cousin tries to seduce her, and she briefly marries an older man who virtually imprisons her out of jealousy. Believing the stories of her mother's friend, Miss Billie, who maintains that women cannot control their own bodies and men cannot control their responses to women, Eva is generally fatalistic and passive, but she does stab a man who grabs her. This eruption of long-suppressed violence foreshadows the crime that culminates in her madness: poisoning then orally castrating her lover.

Eva is identified with three mythical women whose hold on men proves fatal: Medusa, Eve (in Eva's case, the forbidden fruit of knowledge and power is the penis), and a local figure called the Queen Bee. While the Queen Bee believes her love to be deadly for any man and eventually commits suicide to spare her lover, Eva enacts her own version of the Queen Bee's story. Locked in a prison asylum, refusing to explain her motives to anyone—including the reader—Eva weaves her increasingly disjointed narrative out of interrogations, visions, and memories. Through her, Jones dramatizes a woman trapped by the pernicious stereotypes of black women's sexuality.

• Keith Byerman, *Fingering the Jagged Grain: Tradition and Form in Recent Black Fiction,* 1985. Sally Robinson, *Engendering the Subject: Gender and Self-Representation in Contemporary Women's Fiction,* 1991.

—Amy S. Gottfried

EVANS, MARI, poet, dramatist, short fiction writer, children's writer, editor, essayist, and lecturer. Since the 1960s, Mari Evans has produced a body of works unique for its personal sensitivity, political tenor, and precisely crafted diction and structures. Although principally known for her poetry, Mari Evans's dramas have had repeated productions over the years, and her children's books have been noted as models for unobtrusively premising a constructive, nurturing worldview. Her essays and lectures are marked by explicit political commitment, cogent logic, and quiet fervor.

Evans was born in Toledo, Ohio, in 1923. Her father proved to be a tremendous early influence upon her, and she recounts in an autobiographic essay, "My Father's Passage" (1984), how he saved her first story. She had written it while in the fourth grade, and it had appeared in the school paper. Her father not only saved it, but noted with pride his daughter's achievement. "My Father's Passage" is also important because Evans emphasizes her perception of writing as a craft, a professional occupation.

Evans attended public schools in Toledo as well as the University of Toledo. Although she studied fashion design, she did not pursue it as a career option. Her attention turned instead to poetry, almost unintentionally she asserts. Fortuitously she began her professional writing career as an assistant editor in a manufacturing firm where precision and discipline are imperative. Even in her first, intensely personal volume *Where Is All the Music?* (1968), this discipline is evident. These are poems celebrating all aspects of personal love affairs, from love at first sight to the endurance that masters disappointment and loneliness. Also evident is a hallmark of Evans's style: dispassionate language conveying profoundly moving fact and feeling.

Having received a Woodrow Wilson grant in 1968, Evans began the first of what would become a series of appointments in American universities in 1969. She was an instructor at Indiana University at Purdue, where she taught courses in African American literature and served as writer in residence. In 1970 she published *I Am a Black Woman* (incorporating most of the poems from *Music*), a more complex collection divided into titled sections that gradually expand focus to embrace the whole African American community. The first two sections concern romantic love. The next two treat victims of society's injustices and indifference, especially children. The final and longest section, "A Black Oneness, A Black Strength" draws the most overtly political inferences from this exploration of love. The effect of the poems is cumulative; although each poem is a complete, self-sufficient entity, it is enriched by its position among the others. The success of the poetry in 1970 was matched by Evans receiving an award for the most distinguished book of poetry by an Indiana writer.

Between 1970 and 1978 Evans was assistant professor and writer in residence at Indiana University, Bloomington, where she continued to write and publish, and to be recognized for her achievements. She received an honorary degree from Marion College in 1975, and she resided for a time at the MacDowell Colony. She had a visiting assistant professor appointment at Purdue University between 1978 and 1980, the same year she also had an appointment at Washington University in St. Louis, and she has visited at Cornell, SUNY Albany, and Spelman College.

In 1981 she published *Nightstar 1973–1978,* which is also arranged in titled sections that progress from the personal to the communal and political. These poems employ more experimental techniques: more complex exploitation of typography (capitalization, indentations, length of phrase or line); more expansive use of rhetorical figures such as anaphora, reiteration, direct exhortation to the reader (using "we," not "you"); a greater diversity of speakers and portraiture; careful use of African American idiom in ways that foster the reader's respect for and identification with the speaker. Throughout, *Nightstar* reveals rather than claims heroism and grandeur as well as the simple joys of African American life.

Evans has combined teaching, writing, and publishing with many other activities. She directed *The Black Experience,* a television program in Indianapolis, between 1968 and 1973. She has consulted for agencies such as the National Endowment for the Arts (1969–1970), as well as for the Indiana Arts Commission (1976–1977). She is a popular and much-sought lecturer, and she has made repeated appearances at the National Black Writers Festival held biannually at Medgar Evers College.

A Dark and Splendid Mass (1992) represents a new development in Evans's poetic style. The only poems of romantic love celebrate the decisive rejection of perfidious lovers. All the poems are short paeans to the indomitable courage of ordinary suffering people. With a variety of personae, situations, locales, abuse, or deprivations, the poems convincingly convey the emotive perspective of the victim-survivor or hero. The book ends with poems of hard-nosed faith and hope.

Black Women Writers 1950–1980, A Critical Evaluation (1983), edited by Evans, is a unique anthology treating fifteen writers. For each there is an autobiographical statement of artistic intent, two essays of different critical perspectives, and a "bio-selected bibliography." The text holds a wide spectrum of African American critical approaches to very diverse authors.

The kind of professional service that Evans provided by becoming an anthologist is matched by her commitment to community service. She is active in movements for prison reform and against capital punishment, especially in some specific egregious cases. She works with local community organizations and with theater groups. She has a demanding lecture schedule. These activities express in action an implication that pervades her writing: that self-fulfillment for the African American must include identification with the deprived, the oppressed, and efforts to enhance the health and strength of the community.

This emphasis on a wholesome perspective on the African American community is seen in Evans's books for children, *I Look at Me* (1973), *JD* (1973), *Singing Black* (1976), and *Jim Flying High* (1979). Text and illustrations are carefully integrated to reinforce this impression. Unfamiliar words are introduced in self-explanatory contexts, and the stories encourage the reader to exult in selfhood and community.

Among her dramas, *Rivers of My Song* (first performed in 1977), *Portrait of a Man* and *Boochie* (both 1979), and *Eyes* (1979), an adaptation of Zora Neale *Hurston's **Their Eyes Were Watching God*, have all received several productions in various American cities. The first is ritualistic theater combining music, dancers, and actors using both poetry and prose. The form is an excellent example of traditional African American theatrical productions. *Portrait of a Man* uses a divided stage. On one side we see episodes in the experience of a courageous and industrious young African American man, an experience that includes several instances of the perfidy of white Americans. Interspersed among these episodes, on the other side of the stage, we see a querulous old man confronting an impatient, offensive nurse. The two men are, of course, one, and through various allusions, the man's reliance on African American values and culture is demonstrated.

Boochie is mainly a monologue of an old woman preparing dinner for her son, Boochie, a paragon of success, duty, and affection. With deft control of revelations and peripety, the audience is led to recognize very specific consequences of social forces such as welfare, addictions, and unemployment. The drama hangs on an extremely shocking climactic event and our understanding of its causes. As in each of the other plays, vivid characterization, precisely realistic detail, and a strong but assailed African American community provide the basis for the clear political implications of the plot.

Perhaps the genius of Mari Evans centers on her succinct, specific portrayals of the human spirit, and her moral premise that evil is both personal and institutional and must be fought in all its spheres.

• David Dorsey, "The Art of Mari Evans," in *Black Women Writers 1950–1980*, ed. Mari Evans, 1983, pp. 170–189. Solomon Edwards, "Affirmation in the Works of Mari Evans," in *Black Women Writers, 1950–1980*, ed. Mari Evans, 1983, pp. 190–200. Wallace R. Peppers, "Mari Evans," in *DLB*, vol. 41, *Afro-American Poets since 1955*, eds. Trudier Harris and Thadious M. Davis, 1985, pp. 117–123.

—David F. Dorsey, Jr.

EVA PEACE is the protagonist's grandmother in Toni *Morrison's novel **Sula* (1974). Her distinction is due to the claim that she purposely allowed her leg to be cut off by a train so that she could gain the pension that would provide financial support for her children. Desertion by her husband leaves Eva destitute and desperate, and after the loss of her leg, she retreats to her upstairs bedroom and directs the lives of her children, strays, and boarders. Eva is also a mythic character who is unchaste and unwilling to submit to anyone or any God, in opposition to her Christian namesake.

Although Eva is characterized in the narrative as enthralled by "manlove," she demonstrates a contemptuous attitude toward men in her naming. She sets fire to her son Ralph, whom she called Plum, when he returns from war with a heroin addiction and attempts to "crawl back into her womb." She takes in an alcoholic white man and calls him Tar Baby and three homeless boys and calls them all Dewey. After Eva burns her son, she is unable to save her second daughter, *Hannah Peace (Sula's mother), from burning to death.

The community apparently tolerates Eva's idiosyncrasies, but she is challenged and defeated by her equally strong-willed granddaughter, *Sula Peace, who puts her in an old folks' home. Eva, however, gets the last word in the novel, pointing out after Sula's death the similarity between Sula and her former best friend Nel in spite of their deceptive surface differences. Morrison quickly dispatches the assumption that Eva will fall into the traditional "mammy" role, for Eva is a willful, arrogant, independent woman whose strength is based on her sustained hatred for the unfaithful father of her three children.

• Barbara Christian, *Black Feminist Criticism,* 1985. Wilfred D. Samuels and Clenora Hudson-Weems, *Toni Morrison,* 1990. Trudier Harris, *Fiction and Folklore: The Novels of Toni Morrison,* 1991. Rachel Lee, "Missing Peace in Toni Morrison's *Sula* and *Beloved,*" *African American Review* 28.4 (Winter 1994): 571–583.

—Betty Taylor-Thompson

Eva's Man. Like her first novel, **Corregidora* (1975), Gayl *Jones's *Eva's Man* (1976) continues to explore African American women's sexual victimization. The novel's pivotal scene is *Eva Medina Canada's murder and mutilation of her lover. Eva spends a number of days in Davis Carter's apartment, waiting for her menstrual period to end so that they can make love. Jones creates a vaguely repellent, ambivalent feeling of imprisonment and passivity: although he leaves the door open, Davis wants Eva to remain in the apartment, and although Eva seems to feel trapped, she never steps outside the door. With neither remorse nor explanation, Eva murders Davis, bites off his penis, and then calls the police. The book begins with this violent act, moves back to Eva's childhood and adolescence, and ends with her obstinate silence in a prison's psychiatric ward.

Eva's increasingly erratic, first-person narrative shifts from one scene to another, repeating lines of dialogue in different contexts, mingling memory, dream, and fantasy in a story that explores an African American woman's formation of her identity in a culture that devalues her race and her sex. Unlike *Ursa Corregidora, Eva has both a father and mother present throughout her childhood. But she, too, experiences a good deal of sexual abuse, both actual and threatened, in her encounters with men who assume that she is sexually willing. Brought up to believe that women cannot control their own bodies, Eva continually alternates her silent passivity with unexpected moments of violence. When a man follows her into an alley, trying to pay her for sex, she says nothing to dissuade him but then suddenly stabs him with a pocketknife. The older man she marries is psychotically jealous, yet she stays with him for two years. When Davis tries to dominate her, refusing even to let her comb her hair, Eva seems undisturbed by his behavior, even as she secrets away the rat poison that will kill him. She offers no motive for her action, and at one point warns an interrogator not to explain her. While Corregidora's depiction of lesbianism is uneasy at best, *Eva's Man* closes with Eva's being brought to orgasm by her cellmate Elvira—a moment whose simple immediacy might constitute the novel's sole note of redemptive possibility.

Discussions of this book generally focus on Eva's coping with the stereotypical objectifications of black women, especially those that characterize them as faithless or as sexually insatiable. While several critics see Eva's behavior as a rebellion against the racist, sexist structures that posit black women as whores, others argue that Jones refuses to let Eva be so easily explained, even as the character alternately submits to and defies the social system that defines her so rigidly. Also important is the novel's adaptation of African American folklore, especially the communal voice that Eva hears while growing up (that of her mother's friend, Miss Billie), which teaches her about ancestral duties and the fatal power of women's sexuality. Finally, although unreliable, Eva's narrative is truly hers, unlike the rote memorizations of incest and abuse that nearly imprison the protagonist of Jones's first novel.

• Keith Byerman, "Black Vortex: The Gothic Structure of *Eva's Man,*" *MELUS* 7.4 (Winter 1980): 93–101. Melvin Dixon, "Singing a Deep Song: Language As Evidence in the Novels of Gayl Jones," in *Black Women Writers (1950–1980),* ed. Mari Evans, 1984, pp. 236–248. Gloria Wade-Gayles, *No Crystal Stair: Visions of Race and Sex in Black Women's Fiction,* 1984. Keith Byerman, *Fingering the Jagged Grain: Tradition and Form in Recent Black Fiction,* 1985. Sally Robinson, *Engendering the Subject: Gender and Self-Representation in Contemporary Women's Fiction,* 1991.

—Amy S. Gottfried

EVERETT ANDERSON is the six-year-old protagonist of seven children's verse books by Lucille *Clifton, published between 1970 and 1983. Each story-poem is illustrated by pen-and-ink drawings or sepia watercolors that realistically represent the characters' Negroid physicality. In each narrative, Clifton reiterates major themes of her own poetry and of the 1960s Black Arts movement: familial and self-love, ethnic pride, African American masculinity, resistance to racism, the inner city as home, the power of self-referentiality, and the subversion of Euro-American conventions. Moreover, Clifton at once demonstrates allegiance to second-wave feminism and debunks myths of oppressive African American matriarchy through her characterization of Everett's mother as a loving and conscientious single parent–wage earner. In *Everett Anderson's Nine Month Long* (1978), Clifton uses Everett's mother's second marriage and subsequent pregnancy to illustrate parental sensitivity to a son's anxiety about displacement as well as to reveal African Americans' reverence for self-definition. Clifton also explores children's responses to multiculturalism, gender equality, and bilingualism by introducing Everett to Maria, a girl-next-door who beats him at sports and whose Spanish-speaking mother prepares Mexican food. Clifton portrays Everett as a conventional child: he attends school; exults in natural wonders, including his own brown body; sometimes misbehaves; often grieves his dead father. Yet she also insinuates the particular impact of his ethnicity on his experience: the Andersons' tenement apartment functions simultaneously as a site of lessons in self-assertion, charity, security, discipline, and patriotism and as a site of lessons in economic and political injustice and the exclusivity of the mythic American dream.

• Dianne Johnson, *Telling Tales: The Pedagogy and Promise of African American Literature for Youth,* 1990.

—Joycelyn K. Moody

F

FABIO, SARAH WEBSTER (1928–1979), poet, educator, and leading figure and pioneer in the Black Studies and Black Arts movements. Born in Nashville, Tennessee, on 20 January 1928, Sarah Webster Fabio was the precocious daughter of Thomas Webster and Mayme Louise Storey Webster. Fabio graduated from Nashville's Pearl High School in 1943. At age fifteen, she entered Spelman College in Atlanta, Georgia; however, she did not graduate. Returning instead to Nashville, she graduated from Fisk University in 1946, and married Cyril Fabio, a young dental student at Meharry Medical College.

After her husband completed his degree, he joined the military and they were sent to Florida, where her first son was born in 1947. Another son was born in 1948, and a daughter in 1949. Despite the strictures of being a military wife frequently forced to move and mothering small children, Fabio, on one of their moves back to Nashville, enrolled in graduate school. Before she could complete her degree, the family was stationed in Germany. Two other children were born in 1955 and 1956. In 1957, the family settled in Palo Alto, California, where her husband opened a dental practice.

The mothering of five children delayed Fabio's education until 1963, when she enrolled in San Francisco State College. She earned her degree in 1965, on the day that her oldest son graduated from high school, and she landed a job teaching at Merritt College in Oakland, a seed-bed for the Black Power movement in the West. Bobby Seale and Huey Newton of the Black Panther Party, as well as Malauna Ron Karenga of the U.S. Organization, were students at Merritt. These were exciting times for Fabio, who had been writing since high school and had studied poetry under Arna *Bontemps at Fisk. Fabio defined black poetry as works containing themes drawn from and saturated with language, images, and rhythms of the African American experience.

Fabio's training (a master's degree in language arts, creative writing with an emphasis on poetry) enabled her to combine Western metaphor with black realism. Grounding her work in the oral tradition and performing her poetry to jazz accompaniments, Fabio reached a wide and diverse audience. In 1966, she performed at the First World Festival of Negro Art in Dakar, Senegal. Returning home, she lectured at the California College of Arts and Crafts and the University of California at Berkeley, where she worked to create their Black Studies department.

Fabio's first collection of poetry, *Saga of a Black Man* (1968), was followed by *A Mirror, a Soul* (1969). In 1972, she recorded two albums on Folkways Records. Doubleday published *Black Talk: Shield and Sword* (1973). Other books include *Dark Debut: Three Black Women Coming* (1966), *Return of Margaret Walker* (1966), *Double Dozens: An Anthology of Poets from Sterling Brown to Kali* (1966), and *No Crystal Stair: A Socio-Drama of the History of Black Women in the U.S.A.* (1967).

Fabio's poetry reflects the Black Arts movement with its trendy emphasis on the Black Aesthetic, yet is classic in its subtle blending of non-Western and Western literary metaphors. Fabio skillfully handles both traditions.

In 1972, Fabio divorced her husband and accepted a faculty position at Oberlin College in Ohio, where she remained until 1974. In 1976, while teaching and pursuing graduate work at the University of Wisconsin, she was diagnosed with colon cancer. Fabio spent her last two years in California with her oldest daughter. She died 7 November 1979.

Fabio's most impressive collection of poetry is the seven-volume series *Rainbow Signs* (1973). The rainbow symbolized for her a sign of hope following the storms of protest during the turbulent 1960s. "The Hurt of It All" voices the poet's farewell, saying "that's all she wrote."

• Stephen Henderson, ed., *Understanding the New Black Poetry,* 1973. James A. Page, comp., *Selected Black American Authors: An Illustrated Bio-Bibliography,* 1977, pp. 81–82. Nagueyalti Warren, *Notable Black American Women,* vol. 1, ed. Jessie Smith, 1992, pp. 332–333.

—Nagueyalti Warren

FAIR, RONALD L. (b. 1932), novelist, short story writer, and poet. Born in Chicago in 1932, Ronald L. Fair began writing as a teenager. After graduating from public school in Chicago, Fair spent three years in the U.S. Navy (1950–1953) before attending a Chicago stenotype school for two years. While supporting himself as a court reporter and stenographer for the next decade (1955–1966), he produced his first two novels. After then working briefly as an encyclopedia writer, Fair taught for a few years—at Columbia College (1967–1968), Northwestern University (1968), and Wesleyan University (1969–1970). Fair moved to Finland in 1971 and has lived in Europe since that time. He is divorced and has three children.

Ronald Fair's first novel, *Many Thousand Gone: An American Fable* (1965), both fantastic tale and "protest novel," is a satiric re-vision of the South, where, in the mythical Jacobs County, slaves were never freed after the Civil War. Exploring the twin themes of the sexual exploitation of women and the lynching of men from the African American community, the novel concludes with a messianic-like hope rooted in racial purity and revolutionary resistance.

In *Hog Butcher* (1966), the author's critique of racism and hypocrisy turns to the North. Set in Chicago's South Side ghetto, and drawing on Fair's experience as a court reporter, the novel centers on the police shooting of a young African American sports hero-to-be and the trial and cover-up that ensue.

Fair's third major work of fiction, *World of Nothing* (1970), is a pair of novellas. *Jerome,* his most experimental piece, revisits the fantasy genre to explore religious hypocrisy. The second novella, *World of Nothing,* consists of a series of bittersweet episodic sketches related by an anonymous first-person narrator.

We Can't Breathe, published in 1972, after Fair had departed for Europe, is about growing up in 1930s Chicago and is his most autobiographical and documentary work. Versions of the prologue have been frequently anthologized, as have other Fair short stories.

Fair's fiction has generally met with mixed reviews. While he has received praise for his naturalistic accounts in particular, critics have accused his works, variously, of stereotype, weak dialogue, cliché, and a lack of aesthetic unity. Despite the lukewarm critical response, *Hog Butcher* was eventually made into a feature film and reissued as a mass-market paperback, *Cornbread, Earl, and Me* in 1975. Fair also received an award for *World of Nothing* from the National Endowment of Letters in 1971 and a Best Book Award from the American Library Association for *We Can't Breathe* in 1972.

During his self-imposed exile, which began during the decline of the Black Arts movement in America, Fair has continued to explore the settings and themes of his earlier work but primarily through poetry. In addition to contributing to various periodicals, he has published two volumes of poetry: *Excerpts* (London, 1975) and *Rufus* (Germany, 1977; United States, 1980). Fair also received an award from the National Endowment for the Arts in 1974 and a Guggenheim Fellowship in 1975.

Ronald L. Fair's most significant contribution to African American literature has perhaps been the versatility and inventive synthesis of forms with which he has explored communal themes, human types, and the workings and abuses of power.

• "Ronald L. Fair," in *New Black Voices,* ed. Abraham Chapman, 1972, p. 106.

—Sheila Hassell Hughes

FAUSET, JESSIE REDMON (1882–1961), editor, teacher, and writer. The Harlem Renaissance—jazzy, funky, soulful; a time when "Negroes" were "in vogue," when white people descended on Harlem's cabarets to amuse themselves, and when interracial soirees were frequent. One of its leading figures, Langston *Hughes, remembers that Jessie Fauset provided a different social atmosphere in the midst of all that funk, jazz, and soul. At her parties, guests would discuss literature, read poetry aloud, and converse in French. She did not want "sightseers" in her home; therefore, only very distinguished white people were invited to her gatherings, and then only seldomly. Hughes also reports that Fauset used her position as literary editor of the *Crisis* (1919–1926) to feature his talents and those of other young black artists including Countee *Cullen, Claude *McKay, and Jean *Toomer. For this effort, Hughes dubbed her literary "midwife" of the "Negro" Renaissance.

Fauset's considerable accomplishments go far beyond her having hosted social gatherings and nurtured fledgling writers. In keeping with her desire to teach black children pride in their heritage and to encourage their creativity, she cofounded and edited a monthly children's magazine, the **Brownies' Book* (1920–1921). This magazine featured historical biographies of notable black people such as Denmark Vesey and Sojourner *Truth, articles about Africa, current events, games, riddles, and music. Fauset also wrote poetry, numerous essays, and short fiction, which appeared in various periodicals—the *Brownies' Book* and the Crisis among them—as well as in anthologies such as Countee Cullen's *Caroling Dusk* (1927) and Alain *Locke's *The *New Negro* (1925). The most prolific novelist during the period, Fauset wrote four novels that were published over a nine-year span: **There Is Confusion* (1924), *Plum Bun* (1929), *The Chinaberry Tree* (1931), and *Comedy: American Style* (1933).

While the broad range of Fauset's productivity is essential to an understanding of her aesthetics, the novels provide an interesting and significant focus. The content of her first, *There Is Confusion,* was inspired by the publication of T. S. Stribling's *Birthright* (1922). Like so many stereotypical accounts of the "tragic mulatto," Stribling's account depicts a protagonist who is the victim of persistent longing and unattainable desires aroused by his mixed blood. Fauset believed she could tell a more convincing story of black life. Light-skinned, educated blacks, some of whom "pass" for white, are always central figures in her novels, where they not only represent an existing group of black people but also best fulfill Fauset's aim to politicize issues of color, class, and gender. She revises conventional literary forms and themes by using the figure of the mulatto as metaphor to explore identity and difference as they concern blacks generally and black women, specifically. In challenging the myths of mulatto fiction by precursory white writers, in particular, Fauset reveals the fundamentally political nature of her novels.

Until recently, critics have missed the political and subversive aspects of her work. Their misreadings of the novels and of narrative intent stem largely from their using her personal life, real or imagined, to explain her plots and her reasons for creating characters in direct opposition to the kinds of black characters white publishers demanded at that time. The worst of these critiques uses Fauset's marital status and age as reasons for alleged limitations of imagination and creativity—that is, she was unmarried until age forty-seven and "already" thirty-eight by the time she moved to New York and began working at the *Crisis.* She has also been labeled "prim and proper" and criticized for writing so-called "genteel" novels about people too much like herself.

Yet the bare facts of Fauset's background do not support this kind of criticism of her work. On 27 April 1882, she was born in Camden County, New Jersey, not in Philadelphia as has so often been cited. She was the youngest of seven children born to Redmon Fauset, an African Methodist Episcopal minister, and Annie Seamon Fauset. After her mother's death, her father married a widow with three children and together they had three more. Far from "prosperous," the family was "dreadfully poor," according to Arthur Huff Fauset, her half brother and a noted anthropologist.

Indeed, Fauset's early successes are attributable to her intelligence and talent, not to any privilege of birth. She attended Girls' High in Philadelphia, a school noted for high academic achievers. Having been denied admission to Bryn Mawr because of her race, she attended Cornell University and graduated Phi Beta Kappa in 1905. She taught full-time from 1905 to 1919 in Washington, D.C.'s public schools, while earning a master's degree from the University of Pennsylvania (1919). She also studied for six months at the Sorbonne during 1925–1926. After her stint at the *Crisis,* Fauset taught French at DeWitt Clinton High School (1927–1944), and her final teaching position was a brief visiting professorship at Hampton Institute (12 September 1949 to 31 January 1950).

During the period after her last book was published and between teaching jobs, Fauset traveled and lectured, wrote poetry, and contented herself with the duties of "housewife" but published very little. She and her husband, Herbert Harris, an insurance broker, lived in Montclair, New Jersey, until his death in 1958. Fauset then moved to Philadelphia and lived with her stepbrother Earl Huff until her own death on 30 April 1961. Carolyn Wedin Sylvander's book *Jessie Redmon Fauset: Black American Writer* (1981), the most comprehensive study of Fauset's life and writings to date, includes this kind of detailed information, as well as close readings of the novels. Thorough and insightful, Sylvander's book notes and discusses discrepancies, corrects biographical misinformation, dispels many myths about the author and her work, and challenges other critics to take up the task of deeper explications of all of Fauset's writings, but especially the novels.

Fauset once said that she liked to tell a "good story." She insisted, despite the demands of the day, that black middle-class society could be interesting and dramatic. Although her work has been caught in the crossfire of the Black Aesthetic debate then and now, current scholars are beginning to give her the attention and recognition she so richly deserves.

• Abbey A. Johnson, "Literary Midwife: Jessie Redmon Fauset and the Harlem Renaissance," *Phylon* 34 (June 1978): 153. Carolyn Wedin Sylvander, *Jessie Redmon Fauset, Black American Writer,* 1981. Deborah E. McDowell, "The Neglected Dimension of Jessie Redmon Fauset," in *Conjuring,* eds. Marjorie Pryse and Hortense Spillers, 1985. Ann Allen Shockley, *Afro-American Women Writers, 1746–1933: An Anthology and Critical Guide,* 1988. Ann duCille, *The Coupling Convention: Sex, Text, and Tradition in Black Women's Fiction,* 1993. Thadious Davis, introduction to *Afro-American Women Writers, 1910–1940,* ed. Henry Louis Gates, Jr., 1995. Jacquelyn Y. McLendon, *The Politics of Color in the Fiction of Jessie Fauset and Nella Larsen,* 1995.

—Jacquelyn Y. McLendon

FEDERAL WRITERS' PROJECT (FWP), a depression-era New Deal program that employed a number of African American writers and collected significant black folklore and autobiography. When President Franklin Roosevelt's Works Progress Administration (WPA) began hiring out-of-work writers to develop a *Guide to America* series, the "Black Cabinet" or "Brain Trust" of John Davis, William Hastie, and Robert Weaver pressed WPA director Harold Ickes for an Office of Negro Affairs to promote both equal employment of African American writers and black studies. Black representation in the FWP's workforce remained token—only 106 of 4,500 workers in 1937—and inconsistent, with some southern states refusing black applications in order not to spend money for "separate facilities." Yet Virginia, Louisiana, and Florida (as well as New York and Illinois) had active black units, and through the project several African American writers of stature earned necessary income at critical phases of their careers. Richard *Wright, quitting his post office job to write copy for the project in Chicago and New York, found time to write **Native Son* (1940); Zora Neale *Hurston finished three novels while doing field work in Florida; and young Ralph *Ellison in research on trials and folklore discovered what he called the "density" of black experience. The project also employed Claude *McKay, Margaret *Walker, Willard *Motley, and Frank *Yerby.

Beyond his limited success at influencing FWP personnel decisions, Negro Affairs director Sterling A. *Brown was able to intercept biased material intended for the *Guide* series and to instigate important new field studies of black subjects. In Chicago, Katherine *Dunham surveyed cults, including the Nation of Islam, and Arna *Bontemps supervised *The Cavalcade of the American Negro* in conjunction with the city's 1940 Diamond Jubliee. The Georgia project's *Drums and Shadows: Survival Studies among the Georgia Coastal Negroes* (1940) sought cultural parallels between Africa and the Sea Islands. Similar studies remained fragmentary or unpublished when Congress ended support in 1939, although the writers' project survived on the state level until 1943 and some data resurfaced in later texts.

Two African American collections distinguish the project's overall work. *The Negro in Virginia* (1940), a treasury of folklore and history supervised by Roscoe Lewis, won praise from *The Saturday Review* as "one of the most valuable contributions yet made to the American negro's history." The project's greatest monument is the *Slave Narrative Collection,* interviews and testimonies from more than two thousand of one hundred thousand former slaves living in the 1930s. Charles S. Johnson had initiated such research at Fisk University in 1929, and his student Lawrence Reddick launched a pilot program for the Federal Emergency Relief Administration in 1934. Two years later, white folklore editor John Lomax, on loan from the Library of Congress, designed a standard questionnaire for the American Guide Manual. Brown, along with Lomax's successor Benjamin Botkin, later refined this questionnaire, which was used in seventeen states by dozens of FWP workers. From ten thousand pages of manuscript, Botkin excerpted *Lay My Burden Down: A Folk History of Slavery* (1945), remarking that the ex-slaves' stories possess "an essential truth and humanity that surpasses as it supplements history and literature."

• Norman Yetman, "The Background of the American Slave Collection," *American Quarterly* 19 (Fall 1967): 534–553. Monty Noam Penkower, T*he Federal Writers' Project: A Study in Government Patronage of the Arts,* 1977.

—Craig Howard White

Fences. The third play by an African American playwright to be awarded the Pulitzer Prize, August *Wilson's most widely known work won the award in 1987. In addition, it received the New York Drama Critics Circle Award and a Tony Award for best play. Wilson developed the play over more than five years and through, as Joan Fishman discusses ("Developing His Song: August Wilson's *Fences,*" in *August Wilson: A Casebook,* 1994), more than five drafts. First read at New Dramatists in New York in 1982, the play was developed at the Eugene O'Neill Theater in the summer of 1983, produced at the Yale Repertory Theater in 1985, and taken on the road through productions in Chicago, Seattle, and San Francisco. It opened on Broadway at the 46th Street Theater on 26 March 1987. The cast featured James Earl Jones as Troy and Mary Alice as Rose.

The play centers on Troy Maxson and his family, who are posed at the dawn of the civil rights movement in 1959. An ex-con and a former player in the Negro Baseball League who feels racism crippled his athletic career, Troy now works as a garbage man. Convinced that his son Cory, a talented football player who has been promised a college scholarship, will only encounter similar racism, Troy prevents Cory from accepting the scholarship. Perhaps as a further repercussion of his experience of racism, Troy is unfaithful to his wife Rose and, when his girlfriend dies in childbirth, asks for Rose's help in rearing the child. Rose accepts Raynell, the child, but refuses to have any further conjugal relationship with Troy. After Troy's death, Raynell, Cory, and Rose acknowledge their love for this flawed man through the healing ritual of song.

Wilson wrote the play partly in response to conventional critics who had attacked Ma Rainey's *Black Bottom* (1984) for its unconventional structure: he wanted to demonstrate that he could write a unified play that centered around a major character. But more importantly, he wanted to elucidate the indignities that African Americans suffered but hid from their children. As Fishman points out, the character of Troy seems loosely based upon Wilson's stepfather, David Bedford, who had also experienced disappointment in sports, a prison stay, a "new life" with Wilson's mother, and an early death. Brent Staples's review for the *New York Times* suggested that the play presents the life of many other African Americans as well.

The play's conventional husband-wife and father-son conflicts are subservient to its discussion of racism. It illuminates the inherent inequity in America's treatment of African American males and the ways in which this racism becomes internalized and invades the most private of societal units—the family. The title offers the central metaphor for the play, reflecting the dual nature of those structures that people design for their protection but that also become their prisons.

A critical and commercial success, *Fences* broke the record for nonmusical plays when it grossed eleven million dollars in one year. Howard Kissel and Michael Feingold praised Wilson's poetic ability; Clive Barnes called it the strongest American writing since that of Tennessee Williams. The play is generally considered to stand alongside the work of Henry Miller for its insightful portrayal of the problematics of the American dream.

[*See* Piano Lesson, The.]

—Marilyn Elkins

FETCHIT, STEPIN. *See* Stepin Fetchit.

FIELDS, JULIA (b. 1938), poet, short fiction writer, teacher, and dramatist. Growing up on an Alabama farm, Julia Fields imbibed a love of nature, words, and the cadences of biblical language from both parents and a commitment to craftsmanship from her preacher-carpenter father. By age twelve she had already memorized verses from the Bible and poems of Lewis Carroll, William Wordsworth, Robert Burns, William Shakespeare, and even Henry VanDyke. She recited their lines to herself as she knelt over her garden plot. She mused that poets, such as Wordsworth on Toussaint *L'Ouverture, were writing about blacks "before we did."

In seventh grade, her teacher recognized Fields's talent when she assigned the writing of an original poem. The summer she was sixteen, watching the changing colors of the sky while bringing in the cattle for milking, Fields was inspired to write "The Horizon," her first poem to be published (in Scholastic magazine). Fields attended the Presbyterian Knoxville College in Tennessee on scholarship. Dr. Rosey Pool, a concentration camp survivor who had known Anne Frank, visited the school. After hearing some of Fields's poems, she included several in her collection *Beyond the Blues* (1962).

Fields earned her master's degree at Breadloaf and Middlebury College in 1961. She taught in Alabama, then went to the University of Edinburgh in 1963. She was happy in Burns's country because she knew his poems by heart. At Rosey Pool's flat in London she met Langston *Hughes, who introduced her to South African writer Richard Rive, who remembered her as statuesque and as a striking beauty (*Writing Black*, 1981). Fields had taught Rive's story "The Bench" to children in Alabama to calm them during times when white racists were driving by shooting. South Africa's apartheid struck a resonant chord with Americans living in the segregated South.

Influences on Fields were tall, elegant Washington poet Georgia Douglas *Johnson, who reminded her of her great aunt Sally, and Robert *Hayden, whose natural elegance also impressed her and whom she admired for giving readings and trying to get to the heart of poetry despite his poor eyesight and all the criticism against him at one time. She has regretted that mulatto poets such as Sterling A. *Brown and Jean *Toomer wrote so little about living pale, for that would have helped mulatto children.

Feeling split between teaching and writing poetry, Fields searched for insights. She spent two years in the Library of Congress reading John Ruskin, for example. She says that thousands of poems have come to her over the years. One night poems would not let her sleep and she got up twenty-five times to write them down.

Starting with a commonplace subject, Fields strikes out for something of beauty, such as her poem "Vigil" with its turns on Lorraine *Hansberry and Macbeth. A relative commented to Fields on a lady who was a prostitute but got up every Sunday morning to take the neighborhood children to church. Fields considered that anecdote a modern-day Jesus and Mary Magdalene story. She believes that all great cultures have had this particular group of women: the "hopeless young and gifted whores."

Fields interspersed tramping and dancing, words from Greek culture, and the sacred and the profane in "Loose Feet, Skin Tight, and a Place to Dance."She treats with compassionate humor people who change name or religion for ethnic reasons as in "Sin" and "Alabama Suite," but she says that culture cannot be built on invective. Her "Mary" alludes to women in classical history; it reflects dismay that a man will walk farther for sex—("s-x")—than for justice or freedom. "Love Poem," written in an era of swingers, was provoked by Fields's ruminating on what had happened to the love of God.

Her themes are the human condition, God's creation, war, women's survival methods, exploitation, and artists known and unknown. A private person, Fields has lived the roles of wife and mother—her two daughters are now grown—but she deflects questions about herself to her work. In teaching inner-city students she calls on her creativity in order to elicit a recognition that real life is reflected in poetry. For that reason, she contends, poetry should be incorporated into every academic discipline: it gives color to history.

Kenneth Rexroth claimed that Fields represented the arrival of Negritude in America, and she has been praised by such critics as Clarence *Major and Eugene *Redmond. Fields's collection *Slow Coins* (1981) contains gold mined from common life.

• Kenneth Rexroth, "New American Poets," *Harper's*, June 1965, 65–71. Clarence Major, *The Dark and Feeling: Black American Writers and Their Work*, 1974. Mercedese Broussard, "Blake's Bard," review of *A Summoning, A Shining*, by Julia Fields, *Callaloo* 1 (Dec. 1976): 60–62. Eugene B. Redmond, *Drumvoices: The Mission of Afro-American Poetry*, 1976. Richard Rive, *Writing Black*,1981. Mary Williams Burger, "Julia Fields,"in *DLB*, vol. 41, *Afro-American Poets since 1955*, eds. Trudier Harris and Thadious M. Davis, 1985, pp. 123–131.

—Kathleen A. Hauke

Fire Next Time, The. James *Baldwin's well-received 1963 volume *The Fire Next Time* consists of two essays. The first, "My Dungeon Shook: Letter to My Nephew on the One Hundredth Anniversary of the Emancipation," was written on the occasion of the fourteenth birthday of Baldwin's nephew James, who was named after him. The second essay, "Down at the Cross: Letter from a Region in My Mind," recounts Baldwin's experiences growing up in New York, including his unpleasant encounters with the police, his attraction to and rejection of Christianity, his awareness of sexual pitfalls in Harlem, and his later encounter with the Honorable Elijah Muhammad. Filling in the backdrop for these specific comments is Baldwin's ever-spirited indictment of an America in which inequities between the races continue to define people's futures. Recognizing that politics are endemic to life, Baldwin uses the volume for his own political commentary, and that commentary serves to underscore the thoroughly engaging personal and social incidents he relates.

The two essays naturally set up a contrast between past and present, between the sometimes sordid adventures of the older James and the possible revisionist future for the younger James. As powerful expressions from Baldwin at his height as an essayist, the book was a best-seller as well as a popular teaching tool in the 1960s. The much shorter "My Dungeon Shook" takes the form of a letter Baldwin addresses to James. In it, he provides family history and indictments of America for the racism that has pervaded that family history. He indicates that James must remain free of racial prejudice himself, however, in order to be clear-sighted in the fight against racists, for they are themselves frequently "innocent" and "well-meaning." He enlists his nephew's aid in making America "what America must become," that is, receptive to all of its native sons and daughters, allowing the black ones the same opportunities as the white ones.

Baldwin's eloquence continues in the second, much longer essay. "Down at the Cross" is a recounting, first of all, of the perils that Baldwin himself has survived. As survivor, he can serve as example to the young James. Beginning when he himself was fourteen, Baldwin recounts his attraction to the church as a source of possible safety from the evils and fear of the society, as well as his competition with his father, incidents that would form the basis for his first, autobiographical novel, **Go Tell It on the Mountain* (1953). After a short term as a young minister, and extensive commentary on the failures of Christianity, Baldwin leaves the church. He then recounts meeting Elijah Muhammad twenty years later and being saddened that he could not be convinced that Muhammad's way was significantly different from Christianity in its possibilities for failure. He then discusses the position of black people in America and asserts that the country can never be a nation until it solves its color problem. If it does not, he predicts destructive consequences in the image of "the fire next time."

• Therman B. O'Daniel, *James Baldwin: A Critical Evaluation*, 1977.

—Trudier Harris

FISHER, RUDOLPH (1897–1934), novelist, short story writer, and leading figure of the Harlem Renaissance. In his short stories and two published novels Rudolph Fisher was concerned with the development of an urban community with few models to guide it. This was a community that, jazzlike, had to improvise against the history of the rural South and creeping disillusionment with the urban North.

Rudolph John Chauncey Fisher was born 9 May 1897 in Washington, D.C., to the Reverend John W. and Glendora Williamson Fisher. Fisher was the youngest of three children, with an older brother, Joseph, and an older sister, Pearl. In 1903 the family moved to New York, but by 1905 they had resettled in Providence, Rhode Island. Rudolph Fisher attended public schools in Providence and graduated from Classical High School with high honors. By the end of senior year, his interest in both literature and science was established. This was evident throughout his undergraduate career at Brown University (1915–1919). He was elected to Phi Beta Kappa and other honorary societies; he won prizes for performances in his German classes, for public speaking, and for his work in rhetoric and English composition. During his senior year he was elected a commencement-day speaker, and using as his subject the emancipation of science, Fisher attempted to argue for the compatibility of science and religion. In two stories published late in his career, "John Archer's Nose" and "The Conjure Man Dies," he would dramatize if not their compatibility, at least their resigned coexistence. Fisher received an MA in biology at Brown in 1920 and entered Howard Medical School that fall. By the time he finished medical school, Fisher had started at least four short stories, all of which would eventually be published. His first and still one of his most popular, "The City of Refuge," was submitted to *Atlantic Monthly* during the spring of his senior year; it was published the following year. Fisher graduated with highest honors from medical school in 1924, interned for a year at Freedman's Hospital, and won a research fellowship, which supported him from September 1925 to October 1927. In 1926 his lengthy story "High Yaller" won the Amy Spingarn Prize for fiction. In just a few short years, Rudolph Fisher had distinguished himself in the study of medicine and in the writing of short fiction.

While his fiction writing continued steadily, Fisher set up practice as a roentgenologist, working at various New York City hospitals before moving into private practice at his home in Jamaica, Long Island. He was among the few who practiced in the new field of X-ray technology and among the very few African Americans who practiced the specialty between 1920 and 1940.

By 1924 Fisher had met Jane Ryder, a lively and intelligent grade-school teacher in Washington. They married within a year and a half of meeting, and by 1926 a son, Hugh, was born. Fisher promptly and jokingly nicknamed him "the New Negro," the popular term that characterized the pride and assertiveness of many during this period.

Music was always vitally important to Rudolph Fisher and his work. By 1919 he had met and befriended Paul *Robeson, then a student at Rutgers. With Paul singing and Rudolph playing the piano and arranging, they toured the East Coast, hoping to raise money for tuition. Later, while a research fellow, Fisher helped shape some of the skits for a musical revue that was to star Robeson. An avid fan of jazz, "Bud" Fisher, with his wife and friends, often visited Harlem cabarets, speakeasies, and nightclubs. His observations on racially integrated audiences in Harlem and the rage for jazz are wryly presented in his essay "The Caucasian Storms Harlem." In his fiction he was always sensitive to the use of music as more than backdrop or narcotic. He experimented with interesting ways to make the music an essential ingredient in the story. There are fine examples of this in "Common Meter" and "Miss Cynthie" and in the long masquerade ball scene in *The *Walls of Jericho* (1928).

In March, October, and December 1934, Fisher underwent surgeries for a stomach disorder. He died on 26 December 1934 at Edgecombe Sanitarium in New York City. A first lieutenant in the reserve medical corps of the 369th Infantry, Fisher was buried three days later with members of the detachment in attendance.

Fisher's bright, open, comic sense encouraged the development of a Black literary voice that did not avoid the ambiguities and contradictions within the urban community. Whether applied to the specific genre of the mystery story or to literary fiction, his accounts of a group attempting to achieve community were perceptive and helped to deeply enrich as well as suggest fresh directions for a literature entering its modern period.

• Arthur Davis, *From the Dark Tower: Afro-American Writers (1900–1960),* 1974. Robert Bone, *Down Home: A History of Afro-American Short Fiction from Its Beginnings to the End of the Harlem Renaissance,* 1975. Bruce Kellner, *Harlem Renaissance: A Historical Dictionary for the Era,* 1987. John McCluskey, Jr., *City of Refuge: Collected Stories of Rudolph Fisher,* 1987. Charles Heglar, "Rudolph Fisher and the African American Detective," in *Armchair Detective* 30 (1997): 300–05.

—John McCluskey, Jr.

Flight to Canada (1976), Ishmael *Reed's fifth novel, extends his permutation of literary forms such as the Western and the mystery to the foundational genre of African American letters, the slave narrative. In it, Reed turns his historical revisionism, formerly directed at the Crusades, the Old West, and the Harlem Renaissance, to the antebellum South and the Civil War.

The two main protagonists of *Flight to Canada* are Uncle Robin, a house slave who alters his master's will, leaving the plantation to himself, and *Raven Quickskill, a runaway slave whose poem "Flight to Canada" is simultaneously the impetus for his escape and the means for tracking him down—suggesting both the power and the risk of writing. Both of these characters—like the central figures in Reed's previous books—are tricksters. They represent different generations (the old folks and the young "blood") with different strategies for surviving and "getting over." Uncle Robin, a "radical" alternative to Harriet Beecher *Stowe's *Uncle Tom, prefers to turn things his way rather than turn the other cheek; moreover, he stays "home" and works to undermine the slaveocracy from within, instead of "flying" north. Raven does fly (by jumbo jet!), but in the end, the promise of Canada proves illusory, and the novel concludes with his return to the plantation. Among other things, Reed implies that freedom is something we have to create, not simply seek.

Reed's use of anachronism (Lincoln's assassination, for example, takes place on television) is a strategy he has employed before, allowing him to challenge the neat, linear ordering of events that characterizes both our writing of history and our sense of time, of "progress." It also enables him to bring the past into the present in ways that notify us we haven't gone as far as we might think in redressing old problems, in resolving persistent contradictions in the American experiment. Thus, Reed's takeoff on the slave narrative is not just another example of his ongoing effort, begun in his first novel, *The Freelance Pallbearers,* to play with, and assert the play in, the texts of the African American tradition. Published in the year of the American bicentennial, this story of a runaway slave serves as a reminder that, two hundred years after the establishment of the nation, there still is something "fugitive" about black writing and the experience it articulates.

As has been the case with the majority of Reed's novels, some commentators have persisted in employing a laugh meter to evaluate his work—that is, assessing the degree to which Reed is funny or not. Still, with the exception of **Mumbo Jumbo, Flight to Canada* is Reed's most critically acclaimed work of fiction. Henry Louis *Gates, Jr., in his essay on Reed in the *Dictionary of Literary Biography* (vol. 33, 1984), considers *Flight to Canada* to be a major work, while Edmund White, reviewing the novel for the *Nation* (18 September 1976), went so far as to call it "the best work of black fiction since **Invisible Man.*"

• Hortense Spillers, "Changing the Letter: The Yokes, the Jokes of Discourse, or, Mrs. Stowe, Mr. Reed," in *Slavery and the Literary Imagination,* eds. Deborah E. McDowell and Arnold Rampersad, 1989, pp. 25–61. Ashraf H. A. Rushdy, "Ishmael Reed's Neo-HooDoo Slave Narrative," *Narrative* 2.2 (May 1994): 112–139.

—Robert Elliot Fox

FLOWERS, A. R. (b. 1951), novelist, essayist, and cultural activist. A native Memphian, Arthur Flowers's writing integrates regional African American culture, including blues music, hoodoo spirituality, Delta dialect, and oral traditions. His delving into the local, linguistically and culturally, is evocative of Zora Neale *Hurston (who makes a cameo appearance in his first novel), Langston *Hughes, and Ishmael *Reed. Moreover, attending John O. *Killens's (founder of the Harlem Writer's Guild) writing workshop at Columbia University over a span of thirteen years has clearly influenced Flowers. Killens believed that art is a form of propaganda and that it can have decolonizing uses. The workshop inspired Flowers to cofound (with others, including Doris Jean *Austin and B. J. Ashanti) and to act as executive director of the New Renaissance Writer's Guild in New York. Flowers also founded a literary workshop in Memphis called the Griot Shop.

Flowers's writings can be placed in a historical continuum of activism: for him, writing is political because it is a powerful factor in shaping values and behavior. His novels and workshops therefore provide an arena for reconceptualizing African American identity; they are linked to notions of the social responsibility of the artist as an ideological orchestrator. It is in this vein that Flowers describes himself as a literary hoodoo man and as a literary blues man.

His first novel, *De Mojo Blues* (1985), describes the physical and emotional journeys of three dishonorably discharged Vietnam veterans. Each character chooses a different path in his quest to redefine both masculinity and power: Mike attends law school and becomes active in business and politics; Willie D. works as a community activist in New York; and Tucept HighJohn apprentices hoodoo in Memphis in order to learn how to influence the mental and spiritual energies in others. Flowers's prose and dialect evoke the authenticity of place and character of the Black Power era. He captures a part of the African American community in a moment of transition and restructuring, and his use of arhythmic bluesy prose allows the reader to view both the characters and the culture from within.

Another Good Loving Blues (1993) captures another period of transition—the Great Migration—and, again, Flowers emphasizes creative survival in the face of change. Narrated by a griot named Flowers, the novel focuses on Melvira Dupree (a conjure woman) and Lucas Bodeen (a blues man). It is part love story, part fable (Flowers integrates oral traditions of parable, folktale, and toasts), and part quest for artistic authenticity. The subtext reveals many of the difficulties facing African Americans during this period of increased racial tension and violence. Flowers's prose again evokes blues music and the region.

Flowers identifies with his characters because his writing is based in his lived experiences (in Vietnam and as a blues musician, for example). Most importantly, however, in both his novels and his writing workshops, Flowers directly links participation in and knowledge of African American cultural heritage to racial consciousness.

—Vivian M. May

Folks from Dixie. The first collection of short stories written by Paul Laurence *Dunbar, *Folks from Dixie* (1898) is also considered the first volume of short stories by an African American to be published in the United States. Most of the twelve stories in *Folks from Dixie* had been published previously in popular magazines; the volume sold well and was reprinted in England in 1899. Setting the tone for the short fiction that Dunbar collected in three subsequent volumes, the stories in *Folks from Dixie* celebrate the simple pleasures of "down-home" living for African Americans, who find fulfillment in their own communities apart from and seemingly unmindful of the world of whites. Only a comparative few of Dunbar's stories offer candid assessments of social problems occasioned by race.

Five stories in *Folks from Dixie* are set in the antebellum era and portray slaves according to the myths of the plantation tradition. "The Colonel's Awakening" and "The Intervention of Peter," for instance, represent the loyalty of slaves and ex-slaves to whites in ways that substitute sentimentality for thoughtful reflection on the relationships of whites and blacks in the South. In "The Trial Sermon on Bull-Skin" Dunbar employs stock characters from the plantation tradition but also offers insight into the folkways and superstitions of a rural southern black community as it seeks a pastor.

More noteworthy in *Folks from Dixie* are Dunbar's studies of the social and economic realities of life for ordinary African Americans at the turn of the century. "Aunt Mandy's Investment" warns that African American self-help and solidarity can be betrayed as much by misplaced trust in black shysters as by dependence on white patrons. "At Shaft Eleven" speaks frankly about labor strife in a coal-mining town and focuses on a heroic African American foreman, although some critics have felt that Sam Bowles's loyalty to white bosses is troublingly similar to that displayed by ex-slaves to their former masters in plantation fiction. "Jimsella" anticipates Dunbar's *The *Sport of the Gods* (1902) in describing the plight of a working-class African American couple who have migrated from the South to New York in the hope of finding better opportunities. "The Ordeal at Mt. Hope" offers a distinct critique of racial discrimination, demythologizes slavery, and explores the social and political philosophies of Booker T. *Washington and W. E. B. *Du Bois. Typically, however, the difficulties that African Americans face in Dunbar's short stories arise from their own self-deceptions and misplaced priorities, not from deeper causes, such as white racism, that would require a profounder analysis of social and economic forces.

• Arlene A. Elder, *The "Hindered Hand": Cultural Implications of Early African-American Fiction,* 1978. Robert A. Bone, *Down Home: Origins of the Afro-American Short Story,* 1988.

—William L. Andrews and Patricia Robinson Williams

FORBES, CALVIN (b.1945), poet, lecturer, and educator. Calvin Forbes was born the seventh of eight children in Newark, New Jersey, to Jacob and Mary Short Forbes. He was the first of the six boys in his family to graduate from high school, and he attended Rutgers University briefly before entering the New School for Social Research in New York City. There Forbes studied with poet José García Villa, who taught him the fundamentals of writing.

Forbes continued to educate himself through travel, and he was on the move frequently throughout the 1960s. He traveled widely in Europe and hitchhiked from coast to coast in America with only a suitcase, a sleeping bag, and a portable typewriter as his baggage. Forbes also lived in Hawaii for a short time; his stay there was instrumental to his writing the poems for his first volume, *Blue Monday* (1974). Observing Hawaii's Asian American culture, Forbes began to think of his own African American heritage as a culture that belonged to him, and as an element that belonged in his writing.

Not surprisingly, then, many poems in *Blue Monday* are autobiographical in their nature. "The Middle Life," for example, reflects Forbes's background in the church, and "For My Mother" tells the story of his parents' courtship and their migration from Greenville, North Carolina, to the North. In addition to drawing on family stories and memories in his writing, Forbes also culls stories and phrases from African American oral tradition and frequently employs colloquial and idiomatic language in his poetry. Further, Forbes puts his love for blues music to work in *Blue Monday,* threading the mood and wry philosophy that underpin blues lyrics throughout his poems.

Critics have praised Forbes's first book for its metaphoric complexity, noting that he successfully employs synecdoche to make individual images represent the whole of the poem, like the poets John Donne and Gwendolyn *Brooks—writers whose work he admires. Detractors, on the other hand, have argued that elements of blues singing work against Forbes when he tries to incorporate them into poetry: they suggest that blues music allows for a shifting of imagery and an emotional distance that sometimes weaken his work. The critics agree, however, that *Blue Monday* represents an innovative attempt to find an original poetic voice.

Forbes's second book, *From the Book of Shine*, was published in 1979 as a limited edition text (the book was also published in 1980 by Razorback Press in Wales as a limited edition). He creates a number of poems based on an African American folk character named *Shine about whom he heard stories as a young boy; Forbes expands on the folk story by giving Shine a female counterpart, Glow, and poems like "Blind Date with a Voice" and "A Post Card from Colorado" plot the development of their relationship. Here Forbes's work shows the influence of writers such as Sterling A. *Brown; like Brown, Forbes uses the African American folk hero to create poems filled with irony and subtle humor. However, in contrast with Brown's work, throughout the volume humor gives way to a strong sense of despair about living in a racist society.

Forbes's career as a writer is paralleled by a distinguished career as an educator. He taught African American literature at Emerson College in Boston from 1969 to 1973, then left to become an assistant professor at Tufts University in Medford, Massachusetts, for a year. He subsequently took a leave of absence and traveled to Denmark, France, and England as a Fulbright scholar. In 1975, Forbes returned to Tufts and continued to teach there until 1977, when he again departed to finish an MFA at Brown University in Providence, Rhode Island. Forbes accepted a position at Howard University in Washington, D.C., in 1978. He won a National Endowment for the Arts fellowship in 1982 and moved to Jamaica, where he worked on an unpublished novel and lectured at the University of the West Indies in Kingston. After returning to teach at Howard and other neighboring colleges and universities, Forbes moved to Chicago. He currently teaches literature and writing at the School of the Art Institute of Chicago.

Forbes has not produced a large body of work. However, he aspires, like the British poet Philip Larkin—another of his favorite writers—to concentrate on the quality of his writing rather than the quantity. His poetry continues to be anthologized, and even without further publications Forbes maintains an important position in the African American literary tradition.

• David Huddle, "Book Reviews," *Georgia Review* 28 (Fall 1974): 535–540. Joseph Parisi, "Personae, Personalities," *Poetry* 126 (July 1975): 219–241. Robert A. Coles, "Calvin Forbes," in *DLB,* vol. 41, *Afro-American Poets since 1955,* eds. Trudier Harris and Thadious M. Davis, 1985, pp. 131–134. Calvin Forbes, "Calvin Forbes," in *Contemporary Authors Autobiography Series,* ed. Joyce Nakamura, vol. 16, 1992, pp. 105–120.

—Allison Kimmich

for colored girls. Ntozake *Shange's *for colored girls who have considered suicide / when the rainbow is enuf* is a feminist drama with unique origins. Called a choreopoem by its author, the twenty-poem drama tells the stories of the joy, pain, suffering, abuse, strength, and resilience of African American women. Its seven female characters dress in colors representing the rainbow plus brown. Each speaks individual poems and is intermittently aided and joined by other characters in collective poems, producing a choral effect. This comes directly from the work's beginning: In various cafés, bars, and poetry houses in California and New York, Shange performed and presented the poems that eventually became a dramatic unit. It was first performed in December 1974 at a women's bar outside Berkeley, California.

Music, dancing, and lighting are used with creative significance in *for colored girls,* with the characters often singing and dancing together to satisfy their collective need for female support. There are no props, scenery, or furniture, so lighting is used to emphasize or isolate particular characters as needed. Throughout the performance, women move in and out of the spotlight and on and off the stage. These dramatic techniques place the burden of interpretation on the actresses, who must assume different narrative personas, and require the audience members to use their imaginations.

The author notes in her stage directions that the characters live outside of large metropolitan areas in the United States, stressing their isolation from mainstream society; the "ladies" have no names for they represent all oppressed women of color. The colors of their dresses represent various degrees of emotion, with the brighter ones symbolizing vivaciousness and youth and the cooler colors designating frustration and despair. The lady in red, the most vibrant color, interprets the most violent, forceful, and memorable poem, dramatizing the plight of African American women with two significant personas. In "one," near the beginning of the drama, she portrays a lively and glittering seductress who turns into a "regular" colored woman who cries herself to sleep in the early hours of the morning. In "of no assistance," she rails against a lover who failed to assist her in maintaining a loving relationship, angrily disposing of him and sending him away with a heated explanation of her reason for remaining in the heretofore unsatisfying relationship. The lady in red's most violent and heartbreaking poem is "a nite with beau willie brown," in which she tells a horrible story of physical and emotional violence perpetuated by a demented black man against his girlfriend and children; it ends in the children's murder when he throws them from a fifth-story window. Contrastingly, the lady in brown, the only color not associated with the rainbow, interprets poems on more serious and meditative subjects that represent earthly concerns and history, such as "Toussaint," concerning the leader of the Haitian Revolution. In "pyramid," three characters join before and after a disastrous relationship with the same man who betrayed them all and endangered their friendship; however, the poem ends with the women again turning to each other for support and consolation. Shange demonstrates and defines the assertiveness that oppressed women of color must possess in order to fulfill themselves. Her characters begin as fragmented voices but end as supported ones as their isolation diminishes through the support and consolation they give one another.

The work is one of the most critically acclaimed of all African American dramas. It has been produced countless times, in high schools and colleges as well as on commercial stages. It is taught in American literature courses and has been incorporated into master's theses and doctoral dissertations. The work has also influenced younger writers such as Elizabeth Alexander, who draws upon Shange's work in her play *Diva Studies* (1996). Shange is thus an influencing and influential playwright.

• Jeffrey Elliott, "Ntozake: Genesis of a Choreopoem," *Negro History Bulletin* 41 (Jan. 1978): 797–800. Carolyn Mitchell, "'A Laying on of Hands': Transcending the City in Ntozake Shange's *for colored girls . . .*," in Women Writers and the City: Essays in Feminist Literary Criticism, ed. Susan Merrill Squier, 1984, pp. 230–248. Claudia Tate, *Black Women Writers at Work*, 1984. Elizabeth Brown-Guillory, "Ntozake Shange," in *DLB*, vol. 38, *Afro-American Writers after 1955: Dramatists and Prose Writers*, eds. Thadious M. Davis and Trudier Harris, 1985, pp. 240–250. Betty Taylor-Thompson, "Female Support and Bonding in *for colored girls . . .* ," *Griot* 12.1 (Spring 1993): 46–51. Neal A. Lester, *Ntozake Shange: A Critical Study of the Plays*, 1995.

—Betty Taylor-Thompson

For Love of Imabelle. *See Cotton Comes to Harlem.*

For My People. Although Margaret Walker has published three volumes of poetry since the 1970s—*Prophets for a New Day* (1970), *October Journey* (1973), and *This Is My Century* (1989)—her reputation as one of the most accomplished African American poets of the twentieth century was established with the 1942 publication by Yale University Press of her first book of poems, *For My People.* As the winner of the Yale University Series of Younger Poets Award, Walker became the first black woman to be so honored. That the book belongs to the category of first black American achievements is less significant than the craft and historical consciousness that give the poems enduring value and secure their special place in the literary history of African American poetry and in the cultural narrative of African American people.

For My People, particularly its title poem, can be read as a successful fulfillment of the yearning expressed in the early poem "I Want to Write" (1934). It is also, within the evolution of African American poetry, a model of how the individual locates herself in foundational orality and the tradition of formal verse, blending folk speech and fluid lyricism, biblical typology, and the disciplined genres of ballad and sonnet with the freer forms of modernist sensibility to construct a collection that is governed by the logic of response to a people's special history. Also very important for literary study is Walker's heeding of James Weldon *Johnson's call for a poetry that judiciously represented the souls and gifts of black folk, as well as her building on the antecedents of Harlem Renaissance poetry to create works that at once demonstrate mastery of language and the revolutionary vision of the 1930s. Less overtly political than contemporaneous work by Langston *Hughes, for example, such poems as "We Have Been Believers," "Since 1619," and "Delta" illustrate Walker's unyielding commitment to the themes of liberation and social justice. Stephen Vincent Benét was perceptive in noting in his preface to *For My People* that the poet's voice was living, passionate, and replete with "lasting music."

"For My People," which had been published in *Poetry* in 1937 and in the landmark anthology *The Negro Caravan* (1941), and the twenty-five other poems in the book are divided into three sections that focus on the South as place of origin and lineage, on the tragicomic existentialism of folk characters, and the redemptive qualities of belief. As critics such as Eugenia

Collier, Eleanor Traylor, and R. Baxter Miller have asserted, the distinguishing features of this volume are Walker's historical and prophetic vision, deft handling of symbols and biblical rhetoric, and use of myth and lore.

For My People endures as a poetic model of the signal emphasis in African American literature on matters of history, and it is the use of history that links Walker's poetic vision with those of her contemporaries Gwendolyn *Brooks, Robert *Hayden, and Melvin B. *Tolson. The iconic status "For My People" has achieved in African American cultural life serves as one warrant for continuing study of this book. Margaret Walker's lyric and narrative poems resonate with the deep structures of African American philosophy and humanism as they imaginatively look forward to the future of her people.

• Richard K. Barksdale, "Margaret Walker: Folk Orature and Historical Prophecy," in *Black American Poets between Worlds, 1940–1960,* ed. R. Baxter Miller, 1986, pp. 105–117. R. Baxter Miller, "The 'Etched Flame' of Margaret Walker: Biblical and Literary Re-Creation in Southern History," in *Black Southern Voices,* eds. John Oliver Killens and Jerry W. Ward, Jr., 1992, pp. 591–604.

—Jerry W. Ward, Jr.

FORREST, LEON (1937–1997), novelist. Leon Forrest was born in Chicago, Illinois, on 8 January 1937. An only child, he grew up in the largely segregated South Side in a family whose heritage was shaped by his mother's New Orleans, Creole, and Catholic origins and his father's Mississippi Protestant roots. This dual religious heritage is an important influence in his fiction. He attended Wendell Phillips School in his neighborhood, then became one of the few black students to attend Hyde Park High School during the years 1951–1955. He attended Wilson Junior College (1955–1956), Roosevelt University (1957–1958), and the University of Chicago (1959–1960), and served in Germany in the U.S. Army. After his term in the service, Forrest returned to Chicago determined to pursue a career as a writer. He resumed taking courses at the University of Chicago and supported himself for a while by working in a bar and liquor store managed by his mother and stepfather—the setting that inspired many of the scenes in *Divine Days* (1992). In the mid-1960s, while working on his first novel, Forrest became a journalist, working initially for a neighborhood newspaper, the *Woodlawn Observer,* and later for *Muhammed Speaks,* the newspaper of the Nation of Islam. He was promoted to associate editor of *Muhammed Speaks* in 1969 and managing editor in 1972. In 1973, Forrest's first novel, *There Is a Tree More Ancient than Eden,* was edited by Toni *Morrison and published by Random House with an introduction by Ralph *Ellison. Forrest received high praise and was immediately hailed as a major talent. Shortly after the novel's publication, he was appointed to the faculty of Northwestern University, where he was professor and chair of African American Studies.

A highly experimental and symbolically dense novel, *There Is a Tree More Ancient than Eden* introduces the fictional universe of Forest County, a world strikingly similar in its texture to Cook County, Illinois, where Chicago is located. Forrest shares with William Faulkner an intense concern with geographical settings, with history and culture as they unfold through family chronicles, and with the burden of personal and historical consciousness. His novels are linked by their shared location, by interlocking family genealogies, and by their exploration of the experiences and developing consciousness of Nathaniel Witherspoon, who grows to maturity over the course of Forrest's first three novels.

There Is a Tree More Ancient than Eden is a highly lyrical novel that explores the multiple layers of Nathaniel Witherspoon's consciousness in the context of his mother's death during the early 1950s. In *The Bloodworth Orphans* (1977), Forrest creates a crowded canvas of characters, all of whom are connected by their orphanhood and their sometimes destructive quests for father images. In this novel, Nathaniel often functions as an auditor and observer of the nightmarish saga of the black descendants of the southern white Bloodworth family, a collector of the memories, stories, and legends he hears. Similarly, *Two Wings to Veil My Face* (1984) begins with Nathaniel, now twenty-one, being called to the bedside of his grandmother Sweetie Reed. The stories she tells him—about her life and her slave father's—trigger a multilayered journey through time and space, history and myth. *Divine Days,* an epic novel of over one thousand pages, signals a shift in direction from Forrest's earlier novels. Set during one specific week in 1966, *Divine Days* revolves around a turning point in the life of Forrest's protagonist, Joubert Antoine Jones. Like so many of Forrest's characters, Joubert is an orphan; like Leon Forrest, he has returned to Forest County after a stint in the U.S. Army and aspires to be a writer. Like all of Forrest's novels, however, *Divine Days* gives free rein to his formidable creative gifts. In 1994, Forrest published *Relocations of the Spirit: Essays.*

If Leon Forrest was concerned with the themes of historical and cultural disruption, with orphanhood as a metaphor for the African American—and human—condition, he was equally concerned with the quest for redemption. Like Ralph Ellison, whom he clearly claimed as an important literary ancestor, Forrest saw African American oral traditions as rich repositories of ritual and value, sources of meaning in the face of suffering and tragedy. Storytelling, music, religion, and a highly developed comic sense are inextricably woven into the fabric of his fiction. A major stylistic innovator, Forrest also claimed his place among other major twentieth-century literary modernists. Although his restless experimentation and complex, allusive style often prove difficult on first reading, his novels possess a complexity and depth that reward the demands he makes upon his readers.

• Keith E. Byerman, *Fingering the Jagged Grain: Tradition and Form in Recent Black Fiction,* 1985, pp. 238–255. John G. Cawelti, introduction to *The Bloodworth Orphans,* 1987. John G. Cawelti, "Earthly Thoughts on Divine Days," *Callaloo* 16.2 (Spring 1993): 431–447. Danille Taylor-Guthrie, "Sermons, Testifying, and Prayers: Looking Beneath the Wings in Leon Forrest's *Two Wings to Veil My Face,*" *Callaloo* 16.2 (Spring 1993): 419–430. Kenneth W. Warren, "Thinking Beyond Catastrophe: Leon Forrest's *There Is a Tree More Ancient than Eden,*" *Callaloo* 16.2 (Spring 1993): 409–418.

—James A. Miller

FORTEN, CHARLOTTE (1838–1914), diarist. As an African American diarist in antebellum and postbellum America, Charlotte Forten was a privileged individual by birth and endowment. Born 17 August 1838 in Philadelphia, Forten was a toddler when her famous grandfather died. James Forten, Sr., who had been a powder-boy during the American Revolution and a former student of Anthony Benezet, the Quaker abolitionist, was an ingenious man who amassed a fortune by inventing and patenting a practical sailing device. Because of his brilliant mind and rebellious spirit, he was a leading abolitionist among free Negroes in Philadelphia. Robert Forten, his son and Charlotte's father, an antislavery lecturer, hired private tutors to instruct his daughter at home before she moved to Salem, Massachusetts, in protest of Philadelphia's strictly segregated schools. Her aunts, Margaretta, Sarah, and Harriet, were active socially and politically in the women's rights and antislavery movements. Harriet Forten, Charlotte's favorite aunt, was married to Robert *Purvis, an original signer of the American Anti-Slavery Society charter and later the president of that organization.

A product of this environment of revolutionary fervor and commitment, Charlotte Forten was immersed in the spirited politics of renewal. Her own sufferings, however, personalized her involvement in the campaign to end slavery and racism. She may well have been an aristocratic member of the Forten clan, but her status was no protection from the discrimination that she experienced as a person of color connected irremediably to a subjugated group of people. Her journals reveal her anguish and pain as she and her friends were barred from ice cream parlors in Philadelphia and museums in Boston. Indeed, even her white classmates from the "liberal" Higginson Grammar School were capable of ostracizing her at their convenience. She confides to her diary, "I have met girls in the schoolroom—they have been thoroughly kind and cordial to me—perhaps the next day met them in the street—they feared to recognize me; these I can but regard now with scorn and contempt." Charlotte Forten was a victim of a psychic conflict of identity: she was both a blue blood and a member of an oppressed minority at the mercy of a racialized society and its racist whims.

Forten's diaries were written over a period of thirty-eight years from 1854 to 1892, time enough for her and her society to change. The journals capture these changes. There are five diaries, and each one permits Charlotte Forten to develop a new image of herself. The first diary is written from 24 May 1854 to 31 December 1856, when Charlotte Forten is a brooding teenager attending antislavery rallies in Boston, Framingham, and Salem. Written from 1 January 1857 to 27 January 1858, diary 2 mirrors the transformation of Charlotte Forten, a young adult, into an abolitionist snob. After receiving a caller who had failed to embrace the doctrine of radical abolitionism, she writes of him, "intelligent on some subjects—ignorant of true [radical] anti-slavery. I soon wearied of him." Journal 3 is the core of the diaries, for it is here that a twenty-four-year-old Charlotte Forten (upon John Greenleaf Whittier's advice) applies for a commission to travel like a soldier to South Carolina as a New England schoolmarm to teach contraband slaves and nurse Union soldiers during the Civil War. This diary covers five years, 28 January 1858 to 14 February 1863. Two of the most important events recorded here are her involvement in the Port Royal Social Experiment and her eyewitness account of the official reading of Abraham *Lincoln's Emancipation Proclamation statement to South Carolina slaves and black soldiers. Charlotte Forten left Philadelphia for the Sea Islands on 22 October 1862; excluding a two-month northern vacation, she stayed on the coast for approximately seventeen months. She taught at the Penn School, under the supervision of its founder, Laura Towne, and her assistant Ellen Murray, both New Englanders.

Forten travelled to nearby Beaufort, South Carolina, to meet Harriet *Tubman. When former slave Harriet Tubman describes her adventures in assisting fugitive slaves, the diarist writes, "My own eyes were full as I listened to her." Harriet Tubman has been called the *Moses of her people for leading, single-handedly, approximately three hundred men, women, and children to freedom in Canada and the North. When "Moses" and the "soldier" Charlotte Forten come face to face, a symbolic union takes place: the old world of slavery and "ordinary" heroism and the new world of independence and acknowledgment that Americans of African descent, regardless of their place in society, have a shared racial heritage of oppression that makes differences of birth and education of secondary importance in a racialized country.

In diary 4, written from 15 February 1863 to 15 May 1864, Charlotte Forten has settled into her role as nurse to contraband slaves and Union soldiers, at first relishing her relations with the all-black Fifty-Fourth Regiment (she is called the "Daughter of the Regiment") and its leader, Robert Shaw. But her happiness is turned to grief upon their defeat at Fort Wagner.

The last journal, November 1885 to July 1892, was written approximately twenty-one years after diary 4. Although she had been married to the Princeton-educated minister Francis J. Grimké (the mulatto nephew of white feminists-abolitionists Angelina and Sarah Grimké) for seven years, Charlotte Forten gives no details about the marriage. Her diaries were written in secrecy, but she must have been aware of their public historical importance and apparently refused disclosure of her intimate relations. In diary 3 she asks, "What name shall I give to thee, oh ami inconnu? It will be safer to give merely an initial—A. And so, dear A." By giving the journal an initial rather than a full name, Charlotte Forten shows her consciousness of an implied audience and her desire to keep some privacy.

She is wistful and pleased as she reviews past events. Having lost an infant daughter, Theodora, she does not wallow in self-pity and merely cites the age the child would have been had she lived—six years old. On Christmas Day 1885, she recalls dining with the aging Frederick *Douglass one year earlier in Washington, D.C., at his "beautiful home." She takes delight in the "Normal School," managed by Booker T. *Washington, and in the emergence of "colored people of the better class." The old missionary spirit, however, is still evident, as she expresses regrets about the impending move again to Washington, D.C., from Florida, in 1889, because the latter "is a good field for missionary work."

Her last entry is dated July 1892; she is in Massachusetts, having left Washington because of its "intense heat" and her constant illnesses. During the last twenty-two years of her life, Charlotte Forten was silent, dying in 1914. But her journals supersede the status of "mere diaries." For Charlotte Forten captured the zeitgeist of the Civil War epoch, which she helped to transform into something noble and meaningful for all Americans.

• Charlotte Forten, *The Journals of Charlotte Forten,* ed. Ray Allen Billington, 1953. Esther M. Douty, *Forten the Sailmaker,* 1968. Eric Foner, *Reconstruction,* 1988. Charlotte Forten Grimké, *The Journals of Charlotte Forten Grimké,* ed. Brenda Stevenson, 1988. Carla L. Peterson, *Doers of the Word: African-American Women Speakers and Writers in the North (1830–1880),* 1995.

—Geneva Cobb-Moore

FORTUNE, T. THOMAS (1856–1928), African American journalist and editor. Born a slave in Marianna, Florida, T. Thomas Fortune was the son of a prominent Republican politician during Reconstruction, which enabled him to hold various patronage positions during his adolescence. He studied at Howard University, leaving after a year to pursue a career in journalism. He arrived in New York City in the early 1880s, writing for various black and white publications, most notably as the editor of the *Globe.* He established himself as a militant, prodding African Americans to abandon their unquestioned loyalty to the party of Lincoln. His near-endorsement of Grover Cleveland for president in 1884 led to management conflicts and the demise of the *Globe,* though the paper reemerged first as the *Freeman* and then the *Age.* Under his proprietorship, the *Age* would become the leading black paper of the era, and he would become the "most noted man in Afro-American journalism." As one contemporary observed, "he never writes unless he makes someone wince."

Fortune's enthusiasm for the Democrats soon waned, while his 1884 book, *Black and White: Land, Labor and Politics in the South,* cemented his reputation as a civil rights militant. In a typical vein, Fortune vowed, "let us agitate! Agitate! AGITATE! until the protest shall awake the nation from its indifference." He was widely condemned in the white press as a firebrand. In the early 1890s, Fortune also established the Afro-American League, an ideological precursor to the NAACP, which lapsed into inactivity after a few years.

Growing prominence brought few financial rewards for Fortune, which may have contributed to his support of Booker T. *Washington after 1895. Fortune defended Washington while distancing himself from his accommodationist approach, thus lending Washington useful journalistic cover from an established militant. Fortune also acted as his ghostwriter, and Washington's subsidies to the *Age* and personal loans became essential to Fortune's financial survival. Increasing criticism of Washington from fellow radicals like W. E. B. *Du Bois and Monroe Trotter placed Fortune in an uncomfortable position. After the turn of the century, the relationship with Washington became strained, both personally and politically, and Fortune denounced Washington's support for President Theodore Roosevelt's actions after the Brownsville affair in 1906. Marital discord and alcoholism culminated in a mental breakdown in the following year, whereupon Fortune lost control of the *Age* to Washington allies.

Fortune spent the next decade destitute and depressed, writing occasional columns for the *Age* and editing several short-lived newspapers. In 1923, Fortune assumed the position of editor of the *Negro World,* vacated by Marcus *Garvey upon his imprisonment. Though he had opposed back-to-Africa notions and apparently never joined Garvey's Universal Negro Improvement Association, Fortune praised the "dramatic element" in Garvey's message and his skill in securing the support of the masses. He also defended Garvey against government charges of stock fraud, and he generally shared Garvey's resentment against Du Bois and the NAACP leadership. Fortune's reputation as a journalist had recovered somewhat by the time of his death.

• Emma Lou Thornbrough, *T. Thomas Fortune: Militant Journalist,* 1972.

—Michael W. Fitzgerald

Foxes of Harrow, The. Set in the antebellum South between 1825 and 1865, *The Foxes of Harrow* (1946) is a historical romance that chronicles the adventures of Stephen Fox, an Irish immigrant who rises from poverty to wealth in New Orleans society. The novel, which was written by Frank *Yerby, opens with Fox being thrown off a steamboat on the Mississippi River and ends with the destruction of his plantation, Harrow. Between 1825 and 1865, however, he wins recognition among aristocrats by amassing a fortune from gambling and selling cotton and marrying into a prominent family. An outcast in an alien culture, Fox lives on the margins, neither accepting nor adhering to its beliefs and traditions.

Unlike many protagonists in antebellum southern fiction, Fox is not magnanimous. He comes from a disreputable background, holds nonsouthern views, and succeeds by less than admirable means. Thus, while *The Foxes of Harrow* compares favorably to such historical romances as *Gone with the Wind* (1935) and *Anthony Adverse* (1933), it is in actuality a throwback to the picaresque tradition. Yerby's skillful adaptation and manipulation of the picaresque genre create a vehicle for him both to write entertaining fiction and debunk southern myths.

With the publication of *The Foxes of Harrow,* his first novel, Yerby made an abrupt transition from protest to popular fiction. Sales of the novel skyrocketed, magazines reprinted condensed versions of it, Twentieth Century Fox purchased the screen rights, and by the end of 1946, it had sold more than one million copies. Yerby would subsequently produce an impressive list of best-sellers, but in many ways, *The Foxes of Harrow* remains his most defining novel. It catapulted him to national recognition as a writer, it established the commercially successful formula for all of his succeeding novels, and it charted a course for him to gain distinction as the first African American to become a millionaire writing fiction.

• Ann Bontemps, "From Lad of Ireland to Bayou Grandee," *Chicago Sun Book Week,* 10 Feb. 1946, 1. Alice Hackett, "New Novelists of 1946," *Saturday Review of Literature* 30 (15 Feb. 1947): 11–13.

—James L. Hill

FRADO. By the time Harriet *Wilson wrote **Our Nig* (1859) and introduced Frado to the fictional world, many mulattas, with "glossy ringlets" and "creamy" skin, had graced the pages of American fiction. Frado joined William Wells *Brown's Clotel and Harriet Beecher *Stowe's Eliza Harris, anticipated Frances Ellen Watkins *Harper's *Iola Leroy, Nella *Larsen's *Helga Crane, and Zora Neale *Hurston's *Janie Crawford, and initiated a pattern in African American women's writing that wasn't challenged until Ann *Petry's brown-skinned *Lutie Johnson emerged in 1946. Yet Wilson creates an isolated rather than an alienated mulatta character. Moreover, unlike the vast majority of such characters, Frado's mother is white, and maternal abandonment rather than paternal legitimation is at issue. Indeed, through Frado's eyes, we see the most scathing critique of white mothers offered by an African American woman writer in the nineteenth century.

Abandoned when she is six, Frado is forced to work in New Hampshire as a virtual slave for the Bellmont family, who call her "our nig." Although Mrs. Bellmont's brutal treatment cannot break the spunky girl's spirit, it does ruin her health. When Frado leaves, the abuse she has endured has taken its toll and the eighteen year old can no longer work. After an unsuccessful marriage, she writes *Our Nig* to raise money to support herself and her son. We now know that Wilson's son died five months after the novel's publication. While Wilson's tale seems tragic, she successfully creates a spirited, if abused, protagonist who struggles with her captors, her identity as an isolated black child, and her readers' expectations.

• Henry Louis Gates, Jr., ed., introduction to *Our Nig,* 1994.

—P. Gabrielle Foreman

FRANKLIN, ARETHA (b. 1942), gospel, jazz, pop, and rhythm and blues singer. Aretha Franklin was born in Memphis, Tennessee, and grew up in Detroit, Michigan. Her father, Rev. Clarence LaVaugh Franklin, was a gospel singer. Aretha was raised by him and a household of housekeepers and family friends including Clara Ward, James Cleveland, and Mahalia Jackson. She began singing in her father's church choir at the age of twelve. She recorded her first album, *Songs of Faith,* when she was fourteen years old. At an early age she was labeled a "young genius" because of the strength and unique quality of her voice. In 1960, Franklin moved to New York City to pursue a career as a rhythm-and-blues singer. Although she refuses to discuss intimate details of her personal life, her music itself is autobiographical. Songs like "Respect," "Think," and "Try a Little Tenderness" reveal the pain and frustration she has experienced in her life. (She recorded "Respect" after separating from her first, abusive husband, Ted White.) Today Franklin is one of the most celebrated singers in American music. She has won at least fifteen Grammy Awards, including the 1993–1994 Grammy Lifetime Achievement Award. In 1985, the state of Michigan declared her voice a "natural resource"in honor of her twenty-fifth year in the music business. In 1987, she became the first woman to be inducted into the Rock and Roll Hall of Fame. The "Queen of Soul" has been compared to other great blues singers like Dinah Washington, Bessie *Smith, and Billie *Holiday. Blues singers maintain an iconic importance in African American poetry, drama, and fictive narrative. In African American literature they often figure as sensual women who utilize music as a liberating tool to communicate pain, suffering, desire, sexuality, and joy in an environment that normally represses female expression. Nikki *Giovanni's "Poem for Aretha," for example, is included in *Re: Creation* (1970), a book of poetry that advocates African American women's need for self-empowerment and self-sustenance in a spiritually destructive world. Part of "Poem for Aretha" refers to the way "we [society] eat up artists like there's going to be a famine." Writers like Giovanni are inspired by Franklin's signature voice and strive to project their own distinctive voices in their work.

• Mark Brego, *Aretha Franklin, the Queen of Soul,* 1989. Virginia C. Fowler, *Nikki Giovanni,* 1992.

—Alisha R. Coleman

FRANKLIN, J. E. (b. 1937), writer, playwright, and educator. Jennie Elizabeth Franklin was born in Houston, Texas; she began writing her impressions as a child and received a BA from the University of Texas. She was a primary school teacher in the Freedom School in Carthage, Mississippi (1964); served as a youth director at the Neighborhood House in Buffalo, New York (1964–1965); worked as an analyst in the U.S. Office of Economic Opportunity in New York City (1967–1968); and was a lecturer in education at the Herbert H. Lehman College of the City University of New York (1969–1975).

In 1964, while working with CORE in Mississippi, she engaged in an effort designed to interest students in reading. Her techniques led to her playwrighting career and her first full-length play, *A First Step to Freedom* (1964), which was performed in Harmony, Mississippi, at Sharon Waite Community Center. Other produced plays include *Prodigal Daughter,* a street theater project performed at Lincoln Center and on a Bronx street corner; *The In-Crowd* (1965), performed at the Montreal Expo in 1967; *Mau Mau Room,* performed by the Negro Ensemble Company Workshop; *Two Flowers,* produced at the New Feminist Theatre; and *The Prodigal Sister,* produced at Theatre de Lys (1976). The last was a musical, with book and lyrics by Franklin and music by Micki Grant, about an unwed mother-to-be who leaves home to escape parental displeasure; this was her second major New York production.

However, it was the play *Black Girl* (1971) that earned her acclaim and a following; it later became a movie with Ossie *Davis as director and Franklin as screenwriter. Initially, the play was produced by Woodie *King, Jr., at the New Federal Theatre and later moved to the Theatre de Lys. It ran for an entire season, and each performance opened to a full and enthusiastic house. It is the story of Billie Jean, the baby of the family, who is a high school dropout with talent and the desire to become a ballet dancer, and of her family's attempt to thwart her advancement. It is a deceptively simple play that addresses intraracial oppression, family dynamics, choices, and becoming.

In addition to her produced plays, Franklin has many unpublished and unproduced works. She has contributed articles to periodicals and written a book entitled *Black Girl, from Genesis to Revelations* (1977), which details the writing of the play, her confrontation with the theater world, and the pains and promises of converting the play into a television production and later a film.

Franklin's talent has been rewarded with the Media Women Award (1971); the New York Drama Desk Most Promising Playwright Award (1971); the Institute for the Arts and Humanities Dramatic Award from Howard University (1974); the Better Boys Foundation Playwrighting Award (1978); the Ajabei Children's Theater Annual Award (1978); the National Endowment for the Arts Creative Writing Fellowship (1979); and the Rockefeller Grant (1980). In her works, she is realistic, presents multifaceted African American life from a female perspective, and demonstrates her belief that the theater should educate, be socially aware, and present feelings and options to the viewers.

• Fred Beauford, "A Conversation with *Black Girl*'s J. E. Franklin," *Black Creation* 3 (Fall 1971): 38–40. Carole A. Parks, "J. E. Franklin, Playwright," *Black World* 21 (Apr. 1972): 49–50.

—Helen R. Houston

Frederick Douglass's Paper. *See* Douglass, Frederick.

FULLER, CHARLES H., JR. (b. 1939), playwright, writer of fiction, and essayist. As a playwright, Charles H. Fuller, Jr., is one of America's most innovative and provocative voices. He was born on 5 March 1939 in Philadelphia, Pennsylvania, son of Charles H. and Lillian Anderson Fuller. Because of his father's occupation as a printer, Fuller developed early on a love of reading and writing, particularly when Fuller's father asked him to proofread some of his work. Parental influence combined with a love of life's expression through art has inspired Fuller to greatness as a dramatist. Fuller's life as a child was filled with exposure to different personalities and lifestyles because of the constant stream of foster children coming through his Philadelphia home. His initial infatuation with drama occurred after seeing a play at a Yiddish theater. Fuller's contributions range from cofounding and directing the Afro-American Arts Theatre in Philadelphia, and writing and directing "Black Experience" on WIP Radio in Philadelphia, to writing Pultizer Prize–winning plays. Although the literary world recognizes Fuller as a great playwright, his literary career began with poetry, short stories, and essays. Theater came after he realized that his short stories were filled with dialogue. From creating skits, he moved into writing one-act plays and finally into creating full-length dramas.

His realistic treatment of his subject matter and his humanistic approach to many of society's atrocities makes his a sensitive but forceful voice in the African American literary community. For instance,

Fuller's *The Village: A Party,* produced at Princeton's McCarter Theatre (1968), focuses on a community of racially mixed couples who, through murder, attempt to maintain their peaceful, protective society. In this play, Fuller examines integration and implies that it often magnifies racial tension.

Another work, *The Brownsville Raid,* produced in New York City at the Negro Ensemble Company in December 1976, was based on a true occurrence of 1906. This play is another depiction of racism and injustice in America, stemming from the paradoxical existence of black soldiers in a white man's army. Fuller's four-year experience in the U.S. Army in Japan and Korea created the images of military life revealed in many of his works, including this one and especially in the Pulitzer Prize–winning *A *Soldier's Play.*

Fuller's *Zooman and the Sign* was also produced in New York City at the Negro Ensemble Company, in November 1979. It won Fuller an Obie and proved to many critics Fuller's talent as a playwright. As in *A Soldier's Play, Zooman* opens with a death that becomes the center from which all the action evolves. Many critics considered Fuller's attempts to handle the complexity of such themes ambitious.

Not allowing critics to determine his genius, Fuller next wrote *A Soldier's Play* (1984), a dramatic presentation of institutional racism and self-hatred set in the 1940s that explores the psychological effects of oppression on African Americans. The setting of the play is in 1944 during World War II on an Army base in Fort Neal, Louisiana. The tragic hero, Sergeant Vernon C. Waters, takes upon himself the role of savior of all African Americans in a racist society.

This highly acclaimed commentary on the ills and trials of military life for African Americans is built on a foundation of intricate characterizations and tone. The character of Captain Richard Davenport, an investigating officer, discloses to the audience each enlisted man's story through a series of interviews. Fuller often allows one character to tell another's story. At a time when camaraderie among men is essential, Fuller creates dichotomies: Waters and his enlisted men form one, and later Davenport creates another in his leadership role.

Fuller, only the second black playwright to win a Pulitzer Prize for drama, has had an impact on the subjects discussed in theater, and his work is increasingly appreciated by audiences who cross traditional cultural boundaries.

• Walter Kerr, "A Fine Work from a Forceful Playwright," *New York Times,* 6 December 1981, 3:1. "Charles Fuller," in *CA: New Revision Series,* eds. Linda Metzger et al., 1990, pp. 206–208.

—Wanda Macon

FULLER, HOYT (1923–1981), editor, critic, and leading figure of the Black Arts movement. Born in Atlanta but reared in Detroit where he graduated from Wayne State University, Hoyt Fuller embarked on a career in journalism and editing. He held positions with the *Michigan Chronicle,* the *Detroit Tribune,* and *Collier's Encyclopedia,* among others. Increasingly frustrated by American racism, he went abroad in 1957, living in France and in Spain; later, attracted by the anticolonial stance of Sekou Toure of Guinea, he travelled in Africa, an experience evoked in his only book, a collection of essays, *Return to Africa* (1971). Fuller returned to the United States in 1960.

Fuller had worked briefly as an associate editor at the monthly *Ebony* in 1954 before going abroad, and when *Ebony* publisher John Johnson decided to revive the periodical *Negro Digest* in 1961, he offered Fuller the job of editing it. Fuller accepted the position but rejected the digest format, instead casting the revived periodical as a journal of creative expression and opinion. In the course of a few years, Negro Digest became the leading forum of the emerging Black Arts movement. In 1970, the periodical was renamed Black World to more accurately reflect its scope, which extended to Africa and the African diaspora.

Negro Digest/Black World (*ND/BW*) reflected Fuller's concerns with politics, social action, the spiritual and economic health of the black world, as well as with a wide range of artistic expression. The monthly journal was, however, open to a variety of opinions, in spite of its nationalist editorial position. By 1970, a typical issue contained approximately eight articles, a couple of short stories, poems from several bards, and a section called "Perspectives," which was a roundup of cultural information prepared by Fuller. A short reflective essay by Fuller frequently occupied the back cover. These were occasionally replicated, as was the piece "When Is a Black Man Not an African?" In April, the "Annual Theatre Issue" appeared, eagerly awaited by a large component of the readership. In 1976, *ND/BW* was abruptly terminated by the publisher, occasioning widespread protest in the Black Arts community. Fuller left Chicago, reestablishing himself in Atlanta, and busying himself with the creation of a successor journal, *First World.* Though several issues appeared, beginning in 1977, the journal was not fated to be a success.

One of Fuller's most notable activities in the 1960s had been the creation in Chicago of OBAC (Organization of Black American Culture), which functioned primarily as a writers' collective. OBAC participants included Haki R. *Madhubuti (Don L. Lee), Carolyn M. *Rodgers, Nikki *Giovanni, and Angela *Jackson. Directly influenced by OBAC was the visual arts collective AFRICOBRA, coordinated by Jeff Donaldson, a longtime associate of Fuller.

Fuller also taught creative writing and African American literature part-time at a number of colleges and universities. Over time these included Columbia College, Chicago; Northwestern University; Indiana University; Cornell University; and Metropolitan Community College, Atlanta.

Fuller attended and reported extensively on the First World Festival of Negro Arts and Culture held in Dakar in 1966, under the patronage of the president of Senegal, Léopold Sédar Senghor. In 1971, Fuller attended the Colloquium on Negritude in Dakar, at which Senghor announced a forthcoming second festival to be held in Nigeria. Fuller convened a North American assembly in Chicago to prepare for participation in this second festival, FESTAC, which was finally held in 1977. He was also active in a series of New World Festivals of the African diaspora, initiated in 1978.

Fuller's impact was strong and incisive throughout the development and expansion of a number of interrelated movements of the 1960s and 1970s: black consciousness, Black Arts, and the Black Aesthetic. Black consciousness was directed to and concerned with the entire African American community and had to do with the affirmation of identity and the sense of self-worth; its slogans included "Black Pride" and "Black Is Beautiful." The Black Arts movement proposed the participation of artists of all categories in letters, music, and theater in the exemplification of the experience and values of African and African American life. The Black Aesthetic embodied a program for critics that would guide their judgment of art works and performance. The major document of this movement, *The Black Aesthetic* (1971), edited by Addison *Gayle, Jr., was heavily dependent on Fuller and authors associated with *ND/BW,* such as Carolyn Fowler, who later prepared an important bibliography of the movement.

Fuller focused increasingly on what he perceived as the wider contexts of African American life and was harsh in his criticism of whites and blacks alike. In his 1972 pamphlet for the Institute of the Positive Education, "The Turning of the Wheel," he declared,

> Whites maintain . . . that Blacks are strangers here, that they are not fully admitted to the human family, and Blacks are tolerated in this land as long as their energies are directed—"responsibly"—toward the eventual achievement of citizenship, the evolution of their humanity. And Blacks, understanding the terms of their toleration, accede—quietly or raucously, the accession is complete—translating their rage and shame into rhetoric.

While many found Fuller unduly strident, and while a later generation of critics and writers turned to a more nuanced, if not more benign, assessment of the American reality, Fuller's voice was a widely heralded one. His literary and cultural interactions were vast, comprising in the last two decades of his life a broad and extensive network of prominent African Americans. In addition to persons already mentioned, one notes among a numerous roster such eminent writers as James *Baldwin, Gwendolyn *Brooks, and Sterling A. *Brown; critic/scholars such as George Kent, Stephen Henderson, and Houston A. *Baker, Jr.; and theater personalities such as Woodie *King, Jr., Abera Brown, and Val Gray Ward.

Hoyt Fuller's papers are deposited at the Woodruff Library of the Atlanta University Center.

• Dudley Randall, ed., *Homage to Hoyt Fuller*, 1984.

—Richard A. Long

FULTON, DAVID BRYANT (c. 1863–1941), journalist and fiction writer. David Bryant Fulton was born in Fayetteville, North Carolina, and grew up in Wilmington, North Carolina, where he attended school. In 1887, he moved to New York, finding employment as a porter with the Pullman Palace Car Company. With his wife, Virginia Moore, Fulton settled in Brooklyn, New York, and later worked for Sears, Roebuck; the Brooklyn YMCA; and a music publisher. In 1895, he founded the Society of Sons of North Carolina, a social and benevolent organization in Brooklyn. He was also a member of the Prince Hall Masonic Lodge of Brooklyn and an active contributor to the Yonkers-based Negro Society for Historical Research.

Fulton began his writing career as a correspondent to the Wilmington *Record,* an African American newspaper whose editor solicited Fulton's observations about his travels as a Pullman porter. In 1892, Fulton published a selection of these articles in a pamphlet entitled *Recollections of a Sleeping Car Porter,* in which he used his pen name "Jack Thorne" for the first time. Fulton's second book, also self-published, was a loosely constructed novel, *Hanover, or The Persecution of the Lowly* (1900), a blend of fact and fiction designed to set the record straight about the causes and outcome of the infamous Wilmington Massacre of 1898.

Between 1903 and 1906, Fulton, writing under his pen name, became popular and respected in the Brooklyn African American community as a vigorous journalistic defender of his people. Most of the pieces in his *Eagle Clippings* (1907) show Jack Thorne attacking racial slander in books and periodicals and criticizing political and social developments that he judged hostile to African Americans. After 1907, Fulton gave his attention to a variety of literary projects. Except for a handful of short stories published in magazines and in *Eagle Clippings,* the fiction Fulton wrote did not find its way into print. A 1913 poem, "De Coonah Man" (*African Times and Orient Review,* Dec. 1913) relates in dialect verse the poet's memories of the John Cooner (or John Canoe) African American Christmas customs in North Carolina. "Mother of Mine; Ode to the Negro Woman" was commissioned to be read at the annual convention of the New York Colored Women's Club in 1923. Fulton's 1912 pamphlet *Plea for Social Justice for the Negro Woman* was praised by African American women's groups for its denunciation of both African American concubinage in the antebellum South and the persistence of prostitution for white patrons in the contemporary North.

Fulton stated his racial views in "Race Unification; How It May Be Accomplished" (*African Times* *and Orient Review,* Dec. 1913). In this essay he rejected the amalgamation of blacks with whites as a solution to the race problem, favoring instead a knowledge of "race history," "race achievement," and "race literature" as the stimulus necessary to "race pride" and advancement. Though not original, Fulton's espousal of race consciousness and solidarity testifies to the vitality of nationalistic thinking among African Americans in New York before Marcus *Garvey. With his associates in the Negro Society for Historical Research, John E. *Bruce and Arthur A. *Schomburg, Fulton worked to exemplify and foster a combative, community-oriented intellectual activism among African American writers in the urban North of the early twentieth century.

• David Bryant Fulton, *Hanover,* 1969. Dickson D. Bruce, *Black American Writing from the Nadir,* 1989.

—William L. Andrews

Funnyhouse of a Negro. A one-act play written by Adrienne *Kennedy in 1960, *Funnyhouse of a Negro* was first produced professionally at New York City's East End Theatre beginning 14 January 1964. The director was Michael Kahn, and Billie Allen played the lead role of Sarah. The other roles were played by Ellen Holly, Cynthia Belgrave, Gus Williams, Norman Bush, Ruth Volner, Leslie Rivers, and Leonard Frey. The play closed after thirty-four performances, but went on to win the Village Voice Obie for most distinguished play of 1964. It has since been produced professionally in a number of other cities including Boston (1965), London (1968), and in Paris (1968) as *Drôle de baraque.*

Funnyhouse was published in 1969 by Samuel French and has been included in the following anthologies: *Black Drama: An Anthology* (1970), *The Best Short Plays of 1970, Contemporary Black Drama: From "A Raisin in the Sun" to "No Place to Be Somebody"* (1971), and *Adrienne Kennedy in One Act* (1988).

Kennedy submitted *Funnyhouse* as a writing sample along with her 1962 application for admission to Edward Albee's workshop, where the play was first performed at the Circle in the Square Theatre. Best defined at the time as experimental theater, the play exudes the surrealistic qualities of a nightmare. Its protagonist is described as a young, light-skinned Negro woman named Sarah. Sarah enters the play with a bloodied, featureless face; her head is missing hair, which she carries in her hand. She is described as someone who is simultaneously young and ancient. A rope tied in a hangman's noose drapes her neck. She delivers a repetitive monologue describing her various ethnic selves, recounting her educational background, her lineage, and her desire to become an "even more pallid Negro"; she includes a denunciation of her blackness, pronouncing that black is, and has always been, evil.

Sarah is in the final phase of a state of acute schizophrenia brought on by a history of various physical and emotional abuses and, in a larger conception, colonization. Four personas coexist in her mind: Patrice Lumumba, Jesus, Queen Victoria, and the Duchess of Hapsburg. Patrice Lumumba represents the African aspect of Sarah's multiethnic and multicultural heritage. The other three personas are antagonistic toward the African presence, who is charged in several mad monologues with the rape of Sarah's white-looking mother. They are informed by an irrational logic that all ensuing problems have emanated from that signal event. Blackness has infected and tainted Sarah's existence.

In her opening monologue, Negro-Sarah asserts that there is no logical relationship among her selves, no theme, and this assertion about the play was generally echoed by some early critics who panned *Funnyhouse* for being too abstract. A funnyhouse is a place of grotesque distortions, and Kennedy's play is rife with metaphor, surreal visual imagery, and allegorical complexity. Still, the relationship among madness, irrationality, discrimination, and oppression is clearly implicated. The creation of a schizophrenic character embodying ethnic and cultural diversity allows Kennedy to engage in simultaneous discourses on racial, sexual, and political matters. Early criticisms of her work as incoherent and flawed may reflect more upon a lack of preparedness by individual critics than upon Kennedy's abilities.

Although Kennedy wrote the play in 1960, the historical context for its first professional production places it in the middle of a most violent decade in United States history, a time when the country was being forced to come to terms with its African American presence. Thematically, *Funnyhouse* takes up several issues that have since become the topics of study and discussion in academic and other settings. Social justice, the psychosocial consequences of integration, gender issues like the trauma associated with the systematic rape of African American women under slavery, colonization in a postcolonial era, and various forms of oppression are all explored to varying degrees.

Multicultural conflict is played out within Sarah as a unit divided against itself. European and Christian personas in Sarah's mind can only define the African persona as something undesirable and lacking value; but when they follow the African into the jungle to bludgeon him to death, they also obliterate themselves. Sarah's suicide is commented upon offhandedly and callously at the end of the play by her white, Jewish boyfriend and her white landlady. These two characters serve also as the grotesque and bobbing figures typically located at the door to the funnyhouse. The contrast between their indifferent treatment of Sarah's suicide and what has been revealed only moments before as the horribly tormented quality of her existence is only one among many disturbing effects carefully created by the playwright.

Early reviews of Funnyhouse are contained in the *New York Times* and *Newsday* (15 January 1964), *New*

Yorker (25 January 1964), *Boston Globe* (12 March 1965), *Le Monde* (19 March 1968), and *Figaro Littéraire* (25 March 1968). The play was produced as part of Kennedy's September 1995 through May 1996 residence at the Signature Theatre at the Joseph Papp Public Theatre in New York.

• Susan E. Meigs, "No Place but the Funnyhouse: The Struggle for Identity in Three Adrienne Kennedy Plays," in *Modern American Drama: The Female Canon,* ed. Jane Schlueter, 1990, pp. 172–183. Werner Sollors, "Owls and Rats in the American Funnyhouse: Adrienne Kennedy's Drama," *American Literature* (Sept. 1991): 507–532. Robert Scanlan, "Surrealism as Mimesis: A Director's Guide to Adrienne Kennedy's *Funnyhouse of a Negro*," in *Intersecting Boundaries: The Theatre of Adrienne Kennedy,* eds. Paul K. Bryant-Jackson and Lois More Overbeck, 1992, pp. 93–109.

—Lovalerie King

G

GABRIEL GRIMES. One of African American literature's most famous antagonists, Gabriel Grimes of James *Baldwin's **Go Tell It on the Mountain* (1953) remains one of the author's most compelling characters. Modeled after Baldwin's own stepfather, Gabriel futilely attempts to exorcise demons from his reckless southern past.

The novel's opening section introduces Gabriel as a frustrated deacon in a Harlem Pentecostal church. Obsessed with control, he clashes with his entire family, especially with his stepson, John. Meanwhile, Gabriel embraces his and Elizabeth's son, Roy, who attacks Gabriel for slapping Elizabeth. Though Gabriel sees Roy as his hallowed son, the wayward youth is merely a replica of young Gabriel.

"Gabriel's Prayer," the second section in part 2 of the novel, presents his past via flashback. Gabriel spent his youth drinking and whoring, though his mother attempted to reform him. He ostensibly repents, and Baldwin cleverly alludes to the Judgment Day in portraying his conversion. Although he attempts to expiate his sins by becoming a minister and marrying the barren Deborah, Gabriel quickly falls: his affair with Esther, a maid in the home of a white family for whom Gabriel also works, produces a son, Royal. Gabriel repudiates both lover and son and moves to Harlem after Deborah's death. Again, he vows to do penance by marrying Elizabeth and accepting her illegitimate son. Instead Gabriel continues to use religion to denigrate others and minimize his own transgressions.

Sin and guilt haunt Gabriel throughout his life. Reminiscent of Abraham and David, he can never claim the heir he so fervently desires: Royal dies violently, Roy continues his profligate legacy, and John reciprocates his hatred. The redoubtable Reverend Grimes remains one of American literature's most memorable ministers, a descendent of Nathaniel Hawthorne's Reverend Dimmesdale and Ralph *Ellison's Homer Barbee.

[*See also* John Grimes.]

• Michel Fabre, "Fathers and Sons in James Baldwin's *Go Tell It on the Mountain*," in *James Baldwin: A Collection of Critical Essays*, ed. Keneth Kinnamon, 1974, pp. 120–138. Trudier Harris, *Black Women in the Fiction of James Baldwin*, 1985.

—Keith Clark

GAINES, ERNEST J. (b. 1933), novelist, short story writer, and teacher. Ernest J. Gaines is among the most widely read and highly respected contemporary authors of African American fiction. Born on a Louisiana plantation, where, at age eight, he worked in the fields cutting sugarcane for fifty cents a day, he experienced the racism of the Deep South firsthand. He was largely raised by a handicapped aunt, whose courage and determination are reflected in the many strong-willed women who appear in his books. At age fifteen Gaines moved to California, joining his mother and stepfather there, because his Louisiana parish had no high school for African Americans. Homesick, he unsuccessfully sought books about the kinds of people he knew in "the quarters." His reading led him to French, Russian, and Anglo-Irish authors who dealt with rural life, and to the novels of William Faulkner, a major literary influence. But the most important influence on his work seems to have been the "porch talk," the oral folk culture in which he was raised.

All of Gaines's fiction is set in Louisiana, with its unique mixture of white, African American, Creole, and Cajun cultures. The conflicts among these groups are central to his books. Like Faulkner's Yoknapatawpha County, Gaines's rural St. Raphael Parish, with its principal town of Bayonne, gives his fiction a unifying setting and reinforces his characteristic social realism. That realism is intensified by his extensive use of the speaking voice and by his remarkable ear for the subtle variations in Louisiana dialects. Finding a voice, achieving the power of speech, is both one of Gaines's major themes and one of his most effective artistic devices. The impressive range of first-person narrators he has created is among his finest achievements, one that reflects his profoundly democratic commitment to human dignity. That commitment permeates Gaines's fiction and suggests another of his central themes: the quest for identity in a society scarred by racism.

Catherine Carmier (1964) and *Of Love and Dust* (1967), his first two novels, are stories of thwarted love that focus on the destructive barriers dividing white from African American and African American from Creole. The male protagonist of Catherine Carmier, Jackson Bradley, having fled Louisiana, returns from California and rekindles his earlier love for Catherine, a Creole. Her father, both victim and practitioner of racism, opposes their relationship. Though Catherine loves Jackson, she cannot leave her father, knowing the hostility he faces from the Cajuns who covet his land. Among the most striking features of this book is the brooding silence that afflicts Jackson, who apparently finds much of his past literally unspeakable. This motif of self-imposed silence, of unarticulated anguish, reappears in other of Gaines's novels and is made all the more prominent by his customary emphasis on the speaking voice.

While *Catherine Carmier* is told from a third-person point of view, *Of Love and Dust* employs the first-person narration that has become Gaines's hallmark. This novel's narrator is not, however, the book's protagonist. Instead, Jim Kelly tells the story of Marcus Payne, a young African American convicted of murder who is released to the custody of Marshall Herbert, whose Cajun overseer, Sidney Bonbon, aims to break Marcus's spirit. To gain revenge, Marcus initiates an affair with Bonbon's wife, herself neglected by Bonbon in favor of his African American mistress. When Marcus and Louise unexpectedly fall in love, their relationship violates the South's gravest taboo and precipitates Marcus's death. By juxtaposing these two biracial love affairs, Gaines emphasizes the destructiveness of the South's racial codes not only for African Americans but for whites themselves (as he also does in his portrait of Tee Bob in *The *Autobiography of Miss Jane Pittman*). The novel's events alter the narrator's—and the reader's—initial assessment of Marcus, who gradually assumes heroic stature by opposing the "fate" decreed by racism.

With the publication of *Bloodline* (1968), a collection of five diverse first-person narratives, and *The Autobiography of Miss Jane Pittman* (1971), his best-known novel, Gaines earned the wide readership and critical acclaim that have attended the remainder of his career. While he has sometimes been criticized for not embracing the tradition of social protest literature represented by Richard *Wright's fiction, these two books—and indeed Gaines's total canon—make his political commitments clear. Implicit throughout are a critique of racism and an insistence upon the need for social change. Firmly rooted in the folk culture of the African American community and the oral traditions by which that community has sustained itself, Gaines typically portrays ordinary people whom he endows with heroic potential. His characters achieve dignity despite attempts to oppress them, and they affirm not only themselves as individuals but also the value of family and community, the importance of responsibilities to others.

Like most southern writers, Gaines has a strong sense of history and of the past's continuing impact on the present. Nowhere is that historical sense more evident than in *The Autobiography of Miss Jane Pittman,* for the novel's 110-year-old narrator has lived from slavery into the civil rights struggle of the 1960s. Miss Jane's story is both personal and communal, a "folk autobiography," as Gaines terms it. The qualities she exhibits—pride, resourcefulness, love, honor, and endurance—are those Gaines celebrates throughout his work. Miss Jane is his most memorable character, a tribute to the aunt who raised him. More than any other single book, this novel helped white Americans understand the personal emotions and the historical events that had produced the civil rights revolution.

Gaines's subsequent novel, *In My Father's House* (1978), proved far less successful. His only book, other than his first, to use third-person narration, it is also his only book set primarily in a town rather than in the countryside. Both *A Gathering of Old Men* (1983) and *A Lesson Before Dying* (1993), in contrast, reveal an author at the height of his powers. The former, drawing on the popular genre of the detective novel, is particularly effective in creating a sense of community through the fifteen different narrators it employs. The speaking voice dominates this novel, recording both the region's long history of racial injustice and the recognizable improvement in race relations during the 1970s. Gaines's old men, in accepting responsibility for the murder of Beau Boutan, affirm not only their capacity to speak but their ability to act. As in other works, so here Gaines augments his plot's dramatic power by limiting the main action to a single day's events. Yet the memories voiced by the community enable the reader to experience the past as well, with all its brutal injustice. Racism persists, of course, but in this novel Gaines ameliorates the African American/Cajun rivalry by having Beau's brother, Gil, refuse to participate in the family's traditional vigilante vengeance. At the same time, Gaines underscores the repressive nature of the past by noting that it took Charlie Biggs, who killed Beau in self-defense, fifty years to assert his manhood.

Whereas *In My Father's House* and *A Gathering of Old Men* are set in the 1970s, *A Lesson Before Dying* is set in 1948, the year the fifteen-year-old Gaines moved to California. Yet this novel clearly functions not only to remind readers of the maltreatment of African Americans in the pre-civil rights South but also to highlight the continuing effects of institutionalized racism. Gaines's predominant theme, the quest for human dignity, recurs in this book when the first-person narrator, Grant Wiggins, a teacher, is compelled by his aunt to aid her best friend's godson, who is awaiting execution for a crime he neither planned nor committed. Jefferson's attorney has attempted to save his client by equating Jefferson's mental development with that of a hog. When Jefferson's godmother pleads with Grant to teach her godson his human identity, Grant grudgingly agrees. Despite Jefferson's initial resistance, he ultimately succeeds, as the journal Jefferson produces testifies, a journal that also attests to America's deplorable failure to provide equal educational opportunities to African Americans—in the present as well as in 1948. Gaines's choice of Jefferson's name serves to suggest the ongoing betrayal of democratic political ideals that racism represents.

Throughout his career, Gaines has sought to make his fiction widely accessible. The clarity and directness of his prose, the array of engaging characters he depicts, and the effective use he makes of the speaking voice all reflect this commitment, as do the humor and compassion that mark his novels. Gaines's books give voice to individuals long silenced by racial oppression. Like Ralph *Ellison's *Invisible Man (1952), they also articulate fundamental human values that transcend racial differences. His best novels and short stories are likely to remain among the enduring contributions not just to African American but to world literature.

• Jerry H. Bryant, "Ernest J. Gaines: Change, Growth, and History," *Southern Review* 10 (Fall 1974): 851–864. Charles H. Rowell, ed., *Callaloo* 3 (May 1978), special Gaines issue. Jack Hicks, *In the Singer's Temple,* 1981. Frank W. Shelton, "In My Father's House: Ernest Gaines after Jane Pittman," *Southern Review* 17 (Spring 1981): 340–345. Keith E. Byerman, *Fingering the Jagged Grain: Tradition and Form in Recent Black Fiction,* 1985. Charles H. Rowell, "The Quarters: Ernest Gaines and the Sense of Place," *Southern Review* 21 (Summer 1985): 733–750. John F. Callahan, *In the Afro-American Grain: The Pursuit of Voice in Twentieth-Century Black Fiction,* 1988. Marcia Gaudet and Carl Wooton, *Porch Talk with Ernest Gaines: Conversations on the Writer's Craft,* 1990. Valerie Melissa Babb, *Ernest Gaines,* 1991. Akiko Ochiai, "So Far Apart: African American Men in *A Lesson Before Dying*," *Griot* 16:1 (Spring 1997): 39–47. Charles J. Heglar and Annye L. Refoe, "Aging and the African-American Community: The Case of Ernest J. Gaines," in *Aging and Identity: A Humanities Perspective,* ed. Sara Munston Deats, 1999, pp. 139–147.

—John Lang

GARNET, HENRY HIGHLAND (1815–1882), orator, minister, and abolitionist. An antislavery radical, Henry Highland Garnet is best known for "An Address to the Slaves of the United States of America" (1843), a speech delivered in Buffalo at the National Convention of Colored Citizens. In the "Address" and later texts, he advocated active resistance to slavery, urging slaves to take freedom for themselves. Deeply influenced by **David Walker's Appeal* (1829), Garnet argued that slaves had a moral obligation to resist slavery, using violence when necessary.

Garnet's thinking emerged from an activist-nationalist tradition within African American culture passed on to him by his family. In 1815, he was born into an enslaved family living on a Maryland plantation. His father, the son of a Mandingo leader, took enormous pride in his family's heritage. When Garnet was nine, they escaped to New York City. In 1829, while he was at sea serving as a cabin boy, slave catchers pursued his family, apprehending his sister and forcing the rest to scatter. The event had a profound impact on Garnet, who thereafter began carrying a large knife.

After studying with Theodore Wright, an eminent African American Presbyterian minister and abolitionist, and attending the New York African Free School, Garnet continued his schooling and further established his abolitionist ties by attending the Noyes Academy (an interracial school in Canaan, New Hampshire) and the Oneida Institute, where he graduated in 1840. During the 1840s Garnet developed a busy career as a minister and antislavery activist, editing and writing for newspapers, lecturing, working in the convention movement, and campaigning for the Liberty Party. In 1848, he published *The Past and Present Condition, and the Destiny, of the Colored Race,* elaborating his ideas on abolition and emigration.

Following his departure in 1850 for antislavery lecturing in Great Britain and Germany and missionary work in Jamaica, Garnet's ideas about slave resistance, violence, and emigration gained growing acceptance among abolitionists, influencing militants like John *Brown. Garnet returned in 1855 to pastor Shiloh Presbyterian Church in New York City, succeeding his former mentor, Theodore Wright. During the Civil War, he pastored the Fifteenth Street Presbyterian Church in Washington, D.C., and recruited African Americans for the Union Army. In 1865, he became the first African American to deliver a sermon before the U.S. House of Representatives.

After the war, Garnet campaigned for civil rights, championed Cuban independence, and developed his always keen interest in Africa and the West Indies. In 1881, he accepted an appointment as Minister Resident and Consul General to Liberia, where he died the following year.

• Joel Schor, *Henry Highland Garnet: A Voice of Black Radicalism in the Nineteenth Century,* 1977. Sterling Stuckey, "A Last Stern Struggle: Henry Highland Garnet and Liberation Theory," in *Black Leaders of the Nineteenth Century,* eds. Leon Litwack and August Meier, 1988, pp. 129–147. Martin B. Pasternak, *Rise Now and Fly to Arms: The Life of Henry Highland Garnet,* 1995.

—Gregory Eiselein

GARVEY, MARCUS (1887–1940), social activist and journalist. As a major figure of the Harlem Renaissance, Marcus Garvey was in the vanguard of the new awakening among African Americans. Although his philosophy was at odds with other leading figures of the era, such as W. E. B. *Du Bois, his influence could not be abated. Promoting his ideals in the art of oratory and through his newspapers, first *Negro World* and later the *Blackman*, Garvey has influenced almost every generation of African American writers since.

Images depicting the destructive element in racial prejudice, one of the cornerstones of Garvey's ideology, were initially seen when major fiction writers of the Harlem Renaissance, such as Nella *Larsen, grappled with the infirmities of "color" prejudice. In Larsen's so-called passing novels, *Quicksand* (1928) and **Passing* (1929), mulattoes move into the white world to escape personal oppression and limited opportunity. As is typical in Garveyism, this social mobility leads to self-hate and racial ambivalence.

Richard *Wright and his school of fiction writers was the next group to depict the struggle of African Americans against social and political forces. Richard Wright's *Bigger Thomas in **Native Son* (1940), for example, is an "Everyman" motif for social, political, and cultural disenfranchisement of African Americans. Bigger acquires self-pride and faces his troubles through the aid of two white males, both unlikely cohorts, and becomes the folk hero often created through the use of Garveyism.

The next generation of writers displaying Garveyism might be termed the precursors of the Black Arts Movement. Extending James *Baldwin's protest themes in *Nobody Knows My Name* (1960) and **The Fire Next Time* (1963), the aggressive poets of the sixties, such as Amiri *Baraka (LeRoi Jones), decry the destructive environment of the northern ghetto and portray Garvey's contempt for such dehumanizing existence. Beyond the 1960s, an aesthetic perspective that embraces the racial loyalty and pride found in Garveyism is seen in works such as Toni *Morrison's **The Bluest Eye* (1970). Thus, the influence of the Garvey social and political movement continues.

• Tony Martin, *Literary Garveyism: Garvey, Black Arts and the Harlem Renaissance,* 1983. James de Jongh, *Vicious Modernism: Black Harlem and the Literary Imagination,* 1990.

—Patricia Robinson Williams

GATES, HENRY LOUIS, JR. (b. 1950), scholar, critic, essayist, editor, professor, and chair of Afro-American studies at Harvard University. Arguably the most influential black literary scholar of the 1980s, Henry Louis Gates, Jr., who earned his PhD at Cambridge University, has been the recipient of a MacArthur Prize Fellowship and the American Book Award. In his early textual scholarship, Gates achieved prominence by establishing Harriet E. *Wilson's **Our Nig, or Sketches from the Life of a Free Black* (1859) as the first novel published in the United States by an African American. At the same time, Gates, along with such other scholars as Robert Stepto and Dexter Fisher, who together coedited *Afro-American Literature: The Reconstruction of Instruction* (1979), were laying the groundwork for a critical approach to African American literature that sought to focus on its literariness, breaking with, as Gates argued, the social realist preoccupation of critics of previous generations.

Central to Gates's establishment of this intended break was, first, an exploration of what the advent of structuralist and poststructuralist critical theory portended for the study of African American literature, and second, an attention to the way that the formal and rhetorical features of black-authored texts could enable the positing of a distinctly black literary tradition. As an editor Gates addressed the first half of his agenda, bringing together a host of scholars in *Black Literature and Literary Theory* (1984) and *"Race," Writing, and Difference* (1986), which was first published as a special issue of the journal *Critical Inquiry.* These essays sought to demonstrate the applicability of literary theory to a responsible reading of black-authored texts and to reconcile a commitment to a black racial difference with an awareness that race exists as a social construction rather than a biological fact. In his own work of the period, *Figures in Black: Words, Signs and the "Racial" Self* (1987) and *The Signifying Monkey: A Theory of Afro-American Literary Criticism* (1988), Gates continued his effort to define the distinctly black rhetorical tropes and figures in literary texts. *The Signifying Monkey* argued for continuities between African—specifically Yoruban—vernacular and folk traditions, and African American vernacular speech. These continuities, Gates claimed, were to be found in the practice of "signifyin(g)" (self-reflexive linguistic play in everyday language) and in folk tales about the signifying monkey.

Gates's work has not been without its critics. Some readers have discerned a strain of racial essentialism in his putatively social constructionist stance. Others have charged his work with being apolitical or neoconservative in orientation. Even so, Gates's larger editorial projects may be his most enduring contribution to African American literary study. He helped focus attention on the work of Nobel Prize–winner Wole Soyinka, and through serving as general editor for the Schomburg Library of Nineteenth-Century Black Women Writers, has made readily available crucial texts for scholars and general readers in the field. He is also general editor of the *Norton Anthology of African American Literature.*

Gates's publications have extended beyond his specialty in literary criticism. His 1994 memoir, *Colored People,* chronicles fondly and humorously what it was like growing up in segregation-era Mineral County, West Virginia. His writings for the *New Republic,* the *New Yorker,* and the *New York Times* have ranged widely over cultural and political issues. In 1997, with his co-editor, Nellie McKay, and a team of nine editors, Gates saw into print the *Norton Anthology of African American Literature,* a text that received unprecedented attention in the popular media before becoming a widely used college and university textbook. In 1999, Gates, in collaboration with Kwame Anthony Appiah and funded by the Microsoft Corporation, brought out the *Encarta Africana,* the first encyclopedia of Africana to appear on CD-ROM.

[See also Literary History, article on Late Twentieth Century.]

• Theodore O. Mason, Jr., "Between the Populist and the Scientist: Ideology and Power in Recent Afro-American Literary Criticism; or, 'The Dozens' as Scholarship," *Callaloo* 11 (Summer 1988): 606–615. Kwame Anthony Appiah, "The Conservation of 'Race,'" *Black American Literary Forum* 23 (1989): 37–60. Diana Fuss, "'Race' Under Erasure? Poststructuralist Afro-American Literary Theory," in *Essentially Speaking: Feminism, Nature and Difference,* 1989, pp. 73–96.

—Kenneth W. Warren

GAYLE, ADDISON, JR. (1932–1991), literary critic, educator, lecturer, essayist, and biographer. One of the chief advocates of the Black Aesthetic, Addison Gayle, Jr., was born in Newport News, Virginia, on 2 June 1932. Inspired by the growing example of Richard *Wright, young Gayle became a fastidious reader and hoped that a writing career would enable him to overcome the strictures of poverty and racism. By the time he graduated from high school in 1950, Gayle had completed a three-hundred-page novel.

Unable to attend college or secure profitable employment, Gayle joined the air force. During his short stint, he wrote copious drafts of his novel, short stories, and poetry and submitted them for publication. After an honorable discharge and several rejection letters from publishers, Gayle reluctantly returned to Virginia.

In 1960, Gayle enrolled in the City College of New York and received his BA in 1965. The following year he earned an MA in English from the University of California, Los Angeles. He taught at City College, where he participated in the SEEK (Search for Education, Elevation, and Knowledge) program and worked to increase the enrollment of African American and Latino students and to diversify the school's curriculum.

A frequent contributor to Hoyt *Fuller's journal *Black World,* Gayle edited *Black Expression: Essays By and About Black Americans in the Creative Arts* (1969), an anthology of critical writings on African American folk culture, poetry, drama, and fiction. His subsequent publication, *The Black Situation* (1970), contains a collection of personal essays that chronicle his intellectual development and emerging political militancy in the wake of the civil rights movement and the Black Power struggle.

Gayle's best-known work, *The Black Aesthetic* (1971), is a compilation of essays written by prominent African American writers and leading Black Aesthetic theorists. In both the introduction and an essay entitled "Cultural Strangulation: Black Literature and the White Aesthetic," Gayle championed cultural nationalism and argued that the central aim of the African American artist was to address and improve social and political conditions. Gayle continued his advocacy of the Black Aesthetic tradition in *Way of a New World* (1975), a literary history of the African American novel, and his three biographies: *Oak and Ivy: A Biography of Paul Laurence *Dunbar* (1971), *Claude *McKay: The Black Poet at War* (1972), and *Richard Wright: Ordeal of a Native Son* (1980). Gayle's autobiography, *Wayward Child: A Personal Odyssey* (1977), offers a frank and sobering account of his life, which painfully details the exacting price of his indefatigable pursuit of literary excellence.

Gayle also distinguished himself as a professor of English at the City University of New York's Bernard M. Baruch College, where he taught until his death in October 1991. A passionate teacher and writer, Addison Gayle remained a strong supporter of the Black Aesthetic movement and continued to affirm a fundamental link between artistic creativity and the social and political advancement of African Americans.

• Donna Olendorf, "Addison Gayle, Jr.," in *CA,* vol. 13, ed. Linda Metzger, 1984, pp. 207–208. Eleanor Blau, "Addison Gayle, Jr., Literary Critic, Is Dead at 59," *New York Times,* 5 Oct. 1991, 10.

—Bobby Donaldson

GAY LITERATURE. Gay writing was an important element of the Harlem Renaissance. Gay and bisexual men—such as Alain *Locke, Countee *Cullen, Wallace *Thurman, Richard Bruce *Nugent, Langston *Hughes, and Claude *McKay—were vital presences in this literary movement. Locke, a professor of philosophy, mentored some of these men and published their work in his landmark anthology *The *New Negro* (1925), including Nugent's short story "Sadji," the earliest known gay text by an African American. A year later Thurman's *Fire!!* (1926)—a magazine whose explicit purpose was to shock the black reading public—appeared. According to folklore, Thurman and Nugent tossed a coin to choose as a subject either homosexuality or prostitution. Thurman got prostitution and produced the story "Cordelia, the Crude," while Nugent contributed the semiautobiographical "Smoke, Lillies, and Jade," the most explicit homoerotic text of the Renaissance. In 1932 Thurman published *Infants of the Spring,* which included several gay characters. Decades later the black gay British film director Isaac Julien used several texts by these writers in his controversial film *Looking for Langston* (1989), an exploration of homosexuality in the Harlem Renaissance.

Most Harlem Renaissance writers were not as explicit about homosexuality as Nugent or Thurman were. Instead, homosexuality is often referred to in code. Those readers familiar with homosexual coding might detect it in poems such as "Young Sailor" or "I Loved My Friend" by Langston Hughes and others might conjecture homosexuality in the recurring pagan imagery in Cullen's poems. However, it is often difficult to detect homosexual coding because the settings in which gay life occurred in the 1920s no longer exist. For instance, the now extinct bachelor subcultures that provide the setting for McKay's **Home to Harlem* (1928) were sites for gay life in the 1920s and 1930s. Analyses of this novel and others by McKay have yet to consider the full significance of the homoerotic settings in which they take place.

Gay writing was even more concealed after the Harlem Renaissance ended. The economy collapsed bringing on the Great Depression, the Second World War raged, and, after the war ended, the persecution of homosexuals increased. During the Cold War, in particular, the FBI targeted homosexuals as enemies of the state and many were imprisoned, fired from jobs, or forced to hide their identities. Nevertheless, during this period Langston Hughes denounced the persecution of gays and lesbians in his poem "Cafe 3 A.M.," which first appeared in the 1951 collection **Montage of a Dream Deferred.* Hughes's 1963 *Something in Common and Other Stories* also contained "Blessed Assurance," his first short story with gay characters. During this post-war period Owen *Dodson, a professor at Howard University, published plays, poetry, and the semiautobiographical novel *Boy at the Window* (1951).

James *Baldwin's emergence in the 1950s as a leading writer was a watershed event for black gay writing. Shortly after emigrating to Paris, he wrote a defense of homosexuality, "The Preservation of Innocence" and published it in *Zero* (1949), a little-known Moroccan journal. He explored adolescent homosexual yearnings in the short story "Outing" and in **Go Tell It on the Mountain* (1953). In his next novel Baldwin took a strange course for an African American writer, and particularly for one well-known as a critic of American racism. In **Giovanni's Room* (1956) all the major characters were white, the setting was in Europe, and the plot concerned a bisexual love triangle. Giovanni's Room created controversy, but it earned Baldwin a major place in the gay literary tradition. He would explore gay and bisexual themes in future novels **Another Country* (1962), T*ell Me How Long the Train's Been Gone* (1968), and *Just above My Head* (1979).

Since Baldwin, black gay writing has increased significantly. The reasons for this increase are that the gay and lesbian rights movement has had some important successes: the creation of gay publishing houses, the growth of gay-owned independent bookstores, and—in the 1980s—the discovery of a reading public, not exclusively African American, interested in black gay writing. These reasons bear on two seminal works published in the 1980s. Although ideologically dissimilar, Michael J. Smith's *Black Men/White Men: A Gay Anthology* (1983) and Joseph Beam's *In the Life: A Black Gay Anthology* (1986) were published by small gay presses. The fact that both were anthologies is significant. Contributors such as Essex Hemphill, Larry Duplechan, and Melvin *Dixon, who would later publish with mainstream houses, gained attention in these pioneering anthologies.

The black gay anthology is also informative about how black gay writing gets published. Much of the published black gay writing comes out of grassroots community organizing. Importantly, that has enabled the establishment of a variety of black gay-owned publishing concerns. The New York City–based Other Countries writing collective released two critically praised anthologies, *Other Countries Journal: Black Gay Voices* (1988) and the award-winning *Sojourner: Black Gay Voices in the Age of AIDS* (1993). The poet and playwright Assotto Saint founded his own Galiens Press and published his poetry *Stations* (1989), the elegiac *Wishing for Wings* (1995), and also the work of others in *The Road Before Us: One Hundred Gay Black Poets* (1991) and *Here to Dare: Ten Gay Black Poets* (1992). The arrival of the personal computer and widespread use of desktop publishing also increased the proliferation of black gay writing such as "fanzines" and periodicals. A notable instance of a desktop publishing venture that attracted national attention is E. Lynne *Harris's first novel, *Invisible Life* (1991), which a major press reprinted in 1994.

Despite incalculable losses due to the AIDS pandemic, black gay writing is in a healthy state. The writing exists in a variety of genres, notably poetry, short fiction, autobiography, essay, and the novel, and publishers seem eager to release works by black gay writers. Small (white) gay-owned presses such as Alyson Publications in Boston, for instance, released Essex Hemphill's anthology *Brother to Brother: New Writings by Black Gay Men* (1991) and novels by Steven Corbin (*Fragments That Remain,* 1993; *A Hundred Days from Now,* 1994), Larry Duplechan (*Captain Swing,* 1993), James Earl Hardy (*B Boy Blues,* 1994), and Canaan Parker (*The Color of Trees,* 1992). Still, within the last decade both mainstream and university presses published an astonishing array of black gay literature: Don Belton (*Almost Midnight,* 1986), Cyrus Cassells (*Soul Make a Path Through Shouting,* 1995), Steven Corbin (*No Easy Place to Be,* 1989), Samuel R. *Delaney (*The Motion of Light in Water,* 1988; *The Mad Man,* 1994; *Atlantis,* 1995), Melvin Dixon (*Trouble the Water,* 1989; *Vanishing Rooms,* 1991), Larry Duplechan (*Blackbird,* 1986; *Tangled Up in Blue,* 1989), E. Lynn Harris (*Just as I Am,* 1994), Gordon Heath (*Deep Are the Roots: Memoirs of a Black Expatriate,* 1992), Essex Hemphill (*Ceremonies,* 1992), Bill T. Jones (*Last Night on Earth,* 1995), Randall *Kenan (*A Visitation of Spirits,* 1989; *Let the Dead Bury the Dead,* 1992), and George C. *Wolfe (The Colored Museum, 1987).

• Faith Berry, *Langston Hughes: Before and Beyond Harlem,* 1983. Gerald Early, introduction to *My Soul's High Song: The Collected Writings of Countee Cullen; Voice of the Harlem Renaissance,* 1991. Emmanuel Nelson, "Critical Deviance: Homophobia and the Reception of James Baldwin's Fiction," *Journal of American Culture* 14 (Fall 1991): 91–96. James V. Hatch, *Sorrow Is the Only Faithful One: The Life of Owen Dodson,* 1993. George Chauncey, *Gay New York: Gender, Urban Culture, and the Making of the Gay Male World, 1890–1940,* 1994.

—Charles I. Nero

GAY MEN. The image of gay men in black writing is complicated by homophobic values in society that make homosexuality unspeakable and gays invisible. Contributors to black gay anthologies such as *In the Life* (1986) and *Brother to Brother: New Writings by Black Gay Men* (1991) both challenge and document homophobic images of gays in black literature, social theory, and popular culture. In the most virulent homophobic works gays are effeminate, sarcastic males who lead meaningless lives; they disrupt families, are misogynists, and are marginal to black communities and institutions. Sometimes such works also offer homophobic explanations for the origins of homosexuality among black men. They argue erroneously that homosexuality originates in decadent European cultures, to which black men are then exposed, or that it is an unfortunate condition caused by racial oppression, such as imprisonment or psychological obstacles created by whites to prevent black males from becoming men.

Fortunately, in black writing gays are not always figures for debased or wasted masculinity. Writers associated with the Harlem Renaissance sometimes depicted homosexuality as an exhilarating component of human nature. Writings by black gays since the 1950s debunk homophobic images by ending the silence about homosexuality and presenting a variety of gay experiences. For instance, James *Baldwin made men's sexuality a central issue in American literature through his depictions of homosexual lovers and bisexual men; although he did not always avoid the old stereotypes, he nevertheless presented complex characters in a positive light. Since the 1980s black gay writers have been presenting gays in a variety of literary genres and media. Images of gay life involve AIDS, racism, interracial and intraracial love and sex, feminism and sexism, activism, the negotiating of identity in the American mainstream, coming out, the Christian church, bisexuality, and a marked preoccupation with the well-being of black families and communities.

• Joseph F. Beam, ed., *In the Life: A Black Gay Anthology*, 1986. Essex Hemphill, ed., *Brother to Brother: New Writings by Black Gay Men*, 1991.

—Charles I. Nero

GENDER. It is important to understand gender as different from sexuality. Sexuality concerns physical and biological differences that distinguish males from females. Cultures construct differences in gender. These social constructions attach themselves to behaviors, expectations, roles, representations, and sometimes to values and beliefs that are specific to either men or women. Gendered differences—those that society associates with men and women—have no necessary biological component. Instead of biology, socially agreed upon and constructed conduct, and the meanings cultures assign to that conduct, constitute the area of gendered difference.

Labels of "essentialism" can attach themselves to arguments that gender and sex have an inherent relationship. However, a cultural essentialist, who is interested in issues of gender, may argue that a historical relationship exists between gender, a culture's experience, and its public identity and representation that is so pervasive and so intimate that it seems nearly inherent.

The study of gender in African American literature considers the way in which the texts of black writers have distinctive and unique expressions in men and women writers. Critical and theoretical studies may explore the consequences of gendered identity upon the structure, theme, or style of African American texts. The historical development of these textual markers of gender across the tradition of the literature may also be a focus. Cultural essentialism has some place in such studies because African American literature has a racial identity. Discussions of gender and racial identity provoke vigorous argument because socially constructed differences are a matter of debate and discrimination and because essentialism of any design holds a pejorative context among many theorists.

In the 1960s and 1970s, the insistent surge of the civil rights movement and Black Power movement into the political fabric of life in the United States made the issue of race and its political and social stratifications the signal cultural issue for these decades. Dramatic political activity within the women's movement during the same era eventually matched the intensity of the critical attention to race. Contention surrounds the attention garnered by each agenda. Many identify white women as the women's movement's targeted beneficiaries. In an often competitive play for power and visibility, white women arguably shadowed and dominated the movement for racial equity and authority. Notably, contemporary reflections on the civil rights and Black Power movements launch equally critical challenges to the masculinist authority of these organizations.

Among the most significant and prolific in establishing the cultural text of gendered studies has been bell *hooks in her penetrating analyses of culture and gender. In Ain't I a Woman (1981) hooks established the parameters of the debate asserting that conversations about black people "tend to be on black men; and when women are talked about the focus tends to be on white women." Hooks returned to this forceful declaration of the frames of the eventual debate in *Feminist Theory from Margin to Center* (1984), a conversation about radical social and political change that obligated a confrontation with intersecting dynamics of gender constructions and cultural identity. Her work vigorously engages the complicated spheres of power within the domains of race, class, and feminist thought and in many ways is a disciplinary standard and touchstone for contemporary cultural studies.

Given the national political conversations and confrontations of the latter half of the twentieth century, where the rights of those on the margin—women and people of color—have determined a national discourse, it would have been difficult to emerge from this era without the coalescence of these dual issues of race and gender. Consequently, the activity of the women's rights, civil rights, and Black Power movements anticipate the eventual turn to a critical focus on black women.

As social and political scientists looked critically at the activity of the women's rights and Black Power movements, literary critics and theorists turned their attention to the intersection of race and gender in the literary tradition of the United States. Prior to this historical moment, the study of the African American tradition largely concerned the history and development of its cultural presence and identity within the American literary tradition. In other words, "difference"—as a critical category—focused on the difference of race. Initially, literature's critical studies focused on determining the ways that race and gender revealed significant differences in the writing of African American women.

Even though critical studies did not directly address gender construction in African American literatures prior to the twentieth century, it would be a mistake to assume that these cultural representations were not an expressed concern in the individual works of creative writers and scholars. Frederick *Douglass, for example, certainly made it clear that he understood the differences of gender in his narrative and in "The *Heroic Slave" (1853). Contemporary scholars have noted the rigidity in men's and women's identities in his autobiography and the troubled associations these rigid constructions enured. Similarly, women writers such as Harriet E. *Wilson, Julia A. J. Foote, and Frances Ellen Watkins *Harper made the difficulties of women's gender a focus in their works and underscored how it often constrained their struggles for equity and respect. In other words, although an intertextual collaboration of gender issues was neither the means nor the focus of scholarly critique prior to the mid-twentieth century, individual writers certainly made it clear that gender identities were part and parcel of the struggle for equity in African American cultures.

Issues of "manhood" and the challenges that U.S. culture presented to black males are evident in the literature of William Wells *Brown, Martin R. *Delany, W. E. B. *Du Bois, Charles Waddell *Chesnutt, and James Weldon *Johnson. Ralph *Ellison, Richard *Wright, and Claude *Brown made men's and boy's lives a thematic focus in their works prior to the theorizing of gender constructions that characterizes the turn of the century and the end of the millennium. Similarly, dilemmas of "womanhood" clearly complicate the fiction and prose by Jarena *Lee, Harriet A. *Jacobs, Ida B. *Wells-Barnett, and Sojourner *Truth, as well as Jessie Redmon *Fauset, Nella *Larsen, Zora Neale *Hurston, Lorraine *Hansberry, and Gwendolyn *Brooks. All of these writers' works, and a host of others, create the body of literatures that is the focus of contemporary critical studies of gender.

Although, as noted, these first critical studies focused on black feminism, the end of the millennium finds a parallel interest in representations of a black masculinist presence in the arts, literature, and popular cultures of the United States emerging as a sustained and coherent critical project.

Since the 1970s and through the early 1990s, the popularity of women's writing and issues of feminist theory have been at the fore of gendered studies in literature. However, because feminist politics did not initially demonstrate concern for issues of race and culture, it was necessary for literary study to address this absence as it focused on black women writers.

In the preface to **In Search of Our Mothers' Gardens: Womanist Prose* (1983) Alice *Walker argues for a "feminist of color"—a "womanist" for whom culture and gender are both essential. Although this was likely not her intent, Walker's term "womanist" underscores the tension between the feminist agendas of a woman's movement that was initially inattentive to cultural difference and to black women's issues. It has encountered contestation and some debate. In *Talking Back* (1989), bell hooks argues that "womanism" does not engage the dynamics of radical and transformative political struggle and change. Others argue that its separatist agenda underscores potentially divisive problematics of race in gender studies. In this latter sense, womanism has a clearly historical evolution as it calls for attention to the discrete cultural issues of the tradition that do not only implicate gendered differences. In some ways, it may even be considered as a response to Barbara Smith's 1977 argument in what is widely held to be the generative essay for critical attention to women writers in the African American literary tradition.

In that 1977 essay, "Toward a Black Feminist Criticism," Barbara Smith writes that the "politics of sex *as well as* the politics of race and class are crucially interlocking factors in the works of Black women writers" (emphasis added). Smith's essay provoked great controversy in the emergent studies of black feminism. Her arguments concerning a black woman's language and cultural experience that were evidence of "an identifiable literary tradition" seemed problematically essentialist to many readers. What is a black woman's language? How does language indicate a gender and a culture? Do all black women writers "inherently" (i.e., biologically) use this language? These difficult questions raised within the essay's thesis were not, however, its most debatable aspect. More bothersome to some was Smith's insistence on bringing a black female lesbian voice into the discourse of black feminism. Smith's thesis concerned both gender and sex, and for each of these differences the issue of culture was critical. At this point in the developing field of black feminist literary studies, the complications and controversies inherent to the intersecting relationships of culture, sexuality, and gender were riveted to its disciplinary identity. Of these issues, culture and gender have received the most sustained academic study.

A pivotal anthology for the development of and attention to black feminist criticism preceded Smith's essay. Toni Cade *Bambara's *The Black Woman* (1970) gathered prose and poetry of black women writers of the era and forced a focused consideration of their presence in American arts and letters. Bambara's work lay the ground for the 1982 publication edited by Gloria Hull, Patricia Bell-Scott, and Barbara Smith—*All the Women Are White, All the Blacks Are Men, But Some of Us Are Brave.* This text would fix a disciplinary home-place for black women's studies in the academy.

Both the archival projects of critics and theorists' figurative constructions of a poetics of women's writing find distinctions that are apparent and consistent in the voice, structure, and language of African American women writers' texts. Issues of language have a discrete configuration in black women writers according to the work of several theorists, including Mae Henderson's "Speaking in Tongues: Dialogics, Dialectics, and the Black Women Writer's Literary Tradition" (in *Changing Our Own Words,* ed. Cheryl Wall, 1989), Houston A. *Baker, Jr.'s *Workings of the Spirit: The Poetics of Afro-American Women's Writing* (1991), and Karla Holloway's *Moorings and Metaphors: Figures of Culture and Gender in Black Women's Writing* (1992). Hazel Carby's *Reconstructing Womanhood: The Emergence of the Afro-American Woman Novelist* (1987) reconstructs the cultural history "of the forms in which black women intellectuals made political [and] literary interventions" in their social domains. Roseann Bell, Mari *Evans, Gloria Wade-Gayles, Barbara Christian, Joanne Braxton, and Andree McLauglin, Henry Louis *Gates, Jr., and Cheryl Wall explore generational continuities of thesis, character, and language as well as complex intersections of these issues in the literature of nineteenth- and twentieth-century women writers in rich and provocative critical essays. Finally, the 1988 publication of *The Schomburg Library of Nineteenth-Century Black Women Writers*—a project of massive archival documentation and recovery—places back into print heretofore lost volumes of African American women writers. The Schomburg Library collection stands as testament to the scholarly interest in African American women's writing and to the significant and perceptive initiative of Bambara's *The Black Woman.*

As in the developmental history of black feminism, the intersection of race and gender in U.S. sociopolitical discourse is also the likely impetus for the late-twentieth-century focus on black male writers. A critically significant moment in this encounter was the 1994 New York City exhibition at the Whitney Museum of American Art—*Black Male: Representations of Masculinity in Contemporary American Art.* The Whitney exhibit honed in upon this discourse as it indicated, through its collective and eclectic sweep, the newly pervasive subjectivity of the black male. *Black Male,* the exhibit catalog, brings together what seem to be disparate aesthetic commentaries regarding black male representations—from visual art, film, music, literature, and popular culture. The collagelike structure of both the exhibit and the catalog make it apparent that the "invention" of the black man, in public cultures and in private literary/artistic cultures, is a force that dramatically patterns the history and progress of America's racial and sexual stereotype of black masculinity.

To some degree, the sustained interest in black women's writing has been a provocative agent in the recently focused attention on black male writers. In a gendered critique that represented vigorously negative assessments of their work, some black male writers and critics launched bitterly aimed diatribes against black women writers and the attention, celebrity, and publishing opportunities lavishly available to them. Ishmael *Reed, Charles R. *Johnson, David *Bradley, and Stanley *Crouch have been among the most vocal. These writers and critics present what they identify as the selective politics of corporate publishing decisions. Their contentions? First, that black feminist politics have made the contemporary works of black male writers, especially in the 1970s and 1980s, less visible and therefore less important than the work of black women writers; and second, that black women writers' celebrity is constructed by a parallel denigration of black males within the characterizations of their texts. Much of this debate began with the publication of Alice Walker's *The *Color Purple* (1982)—a text in which her black male characters were read, by an American public, as being representative of an abusive black masculine ethos.

However, of more significance than the factional and fracturing disputes about publishing and celebrity are the issues that emerge once expressions of black male cultures come under critical and theoretical scrutiny. Critical interest in individual male writers' characterizations, themes, and issues has not been absent from literary studies of the tradition. Although Edward Margolies's 1968 *Native Sons* critically studies sixteen twentieth-century "Negro American Authors," all of whom are male, his is not a gendered study. The male collective of Margolies's anthology of essays expresses selective bias rather than critical methodology. There is a similar absence of intertextual gendered study in Charles Johnson's 1988 *Being and Race: Black Writing since 1970.* Following an impressive and widely ranging discussion on the philosophy of being and its expressive impact on race, fiction, and novelistic form, *Being and Race* has two sections: "The Men" and "The Women." However, despite the promise of these categorical dividers, Johnson's project does not develop an intertextual conversation concerning thematic exchange or stylistic patterns that are consistent in black men's literature nor does it concern the collective effects of gendered issues in black male writing.

A gendered critique of the literary and intellectual history of African American writing would address lingering issues and questions about the male writers of various eras in the tradition and the male-identified gender associations within those literary periods. Hazel Carby's study accomplishes such a perspective for women novelists. However, critical studies have yet to address, in a sustained manner, questions that concern male writers and their works. In what ways does gender identify the earliest writing of enslaved Africans in America? Why is protest literature male identified? What differences and critical perspectives do gendered studies of the Black Arts Movement reveal? Does the writing from the era known as Black Aesthetics contradict the sexism of the Black Power movement or does it reify those stereotypes?

In the 1990s, interest in the study of gendered intertextualities that focus exclusively on representations of males seems to bear some relationship to a contemporary swell in autobiographical writings by contemporary African American men. This literature, creatively expressed in a variety of personal narrative forms (autobiography, biography, memoir, and reflection), forces a sustained attention to the shared experiences of black male bodies in the United States and to the visceral qualities and exchangeable expressions of those experiences in writers from the beginnings of the tradition to the present. Within this frame, early writers such as Martin Delany and Frederick Douglass, turn-of-the-century authors such as Charles Chesnutt and James Weldon Johnson, the protest literature of Richard Wright and Ralph Ellison, the public courage and challenge recorded in *The *Autobiography of Malcolm X* (1965) as well as the quietly courageous, yet fiercely intimate passion of John Edgar *Wideman's *Fatheralong: A Meditation on Fathers and Sons, Race and Society* (1994) benefit from the discrete attention of a gendered critique. Considering the rich history of critical and theoretical work about gender and women's writing in the tradition, it is probable that the developing scholarly attention to the intersections of culture and masculinity in African American literature will follow a similar trajectory as it defines and theorizes along the lines of gender.

Representing Black Men (eds. Marcellus Blount and George Cunningham, 1995) indicates this developing trajectory. It argues that the social sciences have defined African American men as "absences" and therefore chooses to explore "constructions of African American masculinities as presences" in theories of the culture and its literature. Certainly the 1995 publication of *Brotherman: The Odyssey of Black Men in America* (eds. Herb Boyd and Robert Allen), a hefty anthology of black men's writing, echoes back a quarter of a century and recalls Bambara's 1970 publication, *The Black Woman.* The publication of *Brotherman* augurs an era when the intellectual history of the literature of African American writers, fully attentive to the cultural critique of gendered representations, comes full circle.

• Roseann P. Bell et al., eds., *Sturdy Black Bridges: Visions of Black Women in Literature,* 1979. Barbara Christian, *Black Women Novelists: The Development of a Tradition,* 1980. Mari Evans, ed., *Black Women Writers, 1950–1980: The Development of a Tradition,* 1984. Gloria Wade-Gayles, *No Crystal Stair,* 1984. Joann Braxton and Andree McLaughlin, eds., *Wild Women in the Whirlwind: Afra-American Culture and the Contemporary Literary Renaissance,* 1989. Cheryl Wall, ed., *Changing Our Own Words: Essays on Criticism, Theory, and Writing by Black Women,* 1989. Henry L. Gates, Jr., ed., *Reading Black, Reading Feminist,* 1990. France Smith Foster, *Written by Herself: Literary Production by African American Women, 1746–1892,* 1993. Thelma Golden, ed., *Black Male: Representations of Masculinity in Contemporary American Art,* 1994.

—Karla FC Holloway

GIBSON, PATRICIA JOANN (b. ?), playwright, teacher, and lecturer. P. J. Gibson has demonstrated her talent in writing ranging from poems and short stories to public service announcements and media publications. However, she is best known for her plays, three of which have been anthologized.

Gibson was born in Pittsburgh, Pennsylvania, and grew up in Trenton, New Jersey. While in her early teens, she studied under J. P. Miller (*The Days of Wine and Roses,* 1973). In the early 1970s, she earned a BA in drama, religion, and English from Keuka College in New York. She was then awarded a Shubert Fellowship to study playwriting at Brandeis University in Massachusetts, where she completed her MFA in 1975. Aside from J. P. Miller, Gibson's mentors include Don Peterson (*Does a Tiger Wear a Necktie?,* 1969) and Israel Horovitz (*Indian Wants the Bronx,* 1968).

Although Gibson has had several mentors, Lorraine *Hansberry is one of her primary influences. In fact, in the late 1960s, after seeing a play based on Hansberry's life and writing, *To Be Young, Gifted and Black* (1969), Gibson was inspired to start writing plays. Since that time, she has written twenty-six, a number of which have been produced in various countries. She is quite prolific and explains that "If I live to be 150, I still won't have enough time to write about all the black women inside of me" (Margaret B. Wilkerson, *Nine Plays by Black Women,* 1986).

Gibson's commitment to creating substantial roles for African American women is evident in her first play, *The Black Woman,* which debuted in a one-act version in 1971 and was later produced in a three-act version in 1972. The play consists of a chronological sequence of monologues spoken by twenty African American women characters who live during different periods of history.

The Black Woman was followed by *Void Passage* and *Konvergence,* two one-acts produced as companion pieces in 1973 by Players Company of Trenton, New Jersey. *Void Passage* focuses on the conflicts of two women who have been labeled "strong Black women" while *Konvergence,* published in Woodie *King, Jr.'s *New Plays for the Black Theatre* (1989), depicts the turbulent reunion of a married couple after a year's separation. This upwardly mobile couple struggles with whether or not to assimilate into middle-class society and "become another chocolate-covered android of the system," yet another statistic of the vacuous, materialistic American dream.

The failure of the American dream returns as a theme in *Miss Ann Don't Cry No More* (1980), the play that earned an NEA grant for Gibson. In this, Gibson reveals the failed dreams of the inhabitants of an apartment house and again presents the challenges and struggles urban America presents to African Americans. *Miss Ann* was first performed as a reading at the Frank Silvera Writer's Workshop in 1977 and later mounted as a full production at the Frederick Douglass Creative Arts Center in 1980.

The next year, the Arts Center also staged a reading of one of Gibson's most compelling plays, *Brown Silk and Magenta Sunsets.* Later published in Margaret Wilkerson's *Nine Plays by Black Women* (1986), this play details the tragic results of obsessive love. The plot revolves around Lena Larson Salvinoli, the attractive and affluent widow of an Italian man she did not love. As a teenager Lena was fascinated by a much older musician who lived in the same apartment building and she desperately tries to recover the passionate intensity of this first and only true love. Her obsession for him led to his death and the death of their daughter, and finally leads to Lena's own suicide in the play.

Death also figures prominently in *Long Time since Yesterday,* Gibson's play about the reunion of a group of middle-aged women after the suicide of one of their college girlfriends. Published in *Black Thunder: An Anthology of Contemporary African American Drama* (William Branch, 1992), the play ran twice at the New Federal Theatre in 1985 and won five Audelco awards, including those for the best dramatic production and playwright of the year. Thematically, the play reveals "that strange closeness women have with women," as well as the delicate boundaries between friendship and romantic love.

Gibson has taught as an assistant professor of English at the John Jay College of Criminal Justice in New York City, where she earned a teaching award in 1987. Two stories and one poem of hers have appeared in *Erotique Noire/Black Erotica* (Miriam Decosta-Willis et al., 1992). She is currently writing a novel entitled *Neidyana* as well as a collection of short stories.

• Bernard L. Peterson, Jr., "Gibson, P. J.," in *Contemporary Black American Playwrights and Their Plays,* 1988, pp. 189–193. Margaret B. Wilkerson, "Music as Metaphor: New Plays of Black Women," in *Making a Spectacle: Feminist Essays on Contemporary Women's Theatre,* ed. Lynda Hart, 1989, pp. 61–75. Donna Olendorf, "Gibson, P. J.," in *CA,* vol. 142, 1994, pp. 146–147.

—E. Barnsley Brown

GIOVANNI, NIKKI (b. 1943), poet, essayist, lecturer, and educator. Born Yolande Cornelia Giovanni, Jr., on 7 June in Knoxville, Tennessee, to Jones and Yolande Giovanni, Nikki Giovanni became one of the most prominent young poets to emerge from the Black Arts Movement of the late 1960s and early 1970s. Her initial achievement of national recognition grew out of the militant, revolutionary poems included in her first two volumes, *Black Feeling, Black Talk* (1968) and *Black Judgement* (1969); this early success became the foundation for a sustained career as an important, often controversial, writer, the recipient of numerous honors and awards, including ten honorary doctorates.

Although she grew up in Cincinnati, Ohio, Giovanni was profoundly influenced by and has consciously identified with the values and traditions of the South. She spent many summer vacations with her maternal grandparents in Knoxville and lived with them during her high school years (1957–1960). Her grandmother, Emma Louvenia Watson, helped shape Giovanni's belief in the power of the individual and her commitment to serving others, values important in both her poetry and her conception of herself as a writer. Like Langston *Hughes, Giovanni has identified herself throughout her career as a "poet of the people," and she has consistently addressed ordinary people, rather than literary scholars or critics, in her poetry and essays.

At age seventeen, Giovanni entered Fisk University as an early entrant but was dismissed at the end of her first semester because, as she states in *Gemini* (1971), her "attitudes did not fit those of a Fisk woman." She returned to Fisk four years later and graduated magna cum laude in February 1967 with a degree in history. While she was a student, she participated in the Fisk Writing Workshops directed by John O. *Killens and reinstituted the campus chapter of the Student Nonviolent Coordinating Committee. She briefly pursued graduate study, first in social work at the University of Pennsylvania (1967–1968) and then in fine arts at Columbia University (1969). By 1970, she had given birth to a son (Thomas Watson Giovanni), combined and published with William Morrow her first two volumes (originally self-published) under the title *Black Feeling, Black Talk/Black Judgement,* and distributed through Broadside Press a third volume, *Re: Creation* (1970). Some of the poems in these early volumes gained even wider recognition when, in 1971, she recorded them in juxtaposition to gospel music on the award-winning album *Truth Is on Its Way.* Although Giovanni was not the first of her generation to combine poetry and music, her album enjoyed an unprecedented success. Along with the hundreds of readings and lectures she gave during the early 1970s on college campuses and in churches and civic centers throughout the country, *Truth* helped establish her as an oral poet whose work was intimately connected to its performance.

Many of the poems that led to Giovanni's identification as an angry, militant poet appear in *Black Feeling, Black Talk/Black Judgement,* including such well-known poems as "The True Import of Present Dialogue, Black vs. Negro" and "The Great Pax Whitie." These poems are matched, however, by short lyric poems that explore more private concerns or celebrate personal and familial relationships, such as the well-known poems "Knoxville, Tennessee" and "Nikki Rosa." This division between political and revolutionary themes, on the one hand, and more personal themes, on the other, continues, in different permutations, throughout Giovanni's later volumes of poetry and prose. The anger at injustices perpetrated by the forces of racism that is expressed in "And the word was death to all niggers" ("The Great Pax Whitie") continues to be counterpointed by the celebration of African American people so eloquently captured in the famous line from "Nikki Rosa," "Black love is black wealth."

Perhaps because Giovanni eventually abandoned the rhetoric of militancy, and perhaps because she insisted on her own independence and autonomy, her critics and reviewers voiced increasing disapproval of her poetry. Margaret B. McDowell, analyzing reviews of Giovanni's work between 1969 and 1974, has shown that "critics have allowed personal and political attitudes not merely to affect their judgment but to dominate it." In fact, although the poems in *Re: Creation* and the pivotal *My House* (1972) do not employ the kind of explosive language characteristic of *Black Feeling, Black Talk/Black Judgement,* many of them do concern themselves with subjects that today are recognized as socially and politically significant. As an African American woman and single mother, Giovanni confronts in these volumes questions concerning female identity and female autonomy. She rejects the male constructions of female identity that have led to the double oppression of African American women and asserts instead the right and the necessity for African American women to shape their own identities. Included in *Re: Creation,* for example, is the now classic "Ego Tripping"; through a sustained use of hyperbole, the poem celebrates the African American woman as the creator of the universe and all the treasures within it. The concluding lines of the poem reveal why Giovanni's work has had an empowering effect on the lives of many young African American women: "I am so perfect so divine so ethereal so surreal / I cannot be comprehended / except by my permission / I mean . . . I . . . can fly / like a bird in the sky."

The poems in *My House* similarly offer a series of statements about Giovanni's conception of herself as an African American woman and as a poet. The volume opens with "Legacies," which acknowledges the importance of one's past and one's ancestors in the creation of identity, and concludes with "My House," which uses the house as a symbol of the female poet and the domestic activities within the house as figures to express the authority and power of the poet. The poem insists—as do others in the volume—on the poet's right to decide the meaning of "revolution," her right to decide the appropriate subject matter of her poetry, and, ultimately, her right to create her own identity.

My House is divided into two sections, "The Rooms Inside" and "The Rooms Outside"; the first group charts the poet's individual, personal growth, while the second provides the social, historical, and cultural contexts in which that self has been shaped. In "The Rooms Outside," for example, three short poems about the poet's visits to Africa explore the ambivalent relationship of African Americans to Africa. "Africa I" sounds the keynote of the volume as well as of Giovanni's work in general. The question facing the speaker is whether to trust her own vision of Africa or to allow that vision to be "corrected" by others apparently more knowledgeable: "but my grandmother stood up / from her rocker just then / and said you call it / like you see it / john brown and i are with you." These lines might almost function as Giovanni's credo in their insistence that the writer, supported and empowered by her ancestors, must trust the authority of her own vision.

In her subsequent volumes of adult poetry—*The Women and the Men* (1975), *Cotton Candy on a Rainy Day* (1978), and *Those Who Ride the Night Winds* (1983)—Giovanni continues to write both introspective poems and poems addressing social and political issues. Also apparent in all her poetry, from *Re: Creation* onward, is the influence of music—the blues, rhythm and blues, and jazz—on her poetic forms and figures. Students can now more readily trace the development of Giovanni's poetic career in the recent collection of her poetry, *The Selected Poems of Nikki Giovanni* (1996), which brings together some 150 poems. The alternation between personal and social concerns is also evident in *Gemini,* a collection of autobiographical essays, some written in a private voice remembering the personal past, and others written in a public voice responding to larger social issues. This duality continues in Giovanni's essay collections, *Sacred Cows . . . And Other Edibles* (1988) and *Racism 101* (1994). In the latter volume, Giovanni alternately fuses and juxtaposes these two voices, often with brilliant results.

Giovanni's early success led to two important "conversations" with other writers: *A Dialogue: James Baldwin and Nikki Giovanni* (1972) and *A Poetic Equation: Conversations Between Nikki Giovanni and Margaret Walker* (1974). Giovanni has also written several volumes of poetry for children: *Spin a Soft Black Song* (1971), *Ego Tripping and Other Poems for Young Readers* (1973), and *Vacation Time* (1979). Several of her poems have been published as illustrated children's books: *Knoxville, Tennessee,* illustrated by Larry Johnson (1994), *The Genie in the Jar,* illustrated by Chris Raschka (1996), and *The Sun Is So Quiet,* illustrated by Ashley Bryan (1996). Giovanni's poems for children are characterized by a playfulness with language and rhythms that appeals to children of all ages; in their re-creation of the sounds and smells and sights of childhood, many of these poems clearly have appeal to both children and adults. Her commentary on Harlem Renaissance poets in the anthology *Shimmy Shimmy Like My Sister Kate* (1996) is similarly of interest to both young and mature readers. Giovanni published *Love Poems* in 1997 and *Blues: For all the Changes: New Poems* in 1999.

While the guardians of literary history have often been puzzled by the sometimes dizzying contradictions posed by Giovanni's poetry and prose, ordinary people—the people for whom she states she has always written—continue to keep her works in print, continue to fill the auditoriums in which she reads and lectures. Her place in literary history is undisputed because her voice speaks to and for people—about their joys and their sorrows, the forces arrayed against them and the strengths they bring as resistance—in tones and language they can understand.

• Suzanne Juhasz, *Naked and Fiery Forms: Modern American Poetry by Women, A New Tradition,* 1976. Eugene B. Redmond, *Drumvoices: The Mission of Afro-American Poetry,* 1976. Anna T. Robinson, *Nikki Giovanni: From Revolution to Revelation,* 1979. Claudia Tate, *Black Women Writers at Work,* 1983. William J. Harris, "Sweet Soft Essence of Possibility: The Poetry of Nikki Giovanni," in *Black Women Writers 1950–1980,* ed. Mari Evans, 1984, pp. 218–228. Margaret B. McDowell, "Groundwork for a More Comprehensive Criticism of Nikki Giovanni," in *Belief vs. Theory in Black American Literary Criticism,* eds. Joe Weixlmann and Chester J. Fontenot, *Studies in Black American Literature,* vol. 2, 1986, pp. 135–160. Martha Cook, "Nikki Giovanni: Place and Sense of Place in Her Poetry," in *Southern Women Writers: The New Generation,* ed. Tonette Bond Inge, 1990, pp. 279–300. Virginia C. Fowler, *Nikki Giovanni,* 1992. Ekaterini Georgoudaki, "Nikki Giovanni: The Poet as Explorer of Outer and Inner Space," in *Women, Creators of Culture,* ed. Georgoudaki and Domna Pastourmatzi, 1997, pp. 153–170.

—Virginia C. Fowler

Giovanni's Room. A groundbreaking novel for its exploration of homosexuality, James *Baldwin's *Giovanni's Room* (1956) holds a unique place in the American and African American literary traditions. Baldwin published it against the advice of Alfred Knopf, who published his acclaimed debut novel, **Go Tell It on the Mountain* (1953); editors warned Baldwin that he would jeopardize his potential as a "Negro" author by writing a book about white male sexual and cultural identity. However, the determined Baldwin found a British publisher, Mark Joseph, and Dial Press eventually published *Giovanni's Room* in America.

The first-person narrative centers around David, a white American attempting to "find himself" in France. The novel opens in the present with David recalling his internecine upbringing and an adolescent homosexual encounter. In Paris awaiting the return of his girlfriend and possible fiancée, Hella, David engages in a torrid affair with Giovanni, an Italian bartender. Giovanni loves him unashamedly, and they live together for two months; however, David transforms Giovanni's room into a symbol of their "dirty" relationship. Upon Hella's return from Spain, David abruptly leaves the destitute Giovanni, who has been fired by bar owner Guillaume, a "disgusting old fairy." David's desertion psychologically destroys Giovanni, who enters a sexually and economically predatory gay underworld. Giovanni eventually murders Guillaume, who reneges on a promise to rehire him in exchange for sex; he is later caught and sentenced to death.

Meanwhile, David, despondent over his mistreatment of Giovanni and the truth about his homosexuality, attempts to rejuvenate himself via marriage. But upon discovering him and a sailor in a gay bar, Hella vows to return to America, wishing "I'd never left it." The novel's closing tableau replicates its opening: David ponders Giovanni's impending execution and his complicity in his erstwhile lover's demise.

Giovanni's Room fuses the personal, the actual, and the fictional: Baldwin exorcises demons surrounding his own sexual identity while simultaneously capturing the subterranean milieu he encountered in Paris during the late 1940s and early 1950s; he bases the murder plot on an actual crime involving the killing of an older man who purportedly propositioned a younger one; and he weaves a Jamesian tale of expatriate Americans fleeing their "complex fate" in search of their "true" selves. The novel received favorable reviews, many critics applauding Baldwin's restrained yet powerful handling of a "controversial" subject. Ultimately, the book is more than a study of sexual identity, as Baldwin himself posited: "It is not so much about homosexuality, it is what happens if you are so afraid that you finally cannot love anybody." *Giovanni's Room* maintains a seminal place in American, African American, and gay and lesbian literary studies.

• Georges-Michel Sarotte, *Like a Brother, Like a Lover: Male Homosexuality in the American Novel and Theatre from Herman Melville to James Baldwin,* trans. Richard Miller, 1978. Horace A. Porter, *Stealing the Fire: The Art and Protest of James Baldwin,* 1989.

—Keith Clark

God Sends Sunday. A novel by Arna *Bontemps, *God Sends Sunday* was published in 1931. According to local legend, Little Augie, born with a caul over his face, is blessed with the double gifts of luck and clairvoyance, but the notion is small solace for the timid, frail, undersized youngster who firmly believes his destiny lies in wandering until he exhausts his luck and meets his destruction.

When Little Augie attains manhood and becomes a full-fledged jockey, success transforms him into a swaggering, cigar-smoking gallant with a relish for mulatto women, only to find himself in hopeless rivalry with Mr. Woody for voluptuous Florence Dessau. First Augie turns to drinking whiskey and singing the blues, then he departs for St. Louis in search of a substitute for Florence and finds Della Green, a "fancy woman" on the infamous Targee Street. They thrive famously until Augie kills his impulsive competitor Biglow Brown who had challenged Augie's courage.

Some thirty years later, withered with age, wearing a frayed Prince Albert outfit, Little Augie wends his way to Mudtown, a black country neighborhood in southern California and new home of his sister Leah and her teenaged grandchild, Terry. His battered traveling bag, a bottle of whiskey, and his old accordion represent the complete remains of his character. Soon Augie is reanimated by handling Leah's livestock—especially her worn-out old racehorse—and dares to dream of new beginnings. His schemes, however, are disturbed by menacing signs and dark forebodings. When Little Augie gravely wounds a man in a fight, once again he must move on, and he is last seen making his way to Mexico.

This novel was praised for its poetic style and challenged for its racy content, but Hugh Gloster perceived it as setting a new trend in African American fiction because of its abandonment of Harlem for its background. Countee *Cullen joined Bontemps in a dramatization of the story that subsequently became the controversial yet successful 1946 Broadway musical entitled *St. Louis Woman.*

—Charles L. James

God's Trombones. James Weldon *Johnson's major contribution to the Harlem Renaissance explosion of black American writing was his book of poems, *God's Trombones: Seven Negro Sermons in Verse,* published in 1927. For almost ten years Johnson worked on these folk sermons in verse whenever the demands of NAACP work relented enough to make writing possible. "The Creation" was published in 1918, and two others were published in magazines during the mid-1920s. In this work he followed the principles he had developed in writing the long preface to *The Book of American Negro Poetry:*

> What the colored poet in the United States needs to do is something like what Synge did for the Irish; he needs to find a form that will express the racial spirit by symbols from within rather than symbols from without, such as the mere mutilation of English spelling and pronunciation. . . . He needs a form that is freer and larger than dialect . . . a form expressing the imagery, the idioms, the peculiar terms of thought and distinctive humor and pathos, too, of the Negro. (Quoted in Johnson's introduction to *God's Trombones*)

The completed book presents seven sermons—"The Creation," "The Prodigal Son," "Go Down Death—A Funeral Sermon,""Noah Built the Ark,""The Crucifixion," "Let My People Go," and "The Judgment Day"—preceded by an opening poem, "Listen, Lord—A Prayer." While the book as a whole does not have a narrative structure, as the sermons stand independent of one another, the sermons as poems bring together the narrative element of the stories from the Bible on which they are each based, the narrative/dramatic moment of the sermon, and the lyric quality of the folk preacher's language.

God's Trombones is a radical departure from the beaten pathway for Johnson the aesthetic conservative. While remaining connected to the late Romantic dramatic monologue form that Paul Laurence *Dunbar and other black American poets had long favored, Johnson here admits the free verse tradition of Walt Whitman to mingle with the rhetorical imagery and verbal excitement of the folk preacher. Not forced to represent speech rhythms with mechanical metrics or distracting rhymes, Johnson is able to focus attention on the metaphoric and ironic creativity of the African American oral tradition. His preacher connects a world of Bible-based ideas to the congregation/reader's mundane reality.

Johnson is remarkably successful in creating a poetic equivalent of the language of what he calls in the introduction "the old time Negro preacher." In "The Creation," the first and most famous of these poems, he creates that old-time preacher's voice as a mixture of vibrant folk idiom, King James version grandeur, and apt metaphor. Thus God makes man of the clay from the riverbed while kneeling "like a mammy bending over her baby." The rather abstract and distant creator of the Bible text is humanized by the preacher's narrative details and poetic touches.

The imagery and rhetoric of the poems draw upon the traditions of sacred song as well as sermons. In "Let My People Go" Johnson echoes his favorite spiritual, while at the same time addressing both black readers and white.

Commonly accepted as James Weldon Johnson's highest achievement in poetry, *God's Trombones* demonstrated in art the dignity and power of African American folk culture. With its illustrations by Aaron Douglas, the collection has enjoyed continuous popularity among scholars and general readers alike.

• Jean Wagner, *Black Poets of the United States,* 1973.

—Joseph T. Skerrett, Jr.

Goin' a Buffalo. One of the Black consciousness plays of Ed *Bullins's *Twentieth-Century Cycle, Goin' a Buffalo* first appeared as a staged reading at the American Place Theater in June of 1968.

The play features the tough, streetwise Curt and his nubile wife Pandora, who sells her body to bring Curt money; Curt's friend Rich; Mamma Too Tight, a young white woman who is wholly dependent upon her pimp, Shaky; and Art, a quiet, seemingly naive sort who, after having saved Curt in a prison fight, is befriended by him. Though some of these decide to leave the hostility of Los Angeles, it is Curt who decides on Buffalo as an actual destination, hoping that he and Pandora can start a legitimate business there. As the play proceeds, however, this goal dissolves in a mixture of violence, manipulation, and deception.

Leitmotifs of prison, money, drugs, and sex expose the gritty urban life and fragmented individual lives of the characters. Money for a sexuality based in violence (e.g., the play's manifold sexual connotations based on "Pandora's 'box'") is the governing equation in a world without love. The play moves through a long middle sequence in a neighborhood nightclub where Pandora sings; there, the Bullinsian element of violence controls every interaction between characters, the cast by now having been augmented by unpaid, disgruntled musicians who are both white and African American. This sequence ends in a bloody brawl as Deeny, the club's disreputable manager, arrives to announce that the show is closing and that no one will be paid. Though the issue of racial tension is obvious in a play about African Americans at odds with poverty and with the criminal justice system, Bullins as playwright interestingly adds greater dramaturgical possibilities by writing stage directions that allow Deeny, the Bouncer, and a customer to be cast as whites—possibilities through which, Bullins writes, "there might be added tensions."

The game of chess is also a metaphor; it opens the play as Curt customarily beats Rich. Art, too, prevails at chess but also deftly manipulates the feelings, fears, and aspirations of these desperate characters, especially Mamma and Pandora. Through his machinations, the city of Buffalo itself becomes the object of the endgame in the play's surprise ending.

The scenes in Curt's apartment and in the nightclub are enclosed spaces from which the stricken African American spirit must emerge; Buffalo represents the unrealizable wide-open space of freedom. Robert Tener finds that these spatial boxes are themselves placed within the larger "box" of the American metropolis, which is itself a construction of whiteness that engulfs these characters. Geneva Smitherman sees instead a conscious self-awareness in these and other Bullins characters, one in which their humanity sometimes leads to heroism. This divergence of views is almost certainly due to the fact that Bullins, rather than determining a moral perspective in presenting the lives of his characters, instead allows their movement in and through their particular milieu, thus revealing his execution of naturalistic technique.

• Geneva Smitherman, "Everybody Wants to Know Why I Sing the Blues," *Black World* 23 (Apr. 1974): 4–13. Robert L. Tener, "Pandora's Box: A Study of Ed Bullins' Dramas," *CLA Journal* 18 (1974–1975): 533–544.

—Nathan L. Grant

GOINES, DONALD (1937–1974), novelist. Donald Goines spent his writing career exploring the underbelly of black urban life in what his publisher dubbed "black experience novels." He wrote and published sixteen novels in the span of his five-year career and is still touted by his publisher as "America's best-selling black author."

Born 15 December 1937 in Detroit to parents who owned their own dry-cleaning business, and a product of Catholic elementary school, Goines spent his formative years outside the world he treats in his novels. This began to change during his midteens, however, when he falsified his age to join the U.S. Air Force, served in Japan during the Korean War, and returned to Detroit a heroin addict at the age of seventeen.

After leaving the air force, Goines's range of experiences provided the background for his novels. At various times he was a pimp, professional gambler, car thief, armed robber, and bootlegger. These illegal activities landed him in jail several times, which proved to be productive: Goines was heroin-free only while in prison and focused on his literary talents there as well. During a term in Jackson State Prison in 1965, Goines wrote his first novels, which were Westerns. After being discouraged from writing in this genre and being inspired by *Iceberg Slim's *Trick Baby,* Goines began to write in earnest and produced the first of his ghetto novels during another prison term at Jackson in 1969. After a fellow inmate gave the work his approval and suggested Goines submit it to Slim's publisher, Goines sent *Whoreson, The Story of a Ghetto Pimp* to Holloway House and the manuscript was accepted. *Whoreson* (1972) is Goines's most autobiographical novel and the only one written in the first person. He uses his own experiences as a pimp and multifaceted hustler to paint a vivid portrait of a ghetto pimp and the types of street characters who surround him.

His second novel, but the first to be published, is *Dopefiend: The Story of a Black Junkie* (1971). In this Goines explains the power dynamics between dealer and junkie and illustrates how a perverted, cowardly, black drug dealer in a dilapidated ghetto house can exert his influence across socioeconomic boundaries over anyone who becomes addicted to heroin. Goines emphasizes that no heroin user can emerge from the experience unscathed.

He lived his own lesson. After leaving prison with an advance from his publisher in 1970, Goines resumed his life as a heroin addict. He did continue writing, however, and his next novel, *Black Gangster,* appeared in 1972. This novel tells the story of a gang leader named Prince who uses his organization, the Freedom Now Liberation Movement, as a front for illegal activity. Although Prince's ability to mobilize his community is admirable, Goines illustrates how the positive efforts of the black community are often stunted by the American system that continually proves individual capitalistic gain the only insurance for survival, while it blocks the path that leads to legitimate economic success.

Goines's next significant novel (which follows *Street Players,* 1973) is *White Man's Justice, Black Man's Grief* (1973), framed by Goines's "An Angry Preface," which exposes the racial and economic inequities in the bail-bond system and urges politicians to make changes. The story that follows personalizes the issue and demonstrates how this type of discrimination targets mostly poor black men who become hopelessly tangled in the "justice" system once they have entered it.

Goines's next novel, *Black Girl Lost* (1973), is his most sustained treatment of the black ghetto experience from a woman's perspective. It is also the last novel Goines published before Holloway House requested that he use a pseudonym. The next nine novels, *Cry Revenge!, Eldorado Red, Swamp Man, Never Die Alone, Daddy Cool, Crime Partners, Death List, Kenyatta's Escape* (all published in 1974), and *Kenyatta's Last Hit* (1975), were published under his friend Al C. Clark's name. In these novels, Goines continues to write what critic Greg Goode calls "ghetto realism" without the kind of glamorization one might expect in the era of "blacksploitation."

The last four of these novels comprise a series that features the militant leader Kenyatta. In these novels Kenyatta's army of revolutionaries mounts a campaign to kill white policemen and remove drugs and prostitution from the black ghetto. As the series progresses, Kenyatta comes closer to his goal but is ultimately killed as he is about to assassinate a Los Angeles drug kingpin.

Goines's last novel, *Inner City Hoodlum,* was published posthumously in 1975 after he and his common-law wife, Shirley Sailor, were shot and killed in their Detroit home. Goines's novels have never been out of print and have been embraced by the hip-hop generation of the 1990s.

• Eddie Stone, *Donald Writes No More: A Biography of Donald Goines*, 1974. Greg Goode, "Donald Goines," in *DLB*, vol. 38, *Afro-American Fiction Writers after 1995,* eds. Thadious M. Davis and Trudier Harris, 1984, pp. 96–100. Greg Goode, "From Dopefiend to *Kenyatta's Last Hit:* The Angry Black Crime Novels of Donald Goines," *MELUS* 2 (Fall 1984): 41–48.

—Valerie N. Matthews

GOLDEN, MARITA (b. 1950), novelist, poet, and educator. Marita Golden's works, especially her fiction, present some of the problems faced by contemporary African American women. They also capture the turbulent but exhilarating milieu of the civil rights era with its challenges and opportunities for commitment.

Her first work, *Migrations of the Heart* (1983), was a well-received memoir begun when she was just twenty-nine. It recounts, for example, her involvement in the black consciousness movement while attending American University as a scholarship student from Washington's inner city. It also describes her life as an expatriate in Lagos, Nigeria, where she lived in the mid-1970s, and the failure of her marriage to the Nigerian architect with whom she had fallen in love as a student at the Columbia School of Journalism.

Her first novel, *A Woman's Place* (1986), chronicles a fifteen-year period in the lives of three African American women, Faith, Crystal, and Serena, who meet and become lifelong friends at an elite Boston college during the 1970s. After dropping out of college as a casualty of its new open admissions policy and suffering the death of a child, Faith becomes the wife of an orthodox Muslim nearly twenty years her senior. This relationship deteriorates as her husband becomes increasingly jealous and possessive. Crystal, who becomes a professional poet, enters into a rocky marriage with a white documentary filmmaker. This marriage to a white man alienates her from her father and brother. Serena makes her way as a women's rights advocate in a newly independent African nation. The novel employs multiple narrators, including not only the three major characters but also their husbands, children, and parents.

Golden's second novel, *Long Distance Life* (1989), chronicles the lives of four generations of an upwardly mobile African American family in Golden's hometown of Washington, D.C. The story takes place against the background of the Great Migration, the Marcus *Garvey movement, Washington, D.C., history, and the civil rights movement. It begins with the relocation of the matriarch of the family, Naomi, from her North Carolina farm to Washington to better her prospects. The inspiration for this character was Golden's own mother, Beatrice Lee Reid, who left the poverty of Greensboro, North Carolina, for Washington, D.C., in the late 1920s. Golden says, "It's not conscious, but I find that the women in my work find themselves negotiating the tension between personal and political choices and are compelled to leave home to further their self-definition" (*Essence,* Nov. 1989). Forty years after Naomi leaves the South, her daughter Esther returns there to work in the civil rights movement. One of Esther's sons becomes a physician and the other a drug dealer whose murder is drug-related. The novel employs a third-person narrative interspersed with Naomi's first-person reflections on her life and those of her loved ones. It ends with an eighty-year-old Naomi reflecting that in spite of such tragedies as her grandson's untimely death, she has lived a rewarding, full life and wouldn't have changed any of it.

Golden's third novel, *And Do Remember Me* (1992), traces the lives of two African American women, Jessie and Macon. Jessie escapes from a dysfunctional family in Mississippi, where she is a victim of father-daughter incest, into the civil rights movement. She forms a close friendship with the civil rights activist Macon, the only person with whom she can unburden herself about her incestuous past. Jessie becomes addicted to alcohol, but with the help of an activist-playwright lover, she finds recovery and success in a professional acting career. Macon becomes a professor at a predominantly white college, where she tries to help African American students cope with campus racism. This work is suitable for both adults and young adults.

Golden has edited and introduced a collection of essays, *Wild Women Don't Wear No Blues: Black Women Writers on Love, Men, and Sex* (1993). In her introduction she asserts that if, according to W. E. B. *Du Bois, racism is the basic problem of the twentieth century, sex, as revealed in the ongoing abortion controversy and the worldwide AIDS epidemic, may be the "defining metaphor" for the twenty-first.

Saving Our Sons: Raising Black Children in a Turbulent World (1994) is Golden's personal account of raising her son Michael in a crime-ridden neighborhood in Washington, D.C. This work shows how it takes not only parents but a support network of friends, relatives, and teachers for the African American male child to make a successful passage to manhood. In 1998, Golden published *The Edge of Heaven.*

Golden's novels are in the tradition of contemporary African American women's fiction in her heroines' quests for self-definition and fulfillment. Also like characters in such works as *Waiting to Exhale* (1992) by Terri *McMillan, *The *Color Purple* (1982) by Alice *Walker, and *The *Women of Brewster Place* (1982) by Gloria *Naylor, they find strength and sustenance in the female relationship.

• Thulani Davis, "Don't Worry, Be Buppie: Black Novelists Head for the Mainstream," *Village Voice Literary Supplement,* May 1990, 26–29. Sharon Malinowski, ed., *Black Writers,* 2d ed., 1994. Mary Grimley Mason, *American Women Writers,* vol. 5, supplement, ed. Carol Hurd Green, 1994. Susan M. Trotsky, ed., *CA,* vol. 42, 1994. Ineke Bockting, "Betrayal, Guilt, and 'Unreality' in Southern Civil Rights Novels," in *Twelfth International Conference on Literature and Psychoanalysis,* ed. Frederico Pereira, 1996, pp. 133–144.

—Phiefer L. Browne

GOMEZ, JEWELLE (b. 1948), poet, novelist, short story writer, essayist, teacher, and political activist. Jewelle Gomez contributes to the growing genre of gay literature and lesbian literature by African Americans. Born in Boston, daughter of John ("Duke") Gomes, a bartender of Portuguese descent, and Delores Minor LeClair, a nurse, she lived on welfare with her Native American great-grandmother, Gracias Archelina Sportsman Morandus, until the age of twenty-two.

After receiving her BA from Northeastern University in 1971 and her MS from Columbia University School of Journalism in 1973, she worked as a television production assistant in Boston and New York and as a stage manager for Off-Broadway plays from 1971 to 1981. She was director of the Literature Program for the New York State Council on the Arts from 1989 to 1993 and taught creative writing and women's studies.

Upon hearing the revolutionary poetry of Nikki *Giovanni and Audre *Lorde and seeing Ntozake *Shange's play **for colored girls,* she was inspired "to write about women's lives" and "the women she had known." She self-published two books of poetry, *The Lipstick Papers* (1980) and *Flamingoes and Bears* (1987), that extolled love and sexuality. The Gilda Stories (1991), a first novel, introduces through fantasy/science fiction the first black lesbian vampire. The book won two Lambda Literary Awards for Lesbian Fiction and Lesbian Science Fiction/Fantasy in 1991. This was her third award for fiction, following the Beard's Fund (1985) and Barbara Deming (1990) awards.

Gomez's essays, *Forty-three Septembers* (1993), reflect on family members, childhood, self-discovery as a lesbian, and social and feminist issues. Despite her productivity and recognition as a literary critic, Gomez wavers on the outer edge of the writing mainstream because of her unconventional gay and lesbian subjects. To her, the nontraditional themes in her works contribute "to support the idea that African American is not simply one way of being."

• Lisa L. Nelson, "An Interview with Jewelle Gomez," *Poets & Writers* 21 (July–Aug. 1993): 34–45. Michael Bronski, "Jewelle Gomez," in *Gay and Lesbian Literature,* ed. Sharon Malinowski, 1994, pp. 163–164.

—Ann Allen Shockley

GORDONE, CHARLES (1925–1995), playwright, actor, director, screenwriter, lecturer, and Pulitzer Prize recipient. When Charles Gordone became the first African American to receive a Pulitzer Prize for drama in 1970 for **No Place to Be Somebody* (1969), *New York Times* drama critic Walter Kerr described him as "the most astonishing new American playwright since Edward Albee." The NAACP's *Crisis* remarked that "Charles Gordone has definitely arrived." Although *No Place* was by far Gordone's most successful project, it marked the middle of an extensive career, spanning well over forty years, in writing, acting, directing, and teaching.

Gordone, born in Cleveland, Ohio, on 12 October 1925, grew up in Elkhart, Indiana. Excelling in academics and athletics, he still struggled to gain acceptance in a predominantly white section of town where he lived and among African Americans in the town who questioned his racial allegiance. Though his diverse racial heritage excited an early preoccupation with identity that extended throughout his life and works, Gordone later, on numerous occasions, boasted of being "part Indian, part French, part Irish, and part nigger." Following a semester of study at UCLA and some time in the air force, Gordone studied music at Los Angeles City College and subsequently received a degree in drama from California State University at Los Angeles in 1952.

After graduation Gordone moved to New York City to pursue acting and soon joined a Broadway production of Moss Hart's *Climate of Eden,* portraying the racially mixed character, Logan—a role he later revisited in 1961. In the 1950s and 1960s, while working in local theaters and managing Vantage, his own theater in Queens, Gordone directed several plays and continued a stage acting career. With few acting jobs available to African Americans, Gordone began writing out of necessity and, between performance engagements, worked as a waiter at Johnny Romero's, a Greenwich Village bar that later served as the framework for *No Place.* In 1961 Gordone performed in Jean Genet's *The Blacks* and shared the stage with a cast including Maya *Angelou, Godfrey Cambridge, James Earl

Jones, and Cecily Tyson. He later cited this six-year experience as a cornerstone in his personal and artistic development. At another notable juncture in his acting career, Gordone, in an all–African American cast of John Steinbeck's *Of Mice and Men,* received an Obie Award for Best Performance in 1964.

Although he continued to distinguish himself as an actor and director, Gordone increased his political involvement off the stage. During the convulsant climate of the 1960s, Gordone served as chairman of the Committee for the Employment of Negro Performers, established in 1962 by the Congress of Racial Equality (CORE). A year later, he worked as the production manager for *The Negro in America,* a documentary funded by the United States Information Agency, and he accepted an appointment by President Lyndon Johnson to the Presidential Commission on Civil Disorders in 1968.

With the release of his first play *No Place* shortly thereafter, Gordone, like his contemporaries in the Black Arts Movement, converged political activism and artistic production. Between 1970 and 1977, Gordone directed national tours of *No Place* and, despite the accolades the play received, claimed the success of the play interrupted his creative momentum. However, Gordone continued to work against racial injustice and social disparity in the late 1970s as an instructor in the Cell Block Theatre Program, an effort to rehabilitate inmates in the New Jersey state prison system. As cofounder, along with Susan Kouyomijian, and director in residence of American Stage (1982–1985) in Berkeley, California, Gordone continued to challenge racial and cultural conceptions of the American theater and broadened the acting opportunities of African Americans, Latinos, and Asians by casting them in traditionally white roles.

In 1987 Gordone accepted a position as a distinguished lecturer at Texas A & M University, where he taught English and theater until his death in November 1995. In his later years Gordone remained active on stage as a playwright, director, and screenwriter. Through his work, Gordone probed the complexity of racial and cultural identity. Attempting to forge an inclusive American identity and to offer a poignant analysis of the place of African Americans in American society, Gordone emphasized the contiguity of human experience while underscoring the importance of an acknowledgment of racial and cultural difference. Works to his credit include *No Place to Be Somebody* (1969), *Gordone Is a Mutha* (1970), *Baba Chops* (1975), *The Last Chord* (1976), *Anabiosis* (1979), and two incomplete works, "Roan Brown and Cherry" and "Ghost Riders."

• Warren Marr, "Black Pulitzer Awardees," *Crisis* 77 (May 1970): 186–188. Jean Ross, "Charles Gordone," in *DLB,* vol. 7, *Twentieth Century American Dramatists,* ed. John MacNicholas, 1987, pp. 227–231. Charles Gordone, "An Interview with Charles Gordone," interview by Susan Harris Smith, *Studies in American Drama, 1945–Present,* vol. 3, eds. Philip C. Kolin and Colby H. Kullman, 1988, pp. 122–132. Bernard L. Peterson, Jr., *Contemporary Black American Playwrights,* 1988. Susan Harris Smith, "Charles Gordone," in *Speaking on Stage: Interviews with Contemporary American Playwrights,* ed. Philip C. Kolin and Colby H. Kullman, 1996, pp. 167–175.

—Charles Leonard

Go Tell It on the Mountain (1953) remains James *Baldwin's most critically acclaimed novel. Its working titles—"In My Father's House" and "Crying Holy"—reflect its central concerns, as Baldwin himself explains: the novel "was about my relationship to my father and to the church, which is the same thing really. It was an attempt to exorcise something, to find out what happened to my father, what happened to all of us" (*Conversations with James Baldwin*). Lyrically autobiographical, the book represents Baldwin's wrenching attempt to reconcile religion, family, and sexuality. Ten years in the making, Baldwin finished the first draft in 1952 in Switzerland. Upon revision, Knopf published the novel in May 1953.

The tripartite novel innovatively tells the story of the Harlem-based Grimes family. Told from *John Grimes's perspective, "The Seventh Day" establishes his social and familial marginalization; the section opens with the plaintive boy wondering who will remember his fourteenth birthday. Based on the young Baldwin, John is berated constantly for his "ugliness," unmanliness, and intellect. We also witness the family's domestic strife: *Gabriel Grimes, John's stepfather, dominates his wife Elizabeth, John, and his siblings. The Pentecostal church provides the battlefield on which John wrestles with his hatred of Gabriel, his nascent homosexuality, and his estrangement.

Part 2, "The Prayers of the Saints," consists of flashbacks involving John's aunt, father, and mother. "Florence's Prayer" conveys how the uncaring mother prefers her son, Gabriel, to her daughter, Florence. Rejecting a constricting southern ethos, Florence flees to Harlem and marries Frank, a hard-drinking blues singer; subsequently, she repudiates him for rejecting her middle-class American values. Ill and alone, Florence ultimately seeks refuge in the church while thwarting Gabriel's mistreatment of his family. "Gabriel's Prayer" exposes the minister's profligate past. Attempting to expiate for his sins and to attain power, he outwardly embraces the Lord and the barren Deborah, who was raped by white men. However, Gabriel engages Esther in an adulterous liaison, only to deny his own culpability by rejecting their son. "Elizabeth's Prayer" concludes the middle section, revealing how her life parallels John's. Reared by a "religious" aunt whom she despises, Elizabeth finds solace with Richard, one of Baldwin's archetypal sensitive, angry young men. After Richard's suicide, Elizabeth bears John and seeks atonement by marrying God's messenger, Gabriel.

Part 3, "The Threshing-Floor," recounts the Herculean struggle for John's soul. During a series of surrealistic visions, John hears voices summoning him to the Lord. However, his conversion is spurious: like Gabriel, he uses religion to reinvent himself and to control others. John metaphorically "kills" Gabriel and replaces him with God. However, John's transformation brings little relief from the squalid Harlem life that mocks him mercilessly. John's hope rests in his budding love for Brother Elisha, an older adolescent who conducts his spiritual pilgrimage.

In this resplendent text Baldwin synthesizes a black American family's struggles and innovative modernist techniques. His African American and Anglo-American influences are myriad: the cadences of black sermons and preaching and spirituals; the Joycean adolescent experience in which a boy must negotiate religion and the attendant sexual guilt; biblical stories such as Abraham's quest for an heir; and the Jamesian psychological novel that utilizes a free indirect narrative device. *Go Tell It on the Mountain* maintains a seminal place in Baldwin's oeuvre, with critic Bernard Bell calling it Baldwin's "most carefully wrought novel."

• Louis Pratt, *James Baldwin,* 1978. Horace A. Porter, *Stealing the Fire: The Art and Protest of James Baldwin,* 1989. Fred L. Standley and Louis H. Pratt, eds., *Conversations with James Baldwin,* 1989.

—Keith Clark

GRAHAM, LORENZ (1902–1989), novelist, short story writer, folklorist, educator, lecturer, and award-winning children's and young adult's author. Lorenz Bell Graham was born on 27 January 1902 in New Orleans, Louisiana, to Elizabeth Etta Bell Graham and David Andrew Graham, an African Methodist Episcopal (AME) minister whose duties led the family to various parts of the country. After attending and completing high school in Seattle, Graham pursued undergraduate study at the University of Washington in 1921; the University of California, Los Angeles from 1923 to 1924; and Virginia Union University in Richmond, Virginia, from 1934 to 1936, where he received his bachelor's degree.

One of the consequential events of Graham's life came when he interrupted his college studies at UCLA in 1924 in order to travel to Liberia, West Africa. The decision was initiated by a bishop of the AME Church who had established a school in Liberia and whom Graham had heard make a plea for the help of trained young people. He soon thereafter volunteered and was accepted to go to Liberia and teach, which he did from 1924 to 1928 at Monrovia College. While in Liberia, Graham met Ruth Morris, another missionary-teacher, and they were married on 20 August 1929. Before his exposure to Africa as a teacher and missionary, Graham was unfamiliar with African culture and admittedly held many misperceptions about what he would find. Shortly after his arrival, he began to see the uninformed and false nature of his views and came to the realization that the people of Africa were very much like the people in other lands.

As a result, Graham's tenure in West Africa provided a solid foundation for the kind of writing that he was to pursue upon his return to the United States. Graham often stated that his teaching experience in Africa gave him new insight on human diversity. He also became keenly aware of the "gap" in representations of Africans, and consequently of African Americans, in literature. He was increasingly convinced that writing could promote understanding and more truthful images of people of African descent, both in Africa and the United States. These experiences became the impetus and subject matter for much of his writing.

Graham's first major work, *How God Fix Jonah* (1946), recounts twenty-one stories of the Bible as told in West African idiom. Graham's use of biblical stories provided a way for him to encourage greater understanding of the African people and their common link with the American reader, both child and adult. Graham followed *How God Fix Jonah* with other African tales, namely *Tales of Momolu* (1946) and *I, Momolu* (1966), which observe the protagonist, Momolu, as he is initiated into manhood and experiences events that mark his maturation process. Through these stories, the reader comes to know Momolu's family and the importance of the entire tribe to his development.

Graham's most acclaimed work is his South Town series, a succession of novels for young adults. In *South Town* (1958), Graham follows the Williams family through the various trials and obstacles that racism presents in their lives. *South Town* is followed by three installments: *North Town* (1965), *Whose Town* (1969), and *Return to South Town* (1976). The series focuses attention on David Williams as he and his family seek fairness of treatment and better opportunities in America. Graham stated that he was trying to establish with young people the idea that in every person is potential, and there is a need for struggle and courage and movement toward definite goals. Graham also parallels many of his characters' plights with those of his own lived experiences with racism and discrimination.

Included in his varied written work is a historical biography of John *Brown entitled *John Brown: A Cry for Freedom* (1980) and four novelettes for and about juveniles published in 1972. Graham received numerous awards for his work, including the Follett Award in 1958, the Child Study Association of America Award in 1959, and the Association for Study of Negro Life and History Award in 1959.

Graham's writing has a distinguished and substantial place in the history and production of multicultural literature for children and adolescents, as well as within the production of African American literature. Through his honest and moving portrayals of both

African and African American life, Graham has contributed to the representation of these communities as self-determinant and courageous actors in the struggle for civil rights, human dignity, and the recognition and respect of human diversity.

• Lee Bennett Hopkins, *More Books by More People,* 1974. Rudine Sims, *Shadow and Substance: Afro-American Experience in Contemporary Children's Fiction,* 1982. Charles Irby, "A Melus Interview: Lorenz Bell Graham—Living with Literary History," *Melus* 12.2 (1985): 75–86. "Lorenz B. Graham," in *Children's Library Review,* ed. Gerard J. Senick, vol. 10, 1986, pp. 101–112. Ora Williams, "Lorenz Graham" in *DLB,* vol. 76, *Afro-American Writers, 1940–1955,* ed. Trudier Harris, 1988, pp. 57–66.

—Kim D. Hester Williams

GRAHAM, SHIRLEY (1896–1977), author, political activist, musical director, composer, and multitalented recipient of the National Academy of Arts and Letters Award for contributions to American literature. Shirley Lola Graham, the only daughter of Etta Bell Graham and Reverend David A. Graham, was born on 11 November 1896 in Indianapolis, Indiana, the oldest of five children. Free-spirited, talented, and ambitious, Graham resisted the shackles of race and gender. She divorced her first husband, worked to support two sons, and established a career for herself at a time when women had only recently gained the right to vote.

In 1926, Graham studied music and French at the Sorbonnne. Although her tenure there predates the Negritude movement, her musical training was enriched by interaction with African and Afro-Caribbean students in Paris. In 1931, she enrolled with advanced standing as a sophomore at Oberlin College in Ohio. Her statement of intent there, recorded in the college's archives, made clear her goals of doing "constructive work with Negro music" and research in Africa.

Graham's breakthrough in musical theater came when she turned her one-act play, *Tom-Tom,* into an opera. Billed as *Tom-Tom: An Epic of Music and the Negro* with an all-black cast, the widely publicized opera opened in June 1932 at Cleveland Stadium. It received mixed reviews, though most were positive. While not the first "all-Negro" opera some sources reported, it was the first produced by an African American woman.

Completing a bachelor's degree in 1934, and a master's in music history and fine arts at Oberlin in June 1935, Graham worked with the Federal Theater Project directing, designing sets, and composing musical scores that included the theme songs for John Brownwell's *Mississippi Rainbow* (1936) and Theodore *Ward's *Big White Fog* (1937). In 1938, a Rosenwald Fund grant financed two years of study at the Yale School of Drama, where she composed the music for Owen *Dodson's *Garden of Time* and then turned to writing plays. Her works include a musical entitled *Deep Rivers* (1939); *It's Morning* (1940), a one-act tragedy about a mother who contemplates infanticide; *I Gotta Home* (1940), a one-act drama; *Track Thirteen* (1940), a comedy for radio and her only published play; *Elijah's Raven* (1941), a three-act comedy; and *Dust to Earth* (1941), a three-act tragedy.

Graham's inability to make the plays commercially successful Broadway shows frustrated her, as a letter to W. E. B. *Du Bois (25 Apr. 1940) indicates, "If I had no responsibility other than myself I'd feel perfectly safe to strike out into the professional world and take what comes." Her positions became increasingly political. As director of the YWCA-USO at Fort Huachuca, Arizona, her politics against racism caused her dismissal. She went on to become NAACP field secretary in New York.

In 1951, Shirley Graham married Du Bois and moved to Ghana with him in 1961. While some biographers note that in Du Bois's shadow her work suffered or that her creative aspirations were submerged to his causes, closer observation reveals his causes were hers. She merely switched genres, using language instead of music. Her intent changed little from that articulated in 1931—to do research in Africa and to bring the achievements of African Americans to the attention of the world. The critical biographies she wrote accomplish this goal.

Graham authored the following works: *Dr. George Washington Carver, Scientist* (1944), a biography for young readers; *Paul *Robeson: Citizen of the World* (1946), also for young readers; *There Once Was a Slave* (1947), the Messner Prize–winning historical novel on the life of Frederick *Douglass; *Your Most Humble Servant* (1949), the Anisfield-Wolf Prize–winning biography of Benjamin *Banneker; *The Story of Phillis *Wheatley* (1949); *The Story of Pocahantas* (1953); *Jean Baptiste Pointe duSable: Founder of Chicago* (1953); *Booker T. *Washington: Educator of Hand, Head, and Heart* (1955); *His Day Is Marching On* (1971), a memoir of W. E. B. Du Bois; *Gamal Abdel Nasser, Son of the Nile* (1972); *Zulu Heart* (1974), a novel set in South Africa; *Julius K. Nyerere: Teacher of Africa* (1975); and *A Pictorial History of W. E. B. Du Bois* (1976). Her most important political essays include "Egypt Is Africa," "The Struggle in Lesotho," and "The Liberation of Africa: Power, Peace and Justice," all published in the *Black Scholar* (May, Sept., and Nov. 1970). She also was founding editor of *Freedomways.*

Shirley Graham Du Bois died 27 March 1977 in Beijing, China, where she was undergoing treatment for cancer. Her music, plays, meticulously researched biographies for young people, her one novel unique in its portrayal of South African whites, and the political essays seasoned with firsthand experiences secure her place in African American arts and letters.

• Herbert Aptheker, ed., *The Correspondence of W. E. B. Du Bois,* 2 vols., 1976. Kathy Perkins, "The Unknown Career of

Shirley Graham," *Freedomways* 25 (1985): 6–18. Elizabeth Brown-Guillory, ed., *Women of Color: Mother-Daughter Relationships in 20th Century Literature*, 1996.

—Nagueyalti Warren

GRAVE DIGGER JONES is the constant partner of *Coffin Ed Johnson in the detective novels of Chester *Himes. Though the two African American detectives are very much alike, Grave Digger is often the more philosophical of the two, and he frequently acts as spokesperson for the pair. It is Grave Digger who offers most of Himes's commentary on U.S. racism and on the plight of urban African Americans living in poverty-stricken ghettos. Though Grave Digger is usually portrayed as the more rational of the two detectives, he can be brutal in his investigative tactics. His gun, a custom-made long-barreled nickel-plated .38, is feared by all Harlemites inhabiting Himes's novels. Paradoxically, Coffin Ed and Grave Digger have hero/legend status among the citizens of their beat even though they work for a white-dominated police force and therefore are seen by many as upholding a white power structure that oppresses African Americans.

Grave Digger's comments throughout the novels show that the two detectives are keenly aware of the racial politics of police work in urban America. In several of the books, the arch criminal is a white man who is not a member of the Harlem community but who has entered the neighborhood to exploit its citizens. In such cases Grave Digger and Coffin Ed's ultimate aim is to restore order and protect the Harlem community from further invasion by the white police force. It is this double-edged nature of their characters, at once protectors and violent enforcers, that makes them complex literary creations.

• Gilbert H. Muller, *Chester Himes*, 1989. Robert E. Skinner, *Two Guns from Harlem: The Detective Fiction of Chester Himes*, 1989.

—Wendy W. Walters

GREEN, J. D. (1813–?), slave narrator. Jacob D. Green was born a slave in Queen Anne's County, Maryland, and during his boyhood served as a house servant on a large plantation owned by Judge Charles Earle. When he was twelve years old his mother was sold; he never saw her again. He began thinking of escape while a teenager but did not attempt it because religious teachings convinced him that running away from his master would be a sinful act. When his wife was sold away from him in 1839, however, Green made the first of three escape attempts, the last of which took him from Kentucky to Toronto, Canada, in 1848 and soon thereafter to England. Working as an antislavery lecturer, Green published his forty-three page *Narrative of the Life of J. D. Green, a Runaway Slave in England* in 1864. According to its title page, eight thousand copies of Green's *Narrative* were printed. The *Narrative* is notable for its depiction of Green as a wily and unapologetic slave trickster who exploits whites and blacks alike to achieve his ends. Green's unsentimental, rough-and-tumble portrayal of life on the plantation is one of several distinctively unconventional features of his *Narrative.*

• William L. Andrews, *To Tell a Free Story: The First Century of Afro-American Autobiography, 1760–1865*, 1986. William L. Andrews and Henry Louis Gates, Jr., eds. *Slave Narratives*, 2000.

—William L. Andrews

GREENFIELD, ELOISE (b. 1929), author of prize-winning children's books. Eloise Greenfield was born 17 May 1929, the second oldest of five children, in Parmele, North Carolina, during the early days of the Great Depression. Though money was scarce, Greenfield has fond memories of how family and neighbors made her childhood enjoyable. Influenced by her personal childhood memories and experiences, by observations, and by other stories she has read and heard about, Greenfield has created lively, humorous, rhythmic books and stories that are deeply rooted in reality. Her stories are for children ranging in age from prekindergarten to junior high school. One of her books, *Honey I Love* (1978), which is a collection of love poems, crosses age groups and is enjoyed by kindergartners, teens, and adults. In her stories, Greenfield tries to create what she describes as "word madness," or that feeling of excitement that one gets when reading (interview by Jean Ross in *Contemporary Authors,* 1987). To attain this "word madness" Greenfield explains that she tries to "choose and order words that children will celebrate." She wants children to "celebrate" such issues as family solidarity, relationships, Black heritage, and the joys and turmoils of everyday life.

Familial and platonic relationships are central themes in Greenfield's works. Several stories revolve around her idea that there is no monolithic, typical family and that friendships are crucial to a child's growth and development. Presenting stories with families that are extended, that have single or both parents, and that have experienced divorce and sometimes death, several of Greenfield's works depict families coping with bad and good aspects of life. For example, in *Sister* (1974) a young girl copes with the death of a parent, and through the help of other family members, she attains the strength she needs to survive this ordeal. *Daddy and I* (1991) highlights the relationship between father and son and how they enjoy each other's company playing basketball and doing the laundry together. *Me and Nessie* (1975) is about best friends who want to play with each other all the time. *Big Friend, Little Friend* (1991) is the story of a child learning from an older friend who then teaches what he has learned to one of his younger friends.

Equally important to Greenfield is the significance of Black history and heritage to Black children. She has created books that provide true and positive portrayals of Black historical figures, heritage, and experiences. Greenfield feels that such portrayals instill in young Black readers a sense of self awareness and confidence that is threatened by superficial, stereotypical, and empty depictions of Blacks in television. Some positive images that Greenfield feels "children needed to meet" are seen in her accessible autobiographies of Rosa Parks, Paul *Robeson, and Mary McLeod Bethune.

Greenfield wants her stories to provide "emotional sustenance" for children readers. Her stories tap into those emotions that are created by everyday experiences of playing, death, accidents, and divorce. Her stories help children better understand their emotions as legitimate and common. For instance, in *She Come Bringing Me That Little Baby Girl* (1974), Kevin must cope with feelings of envy and jealousy brought about by having to share his parents' love and attention with his new baby sister. *Alesia* (1981) is one of Greenfield's most poignant and touching stories. It speaks to the courage and strength of a young girl handicapped by a tragic childhood accident. Based on a true story, it shows Alesia's commendable determination to lead a normal life as an adolescent. A collection of poems, *Night on Neighborhood Street* (1991), deals with everyday life issues of young Black children in urban communities. *Night on Neighborhood Street* depicts children playing with and missing their friends, confronting and avoiding drug dealers, attending church, entertaining parents, and participating in other typical everyday activities.

Greenfield has received several awards for her works, including the Carter G. Woodson Book Award; the Coretta Scott King Award; the American Library Association notable book citation; and the National Black Child Development Institute Award.

Greenfield's books add to the body of African American literature in several genres (poetry, biography, semiautobiography, and novels) that provide insight into the life, history, and everyday experiences of Blacks and Black children. Her works instill in Black children a sense of self-confidence and awareness and an appreciation of Black art and writing.

• Eloise Greenfield, interview by Jean Ross, in *Contemporary Authors: New Revision Series*, vol. 19, ed. Linda Metzger, 1987, pp. 215–218. "Greenfield, Eloise," in *Something About the Author*, vol. 105, Alan Hedblad, ed., 1999.

—Chanta M. Haywood

GREENLEE, SAM (b. 1930), poet, fiction writer, novelist, essayist, screenwriter, producer, director, actor, and teacher. Sam Greenlee has employed the Black literary tradition to produce such masterpieces as *The *Spook Who Sat by the Door* (1969) and *Baghdad Blues* (1976). Greenlee was born on 13 July 1930 in the heart of Chicago, Illinois. As a young man he attended the University of Wisconsin, where he received his BS in 1952. Greenlee further studied at the University of Chicago (1954–1957) and the University of Thessaloniki, Greece (1963–1964). His career started as a United States Information Agency Foreign Service Officer in Iraq, Pakistan, Indonesia, and Greece. His military service included time in the U.S. Army Infantry from 1952 to 1954. Greenlee received the *London Sunday Times* book of the year award in 1969 for *The Spook Who Sat by the Door*, and the Meritorious Service Award from the United States Information Agency. He currently resides in Chicago, Illinois.

In *The Spook Who Sat by the Door*, Greenlee presents a satirical novel that criticizes the racist atmosphere of the United States by examining the life of a fictitious black CIA agent, Dan Freeman. It is evident that Greenlee creates his images from his experience in the military and United States Information Agency.

References to Freeman as a "spook" in both the title and the novel possess a sense of duality or double consciousness: spook is used as a racial insult directed toward Blacks, in addition to being a slang term for spies. Greenlee uses this duality to establish a connection between Freeman's character and the African American experience during the turbulent 1960s, which parallels Greenlee's service time. With this multifaceted character, Greenlee begins to examine the mask that has been worn by African Americans for generations to hide their true feelings.

Greenlee is also known for such works as *Blues for an African Princess* (1971), a collection of poems. His novel *Baghdad Blues* (1976) and *Ammunition: Poetry and Other Raps* (1975) both deal with African Americans' pain, anger, and fear, particularly that of those who are caught up in the racism and oppression of government agencies.

Greenlee's contributions to the literary tradition in African American literature have caused his readers to examine closely the racial awareness or unawareness within agencies and institutions that are designed to serve all Americans. His presentation of African Americans' duality and paradoxical existence in a racist society is still providing scholars with text to investigate the themes of racism. Greenlee is masterful in his presentation of characters and community; his work is saturated with the African American literary tradition.

• Walter Burrell, "Rappin' with Sam Greenlee," *Black World* 20.9 (1971):42–47. Catherine Starks, *Black Portraiture in American Fiction*, 1971.

—Wanda Macon

GRIGGS, SUTTON E. (1872–1933), novelist, essayist, biographer, publisher, Baptist minister, and pastor. Born in Chatfield, Texas, on 19 June 1872, the son of Reverend Allen R. Griggs, a pioneer Baptist preacher in Texas, Sutton Elbert Griggs attended public schools in Dallas, graduated from Bishop College in Marshall, Texas, and trained for the ministry at the Richmond Theological Seminary. While he held pastorates in Virginia and Tennessee he produced the thirty-three books (including five novels) urging African American pride and self-help that garnered him widespread renown among African American readers. Because he established the Orion Publishing Company in Nashville, Tennessee, which promoted the sale of his books from 1908 until 1911, his works were probably more widely circulated among African Americans than the works of contemporaries Charles Waddell *Chesnutt and Paul Laurence *Dunbar. During the height of his creative production, both his writings and sermons militantly protested injustices and espoused the rights of his people. By 1920, however, when Griggs moved to Memphis and took up the pastorate of the Tabernacle Baptist Church, he had begun to temper his earlier fiery rhetoric and insistence upon African American self-determination and to emphasize instead interracial trust. In this spirit of cooperation, Griggs worked during World War I as a speaker in black communities in support of the purchase of Liberty Bonds. Increasingly during the last decade of his life, he devoted his energies to the church. He served as president of the American Baptist Theological Seminary from 8 April 1925 to 1 October 1926, resigning to accept his father's former pastorate in Texas, where he died in Houston on 3 January 1933.

Griggs's novels reflect the aesthetic dilemmas of his predecessors in their attempts to sound an authentic African American voice through the strategies of nineteenth-century popular fiction; his novels also set the stage for twentieth-century political analyses and symbolic interpretations of slavery and neoslavery experiences. Like earlier fictional representatives of their race in African American literature, Griggs's heroes and heroines are counterstereotypes designed to refute racist images of African Americans in the public mind. All are extremely handsome or beautiful, cultured, talented, intellectual, virtuous, politically aware, and most are committed to either subversive or overt revolutionary action. Despite the complicated love entanglements of his novels, Griggs's focus is not on romance or adventure, but on the political realities and theories that his characters express. His fiction's primary function is to embody conflicting political possibilities for the "New Negro" of the turn of the century and to highlight the consequences of miscegenation, especially for African American women.

Griggs's first novel, **Imperium in Imperio* (1899), is a visionary, political work positing the establishment of a national, secret organization of revolutionary African Americans demanding either a complete redress of grievances or the formation of a separate state for their people. While sympathetic with this frustration and desire for autonomy, Griggs warns against self-serving political leaders whose quest for personal power guarantees the failure of the community's efforts. The Imperium and a selfless leader, Belton Piedmont, are both sacrificed by just such a demagogue, the mulatto Bernard Belgrade. The personal destruction also intrudes into the domestic sphere; accepting racist, "scientific" theories of the time, Viola Martin, in love with Bernard, commits suicide rather than weaken the African American blood line by marrying a mulatto. In his second novel, *Overshadowed* (1901), Griggs lowers his sights from utopian plans for racial organization and nationhood to focus upon the destructive conflicts within the emerging African American middle class. His tone is satiric, ridiculing in particular the group's insecurity, which causes it to sacrifice its own members, like the hard-working Erma Wysong, on the altar of white social standards. This novel is Griggs's most pessimistic and Astral Herndon the most pitiful of his protagonists. Astral is merely representative of the personal frustrations of the new generation, with none of the necessary energy and perception to save either his people or himself. While also reflecting liberal rather than radical values, Dorlan Warthell in *Unfettered* (1902) is a clear contrast to the demoralized Astral. He severs his ties with the Republican party over the issue of imperialism, but when convinced by the expansionist-minded Morlene that America's presence in the Philippines will lead to cultural uplift for the Filipinos, he accepts the decisions of the national administration. Choosing to work with the African American masses, he rejects the opportunity to travel to Africa as the long-sought descendant of an African prince and, at Morlene's urging, develops "Dorlan's Plan" for ethnic cooperation based upon his people's economic self-determination. *The Hindered Hand* (1905) focuses on Ensal Ellwood who, like Dorlan, publishes a self-help essay offering practical methods of African American betterment. The novel also involves its heroine, Tiara Marlow, in an incredibly convoluted plot designed to demonstrate the fallacy Griggs saw in the schemes of the time to use light skin color to infiltrate the white power structure. Ensal reflects the ambivalence present in many turn-of-the-century African Americans who vacillated between feeling connected with, even dependent upon, Africa and, on the other hand, judging themselves superior to it. Baug Peppers of *Pointing the Way* (1908) is Griggs's final development of his New Negro. The young lawyer attempts to ensure aid for African American success by urging support of liberal, white southern politicians also desirous of such cooperation. Professionally more successful than any of Griggs's other leaders, Peppers appears before the Supreme Court to argue for African American voting rights. Although the outcome of this case is ignored by Griggs at the book's end in favor of a focus on romantic intrigue between Peppers andthe victimized Eina, the work's final political view appears optimistic. Griggs's new professional has moved from Belton Piedmont in *Imperium in Imperio,* who is killed by his own people for his "treasonous" refusal to participate in a violent attack on the government, to Baug Peppers who is so honored by his fellows in *Pointing the Way* that he is allowed to represent their case for full citizenship before the country's highest court.

Like the characters he portrays, Sutton Griggs is a transitional figure. His allegiance to the modes of sentimental fiction and flashes of Emersonian optimism and trust in ethnic cooperation blunt the edge of his protest and dim his utopian vision. Nevertheless, his promotion of political activism and self-determination clearly establish Griggs, like Martin *Delany, as a middle-class forerunner to the revolutionary artists of the 1960s.

• Ruth Marie Powell, *Lights and Shadows, The Story of the American Baptist Theological Seminary, 1924–64,* 1964. Arlene A. Elder, *The "Hindered Hand": Cultural Implications of Early African American Fiction,* 1978. Wilson J. Moses, "Literary Garveyism: The Novels of Reverend Sutton E. Griggs," *Phylon* 40.3 (Fall 1979): 203–216. James Kinney, *Amalgamation!: Race, Sex, and Rhetoric in the Nineteenth-Century American Novel,* 1985. Steven C. Tracy, "Saving the Day: The Recordings of the Reverend Sutton E. Griggs," *Phylon* 47.2 (1986): 159–166.

—Arlene A. Elder

GRIMKÉ, ANGELINA WELD (1880–1958), poet, playwright, essayist, and short fiction writer of the Harlem Renaissance. Although Angelina Weld Grimké's writings appeared in many leading publications of the Harlem Renaissance, such as Alain *Locke's *The New Negro* (1925), Countee *Cullen's *Caroling Dusk* (1927), and Charles S. Johnson's *Ebony and Topaz* (1927), she was not a highly visible member of the literary movement, perhaps because of her retiring personality. The product of a biracial marriage, Grimké grew up in the progressive, aristocratic society of old Boston. Named for her white great-aunt, Angelina Grimké Weld, the famous abolitionist and advocate of women's rights, young Angelina was reared by her devoted but demanding father, Archibald Grimké, the son of Charleston aristocrat Henry Grimké, and his slave, Nancy Weston. Angelina's white mother, Sarah Stanley Grimké, separated from her father in Angelina's early childhood, presumably because of mental and physical illness. Angelina's family background informed the style and content of her literary works. Her father's high standards impelled her to aspire toward the "talented tenth" and to create poetry that was polished and formal. Her heritage of social activism influenced her to use her fiction and drama as propagandist tools. The absence of her mother during her early childhood accounts for her interest in motherhood in much of her drama and fiction.

Angelina's initial writings and publications occurred in verse, with poems appearing in the early 1900s in such periodicals as the *Colored American Magazine,* the *Boston Transcript,* and the *Pilot.* Turning from poetry and fiction to drama, she produced her most prominent work, *Rachel,* a sentimental social protest play performed in Washington, D.C., in 1916 and then published in 1920. Depicting the effects of lynching on an African American family and the sadness of having children in a racist society, this drama was the first by an African American playwright to be performed by African American actors for a white public. Although some critics praised it for its dramaturgical skills, others faulted its sentimentality, a feature that was less pronounced in Grimké's second and last, but unpublished, drama, "Mara," which explored similar themes. Considered the least impressive of her works, her short stories also probed the subject of racial injustice, notably in "The Closing Door," a tale of lynching and infanticide published in *The Birth Control Review* of 1919. Grimké is best known for her poetry, whose hallmark is its brevity, well-wrought images, and pensive moods. Its themes range from the loss of love, especially that of a woman, to tributes to famous people, to the contemplation of nature, to philosophical and racial issues. Grimké's love sonnets, addressed to women from the perspectives of white male personae, have led feminist scholars to reclaim her as a lesbian poet. Unfortunately, much of her work has been ignored, partly because she was eclipsed, as a woman, by the male literati of the Harlem Renaissance.

• Gloria T. Hull, *Color, Sex, and Poetry: Three Women Writers of the Harlem Renaissance,* 1987. Helene Keyssar, "Rites and Responsibilities: The Drama of Black American Women," in *Feminine Focus: The New Women Playwrights,* ed. Enoch Brater, 1989. Carolivia Herron, ed., *Selected Works of Angelina Weld Grimké,* 1991.

—Mary C. Carruth

GRIMKÉ, CHARLOTTE FORTEN. *See* Forten, Charlotte.

GRIT, BRUCE. *See* Bruce, John E.

GRONNIOSAW, JAMES ALBERT UKAWSAW (c. 1710–?), spiritual and slave autobiographer. *A Narrative of the Most Remarkable Particulars in the Life of James Albert Ukawsaw Gronniosaw, An African Prince* appeared in London in 1770, related by a former slave from America in need of financial support for his family. In the work, Gronniosaw mentions how the Puritan spiritual writers John Bunyan and Richard Baxter influenced him. Thus, he tells his life story in accordance with the spiritual autobiography's traditional pattern of sin, conversion, and subsequent rebirth.

The narrative deals with Gronniosaw's remembrance of Africa, where he was kidnapped and sold into slavery. Transported to Barbados, he was resold to a young gentleman in New York and later to a minister who taught him about Christianity. A schoolmaster generously offered instructional services to the young slave, who gained freedom when his master died. Gronniosaw then worked aboard various ships until he settled in England. There he married "white Betty" and, some years later, took his family to live in a religious community. However, their lives were marred by poverty and misfortune due in large part to racial discrimination and prejudice.

A popular work that ran through many editions, Gronniosaw's narrative was known by other ex-slave writers. By using the spiritual autobiographical form to relate his life experience, he no doubt influenced the pattern of slave writing that emerged in England and America. Gronniosaw is mentioned by Olaudah *Equiano in his 1789 two-volume autobiography, which became the model for the slave narrative genre that developed in the nineteenth century during the abolitionist era.

• Henry Louis Gates, Jr., "James Gronniosaw and the Trope of the Talking Book," *Southern Review* 22 (April 1986): 252–272. Angelo Costanzo, *Surprizing Narrative: Olaudah Equiano and the Beginnings of Black Autobiography,* 1987. William L. Andrews and Henry Louis Gates, Jr., eds. *Slave Narratives,* 2000.

—Angelo Costanzo

GUY, ROSA (b. 1925), internationally acclaimed writer of adult and young people's fiction centering on the African diaspora and cofounder of the Harlem Writers Guild. Rosa Cuthbert Guy is of dual heritage—born in Trinidad, she grew up in Harlem, where events in her own life shaped her creative outlook, forming her unforgettable themes and characters. Rosa and her sister Ameze were left with relatives when their parents Audrey and Henry Cuthbert emigrated to the United States in 1927. The girls joined their parents in 1932, and briefly the family was united; however, in 1933, Rosa's mother became ill and the children were sent to Brooklyn to live with a cousin. The cousin was a Garveyite whose politics of black nationalism profoundly affected young Rosa. In 1934, Rosa's mother died and she and her sister returned to Harlem to live with their father who remarried. The girls lived briefly with a stepmother until 1937, when their father died.

Poised on the threshold of adolescence, then orphaned in New York, Guy's experiences breathe life into her works for young people. Guy's maturation process, made difficult by her outsider status in the African American community because she was West Indian, produced a vision that scrutinized both worlds. Following their father's death, Rosa and her sister lived in an orphanage. At age fourteen, Guy left school to work in a brassiere factory in the garment district.

In 1941, Rosa met and married Warner Guy. She was sixteen. While her husband served in World War II, Guy continued to work in the factory but sought creative ways to express herself. A coworker introduced Guy to the American Negro Theater (ANT). ANT, established in 1940, proved a launching pad for such actors as Sidney Poitier and Ruby Dee. Guy did not perform in any of the theater productions but studied acting there. In 1942, she gave birth to Warner, her only child.

When the war ended, Guy moved with her husband and son to Connecticut. Five years later her marriage dissolved and she returned to New York and resumed her factory job. Again she sought the artistic community, but the thriving theater group had vanished. Another organization, the Committee for the Negro in the Arts, had replaced it. The committee's purpose was to eliminate racial stereotypes in the arts. Interaction with this group resulted in Guy writing and performing in her first play, *Venetian Blinds* (1954), a successful one-act play produced Off-Broadway at the Tropical Theater.

The committee enabled Guy to meet many artists, some of them writers, including John O. *Killens. Killens and she shared similar aims, wanting to project an authentic black voice in their works. Guy's artistic orientation predates the Black Arts Movement and probably owes a debt to the Garvey movement. In 1951, Guy and Killens formed a workshop that became the Harlem Writers Guild. With such participants as Paule *Marshall, Audre *Lorde, Douglas Turner *Ward, and Maya *Angelou, the workshop achieved fame long before Guy ever published her first work. Between 1951 and 1970, more than half of all successful African American writers were associated with the workshop.

The workshop and Killens provided the encouragement Guy needed to perfect her craft. In spite of her limited schooling, working, and single-parenting, Guy had no choice but to write. Although she never directly said so, her works seem to indicate that she was, in fact, writing to save her life—or more specifically, writing herself into being. She states that writing "was a driving force in that orphan, out there on the streets . . . who needed something through which to express herself, through which to become a full-bodied person" (Jerrie Norris, *Presenting Rosa Guy,* 1988).

Guy's first published works consist of two short stories of which there are no surviving copies. "The Carnival," reflecting her West Indian heritage, and another her New York experience, were published in a Trinidadian newspaper by C. L. R. James, who in 1960 was editor. *Bird at My Window* (1966), Guy's first novel, received mixed reviews. J. Saunders *Redding's now famous remark was the most negative criticism, claiming that "preoccupation with repossessing a heritage had led to distortion of values and reality . . . making heroes out of heels" (*Crisis,* Apr. 1966). Guy's protagonist, Wade Williams, like her former husband who was murdered, was destroyed by poverty and racism. She dedicated the novel to *Malcolm X, calling him "pure gold salvaged from the gutter of the ghettos."

The assassinations of Malcolm X and Martin Luther *King, Jr., prompted Guy to embrace another genre. She wanted to know how violence affected young people and traveled South for the first time in her life to interview her subjects. *Children of Longing* (1970), a collection of essays, resulted from her investigations. However, the work upon which Guy's reputation as a writer is based is her trilogy for young adults: *The Friends* (1973); *Ruby* (1976); and *Edith Jackson* (1978). The trilogy gives new meaning to the bildungsroman tradition, including race, gender, culture, and class previously missing from this genre.

Guy's other books include *The Disappearance* (1979), the first in a series about young detective Imamu Jones; *Mirror of Her Own* (1981), which focuses on white characters and received mixed reviews; *Mother Crocodile* (1981), an adaptation of an African fable for younger readers; *New Guys Around the Block* (1983), the second Imamu Jones book; *A Measure of Time* (1983), an adult novel that reached number one on the best-seller list in England; *Paris, Peewee, and Big Dog* (1984), another highly praised novel; *My Love, My Love, or The Peasant Girl* (1985), a novel based on "Little Mermaid"; *And I Heard a Bird Sing* (1987), the third in the Imamu Jones trilogy; *The Ups and Downs of Carl Davis III* (1989); *Billy the Great Child* (1991); *The Music of Summer* (1992); and *Caribbean Carnival: Songs of the West Indies* (1992), a collection of songs for children; and *The Sun, The Sea, A Touch of the Wind* (1995).

Guy's approach to her audience, adults as well as young readers, is sincere and honest. She says "a novel . . . is an emotional history of a people in time and place" ("Young Adult Books," *Horn Book Magazine,* 1985). Her works expose her own emotional history as the young West Indian woman, dislocated and marginalized, often longing for love and acceptance. We see also Guy's understanding of the African American urban experience. Utilizing her particular emotional history, loneliness, and pain she speaks to readers over chasms of generations and cultures about the experiences of life.

• J. Saunders Redding, review of *Bird at My Window, Crisis* 103.3 (Apr. 1966): 225–227. Jerrie Norris, *Presenting Rosa Guy,* 1988.

—Nagueyalti Warren

H

HALEY, ALEX (1921–1992), journalist and novelist. Born on 11 August 1921 in Ithaca, New York, Alexander Murray Palmer Haley grew up in Henning, Tennessee, the first of three sons to Simon Henry Haley, a professor of agriculture, and Bertha George Palmer, a schoolteacher. In 1937, he attended Hawthorne College in Mississippi, and then transferred to Elizabeth City State Teachers College in North Carolina, which he attended for two years. He enlisted in the U.S. Coast Guard in 1939 and completed a twenty-year tour of duty, first as a messboy, and then, in 1950, as Chief Journalist. He married three times, fathering three children. During the 1940s, Haley began writing short anecdotal sketches about the coast guard, some of which he published in *Coronet* magazine. In the 1950s, he continued to publish short, mostly biographical pieces in *Coronet,* as well as in *Readers Digest, Atlantic,* and *Harper's.* He retired from the coast guard in 1959 to become a freelance writer.

In the early 1960s, he continued to publish short articles, among them an exposé of Elijah Muhammad and the Nation of Islam for the *Saturday Evening Post.* At the same time, he began a series of interviews for Playboy magazine, including ones with Miles *Davis, *Malcolm X, Martin Luther *King, Jr., Cassius Clay (later Muhammad *Ali), Jim Brown, and Quincy Jones. His interview with Malcolm X led to their collaboration on *The *Autobiography of Malcolm X* (1965). Haley's probing questions of Malcolm X and editorial skills helped shape what has undoubtedly become the most influential twentieth-century African American autobiography.

Almost immediately after his work on the *Autobiography,* Haley initiated research into his own family's genealogy, eventually discovering his maternal great-great-great-great-grandfather, *Kunta Kinte, who, he claims, was captured in West Africa in 1767 and transported to and enslaved in Virginia. Haley incorporated this narrative in **Roots* (1976), a Pulitzer Prize–winning, seven-generation family chronicle that ends with Haley's own life and research. The publication of *Roots,* along with two enormously popular televised versions of it—*Roots* in 1977 and *Roots: The Next Generations* in 1979—made Haley an international celebrity and lecturer. An estimated 80 to 130 million viewers watched the last episode of *Roots,* generating greater interest in the novel and prompting thousands of Americans to investigate their own family genealogies. The novel and the television series also provoked a national discussion about the history and legacy of racism and slavery.

In the 1980s, Haley continued to publish short pieces, although most of his creative energy was directed into television productions. He also wrote *A Different Kind of Christmas* (1988), a historical novella about the political transformation of a slaveower's son into an abolitonist. When Haley died on 21 February 1992 he left several unfinished manuscripts, one of which, *Alex Haley's Queen* (1993), was completed by David Stevens.

Haley's ultimate historical impact has been perhaps more cultural than literary. Roots was criticized for its historical inaccuracy and lack of originality. Nonetheless, it undeniably sparked a popular interest and pride in African American history and in the African ancestry of African Americans.

• Alfred Balk and Alex Haley, "Black Merchants of Hate," *Saturday Evening Post* 236 (26 Jan. 1963): 68–73. Alex Haley, "My Furthest-Back Person—'The African,'" *New York Times Magazine,* 16 July 1972, 12–16. Alex Haley, "In Search of 'The African,'" *American History Illustrated* 8 (Feb. 1974): 21–26. Alex Haley, "There Are Days When I Wish It Hadn't Happened," *Playboy,* March 1979, 115+. Murray Fisher, ed., *Alex Haley: The Playboy Interviews,* 1993. Harold Bloom, ed., *Alex Haley & Malcolm X's The Autobiography of Malcom X,* 1999.

—Roger A. Berger

HAMILTON, VIRGINIA (b. 1936), writer for children and young adults, first African American to win Newbery Medal (1974), and first American to win Hans Christian Andersen Medal (1992). Since the 1970s, the number of children's books featuring African American characters has declined; however, the continuous publication of Virginia Esther Perry Hamilton's provocative works reminds the public that artistic integrity in African American–authored children's and young adult literature has not been relinquished. Hamilton maintains this integrity by uniting politics and art and by continuing to capture the universal in the particulars and complexities of the African American experience. Hamilton, who has published more than thirty books, generally satisfies her goal "to find a certain form and content to express black literature as American literature and perpetuate a pedigree of American black literature for the young," as stated by Violet Harris (*Black Women in America*).

Within this pedigree, Hamilton has published African American children's fiction in more genres than any other writer. She remains the only African American who has written science fiction/fantasy featuring African American children, in the *Justice* trilogy. This pedigree also includes contemporary realistic fiction such as *Plain City* (1993), historical fiction such as *Cousins* (1989), folk tales, fantasy, slave narratives like *Many Thousands Gone* (1993), mysteries such as *House of Dies Drear* (1973), and biographies that include Hugo Black, Paul *Robeson, W. E. B. *Du Bois, and Anthony Burns.

Hamilton's work captures unconventional themes and multitextured characterizations in African American children's literature, addressing such issues as the environment in **M. C. Higgins, the Great* (1974) and *Drylongso* (1992). Her use of unconventional stream of consciousness and language in *Arilla Sun Down* (1976) is also noteworthy. Perhaps most important, though, is Hamilton's string of "firsts": the first young adult novel to feature a black–Native American family; the first modern urban African American trickster, in the *Jahdu* books (1969, 1973, 1980); the first modern African American myth of ancestral origins for African American children as seen in *The Magical Adventures of Pretty Pearl* (1984), as well as superbly revisioning African American folk heroes such as *John Henry and *High John the Conqueror; the first to create a young adult novel featuring the ties between African Americans and Caribbeans, in *Junius Over Far* (1985); the first African American children's novel based on slave history, *The House of Dies Drear* (1970); the first to capture the theme of homelessness in African American children's novels, in *The Planet of Junior* (1974); and the first author to examine the theme of interracial (black/white) dating among teenagers, in *A White Romance* (1987). For all of this, Hamilton has received an unprecedented number of awards: the Newbery Medal, several Newbery Honor awards, three Globe–Horn Book Awards, the Regina Medal, the Edgar Allen Poe Award, the Laura Ingalls Wilder Award for Lifetime Achievement, and honorary doctorates. She was also the first children's author to receive the prestigious MacArthur Prize Fellowship. Since the 1980s, Kent State University has had an annual conference named after her.

Born in Yellow Spring, Ohio, 12 March 1936, the fifth and youngest child of Kenneth James and Ette Belle, Hamilton still lives on land her family purchased in the 1850s after her great-great-grandmother escaped with her son from slavery in Virginia. Coming from a family of storytellers, Virginia knew she wanted to be a writer. At age nine she wrote her first novel, entitled *The Novel,* which was her juvenile collection of gossip. She later lost it and once commented that psychologically her writing may be an attempt to gain back her "lost novel."

As a child she freely explored the surrounding rural area of Glen Helen, which served as a model for the setting of several of her books. She remembers as a child a strange big house that served as a model for the abolitionist house in *The House of Dies Drear.* Although she did not encounter overt racism as a child, she was aware that after her father earned a degree in business, he dressed impeccably in a suit and tie, went to the bank to apply for a job as a teller, and was instead handed a mop and bucket.

Virginia Hamilton enrolled in Antioch College with a five-year scholarship. There Hamilton wrote short stories that she remembers being asked to revise for their unusual plots and characterizations. Her first novel, **Zeely,* nominated for the Newbery Medal in 1968, was begun at Antioch. She later attended Ohio State University (1957–1958) and the New School for Social Research. At the latter she took a writing course taught by Hiriam Hayden, founder of Atheneum Publishers, who unsuccessfully encouraged publishers to print her first adult novel, *Mayo.*

She worked in New York for fifteen years at various jobs including bookkeeping and singing, and married Arnold Adoff, a poet and anthologist, on 19 March 1960. *The Planet of Junior Brown* and the *Jahdu* books, whose settings are Harlem, reflect her New York experiences.

Returning to Yellow Spring with her husband, son, and daughter, Hamilton bought land from her mother and built a home. She was later to say home was freedom and internment—dominant binary oppositions in her fiction that was early influenced by Edgar Allen Poe, William Faulkner, Zora Neale *Hurston, and Carson McCullers.

Hamilton has said she considers *The Magical Adventures of Pretty Pearl* her magnum opus. It connects well with African American literary tradition in its superb development of African American folklore. With *Pretty Pearl,* Hamilton pioneered the demonstration of African mythological influences on African American mythology to young readers. Like Alice *Walker, Paule *Marshall, and Toni *Morrison, Hamilton too has planted her folk roots, soared her mythic wings, and elevated rituals of storytelling in a way to provoke a child's or young adult's imagination.

Critics have criticized yet applauded Hamilton for her divergence from the conventional, her complexities in language, characters, and narrative style.

Hamilton resides in Yellow Spring, Ohio. Manuscripts of her work can be found at Kent State and the Kerlan collection of the University of Minnesota.

• Ann Commire, ed., "Virginia Hamilton," in *Something about the Author,* 1989, pp. 19–21. Margaret Bristow, "The Analysis of Myth in Selected Novels of Virginia Hamilton," PhD diss., University of Virginia, 1990. Darlene Hines, ed., *Black Women in America,* 1993. Nina Mikkelson, *Virginia Hamilton, A Critical Biography,* 1994. Wheeler, Jill C. *Virginia Hamilton, ABDO & Daughters,* 1997.

—Margaret Bernice Smith Bristow

HAMMON, BRITON (?–?), autobiographer. *The Narrative of the Uncommon Sufferings and Surprizing Deliverance of Briton Hammon, a Negro Man* (1760), which recounts almost thirteen years of Hammon's adventures at sea, contains all that is known about Briton Hammon.

Covering a mere fourteen pages, Hammon's account opens with a humble introduction expressing the hope that the reader will overlook any flaws in the text, since the author's "Capacities and Condition of Life are very low." It turns into a tale of amazing events that occur after Hammon obtains permission from his master, General Winslow, to leave Marshfield, Massachusetts, to go to sea. On Christmas day 1747, he sails from Plymouth on a sloop bound for Jamaica; in due course, he arrives safely on the island. Returning from it, however, his vessel catches on a reef off the coast of Florida. Hostile natives attack the ship and kill everyone on board save Hammon; they hold him captive until Spaniards help him to escape. His release brings little relief because his rescuers subject Hammon to a Cuban prison. Eventually, he breaks free once again, takes passage on other ships, and at last lands in England, where, after getting a job on a boat to Boston, he gladly finds that one of its passengers is his old master. Hammon ends his story with an expression of gratitude to "Providence" for delivering him from trying times.

Hammon's *Narrative* was printed in Boston in 1760. It is generally recognized as the first African American autobiography, although Hammon's authorship of the text is uncertain. The *Narrative* is also generally regarded as the first American slave narrative.

• Dorothy Porter, ed., *Early Negro Writing 1760–1837,* 1971. Blyden Jackson, *A History of Afro-American Literature,* volume I, 1746–1895, 1989.

—Roland L. Williams, Jr.

HAMMON, JUPITER (1711–c. 1806), poet, essayist, preacher, and the first published African American writer. Jupiter Hammon gave birth to formal African American literature with the publication of *An Evening Thought, Salvation, by Christ, with Penitential Cries* (1760). Hammon was born on 17 October 1711 at the Lloyd plantation in Oyster Bay, Long Island, New York. He was almost fifty years old when he published his first poem, "Salvation Comes by Christ Alone," on 25 December 1760.

Hammon was a slave to the wealthy Lloyd family. It is evident that he received some education, and he was entrusted with the family's local savings and worked as a clerk in their business. There is no record of his having a wife or child.

By the time he was eighty, Hammon had published at least three other poems—"An Address to Miss Phillis Wheatly [sic], Ethiopian Poetess," "A Poem for Children with Thoughts of Death," and "A Dialogue Entitled the Kind Master and the Dutiful Servant"—and three sermon essays—*A Winter Piece: Being a Serious Exhortation, with a Call to the Unconverted; A Short Contemplation on the Death of Jesus;* and *An Evening's Improvement, Showing, the Necessity of Beholding the Lamb of God.* He wrote several other works that have not yet been found, including a poem celebrating the visit of Prince William Henry to Oyster Bay and *An Essay on the Ten Virgins,* advertised in the Connecticut *Courant* in December of 1779.

Hammon's first poem declares that Christ offers redemption to "everyone" of "every nation" of "all the world." He calls his fellow slaves "Africans by nation" or "Ethiopians," and refers to his brethren as "ancient," uplifting them with a sense of a history older than that of their British masters.

Hammon died around the year 1806. Born before the antislavery movement had gained momentum, he did not have the opportunities afforded to Phillis *Wheatley or Olaudah *Equiano, but he left them a legacy of survival, subtle protest, and living witness.

• Jupiter Hammon, *America's First Negro Poet: The Complete Works of Jupiter Hammon of Long Island,* 1970. Sondra O'Neale, *Jupiter Hammon and the Biblical Beginnings of African-American Literature,* 1993.

—Sondra O'Neale

HANNAH PEACE is *Eva Peace's second daughter and is the mother of the eponymous protagonist in Toni *Morrison's novel **Sula* (1974). Described as a lovely woman who is widowed young and has no intention of marrying again, it is suggested that she inherited from her mother the love of maleness or "manlove," and that she desires and requires touching every day. Still, Hannah is careful about whom she sleeps with, because "sleeping with someone implied for her a measure of trust and definite commitment." Thus, she is "a daylight lover" for whom sex is an ordinary, pleasurable part of life.

*Sula Peace, her daughter, hears Hannah say that she loves her but does not like her and so watches with interest and curiosity as her mother burns to death because of a shift of the wind. One-legged Eva jumps out of a window in an unsuccessful attempt to save her. Years before, Hannah had asked Eva why she had burned Plum, Hannah's drug-dependent younger brother, to death and if Eva had ever loved her children. Now, ironically, Eva shows her love by trying to save Hannah from the same element that she used to destroy her son. On the day prior to Hannah's burning, Sula had acted unusually crazy, distracting Eva and Hannah from seriously contemplating their dreams—which foreshadowed death according to the dream books. Hannah's personality and lifestyle had impressed her young daughter, and the two fiery deaths that Sula witnesses ultimately scorch all the women in the novel.

Like her mother and her daughter, Hannah defied stereotypes, and she cannot be quietly assigned the role of seductress; rather, Hannah has a natural sensuality and remains independent although she would make love to practically any man.

• Barbara Christian, *Black Feminist Criticism,* 1985. Wilfred D. Samuels and Clenora Hudson-Weems, *Toni Morrison,* 1990. Trudier Harris, *Fiction and Folklore: The Novels of Toni Morrison,* 1991.

—Betty Taylor-Thompson

HANSBERRY, LORRAINE (1930–1965), playwright, essayist, poet, and leading literary figure in the civil rights movement. Lorraine Vivian Hansberry was twenty-eight years old when her first play, *A *Raisin in the Sun,* opened on Broadway to instant success. Capturing the spirit of the civil rights movement, this play won the 1959 New York Drama Critics Circle Award and made Hansberry the first black, youngest person, and fifth woman to win that prize. *A Raisin in the Sun,* the first play by an African American woman produced on Broadway, has become a classic of the American theater and has enjoyed numerous professional revivals.

The roots of Hansberry's artistic vision and activism are in Chicago. Born into a family of substantial means, Hansberry was the youngest of four children—Carl, Jr., Perry, and Mamie. Her father, Carl Augustus Hansberry, Sr., was from Gloucester, Mississippi, moved to Chicago after attending Alcorn College, and became known as the "kitchenette king" after subdividing large homes vacated by whites moving to the suburbs and selling these small apartments or kitchenettes to African American migrants from the South. Hansberry's mother, Nannie Perry, a schoolteacher and, later, ward committeewoman, was from Tennessee. At the time of Lorraine's birth, she had become an influential society matron who hosted major cultural and literary figures such as Paul *Robeson, Langston *Hughes, and Joe *Louis. Although Lorraine and her siblings enjoyed privileges unknown to their working-class schoolmates, the parents infused their children with racial pride and civic responsibility. They founded the Hansberry Foundation, an organization designed to inform African Americans of their civil rights, and encouraged their children to challenge the exclusionary policies of local restaurants and stores.

Carl and Nannie Hansberry challenged restrictive real estate covenants by moving into an all-white neighborhood. A mob of whites gathered in front of the house and threw a brick through the front window, narrowly missing eight-year-old Lorraine and forcing the family to move out. Her father won a narrow victory over restrictive covenants from the Supreme Court, but the decision failed to set precedent on this issue.

Hansberry attended public schools: Betsy Ross Elementary and Englewood High School, where she encountered the children of the working class whose independence and courage she came to admire. Their struggle would become the subject of her first major play. Departing from the family tradition of attending black colleges, Hansberry enrolled at the University of Wisconsin at Madison, a predominantly white university, to study journalism, but was equally attracted to the visual arts. She integrated an all-white women's dormitory and became active in the campus chapter of the Young Progressive Association, a national left-wing student organization, serving as its president during her sophomore year. After seeing a moving performance of Sean O'Casey's *Juno and the Paycock,* she decided to become a writer and to capture the authentic voice of the African American working class.

Hansberry left Wisconsin after two years and moved to New York City in 1950. She took a job with *Freedom,* a newspaper founded by Paul Robeson, whose passport had been revoked by the U.S. State Department. She soon became associate editor, working closely with Louis Burnham, who became her mentor. In 1952, she replaced Robeson at a controversial, international peace conference in Montevideo, Uruguay, and subsequently spoke at public rallies and meetings, often critiquing U.S. policy. Hansberry's association with *Freedom* placed her in the midst of Harlem's rich cultural, artistic, and political life. She read avidly and widely in African American history and culture, politics, philosophy, and the arts, and was especially influenced by the works of W. E. B. *Du Bois, Frederick *Douglass, William Shakespeare, and Langston Hughes.

While participating in a demonstration at New York University, she met Robert Barron Nemiroff, son of progressive Russian Jewish immigrants, and after a short courtship, married him on 20 June 1953. Having earned his master's degree four months earlier at New York University, he had begun writing a book on Theodore Dreiser, his thesis topic. The young couple moved to Greenwich Village and Hansberry began to write extensively about the people and lifestyles that she observed around her. She was already an experienced writer and editor, having published articles, essays, and poetry in *Freedom, New Challenge,* and other leftist magazines.

After leaving *Freedom* in 1953 to concentrate on her writing, Hansberry worked various odd jobs including tagger in the garment industry, typist, program director at Camp Unity (an interracial summer camp), recreation leader for the physically disabled, and teacher at the Marxist-oriented Jefferson School for Social Science. When her husband cowrote "Cindy Oh Cindy" (1956), a ballad that became an instant hit, the revenue freed Hansberry to devote her full energies to a play about a struggling, working-class black family, like the families who rented her father's properties on Chicago's South Side—*A Raisin in the Sun.*

A Raisin in the Sun depicts the frustrations of a black family whose dreams of economic progress have been thwarted. After a pre-Broadway tour, it opened at the Ethel Barrymore Theatre in New York City on 11 March 1959 to instant critical and popular success. In 1961, it was produced as a film with most of the original cast and won a special award at the Cannes Film Festival. During this period, Hansberry was much in demand as a public speaker. She articulated her belief that art is social and that black writers must address all issues of humankind. As the civil rights movement intensified, she helped to organize fund-raising activities in support of organizations such as the Student Nonviolent Coordinating Committee (SNCC), called for the abolition of the House Un-American Activities Committee, and declared that President John F. Kennedy had endangered world peace during the Cuban Missile Crisis.

During the last four years of her life, Hansberry worked hard on several plays. *The Sign in Sidney Brustein's Window* was produced on Broadway in 1964, but critics were less receptive to this play that challenged the ennui of Greenwich Village intellectuals. During its short run, Hansberry battled pancreatic cancer, diagnosed in 1963. She died on 12 January 1965, the same night that her play closed.

Hansberry left a number of finished and unfinished writings that indicate the breadth of her social and artistic vision. Robert Nemiroff, whom she had divorced in 1964 but designated as her literary executor, adapted some of her writings for the stage under the title *To Be Young, Gifted and Black,* a show that became the longest-running drama of the 1968–1969 Off-Broadway season and toured colleges and communities in the United States during 1970 and 1971. He also edited and published an anthology of her work (reissued in 1994) that included *Les Blancs,* a play about liberation movements; *The Drinking Gourd,* a television play commissioned by NBC but shelved as too controversial to produce; and *What Use Are Flowers?,* a fantasy on the consequences of nuclear holocaust. Among her other writings were a musical adaptation of Oliver LaFarge's *Laughing Boy;* an adaptation of *The *Marrow of Tradition* by Charles Waddell *Chesnutt; a screenplay based on Jacques Romain's novel about Haiti, *Masters of the Dew;* and a critical commentary on Simone de Beauvoir's *The Second Sex,* a book that had significant impact on Hansberry's thinking. Until 1991 when he died, Robert Nemiroff devoted his life to editing, promoting, and producing Hansberry's works on stage and television.

Hansberry's *A Raisin in the Sun* is a classic of the American theater, frequently produced and an inspiration for young writers and artists. In recent years, a feminist revisioning of her plays and some of her unpublished writings affirm her politically progressive views, her sophistication about gender issues, and her sensitivity to homosexuality and opposition to homophobia. As more of her work is made accessible, the full extent of Hansberry's vision and contribution to American letters will be revealed.

[*See also* Beneatha Younger; Mama Lena Younger; Walter Lee Younger.]

• *To Be Young, Gifted and Black: Lorraine Hansberry in Her Own Words,* adapted by Robert Nemiroff, 1969. *Freedomways,* special issue, "Lorraine Hansberry: Art of Thunder, Vision of Light" 19.4 (1979). Ernest Kaiser and Robert Nemiroff, "A Lorraine Hansberry Bibliography," *Freedomways* 19.4 (1979): 285–304. Lorraine Hansberry, "All the Dark and Beautiful Warriors," *Village Voice,* 16 Aug. 1983, 11–19. Stephen R. Carter, "Lorraine Hansberry," in *DLB,* vol. 38, *Afro-American Writers after 1955: Dramatists and Prose Writers,* eds. Thadious M. Davis and Trudier Harris, 1985, pp. 120–134. Stephen R. Carter, *Hansberry's Drama: Commitment amid Complexity,* 1991. Herb Boyd, "Lorraine Hansberry," in *Encyclopedia of the American Left,* eds. Mari Jo Buhle, Paul Buhle, and Dan Georgakas, 1992, pp. 288–289. Margaret B. Wilkerson, "Lorraine Hansberry," in *Black Women in America: An Historical Encylopedia,* ed. Darlene Clark Hine, 1993, pp. 524–529. Lorraine Hansberry, *The Collected Last Plays: Les Blancs, The Drinking Gourd, What Use Are Flowers?,* ed. Robert Nemiroff, 1994.

—Margaret B. Wilkerson

HANSEN, JOYCE (b. 1942), novelist and educator. Joyce Hansen's interest in writing was influenced by her mother, who had wanted to become a journalist, and her father, whose photography and storytelling fueled her appreciation of the beauty in the lives of ordinary people. After graduating from Pace University with a bachelor's degree in English, New York native Joyce Hansen became a teacher at a school for adolescents with learning disabilities. Confronted with the evidence that even poor readers would complete books that were interesting to them; believing that literature was a way of helping young people have hope, develop responsibility, and understand their environments; and knowing that positive stories of everyday heroism, of those who lived in less than ideal environments but who grew up healthy and whole in loving families and communities, particularly those who were black and Hispanic, were few and far between, Hansen decided to write stories for middle school students such as those she taught. Membership in the Harlem Writers Guild supplemented her careful reading of other writers and conscientious attempts to find her own artistic voice. Using her own life experiences and names, stories, and perspectives from her family, friends, and students, Hansen began to publish novels that reviewers praised for their convincing characters, authentic language, realistic settings, and optimism tempered with common sense. In *The Gift-Giver* (1980), Amir, a foster child, living in the same crime-ridden Bronx neighborhood as Doris, the underachieving daughter of overprotective parents, gives Doris greater understanding of the importance of friendship, of seeing "into" things in order to understand one's world, and of self reliance. In the sequel, *Yellow Bird and Me* (1982), Doris passes on Amir's lessons when she discovers that Yellow Bird plays class clown in an effort to mask his learning disability. While these and other sociopolitical themes inform her writing, Hansen's books are not didactic. Hansen fleshes out the elements that she believes are intrinsic to the African American experience—the importance of family, self-esteem, determination, and optimism—through characters, dialogue, and settings that are well drawn and credible. When Marcus, the protagonist of *Home*

Boy (1982), stabs another student, scenes of his fearful flight are juxtaposed against scenes of his earlier life in St. Cruz, the destruction of the American dream for his emigrant family, and reconciliation with his father as he turns his son in to the police. Marcus, the social delinquent, is also Marcus the troubled and loved son, friend, and neighbor whose own will to reform is supported by members of his community.

In 1986, Hansen began publishing young adult novels about slavery and the Civil War in an attempt to make history come alive for her students. *Which Way Freedom?* (1986) and its sequel *Out from This Place* (1988) give detailed descriptions of slave life in the Gullah area of South Carolina during the Civil War for Obi, Easter, and Jason, three youngsters who come to love and depend upon one another when sold to the same owner. They provide examples of strength, courage, and resilience that can inspire and teach contemporary readers; however, the characters are not larger than life and do not always behave in stereotypical heroic fashion. Obi, for example, knows that Easter and Jason would slow him down so he plans to escape without them. Contrary to many depictions, the Union soldiers do not welcome the fugitive slaves but often return them to their slave owners or force them to do menial and backbreaking work without pay. The novels aptly illustrate why escape plans were fraught with failure and why some slaves chose to remain in bondage. Hansen's interest in the Civil War period led to nonfiction with the publication of *Between Two Fires: Black Soldiers in the Civil War* (1994). In 1995, the African Studies Association awarded Joyce Hansen its Children's Book Award for *The Captive* (1994), a historical novel that considers the problematic concepts of African participation in the slave trade and Puritans who owned slaves. Among her other historical based works are *Breaking Ground, Breaking Silence: The Story of New York's African Burial Ground* (1997) and *I Thought My Soul Would Rise and Fly: The Diary of Patsy, a Freed Girl* (1997). Joyce Hansen believes that writers have the enormous responsibility of arresting ignorance, of providing insight and perspective, and of entertaining. Her work is praised for its powerful use of language to those ends.

• "Joyce Hansen," in *Children's Literature Review* 21 (1990): 149–152. "Joyce Hansen," in *Major Authors and Illustrators for Children and Young Adults,* eds. Laurie Collier and Joyce Nakamura, vol. 3, 1993, pp. 1055–1058. "Joyce Hansen," in *Something About the Author,* vol. 101. Alan Hedblad, ed. 1999.

—Frances Smith Foster

HARPER, FRANCES ELLEN WATKINS (1825–1911), novelist, poet, essayist, journalist, orator, and activist. Born free in the slave state of Maryland, Frances Ellen Watkins was orphaned at an early age. She attended the William Watkins Academy for Negro Youth in Baltimore, an institution noted for rigorous training in a classical curriculum of languages, biblical studies, and elocution, and for developing professional and religious leaders of unusual personal integrity and political activity. Harper was an exemplary alumna. At age twenty-five, she moved to Columbus, Ohio, to become the first woman professor at the newly formed Union Seminary (later Wilberforce University). Exiled from Maryland by state laws that prohibited entry of free blacks into the state and frustrated by the increasing power of slaveholders, in 1853 Harper moved to Philadelphia, where she lived at an Underground Railroad station and devoted her life and literature to abolition and other social reform movements. Her literary production at that time included poems and essays such as "The Dying Christian," "Ethiopia," "Eliza Harris," "Christianity," and "Women's Rights." Reportedly, she published a book, *Forest Leaves,* but no known copies have survived.

In 1854, Watkins accepted a position with the Maine Anti-Slavery Society thereby becoming one of the first professional woman orators in the United States. Traveling throughout New England, southern Canada, and the western states of Michigan and Ohio, Watkins earned accolades for highly articulate and "fiery" speeches that were "marked by dignity and composure" and delivered "without the slightest violation of good taste." Her presentations often included recitations of original poetry and this, combined with regular publication in abolitionist periodicals, earned her a national reputation. Consequently, when she combined her poetry and essays into the 1854 volume *Poems on Miscellaneous Subjects,* it merited dual publication in Boston and Philadelphia. By 1871, this book was in its twentieth edition. Though modern anthologists favor its antislavery poems such as "The Slave Mother—A Tale of Ohio," "The Slave Auction," and "Ethiopia," the volume was, as its title indicates, "on Miscellaneous Subjects," including religion, heroism, women's rights, African American history, and temperance. In an 1859 letter, Watkins outlined the philosophy that informed her writing throughout her sixty-eight-year professional career: "The nearer we ally ourselves to the wants and woes of humanity in the spirit of Christ," she wrote, "the closer we get to the great heart of God; the nearer we stand by the beating of the pulse of universal love."

While she earnestly tried to "teach men and women to love noble deeds by setting them to the music, of fitly spoken words," Watkins understood that universal love realized through devotion to humanity required courage and sometimes decidedly aggressive behavior. In 1858, she protested the segregated streetcars of Philadelphia by staging a personal sit-in and in 1859, when John *Brown's raid on Harpers Ferry failed, she solicited aid for the captured revolutionaries and moved in with Mary Brown until after her husband's execution.

During the antebellum period, Frances Ellen Watkins regularly contributed to national and international abolitionist journals such as the *Provincial Free-*

man, the *Liberator,* the *National AntiSlavery Standard,* and *Frederick Douglass's Monthly.* At the same time, she was active among the African American literati, publishing poems, letters, and essays regularly in African American periodicals such as the *Christian Recorder,* the *Repository of Religion and Literature and of Science and Art,* the *Aliened American,* and the *Weekly Anglo African.* Along with Martin R. *Delany, Frederick *Douglass, William C. *Nell, Mary Shadd Cary, and Sarah M. Douglass, Frances Ellen Watkins is listed as an editor and contributor to what is considered the earliest African American literary journal, the *Anglo-African Magazine.* It was there that in 1859 she published what is generally considered the first short story by an African American, "The *Two Offers."

After marrying Fenton Harper in 1860, the duties of wife, mother, and homemaker slowed but did not stop her social and literary activity. During the Civil War, Frances Harper's lectures and writings carried such titles as "To the Cleveland Union Savers," "Lincoln's Proclamation," and "The Mission of War." She was one of the first to go South to aid the freed slaves. Her husband died in 1864 and within months, Frances Harper was again on the lecture circuit. Between 1865 and 1870, she traveled in every southern state except Texas and Arkansas, lecturing to white, black, and integrated audiences on topics such as "The Claims of the Negro" and "The Work Before Us"; teaching the former slaves reading, writing, home management, and politics; and writing letters back to northern newspapers urging their moral and physical support for the Reconstruction of the United States.

Her newspaper contributions made her "the journalistic mother" of emerging writers such as Ida B. *Wells-Barnett, for whom she was a model and a mentor. Harper's influence was not confined to the postbellum era,, however. Her columns, "Fancy Etchings" and "Fancy Sketches," with their ongoing conversations between Jenny and Aunt Jane about economic, artistic, and social issues prefigure Olivia Ward Bush-Banks's Aunt Viney and Langston *Hughes's **Simple* series in the mid-twentieth century.

Harper's southern travels furnished material for more than newspaper columns that mirrored and guided African American culture of the Reconstruction era, however. Harper had a particular gift for combining social issues, Afro-Protestant theology, and literary innovations. Using the biblical *Moses as a model, for example, Harper represented postbellum United States as a modern biblical narrative in her third book, a dramatic epic called *Moses, a Story of the Nile* (1868), and in her serialized novel *Minnie's Sacrifice* (1867–1868). In 1870, she published *Sketches of Southern Life,* a collection of poems that introduced the wit and wisdom of *Aunt Chloe Fleet and helped shape the emerging interests in literary realism and local color by incorporating African American dialect, folk characters, and cultural experiences.

Frances Harper, like William Wells *Brown and others, was a strong supporter of the temperance movement. Serialized in the *Christian Recorder,* her 1867 novel, *Sowing and Reaping: A Temperance Story,* was one of many stories, poems, and essays that she contributed to this crusade. Joining words and deeds, Frances Harper worked tirelessly in this effort and became one of the first African American women to hold national office in the Women's Christian Temperance Union.

During her career, Frances Harper published several other books, including the novel *Trial and Triumph* (1888) and three 1895 poetry collections: *Atlanta Offering, Martyr of Alabama and Other Poems,* and *Poems.* But, it is for **Iola Leroy* (1892) that she is best known. Harper wrote this tale of slavery, the Civil War, and Reconstruction both in opposition to the inaccurate but increasingly popular plantation school novelists such as Thomas Nelson Page and in answer to the need for more books that would inspire and instruct African American students. *Iola Leroy,* a culmination of the themes and techniques that guided Harper's long career, focuses upon issues of race, gender, and class. Its characters represent the diversity of African American culture and heroic expression. Iola, Dr. Gresham, Robert Johnson, Aunt Linda, Dr. Latimer, Harry, Lucy, Marie, and the others are based, in part, upon actual people and many of their experiences are reincarnations and versions of those who appeared in earlier Harper poems, essays, and stories. As William *Still predicted in his introduction to the first edition, *Iola Leroy* met "with warm congratulations from a goodly number" of readers. Today it is considered a "classic" among African American novels.

Frances Ellen Watkins Harper was a prolific and popular writer who published in practically every genre. She appreciated beauty, she experimented with form and technique, and she enjoyed the accolades of a successful writing career. She believed, however, that literature was to be used to represent, to reprimand, and to revise the lives and aspirations of readers. She was a pragmatic, courageous, and lyrical writer whose major goal was to "make the songs for the people." Frances Harper died on 20 February 1911.

• Maryemma Graham, ed., *The Complete Poems of Frances E. W. Harper,* 1988. Frances Smith Foster, ed., *A Brighter Coming Day: A Frances Ellen Watkins Harper Reader,* 1990. Melba Joyce Boyd, *Discarded Legacy: Politics and Poetics in the Life of Frances E. W. Harper, 1825–1911,* 1994. Frances Smith Foster, ed., *Minnie's Sacrifice, Sowing and Reaping, Trial and Triumph: Three Rediscovered Novels by Frances E. W. Harper,* 1994. John Ernest, *Resistance and Reformation in Nineteenth-Century African-American Literature,* 1995.

—Frances Smith Foster

HARPER, MICHAEL S. (b. 1938), poet, scholar, teacher, and critic. Michael S. Harper was born in Brooklyn, New York, to Walter Warren Harper, a postal worker, and Katherine Johnson Harper, a medical stenographer. Harper recalls his family's move in 1951 to a predominantly white Los Angeles neighborhood grappling with racial tension as a traumatic enough experience to "make" him a poet. Also, his family had an extensive record collection that profoundly affected Harper's poetry. Encouraged to pursue medicine, Harper became only a marginal student after an asthma condition kept him from participating in a junior high gym class, which earned him a failing grade and kept him off the honor roll. At Dorsey High School in Los Angeles, Harper was placed on the vocational track, a situation his father had to "straighten out" so that his son could be on track toward a medical career. During high school, Harper avoided preparing to become a doctor, and he even got significant encouragement from a college zoology professor who told him that black people could not get into medical school. During his high school years Harper wrote a few poems, but he had not yet considered writing as an option for a career.

In 1955, he enrolled at Los Angeles City College, and then Los Angeles State College, which he attended until 1961, during which time he was also employed as a postal worker. He says that his life began here. Many of his coworkers were educated black men like Harper's father who had bumped against the glass ceiling of advancement in the American workplace. Their experiences, which they shared freely, and his own experience of segregated housing at the Iowa Writer's Workshop formed the foundation of Harper's assessment of America as a schizophrenic society. Nonetheless, Harper credits his years at Los Angeles State, where he read John Keats's letters and Ralph *Ellison's **Invisible Man,* for preparing him for the Iowa Writer's Workshop, which he began in 1961. After a year there, Harper taught at various schools, including Pasadena City College (1962), Contra Costa College (1964–1968), and California State College (now University, 1968–1969).

The only black student in both his poetry and fiction classes at Iowa, Harper encountered painter Oliver Lee Jackson, who would influence Harper's thinking. Moreover, he lived in segregated housing, which runs counter to the democratic principles of this nation and best illustrates what Harper calls the schizophrenia of this society. This idea encompasses more than the politics and legacy of racial segregation; it is involved in the very English we speak and the logic we follow. Such binary oppositions as white and black, hot and cold, set the language against itself through a mode of thinking that separates and opposes, contrary to what Harper sees as a holistic universe where humanity is a reflection of the universe, and the universe is a reflection of humanity. This philosophy serves as a basis for the themes, aesthetics, and strategies of his poetry, which include music, kinship, history, and mythology.

For Harper, history and mythology are similar in that neither is fully constituted or contained by its written or commonly understood versions. Such mythologies as white supremacy, and the marred history it engenders, too rigidly encase humanity in static categories. Manipulating old European and American myths and creating new ones illustrates a goal and technique Harper uses throughout his poetry, beginning with his first volume, *Dear John Dear Coltrane* (1970). In the volume, John *Coltrane, who Harper knew, is both the man and his jazz, the talented and tragic musician, and his wholistic worldview and redemptive music. With an understanding of black music similar to W. E. B. *Du Bois's in his description of the African American "sorrow songs," Harper includes the music of poetry as similar affirmation of the importance of articulating suffering to gain from it and survive it. Here, as in Harper's later volumes, musical rhythm replaces traditional metrics in the poetry without sacrificing craft. Coltrane becomes a link between the personal and historical, pain and its expression, suffering and love. To extend these themes, Harper devotes a section of the volume to poems about his own kin, thematically and literally personalizing history so that family ties become continuities of humanity as they link the individual with both a personal and collective history. This opening and overlapping of historical and personal possibility, in the context of Harper's interest in music, seems to provide a handle on Harper's difficult and abstract concept of musical and poetic modality.

In his subsequent volumes, Harper built upon and expanded his philosophy and repertoire of themes and strategies. In 1971, *History Is Your Own Heartbeat* garnered Harper the Poetry Award of the Black Academy of Arts and Letters. Instead of famous musicians, the volume focuses on Harper's family to explore similar issues as Harper's previous volume. Next, *Song: I Want a Witness* (1972) uses black religion as a subtext for its meditations on black history, while, in the second section, the volume dialogues with William Faulkner's short story "The Bear," adding an element of literary history to Harper's thematics. From this volume also comes the limited edition *Photographs: Negatives: History as Apple Tree* (1972). *Nightmare Begins Responsibility,* a volume published in 1975, is another variation on the poet's philosophy of kinship, history, the wholistic universe, and an individual's responsibility to all of these. In many ways, it serves as the sequel to both *Song: I Want a Witness* and *Debridement* (1973), and is considered Harper's richest volume. In it, Harper uses poems to address kinship in a jazz-blues idiom; to consider the death of his friend Ralph Albert Dickey; to affirm responsible action, like Jackie *Robinson's, in the face of a racist nightmare; and to establish the poet's literary, personal, and historical ties to other African American literary and historical figures. *Images of Kin* (1977) earned Harper the Melville-Cane Award and a nomination for the 1978 National Book Award. Four other volumes, *Rhode Island: Eight Poems* (1981), *Healing Song for the Inner Ear* (1985), a limited edition entitled *Songlines: Mosaics* (1991), and *Honorable Amendments : Poems* (1995) have since been published.

By the mid 1970s, Harper's reputation as a poet, scholar, and teacher was firmly established. Among many other awards, such as the National Institute of Arts and Letters Creative Writing Award (1972), a Guggenheim fellowship (1976), and a National Endowment for the Arts grant (1977), Harper received an American specialist grant in 1977, with which he traveled to Ghana, South Africa, Zaire, Senegal, Gambia, Botswana, Zambia, and Tanzania. In several published interviews, Harper affirms the influence this trip had on his thinking and writing. Among Harper's former students are Gayl *Jones, Melvin *Dixon, and Anthony Walton. As a scholar, Harper has made several contributions, including a collaboration with Robert Stepto entitled *Chant of Saints: A Gathering of Afro-American Literature, Art, and Scholarship,* an edition of Sterling A. *Brown's poetry, a limited edition of Robert *Hayden's *American Journal,* and *Every Shut Eye Ain't Sleep,* an anthology of African American poetry since 1945. Harper, poet laureate of the state of Rhode Island, is currently a professor at Brown University, where he teaches literature and creative writing.

• John O'Brien, "Michael Harper," in *Interviews with Black Writers,* 1973, pp. 95–107. Edwin Fussell, "Double-Conscious Poet in the Veil," *Parnassus* 4 (Fall/Winter 1975): 5–28. Robert B. Stepto, "Michael S. Harper, Poet as Kinsman: The Family Sequences," *Massachusetts Review* 17 (Autumn 1976): 477–502. Robert B. Stepto, "After Modernism, After Hibernation: Michael Harper, Robert Hayden and Jay Wright," in *Chant of Saints: A Gathering of Afro-American Literature, Art, and Scholarship,* eds. Michael S. Harper et al., 1979, pp. 470–486. Michael S. Harper, "My Poetic Technique and the Humanization of the American Audience," in *Black American Literature and Humanism,* ed. R. Baxter Miller, 1981, pp. 27–31. Gunter H. Lenz, "Black Poetry and Black Music: History and Tradition: Michael Harper and John Coltrane," in *History and Tradition in Afro-American Culture,* 1984, pp. 277–319. Joseph Brown, "Their Long Scars Touch Ours: A Reflection on the Poetry of Michael Harper," *Callaloo* 9.1 (1986): 209–220. "Michael S. Harper: American Poet," *Callaloo* 13.4 (Fall 1990): 749–829. Elizabeth Dodd, "Another Version: Michael S. Harper, William Clark, and the Problem of Historical Blindness," *Western American Literature* 33:1 (Spring 1998): 61–72.

—Keith D. Leonard

HARRIS, E. LYNN (b. 1955), novelist. Developing a Black male homosexual canon empowers E. Lynn Harris to testify to his experiences and spark conversation on an often taboo topic. Growing up in Little Rock, Arkansas, during the integrationist period, Harris discovered that interracial interaction could be natural and easy, but it also made him realize that Little Rock represented a minute part of the world. His desire to broaden his narrow perspective caused him to dream; through frequent trips to the Little Rock public library, he developed an active imagination that spurred his quest to move beyond Little Rock.

Harris was born in Flint, Michigan, the oldest of four children (he has three sisters). Raised by a single mother, he was taken to Little Rock at the age of three and attended the Little Rock public schools. His interest in writing emerged in the ninth grade when, despite bad grades, he was picked for the newspaper staff. It was the first time that he had to write something, and when his first effort was accepted, he was stunned but inspired.

Harris pursued his education and exploration of the intellect as he escaped from Little Rock. He graduated with honors and a BA in journalism from the University of Arkansas at Fayetteville in 1977. He then attended Southern Methodist's Cox School of Business part-time and was recruited by IBM as a computer salesman. In 1990, however, Harris decided to become a professional writer even though the only writing connection he had had since ninth grade was working on the college yearbook, where he preferred managing to editing. So he moved from Washington, D.C., to Atlanta to try to focus more on writing. James *Baldwin's **Go Tell It on the Mountain* (1953) and Maya *Angelou's **I Know Why the Caged Bird Sings* (1969) mesmerized Harris and inspired him to write. He was particularly impressed with Baldwin's role in the creation of the much-needed Black gay male canon. He also admires the works of Tina McElroy *Ansa, Bebe Moore Campbell, and Terry *McMillan, but his main developmental influence was his mother, not his literary mentors.

His mother does not mirror any of the characters in his books, but she instilled in Harris a preference for goodness, decency, and self-love that shines through his literature. Not only is he recreating the images of Black males and gay males in literature, but Harris refuses to disrespect or devalue Black women in his novels. Through the influence of his mother and his sisters, as well as his extended family, Harris refuses to conceive of Black women as failures or victims. He witnessed his mother leaving an abusive marriage with four children and providing her children with love and opportunity. Harris is also proud of the fact that his late grandmother, a domestic, represented the "seed" to forty-four grandchildren who have never been in jail or on drugs and who range in occupation from professional writers to lawyers.

The needs to be honest to and to testify to his own story through literature remain Harris's primary concerns. His writing represents complete honesty about Black male sexuality for heterosexual and homosexual men. He regards these men as complex and more fearful of showing their feelings than other groups. He does not classify Black male sexuality as an issue because men want to be sensitive and honest with their feelings but they do not know how. He works through these issues in his two published novels.

Invisible Life (1991) functions as Harris's continuation of the Black gay male canon. Playing on the theme of invisibility in Ralph *Ellison, Harris presents the coming-of-age story of Raymond, who defies the invisible ties of sexuality by growing to accept and embrace his own sexual preference. Harris is careful to avoid stereotyping his characters based on the media's interpretation of gay men; instead, he presents a male who is realistic and timeless. The text focuses mainly on Raymond and his journey, while Harris's second novel, *Just as I Am* (1994), explores several interpersonal relationships. Harris continues to testify with honesty and conviction by broadening the representation of homosexuality and AIDS in Black communities. The second novel represents a complex journey of all its characters who face realistic and timeless dilemmas in a world that is quickly changing. In some respects, *Just as I Am* acts as a sequel to *Invisible Life,* as Raymond remains the central character who bridges the lives of characters who journey past their sexual orientation to self-acceptance. And *This Too Shall Pass* (1996) testifies in the same spirit as his previous novels and completes a trilogy dedicated to strengthening the gay literary canon. Harris's latest novels continue this trend. They are *If This World Were Mine: A Novel,* published in 1997, and *Abide With Me: A Novel,* published in 1999.

Harris is currently working on his memoirs, which he stopped writing in 1992 when his literary career took off. The process of recording these memories has been extremely painful but has enabled him to dispel his own myths. Also, through public speaking, he provides support to younger Black gay males confronting their own sexuality.

Ellison's **Invisible Man* remains a model for Harris as he explores the invisibility of Black men and their often secret lives. Similar to Ellison's, Harris's texts travel in a circular motion where the beginning is in the end; he writes the beginning last to ensure this circular movement. He also draws upon W. E. B. *Du Bois's concept of double consciousness to represent the realistic fear of Black men to reveal and live their gay lifestyles. For his daring representations, many Black men identify with Harris and his characters and find reinforcement in their efforts to escape the pain of denial. Harris continues to assist in the creation of the African American gay literary canon by self-healing and telling the truth. His testimony inspires others to tell their stories and leave their personal worlds of denial.

• Traci Carroll, "Invisible Sissy: The Politics of Masculinity in African American Bisexual Narrative," in *RePresenting Bisexualities: Subjects and Cultures of Fluid Desire,* ed., Donald E. Hall and Maria Pramaggiore, 1996, pp. 180–204. Alissa Quart, "E. Lynn Harris: Tales of the Good Life, " *Publishers Weekly* 246: 16 (April 19, 1999) : 44–45.

—Kimberly Weaver

HASKINS, JAMES (b. 1941), author of nonfiction books for juveniles and adults, biographer, educator, critic, editor, and educational consultant. Born into a large family in a racially segregated middle-class section of Demopolis, Alabama, where he was not allowed to visit the town's public library, James S. Haskins was deeply affected by the swirl of events related to the mid-century civil rights movement. He received his bachelor's degree in history at Alabama State College, but limited career opportunities in the South in the early 1960s led him to seek employment in New York City. Two years of selling newspaper advertisements and working as a Wall Street stockbroker brought him to the realization that he was better suited for a career in education and thus he applied for a position in the New York City public school system. After teaching music at several locations, he found a job teaching a special education class at P.S. 92. Obsessed with the plight of his inner-city pupils, he was glad to discuss their problems with anyone who would listen, including a social worker who encouraged him to write his thoughts and experiences in a diary. This resulted in the publication of his first book, *Diary of a Harlem Schoolteacher* (1969), which was widely acclaimed. This initial success attracted the attention of major publishers who approached him to write books for children and adolescents.

An admitted need to reconcile social disparities and a desire to interpret events to young people and to motivate them to read and be influenced by accomplished individuals—particularly deprived youth whom he felt had far too few role models to read about—led him to author more than one hundred books on a diverse array of topics. Written for a general audience of juveniles, his titles include *The War and the Protest: Viet Nam* (1971), *Religions* (1973), *Jobs in Business and Office* (1974), *The Consumer Movement* (1975), *Your Rights, Past and Present: A Guide for Young People* (1975), *Teen-age Alcoholism* (1976), *The Long Struggle: The Story of American Labor* (1976), *Who Are the Handicapped* (1978), *Gambling—Who Really Wins* (1978), *Werewolves* (1981), and *The New Americans: Cuban Boat People* (1982).

Haskins launched his college teaching career in 1970 and continued lecturing on psychology, folklore, children's and young adult literature, and urban education at schools in New York and Indiana before landing a full-time professorship in the English department at the University of Florida at Gainesville in 1977. That same year he authored *The Cotton Club,* a pictorial and social history of the notorious Harlem night club, which seven years later was transformed into a motion picture of the same name directed by Francis Ford Coppola.

Among his books intended for adults or college-level readers are *The Psychology of Black Language* (1973) with Dr. Hugh Butts; *Black Manifesto for Education* (1973), which he edited; *Snow Sculpture and Ice Carving* (1974); *Scott Joplin: The Man Who Made Rag-*

time (1978); *Voodoo and Hoodoo: Their Tradition and Craft as Revealed by Actual Practitioners* (1978); *Richard Pryor, A Man and His Madness* (1984); and *Mabel Mercer: A Life* (1988). He has contributed numerous critical essays and reviews to periodicals. Still, he is best known for his biographies, tailored for elementary and high school students. Most of these recount the triumphs of well-known contemporary African Americans, with whom many young people readily identify. The long list of persons he has profiled (often using the pen name Jim Haskins) include Colin Powell, Barbara Jordon, Thurgood Marshall, Sugar Ray Leonard, Magic Johnson, Diana Ross, Katherine *Dunham, Guion Bluford, Andrew Young, Bill Cosby, Kareem Adbul-Jabbar, Shirley Chisholm, Lena Horne, and Rosa *Parks. Biographies of prominent individuals who are not African American include Indira and Rajiv Gandhi, Shirley Temple Black, Corazón Aquino, Winnie Mandela, and Christopher Columbus.

One of the country's most prolific authors of nonfiction for children and young adults, he has demonstrated unusual versatility in both his selection of subject matter and in gearing his material and writing to interest readers of varying levels of maturity. Critics have noted his careful research, objectivity, and a lucid and understated but straightforward writing style. Haskins has garnered a host of awards and citations, among them the American Library Association Best Book for Young Adults for The Sixties Reader (1988), the Coretta Scott King Honor Book Award for The Harlem Renaissance (1997), and in 1998 Carter G. Woodson Awards for *I Am Rosa Parks* and for *Bayard Rustin.*

• Jim Haskins, "The Triumph of the Spirit in Nonfiction for Black Children," in *Triumphs of the Spirit in Children's Literature,* ed. Richard Rotert, 1986, pp. 88–96. "Jim Haskins," in *Something about the Author Autobiography Series,* vol. 4, ed. Adele Sarkissian, 1987, pp. 197–209. "Jim Haskins," in *CA,* eds. Hal May and Deborah A. Straub, 1989, pp. 186–188. "Jim Haskins," *Something About the Author.* vol. 105, ed. Alan Hedblad, 1999, pp. 111–18.

—Robert Fikes, Jr.

HAYDEN, ROBERT (1913–1980), poet. Robert Hayden looms as one of the most technically gifted and conceptually expansive poets in American and African American letters. Attending to the specificities of race and culture, Hayden's poetry takes up the sobering concerns of African American social and political plight; yet his poetry posits race as a means through which one contemplates the expansive possibilities of language, and the transformational power of art. An award-winning poet of voice, symbol, and lyricism, Hayden's poetry celebrates human essence.

Born to a struggling couple, Ruth and Asa Sheffey (they separated soon after his birth), Hayden was taken in by a foster family, Sue Ellen Westerfield and William Hayden, and grew up in a Detroit ghetto nicknamed "Paradise Valley." The Haydens' perpetually contentious marriage, coupled with Ruth Sheffey's competition for young Hayden's affections, made for a traumatic childhood. Witnessing fights and suffering beatings, Hayden lived in a house fraught with "chronic angers" whose effects would stay with the poet throughout his adulthood. His childhood traumas resulted in debilitating bouts of depression which he later called "my dark nights of the soul." Because he was nearsighted and slight of stature, he was often ostracized by his peer group. As a response both to his household and peers, Hayden read voraciously, developing both ear and eye for transformative qualities in literature. He attended Detroit City College (Wayne State University), and left in 1936 to work for the *Federal Writers' Project, where he researched black history and folk culture. As this work proved enriching for Ralph *Ellison, Richard *Wright, Margaret *Walker, and many other black writers, Hayden's research provided him with essential material and reading skills that would fuel much of his artistry. So too, his work in the theater at Detroit City College and later at the University of Michigan helped to develop his sense of dramatic voicing, evident in the polyvocality of "Middle Passage," one of his best-known works.

After leaving the Federal Writers' Project in 1938, marrying Erma Morris in 1940, and publishing his first volume, *Heart-Shape in the Dust* (1940), Hayden enrolled at the University of Michigan in 1941. In pursuit of a master's degree, Hayden studied under W. H. Auden, who directed Hayden's attention to issues of poetic form, technique, and artistic discipline. After finishing his degree in 1942, then teaching several years at Michigan, Hayden went to Fisk University in 1946, where he remained for twenty-three years, returning to Michigan in 1969 to complete his teaching career.

Hayden's poetry reflects dramatic growth from imitation to a fully realized and independent artistic vision. Heart-Shape in the Dust, largely apprenticeship work, takes many of its cues from Harlem Renaissance poetry, particularly that of Langston *Hughes and Countee *Cullen. Though largely derivative in concept and style, its attention to social criticism and its use of racially and culturally specific materials would mark much of Hayden's ensuing work. In 1942 Hayden assembled a second collection (it remains unpublished as such, but many of the poems appear in *Selected Poems,* 1966), "The Black Spear," using much of the material unearthed during his work for the Federal Writers' Project. Responding to Stephen Vincent Benét's invitation in *John Brown's Body* (1928) for a black writer to pen the seminal "black epic," Hayden explores the complexities of an African American presence in American history. Revealing Hayden's technical development, the collection effectively uses dramatic voices, juxtaposition, irony, and montage for heightened poetic effect.

Hayden's third collection, The Lion and the Archer (1948), launches the career of a mature, self-possessed artist. *The Lion and the Archer, Figures of Time: Poems* (1955), *A Ballad of Remembrance* (1962), *Selected Poems* (1966), *Words in the Mourning Time* (1970), *Night-Blooming Cereus* (1972), *Angle of Ascent* (1975), *American Journal* (1978 and 1982), and *Collected Poems* (1985) establish Hayden as a major influence in American poetry, effectively bridging modernist and postmodernist eras.

An artist passionately committed to the discipline and craft of poetry, Hayden's symbolic density emerges from his manipulation of technical detail. Much of his poetry is highly economical, relying upon compression, understatement, juxtaposition, and montage, which often create highly textured and nuanced irony. Poems such as "Snow," "Approximations," "The Diver," "The Night-Blooming Cereus," and "For a Young Artist" demonstrate the pressure Hayden applies to specific words or concise phrases in order to release a range of suggestions and symbolic possibilities.

Hayden's command of technique makes possible his innovations both within and against the symbolist tradition. Hayden's thematic movement from racial or experiential specificity to fundamental commonalities relies heavily upon a symbolic system. The sordid and oppressive nature of black political life (often represented through the slave trade or the Vietnam War) finds synthesis and resolution in the symbolic realm. Thus Cinquez in "Middle Passage," or the cereus in "Night-Blooming Cereus," or Bahauallah in "Words in the Mourning Time" offer spiritual emancipation and renewal in a realm over and above the physical and limited. Here Hayden's faith as a Baha'i is central as it reinforced his belief in "transcendent humanity," a spiritual or psychic unity of mankind capable of overcoming divisiveness.

Michael S. *Harper refers to Hayden's poetry as "a real testament to craft, to vision, to complexity and historical consciousness, and to love and transcendence." Readers find Hayden's poetry sustaining and compelling largely because of its struggle with epistemology and language; its celebration of African American oral tradition; its engagement of history; and finally its aesthetics and form. With emotional intensity achieved through technical mastery, Hayden's poetry renders a world fraught with anguish, yet one gesturing toward liberating possibility.

• Michael S. Harper, "Remembering Robert Hayden," *Michigan Quarterly Review* 21 (Winter 1982): 182–186. Fred M. Fetrow, *Robert Hayden,* 1984. Pontheolla T. Williams, *Robert Hayden: A Critical Analysis of His Poetry,* 1987. Norma R. Jones, "Robert Hayden," in *DLB,* vol. 76, *Afro-American Writers, 1940–1955,* eds. Trudier Harris and Thadious M. Davis, 1988, pp. 75–88. Xavier Nicholas, ed., "Robert Hayden and Michael S. Harper: A Literary Friendship," *Callaloo* 17 (1994): 975–1016.

—Mark A. Sanders

HEARD, NATHAN C. (b. 1936), novelist, lecturer, musician, educator, television host, and actor. Born in Newark, New Jersey, on 7 November 1936, to Nathan E. and Gladys Pruitt Heard (a blues singer), Nathan Cliff Heard was reared by his mother and maternal grandmother in Newark's inner city; he dropped out of school at fifteen, drifted into a life of crime, and spent the next seventeen years (1951–1968) in and out of New Jersey State Prison at Trenton where he served time for armed robbery.

While in prison Heard distinguished himself as a talented and award-winning athlete. It was not until fellow prisoner Harold Carrington introduced him to the masters—Langston *Hughes, Samuel Beckett, James *Baldwin, Jean Genet, Amiri *Baraka, and others—that Heard began to write, at first about music and African history. In 1963, encouraged by his fellow inmates, he wrote the manuscript for *To Reach a Dream.* Although the novel did not sell, Heard continued to write and read books on writing. In 1968, he succeeded in publishing Howard Street shortly before his release from prison.

Heard is important in African American literature because of his unique ability to imbue his writing with a keen perception of his particular worlds. He infuses his fiction (especially his characters) with his own sense of the pain and hardship of the ghetto and the prison. For Heard, they are significant landscapes. Against these backgrounds, he created his fiction, one that illuminates the brutal realities, the hardships, and despair of these worlds he knew well. Heard's characters are denizens of one or both of these places. *Howard Street* (1968) is a gripping portrait of hustlers, pimps, prostitutes, and other "streeters," and their lives in the ghetto. Just as Heard exposes the horrors of the urban wasteland, he reveals the brutal, violent experiences of the prison system. Heard's *House of Slammers* (1983) is a graphic exposé of prison life, important because it offers a wider canvas than most prison fiction. In this novel, Heard shows the raw, violent life in the American penal system, especially for the nonwhites who constitute the majority of America's prison population. H. Bruce Franklin, in his book *Prison Literature in America* (1989), tells us that "*House of Slammers* is the most important novel yet published about the American prison."

Richard Yarborough, in an article in the *Dictionary of Literary Biography* (1984), describes Heard as an urban realist. In fact, Heard can be regarded as a "latter-day Richard *Wright." For, like Wright, Heard exploits with unusual skill the harsh, mean realities of the black urban experience in America, drawing sharp, biting portraits of the ghetto and prison life he knows firsthand. His writing is unquestionably an authentic representation of black street life, especially his mastery of ghetto vernacular. Heard's literary reputation rests on his novels—*Howard Street, To Reach a Dream* (1972), *A Cold Fire Burning* (1974), *When Shadows Fall*

(1977), and *House of Slammers*—and articles, which include "Boodie the Player" (in *We Be Word Sorcerers: Twenty-five Stories by Black Americans*, ed. Sonia Sanchez, 1973). In 1996 he was completing another novel, "A Time of Desperation."

In addition to writing, Heard taught creative writing at Fresno State College (now California State University, Fresno) from 1969 to 1970 and was an assistant professor of English at Livingstone College (Rutgers University) from 1970 to 1972. He won the Author's Award from the New Jersey Association of Teachers of English in 1969 and from Newark College of Engineering in 1973, and the Most Distinguished Teacher Award of Fresno State College.

• Noel Schraufnagel, *From Apology to Protest*, 1973. Richard Yarborough, "Nathan C. Heard," in *DLB*, vol. 33, *Afro-American Fiction Writers after 1955*, eds. Thadious M. Davis and Trudier Harris, 1984, pp. 110–115. Linda Metzger, Sr., ed. *Black Writers: A Selection of Sketches from Contemporary Authors*, 1985. Bruce H. Franklin, *Prison Literature in American: Victim as Criminal and Artist*, 3d rev. ed., 1989.

—Marva O. Banks

HELGA CRANE is the protagonist of Nella *Larsen's 1928 novel *Quicksand*. An intelligent, sensual, beautiful, searching, and ambitious woman, Helga's quest for security and satisfaction takes her between black society and white society, between the folk and elite cultures of the rural South, the urban North, and even Copenhagen, Denmark. Many have noted the autobiographical similarities between Crane and Larsen. Both are mixed-race women reared by their white mothers from whom they became estranged and who moved (with ambivalence) into black communities. Helga teaches at Naxos, a school modeled after Tuskegee—where Larsen briefly taught. Though biographers have found no supporting evidence, Nella Larsen claimed to have lived in Copenhagen, where Helga spends two years during her search for self-knowledge. And both Nella Larsen and Helga Crane have been noted as daring representatives of modern African American middle-class women. W. E. B. *Du Bois, for example, wrote that Helga was "typical" of the New Negro woman "on whom the shadow of 'race' sits negligibly and Life is always first."

Contemporary critics recognize Helga Crane as an innovative case study especially open to psychoanalytic interpretations. Some see Crane's quest to be a search for happiness, peace of mind, social status, sexual fulfillment, and racial identity. Others see her as the "marginal black woman of the middle class" and as the embodiment of Du Bois's "double consciousness" that even the "New Negroes" could not reconcile.

—Frances Smith Foster

HEMINGS, SALLY (1773–1835), enduring icon in America's imagination since abolition and Thomas Jefferson's alleged lover for thirty-eight years. Sally Hemings was emancipated in 1828, and her mystique subjected her to legend of the magnitude that posthumously hounds Elvis Presley. Hemings sightings proliferated in antislavery periodicals, and she was fictionalized in fugitive slave William Wells *Brown's novel **Clotel, or The President's Daughter* (1853).

Hemings was half sister to Jefferson's wife, Martha, born to Martha's father, John Wayles, and Betty, a half-white slave. An inheritance from Wayles, the quadroon Hemings was house slave at Monticello. Published documentation of the Hemings-Jefferson affair began with a 1 September 1802 exposé by James Thomson Callender in Richmond's *Recorder*.

Biographers who dispute the relationship, including Dumas Malone and Virginius Dabney, oppose historian Fawn Brodie and novelist Barbara *Chase-Riboud (*Sally Hemings*, 1979), who authenticate it. Virtually dismissed have been oral histories of descendants of Thomas Woodson, Hemings's oldest child; testimony recalled from Hemings herself; African Methodist Episcopal records; and ex-slaves' stories. This forces a confrontation on the relevance and reliability of oral traditions. The dispute emblematizes the diminished value and half-hearted evaluation of dictated, collective, and nonsecular sources in African American literature.

As did two of her children, Hemings could have passed as white. Yet names that the public imposed upon her—"Black Sal," "Dusky Sally," "African Venus"—denoted darkness exclusively, and they denigrated mulattas who threatened white racial purity. In retaliation, abolitionists such as William Wells Brown manipulated Hemings to debunk the rhetoric of unadulterated whiteness and to argue that the Republic only masqueraded as egalitarian. Hemings inspired a satirical song, "Jefferson's Daughter," in Brown's *Antislavery Harp* (1848) and a symbolic, sympathetic reference in **Iola Leroy* (1892), Frances Ellen Watkins *Harper's Reconstruction romance. Her figure asserts the hypocrisy of Jefferson's libertarian politics.

• Minnie Shumate Woodson, "Researching to Document the Oral History of the Thomas Woodson Family: Dismantling the Sable Curtain," *Journal of the Afro-American Historical and Genealogical Society* 6 (Spring 1985): 3–12. Paul Finkelman, "Thomas Jefferson and Antislavery: The Myth Goes On," *Virginia Magazine of History and Biography* 102 (Apr. 1994): 193–228.

—Barbara McCaskill

HENDERSON, GEORGE WYLIE (b. 1904), novelist. Born in Warrior's Stand, Alabama, George Wylie Henderson served a printer's apprenticeship at Tuskegee before moving to New York City and eventually writing for the *Daily News* and other publications.

Henderson's acclaimed work *Ollie Miss*, a 1935 novel of rural southern folklife, centers on an attractive eighteen-year-old, hardworking, female farmhand who accepts the consequences for her own decisions and pursues a romantic relationship with Jule, another worker. Following a nearly fatal attack by Jule's jealous lover, Ollie Miss recovers and learns she is pregnant with Jule's child yet rejects his offer to stay with her. The novel closes with Ollie Miss, serenely pregnant with hope of a new future, working her own plot of land.

Published in 1946, *Jule,* sequel to *Ollie Miss,* focuses on the illegitimate son named for his father. Young Jule moves from Hannon, Alabama, where he attacks a white man for making advances toward Bertha Mae, his teenage girlfriend, and escapes to New York where he encounters numerous characters, black and white. In learning to survive, Jule moves from innocent to experienced and becomes a printer's apprentice and even a member of the printers' union. The novel ends with Jule's return to Alabama for his mother's funeral; he plans to marry Bertha Mae and return to New York.

Ollie Miss was applauded for its authentic portrayal of rural black life through setting and characterization. Though Henderson introduced racial and social protest in *Jule,* the less favorably reviewed sequel was sharply critized for its thin character development.

Although Henderson published no novels after *Jule,* he remains significant because his works span the end of the Harlem Renaissance and the beginning of the social protest literature of the 1940s and 1950s.

• Emmanuel S. Nelson, "George Wylie Henderson," in *DLB,* vol. 51, *Afro-American Writers from the Harlem Renaissance to 1940,* ed. Trudier Harris, 1987, pp. 96–100. Lonnell E. Johnson, "The Defiant Black Heroine: Ollie Miss and Janie Mae—Two Portraits from the '30s," *Zora Neale Hurston Forum* 4.2 (Spring 1990): 41–46.

—Lonnell E. Johnson

HENRY BLACUS. *See* Henry Blake.

HENRY BLAKE. The pure-black hero of Martin R. *Delany's epic novel, **Blake, or The Huts of America* (1859, 1861–1862), is late in assuming his titular name. Born Henrico Blacus in Cuba, he had gone to sea as a young man, had been compelled to work first in the Atlantic slave trade and later as a semifree man in Natchez, Mississippi, where—as *Blake* begins—he calls himself Harry or Henry Holland.

When his wife, a slave, is sold away to Cuba, he rapidly evolves into an anti–*Uncle Tom character—and something more than the familiar fugitive slave. Renaming himself Gilbert Hopewell, he becomes an Odyssean observer and schemer, Mosaic-Christian Gospel reviser and advisor, and Romantic-Victorian revolutionary. He boldly races through North America from Texas to Canada to New York to Cuba, promotes black unity and self-reliance in conspirators awaiting his signal for a coordinated strike against white oppressors, notes sociopolitical conditions and attitudes within and between the races, and respectfully takes in folk songs and sayings.

He returns to his island home, rescues his wife from a wicked suitor, finally identifies himself as Henry Blake, signs on to a slaveship to Africa and back, recruits the cargo for his revolutionary army, and organizes supporters. In such travels to so many corners of the African American world, Black becomes the first Afrocentric, Pan-African, revolutionary ideologue and hero in world literature. The final outcome of his scheming, however, remains unknown because of the loss of the story's last six chapters.

—Allan D. Austin

HENSON, JOSIAH (1789–1883), slave narrator, Methodist preacher, educator, activist in the Underground Railroad, and prototype for the title character in Harriet Beecher *Stowe's *Uncle Tom's Cabin* (1852). Josiah Henson was born a slave in Charles County, Maryland, on 15 June 1789. The details of his life are recorded in *The Life of Josiah Henson, Formerly a Slave, Now an Inhabitant of Canada, as Narrated by Himself* (1849). As a very young child Henson states that he was largely unaware that his life was in any way remarkable. It was not until the death of his master, Dr. McPherson, and the sale of his mother and siblings that the real horrors and anxieties of slave life impressed him. After his family is sold, he recalls earlier times when his mother was sexually assaulted and his father was mutilated. In spite of the cruel treatment his mother received at the hands of so-called Christians, she taught him a sense of religion. In 1828, Henson became a preacher in the Methodist Episcopal Church. In 1830, finally convinced that his present master, Isaac Riley, was a beast, he escaped with his wife and four children, reaching Canada on 28 October. After his escape, Henson helped over a hundred slaves escape from Kentucky to Canada.

Henson's life story was first recorded in his 1849 slave narrative, which received little public attention. Harriet Beecher Stowe, however, appreciated Henson's story and made reference to him in her *Key to Uncle Tom's Cabin.* She wrote the introduction to the enlarged 1858 text, *Truth Stranger than Fiction: Father Henson's Story of His Own Life.* Two other versions of Henson's life story appeared in 1876 and 1878; each of these texts was quite popular because Henson was known as Stowe's inspiration for her Uncle Tom character. Henson died in Dresden, Ontario, Canada, on 5 May 1883.

• Sister Mary Ellen Doyle, "Josiah Henson's Narrative: Before and After," *Black American Literature Forum* 8 (Spring 1975): 176–182.

—Charles P. Toombs

HERNTON, CALVIN C. (b. 1934), poet, novelist, essayist, and educator. Born 28 April in Chattanooga, Tennessee, to Magnolia Jackson, Calvin Coolidge Hernton came of age as a writer in the late 1960s and early 1970s. His poetry, novels, and essays reflect not only his education in the social sciences (a BA from Talladega College, 1954, and an MA in sociology from Fisk, 1956) but the issues predominant at that time as well. Hernton worked as a social worker in New York (1960–1961) and cofounded Umbra magazine in 1963. Hernton studied under R. D. Laing from 1965 to 1969 as a research fellow at the London Institute of Phenomenological Studies. He began his teaching career as an instructor in history and sociology in South Carolina (Benedict College, 1957–1958), Florida (Edward Waters College, 1958–1959), at the University of Alabama (1959–1960), and at Louisiana's Southern University (1960–1961). From 1970 to 1972, he was writer in residence at Oberlin College, where since 1973 he has been tenured as professor of Black Studies and creative writing.

Hernton's major nonfiction works are *Sex and Racism in America* (1965) and *White Papers for White Americans* (1966). In *Sex and Racism* he argues that the complex intertwining of sex and racism begun during slavery persists. According to Hernton, this phenomenon originated with the white male's choices: to elevate the white female beyond sexual desire and to seek the black female for sex, in reaction to his puritan discomfort about sex; and in guilt over his actions, to view the black male as desiring the white female. Hernton explains that this sexual "involvement [is] so immaculate and yet so perverse, so ethereal and yet so concrete, that all race relations tend to be, however subtly, sexual relations." In *White Papers,* a collection of personal essays exploring sociological issues, "Grammar of the Negro Revolution" stands as an early analysis of the nonrevolutionary middle-class aims of the civil rights movement: "The Negro is not yet willing to run the risk of a total assault on the culture, to find that many of the things for which he has fought, and is fighting, will no longer be available, within the socioeconomic and political framework that now characterizes this nation." Written before the development of feminist theory, Hernton's analyses in these two essays presage the critique African American feminists would make in the 1970s of the unracialized, middle-class biases of the feminist "revolution."

The theme of the sexual nature of racism can be found in most of Hernton's work. His novel *Scarecrow* (1974) explores the fatal psychosexual problems of voyagers on board the *Castel Felice* to Europe; and in the free-verse poems of *Medicine Man* (1976), individuals contend with a variety of physical, social, and emotional entrapments in an unloving world. Hernton's poetry as well as his essays on James *Baldwin have been anthologized; his most recent critical work includes *The Sexual Mountain and Black Women Writers* (1987) and "The Poetic Consciousness of Langston *Hughes: From Affirmation to Revolution" (*Langston Hughes Review,* Spring 1993). Hernton's early and acute analyses of the complexities of the history of race relations in America and his insistence on the constructed nature of those relations place him as a significant contributor to African American theory.

—Mary Anne Stewart Boelcskevy

Hero Ain't Nothin' but a Sandwich, A. Alice *Childress's *A Hero Ain't Nothin' but a Sandwich* (1973) is a novel that explores the debilitating effects of drugs on a youngster, Benjie Johnson, his family, and his community. A product of the urban ghetto, Benjie is seduced into taking and selling heroin by neighborhood ne'er-do-wells. The issues of identity and the quest for wholeness that surround Benjie's use of drugs are significant in light of the fact that the novel is set immediately following the civil rights movement of the 1960s, when fragmentation and alienation characterized the period. Childress portrays Benjie as a strong-willed, iconoclastic teenager who believes he has to prove something to the world while simultaneously depicting him as a hurting, confused, overwhelmed, sensitive, and intellectually curious youth who craves love and security.

Childress writes Benjie as an anesthetized youth who is having trouble coping with the fact that his biological father abandoned him and that his mother has found a surrogate father for him in Butler Craig. While Benjie's mother and grandmother do their best to nurture him, it is the men in the novel who have the greatest influence on him. His teachers, Nigeria Greene and Bernard Cohen, try to put Benjie on the right track, but it is only when Butler Craig risks his life for Benjie that he begins to want to beat his drug addiction. Butler Craig proves to be the real hero, not the celebrities that the social worker offers Benjie in her attempt to give him hope. When Butler Craig sees Benjie hanging from the ledge and has to decide whether to put himself at risk to save an arrogant stepchild, he chooses to reach out to Benjie. While the novel ends with Butler Craig waiting for Benjie to show up for a counseling session, the point is well made that Benjie does not stand a chance at surviving without someone like Butler Craig, a strong African American male figure, reminding him daily that he is loved and that he can triumph.

A Hero Ain't Nothin' but a Sandwich illustrates the pervasiveness of drug use not only in urban ghettoes but in society in general. Childress argues that the world has become a place where youngsters and adults rely heavily upon opiates to feel good about themselves. On another level, Childress boldly suggests that women can sometimes be powerless in saving their sons. She certainly implies that women alone cannot teach their sons how to become men. She forthrightly suggests that African American men must take responsibility for their youth and try to shelter them from destructive forces. Childress urges African American men to call for nation time, a coming together of black men and women to help preserve their community and build strong self-esteem in their children.

A Hero Ain't Nothin but a Sandwich gave high visibility to Childress as a skilled author of adolescent fiction. For the first time in her writing career, she was able to reach the masses in a way that she had not been able to do with her Off-Broadway and community theater–produced plays. Childress's novel is a milestone because, unlike many of her female contemporaries, she creates a loving, sensitive, generous African American man, Butler Craig, taking responsibility for his family. Childress uniquely captures the beauty and pain of being African American, and she does so by showing that men as well as women are needed to keep the family viable.

• Ed Bullins, review of *A Hero Ain't Nothin' but a Sandwich, New York Times Book Review,* 4 Nov. 1973, 36–40. Elizabeth Brown-Guillory, "A Hero Ain't Nothin' but a Sandwich," in *Masterpieces of African-American Literature,* ed. Frank N. Magill, 1992, pp. 193–196.

—Elizabeth Brown-Guillory

"Heroic Slave, The." "The Heroic Slave," a novella by Frederick *Douglass, was published in March 1853 and is now recognized as the first work of African American long fiction. Amplifying the history of Madison Washington, leader of the successful 1841 Creole slave ship mutiny, Douglass creates for him a fuller chronicle and voice to articulate his motives and champion his actions. The story opens by insisting that despite his slave origins, Washington deserves a place of honor alongside the American Revolutionary hero evoked by his name. Douglass then introduces him through a soliloquy overheard by a white Ohioan, Listwell, who becomes an abolitionist upon hearing the unseen orator's yearning for freedom. When years later the distinctively African-featured, intellectually keen, physically intimidating yet kind-spirited Washington escapes from Virginia, Listwell assists him in reaching Canada. Listwell next meets Washington years later in Virginia, where Washington, recaptured while attempting to free his wife, is bound for the New Orleans slave market aboard the *Creole.* In the climactic mutiny, narrated by the ship's surviving first mate, Washington displays both militancy and mercy, resolutely initiating violence that leaves two dead but temperately preventing further bloodshed. Coupling the slaves' uprising with a contemporaneous squall, Douglass employs popular romantic sea imagery with his earlier American Revolutionary discourse to fashion a powerful statement about slaves' natural right to freedom. Studied for its rhetorical design, its relationship to Douglass's autobiographical writing, its development of a fictive voice, its gendered conception of ideal manhood, and its endorsement of violent revolt, the tale attests to the complex motives behind early African American fiction.

• Richard Yarborough, "Race, Violence, and Manhood: The Masculine Ideal in Frederick Douglass's 'The Heroic Slave,'" in *Frederick Douglass: New Literary and Historical Essays,* ed. Eric J. Sundquist, 1990, pp. 166–188. Eric Sundquist, *To Wake the Nations: Race in the Making of American Literature,* 1993, pp. 115–124.

—Brad S. Born

HERRON, CAROLIVIA (b. 1947), educator, novelist, and short fiction writer. Carolivia Herron was born in Washington, D.C. She earned her BA in English literature from Eastern Baptist College, an MA in English from Villanova University, and another MA in comparative literature and creative writing and her PhD in comparative literature and literary theory from the University of Pennsylvania. Herron has taught at Harvard University (1986–1990) and at Mount Holyoke College (1990–1992). In 1985, she won a Fulbright Post-Doctoral Research award, and a Folger Shakespeare Library Post-Doctoral Research award in 1989. She edited the *Selected Works of Angelina Weld *Grimké* (1991) as part of the Schomburg Library series on nineteenth-century African American women writers. Her short story, "That Place," was published in *Callaloo* in 1987.

Herron's first and only novel to date, *Thereafter Johnnie* (1991), took eighteen years to complete. Taking place in Washington, D.C., the novel is set against an apocalyptic race war in the year 2000 and chronicles the decline of the black middle-class family. The protagonist, Johnnie, is a product of an incestuous relationship between her mother/sister and her father/grandfather. The novel breaks down the taboos and barriers against openly discussing incest and sexual abuse. Herron herself alleges that she was sexually abused by a male relative when she was three years old. Herron's lyrical style has been compared to Toni *Morrison's. The stream of consciousness technique is reminiscent of James Joyce. Herron has also been compared to Alice *Walker, Gloria *Naylor, and Ralph *Ellison. *Thereafter Johnnie* gained its most critical acclaim for its mythic style. Herron is currently working on a three-volume study of the African American epic tradition.

• Farai Chideya, "Two Tales of the Apocalypse," *Newsweek,* 15 July 1991, 53. Andrea Stuart, "Memory and Prophecy," *New Statesman and Society* 5 (5 June 1992): 40–41. Brenda O. Daly, "Whose Daughter Is Johnnie? Revisionary Myth-Making in Carolivia Herron's *Thereafter Johnnie,*" *Callaloo* 18:2 (Spring 1995): 472–491. Elizabeth Breau, "Incest and Intertextuality in Carolivia Herron's *Thereafter Johnnie,*" *African American Review* 31:1 (Spring 1997): 91:103.

—Alisha R. Coleman

HIGH JOHN THE CONQUEROR, a folk term most often associated with conjuring powers and designated by variable names including "High John de Conker," "Low John de Conker," "John the Conqueror root," and "HighJohn." This term may refer to a plant, or a plant-derived substance, that is believed to have conjuring capabilities. It also is said to be a trickster figure in African American culture.

According to folk belief, High John as a "root medicine" will protect a subject against evil spirits and control potentially conflicting situations including love relationships, gambling, litigation, employment, and financial matters. It is most often associated with success, happiness, and improving one's fortune. This product may be dug directly from the woods or purchased from conjurers and used in a variety of forms, including a nonprocessed root, diced, liquid, or powder state.

The notion of High John as a traditional folk hero is somewhat speculative given that none of the collections of tales includes any reference to a figure by that specific name. Zora Neale *Hurston appears to be the first to claim that the trickster in the cycles of *John and Marster* tales is HighJohn. In these tales, John, a cunning slave, may assume the posture of a rogue, naive rascal, or fool when he encounters an oppressive master who reminds him of his limited possibilities on the plantation. John may outsmart his dumbwitted boss, or he may be the unwilling recipient of a misapplied plan. Hurston eloquently valorizes the slave voice through this association. High John is a symbol of the slaves' indomitable spirit, which Hurston argues began in Africa but assumed a more physical form in the New World through High John who metaphorically becomes the ultimate conjure maker.

It is unclear how widespread the usage of this term is. The identification of High John as a root medicine is dependent upon locale and the expertise of the conjurers. They do not all agree on which particular plant or plant-derived substance "High John" is. There is little documentation to support the claim that High John as a trickster figure is derived from the African American oral tradition. None of the collected tales about John, a trickster figure in slavery and freedom, refers to this hero as "High John." Much more research needs to be conducted on this topic to determine more clearly its application in African American culture.

• Zora Neale Hurston, "High John De Conquer," *American Mercury* 57 (1943): 450–458. Harry Hyatt, *Hoodoo, Conjuration, Witchcraft, and Rootwork,* vol. 1, 1970, pp. 455–457 and 593–595.

—Carol S. Taylor Johnson

HILL, LESLIE PINCKNEY (1880–1960), educator and poet. Reflecting the fundamental goals of the New Negro movement, Leslie Pinckney Hill devoted his professional life to the pursuit of "freedom, justice, and fundamental equality," in short, full citizenship for the African American. After receiving his elementary education in the town of his birth, Lynchburg, Virginia, and his secondary education in East Orange, New Jersey, Hill attended Harvard University, where he earned his BA (1903) and MA (1904) degrees, and began to pursue politics through education. In 1904 Hill began his career in education at Tuskegee Institute, teaching English and education under Booker T. *Washington. He was subsequently appointed principal at the Manassas Industrial Institute in Manassas, Virginia, from 1907 to 1913. In 1913 Hill began his thirty-eight-year administration of the Institute for Colored Youth, which, through his leadership, became Cheyney Training School for Teachers (1914), State Normal School (1920), and Cheyney State Teachers College (1951).

Though Hill emphasizes education as the key to racial progress, his essay "What the Negro Wants and How to Get It: The Inward Power of the Masses" articulates the philosophy that informs his educational models and artistic works. That "the human family is one" for Hill summarizes his vision of universal brotherhood, a vision that ultimately negates racial difference in celebration of transcendent commonalities.

Hill's two artistic publications, *The Wings of Oppression* (1921), a collection of sixty-nine poems in standard verse, and *Toussaint L'Ouverture: A Dramatic History* (1928), a dramatic portrait in verse, reveal his didactic leanings and his commitment to universalities. His collection reviews racial, political, and deeply personal themes, all pointing toward the perpetual resilience of the human spirit. Likewise, Hill's drama celebrates Toussaint *L'Ouverture's heroism and that of black Haitians, while lamenting L'Ouverture's tragic betrayal and demise. Although little known, Hill's works and career effectively illustrate the unequivocal New Negro claim to full participation in American political, social, and intellectual life.

• Milton M. James, "Leslie Pinckney Hill," *Negro History Bulletin* 24 (Mar. 1937): 135–137. Patsy B. Perry, "Leslie Pinckney Hill," in *DLB,* vol. 51, *Afro-American Writers from the Harlem Renaissance to 1940,* ed. Trudier Harris, 1987, pp. 101–105.

—Mark A. Sanders

HIMES, CHESTER (1909–1984), novelist. A prolific writer whose career spans fifty years, Chester Himes is best known for his naturalist and detective fiction. A gambler, hustler, burglar, ex-convict, and expatriate, Himes's Catholic experiences and peripatetic life provided him abundant material for fiction that portrays the near existential "absurdity" of blackness in America. Focusing on violence—physical, political, and psychic—as a ubiquitous dynamic in American culture, Himes's fiction ponders the often futile struggle to resist a relentlessly hostile environment.

Born into a struggling middle-class family in Jefferson City, Missouri, Himes's childhood, and that of his two older brothers, Edward and Joseph, was marked by the chronic tensions between his parents and the perpetual disruptions that occurred due to the family's frequent relocation. Himes describes his father, Joseph Sandy Himes, as a dark-skinned man plagued by the internalized stigma of his blackness. Conversely, Himes saw his mother, Estelle Bomar, fair-skinned, as a woman who privileged her white heritage and aspired toward genteel refinement. Exacerbating their differences, Joseph, Sr., worked and taught machinery at several industrial schools across the South, placing Estelle Bomar in contact with rural and poorly educated black communities. After Joseph, Jr.'s accidental blinding in 1923, the family moved several times in search of medical treatment, ending up in Cleveland, Ohio, where the family finally broke up. This break up, in the middle of Himes's adolescence, coupled with a debilitating back injury (for which he was forced to wear an embarrassing brace for several years), left Himes withdrawn and profoundly alienated.

Himes enrolled at Ohio State University in the fall of 1926 to study medicine, but because of his sense of anger and alienation spent his opening quarter exploring Columbus's night life and underworld. After withdrawing from school and returning to Cleveland to live with his father, Himes committed a series of crimes resulting in a 1928 conviction for armed robbery. Facing twenty years of hard labor, Himes entered prison at age nineteen and began his writing career there. His first short stories, "Crazy in the Stir" and "To What Red Hell," portray the hardships of prison life and reveal his preoccupation with the capricious nature of black life. The arbitrariness of persecution coupled with the severely limited means of recourse available to his black protagonists would mark Himes's early naturalist fiction.

Upon parole in 1936 Himes attempted to make a living as a writer. His career divides roughly into three phases, each emphasizing different dimensions of the fundamental predicament of black selfhood in the midst of ubiquitous racism. From 1945 to 1955, the first phase of his career, he published five naturalist novels, all largely autobiographical: **If He Hollers Let Him Go* (1945), *Lonely Crusade* (1947), *The Third Generation* (1947), *Cast the First Stone* (1952), and *The Primitive* (1955). His first two novels render a fatalistic vision of black masculinity, as the respective protagonists, Bob Jones and Lee Gordon, struggle to resist the overdetermination of their racist environments. Ralph Reckly interprets these novels as demonstrating "that the black male who does not subjugate his will to the mainstream cannot survive in America." *Cast the First Stone* reconfigures a totalizing environment in terms of prison. Drawing heavily from his own experiences, Himes presents his white protagonist, Jim Monroe, in a constant state of peril as he attempts to survive interpersonal and institutional brutality. Although Monroe is white, Himes remains focused upon the tenuous proposition of autonomous selfhood.

Completing the first phase of his career, Himes reenvisions the trauma of his childhood family life in *The Third Generation,* and examines the complexities of interracial sexual attraction in *The Primitive. The Third Generation* explores the ways in which adults act out their imbibed racial self-hatred, and the ways in which they transmit their neuroses to their children. *The Primitive* uses a murderous interracial relationship in order to portray the overdetermination of racial stereotypes. That Jesse Robinson, a black male, can see Kriss Cummings, a white female, only as the icon of white virtue, and that Kriss can see Jesse only in terms of primitivist sexuality predetermines a profoundly destructive relationship. Here, as with most of the early fictions, the overarching cultural conceptions of race relegate Himes's characters to severely circumscribed social and psychological spaces. Invariably violence and destruction result.

Following Richard *Wright's example, in 1953 Himes left the United States for France, becoming an expatriate in pursuit of wider personal freedoms and greater publishing opportunities. Both *If He Hollers Let Him Go* and *Lonely Crusade* had already garnered a substantial readership in France, initiating a trend that would outlast Himes's life. Upon the suggestion of an editor, Himes began writing detective fiction, originally to make quick money. From 1957 to 1969, the second phase of his career, he wrote perhaps his most famous novels, eight detective novels setin Harlem: *For Love of Imabelle* (1957), *The Real Cool Killers* (1959), *The Crazy Kill* (1959), *The Big Gold Dream* (1960), *All Shot Up* (1960), **Cotton Comes to Harlem* (1965), *The Heat's On* (1966), and *Blind Man with a Pistol* (1969). Featuring the duo *Grave Digger Jones and *Coffin Ed Johnson, Himes adopts standard detective fiction formula, but uses it to posit black violence as a response to oppressive conditions. Jones and Johnson, like most heroes of the genre, are entrusted with the protection and maintenance of the community. But the means by which they solve crimes, right wrongs, and bring criminals to justice suggest an agency and independence wholly negated in Himes's earlier fiction. The duo uses violence according to their own sense of propriety, and mete out justice in ways often independent of conventional, legal, or judicial practices.

Attesting to the popularity of Himes's detective fiction, *The Heat's On (Come Back Charleston Blue)* and *Cotton Comes to Harlem* were made into movies, and many of the novels remain in print.

During the same period Himes wrote two novels that deviate from the trend: *Pinktoes* (1961) and *Run Man Run* (1966). *Pinktoes* satirizes interracial sexual attraction, presenting self-absorbed characters acting upon their sexual desires for the racial "other." *Run Man Run,* though still detective fiction, does not feature the standard heroes or celebrate their abilities, but ponders the threat of unbridled police brutality. Jimmy Johnson, a poor black student, witnesses the second of two murders perpetrated by a black detective, Matt Walker. Attempting to cover up his crime, Walker stalks Johnson and eventually kills him. Although Walker's crimes are discovered by a fellow detective, Sergeant Brock, Brock protects Johnson out of a warped sense of familial and professional loyalty.

By the beginning of the 1970s, Himes embarked upon the final phase of his career. Along with a volume of collected works—*Black on Black: Baby Sister and Selected Writings* (1973)—and several short novels, Himes published an autobiography in two volumes: *The Quality of Hurt* (1972) and *My Life of Absurdity* (1976). Both volumes propose a life profoundly marked by cultural and institutional racism. Himes's autobiographical hero acts and reacts according to the political and psychic violence that surrounds him, only momentarily claiming for himself a tenuous sense of peace and stability. Read as a final statement responding to both his life and art, Himes's autobiography reiterates his central concern for the random, near chaotic nature of African American life in Western culture. Several critics have commented on the compelling tension between near futility and the individual's defiant responses to such daunting environments found in Himes's work. Just short of naturalism's totalization, Himes's fiction perpetually explores the efficacy of black male agency.

• Michel Fabre and Robert E. Skinner, eds. *Conversations with Chester Himes,* 1995. Michel Fabre and Edward Margolies, *The Several Lives of Chester Himes,* 1997. Bruce A. Glasrud and Laurie Champion, "Chester B. Himes, In *Contemporary African American Novelists,* ed. Emmanuel S. Nelson, 1999, pp. 203–210.

—Mark A. Sanders

His Own Where. The first novel of poet and essayist June *Jordan, *His Own Where* (1971) made the *New York Times* List of the Most Outstanding Books of 1971 for young adults and the American Library Association List of Best Books; it was also nominated for the National Book Award.

His Own Where is the love story of sixteen-year-old Buddy Rivers and fourteen-year-old Angela Figeroa, two African American adolescents struggling with parental abandonment and violence, an intimidating urban environment, and social institutions indifferent to human need. The young characters define their own world and establish their own values, which are often at variance with society's and their parents' demands. Their story's unsparing depiction of society's slow extinction of youthful hopes and dreams warns about the effects of prejudice and sexism, and champions freedom over constriction, sensuality over puritanism, living for others over living for success. Narrated from Buddy's perspective, it is told in flashbacks and dream sequences in an African American spoken English whose rhythms poeticize Buddy's often heroic conflicts with his environment to change situations he finds physically or emotionally confining. At school he agitates for free sex, contraceptives, coeducational classes in anatomy, and dancing and music in the lunchroom; he helps Angela escape her abusive parents as well as an oppressive girls' home. Refusing to be trapped by the hopelessness of indifferent and cruel environmental elements, Buddy takes Angela to a deserted cemetery toolshed, determined to make a new life for them, which includes the prospect of a baby; he seeks "His own where, own place for loving made for making love."

His Own Where makes central June Jordan's interests in architecture and urban design and her commitment to African American English. The novel shows that space and language, vital means by which environment is shaped, bear directly on personal development and community health. Buddy's work on the house he and his father have renovated and on the toolshed he and Angela inhabit suggest that urban redesign should be enlisted to create environmental conditions that can foster African American life. The novel's poetic stream of consciousness style closes the gap between words and experience, with the result of a striking verbal immediacy that realizes the integrity of African American English as well as its energy and creativity. This reflects Jordan's educational and artistic goals to defend and preserve the language while luxuriating in its lyricism, rhythm, and poetic idiom.

His Own Where is an exemplary work from the "second renaissance" of African American culture of the 1960s and 1970s. Blending elements of fantasy and realism, the novel suggests a reconceptualization of realism from the perspective of poetic vision; its dreamlike quality and impressionistic style evoke the grittiness of urban life and the energy of being young and African American. In its emphasis on activist urban redesign and its pride in African American English, *His Own Where* is a novel of political protest that fits in a tradition of works by Alice *Walker, Toni *Morrison, and other socially conscious African American novelists of the 1970s.

• Sarah Webster Fabio, review of *His Own Where, New York Times Book Review,* 7 November 1971, 6, 34. June Jordan, "White English/Black English: The Politics of Translation (1972)," in *Civil Wars,* 1981, pp. 59–73. Peter B. Erikson, "June Jordan," in *DLB,* vol. 38, *Afro-American Writers after 1955: Dramatists and Prose Writers,* eds. Thadious M. Davis and Trudier Harris, 1985, pp. 146–162.

—Ronna C. Johnson

HOLIDAY, BILLIE (1915–1959), jazz singer and lyricist. Like many jazz musicians, Billie Holiday ("Lady Day") began her career in brothels and afterhours clubs. After an apprenticeship at late-night jam sessions, she became one of the most significant figures in the history of jazz. Since her death she has become an American icon, perhaps better known for the stories surrounding her drug addiction and her personal life than for her artistry.

Her autobiography, *Lady Sings the Blues* (1956), coauthored with William Dufty, has become a classic African American autobiography. The text is one of the first to contribute to the myth of Holiday as the tortured but talented jazz and pop singer. The myth is elaborated on the pages of the autobiographies of some of the twentieth century's most significant

African Americans including *Malcolm X's *The *Autobiography of Malcolm X* (1965), Lena Horne's *Lena* (1965), and Maya *Angelou's *The Heart of a Woman* (1981). In these texts Holiday alternates from a hip but generous big sister to a vulgar, mean-spirited, aging woman; however, in all of them she is portrayed as a highly talented, sensitive musician who is the victim of America's racism and the sexism of black and white men.

The most exquisite evocations of Holiday appear in poetry. Alexis *De Veaux's narrative poem, "Don't Explain: A Song of Billie Holiday" (1980); "The Day Lady Died" (1959), by white American poet Frank O'Hara; and "Sometimes You Look Like Lady Day" (1973), by Filipino American poet Jessica Tarahata Hagedorn, all immortalize Holiday in her breathtaking beauty and artistry.

Holiday is the subject of numerous biographies. The most significant include *The Many Faces of Lady Day* (1991), by literary critic Robert O'Meally, and Donald Clarke's *Wishing on the Moon: The Life and Times of Billie Holiday* (1994). O'Meally seeks to turn attention away from the various myths of Holiday's personal life and instead to focus on her development and achievement as an extraordinary jazz artist. In so doing, he moves Holiday beyond her status as victim and situates her in the space of her agency—her music. Clarke's is the most extensive and well researched of the Holiday biographies to date and includes a chapter on her emergence as an American icon.

—Farah Jasmine Griffin

HOLMAN, JOHN (b. 1951), short story writer, essayist, and educator. John William Holman, an associate professor of English at Georgia State University in Atlanta, was born in Durham, North Carolina. He received his BA in English from the University of North Carolina at Chapel Hill in 1973, his MA in English from North Carolina Central University in Durham in 1977, and his PhD in English and creative writing from the University of Southern Mississippi in 1983.

He has published one book, *Squabble and Other Stories* (1990), a collection of eleven short stories that originally appeared in such journals and magazines as the *New Yorker, Crescent Review,* and *Mississippi Review.* These stories are about African Americans in the New South who do not quite fit into mainstream society. Holman's own phrase, "distant weirdness" taken from his short story "Swoosh," published in the fall 1992 issue of *Appalachee Quarterly,* accurately describes his stories and characters, seemingly ordinary yet surreal people whose dialogue and whose lives do not seem to connect. They have strange—though perfectly suited—names like Grim, Cola, and Joyless.

The major character in "Squabble," Aaron, is a retrenched geography professor who gets a job tending bar at a dive called the Bellaire in his neohick hometown. The star attraction at the bar is Dog, a man with half a face. There is the story of Todd in "Pimp," who is an ex-pimp, bouncer, and bodyguard who once faked his own hanging as a Halloween joke. When he returns home for a visit, he thanks his neighborhood friend for writing him while he was away and explains to her that he did not respond because he "didn't know how to talk like [he] still lived here." In "The Story of Art History," two people dance around on red lingerie that has been thrown on the floor. Monroe, who is getting married in "Monroe's Wedding," asks Thompson, his boss of three weeks, to be his best man: "It's you or some joker I can bribe."

Holman has a deft ear for dialogue. He exercises economy in his use of words, with his predominantly short sentences. He writes in the style of Frederick Barthelme, under whom he studied at Southern Mississippi, and Raymond Carver. He uses rich, colorful, vivid, and very descriptive language. In the story "I and I," drug dealers making a stop in a small Mississippi town stay in an unfurnished house where "Every room is a different color—carpets purple, pink, blue, green. Matching drapes shaped like suffocation hang in the windows. They have funeral parlor folds, garish colors of Dracula lips."

In 1991 Holman received the Whiting Writer's Award, a prestigious annual literary prize given to ten American writers of promise. His most recent fiction, *Luminous Mysteries* (1998), is a series of interlinking stories. They, like *Squabble,* will help to firmly establish Holman as a noteworthy writer of short fiction.

• John William Holman, "Scuff," *Alabama Literary Quarterly* 6.1 (Fall/Winter 1992): 41–48. John William Holman, "Immaterial," *Forum* 27.2 (Fall/Winter 1993): 22–27.

—Elwanda D. Ingram

Home: Social Essays. The entries of Amiri *Baraka's *Home: Social Essays* (1966) chronicle the writer's rapidly emerging nationalistic posture. Including a number of essays that were originally published in such journals as *Evergreen Review, Liberator, Kulchur, Cavalier, the Nation, Poetry,* the *Saturday Review,* the *New York Sunday Herald Tribune,* and *Midstream,* this collection is also representative of the collective consciousness of much of the African American populace of the period. Written in the wake of the global liberation struggles of Africans, African Americans, and people of color in general, these essays reflect a growing impatience with the gradualism of the American civil rights movement, a contempt for liberalism, a passion for moral engagement, and a fervent embracing of African American history and culture.

As with much of Baraka's work, there is little middle ground in appraisal of these essays. William Harris notes in the introduction to *The LeRoi Jones/Amiri Baraka Reader* (1991) that *Home* is "an important book of essays written at its author's fullest powers." A reviewer from *Newsweek* (May 1966), on the other hand, notes in an examination of *Home* that

"[Baraka] writes and harangues himself out of the company of civilized men; and forfeits all claim to serious attention."

In "Cuba Libra," the longest essay in *Home*, all of the aforementioned themes are apparent. An accounting of a visit to Castro's newly liberated Cuba, this essay reflects strongly the writer's growing dissatisfaction with the "art-for-art's sake" posture of the Beats. In recounting the dialogue between himself and the more engaged Latin American poets also visiting Cuba, the writer reveals the roots of his politically charged later verse. Although this experience predates the writer's avowal of communism by a good number of years, the idealism that made his ideological conversion possible was abundantly present at the time of this visit.

In a number of these essays, Baraka delves deeply into the roots of African American folkways. Mixing a good bit of humor with the more tragic elements of the collective experience of his people, he celebrates those things that have become emblematic of the African American weltanschauung and style ("Soul Food," "City of Harlem," and "Expressive Language").

Much of *Home* reflects Baraka's impassioned struggle with the idea of a Black Aesthetic. "The Myth of a 'Negro Literature,'" "A Dark Bag," "LeRoi Jones Talking," and "The Revolutionary Theater"are all fundamentally concerned with the African American writer's finding his or her authentic, morally engaged voice. The first of these essays, originally presented as an address to the American Society for African Culture in March 1962, is most notable for its castigation of most African American writing in terms of its derivative and apologetic nature. While attacking the literature, however, he exalts the bona fide artistry of African American music. Referring to jazz and blues as the only "consistent exhibitors of 'Negritude' in formal American culture," Baraka evidences embryonic patterns of thought that would appear fully developed in his monumental *Blues People* (1963). The essays referred to here, especially the hortatory "The Revolutionary Theater," served as touchstones for the many young writers who would ally themselves with the Black Arts movement of the late 1960s.

The remaining essays evidence Baraka's progression from the posture of the cultural nationalist to that of literal black nationalist. In "American Reference: Black Male," "Blackhope," and "The Legacy of Malcolm X," each increasingly apocalyptic, hyperbolic, and darker, we observe Baraka's rationalization for the African American's separation from a dying Western culture.

• James B. Gwynne, ed., *Amiri Baraka: The Kaleidoscopic Torch*, 1985.

—Henry C. Lacey

Home to Harlem, a picaresque novel by Claude *McKay, appeared in 1928, at the height of the Harlem Renaissance. Its unabashed celebration of Harlem lower-class life generated great controversy among black critics and reformers, some of whom believed McKay was catering to stereotyped portrayals of blacks. The controversy helped propel *Home to Harlem* onto New York's best-seller lists, the first novel by a black to achieve such popularity.

Home to Harlem is the story of Jake Brown, McKay's natural man, whose primitive virtues and folk wisdom sustain him in the unnatural industrial world of the urban northeast. McKay's vision of an essentially healthy rural black folk struggling to stay afloat in a hostile sea of urban capitalism owed much to his own rural Jamaican background and to his interest in the works of D. H. Lawrence. McKay had also been strongly influenced by African and other "primitive" folk arts, as well as the revivals of peasant and folk themes in Jewish, Russian, and Irish literatures.

In *Home to Harlem,* Jake Brown deserts the American Army in wartime France. After the war, he returns to Harlem and works as an assistant cook on the Pennsylvania railroad. He befriends Ray, a Haitian waiter on his dining car. Ray's formal education and literary aspirations provide a contrast to the highly intense but limited activities of Jake and the other characters, almost all of whom are single working people. There are no families or children in *Home to Harlem.*

McKay's often lyrical descriptions of lower-class Harlem and its types are discordantly offset by a strong autobiographical element in *Home to Harlem* that depicts a harsher, more brutal world of loneliness, labor exploitation, violence, and frustration. For example, Ray, McKay's fictional alter-ego, thinks of segregated Harlem as a congested "pig-pen," no fit place in which to marry or to start a family. The cumulative evidence of *Home to Harlem,* with its contradictory mixture of primitivism, autobiography, and social realism set within a picaresque mode, suggests that the enormous disorder and despair found in today's "underclass" has a history that goes back decades further than critics often suggest.

Home to Harlem was the first of four volumes (*Banjo,* 1929; *Gingertown,* 1932; and *Banana Bottom,* 1933) in which McKay progressively defined the nature of the modern world, the position of blacks in it, and his own wanderings as an expatriate poet and writer. In all his fiction, rural black folk culture stands upon its own foundations, in some sense independent of and in opposition to an urbanized, industrialized, mechanistic, and denatured Western civilization. Few African American works have aroused more unease among black middle-class reformers and critics than *Home to Harlem.* The literary primitivism of the 1920s, of which McKay was a part, largely expired with the decade, and his novels were little read in succeeding years. But the relevance of the various issues raised in *Home to Harlem* and McKay's other fictional works remain pertinent.

• James R. Giles, *Claude McKay,* 1976. Wayne F. Cooper, *Claude McKay: Rebel Sojourner in the Harlem Renaissance, a Biography,* 1987.

—Wayne F. Cooper

HOOKS, BELL (b. 1955), writer, teacher, and cultural critic. With her first two books, *Ain't I a Woman: Black Women and Feminism* (1981) and *Feminist Theory: From Margin to Center* (1984), bell hooks (born Gloria Watkins) joined a generation of black feminists whose political perspective was explicitly forged in a consciousness of their marginality to the Black Power, civil rights movement, and feminist movement of the 1960s. Unlike some of her contemporaries, hooks did not feel that black women's double oppression warranted advocating a separate black feminist agenda, but instead saw black women's special historical situation as relevant both for a feminist movement that had stumbled over its implicit class and race biases, and for a black liberation movement that remained committed to the patriarchal values of the racist society it denounced. Challenging feminist and antiracist movements to become accountable for the lives and experiences of black women, hooks envisioned black feminism as a catalyst for transforming the historically antagonistic relationship between the two political groups.

Since the publication of her first two books, bell hooks has increasingly centered her reflections on feminism and the politics of race in the areas of popular culture and pedagogy. *In Talking Back: Thinking Feminist, Thinking Black* (1989), *Yearning: Race, Gender and Cultural Politics* (1990), *Black Looks: Race and Representation* (1992), *Outlaw Culture: Resisting Representations* (1994), *Teaching to Transgress: Education as the Practice of Freedom* (1994), and *Art on My Mind* (1995), hooks explores questions concerning black style and commodity culture, the pedagogical implications of multicultural classrooms, and the development of African American artists and of critical methods proper to their work. With *Wounds of Passion: A Writing Life* (1997), *Bone Black: Memories of Girlhood* (1997), and *Remembered Rapture: The Writer at Work* (1999), hooks joined the ranks of contemporary African American memoirists.

The writing of bell hooks is characterized by a concern with the ethics of criticism. In many of her essays, hooks frankly interrogates her own position as a black woman from a working-class background writing and teaching within a professional academic context. In *Breaking Bread: Insurgent Black Intellectual Life* (1991), she addresses this issue through a dialogue with her coauthor, Cornel *West. She complicates West's well-known formulation of the dilemma of the black intellectual by noting some of the ways in which an intellectual identity is uniquely problematic for black women. As an example hooks cites her long struggle to claim the time and space necessary to think and write when those around her regarded her need for privacy as a selfish withdrawal from the community. The format of *Breaking Bread,* which consists of interviews and paired essays, is exemplary of hooks's political strategy as a writer and a teacher. By representing her work in dialogue with the work of other black intellectuals (including filmmaker Isaac Julien and British cultural critic Paul Gilroy), by writing short anecdotal essays rather than conventional academic papers or books, and by publishing in a variety of popular and scholarly journals, from *Artforum* and *Essence* to *Black American Literature Forum* and *Zeta,* hooks appeals to a popular and a professionalized readership to become responsible members of a common intellectual community.

• bell hooks, "Black Woman Artist Becoming," in *Life Notes: Personal Writings by Contemporary Black Women,* ed. Patricia Bell-Scott, 1994, pp. 151–159.

—Deborah G. Chay

HOPKINS, PAULINE E. (1859–1930), editor, novelist, and leading proponent of activist black journalism during the post-Reconstruction era. Pauline Elizabeth Hopkins was born to William A. Hopkins, a veteran of the Civil War, and Sarah A. Allen in Portland, Maine, in 1859. The family moved to Boston when Hopkins was an infant. She graduated from the renowned Boston's Girls' High School and shortly thereafter pursued stenography for a livelihood. In 1892 she worked for Henry Parkman and Alpheus Sanford, prominent Boston-area Republicans, and in 1895 she was appointed stenographer in the Bureau of Statistics for the Massachusetts Decennial Census. When she died in 1930, she was working as a stenographer for the Massachusetts Institute of Technology.

Although Hopkins wrote essays, poetry, and musical dramas before she was twenty, she did not try her hand at fiction until 1900, probably because there were few African American outlets for this genre until the advent of the *Colored American Magazine.* The Boston-based *Colored American* was founded by Walter Wallace, Jesse W. Watkins, Harper S. Fortune, and Walter Alexander Johnson, who also established the Colored Co-operative Publishing Company. An editorial statement, appearing in the inaugural issue (May 1900), expressed the magazine's intentions to strengthen the bonds of "brotherhood" among "the colored people of the United States" and to demonstrate "their ability and tastes, in fiction, poetry, and art, as well as in the arena of historical, social, and economic literature." This issue also published Hopkins's short story "The Mystery Within Us," and the Co-op issued her protest novel **Contending Forces* in 1900 (the subtitle is *A Romance Illustrative of Negro Life North and South*).

Hopkins became one of the most frequent contributors to the magazine during its formative years, often writing under her mother's name—Sarah A.

Allen. Over the next four years she published three serial novels—*Hagar's Daughter: A Story of Southern Caste Prejudice, Winona: A Tale of Negro Life in the South and Southwest,* and *Of One Blood, or The Hidden Self*—seven short stories, two series of biographical articles on famous black men and women, numerous editorials, and social and political commentaries. Hoping that fiction could reawaken the political zeal of the abolitionist period, she used her fiction to persuade her readers to protest the encroachment of Jim Crow racism and restrictive gender prescriptions.

By 1902 Hopkins was an editor of the magazine, although her name did not appear on the masthead until 1903. As Hazel Carby explains (introduction to *The Magazine Novels of Pauline Hopkins,* 1988), Hopkins's editorial influence has been vastly underestimated, undoubtedly because of her sex. As a woman operating in what was assumed to be a male professional arena, Hopkins's influence extended well beyond the female sphere. Even though she routinely masked her editorial authority, many of her male colleagues resented her position. Nevertheless the breadth of her interests in literature, history, journalism, and domestic and international politics, all in the service of Du Boisian–styled racial uplift, characterized the magazine until 1904.

In 1904, Booker T. *Washington gained control of the *Colored American.* During the summer of 1904, Fred R. Moore, the new owner and general manager, moved the Co-op and the magazine to New York. Moore's editorial in the November 1904 issue emphatically endorsed Washington as "the greatest living Negro," proclaimed him as the leader of the race, and embraced his position of racial conciliation.

Contention between the political positions of Moore and Hopkins led to her disassociation from the magazine sometime in 1904, and she was forced to seek other outlets for her political journalism. In 1905 she became a regular contributor to the **Voice of the Negro,* edited by J. Max Barber and T. Thomas *Fortune, and began a series of articles entitled "The Dark Races of the Twentieth Century." Here she vigorously refuted the presumption of Anglo-Saxon superiority, challenged the binary system of racial classification, and argued that the crises of the twentieth century would be the "Negro Problem" and the conflict between "Capital and Labor." In 1905 Hopkins launched her own publishing company—P. E. Hopkins and Co.—with the publication of *A Primer of Facts Pertaining to the Early Greatness of the African Race.* In this project she focused on recovering the record of plundered African civilizations. In the last line of the *Primer,* Hopkins directs her attention to Africans in the United States, exhorting "NEVER GIVE UP THE BALLOT." Hopkins attempted another publishing venture with the launching of the *New Era* magazine in 1915. She saw this publication as a medium for agitating for equal rights, presenting the history of racial progress, and promoting black literature and arts. This serial was basically a duplication of the format and concerns of the early *Colored American.* Unfortunately the magazine failed after two issues.

Hopkins's publication record was as impressive as that of Paul Laurence *Dunbar, Charles Waddell *Chesnutt, or Sutton E. *Griggs. As an editor she was as influential as Barber and Fortune of the *Voice of the Negro* and W. E. B. *Du Bois of the *Moon* and the *Horizon.* Like these men and long before Richard *Wright claimed the printed word as a weapon, Hopkins clearly understood the political power of narrative. By intersecting the "rags to riches" stories of her age with African American culture, and the popular genres of the romance, the Western, and detective fiction with racial protest, Hopkins hoped to intervene in the racist discourses of the early twentieth century. And yet, until the 1980s, this most prolific black woman was routinely disregarded by literary scholars. Gender politics effaced the record of her commitment to make fiction and journalism a part of the reformist dialogues about race, gender, and class. Although gender politics problematized female participation in the intellectual discourse of the post-Reconstruction era, Hopkins (like Anna Julia *Cooper, Ida B. *Wells-Barnett, Gertrude Mossell, and Victoria Earle *Matthews, to mention but a few) nevertheless offered forceful and impassioned opposition to the prevalent imperial discourses of the inferiority of people of color.

• Abby Arthur Johnson and Ronald Maberry Johnson, *Propaganda and Aesthetics: The Literary Politics of Afro-American Magazines in the Twentieth Century,* 1979. Hazel V. Carby, *Reconstructing Womanhood,* 1987. Hazel V. Carby, introduction to *The Magazine Novels of Pauline Hopkins,* 1988. Richard Yarborough, introduction to *Contending Forces,* 1988. Claudia Tate, *Domestic Allegories of Political Desire: The Black Heroine's Text at the Turn of the Century,* 1992. John Cullen Gruesser, ed., *The Unruly Voice: Rediscovering Pauline Elizabeth Hopkins,* 1996.

—Claudia Tate

HORTON, GEORGE MOSES (c. 1797–c. 1883), poet. The "Colored Bard of North Carolina" was the only man to publish volumes of poetry while in bondage and the first African American to publish any book in the South. Born on the tobacco farm of William Horton in Northampton County, North Carolina, George Moses Horton moved with his master to Chatham and worked as a "cow-boy" and farm laborer throughout his teens. During these years he taught himself to read—he could not write until 1832—and began composing verses and hymns in his head. From about 1817, Horton took weekly Sabbath walks of eight miles to the Chapel Hill campus of the University of North Carolina to sell fruit, soon winning the students' admiration by composing love lyrics and acrostics to order. He sold a dozen poems a week, dictating them to the collegians, who furthered their bard's education by giving him books of poetry, geography, history, and oratory. As

Horton's fame as a poet spread through Chapel Hill in the 1820s, the novelist Caroline Lee Hentz transcribed his verses for his first volume, *The Hope of Liberty, Containing a Number of Poetical Pieces* (1829). In the next few years many notables, including Hentz, the university president, and the governor of North Carolina, launched several campaigns to purchase Horton's freedom, but all appeals failed. Earning over three dollars a week in the early 1830s from sales of his love lyrics, Horton arranged to hire his time from his master to become a full-time poet, handyman, hotel waiter, and servant to the university students and staff. He married a slave of Franklin Snipes and fathered two children.

For over thirty years until emancipation, Horton was a daily fixture at the university, prodigiously writing poetry, seeking publication, and futilely appealing for his freedom. His poems appeared in antislavery periodicals as well as in a second collection, *The Poetical Works* (1845); in 1859 at Chapel Hill, he delivered an oration, "The Stream of Liberty and Science." When Union troops occupied Raleigh in April 1865, Horton found a patron in William H. S. Banks, a young captain with whom he traveled in North Carolina, composing dozens of new poems that commemorated northern and southern leaders, events of camp life, dying and homesick soldiers, as well as a substantial batch of verses on love, slavery, religion, and the art of poetry. Banks selected ninety of these poems (plus forty-four from *Poetical Works*) for Horton's third and final volume, *Naked Genius* (1865). In 1866, Horton traveled to Philadelphia, where he probably resided for the seventeen years until his death.

Horton's three collections contain over 150 poems, many of which show remarkable skill with meter and rhyme, firm control over content, sensitivity to language, and a tender, though sometimes cynical, appreciation of what life, and thus poetry, is all about. Horton's verse before 1865 is his best, enlivened by a joyous sense of life that originates in his enthusiasm for nature and for his muse. Although many made-to-order acrostics and love verses are formulaic, a few like "Lines to My——and "Early Affection" share merits of rhythmic repetition, melodious phrasing, and elegantly simple language. Several neatly crafted religious verses, including "The Gad-Fly," "On the Truth of the Savior," and "Pride in Heaven" reveal Horton's undogmatic, humanistic piety, often combined with love of poetry and nature, as in "Praise of Creation." He excels in evoking rural sights and sounds of the seasons, as in "On Summer": "The bee begins her ceaseless hum." The scene swells with noisy birds and insects, "sportive children," overheated farm animals, and bountiful fruit trees and fields. Horton also wrote a few deeply felt antislavery poems, such as "Liberty and Slavery." Other uniquely personalized appeals for manumission include "The Slave's Complaint" and "On Hearing of the Intention of a Gentleman to Purchase the Poet's Freedom," where the poet identifies his physical liberty with the creation of poetry. Outstanding, too, are four earthy folk verses (1845), lively with colloquial detail and wry humor, such as "Troubled with the Itch and Rubbing with Sulphur." Most of Horton's verse after *Hope of Liberty* has more historical than aesthetic value; nevertheless, his lifelong struggles for literacy, freedom, and the art of poetry make his achievements as "Poet Horton" extraordinary.

• George Moses Horton, "Life," in *Poetical Works,* 1829, pp. iii–xx. Collier Cobb, "An American Man of Letters," *The University [of North Carolina] Magazine,* n.s., 27 (Oct. 1909): 3–10. Richard Walser, *The Black Poet,* 1966. Merle A. Richmond, *Bid the Vassal Soar: Interpretive Essays on the Life and Poetry of Phillis Wheatley and George Moses Horton,* 1974, pp. 81–209. Joan R. Sherman, *Invisible Poets: Afro-Americans of the Nineteenth Century*, 2d ed., 1989. Joan R. Sherman, ed., *The Black Bard of North Carolina,* 1997.

—Joan R. Sherman

House behind the Cedars, The. This powerful exploration of passing is both Charles Waddell *Chesnutt's first novel and the first African American novel published by a major American press. Originally titled "Rena Walden," Chesnutt's text went through more than a decade of revision before appearing serially in *Self-Culture Magazine,* beginning in August 1900, then in book form, from Houghton Mifflin, in October of that year. Despite modest sales, *The House behind the Cedars* gained the widest readership of any African American novel up to 1900. From 1921 to 1922, after falling out of print, it was reserialized in the *Chicago Defender.*

The novel tells the story of John and *Rena Walden, the mixed-blood children of a white Southerner and his antebellum mulatto mistress. John—who has passed successfully for ten years—returns home to coax Rena into the white world. Eager to experience the social and economic opportunities denied African Americans after the war, Rena follows John to South Carolina, where (as the strikingly beautiful "Rowena Warwick") she quickly wins the affection of aristocrat George Tryon. Convincing herself that Tryon cares nothing for her past, and anxious to protect her brother's position, Rena decides not to reveal her secret. But to little avail: Tryon accidentally discovers Rena's "true" identity and repudiates her; Rena collapses in shock and takes seriously ill. Deciding during her convalescence to devote herself to African American uplift, Rena accepts a position as a rural schoolteacher, only to find herself besieged by both a mulatto school official and her former fiancé. One night as Rena walks home she finds each man stalking her. Fleeing in terror, she is soon lost in the woods, where she is later found unconscious. Upon waking she becomes delirious; within days she is dead.

Though in certain ways similar to conventional "tragic mulatto" fiction—particularly in its staging of Rena's demise—Chesnutt's novel refuses to portray either sibling as a stereotypically degenerate, self-loathing mulatto. Nor does it criticize their decisions to pass; indeed, Chesnutt's sympathetic depiction of the factors that compel the Waldens across the color line breaks new ground. Certainly John is an original figure: an African American who not only considered his passing justifiable but who married a white Southerner. Early reviewers, focusing on Rena's tale, generally admired the novel's restraint, although some were uncomfortable with its seeming approval of miscegenation, and still others interpreted its stock ending as evidence that Chesnutt favored segregation. Later critics, while often faulting the novel's sentimentality and plot contrivances, have praised Chesnutt's indictment of racial barriers. By showing Tryon's tragically belated determination to love Rena regardless of her race, moreover, Chesnutt demonstrates the pain that racism causes both African Americans and whites.

One character whose representation has divided recent critics is Frank Fowler, the dark-skinned neighbor who loves Rena from a distance. While some have seen Frank's subservient devotions as a nod to more conventional fictions, others have read his complacent acceptance of inferiority as a sign of Chesnutt's inability to escape what may have been his own color prejudices.

• William L. Andrews, *The Literary Career of Charles W. Chesnutt,* 1980. Dickson D. Bruce, Jr., *Black American Writing from the Nadir: The Evolution of a Literary Tradition, 1877–1915,* 1989.

—William A. Gleason

HUGHES, LANGSTON (1902–1967), poet, novelist, essayist, playwright, autobiographer, and writer of children's books. Born in 1902 in Joplin, Missouri, Langston Hughes grew up mainly in Lawrence, Kansas, but also lived in Illinois, Ohio, and Mexico.

By the time Hughes enrolled at Columbia University in New York, he had already launched his literary career with his poem "The *Negro Speaks of Rivers" in the *Crisis,* edited by W. E. B. *Du Bois. He had also committed himself both to writing and to writing mainly about African Americans.

Hughes's sense of dedication was instilled in him most of all by his maternal grandmother, Mary Langston, whose first husband had died at Harpers Ferry as a member of John *Brown's band, and whose second husband (Hughes's grandfather) had also been a militant abolitionist. Another important family figure was John Mercer Langston, a brother of Hughes's grandfather who was one of the best-known black Americans of the nineteenth century. At the same time, Hughes struggled with a sense of desolation fostered by parental neglect. He himself recalled being driven early by his loneliness "to books, and the wonderful world in books."

Leaving Columbia in 1922, Hughes spent the next three years in a succession of menial jobs. But he also traveled abroad. He worked on a freighter down the west coast of Africa and lived for several months in Paris before returning to the United States late in 1924. By this time, he was well known in African American literary circles as a gifted young poet.

His major early influences were Walt Whitman and Carl Sandburg, as well as the black poets Paul Laurence *Dunbar, a master of both dialect and standard verse, and Claude *McKay, a radical socialist who also wrote accomplished lyric poetry. However, Sandburg, who Hughes later called "my guiding star," was decisive in leading him toward free verse and a radically democratic modernist aesthetic.

His devotion to black music led him to novel fusions of jazz and blues with traditional verse in his first two books, *The *Weary Blues* (1926) and *Fine Clothes to the Jew* (1927). His emphasis on lower-class black life, especially in the latter, led to harsh attacks on him in the black press. With these books, however, he established himself as a major force of the Harlem Renaissance. In 1926, in the *Nation,* he provided the movement with a manifesto when he skillfully argued the need for both race pride and artistic independence in his most memorable essay, "The Negro Artist and the Racial Mountain."

By this time, Hughes had enrolled at the historically black Lincoln University in Pennsylvania, from which he would graduate in 1929. In 1927 he began one of the most important relationships of his life, with his patron Mrs. Charlotte Mason, or "Godmother," who generously supported him for two years. She supervised the writing of his first novel, *Not Without Laughter* (1930), about a sensitive, black midwestern boy and his struggling family. However, their relationship collapsed about the time the novel appeared, and Hughes sank into a period of intense personal unhappiness and disillusionment.

One result was his firm turn to the far left in politics. During a year (1932–1933) spent in the Soviet Union, he wrote his most radical verse. A year in Carmel, California, led to a collection of short stories, *The Ways of White Folks* (1934). This volume is marked by pessimism about race relations, as well as a sardonic realism.

After his play *Mulatto,* on the twinned themes of miscegenation and parental rejection, opened on Broadway in 1935, Hughes wrote other plays, including comedies such as *Little Ham* (1936) and a historical drama, *Emperor of Haiti* (1936). Most of these plays were only moderate successes. In 1937 he spent several months in Europe, including a long stay in besieged Madrid. In 1938 he returned home to found the Harlem Suitcase Theater, which staged his agitprop drama *Don't You Want to Be Free?* The play, employing several of his poems, vigorously blended black nationalism, the blues, and socialist exhortation. The same year, a socialist organization published a pamphlet of his radical verse, "A New Song."

With World War II, Hughes moved more to the center politically. His first volume of autobiography, *The *Big Sea* (1940), written in an episodic, lightly comic manner, made virtually no mention of his leftist sympathies. In his book of verse *Shakespeare in Harlem* (1942) he once again sang the blues. On the other hand, this collection, as well as another, his *Jim Crow's Last Stand* (1943), strongly attacked racial segregation.

Perhaps his finest literary achievement during the war came in the course of writing a weekly column in the *Chicago Defender* that began in 1942 and lasted twenty years. The highlight of the column was an offbeat Harlem character called Jesse B. Semple, or *Simple, and his exchanges with a staid narrator in a neighborhood bar, where Simple commented on a variety of matters but mainly about race and racism. Simple became Hughes's most celebrated and beloved fictional creation, and the subject of five collections edited by Hughes, starting in 1950 with *Simple Speaks His Mind.*

After the war, two books of verse, *Fields of Wonder* (1947) and *One-Way Ticket* (1949), added little to his fame. However, in **Montage of a Dream Deferred* (1951) he broke new ground with verse accented by the discordant nature of the new bebop jazz that reflected a growing desperation in the black urban communities of the North. At the same time, Hughes's career was vexed by constant harassment by right-wing forces about his ties to the Left. In vain he protested that he had never been a Communist and had severed all such links. In 1953 he suffered a public humiliation at the hands of Senator Joseph McCarthy, who forced him to appear in Washington, D.C., and testify officially about his politics. Hughes denied that he had ever been a party member but conceded that some of his radical verse had been ill-advised.

Hughes's career hardly suffered from this episode. Within a short time McCarthy himself was discredited and Hughes was free to write at length about his year in the Soviet Union in *I Wonder as I Wander* (1956), his much-admired second volume of autobiography. He became prosperous, although he always had to work hard for his measure of prosperity and sometimes called himself, with good cause, a "literary sharecropper."

In the 1950s he constantly looked to the musical stage for success, as he sought to repeat his major coup of the 1940s, when Kurt Weill and Elmer Rice had chosen him as the lyricist for their *Street Scene* (1947). This production was hailed as a breakthrough in the development of American opera; for Hughes, the apparently endless cycle of poverty into which he had been locked came to an end. He bought a home in Harlem.

The Simple books inspired a musical show, *Simply Heavenly* (1957), that met with some success. However, Hughes's *Tambourines to Glory* (1963), a gospel musical play satirizing corruption in a black storefront church, failed badly, with some critics accusing him of creating caricatures of black life. Nevertheless, his love of gospel music led to other acclaimed stage efforts, usually mixing words, music, and dance in an atmosphere of improvisation. Notable here were the Christmas show *Black Nativity* (1961) and, inspired by the civil rights movement, *Jericho–Jim Crow* (1964).

For Hughes, writing for children was important. Starting with the successful **Popo and Fifina* (1932), a tale set in Haiti and written with Arna *Bontemps, he eventually published a dozen children's books, on subjects such as jazz, Africa, and the West Indies. Proud of his versatility, he also wrote a commissioned history of the NAACP and the text of a much praised pictorial history of black America. His text in *The Sweet Flypaper of Life* (1955), where he explicated photographs of Harlem by Roy DeCarava,was judged masterful by reviewers, and confirmed Hughes's reputation for an unrivaled command of the nuances of black urban culture.

The 1960s saw Hughes as productive as ever. In 1962 his ambitious booklength poem *Ask Your Mama,* dense with allusions to black culture and music, appeared. However, the reviews were dismissive. Hughes's work was not as universally acclaimed as before in the black community. Although he was hailed in 1966 as a historic artistic figure at the First World Festival of Negro Arts in Dakar, Senegal, he also found himself increasingly rejected by young black militants at home as the civil rights movement lurched toward Black Power. His last book was the volume of verse, posthumously published, *The Panther and the Lash* (1967), mainly about civil rights. He died in May that year in New York City.

In many ways Hughes always remained loyal to the principles he had laid down for the younger black writers in 1926. His art was firmly rooted in race pride and race feeling even as he cherished his freedom as an artist. He was both nationalist and cosmopolitan. As a radical democrat, he believed that art should be accessible to as many people as possible. He could sometimes be bitter, but his art is generally suffused by a keen sense of the ideal and by a profound love of humanity, especially black Americans. He was perhaps the most original of African American poets and, in the breadth and variety of his work, assuredly the most representative of African American writers.

[*See also* Hurston, Zora Neale; Madam Alberta K. Johnson; Mule Bone.]

• Arnold Rampersad, *The Life of Langston Hughes,* 2 vols., 1986–1988. Langston Hughes, *Collected Poems,* 1994.

—Arnold Rampersad

HUNTER, KRISTIN (b. 1931), novelist, short story writer, and journalist. Kristin Hunter was born on 12 September 1931 to George Lorenzo and Mabel Eggleston, two schoolteachers, who planned for their only child to pursue a teaching career. However, she wanted to be a writer. After completing the BS in education from the University of Pennsylvania in 1951, Hunter taught third grade for less than a year before resigning to pursue a writing career. Currently, she lectures in the English department at the University of Pennsylvania.

Before Hunter defined herself as a novelist, she commanded notice as a screenwriter and playwright. In 1955 Hunter won first place in a national contest sponsored by CBS for her television documentary, "Minority of One," about the integration of an all-black Catholic school in Camden, New Jersey. In 1965 her play *The Double Edge* was produced in Philadelphia.

Hunter's first novel, *God Bless the Child,* published in 1964, won the Philadelphia Athenaeum Award. The novel recalls the tragic story of Rosie Fleming, an ambitious young woman who struggles to climb the ladder of success and to redeem what she believes is her inferior dark skin by rescuing her octoroon grandmother and her light brown mother from ghetto life. Rosie's invincible spirit cannot overcome the exploitation of those who capitalize on the dreams of young black women. She literally works herself to death to achieve false symbols of success.

The Landlord, published in 1966, continued Hunter's exploration of ghetto life. Whereas *God Bless the Child* is a tragedy, *The Landlord* is a comic novel of social optimism. The story is about the neurotic Elgar Enders, a wealthy white man who purchases an apartment building in a black ghetto and subsequently attempts to reform the tenants. His success is at best modest. What is more important is the effect on him of the tenants, who form a surrogate family for the emotionally vulnerable Enders. The novel's critics were put off by such idealism. Indeed, as Sondra O'Neale explains (*DLB,* vol. 33, 1984), the 1970 United Artists movie version of the novel repudiated the novel's social optimism for a more jaded version of ghetto realism. The movie transformed Enders into a ruthless individualist.

In the late 1960s Hunter turned to a younger audience. She published *Boss Cat* in 1971 for juvenile readers and a series of novels for young adults: *The Soul Brothers and Sister Lou* (1968); *The Pool Table War* and *Uncle Daniel and the Racoon* (both 1972); and *Lou in the Limelight* (1981). *Guests in the Promised Land,* a collection of short stories for young adults, appeared in 1973. *Guests* earned her the 1973 Chicago Tribune Book World Prize for juvenile literature. These works define urban black communities as sites for possible success rather than as containers for social dysfunction. For example, Louetta (Lou) Hawkins in the "Lou" series sings herself out of the ghetto. Hunter's young audience appreciated the spirited optimism of *Soul Brothers and Sister Lou* and made it Hunter's most popular book. It sold over a million copies and won the Children's Prize of the Council on Interracial Books in 1968.

Hunter's novels for adults also draw upon her resolute social optimism. *The Survivors* (1975) and Lakestown Rebellion (1978) feature protagonists who are mature black women. Each speaks her mind, demands respect, and insists that black people be responsible for their own fates. Lena Rich of *The Survivors* is a middle-aged dressmaker who abandons a life of hard-won self-sufficiency to become the surrogate mother of B.J., a thirteen-year-old streetwise boy. *Lakestown Rebellion's* Bella Lakes's rejection of her husband Abe's desire to make her into "a mock-up of some painted white doll" incites the novel's political rebellion. She insists that the residents of the small black town of Lakestown reassert their pride in their black identities and resist the plans of the corrupt representatives of the state planning commission to build a highway that will destroy the town.

Throughout her career and long before the majority of contemporary readers had been conditioned to appreciate black women writers or their black female protagonists, Hunter wrote about black women who rely on their own convictions and fortitude to survive and sometimes prosper. Her novels depend on the comic conventions of satire, parody, caricature, and somewhat implausible plots to depict optimistic portraits of inner-city black people. Because these works reject the pathology generally associated with inner-city black people (see Hunter's article on stereotypes in movies and on television, "Why Buckwheat Was Shot," *MELUS,* Fall 1984) and because juvenile fiction preserves this viewpoint to its advantage more so than adult fiction, Hunter is better known and more applauded as an author of children's and young adult literature.

• Claudia Tate, *Black Women Writers at Work,* 1983. Sondra O'Neale, "Kristin Hunter," in *DLB,* vol. 33, *Afro-American Fiction Writers after 1955,* eds. Thadious M. Davis and Trudier Harris, 1984, pp. 119–124. Rennie Simson, "Kristin Hunter," in *Contemporary African American Novelists,* ed. Emmanuel S. Nelson, 1999, pp. 211–214.

—Claudia Tate

HURSTON, ZORA NEALE (1891–1960), novelist, anthropologist, folklorist, and genius of the South. In February 1927, Zora Neale Hurston left New York City aboard a southbound train. Her destination was Eatonville, Florida, her hometown, where she began collecting folktales, spirituals, sermons, work songs, blues, and children's games. To Hurston this frequently disparaged folklore was priceless; it constituted the "arts of the people before they find out that there is any such thing as art." At a time when the Great Migration, the movement that brought blacks by the hundreds of thousands from the rural South to the urban North, seemed a sign of racial progress, as did the poetry and fiction of the burgeoning Harlem Renaissance, Hurston moved against the tide. Crisscrossing Florida, Alabama, and Louisiana, Hurston spent the next six years documenting the art of "the Negro farthest down," who, she contended, had made the greatest contribution to American culture.

Her years in the field culminated with the 1935 publication of *Mules and Men,* the first volume of black American folklore published by an African American. A self-styled "literary anthropologist," Hurston blurs the boundaries of literature and ethnography in her writing. She employed fictional techniques to shape the narrative of *Mules and Men.* Her theories about language and culture, which she summarized in a 1934 article, "Characteristics of Negro Expression," inspired the technical innovations of her fiction. Her effort was not merely to interpolate folk sayings in her novels; it was to write fiction according to the aesthetic principles that undergirded oral culture. Consequently, Hurston strove to re-create the sense of drama and "will to adorn" she admired in the oral culture and to create a literary language informed by the poetry as well as the perspective of rural black Southerners.

This she did in four novels: **Jonah's Gourd Vine* (1934), **Their Eyes Were Watching God* (1937), *Moses, Man of the Mountain* (1939), and *Seraph on the Suwanee* (1948); a second volume of ethnography based on field work in Jamaica and Haiti, *Tell My Horse* (1938); a memoir, **Dust Tracks on a Road* (1942); and more than fifty published short stories, essays, and plays. No black woman writer had been as prolific. But unstinting devotion to her artistic vision and iconoclastic political views exacted a price. Despite the excellent quality of her writing, none of Hurston's books were in print when she died on 28 January 1960.

Even without her frequent embellishments, Hurston's life was as dramatic as any story she wrote. Born 7 January 1891 in Notasulga, Alabama, a small hamlet near Tuskegee, Zora was the fifth of eight children of John and Lucy Ann Potts Hurston. The family resettled in Eatonville, the first incorporated black community in America, where John served three terms as mayor. Lucy, a former country schoolteacher, encouraged her children to "jump at de sun." A bright pupil, Zora loved fanciful play and the "lies" (stories) adults told on the porch of Joe Clarke's store. But the idyll of her childhood ended with Lucy's death in 1904. Sent to school in Jacksonville, no longer "Eatonville's Zora," she "became a little colored girl."

During the next few years Hurston did domestic work as she lived with relatives in neighboring Sanford and in Memphis; she then joined a Gilbert and Sullivan troupe as a lady's maid. Leaving the troupe in Baltimore, she enrolled in the high school division of what is now Morgan State University in September 1917. The following fall she registered at Howard University in Washington, D.C. Working as a waitress and manicurist, she attended Howard intermittently from 1918 to 1924. An English major, Hurston joined the campus literary club; her first published story, "John Redding Goes to Sea," evoked her memories of Eatonville. Off campus, Hurston attended poet Georgia Douglas *Johnson's literary salon. Two of her poems appeared in *Negro World,* the official newspaper of Marcus *Garvey's Universal Negro Improvement Association. After *Opportunity* published the story "Drenched in Light" in December 1924, Hurston decided to ply her luck in New York.

Her luck held. Alain *Locke selected her short story "Spunk" for the landmark anthology *The New Negro* (1925). Attending the *Opportunity* awards dinner in May 1925, she took two second-place prizes and met poets Langston *Hughes and Countee *Cullen and novelists Fannie Hurst, Annie Nathan Meyer, and Carl Van Vechten. Hurst employed her as secretary, then chauffeur, and Meyer secured her a scholarship to Barnard College in September 1926. Hurston was thirty-five years old; everyone she met in New York believed she was at least ten years younger. The only black student at Barnard, Hurston studied anthropology with Franz Boas, who pioneered the discipline in the United States. Although she continued to write, and joined Hughes and other young artists to plan the first and only issue of *Fire!!,* Hurston determined to pursue a career as a social scientist. With Boas's assistance, she obtained a research fellowship from the Association for the Study of Negro Life and History (ASNLH) and made her journey South.

Her introduction to *Mules and Men* proclaims: "I was glad when somebody told me, 'You may go and collect Negro folklore.'" But gaining the wherewithal to pursue the mission was complicated. Hurston needed more consistent funding than the ASNLH could provide. She needed a patron. Charlotte (Mrs. R. Osgood) Mason had bloodlines and bank accounts traceable to the founding of the Republic. Indians of the Southwest had been Mason's enthusiasm before Harlem's black artists caught her fancy. In December 1927 she contracted Hurston to compile and collect the "music, poetry, folk-lore, literature, hoodoo, conjure, manifestations of art and kindred subjects relating to and existing among the North American Negroes." If the list reflected Hurston's sensibility, the clause asserting that the material collected would belong to Mason was alien both to Hurston's assertive spirit and her understanding that folklore cannot be owned. Yet, in return for a two-hundred-dollar monthly stipend, Hurston agreed not to share the fruits of her research without Mason's permission.

Hurston signed on in lumber camps in Florida, apprenticed herself to hoodoo doctors in New Orleans, and learned Bahamian dances on a research trip to Nassau. Gaining people's confidence could be difficult. In one turpentine camp the workers thought she was a government agent until she alleviated their suspicions by pretending she was a bootlegger's girlfriend on the lam. To learn work songs, she had to sing them. To understand hoodoo curses and cures, she had to undergo harrowing initiation rituals, which she described in

Mules and Men. Hurston's dedication contributed to the failure of a short-lived marriage to Herbert Sheen, a physician and Howard classmate, in 1927.

After compiling the lore, Hurston's challenge was to find an appropriate mode for its presentation. Although she wrote scholarly articles, notably the hundred-page "Hoodoo in America," published in the *Journal of American Folklore* in 1931, she believed black folklore was too vital to collect dust on library shelves. Instead she was convinced the lore could form the basis for "the real Negro theatre." **Mule Bone*, written in collaboration with Hughes, is the best known of her theatrical ventures, but it was never performed in their lifetimes. More successful were the folklore concerts Hurston produced, beginning in 1932, after she left Mason's payroll. Dramatizations of a day in a railroad camp, the concerts presented work songs, folktales, and other expressions in context, as part of a lived culture. The concerts helped Hurston devise a format for *Mules and Men*. By placing folklore texts in context and demonstrating the process of their creation, Hurston anticipated what is now common practice among ethnographers. She was years ahead of her time.

Some of Hurston's field work saw print first in *Jonah's Gourd Vine*. Based in part on her parents' lives, the novel told the story of a preacher-poet, who defines himself through his art; its centerpiece is a sermon Hurston transcribed from her field notes. Her research had revealed how women were denied access to the pulpit and the store porch, the privileged site of storytelling, and consequently denied the commensurate possibility of self-definition. Throughout her writing, she revised and adapted vernacular forms to give voice to women.

In Hurston's finest novel, *Their Eyes Were Watching God*, the protagonist *Janie Crawford must reject the racist and sexist definitions society would impose on her. As her knowledge of her culture deepens, she gains the wisdom and strength to claim her voice and her self. Many vibrant voices speak through the novel; some seek to silence Janie, while others inspire her. Hurston writes the oral culture brilliantly. "Words walking without masters" is an apt metaphor for both the novel's folk speech and its singular prose.

Their Eyes was written while Hurston was in Haiti conducting ethnographic research on a Guggenheim Fellowship. The account of her field work, *Tell My Horse* (1938), is notable for its investigation of African survivals, such as "The Nine Night" in Jamaica and vodun rituals in Haiti. Songs appended to the volume were perhaps the first published transcriptions of Haitian Creole.

When she returned to the United States, Hurston worked for the Works Progress Administration (WPA), drafting sections on folklore for a proposed volume on "The Florida Negro." In time stolen from the job, she wrote the novel *Moses, Man of the Mountain* (1939). Here she explored the myth of *Moses, as recorded in the Bible and in the oral traditions of Africa, and as appropriated by American slaves. Although written in a comic mode, *Moses* was an allegorical history of black Americans and a serious meditation on liberation and leadership. As Hurston realized, her reach in *Moses* exceeded her grasp. In another disappointment, her 1939 marriage to Albert Price, a twenty-three-year-old WPA employee, lasted only months.

Hurston had been a highly productive writer—*Dust Tracks* was her sixth book in eight years—but the quantity and quality of her work began to wane. Although her byline appeared frequently in the 1940s in such mainstream journals as *American Mercury* and the *Saturday Evening Post*, few pieces captured the verve and flair of her earlier writing. When she essayed political analysis, she wrapped sophisticated critique in the glove of folk humor. Folk humor was passé after Richard *Wright's searing 1940 novel **Native Son* transformed the black literary landscape. Social realism and political protest were the black writers' mandate. Critics missed the protest implicit in Hurston's art: by rejecting the definitions of themselves the dominant society attempted to impose and by preserving, adapting, and creating their own cultural practices, Hurston asserted, African Americans waged a heroic struggle of resistance.

Her last novel, *Seraph on the Suwanee*, a turgid melodrama of white Floridian life, did little for Hurston's literary reputation. Worse, just as the novel was published, Hurston's personal life was shattered by scandal. She was falsely accused of molesting a ten-year-old boy. Devastated both by the charges and the scurrilous press coverage, Hurston presented her passport as evidence that she was in Honduras on an ethnographic expedition when the alleged crime occurred. The case was dismissed in March 1949.

By 1950 Hurston was working as a maid in Miami. Seeking to recover happier times, she moved to Eau Gallie, Florida, where she had written *Mules and Men*. What she wrote now, a novel fictionalizing the life of entrepreneur Madame C. J. Walker and a biography of Herod the Great, was unpublishable. Hurston's political views grew more reactionary. Long a critic of civil rights organizations, she concluded that their struggle for integration was predicated on a belief in black inferiority. She wrote the editor of the Orlando *Sentinel* condemning the 1954 Supreme Court decision in *Brown v. Board of Education*, which declared segregation unconstitutional. The sensation the letter caused marked Hurston's last public notice. Forgotten and penniless, she died in a Fort Pierce, Florida, welfare home.

Hurston's rediscovery is among the most dramatic chapters in African American literary history. It was inspired first by writers and critics such as Alice *Walker, who went "in search of our mothers' gardens." For many black women writers, Hurston is a foremother. Critics investigating the impact of oral forms on African American literature find a theoretical foundation as well as a wealth of material in Hurston's writings. Readers respond to the laugh-out-loud humor, the poetry, and the pleasure of her texts.

[*See also* Nanny.]

• Robert Hemenway, *Zora Neale Hurston: A Literary Biography,* 1977. Alice Walker, ed., *I Love Myself: A Zora Neale Hurston Reader,* 1979. Karla F. C. Holloway, *The Character of the Word: The Texts of Zora Neale Hurston,* 1987. Mary Helen Washington, *Invented Lives: Narratives of Black Women 1860–1960,* 1987. Michael Awkward, ed., *New Essays on Their Eyes Were Watching God,* 1990. Henry Louis Gates, Jr., and Anthony Appiah, eds., *Zora Neale Hurston: Critical Perspectives Past and Present,* 1993. John Lowe, *Jump at the Sun: Zora Neale Hurston's Cosmic Comedy,* 1994. Cheryl A. Wall, *Women of the Harlem Renaissance,* 1995.

—Cheryl A. Wall

I

ICEBERG SLIM (1918–1992), novelist, autobiographer, essayist, and most prominent author of the street genre, which emerged in the 1960s. Born in Chicago, Iceberg Slim (the street and later pen name of Robert Beck) spent the happiest years of his childhood in Rockford, Illinois, where he lived between 1924 and 1928 with his mother and stepfather. Abandoned by her husband, Slim's mother had supported her infant son in a variety of jobs, including door-to-door hairdressing. Slim's stepfather, a kind and loving man, lifted his new family to economic security until Slim's mother left him for a violent gambler. For the three and a half years that they lived together, Slim hated the new man in his mother's life and resented her betrayal of his stepfather. In his book of essays and vignettes, *The Naked Soul of Iceberg Slim* (1971), he asserts his belief that the drive to become a pimp derives from a disturbed mother-son relationship: "I am convinced that most pimps require the secretly buried fuel of Mother hatred to stoke their fiery vendetta of cruelty and merciless exploitation against whores primarily and ultimately all women." The name Iceberg Slim reflects his ability to be emotionally frigid and physically brutal to the women who worked as prostitutes for him.

Although Slim's adolescence was strongly influenced by his involvement with street hustlers, his superior intelligence allowed him to graduate from high school at fifteen and to win an alumni scholarship to Tuskegee Institute. Interestingly, he attended Tuskegee in the mid-1930s, the same time that Ralph *Ellison studied there, although they were not acquainted. After two years at college Slim was expelled for selling bootleg whiskey to other students. Back in Chicago by the time he was seventeen, he began his career by convincing his girlfriend to prostitute herself. The twenty-five years that followed were spent either pimping, taking drugs, or serving time in jail.

After his return to straight life, Iceberg Slim married, fathered four children, and began writing the books that assured his reputation as the most-read practitioner of the African American street novel. Between 1967 and 1977, Slim authored seven books including his autobiography, *Pimp: The Story of My Life* (1967). One novel, *Trick Baby* (1967), chronicles the adventures of a light-skinned African American who chooses not to pass. This story was subsequently made into a movie and released by Universal Studios. Of all his fiction, *Mama Black Widow* (1969), a sensitive portrayal of a tortured, cross-dressing, gay male, is considered his most masterful book. Slim's works are marked by their deep criticism of the American justice system, devotion to the politics of the Black Panthers, very frank language, and a combination of violence and sexuality. These books as well as *Airtight Willie and Me* (1979), *The Long White Con* (1977), and *Death Wish* (1976) have gained popularity on college campuses. Between 1985 and 1995, his books were translated into both German and French. The works of Iceberg Slim have their greatest readership in prisons, where they are admired for their recognition of the plight of the criminal.

• Paul Carter Harrison, *The Drama of Nommo,* 1972, p. 164. William Henry Robinson, comp., *Nommo: An Anthology of Modern Black African and Black American Literature,* 1972, p. 475. D. B. Graham, "'Negative Glamour': The Pimp Hero in the Fiction of Iceberg Slim," *Obsidian* 1.2 (1975): 5–17.

—Terri Hume Oliver

If He Hollers Let Him Go (1945) is Chester *Himes's first published novel. Set in Los Angeles during World War II, the novel is narrated in the first person by its African American protagonist, Bob Jones. Himes based details of his novel on his own experiences working in shipyards in both Oakland and Los Angeles in the 1940s. Written in a style many critics find similar to 1930s and 1940s American hard-boiled or tough-guy fiction, the book chronicles five working days in Bob's life, framed by a vision of urban Los Angeles. Other critics see the novel as more closely aligned with a tradition of protest novels, and notably, as being a literary descendant of Richard *Wright's **Native Son* (1940) and Ann *Petry's *The *Street* (1946).

Bob Jones is an intellectual who continually reflects on the ways his options and his actions are circumscribed by the overall systemic violence of American racism. The reader also sees a graphic picture of 1940s Los Angeles, a city fraught with racial conflict as a result of the large influx of white Southerners and African American workers coming to labor in the defense industries. Though Bob is a leadman in the Atlas Shipyard, supervising a crew of African American workers, his actual authority is ineffective since white leadmen refuse to assist him by loaning their white workers to him for job projects.

One such white worker is Madge Perkins. After Madge calls Bob a nigger he returns the insult and is immediately demoted, while she goes unpunished. Through Bob's interactions with and thoughts about Madge, the novel exposes the complex intersections of race and sexual attraction as Bob at once despises and desires Madge.

When Bob accidentally encounters Madge in a small deserted bunkroom, his impulse is to flee, but he hesitates a bit too long. Madge locks the door and screams "rape," thereby inciting the furor of the white workers. Bob escapes lynching but is sentenced by a judge to enlist in the armed forces. Himes points out the irony in U.S. soldiers, many of them African American, being sent abroad to fight fascism in Europe while racial oppression flourishes at home.

Counterposed to Madge's uncouth nature is Bob's girlfriend, Alice Harrison, a social worker and the daughter of one of the wealthiest African American men in Los Angeles. She has no sympathy for Bob's feelings of racial oppression and encourages Bob to stop struggling against white people and instead carve out an upper-middle-class domestic niche within the bounds of societal discrimination. This type of compromise is precisely what Bob cannot do. Himes's critique of such compromises is visible in his portrayal of Alice's father as corrupt and venal.

Bob Jones is represented as an everyman who desires nothing more and nothing less than equal participation in the democratic ideals he was taught as a boy in school. For Himes, Bob's naive belief in the promise of such ideals creates his angst as an adult living in a racist culture.

• Gilbert H. Muller, *Chester Himes,* 1989. Michel Fabre, Robert E. Skinner, and Lester Sullivan, *Chester Himes: An Annotated Primary and Secondary Bibliography,* 1992.

—Wendy W. Walters

"I Have a Dream." From the steps of the Lincoln Memorial, Martin Luther *King, Jr., delivered "I Have a Dream" to over two hundred thousand people on 28 August 1963. Watching on television, millions heard all or part of King's speech, which served as the climax of the March on Washington, the largest rally of the civil rights movement.

Tepid about racial equality for over two years, President Kennedy proposed major civil rights legislation after King's Birmingham crusade in spring 1963. Many viewed the 1963 March as a rally to support that legislation—an interpretation that several speakers at the March encouraged even though labor leader A. Philip Randolph and activist Bayard Rustin had begun organizing the event in 1962.

When supporters rallied at the Lincoln Memorial, they heard singers and a series of measured and unexceptional addresses by Roy Wilkins, director of the NAACP, Whitney Young, head of the Urban League, Walter Reuther, president of the United Auto Workers, and others. Although the Kennedy administration applied intense pressure to make John Lewis, leader of the Student Nonviolent Coordinating Committee, sound more moderate, he delivered a scorching oration that castigated both major political parties.

Marian *Anderson and Mahalia Jackson appeared separately to revive the wilting crowd with spirituals and set the stage for the last speech of the day.

In seventeen minutes, King called for racial equality by presenting an inventory of religious and nationalistic themes. He opened by sketching an American nightmare. One hundred years after emancipation, he announced, "the Negro is still sadly crippled by the manacles of segregation." Attacking institutionalized racism, he contended that Thomas Jefferson, Abraham *Lincoln, and the American government had failed African Americans by issuing a check for freedom marked "insufficient funds." Melding patriotic and religious authorities, King invoked the Declaration of Independence, the Gettysburg Address, ancient Hebrew prophets, and Christianity to argue that racial injustice was un-American and unacceptable. He championed militant nonviolence—or "soul force"—as the route between moderation and extremism.

King dedicated the second half of "I Have a Dream" to a vision of what America could become: a land of equality and peace. In his climactic "Let Freedom Ring" litany, he projected a future in which Isaiah's vision of exalted valleys, which he cited earlier, is realized in a racially harmonious America. He concluded by reciting the lyrics of "America" ("My country 'tis of thee") that Marian Anderson had sung at the memorial during her celebrated Easter concert in 1939. He borrowed and refined the entire "Let Freedom Ring" peroration from a speech by Archibald Carey, an African American pastor from Chicago.

Throughout "I Have a Dream" King and his listeners engaged in a call-and-response interaction common in African American Baptist churches. (He later stated that he extended "I Have a Dream" because of the warm response of his audience.) His rolling cadences and parallelisms also reflected African American pulpit traditions.

King concluded by prophesying a future in which everyone would sing the spiritual: "Free at last! Free at last! Thank God Almighty, we're free at last!" The crowd roared its approval.

More moderate than King's orations in 1967 and 1968, "I Have a Dream" is the most beloved speech of his career and the most famous American oration of the twentieth century.

• Archibald Carey, "Address to the Republican National Convention," 1952, in *Rhetoric of Revolt,* ed. Roy Hill, 1964, pp. 149–154. Martin Luther King, Jr., "I Have a Dream," 1963, in *A Testament of Hope: The Essential Writings of Martin Luther King, Jr.,* ed. James Washington, 1986, pp. 217–220.

—Keith D. Miller and Emily M. Lewis

I Know Why the Caged Bird Sings. The bestselling first volume of Maya *Angelou's serial autobiography inaugurated a new era of African American women's writing. Published in 1970, *I Know Why the Caged Bird Sings* contains many of the themes that would become central to feminist theory and practice in the 1980s. Taken from the first verse of Paul Laurence *Dunbar's poem "Sympathy," the title articulates the woman writer's empowering recognition of her ability to sing her own song despite the cultural odds against her. "If growing up is painful for the Southern Black girl, being aware of her displacement is the rust on the razor that threatens the throat," Angelou writes. "It is an unnecessary insult."

Set mostly in Stamps, Arkansas, *I Know Why the Caged Bird Sings* traces the events in the lives of Marguerite Johnson and her brother, Bailey, who are raised by their grandmother, Momma Henderson, the owner of a general store, and their crippled Uncle Willie. Angelou paints a vast historical fresco of life in the segregated South and in the cities of St. Louis and San Francisco during the 1930s and early 1940s. Part autobiography, part fictional picaresque narrative, part social history and commentary, this story confers an exemplary quality to the experiences of the narrator whose childhood is spent shuttling back and forth between rural and urban America. She undergoes the loss of innocence characteristic of the protagonist of picaresque tales. In St. Louis, she is raped at the age of eight by her mother's boyfriend, and having denounced him, blames herself for his murder. She loses the ability to speak until her return to Stamps, where a friend, Mrs. Flowers, inspires her to rediscover the beauty of the "human voice." Later she moves to California, and after graduating from high school at the age of seventeen, she gives birth to a son. The book begins and ends with intense physical experiences that teach the narrator that she can trust her body, that it is a source of power and knowledge rather than the liability that her racist and sexist society dictates.

George E. Kent has shown that there are two main areas of African American life that give depth to the narrative. The grandmother represents the religious influence and the gospel tradition, and the mother, "the blues-street" tradition, the fast life. Both elements of the black vernacular inform the development of the story, and show the protagonist's complex relationship to the conflicting yet complementary influences that shape her life story. A third element consists in the vast intertextual network of literary allusions and references that Angelou uses. Her narrator is an avid reader who is as familiar with Shakespeare and Molière, Defoe, Brontë, and Dickens as with Dunbar, Langston *Hughes, and Frederick *Douglass. She situates her storytelling within a specifically literary context, and develops a double-voiced message, directed toward both a white audience and the black community. This strategy is characteristic of the genre of the slave narrative. Angelou builds upon and transforms the major tropes that define the tradition of African American letters, and she does so, as Sidonie A. Smith has argued, with a keen sense of style, as well as a rich use of poetic idioms and idiosyncratic vocabulary.

• Sidonie A. Smith, "The Song of a Caged Bird: Maya Angelou's Quest after Self-Acceptance," *Southern Humanities Review* 7 (Fall 1973): 365–375. George E. Kent, "Maya Angelou's *I Know Why the Caged Bird Sings* and Black Autobiographical Tradition," *Kansas Quarterly* 7 (Summer 1975): 72–78. Françoise Lionnet, "Con Artists and Storytellers: Maya Angelou's Problematic Sense of Audience," in *Autobiographical Voices: Race, Gender, Self-Portraiture,* 1989, pp. 130–166.

—Françoise Lionnet

Imperium in Imperio. Sutton E. *Griggs's first novel, *Imperium in Imperio* (1899), is a visionary work positing the establishment of an underground organization of educated and militant African Americans bent on either an elimination of injustice in America or the establishment of an autonomous state. Functioning in the same manner as the U.S. government, the Imperium's program, however, is revolutionary, not reactionary. Its leaders organize a highly disciplined army, determined to publicize their grievances to the world. Throughout the novel, Griggs warns against demagogues who would sacrifice the African American cause for political gain. The Imperium is in the hands of such a leader, the pampered mulatto, Bernard Belgrade, who enters politics primarily out of personal ambition. Belton Piedmont, on the other hand, modeled upon Booker T. *Washington, rejects Bernard's plot for all-out war both because he recognizes the futility of a military attempt but, also, because he believes some whites are enlightened and wish to help. Belton counters Bernard's declaration of war with a more conservative proposal. Whites need to be educated about the new African American militancy, he asserts. If after four years, however, a positive change has not occurred, Belton urges a radical solution—the Imperium's takeover of Texas and establishment of a separate government prepared to fight off invasions from foreign powers, notably the United States. Bernard immediately declares Belton a traitor to the Imperium and orders his execution. As the book ends, the organization is about to be crushed and Belton to be killed by one of his own ethnic kinsmen in a raw power play for political control. The hope for unity and progress seems, therefore, farther away than ever because of African Americans' own blindness in allowing hatred of whites to dupe them into following a self-serving, untrustworthy leader.

Despite his acute awareness of America's failures, Sutton Griggs condemns both African American and white failure to fulfill the country's professed ideals. He depicts his people's severe economic dilemma as a warning to the nation of the presence of bitterness in a growing number of frustrated, young African Americans whose energy either could explode into a suicidal attack upon the racist system or could be channeled into constructive methods of helping their people. *Imperium in Imperio* is the earliest of Griggs's five political statements in fictional form intended to arouse his readers' awareness of the vastly different directions in which turn-of-the-century African Americans might move.

• Hugh M. Gloster. "The Negro in American Fiction: Sutton E. Griggs, Novelist of the New Negro," *Phylon* 4.4 (1943): 335–345. Addison Gayle, Jr., *The Way of the New World: The Black Novel in America*, 1976.

—Arlene A. Elder

Incidents in the Life of a Slave Girl. Harriet A. *Jacobs's slave narrative *Incidents in the Life of a Slave Girl: Written by Herself* is a first-person account of Jacobs's pseudonymous narrator "Linda Brent." Her story is extremely carefully shaped, and although it changes names and omits dates and places, Jacobs's "Linda" transforms the slave narrative by including not only elements of the male-authored narrative but also elements of the captivity narrative and of domestic fiction. Focusing on the forbidden topic of a woman's sexual history in slavery, Linda presents herself as both a "fallen woman" and as a "heroic mother." In doing so she advances a fundamental critique of the nineteenth-century ideology of true womanhood that fostered all such race and gender stereotypes.

Jacobs's Linda writes that although born a slave in the South, she enjoyed a happy childhood with her family until, when she was six, her mother died. Taken in by her mistress, she was taught to read and sew. In adolescence she was moved into the nearby home of the lecherous Dr. Flint, who subjected her to unrelenting sexual harassment. She reveals her sexual involvement with a white neighbor—which she characterizes as a desperate attempt to avoid Flint—and records the birth of her two children. Explaining that Flint's threat to make them plantation slaves prompted her decision to run away in hopes that the children's father would buy and free them, she describes her seven years hiding in town in the space above her grandmother's storeroom. Finally escaping to the North, she writes that she was reunited with her children and met the abolitionists. She ends her book by reporting that when kidnappers followed her to New York and continued to threaten her and her children, Linda's New York employer bought her freedom.

Harriet Jacobs spelled out the conception, composition, and publication of *Incidents* in letters she wrote to her abolitionist feminist friend, the Quaker Amy Post, between 1853 and 1860. Her first idea was to convince Harriet Beecher *Stowe to become her amanuensis. When this failed, she determined to write her story herself. She began in secret and finished a half-dozen years later. Carrying letters of introduction from Boston abolitionists to their British colleagues, she sailed to England to find a publisher. Unsuccessful, she returned home, where, with the help of the African American activist-writer William C. *Nell, she met the white abolitionist author Lydia Maria Child, who agreed to act as her editor and agent. In 1860 Child began editing the manuscript, arranged for financial support from abolitionists, and signed a contract with a Boston publisher. When the firm went bankrupt, Jacobs brought out the book herself in January 1861. *Incidents* was advertised and reviewed in the African American press and in reform publications in the North and in Britain. In 1862, retitled *The Deeper Wrong: Incidents in the Life of a Slave Girl: Written by Herself*, it was published in London by William Tweedie.

Although Jacobs's name was openly connected with the book from the first, its title page names only Child as editor. Perhaps because of this, throughout much of the twentieth century both the authorship and the genre of *Incidents* were disputed. Since the appearance of the Harvard edition in 1987, however, *Incidents* has been hailed as the most comprehensive antebellum autobiography by an African American woman.

• Hazel Carby, *Reconstructing Womanhood: The Emergence of the Afro-American Woman Novelist*, 1987. Harriet Jacobs, *Incidents in the Life of a Slave Girl*, ed. Jean Fagan Yellin, 1987.

—Jean Fagan Yellin

In New England Winter. In the play *In New England Winter*, the second of Ed *Bullins's *Twentieth Century Cycle*, Cliff Dawson returns from *In the Wine Time*. Here, he is older and more subdued; though still stung by a failed marriage, he seeks to shore up ties with his estranged half-brother Steve, who caused the divorce. It is Steve's character, however, that occupies much of the play's emotional energy; his meticulousness in plotting a robbery that he, Cliff, and two cohorts are about to commit, is entirely directed toward obtaining "traveling money" for a return to New England in winter and for Liz, the woman he had long ago left there.

The play's seven sections are divided more or less evenly between a present of 1960, in which the four men are planning the robbery, and flashbacks to 1955, when Liz, Steve, and their alcoholic friends while away the time in New England. Liz, recovering from a severe breakdown, articulates a daydream about the love that she and Steve share and the children it will produce, but her fears that Steve's AWOL status from the navy may suddenly mean their separation suggest a relapse. Additionally, a drunken misunderstanding that finds Steve sleeping innocently in the arms of Liz's sister Carrie causes Liz's fears to become reality as Oscar, Carrie's angered husband, threatens to kill Steve, and Crook, another drinking partner who has been waiting for an opportunity to steal Liz, betrays Steve to the authorities.

Though Steve manages to escape, his efforts in 1960 to get back to Liz are hampered by an oppressive summer heat, the difficulty of planning the robbery, and the differences between himself and Cliff. Principally at issue is Steve's affair with Cliff's wife Lou and the child they produced while Cliff was in jail for murder; one of the cohorts, Bummie, knew of the liaison. But Cliff's prior knowledge of this is a measure of Cliff's magnanimity unknown to Steve, who kills Bummie before he can be betrayed. The brothers reconcile, and Steve resumes his plan to return to New England, but the audience's poignant understanding is that a confused and frightened Liz, after Steve's departure in 1955, had already succumbed to the charms of the serpentine Crook.

Warren R. True notes that because the play's tension seems to emanate entirely from Steve, Cliff, and the two cohorts, Steve's stabbing of Bummie does not appear to be a logical climax. That the tautness among these four grows steadily throughout the play, however, renders the crisis static and unobtrusive, and in this light the play's structure invites comparison to Chekhovian dramaturgy. Genevieve Fabre, however, finds that the folkloric aspects of Bullins's earlier plays are not in evidence here. The symbolism of snow seems gratuitous, and the simple episodic construction forces the play to depend on Bullins's preceding plays for its vigor. Additionally (and unlike Chekhov), this play, like the rest of Bullins's dramas, depends not on tragedy but rather on melodrama, an element that appears often in African American theater.

• Warren R. True, "Ed Bullins, Anton Chekov, and the 'Drama of Mood,'" *CLA Journal* 20.4 (June 1977): 521–532. Genevieve Fabre, *Drumbeats, Masks and Metaphor,* 1983.

—Nathan L. Grant

In Search of Our Mothers' Gardens (1983) brings together a collection of essays, articles, reviews, and commentaries written by Alice *Walker between 1966 and 1982. The collection defines and expresses a womanist worldview with all of the love, respect, spiritual commitment, and demands for change that the term "womanist" implies. *In Search of Our Mothers' Gardens* offers hope, healing, and wholeness to a world that often forgets that these things are possible. At the same time, the book highlights a historical past that includes many of the pioneers who forged the road of female creative expression and freedom.

The opening essay comments upon the importance of role models. Citing the example of Vincent Van Gogh's suicide, Walker states that the absence of role models can be fatal. For an artist, Walker claims, finding role models is essential to appreciating one's own creative abilities and developing a vision for living. Throughout the book she suggests an array of models—many silent and unheralded (mothers whose gardens or hand-crafted quilts were their art) and many long-standing favorites. Walker discusses with fondness and admiration the works of Flannery O'Conner, Jean *Toomer, Langston *Hughes, and of course, Zora Neale *Hurston. Without a doubt Hurston emerges as "queen bee." In a moving article titled "Looking for Zora," Walker describes her 1973 journey to find and mark the grave of her ancestral mentor. In a second essay, "Zora Neale Hurston: A Cautionary Tale and a Partisan View," she argues the importance of recovering and remembering Hurston as a major American writer, anthropologist, and folklorist.

Walker's major concern in each essay is for wholeness and continuity, not only for African American women but for all people. Because of this concern, the collection of nonfiction is simultaneously inspiring and difficult, even painful, to read. *In Search of Our Mothers' Gardens* discusses several subjects important to positive change in our present society (from nuclear weapons and anti-Semitism to child bearing). Almost every essay, however, is accented with Walker's memories of her life—so much so that the book often reads like a memoir. One of the most powerful of these memories is presented in the final essay, "Beauty: When the Other Dancer Is the Self." In prose that reads like poetry, Walker shares the story of how an accident that disfigured her right eye and left it blind affected both her self-confidence and her inner vision.

In Search of Our Mothers' Gardens speaks to every woman and offers a concept for achieving wisdom, hope, and change called womanism. During the years since the book's publication, womanism has become a way of life for many women (and men). Womanist theories and commentaries appear in many areas of academia and popular culture, including film, education, theology, and literature. Distinguishing between womanism and feminism, however, has often been a subject of debate. In Walker's own words: "Womanist is to feminist as purple to lavender." The intensity and sensitive inclusiveness of the essays in *In Search of Our Mothers' Gardens* exemplify and expand Walker's comparison.

• Alma S. Freeman, "Zora Neale Hurston and Alice Walker: A Spiritual Kinship," *SAGE* 2 (Spring 1985): 37–40. Dorothy G. Grimes, "'Womanist Prose' and the Quest for Community in American Culture," *Journal of American Culture* 15.2 (Summer 1992): 19–24.

—Debra Walker King

In the Mecca. It is perhaps ironic that *In the Mecca* (1968), Gwendolyn *Brooks's first overt attack on Chicago, appeared in the same year that she was appointed poet laureate of Illinois. The Mecca was one of the earliest examples in the United States of a multifamily dwelling for the wealthy. Located a few blocks from Prairie Avenue (the city's original "gold coast"), no luxury was spared in its construction. During the World's Columbian Exposition of 1893 it was a tourist attraction. Enclosed courtways served as entrances to the elaborate apartments of the few elite families who lived in the much-visited Mecca, but in time the neighborhood changed and the Mecca fell into disrepair. Before it was finally torn down, all that remained was an unbelievably squalid tenement where thousands actually lived, and it became a symbol for a failure in urban living patterns. Furthermore, the building was a symbol for much that was wrong in the city.

Linguistically, *In the Mecca* juxtaposes standard English with the vernacular and the language of the streets. This collection of primarily free verse poems is dominated by the long title poem, "In the Mecca," which begins with biblical overtones: "Now the way of the Mecca was on this wise." On one level, the narrative poem is relatively simple. Mrs. Sallie, after a hard day as a domestic worker, comes home and finds one of her children missing. She begins to search for Pepita only to eventually discover that the child has been murdered by a fellow resident. Mrs. Sallie's life is filled with unpleasantness, and her discovery is just one more adversity that she must face.

Mrs. Sallie's search for Pepita is a framework by which Brooks is able to recount the stories of some of the fragmented lives in an overcrowded building in a city that does not particularly care about what happens to the dispossessed. Many of her characters recognize their predicament but are powerless to do little more than lash out at each other. Brooks captures the pervasive misery of the place and implicitly contrasts what is with what was, demonstrating that class and race do make a difference.

Following the title poem are other predominantly free verse selections that appear under the heading "After the Mecca." They include not only the ode to Chicago's famous outdoor Picasso sculpture but also the dedicatory poem to the Wall of Respect, a wall painted with likenesses of role models and heroes of various persuasions. Of special interest in this section is the three-part poem entitled "The Blackstone Rangers" concerning the Blackstone P. Nation, a ghetto gang. The group is so highly organized that simply its name creates terror in those who hear it; yet, this is a gang whose "country is a Nation on no map." In the final analysis, black on black crime is explained as a result of the futility that often accompanies the barrenness of urban life.

• Maria K. Mootry and Gary Smith, eds., *A Life Distilled: Gwendolyn Brooks, Her Poetry and Fiction,* 1987.

—Kenny Jackson Williams

Invisible Man has been an auspicious novel since its publication. During the summer of 1945 while Ralph *Ellison was working on a war novel, he was forcefully drawn to type the first sentence of his now famous novel: "I am an invisible man." He then stopped writing his war novel and began *Invisible Man.* The novel took seven years to complete, and during that period two of its sections were published—the battle royal episode in 1947 in the English magazine *Horizon,* and the prologue in *Partisan Review* shortly before the novel's publication. When the novel came out in 1952, it received mostly positive reviews. However, Communists attacked it as being affected and pretentious, written to please "the white supremacy," and John O. *Killens called it "a vicious distortion of Negro life." Scholars such as Robert Bone and Richard Barksdale later praised the novel as embodying the American ideal. However, Irving Howe, who had earlier praised the work, attacked it so keenly in 1963 that Ellison felt it necessary to defend himself. Howe's argument was that the novel did not reflect the experiences of the Black American as did Richard *Wright's **Native Son* (1940), and Ellison responded by asking that his novel be judged as art: "If it fails, it fails aesthetically, not because I did or did not fight some ideological battle." Addison *Gayle, Jr., in *The Black Aesthetic* (1971) argues that the novel is of the assimilationist tradition and that such a tradition "belongs to the period of the dinosaur and the mastodon."

The novel centers on the activities of the title character, a nameless Black male who in his junior year at a southern Black college is expelled for taking a white trustee, Mr. *Norton, into a squalid settlement near the college. The narrator is an idealist who believes that if he cooperates and acquiesces to the demands of others he could become a race leader like the college's president, Dr. *Bledsoe. As he experiences a series of initiation rites that bring him closer to understanding himself and his environment, he realizes that unless he acts out of his own convictions he will become a voiceless, invisible tool in the hands of others. The first rite occurs just before he enters college, in the battle royal episode, from which he learns little about the real world. The second occurs with his expulsion and going north. Though Bledsoe and a veteran from the Golden Day explain to him that he should not be so gullible, the narrator has to be ritualized into the worlds of work (the factory) and politics (the Brotherhood) before he realizes that he alone is responsible for his self-definition. After his final initiation he realizes that "I was material, a natural resource to be used . . . except now I recognize my invisibility."

Because of its use of symbols and metaphors, its adherence to the folk tradition, and its allusion to jazz and blues idioms, *Invisible Man* transcends what Ellison refers to as the "hard-boiled novel." Ellison maintains that in writing *Invisible Man,* his models were Ernest Hemingway, T. S. Eliot, Fyodor Dostoevsky, Mark Twain, and William Faulkner, and that he did not imitate Richard Wright and other Black authors because they were too "ideological." But whatever Ellison owes to his white literary "ancestors," he owes just as much, if not more, to his Black experiences. When, for example, the narrator hides underground to write his memoirs, Ellison might have had Dostoevsky in mind, but, as many critics have pointed out, he was following the tradition of the slave narrative—that of Frederick *Douglass, Olaudah *Equiano, and Harriet A. *Jacobs. Many of the narrator's dilemmas have their origin in what W. E. B. *Du Bois calls the double consciousness that plagues all African Americans. Ellison admits that he relied heavily on the Black folk tradition in writing the novel.

In a 1955 interview Ellison was asked whether his novel would be remembered in twenty years. He responded:" I doubt it. It's not an important novel. I failed of eloquence and many of the immediate issues are rapidly fading away." Perhaps he was being modest, for *Invisible Man* has maintained its popularity and is now billed as an American classic.

[*See also* Mary Rambo; Ras the Destroyer; Rinehart; Todd Clifton; Trueblood.]

• Ralph Ellison, *Shadow and Act,* 1964. Archie D. Anders, "Odysseus in Black: An Analysis of the Structure of *Invisible Man,*" *College Language Association Journal* 13 (Mar. 1970): 217–228. Ronald Gottesman, ed., *Merrill Studes in* Invisible Man, 1971. Joseph F. Trimmer, ed., *A Casebook on Ralph Ellison's* Invisible Man, 1972. John M. Reilly, ed., *Twentieth Century Interpretations of* Invisible Man: *A Collection of Critical Essays,* 1974. Robert O'Meally, ed., *New Essays on* Invisible Man, 1988.

—Ralph Reckley, Sr.

Iola Leroy, or *Shadows Uplifted* by Frances Ellen Watkins *Harper was first published in 1892. Until recently it was considered the first novel by an African American woman published in the United States. Since the novel appeared in the 1890s, a time when Black women's organizations surfaced throughout the country, it was widely read because it addressed pressing social and political issues affecting the Black American community; in particular, lynching, race consciousness, suffrage, women's rights, and temperance are presented as key themes.

Iola Leroy was published during the latter years of Harper's prolific career as a poet, essayist, and short story and prose author. Her earlier novels, *Minnie's Sacrifice* (1869), *Sowing and Reaping: A Temperance Story* (1876–1887), and *Trial and Triumph* (1888–1889), appeared in serialized form in the *Christian Recorder,* a periodical published by the African Methodist Episcopal Church. Harper's novels were designed for political and religious advocacy, and were especially concerned about racial identity and commitment to social change.

The main character, Iola Leroy, embodies race, gender, and class contradictions in American society when she realizes she is black, is enslaved, and loses her status as a wealthy white woman. But unlike the tragic mulattoes of nineteenth-century literature, Iola does not become a victim. She transcends the oppressive dynamics of historical circumstances. After she is freed from slavery, she becomes a teacher, writer, and activist for the black race and for women's rights.

The setting of the novel begins during the Civil War and extends into Reconstruction. In the broader sense the novel is the slave narrative of Iola, and other slave narratives incorporated as prayer meetings, provide settings for other slaves to voice their perspectives and opinions about their experiences and reality. The war activities of the enslaved and runaways refute the prevailing myth that blacks did not fight for their freedom, and critical debates about Ku Klux Klan lynchings as well as the existence of racial discrimination in the North further demonstrate the dangers and difficulties blacks faced during Reconstruction.

In form, this novel is considerably dependent upon the interplay of dialogue to advance its thematic complexity, a format that is typical of nineteenth-century prose. At the same time, the work further demonstrates Harper's talent for capturing and contextualizing voice. Harper combines the politicized slave narrative with the episodic romanticism of the Victorian utopian novel to produce a unique prose style. Oftentimes Harper intersperses descriptions of historical settings with didactic political commentary, which disrupts the creative flow of the plot. Such commentary characterized proletarian literature of the times and is seen in Harper's earlier poetry and prose. The interjection of political analysis diffuses any tendency on the part of the audience to idealize the characters and draws direct associations between the story and historical circumstances.

The novel is firmly grounded in history. Harper uses the surnames of famous and important black cultural, political, and historical figures for her characters. In particular, the first name of the protagonist is the nom de plume of Ida B. *Wells-Barnett, a well-known black woman radical of the 1890s. The purpose of the novel is multifaceted, and the disruption affected by the author's stylistic techniques accomplishes her objectives. Throughout the novel, the characters confront, engage, and dispel illusions in order to free their minds and to determine and renew a liberated vision.

• Hazel V. Carby, "On the Threshold of Women's Era: Lynching, Empire, and Sexuality in Black Feminist Theory," *Critical Inquiry* 12 (Autumn 1985): 262–277. Melba Joyce Boyd, *Discarded Legacy: Politics and Poetics in the Life of Frances E. W. Harper 1825–1911,* 1994.

—Melba Joyce Boyd

Iron City, a realist novel by Lloyd *Brown, was published in 1951 and reprinted with a critical introduction in 1994. *Iron City* is based on Brown's experiences in Pittsburgh's Allegheny County Jail in 1941. In the novel, Paul Harper, Henry Faulcon, and Isaac L. (Zach) Zachary, three African American communist political prisoners, lead a campaign to free Lonnie James, a framed African American youth on death row. As Alan Wald points out in his critical introduction to the 1994 edition, *Iron City* is possibly the first African American prison novel, and probably the first novel to depict the activities of political prisoners in the United States.

In addition to the fight to save Lonnie James, both the inner world of the characters, and the "outside" world—an ironic term to use when talking of a prison novel—are strikingly portrayed. The action of *Iron City* may be confined to the jail, but through the telling of the life stories and testimonies of the three main characters, the novel is able to move from criticizing the racism and injustice in one American institution to a critique of the American capitalist system as a whole. Through the novel's use of autobiographical, biographical, and historical materials, the novel offers a critique of racist, oppressive capitalist America and offers communism as the answer to the American racial question.

Brown's novel was written in response to the tendency for African American writers of the 1940s and 1950s to create dark and negative portrayals of their people in such works as Richard *Wright's *N*ative Son* (1940). *Iron City* was a conscious attempt to introduce positive working-class African American protagonists into African American literature.

• Alan Wald, foreword to *Iron City*, 1994.

—Karen Ruth Kornweibel.

J

JACKMON, MARVIN E. *See* Marvin X.

JACKSON, ANGELA (b. 1951), poet, dramatist, and fiction writer. Angela Jackson was born in Greenville, Mississippi. Her family moved to Chicago, Illinois, while she was a child. The impact of the two locations is evident in her poetry, which evinces southern and midwestern language influences. While at Northwestern University, Jackson emerged as a poet during the Black Arts movement. One of the talented participants in the writer's workshop of Chicago's Organization of Black American Culture (OBAC), Jackson produces work reflective of the Black Arts movement and OBAC's aesthetic thrust. OBAC was one of the many organizations that successfully promoted art for an African American audience that was representational and functional in form and was a major influence on Jackson's style and philosophy. She entered the writer's workshop in 1970 and participated with founding members Haki R. *Madhubuti (Don L. Lee), Carolyn M. *Rodgers, and Johari *Amini (Jewel Lattimore). In 1976 she succeeded Hoyt *Fuller as coordinator. The organization's and the artists' objectives were production of high-quality literature reflecting the black experience, definition of standards by which such literature was to be judged, and development of black critics qualified to evaluate black literature accordingly while conscious of the dynamics of Western literary standards.

Jackson's creative style is distinctive yet representative of the OBAC school. Her work is not necessarily polemical but states the need for a strong African American community. Jackson has written on various aspects of the African American experience: northern and southern black life, African heritage, cultural connectivity and integration, and the wide-ranging experience of love. *Voodoo/Love Magic* (1974) is a collection of poems that explore family, love as a powerful force, and African American identity. She has written in African American vernacular in a creative and authentic manner, with an emphasis on rhythm and sound, particularly inflection, and metaphor to convey layered meaning. This style was honed in work that followed. *The Greenville Club* (1977), collected in *Four Black Poets,* presented multiple voiced perspectives of black urban community life. *Solo in the Boxcar* (1985) is composed of the voices of residents of an apartment building.

In the late 1970s and the 1980s Jackson turned to fiction, publishing the short stories "Dreamer" (1977) and "Witch Doctor" (1977) and a piece from a novel in progress, *Treemont Stone* (1984). In this period she adapted her poetry for the stage in *Witness!* (Chicago Showcase Theater, 1978), *Shango Diaspora: An African-American Myth of Womanhood and Love* (Chicago, Parkway Community House Theatre, 1980), and *When the Wind Blows* (Chicago, 1984).

Jackson is the recipient of many literary prizes and fellowships. Her work has taken her from Chicago, where her works were included in the Dial-a-Poem and Poetry-on-the-Buses campaigns and she participated in the Poets in the Schools program to Lagos, Nigeria, as an elected representative of the United States at the second World Festival of Black and African Arts and Culture (FESTAC) in 1977. In 1984 Jackson was appointed chair of the board of directors for the Coordinating Council of Literary Magazines, and in 1985 she became a writer in residence at Stephens College in Columbia, Missouri. Her most recent publications are *Cowboy Amok* (1992), *Dark Legs and Silk Kisses: The Beatitudes of the Spinners* (1993), a full-length collection of poems that focus on the spider as a symbol of African American womanhood, and *And All These Roads Be Luminous: Poems Selected and New* (1998).

• D. L. Smith, "Angela Jackson," in *DLB*, vol. 41, *Afro-American Poets since 1955,* eds. Trudier Harris and Thadious M. Davis, 1985, pp. 176–183. *Review of Dark Legs and Silk Kisses: The Beatitudes of the Spinners,* Publishers Weekly, 20 Sept. 1993, 68.

—Tracy J. Patterson

JACKSON, ELAINE (b. 1943), playwright and educator. Elaine Jackson emerged as a playwright in the 1970s, a socially and politically dynamic moment in the nation's history and a renascence decade for black theater. Beginning with her early play *Toe Jam* (1971) and continuing through her later plays of the 1970s and 1980s, Jackson presents a sometimes dark but inevitably celebratory vision of women in the process of confronting their lives and reenvisioning them. She, along with other black female dramatists of the period, working within the unique cultural climate created by the Black Power movement and the women's movement, helped to forge a vitally important theatrical space in which the lives of women of color found not only a stage presence but an authentic voice.

Born in Detroit to Essie and Charlie Jackson, the playwright began her theatrical career as an actress. After attending Wayne State University, where she majored in speech and education, Jackson moved to

California to pursue her acting career. She performed in more than forty plays in Michigan, California, and New York (Off-Broadway).

In 1972, while Jackson was still working as an actress on the West Coast, two of her former theater colleagues from Detroit, Woodie *King, Jr., and Ron *Milner, published *Toe Jam* in the *Black Drama Anthology,* a seminal collection of works by twenty-two black dramatists, including Langston *Hughes and Amiri *Baraka. Jackson followed with *Cockfight* (1976), *Paper Dolls* (1979), and *Birth Rites* (1987). Her work has met with both public applause and critical recognition. She was the recipient of the Rockefeller Award for Playwriting for 1978–1979 and the Langston Hughes Playwriting Award in 1979. In 1983, she received a National Endowment for the Arts Award for playwriting. An educator since the late 1970s, Jackson served as playwright in residence at Lake Forest College in 1990 and at her alma mater, Wayne State University, in 1991. She lives with her husband, William Sparrow, and son, Dylan, in New York, where she teaches high school theater and playwriting. Currently collaborating with composer-lyricist Martin Weich on a musical version of her play *Birth Rites,* she is also working on a new play entitled *Puberty Rites.*

Jackson started writing plays as a means of creating acting roles for herself but eventually turned to writing as her primary means of expression. Often her female characters undergo a similar shift in artistic endeavor. *Toe Jam* and *Paper Dolls* both present female protagonists who, acutely aware of themselves as actors in self-negating, socially scripted dramas, become writers in an attempt to create new roles and new life stories for themselves. In Jackson's two other works, the female characters contemplate life's critical turning points; in *Cockfight,* a couple faces the dissolution of their marriage, while in *Birth Rites* several expectant mothers anxiously await the births of their babies. Whether dealing with endings and beginnings or redefining the spaces in between, Jackson's work further opened the stage door for black playwrights and helped to set a standard in mainstream theater for richly textured portrayals of black characters and their stories.

• *Paper Dolls,* in *Nine Plays by Black Women,* ed. Margaret B. Wilkerson, 1986, pp. 347–423. Bernard L. Peterson, Jr., "Jackson, Elaine," in *Contemporary Black American Playwrights and Their Plays: A Biographical Directory and Dramatic Index,* 1988, p. 266.

—Yolanda M. Manora

JACKSON, JESSE (1908–1983), children's book author, journalist, and lecturer. Born 1 January 1908 in Columbus, Ohio, Jesse Jackson attended local schools and completed three years at Ohio State University's School of Journalism (1927–1929) before dropping out to work on the Ohio State Press. Jackson experienced a wide variety of jobs, including stints as an Olympic hopeful in boxing, a boxer in a carnival, a soda-jerk in Atlantic City, a juvenile probation officer, an employee of the National Bureau of Economic Research (1951–1968), and a lecturer at Appalachian State University (from 1974).

While working as a juvenile probation officer, Jackson realized the need for books that would interest nonreaders, as well as address the social issues facing African American teenagers. Jackson was assigned the case of three fourteen- to sixteen-year-old African American youths who had been sentenced to life terms in the Ohio State Penitentiary for robbing a restaurant and killing the owner for five dollars. While investigating their case, Jackson discovered that the boys had dropped out of school because they were too embarrassed to tell their teachers that they could not read. *Call Me Charley,* Jackson's first and most popular novel, was published in 1945 as a result of his perception of a lack of appropriate reading material for African American youths. In the novel, Jackson addresses the problems faced by one African American teenager, Charles Moss, and his attempts to be accepted by his white classmates after he and his parents move to an all-white suburb. *Call Me Charley* predated the *Brown v. Board of Education* Supreme Court decision by nine years and focused on the need for people of different races to get to know each other as individuals in order to eliminate stereotypes. Many of Jackson's other books addressed the issue of relations between African American and white youths as well. Jackson wrote two sequels to *Call Me Charley, Anchor Man* (1947) and *Charley Starts from Scratch* (1958), as well as other works of fiction, *Room for Randy* (1957), *Tessie* (1968), and *Tessie Keeps Her Cool* (1970). Jackson also wrote several biographies for children, including two about Stonewall Jackson, *The Sickest Don't Always Die the Quickest* (1971) and *The Fourteenth Cadillac* (1972). Jackson received the National Council for Social Studies Carter G. *Woodson Award twice, in 1973 for *Black in America: A Fight for Freedom* (1971) and in 1975 for *Make a Joyful Noise unto the Lord: The Life of Mahalia Jackson, Queen of Gospel Singers* (1974). Jackson's novels and biographies paved the way for more explicit writing about race relations in children's and young adult literature and gave African American writers an audience that had, in large measure, previously been denied them. Jackson died on 14 April 1983 in Boone, North Carolina.

• Ruby J. Lanier, "Profiles: Call Me Jesse Jackson," *Language Arts* 54.3 (Mar. 1977): 331–339. "Jackson, Jesse" in *Something about the Author,* vol. 29, ed. Anne Commire, 1982, pp. 111–114.

—Barbara Lowe

JACOBS, HARRIET A. (c. 1813–1897), slave narrator, fugitive slave, and reformer. Harriet Ann Jacobs's major literary contribution is her slave narrative **Incidents in the Life of a Slave Girl* (1861), the most comprehensive antebellum autobiography by an African American woman. *Incidents* is the first-person account of Jacobs's pseudonymous narrator "Linda Brent," who presents a remarkably accurate, although highly selective, story of her life. Breaking taboos to present her sexual history in slavery, Jacobs wrote a woman-centered slave narrative that, emphasizing family relationships and incorporating the forms of the domestic novel, reshaped the genre to encompass female experience.

About 1813, Harriet Jacobs was born into slavery in Edenton, North Carolina, to Delilah and a skilled house carpenter probably named Elijah, apparently the son of Henry Jacobs, a white farmer. Her brother John was born two years later.

In *Incidents,* Jacobs writes of the happy family life she enjoyed until the death of her mother. Then at age six she was taken into the home of her mistress, who taught her to read and to sew. At adolescence sent into the home of Dr. James Norcom, whom she characterizes as the licentious "Dr. Flint," she was subjected to unrelenting sexual harrassment. Jacobs's "Linda" confesses that to prevent "Flint" from forcing her into concubinage, at sixteen she established a liaison with a young white neighbor. This alliance produced two children, Joseph (born c. 1829) and Louisa Matilda (c. 1833–1913). Jacobs describes her master's renewed threat of concubinage, her fear that he will make her children plantation slaves, and her decision to run away in hopes that, in her absence, he will sell the children and that their father will buy and free them. She chronicles her 1835 runaway and her seven years in hiding in a tiny attic crawlspace in the home of her grandmother, a freedwoman.

Jacobs recounts her 1842 escape to New York, her reunion with her children in the North, and her 1849 move to Rochester, where she joined her activist brother, a member of Frederick *Douglass's circle. There Amy Post, a feminist Quaker, urged her to write her life. Returning to New York City after passage of the 1850 Fugitive Slave Act, she became the target of kidnappers. Although determined not to comply with slavery by allowing herself to be bought, in 1853 she was purchased from the Norcoms by her employer, Cornelia Grinnell Willis. Like other slave narratives, her book ends with freedom.

From 1853 to 1861 Jacobs recorded the conception, composition, and publication of *Incidents* in a series of letters to her friend Amy Post. This correspondence reveals that after an unsuccessful effort to enlist Harriet Beecher *Stowe as her amanuensis, she wrote her life herself. She could not find a publisher, however, until in 1860 the African American author William C. *Nell introduced her to the white abolitionist writer L. Maria Child, who agreed to act as her agent and her editor. Early in 1861, Jacobs published *Incidents* pseudonymously with only Child's name on the title page as editor.

Jacobs's name was initially connected with her book, although later, before the 1987 appearance of the Harvard University Press edition, both its authorship and its autobiographical status were disputed. When the Civil War began, she used her newfound celebrity among abolitionists to establish a public career. Joining Elizabeth *Keckley, Sojourner *Truth, and others aiding the "contraband," black refugees crowding behind the lines of the Union Army, Jacobs returned South. From 1863 to 1865, supported by Quakers and reformers, she and her daughter supplied emergency relief and established the Jacobs Free School in occupied Alexandria, Virginia. In 1866 the mother-daughter team continued their efforts in Savannah.

Throughout these years, Harriet and Louisa Jacobs were known to reformers through their reports on their work in the northern press. In 1864 Jacobs was named to the executive committee of the feminist Women's Loyal National League. Two years later Louisa lectured for the radical American Equal Rights Association. In 1868 mother and daughter went to England, where *Incidents* had been published in 1862, to raise money for Savannah's black community. Although successful, back home they were confronted with the increasing antiblack violence in the South, and mother and daughter retreated to Cambridge, Massachusetts.

By 1877 they had moved to Washington, D.C., where, in her declining years, Jacobs continued her mission among the freed people. In 1896 she was confined to a wheelchair when her daughter apparently attended the organizing meetings of the National Association of Colored Women held in Washington, D.C. Harriet Jacobs died in Washington on 7 March 1897.

• Jean Fagan Yellin, "Written by Herself: Harriet Jacobs's Slave Narrative," *American Literature* 53 (1981): 479–486. William L. Andrews, *To Tell a Free Story: The First Century of Afro-American Autobiography,* 1986. Hazel V. Carby, *Reconstructing Womanhood: The Emergence of the Afro-American Woman Novelist,* 1987. Jean Fagan Yellin, introduction to *Incidents in the Life of a Slave Girl: Written by Herself,* 1987. Joanne M. Braxton, *Black Women Writing Autobiography,* 1989. Frances Smith Foster, *Written by Herself: Literary Production by African American Women, 1746–1892,* 1993. Karen Sanchez-Eppler, *Touching Liberty: Abolition, Feminism, and the Politics of the Body,* 1993. Deborah M. Garfield and Rafia Zafar, eds., *Harriet Jacobs and* Incidents in the Life of a Slave Girl, 1996. Jennifer Fleischner, *Mastering Slavery,* 1997.

—Jean Fagan Yellin

JADINE CHILDS. In Toni *Morrison's **Tar Baby* (1981), Jadine Childs is the orphaned niece of Ondine and Sydney, black servants in the wealthy white household of Margaret and Valerian Street. The Streets provided for Jadine's formal education, but she received little cultural or parental nurturing. Called the "Copper Venus" by the fashion world, Jadine works as a model in Paris. She has become completely Europeanized and is engaged to a white

Frenchman. She sees herself as an independent, successful, professional woman who happens to be black but has no appreciation of her black cultural heritage. That her state of identity is confused, however, becomes apparent during her visit to the Streets by her confrontation with *Son Green—a black man hiding on the Streets' property—and an unknown African woman in a yellow dress.

Jadine and Son's relationship is doomed to failure because they represent worlds, ideals, and values that cannot be reconciled. Jadine, in fact, feels more comfortable with the Streets than with the black Floridians she visits with Son, and she is frightened by the vision of the African woman, for she represents authentic African culture and heritage and makes Jadine feel lonely and inauthentic. Jadine's expressed goal is to not belong to anyone but herself; nevertheless she is shaped by the culture of the Streets' household. Morrison paints Jadine as a woman who has forgotten her "ancient properties," that is, her ties to African American heritage and specifically to a community of black women made up of people like her Aunt Ondine. By returning to Paris and to a man she does not love, Jadine effectively opts for materialism rather than heritage. This makes it clear that she is unsentimental in choosing all that the American dream has to offer and leaving her people and culture behind. While her mulatto status does not make her a new character in the literature, her conscious, deliberate rejection of black people does.

• Barbara Christian, *Black Feminist Criticism,* 1985. Craig Werner, "The Briar Patch as Modernist Myth: Morrison, Bartes and *Tar Baby* As-Is," in *Critical Essays on Toni Morrison,* ed. Nellie Y. McKay, 1988, pp. 150–167. Wilfred D. Samuels and Clenora Hudson Weems, *Toni Morrison,* 1990. Trudier Harris, *Fiction and Folklore: The Novels of Toni Morrison,* 1991.

—Betty Taylor-Thompson

JANIE CRAWFORD. The protagonist of Zora Neale *Hurston's novel **Their Eyes Were Watching God* (1937), Janie Crawford is sixteen years old when, lying beneath a pear tree, she experiences a sexual and spiritual awakening. Before she can contemplate its meaning, her grandmother *Nanny forces her to follow the "text" she has saved for her life. For twenty years, Janie lives someone else's dream.

She marries Logan Killicks, an older man who owns a sixty-acre farm. Disillusioned when she finds that marriage does not compel love, Janie leaves Logan for a citified, stylishly dressed stranger. Joe Starks takes Janie to Eatonville, Florida, where he becomes storekeeper, postmaster, and mayor; Janie becomes his ornament. Denied the right to speak in public or even to listen to the "lying sessions" where the wit and wisdom of the culture are performed, Janie claims her voice slowly. In a dramatic confrontation, she talks back to Joe. After Joe's death, she resolves to follow her dream to journey to the horizon in search of people. She meets and marries *Tea Cake, a traveling bluesman. Living in a migrant workers camp, she works alongside Tea Cake and learns to tell stories herself. As he saves Janie during a hurricane, Tea Cake is bitten by a rabid dog. Subsequently, Janie kills him in self-defense.

Critics disagree about whether Janie becomes an articulate heroine. The novel does not record her testimony when she goes to trial for murdering her husband. But after her acquittal, Janie returns to Eatonville and tells her tale to her "kissin'-friend."

—Cheryl A. Wall

Jazz. Toni *Morrison's sixth novel, *Jazz* (1992) takes place in 1926, when the Harlem Renaissance was at its peak, a special time of success and attention for African American artists in all genres, including literature, art, and music, especially jazz. Its story line was inspired by an event that Morrison learned about in *The Harlem Book of the Dead* (1978), in which Camille Billops records the story behind James Van Der Zee's photograph of a young woman's corpse; she was shot yet refused to identify her assailant before she died.

The novel is a multifaceted narrative evolving from the early-twentieth-century migration to New York of a seemingly uncomplicated southern couple. They appear to join the hundreds of thousands of black people who left rural areas for urban areas, the South for the North, between 1890 and 1930; that migration led in part to the Harlem Renaissance. Violet and Joe Trace are thus expecting to improve their economic condition just as other migrants so hoped. The unexpected stresses of the city, however, complicate their lives.

At the beginning of the novel, Morrison relates that the over-fifty-year-old Joe, in a morose and jealous state, had murdered a seventeen-year-old girl, Dorcas, with whom he was having an affair; she had finally turned her attention to a younger man. The narrative ties in to T*he Harlem Book of the Dead* because Dorcas, lying shot by Joe, refuses to allow those surrounding her to call for an ambulance until Joe has disappeared; by then, she is too near death to be revived. Violet disrupts the funeral and has to be wrestled to the floor when she attempts to attack Dorcas's corpse with a knife. She thus becomes known as "Violent" Trace. The novel then focuses on Violet and Joe's past and their continuing fascination with the dead girl as well as upon their own reconciliation. During this healing process, Violet develops relationships with Dorcas's aunt and Dorcas's best friend.

Jazz is narrated by an alternately objective, omniscient, and confused voice that reveals the consciousnesses and personal histories of the characters and their historic setting, and also gives the novel its improvisatory, jazzlike feel. During 1992, *Jazz* achieved best-seller status along with Morrison's nonfiction critical work *Playing in the Dark.* While most critics responded favorably to the novel, others complained of its structure and narrative technique, and many were simply puzzled by what Morrison was trying to accomplish. Initial detractors, however, seem now to be more appreciative of the novel.

• Henry Louis Gates, Jr., and K. A. Appiah, eds., *Toni Morrison: Critical Perspectives Past and Present,* 1993. Paula Gallant Eckard, "The Interplay of Music, Language, and Narrative in Toni Morrison's *Jazz,*" *CLA Journal* 28.1 (Sept. 1994):11–19. Sarah Aguiar Appleton, "'Everywhere and Nowhere': Beloved's 'Wild' Legacy in Toni Morrison's *Jazz,*" *Notes on Contemporary Literature* 25.4 (Sept. 1995): 11–12.

—Betty Taylor-Thompson

JEFFERS, LANCE (1919–1985), poet, short fiction writer, and novelist. Lance Jeffers might accurately be described as a black nationalist without a movement. While he spanned the decades identified with the Black Aesthetic and writers of the 1960s, he was not included in the circles of those most associated with those militant times (though Broadside Press, which published many writers of the 1960s, did publish a couple of his volumes). Yet Jeffers's political stances as a poet are culturally nationalistic and informed by a consistent appreciation of the beauty and possibilities in black people. Though a few critics have paid attention to his work, he is among many less well-known African American writers whose works have not been incorporated into the mainstream of critical commentary on African American or American literature. In addition to singly published volumes, however, his works have appeared in anthologies such as *The Best Short Stories of 1948, Burning Spear, A Galaxy of Black Writing, New Black Voices,* and *Black Fire,* as well as in journals such as *Phylon, Quarto,* and the *Tamarack Review.*

Lance Jeffers was born in Fremont, Nebraska, on 28 November 1919 to Henry Nelson and Dorothy May Flippin; he was their only child. His grandfather, Dr. George Albert Flippin, raised him in Stromburg, Nebraska, from the time Lance was one year old; it was this relative who inspired *Grandsire,* one of Jeffers's volumes of poetry. Lance lived in Nebraska until his grandfather died in 1929. These years turned out to be the most formative of his career, and his grandfather proved to be perhaps the strongest influence on his life, but Lance was in essence separated from large numbers of black people. Reclaiming ties to African heritage and African peoples would occupy Jeffers for the rest of his life. At the age of ten, Lance moved to San Francisco to join his mother and stepfather, Forrest Jeffers, who was a janitor in a building whose tenants were white. Thus Jeffers did not immediately encounter many more black people than he had living with his grandfather and his white wife in Nebraska. Forrest Jeffers encouraged Lance to seek out other blacks, and he taught Jeffers the value of endurance under racially difficult circumstances.

Lance attended three high schools before graduating in 1938, then a succession of colleges before he joined the army in 1942 and served in Europe. When he left the military in 1946, he married Camille Jones, a social worker he had met in England, and, over the next few years, completed his undergraduate (cum laude) and master's work at Columbia University. Jeffers divorced Camille and married Trellie James in 1959; he had a son with Camille and three daughters with Trellie.

Like many practicing African American writers, Jeffers did not support himself exclusively through his writing. He taught at colleges and universities throughout the country, beginning in 1951 and including California State College at Long Beach and North Carolina State University in Raleigh, where he joined the faculty in 1974 and was still there at the time of his death on 19 July 1985. Trellie Jeffers continues her career as a college professor.

Jeffers's published volumes of poetry include *My Blackness Is the Beauty of This Land* (1970), *When I Know the Power of My Black Hand* (1974), *O Africa, Where I Baked My Bread* (1977), and *Grandsire* (1979). He dedicated three of the volumes to his wife Trellie, about whom he has written more than twenty poems, including the entire second section of *Grandsire,* and who served as a touchstone and constant source of inspiration to Jeffers. Other poems focus on racism, the beauty of blackness, the power of human beings to endure oppression, ancestry and homeland, topical issues such as the Vietnam War and the civil rights movement, and global issues such as the Holocaust. *Witherspoon* (1983) is Jeffers's one and only novelistic venture. It is the story of a black minister who, during a racial crisis, learns the value of revolution.

A few critics have appreciated Jeffers's mastery of language and metaphor, his exquisite attention to the possibilities of linguistic expression, and his aggressive pride in blackness, but more expansive and sustained scholarly studies of his works have yet to appear.

• Lance Jeffers, "A Black Poet's Vision: An Interview with Lance Jeffers," interview by Doris Laryea, *CLA Journal* 26 (June 1983): 422–433. David Dorsey, "Lance Jeffers," in *DLB,* vol. 41, *Afro-American Poets since 1955,* eds. Trudier Harris and Thadious M. Davis, 1985, pp. 183–190.

—Trudier Harris

JEMIMA. *See* Aunt Jemima.

JOANS, TED (b. 1928), poet, multimedia performer, musician, painter, surrealist, traveling storyteller, Beat writer, and Black Nationalist Manifesto writer. Ted Joans was born in Cairo, Illinois, on 4 July 1928, to African American entertainers working on Mississippi riverboats. He says that by the age of thirteen, he had learned to play the trumpet as well as the crowd and otherwise to fend for himself after his father's death in the Detroit Riot of 1943. Upon earning a bachelor's degree in painting at Indiana University (1951), he headed for New York, where his studio/apartment soon became a famous salon and party site. With other New York bohemians, he attended the New School for Social Research, but the extracurricular activities of Greenwich Village and, increasingly, of Harlem's Black Arts movement, were his preferred teaching and learning venues. After marrying and fathering four children (three of them sons, bio-blurbs remind, with heroic African surnames), he departed conventional life entirely, in order, experientially and textually, to break and reformulate habits of music, art, sex, and politics. His friends and cohorts included Bob *Kaufman, the then LeRoi Jones (Amiri *Baraka), Jack Kerouac, John *Coltrane, Stokely Carmichael, and Allen Ginsberg; the last, according to Joans, turned him from painting to performing his jazz, Beat, and revolutionary poetry at clubs, public readings, and as a "Rent-a-Beatnik" jazzman before well-paying private art consumers.

Joans met and exchanged words, ideas, and influence with many key political thinkers and creative artists in and beyond the United States. His poems, performances, and legendary conversations reflect, by turns, serious, respectful, satirical, and playfully challenging engagement with André Breton ("Nadja Rendevous," "Flying Piranha," named for Breton's parrot), Langston *Hughes ("Passed on Blues: Homage to a Poet"), *Malcolm X ("The Ace of Spades"), Kwame Nkrumah ("PAN AFRICA"), and Frantz Fanon (indirectly, in "Proposition for a Black Power Manifesto"). Typical is his poetic address to Andy Warhol, whose simultaneous exploitation and exposure of popular culture's obsessive yet repressed sexuality Joans improvised into a kind of jazz chant and/or typographically experimental text, in "Pubik Pak." Refusing equally the roles of victim, respectable bourgeois, nationalist, and traditional activist, Joans's work variously assaults assimilationism and guilty white liberalism; "Mau Mau Message to Liberals," "God Blame America," and "For the Viet Congo" are representative. In erotic, angry, dramatic, and often bitterly ironic short poems, he adopts and explodes from within various limiting personae imposed upon black men, especially African Americans. In this regard, "Let's Play Something" is programmatic, while "The Underground Bitch" bears comparison with *Baraka/Jones's *Dutchman.* While he is everywhere complex, ironic, thought-provoking, and deliberately surreal, his recurrent themes of the "virgin-whore" dichotomy and mythic Mother-Africa do not endear him to empirical feminists or mainstream postcolonialists. Nevertheless, his contributions to poetic style and his critiques of identity politics ensure continued relevance.

For his Beat period texts in context, see *The Beat Scene,* ed. Elias Wilentz (1960) and *City Lights Journal #1* (1963), which includes "Afrique Accidentale," his first poem written from Timbuctu, predicting the full range of his continuing surrealist, Marxist, French, and African commitments. In addition to being collected or translated in France, England, Italy, Germany, and South America, Joans's short political and memorial lyrics have also been anthologized by and with African American poets, including Langston Hughes and Arna *Bontemps (*The Poetry of the Negro, 1746–1970,* 1970), Gwendolyn *Brooks (*A Broadside Treasury,* 1971), and Dudley *Randall and Margaret Taylor Goss *Burroughs (*For Malcolm,* 1973, with bio-bibliography). Sonia *Sanchez published his story "A Few Fact Filled Fiction of African Reality" (*We Be Word Sorcerers,* 1973). Major poetry, prose-poems, manifestoes, and collages in English are published or reprinted by Marion Boyars, Ltd., *A Black Manifesto in Jazz Poetry and Prose* (London, 1971); *Black Pow-Wow: Jazz Poems* (London, 1973); *Afrodisia: New Poems* (London, 1976); and, with Joyce Mansour, for Bola Press, *Flying Piranha* (1978). For years he has promised and continues to live, revise, and add to "Spadework: The Autobiography of a Hipster" (sequel to the 1961 *All of Ted Joans and No More*), "I, Black Surrealist," and a novel "Niggers from Outer Space." Splitting residence between Paris and Timbuctu, he remains part of a casual and underground, though current and international poetry scene. Relatively neglected by critics, if not by fellow poets, the few academic essays about him show a surprising range.

• Skip [Henry Louis] Gates [Jr.], "Ted Joans: Tri-Continental Poet," *Transition* (Ghana) 48 (Spring 1975): 4–12. Michel Fabre, "Ted Joans: The Surrealist Griot," in *From Harlem to Paris: Black American Writers in France,* 1992, pp. 309–323.

—Kathryne V. Lindberg

JOHN GRIMES is a central character in James *Baldwin's autobiographical first novel, **Go Tell It on the Mountain* (1953). Modeled after Baldwin himself, John is castigated for being different—intellectually, physically, and sexually. Moreover, John must negotiate a treacherous Harlem terrain where religion becomes a bulwark against the "evils" of the external world.

Part 1, "The Seventh Day," privileges John's perspective. The action commences on his fourteenth birthday, as the plaintive youth contemplates what he considers his smallness, "ugliness," and precociousness. John's stepfather, Reverend *Gabriel Grimes, is especially abusive, blaming him for all of the family's ills; their battle royal is the novel's central conflict. Baldwin skillfully integrates psychosexual tension into this section. John's sexual thoughts are particularly vexing, as he feels guilt for masturbating and having sexual dreams about his mother and father. However, he finds an alternative to his bleak reality in Brother Elisha, an older adolescent at his family's church who mentors him.

The novel's final section, "The Threshing-Floor," marks John's religious conversion. Baldwin weaves biblical imagery deftly into this surrealistic episode, as

John undergoes a trial by fire for his soul. Though ostensibly God's voice wins, John's conversion is equivocal: He clearly appropriates Gabriel's conception of God as a weapon. John accepts Christianity only to counter his stepfather's cruelty; religion holds no intrinsic value, and John's spiritual re-birth brings little solace. Reminiscent of such sensitive young bildungsroman characters as Stephen Daedelus and Invisible Man, John finds his culture asphyxiating, and his tenuous position at the novel's conclusion makes him one of African American literature's most tragic adolescents.

• Michel Fabre, "Fathers and Sons in James Baldwin's *Go Tell It on the Mountain*," in *James Baldwin: A Collection of Critical Essays*, ed. Keneth Kinnamon, 1974, pp. 120–138. Horace A. Porter, *Stealing the Fire: The Art and Protest of James Baldwin*, 1989.

—Keith Clark

JOHN HENRY. The African American blues-ballad John Henry is arguably both the best-known and the greatest traditional American folk song. Its storyline is famous: When a railroad company brings in a steam drill to speed the construction of a tunnel, an African American laborer named John Henry, standing up for his rights as a worker and a human being, challenges the machine to a duel; displaying almost superhuman strength, John Henry wins the contest. In the 1920s two scholars, Guy Johnson and Louis Chappell, determined the song was based on an actual incident that probably occurred between 1870 and 1872 at the Big Bend Tunnel on the Chesapeake and Ohio Railroad in southeastern West Virginia; however, Johnson and Chappell could not trace the exact identity of "John Henry." Regardless, John Henry has endured into the twentieth century as a folk character and popular icon among both African Americans and whites; over the years his legend has intrigued everyone from railroad workers to union organizers to artists. According to Brett Williams (*John Henry, A Bio-Bibliography*, 1983), the most influential rendering of the legend by a white author is Roark Bradford's popular novel *John Henry* (1931), which Bradford later (1939) recast as a short-lived Broadway musical starring Paul *Robeson as John Henry. The most acclaimed interpretation by an African American author is John O. *Killens's novel *A Man Ain't Nothin' but a Man* (1975). Keith Byerman (*Fingering the Jagged Grain*, 1985) identifies John Henry as a prototype for fictional characters like Doc Craft in James Alan *McPherson's short story "A Solo Song: For Doc," Raoul Carmier in Ernest J. *Gaines's novel *Catherine Carmier* (1964), and Joe Pittman in Gaines's novel *The Autobiography of Miss Jane Pittman* (1971). Several African American authors, including Margaret *Walker, Sterling A. *Brown, and Melvin B. *Tolson, have written poems that respond to the John Henry legend.

• Guy B. Johnson, *John Henry: Tracking Down a Negro Legend*, 1929. Louis Chappell, *John Henry: A Folk-Lore Study*, 1933.

—Ted Olson

JOHNSON, AMELIA E. (1858–1922), novelist, short fiction writer, poet, and editor, who wrote under the name of "Mrs. A. E. Johnson." Born in Toronto, Canada, of parents who were natives of Maryland, Amelia Etta Hall Johnson was educated in Montreal. In 1874 she moved to Boston, where in 1877 she married Reverend Harvey Johnson of the Union Baptist Church. They had a daughter and two sons.

Interested in young people and in encouraging African American women's writing, in 1887 Johnson started an eight-page monthly, *Joy*. She contributed poems, short stories, and articles to various periodicals, but her reputation as a writer rests mainly on her three novels. With the publication of *Clarence and Corinne, or God's Way* (1890), she became the first African American and the first woman to write Sunday school fiction for the American Baptist Publication Society of Philadelphia, one of the largest publishing houses of the time.

Like other turn-of-the-century African American writers, including Emma Dunham *Kelley and Paul Laurence *Dunbar, Johnson does not explicitly mention the racial background of the characters in her novels. Nevertheless, contemporary African American reviewers praised her for writing "from affection for the race, and loyalty to it." In her racially indeterminate fiction, poverty, alcoholism, and family violence are discussed as societal, rather than racially specific, problems.

Clarence and Corinne opens on a scene of urban poverty. After their mother's death and their father's abandonment, Corinne is exploited as a domestic servant by her guardian, while Clarence is falsely accused of theft. Eventually all turns out well, as the siblings acquire educations, become financially secure, and marry two childhood friends. Christian teachings dominate the novel: love for one's neighbor and faith in Divine Providence, in "God's way," are proposed as remedies for contemporary social problems.

In *The Hazeley Family* (1894), Johnson emphasizes the Christian value and social usefulness of women's "home-work." She narrates how the self-reliant, spirited performance of her household duties enables Flora Hazeley, the protagonist, to overcome despondency, reunify her family, and become an agent of moral uplift in her community. Also Johnson's last novel, *Martina Meriden, or What Is My Motive?* (1901), focuses on the importance of having a Christian outlook on life, but it is more repetitive and less readable than her previous ones.

After being out of print for almost a century, Johnson has now begun to attract serious critical attention. While all of her novels end happily, they reveal complex underlying tensions between religious orthodoxy, domestic idealism, and a concern for the limited societal opportunities available to African American women. Flora Hazeley's successful evangelical mission, for instance, ultimately leaves her in the volunteer ranks of Sunday school teachers, while her brother's religious call receives societal sanctioning in his profession as a minister. Johnson's often veiled feminist themes offer interesting insight into the literary strategies of indirect argumentation that are characteristic of much of nineteenth-century African American women's literature.

• Barbara Christian, introduction to *The Hazeley Family,* 1988. Ann Allen Shockley, *Afro-American Women Writers, 1746–1933,* 1988. Hortense J. Spillers, introduction to *Clarence and Corinne, or God's Way,* 1988. Claudia Tate, *Domestic Allegories of Political Desire: The Black Heroine's Text at the Turn of the Century,* 1992. M. Giulia Fabi, "Taming the Amazon? The Price of Survival in Turn-of-the-Century African American Women's Fiction," in *The Insular Dream: Obsession and Resistance,* ed. Kristiaan Versluys, 1995, pp. 228–241.

—M. Giulia Fabi

JOHNSON, CHARLES R. (b. 1948), novelist, essayist, critic, philosopher, illustrator, screenwriter, and playwright. Born in Evanston, Illinois, Charles Richard Johnson first manifested his creativity in the graphic arts, which he parlayed into a job as an editorial cartoonist and then into two collections of drawings—*Black Humor* (1970) and *Half-Past Nation Time* (1972)—and a drawing program on PBS (*Charley's Pad,* 1971) before finishing his undergraduate degree at Southern Illinois University, at Carbondale. Having found success with visual art, Johnson turned to fiction, writing six apprentice novels that remain unpublished and that he describes in *Being and Race* (1988) as influenced by James *Baldwin and John A. *Williams. In 1973, while doing graduate work in philosophy at Southern Illinois University Johnson studied with John Gardner, author of numerous innovative novels and influential critical books. Drawing on African American folktales, his interest in philosophy and Buddhism, and the insights he gained from Gardner, Johnson published *Faith and the Good Thing* in 1974. An intriguing amalgamation of folk wisdom and philosophical inquiry, Faith defines the broad parameters of Johnson's aesthetic system and has been compared to **Invisible Man* (1952), an appropriate equation given Johnson's publicly professed admiration for Ralph *Ellison.

Johnson did course work at SUNY-Stony Brook for a PhD in philosophy; he also wrote screenplays for PBS, including the story of the oldest living African American cowboy, *Charlie Smith and the Fritter Tree* (1978), and a program on Booker T. *Washington (*Booker,* 1984). He and his family relocated to Seattle, where he teaches creative writing at the University of Washington. Other publications include the novels *Oxherding Tale* (1982) and **Middle Passage* (1990 National Book Award); a collection of stories, *The Sorcerer's Apprentice* (1986); and a book of criticism, *Being and Race: Black Writing since 1970* (1988). He continues to write in a variety of media, completing a screenplay for the film version of *Middle Passage* in 1993.

Johnson's second and third novels, as well as the short stories, manifest developments in his philosophical-aesthetic system. Both *Oxherding Tale* and *Middle Passage* explore nineteenth-century America from a perspective both resolutely historical and endowed with insights from contemporary philosophy. Both books fuse traditional genres and established texts—*Oxherding Tale* is a slave narrative clearly drawing on Frederick *Douglass's *Narrative,* while *Middle Passage* is a sea story with obvious Melvillian overtones—with a philosophical system founded primarily in phenomenology. Andrew Hawkins, the protagonist of *Oxherding Tale,* and *Rutherford Calhoun, the narrator of *Middle Passage,* are African American males seeking liberation from physical and/or emotional bondage. Each highly educated, they recount self-exploration and adventures that challenge readers to expand their understanding by destroying all preconceptions they may have about the nature and definition of freedom. The philosophical experimentation Johnson carries out in these novels is bolstered by the stories in *The Sorcerer's Apprentice,* a series of examinations and applications of a variety of philosophies, and by the theoretical chapters in his critical work, *Being and Race,* which outline a program for fiction writing, ostensibly for his use in critiquing other writers, that can be read as a clear statement of his own aesthetic goals and principles.

In his experimentation with concepts of factuality and chronology, Johnson shows the influence of John A. Williams, whose *The *Man Who Cried I Am* Johnson acknowledges as an important early inspiration. His philosophical inquiries show the influence of a series of American writers, including but not limited to Herman Melville, Edgar Allen Poe, Douglass, John Gardner, and Ellison. Furthermore, the revisions of history in his work, as well as his own statements, link him with other important contemporary writers such as Ishmael *Reed.

Johnson's contributions to contemporary African American fiction include a heightened awareness of the links between philosophy and fiction; a further development of the postmodernist sensibilities of history and chronology; and the creation of one of the most compelling and interesting contemporary philosophical-fictional tropes, the Allmuseri, his utterly unique tribe of African sorcerers who appear in several stories and in his second and third novels. Through them Johnson most effectively articulates his innovative approaches to time, history, language, and truth as constructs that bear examination; they represent the full embodiment of his ideology and challenge readers' belief systems, providing an opportunity for the reader to experience the intellectual growth the narrators do through contact with the tribesmen.

Johnson's most recent novel, *Dreamer: A Novel* (1998), combines philosophy and history in a depiction of Martin Luther King, Jr., and a King look-alike. This construction allows Johnson to explore the various beliefs that shaped King's nonviolence philosophy and to speculate about what would have happened to the movement he began if the King double had been shot in Memphis instead of the real King. Johnson's other work in the 1990s included an introduction he wrote to *What Is Man?/Mark Twain* (1996) and *Black Men Speaking,* which he edited with fellow writer John McCluskey, Jr., in 1997.

Gaining recognition for his radical and significant innovations, Johnson stands as a major contemporary writer, offering a fascinating outlook on African American history, fiction, and philosophy that will greatly influence future generations.

• Charles Richard Johnson, *Being and Race: Black Writing since 1970,* 1988. William Gleason, "The Liberation of Perception: Charles Johnson's *Oxherding Tale,*" *Black American Literature Forum* 25 (Winter 1991): 706–728. Jennifer Hayward, "Something to Serve: Constructs of the Feminine in Charles Johnson's *Oxherding Tale,*" *Black American Literature Forum* 25 (Winter 1991): 689–703. Jonathan Little, "Charles Johnson's Revolutionary *Oxherding Tale,*" *Studies in American Fiction* 19 (Autumn 1991): 141–152. Ashraf H. A. Rushdy, "The Phenomenology of the Allmuseri: Charles Johnson and the Subject of the Narrative of Slavery," *African American Review* 26 (Sept. 1992): 373–394. Jonathan Little, "An Interview with Charles Johnson," *Contemporary Literature* 34 (Summer 1993): 159–181. Rudolf P. Byrd, ed., *I Call Myself An Artist: Writings By and About Charles Johnson,* 1999.

—William R. Nash

JOHNSON, FENTON (1888–1958), poet, essayist, author of short stories, editor, and educator, who created works that foreshadowed the Harlem Renaissance. Fenton Johnson's first poetry appeared in 1913, and his last was written in the 1930s. He was a midwestern poet, influenced by that region and by the city of Chicago.

Fenton Johnson was born on 7 May 1888 in Chicago. His parents were Elijah and Jesse (Taylor) Johnson; Elijah, a railroad porter, was one of the wealthiest African Americans in Chicago. Johnson described himself as "having scribbled since the age of nine" but originally planned to join the clergy. He attended public school in Chicago and then enrolled at the University of Chicago. Johnson also attended Northwestern University and Columbia University's journalism school. He taught briefly at the State University at Louisville, a private, black Baptist-owned school in Kentucky. After his marriage to Cecilia Rhone, Johnson spent his artistic years primarily in Chicago and New York City.

Johnson produced three books of poetry, *A Little Dreaming* (1913), *Visions of the Dark* (1915), and *Songs of the Soil* (1916). All three books, which received some favorable critical notice, were directly subsidized by the author himself. In the first collection, Johnson uses a lyrical, "Victorian" style reminiscent of Paul Laurence *Dunbar. By the third collection, Johnson is experimenting with dialect poetry in both traditional and personal idioms. Regardless of style, this early poetry provides glimpses of the despairing tone that is so memorable in his later works.

Fenton Johnson did not limit himself to poetry; he published a collection of short stories, *Tales of Darkest America* (1920), and a book of essays, *For the Highest Good* (1920). He founded and edited literary magazines, and was also a playwright. By the age of nineteen, he says, his plays had been "produced on the stage of the old Pekin Theatre, Chicago." His playwrighting continued through 1925 at least, when "The Cabaret Girl" was performed at the Shadow Theatre in Chicago. This title is the only record of Johnson's plays; no scripts are extant.

Fenton Johnson continued producing poetry for anthologies and journals until the 1930s. Critics have judged this later work as among Johnson's best. He increasingly used free verse forms and explored his own urban experiences. Influenced in later years by Carl Sandburg and other midwestern authors, Johnson wrote of the despair and fatalism that was part of his African American experience. Johnson's final literary collection of around forty poems, posthumously published, was created during the Works Project Association's "Negro in Illinois" program. After the 1930s, the only connection Johnson retained to the artistic community in which he was previously so active was a correspondence with Arna *Bontemps. Johnson died in 1958, at the age of seventy.

Although often judged as a minor poet who merely prefigured the Harlem Renaissance, Fenton Johnson always exhibited a keen racial consciousness. His best work goes beyond foreshadowing to consistently give voice to a largely silent strain of despair and realism among American and African American culture.

• Countee Cullen, ed., *Caroling Dusk: An Anthology of Verse by Negro Poets,* 1927; rpt. 1955. James P. Draper, ed., *Black Literary Criticism of the Most Significant Works of Black Authors over the Past 200 Years,* vol. 2, 1992.

—Elizabeth Sanders Delwiche Engelhardt

JOHNSON, GEORGIA DOUGLAS (1880–1966), poet of the Harlem Renaissance. Born in Atlanta, Georgia, Georgia Douglas Johnson made her way to Washington, D.C., where she lived for over fifty years at 1461 S Street NW, site of one of the greatest literary salons of the Harlem Renaissance. Johnson was the most famous woman poet of that literary movement, publishing four volumes of poetry: *The Heart of a Woman* (1918), *Bronze* (1922), *An Autumn Love Cycle* (1928), and *Share My World* (1962).

Johnson's life illustrates the difficulties faced by African American women writers in the first half of the century. A graduate of Atlanta University (1896), where she met her husband, Henry Lincoln Johnson, Georgia Douglas Johnson did not publish her first poem until 1916, when she was thirty-six, and she remained geographically removed from the major literary circles of her day, which were in Harlem, due to her marriage to a Washington lawyer and civil employee. Her husband, moreover, expected her to look after the home and assume primary responsibility for the upbringing of two sons. When he died in 1925, Georgia Douglas Johnson was forty-five years old with two teenagers to support. Holding a series of temporary jobs between 1924 and 1934 as a substitute public school teacher and a file clerk for the Civil Service, she ultimately found a position with the Commissioner of Immigration for the Department of Labor, where hours were long and pay low. Johnson had to create her own supportive environment by establishing the Saturday night open houses that she hosted weekly soon after her husband's death and that included Langston *Hughes, Jean *Toomer, Anne *Spencer, Alain *Locke, Jessie Redmon *Fauset, and others. Although it was hard for her to write, she was able to follow through on her successes with her first two volumes of poetry by completing a third volume in 1928 that is arguably her best. *An Autumn Love Cycle* confirmed Johnson as the first African American woman poet to garner national attention since Frances Ellen Watkins *Harper. Johnson traveled extensively in the late 1920s, giving lectures and readings, meeting Carl Sandburg in Chicago and Charles Waddell *Chesnutt in Cleveland while receiving awards from various organizations, including her alma mater, Atlanta University. She was able to send her sons to Howard University, where they studied law and medicine, while maintaining a demanding work and travel schedule.

Through the pioneering work of Gloria Hull, we now know that Johnson wrote a substantial number of plays during the 1920s, including *Plumes,* which won first prize in a contest run by *Opportunity* in 1927, and *Blue Blood,* performed by the Krigwa Players in New York City during the fall of 1926 and published the following year. Twenty-eight dramas are listed in the "Catalogue of Writings" that Johnson compiled in 1962–1963, but only a handful have been recovered. She also listed a book-length manuscript about her literary salon, a collection of short stories, and a novel, which were lost as well. Of thirty-one short stories listed in her catalog, only three have been located, under the pseudonym of Paul Tremaine (two of these were published in Dorothy *West's journal *Challenge* in 1936 and 1937). Probably much of this material was thrown away by workers clearing out Johnson's house when she died in 1966.

Georgia Douglas Johnson's prolific writing career also included a weekly newspaper column, "Homely Philosophy," that was syndicated by twenty publications from 1926 to 1932; a collaboration with composer Lillian Evanti in the late 1940s that made use of Johnson's earlier music training at Oberlin Conservatory and the Cleveland College of Music; and an international correspondence club that she organized and ran from 1930 to 1965. Her writing was seriously curtailed by the loss of her Department of Labor job in 1934. She then sought any work she could get, including temporary jobs in a clerical pool, while vainly applying for arts fellowships. As late as the 1960s, Johnson was still applying for fellowships that never materialized. Able to survive by living with her lawyer son, Henry Lincoln, Jr., and his wife, Johnson never lost her enthusiasm for the arts nor her generosity to needy artists who came her way. She called her home "Half-Way House" to represent her willingness to provide shelter to those in need, including, at one point, Zora Neale *Hurston. The rose-covered walk at 1461 S Street, created by Johnson fifty years ago, still stands in testimony to the many African American artists she welcomed and to the love poetry for which she is best known. Struggling without the material support that would have helped bring more of her work to light and battling racist stereotypes that fed lynch mobs and race riots in the formative years of her life, Georgia Douglas Johnson left a legacy of indomitable pride and creative courage that has only begun to be understood.

• Erlene Stetson, ed., *Black Sister: Poetry by Black American Women, 1746–1980,* 1981. Gloria T. Hull, *Color, Sex, and Poetry: Three Women Writers of the Harlem Renaissance,* 1987. Ann Allen Shockley, ed., *Afro-American Women Writers, 1746–1933,* 1988. Maureen Honey, ed., *Shadowed Dreams: Women's Poetry of the Harlem Renaissance,* 1989. Elizabeth Brown-Guillory, ed., *Wines in the Wilderness: Plays by African American Women from the Harlem Renaissance to the Present,* 1990. Lorraine Elena Roses and Ruth Elizabeth Randolph, eds., *Harlem, Renaissance and Beyond: Literary Biographies of 100 Black Women Writers, 1900–1945,* 1990.

—Maureen Honey

JOHNSON, HELENE (1906–1995), poet of the late Harlem Renaissance. When Helene Johnson and her cousin, novelist Dorothy *West, moved from their native Boston to Harlem in 1926, Johnson demonstrated particular promise with competent lyrics extolling romance and nature, and with fresh themes of racial self-respect that prefigured the Black Arts movement writings of the 1960s and 1970s. But Helene Johnson never fulfilled early expectations, probably because her poetry replicates to a greater degree than most the aesthetic confusion that beset Harlem Renaissance literature generally.

Johnson's lifetime output amounts to a little over two dozen uncollected poems, appearing mostly in periodicals such as *Opportunity,* the *Messenger,* the *Saturday Evening Quill,* and *Vanity Fair.* Poems such as "Remember Not" and "Invocation" evoke romantic images of nature and death. For example, Johnson portrays the life cycle as returning to mother earth enclosed in a rain-drenched wooden casket, its polished wood and the cadaver becoming equals through the leveling process of death, as both gradually return to a more primordial state of nature in an unmowed plot overrun, "[r]iotous, rampart, wild and free." Such sentimentalism at once reveals Johnson's mastery of outdated poetic forms and her alienation from the aesthetic spirit of those Harlem Renaissance artists who tried to focus concretely and candidly on African American experience.

Johnson tries to deal with distinctively African American material in "Poem," which, while hailed at the time for its bold racial theme, reveals an ambiguous emotional connection to everyday African Americans. Contrary to the claim of Margaret Perry (*Silence to the Drums: A Survey of the Literature of the Harlem Renaissance,* 1976) that Johnson's work lacks artificial expression, Johnson here creates a contrived and idealized "jazz prince," whose tilted head and "patent-leathered feet" show him to be completely at ease with his racial heritage. Nonetheless, his demeanor also evinces the stereotypical image of flashily dressed African Americans often held by white and black racists. She reinforces this hackneyed portrait by evoking African tom-toms. The primitivism and racial condescension expose the conflicted nature of Harlem Renaissance writers, whose middle-class upbringings and poetic visions apparently limited their abilities to capture the lives of the African American masses. Furthermore, Johnson's poetry all too often displays the self-rejection characteristic of many Harlem Renaissance writings. Thus, Johnson's proud African American prince does not wear his hair natural but so greased down that it "shines in the spotlight." By the end of the poem, Johnson's professed joy in race has turned sarcastic with the speaker mocking the admired "boy."

• Raymond R. Patterson, "Helene Johnson," in *DLB,* vol. 51, *Afro-American Writers from the Harlem Renaissance to 1940,* ed. Trudier Harris, 1987, pp. 164–167. T. J. Bryan, "Helene Johnson," in *Notable Black American Women,* ed. Jessie Carney Smith, 1992, pp. 587–591.

—SallyAnn H. Ferguson

JOHNSON, JACK (1878–1946), prizefighter. Despite the tissue of untruths that fill *In the Ring—and Out,* Jack Johnson's 1927 autobiography, there is little doubt that even here he remained unyieldingly the auteur of his own mythology, that is, on the one indisputably true claim he made about the book. He wrote the book himself, without a ghost-writer. He is one of only, at best, a handful of star athletes who can say that.

Born in Galveston, Texas, on 31 March 1878, Johnson was the most charismatic and the most notorious African American figure in the American popular culture of his day.

He became the first black heavyweight champion in 1908. Johnson's fight against great white hope, Jim Jeffries, in July 1910, was the most discussed sporting event in American history at the time. Johnson easily won the fight but race riots broke out all over the country afterward. In Cuba in 1915, he lost the title to Jess Willard, a fight Johnson always claimed he threw.

There are few individuals in African American history who figured more prominently in black intellectual thinking and in black folklore than Johnson. He was discussed in pieces by Booker T. *Washington, W. E. B. *Du Bois, Reverdy Ransom, and others at the turn of the century. James Weldon *Johnson knew him well and talked of him at length in *Along This Way* (1933) and *Black Manhattan* (1930). Writers such as Richard *Wright and Ralph *Ellison used him symbolically in their fiction. Without question, for a time, until the coming of Joe *Louis and World War II, Johnson dominated the thinking of some blacks when they considered a certain type of black rebellion or black masculinity. Indeed, his impact has been such that his name comes up whenever a famous black male is mentioned or connected to scandal or conspicuously displays a sexual preference for white women. Johnson died in Raleigh, North Carolina, in 1946 from injuries sustained in a car accident.

—Gerald Early

JOHNSON, JAMES WELDON (1871–1938), songwriter, poet, novelist, journalist, critic, and autobiographer. James Weldon Johnson, much like his contemporary W. E. B. *Du Bois, was a man who bridged several historical and literary trends. Born in 1871, during the optimism of the Reconstruction period, in Jacksonville, Florida, Johnson was imbued with an eclectic set of talents. Over the course of his sixty-seven years, Johnson was the first African American admitted to the Florida bar since the end of Reconstruction; the cocomposer (with his brother John Rosamond) of *Lift Every Voice and Sing," the song that would later become known as the Negro National Anthem; field secretary in the NAACP; journalist; publisher; diplomat; educator; translator; librettist; anthologist; and English professor; in addition to being a well-known poet and novelist and one of the prime movers of the Harlem Renaissance.

As the first son of James Johnson and the former Helen Louise Dillet, James Weldon inherited his forebears' combination of industrious energy and public-mindedness, as demonstrated by his maternal grandfather's long life in public service in the Bahamas, where he served in the House of Assembly for thirty years. James, Sr., spent many years as the headwaiter of the St. James Hotel in Jacksonville, Florida, where he had moved the family after his sponge fishing and dray businesses were ruined by a hurricane that hit the Bahamas in 1866. James, Jr., was born and educated in Jacksonville, first by his mother, who taught for many years in the public schools, and later by James C. Walter, the well-educated but stern principal of the Stanton School. Graduating at the age of sixteen, Johnson enrolled in Atlanta University, from which he graduated in 1894. After graduation, Johnson, though only twenty-three, returned to the Stanton School to become its principal.

In 1895, Johnson founded the *Daily American,* a newspaper devoted to reporting on issues pertinent to the black community. Though the paper only lasted a year (with Johnson doing most of the work himself for eight of those months) before it succumbed to financial hardship, it addressed racial injustice and, in keeping with Johnson's upbringing, asserted a self-help philosophy that echoed Booker T. *Washington. Of the demise of the paper he wrote in his autobiography, *Along This Way,* "The failure of the *Daily American* was my first taste of defeat in public life. . . ." However the effort was not a total failure, for both Washington and his main rival, W. E. B. Du Bois, became aware of Johnson through his journalistic efforts, leading to opportunities in later years.

Turning to the study of law, Johnson studied with a young, white lawyer named Thomas A. Ledwith. But despite the fact that he built up a successful law practice in Jacksonville, Johnson soon tired of the law (his practice had been conducted concurrently with his duties as principal of the Stanton School). When his brother returned to Jacksonville after graduating from the New England Conservatory of Music in 1897, James's poems provided the lyrics for Rosamond's early songs. By the end of the decade, both brothers were in New York, providing compositions to Broadway musicals. There they met Bob Cole, whom Johnson described as a man of such immense talent that he could "write a play, stage it, and play a part."

The brothers split their time between Jacksonville and New York for a number of years before settling in New York for good. However, their greatest composition, the one for which they are best known, was written for a Stanton School celebration of *Lincoln's birthday. "Lift Every Voice and Sing" was a song that, as Johnson put it, the brothers let pass "out of [their] minds," after it had been published. But the song's importance grew from the students, who remembered it and taught it to other students throughout the South, until some twenty years later it was adopted by the NAACP as the "Negro National Hymn."

It was this kind of creativity under duress, coupled with his connections in the political sphere, that characterized Johnson's life as an artist and activist. Indeed, between the years 1914 and 1931, his desire to explore the limits of both worlds led him to seek a more thorough synthesis of his public and artistic sensibilities. The study of literature, which Johnson began around 1904 under the tutelage of the critic and novelist Brander Matthews, who was then teaching at Columbia University, caused Johnson to withdraw from the Cole/Johnson partnership to pursue a life as a writer. However, this creative impulse coincided with his decision in 1906 to serve as United States consul to Venezuela, a post that Washington's political connections with the Roosevelt administration helped to secure.

During the three years he held this post, Johnson completed his only novel, *The Autobiography of an Ex-Colored Man,* which he published anonymously in 1912. Though many read the novel as a sociological document, its true value lies in the manner in which it recasts the "tragic mulatto" story within the context of Du Bois's metaphor of the veil. The novel sparked renewed interest when Johnson announced in 1927 that he had authored the book as fiction. Indeed, so great was the public propensity to equate the novel's hero with Johnson himself that Johnson felt obliged to write his autobiography, which appeared in 1933 under the title *Along This Way.*

He had, by this time, established himself as an important figure in the Harlem Renaissance. From his post as field secretary of the NAACP, Johnson was a witness to the changes taking place in the artistic sphere. As a prominent voice in the literary debates of the day, Johnson undertook the task of editing *The Book of American Negro Poetry* (1922), *The Book of American Negro Spirituals* (1925), *The Second Book of American Negro Spirituals* (1926), and writing his survey of African American cultural contributions to the New York artistic scene in *Black Manhattan* (1930). His own career as a poet reached its culmination in **God's Trombones, Seven Negro Sermons in Verse,* published in 1927. Though not noted for playing the role of polemicist, through each of these literary enterprises Johnson worked to refute biased commentary from white critics while prodding African American writers toward a more ambitious vision of literary endeavor. It was Johnson's great hope that the contributions of younger writers would do for African Americans, "what [John Millington] Synge did for the Irish," namely utilizing folk materials to "express the racial spirit [of African Americans] from within, rather than [through] symbols from without. . . ." Hence Johnson's attempt to discredit Negro dialect, a literary convention characterized by misspellings and malapropisms, which in Johnson's view was capable of conveying only pathos or humor. Though writers like Zora Neale *Hurston and Sterling A. *Brown would challenge this viewpoint, Johnson's point must be understood within the context of his life as a public figure.

With the arrival of the 1930s, Johnson had seen the NAACP's membership rolls and political influence increase, though the latter failed to produce tangible legislative and social reform in Washington. Retiring to a life as Professor of Creative Literature and Writing at Fisk University, Johnson lectured widely on the topics of racial advancement and civil rights, while completing *Negro Americans, What Now?* (1934), a book that argued for the merits of racial integration and cooperation, and his last major verse collection, *Saint Peter Relates an Incident: Selected Poems* (1934). Though he died in a tragic automobile accident while vacationing in Maine in June of 1938, Johnson continues to be remembered for his unflappable integrity and his devotion to human service.

• James Weldon Johnson, *Along This Way,* 1933; rpt. 1968. Eugene Levy, *James Weldon Johnson,* 1973. Robert E. Fleming, ed., *James Weldon Johnson and Arna Bontemps: A Reference Guide,* 1978. Carolyn Wedin Sylvander, "Johnson, James Weldon," in *Encyclopedia of World Literature in the Twentieth Century,* vol. 2, ed. Leonard S. Klein, 1982, pp. 517–518. Robert E. Fleming, *James Weldon Johnson,* 1987. Joseph T. Skerritt, "James Weldon Johnson," in *African American Writers,* eds. Lea Baechler, A. Walton Litz, and Valerie Smith, 1991, pp. 219–233. Sondra Kathryn Wilson, ed. *The Selected Writings of James Weldon Johnson,* 2 vols., 1995. Kenneth M. Price and Lawrence J. Oliver, eds., *Critical Essays on James Weldon Johnson,* 1997.

—Herman Beavers

JOHNSON, WILLIAM (1809–1851), diarist. William Johnson's thirteen-volume, sixteen-year journal of life in Natchez, Mississippi, is the lengthiest and most detailed personal narrative authored by an African American during the antebellum era in the United States. Out of ordinary account books in which he tallied the daily expenditures and income of his early business ventures, Johnson's diary evolved into an extraordinary record of social, economic, and political life in his hometown of Natchez, Mississippi, as seen through the eyes of a free man of color.

Johnson was born a slave in Natchez, the son of his white master, William Johnson, and his slave, Amy. Johnson's father manumitted him in 1820. He was soon apprenticed to his free brother-in-law, Natchez barbershop proprietor James Miller. At the age of twenty-one, Johnson purchased Miller's barbershop, the first step in the young businessman's rise in the 1830s to a position of affluence as a property-holder, moneylender, land speculator, and slaveowner in the town of his birth. In 1835, Johnson married, completed a three-story brick home for his new family, and began on 12 October the diary he was to keep until the day of his death in 1851, the victim of a shooting over a land-boundary dispute.

In his diary Johnson writes most of the time as a self-appointed unofficial local historian. But on the occasions when he speaks of his own situation he provides a unique personal perspective on what it was like to negotiate daily the social margins of a slaveholding society.

• Edwin Adams Davis and William Ransom Hogan, *The Barber of Natchez,* 1954. William Ransom Hogan and Edwin Adams Davis, eds., *William Johnson's Natchez: The Ante-Bellum Diary of a Free Negro,* 1993.

—William L. Andrews

Jonah's Gourd Vine. When publisher Bertram Lippincott read Zora Neale *Hurston's short story "The Gilded Six-Bits" in *Story* magazine in August 1933, he wrote to inquire whether she was working on a novel. She was, and by early October she sent him the manuscript of *Jonah's Gourd Vine.* It was published the following May. Loosely based on the lives of Hurston's parents, *Jonah* tells the story of Lucy and John Pearson's courtship and marriage, John's swift rise to prominence as a Baptist preacher, his equally swift fall, Lucy's strength and perseverance, and the family's ultimate dissolution. All this takes place against a background of social and technological change occurring in the South at the turn of the century. These changes are subordinate to the cultural traditions that remain intact: the sermons, work songs, courtship rituals, aphorisms, children's rhymes, and hoodoo beliefs and practices. In the foreground are the experiences of Lucy and John.

In their hometown of Notasulga, Alabama, Lucy is a daughter of a well-to-do farmer, while John's family lives "over-the-creek." She excels in the classroom, while he has mastered the arts of the vernacular culture. After marrying Lucy, John decides to move the family to Florida, where his preaching wins him respect and status. But John's philandering costs him that respect and he almost loses his pastorate, until Lucy advises him how to win it back. He does, but resentful of her help, he soon is caught in the same sin. After Lucy dies, he remarries quickly and unwisely. The novel ends when John, married a third time, is killed when his car is hit by a train, the image the novel associates with him.

As Hurston confided to fellow writer James Weldon *Johnson, her protagonist represents the love of eloquence and beauty that she believed was pervasive among African Americans. But John was to represent more: in the pulpit "he becomes the voice of the spirit." As is true throughout Hurston's fiction, the spirit invoked in the novel fuses Christian theology and African belief, imaged here as the drum. Yet the novel never adequately explores the reasons John, the gifted preacher-poet, repeatedly contravenes the dictates of the spirit and misreads his own metaphors.

Lucy is also unable to achieve an identity between word and deed, even though she possesses the insight that her husband lacks. In a passage echoed in the maternal deathbed scene in Hurston's autobiography, **Dust Tracks on a Road* (1942), Lucy Pearson warns her daughter, "Don't you love nobody better'n you do yo'self. Do you'll be dying befo' yo' time is out." Loving John too much, Lucy has acquiesced in her own suppression. At her death, she remains on the threshold of self-discovery.

Jonah brims with the lore Hurston had spent six intensive years collecting. Some critics argue that the folk materials overwhelm the narrative. But others assert that *Jonah* is an experimental novel that dramatizes Hurston's theories of African American culture, particularly its African retentions and the primacy of spirituality.

—Cheryl A. Wall

JONES, GAYL (b. 1949), novelist, poet, playwright, professor, and literary critic. Born in Lexington, Kentucky, a state that surfaces in much of her work, Gayl Jones has forged an eclectic career, marked by periods of silence, and since the early 1980s, a withdrawal from public existence. Jones began merging academic and creative pursuits early in her life; she was writing stories while in second grade and, as an undergraduate at Connecticut College in 1971, received the college's award for best original poem in 1969 and 1970. Her story "The Roundhouse" also won the Frances Steloff Award for Fiction in 1970. By 1975 she had earned an MA and a DA in creative writing at Brown University and had published **Corregidora*, her first novel. (Her editor for *Corregidora* and **Eva's Man*, the novel that followed it in 1976, was Toni *Morrison, then at Random House.) While still a graduate student Jones also published the play *Chile Woman* (1974) and *The Ancestor: A Street Play.* From Brown, Jones went on to become an assistant professor of English and Afro-American and African Studies at the University of Michigan. In 1975 she received the Howard Foundation Award, followed first by a National Endowment for the Arts Fellowship in 1976, and then by a fellowship from the Michigan Society of Fellows for the years 1977 to 1979.

An associate professor when she left Michigan in the early 1980s, Jones has since kept her life exceedingly private. Her reclusiveness is perhaps best illustrated, if not explained, by her once stating that she most wanted to resemble those writers who, like J. D. Salinger, are known solely by their work, not their personal lives.

For Jones that work has taken a diverse array of forms: two plays, two novels, a collection of short fiction, three books of poetry, and, in 1991, a scholarly work examining the intersections between African American oral traditions and African American fiction—intersections for which her own fiction is noted as well. In various interviews Jones has emphasized the role of listening in her formation as a writer. The person to whom she listened first, and most closely, was her mother, herself a fiction writer. Lucille Jones would read to her children the stories she wrote for them. Additionally, because Gayl and her brother were never banished from the room when adults were talking, they grew up hearing the stories of older generations, an experience that probably catalyzed Jones's interest in exploring histories in her own fiction. The stories she listened to intrigued her with their form as well as their content, the myriad dialects, shifts, and cadences of African American voices. In fact, perhaps the single strongest element in Jones's work is its evocation of human speech; she has said that she had to hear something before she could write it.

Not surprisingly, Jones has been influenced by a wide-ranging group of artists whose voices she felt were true, including Alice *Walker, Ernest J. *Gaines, Geoffrey Chaucer, James Joyce, Michael S. *Harper, Miguel de Cervantes, Ernest Hemingway, Carlos Fuentes, Gabriel García Márquez, and Zora Neale *Hurston (although Jones has argued that Hurston's anthropological perspective distanced her from her created dialogue). And, since much of her work sings as well as speaks, musicians like Ma *Rainey, Billie *Holiday, and Ella Fitzgerald are also important to Jones.

The kind of language that stems from the call-and-response of black sermons, the improvisational motifs of jazz, and the repetitions of the blues structures Jones's early play *Chile Woman,* and is particularly evident in the form and "ritualistic" dialogue of *Corregidora.* Composed of bluesy refrains, lyrical monologues, and fantastic dream sequences, *Corregidora*'s form shares much with that of *Eva's Man.* Both works also display Jones's preoccupation with the manifold dimensions of language through their deliberate echoes of African American dialects and colloquialisms. To a lesser extent, *Corregidora*'s combined emphasis on family history and the virulence of racial and sexual persecution recurs in Jones's second novel. Yet it is *Corregidora* that best depicts what Jones has called the "blues relationship" between men and women: a relationship that, like the blues, encompasses both good and bad, both tenderness and violence. Moreover, the blues' acknowledgment of simultaneous opposites helps to define Jones's authorial stance. While she recognizes the importance of political strategies for writers, Jones refuses to allow her work to be hemmed in by a political agenda. In locating the cultural and historical influences at work in the lives she depicts, Jones avoids pigeonholing her characters into politically correct categories—particularly characters that function merely as uplifting African American role models. In fact, some readers have criticized her insistence on creating literature that does not conform to positive images of black women and men (see especially her interview with Claudia Tate in Tate's *Black Women Writers at Work,* 1983).

Jones's fiction often uses violence to illustrate the interconnectedness of public events and personal lives, portraying, for example, the twentieth-century repercussions of slavery in the Americas for black families. Perhaps most notably, her work graphically probes the harsh fusing of racism and sexism, documenting the ways in which sex can be used to degrade and brutalize primarily women (but also men) in *Corregidora, Eva's Man,* and the short-story collection *White Rat* (1977; rpt. 1991). In depicting sexual relationships under the double rubric of power and coercion, both heterosexual and lesbian, Jones gives some of the most unflinching renderings of sex and desire in contemporary fiction, descriptions made all the more striking by her deliberately stark, colloquial language. Yet it could be argued that several of White Rat's stories make up the broadest arena for Jones's writing about sexual relations. In "The Women," a young girl tersely recalls her mother's series of lesbian relationships as she discovers her own heterosexuality, yet the story closes on a troubling note as the choice she makes seems half-forced upon her. Inexplicable and often degrading sexual passions structure "Jevata," while "Persona" deals with a female professor's silenced desire for other women. *White Rat* also gives evidence of Jones's experimentation in forms of the vernacular, ranging from the earthy prose of the title story's narrator to the rich, interior realm of madness in "Version Two," to the deliberate spare opacity of "Your Poems Have Little Color in Them"—a story that examines an artist's difficulties with both speaking and not speaking, and with storytelling. Since, according to Jones, this last is the only piece in the collection that touches on autobiography, it may reveal some motive for the fact that, with *White Rat,* Jones stopped publishing fiction.

Most likely as a result of her mother's strong influence on her, as well as that of her grandmother, playwright Amanda Wilson, Jones has also worked powerful treatments of the relationships between daughters, mothers, grandmothers, and great-grandmothers into her fiction, especially in terms of shared histories, issues of speech and victimization, and accountability for the future. Interestingly, *Corregidora*'s theme of establishing those "generations" who will keep alive a familial history has a parallel in the author's personal life. Jones recalls her mother's asking about her own responsibility for making generations, a responsibility that Jones has said she regards with a combined sense of guilt and ambivalence.

Jones's latest two novels move in slightly different directions from her previous ones, but they are still solidly focused on women. *The Healing* (1998) treats an African American woman, who, after an attempt on her life and her miraculous recovery without medical assistance, gains the mysterious power to heal others. In a very unconventional scenario, she travels by bus from one small "water tower" town to another to extend her gift to those who need it. In *Mosquito* (1999), a more than six hundred page tome of a novel, Jones focuses on an African American woman near the Texas/Mexican border who drives an eighteen wheeler for a living. These depictions may portend an increasingly different locational focus for Jones's fiction.

Jones's poetry has been published in several literary magazines, but also in three separate works: *Song for Anninho* (1981), which was reissued by Beacon Press in 1999, *The Hermit Woman* (1983), and *Xarque and Other Poems* (1985). Some poems echo African American musical traditions, particularly pieces like "Deep Song," a "blues poem" that Jones wrote while listening to the Billie Holiday song of the same name. The Brazilian slave histories that underpin *Corregidora* take center stage in *Song for Anninho,* a prose poem about a love story between two escaped slaves in seventeenth-century Brazil. Like her fiction, much of her poetry is told from the first-person viewpoint, and is concerned with the complexities of love between men and women.

Liberating Voices: Oral Tradition in African American Literature (1991) takes her fictional concerns into the realm of literary criticism and analysis. Her text examines the influence of dialect, folklore, blues, and spirituals in the poetry of Harper, Paul Laurence *Dunbar, Langston *Hughes, and Sherley Anne *Williams; and also in authors like Hurston, Jean *Toomer, Ann *Petry, Ralph *Ellison, and Toni Morrison. The diversity of Jones's influences echoes in her critical focus, which finds in her selected authors a combination of European and American literary traditions and African and African American oral forms.

Like Alice Walker, Jones has been criticized for what some readers see as a recurrent indictment against black men, particularly in her first two novels' bleak portraits of abusive husbands and lovers. Yet such criticism is countered by a recognition of those characters' own troubled legacies of racial injustices, as well as by *White Rat,* which offers several complex renderings of basically good-hearted men. Perhaps a more accurate appraisal of Jones's treatment of African American men—and women—would encompass her resolute account of the ways in which racism and sexism build upon each other, victimizing both sexes. Certainly, her stern gaze makes for grim reading. Yet that grimness is inextricable from the other qualities of Jones's work: vivid delineation of the physical details of sexual desire, and a deliberate implementation of black oral forms stemming from communal speech patterns, folklore, sermons, jazz, and the blues. Together, these qualities place Jones's writing firmly within that literature that melds the substance and the form of African American cultural history.

[*See also* Eva Medina Canada; Ursa Corregidora.]

• Gayl Jones, "Gayl Jones: An Interview," interview by Michael S. Harper, *Massachusetts Review* 18.4 (Winter 1977): 692–715. Gayl Jones, "Gayl Jones Takes a Look at *Corregidora*—An Interview," interview by Roseann P. Bell, *Sturdy Black Bridges: Visions of Black Women in Literature,* eds. Roseann P. Bell et al., 1979, pp. 282–287. Valerie Gray Lee, "The Use of Folktalk in Novels by Black Women Writers," *CLA Journal* 23 (Mar. 1980): 266–272. Trudier Harris, "A Spiritual Journey: Gayl Jones's *Song for Anninho,*" *Callaloo* 5.3 (Oct. 1982): 105–111. Gayl Jones, "An Interview with Gayl Jones," interview by Charles H. Rowell, *Callaloo* 5.3 (Oct. 1982): 32–53. Gayl Jones, "About My Work," in *Black Women Writers (1950–1980),* ed. Mari Evans, 1984, pp. 233–235. Jerry W. Ward, Jr., "Escape From Trublem: The Fiction of Gayl Jones," in *Black Women Writers (1950–1980),* ed. Mari Evans, 1984, pp. 249–257. Mae G. Henderson, foreword to *White Rat,* 1977; rpt. 1991. Patricia Munoz-Cabrera, "(Em)Bodying the Flesh: Mythmaking and the Female Body in Gayl Jones' *Song for Anninho* and *Corregidora,*" *PALARA* 1 (Fall 1997): 106–116. Stelamaris Coser, "Stepping-Stones Between the Americas: The Narratives of Paule Marshall and Gayl Jones," *PALARA* 1 (Fall 1997): 80–88.

—Amy S. Gottfried

JONES, LeROI. *See* Baraka, Amiri.

JORDAN, JUNE (b. 1936), poet, novelist, essayist, playwright, educator, activist, biographer, and anthologist. In addition to her distinguished career as a college professor, June Jordan is a well-known, prolific writer of poetry, children's and young adult literature, and essays. She has earned critical praise and popular recognition for her exceptional literary skill and her social and political acumen. Having come of age as a writer and cultural commentator during the "second renaissance" of African American arts in the 1960s and 1970s, Jordan is among the significant artists of this cultural revival and of the rise of black consciousness in the 1960s.

Born in Harlem, New York, on 9 July 1936, June Jordan is the only child of Granville Ivanhoe Jordan and Mildred Maud (Fisher) Jordan, who came to the United States from Jamaica. Jordan grew up in the Bedford-Stuyvesant section of Brooklyn, but as a teenager she commuted to Midwood High School, where she was the only African American student. After one year at Midwood, her parents transferred her to the Northfield School for Girls in Massachusetts (later joined with Mount Hermon), a preparatory school which she found to be even less hospitable to the development of her African American identity.

After graduating from high school in 1953, Jordan entered Barnard College in New York City. There she met Michael Meyer, a white Columbia University student, whom she married in 1955. Jordan accompanied Meyer later that year to the University of Chicago, where he engaged in graduate study in anthropology, and she also enrolled in the university. She returned to Barnard in 1956 before finally leaving in February 1957. In 1958 the couple's only child, Christopher David Meyer, was born. Prior to the couple's divorce in 1965, Jordan had assumed full responsibility for their son, accepting a position in 1963 as an assistant to the producer for Shirley Clarke's film about Harlem, *The Cool World.*

Jordan established her writing career with the publication in the 1960s of stories and poems (under the name June Meyer) in periodicals including *Esquire,* the *Nation, Evergreen Review, Partisan Review, Black World, Black Creation, Essence,* the *Village Voice,* the *New York Times,* and the *New York Times Magazine.* Her writing came to national attention in 1969, when Crowell published her first book of poetry, *Who Look at Me,* a collection of works that depict interracial relations and African American experiences of self-definition in a white-dominated society. In 1970 Jordan edited *Soulscript: Afro-American Poetry,* a collection of poetry by young adults aged twelve to eighteen and by well-known poets of the 1960s. Jordan has published twenty-one works to date, consisting of poetry, books for children and young adults, and collections of essays, articles, and lectures. These works include *The Voice of the Children,* a reader edited with Terri Bush (1970); *Some Changes* (poems, 1971); **His Own Where* (young adult novel, 1971); *Dry Victories* (juvenile and young adult, 1972); *Fannie Lou Hamer* (biography, 1972); *New Days: Poems of Exile and Return* (1973); *New Life: New Room* (juvenile, 1975); *Things That I Do in the Dark: Selected Poetry* (1977); *Okay Now* (1977); *Passion: New Poems, 1977–1980* (1980); *Civil Wars* (essays, articles, and lectures, 1981); *Kimako's Story* (juvenile, 1981); *Living Room: New Poems, 1980–1984* (1985); *On Call: New Political Essays, 1981–1985* (1985); *High Tide—Marea Alta* (1987); *Naming Our Destiny: New and Selected Poems* (1989); *Technical Difficulties: African-American Notes on the State of the Union* (essays, articles, and lectures, 1992); *Kissing God Goodbye: Poems, 1991–1997* (1997); *Affirmative Acts: Political Essays* (1998). Jordan is also the author of several plays, including In the *Spirit of Sojourner Truth,* produced in New York at the Public Theater (May 1979), and *For the Arrow That Flies by Day,* a staged reading produced in New York at the Shakespeare Festival (Apr. 1981). In addition, Jordan composed the lyrics and wrote the libretto for *Bang Bang Uber Alles* in 1985.

In 1966 Jordan began her academic career as an instructor of English and literature at the City University of New York. In 1968 she moved to Connecticut College in New London, where she taught English and directed the Search for Education, Elevation and Knowledge (SEEK) program. From 1968 to 1974 Jordan was an instructor of English at Sarah Lawrence College in Bronxville, New York. She was a visiting professor of English and Afro-American studies at Yale University from 1974 to 1975 and later in 1975 became an assistant professor of English at the City College of New York. In 1976 Jordan took a faculty position at the State University of New York at Stony Brook, and in 1982 was promoted to tenured full professor. Since 1989 Jordan has been professor of Afro-American studies and women's studies at the University of California, Berkeley.

Themes of power and empowerment, nurturance and pride, survival and advancement for both the community and its members characterize Jordan's African American literary vision across the several genres in which she writes, from her earliest writings to her last. Her work is antiracist, feminist, and avowedly political; it powerfully and skillfully explores African American experience and advocates self-determination and activism for community advancement, as well as for ameliorating interracial relations and those between the sexes. Jordan's writing for and with African American children and young adults attests to the poet's conviction of the healing empowerment of language and self-expression; moreover, her children's books expand the genre by taking on the harsh social realities they face. The award-winning *His Own Where,* a novel for young adults, is distinguished by its use of African American spoken English and its focus on urban redesign to create environmental conditions that can foster African American life. The emphasis on urban planning derives from Jordan's project to collaborate with E. Buckminster Fuller on the architectural redesign of Harlem; *His Own Where* fulfills in fiction what could not be realized in environmental planning.

Jordan is perhaps best known for her poetry and essays. Her verse has been praised for uniquely and effectively uniting in poetic form the personal everyday struggles and political oppressions of African Americans while at the same time masterfully creating art that conveys bitterness and rage at intolerance with a fine irony. She is recognized for her expert craftsmanship, a patterning of sound, rhythm, and image that interweaves disparate emotions and voices in a poetry that is never less than political and never lessened by its politics. Her poetic vision infuses all that she writes, and Jordan's explicitly political essays, especially those collected in *Civil Wars* and *Technical Difficulties,* advocate change through a personal, autobiographical focus and a clear uncompromising voice. Jordan is a witness for her community but also an intellectual with a vision for its future that embraces a feminism inclusive of men and focused on the nurturance of children and freedom of sexual orientation. In her oft-quoted essay "A New Politics of Sexuality" (*Technical Difficulties,* 1992), Jordan draws an analogy between bisexuality and "interracial or multiracial identity," insisting on the complexities of human existence and individuals' "total, always-changing social and political circumstance." Jordan's political, social, and personal artistic vision is comprehensive, humane, and charged with conviction; her poetry and essays are expansive expressions of her wide-ranging aesthetic and human concerns.

Jordan has received many grants, prizes, and fellowships for her writing, including a Rockefeller grant for creative writing in 1969 and the Prix de Rome in Environmental Design in 1970. She was granted a Yaddo fellowship in 1979, a fellowship in poetry from the National Endowment for the Arts in 1982, and a fellowship award in poetry from the New York Foundation for the Arts in 1985. *The Voice of Children* received a Nancy Bloch Award in 1971, and in the same year, *His Own Where* was selected by the *New York Times* for its List of Most Outstanding Books and was nominated for a National Book Award. Jordan is an executive board member of the American Writers Congress, a board member of the Center for Constitutional Rights and the Nicaraguan Culture Alliance, and a member of PEN. She is also a regular political columnist for *Progressive* magazine.

Jordan has been a significant voice in several traditions of African American art and culture. Her socially conscious literary expressions advance contemporary trends also practiced by Alice *Walker and Toni *Morrison; Toni Cade *Bambara has compared Jordan's achievements to W. E. B. *Du Bois's **Dusk of Dawn: An Essay Toward an Autobiography of a Race Concept* (1940). Jordan's talk-poems and her use of spoken African American English in both fiction and poetry indicate her participation in an oral tradition of African American literature exemplified by Nikki *Giovanni and Amiri *Baraka. Her feminist vision, part of her political enterprise, has been influential in the development of an antiracist, antihomophobic U.S. feminism. The political advocacy of her poetry, decidedly activist and aesthetically black, aligns her with Eldridge *Cleaver and *Malcolm X, although she brings to the radical militancy of 1960s African American thought an anger ultimately seasoned by faith, optimism, and vision.

• Toni Cade Bambara, "Chosen Weapons," review of *Civil Wars, Ms.*, Apr. 1981, 40–42. Alexis De Veaux, "Creating Soul Food: June Jordan," *Essence,* Apr. 1981, 82, 138–150. Sara Miles, "This Wheel's on Fire," in *Woman Poet: The East,* eds. Elaine Dallman et al., 1982, pp. 87–89. Peter B. Erickson, "June Jordan," in *DLB,* vol. 38, *Afro-American Writers after 1955: Dramatists and Prose Writers,* eds. Thadious M. Davis and Trudier Harris, 1985, pp. 146–162. June Jordan, "An Interview with June Jordon," interview by Joy Harjo, *High Plains Literary Review* 3.2 (Fall 1988): 60–76. Peter Erickson, "Putting Her Life on the Line: The Poetry of June Jordan," *Hurricane Alice: A Feminist Quarterly* 7.1–2 (Winter–Spring 1990): 4–5. P. Jane Splawn, "New World Consciousness in the Poetry of Ntozake Shange and June Jordan: Two African-American Women's Response to Expansionism in the Third World," *College Language Association Journal* 39:4 (June 1996): 417–432. Jacqueline Vaught Brogan, "From Warrior to Womanist: The Development of June Jordan's Poetry," in *Speaking the Other Self: American Women Writers,* ed. Jeanne Campbell Reesman, 1997, pp. 198–209.

—Ronna C. Johnson

Jubilee was written as Margaret *Walker's PhD dissertation at the University of Iowa. As she typed the final lines of the story of her maternal great-grandmother, Margaret Duggans Ware Brown (on 9 April 1965), Walker brought to conclusion the creative task of transforming the oral history passed on by her grandmother into a sweeping novel of southern life before and immediately after the Civil War. *Jubilee* won the Houghton Mifflin Literary Fellowship and was published in September 1966.

The novel is divided into three major sections, representing the antebellum years, the Civil War period, and Reconstruction as witnessed by the central character, Vyry. Born a slave on a Georgia plantation, she eventually finds a peace she cannot vocalize and hope for a future in the red-clay hills of Alabama. Orphaned by the death of her mother and nurtured by the women of the slave community, Vyry suffers for being her owner's daughter and must use wit and intelligence to survive the wrath of Salina Dutton, who despises Vyry's resemblance to her own daughter, Lillian. Vyry's strengths are tested when her husband, Randall

Ware, escapes to the North; refusing to abandon her two children for the promise of freedom, she remained on the plantation during the Civil War, a model of sanity and generosity as the chaos of war brings irreversible change. The interdependence of slave and slaveowner and the suffering both must endure are foils for Vyry's heroism. Assuming that Ware is dead, Vyry marries Innis Brown and seeks to begin a new life with him in Alabama at the war's end. Life is marked by the poverty, sickness, and persecution of the postwar South, and Vyry must make a hard choice when Ware reappears.

The compassion of *Jubilee* challenged stereotypes about African American historical fiction. Published just as the focus on civil rights was shifting to Black Power and nationalism, its initial critical reception was decidedly mixed. Opinions ranged from Guy Davenport's biting conclusion in the *National Review* that the novel ironically swallowed the myth of a romantic South that never existed to Abraham Chapman's remarks in *Saturday Review* that the novel was faithful to the facts of slave life. Neither facts that might have cast light on the textual tensions, the pull between verifiable data and the author's re-creation of family history, nor the insights of feminist critique about the novel's complexity were available to early commentators. The facts would not be available until Walker published *How I Wrote Jubilee* (1972), thus enabling a more reasoned assessment of the novel within the tradition of African American historical fiction.

Since the 1970s, many critics acknowledge, as does Bernard Bell in *The Afro-American Novel and Its Tradition* (1987), that *Jubilee* is an innovative neo–slave narrative, remarkable for its use of folklore, knowledge of black culture, abundance of carefully researched historical detail, and the prism of woman's vision. Seen now as the precursor of such works as **Dessa Rose* (1986) and **Beloved* (1987), *Jubilee* inspires deeper studies of what it might tell us about the interrelations of memory and literary imagination in the history of African American literature and culture.

• Barbara Christian, *Black Women Novelists,* 1980. Eleanor Traylor, "Music as Theme: The Blues Mode in the Works of Margaret Walker," in *Black Women Writers (1950–1980),* ed. Mari Evans, 1984, pp. 511–525. Minrose C. Gwin, *Black and White Women of the Old South,* 1985. Melissa Walker, *Down from the Mountain Top: Black Women's Novels in the Wake of the Civil Rights Movement, 1966–1989,* 1991.

—Jerry W. Ward, Jr.

K

KAUFMAN, BOB (1925–1986), poet, prose poet, jazz performance artist, satirist, manifesto writer, and legendary figure in the Beat movement. Bob Kaufman successfully promoted both anonymity and myths of his racial identity and class origins. While romanticized biographies ascribe to him such epithets as griot, shaman, saint, and prophet of Caribbean, African, Native American, Catholic, and/or Jewish traditions, respectively, Kaufman was most likely the tenth of thirteen children of an African American and part Jewish father and a schoolteacher mother from an old New Orleans African American Catholic family. After an orderly childhood that probably included a secondary education, he joined the merchant marines and became active in the radical Seafarer's Union. An itinerant drifter and self-taught poet (but for a brief stint at the New School for Social Research and among the Black Arts and Beat literati of New York), he identified with the lives and cryptically quoted the works of poet-heroes such as Herman Melville, Walt Whitman, Arthur Rimbaud, Guillaume Apollinaire, Federico García Lorca, Hart Crane, Gertrude Stein, Langston *Hughes, Frantz Fanon, Aimé Césaire, and Nicholas Guillén, as well as improvisational artists and jazz musicians, including Charlie *Parker, after whom he named his only son. In individual poems he is, variously, an experimental stylist in the Whitman tradition ("The American Sun"), a French surrealist and existentialist ("Camus: I Want to Know"), a jazz poet after Langston Hughes, and in dialogue with bebop and the Black Arts movement ("African Dream," "Walking Parker Home").

Still "minor," compared to his white bohemian contemporaries, as editor of *Beatitude,* a San Francisco literary magazine, Kaufman is credited by some with coining "Beat" and exemplifying its voluntarily desolate lifestyle. He enjoyed an underground existence as a "poets' poet" (in Amiri *Baraka's poem "Meditation on Bob Kaufman," *Sulfur,* Fall 1991) and as a legendary performer in the much memorialized street scenes of San Francisco's North Beach and New York's Greenwich Village during the late 1950s through the late 1970s. Kaufman is best known for short lyric poems in African American (Langston Hughes, ed., *The New Negro Poetry,* 1964, being the first) and avant-garde anthologies (*New Directions in Prose and Poetry, #17,* 1967, covering poetry and prose; *The Portable Beat Reader,* 1992). Works originally published by City Lights Bookstore of San Francisco are collected in two New Directions publications, *Solitudes Crowded with Loneliness* (1965) and *The Ancient Rain: Poems 1956–1978* (1981). Three early broadsides, *Abomunist Manifesto* (1959), *Second April* (1959), and *Does the Secret Mind Whisper?* (1960) extend his eclectic aesthetics into prose fiction and programmatic prose poetry. *The Golden Sardine* (1967) was translated and influential in France (as *William Burroughs, Claude Pelieu, Bob Kaufman,* Paris, 1967). The latter, along with South American and other translations, have earned Kaufman a wider reputation abroad than among mainstream critics in the United States.

Rather than address electoral, protest, or even literary politics in traditional ways, his elusive and allusive writings as well as his tragicomic life sustain a critique of the subtle rules and terrible punishments that, as he knew them, enforce American bourgeois values of race, class, sexuality, and rationality. Answering McCarthyism, Beat, and Black Arts manifestos with Dadaist anarchism and surrealist irrationalism, "Abomunism" (his contraction of, among other things, communism, atom bomb, Bob Kaufman, and abomination), is serious in its "black humor." From the late 1960s onward, through stretches of withdrawal and suffering the ill effects of political blacklisting and harassment, alcohol, drugs, electroshock treatments, and imprisonment, Kaufman recorded both with humor and pathos the pain of society's victims. While no booklength study has yet been devoted to Kaufman, several recent essays affirm his deceptively broad intellectual interests and the ambiguous power of individual acts of cultural resistance in the continuing struggles of oppressed peoples.

• Barbara Christian, "Whatever Happened to Bob Kaufman?" *Black World* 21 (Sept. 1972): 20–29. Maria Damon, "'Unmeaning Jargon' / Uncanonized Beatitude: Bob Kaufman, Poet," *South Atlantic Quarterly* 87.4 (Fall 1988): 701–741. Kathryne V. Lindberg, "Bob Kaufman, Sir Real," *Talisman* 11 (Fall 1993): 167–182. Gerald Nicosian, ed., *Cranial Guitar: Selected Poems by Bob Kaufman,* 1996.

—Kathryne V. Lindberg

KECKLEY, ELIZABETH (c. 1818–1907), seamstress, activist, and author. Elizabeth Keckley became a center of public controversy with the 1868 publication of *Behind the Scenes, or Thirty Years a Slave and Four Years in the White House.*

Born a slave in Dinwiddie Court House, Virginia, Keckley became such an accomplished seamstress that she was able to purchase her own freedom and her son's. After manumission she moved from St. Louis to establish herself in Washington, D.C., in 1860, becoming modiste first to the wife of Mississippi Senator Jefferson Davis and finally to Mary Todd Lincoln during

Abraham *Lincoln's first term. Two-thirds of *Behind the Scenes* concerns Keckley's life with the Lincolns and the difficult period following the president's assassination, especially Mary Lincoln's desperate attempt to raise money through what became known as the "Old Clothes Scandal." A misplaced trust in her editor, James Redpath, and the sensationalist marketing of Carleton and Company culminated in a furor, the as-advertised "literary thunderbolt." Because of revelations about Mary Lincoln and the inclusion of her personal letters, Robert Lincoln pressured the publisher to remove Keckley's book from sale and terminated all relations with Keckley. After serving as Director of Domestic Arts at Wilberforce University, Keckley retired to Washington, D.C.

While antebellum slave narratives treat slavery as an unadulterated evil and slaveowners as devilish, Keckley's and other post–Civil War narratives emphasize slavery as a school for instruction in self-reliance and hard work. Keckley's success, along with an awareness of the South brought low, allows her reconciling visit with the Garlands, her former owners. Although her sexual exploitation in slavery recalls that of her contemporary Harriet A. *Jacobs, Keckley refuses to make black female sexuality an issue in *Behind the Scenes,* preferring instead to stress her achievement as a successful career woman in freedom.

• John E. Washington, *They Knew Lincoln,* 1942. Frances Smith Foster, *Written by Herself: Literary Production by African American Women, 1746–1892,* 1993. Jennifer Fleischner, *Mastering Slavery,* 1997.

—Anne Bradford Warner

KELLEY, EMMA DUNHAM (?–?), novelist. Little is known about the life of Emma Dunham Kelley. She wrote two novels, *Megda* (1891) and *Four Girls at Cottage City* (1895). Kelley used the pseudonym "Forget-Me-Not" for her first novel, publishing the second under the name Emma Dunham Kelley-Hawkins, thus indicating marriage. It is probable that Kelley lived in New England, where she may have been a schoolteacher or attended school: both novels were published and set in New England, and in the preface to *Four Girls* the author acknowledges that much of the text is based on actual people, places, and events. The dedications to Kelley's novels express a sense of debt to a widowed mother who struggled to provide for her daughter and to an aunt whom she calls a "second mother."

Both of Kelley's texts are didactic novels in the tradition of the female Christian bildungsroman, a genre that was sufficiently popular in the 1890s for *Megda* to warrant a second printing. In their rejection of social protest and their avoidance of the subject of race, Kelley's novels are exceptional among the work of African American women publishing in the 1890s. Rather, they are typical of writing by white women in the "girl's fiction" subgenre of the sentimental novel, a category notable for its emphasis on socializing young women into the dominant social order. Yet while Kelley's texts urge acceptance of the status quo and earthly suffering as God's will, their emphasis on personal salvation may have been based in the widespread view that moral reformation of individuals was the necessary precondition for progressive social change.

Each of Kelley's novels features a group of girls whom readers follow from a carefree late adolescence through a process of Christian conversion and concomitant acceptance of the responsibilities of adult womanhood, as defined by late-nineteenth-century evangelical Protestantism. Each text features a particularly spirited, ambitious, and talented heroine who initially resists the Christian path but who in the end claims Jesus as her savior and finds her reward in a traditional marriage and the inner peace that immediately follows upon her conversion.

There is disagreement regarding the precise racial identification of Kelley's characters. The confusionis compounded by the iconography of *Megda,* in which fair skin is almost invariably correlated with virtue, the exception being one very poor, devout young woman described as having skin significantly darker than that of her wealthier peers. Even here, coloring may be an indicator of class status rather than racial difference. The uncertainty regarding the race of Kelley's characters is indicative of the subtle tension her novels reveal on matters of race and gender. Though atypical among African American treatments of these topics, Kelley's texts display numerous marks of strain that suggest the uncomfortable position occupied by middle-class African American women of the period. Their female-centered Christian ethos, while rejecting social protest, anticipates the feminist spirituality found in much late-twentieth-century African American women's writing.

• Molly Hite, introduction to *Megda,* 1988. Deborah McDowell, introduction to *Four Girls at Cottage City,* 1989.

—Meryl F. Schwartz

KELLEY, WILLIAM MELVIN (b. 1937), novelist, short fiction writer, and educator. Born in New York, William Melvin Kelley attended Fieldston School and Harvard University. He has taught literature and writing at the New School for Social Research, the State University of New York at Geneseo, and the University of Paris, Nanterre.

From the beginning of his career in 1962, William Melvin Kelley has employed his distinctive form of black comedy to examine the absurdities surrounding American racial attitudes. His first novel showed the influence of William Faulkner by creating a microcosm in a mythical southern state; his last pays tribute to James Joyce's stylistic innovations. Like Faulkner's, his works are connected by a cast of common characters.

In *A Different Drummer* (1962), multiple narrators tell the intertwined histories of the Willson and Caliban families. Tucker Caliban is the descendant of a giant African king who died rather than face slavery under General Dewey Willson, leaving his infant son to become "First Caliban," slave, and later servant to Willson, governor of his home state. Moved by an unarticulated instinct, Tucker destroys his small farm, kills his livestock, and leaves the state for the North, emancipating not only himself, his wife Bethrah, and his unborn child but the surviving members of the Willson line, who are freed from their heritage as former slaveholders. Tucker's instinctive action is contrasted not only with his ancestor's ineffective physical rebellion but with the intellectual fight against racism waged by "Black Jesuit" leader Bennett Bradshaw, a northern civil rights advocate. Tucker and his family are followed by all the African Americans in the state, which becomes the only state to have an all-white population.

Dancers on the Shore (1964) is a collection of stories that connect *A Different Drummer* with Kelley's later work. The first story, "The Only Man on Liberty Street," features the illegitimate daughter of General Dewey Willson. In the last story, Wallace Bedlow, a character similar to singer Hudie (Leadbelly) Ledbetter, is one of the refugees inspired by Tucker Caliban. In "Cry for Me," Bedlow travels to New York City, where he forms a special bond with his nephew Carlyle, a prominent character in *dem* (1967) and *Dunfords Travels Everywheres* (1970). Wallace Bedlow plays his distinctive music in the coffeehouses of Greenwich Village and dies during a triumphant concert at Carnegie Hall. Several stories—including "A Visit to Grandmother," "Saint Paul and the Monkeys," and "Christmas with the Great Man"—introduce the Dunford family.

Kelley's second novel, *A Drop of Patience* (1965), is the life story of blind saxophone player Ludlow Washington. Ludlow begins his career in a southern juke joint, moves to New York where he backs up a famous blues singer, Inez Cunningham, then joins a traveling band that allows him the freedom to pursue his own groundbreaking style of jazz. Based loosely on Charlie *Parker, Ludlow is conquered not by drugs but by his destructive relationship with a white woman. *A Drop of Patience* is tied to *A Different Drummer* by Bethra Washington, Ludlow's daughter, who becomes the wife of Tucker Caliban.

The narrator of *dem* is Mitchell Pierce, whose wife, Tam, surprises him by bearing fraternal twins, one white and one black. Guided by Carlyle Bedlow and Calvin Johnson, Pierce explores Harlem, looking for his wife's African American lover, whom he has seen once when the man was dating his maid. After visiting Harlem's nightclubs and several rent parties, Mitchell realizes that Calvin (Coolidge) Johnson is the same man he met in his own kitchen, where he was introduced to him under the man's nickname, "Cooley."

If *dem* is often surrealistic, *Dunfords Travels Everywheres* completely abandons reality. Chig Dunford lives in a foreign country where apartheid is rigorously enforced, not on a racial basis but depending on which color scheme—blue or yellow—each individual has chosen for the day. Returning to the United States by ocean liner, Dunford finds the boiler room of the ship filled with chained Africans being transported to America. Parallel to Chig's story are convoluted tales of Carlyle Bedlow's seduction of his dentist's wife and Bedlow's attempt to save a friend who has sold his soul to the devil. The novel is a mixture of straightforward narrative and language reminiscent of *Finnegan's Wake*.

Early in his career, Kelley distanced himself from racial questions, decrying "symbols or ideas disguised as people" (preface, *Dancers on the Shore*), but during the eight-year span of his career—years of turmoil for the nation—he became increasingly involved in political commentary.

• Roger Rosenblatt, *Black Fiction*, 1974, pp. 142–151. Donald M. Weyl, "The Vision of Man in the Novels of William Melvin Kelley," *Critique* 15.3 (1974): 15–33. Jill Weyant, "The Kelley Saga: Violence in America," *CLA Journal* 19 (1975): 210–220. Howard Faulkner, "The Uses of Tradition: William Melvin Kelley's *A Different Drummer*," *Modern Fiction Studies* 21 (1975–1976): 535–542. Addison Gayle, *The Way of the New World: The Black Novel in America*, 1976, pp. 367–376.

—Robert E. Fleming

KENAN, RANDALL (b. 1963), novelist, short story writer, playwright, editor, and educator. Randall Kenan was born in New York City but moved shortly thereafter to rural North Carolina. Growing up in Chinquapin, Kenan received his BA in English and creative writing with a minor in physics from the University of North Carolina at Chapel Hill in 1985. He also studied at Oxford University during the summer of 1984.

Kenan then became an editor at Knopf and began advancing in the publishing profession. In 1989 his writing career gained momentum with the publication of his first novel, *A Visitation of Spirits*. He became a lecturer at Sarah Lawrence College in 1989, and later at Columbia University, and was a visiting professor at Duke University in 1994 and at the University of North Carolina at Chapel Hill in 1995. Kenan's many honors include nomination for the National Book Critics Circle Award, a 1995 Guggenheim Fellowship, and a 1995 Sherwood Anderson Award.

Published by Grove Press, *A Visitation of Spirits* received impressive accolades for a first novel: the dust jacket includes endorsements by Gloria *Naylor and Adrienne *Kennedy. Set in rural Tims Creek, North Carolina—a community clearly modeled after Chinquapin—the novel is divided into five sections, all of which concentrate on the Cross family, specifically sixteen-year-old Horace Cross and his older cousin, the Reverend Jimmy Greene. The focus of *A Visitation of Spirits* is on Horace and his slide into insanity and suicide. Horace's realization that he is homosexual causes him to believe that he is damned and that he can only escape by transforming himself into a red-tailed hawk. When Horace's sorcery fails to achieve this transformation, his despair is so great that he cannot return to reality. Instead, on a terrifying night filled with demons, the deranged and naked Horace revisits sites of earlier significance in his life but finds no redemption. While confronting his cousin Jimmy, Horace shoots himself in the head with his grandfather's shotgun.

Kenan's *Let the Dead Bury Their Dead* (1992) is a collection of short stories that are also based in Tims Creek. A widely ranging group of twelve tales, the work includes some characters from his earlier work, such as Jimmy Greene, who is the "author" of the title story, a pseudoscholarly history of the town. The first selection humorously portrays a clairvoyant five-year-old, a possessed tractor, and a talking hog. Other stories depict such wildly varied topics as an elderly woman learning that her dead grandson was gay and that his lover was white, and a middle-aged lawyer who is obsessed with his incestuous relationship with his half sister. Throughout, the only apparent link among these stories is Tims Creek.

In 1994 Kenan published a biography, *James Baldwin,* which is in the Lives of Notable Gay Men and Lesbians series, edited by Martin Duberman. In 1996, Kenan was working on a travel book that detailed his explorations of black culture throughout the United States and Canada. It was published as *Walking on Water: Black American Lives at the Turn of the Twenty-First Century* (1999). He was also writing another Tims Creek novel, tentatively called "The Fire and the Baptism" and a play, "The Meek Shall Inherit the Earth." In addition to his longer works, Kenan has published several short stories (in periodicals and anthologies), as well as reviews, interviews, and articles on topics ranging from John Edgar *Wideman to hip-hop music. As a promising young writer who openly addresses homosexuality, Kenan's impact on African American literature is significant. While his use of the supernatural is reminiscent of Toni *Morrison, an early inspiration for him, Randall Kenan's journeys through the rural South are uniquely his own. That uniqueness is also apparent in *A Time Not Here: The Mississippi Delta* (1996), a volume of photographs by Norman Mauskopf, for which Kenan wrote the accompanying essay.

• Robert McRuer, "Randall Kenan," in *Contemporary Gay American Novelists: A Bio-Bibliographical Critical Sourcebook,* ed. Emmanuel S. Nelson, 1993, pp. 232–236. Randall Kenan, interview by Susan Ketchin, in *The Christ-Haunted Landscape: Faith and Doubt in Southern Fiction,* by Susan Ketchin, 1994, pp. 277–302. Doris Betts, "Randall Garrett Kenan: Myth and Reality in Tims Creek," in *Southern Writers at Century's End,* ed. Jeffrey J. Folks and James A. Perkins, 1997, pp. 9–20. Charles H. Rowell, "An Interview with Randall Kenan," *Callaloo* 21:1 (Winter 1998): 133–148.

—Kristine A. Yohe

KENNEDY, ADRIENNE (b. 1931), author, lecturer, and prizewinning playwright. Born Adrienne Lita Hawkins on 13 September 1931 to Cornell Wallace and Etta (Haugabook) Hawkins in Pittsburgh, Pennsylvania, Kennedy grew up in Cleveland, Ohio, and attended Cleveland public schools. The future playwright entered Ohio State University in 1949, earning a BA in education in 1953. She also studied at Columbia University (1954–1956), the Theatre Wing of the New School for Social Research, Circle in the Square Theatre School, and Edward Albee's Theatre Workshop in New York City. On 15 May 1953 Kennedy married Joseph C. Kennedy and they have two sons, Joseph C. and Adam. The couple divorced in 1966.

Kennedy was a founding member of the Women's Theatre Council in 1971, a member of the board of directors of PEN (1976–1977), and International Theatre Institute representative in Budapest in 1978. Her numerous awards include a Village Voice Obie for **Funnyhouse of a Negro* in 1964, a Guggenheim Fellowship in 1967, several Rockefeller grants (1967–1969, 1974, 1976), a National Endowment for the Arts grant in 1973, a CBS Fellowship at the School of Drama in 1973, a Creative Artists public service grant in 1974, a Yale Fellowship (1974–1975), a Stanley Award, a New England Theatre Conference grant, and an American Book Award in 1990. In July 1995, she was named playwright in residence for the September 1995 through May 1996 season with the Signature Theater Company in New York. Two of her predecessors for this honor, Horton Foote and Edward Albee, have been awarded the Pulitzer Prize for their respective seasons.

A writer whose work continues to exemplify complexity and independent vision, Kennedy now claims authorship of some thirteen published plays, five unpublished plays, several autobiographical works of nonfiction, a short story, and a novella. Her first published work was the short story "Because of the King of France," published under the pseudonym Adrienne Cornell in *Black Orpheus: A Journal of African and Afro-American Literature* (1963). Her first professionally produced play was *Funnyhouse* in 1964. *A Lesson in Dead Language* (published in *Collision Course,* 1968) was produced along with Funnyhouse in London on 28 April 1968. *A Lesson* features a classroom setting where the teacher is dressed from the waist up as a white dog. Her pupils (or pupil, depending on the production), all adolescent girls, wear white costumes with red stains signifying sexual maturation; the play deals with the accompanying trauma of the bloody rite of passage. *A Rat's Mass,* in which humans regress to the status of rats, was named one of the best plays of the season for 1966. Written in 1963, it was first produced in April 1966 by Theatre Company in Boston, and later in Rome (21 June 1966) and Turin (28 October 1966). It is anthologized in *New Black Playwrights* (1968).

At a time when other African American playwrights were making profound assertions of black pride in their works, and a sort of nationalist movement in African American theater was afoot, Kennedy created African American female protagonists in *Funnyhouse* and *The Owl Answers* (first produced at the White Barn Theatre, Westport, Connecticut, in 1965) who were clearly confounded by their multiethnic origins. Before the advent of postmodernist drama, Kennedy's plays featured nonlinear narratives, dramatic and surrealistic imagery, split characters who existed in dreamlike states, fragmented formats, and unconventional plots. Her routine use of poetic and bouyant language, pregnant with multiple levels of meaning, makes Kennedy a deliberate master of the verbal metaphor. She combines elements of expressionism with a verbal fluidity to evoke a series of profound and provocative effects. Critics of Kennedy's work must be attuned to a variety of critical approaches and traditions to accurately assess her value to the theatrical community.

In her autobiographical memoir, People Who Led to My Plays (1987), Kennedy discloses an aspect of her life that may help to explain her independent vision. Her maternal grandfather was a rich white peach farmer with whom Kennedy interacted during visits to her parents' hometown of Montezuma, Georgia. From her Morehouse-educated father, the playwright learned that whites in Montezuma were of mostly British heritage. In the preface to Deadly Triplets: A Theatre Mystery and Journal (1990), Kennedy points out that her work in *Funnyhouse* and *The Owl Answers* was as "filled with English imagery—Queen Victoria, Chaucer, William the Conquerer—as it was filled with African images—Patrice Lumumba, savannahs, frangipani trees." Kennedy's acknowledgment of, and involvement with, combined African and British aspects of her heritage helps to account for multicultural themes in her plays. She admits to a fascination with England's legendary queens; literary influences on her personal and professional development actually include a plethora of works by authors from around the world. Her 1987 memoir tracks some of the people and images that affected her development as an author. For example, an entry under the heading "Tennessee Williams" includes the pronouncement that the summer evening she saw *The Glass Menagerie* was "when the idea of being a writer and seeing my own family onstage caught fire in my mind." Under "Wagner" she writes that his music "expressed a wild intensity that I felt growing inside me, but that I could not explain or comprehend." There are entries entitled "Checkhov, Dante, Virgil and the Bible," "Langston *Hughes," and "William Faulkner"; and under "James *Baldwin," she writes: "He sharpened my entire vision of America." Such a personal and professional engagement with the worldwide human community may be a contributing factor to the enduring quality of her work as well as her lengthy tenure as a respected writer and lecturer.

Much of Kennedy's work is taken from real-life experiences. She wrote unpublished autobiographical fiction while studying creative writing at Columbia, and an early autobiographical play, *Pale Blue Flowers* (1955), was also written there. *Deadly Triplets* consists of a mystery in novella form and a journal based on Kennedy's experiences in London from 1966 to 1969. She used a sniper incident described in Vietnam War news accounts to write *An Evening with Dead Essex*, a play first produced at New York's American Place Theatre Workshop (directed by Gaby Rodgers) in 1973. The play was also produced at the Yale Repertory Company in 1974 and published in *Theatre* (1978). *Diary of Lights*, produced in 1987 and described as a musical without songs, depicts the youthful idealism of a young black married couple living on the Upper West Side of New York City. Kennedy calls on her early fascination with Hollywood films in *A Movie Star Has to Star in Black and White* (*Wordplay* 3, 1984; *Norton Anthology of American Literature*, 1989) to examine fractured family relationships while looking at the fantasy lives of movie stars in their films (Bette Davis in "Now, Voyager," Marlon Brando in "Viva Zapata," and Montgomery Clift in "A Place in the Sun"). *A Movie Star* was first produced in New York in 1976 by Public Theatre Workshop; Ntozake *Shange directed a production at the University of Houston in 1985. *Sleep Deprivation Chamber* (1991) is based on Kennedy's own quest for justice following the beating of her son Adam by corrupt police. *The Ohio State Murders*, first produced in 1992 and included in the Kennedy volume entitled *The Alexander Plays* (1992), features protagonist Suzanne Alexander reliving and reinventing some troubling incidents from Kennedy's own days as a student at Ohio State. The other three of the Alexander plays are *She Talks to Beethoven* (first produced in 1989), *The Film Club* (a monologue), and *The Dramatic Circle* (a dramatization of *The Film Club*). *She Talks to Beethoven* is also published individually in *Plays in One Act* (1991) and *Antaeus* (Spring 1991).

A number of Kennedy's plays were commissioned. Herbert Blau and Jules Irving commissioned *A Beast's Story for Lincoln Center*, though the first production of the play was with *The Owl Answers* under the title *Cities in Belzique* (published by Samuel French in 1969). The play underscores the relationship between humans and beasts by highlighting the inhumane tendencies of humankind; it is anthologized in *Kuntu Drama: Plays of the African Continuum* (1974). Controversy surrounded the writing of *The Lennon Play: In His Own Write*, a project for which Kennedy was hired, but whose authorship she eventually shared with John Lennon and Victor Spinetti. Real and fictionalized accounts of her experiences while writing this play are contained in *Deadly Triplets*. The play was first produced in 1967 as "Act I Scene 3," opening as *The Lennon Play: In His Own Write* on 18 June 1968 at the National Theater, London. It was published in *Best*

Short Plays of the World Theatre in 1968 and 1973. *Sun: A Poem for *Malcolm X Inspired by His Murder* was commissioned by the Royal Court Theatre in 1968 and published in *Scripts* (1971) and *Spontaneous Combustion* (1972). Productions were in London August 1969 and in 1970 by La Mama Experimental Theatre Club in New York City. *Boats* was commissioned for "An Omnibus of Short Works," and performed in Los Angeles on 12 October 1969. Other commissioned plays include *Black Children's Day* (Brown University, 1980); *A Lancashire Lad* (Empire State Youth Theater Institute, 1980), based on the childhood of Charles Chaplin; and *Orestes* and *Electra* (the Juilliard School, 1980), adaptations from the Euripides plays. *Orestes* and *Electra* are published in Adrienne Kennedy in *One Act* (1988). Kennedy mentions an additional commissioned play, *The Life of Robert Johnson,* on page three of her 1987 memoir. In 1996, she published *Sleep Deprivation Chamber: A Theatre Piece with Adam P. Kennedy.*

Over the years, Kennedy has spent a good amount of time in classroom settings. She has taught and/or lectured at Yale (1972–1974), Princeton (1977), Brown University (1979–1980), University of California, Berkeley (1986), and Harvard (1990–1991). She published "Letter to My Students" in *Kenyon Review* in 1993.

• *Interviews with Contemporary Women Playwrights,* eds. Kathleen Betsko and Rachel Koenig, 1987. Adrienne Kennedy, interview by Elin Diamond, *Studies in American Drama 1945–Present,* eds. Philip C. Kolin et al., 1989, pp. 143–157. Jane Schlueter, "No Place but the Funnyhouse: The Struggle for Identity in Three Adrienne Kennedy Plays," in *Modern American Drama: The Female Canon,* ed. Susan E. Meigs, 1990, pp. 172–183. *Intersecting Boundaries: The Theatre of Adrienne Kennedy,* eds. Paul K. Bryant-Jackson and Lois More Overbeck, 1992. Linda Kintz, *The Subject's Tragedy: Political Poetics, Feminist Theory, and Drama,* 1992. Obododimma Oha, "Her Dissonant Selves: The Semiotics of Plurality and Bisexuality in Adrienne Kennedy's *Funnyhouse of a Negro,*" *American Drama* 6:2 (Spring 1997): 67–80. Carla J. McDonough, "God and Owls: The Sacred and the Profane in Adrienne Kennedy's *The Owl Answers,*" *Modern Drama* 40:3 (Fall 1997): 385–402 (there are other articles on Kennedy in this issue).

—Lovalerie King

KERMIT, S. L. *See* Delany, Samuel R.

KILLENS, JOHN O. (1916–1987), novelist, university professor, essayist, screenwriter, and editor. John O. Killens was born 14 January 1916 in Macon, Georgia, the son of Charles Myles, Sr., and WillieLee (Coleman) Killens. He married Grace Ward Jones and was the father of two children: Jon Charles and Barbara Ellen Rivera. Killens's childhood and life experiences destined him to become a vital voice in African American literature. As a child he listened attentively to his great-grandmother tell outlandish and outrageous tales. He also read extensively. Killens's educational experiences included attending Edward Waters College, Morris-Brown College, Atlanta University, Howard University, Robert Law School, Columbia University, and New York University. After struggling with law school at night and working during the day, Killens emerged as a writer. His first draft of *Youngblood* was shared over a storefront in Harlem with seven other young African Americans who had dreams of becoming writers. They later formed the Harlem Writers Guild, which came to be known and respected by the African American literary world. Killens died of cancer 27 October 1987 in Brooklyn, New York. His contributions to the African American literary tradition began with his integrational approach and became a voice of blackness later with characters like Yoruba and Lumumba in *The *Cotillion.* Killens's concern with racism, classism, assimilation, and hypocrisy is evident in the body of literature he produced.

As in many protest novels of the time, Killens attacks the institution of racism, oppressive economics, and other injustices in *Youngblood.* The novel was published in 1954, a time when the social and civil unrest of a country dominated print media. Although laws were being passed to end segregation, the South refused to accept this change, and Killens captures this struggle in the southern black family who is fighting for survival during these turbulent times. For those readers who possess some romantic view of the South, *Youngblood* exposes the cruel realities of African Americans who tried to remain tied to their southern roots and not flee to the North for better days. The novel, set in Crossroads, Georgia, explores the lives of four characters who collectively fight against the oppressive educational, social, and economic injustices of a Jim Crow existence.

Killens's voice rang loud and clear on the civil ills of America as demonstrated in his novel, *'Sippi* (1967), which addresses the struggles African Americans experienced during the 1960s. William H. Wiggins, Jr., in the *Dictionary of Literary Biography* states that the title originates from a "civil rights protest joke" in which a black man informs his white landlord that he will no longer include mister or miss when addressing others, including the state of Mississippi: "It's just plain Sippi from now on!" In the novel, Killens's realistic approach to many intimidating acts, such as bombings and shootings, divided critics. His response to this polarized group was that he wrote the book because he had to tell the story, not because he thought someone would respond as he had to his great-grandmother's stories.

In *The Cotillion, or One Good Bull Is Half the Herd* (1971), Killens moves away from his social protest novel and steps into a community of African Americans to explore its dark sides. This satirical novel attacks the classism and assimilation that dominated many African American communities. Killens's Lumumba represents that breed of African Americans who attempt to redefine themselves by separating themselves from their Eurocentric standards. In contrast to Lumumba's ideology, there exists a community of women who symbolize the vise-grip Eurocentrism has on the African American. Although most criticism of *The Cotillion* dealt with the theme of Afrocentricity versus Eurocentricity, the text also has a strong commentary on African American adolescence.

Killens's name will forever ring simultaneously with the bells of freedom. Most of his works, including his nonfiction pieces, are commentaries on social protest and blacks embracing their blackness. His significance to the literary tradition remains two-fold, to provide a silenced community with a voice and to produce a history from which a definition of self can evolve.

• Horst Ihde, "Black Writer's Burden: Remarks on John Oliver Killens," *Zeitschrift fur Anglistik and Amerikanistic* 16 (Jan. 1968): 117–137. William H. Wiggins, Jr., "The Structure and Dynamics of Folklore in the Novel Form: The Case of John O. Killens," *Keystone Folklore Quarterly 17* (1972): 92–118. Burney J. Hollis, *Swords upon This Hill: Preserving the Literary Tradition of Black Colleges and Universities,* 1984. William H. Wiggins, Jr., "John Oliver Killens," in *DLB,* vol. 33, *Afro-American Fiction Writers after 1955,* eds. Thadious M. Davis and Trudier Harris, 1984, pp. 144–152.

—Wanda Macon

KINCAID, JAMAICA (b. 1949), short story writer, essayist, and novelist. A leading West Indian writer, Jamaica Kincaid (born Elaine Potter Richardson) left her birthplace, the nine-by-twelve-mile island of Antigua, just after her sixteenth birthday and came to the United States. Although much of her writing concerns itself with the West Indies, Kincaid did not return to the island where she was born until nineteen years after she left. Kincaid has received a good deal of attention and critical acclaim despite the modest body of work to her name: a slim book of short stories (*At the Bottom of the River,* 1983), two short novels (*Annie John,* 1985; *Lucy,* 1990), a longer novel (*The Autobiography of My Mother,* 1996), a nonfiction essay about Antigua (*A Small Place,* 1988), and short sketches, short stories, and columns published in the New Yorker and elsewhere. Kincaid was editor of *Best American Essays 1995.* In 1997, she published *My Brother.*

Kincaid began her career as a writer through an exposure to the New York literary scene in the 1970s. Her growing acquaintance with contemporary writers led then New Yorker editor William Shawn to ask Kincaid to write a piece for "Talk of the Town." Her pithy, lyrical style was so successful that she became a regular contributor to the magazine. Her first book, *At the Bottom of the River* (1983), included seven stories originally published in the *New Yorker* and touched on themes that would be echoed in her later fiction: mother-daughter relationships, the social constraints felt by a young girl coming of age, a sense of listlessness and dissatisfaction despite surroundings of great beauty, sexual fluidity, questions of identity, and the merging of real and imaginary worlds.

Annie John (1985), Kincaid's next work of fiction, has alternately been called a book of short stories and a novel. An episodic bildungsroman, *Annie John* follows the path of an angry and alienated, yet exceptionally bright, ten-year-old girl as she matures. Stifled yet exhilarated by her small life on Antigua, in love with yet furious at her mother, Annie John suffers acutely from growing pains. Her changing body is awkward to her, she is debilitated by an inexplicable illness that makes her behavior border on madness, and although imbued with a sense of her own superiority, Annie John puzzles as much over her place in the world as she does over the question of what world it is that she inhabits. The book ends with Annie John at seventeen when, not yet freed from her parents' domination but on her way off the island, she embarks on a new life in England.

Kincaid's next novel, *Lucy* (1990), centers around a character whose anger and bitterness (her name is short for Lucifer) bear a great similarity to that of Annie John. Critics have remarked that *Lucy* can be read as a continuation of *Annie John,* although the protagonists have different names. Lucy has traveled a long way from her island home (this time the island is not specified) and come to work as an au pair for a blond and smiling, yet deeply divided, white family in the United States. At nineteen, Lucy is already savvy and seemingly imperturbable. Although she rides an elevator for the first time, eats food taken from a refrigerator for the first time (her island home did not have one, and Kincaid herself grew up without electricity), Lucy is a sophisticated and often embittered young woman. Much is familiar in this new world: she recognizes, for example, her father's love of other women (with whom he had children) in the affair her employer has with his wife's best friend.

The Autobiography of My Mother (1996) is the story of a motherless child, Xuela Claudette Richardson. She negotiates her way through a sensual and desperately lonely world on the island of Dominica, suspecting that her father cherishes his bundle of dirty laundry more than he cares for her. Claiming to embody both her mother and the children she decides not to have, Xuela struggles to construct a self out of the bleak, black wind of her mother's absence.

Best known for her fiction, Kincaid has also written a nonfiction, polemical essay about Antigua. When the piece was rejected by the changing guard at the *New Yorker* (they dismissed it as too angry), Kincaid published *A Small Place* (1988) as a slim book. The essay explores Antigua's shameful past, the island's postcolonial legacy, its dilapidated buildings and astounding beauty, and the corruption and abuse of power by present-day politicians. Kincaid wrote it after a visit back to Antigua and a fresh look at her birthplace through the eyes of an adult.

Kincaid and her husband, composer and college professor Allen Shawn, live in Burlington, Vermont, with their two children, Annie and Harold.

• Daryl Cumber Dance, ed., *Fifty Caribbean Writers: A Bio-Bibliographical Critical Sourcebook,* 1986. Selwyn R. Cudjoe, ed., *Caribbean Women Writers,* 1990. Moira Ferguson, *Gender Relations from Mary Wollstonecraft to Jamaica Kincaid: East Caribbean Connections,* 1993. Diane Simmons, *Jamaica Kincaid,* 1994. Kristin Mahlis, "Gender and Exile: Jamaica Kincaid's *Lucy,*" *Modern Fiction Studies* 44:1 (Spring 1998): 164–183. Diane Simmons, "Coming-of-Age in the Snare of History: Jamaica Kincaid's *The Autobiography of My Mother,*" in *The Girl: Construction of the Girl in Contemporary Fiction by Women,* ed. Ruth O. Saxton, 1998, pp. 107–118.

—Jennifer Margulis

Kindred. Octavia E. *Butler's fourth novel, *Kindred* (1979), is a meditation on the impact of public education, popular media, and family lore upon our conceptions of shared legacies, future prospects, and present positions. Variously classified as realistic science fiction, grim fantasy, neo–slave narrative, and initiation novel, the book evades genre labeling. Using the fantastic convention of time travel to move Dana on repeated trips from twentieth-century southern California to antebellum Maryland, Butler narrates the coming of age of an African American woman during the social revolutions of the 1970s, explores the grim realities and legacies of antebellum slavery, and speculates upon future possibilities for human equality.

On her twenty-sixth birthday, Dana is abruptly and involuntarily transported to a Maryland riverbank in order to save a drowning child, Rufus, who will grow up to be a slaveowner and the father of Dana's grandmother, Hagar. Dana makes several trips between the centuries for she is jerked into the nineteenth century every time Rufus believes he is dying and Rufus's temper and lack of discipline often place him in mortal danger. She is returned to the twentieth century when she believes her own life is ending. During her travels into the past, Dana comes to understand slavery as a psychological as well as a physical danger, and she also learns how inadequate the average twentieth-century education is for knowing one's historical past or for surviving without technological aid. As she lives and becomes friends with other slaves, Dana develops a new understanding of heroism and perfidy, of human potential and human limitations. Dana betrays her great-grandmother Alice in order to save Alice's life. With her great-grandfather Rufus, she insists upon mutual respect despite or because of the differences that society affords to race, gender, and condition of servitude.

Butler's juxtapositioning of life in nineteenth- and twentieth-century America deliberately suggests complicated comparisons. For example, Dana, a black unpublished writer, is married to Kevin, a white recently published writer, who she met when they were both working for a temporary labor pool nicknamed the "slave market." Though she loves her husband, Dana recognizes disturbing similarities between their relationship and those of the antebellum period, while Kevin comes to regard Rufus as his rival for Dana's attention and affection.

Kindred was written, Butler says, during the black consciousness period of the early 1970s as her attempt to understand her own identity and the experiences that had shaped her ancestors. It was influenced also by her discovery of slave narratives by writers such as Frederick *Douglass. Though the antebellum slave past marked a distinct subject and era change for Octavia Butler, *Kindred* does continue the explorations of individual heroism, human relations, and social patterns that mark her other writings.

With *Kindred* Octavia Butler was among the first of recent writers, including Virginia *Hamilton, Belinda Hurmance, Charles R. *Johnson, and Ishmael *Reed, to employ techniques of speculative fiction and fantasy in meditations on slavery and the human condition.

• Jewelle Gomez, "Black Women Heroes: Here's Reality, Where's the Fiction?," *The Black Scholar* 17.2 (Mar./Apr. 1986): 8–18. Robert Crossley, introduction to *Kindred,* 1988.

—Frances Smith Foster

KING, MARTIN LUTHER, JR. (1929–1968), orator, political strategist, essayist, and leader during the 1950s and 1960s civil rights movement. Martin Luther King, Jr., was born in Atlanta, Georgia, on 15 January 1929, the child of Rev. Martin Luther King, Sr., and Alberta Williams King. Alberta King's father, Rev. A. D. Williams, helped found the Atlanta chapter of the NAACP and pastored Ebenezer Baptist Church, which King, Sr., commanded after Williams's death. Both preachers rocked the Ebenezer walls with their thunderous folk sermons while Alberta King played the organ and organized the choir. King, Jr., grew up immersed in the doctrine of Christian love and in the music and oratory of African American Baptist worship.

In 1948 King, Jr., earned a bachelor's degree from Morehouse College, where he heard Benjamin Mays, his father's friend and president of the college, preach during chapel services. Electing to become a minister, King studied at Crozer Theological Seminary and at Boston University, where he received a PhD in theology in 1955.

Early in 1954 King assumed his first pulpit at Dexter Avenue Baptist Church of Montgomery, Alabama. When Rosa Parks was arrested in December 1955 for refusing to give up her bus seat to a white man, JoAnn Robinson and the Women's Political Council initiated a bus boycott. As leader of the boycott organization, King gave his initial civil rights address to an overflow crowd at Holt Street Baptist Church, inspiring his audience to continue the boycott. By the time the protest ended a year later, he emerged as a national figure in the struggle for racial equality. Appearing in 1958, his book about the boycott, *Stride toward Freedom,* articulated the politics of nonviolence.

In 1956 King began an oratorical marathon that lasted over twelve years, attacking segregation in approximately two thousand speeches and sermons as he hopscotched the nation.

In 1963, orchestrating a major civil rights campaign in Birmingham, he answered critics with his famous essay "*Letter from Birmingham Jail." His demonstrations served as morality plays in which nonviolent demonstrators met police who used fire hoses, German shepherds, tear gas, or billy clubs to preserve white supremacy. Such brutality shocked millions watching on television. In 1963 he delivered "*I Have a Dream," the climactic speech of a massive March on Washington, the most important American civil rights rally to date. Sometimes helped by ghostwriters, he also wrote many essays and five books, including *Strength to Love* (1963), a collection of sermons.

He consistently advocated nonviolence in the quest for racial equality and peace—an approach drastically different from that of *Malcolm X, a more radical leader whose refusal to eschew violence made King seem more reasonable to whites.

For years scholars attributed King's ideas to his exposure to Euro-American philosophers and theologians, whom he studied in graduate school. Recently, however, a group of researchers led by James Cone has challenged this view, arguing that King's theology and oratory sprang mainly from his boyhood training at Ebenezer Church.

Many of King's sermons echo earlier texts by African American pastor Howard Thurman and by such white Protestant ministers as Harry Emerson Fosdick, Robert McCracken, J. Wallace Hamilton, and George Buttrick. Borrowing sermons was common practice not only for King, but for many other preachers, black and white.

King buttressed arguments with literary quotations. He repeated and elaborated riveting phrases that often incorporated lyrics from patriotic songs and hymns. Enjoying interaction with audiences, he mastered the traditional call and response of African American pastors. His crescendoing baritone voice, rolling cadences, and anticipatory pauses mesmerized not only African American Christians accustomed to such electric delivery, but also millions of others.

Late in his career, King attempted not only to achieve civil rights, but also to stop the Vietnam War and to eliminate American poverty. Facing threats upon his life, he journeyed to a garbage workers' strike in Memphis, Tennessee, to deliver "I've Been to the Mountaintop." He recalled the Exodus and other epochal events in Western history, claiming a similar importance for the present struggle. The mayor of Memphis was a "pharaoh," and his slaves, the garbage workers, could achieve justice only through unity. At the end King dramatically compared himself to *Moses, who, standing atop a mountain, could glimpse the Promised Land. Amid shouts from enraptured listeners, he assured, "I may not get there with you;" but "we as a people will get to the Promised Land."

The next day King died when shot by a hidden gunman.

Like King, James Farmer, Medgar Evers, John Lewis, Fannie Lou Hamer, Diane Nash, and dozens of others volunteered for jail duty, choreographed dramatic confrontations, and risked their lives. King distinguished himself through his language. Simultaneously perfecting and politicizing a robust black pulpit, King translated the traditional African American demand for equality into an idiom that many whites finally tried to understand.

• Harry Emerson Fosdick, *Hope of the World,* 1933. David Garrow, *Bearing the Cross: Martin Luther King, Jr., and the Southern Christian Leadership Conference,* 1986. Martin Luther King, Jr., *A Testament of Hope: The Essential Writings of Martin Luther King, Jr.,* 1986. James Cone, *Martin and Malcolm and America,* 1991. Keith D. Miller, *Voice of Deliverance: The Language of Martin Luther King, Jr., and Its Sources,* 1992. Clayborne Carson, ed., *The Papers of Martin Luther King, Jr.,* 4 vols., 1992 -. Anita Haya Patterson, *From Emerson to King,* 1997.

—Keith D. Miller and Emily M. Lewis

KING, WOODIE, JR. (b. 1937), essayist, short-story writer, anthologist, dramatist, scriptwriter for film and television, producer, director, actor, and contributor to the Black Arts movement. Born in Mobile, Alabama, Woodie King, Jr., moved to Detroit with his parents, Woodie and Ruby King, when he was five. From 1955 to 1968 to help out his family, which was supported by his mother's housework, King worked as a model for church fans and calendars. He attended Michigan's Will-O-Way School of the Theatre on scholarship from 1958 to 1962, studying every element of the theater while immersing himself in black literature. In 1959, he married casting agent Willie Mae Washington with whom he would have three children. From 1959 to 1962, King wrote drama criticism for the *Detroit Tribune.*

Both at Will-O-Way and at Wayne State University and the Detroit School of Arts and Crafts, where he did postgraduate study in theater, King lamented the lack of acting opportunities for blacks and, with Ron *Milner, cofounded the Concept-East Theatre. As its manager and director from 1960 to 1963, King staged plays by white and black playwrights, including Milner's, eventually exchanging the middle class for a neighborhood audience to the enlivenment of the productions.

Negro Digest published his first story, "Ghetto," in August 1962 and his second, "Beautiful Light and Black Our Dreams," in 1963. The latter, republished in Langston *Hughes's *The Best Short Stories by Negro Writers* (1967), explores the poetically expressed thoughts of a black man and his lover and is notably sympathetic toward the woman who has been disillusioned by too many black hustlers yet longs to color her romantic dreams black.

A year after his 1964 move to New York, King won a John Hays Whitney Fellowship to study directing and theater administration and became Cultural Arts Director of Mobilization for Youth. In 1966, King adapted Langston Hughes's poetry for the stage in *The *Weary Blues,* later adapting Hughes's stories in *Simple's Blues.*

After producing in 1969 *Black Quartet,* four one-act plays by Black Arts movement dramatists (including Ron Milner), King founded the New Federal Theatre in 1970. Serving as showcase and inspiration for new black plays, the New Federal Theatre also welcomed works by other ethnic writers.

In the 1970s, King edited several landmark anthologies, including *Black Drama Anthology* (coedited with Ron Milner), *Black Short Story Anthology* (containing his story "The Game"), and *Black Poets and Prophets: The Theory, Practice and Esthetics of the Pan-Africanist Revolution* (coedited with Earl Anthony).

King has also produced, directed, and written several films, including *The Long Night* (based on Julian *Mayfield's 1975 novel) and *The Black Theatre Movement: "A Raisin in the Sun" to the Present,* and scripted teleplays for "Sanford and Son." A collection of his essays on *Black Theater: Present Condition* was published in 1981.

A multitalented man, King has greatly aided the development of contemporary black theater, both through his writings and encouragement of black dramatists widely varied in political and social viewpoints, and black literature through his short stories and anthologies.

• Stephen M. Vallilo, "Woodie King, Jr.," in *DLB,* vol. 38, *Afro-American Writers after 1955: Dramatists and Prose Writers,* eds. Thadious M. Davis and Trudier Harris, 1985, pp. 170–174. Bernard L. Peterson, Jr., "Woodie King, Jr.," in *Contemporary Black American Playwrights and Their Plays,* 1988, pp. 294–297. Kalamu ya Salaam, "Black Theatre the Way It Is: An Interview with Woodie King, Jr.," *African American Review* 31:4 (Winter 1997): 647–658.

—Steven R. Carter

KNIGHT, ETHERIDGE (1931–1991), poet. In the life and work of Etheridge Knight, the theme of prisons imposed from without (slavery, racism, poverty, incarceration) and prisons from within (addiction, repetition of painful patterns) are countered with the theme of freedom. His poems of suffering and survival, trial and tribute, loss and love testify to the fact that we are never completely imprisoned. Knight's poetry expresses our freedom of consciousness and attests to our capacity for connection to others.

Knight was born on 19 April 1931 in Corinth, Mississippi; he was one of seven children. After having dropped out of school in the eighth grade, he joined the army in 1947, saw active duty in Korea, where he suffered a shrapnel wound, and was discharged in 1957. Throughout this time he developed an addiction to drugs and alcohol that caused him to turn to crime to support his habit. While wandering around the United States after his discharge, Knight was arrested for robbery in 1960 and served his sentence in the Indiana State Prison, where by chance Gwendolyn *Brooks visited him and encouraged his writing. He started writing regularly, supported by members of the Black Arts movement such as Sonia *Sanchez and Dudley *Randall, whose Broadside Press published Knight's *Poems from Prison* in 1968, also the year of his release from prison and his marriage to Sanchez.

Poems from Prison attests to the freedom of consciousness that persists in spite of prison. "He Sees Through Stone" portrays a strong, older man in prison whose vision—ability to think, imagine, and dream—survives even behind the stone walls. "The Idea of Ancestry," one of Knight's most critically acclaimed pieces, is a cry of yearning for the freedom to be with his family and to have one of his own.

Black Voices from Prison (1970) is an anthology of writings by men in prison that includes all of Knight's earlier poems and "A WASP Woman Visits a Black Junkie in Prison." In this poem, two people, initially separated by their differences, find common ground when he asks if she has children. The encounter leaves the man touched and softened by the woman, as are many of Knight's male speakers.

The early 1970s were productive years during which Knight gained popularity and recognition across the United States. From 1969 to 1972 Knight held positions at the University of Pittsburgh, the University of Hartford, and Lincoln University. He gave numerous poetry readings and led Free People's Poetry Workshops, which were open to anyone. He received a National Endowment for the Arts grant in 1972 and a Guggenheim Fellowship in 1974. Still, during this time his marriage to Sanchez ended, and battling his addiction, he periodically admitted himself to veterans hospitals for treatment.

The culmination of these first years out of prison was *Belly Song and Other Poems* (1973). Now married to Mary Ann McAnally, with whom he had two children, Knight produced a volume that features some of his finest work, including many hauntingly beautiful love poems and "Belly Song," the poem that gives the volume its name. In this poem the speaker sings of love: all the emotion, pain, memory, and passion of living, which is located in the belly. Belly love comes from the sharing of memories, the common experience of survival.

In December 1978, Knight had a son with his third wife, Charlene Blackburn. Knight's next work, *Born of a Woman* (1980), presents women as healing, life-giving sources to whom men turn in desire and identification. In "The Stretching of the Belly," written for his wife, the woman's stretch marks are contrasted with the male speaker's scars: hers are marks of growth and life; his are scars from war, violence, and slavery. The volume ends with "Con/tin/u/way/shun Blues," a poem that moves from the "I" to the "we" by means of blues rhythms, attesting to the unifying and strengthening power of the blues tradition, which allows us to "keep on keeping on."

The Essential Etheridge Knight (1986) is divided into five sections, which correspond to his five volumes of poetry. Balanced between poems of prison and freedom, the volume attests to the power of each. Freedom's power is forcefully articulated in "Circling the Daughter," for his daughter, Tandi, upon her fourteenth year. The speaker urges his daughter to remember her goodness, signified by her birth, belly, and newly round body, and reminds her to look within for the freedom to counteract the outside world of limit. In 1991, Knight died at age fifty-nine from lung cancer, yet through his poetry, he continues to testify to the power of freedom, and human capacity to envision it even while in prison.

• Patricia Liggins Hill, "'The Violent Space': The Function of the New Black Aesthetic in Etheridge Knight's Prison Poetry," *Black American Literature Forum* 14.3 (Fall 1980): 115–121. Craig Werner, "The Poet, the Poem, the People: Etheridge Knight's Aesthetic," *Obsidian* 7.2–3 (Summer and Winter 1981): 7–17. Etheridge Knight, "A *MELUS* Interview: Etheridge Knight," interview by Steven C. Tracy, *MELUS* 12.2 (Summer 1985): 7–23. Charles H. Rowell, "An Interview with Etheridge Knight," *Callaloo* 19:4 (Fall 1996): 967–980. Joyce Ann Joyce, "The Poetry of Etheridge Knight: A Reflection of an African Philosophical/Aesthetic," *Worcester Review* 19:1–2 (1998): 105–118; this issue contains a special section on Knight.

—Cassie Premo

KOMUNYAKAA, YUSEF (b. 1947), poet. Few African American writers have won national or international literary prizes, and if fortunate enough to do so, they automatically garner extraordinary attention. That was the case with Gwendolyn *Brooks winning the Pulitzer Prize in poetry in 1950, with August *Wilson winning two Pulitzer Prizes in drama (1987, 1990), with Toni *Morrison winning the Nobel Prize in literature in 1993, and with Yusef Komunyakaa winning the Pulitzer Prize for poetry in 1994. Although his poetry had appeared at regular intervals in journals such as *Callaloo,* Komunyakaa remained relatively unknown—in spite of having published eight volumes—before the award. The distinguishing award now places him in a small and unique group of African American writers; it has also elevated his reputation and spurred critical and teaching interest in his poetry.

Komunyakaa was born in Bogalusa, Louisiana, on 29 April 1947, the oldest of five children. His family name, he says, derives from his grandfather, who was probably a stowaway on a ship from Trinidad to the U.S. coast, who arrived wearing a boy's shoe and a girl's shoe, a scene Komunyakaa would depict in "Mismatched Shoes" in the collection *Magic City.* His father, a carpenter, created strained family relationships by being abusive and indulging in extramarital affairs that caused his mother great grief. The poet would portray some of his complicated relationship with his father in various poems. His mother early exposed him to books by buying a set of encyclopedias for him. When he was sixteen, he discovered James *Baldwin's collection of essays, *Nobody Knows My Name,* and credits that volume with inspiring him to write.

In 1968 Komunyakaa began his military duty in Vietnam. As an information specialist, he edited a military newspaper, the *Southern Cross.* He also won a bronze star. After Vietnam he enrolled at the University of Colorado, where he obtained his bachelor's degree. It was in Colorado, in 1973, that he began writing poetry. He did graduate work at the University of California at Irvine, after also having been in the graduate program at Colorado State University. He taught briefly at various universities before moving to New Orleans, where, while teaching at the University of New Orleans, he married Mandy Sayer, an Australian novelist and short fiction writer, in 1985. It was during this period, fourteen years after the experience, that he began composing poems about Vietnam, which would lead to the publication of *Dien Cai Dau* (1988). The violence he encountered in Vietnam and the pain of returning home are recurring themes in the poetry, as is the casual violence in American society, such as young boys hunting rabbits, birds, and other game. Komunyakaa has come to question this so-called pragmatic violence.

His volumes also include *Dedications and Other Darkhorses* (1977), *Lost in the Bonewheel Factory* (1979), *Copacetic* (1984), *I Apologize for the Eyes in My Head* (1986), *Toys in the Field* (1987), *February in Sydney* (1989), *Magic City* (1992), and *Neon Vernacular* (1994), the Wesleyan University Press Pulitzer Prize–winning volume. Komunyakaa's focus centers upon autobiographical details of his life, including his childhood and his tour of duty in Vietnam. He is particularly interested in connecting the abstract to the concrete as a way of drawing readers into his poems. Indeed, he has expressed an occasional wish to be a painter, in order to capture the images that arise in his head and which he tries to capture poetically. His poetry is also undergirded—in form and subject matter—with music, especially blues and jazz. Trips to Australia inform his volume on Sydney.

Komunyakaa was recognized in some literary circles for the quality of his poetry before he won the Pulitzer Prize. He has won two Creative Writing Fellowships from the National Endowment for the Arts (1981, 1987) as well as the San Francisco Poetry Center Award (1986). He taught at Indiana University between 1985 and 1996, where he held the Lilly Professorship in Poetry in 1989–1990. After visiting at Washington University in St. Louis in the fall of 1996, he joined the faculty at Princeton University in 1997. He continued his interest in the publication of jazz poetry with *The Second Set: The Jazz Poetry Anthology,*

Vol. 2 (1996). His most recent volume of poetry, *Thieves of Paradise,* appeared in 1998. With continued interest in his poetry, including his inclusion in *The Literature of the American South: A Norton Anthology* (1998), additional scholarly emphasis upon Komunyakaa's poetry is assured.

• Yusef Komunyakaa, "'Lines of Tempered Steel': An Interview with Yusef Komunyakaa," interview by Vincente F. Gotera, *Callaloo* 13.2 (Spring 1990): 215–229. Bruce Weber, "A Poet's Values," *New York Times,* 2 May 1994, B1+. Jennifer Richter, "Review of *Magic City,*" *Callaloo* 17:2 (Summer 1994): 650–652. Thomas C. Johnson, "Interview with Yusef Komunyakaa," *Worcester Review* 19:1–2 (1998): 119–127. Suzan Sherman, "Paul Muldoon/Yusef Komunyakaa," *BOMB* 65 (Fall 1998): 74–80. Angela M. Salas, "'Flashbacks Through the Heart': Yusef Komunyakaa and the Poetry of Self-Assertion," in *The Furious Flowering of African American Poetry,* ed. Joanne V. Gabbin, 1999, pp. 298–309.

—Trudier Harris

KRANIDAS, KATHLEEN. *See* Collins, Kathleen.

KUNTA KINTE. A major character in Alex *Haley's **Roots* (1976), Kunta Kinte was, according to Haley, his maternal great-great-great-great-grandfather, discovered after extensive genealogical research and several journeys to Gambia.

The first son to Omoro and Binta, Kunta Kinte, a Mandinka, is born around 1750 in Juffure along the Gambia River. After a mostly idyllic youth in which he is schooled in Islam and initiated into the Mandinka ways, Kunta Kinte is captured in 1767 and shipped to the United States. Arriving in Annapolis, he is sold to John Waller and renamed Toby. As punishment for three escapes, his foot is amputated. He is then sold to William Waller, becoming Waller's gardener and driver. His initial disgust with the other slaves eventually turns to admiration for their ability to mask their true feelings and to resist the cruel demands of the slaveowners. Kunta Kinte grudgingly accepts his condition and marries Bell, a domestic slave, with whom he has a daughter named Kizzy. Kunta Kinte teaches Kizzy African words and culture, a legacy handed down through the generations until Haley hears them as a child from relatives. The reader last sees Kunta Kinte grieving for his daughter after she is sold for helping her lover escape.

In the novel, Kunta Kinte is depicted in heroic fashion, intelligent, resourceful, introspective, and courageous, a Mandinka warrior who never abandons his Islamic faith. He is meant to symbolize both the tragedy of American slavery and the heroism of those who endured it.

—Roger A. Berger

L

LANE, PINKIE GORDON (b. 1923), poet. The first African American to be named Louisiana's poet laureate, the unmistakably southern writer Pinkie Gordon Lane was raised in Philadelphia, where she was born in 1923, the only child of William and Inez Gordon. The death of her father led to five years of work in a sewing factory; she subsequently left for Atlanta, where she earned her BA at Spelman College, and married Ulysses Lane. After teaching high school from 1949 to 1954, she earned an MA from Atlanta University. The Lanes subsequently moved to Baton Rouge, where Pinkie soon developed a lyrical, soaring, poetic gift that took much of its ambiance from her new surroundings.

The poetry in her first collection, *Wind Thoughts,* bespoke a mature imagination, as it was published when she was forty-nine, shortly after her husband's early death. It offers ample display of a unique voice, but also demonstrates her admiration for the Black Aesthetic of that time in her inscriptions from LeRoi Jones, Gwendolyn *Brooks, and Sonia *Sanchez, and in poems directly addressed to fellow black poets. On the other hand, while earning the first PhD degree ever granted to a black woman by Louisiana State University, she acquired an equally important classical sense, which produced an unusually formal tone quite different from those of the Black Arts movement poets, along with references to John Milton, John Keats, William Butler Yeats, and e. e. cummings. Her later poems range even further for antecedents; the title poem of *The Mystic Female* cites Lao Tzu. Lane claims the most important influences on her work have been Gwendolyn Brooks, for inspiration, and Anne Sexton, for style.

Lane studs poems with unexpected, arresting images, but also with reassuring visions of nature, sometimes deceptively simple as in "Roasting Grasshoppers," or ominously foreboding as in "Opossom." Her musings about quotidian details can yield sudden insight, as in "On Being Head of the English Department," a cynical yet loving appraisal of duty; so can poems based on shocking incidents, such as "Sexual Privacy of Women on Welfare" or "Flight," which transmogrifies the discovery of a newborn baby in an airplane's toilet. The moods of love and its torments inform many poems, and white-hot heat flares in "Three Love Poems" and "St. Valentine's Eve Poem." But Lane is mainly an autobiographical poet, so her most successful works pay tribute to friends and family members who are mourned and remembered, even for sour moods and evil deeds, as in "Children," and in what may be her most powerful work, "Poems to My Father." She makes art out of the agony of her husband's fatal illness in "Songs to the Dialysis Machine," while the complex fate of her mother emerges in "Prose Poem: Portrait."

More often than not, her poems offer solitary meditations on quiet interstices of existence; the persona may be listening to the furnace crackle on a winter's evening, as in "Breathing," or reacting to music, as in several poems devoted to her drummer son, Gordon. She feels she runs against the grain with reflective poems and suggests in "A Quiet Poem" that African Americans are expected to write from anger.

Still, Lane's artistry frequently proceeds from pain. Although she can conjure love, she eschews cheap romanticism and often prefers harsh images connected by poetic integuments, as in "Bill," her portrait of a saxophone-playing heroin addict. Lane's subtle renditions of oppression can lie in her omissions as well. Her memories of childhood evoke bittersweet creations that also indict an uncaring society, as in "Rain Ditch," where children frolic in filthy water, unable (although the poem never says so) to swim in whites-only pools.

Lane's books of poetry include *Wind Thoughts* (1972); *The Mystic Female* (1978); *I Never Scream* (1985); and *Girl at the Window* (1991). She has won numerous prizes and awards, has lectured nationally and in Africa, and has been nominated for the Pulitzer Prize. She edited *Discourses on Poetry and Poems by Blacks,* volume 3. For years Lane was chair of the English Department at Southern University, and she recently completed a visiting professorship at Bridgewater College.

• Marilyn B. Craig, "Pinkie Gordon Lane," in *DLB,* vol. 41, *Afro-American Poets since 1955,* eds. Trudier Harris and Thadious M. Davis, 1985, pp. 212–216. Violet Harrington Bryan, "Evocations of Place and Culture in the Works of Four Contemporary Black Louisiana Writers: Brenda Osbey Sybil Kein, Elizabeth Brown-Guillory, and Pinkie Gordon Lane," *Louisiana Literature* 4.2 (1987): 49–60.

—John Lowe

LANGSTON, JOHN MERCER (1829–1897), autobiographer, orator, lawyer, abolitionist, politician and public official, and educator. In his third-person autobiography, *From the Virginia Plantation to the National Capitol* (1894), John Mercer Langston recounts his career as one of the most influential African American leaders of the nineteenth century. Born in Virginia and educated at Oberlin, Langston became in

1854 the first African American admitted to the Ohio bar and in 1855 the first elected to public office in the United States (town clerk of Brownhelm, Ohio). Throughout the 1850s he worked within antislavery and civil rights movements, advocating a nationalist, pro-emigration position before becoming a Republican party activist. Heading recruitment of African American soldiers in the West during the Civil War, he rose to national prominence after the war as the president of the National Equal Rights League (a forerunner of the NAACP), an educational inspector for the Freedmen's Bureau, and a Republican party organizer. In 1868, he accepted a professorship at Howard University, where he founded its law school, and eventually became vice president and acting president of the university. In 1871, President Ulysses S. Grant appointed him to the Board of Health for Washington, D.C. In 1877, President Rutherford B. Hayes made him U.S. minister to Haiti. After eight years in Haiti, Langston returned to Virginia and accepted the presidency of the state college for African Americans in Petersburg, Virginia, Normal and Collegiate Institute. Langston crowned his public career in 1890 by serving as the first African American from Virginia in the U.S. House of Representatives.

Like his grandnephew Langston *Hughes, he combined a hope-filled vision of a more just society with insistent opposition to white supremacy. Although readers have found his autobiography unimaginative and self-serving, his speeches—collected in *Freedom and Citizenship* (1883)—remain highly regarded for their compelling and controlled rhetoric and their blending of evangelical, democratic, and African American oratorical traditions.

• William Cheek and Aimee Lee Cheek, "John Mercer Langston: Principle and Politics," in *Black Leaders of the Nineteenth Century,* eds. Leon Litwack and August Meier, 1988, pp. 103–126. William Cheek and Aimee Lee Cheek, *John Mercer Langston and the Fight for Black Freedom, 1829–1865,* 1989.

—Gregory Eiselein

LANUSSE, ARMAND (1812–1867), New Orleans poet, educator, and editor of *Les Cenelles* (1845). Armand Lanusse was born in New Orleans in 1812 and died there in 1867. Literary historians differ on whether he received his education in New Orleans or Paris. He helped found the New Orleans Catholic School for Indigent Orphans of Color in 1848 and served as principal from 1852 until his death.

Lanusse used his position as a free *Créole de couleur* to promote nonwhites in antebellum New Orleans through education and literary activity. Along with other Euro-African Louisianians, he contributed to *Album littérarie, journal des jeunes gens, amateurs de littérature* (*Literary Album, Journal of Young People, Lovers of Literature,* 1843) and to *Les *Cenelles* (1845), a volume of poetry by Creoles of color, which Lanusse also edited.

Ironically, Lanusse served in the Confederate army and initially opposed Union occupation of New Orleans. The increased oppression of blacks in postbellum years led him to despair of racial equality ever becoming a reality in the United States and drew him closer to less privileged blacks.

Heavily influenced by French romanticism, Lanusse's poetry in *Les Cenelles* highlights love, death, and both the pleasures and the general oppressiveness of life. While in his personal and professional life Lanusse championed black civil rights, his poetry, like most of the *Les Cenelles* poems, does not protest racial discrimination. However, Lanusse's social and religious concerns do manifest themselves in poems treating the morality of Creole women of color. Through the comedy of "Epigram" and the serious warning of "To Elora," for example, Lanusse exposes the spiritual, emotional, and ethical predicaments of *plaçage,* a custom whereby Creole girls of color gained protection and material comfort but sacrificed virtue in becoming white men's mistresses.

As educator, poet, and editor, Lanusse played a leading role in encouraging the educational, vocational, and literary activity of nonwhites and championed their civil rights as well.

• Régine Latortue and Gleason R. W. Adams, eds. and trans., *Les Cenelles: A Collection of Poems by Creole Writers of the Early Nineteenth Century,* 1979.

—Germain J. Bienvenu

LARSEN, NELLA (1891–1964), novelist and participant in the Harlem Renaissance. At the end of the 1920s, Nella Larsen emerged as a premiere novelist of the New Negro movement. In rapid succession, she produced *Quicksand* (1928) and **Passing* (1929), both published by the respected New York firm, Alfred A. Knopf. Before the appearance of her novels, Larsen was an active, though minor, presence in the literary and social life of the Harlem Renaissance. She had published little: two brief accounts of children's games (*The *Brownies' Book,* 1920); a book review of *Certain People of Importance* by Kathleen Norris (*The *Messenger,* 1923), and two pseudonymous stories, "The Wrong Man" and "Freedom" (*Young's Realistic Stories Magazine,* 1926). Her success as a novelist had not been foreshadowed by any of her earlier publications. Her life experiences, however, had provided her with rich materials for a modern fictionist.

Born Nellie Walker in Chicago and reared in a visibly white, Danish immigrant family, Larsen was a lonely child whose dark skin separated her from both parents and a sibling. In preparation for a life within an African American world, she entered the Fisk University Normal High School in Nashville. After a year (1907–1908), she left without a diploma. She trained instead at the Lincoln Hospital School of Nursing in New York City (1912–1915) and worked initially for her alma mater, and briefly for Tuskegee Institute's Andrew Memorial Hospital as head nurse, and subsequently for New York City's Board of Health.

In 1919 Nella Larsen married a research physicist, Dr. Elmer S. Imes. With her marriage Larsen moved from the working class and obscurity to visibility within an upwardly mobile, African American middle class, conscious not only of position, but also of possibility. This social world hastened her disillusionment with nursing. She found employment at the 135th Street branch of the New York Public Library, a job that introduced her to the emerging coterie of writers in Harlem and enabled her to enter the Library School of the New York Public Library in 1922. This was the same year that Larsen and two of the emerging Harlem writers, Walter *White and Jessie Redmon *Fauset, agreed to write novels depicting the complex realities of African American life.

Quicksand and *Passing,* Larsen's only published novels, immediately earned her a considerable reputation and prominence as a writer of powerful explorations of female psychology and modern consciousness. *Quicksand* follows the exploits of an educated mixed-race woman, *Helga Crane, as she seeks self-definition, social recognition, and sexual expression. Her movement through evocative contemporary settings in the rural South and urban North, as well as in cosmopolitan Denmark, signals her determined effort to attain a space within which all parts of her identity can coexist. The episodic construction serves to inflect Helga's psychological and emotional states and to illustrate the multiple subjective spaces disallowed in marking identity only within rigid categories. Helga fails in her quest for control over her own identity and body; her failure is represented in terms of reproduction as a part of a psychic and physical quagmire, threatening to erase a woman's autonomy and agency.

Passing, Larsen's second novel, positions two light-skinned women as antagonists and psychological doubles in a drama of racial passing, class and social mobility, and female desire. Irene Redfield demands safety and security in contained, self-sacrificing race and gender roles; Clare Kendry functions in a self-seeking, risk-filled existence on the edge of danger and duplicity. Although Clare's racial passing is one of the novel's concerns, Irene's obsessive desires, represented through her perspective as the central consciousness, expose a range of intense emotions all cloaked by her persistent concerns for social respectability and material comfort.

Both *Passing* and *Quicksand* illustrate Larsen's nuanced modernity. Recent attention to *Passing* has emphasized Larsen's use of passing as a device for encoding the complexities of human personality, for veiling women's homoerotic desires, and for subverting simplistic notions of female self-actualization. Similarly, recent criticism of *Quicksand* has focused on the dialogics of race and gender and the social production of gender, sexuality, and race. Like Jessie Fauset, to whom she is frequently compared, Larsen emphasizes female sexuality as a component of women's identity, but she also challenges the implication that the domestic sphere can satisfy a woman's quest for satisfaction and completion. More pessimistic than Fauset or earlier women novelists, such as Frances Ellen Watkins *Harper, about the work of uplift as an expression of the racialized female's role in society, Larsen concludes her novels with an irreparable breakdown of illusions about emancipatory strategies or possible futures for women.

Larsen received the Harmon Foundation's bronze medal for achievement in literature in 1929 and a Guggenheim Fellowship in creative writing in 1930. However, that same year, she was accused in *Forum* magazine of plagiarizing "Sanctuary" (1930), the only short story published under her own name. She spent her fellowship year in Spain and France researching a novel on racial freedom and writing a novel about her husband's infidelity. Her literary promise, however, did not achieve a full maturity. She was shattered by the reversal of her material condition: a difficult, highly publicized divorce (1933); an inability to publish her third novel and other announced writing projects; a failure of a partnership to produce collaborative novels; and a perceived loss of status in her return to nursing. Larsen stopped writing in the late 1930s. By 1941, when her former husband died, she had severed her connections with her one-time associates among New York's black and white artists. She worked as a nurse in New York City hospitals until March 1964 when she was found dead. Nearly forgotten as a novelist until the recovery of her fiction in the 1970s, Larsen has been returned to prominence as a major novelist, whose expansively complex representations of gender and race resist reductive readings.

• Deborah E. McDowell, introduction to *Quicksand* and *Passing* by Nella Larsen, 1986. Mary Helen Washington, "Nella Larsen," in *Invented Lives: Narratives of Black Women, 1860–1960,* 1987. Ann Allen Shockley, "Nella Marian Larsen Imes," in *Afro-American Women Writers, 1746–1933,* 1988. Thadious M. Davis, *Nella Larsen, Novelist of the Harlem Renaissance,* 1994. Cheryl A. Wall, *The Women of the Harlem Renaissance,* 1995.

—Thadious M. Davis

Last Days of Louisiana Red, The. *The Last Days of Louisiana Red* (1974) is Ishmael *Reed's fourth novel. Set primarily in northern California in the early 1970s, it deals with the efforts of *Papa LaBas, the hoodoo detective first introduced in Reed's previous novel, **Mumbo Jumbo* (1972), to combat the insidious influence of Louisiana Red, symbolizing forces of discord, especially within the black community, that keep people at one another's throats. It is a stress plague and therefore an antidote to Jes Grew, the epidemic of "boogie fever" depicted in *Mumbo*

Jumbo. Other important characters are Ed Yellings, owner of Solid Gumbo Works, who has found a cure for cancer and is murdered by Louisiana Red in order to prevent him from finding a cure for heroin addiction; Ed's son Street, a thug who wraps himself in the mantle of Black Power; Street's sister Minnie, leader of the Moochers, a gang of opportunists posing as radicals; and two personae "borrowed" from Greek drama: chorus, a "characterless character" who bears a striking resemblance to Cab Calloway, and his perennial antagonist, Antigone (Minnie the Moocher's prototype), who constantly seeks to upstage if not silence him. Antigone, whose name means "born against," represents unmitigated energies of opposition in the community—a somewhat ironic target, given that Reed himself has been accused of being excessively "anti"—and she also stands for a too intense womanism that, in Reed's view, unduly victimizes men.

Once again, Reed offers us a divergent interpretation of a classic, for in Sophocles' famous play, Antigone represents a morally superior position to the authoritarianism of Creon, who found it repugnant that a woman should get the better of a man. Reed also puts a negative spin on a canonical work of African American literature, Richard *Wright's **Native Son* (1940), making the surly, loutish Street Yellings a 1970s version of *Bigger Thomas, and having a white character named Max become possessed by the spirit of Bigger, who then causes him to kill. In this novel, Reed seems to be exposing the bad side of the Business (the workings of neohoodoo) that goes under the name of Louisiana Red (the heckler in the audience, too much red pepper in the gumbo, Frankie looking for Johnny with her .44).

Gerald Duff, in his essay on Reed in the *Dictionary of Literary Biography* (vol. 2), notes that in *The Last Days of Louisiana Red,* Papa LaBas—who often serves as Reed's spokesman—takes a "stringently patriarchal" position with regard to women, which, interestingly, resembles that of the black militants Reed is satirizing, and which they claimed to be sanctioned by traditional African values. This novel, indeed, is one piece of evidence cited by those wishing to indict Reed for misogynistic tendencies.

Houston A. *Baker, Jr., who praised *Mumbo Jumbo* as an exemplary work of black consciousness, condemned Reed for his putdown of cultural nationalists in *The Last Days of Louisiana Red,* implying that he was destroying black American culture with his unrestrained satire. This typifies the antithetical nature of Reed's enterprise, which has as its only consistency a refusal to recognize any sacred cows.

• Lorenzo Thomas, "Two Crowns of Thoth: A Study of Ishmael Reed's *The Last Days of Louisiana Red,*" *Obsidian* 2.3 (1976): 5–25.

—Robert Elliot Fox

LATTIMORE, JEWEL. *See* Amini, Johari.

LEE, ANDREA (b. 1953), fiction writer and journalist. Andrea Lee was born in Philadelphia in 1953 and graduated from Harvard University. Her first book, *Russian Journal* (1981), is based upon her experiences in Russia during 1978–1979 and received a National Book Award nomination, as well as the 1984 Jean Stein Award from the American Academy and Institute of Arts and Letters. Currently a staff writer for the *New Yorker,* Lee lives in Europe with her husband.

Andrea Lee is best known for her 1984 novel, *Sarah Phillips,* composed of stories that were first published in the *New Yorker.* Each is a vignette taken from the life of the title character, the daughter of a prosperous Baptist minister and school teacher mother. Set in the 1960s and early 1970s, *Sarah Phillips* comments on contemporary discourses around race, class, and gender and problematizes the meanings of resistance in the postintegration era.

Critic Mary Helen Washington compares *Sarah Phillips* to works such as William Wells *Brown's **Clotel* (1853), Frances Ellen Watkins *Harper's **Iola Leroy* (1892), James Weldon *Johnson's *The *Autobiography of an Ex-Colored Man* (1912), and Nella *Larsen's *Quicksand* (1928), books in which privileged black characters seek to escape the trials and responsibilities that attach to their racial identities. *Sarah Phillips* also invites comparison with the growing number of novels and autobiographies set in the period after court-ordered desegregation: Jake Lamar's *Bourgeois Blues* (1991), Trey *Ellis's *Platitudes* (1988), Lorene Cary's *Black Ice* (1991), Itabari Njeri's *Every Good-bye Ain't Gone* (1990), Darryl Pinckney's *High Cotton* (1992), Stephen L. Carter's *Reflections of an Affirmative Action Baby* (1991), Connie Porter's *All-Bright Court* (1991), and Jill Nelson's *Volunteer Slavery* (1993). These later works explore the covert forms of racism that emerged during the eras of integration and affirmative action, the various responses these social changes produced, and the complex interconnections among constructions of race and class.

Lee's characters are complexly drawn, her descriptions nuanced, her sensibility both haunting and ironic. Yet neither *Russian Journal* nor *Sarah Phillips* is an especially popular work. This is perhaps the case because both books resist generally unspoken constructions of black women's lives. Some readers dismiss her work, considering it insufficiently assertive of a politics of resistance. However, to the extent that both works refuse to conform to conventions of representing "blackness" and "black womanhood," they raise challenging questions for the reader about what we mean when we use those terms. Sarah Phillips prompts fruitful consideration of the ways in which social and economic class position shape the meaning of racial identity.

• W. Laurence Hogue, "The Limits of Modernity: Andrea Lee's *Sarah Phillips,*" in *MELUS* 19 (1994): 75–90. Sarala Krishnamurthy, "Andrea Lee," in *Contemporary African American Novelists*, ed. Emmanuel S. Nelson, 1999, pp. 267–272.

—Valerie Smith

LEE, DON L. See Madhubuti, Haki R.

LEE, JARENA (1783–?), itinerant preacher and autobiographer. Born free in Cape May, New Jersey, on 11 February 1783, Jarena Lee became both the first African American woman to write an extended account of her own life and the first African American woman whose right to preach received official acknowledgment from church authorities. Her autobiography, *The Life and Religious Experience of Jarena Lee* (1836), begins with a few brief references to her family, whom she left at the age of seven to work as a maid, and then quickly focuses on the steps she took to attain Christian salvation. Three sections follow this account of her spiritual awakening and clearly demonstrate her belief in female equality. The second section, titled "My Call to Preach the Gospel," describes the call to preach she received around the year 1807. She sought permission to answer this call from the Reverend Richard *Allen, head of the African Methodist Episcopal Church, who upheld the church's ban against women preachers. The third section of her autobiography, "My Marriage," tells of her union with Joseph Lee, the pastor of a church outside Philadelphia, whom she married in 1811. In about 1818, Joseph Lee died, leaving her with two small children to support. While married, Jarena Lee did not pursue her call to preach, though her autobiography intimates her frustration with the subordinate role of wife. The last section of her work, "The Subject of My Call to Preach Renewed," recounts the final steps she took toward becoming a preacher. Eight years after she first approached Bishop Allen with her request to preach, Lee asked for—and received—his permission to hold prayer meetings in her home and "of exhorting as I found liberty." Soon after acquiring these limited privileges, Lee unexpectedly found herself the last-minute replacement for the minister who had been scheduled to preach. Allen, who happened to be among those who heard her spontaneous sermon, acknowledged her right to preach, enabling her to embark on a career as a traveling minister. Lee wrote another, longer version of her autobiography, *Religious Experience and Journal of Mrs. Jarena Lee* (1849), the last record we have of her life. Lee's autobiographical writings offer invaluable insight into one woman's efforts to overcome the limitations imposed on her by a racist and sexist culture and show the significance of the church to African American literature.

• Jarena Lee, *The Life and Religious Experience of Jarena Lee*, 1836; rpt. in *Sisters of the Spirit: Three Black Women's Autobiographies of the Nineteenth Century*, ed. William L. Andrews, 1986. Nellie Y. McKay, "Nineteenth-Century Black Women's Spiritual Autobiographies," in *Interpreting Women's Lives*, ed. The Personal Narratives Group, 1989. Carla Peterson, *Doers of the Word: African-American Women Speakers and Writers in the North (1830–1880)*, 1995.

—Candis LaPrade

LEE, SPIKE (b. 1957), film director, writer, and actor. Shelton Jackson "Spike" Lee grew up in Brooklyn and earned degrees at Morehouse College (1979) and New York University (1983) before embarking on a career as perhaps the most celebrated and accomplished African American filmmaker. Aside from his major films, Lee has also made music videos (for such artists as Miles *Davis, Anita Baker, and Public Enemy), and television commercials; he produced, for example, campaign advertisements for Jesse Jackson's 1988 presidential bid. An actor as well as a director, Lee has become a major, outspoken public and political figure. Much of his work is politically inflected, provocative, and often controversial, and treats issues of identity and community that resonate throughout African American literature.

Several of Lee's films deal with questions and dilemmas surrounding African American identity, gender, and class. His first full-length release, *She's Gotta Have It* (1986), about an African American woman and her three very different lovers, earned him the Prix de Jeunesse at the Cannes Film Festival. The film features innovative narrative techniques and begins Lee's exploration of the possibilities of African American male identity. His second film, *School Daze* (1988), a musical set in an all-black college, explores questions of color and class lines, as well as sexism, within the African American community. In *Mo' Better Blues* (1990), a jazz musician must choose between two women, and ultimately between his music and fatherhood. *Jungle Fever* (1991) addresses interracial romance and drug addiction and their effects on the black communities. *Clockers* (1995) challenges "gangsta" stereotypes, complicating received narratives of African American poverty and violence.

Lee may be best known for his more broadly political films, *Do the Right Thing* (1989) and *Malcolm X* (1992). The first, a dramatization of complex racial tensions and conflicts in Brooklyn, focuses on the efficacy (and risks) of violence as a response to racism or oppression. Lee situates the film's point of view between the proactive black nationalism of *Malcolm X and the nonviolent philosophy of Martin Luther *King, Jr., quoting from both at the film's end, choosing neither (or both). In his epic treatment of Malcolm X's life, based on Alex *Haley's *The *Autobiography of Malcolm X* (1965), Lee traces Malcolm's political trajectory, including his pilgrimage to Mecca and his split with the Nation of Islam, and presents Malcolm X's legacy as a living symbol of African American struggle. The film, however, raised controversy about what some, including Amiri *Baraka, considered the commercialization of Malcolm's image.

Lee often appears in his own films and commercials (though sometimes as minor characters). The resultant blurring of Lee's public persona with his fictional characters makes him appear more personally implicated in his films than many directors and recalls the similarly ambiguous positioning of the author/narrator in many African American novels, beginning with William Wells *Brown's **Clotel* (1853). In fact, two of his films—*School Daze* and 1994's *Crooklyn*, an episodic, nostalgic portrayal of Lee's Brooklyn childhood—have autobiographical origins. Lee's work thus evokes both the importance of autobiography as well as the tension between the personal and the political in African American literature.

• Spike Lee, *Spike Lee's Gotta Have It: Inside Guerrilla Filmmaking,* 1987. Terry McMillan et al., *Five for Five: The Films of Spike Lee,* 1991. Gwen Sparks, "Shelton Jackson 'Spike' Lee," in *African American Encyclopedia,* ed. Michael Williams, 1993, pp. 952–955.

—Gary Ashwill

LESTER, JULIUS (b. 1939), activist, essayist, journalist, radio broadcaster, folklorist, writer, historian, poet, and professor. Julius Lester was born on 27 January 1939 in St. Louis, Missouri, the son of Woodie Daniel Lester and Julia B. Smith Lester. He received his BA from Fisk University in 1960, with a semester at San Diego State College, and an MA from the University of Massachusetts at Amherst in 1971, where he is currently a professor. He is married to his second wife and has four children. Lester has won the Newbery Honor Award (1969) and the Massachusetts State Professor of the Year Award (1986), and was a finalist for the National Book Award (1972) and the National Jewish Book Award (1988). Lester converted to Judaism in 1982.

Julius Lester's literary career has spanned a broad variety of political events and literary genres. Lester began his career as an activist with the Student Nonviolent Coordinating Committee (SNCC), traveling to Mississippi, Cuba (with Stokely Carmichael), North Vietnam, and Korea. In 1963 Lester coauthored *We Shall Overcome! Songs of the Southern Freedom Movement* with Guy Carawan, Candie Carawan, Ethel Raim, and Joseph Byrd. His first solo work, *Look Out, Whitey! Black Power's Gon' Get Your Mama,* was published in 1968 and followed in the same year by *To Be a Slave.* In 1969 Lester's collection of essays and articles about revolutionary movements in the United States, entitled *Revolutionary Notes,* was published and, in the same year, *Black Folktales and Search for a New Land.* In 1970 Lester divorced his first wife and left activism. He continued his prolific output with *The Seventh Son: The Thought &. Writings of W. E. B. Du Bois* (1971), *The Long Journey Home: Stories from Black History and Two Love Stories* (1972), and a book of poetry, *Who I Am* (1974), followed in 1976 by his first autobiography, *All Is Well.* In 1982 he began another series of books with *This Strange New Feeling* and continuing with *Do Lord Remember Me* (1984), *The Tales of Uncle Remus* (1987), *More Tales of Uncle Remus* (1988), *Lovesong,* his second autobiography (1988), *How Many Spots Does a Leopard Have?* (1989), *Falling Pieces of the Broken Sky* (1990), and *Further Tales of Uncle Remus* (1990). Four books followed in 1994: *The Last Tales of Uncle Remus, And All Our Wounds Forgiven, John Henry,* and *The Man Who Knew Too Much.*

Lester's work is characterized by his interest in education and change. His participation in academia and literature is marked by a concern both with African American culture and the need to break down the institutionalization of education and information that led him to activism in the 1960s and early 1970s. From the beginning of his career, however, Lester's work has been controversial. In the 1970s, he refused to endorse the Black Panther Party or Stokely Carmichael, consistently writing articles that editorial boards were reluctant to publish. Lester's most recent work is still controversial. His essays, courses, and speeches celebrating Judaism and Jews have raised angry responses from some African Americans, who accuse Lester of being a self-hating African American. Lester's most recent collection of essays, *Falling Pieces of the Broken Sky* (1990), continues to explore the intersections of race, religion, and education, addressing issues of personal identity and group identity, the role of spirituality in life, and the nature of formal and informal education and reeducation.

• "Julius Lester," in *Who's Who among African Americans,* 9th ed., Shirelle Phelps, 1994, p. 927. Paula T. Connolly, "Still a Slave: Legal and Spiritual Freedom in Julius Lester's 'Where the Sun Lives,'" *Children's Literature* 26, 1998, pp. 123–139. Lisa W. Nikola, "John Henry: Then and Now," *African American Review* 32:1 (Spring 1998): 51–56.

—Karen R. Bloom

"Letter From Birmingham Jail." In spring 1963, after a failed campaign in Albany, Georgia, Martin Luther *King, Jr., and his Southern Christian Leadership Conference organized a major nonviolent crusade in Birmingham, Alabama. King, Fred Shuttlesworth, Wyatt Walker, and other organizers dispatched hundreds of protestors, including young children, across Birmingham. Recalcitrant city officials ordered police to unleash snarling dogs on the demonstrators and sent firefighters to wash them down the streets with fire hoses. Millions of Americans were horrified when they witnessed these events on television. Hundreds of marchers were arrested, and on Easter Sunday King himself was jailed.

Early in the campaign eight clergy in Birmingham published a statement in the *Birmingham Post Herald* that called for racial harmony and an end to demonstrations, which the clergy deemed "unwise," "untimely," and "extreme." While critical of the role played by "outsiders," they addressed their declaration to the "white and Negro citizenry" of Birmingham, not to King himself, whom they never mentioned by name.

Relieved of his unrelenting schedule, the jailed King used his solitude to respond to the clergy's assertions. Writing a twenty-page letter/essay that was broadly disseminated, he offers what is easily his most lucid analysis of segregation and his most sophisticated defense of his own tactics. He contends that the city's brutal treatment of agitators represents the less dramatic, daily humiliations imposed by racism. Living in jail, he implicitly claims, symbolizes living under segregation.

Although King apparently carried no reading materials into his jail cell, he remembered his earlier orations and reworked several familiar passages and metaphors into "Letter from Birmingham Jail," including material he originally borrowed from unacknowledged sources.

King folds these materials into a careful, complex argument that begins by defending his presence in Birmingham against the charge that he is an "outsider." Explicitly comparing himself to the apostle Paul, who traveled widely to spread the gospel, King claims that, as a Christian minister, his job is to attack injustice wherever it appears. Then, as Malinda Snow explains, he insinuates into his text numerous Pauline allusions, which he reinforces by his simple presence in jail, where Paul also stayed.

As Richard Fulkerson observes, in "Letter" King adopts, with some modification, an ancient Greco-Roman oratorical pattern of introduction followed by proposition, division, confirmation, refutation, and peroration. Like certain classical orators, he persuades through thoughtful digressions; he adjusts classical form by shoving most of his argument into his refutation. Using what Fulkerson calls "multipremise refutation," he expresses an initial disappointment at having his efforts deemed extreme, then layers that expression within a powerful defense of a certain species of extremism. To buttress this contention, he telescopes time and space by writing about Jesus, Paul, Amos, Martin Luther, Abraham *Lincoln, and other "creative extremists" as though they shared his jail cell with him. Such leapfrogging of chronology and geography is a typical maneuver of African American folk preachers, including those King heard as a child.

For King, interlacing all these elements meant creating one of the most widely read and genuinely persuasive American essays of this century. The eight clergy never attempted to answer it.

• Richard Fulkerson, "The Public Letter As a Rhetorical Form: Structure, Logic, and Style in King's 'Letter from Birmingham Jail,'" *Quarterly Journal of Speech* 65 (1979): 121–136. Malinda Snow, "Martin Luther King's 'Letter from Birmingham Jail' As Pauline Epistle," *Quarterly Journal* of Speech 71 (1985): 318–334. Martin Luther King, Jr., "Letter from Birmingham Jail," 1963, in *A Testament of Hope: The Essential Writings of Martin Luther King, Jr.*, ed. James Washington, 1986, pp. 289–302.

—Keith D. Miller and Emily M. Lewis

LEWIS, THEOPHILUS (1891–1974), drama critic for the Messenger during the Harlem Renaissance. Theophilus Lewis was born in Baltimore, Maryland, in 1891, attended public schools, and moved to New York City. He became a manual laborer and later a postal worker, a position that he retained until his retirement. It provided his livelihood during the Harlem Renaissance when he wrote the theater reviews in the *Messenger,* since he received no remuneration for his writing.

Lewis's theater columns, which appeared from 1923 to 1927, chronicled primarily African American stage productions presented in different venues from Harlem to Broadway at a critical stage in African American history. They also championed development of an African American little theater movement. In referring to such groups as the Ethiopian Art Theater, the Tri-Arts Club, the Krigwa Players (founded by W. E. B. *Du Bois), and the Aldridge Players, Lewis reveals his understanding of their importance to the evolution of African American theater and drama. In a 1926 column, for example, he declined to evaluate three plays presented by the Aldridge Players by strict critical standards, arguing that little theater groups afforded necessary opportunities for African American actors to perfect their craft. Lewis's indulgence did not mean that he was overly tolerant; rather that he was not interested in the craft of acting simply for its own sake. He claimed for the actor a central role in raising the standards of the usual fare available on the African American stage.

Lewis advocated the development of a national African American theater that would be clearly distinct from the American theater in materials and audience. This concern, also expressed in later columns written for *Catholic World,* aligned Theophilus Lewis with other intellectuals of the 1920s who called for the creation of a viable African American literary and artistic tradition based on the folk experience, and it anticipated some of the writers of the 1960s who called for the creation of art based on a Black Aesthetic.

Lewis felt that a national theater that would address itself exclusively to an African American audience would assist in the development of the African American playwright, who, according to Lewis, was at the apprentice stage and needed the closeness to familiar material and a sympathetic audience in order to write legitimate drama. Lewis considered drama to be a higher form of expression than comedy, a form that pervaded the African American theater at that time. Lewis also argued against the prevalence of stereotypes, whether present in the works of African American or white playwrights. While he enjoyed the antics of the chorus lines that appeared in the musical revues of the period, he criticized the intraracial bias evident by the light-hued ladies who comprised most of these productions. Lewis's insight and his ability to address important issues are seen particularly in his recurring discussions of the connection between the evolution of the African American theater and the economic level of its desired target audience.

Lewis's most significant contribution was his theater reviews and commentary, but he did write in other forms. He coauthored a satirical column, "Shafts and Darts," with George S. *Schuyler, reviewed books, wrote commentary on general topics, and authored a few short stories. One of these stories, "Seven Years for Rachel," which was seralized in 1923, exhibits Lewis's attempts to put some of his own pronouncements into practice. The story, subtitled "a dramatic story of Negro life," focuses on a love triangle involving Sam Jones, Rachel, and Amelia. It includes elements of African American folk culture that evoke setting and character in a story in which the primary themes are guilt and remorse.

After the Harlem Renaissance, Lewis published only occasionally. "The Frustrations of Negro Art," written in 1942, addresses the connection between the economic stability of the audience and the growth of African American art and warns of the deleterious effects when an artist must write for alien audiences with preconceived images.

Although he came to his avocation an untrained observer, Lewis was a dedicated and influential figure. His columns exhibited an enthusiasm for African American theater, and for his role as critical and moral guide.

• Theodore Kornweibel, Jr., "Theophilus Lewis and the Theater of the Harlem Renaissance," in *The Harlem Renaissance Remembered,* ed. Arna Bontemps, 1972, pp. 171–189. "Theophilus Lewis," in *CA*, eds. Hal May and Susan M. Trosky, 1989, p. 292.

—Johnanna L. Grimes-Williams

"Lift Every Voice and Sing." Although there is, of course, no executive or legislature to so designate it, "Lift Every Voice and Sing" is frequently referred to as the "Negro National Anthem." It was written in 1900 by James Weldon *Johnson and his brother J. [John] Rosamond Johnson for a celebration of Abraham *Lincoln's birthday in Jacksonville, Florida, their hometown. James, who contributed the lyrics, records in his autobiography *Along This Way* (1933) that he and Rosamond taught the song to a chorus of five hundred schoolchildren who, after the event "kept singing the song; some of them went off to other schools and kept singing it; some of them became schoolteachers and taught it to their pupils. Within twenty years the song was being sung in schools and churches and on special occasions throughout the South and in some other parts of the country." After the NAACP unofficially adopted "Lift Every Voice and Sing" as its own anthem, the song appeared in new, more politically charged contexts as well as in school assemblies and church meetings.

Johnson's poem, which he tells us he wrote in "a poet's ecstasy" followed by "that sense . . . which makes artistic creation the most complete of all human experiences," is both a good fit to Rosamond's music and a rhetorically effective post-Romantic lyric. The poem's sentiments are entirely spiritual, locating the sources of strength in the connection to God. Though an agnostic himself, Johnson valorizes the people's religious faith and posits communal hope for the future as founded upon it.

The conservative sentiments of "Lift Every Voice and Sing" are one reason it receded in popularity somewhat during the civil rights movement. In recent years, the song has again become a fixture of African American social events, now as the historically validated anthem of the new cultural nationalism. As cultural icon, it has been explored in an enormously popular recording by Melba Moore in 1990 and in a text with the music, illustrated by Elizabeth Catlett (1993).

• James Weldon Johnson, *Along This Way,* 1933; rpt. 1968. James Weldon Johnson, *Lift Every Voice and Sing,* 1993.

—Joseph T. Skerrett, Jr.

Like One of the Family. Alice *Childress's *Like One of the Family . . . Conversations from a Domestic's Life* (1956) is a collection of sixty-two short conversations that originally appeared in Paul *Robeson's newspaper *Freedom* under the title "Conversations from Life" and were continued in the *Baltimore Afro-American* as "Here's Mildred." The novel's heroine, *Mildred Johnson, recounts for her friend Marge the daily battles she has with her white employers who either treat her like she is invisible or who try to overwork and underpay her for her services as a maid. Childress's novel uniquely celebrates the lives of countless African American women who raised families while working as domestics. Unlike the docile, self-effacing, one-dimensional domestics often found in American literature, Mildred is assertive, intellectually superior, quick-witted, and dignified. Mildred questions authority, confronts her white employers, attacks stereotypes, and challenges the abuse of Black domestics. Childress creates a world in which a poor, Black female takes it upon herself to enlighten her employers about race, class, and gender biases.

Conversations such as "Like One of the Family," "The Pocket Book Game," and "The Health Card" illustrate Childress's skillful manipulation of her heroine. In "Like One of the Family," Mildred corrects her employer who makes the mistake of boasting that Mildred is like one of the family. Mildred reminds her that she eats in the kitchen while her employer's family eats in the dining room. She tells her that if she were to drop dead, she would be replaced within a heartbeat. Mildred also reminds her that after she has worked herself into a sweat, she does not appreciate the low wages. Mildred uses this opportunity, while she has the employer at a point of vulnerability, to ask for a raise. In "The Pocket Book Game," the white employer holds on tightly to her purse as if she is afraid Mildred will steal from her. Mildred turns the tables when she comes running back into the house and snatches her own pocketbook. She reassures her employer that if she paid anyone as little as she did, she would hold on to her purse, too. Childress demonstrates in "The Health Card" the disruptiveness of stereotypes. When Mildred's employer asks for her health records, Mildred in turn requests health cards from each member of the white family. Mildred's humor serves to expose the rampant racism of the 1950s.

Childress's novel makes a serious contribution to African American literature because of the storytelling forms that she makes use of in the conversations. While the use of an omniscient narrator would have earned for Childress the label of didactic or propagandistic, the use of a character who speaks her own mind allows the audience to view racial tensions of the 1950s from the point of view of an impassioned character who relates her own personal experiences. In a sense, Mildred is held accountable for what she says to her white employers, and Childress as author maintains some degree of distance from the experiences.

Like One of the Family, with Mildred at its center, is unique in that it celebrates the experiences of African American women domestics. Childress gives voice to women who on bended knees improved the conditions of their families.

• Trudier Harris, "'I Wish I Was a Poet': The Character As Artist in Alice Childress's *Like One of the Family,*" in *Black American Literature Forum* 14 (Spring 1980): pp. 24–30.

—Elizabeth Brown-Guillory

LINCOLN, ABRAHAM (1809–1865), sixteenth president of the United States. Abraham Lincoln is an ambiguous figure in history and literature, with much disagreement centered on his beliefs and actions regarding African Americans. Lincoln hated slavery but equivocated in public statements about racial equality. He considered his 1863 Emancipation Proclamation the most historic act of his presidency, but many critics interpret the order freeing Southern slaves during the Civil War as a military measure, not a humanitarian one. In a famous 1862 letter to the editor Horace Greeley, Lincoln explained that his "official duty" in the war was to "save the Union" but added that this stance signaled "no modification of my oft-expressed personal wish that all men every where could be free." Near the war's end, Lincoln vetoed a congressional bill to codify emancipation and insisted instead that the permanent end of slavery be written into the Constitution as the Thirteenth Amendment.

Assassination elevated Lincoln to national martyrdom, but his dual incarnations as "Savior of the Union" and "Great Emancipator" have coexisted uneasily. Thomas Dixon's 1905 novel *The Clansman* (filmed as D. W. Griffith's *Birth of a Nation*) portrayed Lincoln as an eager racist. Despite numerous tributes like Langston *Hughes's poem "Lincoln Monument" (1927) and William E. Lilly's *Set My People Free* (1932), many African American writers have expressed ambivalence. Frederick *Douglass knew Lincoln and believed him to be utterly without prejudice but in an 1876 speech declared Lincoln "pre-eminently the white man's President." In 1922 W. E. B. *Du Bois provoked angry letters from readers of the *Crisis* magazine with a critical paragraph calling Lincoln "a big, inconsistent, brave man." Many civil rights leaders effectively used Lincoln as a political symbol, but criticisms continued from *Malcolm X, Julius *Lester, and more recently from Vincent Harding in *There Is a River* (1982). Lincoln remains a compelling presence, but the icon has proved even more ambiguous than the man.

• Arthur Zilversmit, ed., *Lincoln on Black and White: A Documentary History,* 1971. Stephen B. Oates, *Abraham Lincoln: The Man behind the Myths,* 1984.

—Scott A. Sandage

LITTLE, MALCOLM. *See* Malcolm X.

LOCKE, ALAIN (1885–1954), critic, educator, philosopher, and mentor of the Harlem Renaissance. Alain Locke's role as a general factotum of the Harlem Renaissance has tended to overshadow the full dimensions of an active and productive life. John Edgar Tidwell and John Wright list more than three hundred items spanning the period from 1904 to 1953 in "Alain Locke: A Comprehensive Bibliography of His Published Writings" (*Callaloo,* Feb.–Oct., 1981). Born in (or near) Philadelphia to parents who were schoolteachers, Locke came to maturity in the self-conscious genteel ambiance of Philadelphia's black elite. After completing secondary and normal school studies in Philadelphia, he went to Harvard College, where he majored in philosophy. An appointment as a Rhodes scholar in 1907 followed his undergraduate Harvard experience and he spent time at both Oxford and the University of Berlin, returning to the United States in 1911. Shortly after, he began his long career as a teacher at Howard University. He received his PhD at Harvard in 1917.

Locke began to achieve wide attention as an advisor and contributor to *Opportunity,* founded in 1923 by Charles S. Johnson under the auspices of the National Urban League. A by-product of this association was his editing *The New Negro,* the signature anthology of the Harlem Renaissance. During the 1920s, Locke also edited in 1927 *Four Negro Poets* (Claude *McKay, Jean *Toomer, Countee *Cullen, and Langston *Hughes) and in the same year (with Montgomery Gregory) *Plays of Negro Life.* In 1929, Locke began a comprehensive yearly roundup of books relating to Africa and African Americans. These appeared in *Opportunity* until 1943, and thereafter in *Phylon* until 1952. They constitute an important record of the discourse relating to African Americans in the period covered. During the 1930s he established the Associates in Negro Folk Education, which published critical works by Sterling A. *Brown and others. Locke's own contributions to the series were *Negro Art: Past and Present* and *The Negro and His Music* (both 1936). The crowning effort in this project was Locke's landmark illustrated book, *The Negro in Art* (1940).

From his college days, Locke had been interested in issues of race and culture, leading to his embrace of the concepts of cultural pluralism and cultural relativism. Locke's concept of cultural pluralism had its origins in his interactions with a teacher at Harvard, Horace Kallen, then a graduate assistant to the philosopher George Santayana. Cultural pluralism offers a counter to the cultural amalgamation of the "melting pot" paradigm, since that paradigm would clearly exclude African Americans and other distinctive groups. Cultural relativism is the assertion of the parity of different cultures and the rejection of the social Darwinian hierarchy that supported nineteenth-century racial and political theories inimical to African Americans and other groups. Locke's cultural relativism is closely allied to that which became a tenet of American anthropology as it emerged under the aegis of Franz Boas. It is significant that both Kallen and Boas were Jewish. Locke's early interests in race were explored in a series of lectures offered in 1916, against opposition, at Howard University. These lectures were published only in 1992 in an edition by Jeffrey C. Stewart. Locke's more mature reflections on race and culture are perhaps best represented in his commentaries in the anthology (edited with Bernhard Stern) *When Peoples Meet* (1942).

By the late 1920s, however, Locke had also refined and propagated a theory of ancestral and folk tradition, particularly stressing its relevance for the visual and literary artist. At first, he was especially drawn to those young writers who seemed to exemplify the fulfillment of his expectations; of these, Langston Hughes, Zora Neale *Hurston, and Sterling Brown, only the latter retained his confidence in ensuing years.

Locke envisaged summarizing his views in a work to be entitled *The Negro in American Culture.* Ill health prevented his proceeding with it and the task was entrusted to a protégée, Margaret Just Butcher. The work that appeared under this title, although it mentions Locke's notes, owes little to Locke and must be regarded as an independent production.

Locke ranks with W. E. B. *Du Bois and Carter G. *Woodson as a seminal intellectual influence in African American culture; he shares with them political and social interests and a sense of mission in "uplifting the race"; he was unique, however, in the breadth and knowledge of artistic expression and achievement that he brought to their shared larger tasks.

• Russell J. Linneman, ed., *Alain Locke: Reflections on a Modern Renaissance Man,* 1982. Jeffrey C. Stewart, ed., *The Critical Temper of Alain Locke,* 1983. Leonard Harris, ed., *The Philosophy of Alain Locke: Harlem Renaissance and Beyond,* 1989. Alain Leroy Locke, *Race Contacts and Interracial Relations,* ed. Jeffrey C. Stewart, 1992.

—Richard A. Long

LOMAX, PEARL CLEAGE. *See* Cleage, Pearl.

LORDE, AUDRE (1934–1992), poet, essayist, autobiographer, novelist, and nonfiction writer, also wrote under the pseudonym Rey Domini. American writer Audre Lorde names herself as "a black feminist lesbian mother poet" because her identity is based on the relationship of many divergent perspectives once perceived as incompatible. Thematically, she expresses or explores pride, love, anger, fear, racial and sexual oppression, urban neglect, and personal survival. Moreover, she eschews a hope for a better humanity by revealing truth in her poetry. She states, "I feel I have a duty to speak the truth as I see it and to share not just my triumphs, not just the things that felt good, but the pain, the intense, often unmitigating pain." Lorde was a prolific writer who continually explored the marginalizations experienced by individuals in a society fearful of differences.

Audrey Geraldine Lorde was born in New York City to laborer Frederic Byron and Linda Belmar Lorde, immigrants from the West Indies who had hoped to return until the depression dashed their plans. The youngest of three daughters, she grew up in Manhattan where she attended Roman Catholic schools, retreating silently into reading and the discovery of writing poetry. She wrote her first poem when she was in the eighth grade. Rebelling at the isolation and strict rules of her parents, she befriended others at Hunter High School who were also viewed as outcasts. After graduating from high school, she attended Hunter College from 1954 to 1959, graduating with a bachelor's degree. While studying library science, Lorde supported herself working various odd jobs: factory worker, ghost writer, social worker, X-ray technician, medical clerk, and arts and crafts supervisor. In 1954, she spent a pivotal year as a student at the National University of Mexico, a period described by Lorde as a time of affirmation and renewal because she confirmed her identity on personal and artistic levels as a lesbian and poet. On her return to New York, Lorde went to college, worked as a librarian, continued writing, and became an active participant in the gay culture of Greenwich Village. Lorde furthered her education at Columbia University, earning a master's degree in library science in 1961. During this time she also worked as a librarian at Mount Vernon Public Library and married attorney Edward Ashley Rollins; they later divorced in 1970 after having two children, Elizabeth and Johnathan. In 1966, Lorde became head librarian at Town School Library in New York City where she remained until 1968.

A turning point for Lorde was the year 1968. She received a National Endowment for the Arts grant, and in spring of 1968 she became poet in residence at Tougaloo College, a small historically black institution in Mississippi. Her experiences as both teacher and writer of poetry virtually changed Lorde's life. Her first volume of poetry, *The First Cities* (1968), was published by the Poet's Press and edited by Diane di Prima, a former classmate and friend from Hunter High School. This volume was cited as an innovative and refreshing rhetorical departure from the confrontational tone prevalent in African American poetry at the time. Dudley *Randall, fellow poet and critic, asserted in his review of the book that "[Lorde] does not wave a black flag, but her blackness is there, implicit, in the bone." Lorde's second volume, **Cables to Rage* (1970), which was mainly written during her tenure at Tougaloo, addresses themes of love, betrayal, childbirth, and the complexities of raising children. It is particularly noteworthy for the poem "Martha" in which Lorde poetically confirms her homosexuality: "we shall love each other here if ever at all." This collection was published in London but distributed in America by Randall's Broadside Press.

Her next volume of poetry, *From a Land Where Other People Live* (1973), was published by Broadside Press. There exists obvious personal and poetic growth in her expanding thematic scope and vision of worldwide injustice and oppression. Her subtle anger is fully developed yet she addresses other important concerns: the complexities surrounding her existence as an African American and as a woman, mother, lover, and friend. Anger, terror, loneliness, love, and impatience illuminate the pages of *From a Land Where Other People Live* as Lorde's personal experiences have now become universal. This volume was nominated for the National Book Award for poetry in 1973.

Lorde's *New York Head Shop and Museum* (1974) examines political and social issues and was often characterized as her most radical poetry yet. In this volume, Lorde takes the reader on a visual journey through her native New York City while presenting poetic images of urban decay, neglect, and poverty that confront its inhabitants every day. Lorde believed that political action was the necessary ingredient for change: "I have come to believe in death and renewal by fire." Occasionally, *New York Head Shop and Museum* resembles the rebellious yet proud tone of many black poets of the 1960s.

Coal (1976) introduced Lorde to a wider audience because it was her first volume to be released by a major publisher, W. W. Norton. This volume compiles poetry from her first two books, *The First Cities* and *Cables to Rage,* but is significant also because it began Lorde's association with Adrienne Rich, one of Norton's most acclaimed poets, who introduced her to a larger white audience. Coal contains many themes similar to those found in *New York Head Shop and Museum* and demonstrates her superb metaphorical craft. In the title poem "Coal" she asserts and celebrates her blackness. Lorde is painfully aware that many strangers overlook her blackness by "cancelling me out." Many of her poems in *Coal* are also an indictment of an unjust society that allows women to be treated unfairly, sometimes brutally, and this acknowledgment by Lorde intensifies her plea for cooperation and sisterhood among women.

Lorde's seventh book of poetry, *The Black Unicorn* (1978), also published by Norton, is widely considered the most complex yet brilliant masterpiece written during her prolific literary career. In this volume, Lorde spans three centuries of the black diaspora to reclaim African mythology as the basis for her themes about women, racial pride, motherhood, and spirituality. She also affirms her lesbianism and political concerns. Poet Adrienne Rich wrote: "Refusing to be circumscribed by any simple identity, Audre Lorde writes as a Black woman, a mother, a daughter, a Lesbian, a feminist, a visionary." In this remarkable work, Lorde opens up the myths of Africa to American readers and calls upon the female African gods to grant her wisdom, strength, and endurance.

Lorde's first work of nonfiction was *The *Cancer Journals* (1980), which chronicles introspectively a very frightening ordeal with breast cancer from September 1978 to March 1979. The brief introduction and three chapters based on Lorde's personal diary detail the intermittent despair, hopelessness, and fear for her life and art. When confronted with the possibility of death, Lorde writes candidly that she wants "to write a piece of meaning words on cancer as it affects my life and my consciousness as a woman, a black lesbian feminist mother lover poet all I am." After undergoing a radical mastectomy, Lorde's spirit still intact, she decides against wearing a prosthesis, rejecting the female physical ideal as presented by the male-dominated media. *A Burst of Light* (1988) is a continuation of this facet of Lorde's life as it recounts her second battle with the spreading cancer beginning in 1984. This brooding collection discusses Lorde's choice for a noninvasive treatment program utilizing meditation and homeopathy.

In 1982, Lorde cemented her reputation as a poet and expanded her prose writing with the publications of *Chosen Poems: Old and New,* a compilation of selections from her first five books and several new pieces, and *Zami: A New Spelling of My Name,* a fictionalized account of Lorde's life as a child to a young adult. This autobiographical narrative also exhibits the tenuous, difficult relationship between a daughter and her mother.

As a noted feminist, Lorde painstakingly struggled against the limitations of the label, insisting that feminism is important to all factions of African American life. As a perceived outsider on many fronts, Lorde believed that bringing together divergent groups can only strengthen and heal a torn society: "When I say I am a Black feminist, I mean I recognize that my power as well as my primary oppressions come as a result of my Blackness as well as my womanness, and therefore my struggles on both these fronts are inseparable." These views are explored further in *Sister Outsider: Essays and Speeches* (1984), published by Crossing Press. This nonfiction collection explores the fear and hatred existing between African American men and women, feminists, or lesbians and the challenge between African American women and white women to find common ground. Another crucial area of emphasis presented in *Sister Outsider* is the isolation found among African American women and their subsequent rejection of each other's trust, friendship, and gifts. Before her death in 1992, Lorde published *Our Dead behind Us* (1986), an influential volume of poetry that expresses many similar themes although more deeply and more expanded.

Audre Lorde, who wrote at a feverish pace throughout her literary career, remains an influential and serious talent. To Lorde, her writing was more than a choice or a vocation. It was a responsibility that was necessary for her survival and the survival of others. Her emotional precision blends rage, anger, and destruction with a luminous vision of hope, love, and renewal.

• Claudia Tate, ed., *Black Women Writers at Work,* 1983, pp. 100–116. Jerome Brooks, "In the Name of the Father: The Poetry of Audre Lorde," in *Black Women Writers (1950–1980): A Critical Evaluation,* ed. Mari Evans, 1984, pp. 269–276. Joan Martin, "The Unicorn Is Black: Audre Lorde in Retrospect," in *Black Women Writers (1950–1980): A Critical Evaluation,* ed. Mari Evans, 1984, pp. 277–291. Irma McClaurin-Allen, "Audre Lorde," in *DLB,* vol. 41, *Afro-American Poets since 1955,* eds. Trudier Harris and Thadious M. Davis, 1985, pp. 217–222. Margaret Homans, "Audre Lorde," in *African American Writers: Profiles of Their Lives and Works—from the 1700s to the Present,* eds. Valerie Smith et al., 1993, pp. 211–224. Allison Kimmich, "Writing the Body: From Abject to Subject," *A.B. Auto Biography Studies* 13:2 (Fall 1998): 223–234. Anna Wilson, "Rites/Rights of Canonization: Audre Lorde as Icon," in *Women Poets of the Americas: Toward a Pan-American Gathering,* ed. Jacqueline Vaught Brogan, 1999, pp. 17–33.

—Beverly Threatt Kulii

LOUIS, JOE (1914–1981), professional boxer. "We gon do our part, and we will win, because we are on God's side," Joe Louis intoned on 10 March 1942 at a dinner/show sponsored by the Navy Relief Society. In seven years, Louis had transformed himself in the eyes of white America from a sullen, unlettered, somewhat threatening black boy from the ghetto of Detroit to a transcendent symbol of patriotism and democratic nationalism, something more than a mere sports hero or champion boxer, although this transformation would not have been possible had he not become a champion athlete who dwarfed the competitors of his era. Born in Alabama on 13 May 1914, Joseph Louis Barrow migrated with his family to Detroit in 1926. He took to boxing as a teenager, had a successful amateur career, and turned professional in 1934. He won the heavyweight title in 1937 and successfully defended it twenty-five times before retiring for the first time in 1949. Louis became the most talked about black figure in American popular culture during the depression and World War II. He was virtually a nationalist hero among blacks because his opponents were white. His fights with Primo Carnera, an Italian, in 1935, on the eve of Italy's invasion of Ethiopia, and his 1938 rematch against Max Schmeling, the German Nazi who defeated him two years earlier (Louis's only defeat until he returned to boxing after his 1949 retirement), were highly symbolic affairs politically, the latter being the most talked about and anticipated sporting event in American history at that time. Louis was viewed with considerable suspicion by white America when he emerged, largely because it was feared at first that he might be another Jack *Johnson, the first black heavyweight champion who broke a long-standing color line when he defeated Tommy Burns for the title in 1908. Breaking a color barrier that had existed in heavyweight championship fights since Johnson's defeat, Louis deliberately and unerringly convinced the white public that he was not in any way like Jack Johnson and became, by the time of America's entry into World War II, one of the most beloved athletic figures ever produced in America. He did this by being generous to his white opponents, avoiding white women publicly, and being demonstrably loyal to his country. He was a striking contrast to such black public figures as *Stepin Fetchit, Willie Best, and even Louis Armstrong in not seeming, in any way, to pander to whites as "the good, grinning darky." Louis has been written about or mentioned in works by Richard *Wright, James *Baldwin, *Malcolm X, Maya *Angelou, Chester *Himes, Ernest J. *Gaines, Amiri *Baraka, and many others, and has figured symbolically in numerous books and poems. He is largely seen as an icon of an ur-black nationalism and a heroic figure on the order of *John Henry. Louis died in Las Vegas in 1981. The most revealing and honest of Joe Louis's autobiographies is *Joe Louis: My Life,* coauthored with Edna and Art Rust, Jr., and published in 1981.

—Gerald Early

L'OUVERTURE, TOUSSAINT (c. 1743–1803), Haitian patriot and revolutionary leader. A self-educated former slave, François Dominique Toussaint-L'Ouverture joined the Haitian Revolution in 1791 and became its foremost general, defeating both French and British forces. In 1802, he was betrayed and captured, and he died imprisoned in France.

Toussaint figures importantly in the early-nineteenth-century writings of James McCune Smith,

David *Walker, and Henry Highland *Garnet, among others, as a symbol and exemplar of resistance to slavery, and as an example of the potential of the black race. William Wells *Brown, in his pamphlet *St. Domingo: Its Revolution and Its Patriots* (1854), compares Toussaint favorably to Napoleon and George Washington: "Toussaint liberated his countrymen; Washington enslaved a portion of his." George Clinton Rowe's seventy-stanza poem, *Toussaint L'Ouverture* (1890), lauds Toussaint as the "deliverer of his race." Later African American writers such as Carter G. *Woodson and W. E. B. *Du Bois argued for Toussaint's importance in inspiring slave rebellions, in the abolition of the slave trade (1807), and in Napoleon's decision to sell the Louisiana Territory (1803).

In the twentieth century, Toussaint has been the subject of several dramatic treatments. Leslie Pinckey *Hill's *Toussaint L'Ouverture: A Dramatic History* (1928), written in blank verse, aims "to help fill a long-continuing void": the presentation of black heroes. Hill draws explicit parallels between Toussaint and Christ, and sees Toussaint as exemplifying the best of "our universal human nature." Lorraine *Hansberry's unfinished play *Toussaint* (1958–1965), originally conceived as a musical or an opera, similarly aims at portraying Toussaint as a black hero and role model.

Toussaint has inspired several works by Afro-Caribbean writers, including Edouard Glissant's play *Monsieur Toussaint* (1961) and Aimé Césaire's historical work, *Toussaint Louverture* (1960). C. L. R. James's unpublished play *Toussaint L'Ouverture* (revised as *The Black Jacobins,* 1976), which featured Paul *Robeson in the title role in a 1936 London performance, and his historical study, also titled *The Black Jacobins* (1938), both portray Toussaint as a hero tragically flawed by a "neglect for his own people" and an exaggerated respect for the French.

Arna *Bontemps's novel *Drums at Dusk* (1939) sees Toussaint as separated from common Haitians by his literacy, heroic nature, and "god-like authority." Margaret *Walker, in her poem "The Ballad of the Free" (1970), groups Toussaint with other leaders of slave insurrections as an African American hero. In two quite different works, Ralph *Ellison's short story "Mister Toussan" (1941) and Ntozake *Shange's play **for colored girls who have considered suicide / when the rainbow is enuf* (1977), Toussaint becomes a kind of distant, fairytale hero for children.

• J. Michael Dash, *Haiti and the United States: National Stereotypes and the Literary Imagination,* 1988. Alfred N. Hunt, *Haiti's Influence on Antebellum America,* 1988.

—Gary Ashwill

LUTIE JOHNSON. In Ann *Petry's *The *Street* (1946), Lutie Johnson, estranged from her husband and father, is a single mother, alone and struggling to make a better life for herself and her son, Bub. Lutie is one of the first African American urban heroines, breaking away from the tragic mulatto and other southern woman characters.

From her experience as a suburban domestic, she claims Benjamin Franklin as role model and strives to become a successful self-made American. Her obsession with upward mobility creates independence and self-reliance, yet also aloofness, which hinders her from forming coalitions with neighborhood women. Her independence also prevents her from believing that, as an African American woman, she cannot achieve the American dream. Lutie's constant struggle reveals how capitalism, racism, and sexism are intertwined; yet her hope for a better life reassures her struggle. Although she easily recognizes and confronts racism and attempts to overcome the economic oppression faced daily, as "a good-looking brown girl" she is stumped by the sexism and sexual advances of white and African American men who obstruct her upward mobility and offend her virtuous nature.

When Lutie is faced with attempted rape by an African American man, and forced concubinage to a white slumlord, she responds with violence fueled by rage and frustration. Lutie may be the first African American female character to murder an African American male for participating in her oppression. Yet the violent act only makes Lutie lose self-respect, decide to abandon her son, and give up the struggle.

—Adenike Marie Davidson

Lyrics of Lowly Life (1896) was Paul Laurence *Dunbar's first commercially published book and probably the best-selling volume of African American poetry before the Harlem Renaissance. Of the 105 poems in the volume, 97 had been previously published in Dunbar's *Oak and Ivy* (1893) and **Majors and Minors* (1895), suggesting that *Lyrics of Lowly Life* was designed to serve as a showcase anthology of what the poet and his supporters felt was an underrecognized literary achievement. The popular appeal and literary significance of *Lyrics of Lowly Life* was enhanced by the introduction that William Dean Howells, a well-established white literary critic, wrote for the volume. The major literary influences on the poems in *Lyrics of Lowly Life* are British Romantic poets such as John Keats and Percy Bysshe Shelley, and American regional poetry, particularly the work of the Indiana writer James Whitcomb Riley. What made Dunbar's poetry most notable to readers in his own time, however, were his evocations of the flavor of life and the folkways of "down home" black America through the speech and dialect of rural African Americans.

The contents of *Lyrics of Lowly Life* may be conveniently divided between poems written in standard English and the dialect poetry that gained Dunbar international fame. Among the poems in *Lyrics of Lowly Life* written in so-called Negro dialect are such favorites from previous Dunbar volumes as "When Malindy Sings," "A Negro Love Song," "An Ante-Bellum

Sermon," "The Party," and "When de Co'n Pone's Hot." Dunbar's dialect verse displays his talent in rendering melodies associated with popular songs and ballads, such as "The Old Apple-Tree" and "A Banjo Song." In the introduction to *Lyrics of Lowly Life,* Howells reserved special praise for Dunbar's dialect poems, judging them a product of the poet's innate ability to "feel the negro life aesthetically and express it lyrically." Dunbar showed his appreciation of Howells's support by dedicating *Lyrics of Lowly Life* to the white critic as well as to Dunbar's mother, but the poet came to believe that Howells's praise of the dialect poems deflected attention away from his more serious verse in standard English.

Lyrics of Lowly Life contains a wealth of Dunbar's most thoughtful and ambitious verse. "Frederick Douglass" commemorates in a dignified style the life and example of the great freedom orator and abolitionist. Two odes, "Ode to Ethiopia" and "Columbian Ode," adapt a traditional Romantic poetic form to commemorate both racial and national patriotism. Many of Dunbar's poems about Nature, love, and death betray the poet's tendency to indulge in idealized and conventional responses to time-worn themes. But in such classic lyrics as "Not They Who Soar," which cautions that "flight is ever free and rare," and "We Wear the Mask," which warns of "the mask that grins and lies," Dunbar spoke eloquently and individually to the complexity of his struggle to articulate an African American poetic voice to a white American audience.

• Jean Wagner, *Black Poets of the United States,* 1974. Joanne M. Braxton, ed., *The Collected Poetry of Paul Laurence Dunbar,* 1993.

—William L. Andrews and
Patricia Robinson Williams

M

MACKEY, NATHANIEL (b. 1947), poet, novelist, essayist, music critic, editor, lecturer, and educator. Florida-born Nathaniel Mackey was raised in California, graduated from Princeton University with high honors, and earned a PhD in English and American literature in 1975. From 1976 to 1979 he was director of Black studies at the University of Southern California and assistant professor in both the English department and the ethnic studies program. He joined the faculty of the University of California, Santa Cruz in 1979, where he is a professor of American literature.

Evidence of the Black diaspora echoes throughout his writings. His poetry, prose, and essays situate African American poetry in diverse poetic and cultural traditions: North American, African, Caribbean, and, to some extent, Latin American. He argues that these poetic traditions reciprocally influence each other. The formal experimentation in his writing disrupts any notion that either African American poetry or poetry produced by either "white" or "non-white" Americans is created in an ahistorical vacuum, a disruption that in turn complicates the definition of the North American poetic tradition. To illustrate this, Mackey, in his critical meditation on American poetry entitled *Discrepant Engagement: Dissonance, Cross-Culturality, and Experimental Writing* (1993), describes his project as one that situates black writers from the United States and the Caribbean as well as from the so-called Black Mountain school under a common rubric.

He explains that "creative kinship and the lines of affinity it effects are much more complex, jagged, and indissociable than the totalizing pretensions of canon formation tend to acknowledge." Thus, by bringing their "writing into dialogue and juxtaposition with one another" he demonstrates that

> correspondences, counterpoint, and relevance to one another exist among authors otherwise separated by ethnic or regional boundaries. . . . This fact is especially relevant to the current institutionalization of an African-American canon and the frequent assumption that black writers are to be discussed only in relation to other black writers.

Mackey has written scholarly articles on and been influenced by the poetry of Robert Duncan, Edward Brathwaite, Robert Creely, Amiri *Baraka, and Ishmael *Reed. William Carlos Williams, Charles Olson, Denise Levertov, Federico García Lorca, Aimé Césaire, and Pablo Neruda also had an early influence on his work.

Difficult to categorize in academic terms, his writing questions boundaries between prose and poetry, and especially between writing music; his writing particulary speaks out of and back to jazz. He foregrounds the production of both poetry and jazz as an intellectual project.

His books of poetry include: *Four for Trane* (1978), *Septet for the End of Time* (1983), *Eroding Witness* (1985), *Outlantish* (1992), and *School of Udhra* (1993). His prose texts include: *Bedouin Hornbook* (1986), an epistolary novel, and its sequel, *Djbot Baghostus's Run* (1993), as well as a volume of collected essays, *Discrepant Engagement: Dissonance, Cross-Culturality and Experimental Writing* (1993). Edited volumes include *Hambone,* a literary magazine (1974–1992), and *Moment's Notice: Jazz in Poetry and Prose* (1993).

• Nathaniel Mackey, "An Interview with Nathaniel Mackey," interview by Edward Foster, *Talisman: A Journal of Contemporary Poetry and Poetics* 9 (Fall 1992): pp. 48–61. Christopher Funkhouser, "An Interview with Nathaniel Mackey," in *Callaloo* 18 (1995): 321–34. Scroggins, Mark *DLB,* vol. 169, *American Poets Since WWII,* 5th series, ed. Joseph Conte, 1996: pp. 179–191. Peter O' Leary, "An Interview with Nathaniel Mackey," in *Chicago Review* 43 (1997): 30–46.

—Michelle Habell-Pallán

MADAM ALBERTA K. JOHNSON. Alberta K. Johnson, or Madam Alberta K. Johnson, as she insists on being called by all persons other than her family and friends, is the main character in a number of comic poems written by Langston *Hughes. The first piece to be published, "Madam and the Number Runner," appeared in *Contemporary Poetry* (Autumn 1943). At least seventeen more pieces appeared in various publications, including *Poetry, Common Ground,* and *Negro Story.*

Hughes began composing the pieces in the summer of 1943, soon after the major riot in Harlem early in August 1943 and immediately after the composition of a long poem, itself sardonic, "The Ballad of Margie Polite," about the woman whose altercation with a policeman in Harlem led directly to that riot.

The character of Madam may also be placed in the context of Hughes's Jesse B. Semple, or *Simple, who had emerged the previous February in Hughes's weekly column in the *Chicago Defender.* Like Simple, Alberta K. Johnson is an instantly recognizable Harlem type despite her memorable individuality. A middle-aged woman of uncertain means, she is resourceful, self-confident, sassy, and streetwise. Thus she faces down the world, including her lovers past and present, her landlord, her insurance man come to collect his premiums, other bill collectors, or her self-righteous minister anxious to save her independent, fun-loving soul.

—Arnold Rampersad

MADGETT, NAOMI LONG (b. 1923), teacher, poet, publisher, and editor; born Naomi Cornelia Long. In "He Lives in Me," a poem in *Adam of Ifé* (1992) honoring her father, Clarence Marcellus Long, Sr., Naomi Long Madgett states the principles that underlie her own achievements: faith, integrity, and personal and social responsibility. As a child, she had free access to his book-lined study, discovering early her love of poetry. When she was fifteen, her first collection, *Songs to a Phantom Nightingale* (1941), was accepted for publication, though two years had elapsed before it appeared. Two editions, containing additional early poems, have been issued: *Phantom Nightingale, Juvenilia* (1981) and *Remembrances of Spring: Early Collected Poems* (1993). The second of these also includes her second collection, *One and the Many* (1956).

Between her first two collections, Madgett completed a BA (Virginia State University, 1945), married, settled in Detroit, Michigan, worked briefly for the *Michigan Chronicle,* and gave birth to a daughter, Jill (who is also a publishing poet under the name Jill Witherspoon Boyer). The marriage ended in 1948, and Madgett worked for the Michigan Bell Telephone Company until 1954.

In 1955, she completed an MEd degree in English at Wayne State University and began her teaching career, first as a secondary-school teacher in the Detroit public schools (1955–1968), then at Eastern Michigan University (1968–1984). From the beginning of her teaching career, she has championed textbook reform to provide fairer representation to African American authors. She perceives her contribution to the teaching of this literature and of creative writing as her most influential work, her writing as her most personally satisfying.

In the early 1960s, encouraged by Rosey E. Pool, a Dutch scholar interested in African American poets, a group of poets began to meet for informal discussion and workshops. Dudley *Randall, Oliver LaGrone, James W. Thompson, Harold Lawrence, Edward Simpkins, Alma Parks, Betty Ford, Gloria Davis, and Madgett formed the nucleus of the group, which met at Boone House, the home of Margaret Esse *Danner, poet in residence at Wayne State University from 1962 to 1964. A later group included LaGrone, Randall, Davis, Madgett, Joyce Whitsitt, and several white poets. *Ten: Anthology of Detroit Poets* (1968) grew from this association.

Madgett's third collection, *Star By Star* (1965; rpt. 1970, 1972), includes poems from this period. In 1972, she, three friends, and her third husband, Leonard Patton Andrews, established the Lotus Press to publish her fourth book, *Pink Ladies in the Afternoon* (1972). The press, which Madgett and Andrews took over in 1974, has published well-received books for more than twenty years. Its major contribution has been to bring attention to African American poets. Although many of these have been young women, the press has also published established poets such as May *Miller, notably, her *Collected Poems* (1989). In 1993, having published seventy-six titles, Madgett turned over distribution to the Michigan State University Press, which established the Lotus Press Series and named Madgett its senior editor. In the same year, the Before Columbus Foundation presented her with its American Book Award as publisher-editor.

Her fifth collection of poems, *Exits and Entrances* (1978), appeared six years after the book that launched the Lotus Press, and it would be another ten years before her next new collection. While she did write a college-level textbook, *A Student's Guide to Creative Writing* (1980), her dedication to teaching and the prodigious output of what was, with some volunteer help, a one-person publishing venture left little time for her own poems.

But the subject of her next collection, *Octavia and Other Poems* (1988), also demanded time. Madgett's poems are, in the broadest sense, personal, dealing even with major social concerns from an individual rather than a political viewpoint. This book, focused on family life as it reflects community, intensifies her customary lyric individuality. The sequence "Octavia" re-creates from family memorabilia the life of her father's sister, a schoolteacher who died before Madgett was born. As it does so, it re-creates African American life in Oklahoma and Kansas early in the twentieth century, emphasizing family and personal responsibility for the welfare of the community. The collection *Adam of Ifé: Black Women in Praise of Black Men* (1992), edited by Madgett, is similar in its emphasis on strong, positive African American manhood.

Pilgrim Journey, a collection of autobiographical essays near completion, and a number of recent unpublished poems will testify, as have the past five decades of her poems, to Madgett's firm foundation in the faith, integrity, and sense of responsibility she sees as her patrimony.

Naomi Long Madgett's unpublished poems and papers are deposited in the Special Collections Library at Fisk University, Nashville, Tennessee.

• Robert P. Sedlack, "Naomi Long Madgett," in *DLB,* vol. 76, *Afro-American Writers, 1940–1955,* ed. Trudier Harris, 1988, pp. 104–112. Nagueyalti Warren, "Naomi Long Madgett," in *Notable Black Women in America,* vol. 1, ed. Jessie Carney Smith, 1992, pp. 716–719. Alice A. Deck, "Madgett, Naomi Long," in *Black Women in America,* vol. 2, ed. Darlene Clark Hine, 1994, pp. 741–743. Robert P. Sedlack, "Madgett, Naomi Long," in *The Oxford Companion to Women's Writing in the United States,* eds. Cathy N. Davidson and Linda Wagner-Martin, 1995, pp. 535–536.

—George F. Wedge

MADHUBUTI, HAKI R. (b. 1942), poet, critic, essayist, teacher, editor, publisher, and businessperson. Given the name Don L. Lee, Haki R. Madhubuti changed his name in 1973 as a result of the ideological influences of the Black Arts movement, of which he was a highly visible member. He was born 23 February 1942 in Little Rock, Arkansas. In 1943 he and his parents migrated to Detroit, Michigan, where his father deserted the family before the birth of Madhubuti's sister. In order to cope with poverty and feed her two children, his mother worked as a janitor and a barmaid, eventually becoming an alcoholic and a drug addict. When Madhubuti was sixteen, his mother died from a drug overdose.

This woman, Maxine Lee, was the prime mover behind the creative force that Haki R. Madhubuti has become. When Madhubuti was thirteen years old, his mother asked him to check out for her Richard *Wright's *Black Boy* from the Detroit Public Library. He became a reader with his discovery of Wright, who led him to other writers, such as Chester *Himes, Langston *Hughes, Claude *McKay, Melvin B. *Tolson, Jean *Toomer, Gwendolyn *Brooks, Margaret *Walker, and Arna *Bontemps.

After his mother's death, Madhubuti went to Chicago, where he attended Dunbar High School. Because he could not get a job after graduating, he traveled selling magazines, ending up penniless and sick in East St. Louis, Missouri, where he pawned everything he owned and joined the U.S. Army. When Madhubuti was eighteen, a white drill sergeant tore the pages of his copy of Paul Robeson's *Here I Stand*, stimulating in him a commitment to his Blackness, steepening his drive to study Black cultural and intellectual history, and instilling in him the desire to become a writer.

In 1963 Madhubuti left the army, and four years later Dudley *Randall's Broadside Press published Madhubuti's first collection of poetry, *Think Black* (1967), which had been previously published by the author himself. Six books, all published by Broadside Press, followed: five collections of poetry—*Black Pride* (1968), **Don't Cry, Scream* (1969), *We Walk the Way of the New World* (1970), *Directionscore: Selected and New Poems* (1971), *Book of Life* (1973)—and a collection of critical essays, *Dynamite Voices: Black Poets of the 1960s* (1971).

The titles of these early poetry collections demonstrate that he addressed his work to a Black audience and that he was intensely committed to illuminating for that audience the pitfalls of racism in all its psychological, economic, political, and historical guises. The themes and subjects found in these early collections appear in a more sophisticated form in his poetry collections of the 1980s and 1990s, among them the inner beauty and/or environmental difficulties of the Black woman; what it means to be a Black man in America; the importance of Black male–female relationships; political figures who fight racial problems; poets such as Conrad Kent *Rivers, Langston Hughes, Gwendolyn Brooks, Ted *Joans, and Sterling *Plumpp; the problems with Black assimilation into Western culture; how Blacks in the West have allowed themselves to be brainwashed by Christianity; Blacks who lack substance and commitment to their race; the contradiction of Blacks in the military; and the psychological and artistic contributions of Black musicians.

Madhubuti also involves himself in institution building. He took four hundred dollars he made from reading poetry, bought a mimeograph machine, and along with poets Carolyn M. *Rodgers and Johari *Amini, as well as Roschell Rick, founded Third World Press in his basement apartment on Chicago's South Side on 12 December 1967. With Hoyt Fuller as their guide, Madhubuti and a number of his contemporaries founded the Organization of Black American Culture (OBAC), a city-wide group that tried to impact cultural activity in the arts. Around this time he and other members of OBAC met Gwendolyn Brooks in a church. As is demonstrated by the poems Madhubuti dedicates to Brooks, by his editing and publishing a book that celebrates her seventieth birthday (*Say That the River Turns: The Impact of Gwendolyn Brooks*, 1987), and by his now consistent publication of her works, a special bond exists between the two poets.

When Madhubuti met Brooks, he was also a self-described "foot soldier" for the Student Nonviolent Coordinating Committee (SNCC), the Congress of Racial Equality (CORE), and the Southern Christian Leadership Conference (SCLC). He and other members of the Black Arts movement read and sold their poetry at Black Arts conferences and at SCLC gatherings. Like Sonia *Sanchez, Askia M. *Touré, Amiri *Baraka, and Larry *Neal, Madhubuti is as much political activist as he is poet. His role as writer–political activist emerges in *From Plan to Planet* (1973), *Earthquakes and Sunrise Missions: Poetry and Essays of Black Revival 1973–1983*(1984), *Black Men: Obsolete, Single, Dangerous?* (1990), and *Claiming Earth: Race, Rage, Redemption* (1994). While these publications illustrate Madhubuti's skill as essayist and poet, his 1978 collection of essays *Enemies: The Clash of Races* is the most political. In it he demonstrates that the psychological, the economic, and the sociological are all embodiments of the politics that affect Black lives. *Enemies*, which describes the poet's associations with SNCC, CORE, and SCLC, more than any publication that precedes it, illuminates Madhubuti's global interest, highlighting the Nationalist and Pan-Africanist thinking in his work.

Madhubuti's publication of *Black Books Bulletin* (*BBB*) also grew out of his political activity. He and Larry Neal cochaired a workshop on ideas for publishing at the 1970 meeting of the Congress of Afrikan People. Although *Black World, Soulbook*, and the *Liberator* were still being published, no book review journal existed, and in 1971 Madhubuti and Neal founded the *BBB.* It was published as a quarterly for eight years, after which the issues became very erratic because of a low subscriber base and a lack of a full-time staff. *The Challenge of the Twenty-first Century,* volume 8, and *Blacks, Jews and Henry Gates, Jr.: A Response,* volume 16, published in 1991 and 1994, respectively, both address intellectual and political issues controversial at the time among the Black and white intelligentsia.

Madhubuti's edition of *Why L.A. Happened: Implications of the '92 Los Angeles Rebellion,* published in 1993, also attests to his continued involvement in the politics that affect Black lives. This collection includes twenty-nine essays written by Black intellectuals from diverse academic disciplines. This array of writers and scholars underscores Madhubuti's varied interprofessional relationships and the different types of writers he brings to his press. An ability to clarify controversial issues in the Black community is also reflected in Madhubuti's 1990 edition of *Confusion by Any Other Name: Essays Exploring the Negative Impact of "The Blackman's Guide to Understanding the Blackwoman."*

His 1987 collection of poetry, *Killing Memory, Seeking Ancestors,* published by Lotus Press, exemplifies the best of Madhubuti's poetic vision and shows his understanding that the same cultural, political, historical, economic, and educational issues that affected Black lives in the 1960s appear in new guises in the 1990s. "The Great Wait" in this collection beautifully exemplifies both the consistency in Madhubuti's style and the more than twenty years in which he has been honing that style, admonishing Blacks for waiting for others to improve the quality of their lives. In this critique of Blacks' failure to empower themselves, the poet carefully makes it clear that Blacks must overcome the psychological indoctrination that inhibits their taking charge of their lives. The poem progresses perfectly through the repetition of the words "waiting" and "waiters." The use of these words reflects a "jazzy rhythmic effect" that appears periodically throughout Madhubuti's collections of poetry. His love and knowledge of music is a predominant aspect of his poetry; in various poems he merges diverse musical rhythms with narrative voice, aphorisms, and rhetorical devices such as asyndeton, hyperbole, synecdoche, anaphora, anastrophe, litotes, irony, and ellipsis. His heavy staccato rhythm, the dozens, and sharp humor come straight out of Black street language.

Understanding the need to focus on spiritual and physical health at the same time that one confronts political issues, Madhubuti, John Howell (a Black environmental engineer), and David Hall (a lawyer) founded the National Black Holistic Retreat Society in 1980 to address the multifaceted issues that impact Black men's lives. In addition to this work, Madhubuti reads his poetry and gives lectures on educational, political, literary, and historical issues throughout the United States. He has also spoken in Canada, Morocco, Liberia, Ghana, Tanzania, Senegal, Israel, Brazil, Paris, England, and Holland.

Madhubuti is director of the Gwendolyn Brooks Center at Chicago State University and a professor of English. Having received an MFA from the University of Iowa, he has taught as a writer in residence at Cornell, Howard, Morgan State, and Central State universities as well as the University of Illinois in Chicago. In addition to being named author of the year for 1991 by the Illinois Association of Teachers of English, he received an American Book Award for Publishing and Editing in 1991 and the African Heritage Studies Association's Community Service Award in 1994.

In mid-1996 Madhubuti lived in Country Club Hills, Illinois, with his wife Safisha, a published writer and a professor at Northwestern University in Evanston, Illinois, and their family. *GroundWork: New and Selected Poems of Don L. Lee* appeared in 1996 and his collection of love poems, *Heartlove: Wedding and Love Poems,* in 1998. Madhubuti continued his political activism in writing with the publication of *Million Man March/Day of Absence: A Commemorative Anthology: Speeches, Commentary, Photography, Poetry, Illustrations, Documents,* which he edited with Maulana Karenga in 1996. In the late 1990s, he was also working on a collection of critical essays entitled "Gifted Genius: Writings from the Frontline of the Black Arts Movement" and on a book that contains a page each on the hundred books that have most influenced his life.

• David Llorens, "Black Don Lee," *Ebony,* Mar. 1969, 72–80. Paula Giddings, "From a Black Perspective: The Poetry of Don L. Lee," in *Amistad 2,* eds. John A. Williams and Charles Harris, 1971, pp. 299–318. Annette Oliver Shands, "The Relevancy of Don L. Lee As a Contemporary Black Poet," *Black World* 21 (June 1972): 35–48. Catherine Daniels Hurst, "Haki R. Madhubuti (Don L. Lee)," in *DLB,* vol. 41, *Afro-American Poets since 1955,* eds. Trudier Harris and Thadious M. Davis, 1985, pp. 222–232.

—Joyce A. Joyce

MAJOR, CLARENCE (b. 1936), poet, novelist, short fiction writer, visual artist, essayist, lexicographer, editor, and anthologist. Although known best for his metafictional novels, Clarence Major has long demonstrated his versatility in both the artistic forms he uses and the subject matter he selects. He tests boundaries, asserting and enacting the freedom of the artist to explore the full range of human experience. One source of his versatility is his early exposure to both the North and the South. Though born in Atlanta, he moved at the age of ten to Chicago with his mother after his parents were divorced. He maintained his southern connection through summer visits with his relatives. A key Chicago experience for him was exposure to modern art, especially the Impressionists. He studied briefly at the Chicago Art Institute when he was seventeen. Although he decided to focus his artistic efforts primarily on writing, he has made use of his painting and photography in his fiction, especially *Reflex and Bone Structure* (1975) and *Emergency Exit* (1979).

Much of his work, especially the fiction, has been experimental in that it has broken down conventional assumptions about character, plot, and narrative voice. The texts tend to be fragmentary rather than unified in structure; likewise, their principal theme is the impossibility of a coherent identity in contemporary society. This pattern holds in the two novels mentioned above, as well as *All-Night Visitors* (1969), *No* (1973), *My Amputations* (1986), and some of the stories in *Fun and Games* (1988). In these works, he joins Donald Barthelme, Thomas Pynchon, and Ishmael *Reed in challenging the view that fiction either reflects or constructs a meaningful reality. Literature is, in effect, a set of verbal tricks and needs its artificiality to be acknowledged.

But like Reed, Major also sees cultural significance in metafictional storytelling. His fragmented characters exist in a world in which they are rootless and often paranoid, in quest of a meaning that forever eludes them. In two novels that are more "realistic," he examines the same issue. *Such Was the Season* (1987) uses a southern folklike narrative voice that echoes Ernest J. *Gaines's Jane Pittman and Gloria *Naylor's Mama Day in its down-home wisdom as well as its position as a moral center by which to judge others. But Major complicates the narrative by having Annie Eliza draw much of her knowledge not from traditional black experience but from television talk shows and soap operas.

Similarly, *Painted Turtle: Woman with Guitar* (1988) tells the experiences of a Zuni woman who has been forced out of the tribe because she has worked as a prostitute and because she questions the traditional ways. She makes her living as an itinerant folksinger whose songs become her means of trying to claim an identity for herself as a Zuni. The novel is narrated by a man who is himself Hopi-Navajo and thus outside of her experience as well as uncertain about his own identity.

The subject matter of *Painted Turtle* suggests the multicultural nature of Major's work. One of the early influences on his writing was the work of French artists such as Raymond Radiguet and Arthur Rimbaud, and his interest in white European and American literature is reflected in many allusions in both his fiction and poetry. The importance of the Western tradition is clear in a book of poetry, *Surfaces and Masks* (1988), which is entirely about the experiences of Americans in Venice, with literary references to Disraeli, Dickens, Shelley, and Thomas Mann. His exploration of Native American issues is continued in a collection of poems entitled *Some Observations of a Stranger at Zuni in the Latter Part of the Century* (1989).

The range of forms and subjects reflects Major's commitment to artistic freedom made explicit in his essays and interviews, many of which are collected in *The Dark and Feeling* (1974). He insists that it is the quality of the work rather than its ideology that determines its importance. Even in his 1967 manifesto, "Black Criteria," which calls for greater use of African American materials and a rejection of much of Western tradition, he still concludes that the integrity of the artistic vision is the essential criterion. His work as editor and lexicographer has demonstrated his commitment to language and to literary freedom. His *Dictionary of Afro-American Slang* (1970), expanded and updated in *Juba to Jive* (1994), provides a major resource for discussions of African American language use. His two anthologies, *The New Black Poetry* (1969) and *Calling the Wind: Twentieth-Century African-American Short Stories* (1993), offer a wide range of literary expression within the African American tradition. He is a professor of English at the University of California, Davis.

• *Black American Literature Forum,* special issue, 13 (Summer 1979). Larry D. Bradfield, "Beyond Mimetic Exhaustion: The Reflex and Bone Structure Experiment," in *Black American Literature Forum* 17 (Fall 1983): 120–123. Jerome Klinkowitz, "The Self-Apparent Word: Clarence Major's Innovative Fiction," in *Black American Prose Theory,* eds. Joe Weixlmann and Chester J. Fontenot, 1984, pp. 199–214. Keith Byerman, *Fingering the Jagged Grain: Tradition and Form in Recent Black Fiction,* 1986. Charles Johnson, *Being and Race: Black Writing Since 1970,* 1990. *African American Review,* special issue, 28 (Spring 1994).

—Keith E. Byerman

Majors and Minors (1895) was Paul Laurence *Dunbar's second collection of poetry. Unlike the self-published *Oak and Ivy* (1893), *Majors and Minors* was underwritten by two of the poet's white benefactors and, after publication in Toledo, Ohio, achieved sufficiently wide circulation to be noticed by the prominent white literary critic William Dean Howells, who reviewed the volume in the 27 June 1896 issue of Harper's Weekly. Howells's admiring review, in which he praised Dunbar for displaying "white thinking and white feeling in a black man" (which Howells confessed never to have encountered before), gave the obscure twenty-four-year-old poet from Dayton, Ohio, a national reputation. What Howells most enjoyed in Dunbar was his dialect poetry, which was included under the rubric of "Humour and Dialect" in the second and shorter section of Dunbar's book. Most of the verse in *Majors and Minors* appears in the opening section, where Dunbar grouped sixty-nine poems in standard English.

Majors and Minors contains some of Dunbar's best-known poems in so-called Negro dialect. A few of these poems—"The Party" and "The Deserted Plantation," for example—elicit racial stereotypes and nostalgia for preemancipation days that have earned Dunbar criticism for capitalizing on the popularity of the plantation tradition. But other dialect poems, such as "An Ante-bellum Sermon" and "A Negro Love Song," richly evoke the communal lore and vernacular expression of the rural African American South. Although written in dialect, "When Malindy Sings," a paean to the genius of an untutored but magnificently talented black woman singer, scarcely hides the impatience of the black speaker with the uninspired conventionality of white musical idiom.

Among the poems in standard English, *Majors and Minors* reveals Dunbar experimenting early in his career with a variety of styles, forms, and subject matter. Although many of Dunbar's poems on love and Nature evidence his technical competence and his debt to the lyricism of the English Romantic poets, these works often culminate in familiar sentiments and conventional moralizing. On the other hand, among the "majors" of Dunbar's volume are an outspoken celebration of racial pride—"The Colored Soldiers," which memorializes the heroism and nobility of the black men who fought for the Union cause—and some provocative meditations on his situation as an African American poet struggling to negotiate a difficult passage between popularity and literary integrity. Among these brooding meditative verses are "Ere Sleep Comes Down to Soothe the Weary Eyes," which belies any impression of Dunbar as a simple comic poet, and "We Wear the Mask," which warns the reader of the masked character of the poet's expression and of the need to peer behind appearances in order to appreciate Dunbar's complex situation and his achievement.

• Peter Revell, *Paul Laurence Dunbar,* 1979. Donald A. Petesch, *A Spy in the Enemy's Country: The Emergence of Modern Black Literature,* 1989.

—William L. Andrews and Patricia Robinson Williams

MALCOLM X (1925–1965), Nation of Islam minister, orator, and autobiographer. Born Malcolm Little (and later also known as el-Hajj Malik el-Shabazz) in Omaha, Nebraska, on 19 May 1925, Malcolm X was the fourth of eight children of the Reverend Earl Little and his wife, Louise. Soon after Malcolm's birth the Littles moved to the outskirts of East Lansing, Michigan. When Malcolm was six, his father died, presumably murdered by the Black Legion, a violent racist group similar to the Ku Klux Klan, and the Little home life became more and more difficult. Louise was eventually placed in the state mental hospital, and her children were declared wards of the state. In 1941 Malcom moved to Boston to live with his half sister, Ella. He became caught up in the nightlife of Boston and, later, New York. After a few years in the underworld of Harlem, selling drugs and working for call-girl services, Malcolm began a burglary ring in Boston. In 1946, at the age of twenty-one, he was arrested for armed robbery and sent to prison.

During his six years in Charlestown Prison, Concord Reformatory, and Norfolk Prison, Malcolm underwent a spiritual and intellectual transformation. While interred he corresponded with the Honorable Elijah Muhammad, the leader of the African American sect, the Nation of Islam. He converted to the Nation, attracted by its idea that whites are devils. In prison he also undertook a rigorous process of self-education, which included copying every page of the dictionary.

Upon his release he changed his name to Malcolm X, the X representing the unknown name of his African ancestors and their culture that had been lost during slavery. After personal meetings with Elijah Muhammad, Malcolm became a minister for the Nation. From 1952 to 1963 Minister Malcolm X helped build the Nation of Islam from a tiny sect to a significant force in urban black America. His commanding stage presence, quick wit, and erudition, combined with the authenticity of his experience as a street hustler, made Malcolm a remarkable orator and a dynamic leader.

In 1963 jealousy in the Nation of Islam over Malcolm's increasing celebrity, and Malcolm's discovery of violations of the Muslim's strict moral code by the Honorable Elijah Muhammad precipitated a painful and bitter split. Once out from the strict teachings of the Nation of Islam, Malcolm drifted from the primarily spiritual philosophy of the Nation to a more political black nationalism and, tentatively, to a more internationalist philosophy—Pan-Africanism. Malcolm's position on race relations in the United States at the time of his assassination on 21 February 1965 at the Audubon Ballroom in Harlem has not been resolved. His major literary achievement, *The Autobiography of Malcolm X* (1965), composed during the last two years of his life with the writer Alex *Haley, contains a montage of Malcolm's perspectives and only invites speculation as to which direction Malcolm's philosophy would have taken.

The *Autobiography,* published posthumously, stands as a major twentieth-century African American literary work. Its orality, its political intentions and ramifications, and its promise of unspoken truths about the African American experience all place it firmly in African American autobiographical traditions. The *Autobiography,* however, also resembles more general autobiographical models, most notably the spiritual narrative (his documentation of his conversion experience) and the success story of the self-made man. In fact, it is the text's remarkable meshing of so many modes, and so many "Malcolms," that may be its most significant achievement.

Malcolm X's speeches, found in such collections as *Malcolm X Speaks* (1965), edited by George Breitman, and *Malcolm X: The Last Speeches* (1989), edited by Bruce Perry, are his other contribution to African American literature. His enduring speeches, such as "Message to the Grass Roots" (1963), were given in the last two years of his life and center on the political and social conditions of African Americans. In them, Malcolm blends set pieces and improvisation, and he is especially deft at using analogy to express the African American's plight in America.

Malcolm X also carries tremendous weight as a cultural icon, most notably in the films of Spike *Lee. He has been used to symbolize an alternative, more militant vision of social protest than Martin Luther *King, Jr.'s nonviolence, and his name appears in rap and other African American poetry as a symbol of black pride.

• C. Eric Lincoln, *The Black Muslims in America,* 1961. John Henrik Clarke, ed., *Malcolm X: The Man and His Times,* 1969. Peter Goldman, *The Death and Life of Malcolm X,* 2d ed., 1979. James H. Cone, *Martin and Malcolm and America,* 1991. David Gallen, *Malcolm X As They Knew Him,* 1992. Michael Eric Dyson, *Making Malcolm: The Myth and Meaning of Malcolm X,* 1995. Harold Bloom, ed., *Alex Haley & Malcolm X's* The Autobiography of Malcolm X, 1999.

—J. D. Scrimgeour

Mama Day. Gloria *Naylor's third novel, *Mama Day* (1988) details the lives of the title character, also called Miranda Day, and her great-niece, Cocoa (Ophelia). With sections set in New York City and on Willow Springs—a barrier island that is due east of the border between South Carolina and Georgia and actually in neither state—Naylor creates a magical world set against a background of family history and unique geography.

Following an elaborate map of Willow Springs, a family tree of the Day lineage, and a bill of sale for the most important ancestor, Sapphira Wade, *Mama Day* begins with a prologue giving the pedigree of the island and its inhabitants, dating back to 1799. Naylor writes the prologue in the conversational, colloquial voice of Willow Springs itself, a narrator that returns later. From its current vantage point of August 1999, the prologue reaches back to 1823, the time that Sapphira Wade seized power from the white landowner, Bascombe Wade (whom she killed). Sapphira also convinced Bascombe Wade to deed all of Willow Springs to his former slaves and her descendants, who still own the land in 1999.

The first main section of *Mama Day* begins with Cocoa's frustrated job search in New York City just before she returns home to Willow Springs. While interviewing for a clerical position in an engineering firm, Cocoa meets and immediately dislikes George Andrews. However, apparently because of Mama Day's magical intervention, George and Cocoa begin to date. Their courtship starts gradually with George showing Cocoa New York City and also educating her about its ethnic richness. Even after their subsequent marriage, it is not until several years later that Cocoa and George return to Willow Springs together. In the interim Cocoa visits her grandmother Abigail and Mama Day alone each August, and George goes on annual solo vacations following professional football.

When George and Cocoa do go to Willow Springs together, the action that begins part 2 of the novel, the main characters converge, resulting in *Mama Day*'s climax during a violent storm. During this visit, rational George must confront the supernatural elements of the island's force, Mama Day's magical powers, and the idea that Cocoa's sudden desperately ill health comes from conjuring by an enemy. Yet George's upbringing as an urban orphan does not prepare him for the demands of this mythical realm. While his attempts to suspend his disbelief ultimately fail, resulting in his own fatal heart attack, George's sincere efforts help heal Cocoa, and Naylor implies that his sacrifice is necessary for her recovery.

Throughout *Mama Day,* Naylor presents three different narrators. Much of the novel involves Cocoa and George speaking in passages that occur after his death and within their separate and shared consciousness. Naylor narrates other parts of the novel in the omniscient voice of the island—with special emphasis on Mama Day, whose musings involve her premonitions and attempts to "listen" to the messages of her heritage. At the very end of the work Naylor's all-knowing narrator looks forward to Cocoa assuming the matriarchal role after Mama Day passes on.

Mama Day has received substantial critical acclaim, with praise for its folkloric qualities, its use of magic, its poignant characterizations, its Shakespearean model (*The Tempest*), and its treatment of gender, especially focused on generational sisterhood. Some critics have especially commended Naylor's positive depiction of men in the novel, particularly when compared to the more negative portrayals in her first work, *The *Women of Brewster Place* (1982).

• G. Michelle Collins, "There Where We Are Not: The Magical Real in *Beloved* and *Mama Day,*" *Southern Review* 24 (1988): 680–685. Henry Louis Gates, Jr., and K. A. Appiah, eds., *Gloria Naylor: Critical Perspectives Past and Present,* 1993.

—Kristine A. Yohe

MAMA LENA YOUNGER is a domestic worker and matriarch of the Younger family in *A *Raisin in the Sun* (1959) by Lorraine *Hansberry. Played in the original production by Claudia McNeil, a large dark-skinned actress, Lena conjured up the stereotypical image of the asexual, self-sacrificing mammy. She dominates her adult children, all of whom live under her crowded roof, and decides, without consulting them, to purchase a house with the $10,000 insurance benefit paid on her husband's death.

However, Lena is not only the matriarch as immortalized in Langston *Hughes's poem, "The Negro Mother," but is also the revolutionary who sends her children to do battle in the civil rights movement. Shattering the mammy stereotype, Hansberry creates a Mama who dares to move her family into an all-white and hostile neighborhood in order to improve their living situation; who learns to appreciate, if not have faith in, her children's dreams; and who turns over the leadership of the family to her son, *Walter Lee Younger, a transfer of power that implicitly endorses the growing militancy of the next generation. The Mrs. Johnson scene, cut from the original production but restored in the 1987 version, shows a Lena who rejects the accommodationist philosophy of Booker T. *Washington and implicitly aligns herself with W. E. B. *Du Bois. Her repositioning is further affirmed by Asagai, the young African intellectual and revolutionary who declares that Lena is the true visionary because she acts to bring about change.

[*See also* Beneatha Younger.]

• Lorraine Hansberry, "This Complex of Womanhood," *Ebony*, Aug. 1960, 40. Stephen R. Carter, *Hansberry's Drama: Commitment amid Complexity*, 1991.

—Margaret B. Wilkerson

Manchild in the Promised Land. "Where does one run to when he's already in the promised land?" Claude *Brown opens *Manchild in the Promised Land* (1965) with a political challenge framed as religious metaphor. His autobiography explores this question, documenting his childhood in Harlem during the 1940s and 1950s, with a broader focus on an entire generation, the children of southern-born African Americans who had moved north after the depression. More specifically, Brown portrays the generational conflict that resulted when parents tried to impose rural ways of survival on their children, who struggled with the "new ways" of the urban street. As *Manchild* unfolds, Brown's sociological analysis becomes more apparent and his political consciousness emerges as he places his own life, and Harlem more generally, within the broader context of American racial and economic patterns.

Several story lines underlie the many specific and sometimes seemingly random episodes in the narrative. Brown charts his flight from family conflict to the relative emotional security of life on the street with his friends. He finds relief from the street in juvenile detention, again accompanied by his closest friends. He escapes the perils of the drug scene and the real threat of longer incarceration by embracing the intellectual challenge of books, school, and music; this embrace leads to a time of self-imposed exile from Harlem and a struggle with his identity and sense of "home." Finally, he returns to Harlem with a redefined sense of self and community.

Brown's "sociological imagination" takes shape in the form of explicit and analytical social criticism. He documents the emerging "plague" of heroin in excruciating detail, an account remarkable for its harsh condemnation of the drug combined with profound (and intimate) compassion for the addicts, many of whom were his closest friends, including his beloved younger brother. In an autobiography framed by biblical and religious metaphor, Brown criticizes charismatic and "sanctified" Harlem preachers at the same time that he lauds the activism of seminary-trained urban clergy. He gives a sometimes bemused and skeptical analysis of both the Coptic movement and the Black Muslims. Here Brown expresses an impatience with what he calls these "phases" of Harlem Black Nationalism, but also, especially in regard to the Black Muslims, an appreciation for the social and political impact of their work in the community. *Manchild* also offers an interesting analysis of class dynamics in Harlem. Brown is notably unapologetic and brutally honest in re-creating his early attitudes toward women and in showing his emerging personal (and political) maturity in relation to them as he grew older. He also offers revealing commentary on tensions between African American and Jewish communities in New York City.

Manchild in the Promised Land has not been the subject of extensive literary criticism; most book reviews contemporary with its publication focused on the sociological aspects of the book. These mid-1960s reviews varied depending on the political and racial frame of reference of the reviewer. James A. Emanuel and Theodore Gross, the editors of *Dark Symphony* (1968), placed *Manchild* in the long and complex tradition of African American autobiography, citing it as a "modern analogue" to Briton *Hammon's slave narrative of 1760. The book's sociological emphasis crosses several genres: literary autobiography, sociology, and political analysis.

• Stephen Butterfield, *Black Autobiography in America*, 1974. David L. Dudley, *My Father's Shadow*, 1991.

—Sharon Carson

Man Who Cried I Am, The. A landmark work, John A. *Williams's *The Man Who Cried I Am* (1967; rpt. 1987) recounts journalist-novelist Max Reddick's struggles against an oppressive, murderous social structure. Terminally ill with colon cancer, Reddick inherits an enormous burden from his recently deceased friend and literary rival, Harry Ames: knowledge of the King Alfred Plan, an international agenda for annihilating all people of African origin. As he considers how to use the information, he reflects on his life and the events leading inevitably to this dilemma. Unaware of how closely he is being watched, Reddick transmits the information to an ally, Minister Q, over a tapped telephone, setting into motion events leading to his murder.

This synopsis risks oversimplification; part of the text's greatness lies in *Williams's stylistic innovations. A chronological double consciousness controls the narrative, moving simultaneously through a single day in the present and the entire historical range of Reddick's literary and personal experience with racism in America, keying on events in his friendships with other African American writers to inform that movement. The flexibility of the chronological frame, and the subsequent breakdown of received linear preconceptions of history, is one of Williams's most significant contributions to contemporary African American literature. Similarly, his philosophical exploration of the interconnectedness of history and the states of being assigned to African Americans by the power structure sets a standard upon which writers like Charles R. *Johnson, who acknowledges Williams's influence in *Being and Race: Black Writing since 1970* (1988), have built.

Another significant feature of the text that critics note is Williams's inclusion of thinly disguised portraits of actual events and real people. The 1962 Prix de Rome scandal, in which Williams was promised an award and then inexplicably denied it, appears, happening not to Reddick, who arguably represents Williams himself, but to Harry Ames. Ames is unmistakably modeled on Richard *Wright, just as Marion Dawes clearly represents James *Baldwin. Williams does not stop with literary figures, however; Minister Q seems to reflect the ideas and attitudes of *Malcolm X, and Paul Durrell appears to resemble Martin Luther *King, Jr. This revision of the actual historical record indicates Williams's stylistic sophistication; he takes the so-called truth of the era and presents an alternative perspective through the lens of literature, offering in the process an insightful commentary on national and international affairs. Williams's alteration of history and his fusion of "fact" and "fiction" mark *The Man* as a postmodernist work, reflecting the general upheaval regarding definitions of "truth" and "fiction" that characterized American culture in the late 1960s.

Critics generally agree that *The Man* is Williams's finest work, citing the richness of the characterization and the structural complexity of the narrative as reasons. Within the relatively small body of existing criticism, *The Man* has consistently received the most attention. Its postmodern innovations and frank challenging of preconceptions about American history establish it as a crucial work.

• William M. Burke, "The Resistance of John A. Williams: *The Man Who Cried I Am*," *Critique* 15.3 (1974): 5–14. Addison Gayle, Jr., *The Way of the New World: The Black Novel in America*, 1975. Gilbert H. Muller, *John A. Williams*, 1984.

—William R. Nash

Marrow of Tradition, The. Published in 1901, at the nadir of American race relations and the zenith of fictional apologies for the Jim Crow South, Charles Waddell *Chesnutt's second and most ambitious novel offers a complex retelling of the 1898 Wilmington, North Carolina, "race riot." Though somewhat ambiguous in its messages to African Americans—and labeled too "bitter" by former Chesnutt booster William Dean Howells—*The Marrow of Tradition*'s incisive critique of white terrorism, national racial hysteria, and segregationist logic make it one of the most significant African American socioliterary statements of its day.

Chesnutt would have welcomed such a description, for he envisioned the book as his generation's successor to *Uncle Tom's Cabin.* His main plot traces the intersecting fortunes and genealogies of two southern families, the Carterets and Millers. Philip Carteret, the reactionary editor of "Wellington's" white newspaper, campaigns against the supposed domination of the post-Reconstruction South by African Americans. Enlisting the aid of an equally racist aristocrat (General Belmont) and a former overseer (Captain McBane), Carteret engineers a devastating race riot that purges Wellington of most of its African Americans and restores "rightful" power to the white supremacists. Carteret's wife Olivia, for her part, is determined to repudiate the legal and moral claims of her mulatto half-sister—Janet Miller—on their father's estate. Janet's husband, William Miller, is a middle-class, mixed-blood physician whose considerable medical skills are spurned by Wellington whites. At the climax of the novel, after Carteret's rioters have burned Miller's hospital and a stray bullet has killed the Millers' child, the Carterets must plead with the African American doctor to save their own dying son. At first refusing, Miller agrees to see the child only at the direction of his wife. The novel ends with Miller poised at the foot of the Carterets' stairs, ready to try to save the boy's life.

To this principal story Chesnutt adds an array of subplots and secondary characters, including an African American mammy and her obsequious grandson, whose loyalty to whites fails to save them during the riot; an honest aristocrat and his degenerate heir, for whose crimes an innocent African American is nearly lynched; a well-meaning but ineffectual white liberal; and a powerful African American laborer, who vows to kill McBane in revenge for the death of his father. While many of these subordinate characters are drawn stereotypically, the views of Josh Green, the laborer, represent a strong counterphilosophy to Miller's accommodationism and for many early reviewers offered proof that Chesnutt endorsed African American militancy. Later critics, however, generally align the text's (and Chesnutt's) sympathies with Miller, citing Josh's death as evidence that violent resistance—though potentially useful—must finally be sacrificed for more conciliatory methods. Yet even these readers acknowledge the irresolution of the novel's ending; the optimistic image of Miller climbing the Carterets' stairs provides no guarantee that reconciliation will prove an appropriate strategy. Indeed, the tensions implicit at the novel's close aptly represent the volatile historical and literary contexts within which Chesnutt wrote.

• William L. Andrews, *The Literary Career of Charles W. Chesnutt*, 1980. Eric J. Sundquist, *To Wake the Nations: Race in the Making of American Literature*, 1993.

—William A. Gleason

MARSHALL, PAULE (b. 1929), journalist, short fiction writer, novelist, essayist, lecturer, and educator. Paule Marshall (née Burke) is the daughter of second-generation Barbadian immigrant parents Samuel and Ada Burke. Although Marshall was born in Brooklyn, the influence of her West Indian ancestry has been profound in her writing. Even as a little girl, before her "formal" introduction to the world of African American literature, the sounds, the smells, the sights, the entire culture of the West Indies were a part of her future training as a world-renowned novelist, especially through the daily gatherings of her mother and her female West Indian friends around the kitchen table to discuss, in the language of a kind of folk poetry, personal, neighborhood, and world events. Paule Marshall has lovingly deemed her mother and her neighbor-friends kitchen poets. According to her, they are the foundation for all the beauty and skill with which she employs the often colorful and irreverent language of the "Bajan" (Barbadian) community in her novels.

As a young girl, Paule Marshall was a voracious reader. She grew up reading the sweeping English novels of Charles Dickens, William Makepeace Thackeray, and Henry Fielding. However, it was not until her discovery of the great African American poet Paul Laurence *Dunbar that she became aware of another type of literature, one that spoke to her like no other that she had read before and that expressed to her the possibility that she, too, might someday become a great writer.

The road to becoming the kind of writer who would inspire others to follow in her footsteps was long and hard. After graduating cum laude from Brooklyn College in 1953, she worked at various jobs to make ends meet. Even with her high degree of accomplishment, the prospects for a woman, especially an African American, for finding gainful employment were almost nonexistent. As would characterize the remainder of her career as a writer, Paule Marshall was the exception to the rule. She worked as a librarian for the New York Public Library and then, at first as a research assistant and later as a full-time journalist, for the once very influential African American magazine *Our World* (1955–1956). Her writing assignments would take her to parts of the Caribbean and South America, experiences she would later use to write her collection of short stories *Soul Clap Hands and Sing.*

Marshall ended up leaving *Our World* and married her first husband, Kenneth Marshall, in 1957. In 1958, she gave birth to her first and only child, Evan-Keith. Still, Marshall was not satisfied with the role deemed appropriate for her and most other women of the 1950s, that is, wife and mother exclusively; she needed more. A novel was slowly but surely forming in her consciousness, but because of her marriage and the birth of her child, she had very little free time for her writing. She needed, paraphrasing Virginia Woolf, a room of her own. Against the wishes of her husband, she enlisted someone to help with Evan-Keith and rented a small apartment in order to devote more time to her fledgling novel. Two years later, in 1959, her first novel, **Brown Girl, Brownstones,* was published.

At the time of its publication, few African American women were writing, had written, or had works still in print. There were, of course, Zora Neale *Hurston's seminal novel **Their Eyes Were Watching God* (1937), which would later serve as a model for Marshall's novel *Praisesong for the Widow,* Dorothy West's novel *The Living Is Easy* (1948), and Gwendolyn *Brooks's singular novel **Maud Martha* (1953). According to Paule Marshall, Brooks's novel had the most influence upon her as a beginning writer.

Although critically acclaimed, *Maud Martha,* like many of the works by African American women writers during the 1940s and 1950s, was ignored commercially and quickly went out of print. Still, it had a profound influence upon Marshall and her work because for the first time since Hurston's *Their Eyes Were Watching God,* a novel focused on the interior life of an African American female protagonist. It went well beyond the stereotypes of African American women portrayed in the literature of the dominant culture. With the publication of *Brown Girl, Brownstones,* Paule Marshall took up the reigns passed down from Zora Neale Hurston to Dorothy West and Ann *Petry and finally to Gwendolyn Brooks.

Brown Girl, Brownstones is a milestone in African American fiction not only because it goes against stereotype in its portrayal of African Americans but also because for the first time since Claude *McKay, another West Indian immigrant writer, a connection had been made in literature between African American people and their West Indian counterparts. For both writers, the accurate depiction of language is vital for expressing the similarities and differences between the two cultures. The language of *Brown Girl, Brownstones* is exquisitely rendered. The feel and flavor of the West Indies is beautifully expressed through the language of protagonist *Selina Boyce's parents, especially her mother, Silla. Words like "c'dear" (dear), "lady-folks," and "wunna" (you) are sprinkled liberally and lovingly throughout the text. It is testimony to Paule Marshall's power as a writer to have been able to evoke such genuinely oral magic on paper.

Marshall's next literary project, published in 1961, is a collection of short fiction entitled *Soul Clap Hands and Sing.* The collection of four novellas, called "Barbados," "British Guiana," "Brooklyn," and "Brazil" concerns an overall theme heretofore unexplored in African American fiction, that is, the elderly in literature. The central characters in each of the four novellas are aged men who have consciously given up genuine human feeling for materialism and greed. The novellas explore the consequences of renouncing one's humanity for the seeming quiet and comfort of old age.

Because Marshall is an extremely meticulous writer and because of other demands upon her time, such as raising a family and teaching, eight years elapsed between the publication of *Soul Clap Hands and Sing* and Marshall's second novel, *The *Chosen*

Place, the Timeless People (1969). The pressure of being both wife and mother as well as career woman proved to be too much for her marriage, and she was divorced during the writing of this second novel.

The Chosen Place, the Timeless People is a culmination of all the themes and concerns that Marshall had heretofore explored in her fiction. Through the characterization of its unforgettable protagonist, Merle Kimbona, the novel explores the search for and reconciliation of the self with an African diasporic historical past as well as the themes of ageism, sexism, Western hegemony, and nuclear proliferation. After the publication of this novel, Marshall married Nourry Menard in 1970.

The year 1983 was very important to Paule Marshall's career. It marked not only the publication of her third novel, *Praisesong for the Widow,* but also of another collection of short stories entitled *Reena and Other Stories,* which included her most anthologized short story, "To Da-duh, in Memoriam." In *Praisesong for the Widow,* Marshall returns to familiar themes. The story centers around Avatara "Avey" Johnson, a rather prim and proper middle-aged, middle-class, sixty-two-year-old African American woman who journeys on a Caribbean cruise only to find herself in a kind of psychic distress. Almost mystically forced to abandon her cruise, she finds herself drawn into a kind of reverse middle passage to the island of Carriacou, where she will undergo a reintegration of that part of her African heritage that she has allowed to lie dormant within her for so many years.

Marshall's *Daughters* (1991) is also about self-actualization. Marshall was inspired to write this particular novel by an epigraph on a program to an Alvin Ailey Dance Company recital that she attended in 1983. It read, "Little girl of all the daughters, / You ain't no more slave, / You's a woman now." The novel centers upon a young woman, Ursa Beatrice Mackenzie, the only child born to an American mother, Estell, and a West Indian politician father, Primus. She has been almost smothered by the sheer forcefulness of her father's personality, a pattern that continues well into her adult life. Through the course of the novel, Ursa must not only wrest herself from the controlling nature of her father, she must also bring him back to being the sort of decent man he was before he became involved in the corrupt politics of the island of Triunion.

Paule Marshall is without a doubt one of the major and most influential African American writers. She is a pioneer in the exploration of themes such as ageism, sexual harassment, and nuclear proliferation. With a career that spans almost half a century, she continues to garner both critical raves as well as literary success. In 1992 she was awarded the prestigious MacArthur Prize Fellowship for lifetime achievement. Paule Marshall continues to be a writer's writer, both steady and enduring.

• Paule Marshall, "Shaping the World of My Art," *New Letters* 40 (Autumn 1973): 97–112. Helen Ruth Houston, "Paule Marshall," in *The Afro-American Novel 1965–1975,* 1977, pp. 117–122. Paule Marshall, "The Making of a Writer: From the Poets in the Kitchen," *New York Times Book Review,* 9 Jan. 1983, 3, 34–35. Barbara Christian, "Paule Marshall," in *DLB,* vol. 33, *Afro-American Fiction Writers after 1955,* eds. Thadious M. Davis and Trudier Harris, 1984, pp. 103–117. Daryl Dance, "An Interview with Paule Marshall," in *Southern Review,* 28 Jan. 1992, pp. 1–20. Gavin Jones, "'The Sea Ain't Got No Back Door': The Problems of Black Consciousness in Paule Marshall's *Brown Girl, Brownstones,*" *African American Review* 32:4 (Winter 1998): 597–606. Martin Japtok, "Paule Marshall Brown Girl, Brownstones: Reconciling Ethnicity and Individualism," *African American Review* 32:2 (Summer 1998): 305–315. Alma Jean Billingslea-Brown, *Crossing Borders through Folklore: African-American Women's Fiction and Art,* 1999.

—Keith Bernard Mitchell

MARVIN X (b. 1944), poet, playwright, essayist, director, and lecturer. Marvin Ellis Jackmon was born on 29 May 1944 in Fowler, California. He attended high school in Fresno and received a BA and MA in English from San Francisco State College (now San Francisco State University). The mid-1960s were formative years for Jackmon. He became involved in theater, founded his own press, published several plays and volumes of poetry, and became increasingly alienated because of racism and the Vietnam War. Under the influence of Elijah Muhammad, he became a Black Muslim and has published since then under the names El Muhajir and Marvin X. He has also used the name Nazzam al Fitnah Muhajir.

Marvin X and Ed *Bullins founded the Black Arts/West Theatre in San Francisco in 1966, and several of his plays were staged during that period in San Francisco, Oakland, New York, and by local companies across the United States. His one-act play *Flowers for the Trashman* was staged in San Francisco in 1965 and was included in the anthology *Black Fire* (1968); a musical version, *Take Care of Business,* was produced in 1971. The play presents the confrontation between two cellmates in a jail—one a young African American college student, the other a middle-aged white man. Another one-act play, *The Black Bird,* a Black Muslim allegory in which a young man offers lessons in life awareness to two small girls, appeared in 1969 and was included in *New Plays from the Black Theatre* that year. Several other plays, including *The Trial, Resurrection of the Dead,* and In the Name of Love, have been successfully staged, and Marvin X has remained an important advocate of African American theater.

In 1967, Marvin X was convicted, during the Vietnam War, for refusing induction and fled to Canada; eventually he was arrested in Honduras, was returned to the United States, and was sentenced to five months in prison. In his statement on being sentenced—later reprinted in *Black Scholar* (1971) and also in Clyde

Taylor's anthology, *Vietnam and Black America* (1973)—he argues that

> Any judge, any jury, is guilty of insanity that would have the nerve to judge and convict and imprison a black man because he did not appear in a courtroom on a charge of refusing to commit crimes against humanity, crimes against his own brothers and sisters, the peace-loving people of Vietnam.

Marvin X founded El Kitab Sudan publishing house in 1967; several of his books of poetry and proverbs have been published there. Much of Marvin X's poetry is militant in its anger at American racism and injustice. For example, in "Did You Vote Nigger?" he uses rough dialect and directs his irony at African Americans who believe in the government but are actually its pawns. Many of the proverbs in *The Son of Man* (1969) express alienation from white America. However, many of Marvin X's proverbs and poems express more concern with what African Americans can do positively for themselves, without being paralyzed by hatred. He insists that the answer is to concentrate on establishing a racial identity and to "understand that art is celebration of Allah." The poems in *Fly to Allah, Black Man Listen* (1969), and other volumes from his El Kitab Sudan press are characterized by their intensity and their message of racial unity under a religious banner.

Marvin X has remained active as a lecturer, teacher, theatrical producer, editor, and exponent of Islam. His work in advocating racial cohesion and religious dedication as an antidote to the legacy of racism he saw around him in the 1960s and 1970s made him an important voice of his generation.

• Lorenzo Thomas, "Marvin X," in *DLB*, vol. 38, *Afro-American Writers after 1955: Dramatists and Prose Writers*, eds. Thadious Davis and Trudier Harris, 1985, pp. 177–184. Bernard L. Peterson, Jr., "Marvin X," in *Contemporary Black American Playwrights and Their Plays*, 1988, pp. 332–333. "El Muhajir," in *CA*, vol. 26, eds. Hal May and James G. Lesniak, 1989, pp. 132–133.

—Michael E. Greene

MARY DALTON. In Richard *Wright's **Native Son*,* Mary Dalton is the daughter of the wealthy white Chicago realtor Mr. Dalton, who owns the rat-infested slum tenement in which *Bigger Thomas and his family live and who hires Bigger as his family chauffeur. Mary's chief interaction with Bigger occurs during and after the time she involves him, as her chauffeur, in her clandestine love affair with the Communist Jan Erlone. She is oblivious to the discomfort she causes Bigger, who has always known whites only from a distance and who is frightened and intimidated by her socioeconomic class as well as her race. Mary and Jan force Bigger to accompany them to a restaurant in the ghetto for dinner. Later Bigger drives Mary and Jan around the city while they drink and make love in the backseat. Jan leaves the intoxicated Mary with Bigger to be driven home. Bigger half carries her to her room and becomes sexually aroused by this contact with her. The blind Mrs. Dalton enters the room, and Bigger, terrified, forces a pillow down over Mary's face in order to keep her quiet. By the time Mrs. Dalton leaves the room, Mary has suffocated, killed by Bigger's dread of the consequences of a black man being discovered in the bedroom of a white woman. Bigger, terror-stricken, carries Mary's body to the cellar in a trunk that was to accompany her on a trip to Detroit the next day. He forces her body into the blazing furnace, then leaves, imagining a version of the events of the preceding evening that will point to Jan as Mary's murderer. Later on, he feels a sense of exhilaration because in his violence against Mary he has dared to act outside the conventions governing interrelations between the races.

—Donald B. Gibson

MARY RAMBO is both mother and spiritual guide for the narrator in Ralph *Ellison's **Invisible Man* (1952), who at this point in his life is trying to find a new identity. The narrator survived a paint-factory accident that hospitalized him and resulted in a symbolic rebirth after which his character is like a blank page. It is Mary Rambo who writes his new name and nurtures his new awareness of himself. Like Toni *Morrison's Circe in *Song of Solomon (1977), Mary is the preserver of Black life who helps carry on a Black tradition. She becomes physical and spiritual provider/sustainer for the narrator.

When Mary first appears, her speech and physical characteristics (she is a "big dark woman") suggest the stereotypical southern mammy. But Mary is no mammy; she typifies that down-home maternalism that is evident in the extended family of African Americans. And in her own way she is a race-conscious individual who believes strongly that if Blacks are to survive it will be through Black youths. When the narrator becomes unsure of his future it is Mary who encourages him: "It's you young folks what's going to make the changes. Y'all's the ones. You got to lead and . . . move us all on up a little higher."

Finding the narrator on the streets of Harlem, Mary nurses him back to health and then helps him to move from the sterile atmosphere of Men's House to a more fertile environment where he can recognize his African heritage. To this effect the narrator admits that Mary was "a force, a stable familiar force like something out of my past which kept me from whirling off into some unknown which I dared not face." Mary is no Beatrice, guiding the narrator through the underworld of Harlem, but she is a maternal figure and a moral gauge who helps the narrator on his way to self-determination.

—Ralph Reckley, Sr.

MATHIS, SHARON BELL (b. 1937), children's and young adult author, columnist, librarian, and educator. Sharon Bell Mathis's concern for the welfare of young people is evident in her career as a teacher and librarian, but closest to her heart is her role as author. Mathis explains that "I write to salute the strength in Black children and to say to them, 'Stay strong, stay Black and stay alive'" (quoted in *Something about the Author,* vol. 3, 1987).

Born in Atlantic City, New Jersey, Mathis grew up in the Bedford-Stuyvesant area of Brooklyn, where she attended parochial schools. Her parents, John Willie and Alice Mary (Frazier) Bell, exposed her to a vast array of literary works and encouraged her to write poems, stories, and plays. Despite her affinity for this work, however, Mathis decided not to pursue a career as an author, believing that she would neither be able to make a living at it nor be as great a contributor as were Richard *Wright and other authors whom she admired. In 1960, after graduating from Morgan State College (now Morgan State University) in Baltimore with a BA in sociology, Mathis began teaching.

1969 marked the beginning of her literary career when "The Fire Escape" was published in *News Explorer* and she was named director of the children's literature division of the newly formed D.C. Black Writers Workshop. A year later, *Brooklyn Story* (1970) appeared and two of her poems, "Ladies Magazine" and "R.S.V.P.," were included in Nikki *Giovanni's *Night Comes Softly: An Anthology of Black Female Voices.*

Mathis's second book, *Sidewalk Story,* was chosen as one of the Child Study Association of America's Children's Books of the Year. Her third, *Teacup Full of Roses* (1972), was chosen as one of the Child Study Association of America's Children's Books of the Year, one of the New York Times Best Books of the Year, one of the American Library Association's Best Young Adult Books, and was a runner-up for the Coretta Scott King Award. During this period, Mathis was also serving as a writer in residence at Howard University while at work on a biography of Ray Charles. Starting in 1972, she became the author of "Ebony Juniors Speak!," a monthly column in *Ebony Jr!,* and "Society and Youth," a biweekly column in *Liteside: D.C. Buyers Guide.*

The juvenile biography *Ray Charles* (1973) won the Coretta Scott King Award in 1974 and was the inspiration for her next book, *Listen for the Fig Tree* (1974). *The Hundred Penny Box* (1975), in which the main character, like Mathis's own grandfather, keeps a collection of pennies, was chosen as a Boston Globe-Horn Book Honor Book and was the basis for a children's film. *Cartwheels* (1977) focuses on three girls' attempts to change their lives by winning a gymnastics competition. There was a long hiatus until 1991, when *Red Dog Blue Fly* was published.

Sharon Bell Mathis enables the young person to "stay strong, stay Black and stay alive" by infusing her works with references to other notable Black artists and art forms. Excerpts from Black gospel songs and Bible verses, plus quotes from African poet and political leader Léopold Sédar Senghor and African American poets Nikki Giovanni and June *Jordan, salute the heritage to which she attributes her achievements: "My success is due to the glorious African blood which flows throughout my body."

• Frances Smith Foster, "Sharon Bell Mathis," in *DLB,* vol. 33, *Afro-American Fiction Writers after 1955,* eds. Thadious M. Davis and Trudier Harris, 1984, pp. 170–173. *Something about the Author Autobiography Series,* ed. Adele Sarkissian, vol. 3, 1987, pp. 162–163. "Mathis Sharon Bell," in *Something about the Author,* vol. 58, ed. Anne Commire, 1990, pp. 124–132. *Who's Who in America,* vol. 2, 1994, p. 2252.

—Saundra Liggins

MATTHEWS, VICTORIA EARLE (1861–1907), journalist, short story writer, social reformer, lecturer, and editor. Victoria Matthews was born Victoria Earle in Fort Valley, Georgia, to the slave Caroline Smith. Caroline fled to New York in order to escape a vicious master, probably Victoria's father. Saving her wages, the mother returned eight years later and won custody of Victoria and her sister and took them to New York around 1873. Though Victoria was an adept student, family crises prompted her to leave school for domestic service. Yet she soon harvested a rich education from her admiring employer's library. At eighteen, after marrying William Matthews and bearing a son, Lamartine, she applied her self-enlightenment to a thriving journalistic career, which commenced with work as a "sub"-reporter for publications like the *Times, Herald,* and *Sunday Mercury.* A prolific correspondent for African American newspapers, including the *Boston Advocate* and *New York Globe,* she became an authorial celebrity.

Matthews's career was driven by a belief in converting her people's internal devastations into brilliant external accomplishments, literary and civic. In her essay "The Value of Race Literature" (1895), she advocated releasing the "suppressed inner lives" of African American women onto the printed page. An author of children's stories, she wrote a mininovel, *Aunt Lindy* (1893), which counseled against an ex-slavewoman's murder of an ailing former master: By healing him, she heals the diseased soul he fostered in her. Matthews thus repudiated the vengeful African persona of Maurice Thompson's poem "Voodoo Prophecy."

Matthews, too, espoused causes in her articles, causes that she galvanized into political reform. Noted for her lectures on "The Awakening of the Afro-American Woman," she founded the Woman's Loyal Union in 1892. In the same year she joined educator Maritcha Lyons in supporting the antilynching crusade of Ida B. *Wells-Barnett. And in 1893, she spoke eloquently at Chicago's World Columbian Exposition. Matthews helped found the National Federation of Afro-American Women in 1895: occupied the editorial board of its magazine, the *Woman's Era;* and was instrumental in the federation's merger with the National Colored

Women's League into the National Association of Colored Women (1896). In 1898 she edited *Black Belt Diamonds,* selected speeches of Booker T. *Washington.

The death of Matthews's son at sixteen cast her into profound mourning. This time, she transformed her own grief into vigilant social welfare "for other people's boys and girls." Matthews investigated the so-called employment agencies that were really fronts for the internment of migrating rural "colored" girls into urban prostitution. Establishing the White Rose Industrial Association in 1897, Matthews deployed her own agents to deliver these adolescents to the foundation's home, which instructed them in domestic skills and, through a prodigious library, racial history. The subsidiary sections of the White Rose were eventually unified into the National League for the Protection of Colored Women, one of the founding organizations of the National Urban League. The White Rose thus provided an outlet for Matthews's own inner demons—a means by which her lost son could be reborn in the rescue of female children from sexual exploitation. The White Rose allowed her an active means of avenging both her mother Caroline's trauma as her master's abused object and the historical branding of African American women as sexual possessions.

• *Afro-American Women Writers, 1746–1933,* ed. Ann Shockley, 1988, pp. 181–184 (the entry here is followed by Victoria Earle's *Aunt Lindy: A Story Founded on Real Life*). Frank W. Johnson, "Matthews, Victoria [Earle]," in *African-American Women: A Biographical Dictionary,* ed. Dorothy Salem, 1993, pp. 352–354.

—Deborah Garfield

Maud Martha. Maud Martha Brown is the protagonist of Gwendolyn *Brooks's first novel, *Maud Martha* (1953). Set in the 1930s and 1940s, the novel treats the impact of the era on a group of people, but most especially on Maud Martha herself. Through a series of vignettes, the reader follows an impressionistic rendering of Maud's ordinary life from childhood through adolescence to womanhood. The novel runs counter to the historic black female character in fiction who is usually blessed or cursed (depending upon one's point of view) with a series of tragic incidents that render her life remarkable. Maud Martha is so ordinary, having ordinary problems, leading a life that is not beset by periods of great highs or impenetrable lows, that she is almost forgettable if one is accustomed either to the fictional black mammy or the tragic mulatto. Or, for those who are accustomed to some overpowering black woman in fiction or to one who is so pitiful as she suffers in silence or whimpers when no one is around to hear her, Maud Martha seems a fictional aberration. Certainly she seems different from many of the popular fictional female characters.

A dominant concern of the narrative is an examination of the effect of color upon characters. *Maud Martha* is from the days before the "black-is-beautiful" movement of the 1960s, and within the context of this brief, almost quiet, piece of fiction, Brooks comes to grips with issues of color. Through much of the story, the character thinks she is "ugly" because she does not fit a standard accepted by both black and white communities. Her dark skin becomes a defining characteristic for her. She realizes that Helen, her sister who "is beautiful," seems to get more attention. Maud feels inferior to Russell, her first boyfriend, and finally marries Paul Phillips who is as ordinary as Maud. When Paulette (their daughter) is born, Maud is determined to protect her from the hostile world; but even she cannot shield the child from a white Santa Claus who does not feel like petting a black child. Yet, in the midst of her struggles, she demonstrates an ability to hold on to her sense of dignity and exhibits her method of achieving self-esteem through what would be insignificant incidents to most people.

Like Brooks's *A *Street in Bronzeville* (1945), the setting is important in *Maud Martha* (1953). There are the inevitable kitchenette buildings, corner taverns, vacant lots, and crowded streets as well as beauty parlors that are the social centers of the daylight hours and pitiful nightclubs that attempt to provide a night of forgetfulness. Then there are quick glimpses of "white" Chicago. There is a downtown theater and the University of Chicago that abuts the Black Belt but that is as much foreign territory as downtown. Outside of the South Side, Chicago seems almost like a foreign land that one visits as a tourist but not as a resident of the city. By including these contrasts, Brooks gives a sense of the racial polarization in America's major cities, a separation that was very much a part of the era about which she writes. Yet, urban though this novel is, there is a general sense of quiet reflection that seems to prevail in this world. The cacophony of the city does not exist.

In the final analysis, *Maud Martha* accomplishes a number of things. First and foremost, it is a character study that gains its effectiveness from its terse intensity. At the same time it explores—once again—the changing roles of a woman as she moves through various stages from being primarily a daughter to being a wife and mother. And it presents succinctly the kinds of conflicts that prevail within the black community.

• Mary Helen Washington, "'Taming All That Anger Down': Rage and Silence in Gwendolyn Brooks's *Maud Martha,*" *Massachusetts Review* 24 (Summer 1983): 453–466. Barbara Christian, "Nuance and the Novella: A Study of Gwendolyn Brooks's *Maud Martha,*" in *A Life Distilled: Gwendolyn Brooks, Her Poetry and Fiction,* eds. Maria K. Mootry and Gary Smith, 1987, pp. 239–253.

—Kenny Jackson Williams

MAYFIELD, JULIAN (1928–1985), novelist, journalist, playwright, script-writer/producer, Broadway and Hollywood actor, critical essayist, university lecturer, freedom fighter, and advisor to world leaders.

The son of Hudson and Annie Mae Prince Mayfield, Julian Mayfield was born on 6 June 1928 in Greer, South Carolina, but grew up in Washington, D.C., where his parents relocated when he was five. After graduation from high school in 1946 and army service in the Pacific, he attended Lincoln University in Pennsylvania. His choice of political science as a major was a logical outgrowth of his acknowledged fascination with words and the power of words, both written and spoken.

This fascination with words led him into another role, on the stage. Before graduating, he participated in several Off-Broadway productions, including his own one-act play *417;* he later made his Broadway debut playing the lead role in *Lost in the Stars,* a musical about apartheid.

In 1954, he married a physician, Ana Livia Cordero. Relocating to Mexico, his new role was that of cofounder/newscaster for Mexico's first English-language radio station and cofounder and editor/theater reviewer of the Puerto Rico *World Journal.* While in Mexico, Mayfield launched yet another career, this time in the field of creative writing, with the publication of his first novel, *The Hit* (1957). Based on his play *417,* the novel, like his subsequent publication *The Long Night,* is about lost or deferred dreams. Both novels also focus on the hopelessness and desolation of the African American family trapped in the quagmire of poverty, victimization, and oppression in the Harlem ghetto.

The Hit tells the story of the once prosperous Cooley family: Hubert, the father and successful-entrepreneur-turned-janitor; Gertrude, the abused mother; and James Lee, their son. The highlight of the story is the final desperate attempt by Hubert to ease his frustration by playing the "numbers" and his disillusionment when, by a strange twist of fate, he gets none of the money his magic number 417 hit.

The Long Night (1958) is a story of a broken family, the Browns: Paul, the father and law-school-dropout-turned-doorway-bum; Mae, the overworked mother; and ten-year-old Steeley, their eldest son. The story details the long night of adventures of the very courageous Steeley who is robbed by fellow gang members of the numbers hit that his mother sent him to collect. Reluctant to return home for fear of a beating, Steeley tries desperately to recoup the money by begging, stealing, and robbing. The last of these efforts results in his discovery of his long-absent but much loved, missed, and needed father, the drunk he rolls over with the intention of robbing. This discovery also serves as a catalyst for reuniting the Brown family.

The theme of Mayfield's third novel, *The Grand Parade* (1961), is very different from that of the first two. Set in the "nowhere" city of Gainsboro, the story covers a much broader spectrum of American society with a focus on political corruption, interracial conflicts, and public school segregation.

Between 1961 and 1966, Mayfield resided in Ghana serving as an aide/advisor to President Kwame Nkrumah and founder/editor of the *African Review.* He spent the following two years in Europe and Asia. Returning to the United States in 1968, Mayfield spent most of his remaining life in the milieu of academia, lecturing in universities both within the United States and abroad. His only break from academia was the period between 1971 and 1973, which he spent in Guyana where he served as advisor to Prime Minister Forbes Burnham.

Mayfield's many other post-1967 activities include playing the highly acclaimed leading role in the Paramount production *Uptight* (1968), a film about black militants; editing a collection of short stories, *Ten Times Black* (1972); and writing dozens of articles for newpapers, magazines, and periodicals.

The major significance of Mayfield to African American literature lies in his numerous critical essays, and also the important role his first two novels played in keeping the flame of protest alive at a time when few African Americans were published—the transition period between the end of the Harlem Renaissance and the New Renaissance, which followed in the wake of the civil rights movement.

Concluding her moving tribute to Mayfield and four other "great Afro-American souls" ("Ailey, Baldwin, Floyd, Killens, and Mayfield," 1990), Maya Angelou affirmed that we "can be" and are better off, "for they existed." The world is certainly a better place because Julian Mayfield existed.

• "Uptight," *Ebony,* Nov. 1968, 46–48. Holly I. West, "The Goal of Julian Mayfield: Fusing Art and Politics," *Washington Post,* 7 July 1975, B1, B3. Harriet J. Scarupa, "Eyewitness of Power," *New Directions,* Apr. 1979, 12–15. Arthur P. Davis, *From the Dark Tower: Afro-American Writers, 1960–1990,* 1981, pp. 198–203. William B. Branch, "Julian Mayfield," in *DLB Yearbook,* ed. Jean W. Ross, 1984. Estelle W. Taylor, "Julian Mayfield," in *DLB,* vol. 33, *Afro-American Fiction Writers after 1955,* eds. Thadious M. Davis and Trudier Harris, 1984, pp. 174–178.

—Ruby V. Rodney

McCLUSKEY, JOHN A., JR. (b. 1944), novelist, short story writer, educator, and scholar. Born in Ohio, John A. McCluskey, Jr., earned his BA at Harvard (1966) and his MA at Stanford (1972). His first novel, *Look What They Done to My Song* (1974), is a highly episodic first-person narrative told by Mack, a twenty-six-year-old saxophone player. Set in the Boston area around 1970, the book depicts its narrator's search for direction and commitment following the assasinations of *Malcolm X and Martin Luther *King, Jr. In part a portrait of the artist, the novel also draws effectively upon the picaresque tradition. Its sprawling cast of characters voices the diversity of social-political opinions prevalent in the late 1960s. To the idealistic Mack, McCluskey juxtaposes the unprincipled Ubangi, hustler extraordinaire, whose strategems often misfire hilariously, as when the supposedly street-smart Ubangi decides to become a pimp—only to discover that his first whore, a female impersonator named Ova Easy, is already being pimped by the police. One of the novel's central concerns is change, both personal and social, and the function of art as an instrument of change. The closing chapter, set in a church, presents Mack's vision of music as "the spirit-healer." Through Mack, McCluskey expresses his own belief in the common purposes of art and religion: their affirmation of spirit, hope, and love.

Mr. America's Last Season Blues (1983), McCluskey's second novel, is a third-person narrative centered on Roscoe Americus, Jr., an aging athlete. More complex in characterization and structure than its predecessor, the book subverts stereotypes of the black athlete and engages the reader's emotions in the personal crises Roscoe confronts: his separation from his wife, his abortive comeback as player-coach for a semi-professional football team, and his inability to assist his lover's son, unjustly charged with mudering a white youth. Roscoe's efforts to gather evidence that would free Stone are stymied not only by the racism of the all-white jury but by the silence of those within the African American community whose testimony would lead to Stone's acquittal. The problems Roscoe faces enable McCluskey to movingly explore the legacy of racism, the issue of personal responsibility, and the importance of family ties and the past.

McCluskey's novels, like Ralph *Ellison's **Invisible Man,* incorporate social-political concerns without being dominated by them. His principal mode is literary realism, though his second novel invokes the magic realism of a Toni *Morrison work in its portrait of Roscoe's father's ghost. McCluskey draws extensively upon African American oral traditions and such musical forms as jazz and the blues. Some of his best writing can be found in his short stories, particularly "The Best Teacher in Georgia." McCluskey has also edited three volumes of essays on African American historical figures, as well as the collected stories of Rudolph *Fisher (*City of Refuge,* 1987). With Charles R. Johnson, he edited *Black Men Speaking* (1997). Although he has produced few books of fiction, the artistry and moral force of *Mr. America's Last Season Blues* suggest that his work merits continuing attention.

• Frank E. Moorer, "John A. McCluskey, Jr.," in *DLB,* vol. 33, *Afro-American Fiction Writers after 1955,* eds. Thadious M. Davis and Trudier Harris, 1984, pp. 179–181. Charles H. Rowell, "An Interview with John McCluskey, Jr.," *Callaloo* 19:4 (Fall 1996): 911–928.

—John Lang

McELROY, COLLEEN (b. 1935), poet, college professor, short story writer, and speech therapist. Although Colleen McElroy did not start composing poetry until she was in her mid-thirties, she is a prolific writer: she has completed nine books of poetry (of which *Queen of the Ebony Islands,* 1984, and *What Madness Brought Me Here: New and Selected Poems, 1968–1988,* 1990, are probably the best known), two collections of short stories (*Jesus and Fat Tuesday,* 1987, and *Driving under the Cardboard Pines,* 1991), two plays, and three works of nonfiction, in addition to working on a novel. While heralded chiefly as a poet, McElroy's short stories have appeared in several anthologies including Gloria *Naylor's *Children of the Night: The Best Short Stories by Black Writers, 1967 to the Present* (1996), Craig Lesley's *Dreamers and Desperadoes: Contemporary Short Fiction of the American West* (1993), and Terry *McMillan's *Breaking Ice: An Anthology of Contemporary African American Fiction* (1990). In 1997, McElroy published *A Long Way from St. Louie: Travel Memoirs;* and in 1999, *Over the Lip of the World: Among the Storytellers of Madagascar.*

Born Colleen Johnson in St. Louis, Missouri, she received both her BS (1958) and her MS (1963) from Kansas State University, and completed her PhD in 1973 at the University of Washington in Seattle, where she is a professor of English. She married David F. McElroy in 1968 and they had two children, Kevin and Vanessa, before divorcing. The daughter of an army officer, McElroy had to move often with her family when she was young; and being a child who spent a lot of time by herself, she began telling stories to make friends. Her poems are imbued with this storytelling quality—she has a keen sense of the cadence and lyricism of words, and the dialogue in her short fiction has been highly praised.

McElroy's poetry is varied and diverse. She often draws on the mundane—the cracked sidewalk of girlhood ("as veined as the backs of my Grandma's hands"), the runners outside a window loping past like wild deer in season, the flashing lights of an always illuminated and overly watched TV—to address more profound concerns: the lost sensual and hermetic world of childhood, the injustice of a social system prejudiced against black Americans, the loneliness of growing older. Alongside the mundane comes the sudden and the unexpected, the storyteller's twist that makes her poetry both brutal and beautiful.

The world inhabited by McElroy's fictional characters is one that defies easy categorization, one where the effects of racism are portrayed subtly, and one where sensuality and good humor reign (in the first lines of "The Dragon Lady Considers Dinner," the narrator cannot remember her date's name of the previous evening, but she has not forgotten the food: "there was that business with the flaming crepes"). Although McElroy is not as well known as other contemporary black women poets (indeed, she has been described by one critic as neglected), and her poetry has not received much scholarly attention, she has been the recipient of many honors, including two National Endowment for the Arts Fellowships, a Fulbright Creative Writing Fellowship, and a Rockefeller Fellowship.

• Irv Broughton, ed., *The Writer's Mind: Interviews with American Authors,* vol. 3, 1990. Colleen McElroy, "When the Shoe Never Fits: Myth in the Modern Mode," in *Poet's Perspectives: Reading, Writing, and Teaching Poetry,* eds., Charles R. Duke and Sally A. Jacobsen, 1992, pp. 37–46. J. J. Phillips, Ishmael Reed, Gundars Strads, and Shawn Wong, eds., *The Before Columbus Foundation Poetry Anthology,* 1992.

—Jennifer Margulis

McGIRT, JAMES EPHRAIM (1874–1930), poet, editor, short story writer, and publisher. James Ephraim McGirt was born in Robeson County, North Carolina, and brought up on a family farm. He attended public school in Greensboro, North Carolina, and in 1895 graduated from Bennett College, a Methodist institution just outside of Greensboro. In the preface to his first book, *Avenging the Maine, a Drunken A.B., and Other Poems* (1899), McGirt blames exhausting manual labor and a lack of leisure time for the slimness of the volume and the feebleness of the verse within it. In 1900, McGirt published an enlarged edition of his first collection of poetry and brought out in Philadelphia the next year a new collection of lyrics entitled *Some Simple Songs and a Few More Ambitious Attempts.* Moving to Philadelphia gave McGirt a base on which to build a career as a magazine publisher, which he launched in September 1903 with the first issue of *McGirt's Magazine,* an illustrated monthly that dealt with African American art, literature, science, general culture, and politics. In addition to its editor's own poetry and fiction, *McGirt's Magazine* also featured the work of a wide range of skilled African American writers, including articles by Anna Julia *Cooper and W. E. B. *Du Bois, poems by Paul Laurence *Dunbar and Frances Ellen Watkins *Harper, and fiction by John E. *Bruce and Kelly *Miller. Politically, McGirt's Magazine maintained an unswerving faith in the ballot as the key to African American advancement.

In 1906, McGirt published a third volume of verse, *For Your Sweet Sake.* The following year *The Triumphs of Ephraim,* his only short story collection, appeared. In 1909, declining sales compelled McGirt to change his magazine from a monthly to a quarterly. A year later McGirt's ceased publication, its editor having decided to return to Greensboro to go into business with his sister. During the last years of his life McGirt bought property in the Greensboro area and became a successful realtor.

As a writer McGirt's contribution to African American literature was small. His poetry, a few examples of which are reprinted in Joan Sherman's *African-American Poetry of the Nineteenth Century* (1992), is technically amateurish, often sentimental, and tritely didactic. His fiction, which usually deals with romantic problems faced by idealized African Americans, attempts to portray people of color to their advantage. But despite the reprinting of *The Triumphs of Ephraim* in 1972, McGirt's short stories have not attracted more than the passing attention of literary historians. Only as a magazine publisher who struggled for seven years to maintain a periodical of serious literary quality and self-respecting political outlook did McGirt leave a lasting mark on the history of African American literature.

• Hugh M. Gloster, *Negro Voices in American Fiction,* 1948.

—William L. Andrews

M. C. Higgins, the Great. Virginia *Hamilton wrote the first chapter of *M. C. Higgins, the Great* (1974) eleven times. Such meticulous revision reaped phenomenal awards, for this young adult novel was the first by an African American to win the Newbery Medal, and it also garnered the Boston-Hornbook Magazine Award, the National Book Award, the Lewis Carrol Shelf Award, and the International Board on Books for Young People Award.

M. C. Higgins, the Great centers on fifteen-year-old Mayo Cornelius (M. C.), who lives on Sarah's Mountain in southern Ohio. Steeped in stress because a spoil heap left from strip-mining threatens to crash down on his home, he spends most of his time sitting on a bicycle seat atop a 40-foot flag pole. The arrival of a folk song collector kindles his hope that the recording of his mother's singing will make her famous and enable the family to leave Sarah's Mountain. During the story M. C. has his first feelings of love, his first yearning for independence, his first questions about his belief and value system, and his first questions of his father's adamant desire to stay no matter what. In the end, M. C. and the neighborhood outcasts come together to build a wall around the heap, leaving the reader not knowing whether his first love would return, not knowing whether the recording artist would reconsider using his mother's voice, and ultimately not knowing whether the spoil heap of bulldozed trees and subsoil will indeed kill the whole family.

Praised by children's and young adult literature critics Rudine Sims, Zena Sutherland, Betsy Hearne, Sheila Egoff, Virginia Haviland, and Violet Harris, Virginia Hamilton is renowned for her skillful use of nontraditional settings, poetic imagery, unique characterization, impactful dialogue, plot structures, and themes for African American children and young adults. She is also commended for being among the first in African American children's literature to insightfully use African American folklore.

Perhaps the most provocative critical article on M. C. was written by Perry Nodelman, who explains the demanding structure of the novel and notes its binary oppositions, but fails to resolve or interpret them. On a higher level, since little is definitively resolved in Hamilton's works, the novel could reflect the indeterminacy of meaning in modern novels.

Critics praise the book for the linking of the ancestral past with the present and for being an African American young adult novel that has universal appeal, but few have discussed its pioneering ecological theme. No critic has psychoanalyzed M. C.'s character and interior dialogue even though the girl Louretta ironically represents his anima (yin side) and the recording artist and Jones, M. C.'s father, represents his animus side (yang). Few critics have yet tackled the psychological symbolism of the pole even though one critic simplistically reduced it to a phallic symbol. Critics have commended Hamilton for being so intriguingly unconventional, yet she is quite conventional in her use of mythology. No critic has ventured to give M. C. a Marxist interpretation even though the novel clearly hints at the negative effects of capitalism in the mountain exploitation.

As critic Nina Mikkelson has observed, Hamilton at her best is always puzzling and demanding, which sometimes makes her more favored by critics than by the average young reader. Indeed, M. C. has come a long way from the simplistic didactism seen in early African American children's books such as Amelia E. *Johnson's *Clarence and Corinne, or God's Way* (1889).

Hamilton, the first American winner of the Hans Christian Andersen Medal (1992), is to be commended for not writing down to children, but up to them, showing them that like M. C., in the midst of multiple problems, they too can survive. She made this point in her acceptance speech for the Newbery Medal, which was printed in *Hornbook Magazine* (1975).

• Jessie Carney Smith, *Notable Black Women,* 1992. Nina Mikkelson, *Virginia Hamilton,* 1994.

—Margaret Bernice Smith Bristow

McKAY, CLAUDE (1890–1948), poet, novelist, journalist, and social and political radical, commonly associated with the Harlem Renaissance. Born Festus Claudius McKay, he was the son of relatively prosperous peasants living in upper Clarendon Parish, Jamaica. Around the age of seven McKay went to live with and be educated by his brother, Uriah Theodore, a schoolteacher. There McKay studied classical and British literary figures and philosophers as well as science and theology. He was also encouraged to write poetry and, during his youth, favored conventional English forms. In 1907 McKay met Walter Jekyll, a white British expatriate and folklorist residing in Jamaica, who urged McKay to write dialect poetry rooted in the island's folk culture. Jekyll remained McKay's close friend and patron for many years and was instrumental in the publication of McKay's first two volumes of poetry, Songs of Jamaica (1912) and Constab Ballads (1912). Songs of Jamaica attempts to capture peasant life and language; Constab Ballads is based on McKay's experiences during a brief period in 1911 as a policeman. Both are primarily in dialect and reveal McKay's efforts to define his literary voice in form and content.

In August 1912 under the pretext of studying agriculture, McKay migrated to the United States to advance his poetic career. He studied at Tuskegee Institute and Kansas State College, but by mid-1914, McKay abandoned the study of farming and moved to New York City. Between 1914 and 1919 McKay worked at various jobs, including as a dining-car waiter on the Pennsylvania Railroad, an experience later rendered in his first novel, *Home to Harlem* (1929). During this period McKay wrote poetry and became increasingly involved with political and literary radicals. For a short time in 1919 he was a member of the International Workers of the World; he was a close associate of several African Caribbean Socialists including Hubert H. Harrison, Richard B. Moore, and Cyril Briggs, and he was affiliated with the African Blood Brotherhood. He began a lifelong professional and personal relationship with Max and Crystal Eastman, editors of the *Liberator.* McKay's most widely anthologized poem, "If We Must Die," was published in the July 1919 issue of the *Liberator* and brought him immediate fame.

McKay's political associations led him to England, where he began writing for British Socialist Sylvia Pankhurst's *Workers' Dreadnought.* While there, his third volume of poetry, *Spring in New Hampshire* (1920), was published. Containing no dialect poetry, it was divided between poems commenting on race relations in the United States and others nostalgically recalling island life. Upon returning to the United States in 1921, McKay served as a coeditor of the *Liberator,* but due to disagreements about the aesthetic objectives of the magazine, McKay resigned his post in July 1922. In the spring of 1922 McKay's fourth volume of poetry, *Harlem Shadows,* was published and received favorable reviews. Income generated by this volume, combined with McKay's dissatisfaction with left-wing efforts to confront racism in both England and the United States, provoked him to travel to the Soviet Union. In November 1922 he attended the Third Communist International in an unofficial capacity. He was widely embraced by the Russian public and traveled throughout the country for six months, delivering lectures on both art and politics. While in Russia, McKay republished a series of articles he had written for the Soviet press under the title *Negroes in America* (1923); these essays offer a Marxist interpretation of the history of African Americans.

When McKay left the Soviet Union, he unknowingly embarked upon a decade of unsettled travel throughout Europe and Africa. Though he had been diagnosed with syphilis, an event that marks the beginning of health and financial problems that plagued him until his death, during 1923 McKay spent time in Paris and Berlin, meeting both white American expatriates and African American artists including Alain *Locke, Jessie Redmon *Fauset, and Jean *Toomer. In January 1924, with the financial assistance of friends, he moved to southern France to recuperate from repeated illnesses and to complete a novel, "Color Scheme," which was rejected for publication and subsequently burned by McKay. In 1924 Alain Locke, despite significant political differences with McKay, selected some of McKay's poetry for the influential edition of Survey Graphic that served as the foundation for *The New Negro* (1925). In 1928, while still in France, McKay published **Home to Harlem*. Achieving widespread acclaim, Home to Harlem is McKay's most read novel and is often studied within the context of the Harlem Renaissance. His second novel, *Banjo* (1929), is a commentary on colonialism that focuses on the lives of an international cast of drifters living on the Marseilles waterfront. In 1932, having moved to Morocco, McKay published *Gingertown*, a collection of short stories alternately set in Jamaica and the United States. In 1933 he published his final novel, *Banana Bottom*, a romantic tale set in Jamaica that explores both individual and cultural conflict between colonizing and folk forces. Neither book sold well, however.

In 1934, seriously ill and improverished, McKay returned to the United States, where he remained until his death in 1948. During these years McKay struggled to produce more literary works but had difficulty finding publishers; he did, however, write numerous articles for a variety of journals. In 1937 he published his autobiography, *A Long Way from Home*, and in 1940 he published *Harlem: Negro Metropolis*, an anti-Communist treatise calling for stronger, community-based African American leadership. In 1944 McKay converted to Catholicism. During the last years of his life he completed an autobiography of his youth titled *My Green Hills of Jamaica* (1979) and compiled a collection of his poetry for *Selected Poems of Claude McKay* (1953). Both books were published posthumously. McKay died in Chicago on 22 May 1948.

McKay's exploration of the relationship between art and politics, as conveyed in his complex and wide-ranging writings, establishes him as an important pioneer in African American and African Caribbean intellectual, cultural, and literary history. He is considered an influential predecessor of, as well as participant in, the new Negro movement, an instrumental role model for the founders of the Negritude movement and a resonant historical reference for Black Nationalism during the civil rights era.

• Kenneth Ramchand, *The West Indian Novel and Its Background*, 1970. Wayne F. Cooper, ed., *The Passion of Claude McKay: Selected Poetry and Prose, 1912–1948*, 1973. Jean Wagner, *Black Poets of the United States: From Paul Laurence Dunbar to Langston Hughes*, 1973. James Giles, *Claude McKay*, 1976. Wayne F. Cooper, *Claude McKay: Rebel Sojourner in the Harlem Renaissance*, 1987. Tyrone Tillery, *Claude McKay: A Black Poet's Struggle for Identity*, 1992.

—Heather Hathaway

McKISSACK, PATRICIA C. (b. 1944), editor and consultant on minority literature, and writer of children's picture books, short stories, and nonfiction works primarily in the fields of African American history and biography.

Patricia C. McKissack incorporates distinctive African American cultural traits in her fictional works—the supernatural is a familiar companion, heroes are indefatigable in their opposition to oppression, African American communities are generously supportive, and the language of daily interchange is frequently playful and poetic. From this solid base, McKissack employs any genre that suits her purpose as an entertainer, educator, and strong civil rights advocate.

For pure entertainment, McKissack uses the picture book genre combined with African American folk traditions, as in *Mirandy and Brother Wind* (1988) and *Nettie Jo's Friends* (1989). In the former, a conjure woman links "Brother Wind" (a fanciful figure in a young girl's imagination) with a community frolic, a cake-walk contest, and hints of romance. In *Nettie Jo's Friends*, a resourceful black child outsmarts a harried rabbit, a "hip" fox, and a wisecracking panther. The author's use of a southern idiom adds regional charm.

Pleasure is joined with more serious intentions in *The Dark-Thirty: Southern Tales of the Supernatural* (1992). These original short stories are sometimes based on incidents from African American history, and the tragic realities of slavery shape plotlines and emotional tone. "The Legend of Pin Oak," for example, elaborates upon a system in which children in one family were frequently both African American and Euro-American. One brother (the slaveowner's white son) is in a position to sell the other and both perish in the end. The slave-ocracy's wanton waste of human life is vividly conveyed. As a group of ghost stories and tales of transfiguration, this collection is provocatively mock-scary; as a compilation of historical vignettes it is vitally important to educators.

The civil rights advocacy of McKissack is indirectly apparent in *The Dark-Thirty* and openly central to her work as a biographer and nonfiction writer. She has chronicled the lives of such black leaders as Martin Luther *King, Jr., and Jesse Jackson, and in collaboration with her husband, Fredrick, has written biographies of Frederick *Douglass, W. E. B. *Du Bois, Sojourner *Truth, and others. The McKissacks' study of African American porters (*A Long Hard Journey: The Story of the Pullman Porter*, 1989) won both the Coretta Scott King Award and the Jane Addams Children's Book Award.

Patricia McKissack's historical placement is noticeably connected with the nature of her work. On the one hand, she directly experienced the world of Jim Crow tyranny in her home state of Tennessee. On the other hand, she lived through the Kennedy era and being a "Kennedy product," she says, "made me very idealistic." That optimism would soon be tempered by the ensuing backlash to civil rights, but as a young eighth-grade teacher in Missouri, McKissack could aid her students in both opposing and understanding that hostility. Moreover, her dedication to countering racism on the larger world stage was born of these experiences, and her writings bear witness to that inestimable commitment. In 1999, more than forty-five of Patricia C. McKissack's works were in print.

• Diane Telgen, ed., *Something about the Author,* vol. 73, 1993, pp. 147–152. Patricia C. McKissack and Fredrick McKissack, "Sojourner Truth: Ain't I a Woman?" *Horn Book Magazine,* Jan./Feb. 1994, 53–57.

—Donnarae MacCann

McKNIGHT, REGINALD (b. 1956), short story writer, novelist, essayist, and educator. Because his father served in the air force, Reginald McKnight was born in Fuerstenteldbruck, Germany. His family relocated several times, staying briefly in New York, Texas, Alabama, Louisiana, and California, but McKnight considers Colorado, principally Colorado Springs and Denver, his home. He received an AA degree from Pikes Peak Community College (1978), his BA from Colorado College (1981), and an MA from the University of Denver (1987). McKnight taught English as a foreign language for the American Cultural Center in Dakar, Senegal, from 1981 to 1982. He is a former marine, honorably discharged in 1976; an English teacher, currently employed by the University of Maryland, College Park; and the author of the novel *I Get on the Bus* (1990) and three short story collections, *Moustapha's Eclipse* (1988), *The Kind of Light that Shines on Texas* (1992), and *White Boys: Stories* (1998).

Within the six-year span between 1985 and 1991, Reginald McKnight achieved distinction and earned praise as a crafter of excellent fiction, particularly in the short story. In 1985 he won a Thomas J. Watson Fellowship, which permitted him a year in Africa; there he gathered material that became strands in the semi-autobiographical novel *I Get on the Bus.* Also in 1985, McKnight won the Bernice M. Slote Award for Fiction from the University of Nebraska for "Uncle Moustapha's Eclipse." In 1988 he received the Drue Heinz Literature Prize from the University of Pittsburgh Press for stories collected in *Moustapha's Eclipse;* this collection also earned him an Ernest Hemingway Foundation Award from PEN American Center in 1989. He was a Bread Loaf Fellow in 1988; in 1989, he was awarded the Kenyon Review New Fiction Prize and the O. Henry Award for "The Kind of Light that Shines on Texas." McKnight received a National Endowment for the Arts Grant for Literature in 1991.

Reviewers of McKnight's short fiction tend to focus first on his ability to create evocative, richly textured, and often humorous or comic narrative voices. "The Homunculus: A Novel in One Chapter," collected in *The Kind of Light that Shines in Texas,* was also anthologized in *The Year's Best Fantasy and Horror, Sixth Annual Collection* for 1992. McKnight's ability to manipulate a story's structural frame so that it functions as an active evocative dramatic element rather than a mere vehicle has also been noted, as has his use of the swiftly paced narrative and his ear for striking dialogue. An additional aural technique resonating in his fiction is his poetic prose, his skillful deployment of sound to ensnare a reader's immediate attention. It is through an unexpected blending of rhythm and syntax that his prose yields the remarkable or compelling image. Carolyn Megan, in a 1994 essay for the *Kenyon Review* titled "New Perceptions on Rhythm in Reginald McKnight's Fiction," argues that McKnight's writing relies upon a rhythmic sense, upon meter, sound, and rhythm as avenues into fiction.

If Megan's observations apply to McKnight's short stories, they are more applicable when the text examined is McKnight's novel *I Get on the Bus,* a surrealistic tale about black identity and its convoluted forms in the post-civil rights era. Readers sensitive to imagery are seduced by the effects of the staccato rhythms permeating the novel's highly intense opening passage. The novel reflects the peculiar experiences of a young African American male in Africa. Evan Norris, though serving in the Peace Corps in Senegal, must contend with an inner rootlessness and cultural ambivalence that echoes W. E. B. *Du Bois's concept of the divided self, the double consciousness haunting many African Americans.

McKnight's skillful treatment of various narrative techniques, riffing off autobiographical elements, and his creation of the cultural mulatto male protagonist show him to be an ultramodern African American novelist. Thematically, however, through the novel's emphasis on identity, ambiguity, responsibility, deracination, and the quest for self, McKnight shows an allegiance to James Weldon *Johnson's *The Autobiography of an Ex-Colored Man* (1913) and Ralph *Ellison's **In-visible Man* (1952).

• Reginald McKnight, "Confessions of a Wannabe Negro," in *Lure and Loathing,* ed. Gerald Early, 1993. Carolyn E. Megan, "New Perceptions on Rhythm in Reginald McKnight's Fiction," *Kenyon Review* 16.2 (Spring 1994): 56–62. Reginald McKnight, "We Are in Fact a Civilization: An Interview with Reginald McKnight," interview by William Walsh, *Kenyon Review* 16.2 (Spring 1994): 27–42.

—Sandra Y. Govan

McMILLAN, TERRY (b. 1951), university professor, screenwriter, editor, and author. As a novelist, Terry L. McMillan has contributed to the body of literature that opens the doors of communication between African Americans and society at large. Family problems seem to permeate her texts, especially *Mama* and *Waiting to Exhale,* for which she assisted in creating a screenplay. McMillan was born 18 October 1951 in Port Huron, Michigan, the daughter of Madeline Washington Tillman and Edward Lewis McMillan, proletarians. Like Onika, the child of Bernadine in *Waiting to Exhale,* McMillan's parents divorced, and her mother raised her and her four siblings alone, working as a domestic and an auto factory worker. McMillan graduated from the University of California at Berkeley with a BS degree in 1979 and attended the MFA film program at Columbia University in New York City that year.

McMillan's son, Solomon, whom she raised as a single parent, was born in 1984. Dedicated to her writing and her son, McMillan was determined to make it in a man's world. In 1987, while serving as Visiting Writer at the University of Wyoming, Laramie, she published *Mama,* which she had written while working as a typist. She promoted her first novel by contacting colleges and universities and organizing tours, and by publication date, *Mama* had sold out its first printing. *Mama* depicts the often troubled inter- and intrarelationships of a mother, Mildred Peacock, to her family and her community, but most of all to "self." McMillan places Mildred in the middle of social change in society: Feminists are still burning their "pretty bras" from the 1960s, and African Americans are faced with an identity crisis. Society is dealing with civil rights, Black Power, student protests, and opposition to the Vietnam War. McMillan let all of this assist her in creating a text filled with social realism, and the book deals with much more than a woman's struggle in a sexist, antiwomanist society. The text emphasizes, through Mildred's life and her children's, that positive change is possible, and that a black woman and her people need not be limited by the roles society expects them to play, allows them to play, or prohibits them from playing by virtue of their status in their community.

McMillan's second book, *Disappearing Acts* (1989) is a novel that addresses the issues of urban love. The characters Zora Banks and Franklin Swift create a complex love that enables women who have loved and lost or walked away from love to understand Zora's dilemma. These star-crossed lovers tell their stories and create for the readers polarities that, to them, represent their individual struggles. Again, McMillan's use of language and dialogue gives her readers the needed flavor to continue wanting more and more of her characters.

In 1990, McMillan edited *Breaking Ice: An Anthology of Contemporary African American Fiction,* which consists of works by a wide range of post-1960 authors both established and emerging. In her introduction to the text, McMillan states her explanation for such a work: "I wish there hadn't been a need to separate our work from others, and perhaps, as Dr. Martin Luther King Jr. expressed, one day this dream may come true, where all of our work is considered equal, and measured not by its color content, but its literary merit."

In 1995, *Waiting to Exhale* (1992), the story of four intelligent and attractive but unattached middle-class black women, went to the big screen after selling three million copies. Terry McMillan, through dedication, determination, and her vernacular-based literary style, has created a novel that crosses race and gender. In a conversation with Oprah Winfrey, when asked about the surprise of *Waiting to Exhale*'s success, McMillan replied: "It's like having a baby and praying that people think that it's cute."

McMillan's most recent novel, *How Stella Got Her Groove Back* (1996), again chronicles the relationships of women to each other, their families, and the men in their lives. Stella, McMillan's protagonist, is a forty-two-year-old mother struggling in the male-dominated corporate world to find inner peace after her marriage has dissolved. Her two sisters represent polarized versions of womanhood: Angela, married and pregnant, "feels like nothing without a man" and a sense of family, and free-spirited, outspoken, and impulsive Vanessa, a single parent, wants Stella to live again and take risks. Stella finds her groove when she risks all and falls in love with a twenty-year-old Jamaican man she meets while vacationing. The novel is filled with explosive language and humor and portrayals of women's strength.

With her honesty and control of vernacular language, McMillan has paved the way for contemporary voices to emerge with their stories. Her "knotting up" of her characters will serve as ice-breakers in conversations around the world. Readers can definitely view Terry McMillan as the Frank *Yerby of the 1990s.

• Robert G. O'Meally, "The Caged Bird Sings," *Newsday,* 13 Aug. 1986. Thulani Davis, "Don't Worry, Be Buppie: Black Novelists Head for the Mainstream," *Village Voice Literary Supplement* 85 (May 1990): 26–29. Jacqueline Trescott, "The Urban Author: Straight to the Point," *Washington Post,* 17 Nov. 1990. Daniel Max, "McMillan's Millions," *New York Times Magazine,* 9 Aug. 1992. Edward M. Jackson, "Images of Black Males in Terry McMillan's *Waiting to Exhale*," *MAWA Review* 8.1 (June 1993): 20–26. Rita B. Dandridge, "Debunking the Beauty Myth in Terry McMillan's *Waiting to Exhale,*" in *Language, Rhythm, and Sound: Black Popular Cultures into the Twenty-First Century,* ed. Joseph K. Adjaye and Adrianne R. Andrews, 1997, pp. 121–133. Janet Mason Ellerby, "Deposing the Man of the House: Terry McMillan Rewrites the Family," *MELUS* 22:2 (Summer 1997): 105–117. Dandridge, "Debunking the Motherhood Myth in Terry McMillan's *Mama,*" *College Language Association Journal* 41:4 (June 1998): 405–416.

—Wanda Macon

McPHERSON, JAMES ALAN (b. 1943), short story writer and essayist, and winner of the Pulitzer Prize in fiction for *Elbow Room* (1978). James Alan McPherson was born in Savannah, Georgia, son of James Allen and Mable (Smalls) McPherson. He attended Morgan State University (1963–1964), Morris Brown College (BA, 1965), Harvard University (LLB, 1968), and the University of Iowa (MFA, 1969). He has taught English at the University of Iowa Law School (1968–1969), the University of California, Santa Cruz (1969–1970), Morgan State University (1975–1976), the University of Virginia (1976–1981), and the University of Iowa Writer's Workshop (1981–).

McPherson published his first book of short stories, *Hue and Cry* (1969), shortly after graduating from

Harvard Law School, which may explain his lawyerly approach to storytelling. Like a good counsel, he knows how to make the strongest rhetorical case for each of his clients or characters—indirectly, through a balanced presentation of narrative detail, or directly, through the voices of the characters themselves. Like a good judge, he suspends authorial judgment, allowing readers to reach their own conclusions about guilt and innocence.

In his first collection of stories, McPherson dramatizes the themes of isolation, injustice, and self-definition in the dim light of contemporary America. While some reviewers found McPherson's language awkward, verbose, or inappropriately hip, the dust jacket included a statement from Ralph *Ellison commending McPherson for his commitment to craft. Many commentators praised the book as an eloquent study of the effects of racism on African Americans, despite the author's intention to keep race a secondary issue.

In **Elbow Room* (1977) McPherson deals with the theme of selfhood—how it is won, lost, or evaded—and offers a more affirmative vision of human possibility. In this case reviewers generally praised both McPherson's style and ability to see beyond color, yet others continued to insist that McPherson's strengths and thematic concerns derive from his African American identity.

Since 1977, McPherson has written only personal and political essays, attempting through them to define his own background and outline his vision of an America where citizens would be, as he puts it in "On Becoming an American Writer," "a synthesis of high and low, black and white, city and country, provincial and universal." As the title of the essay and the quotation suggest, McPherson seems to be most comfortable thinking of himself as an American writer interested in how the distinctively American issues of identity and diversity might be defined and in how, as values, selfhood and diversity might be achieved and constructively preserved within a country beset by difference.

To be sure, McPherson is an African American and most of his characters are black, but both his fiction and his essays resist simple classification. Racism for him is a problem not only because it is cruel and unjust but also because it restricts humankind's imaginative freedom and therefore its ability to discover better ways of being human.

In both his fiction and essays, McPherson challenges the reader to take the future as well as the past and present seriously.

• Patsy B. Perry, "James Alan McPherson," in *DLB*, vol. 38, *Afro-American Writers after 1955: Dramatists and Prose Writers*, eds. Thadious M. Davis and Trudier Harris, 1985, pp. 185–194. James Alan McPherson, "Chantpleure," in *Contemporary Authors Autobiography Series*, vol. 17, ed. Joyce Nakamura, 1993, pp. 121–136.

—Jon Wallace

MERIWETHER, LOUISE (b. 1923), short fiction writer, essayist, novelist, writer of children's literature, and black activist. Louise Meriwether holds an established place among literati whose writings reassess African Americans' past. Her fiction treats bygone times to revise American history and to record African Americans' tremendous achievements despite overwhelming odds.

Born in Haverstraw, New York, to Marion Lloyd Jenkins (a bricklayer) and Julia Jenkins (a housewife), Meriwether grew up in Harlem during the depression. The only daughter of five children, she remembers her mother applying for welfare because her unemployed father could not sustain the family as a numbers runner. Despite her humble beginnings, she received her BA in English from New York University and her MA in journalism from the University of Los Angeles in 1965. She has worked as a freelance reporter (1961–1964) for the *Los Angeles Sentinel*, a black story analyst (1965–1967) for Universal Studios, and a faculty member at Sarah Lawrence College in Bronxville, New York (1979–1988), and the University of Houston (1985–1988).

In the early 1960s, Meriwether published biosketches of important African American figures: Grace Bumbry, singer; Audrey Boswell, attorney; Vaino Spenser, Los Angeles judge; and Mathew Henson, explorer. Her short stories appeared later that same decade: "Daddy Was a Number Runner" (*Antioch Review*, 1967), "A Happening in Barbadoes" (*Antioch Review*, 1968), and "The Thick End Is for Whipping" (*Negro Digest*, 1969). Three juvenile readers on historical black figures were published in the 1970s: *The Freedom Ship of Robert Smalls* (1971), *The Heart Man: Dr. Daniel Hale Williams* (1972), and *Don't Take the Bus on Monday: The Rosa Parks Story* (1973). Whether for adult or juvenile reading, each work includes some aspect of African American life not usually found in American history texts.

Meriwether's first novel, *Daddy Was a Number Runner* (1970), returns to the depression and captures the disintegration of a struggling African American family during difficult economic times. The novel is not autobiographical in the strictest sense, but parallels do exist between the author's family and that of Francie Coffin, the twelve-year-old protagonist. The depression took a toll on the physical, mental, and social health of both families; the first-person point of view makes plausible the Coffins' demise.

Fragments of the Ark (1994), Meriwether's second novel, recounts the daring escape of Peter Mango, a Charleston slave, to the Union army to achieve his freedom. Based on the real-life adventure of Robert Smalls, the novel changes the name of the historic figure to consider interpersonal relationships. This novel joins other historical fiction, such as Toni *Morrison's **Beloved* (1987) and Alex *Haley's **Roots* (1976), to retell the story of slavery from an African American perspective.

Between the publication of *Fragments of the Ark* and *Daddy Was a Number Runner*, twenty-four years passed. Often Meriwether delayed her writings to engage in political activity. In 1965, Meriwether worked with the Congress of Racial Equality (CORE) in Bogalusa, Louisiana, and with the Deacons, a black coalition that armed itself to protect the community from Ku Klux Klan raids. Two years later, she and Vantile Whitfield, founder of the Performing Arts Society of Los Angeles, formed the Black Anti-Defamation Association to prevent Twentieth Century Fox's producer David L. Wolper from making a film of William Styron's controversial book *The Confessions of Nat Turner* (1967). Styron's book denigrated the Virginia insurrectionist and misinterpreted African American history. The outcome of Meriwether and Whitfield's efforts was that the film was not made.

Whether in her writings or in her militant tactics, Meriwether insists on revising American history to give African Americans a deserving, respectable place in it.

• Rita B. Dandridge, "From Economic Insecurity to Disintegration: A Study of Character in Louise Meriwether's *Daddy Was a Number Runner*," *Negro American Literature Forum* 9 (Fall 1975): 82–85. Rita B. Dandridge, "Meriwether, Louise," in *Black Women in America*, vol. 2, ed. Darlene Clark Hine, 1993, pp. 783–784. Brenda Boudreau, "The Battleground of the Adolescent Girl's Body," in *The Girl: The Construction of the Girl in Contemporary Fiction by Women*, 1998, pp. 43–56.

—Rita B. Dandridge

Messenger, The. *The Messenger*, a monthly journal (1917–1928), was remarkable for its editorials, occasional literature, and varied appeal. Variously subtitled, it was first a spartan *Journal of Scientific Radicalism* or the *Only Radical Negro Magazine in America*, describing itself as the "first publication to recognize the Negro problem as fundamentally a labor problem." Scintillating editorials by A. Philip Randolph and Chandler Owen rebuked President Warren G. Harding for endorsing California's exclusion of Japanese immigrants or lambasted W. E. B. *Du Bois for "demagogy" regarding socialist revolution, while sociopolitical poems by Claude *McKay and the memoirs of Bartolomeo Vanzetti appeared as occasional literature. Beginning in 1923, however, the *Messenger* as *New Opinion of the New Negro* or *World's Greatest Negro Monthly* began to feature what it called "pure literature"—poems by Langston *Hughes, Countee *Cullen, Georgia Douglas *Johnson, and Alice *Dunbar-Nelson. Fashion-plate covers and society photographs dominated until 1926, when muscular workers again appeared on the cover and the *Messenger* became the official organ of Randolph's Brotherhood of Sleeping Car Porters. Thanks, however, to Wallace *Thurman's brief managing editorship, in these last two years the *Messenger* also published Zora Neale *Hurston's "Eatonville Anthology" and Hughes's first short stories.

• Langston Hughes, *The Big Sea*, 1940. Chidi Ikonné, *From Du Bois to Van Vechten: The Early New Negro Literature, 1903–1926*, 1981.

—Craig Howard White

MEYER, JUNE. *See* Jordan, June.

MICHEAUX, OSCAR (1884–1951), director, producer, novelist, and leading director in early independent African American film. Oscar Micheaux was the first major African American director to produce feature films with black characters for black audiences. Over a thirty-year period from 1919 to 1948 he wrote, directed, and produced thirty-four pictures. Among these are *Body and Soul* (1924), a silent film starring Paul *Robeson in his first American movie, and *The Exile* (1931), the first African American talkie made by a black film company. Micheaux was a legendary figure in early African American film, a field that began in earnest after the appearance of D. W. Griffith's controversial *Birth of a Nation* (1915). The great public outcry over the racism in Griffith's film created an underground movement of black filmmakers intent on presenting a more realistic appraisal of African American life.

Micheaux was born in Illinois and after a short period as a farmer and Pullman car porter turned his efforts to writing novels for black audiences. Over a ten-year period Micheaux wrote and self-published ten novels. In 1918 he founded the Oscar Micheaux Corporation in Harlem, New York, and turned to producing and directing films. After a series of short films he made *The Homesteader* (1919), based on his own novel. In rapid succession during the 1920s and 1930s Micheaux made many films, among them: *Sons of Satan* (1922), *Birthright* (1924), *Wages of Sin* (1929), *Underworld* (1936), and *God's Stepchildren* (1937). Micheaux was also an indefatigable promoter of his creations, touring the country to publicize and finance his films. He convinced white theater owners to have special showings for black audiences; he also distributed his films to approximately one hundred black theaters. Filming on a shoestring budget, Micheaux used black actors and actresses anxious for work in films, among them Lorenzo Tucker, Ethel Moses, and Bee Freeman. Reputedly over six feet tall, Micheaux dressed in large black coats and wide-brimmed hats. As a maverick director he often chose his players on a whim and had them work without repeated takes. The films were shot in convenient locations such as friends' homes and hastily constructed sets. Although most films were shot in less than six weeks, Micheaux created films showing black life on realistic terms while also providing entertainment for the black masses. His films contained a range of types and attempted to show that blacks were often just as rich, educated, and cultured as whites.

Recently Micheaux has been criticized for presenting a class system based on color in his movies. Often the most affluent or successful blacks in his films are the lightest-skinned with the straightest hair. Although the nightclub and cabaret scenes in Micheaux's films provide valuable insight into black music and dance, some critics suggest they may have been added to entice white audiences to his films. Nevertheless Micheaux's strongest films confront the race problem head on while presenting the lifestyle and attitudes of the black middle class. His heroes and heroines suffer through conventional romantic and financial crises complicated by the issues of passing and racial prejudice. In their own way Micheaux's films make a plea for black unity and black independence through education and economic competition while presenting a positive image for black audiences.

Micheaux successfully fashioned almost single-handedly a popular black cinema and a black star system that provided a prototype for African American independent cinema in general. He created dynamic roles for aggressive black female actresses and many of his films featured females in the stronger roles. He gave black actors and actresses roles far different from the usual Hollywood stereotype of servants, *Uncle Toms, and buffoons. Micheaux's extravagant personality, great creative flair, and independent vision made him a visionary filmmaker who could connect with the black audiences of the period. He examined and explored the shared, collective attitudes and outlooks of African Americans between the wars in a large body of films, many of which are now lost. Micheaux worked in both silent and sound film, one of the few black directors to bridge this important transitional era in American cinema. His final dream of widespread black and white audiences for his films was not to be. Micheaux'slast film, *Betrayal* (1948), opened in New York at a white theater and received major attention from the press, but the public took little notice and the movie failed. Soon after, Micheaux died in relative obscurity, and his films remained neglected for over thirty years.

• Donald Bogle, Toms, Coons, *Mulattoes, Mammies, and Bucks: An Interpretive History of Blacks in American Films,* 1973. James P. Murray, *To Find an Image: Black Films from Uncle Tom to Super Fly,* 1973. Bernard L. Peterson, "Films of Oscar Micheaux: America's First Fabulous Black Filmmaker," *Crisis* 86.4 (Apr. 1979): 136–141. Kenneth Wiggins Portor, "Oscar Micheaux," in *DANB,* eds. Rayford W. Logan and Michael R. Winston, 1982, pp. 433–434. "Oscar Micheaux" in *World Film Directors 1890–1945,* vol. 1, ed. John Wakeman, 1987, pp. 765–770. Donald Bogle, *Blacks in American Films and Television: An Encyclopedia,* 1988. Marc A. Reid, "Pioneer Black Filmmaker: The Achievement of Oscar Micheaux," *Black Film Review* 4.2 (Spring 1988): 6–7. Jane Gaines, "Fire and Desire: Race, Melodrama, and Oscar Micheaux" in Manthia Diawara, ed., *Black American Cinema,* 1993, pp. 49–70.

—Stephen F. Soitos

Middle Passage, which won the 1990 National Book Award for Fiction, marks the culmination of Charles R. *Johnson's philosophical exploration and formal innovation to date. Taking the form of ship's log entries, the novel recounts the adventures of *Rutherford Calhoun, a freed slave from Illinois who relocates to New Orleans and leads a hedonistic life financed by petty thievery. While there, Rutherford becomes involved with two powerful figures: Isadora Duncan, the proper schoolmistress who treats Rutherford much like her adopted stray animals, and Philippe "Papa" Zeringue, a Creole gangster to whom Rutherford becomes indebted. Isadora learns of and buys Rutherford's debts; in return Zeringue helps her attempt to force Calhoun into marriage. Desperate to escape both oppressors, Rutherford stows away aboard the *Republic,* unwittingly choosing a slave ship in which Zeringue holds a partial interest.

Aboard the *Republic,* Rutherford is torn between the disparate influences of evil captain Ebenezer Falcon, a man literally and figuratively twisted and dissolute who seeks both to bed and subordinate him, and the example of the Allmuseri, the tribe of African wizards who, along with their god, make up the cargo of the *Republic* on her return voyage. Led by the wise and inscrutable Ngonyama, the Allmuseri present an entirely different picture of existence to Rutherford. Living a life characterized by complete harmony and speaking a language that cannot be subdivided into any discrete pieces, the Allmuseri contradict Falcon's rabid individualism. Convinced of the captain's insanity, the crew decides to mutiny and enlists Calhoun's aid, a plot that he reveals to Falcon under duress. His attempts to stop the mutineers are thwarted by the Allmuseri's rebellion, an event that forces Rutherford, one of the few crew members who understands Ngonyama's people, into the position of mediator between rebellious cargo and surviving crew. Enduring a number of painful adventures, Rutherford ultimately returns home in time to prevent Isadora's marriage to Zeringue. He reveals Zeringue's treachery, frees himself from debt, and weds Isadora, settling down to a life he had not previously valued.

The linear plot masks philosophical twists that make the novel quite challenging. Drawing on sources including *The Odyssey,* Edgar Allan Poe's *The Narrative of Arthur Gordon Pym,* Herman Melville's *Moby-Dick* and "Benito Cereno," principles of phenomenology, and the Hegelian slave-master paradigm, Johnson creates a world in which conventional notions of time, language, freedom, and loyalty are tested. Calhoun serves as mediator, both within the text and between audience and text, offering a model for the type of reading necessary to a full comprehension of the fictional landscape's significance.

This novel reinforces many points Johnson makes in *Oxherding Tale* (1982); however, where the philosophical substructure of the former novel is glaringly obvious, *Middle Passage* manages to submerge many of the same concerns in a narrative that easily entertains while offering challenging ideas. As a result, the work has attracted a variety of readers and exposed a large portion of the general public to Johnson's aesthetics, thereby firmly establishing him as an important contemporary author.

• Charles Johnson and Ron Chernow, *In Search of a Voice*, 1991, pp. 1–18. Ashraf H. A. Rushdy, "The Phenomenology of the Allmuseri: Charles Johnson and the Subject of the Narrative of Slavery," *African American Review* 26.3 (Winter 1992): 373–394. Charles Johnson, "An Interview with Charles Johnson," interview by Jonathan Little, *Contemporary Literature* 34.2 (Summer 1993): 159–181.

—William R. Nash

MILDRED JOHNSON in Alice *Childress's **Like One of the Family . . . Conversations from a Domestic's Life* (1956) is one of the most memorable characters ever created in African American literature. A day worker who goes from house to house across New York City, Mildred enlightens her white employers about their own foibles related to race, class, and gender biases. She is motivated by her conscience to help her employers see their condescension and make changes. Mildred, a consummate storyteller, informs her best friend, Marge, about the daily confrontations with her white employers. Each of the sixty-two short conversations that Mildred has with Marge serves to comment on the social tensions of the 1950s while countering myths about African Americans and their place in society. Mildred is bold, witty, vivacious, and intellectually superior. Instead of quietly accepting abuses, she speaks out not only for herself but for all domestics. She uses humor and cunning to insist upon better wages and working conditions. Mildred also serves as the voice of nationalistic pride, which places her in the context of other great African American spokespersons such as Olaudah *Equiano, Martin R. *Delany, Marcus *Garvey, and Langston *Hughes. Mildred, as mouthpiece for Childress, highlights the accomplishments of African Americans. Childress's Mildred, a supermaid, serves as heroine of the Black working class in the tradition of Langston Hughes's Jesse B. *Simple. Childress's Mildred voices with aplomb the frustrations and joys of the little people, the masses of poor, invisible people who have the power to disrupt life if they so choose.

• Trudier Harris, introduction to *Like One of the Family: Conversations from a Domestic's Life*, 1956; rpt. 1986.

—Elizabeth Brown-Guillory

MILKMAN DEAD is the protagonist in Toni *Morrison's **Song of Solomon* (1977). Named by the town gossip because his mother, Ruth, nursed him at her breast far longer than considered socially acceptable, Milkman's real name is Macon Dead III. The novel tells the story of his passage into manhood and the identity crisis that comes from being the son of Macon Dead II, the most "propertied" African American man in their Michigan town. Macon not only intimidates his tenants, who regard him as a slum landlord, but also his wife and children. He forbids Milkman to associate with his aunt, *Pilate Dead, regarding her as the town pariah whose eccentric ways are a source of embarrassment to him and the middle-class identity he has struggled to secure for himself and his family. Milkman decides to give up his middle-class comforts to go south to look for the gold inheritance he has learned about from his father.

The second half of the novel traces Milkman's journey to the South, where he meets his father's people and learns the family history of Solomon, his paternal great-grandfather, who, according to the song he first heard Pilate sing when he was a child, flew back to Africa rather than remain in slavery. The novel also traces Milkman's journey into a new understanding of himself, the African American community, and his relationship to others. At the end of the novel he learns there is no gold, only a sack containing his grandfather's bones. He escorts Pilate to the South and helps her give her father a proper burial. As Pilate dies in his arms, he sings the song he learned from her, having learned that it was not only the song of his people, but also the song that had helped him reclaim a sense of self and his heritage.

• Marilyn Sanders Mobley, *Folk Roots and Mythic Wings in Sarah Orne Jewett and Toni Morrison*, 1992.

—Marilyn Sanders Mobley

MILLER, E. ETHELBERT (b. 1950), poet, essayist, critic, educator, and broadcast journalist. Eugene Ethelbert Miller was born in New York City to West Indian immigrant parents. He attended a predominantly Italian American and Jewish high school in the Bronx. These early cultural influences contribute to the thematic scheme of much of his poetry. Before obtaining a BA in African American Studies from Howard University, Miller had intended to complete a degree in history and begin a career in law. It was during the time Miller reassessed his professional goals that the poetry and song of the 1960s and the Black Arts movement were in full effect and would help him develop his voice.

Miller is a living cultural and literary resource. Since 1974, as director of the African American Studies Resource Center at Howard University, he has maintained an extensive, rare collection of African American literature and history of which he has an amazingly personal knowledge. Numerous young writers continue to benefit from Miller's commitment to cultivating the arts in the District of Columbia. He is founder and director of the Ascension Poetry Series, one of the oldest series in Washington, D.C. Through this series of readings and professional workshops, Miller has introduced the community to the undiscovered talents of many now renowned writers. Miller's insistence that the community respond to and provide encouragement for fresh and diverse new artists is evidenced in the volumes he has edited: *Synergy D.C. Anthology* (1975), *Women Surviving Massacres and Men* (1977), and *In Search of Color Everywhere* (1994).

Along with his informal interpersonal cultivation of advice, ideas, and information, Miller extends himself to academic and policy-making venues. As he expressed in a 1987 interview with the *Washington Post,* Miller is dedicated to involving himself in every aspect of writing. He is an associate faculty member at Bennington College, Bennington, Vermont; a visiting professor at the University of Nevada, Las Vegas; a member of the board of the National Writers Union and Associated Writing Programs; and senior editor of *African American Review* and *Washington Review.*

Miller is essentially a cultural critic whose vision reaches beyond race to examine the human condition. Miller's work captures the poetic struggle of day-to-day living: love, family, manhood, the liberation of women, the politics of protest and inclusion. The lines are quiet and succinct, much like the quickness and quietness that disguise the profundity of daily events. In "Only Language Can Hold Us Together," Miller identifies with the politics involved in a black woman's struggle for beauty, saying she did not understand why no one recognized the "beauty of her hair." In "The Kid," the poet unveils the hidden core beneath a comfortable mask, telling about how the subject talks candidly about his father "sometimes when we ain't talking about baseball."

Miller's collections attest to his twenty-year commitment to the continuing tradition of African American literature: *The Land of Smiles and the Land of No Smiles* (1974), *Andromeda* (1974), *The Migrant Worker* (1978), *Season of Hunger/Cry of Rain: Poems 1975–1980* (1982), *Where Are the Love Poems for Dictators?* (1986), *First Light: New and Selected Poems* (1993), and *How We Sleep on the Nights We Don't Make Love* (1996). In recognition of his talent, Miller has won the O. B. Hardison, Jr., Award for imaginative art and teaching (1995), the Columbia Merit Award (1993), the Public Humanities Award from the D.C. Community Council (1988), and the Mayor's Art Award for Literature (1982).

• Priscilla R. Ramsey, "E. Ethelbert Miller," in *DLB,* vol. 41, *Afro-American Poets since 1955,* eds. Trudier Harris and Thadious M. Davis, 1985, pp. 233–240.

—Elanna N. Haywood

MILLER, KELLY (1863–1939), educator, essayist, and sociologist. The son of Kelly Miller, a free African American cotton farmer, and Elizabeth (Roberts), a slave, Kelly Miller was reared on a backcountry farm near Winnsboro, South Carolina, and attended Howard University and Johns Hopkins, where he studied physics and mathematics. He held jobs in the United States Pension Office and in the Washington, D.C., public schools before joining Howard's faculty in 1890. While there he completed his AM (1901) and LLD (1903) degrees. He remained at his alma mater for forty-four years in a range of teaching and administrative positions, including professor of mathematics, chair of sociology, dean of the junior college, and dean of the College of Arts and Sciences. So closely identified with Howard that it was often known during his tenure as "Kelly Miller's University," he helped to modernize its curriculum, to institute the systematic study of Negro life, to promote the hiring of African American faculty and administrators, and by the 1930s, to champion segregated education. Toward the end of his academic career, he came increasingly into conflict with his junior colleagues, who had been hired by Howard's first African American president, Mordecai Johnson. The scientific and theoretical methods of research pursued by these young professionals, who included Ralph Bunche, Sterling A. *Brown, and E. Franklin Frazier, were, in Miller's view, at odds with his more personal emphasis on self-help and character building.

Equally active outside the university, he wrote an influential column circulated in more than one hundred newspapers across the country, assisted W. E. B. *Du Bois as an editor of the *Crisis* magazine, and authored several important pamphlets, including "The Disgrace of Democracy: An Open Letter to President Woodrow Wilson" (1917), and a series of essays, some of which were compiled and published as books. The best of these include *From Servitude to Service* (1905), *Race Adjustmen*t (1908), *Out of the House of Bondage* (1917), and *The Everlasting Stain* (1924).

As a race leader, Miller was a philosophic moderate critical of both the militant agendas associated with the Niagara Movement (despite holding firm respect for the movement's leader, Du Bois) and the conservative views, especially on education, of Booker T. *Washington. Calling for a measured, middle-of-the-road response to the "oppressive conditions" of African Americans, he observed in *Race Adjustment* that "no thoughtful Negro is satisfied with the present status of his race." But as a pragmatist who sought progress through harmony, he held that African American advancement was a slow, if inevitable, process relying on black achievement and patience, middle-class virtue, economic development, and white goodwill. Later in his life, he was dismayed by the direction of American racial politics, which seemed to him to be driven by young radicals. In contrast to most African American intellectuals, he supported Roosevelt's New Deal, opposed organized labor, and spoke out strongly against African American migration to the urban industrial North, which challenged the roots of his agrarian values. Nonetheless, he will be remembered for typifying the African American intellectual elite of the early twentieth century.

• August Meier, *Negro Thought in America, 1880–1915,* 1963, pp. 213–218. James Young, *Black Writers of the Thirties,* 1973, pp. 3–13. "Kelly Miller," in *Dictionary of American Negro Biography,* eds. Rayford W. Logan and Michael R. Winston, 1982, pp. 435–439.

—Lawrence R. Rodgers

MILLER, MAY (1899–1995), poet and playwright. May Miller was born on 26 January 1889 in Washington, D.C., to Annie May Butler and Kelly Miller, a distinguished professor of sociology at Howard University. At Paul Laurence *Dunbar High School, May Miller studied with prominent African American dramatist Mary Burrill and poet Angelina Weld *Grimké. As a drama major at Howard University, she directed, acted, and produced plays while collaborating with Alain *Locke and Montgomery Gregory in the founding of a black drama movement. Later, she taught speech, theater, and dance at Frederick *Douglass High School in Baltimore, Maryland, and was a lecturer and poet at Monmouth College, the University of Wisconsin–Milwaukee, and the Philips Exeter Academy.

Most of her plays were written between 1920 and 1945. A number won drama prizes, including *Within the Shadows, Bog Guide,* and *The Cuss'd Thing.* Four were published in the anthology she edited with Willis *Richardson in 1935: *Negro History in Thirteen Plays,* a collection that firmly established Miller's national reputation. Of these, *Sojourner *Truth* is notable for its inclusion of white characters who are changed by their contact with a black character, but this play seems somewhat wooden compared to the powerful *Harriet *Tubman,* about a spurned mulatto suitor attempting to betray other slaves in pursuit of money with which to buy his own freedom. The plays set in the African Sudan (*Samory*) and Haiti (*Christophe's Daughters*) lack the verisimilitude of her other work. Miller's *Ridin' the Goat* uses humor to challenge the values of the black middle class and to suggest the importance of community rituals and cultural practices. Other important plays include *Scratches* (1929) and the antilynching *Nails and Thorns* (1933).

By the mid-1940s, Miller devoted most of her attention to poetry. Fairly traditional in their form and language, Miller's volumes of poetry include *Into the Clearing* (1959); *Poems* (1962); *Lyrics of Three Women: Katie Lyle, Maude Rubin, and May Miller* (1964); *Not That Far* (1973); *The Clearing and Beyond* (1974); *Dust of Uncertain Journey* (1975); and *The Ransomed Wait* (1983). *Editor of Green Wind* (1978) and *My World* (1979), she also authored a book of children's poems, *Halfway to the Sun* (1981). Her poems frequently engage in significant spiritual and ethical questions. "Late Conjecture," for instance, questions the meaning of Christ's sacrifice, while Miller's "The Dream of Wheat" envisions "unnumbered rows of ripened wheat" that "March to greedy ovens." The poem ends by demanding starkly "Who will eat? / Who go hungry?" Her poems have been published in *Phylon,* the *Antioch Review,* the *Crisis,* the *Nation,* the *New York Times,* and *Poetry,* and have been praised by Gwendolyn *Brooks as "excellent and long-celebrated" and by Robert *Hayden, who has said of May Miller that she "writes with quiet strength, lyric intensity. She is perceptive and compassionate, a poet of humane vision." Miller read her poetry at the inauguration of President Jimmy Carter, and is included in a 1972 Library of Congress collection of poets reading their own works. May Miller, who died on 11 February 1995, lived to see the manifestation of her own prediction of the importance of the movement she encouraged, the "little one-act play groups that performed in churches and schools [and which were] a forerunner to what we're doing now" (quoted in *DLB,* vol. 41, 1985).

• Winifred L. Stoeling, "May Miller," *DLB,* vol. 41, *Afro-American Poets since 1955,* eds. Trudier Harris and Thadious Davis, 1985, pp. 241–247. James V. Hatch and Leo Hamalian, eds., *The Roots of African-American Theater,* 1991, pp. 307–327. Willis Richardson, *Plays and Pageants from the Life of the Negro,* 1993, pp. 109–177.

—Lynda Koolish

MILLICAN, ARTHENIA J. BATES (b. 1920), poet, educator, short fiction writer, lecturer, and humanist of the rural southern folk. Born Arthenia Bernetta Jackson on 1 June 1920, in Sumter, South Carolina, this African American woman of the South rose above her obscure place in letters in the 1980s. Her parents, Calvin Shepard Jackson and Susan Emma David, were both professionals who embraced education and religion. The mother, however, was extremely class-conscious, a quality Arthenia Bates never adopted. In fact, a hallmark of her writing is her love of the folk, evident in her themes and the dialect and rhythms of her short stories. Her exposure, on an intimate level, to common people came through her two marriages to nonprofessional men, Noah Bates on 11 June 1950, and Wilbert Millican on 14 August 1969. The marriage to Bates ended in divorce in 1956, and Millican's mother never forgave her for marrying the laborer Bates and the dockworker Millican, thus removing herself from the privileged African American middle class.

Millican's early career was as a teacher and department head in South Carolina and Virginia public schools. She finished Morris College in Sumter, South Carolina, in 1941, earned a master's degree from Atlanta University in 1948, and earned a PhD from Louisiana State University in 1972, writing a dissertation on James Weldon *Johnson, "In Quest of an Afro-Centric Tradition for Black American Literature." This was a long-deferred dream. While in Atlanta, she studied the art of poetry writing with Langston *Hughes, a major influence.

In 1969, after a lifetime of writing, Millican published her *Seeds Beneath the Snow: Vignettes from the South.* Much of her literary reputation is based on this work, a collection of short stories that has steadily gained a national reputation. Millican thought of the people of Virginia as late-blooming seeds that survived in spite of a blanket of snow.

Critical reception of *Seeds Beneath the Snow* was highly favorable, and Millican was compared to Paul Laurence *Dunbar, Charles Waddell *Chesnutt, Zora Neale *Hurston, and Thomas Hardy. The *Washington Post,* in a 1970 review, praised Millican for her "primitive themes." *CLA Journal,* in 1973, cited the writer for her unusual ability as a "local colorist." Millican's ability to sketch characters may be attributed to her immersion in Henry James and her direct involvement on the front porches with people of the community during her first marriage.

Millican's critical and scholarly articles have appeared in the *Southern University Bulletin, Negro American Literature Forum,* and *CLA Journal. Harlo Press* of Detroit published her *The Deity Nodded* in 1973, and Millican published *Such Things from the Valley* in 1977. Her fiction has appeared in *Black World* (July 1971), *Obsidian* (1975), and *Callaloo* (December 1975).

As an educator, Millican gave most of her career to Southern University in Baton Rouge, Louisiana, where she taught from 1956 until her retirement in 1980. In an unusual town-gown initiative, she and others at Southern University formed a group called the Academic Humanists in order to bridge the wide gap between college and community.

In July 1976, Millican received a $6,000 fellowship from the National Endowment for the Arts for her story "Where You Belong." Ignored by major anthologists until *Sturdy Black Bridges* (Bell et al., 1979), Millican is finally getting her due.

• Virginia Whatley Smith, "Arthenia J. Bates Millican," in *DLB,* vol. 38, *Afro-American Writers after 1955: Dramatists and Prose Writers,* eds. Thadious M. Davis and Trudier Harris, 1985, pp. 195–201.

—Glenda E. Gill

MILNER, RON (b. 1938), playwright, writer, editor, critic, and director. Born in Detroit, Michigan, Ron Milner graduated from Detroit's Northeastern High School. He attended Highland Park Junior College, Detroit Institute of Technology, and Columbia University in New York. In the early 1960s, Milner received two prestigious literary grants, the John Hay Whitney Fellowship (1962) and a Rockefeller Fellowship (1965), to work on a novel, *The Life of the Brothers Brown.* Milner is one of the most significant figures to emerge from the Black Arts movement. He is known affectionately as the "people's playwright" for his ongoing commitment to using Black theater for the advancement of Black people. Milner has taught widely and was writer in residence at Lincoln University (Pennsylvania) from 1966 to 1967, where his friendship with Langston *Hughes, who urged him to use a personal voice in his writing, matured.

A "born writer," Milner is a prolific playwright. His first major play, *Who's Got His Own,* premiered in Harlem in 1967. Milner went to New York with friend and producer-director Woodie *King, Jr., as part of a touring production of three plays by Malcolm Boyd in 1964. He and King joined the American Place Theatre, where *Who's Got His Own* and *The Warning: A Theme for Linda* (1969, published in *A Black Quartet: Four New Black Plays,* 1970) were conceived and performed. Other published plays include *The Monster* (*Drama Review,* 1968), *(M)Ego and the Green Ball of Freedom* (*Black World,* 1968), and *What the Wine-Sellers Buy* (*Samuel French,* 1974).

From 1979 to 1981 Milner lived in California, teaching creative writing at the University of Southern California and doing community work. Milner has since returned to Detroit, where he remains and where he feels he can better visualize the chronology of his stories. Milner feels his creative energy can feed on the unique experience of life in his hometown.

Milner's life and art reflect the driving force he calls for in his critical writing. In "Black Magic, Black Art" (*Negro Digest,* Apr. 1967; *Black Poets and Prophets,* 1972), Milner proclaimed that Black Art must affirm, inspire, and touch the souls of Black people. Milner's *Roads of the Mountaintops* (1986) deals with the internal struggle of Martin Luther *King, Jr., following his receipt of the Nobel Peace Prize in 1964. *What the Wine-Sellers Buy,* which earned over a million dollars in 1974, deals with a young Black man choosing between good and evil while simultaneously addressing the issue of Black male responsibility. *Checkmates* (1987), which starred Denzel Washington, portrays the potential strength of Black love. *Don't Get God Started* (1988) is a gospel-tinged musical play done for the family singing group the Winans.

A lesser-known work from Milner's career is his short story "Junkie Joe Had Some Money," which was anthologized in Langston Hughes's *Best Short Stories by Negro Writers* (1967). Perhaps Milner's most significant contribution to the field of African American letters is *Black Drama Anthology* (1972), coedited with Woodie King. One of the earliest and certainly one of the most respected anthologies of Black plays, it documented important works by Milner, Amiri *Baraka, Ed *Bullins, and Langston Hughes, among others.

Twice married and twice divorced, Milner is the father of four children. His son Raymarc is a filmmaker with whom Milner wishes to collaborate in the future. Milner currently writes film and television scripts in addition to teaching playwriting to younger Blacks.

Much of Milner's life revolves around working with children and using theater to educate them. This "functional writing," as Milner calls it, brings young African Americans into a dialogue with his plays and raises critical concerns as a vehicle for their self-improvement. Milner currently persists in his endeavor to establish regional-level Black theater in Michigan.

• Jeanne E. Saddler, "Ron Milner: The People's Playwright," *Essence*, Nov. 1974, 20. Geneva Smitherman, "'We Are the Music': Ron Milner, People's Playwright," *Black World* 25.6 (Apr. 1976): 4–19.

—Derek A. Williams

MINNIE RANSOM. The "fabled healer" of Claybourne, Georgia, Minnie Ransom is the stimulus for *Velma Henry's healing in Toni Cade *Bambara's *The *Salt Eaters* (1980). A multifaceted character, Minnie communes with her spirit guide, Old Wife; plays jazz recordings; and has a "voluptuous eye" cast on a young doctor, all while guiding Velma in her healing journey.

Minnie's characterization is a departure from the usual representations of conjure women, healers, or mammies in African American literature. Wearing a red dress, hot pink headwrap, kente cloth, a silk fringed shawl, and an armful of bangles, she is fully sexual, a celebration of African American womanhood. While deeply committed to her community and its collective as well as individual well-being, she refuses to take responsibility for the health of others, insisting, for example, that Velma be sure she is ready for the "weight" of being well.

Although Minnie's spirit guide, Old Wife, is a "good Christian," Minnie's spiritual system is more syncretic. She draws on the powers of the loa and astrology, as well as the "chapel" she visits with Old Wife. As able to read auras as she is to cure disease, Minnie came to her gift reluctantly, nearly going crazy as she realized what was happening to her. Seeing their "educated, well-groomed, well-raised" daughter eating dirt prompted her family to send Minnie off to a seminary. Like her patient Velma, however, Minnie grows and becomes wise, knowing that healing is not about being good or righteous, but being "available" to the powers and gifts within and around her.

—Ann Folwell Stanford

Montage of a Dream Deferred. In a prefatory note to *Montage of a Dream Deferred* (1951), Langston *Hughes wrote about his artistic influences, concerns, and aims in the book, which he saw as a single poem rather than as a collection of poems: In terms of current Afro-American popular music and the sources from which it has progressed—jazz, ragtime, swing, blues, boogie-woogie, and bebop—this poem on contemporary Harlem, like bebop, is marked by conflicting changes, sudden nuances, sharp and impudent interjections, broken rhythms, and passages sometimes in the manner of the jam session, sometimes the popular song, punctuated by the riffs, runs, breaks, and disc-tortions of the music of a community in transition.

The volume appears to have sprung from a momentous occasion in his life: his moving into his own home in 1948 after a lifetime of rented or borrowed rooms and houses. (With the royalties from the 1947 musical play *Street Scene*, on which he had served as lyricist with Kurt Weill and Elmer Rice, he had purchased a rowhouse in Harlem.) In September 1948 he wrote to a friend: "I have completed a new book I wrote last week!" Hughes called it "a full book-length poem in five sections," and characterized it further as "a precedent shattering opus—also could be known as a tour de force."

If the aggressive discordancies of bebop music as played by musicians such as Dizzy Gillespie and Charlie *Parker shaped the form of the book, its central idea is that of the "dream deferred." The dream had always been perhaps the central motif in Hughes's poetry, and especially the dream of political and social empowerment for blacks. But Hughes now faced the fact that the hopes that had drawn thousands of blacks to the northern cities had led many of them to disappointment, alienation, and bitterness. Some of these poems depict blacks still able to hope and dream, but the most powerful pieces raise the specter of poverty, violence, and death. In "Harlem," a dream deferred can "dry up," or "fester," or "crust and sugar over—or does it explode?"

At various times witty, sardonic, ironic, documentary, loving, or tragic, the volume touches on virtually every aspect of daily Harlem life, from the prosperous on Sugar Hill to the poorest folk living down below; it touches on the lives of Harlem mothers, daughters, students, ministers, junkies, pimps, police, shop owners, homosexuals, landlords, and tenants; its aim is to render in verse a detailed portrait of the community, which Hughes knew extremely well. Eventually he would take pride in the fact that of all major black writers, he alone still lived in the midst of a typical urban black community.

Despite Hughes's enthusiasm, his longtime publisher, Knopf, rejected the manuscript. The response when it appeared from Henry Holt in 1951 was lukewarm at best. To J. Saunders *Redding in the black *Pittsburgh Courier*, the book probed old emotions and experiences "but they reveal nothing new." In the *New York Times Book Review*, Babette Deutsch attacked Hughes's "facile sentimentality," his "cultivated naivete," and saw the work revealing "the limitations of folk art." Nevertheless, the volume ranks among his finest works of art, a major product of his intimate, ongoing engagement with African American life and culture.

[*See also* Raisin in the Sun, A.]

—Arnold Rampersad

MOODY, ANNE (b. 1940), civil rights activist and writer. Anne Moody was born in 1940, the daughter of sharecroppers. In *Coming of Age in Mississippi* (1968), Moody describes growing up in rural Mississippi where racism, lack of opportunity, and economic failure devastated her family and others in the African American community. The autobiography also chronicles the growth of the civil rights movement in Mississippi in the 1950s and 1960s, thus making the work a record of personal and political importance.

Coming of Age in Mississippi emerges out of a long tradition in African American literature, dating back to the slave narratives of the nineteenth century and continuing with autobiographies of the twentieth century. Moody's work has been compared to Harriet A. *Jacobs's **Incidents in the Life of a Slave Girl* (1861), Mary Church *Terrell's *A Black Woman in a White World* (1940), and Richard *Wright's **Black Boy* (1945).

Part 1 ("Childhood") concerns Moody's early years and her family's struggles and instability. While Jacobs and Terrell recalled Edenic periods in their early lives, Moody's did not contain such innocence. Even at a young age, Moody recognized the social and economic forces impacting on her family. Like Richard Wright, she questioned the position of superiority and privilege granted to whites, but met with fear and silence from the adults around her. Moody was angered by the apathy and seeming indifference that the black community had toward the inferior social and economic positions assigned to them. The eldest of six children, Moody was particularly aware of the plight of poor black women and their children. Her own mother's struggle to endure harsh field work, equally difficult domestic work, poverty, repeated childbearing, and desertion by her husband becomes an important subject in Moody's autobiography.

Parts 2 and 3 ("High School" and "College") describe the important role that school and education had in Moody's life. In high school, Moody channeled her anger and confusion into academic achievement and playing basketball. However, high school brought a deepening awareness of the realities of black life in Mississippi. The murder of Emmet Till the week before high school began initiated Moody into these truths. It also brought her a new and devastating fear: "the fear of being killed just because I was black."

Moody continued her education at Natchez College for two years on a basketball scholarship. She then received a full academic scholarship to Tougaloo College. Here Moody became involved in the NAACP and the Student Nonviolent Coordinating Committee. Such involvement was fraught with danger for both Moody and her family. However, this did not prevent her full immersion in civil rights activities during her senior year at Tougaloo, described in part 4, "The Movement."

Moody served as a canvasser and church speaker for the NAACP, participated in boycotts of downtown Jackson, Mississippi, stores, led a sit-in team at a Woolworth's lunch counter, registered voters for the Committee on Racial Equality, and taught workshops on self-protection to potential demonstrators. With vivid detail Moody recounts these activities, as well as the demoralizing impact of the assassinations of Medgar Evers and John F. Kennedy. All told, *Coming of Age in Mississippi* bears poignant witness to the injustices and evils of segregation in the South and portrays the growth and development of individual social conscience.

• Lynn Z. Bloom, "Coming of Age in the Segregated South: Autobiographies of Twentieth-Century Childhoods, Black and White," in *Home Ground: Southern Autobiography,* ed. J. Bill Berry, 1991, pp. 110–122. Nellie Y. McKay, "The Girls Who Became Women: Childhood Memories in the Autobiographies of Harriet Jacobs, Mary Church Terrell, and Anne Moody," in *Tradition and the Talents of Women,* ed. Florence Howe, 1991, pp. 105–124.

—Paula Gallant Eckard

MOORE, OPAL (b. 1953), poet, short story writer, essayist, educator, and critic of children's literature. Born and raised in Chicago, Illinois, Opal Moore was influenced from childhood by the particular dynamics of the Pentecostal church; echoes of that institution reverberate in her plots, themes, characters, tone, and language. When Moore entered Illinois Wesleyan University's School of Art in 1970, she was so shocked by her first real encounter with racism and her sense of powerlessness in the face of it that she sought some control over what was happening to her by writing, thus initiating her first journals. She also turned to writing poetry. After receiving a BFA from Wesleyan in 1974, she enrolled in the graduate program at the University of Iowa, where she began writing fiction. She earned an MA from the University of Iowa's School of Art in 1981, and an MFA from the University of Iowa's Iowa Writers' Workshop in 1982. She has taught creative writing and African American literature at Virginia Commonwealth University, Virginia State University, Hollins College, Kassel University (Germany), Johannes Gutenberg-Universität Mainz (Germany), and Radford University. She joined the English faculty at Spelman College in 1997.

Moore studied with Paule *Marshall and James Alan *McPherson, both of whom taught her much about the craft of writing. Long after she left Marshall's workshops, the novelist continued to critique Moore's drafts for her, persistently encouraging her to refine her sense of style and structure and to give thorough and legitimate handling to her male characters. Moore asserts that her first idol was Gwendolyn *Brooks. After reading Brooks and being capitivated by her language, she concluded that the only real writing had to be poetic. Moore was also profoundly affected by her reading of Toni *Morrison's **Sula*, with its protagonist's rebellion against communal values and generally accepted assumptions.

In her 1989 short fiction, "A Happy Story" (published in *Callaloo*), Moore portrays a somewhat cynical female writer wrestling with questions such as, "How do we achieve happiness? How do we define it?" Presenting her story through sometimes humorous debates with her more optimistic husband, the narrator tries and rejects many different story lines, but from beginning to end, there remains the same germ of a plan for her story: "It's about a woman, . . . Intelligent. Attractive. Educated." This story reflects some of Moore's major concerns in her poetry and short stories, which frequently focus on a black female child or adult who is unable to find happiness in a world with so many restrictions based on religion, race, and gender. In this problematic world there is little happiness (the character in "A Happy Story" doesn't believe there is such a thing as a happy story and can't recall a truly happy moment in her life), little humor, little freedom, little real love, little true communication.

Communication (or the lack thereof) is a frequent concern in Moore's work. Often, she insists that silence is an effective, potentially revolutionary form of communication. This revolution through silence, through the unspoken word, is something that the author early learned: Ordered to sit at the Sunday dinner table until she asked to be excused, the six-year-old Opal silently faced her mother for hours, refusing to utter the phrase, "Excuse me"; she had, after all, done nothing to require her to ask to be excused. Similarly, her characters are constantly refusing in subtle and varying ways to comply with rules that do not make sense to them. And Moore, as a writer, is constantly wrestling with the possibility of writing honest stories that obviously go against the grains of someone's taboos.

Moore's work is very intense and often painful. There is little relief in the occasional humor, which tends to be caustic and sardonic, as in "Freeing Ourselves of History: The Slave Closet" (*Obsidian II,* 1988), in which a modern assimilationist, proud of his "freedom," is confronted by a slave. Satirical treatment of this individual who never reaches self-realization ends with him wondering what use a dead slave is to "a modern free man."

Though Moore claims to have given up poetry for short fiction, the poet is evident in everything she writes. Words on a page magically evoking felt life is the essence of her best work. Marked by a mesmerizing, rhythmic beauty, her work paints poetic word pictures (Moore is also an artist) in unexpected but tantalizing images and metaphors. A master stylist, Moore, like Toni Morrison, grabs us with the opening phrase and has us pausing frequently to reflect, to relish some particularly apt description, some poignant picture, some surprising turn of phrase, some amazing use of language, some unusually melodic line.

Moore, whose fiction and poetry have appeared in a variety of journals and collections, is preparing a volume of short stories for publication. She has also published a number of critical and pedagogical essays, in which she frequently focuses on literature for children.

• "Picture Books about Blacks: An Interview with Opal Moore," interview by Donnarae MacCann and Olga Richard, *Wilson Library Bulletin* 65 (June 1991): 24–28.

—Daryl Cumber Dance

MORRISON, TONI (b. 1931), novelist, essayist, editor, short fiction writer, lecturer, educator, and Nobel Prize laureate. From "Quiet as it's kept," the phrase that begins the narrative of *The Bluest Eye* (1970), her first novel, to "Look where your hands are. Now," the final phrase of *Jazz* (1992), her sixth novel, Toni Morrison has distinguished herself as an author, editor, and critic who has transformed the American literary landscape with her presence in the African American literary tradition. When she won the 1993 Nobel Prize in Literature, the Swedish Academy referred to her as one "who, in novels characterized by visionary force and poetic import, gives life to an essential aspect of American reality." Indeed, in her Nobel lecture, delivered on 7 December 1993 in Stockholm, she eloquently demonstrated that the visionary force and poetic import of her novels reflect her worldview and understanding of how language shapes human reality. Through her own use of the spoken and written word, she has created new spaces for readers to bring both their imaginations and their intellects to the complex cultural, political, social, and historical issues of our time. Moreover, through her work as an editor and novelist, she has made it possible for the texts of both African American and feminist writers to reshape the contours of what we call American literature.

Toni Morrison was born Chloe Anthony Wofford on 18 February 1931 in Lorain, Ohio, the second of four children of Ramah Willis Wofford and George Wofford. Having grown up in a family of storytellers and musicians, she developed an early appreciation for language, folk wisdom, and literature. Formative influences in her life not only include listening to family history through the stories of her relatives, but growing up in an ethnically and racially diverse community whose coherence seemed to come from its identity as a poor steel town twenty-five miles west of Cleveland. Despite the sense of cooperation that class consciousness created in Lorain neighborhoods, Morrison learned from her parents that racial politics were a reality with which African Americans had to contend. She tells of her father's blatant hostility toward white people and her mother's somewhat optimistic belief that over time race relations in America would improve. It is no surprise, therefore, that her novels reflect both the pessimism that racism produces and the optimism that has empowered African American people to survive and thrive in spite of racism.

After graduating from Lorain High School, Morrison attended Howard University, where she earned a BA degree in 1953. While at Howard, where she changed her name from Chloe to Toni, she appeared in campus productions as a member of the Howard University Players, a campus theater company, and she toured the South with a faculty-and-student repertory troupe. From Howard she went on to Cornell University, where she earned an MA in English in 1955, with a thesis on the theme of suicide in the works of William Faulkner and Virginia Woolf. After working for two years as an instructor at Texas Southern University in Houston, she joined the faculty of Howard University where she taught in the English department from 1957 to 1964. A year after going to Howard to teach, she married a Jamaican architect, Harold Morrison, with whom she had two sons, Harold Ford and Slade Kevin. Morrison regarded the marriage as part of the stifling situation that led her to turn to writing for solace during the early 1960s. She joined a writers' workshop and began work on a short story about a black girl who wanted blue eyes. This short story would later become her first novel, *The Bluest Eye.* In 1964 she resigned from her teaching post at Howard, divorced her husband, and returned with her two sons to her parents' home in Lorain, where she stayed for eighteen months before moving to Syracuse,New York, to accept a position as a textbook editor for a subsidiary of Random House. Though she admits she began writing at night after her sons were asleep as a way to combat her own loneliness, it is clear that this activity was well on its way to reshaping her identity and her entire life. As she says, she realized, "Writing was . . . the most extraordinary way of thinking and feeling. It became the one thing I was doing that I had absolutely no intention of living without."

In 1968 Toni Morrison moved to New York City, where she became a senior editor at Random House. Her significance in this role cannot be overestimated because she was assigned to working, almost exclusively, on black writers. Authors who were published as a result of her work include Angela *Davis, Henry *Dumas, Toni Cade *Bambara, Muhammad *Ali, and Gayl *Jones. One of the most important books she edited during her time at Random House was *The Black Book,* published in 1974. An eclectic collection of more than three hundred years of history that attempts to record what it has been like to be of African descent on American soil, this book contains documents pertaining to slavery (such as bills of sale and announcements of searches for runaway slaves), pictures of slave quilts, photographs from family albums, recipes, songs, newspaper clippings, advertisements, and other miscellaneous memorabilia. Viewing the book as a representation of "Black life as lived," Morrison considered *The Black Book* an antidote for the unhistorical sense of self she felt was emerging from the Black Power movement of the late 1960s and early 1970s. She integrates this same concern for the African American past, history, and cultural memory into each of her novels.

During her early years as an editor at Random House, she developed the short story she began at Howard into her first novel, *The Bluest Eye,* and thus established her reputation as a writer with its publication in 1970. From 1970 to 1992, Morrison published five more novels, a play, a book of literary criticism, and an anthology of social criticism. In the midst of her already demanding schedule of editing and writing, she also began teaching part-time at various places on the East Coast, taking positions at SUNY-Purchase in 1971, at Yale in 1976, at SUNY-Albany in 1984, and at Bard College in 1986. Since 1988 she has been the Robert F. Goheen Professor of the Humanities at Princeton University, where she teaches in the Afro-American Studies and creative writing programs.

The rewards for deciding to devote her life to writing have been great. In 1975 Morrison received the National Book Award nomination for **Sula*, published in 1973. With **Song of Solomon,* published in 1977, she received even greater acclaim in the form of a Book-of-the-Month Club selection, the National Book Critics Circle Award, and the American Academy and Institute of Arts and Letters Award. Following the publication of **Tar Baby* in 1981, she wrote the play *Dreaming Emmett,* which was first produced in Albany, New York, in 1986. In 1988 she won the Pulitzer Prize and the Robert F. Kennedy Award for **Beloved,* the novel she published in 1987. She received her most prestigious award, the Nobel Prize in literature, in 1993 after the publication of *Jazz* in 1992.

Toni Morrison has not only established herself in American and African American literature as a first-rate novelist but also as a popular lecturer and first-rate literary and cultural critic. On 7 October 1988 she delivered the Tanner Lecture on Human Values at the University of Michigan, a presentation entitled "Unspeakable Things Unspoken: The Afro-American Presence in American Literature." This often-quoted lecture is noteworthy for the ease with which she engages in the literary critical discourse about canon formation and curriculum revision at the precise moment that these were central issues on campuses throughout the nation; for its meticulous, close reading of the first line of each of her first five novels, which places her in company with other African American writers such as Ralph *Ellison, Richard *Wright, and Sterling A. *Brown, who were also critics and theorists of their own writing; and for the way it introduces the commentary that becomes the focus of *Playing in the Dark: Whiteness and the Literary Imagination* (1992), Morrison's first book of literary criticism. In this book, she argues that canonical texts in American literature are long overdue for an analysis of how they are structured in subtle and not so subtle ways by their antithesis to blackness. With the publication of Race-ing Justice, *En-Gendering Power: Essays on Anita Hill, Clarence Thomas, and the Construction of Social Reality,* a book she edited in 1992, Morrison offers insightful social commentary on the race and gender politics of one of this nation's most significant moments in recent history. In 1997, Morrison published Birth of a *Nation'-hood: Gaze, Script, and Spectacle in the O.J. Simpson Case,* ed., with Claudia Brodsky Lacour.

More important than any of her literary and cultural criticism, however, are the six novels that have established her literary reputation as a writer whose work possesses tremendous aesthetic beauty and political power. We first bear witness to this power in *The Bluest Eye,* the novel about *Pecola Breedlove, the black girl whose insatiable desire to be loved is manifested in a desire for blue eyes that ultimately drives her into insanity. The novel's treatment of some tragic dimensions of black life, such as incest and poverty, and the larger racialized context from which some of this tragedy springs reflect Morrison's desire to invite her reader to examine the family values, gender politics, and community secrets that shape individual and collective identity. With her second novel, *Sula,* Morrison ventures into a treatment of female friendship, exploring the dynamics of the relationship between two women, *Sula Peace and Nel Wright, to examine what Deborah McDowell calls the representation of character as process, not essence. The novel not only narrates the story of how Sula and Nel become friends, but also the implications of the rift that separates them when one chooses a traditional life of marriage and family and the other chooses independence from traditional expectations for women. Moreover, through her meticulous treatment of place in her depiction of the Bottom, the neighborhood where Sula and Nel grow up, Morrison illustrates how a black community's identity evolves and shapes itself with its own cultural resources and elaborate social structure.

In her third novel, *Song of Solomon,* Morrison narrates a complex tale of a black man, *Milkman Dead, and his search to understand himself in the context of family history and racial politics. Weaving memories of her own family stories of relatives who lost land during Reconstruction, *Song of Solomon* chronicles Milkman's journey from the North back to the South to the very places and people of his ancestry that his middle-class life had encouraged him to devalue. Morrison uses her fourth novel, *Tar Baby,* to synthesize an interest in racial politics and the African diaspora with gender relations. A love affair between a black upper middle-class model and art historian, *Jadine Childs, and *Son Green, the uneducated stowaway who intrudes in the Caribbean island mansion of her wealthy white benefactors, illustrates Morrison's interest in debates about how blackness and authenticity get defined in the African American community. In *Beloved,* Morrison connects her preoccupation with history with an exploration of how personal and cultural memory operate in the formation of relationships. Using the story of *Sethe Suggs, a slave woman who took her child's life to protect it from slave catchers, Morrison takes the core of a real story recorded in *The Black Book* as the basis of this intricately narrated novel about two former slaves who work their way through remembering the pain of enslavement and dealing with the dead child's ghost, to healing, wholeness, and love. Finally, in *Jazz,* a novel inspired by her reading in *The Harlem Book of the Dead* about a young woman who, as she lay dying, refused to identify her lover as the person who shot her, Morrison combines the history and music of the Harlem Renaissance with a fascination with New York City, the story of a stale marriage, and a fatal love affair. What distinguishes the novel more than its plot is Morrison's innovative telling of it, a telling that is meant to emulate the improvisational techniques of jazz.

In 1998, Morrison published *Paradise,* her seventh novel. Set in an all-black town in the Southwest, it explores the relationships among darker and lighter skinned black people, the efforts of a group to create a sanctuary from discrimination and prejudice, and the complicated ways in which history returns to haunt those who try to make themselves immune from history and racism.

In sum, Toni Morrison's novels reflect her desire to draw on the people, places, language, values, cultural traditions, and politics that have shaped her own life and that of African American people. In so doing, she offers no solutions to problems, nor does she simplify the complex realities of the past or present. Instead, out of respect for the cultural knowledge that black people bring to life and living, she uses the power and majesty of her imagination to address them and anyone interested in the stories that have created a permanent place for her among America's greatest writers.

[*See also* Baby Suggs; Eva Peace; Hannah Peace; Paul D; Pilate Dead; Shadrack.]

• Toni Morrison, "A Slow Walk of Trees (As Grandmother Would Say), Hopeless (As Grandfather Would Say)," *New York Times Magazine,* 4 July 1976, 104. Colette Dowling, "The Song of Toni Morrison," 1979. David L. Middleton, *Toni Morrison: An Annotated Bibliography,* 1987. Nellie Y. McKay, Critical Essays on Toni Morrison, 1988. Claudia Tate, *Black Women Writers at Work,* 1989. Trudier Harris, *Fiction and Folklore: The Novels of Toni Morrison,* 1991. Henry Louis Gates, Jr., and K. A. Appiah, eds., *Toni Morrison: Critical Perspectives Past and Present,* 1993. Denise Heinze, *The Dilemma of "Double-Consciousness": Toni Morrison's Novels,* 1993. Barbara Christian, "Beloved, She's Ours," *Narrative* 5:1 (January 1997): 36–49. Carl Plasa, ed. *Toni Morrison: Beloved,* 1998. Naomi R. Rand, *Silko, Morrison, and Roth: Studies in Survival,* 1999. Patricia McKee, *Producing American Races: Henry James, William Faulkner, Toni Morrison,* 1999.

—Marilyn Sanders Mobley

MOSES. From the days of slavery through the civil rights era, African Americans struggling for freedom from oppression have turned for inspiration to Moses, the biblical leader who guided the Israelites out of slavery in Egypt to the promised land. The slaves were so fascinated by Moses that they often called the South "Egyptland," the North "the promised land," and antislavery leaders like Harriet *Tubman "Moses"; also, slaves praised Moses' heroic deeds in sermons, folktales, and spirituals (such as "Go Down Moses," "Oh, Mary Don't You Weep," and "Little Moses"). Literary works by modern and contemporary African American authors reflect the enduring importance of Moses to the African American community. Some works, such as Zora Neale *Hurston's *Moses, Man of the Mountain* (1939), straightforwardly retell and reinterpret the biblical account of Moses for twentieth-century African

Americans. Other works, writes H. Nigel Thomas, employ Moses as a character type: according to Thomas, such works as Paul Laurence *Dunbar's "The Strength of Gideon" (1900), Ralph *Ellison's **Invisible Man* (1952), and William Melvin *Kelley's *A Different Drummer* (1959), present characters who attempt to help their fellow African Americans escape oppression as their prototype Moses had helped his people. Thomas also identifies a few works, like Toni *Morrison's **Sula* (1973) and Leon *Forrest's *The Bloodworth Orphans* (1977), that present an ironic or satiric interpretation of the Moses character type. In literary works like Ernest J. *Gaines's *The Autobiography of Miss Jane Pittman* (1971) and Margaret *Walker's *Jubilee* (1966) that attempt to chronicle an individual's or a group's particular struggle for civil rights, fictional characters frequently discuss or refer to Moses, in part to provide an example of a people who have already successfully struggled for their civil rights. For similar reasons, twentieth-century African American civil rights leaders have frequently mentioned Moses in their speeches and writings.

• H. Nigel Thomas, *From Folklore to Fiction,* 1988.

—Ted Olson

MOSLEY, WALTER (b. 1952), novelist. Born in 1952 to Leroy and Ella Mosley, Walter Ellis Mosley grew up in South Central Los Angeles, the setting for his first four novels. An intelligent and thoughtful young man but an indifferent student, Mosley eventually earned a degree in political science from Johnson State College in Vermont, then worked as a computer programmer for several years before enrolling in a creative writing program at City College New York. Lauded for his perfectly inflected dialogue, his simple but elegant prose, and his vivid characters, Golden Dagger prize-winner Walter Mosley's primary contributions to the detective genre are his hero, Ezekiel (Easy) Rawlins, and his expansion of the mystery novel to chronicle African American social history.

*Easy Rawlins is a working-class man, a reluctant private eye, prone to sleuthing mistakes and without the usual friends in the profession to ease his way. Easy succeeds because of his common sense, his integrity, and his community ties. Based upon Mosley's father and several acquaintances and created as a realistic black male hero, one who has "flaws that have to be overcome," Easy is divorced, has financial worries, and gets too involved with his clients. Easy has two adopted children: Jesus, a Mexican boy whose muteness testifies to his trauma as a child prostitute before Easy rescued him, and Feather, whose grandfather killed her mother because Feather's father was black. Easy wants what most men want: a house, a good income, a safe and happy family life; but he is also streetwise and capable of cruel vengeance. Easy's best friend, Raymond Alexander, better known as Mouse, is much less admirable and much more violent. Mouse does not hesitate to shoot a hogtied man first in the groin then the head in order to get a reluctant witness to provide information, and several times he almost shoots Easy over trifles. Mosley presents both as black male heroes. "Black male heroes are not sports stars or movies stars," Mosley asserts. Black male heroes are like Easy, "the guys who get up and go to work every day" and like Mouse who "demands and wins, at whatever cost, ultimate respect."

This unlikely duo dominates Walter Mosley's first four of a series recording experiences from post–World War II, when southern blacks optimistically arrived in southern California seeking and finding living wages and livable communities, to the present, which appears to offer less of both for most. Despite due attention to racism, discrimination, corruption, and other poisoners of dreams, Mosley's emphasis is upon resilience in the face of difficulties. As Malcolm Jones, Jr., says, "Easy Rawlins never whines."

Devil in a Blue Dress (1990) introduces Easy Rawlins, an intelligent and thoughtful veteran whose recent firing combined with an impending mortgage payment convinced him in 1948 to take the job of locating the missing Daphne Monet. *I* (1991) finds Easy in 1953 working as a janitor for and secretly buying the Magnolia Street Apartments when IRS troubles force him to spy on members of the First African Baptist Church, a decision that leads to his own investigation for murder. *White Butterfly* (1992) revolves around serial killings in 1956 that fail to interest law enforcement agents until Cyndi Starr, a stripper known as the "White Butterfly," who was also a white UCLA coed, is killed. In *Black Betty* (1994), it is 1961 and Easy, now forty-one years old, needs money to save his proposed neighborhood shopping mall from exploitative but politically powerful competitors. Easy discovers that the missing housekeeper a wealthy Beverly Hills family hires him to find is the same Elizabeth Eady he had a crush on when he was nine years old. Mosley plans to continue the saga until Easy is about seventy years old; but the protagonist of his current project is a jazz musician who travels back in time to study with bluesman Robert Johnson.

Mosley's popularity was not hurt by being named as President Bill Clinton's favorite writer. Readers also respond to his deliberate echoes of Raymond Chandler and Chester *Himes, and reviewers compare him to John D. MacDonald, Dashiell Hammett, Richard *Wright, and Ruldoph *Fisher. Both Valerie Wilson Wesley and Eleanor Brand have black single parent detectives, but they are female. Gar Anthony Haywood and Clifford Mason preceded Mosley with politically aware black private eyes. Playwright August *Wilson and novelist John Edgar *Wideman have created series that attempt to write ordinary black men into American social history. Walter Mosley stands alone, however, in his acclaimed combination of these and other elements as never before.

[*See also* Poinsettia Jackson.]

• Kristina L. Knotts, "Walter Mosley," in *Contemporary African American Novelists,* ed. Emmanuel S. Nelson, 1999, pp. 350–354. Robert Crooks, "From the Far Side of the Urban Fiction: The Detectives of Chester Himes and Walter Mosley" in *Race-ing Representation,* eds. Myrsiades, Kostos and Linda Myrsiades, pp. 175–200. Stephen Soitos, *The Blues Detective: A Study of African American Detective Fiction,* 1996.

—Frances Smith Foster

MOTLEY, WILLARD (1909–1965), novelist, journalist, diarist, and essayist. The second son of a Pullman porter, Willard Francis Motley was raised in the only African American family in a predominantly white middle-class neighborhood on Chicago's South Side. At age thirteen his first short story appeared in the *Chicago Defender.* Unable to attend college during the Great Depression, as a young adult he trekked across the country accumulating real life experiences that informed much of his writing. He moved from his parents' home into a dingy apartment in a Chicago slum to better observe the lower-class whites he intended to portray. Simultaneously, he established contact with and was encouraged by the city's leading proletarian writers: Alexander Saxton, William Shenck, and Jack Conroy. They introduced him to the writings of numerous classic and modern authors.

Cofounding a literary journal, signing up with the WPA *Federal Writers' Project in 1940, and the assistance of two fellowships allowed Motley to focus more of his attention on creative writing. He was determined to humanize and place in social context the characters he researched and of which he had firsthand knowledge via his previous experiences as a hobo, day laborer, and even a jail inmate, among other things. By 1943 he had essentially completed the first of his massive novels, *Knock on Any Door* (1947), the story of the transformation of an Italian American altar boy into a streetwise tough destined for the electric chair, which indicts the criminal justice system while evincing compassion for the denizens of a big city ghetto. The novel received wide critical acclaim and Motley's harsh, unrelenting realism invited comparisons with Richard *Wright and the revered naturalists Theodore Dreiser and Frank Norris. A best-seller, the novel was made into a motion picture starring Humphrey Bogart, as was its sequel, *Let No Man Write My Epitaph* (1958), which featured Shelley Winters. His two other novels—*We Fished All Night* (1951), about societal forces impinging on the lives of three returning military veterans, and *Let Noon Be Fair* (1966), a sprawling tale of the exploitation of a Mexican village—were markedly less successful.

His emphasis on universality and the near absence of African Americans as major characters in his work placed him in the company of several gifted African American authors who flirted with "raceless" or "assimilationist fiction" in the 1940s and 1950s. Unlike the others in this group, though, Motley eschewed writing long fiction concerning those of his race; his reputation and interest in his novels declined in succeeding decades partly as a result. Identifying himself as a member of no particular race save the human race, he publicly rebuked Chester *Himes and James *Baldwin (whom he called a "professional Negro") because he felt they portrayed virtually all whites as racist. Never married, Motley hoped to escape the cage of race, which he found increasingly discomforting, by immigrating to Mexico in 1951, where he adopted a son. At age fifty-five, surviving on meager royalty checks, he died of intestinal gangrene and was buried in Cuernavaca.

• Robert E. Fleming, *Willard Motley,* 1978. Willard Motley, *The Diaries of Willard Motley,* ed. Jerome Klinkowitz, 1979. John Conder, "The City in the Fiction of William Attaway and Willard Motley," in *The City in African-American Literature,* eds. Yoshinobu Hakutani and Robert Butler, 1995, pp. 110–22.

—Robert Fikes, Jr.

Mule Bone. In 1931 Zora Neale *Hurston and Langston *Hughes began to collaborate on a comedy called *Mule Bone.* They worked in secret because their patron, Charlotte Mason, disapproved of theatrical ventures. Hughes and Hurston were exploring a new concept of theater, free of the distortions of minstrelsy, to be based on daily rituals of life in African American communities and performed with music and dance. The collaboration produced bitter recriminations and charges of plagiarism but no play. Hurston and Hughes never spoke again, and their dream of a "real Negro theatre" was stillborn.

Based on a folktale, "The Bone of Contention," which Hurston had collected and Hughes adapted, *Mule Bone* was a series of oral and musical performances connected by the slenderest of plots. Guitar-playing Jim and dancing Dave are rivals for a woman, Daisy. When their musical and verbal dueling turns physical, Jim hits Dave with a mule bone. In the second act a trial divides the loyalties of the Eatonville townspeople: the Baptists versus the Methodists. The Baptist pastor demonstrates Jim's guilt by proving, according to scriptural citation, that a mule bone is a lethal weapon. Jim is expelled from Eatonville. In the final act Jim, Dave, and Daisy meet outside of town, and the two men reaffirm their friendship.

Mule Bone was finally produced by New York City's Lincoln Center in 1991, featuring veteran black performers and directed by Michael Schultz. A Hurston figure, dressed in the coat, hat, and fur skins familiar to many from an often reproduced photograph by Carl Van Vechten, provided a new prologue and coda. Crafted by editor George Bass, these monologues echo the introduction to Hurston's book of folklore, *Mules and Men.* Blues musician Taj Mahal composed the score, with most of the lyrics taken from Hughes's poetry. Reviews were mixed.

—Cheryl A. Wall

Mumbo Jumbo. Ishmael *Reed's third novel, *Mumbo Jumbo* (1972) is generally acknowledged to be his masterpiece. Complex, enigmatic, and ecstatic, it is impossible to summarize coherently with any brevity. Combining elements of collage, Marx Brothers movies, and film noir, illustrated histories, occult books, and the recombinant techniques of jazz improvisation, the novel seems as resistant to complete interpretation, to the extraction of all its "flavors," as a gumbo, that cross-cultural culinary achievement constituting Reed's favorite metaphor for an aesthetic capable of unlimited possibilities and rewards.

The main action takes place in the 1920s, the Jazz Age and time of the Harlem Renaissance when the Negro was "in vogue," but also, significantly, the age of Prohibition. Jes Grew, a "psychic plague" that threatens to free people from their inhibitions, is seeking its Text, the matrix that will give it legitimacy, while the Wallflower Order, agents of the forces of repression, strive to save "civilization as we know it"—that is, white, right, and uptight—from Jes Grew's positive vibrations. Working in this environment of clashing impulses, *Papa LaBas, a hoodoo detective, attempts to trace the missing Text and at the same time outwit the crusaders who are out to destroy it and thereby dissipate Jes Grew.

Reed adopts Nietzsche's vision of human history as a pendulum movement between opposing tendencies symbolized by the Greek gods Apollo (reason) and Dionysus (emotion), but Reed traces this polarity back to ancient Egypt—anterior to Greece—and the conflict between Osiris (the Egyptian Dionysus) and his brother/adversary Set, whom Reed sees as unnatural and obsessed with control. Jes Grew clearly is Osirian/Dionysian, while Set/Apollo are the progenitors of Jes Grew's eternal enemy, Atonism (named after the monotheism of the pharaoh Akhenaton), which in the novel represents rigid singularity of vision and belief, hostility to Nature, and a relentless drive to dominate. The struggle, as Reed portrays it, is one of puritanism versus paganism, knowledge versus "mumbo jumbo," the self-styled "universalism" of Western civilization versus the supposedly parochial cultures of the "underdeveloped" peoples of the world.

In an essay in *Obsidian* (Spring–Summer 1986), Lizabeth Paravisini discusses *Mumbo Jumbo* as a parody of the detective novel, in which crimes are solved by rational processes of investigation, whereas Papa LaBas employs "knockings" and astral procedures. But in a 1991 doctoral dissertation dealing with "detective undercurrents" in the work of several black novelists, Helen Mary Lock asserts that the story of Osiris provides the mythic framework for the African American detective tale, whose purpose is not to reveal "whodunit," but how to undo it. Mystery, moreover, is embraced, rather than dispelled. In this reading, *Mumbo Jumbo* fits into the tradition of the African American detective novel, which begins with Rudolph *Fisher's *The Conjure-Man Dies* (1932). In *Mumbo Jumbo,* the "conjure-man," Papa LaBas, lives and continues to fight the good fight against anti–Jes Grew forces, including the "crabs-in-a-barrel" syndrome found in Reed's next novel, *The *Last Days of Louisiana Red* (1974).

Darryl Pinckney (*New York Review of Books,* 12 Aug. 1989) calls *Mumbo Jumbo* Reed's "most ambitious" book, though Theodore O. Mason, Jr., in *Modern Fiction Studies* (Spring 1988), argues that Reed's elaborate intentions get the better of him. Acknowledging that it has flaws, Houston A. *Baker, Jr., nevertheless considers *Mumbo Jumbo* a work of genius (*Black World,* Dec. 1972). In fact, the book's appeal has been broad, as evidenced by the fact that it is on traditional scholar Harold Bloom's list of works that deserve inclusion in the Western literary canon, in addition to being one of the significant items in pop critic Nelson George's "Chronicle of Post-Soul Black Culture."

• Henry Louis Gates, Jr., "On 'The Blackness of Blackness': Ishmael Reed and a Critique of the Sign," in *The Signifying Monkey: A Theory of Afro-American Literary Criticism,* 1988, pp. 217–238.

—Robert Elliot Fox

MURPHY, BEATRICE M. (1908–1992), poet, editor, columnist, and reviewer. Born in Monessen, Pennsylvania, Beatrice Murphy lived most of her life in Washington, D.C. In 1928 she graduated from Dunbar High School and published her first poem. From 1933 to 1935 she was a columnist and for the next two years an editor at the *Washington Tribune.* Converting to Catholicism in 1938, she also became book review editor that year for the *Afro-American* and published her first poetry anthology, *Negro Voices.* She was also a secretary at Catholic University and part owner of a circulating library and stenography shop. She became a regular columnist for the Associated Negro Press and contributed poetry and reviews to numerous serials and collections. In the 1940s and 1950s she worked for the Office of Price Administration and then the Veterans Administration. In 1954 she was suspended without pay from her job as procurement clerk for supposedly having joined a subversive organization. She disproved the allegations and was reinstated four months later. She reported great bitterness over the incident but succeeded in recovering her fundamental optimism.

Her most important accomplishment in the 1960s was founding the Negro Bibliographic and Research Center and editing its journal, *Bibliographic Survey: The Negro in Print* (1965–1972). Active in charities and clubs, she continued her publishing career with a coauthored book of poems and an edited poetry anthology. She died of heart disease.

Murphy's major work of poetry, *Love Is a Terrible Thing* (1945), dramatizes the stages of love. Many of the poems are conventional in approach, but Murphy has some flair for vivid metaphor and asserts her freedom from her earlier stricter forms. Some of her strongest poems express desire, anger, or bitterness. Many of the later poems in the collection both vindicate youthful candor and lament its vulnerability. One of the most vivid extended images is of a scrapyard ("Salvage"), and one of the most poignant poems is "The Prostitute," in which the speaker welcomes Death into her bed for the price of peace. Murphy's later poems in *The Rocks Cry Out* (1969), while opposing the younger generation's violence, resemble the 1960s' "poetry-as-statement," as she called it, but show less vigor of imagery than her youthful poems.

As an editor of poetry anthologies, Murphy sought above all to give voice to young unknown writers. *Negro Voices* (1938) and *Ebony Rhythm* (1948) are dominated by college students and working amateurs. Perhaps as the result of Nikki *Giovanni's exasperation (expressed in a 1969 Negro Digest review) with her conservatism in *The Rocks Cry Out,* she included several of Giovanni's and Carolyn M. *Rodgers's poems in her last anthology, *New Negro Voices* (1970), and showed respect for the new militancy and black pride (though once again omitting poems with foul language). Her prefaces, essays, and reviews frequently acknowledge the difficulty African Americans have getting published in the white publishing industry, criticize white liberal hypocrisy, and encourage African American education.

Although Murphy wrote some creditable poems on a variety of compelling subjects, her importance may have been more as publicist and midwife to others' work.

• Nikki Giovanni, review of *The Rocks Cry Out, Negro Digest* 19 (Aug. 1969): 97–98. Lorraine Roses and Ruth Randolph, eds., *Harlem Renaissance and Beyond,* 1990, pp. 247–249.

—Larry R. Andrews

MURRAY, ALBERT (b. 1916), essayist, novelist, and cultural critic. Albert Murray's contribution to African American literature has established the value and importance of the blues idiom as the basis for approaching life as an African American. Whether writing fiction, social essays, book reviews, memoirs, aesthetic theory, or music criticism, Murray performs like the best-trained jazz musician. In his essays, Murray turns the basic beliefs of "social science fiction" inside out, exposing and playing on their assumptions just as Billie *Holiday created soul-stirring art out of trite popular tunes. In his fiction, Murray draws from the modernism of Thomas Mann, James Joyce, and William Faulkner in order to interpret the basic raw materials of growing up African American in the South, creating a style as innovative as the harmonically and rhythmically complex improvisations of Charlie *Parker. When his career is examined as a whole, Albert Murray seems similar to Duke Ellington, a modern composer for the entire orchestra of literary genres, capable of creating material suitable for the brassy tonalities of topical journalistic debate, the more somber muted timbres of philosophical reflection, and the soaring glissandos of the memoir and the bildungsroman. Murray's work in each of these genres is motivated by the hard-driving assertive rhythm section of a single idea—that the blues idiom represents an entire set of cultural equipment for living, an expansive range of styles and attitudes and possibilities for creating meaningful art, and a strategy for survival and even victory over racism in American society.

Born in Nokomis, Alabama, on 12 May 1916, Murray received his BS from Tuskegee Institute in 1939. He joined the air force in 1943 and retired with the rank of major in 1962. During his period in the service, Murray earned his MA from New York University (1948) and taught literature and composition to civilians and soldiers both in the United States and abroad. *The Omni-Americans* (1970), Murray's first book, contains reviews, essays, and commentaries that engage and challenge the predominant frameworks within which matters of race and culture were then being discussed. Critiquing what he called "the folklore of white supremacy and the fakelore of black pathology," the book argues that all Americans are multicolored and that social scientific attempts to explain black life in America are fundamentally mistaken. His next book, *South to a Very Old Place* (1971), extends that argument with a series of memoirs, interviews, and reports that document the positive nurturing aspects of the African American community in the South. In 1972, Albert Murray was invited to give the Paul Anthony Brick Lectures on Ethics at the University of Missouri. These lecturers were published as *The Hero and the Blues* (1973). Here Murray develops his concept of literature in the blues idiom, a theory he eloquently practiced in the novel *Train Whistle Guitar* (1974), which won the Lillian Smith Award for Southern Fiction. The hero of this novel receives from his family and neighbors in the segregated South the cultural equipment necessary for leading a successful life—a sense of fundamental individual worth combined with community responsibility akin to the relationship between the improvising jazz soloist and the supporting band. In 1976, Murray turned the concept of the blues idiom back on itself, writing perhaps the best book ever published on jazz aesthetics, *Stomping the Blues.* Murray collaborated with Count Basie on his autobiography, *Good Morning, Blues* (1985), and in 1991 published *The Spyglass Tree,* the long-awaited sequel to his first novel. A catalog essay on the paintings of Romare Bearden (*Romare Bearden, Finding the Rhythm,* 1991), extends Murray's concepts of improvisation, rhythm, and synthesis even to the realm of the visual arts. *Blue Devils of NADA* (1996) contains further meditations on blues and jazz greats, while Murray's third novel, *The Seven League Boots* (1996), brings the hero of *Train Whistle Guitar* and *The Spyglass Tree* to maturity as a bass player in a touring jazz band.

For Murray, the blues idiom functions like classical tragedy, as a means for making the best out of a very bad situation. Like tragedy, the blues idiom contains a stylistic code for representing the most difficult conditions, but it also provides a strategy for living with and triumphing over these conditions with dignity, grace, and elegance. As in any highly developed aesthetic form, the blues idiom enables the artist to transform stylistically the grit of raw experience into art of tremendous and subtle beauty. But the blues idiom is distinguished from tragedy in that it has grown out of the specific historical experiences of, and the cultural resources developed by, African Americans. Whether made manifest in literature, the visual arts, or music, the blues idiom challenges and affirms an individual's basic humanity and higher aspirations "in spite of the fact that human existence is so often mostly a low-down dirty shame."

• James Alan McPherson, "The View from the Chinaberry Tree," *Atlantic* 234 (Dec. 1974): 11, 88, 120–123. John Wideman, "Stomping the Blues: Ritual in Black Music and Speech," *American Poetry Review* 7.4 (1978): 42–45. Elizabeth Schultz, "Albert L. Murray," in *DLB*, vol. 38, *Afro-American Writers after 1955: Dramatists and Prose Writers*, eds. Thadious M. Davis and Trudier Harris, 1985, pp. 214–224. John Gennari, "Jazz Criticism: Its Development and Ideologies," *Black American Literature Forum* 23.3 (Fall 1991): 449–523. Warren Carson, "Albert Murray: Literary Reconstruction of the Vernacular Community," *African American Review* 27.2 (1993): 287–295. Roberta S. Maguire, *Conversations with Albert Murray*, 1997.

—Barry Shank

MURRAY, PAULI (1910–1985), poet, biographer, historian, lawyer, teacher, activist, and priest. Born in Baltimore, Pauli Murray was orphaned at age three and raised by her mother's sister in the home of her maternal grandparents (the Fitzgeralds) in Durham, North Carolina. The Fitzgerald family had a profound influence on Murray throughout her life. The aunt who raised her was a teacher, and Murray learned to read and write at a very early age. Her grandfather, wounded in the Civil War as a Union soldier, and among those who set up the first schools for free blacks in North Carolina and Virginia, and her grandmother, daughter of a prominent white North Carolinian and a slave woman, served as strong examples of fortitude. Education, equal rights, and personal faith and courage are themes connecting the various spheres of Murray's work and life.

Murray received her BA from Hunter College in New York in 1933, with an English major and a minor in history. This was the time of the Harlem Renaissance, and Murray had the opportunity to meet figures such as Dorothy *West, Countee *Cullen, Sterling A. *Brown, and Robert *Hayden, as well as Langston *Hughes, who helped her to publish her first poem, "The Song of the Highway," in Nancy Cunard's 1934 anthology, *Color.* At Hunter she also encountered Stephen Vincent Benét—not in person, but through his poem "John Brown's Body," which strongly affected her. It was seven years, however, before she introduced herself to Benét, sending him an early version of what was to become the poem "Dark Testament." When she did, he offered encouragement and served as her literary mentor until his death in 1943.

Murray's social and spiritual concerns took her beyond writing, however. She received her initial degree in law from Howard University in 1944. Denied entry to the graduate program at Harvard because she was a woman, Murray received her LLM (1945) from the University of California at Berkeley instead. She practiced law in California and New York and earned the JD from Yale (1965), eventually teaching at Yale and Brandeis, and in Ghana. During the 1940s Murray worked briefly for the National Urban League and was one of the original "freedom riders" protesting bus segregation. She worked to further education rights, bringing legal action against universities for denying women admission to their graduate schools. Murray also was one of the founders of NOW, the National Organization for Women, and in 1977 she was among the first ten women ordained in the Episcopal Church—the first African American woman ever to hold that office.

Years of historical research went into Murray's first major literary publication, *Proud Shoes: The Story of an American Family* (1956). Tracing the Fitzgerald family history from the time of slavery, it looks unflinchingly at issues of racism, sexism, and miscegenation. Critics have praised its willingness to address the full range of African American experience, in order to claim a past that is both honest and "usable," and it has been read as a microcosm of African American history as well.

Her second major work, *Dark Testament and Other Poems* (1970), is a collection written over four decades (although most were written in Harlem in the late 1930s). Murray began the long title poem in New York in the 1930s, finishing it during the Harlem riot of 1943. A history of American race relations, it emphasizes imagination as a tool to face and transform a painful past, and draws on religious language and imagery both to encourage the oppressed and to challenge the oppressor. The collection is diverse, and it connects different historical periods and various groups who share "the dream of freedom." The book reflects, in fact, Murray's own breadth of experience and the range of her social and spiritual vision.

In both works Murray demonstrates her lifelong concern for social and spiritual integration, making various connections: between white and African American history; between African Americans and other cultural "outsiders" in America; between literature and activism; between family and nation; and among the past, present, and future. Facing the tension between different perspectives and goals within herself and in her world was sometimes a difficult task. In the poem "Conflict," for example, Murray describes her anxiety over the poet and the warrior grappling in her brain. Consistently, however, she found the encouragement—in history and faith and among activists and poets—to apply her varied gifts to a common cause. When she died in 1985 Murray was preparing another personal history for publication, her memoir *Song in a Weary Throat* (1987; reprinted as *Pauli Murray: The Autobiography of a Black Activist* in 1989), which traces the author's lifelong journey as both political pioneer and spiritual pilgrim. Although this deeply spiritual autobiography ends, rather than begins, with a call to ordained ministry, this conclusion to her final book testifies to the interwoven character of all Murray's previous struggles and vocations.

• Nellie McKay, "Pauli Murray," in *DLB*, vol. 41, *Afro-American Poets since 1955*, eds. Trudier Harris and Thadious M. Davis, 1985, pp. 248–251.

—Sheila Hassell Hughes

My Bondage and My Freedom. Frederick *Douglass's second autobiography, *My Bondage and My Freedom,* published by the New York commercial publishers Miller, Orton, and Mulligan in 1855, is larger, more self-consciously literary, and more self-analytical than the **Narrative of the Life of Frederick Douglass* (1845). From its opening pages, where the African American abolitionist James McCune Smith, known for his vehement criticism of William Lloyd Garrison, supplants Douglass's former mentor as prefacer of the memoir, *My Bondage and My Freedom* shows that it is more than a mere updated installment of the *Narrative.* The second autobiography offers a thoughtful revision of the meaning and goals of Douglass's life.

My Bondage and My Freedom introduces few incidents or figures from Douglass's past that do not appear in the *Narrative.* But the second autobiography says more about Douglass's complex relationship to his environment, particularly in the South, than emerges in the more famous fugitive slave narrative. Douglass's grandmother, who appears in the *Narrative* only in the throes of a pathetic death, becomes the able and self-sufficient Betsey Bailey in the opening chapters of *My Bondage and My Freedom,* respectfully portrayed as the creator of the only real home young Frederick ever knew as a slave. Douglass's master, Aaron Anthony, tersely indicted in the *Narrative* as "a cruel man," is rehabilitated in *My Bondage and My Freedom* into "a wretched man" who could be "almost fatherly" toward Frederick when not tormented by his passions and bad temper. The slave youth engaged in a lonely struggle for direction and dignity in the *Narrative* finds much inspiration and support within the southern African American community as depicted in *My Bondage and My Freedom* and epitomized in Charles Lawson, unmentioned in the *Narrative* but dubbed by Douglass in 1855 his "spiritual father." The high seriousness of the *Narrative*'s rendition of Douglass's climactic hand-to-hand struggle with the satanic Maryland slave-breaker Edward Covey is tempered comically in *My Bondage and My Freedom* so as to emphasize Douglass's common humanity rather than his outsized heroism.

In 1845, Douglass brought his life story to a glorious culmination with an image of himself proclaiming the antislavery gospel from the lecture platform, a fugitive slave fully enlisted in the abolitionist crusade. Ten years later a chastened Douglass testified to the prejudice and paternalism among the Garrisonian abolitionists that caused him eventually to break from their ranks. Whereas the *Narrative* says almost nothing about northern racism, the better to draw a diametric opposition between the "free" North and the slave South, *My Bondage and My Freedom* catalogs the many forms of segregation that Douglass encountered after his escape from slavery. Realizing the subtle bondage of racist paternalism in the North as well as the South, Douglass announces at the end of *My Bondage and My Freedom* his conviction that the best way to attack slavery in the South is to immerse himself in the cause of the quasi-free African Americans of the North. Thus Douglass moves away from the individualism of the *Narrative* and toward a greater communal identification in *My Bondage and My Freedom.*

• William L. Andrews, *To Tell a Free Story: The First Century of Afro-American Autobiography, 1760–1865,* 1986. Frederick Douglass, *My Bondage and My Freedom,* ed. William L. Andrews, 1987. Eric J. Sundquist, *To Wake the Nations: Race in the Making of American Literature,* 1993.

—William L. Andrews

MYERS, WALTER DEAN (b. 1937), poet, editor, and novelist. A versatile and prolific writer, Walter Dean Myers (also Walter M. Myers) has published short fiction, essays, and poetry in such disparate periodicals as the *Liberator, Negro Digest, McCall's, Essence, Espionage,* and *Alfred Hitchcock's Mystery Magazine.* He was a regular contributor to men's magazines until, as he says, "they gave themselves up to pornography." In 1968, he wrote his first children's book as an entry to a contest sponsored by the Council on Interracial Books for Children. He won, *Where Does the Day Go?* was published by *Parent's Magazine* Press, and thus began his career as a writer of children's and young adult literature. To date, Myers has published nearly sixty books, many of which have earned awards and citations such as the American Library Association Best Book for Young Adults, the Newbery Honor Book, the *Boston Globe*/Horn Book Honor Book, and the Coretta Scott King Award. In 1994, Walter Dean Myers was honored by the American Library Association and School Library Journal with a Lifetime Achievement Award.

Myers writes fantasy with black characters (*The Golden Serpent,* 1980, and *The Legend of Tarik,* 1981). He retells his father's and grandfather's ghost stories and legends (*The Black Pearl and the Ghost,* 1980, and *Mr. Monkey and the Gotcha Bird,* 1984). His adventure tales take black adolescents to Peruvian jungles and Hong Kong temples (*The Nicholas Factor,* 1983, and *The Hidden Shrine,* 1985). His nonfiction is often innovative in form and subject matter. In *Sweet Illusions* (1987), Myers examines pregnancy through the stories of fourteen teenage mothers, fathers, and their friends and relatives. Each chapter ends with blank pages for readers to complete the ending. His biography of *Malcolm X (1994) uses actual photographs and inserts from newspapers, interviews, and magazines to create an inspirational and provocative book. Myers pairs poems and commentary to turn-of-the-century photographs of African American children in *Brown Angels* (1993) and Jacob Lawrence's pictures in *The Great Migration* (1994).

Walter Dean Myers is best known, however, for his young adult novels about Harlem residents. Like many black writers, Myers loved to read but rarely encountered books about people like him or his friends and family. This desire to fill a void, to create for other youth that which had been lacking in his own adolescence, was further motivated by his displeasure with the prevalent images of African Americans as exotics, misfits, criminals, victims, and "unserious" people. Having grown up in Harlem, he was particularly upset by the negative and monolithic portrayals of that community. Myers's stories usually take place within a Harlem community of diverse people who love, laugh, work, and dream as much as any other people in the world. Though praised for his natural dialogues, his optimistic endings, and his eccentric but loveable characters, Myers does not romanticize. Drugs and violence, loneliness and indifference, sex, religion, economics, and other oppressive and challenging agencies figure into his plots. In *It Ain't All for Nothin'* (1978), Tippy's grandmother is put into a nursing home and his ex-convict father involves him in a robbery. Steve's parents in *Won't Know Till I Get There* (1982) try to rehabilitate a troubled teen only to have their middle-class child and his friends end up in juvenile court. Lonnie Jackson escapes Harlem with an athletic scholarship but the predominantly white midwestern college presents a new set of problems in *The Outside Shot* (1984). Richie Perry's escape, on the other hand, moves him from the frying pan of Harlem to the fire of Vietnam in *Fallen Angels* (1989). Myers tends to focus upon male relationships but his female protagonists are neither stereotypical nor predictable. *Crystal* (1987) presents a sixteen-year-old fashion model and actress whose meteoric rise does not satisfy her. In *Motown and Didi: A Love Story* (1984), a disciplined and intelligent student's college career is jeopardized by her brother's drug addiction and her mother's mental instability. Each individual works out her or his own destiny, but each comes to recognize and value supportive relationships.

As a member of John O. *Killen's writers workshop, Walter Dean Myers practiced his craft with Wesley Brown, George Davis, and Askia M. *Touré. When he became an editor at Bobbs-Merrill in 1970, Myers learned not only the business of publishing that helped his own career, but he published fellow writers Nikki *Giovanni, Ann Allen *Shockley, and Richard Perry. Among the African American writers who served as his literary models, Myers names Frank *Yerby and his Harlem neighbor and fellow children's book writer, Langston *Hughes. Today, Walter Dean Myers ranks with Virginia *Hamilton and Lucille *Clifton as the foremost writers in children's and young adult literature.

• Rudine Sims Bishop, *Presenting Walter Dean Myers,* 1990. *Something about the Author,* vol. 71, ed. Diane Telgen, 1993, pp. 133–137. Karen Patricia Smith, ed. *African American Voices in Young Adult Literature: Tradition, Transition, Transformation,* 1994. Diane Patrick-Wexler, *Walter Dean Myers,* 1996. Terry Novak, "Walter Dean Myers," in *Contemporary African American Novelists,* ed., Emmanuel S. Nelson, 1999, pp. 360–365.

—Frances Smith Foster

N

NANNY. A character in Zora Neale *Hurston's novel **Their Eyes Were Watching God* (1937), Nanny is protagonist *Janie Crawford's grandmother. A domestic servant who was born a slave, Nanny has raised and sheltered her granddaughter. When sixteen-year-old Janie begins to consider her own dreams and desires, Nanny interposes a different vision. She compels Janie to marry an older man, Logan Killicks, whose sixty acres and a mule constitute his eligibility. For Nanny the marriage represents an opportunity for Janie to sit on the pedestal reserved for southern white women, far above the drudgery that has characterized Nanny's life and made the black woman "de mule uh de world." But by denying Janie the right to follow her dreams, Nanny inhibits her quest for selfhood.

Nanny's history explains her flawed vision. As a slave, Nanny was impregnated by her master. In freedom her best efforts fail to protect her daughter. Using the metaphor of the pulpit, the devoutly Christian Nanny speaks of lost possibilities: "Ah wanted to preach a great sermon about colored women sittin' on high, but they wasn't no pulpit for me." She has saved the text for Janie, who, as long as Nanny lives, cannot resist her commands.

Physically ravaged by age, oppressed, and impoverished, Nanny derives her power from her ability to manipulate African American expressive codes. Even without a pulpit, Nanny is a powerful preacher whose metaphors fuse the biblical and the domestic in arresting ways. She is an accomplished storyteller and skilled slave narrator as well.

[*See also* Tea Cake.]

—Cheryl A. Wall

Narrative of the Life of Frederick Douglass. The epitome of the antebellum fugitive slave narrative, Frederick *Douglass's *Narrative* was published in May 1845 by the American Anti-Slavery Society of Boston. Priced at fifty cents a copy, the *Narrative*'s first printing of five thousand sold out in four months. To satisfy demand, four additional reprintings of two thousand copies each were brought out within a year. By 1850 approximately thirty thousand copies of the *Narrative* had been sold in the United States and Great Britain. In 1846, a Dutch translation and in 1848, a French translation of the *Narrative* helped spread Douglass's fame on the European continent. Sales were helped greatly by positive reviews that compared Douglass's style to that of John Bunyan and Daniel Defoe. The fact that the *Narrative* bore the subtitle "Written by Himself" witnessed powerfully to the capacity of the African American, even when oppressed through years of slavery, to speak eloquently on his own behalf against social and economic injustice.

The self-consciousness of the writing in the *Narrative* attests to Douglass's determination to make his story not merely an exposé of the evils of slavery but also an exploration of the mind of a slave aspiring to freedom. The key to the originality and import of Douglass's rendition of his life, in contrast to that of most other fugitive slave narrators, is his emphasis on the psychological and intellectual struggle that he waged against slavery from his early childhood on Maryland's Eastern Shore. The *Narrative* recounts Douglass's boyhood as a series of challenges to white authorities intent on preventing him from achieving knowledge of himself and his relationship to the outside world. Resistance to slavery takes the form of an early clandestine pursuit of literacy. Armed with the power to read and write, the young slave graduates to a culminating physical rebellion against a slave-breaker, Edward Covey. Douglass's reputation as a fighter gives him a leadership role in the slave community, which he uses to teach other slaves to read and then to engineer a runaway plot. The first attempt for freedom fails, but a second try, in early September 1838, successfully conveys Douglass to New York City. In the last chapter of the *Narrative,* Douglass recounts his marriage, his integration into a new life of independence and self-sufficiency in the North, and, climactically, his discovery of a vocation as a speaker for the American Anti-Slavery Society.

In addition to what it did to open up the minds of whites in the North about the injustice of slavery, Douglass's *Narrative* also inspired a number of major early African American writers, including William Wells *Brown and Harriet A. *Jacobs, to undertake literary careers of their own. The *Narrative* is recognized today as a classic narrative of ascent from South to North in the African American literary canon, and a lasting contribution to the portrait of the romantic individualist in nineteenth-century American literature.

• William L. Andrews, *To Tell a Free Story: The First Century of Afro-American Autobiography, 1760–1865,* 1986. William L. Andrews, ed., *Critical Essays on Frederick Douglass,* 1991.

—William L. Andrews

Native Son. Published in 1940, Richard *Wright's *Native Son* was the first novel by an African American writer to be a Book-of-the-Month Club selection. *Native Son* tells the story of *Bigger Thomas, an angry and vicious young black ghetto dweller who at first has little to recommend him beyond his membership in the human race.

The novel opens early one morning with Bigger killing a huge rat that has invaded the kitchenette in which he, his mother, sister, and brother live. After promising his mother he will keep an interview appointment for a job as a chauffeur, he meets his "gang" and starts a fight with one of them in order to conceal his fear of robbing a white grocer—his fear of whites leads him to believe he will be sought, captured, and severely punished. Later he goes to the interview and is hired as chauffeur to the Dalton family. His first assignment is to drive *Mary Dalton to a lecture at the university, but instead of going to a lecture, she meets her Communist boyfriend, Jan. At dinner in a ghetto restaurant, where Bigger is known, neither Mary nor Jan realizes the extent to which they at once condescend to Bigger and violate his sensitivities. The meal finished, Bigger drives Mary and Jan around the city while they drink and make love in the backseat. Jan leaves and Bigger takes Mary home, but she is too drunk to walk. Bigger carries her into her bedroom. Sexually aroused, he kisses her and fondles her breasts. The door opens and the blind Mrs. Dalton enters the room. Bigger, terrified, holds a pillow over Mary's face to keep her quiet. When Mrs. Dalton eventually leaves the room, Mary has suffocated. Bigger carries her body to the basement and stuffs it in the furnace. He later imagines that her death was intentional, that he is transformed by having stepped beyond the boundaries limiting him, and decides to assert his control by writing a note demanding ransom and signed "Red." When Mary's body is discovered, Bigger flees. Later, afraid of betrayal, he brutally murders his girlfriend Bessie. After a massive manhunt through the city, Bigger is captured and imprisoned.

The final section of the novel, "Fate" (following "Fear" and "Flight"), shows Bigger's trial and the racist outpouring of hatred and bigotry that it elicits. Whereas Bigger's fate is a foregone conclusion, the final disposition of his psyche is not. Through conversations with his lawyer, Max, Bigger mulls over his situation and finally comes to accept himself as the person who killed two people because of his irrational fear of whites. "What I killed for I am," he says at the end of the novel. Thus, prior to his execution he sees that his experience as a black person in his ghetto has created him.

—Donald B. Gibson

NAYLOR, GLORIA (b. 1950), novelist, essayist, screenplay writer, columnist, and educator. Gloria Naylor was born in New York City on 25 January to Roosevelt and Alberta McAlpin Naylor, who had recently migrated northward from their native Robinsonville, Mississippi. Having worked as cotton sharecroppers in Mississippi, her father became a transit worker for the New York City subway system and her mother a telephone operator. Naylor, who was a very shy child, grew up in New York City, where she lived until she graduated from high school in 1968.

From shortly after her graduation until 1975, Naylor worked as a missionary for the Jehovah's Witnesses in New York, North Carolina, and Florida. Eventually deciding that missionary life and the Jehovah's Witnesses were not for her, Naylor returned to New York City and attended college while working as a telephone operator in several different hotels. Although she studied nursing for a short time at Medgar Evers College, she soon decided to pursue a BA in English at Brooklyn College, from which she graduated in 1981. Next Naylor entered Yale University on a fellowship and received an MA in Afro-American studies there in 1983. Having published her first novel, The **Women of Brewster Place*, in 1982, she wrote for her master's thesis at Yale what would become her second novel, *Linden Hills* (published 1985).

In 1983 Naylor's literary career took off mainly because of the attention she received for her first book. *The Women of Brewster Place* was granted the American Book Award for Best First Novel that year, and Naylor received the annual Distinguished Writer Award from the Mid-Atlantic Writers Association. In 1983 she also served as writer in residence at Cummington Community of the Arts and as a visiting lecturer at George Washington University. During the 1980s Naylor had jobs at numerous other institutions, including working as a cultural exchange lecturer in India for the United States Information Agency, and teaching at Yale, the University of Pennsylvania, New York University, Princeton, Boston, Brandeis, and Cornell. Naylor also received several prestigious awards, such as a National Endowment for the Arts Fellowship in 1985, the 1986 Candace Award from the National Coalition of One Hundred Black Women, a Guggenheim Fellowship in 1988, and the 1989 Lillian Smith Award.

Since Naylor began publishing in the early 1980s, she has produced five novels: *The Women of Brewster Place* (1982), *Linden Hills* (1985), **Mama Day* (1988), *Bailey's Cafe* (1992), and *The Men of Brewster Place* (1998). In addition to these primary works, she has also published essays—including a column in the *New York Times* in 1986 and a scholarly piece, "Love and Sex in the Afro-American Novel," which was published in the *Yale Review* in 1988—and has written several unproduced screenplays. Another important publication is "A Conversation" between Naylor and Toni *Morrison, which appeared in the *Southern Review* in 1985. She edited *Children of the Night: The Best Short Stories by Black Writers 1967 to the Present* in 1995.

Naylor's first novel, *The Women of Brewster Place*, consists of the interrelated tales of seven African American women who all end up on a dead-end street in a northern ghetto. Ranging in age from their twenties to their fifties, these characters have often suffered greatly because of the insensitive behavior of men. The protagonist of the novel, Mattie Michael, has found disaster in just about every interaction she has had with a man. Although her father in rural Tennessee is sternly caring during her childhood, his reaction to her later pregnancy is violent. And her son, Basil, who Mattie spoils, betrays his mother when she puts up her house as collateral for his bail: his pretrial flight instead of facing murder charges forces her to move to Brewster Place.

Most of the other women in the novel also suffer male exploitation. For instance, although Etta Mae Johnson, Mattie's childhood friend, sometimes has control in her relations with men, Etta's lifelong dependence on them for support and identity leads to trouble. In addition, Lucielia Louise Turner (Ciel) reluctantly undergoes an abortion to try to hold onto her husband, who is threatening to leave. Indirectly resulting from the neglect created by this upheaval, their toddler daughter sticks a fork into an electrical outlet and dies. Ciel's horrified reaction almost kills her, but Mattie intervenes.

Other women exploited by men in *The Women of Brewster Place* include Cora Lee, whose addiction to having babies leads to her frequent and casual sexual encounters. But the most horrific incident of this sort in the novel occurs when Lorraine is raped by C. C. Baker and his gang of hoodlums. Because of the gang members' homophobia regarding Lorraine's lesbian relationship with Theresa, they feel compelled to teach her a lesson.

Ben, the one partially positive male character in the novel, is nevertheless flawed by his excessive drinking and by his earlier passive complicity when his daughter was repeatedly taken advantage of sexually. Ironically, this relatively likable man is bludgeoned to death beside the Brewster Place wall by Lorraine when she is deranged after being raped. The novel ends when all the women cathartically destroy the wall that has cut them off from the rest of the city—and from their chances for better lives.

Naylor's second novel, *Linden Hills* (1985), is loosely based on Dante's *Inferno,* but the hell she creates is in a middle-class neighborhood. Controlled by the Lucifer-like Luther Nedeed, who is an undertaker, Linden Hills consists of a sloping spiral of streets that become more elite as one nears the bottom of the hill, where Nedeed lives. In a fated pattern of reproduction, several generations of nearly identical Luther Nedeeds are born in Linden Hills, with their primary purposes in life being to continue their lineage and to reign over the growing neighborhood.

During the contemporary time of the novel, Luther Nedeed presides over an affluent, middle-class community where "successful" African Americans essentially sell their souls in order to live there. Luther's grand scheme, however, is thwarted by his wife, Willa, who bears him a son according to plan, but this son is too pale to fulfill his role as his father's replica. Wrongly accusing Willa of infidelity with a white man, Luther locks her up in the cellar, which was originally a morgue, with their son, who eventually dies there. While trapped, Willa explores relics left by her predecessors and eventually learns to assert her right to exist. The resultant action, however, causes the destruction of the Nedeed house by fire and Willa's and Luther's deaths—all on Christmas Eve.

Meanwhile, two young men, Willie and Lester, journey around Linden Hills seeking odd jobs. Their interaction with the neighborhood residents reveals the hollowness of the rich, as well as the comparable depth of those less wealthy. Willie and Lester serve as Naylor's equivalent of Vergil and Dante as they traverse the hellish terrain of Linden Hills. This Dantean parallel is effectively developed, including the two poets' escape over water (the moat around the Nedeed house) at the novel's end.

With her third novel, *Mama Day* (1988), Naylor has received the most praise. As the story of the title character and her great-niece, Ophelia (Cocoa) Day, this work fully develops Naylor's themes of magic, myth, and family. Naylor superimposes the two settings of Willow Springs—an island off the coast between (but not in) South Carolina and Georgia—and New York City, thereby contrasting the philosophical differences between Cocoa and her husband, George Andrews. In a 1989 interview with Nicholas Shakespeare, Naylor said that her purpose in *Mama Day* was to analyze the makeup of individual belief, as well as what constitutes individual definitions of reality. During the course of the novel, she compares her depictions of magic and personal faith with the willing suspension of disbelief that all readers of fiction undergo.

Following a prologue that explains the history of Willow Springs, and which is narrated by the collective consciousness of the island itself, part 1 of the novel primarily consists of exchanges between Cocoa and George. Although George is already dead during the time of these narrated memories, he and Cocoa continue to commune from beyond the grave. Focusing on New York City, where Cocoa and George meet and eventually marry, part 1 also introduces Miranda (Mama) Day, the matriarch of Willow Springs, and her sister, Abigail, Cocoa's grandmother. Mama Day is a midwife, healer, root doctor, herbalist, and, if the reader chooses to interpret Naylor's ambiguous signals this way, a conjure woman.

Part 2 of *Mama Day* depicts the events that occur after George and Cocoa travel to Willow Springs. Following a tremendous storm, the bridge connecting the island to the mainland washes away. Cocoa then becomes dangerously ill, apparently as a result of poisoning and conjuring by Ruby, an intensely jealous woman. In order to save his wife, George must suspend rational thought and fully accept the mystical ways of the island. Although his love for Cocoa almost makes him capable of this leap of faith, ultimately he cannot believe what the island and Mama Day demand of him. George's already weakened heart fails and he dies. Yet, partly because of George's sacrifice, Cocoa recovers. The novel's close in 1999, also the time of its beginning, shows Cocoa poised to succeed the 105-year-old Mama Day as the island's spiritual leader.

Naylor's novel *Bailey's Cafe* (1992) shows her continuing experimentation with patterns of narration, definitions of reality, and depiction of the supernatural. Centered on the New York City restaurant of its title and set in the late 1940s, the novel is orchestrated by the unnamed cafe owner, who is called Bailey. Bailey and his wife, Nadine, run the all-night eatery, which serves as a way station for lost souls of various backgrounds. Behind the cafe is the novel's most mystical realm: a dock on the water that is capable of transforming reality to match the expectations and needs of the wretched folks who come there.

One such character in need is Sadie, whose violent childhood at the hands of a drug-addicted prostitute mother leads her to seek quiet and cleanliness. Yet after Sadie's dream of having a home of her own is hopelessly thwarted, she escapes into alcoholism and works as a whore, earning only enough to support her habit of cheap wine. When Iceman Jones, another cafe customer, offers to fulfill her dream of security, her fantasy back behind the restaurant wins out over reality.

Just down the street from the cafe is Eve's place, a brothel that only takes fresh flowers for payment. Presided over by Eve, who has suffered unspeakable abuse from her godfather in Louisiana, this establishment only accepts the particular women whose horrific backgrounds Eve can relate to. One of its residents, Peaches, is so haunted by her own beauty that she slashes her face in order to curb unwanted male attention. Another inhabitant, Jesse Bell, is a bisexual heroin addict whom Eve helps recover by means of brutal, hellish temptation. This unique boardinghouse is cleaned and protected by Miss Maple (Stanley), a heterosexual transvestite who wears women's clothes simply because he finds them more comfortable. While searching for a job after receiving his doctorate in mathematics from Stanford, Miss Maple discovers the impenetrable wall of racism in corporate America. Eventually giving up, Miss Maple seeks a gun in Gabe's pawnshop, but then stumbles into Bailey's Cafe, meets Eve, and finds his home.

The most startling section of *Bailey's Cafe* concerns Mariam, a fourteen-year-old Ethiopian Jew, who is expecting a baby and who is also a virgin. Having experienced genital mutilation in her homeland, Mariam inexplicably becomes pregnant and still insists on her innocence. After she is expelled from her village, she makes her way to Addis Ababa and then somehow ends up on the doorstep belonging to Gabe, who is a Russian Jew. Eve takes her in and then arranges for Mariam to give birth in a "proper" but fantastical setting behind the cafe, which transforms into the ceremonial hut of her native Ethiopian village. Although Mariam eventually dies, her son, George, survives and is placed in an orphanage. Interestingly, Naylor makes it clear that he is the same character as George Andrews, one of the protagonists of *Mama Day.*

In *The Men of Brewster Place,* Naylor revisits the territory she explored in her 1992 novel. She gives voice to many of the silent and violent men who made miserable the lives of the women in that novel. Noteworthy among her creations is Basil, the young man for whom Mattie Michael lost her house when he jumped bail after having killed a man. Naylor revisits a tortured, guilt-ridden young man who tries to make up for past deeds by allowing himself to be used in the present action. Similar efforts to atone for past actions inform other characterizations, but Naylor also adds a couple of new faces into the mix. Perhaps a response to criticism about her treatment of men in *The Women of Brewster Place* and other works, the companion novel is intriguing but is perhaps ultimately not as well executed.

Naylor's important contributions to African American literature include her expansion of narrative technique and privileging of the supernatural—both approaches similar to those used by Toni Morrison. Naylor's interrelated fictive terrain also resonates with the Yoknapatawpha County of William Faulkner, whose narrative style she has cited as an influence, especially on *Mama Day.* Gloria Naylor's most lasting contribution to literature may well be her vivid portraits of fascinating and fantastic characters.

• G. Michelle Collins, "There Where We Are Not: The Magical Real in *Beloved* and *Mama Day,*" *Southern Review* 24 (1988): 680–685. Larry R. Andrews, "Black Sisterhood in Gloria Naylor's Novels," *CLA Journal* 33 (Sept. 1989): 1–25. Gloria Naylor, interview by Nicholas Shakespeare, *Institute of Contemporary Arts—"Guardian" Conversations,* directed by Fenella Greenfield, 1989. Barbara Christian, "Gloria Naylor's Geography: Community, Class, and Patriarchy in *The Women of Brewster Place* and *Linden Hills,*" in *Reading Black, Reading Feminist,* ed. Henry Louis Gates, Jr., 1990, pp. 348–373. Henry Louis Gates, Jr., and K. A. Appiah, eds., *Gloria Naylor: Critical Perspectives Past and Present,* 1993. Michelle C. Loris and Sharon Felton, eds., *The Critical Response to Gloria Naylor,* 1997. Patricia Hopkins Lattin, "Naylor's Engaged and Empowered Narrative," *College Language Association Journal* 41:4 (June 1998): 452–469. Fred Metting, "The Possibilities of Flight: The Celebration of Our Wings in *Song of Solomon, Praisesong for the Widow,* and *Mama Day,*" *Southern Folklore* 55:2 (1998): 145–168.

—Kristine A. Yohe

NEAL, LARRY (1937–1981), poet, essayist, editor, playwright, critic, filmmaker, folklorist, and one of the Black Arts movement's spiritual journeymen. Born Lawrence Paul Neal to Woodie and Maggie Neal in Atlanta, Georgia, on 5 September 1937, Neal grew up in Philadelphia with his four brothers. Larry Neal graduated from Lincoln University and then completed a master's degree at the University of Pennsylvania. He spent most of his adult life in New York.

Although he was a prolific essayist, Neal is perhaps best known for editing *Black Fire: An Anthology of Afro-American Writing* with Amiri *Baraka. This collection, published in 1968, was among the early attempts to define the aesthetic of the new Black Arts movement. Neal's essays included in *Black Fire* and elsewhere are recognized as some of the most cogent statements of that aesthetic. Neal was committed to politics in his life and writing; but he insisted on artistic rigor as well as revoluntary intent in literature.

Neal produced reviews of artists ranging from Lorraine *Hansberry to Ornette Coleman. His critical essays—on social issues, aesthetic theory, literary topics, and other subjects—appeared in such periodicals as *Liberator Magazine, Negro Digest, Essence,* and *Black World.* Neal wrote two plays, *The Glorious Monster in the Bell of the Horn* (1976) and *In An Upstate Motel: A Morality Play* (1980). He published two collections of poetry: *Black Boogaloo: Notes on Black Liberation* in 1969 and *Hoodoo Hollerin' Bebop Ghosts* in 1974. Much of his poetry engages African American mythology, history, and language, but few poems simplify ideological issues. Instead Neal allowed for complexity and contradiction in his poems. His poems were frequently anthologized during the era but have received little critical attention since then. Some of Neal's work was collected and published posthumously in 1989 under the title *Visions of a Liberated Future: Black Arts Movement Writings.*

Larry Neal also edited several journals and magazines during his career. These include *Journal of Black Poetry,* the *Cricket,* and *Liberator Magazine.* Throughout his career Neal worked closely with Baraka; their collaboration began publicly in 1964 when both men helped to create the Black Arts Repertory Theater in Harlem. Neal's involvement with performance art expanded as he wrote films for television and private companies. Neal taught and lectured at several universities including City College of New York and Yale, Howard, and Wesleyan universities. He made television appearances, gave interviews, and profiled other main players in African American artistic life during his career. As a resident of New York's Sugar Hill section, Neal participated in and shaped the social climate of the city.

Larry Neal died of a heart attack at the age of forty-three on 6 January 1981. His significance in African American letters is primarily established by his influence on and engagement with the Black Arts movement.

• *Callaloo* 8.1 (Winter 1985), a special issue dedicated to Larry Neal.

—Elizabeth Sanders Delwiche Engelhardt

NEELY, BARBARA (b. 1941), short story writer, novelist, feminist, and community activist. While writing and a love for language had been deeply held interests since her childhood, Barbara Neely did not begin to take herself seriously as a writer nor consider earning a living as such until 1980 when the tensions between balancing a career and a stable emotional life lessened. The oldest child of parents Ann and Bernard, Neely grew up in the small Pennsylvania Dutch community of Lebanon. She attended the town's Catholic schools where she was the only African American through both elementary and high school. A nontraditional student who never acquired an undergraduate degree, Neely obtained her master's degree in urban and regional planning from the University of Pittsburgh in 1971. Until the publication of her first novel in 1992, Neely led the very demanding life of a community activist. Formerly the director of the Massachusetts-based Women for Economic Justice, she resigned in 1992, becoming cochair of the organization's board of directors to allow more time for her writing. Neely was also a founding member of Women of Color for Reproductive Freedom and is a member of the Jamaica Plain Neighborhood Arts Council. She lives in Boston.

Neely is the author of several short stories and two novels featuring Blanche White, a black maid who inadvertently becomes involved with murder or suspicious deaths. Yet despite the success of the two Blanche novels, the short story remains Neely's first love. In 1981 "Passing the Word," her first nationally published story, appeared in *Essence;* other tales have been anthologized in *Breaking Ice, Speaking for Ourselves, Things That Divide Us, Angels of Power, Street Talk, World of Fiction,* and *Test Tube Women.* The connecting link between Neely's professional life as an advocate for social issues and women's rights first surfaces in her short fiction. "Passing the Word" involves the dreams of two women about marriage, fulfillment, and taking control of and assuming responsibility for one's own life. A 1990 story, "Spilled Salt," illustrates a single mother's unmitigated pain when she must confront conflicting emotional duress because her son, whom she raised alone, has raped a young woman, gone to prison, and returned home. In both the short story and the novel, Neely's fiction reflects her clear intention of illustrating, often with a measure of humor, the issues of race, class, gender, and social values as these impact on her characters.

Blanche on the Lam (1992) is set in fictional Farleigh (Raleigh), North Carolina. Readers meet the very dark Blanche White, a very capable, articulate, proud, and perceptive African American woman whose very name is a pun. Fleeing from jail on a bad-check charge, Blanche finds work as a cook and maid for a wealthy white family. In the course of her service she uncovers a mystery and identifies a murderer. The true focus of the novel, however, is less about the murder and more about Blanche as distinctive character, as a social commentator and working woman with a very distinct view of her employers and firm ties to her own community. Neely's second novel, *Blanche among the Talented Tenth* (1994), takes Blanche from North Carolina to the Boston area and on to Amber Cove, Maine, an oceanside resort community for wealthy African Americans. Another mystery must be solved, and in the process, Blanche faces the twin barriers of class snobbery and intraracial color consciousness. Although the two novels developed in the mystery/detective mode have been well received, the tag "mystery writer," because it signals adherence to a defined genre format, makes Neely uncomfortable. Her aim was to write social novels, and creating the element of mystery was a means to that end. Indeed, in the second novel, the social commentary sometimes overshadows the mystery; and in her haste to critique lingering vestiges of an absurd class and color bias, the prose is somewhat strained. Neely continued her Blanche series with the publication of *Blanche Cleans Up* in 1998.

Barbara Neely's fiction stems from a drive to write about those whom she believes the larger society shunts aside, those black women whose experiences have been scorned or unappreciated. Yet Neely's talents in the mystery/detective genre have been recognized by others. In 1992 she won the "Go on Girl!" Award for the best debut novel from the Black Women's Book Club; that same year, from three different organizations that support mystery fiction, she won the Agatha, the Anthony, and the McCavity awards for the best first mystery, the latter granted by Mystery Writers International. She also won the 1994 Women of Conviction Award for Arts and Literature from the Massachusetts section of the National Council of Negro Women.

Neely has read writers as diverse as Agatha Christie, P. D. James, Chester *Himes, and Walter *Mosley. It was Toni *Morrison, however, whose evocative fiction created the most lasting impression on her. Morrison served Neely as both model and inspiration, freeing her to use the experiences of black women, illustrating for her the evocative power good writing taps to tell the stories of ordinary people.

• Barbara Neely, interview by Rebecca Carroll, in *I Know What the Red Clay Looks Like: The Voice and Vision of Black Women Writers,* 1994, pp. 174–184. Bonnie C. Plummer, "Subverting the Voice: Barbara Neely's African American Detective," *Clues: A Journal of Detection* 20:1 (Spring-Summer 1999): 77–88.

—Sandra Y. Govan

"Negro National Anthem." *See* "Lift Every Voice and Sing."

"Negro Speaks of Rivers, The." "The Negro Speaks of Rivers" appeared in June 1921 in the *Crisis,* when *Langston Hughes was only nineteen years old. It was the first Langston Hughes poem published in a national magazine.

According to Hughes in *The *Big Sea* (1940, 54–56), the poem was written in the summer of 1920, after his graduation from high school, while he was on a train going from Cleveland, Ohio, to Mexico. He was going to join his father, who lived there, and with whom the poet had a troubled relationship. "All day on the train," Hughes recalled, "I had been thinking about my father and his strange dislike of his own people. I didn't understand it, because I was a Negro, and I liked Negroes very much."

As the train crossed the Mississippi at sunset over a bridge near St. Louis, Hughes began to brood on the historical associations of that river with blacks, slavery, and the myth that Abraham Lincoln had vowed to himself, on a journey in his youth, to free the slaves someday. "Then I began to think about other rivers in our past—the Congo, and the Niger, and the Nile in Africa—and the thought came to me: 'I've known rivers.'" The poem was finished within "ten or fifteen minutes."

The following year, it was accepted for publication by the literary editor of the *Crisis,* Jessie Redmon *Fauset, who had earlier discovered Hughes's talent. Later, when he included the poem in his first published volume, *The *Weary Blues* (1926), he dedicated it to W. E. B. *Du Bois in response to Fauset's request that he honor the venerable editor.

Probably indebted in its basic structure—its long, irregular, unrhymed lines and its dignified but casual language—to the example of Walt Whitman, the poem sounded a note previously unheard in African American poetry. It invokes the subject of the violation of African people by slavery, but rage and the will to revenge are gently subsumed within lyric cadences that capture something of the noble spirit of the black spirituals without ever appealing to traditional ideas about religion.

With its allusions to dusky rivers, soul, blood, the setting sun, and sleep, the poem is fairly suffused with images of death. However, it aims ultimately to affirm the ability of blacks to transcend their historic suffering and affirm their fundamental dignity and beauty. The words "I've seen its muddy bosom turn all golden in the sunset" capture the ability of the poetic vision and the poetic will, accessible to all sympathetic people through the communality of the first-person narrator of the poem, to turn the mud of black life, beset by racism and injustice, into gold.

"The Negro Speaks of Rivers" laid the foundation for the special bond between Hughes and African Americans that led him at one time to be hailed as "the poet laureate of the Negro race."

• Langston Hughes, *Collected Poems,* 1994.

—Arnold Rampersad

NELL, WILLIAM C. (1816–1874), historian, journalist, orator, and abolitionist. Born into a Boston abolitionist family, William C. Nell attended an African American grammar school and graduated from an interracial school. As a student, he earned the right to an academic prize but, because of his race, was denied the award. The experience led him at an early age into battles against race discrimination and segregation in public schools. After studying law, Nell dedicated himself to antislavery work, lecturing, organizing meetings, and assisting fugitive slaves. He helped establish in 1842 the Freedom Association, an organization of African Americans who provided escaped slaves with protection, food, clothing, and shelter. Inspired by white abolitionist William Lloyd Garrison, Nell joined the *Liberator* in the early 1840s. He managed the paper's Negro Employment Office and wrote articles, while continuing to lecture and organize antislavery meetings. Like Garrison, he consistently opposed separate African American antislavery conventions and organizations. In 1847, Nell moved to Rochester where he joined Frederick *Douglass in publishing Douglass's newspaper, the *North Star.* While busy with antislavery work in Rochester, he maintained close ties with abolitionists in Boston. In 1850, he made an unsuccessful Free Soil Party bid for the Massachusetts legislature. In response to the Fugitive Slave Act (1850), Nell and other abolitionists created a Committee of Vigilance to assist and protect escaped slaves.

During a temporary but serious illness in 1851, Nell finished his pamphlet, *Services of Colored Americans in the Wars of 1776 and 1812,* one of the first pieces of historical writing devoted to the experiences of African Americans. Following the breach between Garrison and Douglass, Nell resigned at the *North Star* and in 1852 returned to Boston. In April 1855, after years of struggle led largely by Nell, Massachusetts desegregated its public schools. Later that year, with an introduction by Harriet Beecher *Stowe, Nell published *The Colored Patriots of the American Revolution,* the first comprehensive work of African American history. Less narrowly focused than the title suggested, *Colored Patriots* was a wide-ranging treatment of African American history, containing biographies of "distinguished colored persons," a survey of "Conditions and Prospects of Colored Americans," and a variety of historically significant documents. In 1858, in protest of the Supreme Court's Dred Scott decision, Nell founded the Crispus Attucks celebration to honor the African American patriot killed in the Boston Massacre. During these years, Nell also assisted other African American writers. As early as 1854 he attempted to help Harriet A. *Jacobs find a publisher and in 1860, introduced her to Lydia Maria Child, who edited Jacobs's narrative and secured its publication. During the Civil War, Nell used speeches, meetings, and the pages of the *Liberator* to urge the inclusion of African Americans in the Union army. In 1862, he became a postal clerk, one of the first such federal appointments for an African American, and he held the position until his death in 1874.

Nell was a key figure in antebellum African American letters, in part because of his connections to more famous antislavery writers. More significantly, Nell's historical writings have remained the most important early texts in African American historiography.

• Benjamin Quarles, *Black Abolitionists,* 1969. Robert P. Smith, "William Cooper Nell: Crusading Black Abolitionist," *Journal of Negro History* 55 (July 1977): 182–199. James Oliver Horton and Lois E. Horton, *Black Bostonians: Family Life and Community Struggle in the Antebellum North,* 1979.

—Gregory Eiselein

New Negro, The. An anthology edited by Alain *Locke, *The New Negro* was hailed immediately upon its publication in 1925 as a highly significant exemplar of the burgeoning creativity that came first to be known as the New Negro movement, then as the Negro Renaissance, and finally as the Harlem Renaissance. Behind the publication of this work lay a number of events and activities of which *The New Negro* was the culmination.

In 1923, the monthly magazine *Opportunity* began publication as an organ of the National Urban League. Edited by Charles S. Johnson, *Opportunity* immediately took on the character of a literary and art review. Johnson called to his aid as advisor and mentor Alain Leroy Locke of Howard University, and Locke was to remain a principal collaborator of *Opportunity* throughout its history.

In 1924, Johnson organized a dinner at the Civic Club in New York City in order to celebrate the publication of Jessie Redmon *Fauset's first novel, *There Is Confusion* (1924), and simultaneously to bring some of the younger literary artists into contact with the New York literati. He invited Locke to be toastmaster. This event led to a proposal by Paul Kellogg, editor of the influential magazine *Survey Graphic,* that Locke edit a special Harlem number of the magazine. As the Harlem number took shape, plans evolved to use it as the basis for a book. The Harlem number appeared in March 1925 and *The New Negro* in December of the same year.

The New Negro is divided into two sections—part 1, "The Negro Renaissance," and part 2, "The New Negro in a New World." Part 1 offered Locke's title essay "The New Negro" and articles on African art (by Albert C. Barnes) and literature (by William Stanley *Braithwaite). Fiction and poetry are then presented. Authors of fiction included Rudolph *Fisher, Jean *Toomer, John F. Matheus, Zora Neale *Hurston, Richard Bruce *Nugent, and Eric *Walrond. Poets were Countee *Cullen, Langston *Hughes, Claude *McKay, Anne *Spencer, Toomer, and Angelina Weld *Grimké. There are essays by Jessie Fauset and Montgomery Gregory on theater, as well as Arthur A. *Schomburg's "The Negro Digs up His Past."

In contrast to part 1, devoted primarily to creativity in the arts, part 2 offers social and political analysis. James Weldon *Johnson's essay on Harlem contains the kernel of his later *Black Manhattan* (1931). E. Franklin Frazier provides an early observation of the middle class in an article on Durham, North Carolina. Kelly *Miller and Robert R. Moton respectively portray education in the Howard and the Hampton-Tuskegee traditions. Walter White writes on the "Paradox of color," and W. E. B. *Du Bois provides an article on the international dimensions of color and imperialism.

Portraits of prominent individuals by the German-born artist Winold Reiss and the decorative motifs by Aaron Douglas are striking features of *The New Negro.* Bibliographies by Schomburg, Locke, and Arthur Huff Fauset were appended.

The New Negro inspired other anthologies, including Charles S. Johnson's *Ebony and Topaz* (1927) and Countee Cullen's *Caroling Dusk* (1927). Other successor works were Nancy Cunard's *Negro* (1933) and *The Negro Caravan* (1941), edited by Sterling A. *Brown and others.

• Arnold Rampersad, introduction to The New Negro: Voices of the Harlem Renaissance, 1992 (rpt.). David Levering Lewis, ed., The Portable Harlem Renaissance Reader, 1994.

—Richard A. Long

NEWSOME, EFFIE LEE (1885–1979), children's poet, short fiction writer, and editor of a literary column for children in the *Crisis* from 1925 to 1929.

Effie Lee Newsome (born Mary Effie Lee) was an important link between the **Brownies' Book* (1920–1922) and works for children in the 1930s by such writers as Langston *Hughes and Arna *Bontemps. Under W. E. B. *Du Bois's editorship of the *Crisis,* Newsome was recruited to establish a regular column where she could delight children with nature poetry, nonsense verse, and parables about the unique experience of being young and African American in the racially biased 1920s.

The poem in the *Crisis* (Oct. 1922) entitled "The Bronze Legacy" ("'Tis a noble gift to be brown, all brown") and the fable in the August 1928 issue, "On the Pelican's Back" (a comedy in which an arrogant white bird learns a humbling lesson), are significant examples of an early multicultural literature for the young.

On a personal plane, Newsome was an intellectual surrounded by prominent African Americans of her day. She had extensive university training at Wilberforce, Oberlin, and the University of Pennsylvania. She was the daughter of Dr. Benjamin Franklin Lee, a president of Wilberforce University and a bishop of the African Methodist Episcopal Church. She also married a minister: the Reverend Henry Nesby Newsome. Her poems for adult readers are included in Hughes's and Bontemps's *The Poetry of the Negro, 1746–1949* (1949), and she anthologized some of her poems for children in *Gladiola Garden* (1940).

Newsome decried the dearth of African and African American images in children's books and dedicated herself to giving youngsters two great gifts: a keen sense of their own inestimable value and an avid appreciation of the natural world.

• Effie Lee Newsome, "Child Literature and Negro Childhood," *Crisis* 34.8 (Oct. 1927): 260, 280, 282. Donnarae MacCann, "Effie Lee Newsome: African American Poet of the 1920s," *Children's Literature Association Quarterly* (Summer 1988): 60–65.

—Donnarae MacCann

No Place to Be Somebody. Charles *Gordone's play *No Place to Be Somebody* (1969) recounts the happenings in a New York City bar and the past fifteen years in the life of its African American owner Johnny Williams. As part of the larger theme of the thwarted ambitions of motley bar patrons consisting of ex-convicts, hustlers, prostitutes, politicians, and artists, Johnny, rankled by a history of poor race relations, eagerly awaits the prison release of his mentor Sweets Crane to initiate a racketeering scheme and to claim a share of the organized crime market. However, after ten years of incarceration, Sweets is a reformed old man whose recidivism and "Charlie fever" are tempered by poor health and religion. Framed in all three acts by the multiple voices of Gab Gabriel, who simultaneously serves as writer, chorus, and aspiring actor in the play, *No Place to Be Somebody* examines the individual and communal struggle for identity and the potential destruction and regeneration this enterprise entails.

After numerous revisions and artistic and financial setbacks, *No Place* opened at Joseph Papp's New York Shakespeare Festival Public Theatre on 4 May 1969, moved to the ANTA Theatre on 30 December, and concluded a run of 903 performances Off-Broadway with a third opening at the Promenade Theatre on 20 January 1970. Distinguishing Gordone as the first African American playwright to receive the award, *No Place* was the first Off-Broadway play to win a Pulitzer Prize for drama (1970) and was in the same year the recipient of the Vernon Rice Award, the Drama Desk Award, and the New York and Los Angeles Critic's Circle awards. Directed by Gordone, the play made its Broadway debut on 9 September 1971 at the Morosco Theatre. Subsequently, the play has been revived by several schools and regional theaters and translated into French, German, Spanish, and Russian for productions throughout the world. Though some critics claimed that the play was too dense and that Gordone's artistic vision was unclear, *No Place to Be Somebody* was hailed widely as a critical success for its adept use of language, for its experimentation with varying dramatic forms, and for its candid commentary regarding racial tensions in America.

In the late 1960s and the early 1970s and at a time when there was an increased demand for racially conscious and constructive artistic production and the stage gained great significance as an arena for the exploration, negotiation, and assertion of African American identity, *No Place to Be Somebody* advanced the project of identity by positing what Gordone called an

"American chemistry." In a 1988 interview with Susan Harris Smith in *Studies in American Drama,* Gordone suggests that the formulation of identity in American society emerges from a synthesis of cultural, racial, and religious experiences. This amalgam of cultures, races, and religions, according to Gordone, had profound implications not only in expanding the parameters of African American identity, but also offered a broader understanding of the American experience and ultimately of humanity.

• Jean W. Ross, "Charles Gordone," in *DLB,* vol. 7, *Twentieth-Century American Dramatists,* ed. John MacNicholas, 1981, pp. 227–231. Bernard L. Peterson, Jr., *Contemporary Black American Playwrights and Their Plays,* 1988.

—Charles Leonard

NORTHUP, SOLOMON (1808–1863), free-born resident of upstate New York, whose kidnapping, transport, and enslavement in the deep South are recounted in his 1853 slave narrative, *Twelve Years a Slave.* Solomon Northup's early life took an ordinary course, from youth on the family farm to marriage at age twenty-one to Anne Hampton, followed by the birth of three children. A farmer, semiskilled laborer, but also a part-time fiddle player, Northup accepted an offer in March 1841 from two strangers in Saratoga, New York, to provide music for their traveling circus. But when the tour reached Washington, D.C., the men had him seized, delivered to slave traders, shipped to New Orleans aboard an American coastwise slaver, and sold to a succession of Louisiana slave owners, for whom he worked until returning to New York and freedom in January of 1853.

Though literate, Northup dictated his narrative of captivity to a ghostwriter, David Wilson, who proved less intrusive than many other white amanuenses of slave narratives, allowing Northup to exercise final editorial decisions over the events narrated, but whose mannered style precludes the narrative from being as authentic as autobiographies written by their own subjects. While abolitionist journals had previously warned of slavery's dangers to free African American citizens and published brief accounts of kidnappings, Northup's narrative was the first to document such a case in book-length detail. Dedicated to Harriet Beecher *Stowe, whose *Uncle Tom's Cabin* had appeared in 1852, Northup's narrative promised facts that would surpass Stowe's fiction. The narrative's immediate success (final sales exceeded thirty thousand copies) was boosted by such comparisons, especially that between the Red River region of Northup's enforced slavery and the territory where Uncle Tom suffers the cruelty of Simon Legree. When Stowe published her *Key to Uncle Tom's Cabin* in 1853, she cited Northup's narrative to bolster her novel's credibility, and subsequent reprints of Northup's narrative in turn proclaimed it "Another Key to Uncle Tom's Cabin." Although capitalizing on the popularity of Stowe's fiction, Northup's narrative nevertheless asserts its unique value. In its insistence upon telling the whole ugly truth of slavery it not only departs from Stowe's self-proclaimed rhetorical restraint but also illustrates slave narratives' evolution during the 1850s and 1860s from earlier autobiographies whose authors had found it necessary to moderate their stories in order to win credibility from white audiences.

• William L. Andrews, *To Tell a Free Story,* 1988, pp. 181–183. Marion Wilson Starling, *The Slave Narrative: Its Place in American History,* 2d ed., 1988, pp. 171–174.

—Brad S. Born

NORTON, MR. Mr. Norton is a white man from the North who is a founder and financial supporter of the southern Negro college that the narrator attends in Ralph *Ellison's **Invisible Man* (1952). The narrator unwittingly drives the northern, white philanthropist through the backwash of the college community and, as a result, is expelled from the edenic campus environment. Structurally, Mr. Norton functions as a springboard for launching the Invisible Man on his quest for knowledge and self-identity. It should be understood though that Norton is not the philanthropist that he seems to be. He operates out of self-interest and guilt. If not physically (as Trueblood did), he has psychologically and mentally raped his own daughter, and his philanthropy to Blacks becomes a monument to her memory. Then, too, Norton suffers from delusions of grandeur. He sees himself as a god directing the affairs of Black people for whom he has very little respect. He says of his association with the college: "That has been my real life's work, not my banking or my researchers, but my first-hand organization of human life." His philanthropy is nothing more than a guise for controlling the destiny of others.

Norton, in his self-righteousness, thinks of himself as a master builder. He says to the Invisible Man, "if you become a good farmer, a chef, a preacher, doctor, singer, mechanic—whatever you become, and even if you fail, you are my fate." Over and over again he reminds the Invisible Man that Blacks are associated with his "fate," his "destiny." But it must be remembered that it is the Mr. Nortons of America who are responsible for the Golden Day, the human zoo that is located in the hinterlands of the college community. Many of the patients (political prisoners) at the Golden Day are doctors, lawyers, teachers, civil service workers, preachers, politicians, and artists. The range of human endeavor is represented in the Black men who are detained in this mental facility. They, like the Invisible Man, were probably educated at this Black college or other Black colleges by other Nortons. But once the Blacks were educated and began to compete in the mainstream, the metaphorical Nortons herded them into institutions because they, the Nortons, were afraid of the talented, intellectually competent professionals they had created. In short, all the country's Mr.

Nortons are nothing more than self-righteous hypocrites.

—Ralph Reckley, Sr.

Notes of a Native Son. James *Baldwin's first collection of essays, *Notes of a Native Son* (1955) brought together pieces he had published in *Commentary, Harper's Magazine, Partisan Review,* and other journals. The essays solidified Baldwin's reputation as an essayist as well as his persistence in criticizing America for its racial shortcomings. An autobiographical section precedes the ten essays. Dominant in his own life and in the essays is a recurring theme: what it means to be a black man in America. His status as a writer gives a special twist to that problem and leads him to assert: "I want to be an honest man and a good writer."

Part 1, consisting of three essays, reflects Baldwin's early attempts at literary and cultural criticism. "Everybody's Protest Novel" revisits *Uncle Tom's Cabin* (1852), which Baldwin read so frequently as a child that his mother had to hide it from him. Now thirty-one and reexamining his childhood fascination, Baldwin concludes that the book "is a very bad novel," primarily because of its sentimentality and its protest theme. In "Many Thousands Gone," Baldwin comments on stereotyping and the dehumanization of the Negro, with a particular focus on the problems inherent in Richard *Wright's creation of *Bigger Thomas (**Native Son,* 1940). "Carmen Jones: The Dark Is Light Enough" focuses on the Hollywood production of Carmen Jones.

Part 2 contains some of Baldwin's most recognized and studied essays. As cultural historian and critic in "The Harlem Ghetto," Baldwin comments on familiar territory, giving particular attention to "the Negro press" and to the often tense relationships between blacks and Jews. "Journey to Atlanta" uses political commentary as the backdrop to discussing a disastrous trip Baldwin's brother David made to Atlanta as a member of a quartet. The title essay, "Notes of a Native Son," recounts the death of Baldwin's father, which was on the same day his last sibling was born and a few hours before a race riot in Harlem. For Baldwin, all of these events come together in trying to make sense of his tempestuous relationship with his father, of their identity, of his place in his family, of his family's place in America. The challenge is to claim life and sanity in the midst of bitterness, poison, hatred, and fear, for these are the emotions that tie the disparate pieces of the essay together.

Baldwin moves from the United States to the international scene in part 3 of the volume as he explores his own reactions and those of others to his travels to Paris and other European cities; the concept of strangers underlies all the essays. "Encounter on the Seine: Black Meets Brown" highlights the difficulties of black Americans meeting Africans on French soil. "A Question of Identity" focuses on the American student colony in Paris, while "Equal in Paris" recounts a funny but nonetheless serious incident in which Baldwin was arrested for receiving stolen goods. The eight days he spent in jail were comparable to encountering the familiar institutional dehumanization in America. Finally, "Stranger in the Village," one of the most well-known of Baldwin's essays, relates his visit to a Swiss village in which, as a black man, he was an object of great curiosity among the villagers; that provided yet another opportunity for focusing on the situation of black people in America. Awareness of the central place black people have held in the world leads Baldwin to assert that "this world is white no longer, and it will never be white again."

• Keneth Kinnamon, *James Baldwin: A Collection of Critical Essays,* 1974. Fred L. Standley and Nancy V. Burt, eds., *Critical Essays on James Baldwin,* 1988.

—Trudier Harris

NUGENT, RICHARD BRUCE (1906–1987), popular writer and artist of the Harlem Renaissance era, also known as Bruce Nugent and Richard Bruce. "Shadows," Richard Bruce Nugent's first published poem, on the subject of race, appeared in *Opportunity* and was reprinted in 1927 in Countee *Cullen's *Caroling Dusk.* "Sahdji," published in Alain *Locke's *The *New Negro* (1925), is a pseudo-African story characterized by the use of ellipses and contains the twin themes of homosexuality and biblical imagery that would often determine his later work. In collaboration with Locke this later became *Sahdji—An African Ballet* and appeared in Locke's anthology *Plays of Negro Life* (1927). Scored by William Grant *Still, it was performed at the Eastman School of Music in 1932.

In 1926, with Wallace *Thurman, Langston *Hughes, Zora Neale *Hurston, and Aaron Douglas, Nugent founded the controversial magazine *Fire!!* Nugent's "Smoke, Lilies and Jade," apparently the first tale of explicit homosexuality published by an African American, features Alex, a young artist who resembles the author.

After the failure of *Fire!!,* Nugent coedited, with Wallace Thurman, *Harlem* (1928). His bold illustrations appear here as well as in *Fire!!;* other works are in *Opportunity* and the *Crisis;* his ambitious *Drawing for Mulattoes* series appears in *Ebony* (1927).

Though never widely published, Nugent, as a fund of information and as an aid to other writers and artists, nevertheless had an important impact on art in Harlem. As cofounder in the 1960s with Romare Bearden of the Harlem Cultural Council, Nugent expressed his continuing commitment to African American life and culture.

• David Levering Lewis, *When Harlem Was In Vogue,* 1981.

—Nathan L. Grant

O

OCCOMY, MARITA BONNER. *See* Bonner, Marita.

OLIVER, DIANE (1943–1966), naturalist southern black feminist writer. Diane Alene Oliver lived only twenty-two years, but she left a legacy of short stories to earn her recognition. Born 28 July 1943, Oliver grew up in Charlotte, North Carolina, where her passage into adolescence coincided with the racial upheavals in the Charlotte-Mecklenburg school system. The Supreme Court ruled on *Brown v. Board of Education* in 1954, mandating desegregation of public schools. Oliver never capitulated to notions of racial inferiority and went on to graduate from West Charlotte High School.

In 1960, she enrolled at the University of North Carolina at Greensboro; that marked the beginning of an auspicious writing career. Oliver served as managing editor of *The Carolinian,* the campus newspaper; studied under poet Randall Jarrell; and also began to write short stories. A career break occurred when Oliver won the guest editorship for the June 1964 edition of *Mademoiselle* magazine in its contest to honor outstanding college writers. A year later, she published her first short story in the fall 1965 issue of *Red Clay Reader.* "Key to the City" provided Oliver with a scholarship in 1965 to the University of Iowa, where she enrolled in the Writers' Workshop.

Oliver portrays strong-willed, black women caregivers of her era. As abandoned wives or nurturing daughters, the women struggle to maintain family unity while oppressive social forces work to disintegrate it. They are determined women but subtle in their warfare, as the ironic titles of the works illustrate. These stylistics are evident when Oliver's stories are examined thematically rather than chronologically.

Oliver's first and third stories, "Key to the City" and "Neighbors," published in the spring 1966 issue of *Sewanee Review,* invoke the migration theme of South to North when blacks looked to Chicago as the promised land. Once Nora Murray completes high school in Still Creek, Georgia, she sets her goal to attend college in the North. "Key to the City" centers on Nora's domestic duties: settling the house and preparing her siblings and working mother for the bus trip to Chicago. They trade one dead-end situation for another, arriving in Chicago only to learn that their husband-father has abandoned them and that they must immediately go on welfare.

"Neighbors" continues the regional theme of Chicago to show reality as a racist enclave in the stead of Oliver's predecessors, Richard *Wright and Lorraine *Hansberry. Oliver's story differs, however, by her focus on racial tensions during the era of busing. Eloise Mitchell, a twenty-year-old working girl, resides with her family in a Chicago Housing Project that borders a white district that has been targeted for court-ordered school integration. The conflict concerns the family's responses to the bombing of their home and the welfare of the six-year-old son who is the test case. Eloise dissolves family tension in the most unobtrusive manner by redirecting their fears to the mundane issue of breakfast. Her clever ruse contrasts the disruptive force of the historical moment at hand.

In her second and fourth stories, "Health Service" and "Traffic Jam," published in the November 1965 and July 1966 issues of *Negro Digest,* respectively, Oliver invokes a Faulknerian device. She invents the fictional southern community of Fir Town where Libby, Hal, and their children struggle against the racial oppression of whites. Libby is the reticent, central consciousness of both works who endures derision from both the black and white communities because Hal has abandoned her and their children. The main conflict of "Health Care" concerns Libby's trek to Fir Town with five hungry children all under the age of six in order for Meetrie, the eldest, to get an immunization shot for day camp. The daylong plight ends with no health care and loss of a day's wages. "Traffic Jam" extends the theme of humiliation to Libby's job as a domestic where she daily endures insults from her white female employer for Hal's desertion of them. He returns unexpectedly after a year, but with an automobile instead of money. Libby accepts Hal and his symbol of manhood since she knows that their socioeconomic condition will remain unchanged with or without Hal's car.

Oliver was the daughter of William Robert and Blanche Rann Oliver of Charlotte, North Carolina. She prefigured the black feminist writers of the 1970s. A motorcycle-automobile collision on 21 May 1966 in Iowa took her life just days before graduation. The University of Iowa conferred Oliver's Master of Fine Arts degree posthumously.

• "Remembering Young Talent," *Negro Digest* (Sept. 1966): 88–89. "Oliver, Diane," *Afro-American Encyclopedia,* vol. 7, 1974, p. 1944. "Oliver, Diane," in *Black American Writers Past and Present,* vol. 2, ed. Theresa Gunnels Rush, 1975, p. 573. Mary Pratt, *The Imaginative Spirit,* 1988, p. 77.

—Virginia Whatley Smith

OSBEY, BRENDA MARIE (b.1957), poet. Brenda Marie Osbey, born in New Orleans in 1957, has roots in Creole culture that run deep and give her work a haunting sense of place. No one since Walker Percy has made more memorable music out of the names of the city's streets and the people who throng them. Her poetry offers more than a slice of local color, however, for the metropolis she summons up quickly and magically becomes a backdrop for a display of the ambiance of the black feminine mind. Her women lead lives that often erupt in violence and sometimes end with madness. But alongside all this—and often because of it—we find a riveting poignance and searing beauty.

Osbey has said that her poetry forms a kind of cultural biography and geography of Louisiana, but one finds influences from her travels and sojourns elsewhere. She attended Dillard University, Université Paul Valéry at Montpélliér, France, and received an MA from the University of Kentucky. She has taught at Dillard and the University of California at Los Angeles, and currently teaches at Loyola University in New Orleans. She has received several awards, including the Academy of American Poets' Loring-Williams Prize, an Associated Writing Program Award, and a National Endowment for the Arts Fellowship. Osbey has been a fellow of the Fine Arts Work Center at Provincetown, the Kentucky Foundation for Women, the MacDowell Colony, the Millay Colony, and the Bunting Institute, Harvard University. She has published three volumes of poetry, *Ceremony for Minneconjoux* (1983), *In These Houses* (1988), and *Desperate Circumstance, Dangerous Woman* (1991), and has just completed *All Saints,* a tribute to mythic New Orleaneans and a rich tapestry of the city's history.

Osbey's stunning first collection of poetry offered up the voices and visions of women through a series of vignettes, each framing and telling a story. One sees a fusion of incidents, remembrances, and details that uncoils in a disciplined way, yet somehow remains shrouded in mystery. Accordingly, these poems possess a kind of uncanny tension, as she navigates between the rational and unexplainable. Her saturation in the Afro-Caribbean ambiance of New Orleans's Faubourgs (neighborhoods)—especially Marigny and Tremé—enables Osbey to plunge the reader into the eerie world of the Bahalia women, with their roots and tamborines, to introduce African Gods on the bankettes of the city. The central story of Lenazette of Bayou La Fouche and her Choctaw lover, as narrated to her daughter Minneconjoux, produces a murder; in another poem a woman writes letters to a man long dead; Ramona Veagis "falls off the world" and sits in a chair that erupts from a bathtub full of water. These tumbles into madness arrest and amaze, but also provoke a discomforting set of queries about the relation of madness and beauty, sanity and lies.

Osbey's next collection, *In These Houses,* continued her exploration of these women called "Madhouses," often merging them with swift "easy" women who Circe-like lure men into disaster, men like Diamond, who hangs himself out of desperate love for careless Reva. But there is also Thelma Picou, who runs out naked to eat dirt, crazed with the oppressive dominance of "Darling Henry"; Little Eugenia's Hispanic lover kills her when he mistakes her for lost diamond mines. Over and over again, characters end up in "infirmary," or Jackson, the state institution for the insane. Osbey appends a glossary of Louisiana ethnic expressions and place names, in part an indication of her growing awareness of herself as a kind of Virgil leading the Dante-like reader into "unknown realms." In many of these spectral poems the narration shifts without warning, from the man to the woman, the mother to the daughter, the sane to the insane. But if the reader sometimes loses his or her mooring, the author never does.

Osbey has been influenced by the work of Jean *Toomer in particular, but also by Robert *Hayden, the relatively unknown New Orleans poet Marcus Christian, and the music of Buddy Bolden, Dinah Washington, and Sarah Vaughan.

Her women reflect all ages: "Consuela" grows out of a girl's ring-game song, while "The Old Women on Burgundy Street" hymns an ode to learned resignation. "House of Bones," however, operates in the realm of abstractions, putting forth a recipe for a spiritual dwelling whose construction nevertheless proceeds, in Osbey's alchemy, visibly before you.

Desperate Circumstance, Dangerous Woman: A Narrative Poem was a new departure for Osbey, a single, long, richly evocative story. Ms. Regina, the hoodoo woman of the earlier collection, reappears here, ministering to the magnetically attractive narrator Marie Calcasieu ("Screaming Eagle"), who can "walk" in men's blood, especially Percy's. The Faubourg Marigny setting provides a tale for everything, as we gaze at the life of the quarter and see the bits of history in the debris of the daily. Every detail of life here is ritualistic, spiritual, and embued with meaning, even the empty rooms of Marie's house. The patterns of hoodoo assist here; Osbey sees them as a series of life principles. Generational influences intersect; Marie's life seems linked to the old story of her parents, to the old place out in Manchac swamp, and to the maroon people who live nearby.

Osbey's work in the mid-1990s, *All Saints,* continues her exploration of Louisiana's Creole–African American culture and features a number of meditations on historical and legendary figures. Osbey won an American Book Award for *All Saints: New and Selected Poems* in 1997.

• Violet Harrington Bryan, "Evocations of Place and Culture in the Works of Four Contemporary Black Louisiana Writers: Brenda Osbey, Sybil Kein, Elizabeth Brown Guillory, and Pinkie Gordon Lane," *Louisiana Literature Review* 4.2 (1987): 49–80. Brenda Marie Osbey, interview by John Lowe, in *The Future of Southern Letters,* 1995, pp. 93–118.

—John Lowe

OTTLEY, ROI (1906–1960), foreign correspondent, journalist, and author. Roi Ottley was born in New York City and educated at St. Bonaventure College, the University of Michigan, and St. John's School of Law. He studied playwriting at Columbia University, article writing at the City College of New York, and Negro folk literature under James Weldon *Johnson at New York University. However, at St. John's he decided writing would be his life's work. He began this career at the *Amsterdam Star-News* in Harlem, where he worked for seven years as, successively, a reporter, columnist, and editor. Following this period, he became a freelance writer for the following magazines: *New York Times, Liberty, Mercury, Ebony, Common Ground, Travel, Colliers, The Nation,* and *New Republic.* He became a foreign correspondent for *Liberty, PM* newspaper, the *Pittsburgh Courier,* and the Overseas News Agency. Ottley was the first African American to be employed as a working war correspondent for a nationally known magazine and a major white daily newspaper. He later became a reporter for the *Chicago Tribune* and broadcasted reports for both the Columbia Broadcasting System and the British Broadcasting System. In 1943, he served as publicity director for the National CIO War Relief Committee.

Ottley reported on such events as the Normandy Invasion, the hanging of Mussolini, and the Arab-French conflict in Syria. He interviewed important Allied political leaders and such personalities as Pope Pius XI, Governor Talmadge of Georgia, and Samuel Green, Grand Dragon of the Ku Klux Klan. At the *Chicago Tribune,* he wrote series on the migration of African Americans from the agricultural South to the industrial North and its impact, the voting trends among African Americans, and the war. Topics in the latter series included the plot to remove all African American soldiers from occupied Germany, the desire of the African American to fully participate in the war, the absence of race problems when African Americans were allowed full participation, and the stellar performance of the African American soldier. Additionally, he wrote articles on African American achievers in Chicago, such as Dr. Philip C. Williams, the first African American to be admitted to the Chicago Gynecological Society.

Based on his travels, observations, and interviews, Ottley wrote four books, contributed satirical short stories to *Negro Digest,* and at the time of his death was completing his first novel. His first book, *New World A-Coming: Inside Black America* (1944), presents the African American's history, problems, and hopes. It appeared a few weeks after a wave of race riots; this helped catapult it to best-seller status. According to Ottley, the way in which the African American is responded to will determine the way in which the world will heed America. It was published in Brazil and England as *Inside Black America.* He became the first African American to be published in the Houghton Mifflin Life-in-America series, was recognized for his contribution to interracial understanding by both the *Chicago Defender* and the Schomburg Library, and became the first African American journalist to receive a Rosenwald Fellowship. He won the Peabody Award for his radio dramatization *New World A-Coming,* a series designed to promote racial harmony. Following his overseas tour, he returned to the United States to work on his history of the African American's search for equality in America, *Black Odyssey: The Story of the Negro in America* (1948), which grew out of interviews and records in both America and Europe. This work, which details the origin of African American slavery and other historical occurrences, is marked by its fusion of individuals and events, an emphasis upon the human aspect of history without the omission of facts. His third book, *No Green Pastures* (1951), which was published in England in 1952, cautions the reader not to believe that European racial tolerance and lack of color prejudice are realities, and the African American not to consider Ottley's European treatment as typical. His final book, *Lonely Warrior: The Life and Times of Robert S. Abbott* (1955), is the biography of Robert Sengstacke Abbott, a multifaceted and often contradictory individual, the founder and editor of the *Chicago Defender.* Abbott created a channel through which individuals could speak out on the African American's behalf; lived and wrote history; called for the destruction of American race prejudice; established the Bud Billiken page in the *Defender,* devoted to issues of interest to young people; loved his race; and is considered by many to have initiated the modern African American press.

• "Roi Ottley Dies; Wrote on Negro," *New York Times,* 2 October 1960, 84.

—Helen R. Houston

Our Nig. The year 1859 was a year of important "firsts" for African American women's writing. Frances Ellen Watkins *Harper's short story "The *Two Offers" appeared, and Harriet E. *Wilson's *Our Nig* became the first novel by an African American to be published in the United States. Wilson addressed race relations in the North. She extended the slave narrative's attack on chattel relations below the Mason-Dixon line by offering a scathing revelation of northern racism and a forceful critique of the then-sacred realm of domesticity.

The hybrid form of *Our Nig* reflects the multipronged nature of Wilson's critiques. While a quiet debate has emerged about how to classify *Our Nig,* critics agree that Wilson blends aspects of sentimental fiction, autobiography, and slave narratives. Wilson opens her tale with the seduction of "lonely Mag Smith . . . alone and inexperienced . . . as she merged into womanhood, unprotected, uncherished, uncared for." Her language mirrors, or perhaps parodies, the conventional seduction tale—the isolated young maiden, without a loving family to guide her, falls prey to "the voice" of her ravisher who then leaves her to her fate. Yet, rather than dying, Mag marries a black man in order to survive. While the child born in her seduction narrative dies, her second child, *Frado, lives; it is Frado's story that Wilson narrates.

Throughout the text Wilson makes it clear that Frado's life is based on her own. Indeed, Barbara White has corroborated almost all of the details concerning the Bellmonts, whose nonfictional name is Hayward. Wilson's title itself, *Our Nig, or Sketches of a Free Black in a Two Story White House, North, Showing that Slavery's Shadows Fall Even There; by "Our Nig,"* both modifies the common form of slave narrative titles (*Narrative of the Life of*...) and stresses its own autobiographical nature; *Our Nig* is written by "Our Nig." Likewise, in her closing pages, after referring to "my narrative," Wilson pleads for assistance from her readers, as she further establishes the autobiographical relation to the story she tells.

Wilson's ironic use of "our nig" ties the novel to the slave narrative form as well and shows that others call her this to claim her. In appended letters—themselves a standard convention of slave narratives—readers also find autobiographical confirmation. Margareta Thorn describes Wilson as "a slave, in every sense of the word." After Frado's father dies, her mother abandons the six year old at her wealthier and ill-reputed New Hampshire neighbors'; soon christened "nig," she is showed how her chores are "always to be done . . . any departure to be punished by a whipping."

In the Bellmont house, the principal source of abuse is "Mrs. B.," whose uncontrollable rage parallels depictions of the jealous southern mistress who beats and torments the master's illegitimate offspring. John Bellmont's ostensible affection for Frado, but virtual refusal to stand up to his (metaphorically wronged) wife, points to his symbolic status as a neglectfully benign slave father.

In the final chapters, Frado leaves the Bellmonts and then gets married. Frado's husband's actions echo Mr. Bellmont's—he is a poor protector and also abandons Frado, whose health is broken after years of overwork and beatings. Significantly, despite their legitimate marriage, like Frado herself, their boy is the son of an illegitimate partner. Thomas Wilson is a freeborn man who poses as a slave to lecture for the abolitionists; it is Wilson's need to provide for her son alone that drives her to write a metaphorical slave narrative.

Our Nig has been derided for its affiliations with sentimentality—a genre that asserts a woman's sphere is ruled by affection, love, and submissiveness. Yet arguably Wilson advances the most forceful critique of northern domesticity in nineteenth-century black women's fiction. As an indentured servant, Wilson reveals that when one considers race and class relations, abuse is perpetuated by women and that domesticity is violent. Moreover, in *Our Nig,* violence itself is domesticated. Whipping in slavery is displayed publicly; Mrs. Bellmont tortures Frado privately, in the kitchen, near the hearth. The novel becomes markedly more violent while Frado is within the "two story white house, North," the symbol of true womanhood. In the first novel written by an African American woman, Wilson draws upon different generic conventions to create her own form and exposes multiple layers of northern hypocrisy.

• Elizabeth Ammons, "Stowe's Dream of the Mother Savior: *Uncle Tom's Cabin* and American Women Writers Before the 1920s," in *New Essays on Uncle Tom's Cabin,* ed. Eric Sundquist, 1986, pp. 155–195. Hazel Carby, *Reconstructing Womanhood: The Emergence of the Afro-American Woman Novelist,* 1987, pp. 40–61. Barbara Christian, "Somebody Forgot to Tell Somebody Something: African American Women's Historical Novels," in *Wild Women in the Whirlwind: Afra-American Culture and the Contemporary Literary Renaissance,* eds. Joanne Braxton and Andree McLaughlin, 1990, pp. 326–341. David Ames Curtis and Henry Louis Gates, Jr., "Establishing the Identity of the Author of *Our Nig,*" in *Wild Women in the Whirlwind: Afra-American Culture and the Contemporary Literary Renaissance,* eds. Joanne Braxton and Andree McLaughlin, 1990, pp. 48–69. P. Gabrielle Foreman, "The Spoken and the Silenced in *Incidents in the Life of a Slave Girl* and *Our Nig,*" Callaloo 13 (Spring 1990): 313–324. Barbara White, "Our Nig and the She-Devil: New Information about Harriet Wilson and the Bellmont Family," *American Literature* 65.1 (Mar. 1993): 19–52.

—P. Gabrielle Foreman

P

PAPA LABAS is a major character in Ishmael *Reed's novels *Mumbo Jumbo* (1972) and *The *Last Days of Louisiana Red* (1974). Insofar as these books fit into the detective genre, Papa LaBas is a hoodoo investigator trying to solve crimes; but since these novels also are mysteries in the metaphysical sense, LaBas is, as Gerald Duff notes, a "cultural diagnostician and healer." Tracing his origins back to the plantation, W. E. B. *Du Bois in *The *Souls of Black Folk* (1903) referred to such an individual as "interpreter of the Unknown," "supernatural avenger of wrong," and viewed him as the prototype of the preacher, the "most unique personality" developed by African Americans. On another level, Papa LaBas, like his Haitian counterpart Papa Legba, is descended from the West African deity known as Eshu/Elegbara, lord of transitions, conjoining the real with the unreal, a trickster who is also a communicator. This last connection is especially important because, in *Mumbo Jumbo* and *Louisiana Red,* it is generally Papa LaBas who "runs the voodoo down" by providing crucial explanations and analyses.

If the Loop Garoo Kid (**Yellow Back Radio Broke-Down,* 1969) and **Raven Quickskill* (**Flight to Canada,* 1976) are the alter egos of a youthful, combative Reed, Papa LaBas may be said to be Reed's imaginative counterpart of himself as spiritual elder statesman, wise but still acquiring wisdom, not impulsive in struggle but settled in for the long haul, resolutely rooted in the ancient traditions of his people.

—Robert Elliot Fox

PARKER, CHARLIE (1920–1955), also known as Bird or Yardbird, alto saxophonist and major figure in the development of bebop. The new music known as "bebop" was based on experimentation with harmonic structures, but also possessed a strong political edge, which would make it the inspiration of numerous artists, black and white, who were looking for a means of confronting the sterility of Cold War culture. Charlie Parker's musicianship and skill as an improviser were unmatched, yet due to the exigencies of the jazz music business, he struggled to hold his life together. Parker was famous for his wit and thoughtfulness, but continued problems with drugs and failing physical and mental health led to his death in March 1955.

Parker's brilliance and irreverance made him as much of a legend as an important historical figure. His death led to the seemingly miraculous overnight appearance of the graffitti slogan "Bird Lives." For African American writers, and indeed for many American writers generally, Parker's life and death were resonant with the myth of the romantic artist who dies young, yet leaves an extraordinarily rich body of work behind. Some writers, like Bob *Kaufman, attempted to duplicate or imitate Parker's style in prose or poetry, but more often than not it was the myth of Charlie Parker that captured the imagination of writers. Ralph *Ellison criticized this phenomenon in his essay "On Bird, Bird-Watching and Jazz," included in his **Shadow and Act* (1964). More positively, Parker's legend has led to his being memorialized and celebrated in dozens of memoirs, poems, stories, and novels.

• Robert Reisner, *Bird: The Legend of Charlie Parker,* 1972. Gary Giddins, *Celebrating Bird: The Triumph of Charlie Parker,* 1987.

—James C. Hall

PARKS, GORDON (b. 1912), photographer, journalist, essayist, autobiographer, biographer, novelist, poet, film director, screenwriter, and composer. Gordon Parks's first two publications—*Flash Photography* (1947) and *Camera Portraits: The Techniques and Principles of Documentary Portraiture* (1948)—while written primarily for the professional photographer, reveal an aesthetic and a social commitment that structures the astonishing diversity of his subsequent work. Embodying his conviction that the photographer must combine technical intelligence, especially in the use of light, with a sensitive response to people, both works are photographic portfolios representing a cross-section of American lives—rural and urban, wealthy and leisured, poor and laboring.

Frequently identified as a Renaissance man, given the range of his accomplishments and the variety of media he has used, Parks was also the first African American to work for *Life, Vogue,* the Office of War Information, and the Farm Security Administration and one of the first African Americans to write, direct, produce, and score a film. While the commercial success of his work suggests he has fulfilled the American dream, a recognition of the demoralizing force of racism and poverty and the dignifying force of the struggle against these conditions underlies his entire creative output.

Parks grew up on a Kansas farm, where this defining dialectic was formed. As his autobiographical first novel, *The Learning Tree* (1963), and his subsequent autobiographies demonstrate, here he learned to value his parents' hard work, compassion, integrity, and capacity for hope as well as to fear the brutality and perversity of personal and institutionalized racism. While the young hero of *The Learning Tree* is tormented by a series of deaths, from natural causes and from racist violence, each of Parks's three autobiographies—*A Choice of Weapons* (1966), *To Smile in Autumn, A Memoir* (1979), *Voices in the Mirror, An Autobiography* (1990)—reviews these boyhood incidents, much as Frederick *Douglass returned to his experiences during slavery in his three autobiographies. Parks's autobiographical works record his struggles first to survive and then to succeed in the white world; if he is able to record his relationships with well-known figures of this century, his family relationships always remain paramount.

Set in New York City against a backdrop of labor unrest and an emerging socialism, World War I, and the Depression, his nonautobiographical novel, *Shannon* (1981), is Dickensian in scope. Revealing America to be a racist and classist society, he describes the interdependent lives of Americans from differing racial and class backgrounds. Although European immigrants in *Shannon* rise to attain enormous wealth, their wealth proves either corrupting or immaterial to their happiness, and although college-educated African American war heroes appear doomed by financial failure and injustice, they die with dignity.

Through the interrelation of words and photographs in several other works, Parks continues to reflect on dialectic differences in human life and to contemplate their resolution. Thus powerful black-and-white portraits illuminate essays on African Americans prominent in the 1960s civil rights movement and on a destitute Harlem family in *Born Black* (1971), as well as the story of Parks's personal involvement with a boy in a Brazilian slum in *Flavio* (1978). *Gordon Parks: A Poet and His Camera* (1968), *In Love* (1971), *Gordon Parks: Whispers of Intimate Things* (1971), and *Moments without Proper Names* (1975), however, experimentally juxtapose lyrical poems with impressionistic color photographs. Focusing on nature, romantic love, loneliness, beauty, childhood, aging, and death, both the photographic and poetic images suggest a view of life transcending economic and racial oppression. Given their various settings—Europe, Asia, North and South America—as well as their putative apolitical content, these images show Parks seeking a universal language. Yet, the explicit subject of the first section of *Moments without Proper Names* is the suffering of African Americans. His frequently reprinted poem "Kansas Land" concludes its catalog of pastoral images with an evocation of the violence and fear blacks have endured.

In his films—*The Learning Tree* (1968), *Shaft* (1971), *Shaft's Big Score* (1972), *The Super Cops* (1974), and *Leadbelly* (1976)—and in his ballet, *Martin* (1990), Parks integrates his multiple talents, writing the screenplay and/or the score for several of them. These works explore the African American male experience in addition to celebrating the African American ability to prevail—through violence and peaceful resistance, music and love. In the mid-1990s Parks was at work on a biography of the early-nineteenth-century British painter J. M. W. Turner, with whom he shares an interest in using light to reveal a complex world—one that includes slavery as well as multiple sources of beauty—more clearly. In 1997, to accompany a major traveling retrospective collection, Parks published *Half Past Autumn: A Retrospective*, a memoir illustrated by hundreds of his photographs.

• Martin H. Bush, *The Photographs of Gordon Parks,* 1983. Jane Ball, "Gordon Parks," in *DLB*, vol. 33, *Afro-American Fiction Writers after 1955,* eds. Thadious M. Davis and Trudier Harris, 1984, pp. 203–208. Deedee Moore, "Shooting Straight: The Many Worlds of Gordon Parks," *Smithsonian* 20.1 (Apr. 1989): 66–72, 74, 76–77. "Gordon Parks," in *Black Literature Criticism: Excerpts from Criticism of the Most Significant Works of Black Authors over the Past Two Hundred Years,* vol. 3, ed. James P. Draper, 1992, pp. 1551–1557. Elizabeth Schultz, "Dreams Deferred: The Personal Narratives of Four Black Kansans," *American Studies* 34.2 (Fall 1993): 25–52.

—Elizabeth Schultz

Passing. Nella *Larsen's second novel, *Passing* appeared in 1929 at the peak of the Harlem Renaissance. Many of its characters and occasions resemble other novels written during that era. Indeed, its working title, "Nig," alludes to *Nigger Heaven,* the novel by Larsen's friend and mentor Carl Van Vechten. Passing is more complex and ambitious than many of its predecessors, however, and this may account for the title change and for earning its author the distinction of being one of the first African American women to win a Guggenheim Fellowship for literature.

The central characters of *Passing* are Irene Redfield and Clare Kendry, two African Americans who look like Euro-Americans. These two women had been girlhood friends but separated for years before they accidentally meet when Clare is seated next to Irene in an expensive Chicago restaurant that only serves whites. Although both women are exploiting their appearance and passing for white, for Irene this is an occasional indulgence. She has established an identity as the doting mother of two sons, the wife of a prominent African American physician, and a supporter of appropriately conservative and uplifting community affairs. Clare on the other hand has married a successful white businessman, who not only believes she is white but deeply dislikes black people. From this accidental reunion, the two women's lives become entangled as Clare increasingly seeks opportunities to socialize with, and Irene reluctantly sponsors Clare's entrée into, the African American middle class. Clare's recklessness worries Irene because it threatens her carefully constructed white identity. But Irene also finds Clare's choices and the danger they entail both frightening and fascinating until she discovers that Clare is having an affair with her husband. Thus, when Clare's enraged husband rushes into one of these gatherings and in the confusion Irene reaches toward Clare and Clare suffers a fatal fall from the window, Irene's culpability is unclear.

Passing explores the relationships between appearance and reality, deception and unmasking, manipulation and imaginative management, aggression and self-defense. The novel's epigraph from Countee *Cullen's poem "Heritage" encourages one to read *Passing* as another in the genre that explores the ambiguity and contestations inherent in prevailing constructions of race. When it was first published, many reviewers referred to the novel as a "tragedy," alluding to both its shocking ending and to its obvious similarities to the tragic mulatto genre exemplified by works such as William Wells *Brown's **Clotel* (1853). Larsen's examination of passing, however, is more in the tradition of Frances Ellen Watkins *Harper's *Minnie's Sacrifice* (1868) or James Weldon *Johnson's *The *Autobiography of an Ex-Colored Man* (1912) because it focuses more upon the psychological dimensions than upon the physical acts that the tragic mulatto novels portrayed. Most critics agree that Larsen's novel is also concerned with class and gender identities and the emotional and ethical consequences of their manipulation. Some such as Mary Helen Washington emphasize gender as well as race and argue that Larsen uses passing as a metaphor for "risktaking experiences," or lives lived without the communal support of other black women. Deborah E. McDowell and others have suggested that the text questions the safe and legitimate parameters of sex and flirts with the idea of lesbianism.

• Thadious M. Davis, *Nella Larsen, Novelist of the Harlem Renaissance,* 1994. Cheryl A. Wall, *Women of the Harlem Renaissance,* 1995.

—Frances Smith Foster

PAUL D. In Toni *Morrison's **Beloved* (1987), Paul D is one of six male slaves on Mr. Garner's Kentucky plantation, ironically named Sweet Home. Paul D is described as a man with "peachstone skin; straight-backed. For a man with an immobile face it was amazing how ready it was to smile, or blaze or be sorry with you." Under Mr. Garner, a somewhat humane master, slavery had been bearable; but when he dies, his brother and heir, schoolteacher, is brutal and inhumane. After Paul D's attempted escape is foiled, he is reduced to chattel, has his feet shackled, has a three-spoked collar placed on his neck and a bit placed in his mouth, and is tethered to a buckboard. Later sold, he spends eighty-six days on a chain gang after attempting to kill his new owner. He escapes during a torrential rain and eventually makes his way to Ohio.

When Paul D enters "124"—home of former Sweet Home slave *Sethe Suggs and her child Denver, and tormented by the ghost of baby Beloved, whom Sethe killed rather than see remanded to slavery—he immediately recognizes the ghost's presence and drives it out, only to have an older Beloved physically return and seduce him. Paul D falls in love with Sethe and becomes a support for her, but he abandons her and takes refuge in a church cellar when someone shows him the newspaper accounts of Sethe killing Beloved. He insults Sethe by implying she has acted as an animal—with four feet instead of two. Once the women of the community exorcise Beloved, he becomes sensitized to Sethe's plight and realizes that he had no right to judge her as he did, and he returns to 124 and once again becomes a comfort to her. The life of Paul D represents the continuing effort of African American men to overcome the malevolence of the slave past and a racist society.

• Wilfred D. Samuels and Clenora Hudson Weems, *Toni Morrison,* 1990. Trudier Harris, *Fiction and Folklore: The Novels of Toni Morrison,* 1991. Deborah Ayer Sitter, "The Making of a Man: Dialogic Meaning in Beloved," *African American Review* 26 (1992):17–29. Trudier Harris, "Escaping Slavery but Not Its Images,"in *Toni Morrison: Critical Perspectives Past and Present,* ed. Henry Louis Gates, Jr., and K. A. Appiah, 1993, pp. 330–341. Molly Abel Travis, "*Beloved* and Middle Passage: Race, Narrative and the Critic's Essentialism," *Narrative* 2.3 (Oct. 1994): 179–200.

—Betty Taylor-Thompson

PAYNE, DANIEL A. (1811–1893), minister, poet, historian, educator, and abolitionist. Long recognized as a leading nineteenth-century Christian activist and theologian, Daniel Payne's literary achievements are varied and equally important. From his childhood in Charleston, South Carolina, where he was born to free and deeply religious parents, through his long ministry with the African Methodist Episcopal (AME) Church and eventual presidency of Wilberforce University, Payne pursued a rigorous program of self-directed study. He began to write and teach at an early age, starting his first school in Charleston in 1829 when he was only nineteen years old, and teaching there until 1835, when the South Carolina legislature made it illegal to teach slaves to read or write. Forced to close his school, Payne moved to the North, where he published a collection of poetry in 1850. In *The Pleasures and Other Miscellaneous Poems,* Payne included a poem heralding the emancipation of the West Indies in 1838, several poems concerning his family, and moving tributes to his wife and daughter after their deaths in the late 1840s. Much of Payne's poetry also expresses his concern for "moral purity" and "holy virtue." Payne was very active in the temperance movement and other Christian efforts at social reform.

In 1888, the Publishing House of the AME Sunday School Union printed Payne's autobiography, *Recollections of Seventy Years.* In this work Payne blends theology, personal experience, and political analysis. The autobiography provides a detailed account of important people and events in the antebellum African American abolitionist movement, the AME church, and African American activist communities nationwide through the extended Reconstruction years (1865–1888). Also a historian, Payne completed his exhaustive two-volume *History of the African Methodist Episcopal Church* in 1891. A collection of his sermons was published posthumously in 1972 under the title *Sermons and Addresses,* 1853–1891.

In all of these works, readers can see the unique tensions present in Payne's dual commitments: first, to self-defined freedom for African Americans, and second, to the spread of a form of "moral reform" that sometimes misapprehended the experience of non-Christians. For example, Payne supported missionary efforts to Africa by African American clergy but infused this support with the desire to convert "barbarous and savage men." At the same time, he helped found the Bethel Literary and Historical Association (1881), where he and other African American activists studied not only African American literature and history but also celebrated the cultures of Africa in an effort described by some later scholars as Pan-Africanist and nationalist. Another interesting political tension is Payne's early involvement in the Philadelphia Vigilance Committee (1838–1844), where African Americans challenged the legal status quo of the country by assisting newly escaped fugitive slaves, tempered by his later apparently "assimilationist" claims for the legitimate authority of the U.S. government.

W. E. B. *Du Bois counted Payne among the most important African American leaders and also listed some of his literary work and sermons among the key documents of African American literary tradition. Payne's autobiography, especially, through its rhetorical blend of literary narrative, theology, and political observation, allows readers access to the challenging complexity of nineteenth-century African American culture.

• Benjamin Quarles, *Black Abolitionists,* 1969. Wilson Jeremiah Moses, *The Golden Age of Black Nationalism, 1850–1925,* 1978.

—Sharon Carson

PECOLA BREEDLOVE is the protagonist in Toni *Morrison's *The Bluest Eye* (1970). An African American girl whose family life is in stark contrast to the image of perfection suggested in the epigraph from the primer that opens the novel, Pecola's struggle is to be loved. She craves blue eyes, thinking that if she looked like the blue-eyed girls from storybooks, her parents, teachers, and boys would love her. Her tragedy is one that begins at home. Convinced of her ugliness, and finding no consolation from her parents—her mother works as a domestic and seems to treasure her white employer's daughter more than her own, and her alcoholic father fights with her mother—Pecola is forced into isolation and fantasizes about escaping into whiteness. The narrator of the novel, Claudia McTeer, and her sister Frieda attempt to befriend Pecola when she comes to live with their family, after the Breedlove family has been put outdoors. Pecola's only real consolation comes from occasional visits to three prostitutes who are the only ones who give her any attention aside from Soaphead Church, the bootleg preacher, who out of compassion for her convinces her that he has given her blue eyes. Pecola's story ends with the premature death of her baby, her plunge into insanity, and the community's attempt to deny its role in her tragic demise. The narrator explains that the community is ultimately responsible for Pecola's fate because it has chosen to ignore its own warped values, distorted aesthetics, and obvious shortcomings and to scapegoat her instead.

• Michael Awkward, *Inspiriting Influences: Tradition, Revision, and Afro-American Women's Novels,* 1989.

—Marilyn Sanders Mobley

PEGGY. *See* Aun' Peggy.

PENNINGTON, JAMES W. C. (1807–1870), essayist and slave narrator. James William Charles Pennington was born into slavery on the eastern shore of Maryland. At the age of four, he, his brother, and his mother were given to the son of his master, who moved to Washington County in the western part of the state. In his slave narrative, *The Fugitive Blacksmith, or Events in the History of James W. C. Pennington* (1849), Pennington is particularly attentive to the effects of slavery on black children. Using the special abuses (lack of consistent parental attention, abusive white children, and brutal overseers) that slave children must endure as a gambit for his narrative, Pennington charted his development into an activist minister who witnessed, through word and deed, against slavery in the South and racism in the North.

Pennington escaped slavery in 1828. The next year he moved to Long Island, where he pursued an education in night school. Between 1829 and 1834 as a member of the "General Convention for the Improvement of the Free Colored People," Pennington was instrumental in efforts to improve the conditions of newly freed blacks of New York. His first book, *A Text Book of the Origin and History . . . of Colored People* (1841), was designed to meet the needs of teachers, such as himself, who were dedicated to the inspiration as well as instruction of African Americans.

From teaching Pennington's interests evolved into preaching. On 15 September 1838, Reverend Pennington officiated at the marriage of Anna Murray and Frederick *Douglass. During the 1840s and 1850s, Pennington held pastorates in African Congregational churches in Newtown, Long Island; Hartford, Connecticut; and New York City. A few of his sermons and addresses were published as pamphlets. Pennington's fame as the author of *The Fugitive Blacksmith,* an international antislavery lecturer, and a New York City civil rights leader caused Harriet Beecher *Stowe to single him out in *Uncle Tom's Cabin* (1852) as an exemplary figure in the free African American community.

• William L. Andrews, *To Tell a Free Story: The First Century of Afro-American Autobiography, 1760–1865,* 1986. Herman E. Thomas, *James W.C. Pennington,* 1995.

—Charles E. Wilson, Jr.

PETERSON, LOUIS (b. 1922), film and television screenwriter, and playwright. If one were to summarize the forty-year career of Louis Stamford Peterson, Jr., in one word, it would be "passages." Peterson's play of the 1950s, *Take a Giant Step,* earned him acclaim in American theater. Since that time, he has released a play every decade. He strongly believes that people write out of what they do best, and that "best" means maintaining ethical standards learned from childhood.

Born 17 June 1922 in Hartford, Connecticut, Peterson grew up in a middle-class, multiethnic neighborhood. White immigrants were dominant but Peterson never felt deterred from aspiring for high ideals. He was trained by his parents to value education and the Protestant work ethic. Louis Stamford Peterson, Sr., worked as a bank guard and then as a money roller. His wife, Ruth Conover Peterson, accepted employment at a lunch counter in the same bank during the 1930s to insure that their two sons would acquire college educations. Peterson graduated from Bulkeley High School in 1940 and went south to attend Morehouse College (Atlanta, Georgia) from 1940 to 1944. He acted in collegiate productions, and upon graduation, Peterson spent a year at the Yale School of Drama and then enrolled in drama at New York University, where he earned a master of arts degree in 1947.

Acting classes at New York University eventually led Peterson to playwriting. He performed in *A Young American* and *Our Lan',* the latter taking Peterson to Broadway in 1947. However, he consistently found his character being lynched and became disturbed about these negative portraits of African Americans. He wrote two trial plays after *Our Lan'* and then studied playwrighting under Clifford Odets. While touring with *Members of the Wedding,* Peterson completed *Take a Giant Step.*

The play opened on 28 November 1953 on Broadway and ran for seventy-two performances that left an indelible mark on American theater. This adolescent play is set in New England in the 1950s and is reminiscent of Peterson's childhood of growing up black in white suburbia. Critics of this period interpreted the painful rite-of-passage experience of seventeen-year-old Spencer "Spence" Scott as his sexual awakening and transition into manhood. However, in the 1990s, critics recognize that the social factor of Spence's race is the subtext informing his feeling of ostracism by his white classmates and his precipitating subsequent sexual initiation into manhood. *Take a Giant Step* was listed in *Best Plays of 1953–1954,* ran Off Broadway for 264 performances in 1956, and was made into a film in 1958, which Peterson cowrote with Julius Epstein.

The decades from 1960 to 1980 represent disparate passages during which Peterson attempted to reclaim the scintillating power of subject that he had attained with *Giant.* He became the first African American screenwriter in Hollywood, but he also found himself subject to its vicissitudes and left in the 1960s. Coupled with Hollywood's instability, Peterson found East Coast theatergoers always expecting another *Giant.* One problem of his 1960s and 1970s plays was Peterson's adoption of intricate plots. *Entertain a Ghost,* a dual-plotted story about a self-absorbed young woman determined to become an actress, opened at the Actors Playhouse on 9 April 1962 to poor reviews. *Crazy Horse,* the story of an interracial marriage between a black journalist and white woman during the 1950s, enjoyed a brief stint at the New Federal Theater during November 1979.

In the 1980s, Peterson shifted his theatrical stage to the Theater Department at the State University of New York at Stony Brook. *Another Show* concerns another adolescent—this time a young male who commits suicide on campus—but the focus of the play involves the parent's reactions. This February 1983 student production enjoyed a two-week world premiere that caught the attention of Broadway critics.

The 1990s find Peterson, a widower, assiduously writing. While he retired from Stony Brook as a professor in 1993, he has been cowriting a musical with Ken Lauber over the past several years. *Numbers* concerns a "black gangster and a Jewish boy" involved in the numbers racket in Harlem after World War II. Peterson anticipates a London production. Future projects include writing for television once again.

• Seymour Peck, "The Man Who Took a Giant Step," *New York Times,* 20 Sept. 1953, 2:1. Howard Taubman, "Theatre and Peterson's Work," *New York Times,* 10 Apr. 1962, 1:48. Doris E. Abramson, *Negro Playwrights in the American Theatre, 1925–1959,* 1969, pp. 221–238. Donald T. Evans, "Bring It All Back Home: Playwrights of the Fifties," *Black World* 20 (Feb. 1971): 41–45. Mel Gussow, "Stage: 'Crazy Horse,' Drama by Louis Peterson at New Federal," *New York Times* 12 Nov. 1979, 3:13. Barbara Delatiner, "Playwright Eyes a New Giant Step," *New York Times,* 20 Feb. 1983, 21:19. Steven R. Carter, "Louis Peterson" in *DLB,* vol. 38, *Afro-American Writers after 1955: Dramatists and Prose Writers,* eds. Thadious M. Davis and Trudier Harris, 1985, pp. 134–139.

—Virginia Whatley Smith

PETRY, ANN (b. 1908), novelist, short story writer, author of books for children and juveniles, essayist, poet, and lecturer. Ann Petry was born above her father's drugstore on 12 October 1908 in Old Saybrook, Connecticut. She attended Old Saybrook's public schools, starting at the age of four. In 1931, she earned the PhG degree at the University of Connecticut, and, for more than nine years, worked as a pharmacist in the family-owned drugstores in Old Saybrook and Old Lyme. During these years, she also wrote short stories. These stories remain unpublished.

Following her marriage to George D. Petry in 1938, Ann Petry moved to Harlem, abandoned the family profession, and, for the next eight years, actively pursued a career as a writer. From 1938 to 1941, she worked as a reporter for New York's *Amsterdam News.* From 1941 to 1944, she was a reporter and also the editor of the woman's page for *The People's Voice,* where from 1942 to 1943 she wrote about Harlem's upper middle class in the weekly column "The Lighter Side." During these years, she also enrolled in a writing workshop and a creative writing class at Columbia University. Petry's decision to change her profession to writer was a gamble that paid off. Her first short story, "Marie of the Cabin Club," a suspense-romance that is set in a Harlem night club, was published in 1939 in the Baltimore newspaper *Afro-American.* "On Saturday Night the Sirens Sound" (1943), which is also set in Harlem and focuses on children left home alone, was published in the *Crisis.* This story intrigued an editor at Houghton Mifflin who encouraged Petry to apply for Houghton's fellowship in fiction. Recipients of this fellowship received $2,400 and the publication of their winning work. In 1945, Petry won the fellowship, and in 1946, Houghton Mifflin published *The *Street,* a naturalistic/feminist novel about a mother who tries to provide a better life for herself and her son in an urban environment that foreshadows failure.

Soon after its publication, *The Street* became a best-seller. Reprinted in 1985 as part of the Black Women Writers series at Beacon Press and reissued in 1992 by Houghton Mifflin, this novel has sold close to two million copies and is hailed universally as a "masterpiece" of African American fiction and a "classic" of urban American realism. Other widely acclaimed works by the writer that also continue to be reprinted or reissued are *The Drugstore Cat* (1949), her only children's work; *The Narrows* (1953), a complex novel of psychological realism; *Miss Muriel and Other Stories* (1971), a collection that presents "well-founded" portrayals of characters in both urban and small town America; and *Harriet Tubman: Conductor on the Underground Railroad* (1955) and **Tituba of Salem Village* (1964), juvenile works with convincingly human depictions of well-known slaves Harriet *Tubman and Tituba Indian.

Outstanding works by Petry but with a smaller audience are *Country Place* (1947), a novel that examines class and gender within a white New England community; *Legends of the Saints* (1970), a juvenile work that includes in its documentation of saints an African American; and "The Moses Project" (1988), a short story about house arrest in modern times. Published in anthologies but not bearing Petry's name are five poems that are reminiscent of African American poetry from the 1970s: "Noo York City 1," "Noo York City 2," and "Noo York City 3" (1976) and "A Purely Black Stone" and "A Real Boss Black Cat" (1981). Her essays, which cover topics ranging from how to teach students to write creatively to the novel as social criticism, are mostly lectures revised for collections by other writers.

Critics call Petry's style versatile. Her novels, short stories, and poems evolve from her experiences in Harlem and Old Saybrook. History is the basis of her books for adolescents. When describing settings, Petry has an eye for details, and when creating characters, an ear for dialogue. Because of her sensitivity to landscapes and personalities, readers can almost see and feel with her narrators and characters.

Critics also call Petry a visionary and a humanist. In the 1940s and 1950s, long before feminism became ideological, she had created in *The Street* and *The Narrows* women who might be characterized as feminists. Long before interracial relationships between men of African descent and white women would become accepted in America, she described a love affair between an African American man and a white woman in *The Narrows.* Long before African American and white women in the 1960s would enter into dialogue to oppose patriarchy, she had provided in the 1940s such discourses in subtexts within *The Street* and *Country Place.*

Recognitions of Petry's aesthetics have also come in the form of honorariums, citations, lectureships at universities, library collections, and numerous translations of her novels, short stories, and juvenile works. In 1946, editor Martha Foley dedicated to Petry the collection *The Best American Short Stories, 1946,* which also included Petry's short story "Like a Winding Sheet." That same year, the New York Women's City Club honored her for her contributions to the city as a reporter and novelist; as an organizer of The Negro Women, Incorporated, a consumer watch-group for working-class women in Harlem; as a recreation specialist, particularly for her development of programs for parents and children in problem areas in Harlem; as a writer of skits and programs for children of laundry workers; and as a member of the American Negro Theatre, where during the year 1940 she performed at the Schomburg Center for Research in Black Culture as Tillie Petunia in *On Striver's Row.* Since the 1970s, Petry has appeared in *Who's Who of American Women, Who's Who among Black Americans,* and *Who's Who in Writers, Editors and Poets.* She has received citations from the Greater Women in Connecticut History, the United Nations Association, the city of Philadelphia, the Connecticut Commission on the Arts, and from literary groups such as the annual Celebration of Black Writing Conference in Philadelphia and the Middle Atlantic Writers Association. She has lectured at Miami University of Ohio and was a visiting professor at the University of Hawaii. She has received honorary degrees from Suffolk University (1983), the University of Connecticut (1988), and Mount Holyoke College (1989). All of her novels, several short stories, and one juvenile work have been translated, together, into at least twelve different languages. Collections of her manuscripts, letters, first editions, and translations have been compiled at Boston University, Yale University, and the Atlanta University Center.

Petry has said often that she wants to be remembered for not only *The Street,* her most celebrated work, but for everything she has written.

• Theodore L. Gross, "Ann Petry: The Novelist as Social Critic," in *Black Fiction: New Studies in the Afro-American Novel since 1945,* ed. A. Robert Lee, 1980, pp. 41–53. Trudier Harris, "On Southern and Northern Maids: Geography, Mammies and Militants," in *From Mammies to Militants: Domestics in Black American Literature,* 1982, pp. 88–100. Gloria Wade-Gayles, "Journeying from Can't to Can and Sometimes Back to 'Can't,'" in *No Crystal Stair: Visions of Race and Sex in Black Women's Fiction,* 1984, pp. 148–156. Marjorie Pryse, "'Patterns Against the Sky': Deism and Motherhood in Ann Petry's *The Street,*" in *Conjuring: Black Women, Fiction and Literary Traditions,* eds. Majorie Pryse and Hortense J. Spillers, 1985, pp. 116–131. Suzanne Poirier, "From Pharmacist to Novelist," in *Pharmacy in History,* 1986, pp. 27–33. Gladys J. Washington, "A World Made Cunningly: A Closer Look at Ann Petry's Short Fiction," *CLA Journal* 30 (Sept. 1986): 14–29. Nellie McKay, introduction to *The Narrows,* 1988. Calvin Hernton, "The Significance of Ann Petry," in *The Sexual Mountain and Black Women Writers, Adventures in Sex, Literature and Real Life,* 1987; rpt. 1990, pp. 59–88. Hazel Arnett Ervin, introduction to *Ann Petry: A Bio-Bibliography,* 1993.

—Hazel Arnett Ervin

PHARR, ROBERT DEANE (1916–1992), novelist. Rediscovered in the late 1960s after an interrupted career, Robert Deane Pharr constructs a critique of the American dream and the African American community's ability to attain it. By handing his manuscript from one professor to another at the Columbia Faculty Club (where he worked as a waiter), he eventually saw the publication of his first novel, *The Book of Numbers,* in 1969. As Pharr's most widely respected and successful novel, this first major work relates the role crime and fate play in the African American attainment of the American dream.

Charting the rise and fall of a numbers runner named David Greene, Pharr suggests that in order to break into the restrictive confines of the American dream, an African American must work outside the bounds of legitimacy. This novel, set in a small southern city during the Depression, combines this critique with an overlay of biblical prophecy to paint a portrait of a community and a people caught between their hopes for success and the limited possibility that they might be realized. His characters (Blueboy Harris, Althea Goines, Delilah Mazique) defy the law and risk all for the illusion of certainty. Flawed by excessive length (a quality that would also plague his second novel, *S.R.O.*) and didacticism, *The Book of Numbers* nonetheless demonstrates Pharr's talent for relating dialect and dialogue. His evocative exploration of the ways in which chance bolsters human endurance established a framework for depicting the urban experience of African Americans that persists today. The book's success—eventually leading to an Avco film of the same title (1973)—buoyed Pharr's career and motivated the process of self-reflection and imagination that his succeeding works described.

Pharr's second novel, *S.R.O.* (1971), moves his exploration of the dream to Harlem, where a picaresque parade of lesbians, drug addicts, and would-be artists explore the paths of fulfillment left open to them. This most autobiographical and self-reflexive of Pharr's works documents Sid Bailey's relationships with beautiful recovering addict Gloria Bascomb and with his writing (which he calls "his woman"). In particular, critics have praised the use of structural interchapters that alleviate and focus the first-person energies of the primary narrative. Once again, however, it is an extraordinarily long, didactic novel that harbors moments of exquisite dialogue and insight.

Pharr continued to write after *S.R.O.* (producing *The Welfare Bitch* in 1973 and *The Soul Murder Case: A Confession of a Victim* in 1975), but he never achieved the kind of success he tasted with *The Book of Numbers.* Relating its protagonist's unwilling protection of a relative's crime empire, *Giveadamn Brown* (1978), Pharr's final work, combines brevity of expression and the author's enduring skill with dialogue and quickly paced action. Of the late works, it comes closest to enacting the promise of his critical perspective on ambition and success in the United States.

The Book of Numbers is an important, groundbreaking analysis of the ironies that persist within the African American experience. As a social critic, literary realist, and pioneer in the exploration of the mechanics of writing, Robert Deane Pharr stands as an exemplar for authors who followed him.

• John O'Brien and Raman K. Singh, "Interview with Robert Deane Pharr," *Negro American Literature Forum* 8 (Fall 1974): 244–246. Garrett Epps, "To Know the Truth: The Novels of Robert Deane Pharr," *Hollins Critic* 13 (1976): 1–10.

—Daniel M. Scott III

Philadelphia Fire (1990) is John Edgar *Wideman's seventh novel and the second of his books to receive the prestigious PEN/Faulkner Award (*Sent for You Yesterday* won in 1984). A work that combines public events, personal history, and the imagination, *Philadelphia Fire* has been referred to as "docufiction" (documentary fiction). It also could be called a metafiction because it deals in part with the circumstances of its own composition.

The book concerns the aftermath of the 13 May 1985 bombing by the city of Philadelphia of a house occupied by a militant African American organization known as MOVE, which had resisted an eviction order. Nearly everyone in the house died and an entire city block was consumed in the resulting conflagration. This event and Wideman's personal response to it are described in the middle section of the book, which also deals with the author's anguish over the conviction and imprisonment for murder of his youngest son, Jake.

In the main narrative, a writer named Cudjoe returns from self-imposed exile on a Greek island to attempt to trace the whereabouts of Simba Muntu, a child who is supposed to be the sole survivor of the fire. Precisely what motivates Cudjoe to return so precipitously to the United States is not clear, but it appears to have something to do with his growing sense of betrayal: of himself, his sons (from whom he has estranged himself since his divorce), his talent, and his former commitment to changing the world. Cudjoe's separation from his sons parallels Wideman's loss of his own son to prison, and Cudjoe's quest to find Simba Muntu counterpoints Wideman's quest to free his son. But Simba isn't found, and Wideman's son remains imprisoned, underscoring the tragedy of a lost generation of American youth, one of the book's principal themes.

Views of the book have been divergent. Celebrated African American writer Charles R. *Johnson, in a 1990 review in the *Washington Post,* calls Wideman "the most critically acclaimed black male writer of the last decade" and declares himself a fan, yet he finds *Philadelphia Fire* to be confusing and disappointing. For Darryl Pinckney, writing in 1991 in the *Times Literary Supplement,* the book is disorganized, a "parable" that "attempts too much." On the other hand, Mark Hummel, assessing the book in the same year for the *Bloomsbury Review,* finds it to be "difficult but immensely important and always eloquent." Ishmael *Reed in *Airing Dirty Laundry* (1993) blames the metafictional form for some of *Philadelphia Fire*'s problems—overdone details, uncertainty of plot—but he praises Wideman's courage as an artist and compares the novel to a Miles *Davis concert, finding the performance to be "terrific."

In an interview in *Callaloo* (Winter 1990), Wideman stated that in *Fever* and in *Philadelphia Fire,* he was forcing himself to stop and assess "what's happening to us." This "urgent desire to bear witness," as Darryl Pinckney calls it—also a principal motive in **Brothers and Keepers* (1985)—is one in which personal concerns converge with a concern for the state of the nation as a whole. Jan Clausen's description of *Philadelphia Fire* (in *The Kenyon Review,* Spring 1992) as "anguished, apocalyptic" underscores the unsettling nature of Wideman's testimony, the unsettled nature of our social being.

• Doreatha Drummond Mbalia, *John Edgar Wideman: Reclaiming the African Personality,* 1995, pp. 63–67, 107–112.

—Robert Elliot Fox

Piano Lesson, The. The winner of the 1990 Pulitzer Prize, *The Piano Lesson* is August *Wilson's second play to receive that award (**Fences* won in 1987). With this selection, Wilson became the first African American to receive the award twice and joined the select company of only seven American playwrights to be so honored. In addition, *The Piano Lesson* received the Drama Critics' Circle Award and the Tony Award for best play. Like Wilson's other plays, it was given a staged reading at the Eugene O'Neill National Playwrights Conference (1987) and directed by Lloyd Richards, the dean of the Yale Drama School, where it was first performed (1988) before, subsequently, touring other cities prior to its Broadway opening at the Walter Kerr Theatre on 16 April 1990. The cast included Charles S. Dutton in the role of Boy Willie and S. Epatha Merkerson as Berniece.

Set in 1936 in Pittsburgh, the play looks at the displacement of African Americans from Mississippi who have migrated north without coming to terms with their southern past. This struggle is objectified in the brother-sister conflict between Berniece and Boy Willie. They fight over a piano that their great-grandfather carved for a white man, which the brother and sister have now inherited.

Bringing along a truckload of watermelons to sell to finance his trip to see Berniece and reclaim his family legacy, Boy Willie wants to sell the piano and use the money to buy the farmland that his ancestors worked as slaves and sharecroppers. Berniece, however, does not want to part with this symbol of her family past; their father died stealing the piano—and its artistic legacy—from the white man who had exploited his family. The piano is a concrete representation of the still-existing conflicts and connections between the past and present; it works on several levels to suggest that white exploitation of blacks' artistic and manual accomplishment is an American tradition underlying the reality of the American dream. The play's resolution, which comes with the assistance of a ghost, suggests that claiming and transforming the suffering of the past into cultural artistry is necessary before Americans can begin to participate creatively in the present. As a result of their discussions and the activity of the ghost, the brother and sister achieve a family unity and closeness. Berniece's daughter and Boy Willie's niece, Maretha, will use the ancestral piano to produce music and as a source of pride in her heritage.

Richard Hummler praised the play for its powerful and accurate rendering of black dialogue, and Frank Rich lauded Wilson for his ability to infuse the play with history lessons. While critics were also quick to point out that the success of this play helped cement Wilson's phenomenal rise to theatrical prominence, Robert Brustein, writing in the *New Republic,* questioned the play's commercialism and suggested that it lacked artistic merit. The drama critic for *Time,* however, argued that the play established Wilson as the "richest theatrical voice to emerge in the U.S. since . . . the flowering of Tennessee Williams and Arthur Miller."

—Marilyn Elkins

PICKENS, WILLIAM (1881–1954), orator, journalist, essayist, and autobiographer. William Pickens, one of the most popular African American speakers of his era, was born in Anderson County, South Carolina, on 15 January 1881, the son of former slaves who worked as tenant farmers. His parents moved their family to Arkansas in 1888 in search of better economic and educational opportunities. From the beginning a zealous student, Pickens's first systematic schooling came in 1890 in Argenta, across the river from Little Rock. With funds earned from a variety of manual labor jobs, Pickens paid his way to attend the Little Rock High School, from which he graduated at the top of his class in 1899. He then obtained admission to Talladega College in Alabama, where he studied for three years before entering Yale University in 1902. At Yale Pickens won the Henry James Ten Eyck prize in oratory for a speech on Haiti and was elected to Phi Beta Kappa. After completing his bachelor's degree in classics in 1904, Pickens rejected an offer to tour the country as a platform lecturer, choosing instead to return to the South to teach classics, literature, and sociology at Talladega (1904–1914), Wiley University in Texas (1914–1915), and Morgan College in Baltimore (1915–1920), where he served as dean and later vice-president.

Having been active as an organizer and recruiter for the NAACP since its founding in 1910, Pickens readily accepted an offer in 1919 to become assistant to James Weldon *Johnson, field secretary of the NAACP. When Johnson was elevated to executive director of the NAACP the following year, Pickens became associate field secretary. In this capacity and later as director of branches, Pickens made a major contribution to the expansion of the NAACP, especially in the South, between 1920 and 1940. As a contributing editor of the Associated Negro Press for twenty-one years, Pickens helped publicize NAACP positions and activities in more than one hundred African American newspapers. After leaving the NAACP in 1942, Pickens went to work for the U.S. Treasury Department. During World War II, his efforts centered on selling war bonds in the African American community. After retirement from his government job in 1950, Pickens and his wife traveled internationally. He died aboard a ship off the coast of Jamaica on 6 April 1954 and was buried at sea.

Pickens first made a name for himself as a writer in 1904, when he began publishing increasingly blunt and controversial articles in the *Voice of the Negro.* "Choose!" (June 1906) demanded that every African American take an unequivocal stand against the philosophy and tactics of Booker T. *Washington and in favor of those of W. E. B. *Du Bois. Readers of Pickens's 1911 autobiography, *The Heir of Slaves,* however, found only hints as to Pickens's public differences with Washington. Patterned after Washington's much celebrated **Up from Slavery* (1901), *The Heir of Slaves* emphasizes a young African American's devotion to education and to the dedication of his learning and experience to the uplift of his people in the South. But with the 1916 publication of *The New Negro: His Political, Civil and Mental Status,* a collection of his essays dedicated to the "essential humanity and justice" of "the white and the black men of tomorrow," Pickens made plain his uncompromising views on civil rights. The fundamental right Pickens demanded for African Americans in *The New Negro* was "full citizenship," by which he meant an end to all forms of segregation and a guarantee of the right to vote. In 1922, Pickens published *The Vengeance of the Gods and Three Other Stories of the Real American Color Line,* in which he denounces through highly didactic fiction the stereotyping of African American men and the illusory notions of superiority entertained by white Americans. A year later an expanded version of Pickens's autobiography appeared under the title *Bursting Bonds.* Retaining the nine chapters of *The Heir of Slaves,* Pickens added five new ones to create *Bursting Bonds,* the title of which implied its author's determination to speak freely about matters on which he had previously been circumspect. *Bursting Bonds* exposes the mystique of white power and paternalism at Talladega, details the explosive intricacies of Jim Crow in east Texas, and recalls Pickens's lonely, defiant ride in a forbidden Pullman car through Arkansas. By the end of the book, Pickens exemplifies in himself a model of what the New Negro of the 1920s stood for and wrote about. In its candor about the contemporary color line and sensitivity to its author's transition from conservative to militant, *Bursting Bonds* marks a turning point in the evolution of African American autobiography away from the deferential posture of *Up from Slavery* and toward the confrontational rhetoric of **Black Boy* (1945).

• Rebecca Chalmers Barton, *Witnesses for Freedom,* 1948. Sheldon Avery, *Up from Washington: William Pickens and the Negro Struggle for Equality,* 1989. William Pickens, *Bursting Bonds,* ed. William L. Andrews, 1991.

—William L. Andrews

PILATE DEAD is the aunt of *Milkman Dead, the protagonist in Toni *Morrison's **Song of Solomon* (1977). Represented in the novel as the eccentric sister of Macon Dead II, who like her daughter Reba and her granddaughter Hagar has no navel, Pilate wears an earring made of a little box that contains her name and makes bootleg wine for a living. For these reasons and because he believes she tricked him out of the family inheritance of gold, Macon forbids Milkman to have any dealings with Pilate. Yet she is a part of his life from the beginning. The novel opens with her singing the song of her grandfather's flight back to Africa to escape from slavery on the day before Milkman's birth. The fact that his mother even conceives him is supposedly attributed to a green potion Pilate, described as a "natural healer" and a "root worker," gives her. Described as her own person, Pilate is a woman who "threw away every assumption she had learned and began at zero." When Milkman starts to have questions about his identity and where he fits in, he ignores his father's command and consults Pilate about his family history. As the family griot and ancestor who knows the past, Pilate becomes the key to Milkman's quest to understand himself and his heritage. On his trip from Michigan to the South, he learns that the sack she keeps is really a sack of her father's bones. He escorts her back to the South to give her father a proper burial, and as she dies in his arms, he sings to her the song of his ancestors, the song he learned from her and that he had once regarded as a nonsense rhyme. Pilate is representative of the ancestor figure and griot in many of Morrison's novels, that member of the African American community who is both a link to the past and a key to the future.

• Marilyn Sanders Mobley, *Folk Roots and Mythic Wings in Sarah Orne Jewett and Toni Morrison,* 1992.

—Marilyn Sanders Mobley

PLATO, ANN (?–?), essayist and poet. Little is known about the life of Ann Plato. Apparently, she was a free black in Hartford, Connecticut, at a time when the city's free black residents outnumbered the town's slave population. She was also a member of Hartford's Colored Congregational Church. Knowledge about her is limited to the one book that she published. Entitled *Essays: Including Biographies and Miscellaneous Pieces of Prose and Poetry* (1841), it contains four biographical compositions, sixteen very short essays, and twenty poems.

Her minister, the Reverend James W. C. *Pennington, wrote an introductory notice "To the Reader." After identifying Ann Plato as one of his parishioners, he repeatedly says she is young but does not make clear exactly how old she is. He says nothing about her family except to indicate that she is "of modest worth." Neither does he tell how long she had been a member of his church, but he does record she is "of pleasing piety."

If Pennington tells little about Ann Plato, she told even less about herself. There is some evidence that she was either a young teacher or preparing to be one. Her essays are conventional. Designed as didactic renderings of issues that she found important, they focus primarily on religious and educational matters. Her attitude toward Africa appears in an essay entitled "Education" in which she commends those Christian missionaries who were willing to forsake the comforts of home in order to take "a message of love to the burning clime of Africa." In keeping with an eighteenth-century tendency to eulogize one's friends, Plato mourns—in the four biographies—the early deaths of some friends, one of whom was apparently a slave.

Although Plato's poetry seldom deals with racial issues, she apparently was not totally oblivious to the concerns of her day. One of her poems, "To the First of August," celebrates the ending of slavery in the British West Indies and may have been written shortly after that law went into effect on 1 August 1838. At the time there were a number of poems written by a variety of poets on the subject, and she presumably joined this contemporaneous group. "The Natives of America" is a dramatic poem which relates her consideration of the plight of Native Americans in the United States. But for the most part, her subjects seem to have little to do with the specific problems faced by African Americans in everyday life.

One might conclude her only value is as a link between Phillis *Wheatley, whose work she apparently knew, and later women writers. On the other hand, Plato does show in *Essays* some tendencies toward a lyricism not associated with Phillis Wheatley. For example, her elegaic "Reflections, Written on Visiting the Grave of a Venerated Friend" goes beyond the expected neoclassical tradition and shows real feeling about death. Her love poem "Forget Thee Not" is another example of a stylized lyric that conveys a sense of emotion. But in following neoclassical conventions, she did not write about herself. As a result, much about Ann Plato has—so far—been lost to history. Yet, one wonders how autobiographical are such poems as "On Examination for a Teacher," "I Have No Brother," or "The Residence of My Fathers."

• "Ann Plato" in *Afro-American Women Writers, 1746–1933,* 1988, ed. Ann Allen Shockley, pp. 26–28. Kenny J. Williams, introduction to *Essays,* by Ann Plato, 1988.

—Kenny Jackson Williams

PLUMPP, STERLING (b. 1940), poet, educator, editor, and critic. Writing "tales of who I am" (*Contemporary Authors Autobiography Series,* vol. 21, 1995), Sterling Plumpp struggles to create the homeland of the spirit that accidents of birth—racial and economic—and what might be called accidents of destiny—the deaths of loved ones, the historical changes that have swept the African American and world community since his birth—have denied him. Yet his poems have far more than autobiographical resonance, not only because of the allusive, lyrical language in which he writes his best work, but because his quest for identity resonates with the surrounding struggle for freedom of the African American community during the civil rights movement and its aftermath, and, especially in poems chronicling his experiences in Africa, with the struggle during the same years of colonized peoples for national sovereignty.

Sterling Plumpp was born to unmarried parents on 30 January 1940 in Clinton, Mississippi. His maternal grandparents raised him on the cotton plantation where his grandfather, Victor Emmanuel Plumpp, labored as a sharecropper. At age seven, a year before he started school, he joined his grandfather, an older brother, and other relatives in the fields picking cotton, but no amount of work was sufficient to raise the family out of debt. Listening to his grandparents' nightly prayers, Plumpp learned that one "could use words to petition for a different reality."

The full power of religion struck him in 1951 in a local evangelical church, when the force of a singer's voice prompted him to march to the altar to signify a conversion that soon, however, had to compete with budding adolescent interests. One of the abrupt psychological blows the South could deliver came in 1954, when news of Emmett Till's murder for flirting with a white woman traumatized Plumpp and others of his generation. At sixteen, Plumpp converted to Catholicism, and, throughout high school, cast about for a way to escape the dangers of Jim Crow. Success took the form of an academic scholarship to St. Benedict's College in Atchison, Kansas.

There he had a new kind of conversion experience when he discovered Greek literature and James *Baldwin, whose "Sonny's Blues" inspired Plumpp to become a writer. After two years, yearning to write and feeling cut off from black culture, Plumpp left St. Benedict's and traveled north to Chicago.

He found work there in the main post office, read and tried to write in his off hours, and eventually enrolled at Roosevelt University, where he majored in psychology. After completing his bachelor's degree, he enrolled in a graduate program in clinical psychology, but continued to read widely—everything from Amiri *Baraka to Jean-Paul Sartre, and, of course, Baldwin, whose *The Fire Next Time* (1963) struck Plumpp like a thunderbolt—and immersed himself in music. During a "nightmarish" 1964–1965 interlude in the U.S. army, such books were his window to the outside world.

He published his first book, *Portable Soul*, in 1969, offering poems that drew on the language of the Black Power movement, but also began to construct the vocabulary for Plumpp's tales of identity. Publication led to a job teaching African American studies at the Chicago campus of the University of Illinois, where Plumpp became a full professor teaching both literature and creative writing.

His second book, *Half Black, Half Blacker* (1970), continues his simultaneous grappling with late 1960s upheavals in African American identity, and with his ongoing self-creation. Every black man, he writes in "Daybreak," "is an epic." The fusion of personal and public struggles is expanded into an impressionistic psychological treatise in Plumpp's 1972 book, *Black Rituals.* Confronting what he calls the "dragons" of his existence—his sharecropping youth in the Jim Crow South, the saving power of black music as a conduit of the divine, and the centrality of the black church as a repository of African American culture and engine of change—Plumpp created in this book a rough theory of his own and his people's existence.

The theory continued to develop in two long poems, "Steps to Break the Circle" and "Clinton," published as pamphlets in 1974 and 1976, respectively, and later included in Plumpp's 1982 volume, *The Mojo Hands Call / I Must Go.* Plumpp's growing interest in international liberation movements also bore fruit in 1982 when he edited an anthology of South African poetry, *Somehow We Survive.* With the anthology and the new collection, which won the 1983 Carl Sandburg Award, Plumpp established himself as a significant voice in American letters. The new collection's reference to irresistible "Mojo hands," furthermore, spotlights Plumpp's arrival at a new conceptual plateau in the collection. In "Steps to Break the Circle: An Introduction," for instance, Plumpp casts a critical, evaluative eye on 1960s poetry and politics, and on his own evolution. He expresses doubts about whether the "answer" that will break the circle of African American pain is 1960s-style black nationalism, and not something at once more "coldly programmatic" and more open to a poetics of individuality.

In *Blues: The Story Always Untold* (1989), Plumpp firmly attaches himself to the blues as the root of African American poetics. An increasing faith in words as arbiters of reality is expressed in poems celebrating the power of blues singers and of the music that passes through them like a god: When the protagonist of his poem "Mississippi Griot" bent guitar strings, Plumpp writes that his grandfather's "fields were flooded."

The parallel between African American and South African experience is the force behind Plumpp's 1993 volume, *Johannesburg and Other Poems,* which grew out of a 1991 visit Plumpp made to South Africa. His observations there taught him, he says, the centrality of class as well as race in African and African American experience. Yet his spiritual repatriation is also a repatriation in suffering. In the title poem, the Johannesburg he experiences is both a song-rich African Harlem, and a dehumanizing "Cold Steel Mountain." Thus in his "homeland," Plumpp is cast back on his career-long sifting of memory and history for the elements of identity: "I ask, Johannesburg, if your streets know my name." In his volume, *Hornman* (1995), Plumpp returns to his abiding balm, music, seeking the link between his "blues roots" and jazz improvisation. Plumpp published *Ornate With Smoke* in 1997, and *Blues: Narratives* in 1999. His importance lies in his ability to communicate the excitement of such quests, and to fix ready-made concepts such as race—inevitable broadcaster of racism that it is—in the way the late Richard Feynman was said to fix radios: by thinking. In his best work, Plumpp makes mind-dimming concepts transmit vision, not hate.

• James Cunningham, "Sterling Plumpp," in *DLB*, vol. 41, *Afro-American Poets since 1955*, eds. Trudier Harris and Thadious M. Davis, 1985, pp. 257–265. "Plumpp, Sterling D(ominic)," in *Contemporary Authors: New Revision Series*, vol. 24, ed. Deborah A. Straub, 1988, pp. 371–372. James Cunningham, "Baldwin Aesthetics in Sterling Plumpp's Mojo Poems," *Black American Literature Forum* 23 (Fall 1989): 505–518. Sterling Plumpp, "Sterling Plumpp," in *Contemporary Authors Autobiography Series*, ed. Joyce Nakamura, vol. 21, 1995, pp. 165–178.

—Michael Collins

Poems on Various Subjects, Religious and Moral, the first book published by an African American on the North American continent, first appeared early in September of 1773. Printed in London and backed by the British philanthropist Selina Hastings, Countess of Huntingdon, an earlier version of this book, which was to have been printed in Boston, was rejected for racist reasons. This projected volume of 1772 would have been quite different from that which actually did come out in September of the next year. Of the twenty-eight poems slated to appear in the planned 1772 volume, six are decidedly political and patriotic in subject, while only two poems of the 1773 volume's thirty-eight pieces by Phillis *Wheatley (the thirty-eighth poem, by James Bowdoin, is a riddle that Wheatley "solves" in the thirty-ninth and final poem of the volume) specifically deal with patriotic topics.

While the 1772 proposals promise a volume that would probably have propelled Wheatley into the limelight as first poet for American Independence, eclipsing Philip Freneau's later claim to this distinction, the 1773 *Poems* is much less obviously political in nature. "To the King's Most Excellent Majesty. 1768" and "To the Right Honourable William, Earl of Dartmouth" both state Wheatley's preoccupation with freedom, the central subject of her oeuvre. The former poem celebrates George III's repeal of the Stamp Act and concludes with the arresting line, "A monarch's smile can set his subjects free!" "To . . . the Earl of Dartmouth" opens with the enthusiastic couplet, "Hail, happy day, when smiling like the morn, / Fair Freedom rose New-England to adorn," but contains the affecting story of Wheatley's seizure by slavers from her father's embrace.

Such poems as "To Maecenas," "On Recollection," and "On Imagination" appear to take up aesthetic concerns. "To Maecenas," for example, ostensibly addresses the issue of literary patronage, paralleling Horace's dedication of his first *Book of Odes* to Maecenas. Yet Wheatley's structure is much more complex than that of her Latin predecessor. Expanding her poem from Horace's thirty-six lines of Latin to fifty-five of neoclassical American colonial verse, Wheatley introduces the classical pastoral mode ("myrtle shade" and shepherds piping in sunny meadows), which she exploits as a major part of her subversive style; declares she longs to emulate Homer and Virgil, which she later attempts in her two epyllia (short epics), "Goliath of Gath" and "Niobe in Distress"; specifies her personal struggle for freedom by calling Terence, the Latin comedic dramatist and former slave from North Africa, "happier" than she because his pen has effectually freed him; and states that she will sing the virtues of Maecenas and at the same time praise "him [God] from whom those virtues sprung," hence signaling the religious and moral subjects of her volume's title that she will explicate in her frequent use of myth and symbol adapted from the King James Bible. Wheatley also asserts her own poetic maturity, manifested by attainment of the poet's laurel (as does Horace, yet whereas what the Latin poet affirms comes to him by acknowledged right, the black woman poet must "snatch . . . While [others] indulgent smile upon the deed").

In a similar manner "On Recollection" and "On Imagination," seeming to address central issues of the aesthetic categories of the time, actually serve as vehicles for Wheatley's demonstration of power over words and permit her to break the "iron bands" of oppression and to move freely "through the unbounded regions of the mind."

The 1773 *Poems* is prefaced by several items, including a frontispiece or woodcut of Wheatley before a writing desk, a "Dedication to the Right Honourable the Countess of Huntington," a letter by Wheatley's master, John Wheatley, and a second letter, "To the Publick," attesting to Wheatley's authenticity as author of the volume's poems and signed by the best-known dignitaries in Boston. Of these materials, the letter of attestation and the portrait are of particular interest.

The letter of attestation is a remarkable document. This testimony marks the first occasion that the authentication procedure, to which so many African Americans subsequently found themselves subjected, was applied to verify either the literacy of the African American author, as in this case, or the veracity of the African American who recited her or his "narrative" to an amanuensis.

While the frontispiece of Wheatley may look innocuous to today's audience, it cannot have seemed so to Wheatley's. The presentation to the world of an obviously black woman, holding a quill pen resting on paper on which one can see writing, striking a meditative pose promising still more writing, definitely denies all notions that black people cannot participate in the creation of literate artifacts; in short, this portrait enacts rebellion. This rebellion against white oppression occurs at the beginning of the African American literary tradition, a moment whose significance cannot be exaggerated.

[*See also* Literary History, article on Colonial and Early National Eras.]

• William H. Robinson, *Black New England Letters: The Uses of Writings in Black New England,* 1977. Houston A. Baker, Jr., *The Journey Back: Issues in Black Literature and Criticism,* 1980. Sondra A. O'Neale, "A Slave's Subtle War: Phillis Wheatley's Use of Biblical Myth and Symbol," *Early American Literature* 21.2 (Fall 1986): 144–165. John C. Shields, ed., *The Collected Works of Phillis Wheatley,* 1988. Philip M. Richards, "Phillis Wheatley and Literary Americanization," *American Quarterly* 44.2 (June 1992): 163–191. Frances Smith Foster, *Written by Herself: Literary Production by African American Women 1746–1892,* 1993.

—John C. Shields

POINSETTIA JACKSON, character in *A Red Death* (1991) by Walter *Mosley. Poor, sick, but still sexy as the novel opens, and soon thereafter dead, Poinsettia Jackson is more catalyst than character in Walter Mosley's second *Easy Rawlins mystery, set in Los Angeles in Red-scared 1953. Her murder provides the key to subsequent murders, a window into other characters, and the novel's thematic center. In their reactions to Poinsettia's murder, unorthodox amateur investigator Easy Rawlins and uptight black police detective Quinten Naylor reveal what they have in common—a special sense of responsibility toward black people. When Easy finds Poinsettia hanging in her apartment in one of the buildings he pretends not to own, he thinks she has committed suicide for fear of eviction and blames himself. When Naylor's white partner, accepting too easily the evidence of suicide, asks, "Who's gonna care about this one girl, Quint?" Naylor replies, "I care." The process of solving the murder shifts the blame from Easy to another black man, his rental agent Mofass, to a racist Internal Revenue agent who has exploited blacks' fear of the law in a racist society to extort money from them. As Easy is cleared of blame, however, he realizes he still bears responsibility, for Poinsettia is the victim not simply of murder but of a chain of victimization in which he, too, has participated. When targeted by the corrupt IRS agent, Easy had betrayed a more vulnerable friend of black people, Jewish labor organizer and alleged Communist Chaim Wenzler, just as Mofass had used Poinsettia, more vulnerable than he because of her sex and poverty, to save himself. Thus, though she plays little active role in the novel, Poinsettia is central to its unfolding of the process by which racism can make its victims participate in their own victimization.

• Theodore O Mason, Jr., "Walter Mosley's Easy Rawlins: The Detective and Afro-American Fiction," *Kenyon Review* 14.4 (Fall 1992): 173–183.

—Susan L. Blake

POLITE, CARLENE HATCHER (b. 1932), novelist, essayist, dancer, activist, and educator. Carlene Hatcher Polite is among the important artists to emerge from the "second renaissance" of African American culture in the 1960s and 1970s. The author of two experimental novels, *The Flagellants* (1966) and *Sister X and the Victims of Foul Play* (1975), Polite forged a unique prose style that helped establish innovative modes popularized by later writers. In addition to writing, her widespread career has included professional dance training, performance, and instruction; political organizing; civil rights activism; and academic appointments. Born in Detroit to John and Lillian (Cook) Hatcher, international representatives of UAW-CIO, Polite attended Sarah Lawrence College and the Martha Graham School of Contemporary Dance. From 1955 to 1963, she pursued a career as a professional dancer. Polite performed with the Concert Dance Theater of New York City (1955–1959) and the Detroit Equity Theatre and Vanguard Playhouse (1960–1962), and taught modern dance in the Martha Graham technique as a guest instructor at the Detroit YWCA (1960–1962), the Detroit YMCA (1962–1963), and as a visiting instructor at Wayne State University.

In the early 1960s Polite turned from dance to political organizing and civil rights activism, joining in the cause with many African American artists and intellectuals. In 1962 she was elected to the Michigan State Central Committee of the Democratic Party. She was coordinator of the Detroit Council for Human Rights and participated in the historic June 1963 Walk for Freedom and the November 1963 Freedom Now Rally to protest the Birmingham church bombings. In 1963 Polite organized the Northern Negro Leadership Conference and was active in the NAACP throughout this time.

In 1964 Polite moved to Paris, where she lived until 1971. The influential French editor Dominique de Roux encouraged Polite's writing, and in 1966 *The Flagellants* was published in French by Christian Bourgois Editeur; Farrar, Straus and Giroux brought the novel out in English the following year. Polite received a National Foundation on the Arts and Humanities Fellowship in 1967 and a Rockefeller Foundation Fellowship in 1968. *Sister X and the Victims of Foul Play* was published in 1975, four years after Polite's return to the United States. As of the mid-1990s she is a full professor of English at the State University of New York at Buffalo, where she began as an associate professor in 1971. Polite continues to work on two other novels.

The Flagellants protests limited gender roles for African American women and men in a racially oppressive society and, by a series of interior monologues and exchanges, explores existential questions of identity that transcend yet must be part of racial cultural liberation. Sister X recounts the life of a dead black dancer in Paris who was a victim of foul play, racial stereotypes, and discrimination. Both novels have been underappreciated, though Polite's experimentation with form and attention to the rhythms and dialects of African American oral expression influenced the development of postmodern black fiction, especially the work of later innovators such as Gayl *Jones and Ishmael *Reed.

• Hammett Worthington-Smith, "Carlene Hatcher Polite," in *DLB*, vol. 33, *Afro-American Fiction Writers after 1955*, eds. Thadious M. Davis and Trudier Harris, 1984, pp. 215–218. Claudia Tate, introduction to *The Flagellants*, 1967; rpt. 1987. Margaret A. Reid, "The Diversity of Influences on Carlene Hatcher Polite's *The Flagellants* and *Sister X and the Victims of Foul Play*," *Connecticut Review* 18:1 (Spring 1996): 39–50.

—Ronna C. Johnson

Popo and Fifina. A juvenile novel by Arna *Bontemps and Langston *Hughes with illustrations by E. Simms Campbell, *Popo and Fifina: Children of Haiti* was published in 1932. Papa Jean and Mamma Anna, peasant farmers grown tired of farming on the hillsides of

Haiti, decide to pursue Papa Jean's dream to own a fishing boat, a decision that means moving the family from the interior to the coast. The story opens with a procession wending its way to the port village of Cape Haiti, parents leading the way with baby Pensia, followed by two burros laden with the family possessions, ten-year-old Fifina, and eight-year-old Popo.

Their new home is a single-room, windowless shack with a tin roof and a rickety door in a yard that includes fruit trees and fuel for cooking at their fingertips. Papa Jean secures work as a fisherman right away, and he is at sea over the succeeding days, but the reader-spectator is accorded a cultural excursion through home and village by accompanying Mamma Anna and the eager-eyed children through their daily routines.

Before the appeal of newness in Cape Haiti wears thin for the children, Mamma Anna is overtaken with homesickness for her birthplace, and the children join her for a holiday in the hills with Grandma Tercilia and other relatives, providing a brief view of the country Creole culture the family left behind. For Popo the high point of this visit occurs when he steals from his bed one evening, lured by the drums, to follow his young grown-up cousin André to the dance of the Congo.

Back at Cape Haiti, Fifina and Popo are thrilled one afternoon by the sight of a sky full of kites with long tails and singing strings in the hands of children like themselves. Owning a kite becomes their dream, and Fifina suggests a plan to gain their parents' approval. The strategy succeeds, and for several days the children are solely preoccupied with the joy of flying. But just as Fifina predicts, their parents eventually determine that the children are neglecting their other responsibilities. They must set aside the kite so that Fifina can help Mamma Anna at home and Popo can become an apprentice in Uncle Jacques's woodworking shop.

Besides Uncle Jacques, Papa Jean's older brother, the small wood shop employs old Durand, his helper, and cousin Marcel, his youngest son, who is near Popo's age. In no time, Popo focuses approval on a beautiful tray cousin Marcel is fashioning and, because he longs to craft one of his own, wonders if it is not modeled after an established pattern. The surprising knowledge that each tray is of a singular design provokes Popo's difficult question: How can anybody make a design without a pattern? His wonder about the sources of imagination prompts old Durand to observe the "riddle" that you have to put yourself into the design. Popo discovers both the pleasure and the pain of the act as he works his own tray, accompanied by the sad tale of the great King Christophe related by Uncle Jacques.

Later, when the two families picnic together along the coast, a more sober Popo climbs the steep cliffs to visit the lighthouse with Papa Jean, Uncle Jacques, Fifina, and Marcel. En route they pass several abandoned forts that remind Popo of the sad history of Christophe. The perspective from the lighthouse resonates in Popo's and Fifina's first approach to Cape Haiti, but now there are intimations that they are more grown up.

This juvenile narrative once represented a new genre in African American writing, and it was unanimously praised for its simple charm, its attention to informative details, and its poetic style. It was translated into many languages and remained in print for twenty years.

• Violet J. Harris, "From *Little Black Sambo* to *Popo and Fifina:* Arna Bontemps and the Creation of African-American Children's Literature," *The Lion and the Unicorn: A Critical Journal of Children's Literature* 14 (June 1990): 108–127.

—Charles L. James

PORTER, DOROTHY (1905–1995), bibliographer and curator. In the introduction to Richard Newman's *Black Access: A Bibliography of Afro-American Bibliographies* (1984), Dorothy Burnett Porter Wesley writes that her appointment in 1930 as "librarian in charge of the Negro Collection" at Howard University Library in Washington, D.C., was the turning point in her life. She had recently been one of the first two African Americans to receive the master's degree in library science from Columbia University. In accepting the Howard position, she brought the energy and intelligence necessary to make what would become the Moorland-Spingarn Research Center the renowned repository it is today. She has spent nearly six decades collecting, cataloging, and writing about the works of African Americans, Africans, Afro-Brazilians, Afro-Cubans, West Indians, and people of African descent living in the Spanish-speaking countries of South America. Moreover, her own scholarly publications about African American culture and people provide further evidence of her resourcefulness.

In 1914, Jesse E. Moorland gave Howard University most of his private collection about people of African descent, but it and many other items of Africana remained unavailable to readers until Dorothy Porter set about ripping open boxes and cataloging their contents. She determined that the Moorland donation amounted to about three thousand pieces, and eventually edited and annotated one segment of it in *A Catalogue of the African Collection in the Moorland Foundation Howard University Library* (1958). When she retired in 1973, the Moorland gift had grown to over one hundred and eighty thousand items, including those bequeathed to Howard University by bibliophile Arthur B. Spingarn. In fact, the Moorland-Spingarn Research Center has developed into the largest and most comprehensive repository on African Americans at an academic institution. Porter's collecting techniques ranged from buying and trading books, to encouraging donations, to actually picking up texts wherever they were available. She saved from the trash heap files from the Washington, D.C., chapter of the NAACP. Indeed, Porter was nicknamed "bag lady" because she made "salvage excursions" to basements and attics owned by the educator Mary Church *Terrell and other distinguished African Americans.

Perhaps Porter's greatest influences on African American literature have been her numerous published bibliographies and one anthology. *North American Negro Poets: A Bibliographical Checklist of Their Writings 1760–1944* (1945) expands on the first notable bibliography of African American poetry, *A Bibliographical Checklist of American Negro Poetry* (1916), published by Arthur A. *Schomburg. Porter's volume includes annotated entries on books and pamphlets by individual poets, anthologies, as well as other annotated listings. Her anthology, *Early Negro Writing 1760–1837* (1971), reprints such items as books, pamphlets, broadsides, and parts of books that document the economic, social, and educational improvement societies founded by mostly northern African Americans. More specifically, the anthology includes constitutions and bylaws of beneficial societies, speeches, reports, debates about colonization outside America, and sermons. Porter has also published several scholarly articles in journals, such as "Early Manuscript Letters Written by Negroes" in *Journal of Negro History* (1939), "A Library on the Negro" in *American Scholar* (1938) and "Bibliography and Research in Afro-American Scholarship" in *Journal of Academic Librarianship* (1976).

• Esme E. Bhan, "Dorothy Porter," in *Notable Black American Women,* ed. Jessie Carney Smith, 1992, pp. 863–864. Arthur C. Gunn, "Dorothy Burnett Porter Wesley," in *Black Women in America: An Historical Encyclopedia,* 1993, pp. 1246–1248.

—SallyAnn H. Ferguson

Possessing the Secret of Joy. Dedicated "With Tenderness and Respect to the Blameless Vulva," Alice *Walker's *Possessing the Secret of Joy* (1992) has raised the consciousness of the Western world concerning ritual clitoridectomy or female genital mutilation (also called circumcision or infibulation). The novel indites the centuries-old African tradition for its role in the torture, enslavement, and destruction of women. It announces with a vengeance that the secret of joy (that is, the secret of survival) is resistance.

Introduced first in *The *Color Purple* (1982), female genital mutilation emerges in graphic detail in Walker's fifth novel. Tashi, a minor character in both *The Color Purple* and *The *Temple of My Familiar* (1989), is set at center stage. Saved from what the Olinka call "baths" by the presence of Christian missionaries, the adult Tashi (whose Americanized name is Evelyn Johnson) feels a need for a deeper bond with her African roots, her heritage. To achieve this bond she chooses to become a victim of her people's ceremonious rite of passage, a rite that years earlier left her sister dead in a pool of blood.

Again Walker breaks a taboo and speaks of the unspeakable and again some critics condemned her for doing so—claiming that she had no right to judge or condemn African culture and tradition. But, like one hundred million other women, Tashi's submission to the dominating power of the tsunga's (the circumciser's) knife leaves her incapacitated both physically and psychologically (a confirmed reality that quieted Walker's most insistent opposing critics).

The novel details Tashi's battle with madness. Although she visits several therapists (among them Carl Jung and a student of Freud), she is unable to reconcile her loss. Tashi's act of resistance falls ironically within the guidelines of Olinka tradition: she murders the tsunga M'Lissa for her bloody betrayal of thousands of African girls and burns her body.

• Alice Walker and Pratibha Parmar, *Warrior Marks: Female Genital Mutilation and the Sexual Blinding of Women,* 1993.

—Debra Walker King

POSTON, TED (1906–1974), award-winning journalist, short fiction writer, and unionist. Born Theodore Roosevelt Augustus Major in Hopkinsville, Kentucky, Ted Poston was the youngest of eight children. His parents, Mollie and Ephraim Poston, were educators, a distinction that earned his family a leadership role within the African American community and some access to the white leadership of the town. It was the family's weekly paper that started Ted Poston on his journalistic career: as a teenager he wrote copy for the *Contender* until it became too radical and had to be moved out of town in 1921. After graduating from the Tennessee Agricultural and Industrial College in 1928, Poston became one of many to move north, settling in New York City.

Initially employed as a speech writer for presidential candidate Alfred E. Smith, by 1929 he was writing for one of the city's African American papers, the *New York Amsterdam News,* where he covered such explosive topics as the *Scottsboro boys trials. By 1932, when he went to Moscow to act in a never-completed Soviet film about American race relations, Poston had advanced to become the city editor for the *News,* a position he held until 1936, when he was fired after leading a successful effort to unionize the paper. Struggling to find work, in 1937 Poston interviewed for a position at the *New York Post,* only to be told that they would not hire him unless he could produce a front page story for the next day's edition. Rising to this seemingly impossible challenge, Poston got the job and worked at the *Post* for the next thirty-five years. As one of the first and only African American reporters employed by a white daily paper, Poston repeatedly traveled undercover to the South, where he risked his life reporting on several high-profile prosecutions of African Americans and providing early coverage of the civil rights movement. He also pursued other stories and landed exclusive interviews with major public figures; he's credited with proving that African American reporters need not be restricted to "race issues."

In the early 1940s Poston began to write short fiction that was published in journals such as the *New Republic* and later anthologized in several collections of African American writing. Loosely autobiographical, Poston's stories explicitly addressed the contradictions of race in America, exploring with particular immediacy the inner costs exacted by racism upon its targets. In "You Go South" (1940), for example, he traces the psychological states "you" experience during a two-week return to the South: initially warily determined, arguing calmly with the train conductor as you are forced into the crowded Jim Crow car, you move quickly into rage and confusion, and it is only the last-minute realization that you will soon be back in Harlem that stops you from buying a pistol in helpless desperation. In one of his many childhood tales ("The Revolt of the Evil Fairies," 1942), Poston tackles the taboo issues of class and color-based divisions within the African American community.

• Ted Poston, *The Dark Side of Hopkinsville: Stories by Ted Poston*, ed. Kathleen A. Hauke, 1991. Kathleen A. Hauke, *Ted Poston: Pioneer American Journalist*, 1998.

—Melanie Boyd

Preface to a Twenty-Volume Suicide Note. Appearing in 1961, *Preface to a Twenty-Volume Suicide Note* is Amiri *Baraka's (LeRoi Jones) first published collection of verse. Published by Totem Press in association with Corinth Books, *Preface* contains a number of poems that had appeared earlier in such little magazines as the *Naked Ear, Swank, White Dove Review, Evergreen Review, Beat Coast East, Nomad, Provincetown Review,* and others. It is in this spare volume that Baraka first received the notice of serious critics, as evidenced in Denise Levertov's fairly typical review. Noting the "sensuous and incantatory" beauty of the poems, she says, "his special gift is an emotive music" (*Nation,* 14 October 1961). Critics of Baraka also took note of the extent to which various modern masters had influenced his early verse. Baraka himself acknowledges in a 1959 essay entitled "How You Sound" (*New American Poetry 1945–1960,* ed. Donald M. Allen) and in a *Nomad/New York* interview (Autumn 1962) his debt to, among others, Charles Olson, William Carlos Williams, T. S. Eliot, Ezra Pound, and García Lorca.

Despite the acknowledgments, the young Baraka was even more pervasively influenced by the writers of the Beat Generation, a group characterized by its scorn for the forces of convention, pretense, and materialism, as well as its posture of cool disengagement. An index of the poet's attachment to the concerns of these writers is apparent in the dedication of several selections to such members of the Beat coterie as Allen Ginsberg, Gary Snyder, John Wieners, and Michael McClure. The poems uniformly reflect the angst of a thoroughly drained soul in search of meaning and commitment.

The title poem of the volume introduces the recurring themes of despair, alienation, and self-deprecation. "Preface to a Twenty-Volume Suicide Note" lays bare the weary psyche of the hipster, or Beatnik. Filled with images of the stultifying life of convention and respectability, the poem concludes on a profoundly pessimistic note that is intensified in the death-haunted lyrics of "The Bridge" and "Way out West."

The poems of *Preface* evidence yet another notable characteristic of Beat artistry in the frequency of reference to images from American popular culture. Allusions to jazz and popular music and references to characters from radio, film, and comic strips are present in a good number of the works. The fascination with jazz music and musicians, evident in "The Bridge," is, in large part, a reflection of the Beat poet's reverence for an improvisational orientation to life as well as music. The attraction to the heroes of popular culture—most apparent in "In Memory of Radio," "Look for You Yesterday, Here You Come Today," "The Death of Nick Charles," and "Duke Mantee"—is evidence of the cynical, disengaged artist's hunger for commitment and positively directed action.

The remaining poems of *Preface* focus sharply on the related themes of racial identity and artistic engagement, matters that would receive ever growing attention in the later poems, plays, essays, and fiction of Baraka. Although minimally present in the previously cited poems, the question of the proper uses of poetry receives its strongest evocation in works such as "Betancourt" and "One Night Stand." The racial identity theme is addressed most directly in the long, sardonic "Hymn for Lanie Poo." In the final poem of *Preface,* "Notes for a Speech," the poet effects an uneasy marriage of these two themes.

• Lloyd Brown, *Amiri Baraka,* 1980. Henry C. Lacey, *To Raise, Destroy and Create: The Poetry, Drama and Fiction of Imamu Amiri Baraka,* 1981.

—Henry C. Lacey

PRINCE, MARY (c. 1788–?), West Indian slave narrator, also known as Molly Wood, Mary James, or Mary, Princess of Wales. Mary Prince was born in Bermuda. She worked as a household slave there and in Antigua and in the salt mines of Turk Island under the most brutal of conditions. In 1828, she went to England with her owners hoping to secure manumission. Unable to purchase her freedom and return to Antigua as a free woman, Prince dictated her story to Susanna Strickland, an abolitionist and poet. With Prince's approval, her narrative was pruned and edited for publication in accordance with the legal and social conventions governing the publication of such a controversial narrative. Little is known about Mary Prince beyond what is recorded in *The History of Mary Prince, a West Indian Slave, Related by Herself,* first published as an antislavery tract in England in 1831, with supporting documentation furnished by Thomas Pringle, Prince's employer, editor, publisher, and secretary of the Anti-Slavery Society. After testifying before the London Court of Common Pleas in a suit brought by Pringle against Thomas Cadell of *Blackwoods Magazine,* on 21 February 1833, Prince disappeared from public record.

The recovery and republication of Prince's *History* (1987) reconfigures assumptions about race, gender, and cultural production in modern Caribbean literature. It illuminates the oral beginnings of the literature, and anticipates its defining paradigms, such as the relationship between written and oral narrative, metropolis and colony, elite and subaltern, exile and return. This unique document elucidates the discourse of struggle versus memory in African American literary circuits in respect to the autobiographies of those who do not write, and in respect to literature as a sanctioned space for the expression of social dissidence and marginality, especially among women.

• Sandra Pouchet Paquet, "The Heartbeat of a West Indian Slave: The History of Mary Prince," *Black American Literature Forum* 26.1 (1992): 131–146. Moira Ferguson, introduction to *The History of Mary Prince, a West Indian Slave, Related by Herself,* 1993. Brenda F. Berrian, "Claiming an Identity: Caribbean Women Writers in English," *Journal of Black Studies* 25.2 (1994): 200–216.

—Sandra Pouchet Paquet

PURVIS, ROBERT (1810–1898), lecturer, pamphleteer, and antislavery activist. Born in Charleston, South Carolina, to a wealthy English businessman and the free-born daughter of a slave, Robert Purvis was sent to Philadelphia at the age of nine for private schooling. When his father died in 1826, Purvis inherited $120,000, which gave him financial independence and allowed him to devote the rest of his life to reformist causes.

In 1830, Purvis met Benjamin Lundy and William Lloyd Garrison whose crusade against slavery focused Purvis's sympathies for less-privileged African Americans and offered him a means of striking back at the racial discrimination he experienced firsthand. Purvis joined Garrison in the founding of the American Anti-Slavery Society in 1833. In the same year, he led in the organization of the Philadelphia Library Company of Colored Persons, dedicated to "promoting among our rising youth, a proper cultivation for literary pursuits." When the Pennsylvania legislature proposed to disfranchise the African American voters of the state, Purvis headed a convention of blacks in 1838 to protest the measure. As chair of a committee selected to speak for the convention, Purvis drafted an eighteen-page pamphlet entitled *Appeal of Forty Thousand Citizens, Threatened with Disfranchisement, to the People of Pennsylvania* (1838), which stressed the accomplishments and contributions of the African American citizenry to the economic, political, and cultural life of the state and invoked the "no taxation without representation" theme of the Declaration of Independence as a precedent for opposition to disfranchisement. Despite the vigor and logic of Purvis's argument, the *Appeal* did not succeed. But the *Appeal* was widely admired in antislavery circles and often reprinted and cited in the abolitionist press. Purvis's speeches denoucing the U.S. Supreme Court's Dred Scott decision in 1857 cemented his reputation as an important antislavery orator. In 1883, he coedited the *History of the Underground Railroad in Chester and the Neighboring Counties of Pennsylvania,* including a detailed autobiographical narrative.

• Carter G. Woodson, ed., *The Mind of the Negro as Reflected in Letters Written During the Crisis 1800–1860,* 1926. Benjamin Quarles, *Black Abolitionists,* 1969.

—William L. Andrews

Q

Quest of the Silver Fleece, The. W. E. B. *Du Bois's first novel, *The Quest of the Silver Fleece* (1911), shifts its action from rural Alabama to Washington, D.C., and back again, achieving its narrative unity through a carefully constructed framework of contrasting symbols and the maturation journeys of its young protagonists, Zora and Bles. Identified by Addison *Gayle, Jr., as "the first Bildungsroman in African-American literature," *The Quest* traces the growth of the young, rural heroes from ignorance and exploitation (in Zora's case, sexual use by the wealthy landowners, the Cresswells); to their encounter in Washington, D.C., with political deception by urban, talented tenth Africans, like the savvy, self-serving Carry Wynn; to the resulting appreciation of their own strengths and the potential of their people, and their return to Alabama to create a black-owned farming commune to develop the lucrative cotton crop, the "silver fleece."

Adding an African American voice to popular novels at the turn of the century such as Frank Norris's The Octopus (1901) and The Pit (1903) and Upton Sinclair's The Jungle (1906), which explored the consequences of unregulated, free market forces, Du Bois's primary concern is to demonstrate the physical and mental serfdom that trapped blacks in ignorance and poverty after emancipation, and to suggest effective courses of action to overcome this new kind of slavery. To examine these economic issues and their personal results, he structures his work on the clash of two opposing world views, those of the Swamp and the Plantation.

The swamp represents all that is free, wild, joyful, and loving, but also the fear, jealousy, ignorance, and poverty fostered by racism, slavery, and the tenant farming system. The plantation, symbolic of a materialistic attitude clearly not confined to the southern locale, encourages all that is self-serving, cruel, and exploitative of humans and nature, but also thrives on knowledge, talent, and ambition, qualities Zora comes to recognize as essential for the self-reliance of rural workers, black or white. Throughout the first part of the narrative, the story of Jason and the Golden Fleece—with its correspondence of the valuable fleece with the special cotton Zora grows in the swamp and is cheated out of by Colonel Cresswell; Medea with the witch, Elsbeth, Zora's mother; and Jason with the thieving southern land owners and northern capitalists—appears as a mythic reference for Du Bois's complex plantation/swamp dichotomy.

The improvement of the situation of black farmers is intrinsically linked in *The Quest* to the development of Zora, who begins as the wild "elf-girl," her creativity inspired by the beauty of the swamp where she was born, but her early powerlessness also linked to its other side, the "gray and death-like wilderness" symbolized by Elsbeth, in whose hut the local white men drink and sexually exploit black women. Nellie McKay believes "the 'black' heroine was born in this novel, marking a major breakthrough in the overthrow of the stereotypical use of near-white" heroines in earlier African American fiction. In **Dusk of Dawn* (1940), Du Bois referred to the novel simply as "an economic study of some merit."

• Addison Gayle, Jr., *The Way of the New World, The Black Novel in America,* 1976. Nellie McKay, "W. E. B. Du Bois: The Black Women in His Writings—Selected Fictional and Autobiographical Portraits," in *Critical Essays on W. E. B. Du Bois,* ed. William L. Andrews, 1985. David Levering Lewis, *W. E. B. Du Bois, Biography of a Race, 1868–1919,* 1993.

—Arlene A. Elder

Quicksand, Nella *Larsen's first published novel, appeared in 1928 and won the Harmon Foundation's bronze medal. The New York Times Book Review proclaimed it had more "dignity" than most first novels and praised it for having a "wider outlook upon life" than writings by most African Americans. W. E. B. *Du Bois declared she had published "the best piece of fiction" by an African American since Charles Waddell *Chesnutt.

Quicksand is the story of *Helga Crane, whose mixed heritage (she is the daughter of a Danish American mother and an African American father) complicates her quest for security and self-realization. When the novel begins, Helga Crane has achieved high status as a teacher at Naxos (an African American college modeled after Tuskegee) and seems set for social success as the fiancée of James Vayle, a solid member of the Atlanta African American bourgeoisie. But she is dissatisfied. She quits her job, breaks off her engagement, and travels to Chicago hoping to be welcomed into the family of her Danish American uncle. Uncle Peter's new wife rebuffs Helga at the door. Alone and nearly broke, Helga finally obtains employment as a travel companion to Mrs. Hayes-Rore, an African American activist en route to New York. Hayes-Rore introduces Helga to Anne Gray, a wealthy Harlem widow who becomes her next benefactor. Though Helga lands a respectable job and is welcomed into Harlem middle-class society, she soon becomes dissatisfied again. Her quest this time takes her to Copenhagen, where her Danish relatives not only welcome but flaunt their dark family member, and for two years, Helga is feted. Alex

Olsen, a socially prominent Danish artist, asks Helga to become his mistress, and when she rejects this proposition he proposes marriage; but Helga is now tired of being an exotic, rare specimen and returns to Harlem. Not long after her return, she discovers that Anne Gray is going to marry Dr. Robert Anderson, a man who has always provoked ambiguous but powerful passions in Helga. After an embarrassing incident with Robert, Helga despairs of ever finding happiness. Wandering about in a stormy night, she seeks refuge in a storefront church, where she has a conversion experience and meets the Reverend Mr. Pleasant Green. She marries this uneducated country preacher and returns with him to Alabama, where she has three children in twenty months.

Some critics find the novel's conclusion weak and ambiguous, but they generally praise its narrative unity and lush, evocative detail. They variously describe the tone of *Quicksand* as "wistful," "zestful," and "bitter" but generally agree that the book offers a pioneering psychological portrayal of a modern woman from a perspective that recognizes the inextricability of race, class, and gender. Scholars recognize the book as revising the stereotypes of the tragic mulatta and as providing one of the first serious considerations of both the limitations and the privileges of aspiring to the African American middle class. In her concern with gender and class, Larsen is often compared to Jessie Redmon *Fauset and Dorothy *West. Her interest in the particularities of race and sexuality also places her in conversation with Jean *Toomer and Claude *McKay.

• Deborah E. McDowell, introduction to *Quicksand and Passing*, ed. Deborah E. McDowell, 1986. Thadious M. Davis, *Nella Larsen, Novelist of the Harlem Renaissance*, 1994.

—Frances Smith Foster

R

RAHMAN, AISHAH (b. 1936), professor and avant-garde surrealistic playwright whose works are performed mostly at small theaters and on college campuses. A native of New York City, Aishah Rahman (born Virginia Hughes) has traveled and worked in Africa and Latin America. She graduated from Howard University with a BS in political science in 1968 and received an MA in playwriting and dramatic literature from Goddard College in 1985. Rahman, who started writing plays professionally in the 1970s, is an associate professor of English at Brown University, where she is also founder and editor in chief of *NuMuse,* an annual journal of new plays. Before joining the faculty at Brown, she spent ten years teaching at Nassau Community College on Long Island and was director of the Henry Street Settlement's Playwrights Workshop at the New Federal Theater for five years.

Rahman's plays are often rooted in the lives of historically important African American figures. Rahman's first play, *Lady Day: A Musical Tragedy,* originally produced in 1972, takes place on the stage of New York City's famed Apollo Theater and is based on the life and career of Billie *Holiday. Rahman's best-known work, *Unfinished Women Cry in No Man's Land While a Bird Dies in a Gilded Cage,* first produced by the New York Shakespeare Festival in June 1977, takes place on 12 March 1955 on the day of jazz saxophonist Charlie *Parker's death. While five teenage girls, confined to the Hide-A-Wee Home for unwed mothers, must decide whether to keep their babies or put them up for adoption, Charlie Parker, wasted by years of drug abuse and exploitation, dies in "Pasha's Boudoir," the lavish apartment of a wealthy European baroness who was once his lover. The play juxtaposes the pain of these ordinary "unfinished women" with the suffering of a jazz musician of almost mythical status who has touched the girls' short lives.

Rahman's next play, *The Tale of Madame Zora* (1986), is a blues musical based on the life of author and folklorist Zora Neale *Hurston. Rahman then turned to another genre, opera, and wrote *The Opera of Marie Laveau* (1989) with composer Akua Dixon Turre, expanding on the traditional form and content of the European opera. A pastiche of folklore and history about the nineteenth-century French, Native American, and African New Orleans voodoo queen, Rahman renamed the libretto *Anybody Seen Marie Laveau?*

Rahman's most recent plays are *The Mojo and the Sayso* (1987) and *Only in America* (1993). *The Mojo and the Sayso,* which has received excellent reviews, revolves around the lives of a working-class family devastated by the murder of the ten-year-old son, Linus, who was shot in the back by police. The paralyzing guilt that has gripped the Benjamin family since the boy's death is explored in this short (the running time is seventy minutes) play through surreal and often intentionally nonresponsive dialogue. *Only in America* is a farcical allegory in which the Greek prophetess Cassandra reappears as a contemporary victim of sexual harassment.

Rahman's plays are heavily symbolic and suggestive. While fictionalizing the lives of important historical figures, Rahman creates a surreal atmosphere by emphasizing the unexpected and the nonrational, and by exposing the fetishes and subconscious desires of her characters. She has been compared to award-winning playwrights August *Wilson and Eugene O'Neill, and she cites Adrienne *Kennedy, Amiri *Baraka, Sam Shephard, Federico García Lorca, and Bertolt Brecht as her literary influences. In 1996, Rahman was writing a novel, "Illegitimate Life," and an anthology of her plays, *Three Plays by Aishah Rahman,* was scheduled to be published. Often described as underground classics, Rahman's work has yet to be accepted in commercial mainstream theater but has unquestionably enjoyed wide circulation, influence, and appeal.

• Aishah Rahman, "To Be Black, Female and a Playwright," *Freedomways* 19 (1979): 256–260. Bernard L. Peterson, Jr., ed., *Contemporary Black American Playwrights and Their Plays,* 1988. Alicia Kae Koger, "Jazz Form and Jazz Function: An Analysis of *Unfinished Women Cry in No Man's Land While a Bird Dies in a Gilded Cage,*" *MELUS* 16.3 (Fall 1989–1990): 99–111.

—Jennifer Margulis

RAINEY, MA (1886–1939), blues singer, comedienne, songwriter, and theater owner. Born Gertrude Pridgett on 26 April 1886 in Columbus, Georgia, Ma Rainey began performing at the age of fourteen at the Springer Opera House in Columbus. In 1904 she married William "Pa" Rainey. Early in her career Rainey became leader of her own show and proved herself to be both an exciting blues performer and a capable manager. In 1923 she began her recording career with Paramount Records; she stayed with the company until 1928. Rainey's performances and records incorporated rural as well as jazz elements. She recorded with jug bands as well as with jazz greats. One of her most well-known songs, "See See Rider," exemplifies her style. Her biographer, Sandra Lieb, characterized Rainey's style as a rich contralto filled with slurs and moans and "lisping diction" (*Ma Rainey,* 1959).

Throughout her career Rainey appealed most to southern audiences—both black and white. She returned south to Columbus in 1935, when she retired from active performing. At that time, Rainey purchased and operated the Lyric and Airdome theaters in Rome, Georgia.

Rainey's power as a performer and her success as a businesswoman have inspired African American writers. Sterling A. *Brown's poem "Ma Rainey" is a poetic portrayal of Rainey's impact upon her poor, southern black audience. Brown's Rainey is a charismatic spirit worker who is capable of articulating her audience's joy and sorrow. For the persona of Al *Young's poem "A Dance for Ma Rainey" (1969), Rainey continues to give voice to "that sick pain" he says he knows so well yet is forced to hide. In 1984 August *Wilson's Broadway play *Ma Rainey's Black Bottom* presented Rainey as a tough manipulator of the racist recording industry. Though the play focuses on the men in the band, Rainey emerges as the wise, powerful leader of the group. She also recognizes the limitations of her authority given the presence of racism, working what authority she does have to her advantage.

Like other classic blues singers, Ma Rainey has recently come to the attention of black feminist literary and cultural critics as the embodiment of black female independence, sexuality, and creativity.

• Sandra Lieb, *Mother of the Blues: A Study of Ma Rainey,* 1981. Sandra Lieb, "Ma Rainey," in *Black Women in America: An Historical Encyclopedia,* 1992, pp. 958–960.

—Farah Jasmine Griffin

Raisin in the Sun, A. Lorraine *Hansberry's *A Raisin in the Sun* won the 1959 New York Drama Critics Circle Award after opening on Broadway, 11 March 1959, at the Ethel Barrymore Theatre to instant critical and popular success. Hansberry's first produced play, realistic in style, dramatizes the struggles and frustrations of a multigenerational, African American, working-class family living in a cramped apartment on Chicago's South Side. An insurance benefit of ten thousand dollars paid on the death of Walter, Sr., becomes the source of conflict within the Younger family, as *Mama Lena Younger, his widow/beneficiary and matriarch, and her son, *Walter Lee Younger, argue over its use. Their debate reveals fundamental differences in values and ponders the relationship of material wealth to human dignity. An authentic portrayal of the economic dilemma and spiritual resilience of African Americans, the play captured the urgent voice of the civil rights movement and catapulted its author into instant fame. The original cast, led by film star Sidney Poitier, was outstanding, and many of the cast members went on to highly successful theater careers: Claudia McNeil, Ruby Dee, Lou Gossett, Jr., Glynn Turman, Diana Sands, and director Lloyd Richards. The play ran for 538 performances on Broadway and was made into a film, which won a special award at the Cannes Film Festival in 1961.

Now a classic of the American theater, *A Raisin in the Sun* is one of the nation's most frequently produced plays, has been translated into over thirty languages on every continent, and has been produced in such diverse countries as the former Czechoslovakia, England, the former Soviet Union, and France. The play has been published in several editions since its inaugural production. The late Robert Nemiroff, Hansberry's former husband and literary executor, actively promoted this play and her other works after her death in 1965. In 1974, he produced *Raisin,* a musical based on the play, which won a Tony Award. In 1987, he restored scenes and dialogue cut from the original script and promoted a production of the uncut version that ran at the Kennedy Center in Washington, D.C., and was subsequently produced on television's American Playhouse with actors Danny Glover and Esther Rolle in the lead roles.

The play is regarded as a model of stage realism whose authenticity, candor, and timeliness have made it one of the most popular plays ever produced on the American stage. Critics were nearly unanimous in praising the "honesty" and craft of the original production, although a few disparaged it as a "black soap opera." The play, whose strong affirmation of human potential opposed the drama of despair popular at the time, anticipated the Pan-Africanism and growing militant mood of blacks soon to sweep the arts as well as the country in the 1960s. *A Raisin in the Sun* continues to have currency because of its evocation of the African American struggle and its poignant exploration of human values.

[*See also* Beneatha Younger.]

• Lorraine Hansberry, *A Raisin in the Sun and The Sign in Sidney Brustein's Window* (contains restored materials to both scripts), 1987. Margaret B. Wilkerson, "*A Raisin in the Sun:* Anniversary of an American Classic," in *Performing Feminisms: Feminist Critical Theory and Theatre,* ed. Sue-Ellen Case, 1990. Stephen R. Carter, *Hansberry's Drama: Commitment Amid Complexity,* 1991, pp. 119–130.

—Margaret B. Wilkerson

RAMPERSAD, ARNOLD (b. 1941), scholar, literary and cultural critic, educator, winner of the American Book Award, and MacArthur Fellow. Born in 1941 in Trinidad, Arnold Rampersad received a BA and MA from Bowling Green State University and an MA and PhD from Harvard. He has held teaching positions at Stanford, Rutgers, and Columbia. Rampersad has been Woodrow Wilson Professor of Literature at Princeton since 1990.

Although he began his career specializing in Herman Melville, Rampersad is best known for biographies of W. E. B. *Du Bois and Langston *Hughes. In *The Art and Imagination of W. E. B. Du Bois* (1976),

Rampersad sought to trace the intellectual development of one of this century's preeminent black political and social leaders. He achieved this by presenting the complete scope of Du Bois's complex and paradoxical beliefs and opinions. By bringing the conservative Du Bois into relation with the radical Du Bois, Rampersad made sense of what might appear to be a contradictory career.

In the two-volume *Life of Langston Hughes* (1986–1988), Rampersad again illuminated the life of a central figure in African American literary and cultural studies. As was the case with Du Bois, Hughes presented an instance of a writer whose complexities had been insufficiently revealed. Well known was Hughes's affection for "common everyday" African Americans. Less well known were the psychological and cultural groundings of this affection, subjects Rampersad sought to illuminate. Revealed, too, was the historical background against which Hughes so frequently reacted, such that *The Life of Langston Hughes* is not only concerned with the life of one person but also with the life of a culture and a nation. It is considered the authoritative biography of this central African American poet.

Rampersad is rightly credited with rehabilitating biography as a valued form of literary and cultural criticism in the face of the influence of literary theory in the late 1980s and the 1990s. While literary biography is not intended to replace literary or cultural criticism, per se, or literary theory, Rampersad's contribution is to restore a neglected mode of intellectual and scholarly discourse to its previous prominence. In *Days of Grace* (1993), tennis star Arthur Ashe's autobiography, which Rampersad coauthored, and in the biography *Jackie Robinson* (1997), Rampersad brought the craft of the scholar to the enterprise of popular biography, illuminating the life of an instrumental figure in African American cultural life during the last quarter of the twentieth century. In dealing with all these subjects—Du Bois, Hughes, and Ashe—Rampersad sought to bring the individual life into relation with the life of the culture. The title of the second volume of *The Life of Langston Hughes, I Dream a World* powerfully indicates the extent to which Rampersad seeks to negotiate the connection between the visionary aspects of individual greatness and the demands of cultural representativeness by means of scholarly biography.

• Arnold Rampersad, *Melville's Israel Potter: A Pilgrimage and Progress*, 1969. Arnold Rampersad, *The Art and Imagination of W. E. B. Du Bois*, 1976. Arnold Rampersad, *The Life of Langston Hughes*, 2 vols., 1986–1988. Arthur Ashe and Arnold Rampersad, *Days of Grace*, 1993.

—Theodore O. Mason, Jr.

RANDALL, DUDLEY (b. 1914), poet, publisher, editor, and founder of Broadside Press. Dudley Randall was born 14 January 1914 in Washington, D.C., but moved to Detroit in 1920. His first published poem appeared in the *Detroit Free Press* when he was thirteen. His early reading included English poets from whom he learned form. He was later influenced by the work of Jean *Toomer and Countee *Cullen.

His employment in a foundry is recalled in "George" (*Poem Counterpoem*), written after encountering a once vigorous coworker in a hospital years later. His military service during World War II is reflected in such poems as "Coral Atoll" and "Pacific Epitaphs" (*More to Remember*).

Randall worked in the post office while earning degrees in English and library science (1949 and 1951). For the next five years he was librarian at Morgan State and Lincoln (Mo.) universities, returning to Detroit in 1956 to a position in the Wayne County Federated Library System. After a brief teaching assignment in 1969, he became librarian and poet in residence at the University of Detroit, retiring in 1974.

His interest in Russia, apparent in his translations of poems by Aleksander Pushkin ("I Loved You Once," *After the Killing*) and Konstantin Simonov ("My Native Land" and "Wait for Me" in *A Litany of Friends*), was heightened by a visit to the Soviet Union in 1966. His identification with Africa, enhanced by his association with poet Margaret Esse *Danner from 1962 to 1964 and study in Ghana in 1970, is evident in such poems as "African Suite" (*After the Killing*).

When "Ballad of Birmingham," written in response to the 1963 bombing of a church in which four girls were killed, was set to music and recorded, Randall established Broadside Press in 1965, printing the poem on a single sheet to protect his rights. The first collection by the press was *Poem Counterpoem* (1966) in which he and Danner each thematically matched ten poems on facing pages. Broadside eventually published an anthology, broadsides by other poets, numerous chapbooks, and a series of critical essays. These publications established the reputations of an impressive number of African American poets now well known while providing a platform for many others whose writing was more political than literary.

Following the 1967 riot in Detroit, Randall published *Cities Burning* (1968), a group of thirteen poems, all but one previously uncollected. This pamphlet, like the first, contains poems selected on the basis of theme and does not follow a chronological development in the author's work. Fourteen love poems appeared in 1970 (*Love You*), followed by *More to Remember* (1971), fifty poems written over a thirty-year period on a variety of subjects, and *After the Killing* (1973), fifteen new poems that comment on such contemporary topics as contradictory attitudes during a period of racial pride and nationalism.

Publication of *A Litany of Friends* (1981; rpt. 1983) followed several years of suicidal depression that incapacitated Randall and put Broadside Press temporarily at risk. This period of recovery was his most productive, comprising some of his most original—though not necessarily his best—work. Included are eighty-four poems, thirty very recent ones and forty-six previously uncollected.

On the basis of "Detroit Renaissance," published in *Corridors* magazine in 1980, the mayor of Detroit named Randall poet laureate of that city in 1981.

A distinctive style is difficult to identify in Randall's poetry. In his early poems he was primarily concerned with construction. Many of those in *More to Remember* are written in such fixed forms as the haiku, triolet, dramatic monologue, and sonnet while others experiment with slant rhyme, indentation, and the blues form. He later concentrated on imagery and phrasing, yet some of his more recent work continues to suggest the styles of other poets. Although many of these move with more freedom, originality, and depth of feeling, and encompass a wider range of themes, others identifiable by printed date demonstrate a return to traditional form.

While Dudley Randall's reputation as a pioneer in independent African American book publishing is secure, he is sure to be remembered for his poems as well, including "Booker T. and W.E.B.," which succinctly summarizes philosophical differences between Booker T. *Washington and W. E. B. *Du Bois in a simple dialogue; "Ballad of Birmingham," "Southern Road," and "Souvenirs," all from *Poem Counterpoem;* "Roses and Revolutions," "Primitives," and "A Different Image" (*Cities Burning*); "Faces" and "Perspectives" (*More to Remember*); "The Profile on the Pillow" and "Black Magic" (*Love You*); "Frederick Douglass and the Slave Breaker" (*After the Killing*); and "A Poet Is Not a Jukebox" (*A Litany of Friends*).

• A. X. Nicholas, "A Conversation with Dudley Randall," in *Homage to Hoyt Fuller,* ed. Dudley Randall, 1984, pp. 266–274. R. Baxter Miller, "Dudley Randall," in *DLB,* vol. 41, *Afro-American Poets since 1955,* eds. Trudier Harris and Thadious M. Davis, 1985, pp. 265–273.

—Naomi Long Madgett

RAS THE DESTROYER. In Ralph *Ellison's **Invisible Man* (1952) Ras the Exhorter (turned Ras the Destroyer) represents the nationalistic view of the African American. He is a foil to the narrator in that where the narrator seeks an integrated universe, Ras's major concern is nation-building for the Black American. As a result of his experiences the narrator has come to suspect any organization or group that is exclusive. He believes that the Blacks who do not become a part of the mainstream are "outside of history," and he therefore rejects Ras's nationalist rhetoric as nonsense. Ras has been linked to Marcus *Garvey. Certainly both the fictional character and the historical figure share a compelling view of Black nationalism, and they both demanded social justice for Blacks. Also, like Garvey, Ras has strong ties with Africa.

Ras, patrolling the streets of a riot-torn Harlem in his ancestral attire, astride a great black horse, is "dressed in the costume of an Abyssinian Chieftan." Ras is also the short term for Rastafarian, originally a Jamaican religious group whose members trace their roots back to Ethiopia and to Haile Selassie. When Ras urges Blacks to unite, he, like Garvey, is not limiting his national movement to Harlem; he is pleading for nationalism throughout the Black diaspora. While Ellison (through the narrator) might reject Black nationalism as disruptive, Ras stands as a symbol of the malignant force that comes as a result of America's blindness (a blindness represented in the organization of the brotherhood and in the philanthropy of Mr. *Norton) to the needs of oppressed minorities.

While Ras is a powerful character in the novel, Ellison, through his use of the comic, undercuts Ras's dignity and makes him appear clownish at times. Even in the scene where he appears majestic, Ellison uses the comic to downplay his regality. Despite Ras's proud bearing on this occasion, Ellison says he had "a hauty, vulgar dignity." Instead of being robed in the skin of a lion or a leopard that is customary for African royalty, Ras is clad in a cape "made from the skin of some wild animal" that makes Ras himself look wild. And while Ras's appearance is "real, alive, [and] alarming," the narrator insists that it was "more out of a dream than out of Harlem." Ellison's depiction of Ras prefigures the negative images of the West Indian male that later appears in works by writers such as Toni *Morrison and Chester *Himes. One must add, however, that elements of the surreal and the comic pervade the novel, and Ras suffers no more from Ellison's pen than do other characters.

—Ralph Reckley, Sr.

RAVEN QUICKSKILL. A poet and runaway slave, Raven Quicksill is the principal protagonist of Ishmael *Reed's fifth novel, **Flight to Canada* (1976). He is an activist, aesthetician, and a master of the arts of resistance in the lineage of the tricksters celebrated in African American oral tradition.

Raven is a synonym for black, but the raven also figures significantly in various Native American myths—especially those of the Tlingit people of Alaska—underscoring Reed's concern with multiculturalism. Quickskill resembles a Native American name (like many African Americans, Reed has Native American ancestry) but it functions here to highlight the creativity and resilience of all oppressed or "marginal" peoples. Quickskill suggests speed and dexterity, quick-wittedness, the ability to improvise on the spot. Quick also means living; thus, Quickskill possesses life-skill: he knows how to stay alive and he knows how to live. In connection with speech or writing, quick also means sharp or caustic. Like Ishmael Reed, Raven Quickskill is a satirist whose words are weapons.

Raven also brings to mind Edgar Allen Poe's famous poem "The Raven," especially since *Flight to Canada* contains many obvious allusions to Poe's work. While the "Nevermore!" of Poe's raven signals an end to being, Ishmael Reed's Raven says "nevermore" to slavery and all that is antilife; he is "free as a bird." The appropriateness of bird imagery is reinforced by the fact that Yardbird, or simply Bird, was the nickname of saxophonist Charlie *Parker, who is for Reed one of the prime exemplars of neohoodooism, his name for the aesthetic practices he champions and that Raven Quickskill personifies.

—Robert Elliot Fox

REDDING, J. SAUNDERS (1906–1988), literary critic and historian. Taught by Alice Moore *Dunbar-Nelson at his Wilmington, Delaware, high school, J. Saunders Redding earned an advanced degree in English at Brown University (1932) and was a professor at various colleges and universities, including Morehouse, Hampton, and Cornell. In 1949, his stint as a visiting professor at Brown made him the first African American to hold a faculty position at an Ivy League university. He wrote many books and articles on African American culture and other topics, including *To Make a Poet Black* (1939), a landmark history of African American literature; *No Day of Triumph* (1942), an autobiographical account of a journey through southern black communities; and *Stranger and Alone* (1950), a novel, as well as several more general historical and sociological works. He also edited with Arthur P. Davis an important anthology, *Cavalcade: Negro American Writing from 1760 to the Present* (1971).

Redding was an exponent of individual achievement as symbol and inspiration for all African Americans. He maintained the classical civil rights posture against segregation, thus opposing both black and white establishment interests in the 1930s and 1940s. Redding explicitly favored the "liberal" W. E. B. *Du Bois over the "conservative" Booker T. *Washington, and in fact lost his position at Morehouse (1931) because of his "radical" beliefs; yet he was later criticized by such 1960s black nationalists as Amiri *Baraka for his opposition to cultural separatism and racial essentialism.

Redding's best-known and most influential book is his first, *To Make a Poet Black,* one of the earliest important works of African American literary criticism. In this book, Redding works to establish a canon of African American literature, from Jupiter *Hammon to Zora Neale *Hurston, pointedly excluding writers he regards as less central to the tradition. He rejects earlier, simplistic notions of racial identity, such as Benjamin *Brawley's theory of "Negro genius," emphasizing instead what he calls "the pressure of the age," or social and historical forces, in shaping the racial consciousness and literary careers of the writers he treats in his study.

Redding's concern is with the historical development of a black aesthetic, and he evaluates poets and novelists according to their contribution to this development. African American literature, in his view, has always been politically involved, "literature either of purpose or necessity." Necessity sometimes demands that the writer become a "propagandist," a development Redding applauds if, as in the case of Du Bois, it is "inspired" by "righteous wrath" and a selfless desire to further the interests of African Americans. Du Bois, in Redding's view, possessed "the rarest gift of all," the "power of setting forth the abstract concretely."

African American writers also contend with a split between black and white audiences: "Negro writers have been obliged to have two faces," he writes. Sometimes the "white" becomes dominant, with artistically unhealthy consequences: Redding, for example, deplores the "cheerful, prideless humility" of certain nineteenth-century dialect poets, such as Daniel Webster Davis, who "wrote for a white audience in a way that he knew would please them." Redding's novel, *Stranger and Alone,* dramatizes the psychological and moral costs of denying one's racial identity and allowing one's "white face" to predominate. Striving for individual success through rejection of one's people, the novel implies, amounts to a betrayal of oneself, as well as a futile striving against history, "the time on the clock of the world." In *No Day of Triumph,* Redding begins with a chapter about his family, then records the results of a journey through African American communities in the South. He ultimately finds value in the lived experience of the community.

A similar concern with the language and experiences of the people is evident in *To Make a Poet Black,* which covers the evolution of literary uses of the black vernacular, from James Edwin *Campbell and Paul Lawrence *Dunbar to James Weldon *Johnson and Zora Neale Hurston. For Redding, the most important development in African American letters of the 1920s and 1930s was not necessarily the better-known, urban-centered writing of the Harlem Renaissance but rather writing, such as Johnson's *God's Trombones (1927), that acknowledged its debt to folklore, spirituals, and sermons and preaching. The book concludes with a call for "a spiritual and physical return to the earth." Aside from his contributions to the development of the African American canon, the lasting importance of Redding's work for black theory and criticism lies here, in his recognition and celebration of the importance of the black vernacular in literary and social history, and in his view of African American literature as a self-contained tradition.

• Henry Louis Gates, Jr., introduction to *To Make a Poet Black,* 1988.

—Gary Ashwill

REDMOND, EUGENE (b. 1937), poet, playwright, critic, editor, educator, and important figure in the 1960s black arts movement. Eugene Redmond was born 1 December 1937 in St. Louis, Missouri. Orphaned at age nine, he was raised by his grandmother and "neighborhood fathers," made up of members of the Seventh Day Adventist Church and friends of his older brother. During high school he worked on the newspaper and yearbook, performed in school and church plays, and composed for neighborhood singing groups.

From 1958 to 1961 Redmond served as a U.S. Marine in the Far East, acquiring a speaking knowledge of Japanese. He was an associate editor of the *East St. Louis Beacon* from 1961 to 1962. In 1963 Redmond cofounded a weekly paper in East St. Louis, the *Monitor*, working at different times as a contributing editor, executive editor, and editorial page editor.

At Southern Illinois University he was the first African American student editor of the university newspaper. After receiving his bachelor's degree in English literature in 1964, he earned a master's degree in English literature from Washington University in 1966.

In 1965, while still in graduate school, Redmond won first prize in the Washington University Annual Festival of the Arts for his poem "Eye in the Ceiling." In 1968 he published his first volume of poetry, *A Tale of Two Toms, or Tom-Tom (Uncle Toms of East St. Louis and St. Louis)*. Subsequent volumes include *A Tale of Time & Toilet Tissue* (1969), *Sentry of the Four Golden Pillars* (1970), *River of Bones and Flesh and Blood* (1971), *Songs from an Afro/Phone* (1972), *Consider Loneliness as These Things* (1973), *In a Time of Rain & Desire* (1973), and *Eye on the Ceiling* (1991). Three of these collections were published by the Black Writers Press, which Redmond founded with Henry *Dumas and Sherman Fowler. He has been poet in residence at Oberlin College, California State University, University of Wisconsin, and Wayne State.

From 1967 to 1969 Redmond was a senior consultant to Katherine *Dunham at Southern University's Performing Arts Training Center, where he acted, directed, wrote plays, and supervised the drama and writing departments. Twelve of Redmond's plays, ballets, and choral dramas have been produced on university campuses and on California television. Redmond's one-act *Will I Still Be Here Tomorrow* was also produced Off-Broadway at the Martinique Theatre in New York in 1972. Redmond combined writing with performance with a 1973 recording of his poems, *Bloodlinks and Sacred Places*.

Redmond's poetic style displays his knowledge of the spoken word and performance. He sees basic rhythms and music as a key to a style of African American writing. Many of his poems have a rap-like beat and contain direct references to jazz, blues, spirituals, soul music, and black musicians.

Frequent allusions to African heritage also convey pride in African American culture and history and a black consciousness characteristic of the Black Arts movement. Some of his other poems explore the bleakness of urban existence while some depart from the overtly political style of the period, lyrically exploring introspective or romantic themes.

Redmond's commitment to the concept of an "African continuum" is evident in his influential study, *Drumvoices: The Mission of Afro-American Poetry, A Critical History* (1976). A survey of poetry from 1746 to 1976 that took eight years to research, *Drumvoices* explores the "complex web of beliefs, customs, traditions and significant practices that tie diasporan black cultures to their African origins."

Redmond has also contributed significantly to African American letters by editing volumes of African American writing, establishing multi-cultural literary journals—including *Literati Internazionali* and *Drumvoices Revue*—and training young writers. He is Henry Dumas's literary executor and has edited seven volumes of Dumas's work, including *Goodbye Sweetwater* (1988) and *Knees of a Natural Man* (1989).

Redmond has been a professor at Southern Illinois University since 1990. He also works in the public schools and has established a feeder system, following some writers from elementary school through high school as a way of bringing "literacy to the many and the literary to the few." His other community activities include organizing the annual "Break Word with the World" event in East St. Louis, a month-long "mock trial of the media" culminating in a reading and publication.

Redmond has received wide recognition as a poet and teacher. In 1976 he became poet laureate of East St. Louis, the first poet laureate named by a municipality. He was awarded a National Endowment for the Arts creative writing fellowship in 1978. The Eugene B. Redmond Writers Club was founded in 1986, with writers such as Maya *Angelou and Amiri *Baraka on the board of directors. *Eye on the Ceiling* (1991) won an American Book Award. In 1993 Pan-African Movement USA awarded him a Pyramid Award for lifetime contributions to Pan-Africanism through poetry. He received a "Tribute to an Elder" award from African Poetry Theater in 1995.

• "Eugene B. Redmond," in *Contemporary Authors, New Revision Series*, vol. 25, eds. Hal May and Deborah A. Straub, 1985, pp. 375–377. Joyce Pettis, "Eugene B. Redmond," in *DLB*, vol. 41, *Afro-American Poets since 1955*, eds. Trudier Harris and Thadious M. Davis, 1985, pp. 274–281. Joyce Mercer, "A Contagious Enthusiasm for Life and Literature," *Chronicle of Higher Education* 40.29 (23 Mar. 1994): A5. Tess Onwueme, "Another African Artist's Wayward Thoughts on Eugene Redmond's Poetry," in *Dreams Deferred, Dead or Alive: African Perspectives on African-American Writers*, 1996, pp. 83–95.

—Jennifer Burton

REED, ISHMAEL (b. 1938), poet, novelist, essayist, teacher, anthologist, publisher, and cultural activist. Ishmael Reed is one of the most original and controversial figures in the field of African American letters.

Reed was born in Chattanooga, Tennessee, on 22 February 1938, but he grew up in Buffalo, New York. After graduating from high school in 1956, he enrolled as a night student at Millard Fillmore College but transferred to the University of Buffalo as a day student with the assistance of an English teacher who was impressed with a story Reed had written. For financial reasons, however, Reed eventually withdrew without taking a degree. He remained in Buffalo for some time, working as a correspondent for the *Empire Star Weekly,* a black community newspaper, and serving as cohost of a local radio program that was canceled after Reed conducted an interview with *Malcolm X.

Moving to New York City in 1962, Reed served as editor of a Newark, New Jersey, weekly and helped establish the legendary *East Village Other,* one of the first and best-known of the so-called underground newspapers. Reed also was a member of the Umbra Writers Workshop, one of the organizations instrumental in the creation of the Black Arts movement and its efforts to establish a black aesthetic.

Reed's first novel, *The Freelance Pallbearers,* was published in 1967. That same year he moved to Berkeley, California, later relocating to the adjacent city of Oakland, where he currently resides with his wife, Carla Blank, a dancer and choreographer. They have a daughter, Tennessee. Reed also has a daughter, Timothy Brett, from a previous marriage.

Reed has taught at the University of California at Berkeley since the late 1960s, even though he was denied tenure in 1977 (a circumstance he wrote about in his first collection of essays, *Shrovetide in Old New Orleans,* 1978). He also has held visiting appointments at many other academic institutions, including Yale, Harvard, Dartmouth, Washington University in St. Louis, and SUNY Buffalo. In addition to winning several awards for his writing, Reed has been nominated for the Pulitzer Prize and was twice a finalist for the National Book Award (once in poetry and once in fiction).

As of 1995, Reed had published nine novels, five books of poems, and four collections of essays; he also had authored four plays, three television productions, and two librettos, four anthologies, and one collection of essays. In 1997, Reed edited *MultiAmerica: Essays on Cultural Wars and Cultural Peace.* His publishing and editing enterprises have included Reed, Cannon and Johnson Publications, I. Reed Books, and the journals *Yardbird Reader, Y'Bird, Quilt,* and *Konch.*

In 1976, Reed cofounded what is—outside of his writing—perhaps his most significant venture, the Before Columbus Foundation, a multiethnic organization dedicated to promoting a pan-cultural view of America. One of Reed's outstanding attributes is his consistent advocacy of powerful, innovative, and neglected writing—not just by people of color but by white people as well. This might seem surprising to those who associate Reed with the combative, antiwhite aesthetics and politics of the cultural nationalist program, but it is important to understand that Reed's involvement with the Black Arts movement, through his membership in the Umbra Workshop, was a complex one that can be described as both participatory and adversarial. True, Reed is a vigorous promoter of African-originated modes of being and performance, which he uses to challenge established canons of judgment and achievement, but a careful assessment of his work over three decades reveals that his problack position never was a dogmatic one. If much of Reed's work constitutes an intertext through which "the blackness of blackness" can be read, he nevertheless insists that this "blackness of blackness" cannot be categorized or prescribed. For Reed, as his masterpiece **Mumbo Jumbo* (1972) signifies, this indefinable but irresistible something "'jes grew.' It may indeed be "mumbo jumbo"—an enigma to the ignorant, a function of "soul" to those who know—but it is not reducible to skin color alone or to a militant creed.

In Reed's view, the black element reveals the permeable nature of American experience and identity, but he also acknowledges the permeable nature of blackness; thus Reed actually belongs in the company of those for whom notions of "mainstream" and "margins" are falsely dichotomous. Reed insists, for example, that a black writer steeped in tradition is a "classical" writer. At the same time, Reed's postmodernism enables him to take in everything at once, so to speak, so that conventional ideas of form and genre are contested, as well as canonical considerations.

Neohoodooism is the name Reed gave to the philosophy and aesthetic processes he employs to take care of business on behalf of the maligned and the mishandled. Hoodoo—the African American version of voodoo, a misunderstood term that actually refers to traditional African religious practices as they have reasserted themselves in the diaspora—appeals to Reed because of its "mystery" and its eclectic nature, thus providing him with an appropriate metaphor for his understanding and realization of art. Reed's best statements concerning the workings of neohoodooism can be found in his first book of poetry, *Conjure* (1972)—especially "Neo-HooDoo Manifesto," "The Neo-HooDoo Aesthetic," and "catechism of d neoamerican hoodoo church"—while the most successful actualizations of neohoodooism as a practice are his novels **Yellow Back Radio Broke-Down* (1969), the aforementioned *Mumbo Jumbo,* and **Flight to Canada* (1976).

Neohoodooism is, in many ways, a truly "black" art, but at the same time, due to the undeniable mix of ingredients in the New World, it is also "something else." Unlike those who argue for a black essentialism, Reed sees this hybridity as a virtue, rather than a defect or betrayal. A deep immersion in blackness is simultaneously an immersion in Americanness, given the extent to which, as a result of slavery and its aftermath, Africa helped to make America; and, considering the give-and-take of many other cultural influences, an immersion in Americanness is also an experience of the unfolding of multiculturalism.

Leaving aside for a moment his contributions as an author to American literature, it seems safe to say that when the history of multiculturalism in the late twentieth century is written, Ishmael Reed's entrepreneurial and promotional efforts will be seen to have played a meaningful role in demonstrating the degree to which we are—artistically as well as demographically—a nation of nations.

In his writing, Reed is a great improviser, a master of collage with an amazing ability to syncretize seemingly disparate and divergent materials into coherent "edutainments"—forms of surprise, revelation, and frequent hilarity. However, those who focus primarily on how funny or unfunny his works are miss the point of Reed's rollicking revisions, his apparently loony "'toons"—which is to employ humor as a weapon in the very serious enterprise of exposing human excesses and absurdities, and, at the same time, to remind us of the dangers of taking ourselves and our cherished opinions too seriously. (One of Reed's consistent gripes about militants of all perusasions is that they lack a sense of humor.)

From the start, Reed's iconoclasm has been aimed not only at the Western tradition, which has attempted to monopolize the world at the expense of other versions of experience, but at the black tradition as well. Reed's first novel, *The Freelance Pallbearers,* parodied Ralph Ellison's **Invisible Man*—for many critics, the masterwork of African American fiction and black autobiography in general—at a moment when black studies was just being established and the principal critical approach was a documentary one that emphasized black art's sociopolitical aspects. For Reed to be seen as satirizing the black literary tradition in a period of Black Power and the long overdue recuperation and reassessment of that very tradition was not likely to endear him to either white liberals or black cultural nationalists.

The risk of censure and ridicule notwithstanding, Reed always has gone against the grain of the prevailing critical-polemical fashion—a sign of his fierce independence as an artist and thinker. He has insisted continually on his right to do things his own way, and possesses an uncanny skill at pinpointing the follies and inconsistencies of many aspects of our consensus reality. Although Reed prefers to ride ahead of the herd, he is viewed in certain quarters as conservative, even reactionary—a judgment of his own position that he satirized in "The Reactionary Poet" in his third collection of poems, *Secretary to the Spirits* (1978).

Using analogies from comedy and music, one could argue that Ishmael Reed is much closer to Richard Pryor and *In Living Color* than he is to Bill Cosby, more akin to George Clinton or Sun Ra than to Wynton Marsalis. Does this help us to place him within the black tradition? At the least, it forces us to relinquish any notion of "the" black tradition; there are, and always have been, several black traditions, sometimes conflicting, sometimes intersecting, but nonetheless coexistent. One of the reasons Reed's reputation has suffered over the years is that he has steadfastly refused to toe any party line with regard to African American authenticity, aspiration, and achievement. Moreover, as the title of his 1993 essay collection, *Airing Dirty Laundry,* indicates, Reed believes in "outing" what others wish to keep closeted. Rather than working toward closure, he vigorously engages in disclosure. Some critics have interpreted the openness (and occasional open-endedness) of Reed's works as indeterminacy. For example, Michael G. Cooke, in *Afro-American Literature in the Twentieth Century* (1984), while emphasizing Reed's importance based upon the distinctiveness of his vision, style, and scope, believes nonetheless that his work is "affected by an instinct of irresolution." Reed's target, however, is the overdetermined, which he combats by accentuating chance, spontaneity, and instinct, deliberately embracing what amounts to an uncertainty principle that acknowledges "other" positions, myriad possibilities.

Given Reed's chosen task of providing revelatory "readings" of, and putting operative "writings" on, both black and white mischief and miscreants, it would have been impossible for him to have received only praise for his efforts. Reed does, in fact, have his share of enemies and detractors, who, in a real sense, are as much of a defining presence for his career as the endorsements of his many admirers. Indeed, Reed made the negative pronouncements of some of his critics part of the "problem" to be solved by the proper decoding of *Mumbo Jumbo* when he included them on the back of the dust jacket of the original hardcover edition of the novel.

The impressive commercial success attained by some African American authors has eluded Reed; yet, over the course of a distinguished and turbulent career, he has received numerous, frequently potent, critical accolades. Musician Max Roach is said to have called Reed the Charlie *Parker of American fiction, while Fredric Jameson has judged him to be one of the principal postmodernists. Nick Aaron Ford, in *Studies in the Novel* (vol. 3, 1971), referred to him as the "most revolutionary" African American novelist to have appeared thus far, and Addison *Gayle, Jr., in *The Way of the New World* (1975), called Reed the best satirist in the black tradition since George S. *Schuyler. Acknowledging that his satire does derive in part from Schuyler, Wallace *Thurman, and Rudolph *Fisher, Henry Louis *Gates, Jr.'s essay on Reed in the *Dictionary of Literary Biography* (vol. 33), argues that he really has "no true predecessor or counterpart." For Gates, Reed's situation in the African American literary tradition is both "unique" and "ironic" because the conventions and canonical texts of the tradition itself are the principal targets of Reed's satire. It is crucial to insist, however, that Reed is in no way indulging in a gratuitous put-down of black writers and writings;

rather, he is engaged in a project of emancipating an artistic heritage from predictable or predetermined forms and norms imposed by those who fail to fully comprehend the depth and complexity of that heritage, including its folkish inventiveness, hilarious undercurrents, and seasoned extravagances. Reed, in short, uses tradition to illuminate and reinvigorate tradition, combining continuity and improvisation in a cultural dynamic that Amiri *Baraka has astutely dubbed "the changing same."

[*See also* Last Days of Louisiana Red, The; Raven Quickskill.]

• Neil Schmitz, "Neo-Hoodoo: The Experimental Fiction of Ishmael Reed," *Twentieth Century Literature* 20.2 (Apr. 1974): 126–140. John O'Brien, ed., Juan Goytisolo/Ishmael Reed Issue, *The Review of Contemporary Fiction* 4.2 (Summer 1984): 176–244. Robert Elliot Fox, "Ishmael Reed: Gathering the Limbs of Osiris," in *Conscientious Sorcerers: The Black Postmodernist Fiction of LeRoi Jones/Amiri Baraka, Ishmael Reed, and Samuel R. Delany,* 1987, pp. 39–92. Reginald Martin, *Ishmael Reed and the New Black Aesthetic Critics,* 1988. Darryl Pinckney, "Trickster Tales," *New York Review of Books,* 12 Oct. 1989, 20–24. Kathryn Hume, "Ishmael Reed and the Problematics of Control," *PMLA* 108.3 (May 1993): 506–518. Bruce Dick and Amritjit Singh, eds., *Conversations With Ishmael Reed,* 1995. Robert Elliot Fox, "Blacking the Zero: Toward a Semiotics of Neo-Hoodoo," in *Masters of the Drum: Black Lit/oratures Across the Continuum,* 1995, pp. 49–62. Patrick McGee, *Ishmael Reed and the Ends of Race,* 1997. Sami Ludwig, "Ishmael Reed's Inductive Narratology of Detection," *African American Review* 32:3 (Fall 1998): 435–444.

—Robert Elliot Fox

RENA WALDEN, the stately, beautiful, and light-complexioned mulatta heroine of Charles Waddell *Chesnutt's *The *House Behind the Cedars* (1900), attempts to pass for white in the Reconstruction South only to see her secret inadvertently revealed and her young life cut tragically short. In certain ways an alter ego for Chesnutt himself (who was light enough to pass but chose not to), Rena embodies the aspirations and frustrations of those African Americans barred by the color line from the social, intellectual, and economic rewards available to "pure" whites. In comparison to her brother John, a mulatto who has passed successfully for ten years, Rena also illustrates the special constraints on the mobility of African American women, as her prospects appear limited to those conferred by marriage. Although Rena's own limitations—particularly her lack of imagination—may contribute to her downfall, she is in general more sympathetically portrayed as an innocent woman punished for the sins of her African American mother and white father. Yet Rena is no mere pathetic symbol of the supposed destructiveness of interracial sexuality. Despite her tragic end, at the close of the novel Rena is earnestly (if belatedly) sought by her former white fiancé, who has struggled to rid himself of his preconceptions about racial mixing. Rena's tale thus partially transcends the late-nineteenth-century conventions of the "tragic mulatto" formula and in so doing anticipates the powerful explorations of passing and assimilation in the works of such later writers as James Weldon *Johnson, Jessie Redmon *Fauset, and Nella *Larsen.

• William L. Andrews, *The Literary Career of Charles W. Chesnutt,* 1980. SallyAnn H. Ferguson, "Rena Walden: Chesnutt's Failed 'Future American,'" *Southern Literary Journal* 15 (Fall 1982): 74–82.

—William A. Gleason

RICHARDSON, WILLIS (1889–1977), playwright, director, teacher, magazine contributor, and government worker, began writing during the Harlem Renaissance. Willis Richardson's interest in the theater was encouraged when he viewed a production of Angelina Weld *Grimké's *Rachel* and by his belief that African American life was richer in theme and character than was being portrayed on the stage in musicals, comedies, and "serious" plays by whites. These were limited to stereotypical roles and one-dimensional representations. Added to this, theatrical groups were without plays by African American writers. With Richardson, all of this changed.

He began to write one-act plays; his early plays presented heroes such as Crispus Attacks, Antonio Maceo, and Simon the Cyrenian for children's edification and were published in *The *Brownie's Book.* In 1920, he published his first adult play, *The Deacon's Awakening,* in the *Crisis.* In 1923, he became the first African American playwright to have a nonmusical production on Broadway: *The Chip Woman's Fortune;* and in 1924 with *Mortgaged,* the first African American playwright produced by the Howard players. Richardson was the first to win the drama contest established by W. E. B. *Du Bois in the pages of the *Crisis* to encourage and extend African American theater; Richardson won with his *Broken Banjo, A Folk Tragedy* (1925) and again with *The Bootblack Lover* (1926). In these plays and others (he wrote more than thirty), he presented the everyday African American and such concerns as manhood, family, middle-class behavior, and intraracial relations.

His recognition of the need for a national theater that would serve as a testing ground and an outlet for drama by and about African Americans and his belief that the theater should serve as a vehicle for education anticipated the black aesthetic of the 1960s. His work increased the quantity and quality of African American drama. Even more, as playwright and director, he was influential in high school, college, and community African American theater groups. His plays provided production material for such groups as the Krigwa Players, the Ethiopian Art Players, and the Gilpin Players. Richardson also made plays accessible to theatrical groups and students by editing three anthologies over his lifetime: *Plays and Pageants from the Life of the Negro* (1930); *Negro History in Thirteen Plays* (1935), coedited by May Miller and including five of his history plays; and *The King's Dilemma and Other Plays for Children* (1956), containing six of his plays. These represent only a portion of his published works. He has unpublished plays at the Schomburg and Howard University libraries.

Richardson was the most prolific and recognized African American playwright of the 1920s; in addition to the prizes awarded by the *Crisis,* he won the Spingarn award, the Public School Prize in 1926, and the Edith Schwarb Cup from Yale University in 1928. He continues to be anthologized and recognized: Wilmington, North Carolina, his birthplace, established the Willis Richardson Players, a community group, in 1974, and his work is part of the Hatch-Billops Collection at City College, New York.

• Bernard L. Peterson, Jr., "An Evaluation—Willis Richardson: Pioneer Playwright," *Black World* 26 (Apr. 1975): 40–48, 86–88. Patsy B. Perry, "Willis Richardson," in *DLB,* vol. 51, *Afro-American Writers from the Harlem Renaissance to 1940,* ed. Trudier Harris, 1987, pp. 236–244.

—Helen R. Houston

RINEHART. Bliss Proteus Rinehart, a con artist in Ralph *Ellison's **Invisible Man* (1952), takes his middle name from the sea god Proteus, who had the power to assume many different shapes and disguises in order to elude those who would capture him and compel him to answer their questions. Like his namesake, Rinehart assumes many disguises: "Rine the [numbers] runner and Rine the gambler and Rine the briber and Rine the lover and Rinehart the Reverend." Ellison maintains that Rinehart's major function is to provide a mode of escape for the narrator. In truth, like Joseph Conrad's Lord Jim, everyone talks about Rinehart, but no one ever sees him. He is the trickster par excellence.

Despite the fact that Rinehart never appears physically he is a powerful force in the novel because he represents a particular type of male. His first name, Bliss, his big hat, his dark shades, his Cadillac, his zoot suit, and his jive talk suggest a ghetto-specific culture that has always been associated with the Black males of America's inner cities. But in these stereotypical images of Black men Ellison sees the possibility of freedom and growth. The narrator, through his education and his association with the Brotherhood, has been molded into a being still limited in his vision of himself and his universe, still limited in recognizing the potential of Blacks. Rinehart represents chaos, but he also represents freedom and growth. Through Rinehart, Ellison suggests that there are both negative and positive aspects of all cultural traditions and that instead of rejecting those traditions because we do not understand them or because they are outside of the traditional value system, we should embrace them and make them a part of the traditional culture. Through Rinehart, Ellison suggests that Blacks should not forget or deny their culture, their experience, their history.

—Ralph Reckley, Sr.

River Niger, The. Joseph A. *Walker's *The River Niger* (1973) is the dramatic emblem of an important era in African American theater and literary history. The renowned Negro Ensemble Company first produced the play, which was to become its biggest hit, Off-Broadway in 1972. The play then moved on to Broadway, continuing to draw large crowds and rave reviews. It won numerous awards, including the Drama Desk Award for best playwright, a Tony Award for best play, an Obie Award, a Burns Mantle Theatre Yearbook selection as best play, and an Audelco Black Theatre Recognition Award. In addition, Douglas Turner *Ward and Roxie Roker both won Obies for their performances. In 1976 the play was adapted as a full-length feature film.

Although white viewers and critics received the play warmly, finding a certain "universality" of characters and themes with which to identify, it was the response of African American theatergoers that truly marked and measured the play's significance. For the first time African Americans comprised the majority of the ticket-buying audience, lending unanimous praise and major financial support to the world-class production. What they found unique and satisfying in Walker's play were realistic portrayals of working-class characters struggling with what it meant to be African Americans in contemporary society. And, despite the violence of the plot, Walker's script incorporated a poetry representative of the black aesthetic of the time, which inspired audiences with pride and hope.

Like Walker's previous work, *The River Niger* addressed the dilemma of "the black man," a figure struggling to assert his manhood in the face of racism, violence, impending poverty, alcoholism, and the problematic women in his life. Although Walker has said that his own father's ghost haunted all of his work, this realistic play is especially autobiographical. The air force dropout son and the alcoholic poet father in *The River Niger* are modeled after Walker and his own father, and the stoic, cancer-stricken mother is taken from the playwright's family as well.

In the play, set in Harlem, the two heroic men, surrounded by a predominantly supportive group of women relations and a divided male group, struggle with and against each other to determine the site and means of revolution. John, the father, finds meaning, joy, pride, and resistance primarily through his poetry. The son, Jeff, has tried integration, playing the "Super Culludguy," but now, turning instead to search for a racially identified integrity and self-possession, he walks the line between his father's artistry and his friends' militancy.

Although *The River Niger* continues to be viewed as a landmark of African American theater history, it is not without its historical limitations. It has drawn negative criticism more recently for its treatment of gender and sexuality, for instance. It seems that some of the very factors that contributed to its success in the 1970s—the valorization of "the [heterosexual] black man" at the expense of gay and female African Americans—are what might make it somewhat dated and troubling decades later. The play remains significant, however, as a theatrical and cultural icon of African American life in the 1970s.

• Maurice Peterson, "Taking Off With Joseph Walker," *Essence,* Apr. 1974, 55, 74, 78, 82. Clark Taylor, "In the Theater of Soul," *Essence,* Apr. 1975, 48–49. Anthony Barthelemy, "Mother, Sister, Wife: A Dramatic Perspective," *Southern Review* 21.3 (Summer 1985): 770–785.

—Sheila Hassell Hughes

RIVERS, CONRAD KENT (1933–1968), poet, fiction writer, and dramatist. In 1951, when he was in high school, Conrad Kent Rivers won the Savannah State Poetry Prize for his poem "Poor Peon." In 1959, when he was a senior at Wilberforce University, his first book of poetry, *Perchance to Dream, Othello,* was published. The collection, which features a series of conversations with Othello, Harlem, and the United States, probes racism, alienation, and death—themes that would also dominate his later works. Rivers attended graduate school at Chicago Teacher's College and Indiana University, and taught high school in Chicago and in Gary, Indiana, all the while publishing poems in periodicals such as the *Antioch Review, Negro Digest, Ohio Poetry Review,* and *Kenyon Review.* Rivers is generally considered a poet of the black aesthetic and his concern with issues such as racism and violence, black history and black pride, self-love and self-respect are part and parcel of that movement. However, he was also fascinated with traditional poetic forms and techniques and his work evidences the influence of established writers such as his uncle Ray McIvers, James Weldon *Johnson, Langston *Hughes, Richard *Wright, and James *Baldwin. The title of his second book of poems, *These Black Bodies and This Sunburnt Face* (1962), alludes to William Blake and continues the intertextual conversations begun in his first. The poems in *Dusk at Selma* (1965) and *The Still Voice of Harlem* (1968) demonstrate increasing artistry; however, Rivers died a few weeks before the fourth volume appeared. According to Paul Breman, who published *The Wright Poems* (1972), a posthumous collection of poems Rivers wrote about or dedicated to Richard Wright, Rivers authored several short stories and a play about Paul Laurence *Dunbar that still await "the sympathetic hand of a publisher or producer."

• Eugene B. Redmond, *Drumvoices: The Mission of Afro-American Poetry: A Critical History,* 1976. Edwin L. Coleman II, "Conrad Kent Rivers," in *DLB,* vol. 41, *Afro-American Poets since 1955,* eds. Trudier Harris and Thadious M. Davis, 1985, pp. 282–286.

—Frances Smith Foster

ROBESON, PAUL (1898–1976), influential African American singer, actor, and social activist. Paul Robeson was born in Princeton, New Jersey, and was the child of a clergyman who had been born a slave. After winning a scholarship competition, Robeson attended Rutgers University, distinguishing himself as both scholar and athlete. While at Rutgers he augmented his scholarship income by offering concerts and dramatic performances. After graduating from Columbia Law School in 1923, Robeson turned to dramatic and musical theater where he became internationally celebrated. His roles in Eugene O'Neill's *All God's Chillun Got Wings* (1924) and *Emperor Jones* (1924 in New York and 1925 in London) catapulted him to prominence as a serious actor when opportunities for African Americans on stage were generally limited to the comic or to racist stereotypes. Robeson's performances in productions of Shakespeare, particularly Othello, were enormously popular and won him enthusiastic critical acclaim.

Robeson was always acutely conscious of the complex racial politics of the American scene (even as early as his Rutgers years). From the mid-1930s on Robeson became increasingly interested in Communism, particularly as it seemed to speak to the plight of African Americans. In this respect, the trajectory of Robeson's life mirrors that of many African American artists and intellectuals, such as Richard *Wright and Ralph *Ellison. Robeson's interest in radical politics deepened over the years, even as it limited his opportunities to perform. This limitation became especially pronounced in the early 1950s, given the advent of explicit conflict between the United States and the Soviet Union. Unlike Wright, who renounced Communism in favor of a more generalized anticolonialism, Robeson continued his interest in the politics of Communism, bringing him into conflict with the government of the United States, which revoked his passport (in 1950), though it was restored in 1958. Robeson spent the latter years of his life in ill health, living in Europe and later in the United States.

• Paul Robeson, *Here I Stand,* 1958. Martin Duberman, *Paul Robeson,* 1988.

—Theodore O. Mason, Jr.

ROBINSON, JACKIE (1919–1972), athlete and autobiographer. Jack Roosevelt Robinson was born in 1919 in Cairo, Georgia, and grew up in Pasadena, California. He was a star athlete in high school and junior college before becoming an athletic legend at the University of California at Los Angeles from 1939 to 1941, playing football, baseball, basketball, and competing in track and field. He joined the army in 1942 and was discharged as a lieutenant in 1945 after breaking a white bus driver's jaw in a disagreement about moving to the back of the bus.

Robinson was selected by Branch Rickey, general manager of the Brooklyn Dodgers, to become the first

African American to play Major League baseball in the twentieth century. Entering the big leagues in 1947, Robinson had to abide by an agreement he made with Rickey not to be provoked to retaliation by taunts from white players and fans. Robinson endured racial epithets shouted by opposing players and patrons, segregated hotel and restaurant accommodations, balls thrown at his head by opposing pitchers, spiking incidents by opposing runners, volumes of hate mail, and a threatened strike by some white players including several on his own team. Nontheless, he performed brilliantly in the field and earned Rookie-of-the-Year honors in 1947. During his nine years with the Dodgers, Robinson also won a Most Valuable Player award and a batting title. He was elected to baseball's Hall of Fame in 1962.

Robinson's influence can be most easily seen in the film persona of Sidney Poitier in the 1950s and 1960s, who tended to play black characters who were forced to function under great pressure and stress in the white world, maintaining his dignity and poise while pacifistically revealing his contempt when he is mistreated. Robinson's behavior in his first few years in the big leagues became the model, along with Gandhi, for the nonviolent civil rights marchers in the 1950s and 1960s. Robinson died in 1972 at the age of fifty-three. Many believe that what he endured in his days as a player took a dramatic toll on his health. Robinson coauthored several autobiographies including *Breakthrough to the Big Leagues* (with Alfred Duckett), published in 1965; *Jackie Robinson: My Own Story* (with black sportswriter Wendell Smith), published in 1948; and *I Never Had It Made* (with Alfred Duckett), published in 1974.

—Gerald Early

ROBINSON, SUGAR RAY (1921–1989), professional boxer. World welterweight champion and five times world middleweight champion, bon vivant, stylish dresser, night club owner, believed by many to be pound-for-pound the best boxer in the history of the sport, Sugar Ray Robinson, more than any other black public figure between World War II and the 1960s, epitomized black masculinity and the cool. He was unquestionably the most admired black male among African American males in the 1950s.

Born Walker Smith in Detroit on 3 May 1921, he borrowed the amateur card of a friend, Ray Robinson, and was known under that name for the rest of his life. "Sugar" was the signifying acknowledgment of the refulgence of his grace and overall athletic ability. With his processed hair, his smooth moves (he danced professionally for a time), his defiance of the Mob when he refused to "carry" Jake LaMotta in their sixth fight, his silk shirts, his apolitical aplomb, Robinson strikingly melded the personas of the street or underworld Negro, the working class black, and the gifted, aloof artist, representing a sense of the hip black male elegance and tough poise that was widely admired. Certainly, Norman Mailer had Robinson in mind for some portions of his 1957 essay, "The White Negro," just as Albert *Murray must have been thinking of him in certain parts of his 1970 book, *The Omni-Americans.* Ralph *Ellison surely had him in mind in describing the three cool-walking black boys with conked hair in his 1952 novel **Invisible Man.* It was not until the rise of Muhammad *Ali in the middle 1960s and the new era of Black Power and African American militancy that Robinson's influence as a major African American cultural icon began to fade, tarnished, in part, by his lack of political engagement. Robinson died on 12 April 1989 in Culver City, California, after a lengthy bout with Alzheimer's disease. With Dave Anderson, he coauthored *Sugar Ray,* an autobiography published in 1970.

—Gerald Early

RODGERS, CAROLYN M. (b. 1945), poet, short-fiction writer, literary critic, and lecturer. A Chicago native, Carolyn Marie Rodgers was influenced artistically in young adulthood by Gwendolyn *Brooks and by the Organization of Black African Culture, a writers' group concerned with articulating the black aesthetic. In the late 1960s, she emerged from the Black Arts movement in Chicago as one of the "revolutionary poets" who created a profoundly black poetry in terms of language, technique, and theme.

Her early poems, collected in *Paper Soul* (1968), *2 Love Raps* (1969), and *Songs of a Black Bird* (1969), deal with her advocacy of African American cultural revolution and with the conflicts between militancy and the traditional African American life that nurtured her. Her identity as an African American female poet is also a prominent concern in these poems, particularly as she tries to reconcile complex relationships between mothers and daughters and men and women. Attempting to break away from the conventional forms, especially those considered appropriate for female poets, she uses a "hip" style that consists of free-verse form and street language, and that also features nonstandard structure, spelling, capitalization, and punctuation. There is some feeling that her work has been underappreciated because of criticism by the revolutionary male poets whose dominant positions in the Black Arts movement gave credence to their public devaluation of her uncommon poetic style.

Rodgers's mature and more accomplished poetry appears in two later volumes, *how i got ovah: New and Selected Poems* (1975) and *The Heart as Ever Green* (1978). These poems deal with feminist issues, especially the act of defining self. Many are autobiographical, portraying a militant woman who has begun to question the revolution and her relationship to it, and who now embraces her mother and the church as the solid foundations in her life. The issue guiding the latter collection, expressed metaphorically in the title, is that the freedom to grow and create, particularly for the woman and poet of African descent, is a feasible reality. Her latest volumes of poetry include *Translation* (1980) and *Eden and Other Poems* (1983).

The same insight and searching analysis that distinguish her poetry are integral to Rodgers's short fiction and her literary criticism. She portrays in her short fiction the ordinary and overlooked people in everyday African American life and emphasizes the theme of survival. Many consider her critical essay "Black Poetry—Where It's At" (1969) to be the best essay on the work of the "new black poets." In it, she aesthetically evaluates contemporary African American poetry and sets up preliminary criteria of appraisal.

Although her reputation rests on her militant poetry of the late 1960s, Rodgers has continued to write, progressively moving from militant liberationist to religious believer. She holds a bachelor's degree from Roosevelt University and a master's degree in English from the University of Chicago. She has taught writing in colleges across the country, and has continued to publish poetry in magazines and anthologies.

• Bettye J. Parker-Smith, "Running Wild in Her Soul: The Poetry of Carolyn Rodgers," in *Black Women Writers (1950–1980): A Critical Evaluation,* ed. Mari Evans, 1984, pp. 393–410. Jean Davis, "Carolyn M. Rodgers," in *DLB,* vol. 41, *Afro-American Poets since 1955,* eds. Trudier Harris and Thadious M. Davis, 1985, pp. 287–295.

—Marsha C. Vick

Roll of Thunder, Hear My Cry. In *Roll of Thunder, Hear My Cry,* a highly acclaimed novel that was a Newbery Medal winner and an American Library Association Notable Book, Mildred D. *Taylor created an African American saga for young people with her vivid portrayal of the Logan family.

The novel chronicles one traumatic year in the heroic lives of David Logan; his wife Mary; their children Cassie, Stacey, Little Man, and Christopher-John; and their extended family. Nine-year-old Cassie's narration enables Taylor to juxtapose childhood innocence and wonder with bigotry and racism. She creates a realistic world of rural Mississippi through the eyes of a child, without bitterness and polemics, but with surprise and growing disillusionment.

In 1933, the Great Depression grips the entire country, but what Cassie knows is that the price of cotton has dropped, forcing her father to leave home and find work on the railroad. Cassie learns what it means to be African American. She witnesses discrimination in her segregated school, feels terror when the Ku Klux Klan rides through the night, witnesses crimes against African Americans go unpunished, and is humiliated when she is forced to step off the sidewalk for Lillian Jean to pass, invoking white privilege.

The Logan family struggles to maintain its economic independence, symbolized by their ownership of four hundred acres of land. The land is their hope, representing, as it were, all of America's promises to its huddled masses longing to be free. The Logans, not sharecroppers, not illiterate, and not poverty-stricken, are educated, proud, and industrious. Their very presence threatens white supremacy, marking them for victimization. But the Logans are not victims—they are survivors. Their love for each other and for the land shelters them from the storm of aggression aimed to destroy them and take their land.

The author's angle of vision is unflinching. Taylor does not look away or soften the impact of racism for young readers. Instead, Cassie's movement from innocence to awareness to bitterness and disillusionment enables readers to experience vicariously these feelings and Taylor to show the influence events of the 1930s had on shaping the civil rights and Black Power movements of the 1950s and 1960s.

Most critics have praised Taylor's novel. However, Margery Fisher's review (*Growing Point,* Apr. 1978) claimed the book was altogether too natural and crowded with details and raw emotionalism. David Rees ("The Color of Skin: Mildred Taylor," *Horn Book,* 1980) complained that Taylor loses the excitement of direct action by forcing the children to overhear or eavesdrop on their parents' conversations. In her Newbery Award acceptance speech (18 June 1977), Taylor recalled her temptation to place Cassie at the heart of all the adult action, but explained that she felt compelled to maintain Cassie in a child's place. Whatever is lost to excitement is offset by the realistic portrayal of parental efforts to shelter children from danger and life's unpleasant realities.

• Emily R. Moore, review of *Roll of Thunder, Hear My Cry,* in *Interracial Books for Children,* vol. 7, 1976, p. 18. Gerard Senick, ed., *Children's Literature Review,* vol. 9, 1985, pp. 223–229.

—Nagueyalti Warren

Roots. This 1976 Alex *Haley novel narrates a seven-generation story about his own family. It begins with the birth of West African *Kunta Kinte, Haley's maternal great-great-great-great-grandfather, and ends with Haley's own research and dramatic discoveries about his genealogy. Because it purports to be the first African American text to definitively locate an African ancestor and because of two widely watched television miniseries—"Roots" (1977) and "Roots: The Next Generations" (1979)—loosely based on the novel, the book became an immensely popular cultural phenomenon. In 1977 *Roots* received a special citation Pulitzer Prize and the National Book Award.

Haley termed the narrative strategy in Roots "faction." While Roots is based on what he claims is factual material, Haley fictionalizes and enhances the story, adding imagined dialogue and incidents to flesh out the story and relay the horrific nature of American slavery. The first half of the novel focuses on Kunta Kinte, his birth and often paradisical childhood in Juffure, his West African village, and his capture in 1767 and Middle Passage journey to Maryland and then Virginia where he is enslaved. Eventually, after several unsuccessful escapes (he ultimately had his foot amputated to stop him), Kunta Kinte, now renamed Toby, settles down and marries Bell, a domestic slave, and they have one daughter, Kizzy.

Kunta Kinte's ultimate legacy is his own story and culture, parts of which he conveys to his daughter. In the novel's second part, when Kizzy is sold off to a North Carolina slaver, she is able to pass on her father's narrative to her son, Chicken George, an accomplished gamecock trainer, who does the same with his children. After the Civil War, George's fourth child, Tom, a blacksmith, moves the family to Henning, Tennessee. Tom's youngest daughter Cynthia marries Will Palmer, whose daughter Bertha George marries Alex Haley's father, Simon Alexander Haley.

Perhaps the most compelling part of *Roots* is Haley's chronicle of his own search for his family's genealogy. Starting with his recollections of his grandmother Cynthia's family stories about an African ancestor, Haley tells of his relentless, ten-year search through various American and British genealogical archives, discussions with Africanist scholars, and dramatic journeys back to Gambia, where he learns from a griot the history of the Kinte family, especially the late-eighteenth-century disappearance of Kunta Kinte.

Almost from the beginning, Haley and *Roots* have been criticized for historical inaccuracy and plagiarism. Mark Ottaway, Willie Lee Rose, and Gary B. and Elizabeth Shown Mills have challenged, respectively, Haley's Gambian story, his historical accuracy, and his genealogical research. More troubling are the accusations of plagiarism by Margaret *Walker and Harold Courlander. While Walker's suit was dismissed, Haley settled with Courlander for $500,000, admitting that parts of Courlander's *The African* (1967) inadvertently found their way into *Roots*.

Nevertheless, *Roots* provoked a renewed interest by many Americans in their own genealogy and instilled a new pride for African Americans about their African ancestry. It has also had a profound impact on the teaching of African American history.

• Willie Lee Rose, "An American Family," *New York Review of Books*, 11 Nov. 1976, 3–4, 6. Mark Ottaway, "Doubts Raised over Story of the Big TV Slave Saga," *Sunday Times*, 10 Apr. 1977, 1, 17, 21. Harold Courlander, "'Roots,' 'The African,' and the Whiskey Jug Case," *Village Voice*, 9 Apr. 1979, 33–35, 84–86. Gary B. and Elizabeth Shown Mills, "Roots and the New 'Faction': A Legitimate Tool for Clio?" *Virginia Magazine of History and Biography* 89 (Jan. 1981): 1–26. Philip Nobile, "Uncovering Roots," *Village Voice*, 23 Feb. 1993, 31–38.

—Roger A. Berger

RUFEL, MISS. In Sherley Anne *Williams's **Dessa Rose* (1986), Miss Rufel—a southern white lady and mistress of an unfinished plantation—serves as a revisioning of the abolitionist. In her home, which is an unfinished replica of a stop on the Underground Railroad, she is first antithesis, then coconspirator, and ultimately friend to the novel's protagonist, the runaway slave *Dessa Rose. Through Miss Rufel, Williams deconstructs the stereotype of slave and mistress and suggests that the traditional roles that white and black women play cannot hold together when the economic structure of slavery falls apart.

Williams deconstructs Miss Rufel conceptually and spatially by divesting her of those agents that ensure her place as mistress, including her husband Bertie, who as master of their plantation represents the rigid constraints of southern society. When the terms by which slave relates to mistress are redrawn in this manner, what results is an equation of mistress with slave. Miss Rufel can see how she is a slave to the castes of economics, class, gender, and color. Yet hers is a precarious position: She cannot function as mistress without the runaways who run her farm, providing economic security in exchange for food and shelter from reenslavement. Therefore Miss Rufel as ex-mistress and revisioned abolitionist is a fitting metaphor for Williams's economic, spatial, and conceptual deconstruction and reconstruction of slavery, for it is primarily through the interactions between Rufel and the runaways that slaves and mistress become free.

• Marta E. Sanchez, "The Estrangement Effect in Sherley Anne Williams' *Dessa Rose*," *Genders* 15 (Winter 1992): 21–36.

—Mildred R. Mickle

RUFUS SCOTT. Arguably James *Baldwin's most tortured protagonist, Rufus Scott of **Another Country* (1962) reflects the author's view of the artist as prophet. Baldwin based him on Eugene Worth, a friend who committed suicide; like Worth, Rufus jumps from the George Washington Bridge. Ironically, Rufus's premature suicide catalyzes the other characters' physical and spiritual journeys.

A fledgling Greenwich Village jazz drummer, Rufus symbolizes American and existential loneliness; we first encounter him "peddling his ass." Psychologically and physically eviscerated, he is rescued temporarily by Vivaldo Moore, his Italian American best friend. Rufus also finds momentary solace with Leona, a white southerner. However, hegemonic oppression engenders an acute malaise in Rufus. Leona becomes the receptacle for his racial and self hatred and goes insane. We also learn of Rufus's former lover—another southerner, Eric Jones. Because of society's constricting definitions of manhood, Rufus repulsed Eric's affection. Ultimately, Rufus's multiple demons compel his suicide, which concludes the opening section.

Rufus's spiritual deformity is symptomatic of an American ethos that constructs racial and sexual barriers. Only when characters such as Vivaldo vitiate society's restrictions can they enter "another country," a metaphorical haven where love can exist. Rufus remains a groundbreaking figure in African American literature as one of the few suicides. Baldwin's characterization also signifies upon the discursive treatment of black men as archetypal victims, for Baldwin makes Rufus "partly responsible for his doom" (*Conversations with James Baldwin,* 1989).

• Therman B. O'Daniel, ed., *James Baldwin: A Critical Evaluation,* 1977. Trudier Harris, *Exorcising Blackness: Historical and Literary Lynching and Burning Rituals,* 1984. Fred L. Standley and Louis H. Pratt, eds., *Conversations with James Baldwin,* 1989.

—Keith Clark

"Runagate Runagate." One of Robert *Hayden's most successful historical poems, "Runagate Runagate" (first published in 1962), employs a montage of voices to portray the tumultuous world of escaped slaves, and ultimately the fundamental human impulse toward freedom. "Runagate," a term for a runaway slave, refers specifically to Harriet *Tubman and by extension to a series of symbols suggesting freedom and emancipation. Divided into two sections, the poem's opening stanza strikes a particularly high level of dramatic tension, impressing upon the reader the visceral immediacy of escape. Entirely free of punctuation, the first stanza both describes and effects flight, rendering a sense of perpetual motion, tumult, and omnipresent threat. The ensuing stanzas reconfigure this sense of motion and confusion through the juxtaposition of voices. Employing multiple voices (and their implicit sense of contrast) in a manner reminiscent of T. S. Eliot and very similar to Hayden's "Middle Passage," Hayden echoes hymns, spirituals, protest songs, wanted posters, slave voices, and ultimately Harriet Tubman. Though these voices appear in sequential fashion, the compression, typography, and absence of transitions suggest a simultaneity, a montage of personae and perspectives. Thus as multiple voices vie for visibility and ultimate control over the reader's attention, Hayden creates a complex signifying text whose multiple possibilities discourage unitary or rigid interpretations.

In order to hold these highly discursive voices in check, the poem relies upon the progression of its central symbols signifying freedom and possibility. In the first section the refrain "Runagate Runagate," strategically placed between disparate voices, reasserts the symbolic and thematic focus of the poem. The second section reconfigures the relatively abstract runagate as the historically concrete Harriet Tubman. Her voice dominates the first half of the second section, anticipating and effectively neutralizing oppositional voices that call for her incarceration or destruction. Tubman's final call to ride her train presents trains as the poem's final symbol. Sustaining her sense of defiance and affirmation, trains, here, reassert perpetual agitation through the historical specificity of the Underground Railroad, and more broadly suggest the pan-historical struggle for freedom. The final line of the poem condenses and transforms the competing voices into a singular voice and impulse ultimately transcendent of its own immediate circumstances. One of Hayden's best uses of history and montage, "Runagate Runagate" aptly illustrates one of his chief tenets expressed in his manifesto "Counterpoise," the unity of humanity and the crucial role the arts play in the struggle toward lasting peace. As the poem affirms physical, political, and psychic freedom, it suggests peace and resolution in the very act of resistance.

Hayden's focus on slavery and on the literal and symbolic act of escape revisits a theme important to a number of African American writers, particularly Octavia E. *Butler. Her novel **Kindred* (1979), perhaps her best-known work, also explores the physical and psychic perils of slavery, and the irrepressible impulse toward freedom.

• Wilburn Williams, Jr., "The Covenant of Timelessness and Time: Symbolism and History in Robert Hayden's Angle of Ascent," *Massachusetts Review* 18 (Winter 1977): 731–749. Howard Faulkner, "'Transformed by Steeps of Flight': The Poetry of Robert Hayden," *CLA Journal* 21 (June 1978): 96–111.

—Mark A. Sanders

RUSSWURM, JOHN BROWNE (1799–1851), journalist and editor. Born a slave in Jamaica, John Browne Russwurm was sent by his white father to Quebec in 1807 to go to school. In his early teens Russwurm rejoined his father in Portland, Maine, where he was given an opportunity to continue his intellectual development. In 1824, Russwurm enrolled in Bowdoin College in Brunswick, Maine, from which he graduated in 1826 with one of the first bachelor's degrees earned by an African American in the United States.

Migrating to New York, Russwurm formed a partnership with Samuel *Cornish, a black Presbyterian minister, to found a newspaper. The result of their partnership was *Freedom's Journal,* the first African American newspaper in the United States, launched on 16 March 1827. *Freedom's Journal* was offered for sale in the United States, Canada, England, and Haiti. David *Walker, one of the newspaper's agents, first published his powerful *Appeal in Freedom's Journal,* lending support to the paper's editorial contention that the time had come for black Americans to plead their own cause in their own way.

In September 1827, Cornish resigned from his editorial duties to devote himself to the ministry. Russwurm continued as sole editor until March 1829, when he turned the newspaper over to Cornish, who renamed the paper the *Rights of All* and kept it financially afloat for another year. By the time the newspaper ceased publication in 1830, Russwurm had moved to Liberia, where he became editor of the *Liberia Herald* and superintendent of education in Monrovia, the capital of Liberia. Russwurm's decision to emigrate to Liberia angered some of his black compatriots in the

American antislavery movement, who felt he was deserting the cause. To Russwurm, however, Liberia offered a genuine opportunity for African Americans to put racial prejudice behind them and build a just and workable society. Russwurm remained a committed African colonizationist for the rest of his life.

• Martin E. Dann, *The Black Press, 1827–1890,* 1971.

—William L. Andrews

RUTHERFORD CALHOUN. The protagonist of Charles R. *Johnson's novel **Middle Passage* (1990), Calhoun acts as interpreter for the Allmuseri, a tribe of African wizards Johnson created as a representation of his philosophical-aesthetic program. In the aftermath of a shipboard rebellion, Calhoun keeps the slave ship *Republic's* logbook, simultaneously informing the reader of his history and tracing his further development. Presenting a people's alternative senses of time, history, language, and fidelity, Rutherford becomes like the Allmuseri as he grows to understand them. His is the sole perspective offered; as he grows through contact with the Allmuseri, the reader's consciousness evolves as well.

Calhoun's position in the text identifies him with a host of protagonists; three significant predecessors are Herman Melville's Ishmael, Ralph *Ellison's Invisible Man, and Johnson's own Andrew Hawkins of *Oxherding Tale* (1982). Like his forebears, Rutherford seeks self-knowledge through a series of adventures. Also like them, Rutherford must face a number of hostile forces that would limit his search and destroy him; furthermore, he must expand his definition of evil in the process. Drawing on the legacy of earlier writers and his own work, Johnson in Rutherford offers the fulfillment of his program, moving the reader from a look at an alternative mind-set to a chance to experience it. In *Oxherding Tale,* the reader learns a great deal from the solitary Allmuseri character; in *Middle Passage* Johnson expands his initiation and makes the reader part of the tribe. Johnson thereby achieves his goal of expanding people's consciousnesses through hermeneutical reading, a "real-life" process modeled in his fictional universe.

—William R. Nash

S

SALAAM, KALAMU YA (b. 1947), poet, playwright, essayist, literary and cultural critic, short story writer, editor, and activist. Kalamu ya Salaam was born Vallery Ferdinand III on 24 March 1947 in New Orleans. He attended Carleton College in Minnesota and Southern University in New Orleans in the 1960s but did not graduate from either school. He was expelled from Southern University for his student protests against the university administration in 1969. From 1965 until 1968 he served in the U.S. Army. He eventually received an associate degree from Delgado Junior College. After completing his formal education, Salaam moved into the next and most important phase of his life's work, social and political activism, and liberation of African Americans and Africans. His community-based work includes participation in such organizations as the World Black and African Festival of Arts and Culture, Free Southern Theater (which in 1969 changed its name to BLKARTSOUTH), and Ahidiana (a New Orleans Pan-African Nationalist Organization), and he was a founding member and editor of the *Black Collegian* and executive director of the New Orleans Jazz Heritage, among many other organizations.

His literary productions, whether as poet, playwright, short story writer, or cultural critic, all address his fundamental position that art must be a vehicle to assist in the liberation of African people. To this end, a great deal of his work opposes Western cultural hegemony. His first plays, produced by the Free Southern Theater, reflect both in style and subject matter the nuances of the Black Arts movement and the black aesthetic of the 1960s and early 1970s. Salaam's *The Picket* (1968), *Mama* (1969), *Happy Birthday Jesus* (1969), *Black Liberation Army* (1969), *Homecoming* (1970), and *Black Love Song* (1971) were his attempts to capture the communality of black life in drama. His first volumes of poetry, *The Blues Merchant* (1969), *Hofu Ni Kwenu* (1973), and *Pamoja Tutashinda* (1974), not only created powerful and laudatory images of black people and their life in America but emphasized the need for art to serve a number of political and liberating functions for the black masses. His best-known volume of poetry is *Revolutionary Love* (1978), which connects the black liberation struggle to the notion of kinship in the black cultural heritage.

His literary and scholarly works since the mid-1970s include *Ibura* (1976), *Tearing the Roof off the Sucker* (1977), *South African Showdown* (1978), *Nuclear Power and the Black Liberation Struggle* (1978), *Who Will Speak for Us? New Afrikan Folktales* (1978, coauthored with his wife, Tayari kwa Salaam), *Herufi: An Alphabet Reader* (1978), *Iron Flowers: A Poetic Report on a Visit to Haiti* (1979), *Our Women Keep Our Skies From Falling* (1980), and *"He's the Prettiest": A Tribute to Big Chief Allison "Tootie" Montana's 50 Years of Mardi Gras Indian Suiting, July 12-August 31, 1997* (1997). His works are published in major African American literature anthologies. These works continue earlier themes and subjects of empowering black people at the cultural and political levels. The communal thrust of Salaam's vision extends to his cultural criticism of literature, music, and politics, as announced in his many essays, reviews, and interviews, published in such forums as *Negro Digest, Black World, Black Collegian, First World, Black Scholar,* and *Black Theatre.* Salaam is one of the most prolific writers and creators of African American discourse in the late twentieth century. He continues to reside in New Orleans and to carry on his artistic and cultural work.

• Vincent Hardy, "The Seventies," *Black Collegian* 10 (Oct./Nov. 1979): 86–99. J. O. Lockhard, "An Ideology for Black Artists," *First World* 2 (1980): 20–22, 67. Jerry W. Ward, Jr., "Kalamu ya Salaam: A Primary Bibliography (in Progress)," *Mississippi Quarterly* 51:1 (Winter 1997–1998): 105–148.

—Charles P. Toombs

Salt Eaters, The. Toni Cade *Bambara's important multilayered novel *The Salt Eaters* (1980) is set in the community of Claybourne, Georgia, during the late 1970s. The novel centers on the attempted suicide and healing of the main character, *Velma Henry, as she comes to grips with the fragmentation, rage, and self-will that have driven her in the past. In the Southwest Community Infirmary, after her wounds are bandaged, Velma sits with the fabled healer, *Minnie Ransom, surrounded by a circle of twelve spiritual adepts (The Master's Mind); a group of nervous medical students; the clinic physician, Dr. Julius Meadows; and an assortment of casually interested clinic patients. Also surrounding Velma and Minnie, beyond the clinic itself, are a dazzling constellation of characters, institutions, and situations: Fred Holt, the bus driver nearing retirement and grieving the death of his friend, Porter; Velma's husband, Obie, who heads the also fragmented Academy of the Seven Arts; the Seven Sisters performing arts group who travel toward Claybourne for the annual Mardi Gras festival.

Boundaries of time and space, imagination and reality are frequently blurred, as when Minnie Ransom and her spirit guide, Old Wife, freely commune throughout Velma's healing and even "travel" to a chapel for prayer. Jazz-inflected rhythms, lyrical language, flashbacks, digressions, and a panoply of characters and subplots create a novel that many reviewers initially found difficult—but ultimately worthwhile—to read. Gloria Hull, calling the novel "daringly brilliant," describes its structure as one of widening circles, and provides a diagram of how those many circles and characters connect. While the novel was enthusiastically received, some felt that its strength—its panoramic sweeps and encompassing themes—eclipsed character development, leaving readers little connection with individual characters.

All of the main characters are related in some way to Velma, whose fractured psyche serves as a trope for the splinterings and fractures of the community, where fundamental values (like connections with the best of people's traditions and attention to spiritual well-being) have been left behind in the wake of the civil rights movement. Like other African American women's novels of the 1970s and 1980s, *The Salt Eaters* deals with the gender oppression that African American women experienced before, during, and after civil rights. Minnie Ransom repeatedly asks Velma if she is ready for the "weight" of being well, a question the novel implicitly directs to the entire community.

The Salt Eaters integrates African and Afro-Caribbean spiritual and healing traditions with those from Western religion and other spiritual practices. The novel includes references to prayer, tarot, cowrie shells, herbal and folk medicines, loa, rootwork, and obeah, among others. Under Minnie's guiding hand, Velma will move backward in time to relive her fear and rage, as well as to recover lost wisdom and rootedness. Illness, however, becomes a matter of community as well as individual healing; as Velma returns to health, she is also restored to a community badly in need of its own healing. The novel ends apocalyptically, with the culmination of preparations for a local Mardi Gras festival and a cataclysmic storm that signals changes in the characters who need them the most, including Velma, who rises from the stool as though from a "burst cocoon."

• Gloria Hull, "What It Is I Think She's Doing Anyhow: A Reading of Toni Cade Bambara's *The Salt Eaters*," in *Home Girls: A Black Feminist Anthology*, ed. Barbara Smith, 1983, pp. 124–141. Margot Anne Kelly, "'Damballah Is the First Law of Thermodynamics': Modes of Access to Toni Cade Bambara's *The Salt Eaters*," *African American Review* 27.3 (1993): 479–493.

—Ann Folwell Stanford

SAMBO. Variants of the name Sambo can be found in several African cultures, including Samba in Bantu; Samb and Samba in Wolof; Sambu in Mandingo; and Sambo in Hausa, Mende, and Vai. Throughout census materials and assorted other eighteenth-century documents, these names emerge as those of new world slaves. The name also has possible Hispanic antecedents: the sixteenth-century word "zambo" refers to a bowlegged or knock-kneed individual.

By the late eighteenth century, whites had begun to use the name in a generic fashion to refer to male slaves. Before long, comic associations were commonplace; childishness, sloppiness, and a propensity to mispronounce multisyllabic words were the key traits of a Sambo figure. Such characters emerged in late eighteenth-century plays and sheet music, and became mainstays of nineteenth-century minstrelsy. By the time Helen Bannerman's *The Story of Little Black Sambo* was published in 1898, the name was thoroughly linked with the image of an immature, fun-loving, inept, black male. The hero of her popular children's story was, in fact, from India and his cleverness is the cornerstone of the tale.

Throughout the twentieth century, African Americans have had to grapple with the tenacious Sambo image. The white public's love affair with Sambo-inspired characters undermined the efforts of African Americans to achieve equality. Black author Ralph *Ellison addressed the insidiousness of the Sambo image in his masterpiece **Invisible Man* (1952). Nonetheless, advertisers, filmmakers, and others continued to depict black characters in the familiar Sambo fashion. In the mid-1950s, white historian Stanley Elkins caused a furor by using the Sambo label to refer to an actual personality type he believed to be prevalent during the era of slavery. But social critics continued to argue that Sambo was more representative of white wishful thinking than of any genuine personality profile evident within the African American population.

• Joseph Boskin, *Sambo: The Rise and Demise of an American Jester*, 1986. Clarence Major, ed., *Juba to Jive: A Dictionary of African-American Slang*, 1994.

—Patricia A. Turner

SANCHEZ, SONIA (b. 1934), poet, playwright, essayist, and educator. The life and work of Sonia Sanchez mark her progression toward enlightened understanding and expression of what it means to be Black and woman and connected to a larger world. At various periods she has been reborn: as child poet after her grandmother died, as militant revolutionary of the 1960s, as spiritual visionary of the 1970s—all were stages in becoming a self-possessed strong woman. Her writings have served as source and expression of her growth and commitment to harnessing political and spiritual energies to make a better world.

Born Wilsonia Benita Driver in Birmingham, Alabama, to Wilson L. Driver (musician and teacher) and Lena (Jones) Driver, who died when Sanchez was a baby, Sanchez had two siblings: Patricia and Wilson, who died in 1981. Her grandmother, whose strength and unconditional love provided the security Sanchez needed to withstand childhood traumas and adult pain, died when Sanchez was six. After this, possibly to compensate for a stutter she developed and that lasted throughout adolescence, Sanchez began to write poetry. Moving to Harlem at age nine, she attended school, earned a BA in political science at Hunter College, and studied poetry under Louise Bogan at New York University. Sanchez became deeply embroiled with Amiri *Baraka and Larry *Neal in political activism and poetry. She taught at the Downtown Community School in San Francisco (1965–1967), then at San Francisco State University (1967–1969), where she helped found the first Black Studies program.

Sanchez's early work responds to political and personal upheavals of the 1960s with radical experiments in form, style, and theme. "Assassin poems" and "lyrical confessionals" dominate *Homecoming* (1969) and **We a BaddDDD People* (1970). Sanchez targets the enemies—murdering "wite americans," cops, sanctimonious Black puritans, and revolutionary poseurs—and lauds the heroes: *Malcolm X, Bobby Hutton, John *Coltrane, and Billie *Holiday. Like e.e. cummings, whom she parodies, Sanchez disrupts normal typography, word shapes, and the use of space to convey both emotion and clues to performance. *Homecoming*'s title poem epitomizes her theme: the return to blackness—rejection of white values—represents a return to Black speech and rhythms, idioms (dozens, rap), and music (jazz, blues) in a poetry as personal and confessional as it is insurgent. Loneliness and lyricism characterize the personal poems so infused by a blues sensibility and sound that some critics credit Sanchez with placing blues at the center of poetic discourse.

Sanchez's first plays display similar militant themes: *The Bronx Is Next* (1968), dramatizing a plot to burn down a Harlem ghetto, and *Sister Son/ja* (1969), portraying the journey of a sister who is "moving consciously black," despairs, and is reborn. Other plays focus on Malcolm X, Black male and female relationships, and political allegory.

The anger and confrontation of the 1960s were consolidated in the empowering 1970s, when African Americans sensed a new connectedness to the world outside of America. Travels in China, the Caribbean (1973), and Cuba (1979), and membership in the Nation of Islam (1972–1975) broadened Sanchez's vision. She held a succession of teaching positions in the Northeast (University of Pittsburgh, Rutgers University, Manhattan Community College, and Amherst College) before moving to Philadelphia, where she began teaching at Temple University in 1977 and is the Laura H. Cornell Professor of English.

The less strident, pastoral lyrics of *Love Poems* (1973) depict moving moments in Sanchez's life: estrangement from her Puerto Rican husband, indictment of her father for casting her adrift, memories of love's ecstasy and despair. Surrealistic imagery in "Old Words" gives way to anticipation of love in "Welcome home my Prince." An exquisite lyricism informs Sanchez's maturing vision and technique as she distills emotion into ever more restrictive forms: sonnets and ballads, tankas and haikus. Other poems express growing allegiance to Elijah Muhammad, heralding her conversion to Islam, which inspired *A Blues Book for Blue Black Magical Women* (1973), perhaps her strongest achievement before *Homegirls*. Sanchez experienced visions while writing this, her spiritual autobiography in five parts. Exhorting the "Queens of the Universe" to forsake racist Western ways, she invokes the Earth Mother to guide her spiritual journey into the past, tracing her evolution from birth to rebirth; declares her devotion to the Nation of Islam; and returns to her ancestral home to be purified. The last section draws from the Bible and Koran to depict apocalyptic visions and ends with the repeated refrain "in the beginning / there was no end." Chanting rhythms and imagery of Egyptian myth and Swahili praise poem enact the symbolic death and rebirth of all Black women. It is a "mountaintop poem" that transports African American rhythms to the pinnacle, then into deeper self-understanding.

During the 1970s Sanchez also wrote three children's books. *It's a New Day* (1971), *The Adventures of Fathead, Smallhead and Soaphead* (1973), and *A Sound Investment* (1980) address the need to instill in young people pride in their heritage and knowledge of their history and culture.

Throughout the 1980s and early 1990s Sanchez has been a dedicated teacher, mother, and prolific writer. Her work has appeared in numerous magazines, journals, and anthologies, and six records exist of her readings. She has also received prestigious awards, among them a National Endowment for the Arts fellowship (1978–1979), the Lucretia Mott Award (1984), American Book Award (1985), Pennsylvania Governor's Award (1988), and Paul Robeson Social Justice Award (1989).

The 1980s witnessed the production of some of her finest work. In *I've Been a Woman: New and Selected Poems* (1981) earlier poems establish a context for new works. Four poems about her father trace her evolving feelings, from vengeful scorn to forgiveness and reconciliation. Love, "sweet as watermelon juice," pervades the "Haikus and Tankas and Other Love Syllables," which explode with sensual images of color, sound, taste, and touch. "Generations" honors Sterling A. *Brown, "griot of fire," Gerald Penny, a student who died in 1973, and Shirley *Graham. Haki R. *Madhubuti calls this book "a truly earth-cracking contribution," exuding a rage and "urgency" unmatched by most of her peers.

Sanchez's most acclaimed work, *Homegirls and Handgrenades* (1984), received the American Book Award in 1985. "Grenades" are words that explode people's deluding myths about themselves and the world. New poetry and prose poems, interspersed with selections from *Love Poems*, comprise the four sections documenting the lives and longings of people who have loved or betrayed, disappointed or inspired her. Affirmations of "The Power of Love" contrast with the bleak portraits of "Blues Is Bullets," exposing love's power to distort and destroy. Prevailing images of death in "Beyond the Fallout" contextualize tributes to Jesse Jackson, Margaret *Walker, and Ezekiel Mphehlele in "Grenades Are Not Free." Sanchez introduces a series of prose poems reminiscent of Jean *Toomer's *Cane* (1923), describing an encounter in a park between an old woman and an overburdened young mother, the ravages of drug addiction on a family, and meetings with former classmates whose youthful promise has been twisted into self-annihilation. The powerful climax—her letter to Martin Luther *King, Jr., announcing a new day, and "MIAs," commemorating those missing in action in Atlanta, Johannesburg, and El Salvador—exhorts all people to liberate the oppressed and alleviate suffering.

Under a Soprano Sky (1987) interweaves strands of earlier works with new themes and techniques to demonstrate Sanchez's political, spiritual, and artistic growth. The title poem's lyricism, sensuously mingling the body and the natural world, infuses elegies for her brother, for members of the back-to-nature movement MOVE slaughtered by Philadelphia police, and for the city itself. Chronicles of victims—a Hiroshima maiden, a Black man, Vietnam veteran James Thornwell, and Stephen Rinaldo, a murdered boy—inform tributes to heroes like Papa Joe, Paul *Robeson, John *Brown, and "Dear Mama," the grandmother who allowed her to grow. A melange of voices speak in haikus, tankas, and blues, alternating with more prosaic forms portraying a feisty "rough mama" and Mildred Scott Olmstead. The selections in "Endings" look ahead to the rise of a new earth, the work of tomorrow's poets, and the bright promise of her graduating sons.

In the 1990s, Sanchez continued her poetry and essay production with several volumes. They include *Wounded in the House of a Friend* (1995), *Does Your House Have Lions?* (1997), *Like the Singing Coming Off the Drums: Love Poems* (1998), and *Shake Loose My Skin: New and Selected Poems* (1999).

For Sanchez poetry is a "subconscious conversation," a dialogue she has carried on for nearly three decades with the lost, lonely, and oppressed. She has been called a revolutionary, ritual singer, cultural worker, and people's poet—the roles intertwine, unified by an unshakable faith that the world can be changed and that one person can make a difference. She has certainly done her part. The revolutionary has ceaselessly agitated for radical reform, assaulting a morally bankrupt economic system, denouncing a racist agenda that incapacitates and kills, exhorting the "humanitarians" to join the struggle. The ritual singer has chanted the syllables of "ancestral" voices—Orisha, Oshun, Maat, Shirley Graham, Lizzie Driver—making past mysteries sound powerfully in the present. The cultural worker and people's poet has ministered to generations of writers, preaching the virtues of disciplined composition and living language, while celebrating African American sounds and sensibilities, boldness and beauty. Like Langston *Hughes, Sterling Brown, Jean Toomer, and Margaret Walker, with whom she is compared, Sonia Sanchez has opened a space in American letters where the racial self may be heard, affirmed, and strengthened. With her sense of fiery justice and her legacy of love, Sanchez stands as an inspiration, an example of what it means to survive whole and human in a troubled world.

• Claudia Tate, "Sonia Sanchez," in *Black Women Writers at Work,* 1983, pp. 132–148. Haki Madhubuti, "Sonia Sanchez: The Bringer of Memories," in *Black Women Writers (1950–1980),* ed. Mari Evans, 1984, pp. 419–432. David Williams, "The Poetry of Sonia Sanchez," in *Black Women Writers (1950–1980),* ed. Mari Evans, 1984, pp. 433–448. Houston A. Baker, Jr., "Our Lady: Sonia Sanchez and the Writing of a Black Renaissance," in *Black Feminist Criticism and Critical Theory,* eds. Joe Weixlmann and Houston Baker, 1988, pp. 169–202. Zala Chandler, "Voices beyond the Veil: An Interview with Toni Cade Bambara and Sonia Sanchez," in *Wild Women in the Whirlwind,* eds. Joanne Braxton and Andree Nicola McLaughlin, 1990, pp. 342–362. Joanne Veal Gabbin, "The Southern Imagination of Sonia Sanchez," in *Southern Women Writers: The New Generation,* ed. Tonette Bond Inge, 1990, pp. 180–203. D. H. Melhem, "Sonia Sanchez: The Will and Spirit," in *Heroism in the New Black Poetry,* ed. D. H. Melhem, 1990, pp. 132–179. Regina B. Jennings, "The Blue/Black Poetics of Sonia Sanchez," in *Language and Literature in the African-American Imagination,* ed. Carol Aisha Blackshire-Belay, 1992, pp. 119–132. William Cook, "The Black Arts Poets," in *The Columbia History of African-American Poetry,* eds. Jay Parini and Brett C. Millier, 1993, pp. 674–706. Danielle Alyce Rome, "An Interview with Sonia Sanchez," in *Speaking of the Short Story: Interviews with Contemporary Writers,* ed. Farhat Iftekharuddin et al., 1997, pp. 229–236.

—Deborah Ayer Sitter

SANDERS, DORI (b. 1934), novelist. Dori Sanders, the popular storyteller and lifelong peach farmer in Filbert, South Carolina, made her literary debut with *Clover* (1990), a novel about a ten-year-old black farm girl whose widowed father dies only hours after marrying a white woman. Clover Hill and her stepmother, Sara Kate, build a life together in rural South Carolina while coming to terms with their grief, with Clover's extended family, and with their cultural differences. The child's perceptive and humorous first-person narrative depicts their experiences as they learn to live with and love each other.

Her Own Place (1993), Sanders's second novel, traces fifty years in the life of Mae Lee Barnes, a World War II bride who raises five children and runs her own farm in South Carolina after her husband abandons the family. She finds inner strength and meaning through her love of family, community, and the land. After her children are grown, she moves from the farm into town, where she becomes the first black volunteer at the local hospital. Her relationship with her white, upper-class colleagues is awkward, humorous, inspiring, and ultimately successful.

In 1995, Sanders published *Dori Sanders' Country Cooking: Recipes and Stories from the Family Farm Stand.* Throughout this autobiographical work, Sanders's spirited storytelling associates recipes with tales of farm traditions and memories of her family.

The tradition of African American women's writing has been enriched by Dori Sanders's particular insights into the southern rural African American community and its worldview. Her convincing folk vernacular, imaginative metaphor, humor, and keen observations of small details create drama and force in her commentary on the richness of family and community. Refusing to recognize limits to the possibilities of human relationships, Sanders develops in her novels a theme that is uncustomary in contemporary African American fiction: the celebration of everyday people, black and white, who live in the rural South and depend upon each other for personal and economic preservation during the years since the 1940s.

—Marsha C. Vick

SAPPHIRE. One of the most pervasive and persistent stereotypes of African American women, Sapphire is an overly aggressive, domineering, emasculating female. Her origins can be found in *Sam 'n' Henry,* a 1926 radio serial (renamed two years later as *Amos 'n' Andy*) in which two white actors, Freeman Gosden and Charles Correll, portrayed two southern African American men who had migrated to Chicago. Rooted in nineteenth-century minstrel shows and blackface vaudeville acts, in 1929 *Amos 'n' Andy* joined NBC and added the Kingfish and his wife, Sapphire, and became the most popular radio show in the United States.

Ernestine Wade's radio portrayal of the Kingfish's wife catapulted the character of Sapphire into fame as the most popular and most stereotypical female in the series. She was loud-talking, abrasive, overbearing, bossy, controlling, and emasculating. The most memorable scenes of the marriage were Sapphire scolding her husband about his dishonesty, laziness, and unreliability. Their relationship was consistent with the stereotypical matriarchal African American family that Black sociologist E. Franklin Frazier portrayed in his classic *The Negro Family in the United States* (1939). In 1951 *Amos 'n' Andy* premiered on television and etched derogatory stereotypes of African Americans into the national consciousness for more than a decade.

"Sapphire" became, long after the name's association with the program had faded, an unquestioned characterization of the so-called emasculating African American woman. She also became a pervasive image in African American folk culture and one of the most damaging stereotypes in the mass media, one that influences contemporary conceptions of Black womanhood.

• Melvin Patrick Kelley, *The Adventures of Amos 'n' Andy: A Social History of an American Phenomenon,* 1991.

—Beverly Guy-Sheftall

SCHOMBURG, ARTHUR A. (1874–1938), bibliophile, bibliographer, curator, historian, and Pan-Africanist; also wrote under the name Guarionex. Arthur Alfonso Schomburg's vast private collection, now housed in the Schomburg Center for Research in Black Culture (formerly the 135th Street branch of the New York Public Library), is one of the outstanding collections of materials concerning the history and culture of people of African descent.

Schomburg was born on 24 January 1874 to an unwed freeborn mulatta, Maria Josepha, in Saint Thomas, U.S. Virgin Islands, and raised in Puerto Rico by his mother's family. Although he adopted his surname, there is no evidence that Schomburg's father, Carlos Federico Schomburg, a German-born merchant living in San Juan, acknowledged or supported his son. Little is known about Schomburg prior to his emigration to the United States. Upon arriving in New York in 1891, he settled into the Puerto Rican and Cuban community on Manhattan's east side. For most of his professional career, Schomburg worked for Bankers Trust Company in the bank's foreign mailing section. Schomburg became fully immersed in American Black culture in New York and focused his personal and scholarly attentions there.

The segue into African American culture was a natural consequence of Schomburg's personal life. He married three African American women—each named Elizabeth—who altogether bore him six sons and one daughter. Never much of a family man, Schomburg focused his energies on Freemasonry, research societies, community activities, and his passion for research and collecting.

Schomburg dedicated his life to collecting materials that would confirm and affirm the history and contributions of people of color. Thus he became widely known for his prodigious collection and respected for his bibliographic acumen—particularly his ability to find rare or lost materials. Schomburg sold his private collection to the New York Public Library in 1926. While the original inventory has been lost, Schomburg's collection is estimated to have contained over ten thousand books, manuscripts, prints, and pieces of memorabilia. In 1930 Schomburg was asked to establish a collection of resources in Black history and culture for the Fisk University library and to map out a plan for the library's future acquisitions. He served as curator for the Negro Collection in Fisk's Cravath Memorial Library for two years. In January 1932 Schomburg returned to New York to become the curator for his former collection.

While he had no formal education, Schomburg became a respected lay authority on many subjects concerning Blacks around the world. He published a bibliography, an exhibition catalogue, and various articles about Black subjects in the *Crisis, Opportunity, Survey Graphic,* and *Negro World.* He gave frequent public lectures at important cultural events. The Harlem Renaissance—the political, social, and literary movement designed to celebrate the African American's talents and accomplishments—showcased Schomburg's extraordinary collection and his bibliographic genius.

• Arthur Schomburg, "The Negro Digs Up His Past," *Survey Graphic* 6 (Mar. 1925): 670–672; rpt. in *The New Negro,* ed. Alain Locke, 1968. Elinor DesVerney Sinnette, *Arthur Alfonso Schomburg,* 1989.

—Deborah H. Barnes

SCHUYLER, GEORGE S. (1895–1977), satirist, critic, and journalist. George Samuel Schuyler was born in Providence, Rhode Island, to Eliza Jane Fischer and George S. Schuyler. He grew up in a middle-class, racially mixed neighborhood in Syracuse, New York, where he attended public schools until he enlisted in the army at the age of seventeen. He spent seven years (1912–1919) with the black 25th U.S. Infantry and was discharged as a first lieutenant.

From early on, Schuyler possessed a high level of confidence and boasted of his family having been free as far back as the Revolutionary War. In 1921, Schuyler joined the Socialist Party of America, through which he connected with A. Philip Randolph, who hired him in 1923 as assistant editor for the *Messenger;* in that position, from 1923 to 1928, Schuyler also wrote a column entitled "Shafts and Darts: A Page of Calumny and Satire." In 1924, Schuyler became the New York correspondent for the *Pittsburgh Courier,* contributing a weekly commentary, "Views and Reviews." Schuyler led several investigative series while with the *Courier,* including one entitled "Aframerican Today," reporting on race relations in Mississippi in 1925–1926. In 1926, his article "The Negro-Art Hokum," published in the *Nation,* propelled him into the middle of the literary debate of the Harlem Renaissance. While Schuyler was concerned with race difference always being interpreted as inferiority and was trying to refute negative stereotypes, his statement in that essay, "the Aframerican is merely a lampblacked Anglo-Saxon," caused him to be labeled as an assimilationist throughout his career. In 1927, "Our White Folks" was published in H. L. Mencken's *American Mercury;* from this, Schuyler's reputation grew and Mencken published nine more of Schuyler's articles between 1927 and 1933.

By the end of the 1920s, Schuyler began to acquire a national reputation as an iconoclast; despite his constant attacks on white racism, his commitment to exposing fraud, regardless of race, caused some African Americans to doubt his racial loyalty. In 1928, Schuyler married Josephine Cogdell, a white Texan ex-model.

In 1931, Schuyler published his first satirical novel, **Black No More, Being an Account of the Strange and Wonderful Workings of Science in the Land of the Free.* The bulk of Schuyler's reputation rests on the success of this novel, which attacks myths of racial purity and white supremacy and the ways in which the perpetuation of racism serves economic purposes. Also in 1931, Schuyler became the first African American writer to serve as a foreign correspondent for a metropolitan newspaper, when the *New York Evening Post* sent him to assess the controversy of Liberia's slave labor. The articles were condemned by Marcus Garvey supporters, but based on the experience he published *Slaves Today: A Story of Liberia* (1931).

Schuyler also had several literary alter egos. Between 1933 and 1939, he produced fifty-four short stories and twenty novels/novellas in serialized form under such pen names as Samuel I. Brooks and Rachel Call. Until recently, scholars paid no attention to this body of work and Schuyler's own attitude toward his serialized fiction ranged from amusement to disdain. The freedom of a pen name allowed him to explore melodrama, and in contrast to the audience for his satirical essays and his novel, *Black No More,* Schuyler wrote his serialized fiction for an exclusively African American audience. To date, four of his serialized novels have been reprinted into two volumes: *Black Empire* (1991) and *Ethiopian Stories* (1995). *Black Empire* explores the success of the retaking of Africa from European colonial powers; *Ethiopian Stories* explores Ethiopia's wars against Italian occupation.

Schuyler continued his career as a journalist until 1966, when he published his autobiography, *Black and Conservative,* which gives an inside track to the feuds among the leaders of the Harlem Renaissance, as well as a look at Schuyler's own anticommunist/anticapitalist views. While Schuyler saw the major problem of the twentieth century to be the color line, he felt that focusing on race conflict only would lead African Americans into second-class citizenship. George Schuyler is generally considered the most prominent African American journalist and essayist of the early twentieth century.

• Michael W. Peplow, *George S. Schuyler,* 1980. Stacy Morgan, "'The Strange and Wonderful Workings of Science': Race, Science and Essentialism in George Schuyler's *Black No More,*" in *CLA Journal* 42 (1999): 331–52.

—Adenike Marie Davidson

SCOTTSBORO BOYS. Nearly lynched, quickly tried and sentenced to death for supposedly raping two white women in a railroad car near Scottsboro, Alabama, in 1931, the Scottsboro boys symbolized, in literature, law, and the minds of many, the desperate situation of southern African American men. Several writers, including Countee *Cullen and S. Ralph Harlow, wrote in response to this incident, but none more significantly than Langston *Hughes.

In his small volume, *Scottsboro Limited* (1932), Hughes presented this case as an exemplar of larger ethical, moral, and economic issues. In "Justice," Hughes gives infected eyes to the blind Justice of U.S. jurisprudence, reshaping a foundational figure of impartiality and reasoned judgment as an image of physical and ethical decay. In "Christ in Alabama," he casts violent and sexual overtones over the relation of a light-skinned God to a darker-skinned Mary, thereby asserting that the true sexual aggressor is not a martyred, African American Christ, but a powerful white man. In "Scottsboro," the imprisoned boys are joined by a series of other freedom fighters, including John *Brown, *Moses, Jeanne d'Arc, Nat *Turner, and Lenin. In a more upbeat tone, Hughes's play, *Scottsboro Limited,* later staged by Amiri *Baraka in the 1960s, connects the plight of these nine men with that of white working people, using communist understandings of an oppressed underclass to call for solidarity across racial and along class lines. Hughes symbolizes the communist activists who brought the Scottsboro case into the national spotlight with a chorus of Red voices that continually speak to the boys in their cell. The play ends hopefully with white and black workers pouring on stage, smashing the electric chair, and clasping hands while a red flag is rising. Hughes's volume eloquently illustrates the multiple and complex aspects of the African American experience that Scottsboro briefly brought to the fore.

• Hugh T. Murray, Jr., "Changing America and the Changing Image of Scottsboro," *Phylon* 38 (1977): 82–92. Amiri Baraka, "Staging Langston Hughes's *Scottsboro Limited:* An Interview with Amiri Baraka," interview by Veve Clark, *Black Scholar* 10 (1979): pp. 62–69.

—Maggie Sale

SÉJOUR, VICTOR (1817–1874), dramatist, poet, novelist, and recipient of the French Legion of Honor. The most distinguished African American writer of nineteenth-century Louisiana, Victor Séjour's lengthy career as a successful dramatist in Paris makes him a unique figure, important to both the history of African American writing and the history of French theater in the Second Empire (1851–1870).

Juan Victor Séjour Marcouet Ferrand was born a free Creole of color in New Orleans, son of prosperous merchant Juan François Louis Séjour Marcou, a free mulatto from Santo Domingo, and Eloisa Phillippe Ferrand, a free octoroon born in New Orleans. After secondary education under black writer and journalist Michel Séligny at New Orleans's Sainte-Barbe Academy, Séjour departed for Paris, like many other elite Creoles, to pursue further education and a career unencumbered by the racial constraints of American society.

In Paris Séjour entered literary circles where he associated with influential figures Emile Augier, Alexandre Dumas père, and abolitionist editor Cyrille Bisette (like Séjour, Dumas and Bisette were men of color). His first publication, a short story entitled "Le mulâtre" ("The mulatto"), in which a slave murders his master only to discover he has killed his father, appeared in 1837 in Bisette's journal, *La revue des colonies.* References to slavery and American racial dilemmas are overt in this first publication, one of the earliest African American fictionalizations of slavery, but thereafter occur only in allusions and metaphors such as the persecution of Jews (*Diégarias,* 1844; *La tireuse de cartes,* 1860) and class-based separatism in France (*Le martyre du coeur,* 1858). Literary success came in 1841 with *Le retour de Napoléon,* a heroic ode celebrating the return of Napoleon's remains to Paris. *Le retour de Napoléon* was reprinted in the United States in 1845 by editor Armand Lanusse as part of *Les *Cenelles,* the first anthology of poetry by African Americans.

Séjour's run of twenty-five years as a leading figure in Parisian theater, during which he brought over twenty plays to the stage, was extraordinary by any standards. His first plays, *Diégarias* (1844) and *La chute de Séjan* (*The Fall of Sejanus,* 1849), historical verse dramas in the romantic style of Victor Hugo, garnered critical praise. Wide popularity followed during the 1850s as he turned to prose melodramas, adventures, and comedies. During these years he lived well, brought his parents to France, and fathered three children with three mothers outside marriage. His success, however, was linked to precisely the kind of lavishly staged romantic melodrama that fell out of favor in the 1860s, and his personal fortunes declined with the genre's waning popularity.

Struggling in his last years with illness and a changing literary marketplace, further disrupted by the Franco-Prussian War and the Paris Commune (1870–1871), Séjour also produced a serialized novel, *Le compte de Haag* (*The Count of Haag,* 1872), the story of a revolutionary in France, left unfinished because of declining health. Séjour was hospitalized for tuberculosis in 1873 and died in September 1874.

Overall, Séjour's career and significance are closely tied to the Second Empire's culture and values. The world of his writing is that of Bonapartism, emphasizing nationalism, liberalism, the family, and religious life, attempting to steer a middle path between conservative monarchists and radical republicans. Nevertheless, as an African American his racially driven alienation from U.S. culture and career-long concern with ethnic and class conflict are noteworthy, and constitute a precedent for African American cultural expatriates of later periods.

• T. A. Daley, "Victor Séjour," *Phylon,* First Quarter (1943): 5–16. Charles Edwards O'Neill, "Theatrical Censorship in France, 1844–1875: The Experience of Victor Séjour," *Harvard Library Bulletin,* 26.4 (Oct. 1978): 417–441. Charles Edwards O'Neill, "Victor Séjour," in *DANB,* eds. Rayford W. Logan and Michael R. Winston, 1982, pp. 551–552. J. John Perret, "Victor Séjour, Black French Playwright from Louisiana," *The French Review* 57.2 (Dec. 1983): 187–193. Thomas Bonner, Jr., "Victor Séjour," in *DLB*, vol. 50, *Afro-American Writers before the Harlem Renaissance*, ed. Trudier Harris, 1986, pp. 237–241.

—Philip Barnard

SELINA BOYCE, in Paule *Marshall's **Brown Girl, Brownstones* (1953), is one of the most psychologically complex female African American fictional characters since *Janie Crawford in Zora Neale *Hurston's **Their Eyes Were Watching God* (1937) and Gwendolyn *Brooks's Maud Martha (**Maud Martha,* 1953). Selina is a young woman of two worlds, two cultures. Born in the United States of Barbadian parentage, she must somehow bridge the gap between two identities that are often in conflict. Paule Marshall explores Selina's cultural identity crisis through the often ambivalent and volatile feelings she has toward members of the surrounding "Bajan" (Barbadian) community (and especially her mother), who exert strong pressure upon her to conform to their ideas concerning their position as immigrants in American society, as opposed to her father, who rejects the kinds of culturally and spiritually draining behavior that the pursuit of the American dream can inflict upon anyone not strong enough to withstand its pressures.

Selina, as a young woman, must carefully navigate herself between two worlds in order to utilize the best of both. By the end of the novel, she realizes that it was never a question of either/or in terms of her cultural identity. She learns that it is only the best of both her American and Barbadian cultures that has made her strong and that will continue to sustain her.

• Geta J. Leseure, "*Brown Girl, Brownstones* as a Novel of Development," *Obsidian* II 1 (1986): 119–129.

—Keith Bernard Mitchell

SEMPLE, JESSE B. *See* Simple.

SETHE SUGGS. In Toni *Morrison's **Beloved* (1987), Sethe Suggs is the epitome of the slave mother, even more tragic because she loved her children in a system that negated her humanity as well as her maternal instinct.

Purchased by Mr. Garner at age thirteen, Sethe marries Halle Suggs and he fathers every one of her four children—unusual in the slave system. With the death of Mr. Garner, whom the slaves considered humane, his heir schoolteacher takes over and subjects them to the full degradation and inhumanity of the system. Sethe feels she must escape to ensure the safety of her children (the fourth still unborn) and to feed her young daughter Beloved from her milk-laden breasts, but before she can leave, schoolteacher's three nephews hold her down in the barn, milk her like a cow, and beat her. This is the final blow to her sense of who and what she is, and she immediately sets out for the North, walking and crawling to freedom when her feet become mutilated. When schoolteacher comes to reclaim his "property," Sethe kills Beloved with a handsaw rather than see her returned to slavery. After Sethe serves a jail sentence for the murder, she and her children are free but Beloved's venomous and spiteful spirit begins to torment them, disappearing but then returning as a twenty-year-old. Moreover, Sethe is relentlessly haunted by guilt. Beloved's return is a horrible reminder of Sethe's history and, more significantly, of the horrific history of all African Americans.

[*See also* Paul D.]

• Wilfred D. Samuels and Clenora Hudson Weems, *Toni Morrison,* 1990. Trudier Harris, *Fiction and Folklore: The Novels of Toni Morrison,* 1991. Patrick Bryce Bjork, *The Novels of Toni Morrison: The Search for Self and Place within the Community,* 1994.

—Betty Taylor-Thompson

Shadow and Act. When it was first published in 1964, Ralph *Ellison's *Shadow and Act* was hailed as his autobiography. Such critics as George P. Elliot and R. W. B. Lewis took their cue from Ellison himself, who in the volume's introduction wrote that the essays, "whatever their value," were autobiographical. While there are discussions of Ellison's early life in the text, the work is a statement of his literary credo as it had evolved over a twenty-two year period. As biography it is more concerned with the history of a race rather than with the history of a person.

The text has an introduction and three divisions: "The Seer and the Seen," which deals with literature and Ellison's literary career; "Sound and the Mainstream," which deals with music and musicians; and "The Shadow and the Act," which concerns itself with racial issues. Each article has the original date of production at its end, allowing the reader to chart Ellison's development as a writer from 1942, the date of the earliest piece, to 1964.

In "The Seer and the Seen," Ellison uses literature as a vehicle for discussing the social consciousness of Blacks. He contends that whites assume that because Blacks have been brutalized in America they have become brutes and are unable to rise above this condition in life or in art. It is this vision that produces what Ellison calls "ideological" writing. But Blacks, according to Ellison, have been able to "deflect racial provocation and to master and control pain." In short, Blacks have been able through discipline to transcend the negative environment spiritually and artistically and to contribute to the national growth on all levels. The second section of the book is a variation of the first, but instead of using literature as a springboard for his discussion, Ellison uses jazz. Originating in the Black community, jazz has been associated with poverty and low life, but the author contends that like the Black experience itself, the artists and the art form have transcended the limitations of the environment to triumph nationally. The third section is a bit more caustic. Here Ellison examines the effects of racism on Blacks and concludes that not only has it affected the population adversely, causing mental and emotional problems, but that during World War II it was responsible for the death of Blacks. The essays, coming as they did when America was experiencing a great deal of racial turbulence, must have had a sobering effect on the mainstream, for the book clearly indicates it is the Black experience in America that makes the American experience what it is: "It is practically impossible for the white American to think of sex, of economics, of children or women folk, or of sweeping socio-political changes without summoning into consciousness fear-flecked images of black men." For Ellison Blacks have become "the gauge of the human condition in America."

Shadow and Act is anchored in the African American literary canon between W. E. B. *Du Bois and Toni *Morrison. It shares a spiritual kinship with its "ancestor," Du Bois's *The *Souls of Black Folk* (1903). *Shadow* differs in structure and style from *Souls,* but both works demonstrate that despite adversity Blacks have made great artistic contributions to America. Ellison's essays also share a kinship with Amiri *Baraka's *Blues People,* reviewed by Ellison in 1964, and James *Baldwin's **Notes of a Native Son* (1955) and *More Notes of a Native Son* (1961). *Shadow* anticipates such high-profile writers as Toni Morrison and Charles R. *Johnson. Morrison's *Playing in the Dark* (1992), like *Shadow,* inquires into the role Blacks play in the literature of whites. And Johnson's *Being and Race* (1988) questions, as *Shadow* does, the importance of experience in creating a work of art. *Shadow and Act* is an important literary and social document because it not only affirms Black humanity but also states emphatically that despite cultural deprivation Blacks have given much to America in the form of art.

—Ralph Reckley, Sr.

SHADRACK, the shell-shocked ex-soldier in Toni *Morrison's **Sula* (1974), is intimately connected with death. Having lost his sanity after his first battle in World War I, in which he saw a fellow private's face blown off, Shadrack believes that his hands have grown to monstrous proportions and he has no sense of self, "no past, no language, no tribe, no source, no address book, no comb, no pencil, no bed . . . and nothing nothing to do." Following his release from a veteran's hospital, he returns to his home neighborhood, in Medallion, where the novel takes place. He institutes National Suicide Day, in which he walks down the street ringing a cow bell and holding a hangman's rope, thereby offering people a chance to kill themselves in a prescribed period so that death will not be a constant worry to them. The community eventually accepts Shadrack as an eccentric.

After *Sula Peace, the novel's protagonist, and her friend Nel participate in the drowning of a young boy, Sula goes to Shadrack's shack near the river to see if he witnessed anything. In the veteran's hospital he had dreamed of a river and a window, and to Sula he simply replies, "Always." This creates a bond between the two of them, both of whom are viewed as eccentrics by the community. Shadrack remains on the edges of the community physically but is very much a part of it. In an ironic twist, a group of black people follows him on one playful and fateful observance of National Suicide Day. They march out of Medallion and into the white section of town, into an unfinished tunnel on which the black men had been denied work. The tunnel breaks under their weight and they drown—without conscious intent to commit suicide—and Shadrack is one of few survivors. Shadrack, whose name comes from the biblical character who was saved from the fiery furnace by his faith in God, cannot be saved from the madness caused by the catastrophes and inhumanity of men and war.

• Wilfred D. Samuels and Clenora Hudson Weems, *Toni Morrison,* 1990. Trudier Harris, *Fiction and Folklore: The Novels of Toni Morrison,* 1991. Patricia Hunt, "War and Peace:Transfigured Categories and the Politics of *Sula,*" *African American Review* 27 (1993): 443–459. Eileen Barrett, "Septimus and Shadrack:Woolf and Morrison Envision the Madness of War," in *Virginia Woolf: Emerging Perspectives,* 1994, pp. 26–32.

—Betty Taylor-Thompson

SHANGE, NTOZAKE (b. 1948), poet, playwright, novelist, and essayist. Ntozake Shange (En-to-za-kee Shong-gā) was propelled into the national literary and dramatic scene in 1974 with the dramatic debut of **for colored girls who have considered suicide / when the rainbow is enuf* and has since maintained a literary presence, garnering awards and honors for her achievements as a dramatist, poet, and novelist. Her list of creative achievements has steadily increased through the writing of several dramas such as *From Okra to Greens* (1978), *A Photograph: A Still Life with Shadows / A Photograph: A Study in Cruelty,* which was revised as *A Photograph: Lovers-In-Motion* and published with *Spell #7* (1979) and *Boogie Woogie Landscapes* (1979) in *Three Pieces* (1981). Other dramas include *Where the Mississippi Meets the Amazon,* (coauthored with Jessica Hegedorn and Thulani Nkabinda); *Mother Courage and Her Children* (1980); and *Daddy Says* (1989). Her poetry collections include *Nappy Edges* (1978) and *Ridin' the Moon in Texas* (1989), and her books and essays include *Sassafras: A Novella* (1977); *Some Men* (1981); *Sassafras, Cypress and Indigo* (1982); *A Daughter's Geography* (1983); *See No Evil: Prefaces Essays and Accounts, 1976–1983* (1984); and *Betsy Brown* (1985). Shange describes herself as a poet in the American theater, where she sees mostly shallow, stilted, and imitative action taking place on stages.

Shange was reared in a middle-class household in Trenton, New Jersey. Named Paulette Williams, she is the oldest of four children born to Eloise Owens Williams, a psychiatric social worker, and Paul T.

Williams, a surgeon. The author seems to have enjoyed a childhood enhanced by material security and intelligent parents who exposed her to cultural influences, including jazz, blues, and soul, and literary artists such as Paul Laurence *Dunbar, Langston *Hughes, Shakespeare, and T. S. Eliot. She often mentions her family's Sunday afternoon variety shows, which sometimes consisted of her mother offering selections from Shakespeare, her father performing on the congas, and the children dancing or playing instruments. In the introduction to *Nappy Edges,* she indicates that her family members pursued whichever arts struck their fancy. These early artistic and cultural influences obviously affected Shange's life and art.

When she was eight, her family moved to St. Louis, Missouri. There she was among the first black children to integrate the public school system, and experiencing the cruelty and violence of racist whites seems to have caused feelings of anger while strengthening her independence and her fighting spirit. When Shange was thirteen, the family moved back to New Jersey. She published poetry in the Morristown High School magazine, but after derogatory comments were made concerning her choice of African American subjects, she abandoned her poetry as she had once abandoned short story writing in elementary school because of racist comments. She feels that as a young black girl with an artistic bent she had no adequate role models in school.

Shange entered Barnard College in 1966 but became increasingly despondent over a recent separation from her husband and enraged at a society that she felt was unfair to intelligent women, and she attempted suicide four times. She managed, however, to graduate with honors in 1970 and pursued a master's degree in American Studies at the University of Southern California, living with other writers, dancers, and musicians. There she adopted a new name (Ntozake meaning "she who brings her own things," and Shange, "one who walks with lions"), after two South African friends baptized her in the Pacific Ocean. She earned a master's degree in 1973 and moved to the San Francisco Bay Area, teaching humanities and women's studies courses at Mills College in Oakland, the University of California Extension in San Francisco, and Sonoma State College. At Sonoma she worked with poets, dancers, and teachers who allowed her to study women's history, write poetry, and theorize about the oppressive experiences of women.

In all her works, Shange suggests that black women should rely on themselves, and not on black men, for completeness and wholeness. She speaks for women of every race who see themselves as disinherited and dispossessed. The choreopoem (a descriptive name given by the author) for *colored girls* won the 1977 Obie, Outer Critics Circle, Audelco, and *Mademoiselle* awards, and received Tony, Grammy, and Emmy nominations. During 1994, for its twentieth anniversary, theaters around the country (including the Ensemble in Houston, Texas, where Shange once lived and worked), presented the drama, and Shange personally directed and served as consultant for the Houston production.

In an essay titled, "It is not so good to be born a girl" (in *Racism and Sexism,* ed. Paula S. Rothenberg, 1988), Shange discusses the disadvantages and restrictions that hinder a fulfilled life for African American women, noting that females all over the world and throughout history have been victimized and exploited sexually and emotionally from birth. Societies have thrown women away, sold them, and sewn up their vaginas, and in contemporary times, Shange avers, rape and violent crimes against women make even attending midnight mass dangerous. Nevertheless, the author asserts in this essay the same philosophy that she advances in *for colored girls,* namely, that only through finding "god inside themselves and finding meaning and self satisfaction in their own lives—that only by defining and living out their own destinies unsubjected to the whims of the oppressors, no matter their race or sex, can women become whole, self-sustaining humans."

Although *for colored girls* assured Shange's place in the African American dramatic canon and remains her most celebrated piece, the years from 1977 to 1982 were continually productive. *Mother Courage and Her Children* won Shange a second Obie in 1981; *Three Pieces* earned the *Los Angeles Times* Book Review Award in 1981, and that same year she was granted a Guggenheim Fellowship and Columbia University's Medal of Excellence. Shange was appointed to the New York State Council of the Arts and was an artist in residence at Houston's Equinox Theater.

Shange is known for her nonconventional use of English—unorthodox capitalization, punctuation, and spelling, and the use of African American idioms, dialect, slang, and rhythms. Her struggle to come to an articulate resolution in her work is acknowledged in articles such as the prefatory essay to *Three Pieces,* "unrecovered losses/black theater traditions." A preference for tension and complexity in her themes and characters is also displayed in her fiction. She has a predilection to rework and expand her materials, as demonstrated by the expansion of her novella *Sassafras* into the novel *Sassafras, Cypress and Indigo.* Her love of music is clear in the opening sentence of the novel: "Where there is a woman there is music." The novel tells about three sisters—Sassafras is a weaver, Cypress a dancer, and Indigo a midwife—all seeking to find themselves as creative people with a purpose. By the end of the novel they return home to their mother, but the reader doubts whether they can remain because of their need to pursue their own identities and freedom. Shange's poetry also demonstrates her penchant for complexity and emphasizes her unconventional use of English. Much of her artistic philosophy and theories can be found in her prefaces, such as the preface to *Nappy Edges* where she states, "quite simple a poem shd fill you up with something / cd make you swoon, stop in yr tracks, change yr mind, or make it up." Her latest work is *If I Can Cook, You Know God Can* (1998).

Critic Mary Deshazer describes Shange as both writer and warrior. In the preface to *Three Pieces* Shange says her writing is fueled by "combat breath," a term borrowed from social observer Frantz Fanon. She tells the reader that the pieces were excruciating to write because they forced her to continually confront moments that had caused fury and homicidal desires. She says *Spell #7* and *Boogie Woogie Landscapes* contain "leaps of faith / in typical afro-american fashion." In her poetry, novels, and essays, Shange continues to engage readers with her unique literary warfare.

• Sandra L. Richards, "Conflicting Impulses in the Plays of Ntozake Shange," *Black American Literature Forum* 17 (Summer 1983): 73–78. Claudia Tate, *Black Women Writers at Work,* 1983. Elizabeth Brown-Guillory, "Ntozake Shange," in *DLB*, vol. 38, *Afro-American Writers after 1955: Dramatists and Prose Writers,* eds. Thadious M. Davis and Trudier Harris, 1985, pp. 240–250. Stella Dong, "Ntozake Shange," *Publishers Weekly,* 5 May 1985, 74–75. Elizabeth Brown-Guillory, *Their Place on the Stage: Black Women Playwrights in America,* 1988. Serena W. Anderlini, "Drama or Performance Art? An Interview with Ntozake Shange," *Journal of Dramatic Theory and Criticism* 6 (Fall 1991): 85–97. Betty Taylor-Thompson, "Female Support and Bonding in *for colored girls . . . ,*" *Griot* 12.1 (Spring 1993): 46–51. Neal A. Lester, *Ntozake Shange: A Critical Study of the Plays,* 1995. P. Jane Splawn, "'Change the Joke(r) and Slip the Yoke': Boal's 'Joker' System in Ntozake Shange's *For Colored Girls* and *Spell #7,*" *Modern Drama* 41:3 (Fall 1998): 386–398. Maria Damon, "Kozmic Reappraisals: Revising California Insularity," in *Women Poets of the Americas: Toward a Pan-American Gathering,* ed., Jacqueline Vaught Brogan, 1999, pp. 254–271.

—Betty Taylor-Thompson

SHAW, NATE. *See* All God's Dangers; Cobb, Ned.

SHEARER, JOHN (b. 1947), photographer and author of fiction and nonfiction. Known for his books for children, John Shearer was born and raised in New York City and attended Rochester Institute of Technology and School of Visual Arts. In 1970, he became staff photographer for *Look* and *Life,* and contributed photographs to other national magazines, including *Popular Photography* and *Infinity.*

Shearer entered the field of children's and young adult literature with *I Wish I Had an Afro* (1970), a nonfiction essay exploring the challenges of rearing an African American boy in poverty. Shearer's black-and-white photographs contribute to the intense depiction of an urban family's struggle against ignorance, gangs, and drugs. Shearer's talent for illustrating narratives of childhood experience is seen also in *Little Man in the Family* (1972), a double photographic essay exploring the lives of two boys from differing racial and class backgrounds. Louis Berrios is Puerto Rican and lives in a New York City ghetto with his mother and five sisters, while David Roth is white and the son of a suburban dentist. The essay explores the children's life ambitions through dialogue taken from interviews with the boys, their parents, teachers, and friends. The graphic candor of the photographs and the boys' revealing narratives communicate the sharp contrasts of their lives and the similarities of their dreams.

In 1976, John Shearer published *Billy Jo Jive Super Private Eye: The Case of the Missing Ten Speed Bike,* the first of five in the "Billy Jo Jive" fiction series for children. All illustrated by his father, Ted Shearer, *The Case of the Sneaker Snatcher* (1977), *Billy Jo Jive and the Case of the Missing Pigeons* (1978), *Billy Jo Jive and the Walkie Talkie Caper* (1981), and *Billy Jo Jive and the Case of the Midnight Voices* (1982) are mystery stories about a boy detective and his sidekick, Sunset Susie. Pairing up to solve small-time neighborhood crimes, the child "private eyes" recover stolen goods as well as locate the source of eerie noises. Targeted at primary grade readers, the series' fast-paced plots, first-person narration marked by urban vernacular, and vivid illustrations offer visually and textually entertaining yet educational stories. The series became so successful that short films based on the stories were shown regularly on the children's television program *Sesame Street,* produced by the author. In 1978, John Shearer received a Ceba award for the animated film adaptation of *Billy Jo Jive Super Private Eye: The Case of the Missing Ten Speed Bike.*

The recipient of over twenty national awards, John Shearer has had his work exhibited at the Metropolitan Museum of Art and in shows at Grand Central Terminal, the IBM Galleries, and Eastman Kodak. He has also taught photojournalism at the Columbia University School of Journalism. His essays and stories contribute to African American literature by offering young readers characters with whom they can identify, plots to which they can relate, and myriad images of African American children rarely seen in children's literature.

• "Shearer, John" in *Something about the Author,* vol. 43, ed. Anne Commire, 1986, pp. 192–196. "John Shearer" in *Children's Literature Review,* vol. 34, ed. Gerard J. Senick, 1995, pp. 165–168.

—Kim Jenice Dillon

SHINE. Probably the most well-known twentieth-century trickster, Shine is an epic figure in African American folklore. His name could refer to the generic nickname given to black men who shined shoes or it could indicate that his skin was dark enough to literally "shine." In the toasts that celebrate him, the wiry-built Shine begins as the lowest-ranked employee on the ill-fated *Titanic,* the infamous luxury ship that hit an iceberg during its maiden voyage in 1912. Assigned to stoke coal in the ship's bowels, the fictional hero notices the encroaching water and repeatedly warns the captain. Unwilling to heed the lowly black man's advice, the captain waits too long before ordering the passengers and crew to evacuate. Shine's status has risen and many of the passengers seek his assistance in their quest for safety. Concerned only with his own well-being, Shine answers the pleas for help with his bawdy rhymes and emerges, in most versions of the toast, as the ship's only survivor. One version concludes, "When the word got to Washing'times the great *Titanic* was sunk / Shine was on Broadway, one-third drunk."

Tricksters such as Shine or even *Brer Rabbit appeal to African Americans for several reasons. Ostensibly, they are the least powerful characters in a given situation. But they use their cunning to undermine their larger, more powerful opponents. Their social world reflects that of many African Americans, accustomed to making their way in spite of handicaps. Also their verbal dexterity has considerable appeal.

• John Roberts, *From Trickster to Badman: The Black Folk Hero in Slavery and Freedom,* 1989.

—Patricia A. Turner

SHINE, TED (b. 1931), dramatist, television scriptwriter, educator, and contributor to the Black Arts movement and regional theater. Soon after Ted (Theodis) Shine's birth in Baton Rouge, he and his parents, Theodis and Bessie, moved to Dallas where he grew up. At Howard University he was encouraged to pursue satiric playwriting by Owen *Dodson, who tactfully indicated Shine's limits as a tragic writer. His play *Sho Is Hot in the Cotton Patch* was produced at Howard in 1951. Graduating in 1953, Shine studied at the Karamu Theatre in Cleveland on a Rockefeller grant through 1955 and then served two years in the army. Earning his MA at the University of Iowa in 1958, he began his career as a teacher of drama at Dillard University in 1960, moving to Howard University from 1961 to 1967, and then settling at Prairie View A & M University where he became a professor and head of the drama department.

In 1964 Shine wrote *Morning, Noon and Night,* first produced at Howard University, which awarded it the Brooks-Hines Award for Playwriting in 1970 upon its publication in *The Black Teacher and the Dramatic Arts.* Combining humor and horror, Shine's play focuses on Gussie Black, who is manipulating her eleven-year-old grandson into becoming a traveling preacher and poisoning anyone who obstructs her project. Identifying himself as a Baptist, Shine often skewers those who cloak vicious ends in religiosity.

In 1970 Shine's 1969 plays, *Shoes* and *Contribution,* were produced and published together along with *Plantation* under the title *Contributions.* Strikingly different in theme, setting, and characterization, they collectively demonstrate Shine's skill in creating realistic, seemingly meandering, artfully constructed dialog, stunning, appropriate, meaningful plot twists, and thought-filled commentary on the black/human condition. *Shoes* points to the values that lead Smokey, a young waiter, to attempt shooting his benefactor, symbolically named Wisely, for withholding his summer earnings so he can reflect on his decision to blow them on fancy clothes. While warning about dehumanizing, community-undermining materialism, Shine remains sympathetic toward the poverty-striken childhood that drives Smokey to this extremity. *Contribution,* the most popular of Shine's many works, portrays Mrs. Grace Love, a spiritual-singing Christian who is chided by her activist grandson for loving the bigots she works for, but in reality she is contributing to the movement by poisoning them all. The farcical *Plantation* exposes a segregationist who discovers after his black son's birth that he is a mulatto. Following his suicide, a star rises in the east and three wise men appear in El Dorado, hilariously and hopefully hailing a new era.

From 1969 to 1973 Shine wrote over sixty scripts for the Maryland Center for Public Broadcasting's *Our Street* series while earning his doctorate from the University of California, Santa Barbara in 1971. The 1974 seminal anthology *Black Theater USA,* with Shine as consultant to editor James V. Hatch, includes his play *Herbert III,* a humorously insightful study of a couple with contrasting attitudes toward how to raise children amid racism. This play, like those preceding and following it, displays his shining contribution to contemporary black theater.

• Winona L. Fletcher, "Ted Shine," in *DLB,* vol. 38, *Afro-American Writers after 1955: Dramatists and Prose Writers,* eds. Thadious Davis and Trudier Harris, 1985, pp. 250–259. Bernard L. Peterson, Jr., "Ted Shine," in *Contemporary Black American Playwrights and Their Plays,* 1988, pp. 425–428.

—Steven R. Carter

SHOCKLEY, ANN ALLEN (b. 1927), librarian, newspaper columnist, teacher, lecturer, compiler, essayist, and fiction writer. A multitalented professional, Ann Allen Shockley has contributed to various fields, yet her contributions as writer remain invisible to much of America.

Born 21 June 1927, in Louisville, Kentucky, Shockley is the only daughter of Henry and Bessie Lucas Allen, both social workers. To her parents and a devoted eighth-grade teacher, she has attributed her insatiable desire to read and write. She edited her junior high school newspaper, wrote short pieces in the *Louisville Defender,* and penned essays and short fiction for the *Fisk Herald* while an undergraduate at Fisk University (1944–1948)—all before her twenty-first birthday. These early pieces show Shockley's interest in social and cultural issues.

In 1949 Shockley began a weekly column called "Ebony Topics" for the *Federalsburg Times* (Md.). From 1950 to 1953 she penned a similar column for the

Bridgeville News, in Bridgeville, Delaware, where she resided with her husband, William Shockley. Married in 1949 and later divorced, she had two children, William Leslie, Jr., and Tamara Ann. Political, cultural, and social events swelled Shockley's columns, which celebrated African American family unity, praised ebony heroes, and honored those who had excelled in their fields. Some of her pieces defined Thanksgiving, Armistice Day, and Mother's Day; others championed women's issues, a position she would return to again in her later pieces. She also contributed articles to the *Baltimore Afro-American* and to the *Pittsburgh Courier.* During her years as freelancer for newspapers, she held jobs as public school teacher and librarian. In 1959 she received her master's degree in library science from Case Western Reserve University.

Shockley has written several reference books for the library. Her unpublished *History of Public Library Services to Negroes in the South, 1900–1955* gives an overview of the inadequate, segregated public library services that were available to African Americans in southern states during the first half of the twentieth century. *Living Black American Authors: A Biographical Directory* (1973) stands as a significant compilation of African American writers with entries ranging from Russell Adams to Andrew S. Young. *Handbook of Black Librarianship* (1977) identifies for librarians and archivists ways to collect and preserve materials that relate to the history of African Americans. *Afro-American Women Writers, 1746–1933: An Anthology and Critical Guide* (1988) documents the achievements of African American women writers and the effects their sociohistorical environments had on their works.

Most of Shockley's essays complement her books and pinpoint the neglected areas of librarianship related to African Americans. She examines African American librarians' attitudes toward their jobs ("Negro Librarians in Predominantly Negro Colleges"), assesses the need for special collections ("Does the Negro College Library Need a Special Negro Collection?"), and documents the library's role in encouraging students to read ("Reading Encouragement in the Maryland State College Library"). Shockley's essays and books on librarianship reflect her concerns as curator of African American collections at Delaware State College (1959–1960), University of Maryland, Eastern Shore (1960–1969), and at Fisk University (1969–).

Themes related to African American culture continue in Shockley's short stories, which mirror the social and political unrest of the 1960s and 1970s. She explores interracial dating ("End of an Affair"), de facto segregation in public schools ("Monday Will Be Better"), sexism ("To Be a Man"), the hypocrisy of some Black Power advocates ("Is She Relevant?"), the African American brain drain to white universities ("The Faculty Party"), student uprisings on African American campuses ("The President"), the plight of the Vietnam veteran ("The Saga of Private Julius Cole"), and homophobia ("Home to Meet the Folks"). These stories—growing out of the civil rights, Black Power, women's liberation, and lesbian and gay movements—entertain the experiences encountered and choices made by African Americans. Her literary influences—Richard *Wright, Ann *Petry, Lillian Smith, and Dorothy Parker—leave a noticeable tincture of naturalism.

Shockley's major contribution to African American literature is in lesbian literature. *Loving Her* (1970) and *Say Jesus and Come to Me* (1982), Shockley's two novels, and *The Black and White of It* (1980), her collection of ten short stories, focus on lesbian issues. *Loving Her* depicts the abusive marital relationship of Renay Davis, who finds romantic love with a wealthy white woman. *Say Jesus and Come to Me* profiles Myrtle Black, a charismatic lesbian minister whose presence highlights homophobia in the African American church. Influenced by the lesbian and gay movement, *The Black and White of It* explores infidelity ("The Play"), white lesbians ostracizing black lesbians ("A Meeting of the Sapphic Daughters"), the aging lesbian ("A Birthday Remembered"), self-denial ("Holly Craft Isn't Gay)," and homophobia in the African American community ("Home to Meet the Folks"). Reissued by Naiad Press and reviewed in fledging women's magazines, these three volumes have not received adequate attention.

Shockley observes life as it is lived and considers nothing too insignificant or taboo to write about. A pioneer of lesbian themes and protagonists in African American literature, she waits for scholars to embrace fiction that reaches out to all subjects.

• Rita B. Dandridge, *Ann Allen Shockley: An Annotated Primary and Secondary Bibliography,* 1987. Diane Adams Bogus, "Theme and Portraiture in the Fiction of Ann Allen Shockley," PhD diss., Miami University, 1988. Tracye A. Matthews, "Ann Allen Shockley," in *Black Women in America: An Historical Encyclopedia,* ed. Darlene Clark Hine, vol. 2, 1993, pp. 1029–1030.

—Rita B. Dandridge

SHUG AVERY. The symbol of self-determination and self-love in Alice *Walker's *The *Color Purple* (1982) is Lillie, better known as Shug Avery or the Queen Honeybee. Shug is a beautiful, vivacious, and flamboyant blues singer who is considered a "loose woman" by some of the novel's characters. These opinions are of little concern to Shug, however. Unlike the novel's protagonist, *Celie, Shug does not accept imposed definitions of herself, nor does she allow anyone to control her. Instead, she is compassionate toward others and allows herself the freedom to enjoy love wherever she finds it—even in the arms of another woman. Her spirit of determination is the catalyst for Celie's transformation and the vehicle to freedom for Mary Agnes (a younger woman who wants to leave rural Georgia to become a blues singer).

Even though Shug is a positive influence on others, she is also a character in pain. True to her name, this

Queen Honeybee moves from one garden of love to another as if trying to escape something she does not want to face. Her parents reject her because of her adulterous relationship with Albert, a man whose father forbids him to marry her. Although Shug does not want to marry Albert, she believes in their love. Knowing that he will always choose her over his wife, Shug remains his lover, gliding in and out of his life as she pleases. When she discovers Albert's true nature—his cowardliness—she rejects him and develops a relationship with his wife, Celie.

• Om P. Juneja, "The Purple Colour of Walker Women: Their Journey from Slavery to Liberation," *Literary Criterion* 25.3 (1990): 66–76.

—Debra Walker King

SIMPLE, or Jesse B. Semple, first appeared in print on 13 February 1943 in the black-owned *Chicago Defender.* Langston *Hughes first intended Simple as a device to popularize the war effort among blacks, many of whom resented the disparity between racial injustice at home and the alleged democratic goals of the war, but Simple acquired a life beyond propaganda.

The classic setting for a Simple episode is a Harlem bar, with a conversation between the fun-loving, irreverent, but racially committed Simple, on the one hand, and the educated, poised, but dull narrator, on the other. However, Simple's world also includes memorable characters such as his girlfriend, Joyce, later his wife; a less respectable friend, Zarita; and his landlady, who calls him "Third Floor Rear."

Hughes claimed that Simple was based on a man he knew casually in Harlem, but both Simple and the narrator in reality are Hughes himself, who once pronounced Simple "really very simple. It is just myself talking to me. Or else me talking to myself" ("Simple and Me," *Phylon,* Oct.–Dec. 1945). The two voices form a sort of colloquium on Hughes's tensions of beliefs, as well as on his deeper fears and desires. The narrator may be seen as Hughes without love, laughter, and poetry, the man he might have been without his writing in service to black America. Simple himself epitomizes the saving graces of black America, the gift of self-redemption in the face of historic adversity.

Over twenty years, Simple became one of Hughes's most successful artistic creations, admired and beloved by readers who followed his exploits in syndicated columns that eventually included the white *New York Post.* Edited, the columns led to five volumes in Hughes's lifetime: *Simple Speaks His Mind* (1950), *Simple Takes a Wife* (1953), *Simple Stakes a Claim* (1957), *The Best of Simple* (1961), and *Simple's Uncle Sam* (1965). A sixth volume, *The Return of Simple,* appeared in 1994, edited by Akiba Sullivan Harper. Simple is easily the most enduring and endearing creation of a comic character in African American journalism and literature.

—Arnold Rampersad

Sister Outsider (1984), a collection of fifteen essays written between 1976 and 1984, gives clear voice to Audre *Lorde's literary and philosophical personae. These essays explore and illuminate the roots of Lorde's intellectual development and her deep-seated and longstanding concerns about ways of increasing empowerment among minority women writers and the absolute necessity to explicate the concept of difference—difference according to sex, race, and economic status. The title *Sister Outsider* finds its source in her poetry collection *The Black Unicorn* (1978). These poems and the essays in *Sister Outsider* stress Lorde's oft-stated theme of continuity, particularly of the geographical and intellectual link between Dahomey, Africa, and her emerging self.

The subject matter of these essays is remarkably varied, yet homogeneous. The quality of these essays is consistently high and the unity is made possible by Lorde's emphasis on differences as a source of strength rather than divisiveness. In essay after essay, Lorde promotes the unity of difference. In lieu of remaining an isolato, she stresses the necessity of every individual, group, sect, cult, and movement to strive for unity in such diversity. Nowhere is this more clearly articulated than in "The Master's Tools Will Never Dismantle the Master's House," "Age, Race, Class, and Sex: Women Redefining Difference," and in "Scratching the Surface, Some Notes on Barriers to Women and Loving." In a powerful and persuasive manner, Lorde stresses the strengths of empowerment and acceptance as necessary acquisitions.

Perhaps the most well-known essay in *Sister Outsider* is "Uses of the Erotic: The Erotic as Power," an emotional and powerful study of the erotic explicated by Lorde's famous analogy between the World War II practice of mixing yellow food coloring with colorless margarine at home to give the margarine the "proper" popular appearance. Lorde makes this communal experience erotic and, by extension, makes other mundane tasks become erotic and, therefore, highly pleasurable. Moreover, differences are also homogenized.

Another major emphasis of *Sister Outsider* is poetic theory, explored primarily in "An Interview: Audre Lorde and Adrienne Rich" and "Poetry is not a Luxury." The interview with Rich becomes a proving ground for unity in diversity as both women explore their common ground as lesbian poets struggling with voicing their most private concerns while not yet being able to totally trust individuals of other color, political persuasion, or economic status. Conversely, "Poetry is not a Luxury," originally published in 1977, emphatically places poetry in the front ranks as "a vital necessity of an existence." Why? Because poetry gives us access to our dreams, which cause us to keep on keeping on.

One of the most moving essays here is also one of the shortest, namely "An Open Letter to Mary Daly," who is the author of *Gyn/Ecology: The Metaethics of*

Radical Feminism (1978). In the letter Lorde challenges Daly to reexamine some of her statements regarding methods of achieving feminist unity. The last essay in *Sister Outsider* is "Grenada Revisited: An Interim Report," which brings full circle the theme of diversity complementing solidarity. Highly politicized, "Grenada Revisited" allows Lorde to make peace with her mother while simultaneously revealing her views concerning racism/colonialism, noting that the slogan of the Grenadian Revolution was "Forward Ever, Back Never," a spirit evoked by *Sister Outsider.*

Today *Sister Outsider* occupies a unique position in African American literature. The text presents a classic manifesto, one frequently referred to in women's/minority/alternative studies courses. *Sister Outsider* remains one of the few texts to explicate brilliantly and forthrightly the paradigm of racism as it exists in the highest and most influential levels of American society, particularly in educational media. Here Audre Lorde asks her readers to undergo intense self-examination. This is particularly noteworthy since nine of these essays were written after Lorde discovered she had cancer, a mind-numbing discovery she explicates in "The Transformation of Silence into Language and Action."

Sister Outsider is not merely a collection of essays, interviews, and speeches. Every piece requires the reader to rethink bias and negative opinion. It compares quite favorably with Alice *Walker's *In Search of Our Mothers' Gardens* (1983) and Toni *Morrison's *Playing in the Dark* (1992).

• Charles H. Rowell, "Above the Winds: An Interview with Audre Lorde," *Callaloo,* 14 (1991): 83–95.

—Joseph Benson

SLIM, ICEBERG. *See* Iceberg Slim.

SLIM GREER is both a literary character created by Sterling A. *Brown and the term designating his memorable series of satiric poems. In the cycle are five poems: "Slim Greer," "Slim Hears 'the Call,'" "Slim in Atlanta," "Slim in Hell," and "Slim Lands a Job?," all of which were published between 1930 and 1933. These poems reveal Brown's careful study of oral and written literatures, from Molière's satire to Mark Twain's humor, and his absorption of less formal teaching from a gallery of African American raconteurs. After graduation from Harvard University (MA, 1923), he immersed himself in the cultural life and lore of Black folk by frequenting barbershops, "jook-joints," and isolated farms. In these places, "master liars" like "Preacher," Duke Diggs, and an actual Slim Greer transformed mundane, prosaic experiences into performances of high art. The results of their informal instruction are readily discerned in Brown's poems.

The Slim Greer poems represent the principal concern in nearly all of Brown's work: reclaiming the humanity of African Americans to insure the completion of selfhood. To accomplish this purpose, Brown adapts features of the American tall tale, including vernacular language, "deadpan" manner of narration, development from plausibility to frantic impossibility, and the snapper climax or exposure at the end. As in the best tall tales, these poems achieve their success by laughing the reader/listener into an awareness of practices that prevent the self from attaining wholeness, such as religious hypocrisy and the absurdity of racial segregation. In so doing, Brown makes his Slim Greer do in poetry what Langston *Hughes's *Simple does in short fiction.

• Sterling A. Brown, "In the American Grain," *Vassar Alumnae Magazine* 36.1 (Feb. 1951): 5–9. John Edgar Tidwell, "The Art of Tall Tale in the Slim Greer Poems," *Cottonwood Magazine* 38/39 (Fall 1986): 170–176.

—John Edgar Tidwell

SMITH, BESSIE (1894–1937), blues singer. Bessie Smith began her performance career as a dancer with a traveling minstrel troupe. Her vocal talents were quickly recognized, and by the age of nineteen she had begun to establish her reputation as one of the foremost blues singers of her day. By the time she recorded her first record with Columbia Records in 1923, she was an established star on the southern vaudeville circuit.

Smith became known as Empress of the Blues because of her incredible voice, sexually aggressive lyrics, fierce independence, and glamour. These qualities have also endeared her to generations of African American poets, novelists, and critics, particularly black feminists. Literary interpretations of her life and work range from portrayals of a genius victim of American racism to portrayals of a protofeminist icon, an alternative to the fair upper-middle-class heroines of early black women novelists. For Amiri *Baraka's Clay (from **Dutchman,* 1964), Bessie Smith is the quintessential wearer of the mask, saying "Kiss my ass, kiss my black unruly ass." According to Clay, "If Bessie Smith had killed some white people she wouldn't have needed that music." In contrast, the Smith of Sherley Anne *Williams's "Someone Sweet Angel Chile" emerges as a woman who triumphs through her ability to make music and sing the song of her own personal life as well as the collective song of black people. Recently, Smith has been identified by African American feminist critics as an important foremother for black women writers, who celebrate her independence and forthright attitudes about race and sexuality.

• Chris Albertson, *Bessie,* 1972.

—Farah Jasmine Griffin

SMITH, VENTURE (c. 1729–1805), autobiographer. Venture Smith, known as the black Bunyan because of his reputed feats of great strength, was born in Dukandarra, Guinea, West Africa. By Venture's own testimony his father named him Broteer. He was brought to America at the approximate age of eight, having been already sold to an American slaver before he arrived on the shore of Rhode Island. His life for the next twenty-eight years was devoted almost exclusively to his quest for freedom. He achieved what he called his "redemption" in his thirty-seventh year. Most of the remainder of his life was devoted to earning the money, through years of prodigious labor, to free his wife Meg, his sons Solomon and Cuff, his daughter Hannah, and three other black men.

Smith dictated his *A Narrative of the Life and Adventures of Venture, A Native of Africa: But resident above sixty years in the United States of America. Related by Himself* to an amanuensis, who has been identified as the Connecticut schoolmaster Elisha Niles, in 1798. Calling Smith "destitute of all education but what he received in common with other domesticated animals" such that he could hardly "suppose himself superior to the beasts, his fellow servants," Smith's recorder refuses to refer to him as a freed African American but rather chooses to label him "an untutored African slave."

Yet no reader of Smith's narrative can escape this man's bitterness at having not realized "in a Christian land" the promise of reward available to white folks of industry. According to Smith's own testimony, no one could have worked harder to achieve the American dream, undeniable according to St. Jean de Crèvecoeur (in *Letters from an American Farmer*) to whoever would "be just, grateful and industrious."

Even though by his alleged sixty-ninth year Smith had acquired one hundred acres of land, some twenty "boats, canoes, and sail vessels," and three habitable dwelling houses, he found that in the American courts he was unable to exact justice for a white man's crime against him. In his native Africa, Smith protests, this crime would "have been branded . . . highway robbery." But his adversary "was a white gentleman, and I a poor African, therefore it was all right, and good enough for the black dog [sic]." Despite all his bitterness, Smith still avows, "My freedom is a privilege which nothing else can equal."

Smith's *Narrative* is composed of three chapters: the first tracing what he chooses to remember for his largely white audience of his African homeland, the second accounting for his quest to free himself from slavery, and the third revealing his herculean efforts to free his family and others, to participate in the American dream, and to realize for himself and his family a fair share of human dignity. In contrast to the Boston poet Phillis *Wheatley, who recalled little of her African homeland to her white captors, Smith presents substantial and fascinating details of his experiences in West Africa. Venture Smith died on 19 September 1805, and his grave is marked by this fitting inscription: "Sacred to the memory of Venture Smith, African though son of a king he was kidnapped and sold as a slave, but by his industry he acquired enough money to purchase his freedom."

• Dorothy Porter, *Early Negro Writing: 1760–1837,* 1971. William L. Andrews, *To Tell a Free Story: The First Century of Afro-American Autobiography, 1760–1865,* 1986. Sidney Kaplan and Emma N. Kaplan, *The Black Presence in the Era of the American Revolution,* 2d ed., 1989.

—John C. Shields

SNELLINGS, RONALD. *See* Touré, Askia M.

Soldier's Play, A (1981). Charles H. *Fuller, Jr.'s presentation of institutional racism and self-hatred set in the 1940s explores the psychological effects of oppression on African Americans. The setting of *A Soldier's Play* is an army base in Fort Neal, Louisiana, in 1944. Fuller creates an ironic situation with an all-black company eager to fight for justice in World War II for a country that refuses to send the company overseas because of discrimination. The tragic hero, Sergeant Vernon C. Waters, has taken upon himself the role of savior of all African Americans in a racist society. This highly acclaimed commentary on the ills and trials of military life for the African American is built on a foundation of intricate characterizations and tone.

Fuller's use of the mystery plot provides the audience with Waters's identity as a tragic hero. The investigating officer, Captain Richard Davenport, through a series of interviews, discloses to the audience each of the enlisted men's stories. Fuller often allows one character to tell another's story. At a time when camaraderie among men is essential, Fuller creates dichotomies between them: Waters and his enlisted men form one, and later Davenport creates another in his leadership role.

Oftentimes the most powerful force in society is the role of its men. Whether the role is that of a father, follower, or leader, the status of men is closely scrutinized, and Fuller demonstrates how such expectations can become destructive. The African American male may often find himself trapped between the high expectations of his own society in comparison to the low esteem and extensive oppression exerted by his white counterparts. Waters appears to be a victim and worthy of pity when we see him groveling in drunkenness just before he is brutally shot in the head and heart, symbolic of the black man who fails to think for himself, hates himself, and has lost compassion for others.

Fuller does not allow the image of the downtrodden African American male to remain the only one projected. Private C. J. Memphis, a blues-singing country boy, escapes the need to lead by creating lyrics and sounds that ring of following, whether it is a "woman to the dance floor" or Sergeant Waters to a detail. Through his music and strength, C. J. Memphis sings his troubles away and believes in the initial good of man. He feels sorry for Sergeant Waters because "any man ain't sure where he belongs, must be in a whole lotta' pain." In C. J. there are indeed heroic qualities in spite of his eventual suicide.

Charles Fuller did not write *A Soldier's Play* just to offer another glimpse at the ugly face of racism, but to serve as a wake-up call for camaraderie among men; a call for men to accept, love, and support one another. He presents each character and asks the audience to examine each character through history. Because of his intense hatred for those African Americans he considered "inferior," Waters taught African Americans to love Afrocentricity, to increase black sensibility, and to see institutional racism as a part of the whole society rather than individual targets of rage.

Frank Rich writing for the *New York Times* described Fuller as a playwright with a "compassion" for blacks who might be driven to murder their brothers because he sees them as victims of a world they haven't made. Rich views the play as a rock-solid piece of architecture with the right mixture of characters to create a historical literary movement. Walter Kerr saw the piece as tough but filled with honesty.

• Walter Kerr, "A Fine Work from a Forceful Playwright," 6 Dec. 1981, *New York Times*, 3:1. James Draper, *Black Literature Criticism*, vol. 2, 1992, pp. 824–825.

—Wanda Macon

Song of Solomon. Toni *Morrison's third novel, *Song of Solomon* (1977) was immediately acclaimed as one of beauty and power, mythical and magical in proportion and theme. Its protagonist, Macon Dead III, the first black baby born at Mercy Hospital (called No Mercy by the Michigan town's black population), is born on the day that the insurance man attempts to fly from its steeple. He and his family are portrayed in the novel's first section. Known as *Milkman Dead because of his mother's excessive and prolonged nursing, he grows up in a house with a passive mother, a greedy, abusive, and materialistic father, and silent, frustrated sisters. His grandfather, Macon Dead I, was murdered by whites for his property, leaving his son and daughter, Macon and Pilate. They are hunted by the white men who killed their father, and they, in turn, are later forced to kill a white man. This incident sets their values and life goals, for Macon believes the man was hiding money while Pilate rejects material goods. Macon Dead II later scorns his sister and becomes a wealthy property owner at the sacrifice of his family's happiness and psychological health. He abandons his wife spiritually and physically after the birth of Milkman, who is only born through the intervention and magic of Pilate.

The novel's second part involves Milkman's search for gold that he believes was hidden in a cave in Virginia by his aunt and his father in their youth; however, this becomes a search for himself and his family history. Part 2 also focuses on Milkman's aunt, a character embracing mythology and magic, whom Milkman sees despite being forbidden to do so by his father. *Pilate Dead is a natural woman, "born wild" and without a navel, and she has values that directly oppose her brother's—she is moral, responsible, loving, generous, and unpretentious. Also a direct contrast to her sister-in-law Ruth, who is dominated first by her father and then by her husband, Pilate lives free of all materialistic conveniences (i.e., running water and electricity) and she is a bootlegger. She lives with her daughter and granddaughter, Hagar, who develops a destructive and obsessive love for Milkman.

At first Milkman is a selfish, pleasure-seeking young man; however, with Pilate and his childhood friend Guitar Bains as examples, he is guided to achieve self-knowledge and self-sufficiency. Arriving in the South in search of his father's treasure, Milkman is enthralled and overcome by the folklore and myth surrounding his family's history, especially the legend of his paternal great-grandfather (Shalimar or Solomon), who, according to a song Pilate sang to Milkman when he was young, flew like a black eagle back to Africa to escape slavery. When Milkman and Pilate later return to their ancestral home, they are tracked and hunted by Guitar Bains, who has become part of a group that takes revenge for the unjust murder of blacks by whites and who believes Milkman is going to retrieve gold and not share with him. Guitar shoots Pilate when aiming for Milkman, and Milkman notes that she can fly without leaving the ground. He then acknowledges Guitar's presence and leaps into the air, modeling the ability to fly.

Women are the main sources of knowledge in Milkman's world, with Pilate his primary guide and source of understanding. *Song of Solomon* has consistently been praised by critics for its inventiveness and variety of language and its handling of folklore, allegory, magic, fantasy, song, and legend. It won the prestigious National Book Critics Circle Award in 1977 and firmly established Morrison as a major American writer.

• Jacqueline de Weever, "Toni Morrison's Use of Fairy Tale, Folk Tale, and Myth in *Song of Solomon*," *Southern Folklore Quarterly* 44 (1980): 131–144. Charles Scruggs, "The Nature of Desire in Toni Morrison's *Song of Solomon*," *Arizona Quarterly* 38 (1982): 311–335. Susan Blake, "Toni Morrison," in *DLB*, vol. 33, *Afro-American Fiction Writers after 1955*, eds. Thadious M. Davis and Trudier Harris, 1984, pp. 187–199. Wilfred D. Samuels and Cleora Hudson Weems, *Toni Morrison*, 1990. Ja Mo Kang, "Toni Morrison's *Song of Solomon*: Milkman's Limited Moral Development," *Journal of English Language and Literature* (Seoul, Korea) 41.1 (1995): 125–147.

—Betty Taylor-Thompson

SON GREEN. In Toni *Morrison's **Tar Baby* (1981), William (Son) Green has been on the run for eight years (after killing his adulterous wife) when he becomes infatuated with *Jadine Childs, a Sorbonne-educated model who is visiting her benefactors in whose Caribbean-island house he's taken refuge. The affair that develops between them is emblematic of different cultural points of view: Son represents the humanistic African cultural heritage in contrast to the materialistic European culture Jadine has embraced.

They leave the island to continue their relationship in New York. When Son takes Jadine to see his hometown of Eloe, Florida, where buildings are sparse and shabby and tradition and human relationships valued, she feels threatened. In contrast, Jadine feels at home in New York, while Son confesses to feeling "out of place" in the Streets' home. Although Son is attracted to Jadine sexually, he is not completely intellectually or emotionally ensnared and refuses to succumb to her plans for a professional career for him. In fact, it is Son who narrates his version of the tar baby story to Jadine in an emotional tirade against her lifestyle. She leaves him shortly after their trip to Eloe. When he returns to the island to find her, he is diverted by Thérèse, an islander who does yard work. She directs him to the wild side of the island, supposedly inhabited by blind African horsemen, and Son goes to join them. In this clash between folk culture and commercialism, Son represents the black man who can be drawn to the very forces that could destroy him, whether those forces come in the shape of a mulatto woman or a law degree. Although Morrison portrays him sympathetically, it is finally ambiguous as to whether she prefers Jadine's education and mobility or Son's immersion in folk tradition and myth.

• Susan Blake, "Toni Morrison," in *DLB*, vol. 33, *Afro-American Fiction Writers after 1955*, eds. Thadious M. Davis and Trudier Harris, 1984, pp. 187–199. Wilfred D. Samuels and Clenora Hudson Weems, *Toni Morrison,* 1990. Judylyn S. Ryan, "Contested Visitions/Double Vision in Tar Baby," *Modern Fiction Studies* 39.3–4 (Fall/Winter 1993): 597–621. Trudier Harris, "Toni Morrison: Solo Flight through Literature into History," *World Literature Today* 68.1 (Winter 1994): 9–14.

—Betty Taylor-Thompson

Soul on Ice. Widely read and enormously influential, the collection of Eldridge *Cleaver's 1965–1966 prison letters and essays titled *Soul on Ice* (1968) remains one of the most important articulations of 1960s African American revolutionary nationalism. Published in 1968, *Soul on Ice* clearly captures the liberationist spirit of the moment through autobiographical accounts, personal letters, and sociopolitical essays. The volume generally outlines the devastating impact of American racism, especially on African American men, and suggests strategies for healing the profoundly wounded African American sense of identity and for bridging the seemingly irreconcilable racial divide in America.

The opening section, "Letters from Prison," recounts Cleaver's early criminal and prison careers, details the everyday racial tension in the California penitentiary system, and provides vignettes of prison life and portraits of other prisoners, an influential teacher in San Quentin prison, and *Malcolm X. The second section, "Blood of the Beast," perhaps the most important part of the volume, offers sociocultural readings of the state of race relations in 1960s America. Cleaver acknowledges his admiration for the new generation of white youth who had jettisoned an unrealistic version of American history and thus their racist attitudes. He offers an allegorical interpretation of the Muhammad *Ali–Floyd Patterson fight as signifying the Lazarus-like awakening of the African American. Cleaver goes on to attack James *Baldwin for his supposed racial self-hatred and his homosexuality, elevating Richard *Wright as a masculine literary standard. Several essays linking the 1960s African American liberation movement with anticolonial struggles throughout the world, especially the war in Vietnam, conclude the second part of *Soul on Ice.* The last two sections, "Prelude to Love—Three Letters" and "White Woman, Black Man," focus more fully on gender issues, particularly on the psychological emasculation of the African American male and on the pathological impact of racism on human sexuality.

While Cleaver's discussion of sexual roles often seems masculinist and oversimplified, his description of the condition of the African American prisoner remains powerful and timely.

—Roger A. Berger

Souls of Black Folk, The. A collection of fourteen prose pieces by W. E. B. *Du Bois, *The Souls of Black Folk* had a powerful impact on African American intellectual life when it appeared in 1903. Thirty years later, James Weldon *Johnson declared that it "had a greater effect upon and within the Negro race in America" than any book since Harriet Beecher *Stowe's epochal *Uncle Tom's Cabin* (1852).

The collection included nine pieces previously published in some form in magazines, notably the prestigious *Atlantic Monthly.* Five new pieces rounded out this racial portrait, which reflects the remarkable breadth of Du Bois's interests, training, and temperament. Schooled in history and sociology, he also had an abiding personal interest in fiction, poetry, and the essay.

One major concern of the book is the history of blacks from slavery down to the present time of legal segregation. Another is a loosely sociological accounting of their lives, especially in the South, where the vast majority still lived in 1903. Closing the book are Du Bois's elegy for his son, an emblematic short story, and essays on the spirituals and on religion. Here Du Bois concentrates on the psychological and expressive aspects of black culture, but the entire work attempts to probe the black American mind, in keeping with the title of the volume.

The meaning of the title is spelled out early. Blacks, who are prevented by the repressive white culture from ever possessing "true self-consciousness," can see themselves only as whites see them:

> It is a peculiar sensation, this double-consciousness, this sense of always looking at one's self through the eyes of

> others, of measuring one's soul by the tape of a world that looks on in amused contempt and pity. One ever feels his twoness,—an American, a Negro; two souls, two thoughts, two unreconciled strivings; two warring ideals in one dark body, whose dogged strength alone keeps it from being torn asunder.

The book is also memorable for Du Bois's prophecy, first enunciated in the "Forethought," that "the problem of the Twentieth Century is the problem of the color line."

In "Of Mr. Booker T. *Washington and Others," Du Bois challenged the leadership of the most powerful black American of the age. The head of Tuskegee Institute, Washington emphasized industrial training for blacks, rather than the liberal arts. He also urged blacks to surrender to southern whites on the issues of voting rights and racial integration in return for peace and prosperity. Attacking these positions, Du Bois's book split the black intelligentsia into two opposing camps.

Perhaps the most powerful single unifying element in this diverse collection, with its multiplicity of vignettes and approaches, is its portrait of Du Bois himself, so much so that the book is sometimes taken as an autobiography. The record of his personal feelings, rendered in often brilliant language, is made central to his purpose—most notably in his elegy "Of the Passing of the First-Born." The final impression is of a highly intelligent, learned, generous, but deeply wounded individual, unusual and yet profoundly representative of African Americans in his inability, despite his gifts, to find peace in a nation hostile to its blacks.

• Herbert Aptheker, ed., *Annotated Bibliography of the Published Writings of W. E. B. Du Bois,* 1973. Arnold Rampersad, *The Art and Imagination of W. E. B. Du Bois,* 1976. David Levering Lewis, *W. E. B. Du Bois: Biography of a Race, 1868–1919,* 1993.

—Arnold Rampersad

Sounder. When *Sounder* was released in 1972, the film received praise throughout the country as a landmark in its departure from the heretofore typical depiction of blacks on the screen. However, while *Sounder* was hailed by critics and moviegoers alike, that praise was also mixed with criticism of the movie as sentimental, superficial, and oversimplified.

The screenplay for *Sounder* was written by African American playwright Lonne *Elder III, based loosely on an award-winning children's book of the same title by white author William Armstrong. Elder's screen version tells the story of an African American sharecropping family in Louisiana during the Great Depression. Elder shifts the focus from the significance of the relationship between the eldest son and the family dog (for whom the story is named); in the film, the dog is an important "character" but not central. Instead, he provides companionship for the boy and serves a symbolic role as the plot develops around the family's major conflict. Set in 1933, the film stars Paul Winfield as the father, Nathan Lee Morgan; Cicely Tyson as his wife, Rebecca; and Kevin Hooks, in his first major role, as their eldest son, twelve-year-old David Lee. Two younger children (Earl and Josie Mae) are played by Hooks's younger brother, Eric, and a young girl (Yvonne Jarrell) from the Louisiana parish where the movie was filmed.

Nathan Lee shares a close and special father-son relationship with his eldest son, David Lee, which is often characterized by meaningful eye contact and smiles, spontaneous hugs, and solemn handshakes. David Lee has to quickly assume the role of adult when Nathan Lee, unable to feed his family, steals meat from a white neighbor's smokehouse. Following his arrest, Nathan Lee is tried, convicted, and sentenced to one year on a prison chain gang in a distant parish. While Nathan Lee is awaiting trial, Rebecca is rebuffed in her attempt to visit him after making a daylong trek to the jail in town. Following this failed attempt, the family suffers further humiliation and uncertainty as Rebecca is belittled by the plantation owner in his company store and is forced to plant and harvest the season's crop with the assistance of only her children. In an act of private rebellion and self-assertion, Rebecca buys supplies for a chocolate cake from the owner, which she promptly bakes and sends to her husband via David Lee, who, as a boy child, is allowed to visit. A sympathetic white woman for whom Rebecca does laundry, Mrs. Boatwright, promises David Lee that she will find out which prison camp his father has been sent to. Mrs. Boatwright steals an opportunity to rifle through the sheriff's files and finds the information. She is threatened by the sheriff and initially refuses to disclose the information to young David Lee. However, upon seeing his disappointment and utter loss of faith in her, Mrs. Boatwright tells David Lee what she has found. Armed with this information and advice from his mother and family friend, Ike (played by musician Taj Mahal), David Lee embarks on a journey to visit his father on the chain gang. He does not find him but is befriended by a black teacher, Camille Johnson (Janet MacLachlan), who invites him to come back and attend the school she runs for black children. Nathan Lee returns home limping from an injury he suffers in an accident while on the chain gang and attempts to pick up where he left off with his family, resuming the role of head of household. Things have changed, of course, and in a symbolic depiction of the end of one phase of the Morgans' lives and the beginning of another, the movie ends with Nathan Lee driving David Lee back to the parish to attend Miss Johnson's school the following term.

In a 1973 interview, Elder revealed that he hoped *Sounder* would be the first in a permanent movement toward honest, realistic portrayals of blacks on the screen. Sounder can be judged a classic in its ability to transcend time in its artful reflection of a particular experience through understatement and innuendo. The movie depicts the family's humanity in the face of pervasive racism rather than reinforcing or reiterating these ills from an outside or reactionary perspective. In his shift from the focus of Armstrong's book on the heroism of the dog to that of the family, Elder asserts his artistic vision and his desire to portray the humanity of African Americans and provides a film that opened the path for subsequent movies that sought and achieved the same end.

• "The Current Cinema—Soul Food," *New Yorker,* 30 Sept. 1972, 109–111. "Sounder," *Variety,* 16 Aug. 1972, 15. "The South: Movie Sounder is a Modern Rarity," *Ebony,* Oct. 1972, 82–84. Paul Warshow, "Sounder," *Film Quarterly* 26 (Spring 1973): 61–64.

—Karla Y. E. Frye

SOUTHERLAND, ELLEASE (b. 1943), poet, essayist, short story writer, and novelist. Ellease Southerland's works draw mainly from the folk tradition. Frank and deeply personal, she writes about childhood remembrances, the joys of family togetherness, and the sorrows of separation. Folklore, biblical tradition, Egyptology, African history, and lore combine to inform her creative voice.

Southerland was born in Brooklyn, New York, to Ellease Dozier, a housewife, and Monroe Penrose Southerland, lay preacher, both migrants from the South. The third of fifteen children, Southerland received her BA from Queens College (1965) the same year her mother died from cancer. To help support twelve younger siblings, she worked in New York City as a social caseworker from 1966 to 1972. She received her MFA from Columbia University in 1974. She has traveled to Africa six times, has received the John Golden Award for Fiction (1964) for her novella *White Shadows;* and has won the Gwendolyn Brooks Poetry Award (1972) for her poem "Warlock."

The Magic Sun Spins (1975), Southerland's first collection of poetry, is an autobiographical celebration. "Black Is," the title poem, announces the beauty of her being. Another poem, "That Love Survives," affirms the love for her mother four years after her death, and "Ellease" lauds herself as a reservoir of knowledge and experience. The outpouring of her inner nature and the inspiration gathered from family love make Southerland's poems deeply spiritual.

Her short stories, "Soldiers" (*Black World,* June 1973) and "Beck-Junior and the Good Shepherd" (*Massachusetts Review,* Autumn 1975), contain personal ruminations. With a close friend in the Vietnam War and with nine brothers herself, Southerland wrote "Soldiers" to portray the hardships endured by family members and those physically and mentally maimed participants in the war. "Beck-Junior and the Good Shepherd" relates the story of Beck Torch, Southerland's sister, and her experiences at a Catholic school. Originally intended to be a part of a novel, the latter short story was noticed by an editor at Scribner's who published Southerland's novel, *Let the Lion Eat Straw* (1979).

A thinly disguised autobiographical novel, *Let the Lion Eat Straw* was named one of the best books of 1979 by the American Library Association. Based on her parents' relationship, it details the experiences of Abeba, the protagonist born out of wedlock in the South; her journey to Brooklyn, where she rejoins her mother and graduates from high school; her marriage to the mentally unstable Jackson, for whom she gives up a promising career as a concert pianist; and her struggles with their fifteen children. Infused with lilting dialect, haunting spirituals, and southern lore, the novel gained immediate popularity, appearing in four editions within two years.

Southerland's autobiographical pieces extend beyond the geographical limits of America. Her essay "Seventeen Days in Nigeria" (*Black World,* Jan. 1972) recounts her first visit to Africa in search of her heritage. The country's ambience—its friendly roadside vendors, its different foods, unusual manners, and native innocence—add to Southerland's excitement about a place that she had longed to visit. "Ibo Man" and "Seconds," two poems appearing in *Présence Africaine,* 1974 and 1975, respectively, continue her impressions of Nigeria. So do "Blue Clay" and "Nigerian Rain," the latter of which expresses her fulfillment in and oneness with Nigeria, which she calls home.

An engaging writer, Southerland's fame is that she blends her family's history with the folk tradition to tell a rich story.

• Mary Hughes Brookhart, "Ellease Southerland," in *DLB,* vol. 33, *Afro-American Fiction Writers after 1955,* eds. Thadious M. Davis and Trudier Harris, 1984, pp. 239–244. Carolyn Mitchell, "Southerland, Ellease," in *Black Women in America,* ed. Darlene Clark Hine, 1993, vol. 2, pp. 1090–1091.

—Rita B. Dandridge

SPELLMAN, A. B. (b. 1935), poet, music critic and historian, and arts administrator. Alfred B. Spellman has cut a wide swath in the world of the arts as a music critic, poet, administrator, and educator. "It's a function of social consciousness," he said in a 1992 interview (*Dance/USA Journal,* Winter 1992), "to provide art, strong art." The creation, identification, and support of "strong art" have been the alternating currents of Spellman's career, whose highlights include the publication of his book of poems, *The Beautiful Days,* in 1965, the appearance of his classic *Black Music: Four Lives* (as *Four Lives in the BeBop Business*) in 1966, and his two decades of service at the National Endowment for the Arts (NEA).

One of two sons of the schoolteachers Alfred and Rosa Bailey Spellman, Alfred B. Spellman was born 12 August 1935 in his grandmother's house in Nixonton, a hamlet outside Elizabeth City, North Carolina. Perhaps because of his parents' academic focus, Spellman was little challenged by the assignments at the public schools he attended. Some of his early memorable impressions of art and performance were provided by his father's paintings and, during his adolescence, by his success in sliding under the canvas tents of the traveling "Silas Green" blues troupe to see the half-dressed female dancers and ribald comics.

He became seriously interested in writing after entering Howard University in 1952. Classmates such as Amiri *Baraka (then LeRoi Jones) were his sounding boards and fellow cultural explorers. A famed instructor, Sterling A. *Brown, helped develop his interest in jazz and in the relationship between literary and oral traditions in African American culture. In 1958, at Baraka's urging, Spellman left Howard to seek his fortune in New York City. He had earned a BA in political science and history and begun course work in law. He remained in New York until 1967—working in bookstores, writing poetry, and, beginning in the early 1960s, hosting a WBAI radio morning show called "Where It's At."

The Beautiful Days appeared with an introductory note by Frank O'Hara praising Spellman for cutting "through a lot of contemporary nonsense to what is actually happening to him." What actually happens to Spellman in the best poems is extraordinary. In "'64 like a mirror in a darkroom. '63 like a mirror in a house afire," he measures his own vitality by his ability to continue caring about the "newly dead."

Four jazz musicians Spellman appears to have understood by their minds' "flutter" and their style of survival—Cecil Taylor, Ornette Coleman, Jackie McLean, and Herbie Nichols—are the subjects of *Black Music,* which enumerates, on the one hand, the tribulations of working in the jazz world, and, on the other hand, the ferocious will needed to avoid being silenced or destroyed. A reviewer for *Library Journal* found in the four interlocked portraits a "well reasoned statement of the position of the Negro in modern jazz and in modern America as well."

Spellman has said he wrote in defense of his subjects, who struggled variously against the failure of their peers, their reviewers, and existing funding organizations to acknowledge not only their brilliance, but even their competence. The urgency of his project is conveyed by his concluding remarks on Herbie Nichols: "It was typical of Herbie Nichols' life that *Metronome,* the magazine for which I was preparing the first article ever written on him, folded before the article could be published. By the time I placed it elsewhere, Herbie had died."

In 1976, after teaching jazz, literature, and writing at Emory, Harvard, and other universities, Spellman joined the NEA first as director of the Arts in Education Study Project and then as assistant director of the Expansion Arts Program. "We try to solidify and stabilize [arts] organizations, if we can, with the limited funds we have," he told *Dance/USA Journal.* He is currently the endowment's Acting Deputy Chair.

• Carmen Subryan, "A. B. Spellman," in *DLB,* vol. 41, *Afro-American Poets since 1955,* eds. Trudier Harris and Thadious Davis, 1985, pp. 311–315. A. B. Spellman, "Reflecting and Encouraging American Culture," interview by Bonnie Brooks, *Dance/USA Journal* 9.3 (Winter 1992): 16, 17, 26, 27.

—Michael Collins

SPENCER, ANNE (1882–1975), poet, librarian, community activist, and muse and confidante to Harlem Renaissance intellectuals and literati. Anne Spencer was born inauspiciously on a Virginia plantation. Yet the combination of loving, though irreconcilable, parents and an unorthodox, isolated youth formed her extraordinary independence, introspection, and conviction.

Her father, Joel Cephus Bannister, of African American, white, and Native American descent, and her mother, Sarah Louise Scales, the mulatta daughter of a slaveholder, separated when Spencer was six. While her mother worked as an itinerant cook, Spencer roomed with foster parents in Bramwell, West Virginia, where no other black children lived. In insular and parochial Bramwell, she was groomed for the African American bourgeoisie. Her mother dressed her in the finest frocks she could afford and withheld her from an outlying school that enrolled working-class children until she could attend Lynchburg's Virginia Seminary with socially suitable African American students. Spencer entered the seminary at age eleven. At seventeen, she graduated as valedictorian.

Two events there redirected her life. With a sonnet, "The Skeptic" (1896), she began writing poetry; and she met her husband, Edward. They settled in Lynchburg and raised three children. In 1918 Spencer was visited by James Weldon *Johnson (*The *Autobiography of an Ex-Colored Man,* 1912), then field secretary for the NAACP. Their meeting launched a lifetime friendship—and with "Before the Feast at Sushan," submitted to the the *Crisis* (1920), it inaugurated her publishing era.

Such poems as "At the Carnival" (1922), "Lines to a Nasturtium" (1926), "Substitution" (1927), and "Requiem" (1931) share the Romantics' affection for the ordinary and simple, retreat to nature's purity and peace, quest for love, disillusionment with earthly vanities, and passionate contemplation of eternity. Spencer flaunted tradition as much as she acknowledged it, laying claim to a modern poet's signature with sinister rhythms, slanted rhymes, blunt rejection of religious dogma, and enigmatic symbolism. During the 1920s, largely due to Johnson's mentorship, she published in such intellectual race magazines as the *Crisis* and *Opportunity,* in general anthologies of American poetry, in poet Countee *Cullen's *Caroling Dusk* (1927), in Johnson's *Book of American Negro Poetry* (1922), and in Alain *Locke's *The New Negro*

(1925), the official mission declaration of Harlem Renaissance (New Negro movement) writers and artists.

She detested an editorial process that misread her meanings, misunderstood her motives, mercilessly alluded to her inconsistent output, and miscategorized her poems as either much too subtle or too subtly militant. For many poems, including "White Things" (1923) and "Grapes: Still-Life" (1929), Spencer stood at variance with editors and publishers who censored statements of racial and sexual equality and rejected whatever they judged too controversial and/or experimental for American audiences. Consequently, she confined her editorial submissions to a decade, and she never published a poetry collection. Of her thousands of unpublished writings, including a novel and cantos commemorating John *Brown, some fifty remain.

Her paradoxical lifestyle kindled her writing. During the depression and World War II, her salon at 1313 Pierce Street hosted notables from W. E. B. *Du Bois to Paul *Robeson. Yet she so enjoyed the solitude of her garden that Edward erected a cottage for her there, naming it Edankraal, and he hired housekeepers to liberate her from the average southern woman's sentence to domestic drudgery. "The Wife-Woman" (1922), "Lady, Lady" (1925), and "Letter to My Sister" (1927) confide Spencer's ambivalence about matrimony, motherhood, feminism, and the unattainability of gender equality for African American women. They identify the masculine prerogatives of seclusion, intellect, and leisure served by the madonnas found everywhere in productions of the Harlem Renaissance.

Spencer frequently abandoned her privacy to antagonize local racists and class snobs. She organized Lynchburg's NAACP chapter, opened a library at the African American Dunbar High School, and offered sanctuary to the pygmy Ota Benga, who had been exhibited in zoos as a specimen of African inferiority. She infuriated African Americans with her scandalous fondness for pants and stubborn opposition to integration of public schools. Lynchburg's whites, in turn, sniffed their noses at her interracial friendships and scathing editorial disclaimers against the alleged self-evidence of white superiority.

Spencer's overall contribution has been to refocus critical attention on the stake that southern African American writers, virtually dismissed, have held in the enduring legacy of the Harlem Renaissance. At once homespun and urbane, her writings complicate the arbitrary amputation of New Negroes into either the folk, epitomized by Langston *Hughes's *Simple stories, or the bourgeois mulattoes of Jessie Redmon *Fauset's novels. Finally, Spencer's complexity advances our assessment of African American women writers in general, placing her at the center of a feminist renaissance midwifed by her forward vision.

• J. Lee Greene, *Time's Unfading Garden: Anne Spencer's Life and Poetry*, 1977. J. Lee Greene, "Anne Spencer of Lynchburg," *Virginia Cavalcade* 27 (1978): 178–185. Cheryl A. Wall, "Poets and Versifiers, Singers and Signifiers: Women of the Harlem Renaissance," in *Women, the Arts, and the 1920s in Paris and New York*, ed. Kenneth W. Wheeler and Virginia Lee Lussier, 1982, pp. 74–99. William Drake, *The First Wave: Women Poets in America, 1915–1945*, 1987. Charita M. Ford, "Flowering a Feminist Garden: The Writings and Poetry of Anne Spencer," *Sage* 5 (Summer 1988): 7–14. Maureen Honey, *Shadowed Dreams: Women's Poetry of the Harlem Renaissance*, 1989.

—Barbara McCaskill

Spook Who Sat by the Door, The. Sam *Greenlee's satirical novel *The Spook Who Sat by the Door* (1969) criticizes the racist atmosphere of the United States by examining the life of a fictitious black CIA agent, Dan Freeman, who is recruited under the efforts of Senator Gilbert Hennington to integrate the Central Intelligence Agency. For five years Dan Freeman had been the best spook of all as he conned the entire CIA while "he sat by the door." After absorbing a sufficient amount of knowledge, Freeman resigned to "make a greater contribution to his people by returning to Chicago and working among them."

References to Freeman as a "spook" in both the title and the novel possess a sense of duality or double consciousness: spook is used as a racial insult directed toward Blacks, in addition to being a slang term for spies. Greenlee uses this duality to establish a connection between Freeman's character and the African American experience during the turbulent 1960s. With this multifaceted character, Greenlee begins to examine the mask that has been worn by Blacks for generations to hide their true feelings. The author notes, as does Paul Laurence *Dunbar in "We Wear the Mask," that historically Blacks have veiled their emotions to meet white America's archetypes and expectations.

Freeman's persona escapes the boundaries of typical character definition as he openly supplies viewpoints and rationales on a wide range of topics—the Black man's pain, anger, fear, and frustrations. Freeman's multiple personalities leave him lonely: "his cover, his plans had forced him into himself and his loneliness ate at him like a cancer." He understands the paradoxical existence of the black middle class to be a collection of token Blacks who have been allowed to succeed to validate "whitey's integration movement." Greenlee's character represents the "New Negro" mentality; his is assertive, self-respecting, and fed up with racism.

Freeman reaches great heights on the mountain of social analysis as he demarcates the life of a Black man. The novel, first published in Europe and later in the United States, is an explosive exposition that divulges the emotions of the Negro of the 1960s, and continues to demand reaction from the African American of the 1990s.

Freeman's underlying goal in *The Spook Who Sat by the Door* is to facilitate social criticism. Greenlee is masterful in his presentation of characters and community. His honest yet satirical examination of a system created on lies, perpetuated by lies, and often destroyed or brought to terms with the hyprocrisy it advocates is still relevant in the struggle of the African American male. It is often by examining literature such as *The Spook Who Sat by the Door* that readers have an opportunity to analyze life's frustrations and fears.

• Catherine Starks, *Black Portraiture in American Fiction*, 1971.

—Wanda Macon

Sport of the Gods, The. Paul Laurence *Dunbar's *The Sport of the Gods* appeared in the May issue of *Lippincott's* magazine and was published by Dodd, Mead in 1902. The novel traces the dissolution and decline of the Hamiltons, a southern black family prevented from shaping their own fate by forces beyond their control.

Berry Hamilton has been a butler and his wife, Fanny, a cook on Maurice Oakley's prosperous southern plantation, where they have raised two children, Joe and Kitty. Berry's thirty years of loyal service, since before emancipation, have brought the family financial comfort and made them the envy of their black neighbors. But their fortune changes drastically. When Maurice's dissipated brother, Francis, discovers money missing, Berry is wrongly accused of the theft. With no evidence against him, Berry is convicted and sentenced to ten years at hard labor. Evicted from the plantation and ostracized by both blacks and whites, the rest of the family migrates to New York City to make a fresh start.

The provincial Hamiltons are immediately attracted to the lure of the city and soon fall victim to its various temptations. Joe takes up with the lowly denizens of the "Banner Club," a "social cesspool" that feeds his thirst for alcohol and his hunger for urban nightlife. He meets Hattie Sterling, a rapidly aging chorus girl who tries to protect and educate him. In a jealous rage, Joe murders Hattie and goes to prison. Kitty becomes, in her mother's eyes, a fallen woman after being flattered into using her singing talent for a career on the vaudeville stage. Fanny mistakenly believes she is divorced from Berry and marries an abusive racetrack gambler. In a parallel plot Francis Oakley confesses to stealing the money, but in an effort to maintain the family's good name, his brother, Maurice, conceals Francis's guilt and allows Berry to remain in prison. Through a series of plot contrivances, a northern muckraker eventually exposes the cover-up and manages to get Berry freed. He travels to New York only to confront the tragic effect of the city on his family. The timely death of Fanny's second husband allows Berry and Fanny to remarry and return to the South where they take up a sad residence in their former cottage on the Oakley plantation.

The last of Dunbar's four novels, *The Sport of the Gods* is the author's most pessimistic examination of the powerlessness of African Americans. In contrast to his more famous poetry, which positively portrays African American life in rural southern settings, *The Sport of the Gods* undercuts the plantation tradition's assumption that African Americans have a benevolent relationship to white Southerners. As the first African American novel to show characters who participate in the Great Migration from the rural South to the urban North, the novel also examines how ill-prepared unsophisticated Southerners are for the complexities of city life. By calling attention to the limitations of both the South and the North, *The Sport of the Gods* summarizes the deteriorating racial situation of turn-of-the-century America.

• Gregory Candela, "We Wear the Mask: Irony in Dunbar's *The Sport of the Gods*," *American Literature* 48 (1976): 60–72. Houston Baker, *Blues, Ideology, and Afro-American Literature: A Vernacular Theory*, 1984. Lawrence Rodgers, "Paul Laurence Dunbar's *Sport of the Gods:* The Doubly Conscious World of Plantation Fiction, Migration and Ascent," *American Literary Realism: 1870–1910* 24 (Spring 1992): 42–57.

—Lawrence R. Rodgers

STACKOLEE. Other spellings for Stackolee, the name of the notorious black folk bandit abound: Stagolee, Stackerlee, Stackalee, and Stagger Lee have all been collected. The first references to the outlaw emerged in the 1890s. It is important to note, however, that collections of folklore from African Americans were virtually nonexistent before that time, so this tradition may be much older than the evidence suggests.

Stackolee is prominent in folk literature, namely songs, toasts, and folktales. Many of these genres focus on the deeds of thoroughly "bad men." Stackolee is probably the most well-known of these characters. Because he has lost his beloved Stetson hat while gambling, Stackolee engages a hard-living black man Billy (or Bully) Lyons (or Lion) in a gun battle. Citing family considerations, Billy eventually begs for mercy, but Stackolee shows no sympathy. In most versions, Stackolee's reputation for evil is so powerful that law enforcement officials fear him; sheriffs and deputies refuse to pursue him. In some versions, the judge refuses to send Stackolee to jail because he fears the bandit will somehow seek retribution. In others, Stackolee responds to a ninety-nine year sentence by boasting, "Judge, ninety-nine ain't no goddamn time / My father's in Sing Sing doing two ninety-nine." In other versions, the hangman refuses to execute him, or his neck won't snap after the noose has been tightened. Folklorists have argued that Stackolee and other bad black men in folk tradition owe their appeal to the African American public's awe for men who disdain all conventions. So long victimized by the institution of slavery and the second-class citizenship that followed, many African Americans developed a fondness for stories about men who disdain all conventions.

• Lawrence Levine, *Black Culture and Black Consciousness: Afro-American Folk Thought from Slavery to Freedom*, 1977. Cecil Morris Brown, "Stagolee: From Shack Bully to Cultural Hero," PhD diss., University of California at Berkeley, 1993.

—Patricia A. Turner

STEINER, K. LESLIE. *See* Delany, Samuel R.

STEPIN FETCHIT (c. 1902–1985), actor. His name now nearly synonymous with slow-witted, shuffling servility, Stepin Fetchit was a talented comic actor and the first African American movie star. Born Lincoln Theodore Monroe Andrew Perry in Key West, Florida, Fetchit was by 1914 performing in stage revues and vaudeville shows, largely for African American audiences. Fetchit's early work in Hollywood as a lazy, whining clown in films such as *In Old Kentucky* (1927) and *Salute* (1929) got him noticed, but it was *Hearts in Dixie* (1929), an all-black talking picture, that first highlighted his comic gifts. Bald, lanky, and shambling, Fetchit sometimes transcended his persona's stereotypical outlines through impeccable timing and projection of personality. Crafted in African American settings, Fetchit's character was not served well by the white contexts of the movies that made him an international star. He is little more than comic relief in films such as John Ford's *The World Moves On* (1934), the Shirley Temple vehicle *Stand Up and Cheer* (1934), and *Helldorado* (1935); he is whipping-boy and lackey to Will Rogers in *David Harum* (1934), *The County Chairman* (1935), and Ford's *Judge Priest* (1934) and *Steamboat 'Round the Bend* (1935); he is downright foolish in *Charlie Chan in Egypt* (1935). Yet even in the harshest surroundings Fetchit armors himself with a detachment that seems almost wise. His great success pointed the way toward more substantial African American film roles, and his legendary off-screen high life (including spending binges, car accidents, and brawls) only increased his allure. By the end of the 1930s, Fetchit's recklessness and the criticism of civil rights groups brought his stardom to an end; he appeared on film only occasionally in the following decades. In the late 1960s Fetchit was a member of Muhammad *Ali's entourage and in 1968 filed a lawsuit against CBS for broadcasting a documentary that villainized him, the man who opened Hollywood's doors to African Americans.

• Donald Bogle, *Toms, Coons, Mulattoes, Mammies, and Bucks: An Interpretive History of Blacks in American Films*, 1973. Thomas Cripps, *Slow Fade to Black: The Negro in American Film, 1900–1942*, 1977.

—Eric Lott

STEPTOE, JOHN (1950–1989), artist, author, and illustrator of children's books. Born on 14 September 1950 and raised in the Bedford-Stuyvesant section of Brooklyn, New York, John Lewis Steptoe attended the New York School of Design and an afternoon art program sponsored by the Harlem Youth Opportunity Act from 1964 to 1967. In 1968, Steptoe was recruited as a senior in high school by John Torres to attend an eight-week summer program for minority artists at Vermont Academy. There Steptoe met Philip Dubois, who provided him with a place to work at the end of the summer session. While he was a student at Vermont Academy, Steptoe wrote and illustrated his first novel, *Stevie.* Published by Harper in 1969 and reprinted in *Life, Stevie* vaulted the nineteen-year-old Steptoe into the limelight. Written by an inner-city African American teenager and directed at inner-city African American youth, *Stevie* was lauded by the critics for its appeal to white as well as black audiences. Steptoe's use of inner-city dialect and his depiction of an urban setting targeted an audience previously ignored by children's book publishers: urban African American youth. What made *Stevie* so popular, however, was Steptoe's choice of subject matter. His tale of jealousy and reconciliation addressed a universal theme to which readers of all colors could relate.

Throughout his prolific career, Steptoe continued to write and illustrate books that dealt with experiences, issues, and concerns in the African American community. His works include *Uptown* (1970), *Train Ride* (1971), *Birthday* (1972), *My Special Best Words* (1974), *Marcia* (1976), *Daddy Is a Monster . . . Sometimes* (1980), *Jeffrey Bear Cleans Up His Act* (1983), *The Story of Jumping Mouse: A Native American Legend* (1984), *Mufaro's Beautiful Daughters: An African Tale* (1987), and *Baby Says* (1988).

Steptoe also used his considerable artistic talents to collaborate with other authors. His illustration credits include *All Us Come Cross the Water* (with Lucille *Clifton, 1972), *She Come Bringing Me that Little Baby Girl* (with Eloise *Greenfield, 1974), *OUTside/INside Poems* (with Arnold Adoff, 1981), *Mother Crocodile=Maman Caiman* (by Birago Diop, translated and adapted by Rosa *Guy, 1981), and *All the Colors of the Race: Poems* (with Arnold Adoff, 1982).

Steptoe won numerous awards for his work, including the Gold Medal from the Society of Illustrators (in 1970 for *Stevie*), the Irma Simonton Black Award from Bank Street College of Education in New York City (with Eloise Greenfield in 1975 for *She Come Bringing Me that Little Baby Girl*), the Lewis Carroll Shelf Award (in 1978 for *Stevie*), the Coretta Scott King Award for Illustration (in 1982 for *Mother Crocodile=Maman Caiman* and in 1988 for *Mufaro's Beautiful Daughters*), the Caldecott Honor Medal (in 1985 for *The Story of Jumping Mouse: A Native American Legend* and in 1988 for *Mufaro's Beautiful Daughters*), and the Boston Globe-Horn Book Award for Illustration (in 1987 for *Mufaro's Beautiful Daughters*).

In addition to *Stevie,* Steptoe's most well-known work is *Mufaro's Beautiful Daughters: An African Tale.* A retelling of the Cinderella story set in ancient Africa with vivid full-color paintings and fully realized characters, which Steptoe modeled on members of his family, *Mufaro's Beautiful Daughters* embodies Steptoe's conviction that ancient African culture bore no resemblance to the stereotypical view of Africa as a Dark Continent inhabited by savages. During the two and a half years it took him to write and illustrate the book, Steptoe consulted anthropological studies that detailed the technological sophistication of the ruins of Zimbabwe. In *Mufaro's Beautiful Daughters,* Steptoe captures the beauty of Africa and Africans while retelling a tale of sibling rivalry found in all cultures. His choice of such a universal theme echoed the approach he took with *Stevie* and with other works throughout his career.

Steptoe died on 28 August 1989 in New York City.

• Anne Commire, ed., *Something about the Author,* vol. 8, 1976, p. 198. Carolyn Riley, ed., *Children's Literature Review,* vol. 2, 1976, pp. 162–165. Gerard J. Senick, ed., *Children's Literature Review,* vol. 12, 1987, pp. 234–242. John Steptoe, "*Mufaro's Beautiful Daughters,*" *Horn Book* 64.1 (Jan./Feb. 1988): 25–29. Anne Commire, ed., *Something about the Author,* vol. 63, 1991, pp. 157–167.

—Barbara Lowe

STEWARD, THEOPHILUS GOULD (1843–1924), minister, journalist, novelist, historian, and autobiographer. T. G. Steward was born in 1843 in Gouldtown, Pennsylvania, one of the oldest African American settlements in the state. Little is known of his early life. Ordained a minister in the African Methodist Episcopal (AME) church in 1864, he moved to Charleston, South Carolina, immediately after the end of the Civil War to teach and preach among the freed people. His political activities in the late 1860s in Georgia, in particular his published call for federal troops to counteract the rise of the Ku Klux Klan, brought threats on his life. He moved back to the North in 1871, resuming his preaching career in Philadelphia and Wilmington, Delaware, and recording his controversial experience in the South in *My First Four Years in the Itinerancy of the African M. E. Church* (1876). In the 1870s, Steward helped lead protests against inadequate funding for African American Schools in Delaware and Philadelphia. Two of his early theological works, *Divine Attributes* (1884) and *Genesis Re-Read* (1885), reflect his conservative views on biblical interpretation.

In 1886, Steward accepted the pastorate of the Metropolitan AME Church in Washington, D.C., where Federick *Douglass and Blanche K. Bruce were among his parishioners. Appointed chaplain of the 25th U.S. Infantry Division in 1891, Steward traveled considerably in connection with his official duties, which gave him the opportunity to comment in magazines such as the *Social Economist,* the *Colored American Magazine,* and *Frank Leslie's Popular Monthly* on domestic racial issues as well as conditions in Mexico, Haiti, the Philippines, and Europe. In 1899, Steward was assigned by the army to write a military history, *The Colored Regulars in the United States Army,* which was published by the AME church in 1904. The year 1899 also saw the appearance of Steward's *A Charleston Love Story, or Hortense Vanross,* a novel concerned with the deleterious social and moral effects of liberal religion and "free love." Though the central characters of *A Charleston Love Story* are white and the questions at issue do not address race explicitly, the novel's setting, Reconstruction South Carolina, allows for a quietly revisionist perspective on the slaveocracy. The novel also offers brief but respectful portrayals of African American soldiers in the occupying army and observes with confidence the rise of the freemen and -women to citizenship in the South. Although it was published commercially in London and in New York, this early African American novel was unknown until the 1980s.

In 1907, Steward retired from the army to become chair of the history department at Wilberforce University in Ohio. In 1913, J. B. Lippincott published *Gouldtown,* Steward's genealogical history of his hometown. The following year Steward completed *The Haitian Revolution, 1791 to 1804,* which enjoyed enduring popularity as a work of African American history. In 1921, the *A.M.E. Book Concern published Steward's memoir, *From 1864 to 1914: Fifty Years in the Gospel Ministry,* a narrative that attests to Steward's multifaceted professional career and his dedication to social activism as well as preaching the gospel.

• Charles Spencer Smith, *A History of the African Methodist Episcopal Church,* 1922. William L. Andrews, "Liberal Religion and Free Love: An Undiscovered Afro-American Novel of the 1890s," *MELUS* 9 (Spring 1982): 23–36.

—William L. Andrews

STEWART, MARIA W. (1803–1879), essayist, lecturer, abolitionist, and women's rights activist. Maria Stewart was the earliest known American woman to lecture in public on political themes and leave extant copies of her texts. Her first publication, a twelve-page pamphlet entitled *Religion and the Pure Principles of Morality* (1831), revealed her distinctive style, a mix of political analysis and religious exhortation. Her message, highly controversial coming from the pen of a woman, called upon African Americans to organize against slavery in the South and to resist racist restrictions in the North. She invoked both the Bible and the Constitution of the United States as documents proclaiming a universal birthright to freedom and justice.

Influenced by the militant abolitionist David *Walker, Stewart raised the specter of armed rebellion by African Americans. In a lecture at Boston's African Masonic Hall in 1833 she declared, "[M]any powerful sons and daughters of Africa will shortly arise, . . . and declare by Him that sitteth upon the throne that they will have their rights; and if refused, I am afraid they will spread horror and devastation around."

She further advocated the establishment of strong, self-sufficient educational and economic institutions within African American communities. In particular, she called upon women to participate in all aspects of community life, from religion and education to politics and business. "How long," she asked in *Religion and the Pure Principles of Morality,* "shall the fair daughters of Africa be compelled to bury their minds and talents beneath a load of iron pots and kettles?"

Born in Hartford, Connecticut, orphaned at the age of five, Stewart grew up as a servant in the home of a white clergyman. As a young woman she went to Boston, where she married James W. Stewart, a successful ship's outfitter. Widowed after barely three years of marriage, Maria Stewart was left penniless through the legal machinations of unscrupulous white businessmen. An 1830 religious conversion led her to proclaim her distinctive social gospel.

During her public career in Boston, Stewart also published a collection of religious meditations (1832), delivered four public lectures (1832–1833), and saw her speeches printed in *The Liberator.* After moving to New York City, she published her collected works, *Productions of Mrs. Maria W. Stewart* (1835). During the Civil War, Stewart moved to Washington, D.C. There she established a school for children of families that had escaped from slavery during the war, and she later became head matron at Freedmen's Hospital. Her expanded 1879 edition of *Productions* includes an autobiographical sketch, "Sufferings During the War."

Writing to William Lloyd Garrison in March of 1852, historian William C. Nell remarked, "In the perilous years of '33–'35, Mrs. Maria W. Stewart [was] fired with a holy zeal to speak her sentiments on the improvement of colored Americans . . . [H]er public lectures awakened an interest acknowledged and felt to this day." Stewart's essays and speeches presented original formulations of many ideas that were to become central to the struggles for African American freedom, human rights, and women's rights. In this she was a clear forerunner to Frederick *Douglass, Sojourner *Truth, and generations of the most influential African American activists and political thinkers.

• Marilyn Richardson, *Maria W. Stewart, America's First Black Woman Political Writer: Essays and Speeches,* 1987. Carla L. Peterson, *Doers of the Word: African-American Women Speakers and Writers in the World (1830–1880),* 1995.

—Marilyn Richardson

STILL, WILLIAM (1821–1902), abolitionist and historian. Born of free black parents in New Jersey, William Still grew up on a farm, with little opportunity for formal schooling. He moved to Philadelphia in 1844, married in 1847, and in the same year went to work for the Pennsylvania Society for the Abolition of Slavery. In 1851 he became chairman of the society. Later in the decade he campaigned to end racial discrimination on Philadelphia railroad cars. Until the end of the Civil War, Still was involved in aiding fugitives from slavery, an activity that allowed him to meet and interview hundreds of runaways. The records he kept of these interviews, along with numerous other documents, such as biographical sketches of prominent activists and letters from abolitionists and escaped slaves, became the source material for his book, *The Underground Railroad.* Commissioned by the Pennsylvania Society for the Abolition of Slavery, this bulky volume was not published until 1872 because of Still's anxiety about reprisals that might await him because of his work on the Underground Railroad. The book was sold through subscription. Well received, it was reprinted in 1879 and 1883.

The Underground Railroad paid tribute to the generous efforts of white abolitionists on the "liberty line" but also stressed the courage and self-determination of the fugitives themselves in their quest for freedom. Still's motive in writing his book was to encourage other African Americans to write of the heroic deeds of the race during the crisis years of the mid-nineteenth century and, in general, to promote African American literature.

• William Still, *The Underground Railroad,* 1872; rpt. 1968.

—Kenneth W. Goings

STILL, WILLIAM GRANT (1895–1978), composer of symphonic music and opera. William Grant Still's first major symphonic works, *Sahdji* and *First (Afro-American) Symphony,* both completed in 1930, combined a distinctly nationalistic and patriotic character with African American elements. By 1934 he had settled in Los Angeles, where he remained the rest of his life. His compositions received favorable reviews during the late 1930s and throughout the war years.

By the late 1950s, however, American concert music was being composed by and supported by people who considered themselves modernists. Still refused to change his vision to accommodate the changing times. *Troubled Island,* his most important postwar opera, which told the story of the overthrow of Dessalines in Haiti, premiered in 1949 to negative reviews because of his continued use of recurring melodic themes at a time the modernists wanted more experimental music. The fate of *Troubled Island* prefigured the general rejection of Still's work throughout the 1950s and 1960s.

William Grant Still has often been referred to as the dean of African American composers. He was the first African American to conduct a symphony in the South and to have a symphony and opera performed by a major company. Still, however, would have rejected that designation. His purpose in life was to be seen and heard as an American composer. He felt that his blackness was just one part of him and that he should be seen as a whole.

• Robert Bartlett Haas, ed., *William Grant Still and the Fusion of Cultures in American Music,* 1972. Jon Michael Spencer, ed., *The William Still Reader: Essays on American Music,* 1992.

—Kenneth W. Goings

STOWE, HARRIET BEECHER (1811–1896), novelist and abolitionist. Harriet Beecher Stowe wrote the widely popular antislavery novel *Uncle Tom's Cabin,* which was published in 1852 and went on to sell three hundred thousand copies the first year. Credited with mobilizing antislavery sentiment in the North, Stowe was praised, honored, and respected among African Americans both during her lifetime and in the years following.

Uncle Tom's Cabin was based on various slave narratives, including those of Lewis Clarke, Frederick *Douglass, and Josiah *Henson. Legend has it that Henson was the model for *Uncle Tom, and Henson capitalized on this legend by writing two more narratives after *Uncle Tom's Cabin* was published.

The years following the publication of *Uncle Tom's Cabin* saw African American authors publish a number of narratives, novels, plays, and poems inspired by Stowe's work, including William Wells *Brown's **Clotel* (1853), Martin R. *Delany's **Blake* (1859), and Frances Ellen Watkins *Harper's **Iola Leroy* (1892). In addition, Harper published three known poems inspired by Stowe. "Eva's Farewell" and "Eliza Harris" are based on incidents in *Uncle Tom's Cabin,* and "Harriet Beecher Stowe" extols Stowe as a savior to African Americans. Other poets who paid tribute to Stowe in verse include Henrietta Cordelia Ray and Paul Laurence *Dunbar, whose 1898 sonnet praises Stowe as a "prophet and priestess" whose voice "spoke to consciences that long had slept."

With a new century came a more critical look at Stowe. Sterling A. *Brown in his literary history *The Negro in American Fiction* (1937) suggested that Stowe's sentimentalized representations of African Americans paved the way for the more pernicious stereotypes that characterized the works of racist writers such as Thomas Dixon. Richard *Wright indirectly referred to Stowe's most famous work in the names of both his short story collection, **Uncle Tom's Children* (1940), and the main character of **Native Son* (1940), *Bigger Thomas. For Wright, Stowe's novel signified the racist past that continued to influence the present aspirations of young African Americans. Similarly, in "Everybody's Protest Novel" (1955), James *Baldwin called *Uncle Tom's Cabin* a "bad novel" characterized by a "self-righteous, virtuous sentimentality" motivated less by sincere empathy for African Americans oppressed by slavery and more by Stowe's desire for moral salvation and the assimilation of African Americans into her own moral and cultural purview.

Stowe's moral and theological views and domestic discourse were accepted as progressive, indeed radical, in the nineteenth century. It is ironic that in the twentieth century, she has come to exemplify both impotent white liberalism and the source of racist preconceptions about African Americans.

• Jean Ashton, *Harriet Beecher Stowe: A Reference Guide,* 1977. Joan D. Hedrick, *Harriet Beecher Stowe,* 1994.

—Wendy Wagner

Street, The. Ann Petry's first novel, published in 1946 by Houghton Mifflin and winner of the Houghton Mifflin Literary Fellowship, *The Street* follows the tradition of naturalism and protest fiction while rejecting the traditions of the tragic mullato and the southern belle. Critics often compare the novel to Richard *Wright's **Native Son* (1942). At first publication, *The Street* received high acclaim, yet it went out of print for several decades. In 1985 Beacon Press reissued the novel as a part of the African American Women Writers series; and in 1991, forty-five years after the original, Houghton Mifflin reissued *The Street,* because its theme made the book seem pertinent enough to have been written today.

Petry's premise relies on environment being highly influential in determining one's life path. Harlem's 116th Street is the most foreboding character in the novel, and the book both begins and ends with its image, representing the evil in urban ghetto life. Portraying the interrelationships among racism, sexism, and economic oppression—revealed through the struggles of *Lutie Johnson, a beautiful brown woman, struggling as a single mother—*The Street* reveals the dreary despair of a black woman in the urban city whose plight can only end in crime and/or tragedy.

At the beginning of the novel, Lutie and her son, Bub, move to 116th Street, intoxicated with the images of statesman Benjamin Franklin and the self-made individual. These American ideals replace her husband, father, and any sense of community; she isolates herself with this quest for wealth and a house with a white picket fence. This rosy-eyed outlook causes her to become the easy prey of many predators: The building superintendent sees her as the ultimate sexual conquest; Mrs. Hedges, the neighborhood madam, sees in her a great "business" opportunity; Boots Smith, smooth-talking band leader, wants Lutie as a means of easing his own struggles and pains; and Junto, white slumlord, wants Lutie as a personal concubine. The character of Junto is contrasted with her "role model," Ben Franklin; she thinks the latter will lead her to success, and the former only leads her to self-destruction.

Most of the novel's tension comes from Lutie's hopes for a promising future clashing against reality. Because of a lack of options and her unwillingness to face the grim truth, Lutie trusts those she should not—especially Franklin—and rejects building coalitions where she should. She insists on going against the tide in an attempt to break out of despair, but external forces combine to overpower her desires. By the end of the novel, the rosy-eyed outlook faded, Lutie finally understands that the ideals she believed in have always rejected black women and in the process she has lost that which she most valued: her son and her dignity.

—Adenike Marie Davidson

Street in Bronzeville, A. Gwendolyn *Brooks's first book of poetry, *A Street in Bronzeville* (1945), introduced a group of characters in a segregated urban area unknown to many in America's reading public but closely resembling Chicago's South Side.

Bronzeville was an enigma. There were enough examples of successful enterprises and hardworking people who could serve as true role models that "going to Chicago" made sense even when the rest of the country was facing severe economic and social problems. But, Bronzeville had many unlovely places and spaces: back alleys, street corners, vacant lots, and kitchenette buildings with all of the associated odors.

While they collectively represent an intensity unmatched in much urban poetry, the poems in *A Street in Bronzeville* are essentially realistic. In celebrating the life in urban streets, Brooks seems to work like others who create celebratory examinations of ordinary places and people. At the same time, she seems to be in the vanguard of those black writers intent upon looking at black city life. Not only does she present compassionate portraits drawn with skill, understanding, and great sensitivity, but she also does not idealize her characters. Despite the despair of most of them, they are not completely victimized by circumstances over which they have little or no control. They take life as it comes to them; and within these parameters, they exercise a degree of free will. This is not to suggest that there are no elements of protest within the collection. Brooks's protest, however, is often muted and ironic.

Her memorable characters range from workers in service-oriented jobs such as maids and beauty shop operators to the professional classes often represented by preachers. There are gamblers and "bad girls" and those who do not seem to have any visible means of support, but all of them are members of the very crowded urban ghetto. Despite their lack of heroism, there is a quiet dignity that comes to all of them predicated upon their humanity that is often unrecognized by the larger society. While many of the people who live in Brooks's Bronzeville are surrounded by failure, they refuse to succumb completely, and their lives frequently offer glimpses of a pitiful hope.

The irony of life in the ghetto is illustrated by "Gay Chaps at the Bar," consisting of a group of interrelated sonnets dealing with blacks in the military during World War II whose treatment often left much to be desired despite the announced nobility of the cause for which they fought. Like Claude *McKay, Brooks uses the sonnet form to prove that what had historically been a lyric form could also be used as a vehicle for protest.

Brooks's social concerns are etched against the universality of the nondemanding dreams of the young, the limited hopes for the future that mothers and fathers exhibit, and the general need shared by all people to seek and receive not only justice but also love. Sometimes—as in the case of Satin-Legs Smith—it is the hope to exist until the following Sunday when he can dress up and strut around the streets.

A Street in Bronzeville demonstrates social sensitivity while remaining free of the rhetoric of hate. Despite the setting, the problems, and the tragedies, there is an affirmation of life—not on some grand scale but simply in terms of small daily victories.

• Gary Smith, "Gwendolyn Brooks's *A Street in Bronzeville*, the Harlem Renaissance, and the Mythologies of Black Women," *MELUS* 10 (Fall 1983): 33–46.

—Kenny Jackson Williams

Sula (1974), the second novel by Toni *Morrison, is set in an African American neighborhood known as the Bottom even though it is in the hills. This name comes from a "nigger joke" used to trick a slave who had been promised freedom and a piece of bottom land. The narrative begins with the community's destruction to make way for the Medallion City Golf Course and then flashes backward to tell the story of *Sula Peace, who leaves the Bottom only to be perceived as an evil and suspicious force upon her return.

The novel is woven around the friendship between Sula and Nel Wright, two young girls who come from extremely different family environments yet become "two throats and one eye." Nel's mother runs an immaculate, orderly household while Sula's home is filled with disorder and casual or absent moral habits and values. Other characters include *Shadrack, the village madman; *Eva Peace, Sula's grandmother; *Hannah Peace, Sula's mother; the three Deweys, homeless boys taken in by Sula's grandmother; Ajax, Sula's friend and later boyfriend; and Plum, the drug-addicted son of Eva Peace who she burns rather than see degenerate and attempt figuratively to "return to her womb."

Evidence of Sula's detachment displays itself early on: When Nel and Sula are young, they accidentally let a young boy slip into a river and drown. Later Sula watches with curiosity as her mother burns to death. Sula and Nel learn early that in the Bottom they are restricted by race, gender, and economics, and Sula eventually leaves to seek her freedom. Nel stays within the community, subscribing to and being limited by its mores and conventions. When Sula returns to Medallion ten years later, her return is symbolically accompanied by a plague of robins. Seeing Sula perform a series of incomprehensible actions such as casually taking Nel's husband Jude as a lover and later just as casually discarding him, and putting her grandmother in a despicably kept old folks' home, the inhabitants of the Bottom treat her with contempt. Nel's chagrin and Jude's abandonment of his family cause a split in the women's friendship that is only somewhat mended when Sula becomes deathly ill. Sula dies a disinterested observer of her own death, remarking to herself that it does not hurt and that she must tell Nel. More than twenty years later, the elderly Eva Peace reminds Nel of her similarities to Sula, which leads Nel to conclude that all the time she thought she was missing Jude, she was really missing Sula.

Sula is an intriguing novel, not only because of its controversial and shocking protagonist, but because of her amoral actions and values, and the novel probes into the minds and lives of its characters. Sula seeks freedom and the ability to define herself, and her insistence on her own freedom helps others define themselves. The novel was selected as a Book-of-the-Month Club alternate and brought Morrison national recognition because of its distinctive view of African American life and the lives of black females coupled with the detached view of the novelist toward her characters, which some considered unsettling and original. The novel reflects Morrison's view of the importance and relevance of African American history, and her ability to explain the underlying motives for the actions of her creations.

• Naana Banyiwa-Norne, "The Scary Face of the Self: An Analysis of the Character of Sula in Toni Morrison's *Sula*," *Sage* 2 (1985): 28–31. Barbara Christian, *Black Feminist Criticism*, 1985. Deborah E. McDowell, "'The Self and the Other': Reading Toni Morrison's *Sula* and the Black Female Text," in *Critical Essays on Toni Morrison*, ed. Nellie Y. McKay, 1988, pp. 77–89. Maurine T. Reddy, "The Tripled Plot and Center of *Sula*," *Black American Literature Forum* 22.1 (Spring 1988): 29–45. Wilfred D. Samuels and Clenora Hudson Weems, *Toni Morrison*, 1990.

—Betty Taylor-Thompson

SULA PEACE is the character who forms the center of action and controversy in **Sula* (1974), Toni *Morrison's second novel. The only child of *Hannah Peace and granddaughter of *Eva Peace, in whose home Hannah, Sula, and a host of other characters reside, Sula is a restless adolescent who forms a lifelong friendship with Nel Wright, an equally lonely child. Having discovered that they are neither "white nor male," the girls must find ways to grow and explore within the community of the Bottom. They share sexual awakening when Ajax, who will become Sula's lover twenty years later, calls them "pigmeat," his epithet for attractively developing female flesh. They share guilt and failed moral conscience when Sula accidentally lets Chicken Little, a neighbor child, slip to his death in a nearby river; though remorseful, neither girl fully accepts responsibility for the act.

Bored with life in the Bottom, Sula departs as a teenager and sojourns for ten years. Her return marks her as the witchlike personification of evil: she puts Eva in an old folks' home, sleeps with and discards her neighbors' husbands, sleeps with Nel's husband Jude, disrespects the church ladies' social functions, and generally disrupts the community's sense of propriety. More damning than any of her other actions, the belief that she sleeps with white men makes her a pariah. When she becomes ill, all the townspeople except Nel ignore her. Instead of using her brief encounter with Sula as a moment of reconciliation, Nel still blames Sula for Jude's desertion, which only gives way to true pain, the true expression of the loss of this special friend, twenty-five years after Sula's death. With Sula, Morrison explores the impact of an independent female spirit upon a town that can envision such a manifestation only in masculine guise. Members of the community therefore judge Sula harshly, but, true to her refusal to portray absolutes in her works, Morrison makes it difficult for readers to pass similar easy judgment.

—Trudier Harris

System of Dante's Hell, The. According to chapter headings and author Amiri *Baraka's (LeRoi Jones) assertions, *The System of Dante's Hell* (1965) is structured in a manner similar to *The Inferno*. However, the reader of *System* is hard-pressed to find readily apparent parallels between the two works. This difficulty lies primarily in the cryptic, fragmentary style of Baraka's only foray into the domain of the novelist. Like *Tales* (1967), the author's collection of short stories, *System* is a loosely structured, highly suggestive, and strongly autobiographical work of fiction. A vivid montage of scenes and characters from key phases of Baraka's life, this experimental bildungsroman evidences that the author's debt to James Joyce is at least as compelling as that owed to Dante.

Critical reception of this work has reflected the continuing argument between those who favor Baraka's experimentation and the politicizing of his art and those who deem it detrimental. Bernard Bugonzi notes, for example, in a review of *System*, "This is ultimately a political act rather than an imaginative or creative one. And not, I think all that effective" (*New York Review of Books*, 20 Jan. 1966). On the other hand, William Harris, in praise of *System*, refers to Baraka as "the pioneer of black experimental fiction, probably the most important since Jean Toomer" (introduction to *The LeRoi Jones/Amiri Baraka Reader*, 1991).

The early sections of System are reminiscent of the lyrics of **Preface to a Twenty-Volume Suicide Note* (1961) in both tone and sentiment. The narrative voice of the "Heathen" sections, for example, expresses the same self-loathing and despair so powerfully felt in the earlier lyrics.

As in all of Baraka's writings, the most pervasive theme of *System* is that of racial identity. The protagonist's struggle is the same as that faced by Clay of **Dutchman* (1964). He is torn between the path of self-denial on the one hand and the path of authentic black identity on the other. The centrality of this theme is emphatically underscored in Baraka's characterization of those he calls "Heretics," individuals whom he places in "the deepest part of hell" because of their maniacal pursuit of assimilation. The narrator notes, "It is heresy, against one's own sources / running in terror, from one's deepest responses and insights . . . denial of / feeling . . . that I see as basest evil." The narrator's recollection of the Newark of his boyhood, adolescence, and young adult years deals with images of this "heretical" behavior and the sense of guilt thereby engendered. The book abounds with satirical snapshots of leaders and aspiring leaders of the black middle class, all twisted by cultural shame and motivated by the overwhelming desire to distance themselves as far as possible from their black roots.

This theme receives more compelling and direct treatment in the latter sections of the novel. In the section entitled "The Eight Ditch Is Drama," Baraka dramatizes the split psyche of the assimilationist through the creation of two characters, "46" and "64," who represent the warring factions within. Toward the novel's conclusion, the experimental mode gives way to a markedly more accessible, or traditional, story line. Both "Circle 9: Bolgia 1—Treachery to Kindred" and "6. The Heretics" focus on the narrator's interaction with highly symbolic black women, each of whom represents, in almost allegorical fashion, racial authenticity and acceptance of self. Until he is able to embrace these women unconditionally, the narrator relegates himself to "the deepest part of hell," a psychological hell of self-contempt and guilt.

• Robert Eliot Fox, *Conscientious Sorcerers: The Black Postmodernist Fiction of LeRoi Jones/Baraka, Ishmael Reed, and Samuel R. Delany*, 1987.

—Henry C. Lacey

T

Tar Baby. The fourth novel by Nobel Prize–winner Toni *Morrison, *Tar Baby* (1981) is the story of the ill-fated love affair between Jadine Childs and William (Son) Green. The title derives from an African American folktale about a farmer trying to capture a thieving rabbit in his cabbage patch by fashioning a sticky tar baby, enhancing the mythical quality of the work. In this case, *Jadine Childs is the tar baby fashioned by a rich white man, and she is subsequently alienated from her relatives, her history, and her culture.

In *Tar Baby,* Morrison brings together Valerian Street, a retired candy manufacturer who is Jadine's benefactor; his wife Margaret, once a beauty queen in Maine who physically abused their son; and Sydney and Ondine, Jadine's aunt and uncle and Valerian's faithful servants, in L'Arbe de la Croix, the Streets's Caribbean retirement home. Jadine, an orphan educated in Europe through the Streets's charity who has become a successful fashion model, comes to the island to contemplate her impending marriage to a white Parisian. *Son Green, a black man who jumped ship, takes secret refuge on the grounds and, at times, in the home. He and Jadine enter into an attraction/repulsion dance of sorts in which his "funkiness" contrasts sharply with her modeling and middle-class background. They eventually seduce each other and enter into a stormy relationship that takes them from the island to New York and to Son's hometown of Eloe, Florida. Uncomfortable in such a small town, increasingly critical of Son, and uncertain about the future of their troubled relationship, Jadine precedes Son to New York. When Son does not arrive on schedule, Jadine returns to the island, collects her belongings, pushes Son to the back of her mind, and returns to Paris. Shortly thereafter Son comes to the island looking for Jadine. He enlists the aid of Thérèse, the washerwoman with whom he had earlier formed a congenial relationship, but Thérèse purposely leads him to the "wrong side" of the island, where mythical blind African horsemen who escaped from slavery supposedly still reside. Son goes "lickety-split, lickety-split" to join them.

The focal point of the novel is Jadine's conflict with her African American culture, history, and identity, and this identity crisis is not resolved. The novel's overlapping narrative structure, mythological themes, and dependence on dialogue to advance the plot have been criticized by reviewers and readers, and *Tar Baby* is generally seen as Morrison's most difficult novel and a sharp departure from her earlier works. However, this criticism has been refuted as exaggeration since *Tar Baby* has as its themes identity, maternity, ancestral significance, and the sexuality of the African American woman, motifs that Morrison used in her earlier novels.

• Susan Blake, "Toni Morrison" in *DLB,* vol. 33, *Afro-American Fiction Writers after 1955,* eds. Thadious M. Davis and Trudier Harris, 1984, pp. 187–199. Craig Werner, "The Briar Patch as Modernist Myth: Morrison, Barthes and Tar Baby As-Is," in *Critical Essays on Toni Morrison,* ed. Nellie Y. McKay, 1988, pp. 150–167. Terry Otten, *The Crime of Innocence in the Fiction of Toni Morrison,* 1989. Wilfred D. Samuels and Clenora Hudson Weems, *Toni Morrison,* 1990. Margot Gayle Backus, "'Looking for That Dead Girl': Incest, Pornography, and the Capitalist Family Romance in *Nightwood, The Years,* and *Tar Baby,*" *American Imago* 51.4 (Winter 1994): 521–545.

—Betty Taylor-Thompson

TATE, ELEANORA (b. 1948), author of children's and young adult literature, poet, short fiction writer, journalist, storyteller, and media consultant. A former journalist in Iowa and Tennessee, a former president of the National Association of Black Storytellers, and a poet, Eleanora Tate has been most successful as a writer of children's and young adult literature. The film version of her first book, *Just an Overnight Guest* (1980), was aired as a part of PBS's Wonderworks series. *The Secret of Gumbo Grove* (1987) is not only a mystery but a story with a strong message about the importance of history and heritage. *Thank You, Dr. Martin Luther King, Jr.!* (1990) chronicles young Raisin Stackhouse's journey toward self-appreciation. *Retold African Myths* (1993), illustrated by Tate's nephew, Don Tate, demonstrates her storytelling prowess. The same is true of *Front Porch Stories at the One-Room School* (1992) in which a father tells his daughter and niece the stories of his youth in their community.

The value of education is a recurring theme in Tate's work. The novel's front porch is modeled upon the Lincoln One-Room School in Canton, Ohio, that Tate attended as a girl. (She is a graduate of Roosevelt High School and Drake University, both in Des Moines, Iowa.) More important, the father is a central figure in this book, as is also the case in A *Blessing in Disguise* (1995). Tate believes that the need for "father-daughter love" among blacks often goes unrecognized, but that it is connected to black girls' self-image and self-esteem. She is one of the first young people's writers to address openly the issue of self-esteem in the context of skin color and African heritage, accomplishing what Toni *Morrison's *The *Bluest Eye* does in adult literature.

• "Tate, Eleanora E(laine)," in *Something about the Author,* vol. 38, ed. Anne Commire, 1985, pp. 199–201.

—Dianne Johnson-Feelings

TAYLOR, MILDRED D. (b. 1943), writer of children's fiction, hailed for her realistic portrayal of the African American experience. Born in Jackson, Mississippi, at a time when African Americans were fighting overseas for liberties they did not possess at home, Mildred Delois Taylor and her family fled the South when she was scarcely three months old to prevent a violent confrontation between a white man and her father, Wilbert Lee Taylor.

The fleeing family settled in Toledo, Ohio, where Taylor grew up self-confident and loved in the large house her father purchased to shelter relatives and friends escaping the pre-civil rights South. In this house conversation was an art and storytelling a tradition. Taylor has stated that her father was the most influential person in her life. He was a master storyteller, keeping alive southern memories and traditions. Although Taylor visited the South many times with her parents, she never lived in her birthplace. She absorbed the rhythms and the nuances of African American southern speech and culture from her visits and her father's vivid rendering of the stories he told her.

An honor student, Taylor expressed an interest in writing during high school, becoming editor of the school newspaper. In 1960, she entered the University of Toledo and following her graduation, she joined the Peace Corps. After two years in Ethiopia, where she taught history and English, Taylor returned to the United States at the height of the Black Power movement of the late 1960s. She enrolled in a graduate program at the University of Colorado, where she earned an MA in journalism. Taylor, who had always been politically aware, became a student activist lobbying for the creation of a black studies program and helping to establish the Black Student Alliance.

Following her graduation from Colorado, Taylor worked as coordinator of the study skills center. The job was demanding and interfered with her growing urge to write. Taylor decided the time had come for her to inspire others as she had been by the stories of heroic men and women who overcame the obstacles of racial oppression. She resigned her position at the university and moved to Los Angeles, where she found a job that did not interfere with her writing.

Taylor completed her first work in 1973. *Song of the Trees* is a novella of scarcely fifty-two pages. She entered her manuscript in the Council on Interracial Books for Children competition, winning first place in the African American category. *Song of the Trees,* published in 1975, is dedicated "To the Family, who fought and survived," and introduces the Logans, consisting of several generations of grandparents and wise ones "who bridged the generations between slavery and freedom." Taylor patterns the story on her own family history, setting a tone that rings clearly throughout her works, one of pride and perserverance.

Song of the Trees was hailed by critics for its simplicity, its finely rendered characters, and its poetry. Taylor's second novel continues the story of the Logans. Her second book, now considered a children's classic, **Roll of Thunder, Hear My Cry* (1976), was praised for its honest portrayal of racial prejudice and in 1977 won the Newbery Medal. She was the second African American to receive the medal. Taylor continued her chronicle of the Logans with *Let the Circle Be Unbroken* (1981), which won the Coretta Scott King Award in 1982 and was nominated for an American Book Award. The fourth book in the series, *The Friendship,* also won the Coretta Scott King Award, in 1984. Taylor's works compare favorably to such classics as *Huckleberry Finn* and *Little House on the Prairie.*

Other books by Taylor include *The Gold Cadillac* (1987), a humorous and ironic account of an African American family with the chutzpah to visit the South in a flashy, prestigious car. *Mississippi Bridge* and *The Road to Memphis,* both published in 1990, were named Notable Children's Books in the field of social studies.

Taylor's works appeared when Americans had etherized their memories of racial oppression with the promising results of the civil rights movement. Holding the past at bay did not, however, insure a democratic future. Taylor urged understanding and acceptance of a history few would care to repeat. Children, having no painful psychic history to suppress, therefore were the perfect audience. Taylor reaches readers eager to learn about lives of people missing, even today, from history and literary textbooks. Her themes encompass real world problems and her characters are lovable and brave. Taylor's future as a writer is assured because young readers embrace her books so wholeheartedly.

• Mildred Taylor, "Newbery Award Acceptance," *Horn Book Magazine,* Aug. 1977, 401–409. Violet Harris, "Taylor, Mildred," in *Black Women in America: An Historical Encyclopedia,* vol. 2, 1993, pp. 1144–1145.

—Nagueyalti Warren

TAYLOR, SUSIE KING (1848–1912), nurse, educator, domestic, and autobiographer. Susie Reed was born a slave on the Isle of Wight, off the coast of Georgia, in 1848. As a child, she was educated surreptitiously by white schoolchildren and slave neighbors. Once literate, she endorsed counterfeit passes for other slaves, early demonstrating both a defiance against bondage and injustice and a commitment to African American education. During the Civil War, she attained freedom when an uncle took her with his family to St. Catherine Island, South Carolina, then under Union army administration. At age fourteen, she taught island children by day and conducted night classes for numerous adults. Later in 1862, she joined a troop of African American soldiers, under the command of Lieutenant Colonel C. T. Trowbridge, and served them as nurse, laundress, teacher, and cook. After the war, she and her first husband, Sergeant Edward King, returned to Savannah, where King died, leaving her to rear their infant son alone. From 1865 to 1868, she operated a private school, then performed domestic work in both southern and northern states. At age thirty-one, she married Russell Taylor. During Reconstruction, she organized the Women's Relief Corps, gaining national recognition for African American war heroes—men and women alike. In 1902 she published her autobiography.

Reminiscences of My Life in Camp portrays Susie King Taylor as both altruistic and astute; in it, as a representative African American woman of the late nineteenth century, she analyzes race relations and gender roles of her day. By reconstructing her army life, she tacitly demonstrates women's equality with men: while performing such traditional women's duties as sewing, women in the army revealed themselves to be as perceptive, valiant, and hardy as men. More overtly, Taylor condemns the post-Reconstruction racism manifest in Jim Crow groups such as the ex–Confederate Daughters, and American-Cuban relations. Throughout her *Reminiscences,* Taylor emerges brave and benevolent.

• Anthony Barthelemy, ed., *Reminiscences of My Life in Camp: With the 33d United States Colored Troops Late 1st S.C. Volunteers,* 1988. Joanne Braxton, *Black Women Writing Autobiography: A Tradition Within a Tradition,* 1990.

—Joycelyn K. Moody

TEA CAKE. Vergible Woods, known as Tea Cake, is the third husband of *Janie Crawford, the protagonist of Zora Neale *Hurston's novel **Their Eyes Were Watching God* (1937). He is a troubadour, a traveling bluesman dedicated to aesthetic and joyful pursuits, and he presents a vivid contrast to Janie's second husband, Joe Starks, a politician and businessman. Tea Cake is, as his name implies, a veritable man of nature or natural man, who seems at ease being who and what he is. Unlike Joe, Tea Cake has no desire to be a "big voice." Tea Cake and Janie engage in small talk and invent variations of traditional courtship rituals. They play checkers, fish by moonlight, and display their affection freely. An unselfish lover, Tea Cake delights in Janie's pleasure. Janie soon concludes that Tea Cake "could be a bee to a blossom—a pear tree blossom in the spring." Despite the disapproval of her neighbors, she marries this man several years younger than she whose only worldly possession is a guitar. She travels with him to the "muck," where they both work in the field and share household chores.

Though their romance is idyllic, Tea Cake is not a completely idealized character. When he feels their relationship is threatened, he beats Janie. But at the novel's climax, he saves her life during a hurricane. Later, having contracted rabies, he attacks his wife. Janie kills him in self-defense. In the epilogue, Janie cherishes Tea Cake's memory; not only her lover, he has been a cultural mentor and spiritual guide.

—Cheryl A. Wall

Temple of My Familiar, The. To experience the full flavor of Alice *Walker's fourth novel, *The Temple of My Familiar,* a reader must allow him- or herself to expand and collapse within an intensely provocative expression of a womanist world view. In fact, calling *The Temple of My Familiar* a novel is a misnomer. The book, published in 1989, is anything but a novel. It is a collection of loosely related stories, a political platform, a sermon, and a stream of dreams and memories bound together by definitions of (and explanations for) the present state of human affairs.

The book explodes with imagination and presents a past (and a present) in which all things are possible through change, respect, and self-awareness. This optimistic view of the world is presented through the memories of Miss Lissie, a woman who has experienced several incarnations; Zedé and Carlotta, a mother and daughter who share the intimate affections and love of one man; Fanny Nzingha, granddaughter of *Celie from *The *Color Purple* (1982); Suwelo, an American history professor; and an array of other characters (including *Shug Avery from *The Color Purple*).

The Temple of My Familiar is the ultimate expression of womanism. There is virtually no subject that escapes Walker's womanist commentary. The book speaks of homosexuality, AIDS, drug abuse, racism, religion, parenting, marriage, and death. A cascade of memories (ancient and contemporary) connect these issues to the various stories and messages of the book. Within all the stories dignity, honor, and grace are ruthlessly denied to those in spiritual, mental, or physical bondage, making it nearly impossible for them to achieve wholeness. Regardless of financial standing, throughout time the "enslaved" have endured an endless struggle for gracious living. The importance of this theme is summarized by the character Fanny Nzingha who comments that "all daily stories are in fact ancient and ancient ones current. . . . There is nothing new under the sun."

Present in each story is the suppression of individuality by rules of morality and by the power one culture (usually white culture) wills over another. One clear message of this book is that although suffering is not new, it is inflamed by ignorance and freed by determination and change. Although *The Temple of My Familiar* demands respect for the instruments of change (self-awareness, freedom, equality, love, and respect), it does not insist that change is always positive. According to Zedé, the moment prehistoric man sought to emulate woman (and produce life through a physical opening that he did not possess) destruction, disorder, and death were conceived.

If this concept sounds somewhat mythic, that is only because it is. The entire book is a myth—a rewriting of history so that her story, or at least Walker's version of it, can surface and shine. In this book, an acknowledgment of the sacredness of woman, love for her essential nature, and respect of her power is the key to finding healing in a world that has gone wrong.

• Ikenna Dieke, "Toward a Monastic Idealism: The Thematics of Alice Walker's *The Temple of My Familiar*," *African American Review* 26.3 (1992): 507–514. Clara Juncker, "Black Magic: Woman(ist) as Artist in Alice Walker's *The Temple of My Familiar*," *American Studies in Scandinavia* 24.1 (1992): 37–49.

—Debra Walker King

TERRELL, MARY CHURCH (1863–1954), suffragist, humanitarian, and activist for racial equality and women's rights. An articulate lecturer and writer, Mary Church Terrell fought to end lynching, disenfranchisement, employment discrimination, public segregation, and other injustices. Over her long career Terrell's activism evolved from "Woman's Era" refinement to direct action, militant tactics involving picketing, sit-ins, and boycotts. In her late eighties she organized and led demonstrations against Washington, D.C., restaurants that refused to serve blacks. One such effort culminated in the famous Thompson Restaurant case and the 1953 Supreme Court ruling that opened Washington, D.C., eating establishments to all races.

The daughter of former slaves, Terrell was born in 1863 in Memphis, Tennessee. Her father, Robert Reed Church, was a prominent Memphis businessman and the first black millionaire in the South. Nicknamed Mollie, Mary Church Terrell graduated in 1884 from Oberlin College where she followed the "gentlemen's course," studying Latin and Greek and earning a BA degree rather than the two-year certificate women normally acquired. She taught at Wilberforce University and Washington, D.C.'s Colored High School before marrying Robert Terrell, a teacher, lawyer, and district court judge, in 1891. Terrell gave birth to four children, but only a daughter, Phyllis (named for Phillis *Wheatley), survived.

During the late nineteenth century, Terrell was one of the best-educated black women in America. In 1895 she was appointed to the Washington, D.C., board of education, becoming the first African American woman in the country to hold such a position. Terrell was also a founder and first president of the National Association of Colored Women and an early organizer of the NAACP. In 1904 she addressed the International Council of Women in Berlin on the race problem in the United States, delivering speeches in both French and German.

Terrell fought tirelessly for the passage of the Nineteenth Amendment and later became involved in Republican politics. Although she admired Eleanor Roosevelt, Terrell never supported Franklin Roosevelt. In the 1940s, Terrell received doctor of letters degrees from Oberlin, Wilberforce, and Howard, but she was denied membership in the American Association of University Women (AAUW). She appealed to the AAUW's national board, and in 1949 the association admitted Terrell and voted to admit other minority women as well.

A prolific writer, Terrell published articles in over thirty newspapers, magazines, and journals. Her works focused on racial and social injustices, African American life and history, and such notable personages as Frederick *Douglass, Phillis Wheatley, George Washington Carver, Samuel Taylor Coleridge, and Susan B. Anthony. In 1940 Terrell published *A Colored Woman in a White World*, an ambitious, full-length autobiography chronicling her struggles against racial and sexual discrimination. While Terrell's writings have been criticized for failing to grasp the full complexity of the racial struggle in America, they served to boost the morale of African Americans, call attention to important social issues, and educate whites about black life.

• Dorothy Sterling, "Mary Church Terrell," in *Black Foremothers*, 1979, pp. 118–157. Beverly Washington Jones, *Quest for Equality: The Life and Writings of Mary Eliza Church Terrell, 1863–1954*, 1990.

—Paula Gallant Eckard

TERRY, LUCY (c. 1730–1821), poet. Lucy Terry was the creator of the earliest known work of literature by an African American. Her poem, "Bar's Fight," created when the poet was sixteen years old, records an Indian ambush of two white families on 25 August 1746 in a section of Deerfield, Massachusetts, known as "the Bars," a colonial word for meadows. Composed in rhymed tetrameter couplets and probably designed to be sung, Terry's ballad was preserved in the memories of local singers until it was published in Josiah Holland's *History of Western Massachusetts* in 1855. Although Terry had grown up a slave in Deerfield, "Bar's Fight" conveys genuine sympathy for the white men and women who died in the skirmish.

Lucy Terry was born in Africa, kidnapped as an infant, and sold into slavery in Rhode Island. In 1735, when she was about five years old, she became the property of Ensign Ebenezer Wells of Deerfield, Massachusetts. After converting to Christianity she became a member of her master's church in 1744. She remained a slave until Obijah Prince, a wealthy free black, bought her freedom and married her in 1756. In 1760, the Princes moved to Guilford, Vermont, where Lucy's reputation as a storyteller and a strong defender of African American civil rights grew. Committed to an education for her six children, Lucy Terry Prince encouraged her oldest son to apply for admission to Williams College. When he was refused, she traveled to Williamstown, Massachusetts, and delivered a three-hour argument to the college's trustees against Williams's policy of racial discrimination. Though unsuccessful, this effort augmented Lucy Terry Prince's regional reputation as a skilled orator. After her husband's death in 1794, she moved to Sunderland, Vermont, where she died in 1821. "Bar's Fight," though of slight significance from a purely literary point of view, testifies to African American participation, from early colonial times, in the inscription of the cultural memory of the United States.

• Josiah Holland, *History of Western Massachusetts,* vol. 2, 1855. Frances Smith Foster, *Written by Herself: Literary Production by African American Women, 1746–1892,* 1993.

—William L. Andrews

Their Eyes Were Watching God. According to her autobiography, Zora Neale *Hurston wrote *Their Eyes Were Watching God* in seven weeks while she was conducting ethnographic fieldwork in Haiti and recovering from a failed romance. The circumstances were hardly promising, but the novel, published in September 1937, almost exactly a year after she arrived in Port-au-Prince, is her masterpiece. While it presents diverse oral performances—personal narratives, folktales, courtship rituals, speeches, and sermons—the folk material fuses seamlessly with a formal narrative that charts a woman's coming to voice and to selfhood. The protagonist, *Janie Crawford, begins a quest for romance but achieves spiritual fulfillment.

During a plot spanning twenty-odd years, Janie grows from a diffident teenager to a woman in possession of herself. She learns to resist the definitions of "what a woman should be" imposed on her by her grandmother, *Nanny, and by the three men she marries. Nanny chooses Janie's first husband, Logan Killicks, because he can provide protection and support. Janie dreams of love. Joe Starks becomes "a big ruler of things," who dominates his community and his wife. *Tea Cake (Vergible) Woods is a bluesman who guides Janie to a deeper understanding of African American culture even as he betrays its sexism. Through Janie's struggles with and against her husbands, the novel explores the relationship between voice and self-knowledge.

Janie is a master of metaphor. As a girl, she figures her life as a "tree in bloom." Dreaming of a man who will be "bee to her blossom," Janie rejects bourgeois marriage as an ideal. After Joe Starks's death frees her to dream again, she dreams of journeying to the horizon in search of people. She realizes both dreams through Tea Cake.

In the novel's frame tale, Janie returns to Eatonville after completing her quest. Townspeople sit on porches exchanging words full of drama and metaphor. For reasons of gender and class, Janie is excluded from this community; she is the object of its ridicule. Not only is storytelling mainly the province of men in Eatonville, but Mayor Starks has ordered Janie to remain aloof from other women and has forbidden her participation in their verbal rituals. With Tea Cake, Janie has learned the culture's expressive codes, however, and when she tells her story to her friend Pheoby it transforms teller and auditor.

Beginning with an early review by Richard *Wright, critics have faulted *Their Eyes* for its alleged lack of racial militancy. Some find the attacks on racism, present throughout the novel but especially in the scenes on the "muck," too indirect. Others contend that the novel's idealized representation of Tea Cake undercuts its critique of sexism. But Hurston's great accomplishment is the creation of a literary language equivalent to the oral performances she admired as a child and studied as an ethnographer. Vernacular voices speak in and through the novel, informing both its dialogue and narration. Like the oral performances it celebrates and critiques, the novel's words "[walk] without masters." *Their Eyes* is a singular achievement.

• Barbara Johnson, "Metaphor, Metonymy, and Voice in *Their Eyes Were Watching God,*" in *A World of Difference,* 1987. Michael Awkward, ed., *New Essays on* Their Eyes Were Watching God, 1990. Henry Louis Gates, Jr., and Anthony Appiah, eds., *Zora Neale Hurston: Critical Perspectives Past and Present,* 1993.

—Cheryl A. Wall

There Is Confusion (1924), by Jessie Redmon *Fauset, was the author's first novel and was written in direct response to *Birthright* (1922), a novel by a white writer, T. S. Stribling. Fauset, along with renaissance writers Nella *Larsen and Walter *White, believed the mulatto protagonist of Stribling's book to be unrealistic and felt that she was better "qualified" to write about the subject. Thus Fauset deliberately set about revising stereotypical representations of black life.

There Is Confusion centers on two families, the New York Marshalls and the Philadelphia Byes. In delineating their histories, Fauset stresses the significance of kinship and origins. She also shows the interconnectedness of the black and white races within these families in order to challenge the prevailing notion that black is evil and white is good. Making Peter Bye's "strain of white blood" responsible for all his faults reverses the conventional mulatto tales; however, her complicated genealogies sometimes confuse readers. Critics also agree that the book attempts to cover too much ground—too much time and space, too many characters, themes, and subplots.

A particular strength is its focus upon black women's psychological reactions to sexism and racism. Joanna Marshall—beautiful, ambitious, talented, confident, but snobbish—fights to overcome obstacles against her race and gender in her attempt to become a famous singer and dancer. Her attitude that with enough determination "colored" people can be anything they want helps her to achieve at least partial victories. Another woman, Maggie Ellersley, struggles against the same obstacles of race and gender but with the added struggle against classism. Maggie lives in a tenement with her laundress mother and slides further down the social scale when she marries a "common gambler," after her romance with Philip Marshall is thwarted by his sister Joanna. Eventually Maggie leaves her gambling husband, reunites with Philip, and marries him, but happiness is fleeting for Philip soon dies.

Many critics praise the novel for its revelation of middle-class attitudes; however, *There Is Confusion* is also important for its depiction of black women who question normative wife and mother roles by pursuing careers and self-reliance. Joanna believes women who give up everything for love are "poor silly sheep," and Maggie realizes she does not need anyone, not even a man. Maggie describes marriage as not very "interesting" or "picturesque"; and Joanna will not let it interfere with her other interests. By the end, however, Joanna marries Peter Bye and willingly forfeits her career for "pleasure" in "ordinary" things. Maggie, after Philip dies, still feels "bulwarked by the Marshall respectability." Some critics view the novel's conclusion as Fauset's capitulation to the very values she questions.

Rather than capitulating, however, Fauset seems to advocate men and women putting aside their individual desires and joining in love to fight racism. For Fauset, nothing was so difficult as the "problem of being colored in America." The didactic narrative voice that presses this thesis is a flaw in the novel, but the sentiment is a hallmark of the Harlem Renaissance.

• Carolyn Wedin Sylvander, *Jessie Redmon Fauset, Black American Writer,* 1981. Ann duCille, *The Coupling Convention: Sex, Text, and Tradition in Black Women's Fiction,* 1993. Jacquelyn Y. McLendon, *The Politics of Color in the Fiction of Jessie Fauset and Nella Larsen,* 1995.

—Jacquelyn Y. McLendon

Third Life of Grange Copeland, The. Alice *Walker's first novel, *The Third Life of Grange Copeland* (1970), is set in southern Georgia. A theme that dominates much of her writing (the survival whole of African Americans as individuals and as a race) is born within this epic story, setting the tone for Walker's entire body of work. This novel depicts the insurmountable difficulties that faced many uneducated and oppressed African Americans of the 1920s through the early 1960s—people whose hope faded and whose rage flared as each year's injustices fell upon them. Amidst the strife and struggle of life within a society dominated by racism, fear, and rage, three generations of an African American family struggle to survive.

The title character, Grange Copeland, is a sharecropper who beats his wife, Margaret, and has an extramarital affair with a prostitute named Josie. His son, *Brownfield Copeland, is a child whose father abandons him and whose mother commits suicide. At fifteen, Brownfield begins a search for his father that leads him into a world of lust and forbidden sex. At the Dew Drop Inn, he finds the beds of both Josie and her daughter, Lorene, are open to him. This sex triangle is broken, however, when Brownfield falls in love and marries Josie's niece, Mem.

Unfortunately, Brownfield follows his father's footsteps into the mire of the white man's sharecropping system. Feeling defeated and trapped, he turns his rage against his wife and children. Eventually, Mem grows tired of Brownfield's abuse and the unhealthy conditions in which they live. She forces Brownfield, at gun point, to get a factory job and returns to her profession as a schoolteacher. Mem succeeds in raising the family's standard of living until her health fails and Brownfield drags her back to the rat-infested shacks she despises. She takes a second step toward change but is defeated when Brownfield, jealous of her and fearful of any future she might be able to create, kills her.

Meanwhile, Grange returns from the North, marries Josie (for her money), and buys a farm. Together they raise Ruth, Mem's youngest daughter. Unlike his son, Grange has discovered that a cycle of hopelessness can only be broken if mistakes are faced with courage and life-building sacrifices for others are made. Based upon this belief, a bond of love develops between Grange and Ruth that distances Josie (who finds comfort in Brownfield's arms). Later, Brownfield gains legal custody of Ruth. Knowing that Brownfield's only objective is to destroy the possibility of wholeness within the child, Grange stops him. As the novel ends, Grange is hunted and killed for the murder of his only son.

This novel was not received with thunderous applause. Critics objected to the savage-like characterization of Brownfield. But like many African American women writers of the 1970s, Walker's purpose in telling this story is not to pick the sores of the African American male image. Her objective is to remove the blinders from the eyes of history so that the "real" stories of African American women's strengths and weaknesses can reveal themselves.

• Thomas Brooks, "The Third Life of Grange Copeland," in *Masterpieces of African-American Literature,* ed. Frank N. Magill, 1992, pp. 573–576. Robert James Butler, "Alice Walker's Vision of the South in *The Third Life of Grange Copeland,*" *African American Review* 27.2 (Summer 1993): 195–204.

—Debra Walker King

This Child's Gonna Live (1969), the award-winning first novel by Sarah Elizabeth *Wright, was lauded as a prose poem–folk epic for its richness, texture, characterization, heroine of epic proportions, use of the regional vernacular, and graphic depictions of life in a small rural oyster farming community in the 1930s. This is the story of Mariah Upshur, a native of Tangierneck, Maryland, the wife of Jacob and the mother of Skeeter, Rabbit, and Gezee. It centers on her children—born, dead, and about-to-be-born—her husband, and her driving desire to move her children north to a better life to escape the land of death that engulfs them. This life on the eastern shore is rife with racism, violence, brutality, dehumanizing incidents, interracial liaisons, hardships, illnesses (worms, tuberculosis), unrelenting poverty, oppression, calls on a gentle Jesus, dependence on a stern unyielding God, and the struggle of all to survive whole. Like Zora Neale *Hurston, Wright creates a detailed portrayal of a place, which leads to authenticity of language, culture, and community. Wright shows that both Black men and women are limited, measured, defined, and victimized by the same moral and sexual codes. Jacob, in an attempt to follow the code, becomes abusive and oppressive when his situation bars him from living up to the definition of what he should be and do. Mariah also suffers from the code and from an external definition of how she is to act, but she refuses to succumb. She takes hold of her life, defines herself, and with a passionate commitment strives for a better life without apologies or explanations—actions that in the 1990s label her a womanist. There is no evidence that things will change, but there is assurance that Mariah will continue to be her own person in spite of devotion to motherhood and family.

• Anne Z. Mickelson, "Winging Upward: Black Women: Sarah E. Wright, Toni Morrison, Alice Walker," in *Reaching Out: Sensitivity and Order in Recent American Fiction by Women,* 1979, pp. 112–124. Trudier Harris, "Three Black Women Writers and Humanism: A Folk Perspective," in *Black American Literature and Humanism,* ed. R. Baxter Miller, 1981, pp. 50–74.

—Helen R. Houston

THOMAS, JOYCE CAROL (b. 1938), novelist, poet, playwright, and educator. Born in Ponca City, Oklahoma, Joyce Carol Thomas was the fifth child in a family of nine children. As an adult, Thomas moved to San Francisco, where she worked as a telephone operator during the day while raising four children and taking college courses at night. She received a bachelor's degree in Spanish from San Jose State University, and in 1967 she earned a master's degree in education from Stanford University. She has received several awards, including a Danforth Graduate Fellowship at the University of California at Berkeley, the Before Columbus American Book Award (for her first novel, *Marked by Fire,* 1982), and the Djerassi Fellowship for Creative Writing at Stanford University. She has taught creative writing, black studies, and literature at California State University, Purdue University, and the University of Tennessee at Knoxville. In addition to lecturing at several universities and colleges in the United States, she has presented lectures, seminars, and workshops on creative writing and cultural studies in Nigeria and Haiti. Her work has appeared in a number of periodicals such as the *Black Scholar, American Poetry Review, Giant Talk, Yardbird Reader, Drum Voices,* and *Calafia.* She is a former editor of the West Coast black feminist magazine *Ambrosia.*

Before Thomas's first novel, *Marked by Fire,* was published she was known as a poet and playwright. As a poet, Thomas creates works that are commended for their serious themes, honest rendering of human experience, privileging of black people's customs, heritage, and language, and their believable personas. Her poems present vivid portraits of specific families and African American rituals. Her first forays into poetry are contained in three volumes, *Bittersweet* (1973), *Crystal Breezes* (1974), and *Blessing* (1975). In 1982, Thomas's earlier poems, along with new ones, were published in *Inside the Rainbow. Brown Honey in Broomwheat Tea* (1993) is Thomas's most recent volume of poetry. These lyrical poems continue to celebrate the beauty, heritage, and communality that make up a major part of the Thomas creative vision.

African American culture, heritage, and the need to pay homage to it also provide direction for Thomas's fictional canon, which to date includes six novels. Black children, their families, the black community, and the larger world's impingement on them is a key theme in the novels. Although Thomas's novels are accessible to juvenile audiences, and this is how they are usually classified, they offer much to adult readers. The award-winning *Marked by Fire,* the first novel of Thomas's Abyssinia series, signals its author's attention to the importance of community in black people's lives. Her other novels are *Bright Shadow* (1983), *Water Girl* (1986), *The Golden Pasture* (1986), *Journey* (1988), and *When the Nightingale Sings* (1992).

In her fiction and poetry, Joyce Carol Thomas is an important writer whose work is a significant contribution to the African American women's literary tradition.

• Charles P. Toombs, "Joyce Carol Thomas," in *DLB,* vol. 33, *Afro-American Fiction Writers after 1955,* eds. Thadious M. Davis and Trudier Harris, 1984, pp. 245–250.

—Charles P. Toombs

THOMAS, LORENZO (b. 1944), poet, literary and music critic, and educator with roots in the Black Arts movement. Lorenzo Thomas emerged from the Black Arts movement as one of the most prolific poets of the 1970s. Though best-known for his poetry, he also actively promotes the understanding and appreciation of all African American cultural forms, particularly music. Born in Panama to Herbert Hamilton Thomas and Luzmilda Gilling Thomas, Thomas immigrated to New York in 1948. As a native Spanish speaker, Thomas traces his interest in literature to his struggle to learn English in order to fit in with his schoolmates. While attending Queens College in the 1960s, Thomas joined the Umbra workshop, one of several experimental literary groups from which the Black Arts movement grew. Here, Thomas developed a poetic style marked by a wariness of the media and mass culture, pride in the African heritage and history, and a strong sense of political engagement. While Thomas also works powerfully in the lyric mode, such works as "Framing the Sunrise," "Historiography," and "The Bathers" typify his ability to combine heterogeneous source material into a comment on modern life. Underlying the often fragmented form of his poetry is Thomas's belief in the universal qualities of the experience of all people of African descent.

Thomas joined the United States Navy in 1968, serving as a military advisor in Vietnam in 1971. He reflects on the experience of war and the return to civilian life in such poems as "Wonders" and "Envoy." In 1973 he left New York to become writer in residence at Texas Southern University and has lived in the Southwest ever since. From his base in Texas, Thomas expanded his artistic range and increased his work with African American musical forms. He conducted writing workshops at Houston's Black Arts Center from 1974 to 1976 and was one of the first black authors to work in artists-in-the-schools programs in Texas, Oklahoma, and Arkansas. *Blues Music in Arkansas* (1982), cowritten with Louis Guida and Cheryl Cohen, is a product of his association with these programs. He was also an organizer for the Juneteenth Blues Festival. He remains active at both the grassroots and institutional levels, conducting readings, hosting music programs and writing for regional publications as well as working with the Texas Commission of Arts and Humanities and the Cultural Arts Council of Houston. He currently teaches at the University of Houston-Downtown.

Thomas's major collections of poetry are *Chances Are Few* (1979); *The Bathers* (1981), which contains uncollected early work as well as the text from three early publications; *Fit Music* (1972); *Dracula* (1973); and *Framing the Sunrise* (1975). His work also appears in anthologies including *Black Fire* (1968), *New Black Voices* (1972), *The Poetry of Black America* (1973), *Jambalaya* (1974), *American Poetry Since 1970: Up Late* (1987) and *Erotique Noire* (1992). In prose, Thomas has published literary and music criticism for both academic and general audiences including *Sing the Sun Up: Creative Writing Ideas from African American Literature,* which he edited in 1998. As yet, little criticism has been published on Thomas's work.

• Charles H. Rowell, "'Between the Comedy of Matters and the Ritual Workings of Man': An Interview with Lorenzo Thomas," *Callaloo* 4.1–3 (Feb.–Oct. 1981): 19–35. Tom Dent, "Lorenzo Thomas," in *DLB,* vol. 41, *Afro-American Poets since 1955,* eds. Trudier Harris and Thadious M. Davis, 1985, pp. 315–326.

—Jennifer H. Poulos

THOMAS, PIRI (b. 1928), autobiographer, essayist, playwright, poet, filmmaker, and lecturer. Piri Thomas was born Juan Pedro Tomás, in New York City's Spanish Harlem on 30 September 1928 of Puerto Rican and Cuban parentage. His early life was marked by involvement in violence and drugs, culminating in his arrest and imprisonment for attempted armed robbery. Thomas served seven years (1950–1956) of a five-to-fifteen year sentence. Upon his release from prison, he began working in prison and drug rehabilitation programs in New York City and has subsequently written three volumes of autobiography, a collection of short stories for adolescent readers, and a play. Today Thomas travels, presenting a program entitled Unity Among Us, stressing human dignity and people's relationship to the earth.

In 1967 Thomas published *Down These Mean Streets,* a chronicle of his youth. In crude but forceful language, *Down These Mean Streets* recounts Thomas's life on the streets, his experiences with sex, drugs, and crime, and his groping toward empowerment and self-worth through the expression of machismo, an aggressive code of male behavior derived from Hispanic culture.

While noting the autobiography's stylistic flaws, critics praised *Down These Mean Streets* for its powerful depiction of the hellish conditions of inner-city life and hailed Thomas as a chronicler of a previously "silenced" group—the negritos, or black Puerto Ricans, of Spanish Harlem. Thomas was compared favorably with James *Baldwin and Claude *Brown as a writer documenting his successful struggle to achieve personhood despite the dehumanizing conditions of minorities in America.

Savior, Savior, Hold My Hand (1972) recounts how Piri Thomas, newly released from prison, strives to rebuild his life. He converts to Christianity, works with street youths, seeks employment, marries, and starts a family. Critics generally expressed disappointment with *Savior, Savior Hold My Hand* for lacking the emotional intensity of Thomas's first book. *Seven Long Times* (1974), Thomas's account of his prison years, was criticized by some as a tepid retelling of events more forcefully recorded in *Down These Mean Streets* but praised by others as a testament to the human will to survive and as a call for prison reform. Thomas's collection of stories for young adults, *Stories from El Barrio,* appeared in 1978, to mixed reviews.

Piri Thomas continues to write, work in film production, and present his message of self-worth to varied audiences. He will probably be remembered, however, for *Down These Mean Streets,* the one volume of his autobiographical trilogy currently in print. The book provides readers with the satisfaction of seeing Thomas escape from the horror of his early life—a story often told in African American autobiography and fiction—but it speaks a note of warning, as well. More than twenty-five years after its publication, *Down These Mean Streets* reminds us that the conditions under which Thomas grew up are today the same or worse for thousands of young Americans. Tragically, many of them, unlike Piri Thomas, will not be able to leave the street and create new lives.

• "Thomas, Piri," in *CA,* vol. 73–76, ed. Frances C. Locher, 1978, pp. 604–605. "Piri Thomas," in *Contemporary Literary Criticism,* vol. 17, ed. Sharon R. Gunton, 1981, pp. 497–502. Marta E. Sanchez, "La Malinche at the Intersection: Race and

Gender in *Down These Mean Streets,*" *PMLA* 113 (Jan. 1998): 117–128.

—David L. Dudley

Thomas and Beulah (1986), which won the Pulitzer Prize for poetry in 1987, is the most well-known work by U.S. poet laureate Rita *Dove. Loosely based on the lives of Dove's maternal grandparents, this volume of poems opens with instructions that "These poems tell two sides of a story and are meant to be read in sequence." This chronological order gives the poems a novelistic sense of narrative. Details from the chronology included at the end of the poems tell us that Thomas was born in Wartrace, Tennessee, in 1900, and Beulah was born four years later in Rockmart, Georgia. Beulah soon moved to Akron, Ohio, and Thomas met her there almost twenty years later. They marry, have four daughters over the next ten years, and live out their lives in this midwestern town with an African American population of fewer than five percent. The cover sports a photograph of Dove's grandparents, giving a sense of the ordinary people whose quotidian lives will be fleetingly sketched within.

Although they live together for decades, the poem sequences reveal lives that barely intersect, more often the two moving in their own worlds. For example, when Beulah is pregnant for the third time, Thomas plans what he would teach the child if the child were a male. Thomas's poems have revealed so little interest in his children, that his desire for a son whom he can teach to be a man leaps out. Beulah's life, on the other hand, is filled with her daughters.

In two linked poems, Dove continues to explore the disconnection among family. Dove illustrates Thomas's main concern by naming the poem on his daughter's marriage "Variation on Gaining a Son." The poem begins with his focus on his daughter and the "shy angle" of her head, his ignorance of her life—and women's lives—revealed in his wonder: "where did they all learn it?" As he watches her with her bridegroom, Thomas forges a familiar relation from his empathetic response to the groom's fear, nervousness, and wonder. Dove skillfully connects this poem with one in Beulah's sequence, reversing father and daughter. In "Promises" Beulah recalls not her groom, but her father and the advice he whispered during the ceremony. Although her father, unlike Thomas with his daughter, may be focused on wishing her well, his words strike her as hypocrisy. Fathers and daughters, wives and husbands, all inhabit perspectives separated by lack of understanding and common interest. Yet the volume also mediates the sadness of disconnection with the richness of individual lives, imagined as well as lived.

• Helen Vendler, "In the Zoo of the New," *New York Review of Books,* 23 October 1986, 47–52. Ekaterini Georgoudaki, "Rita Dove: Crossing Boundaries," *Callaloo* 14.2 (Spring 1991): 419–433. Maxine Sample, "Dove's *Thomas and Beulah,*" *Explicator* 52.4 (Summer 1994): 251–253.

—Maggie Sale

THOMPSON, ERA BELL (1906–1986), editor, journalist, and autobiographer. Born 10 August 1906 in Des Moines, Iowa, Era Bell Thompson grew up in Driscoll, North Dakota, on her family's farm. Her contact with African Americans limited by regional population composition, she became fully aware of African American life, culture, and problems only after reaching adulthood.

Thompson attended North Dakota State University in Grand Forks, where she wrote for the university paper. Ill, Thompson left the university, and after recovering went to Chicago, working at a magazine, proofreading, writing advertising copy, and reviewing African Americans' books—exposing herself to the artistic outpourings of African Americans for the first time. She was particularly moved by W. E. B. *Du Bois's *The Dark Princess* (1928), which exalted "Negroes" and "blackness." Thompson later moved to Minneapolis, where she wrote features, advertising copy, and straight news for the *Bugle,* a weekly.

Encouraged and subsidized by Dr. Riley, a white minister interested in educating African Americans, Thompson returned to North Dakota State and received her degree in 1933 from Dawn College in Iowa, where she had followed Dr. Riley, who had been elected college president, and his family.

Returning to Chicago, Thompson continued her studies in journalism at Northwestern University and worked as a senior typist at the Department of Public Works, where she produced the humorous newspaper *Giggle Sheet.* Thompson later worked for the Illinois and United States Employment Services, where she deplored interracial, class, gender, and religious prejudice, recognizing the fundamental similarities Americans shared and looking toward a time when the "chasm" would disappear.

Thompson obtained a fellowship from the Newberry Library and published her autobiography, *American Daughter* (1946), a humorous recollection of her past for which she received the Patron Saint's Award (1968). Launched in her literary career, Thompson worked for the *Negro Digest* as an editor (1947) and for *Ebony* as associate editor (1947–1951), co-managing editor (1951–1964), and international editor (1964–1986).

In 1954, Thompson published *Africa: Land of My Fathers,* recounting her attempt to comprehend and reconnect with the land of her "forefathers." In 1963 she coedited *White on Black,* a collection of articles written by whites reflecting their views of African Americans. Thompson's articles can be found in *Phylon,* "Negro Publications and the Writer" (1950), *Negro Digest,* "Girl Gangs of Harlem" (1951), and *Ebony.* These include; "Love Comes to Mahalia" (1964); "Instant Hair" (1965); "What Weaker Sex?" (1966), which denounces men's treatment of women, reflecting her feminist leanings; and "The Vaughan Family: A Tale of Two Continents" (1975), which recounts the maintenance of contact between African and American descendants of a former slave for over a century.

Thompson received honorary doctorates from Morningside College (1965) and the University of North Dakota (1969), was inducted into the North Dakota Hall of Fame, and received the State's Theodore Roosevelt Rough Rider Award (1976).

Thompson died 29 December 1986. Her literary career reflects her quest to understand her people and their heritage as well as to encourage an understanding and cooperation between all Americans as human beings.

• Lorraine Elena Roses and Ruth Elizabeth Randolph, *Harlem Renaissance and Beyond: Literary Biographies of 100 Black Women Writers,* 1900–1945, 1990, pp. 321–352.

—Janet M. Roberts

THURMAN, WALLACE (1902–1934), novelist, editor, poet, playwright, and literary critic. After leaving his native Salt Lake City, Utah, for the University of Southern California, Wallace Thurman established the *Outlet,* a magazine similar to those being published as part of the artistic renaissance then blossoming in Harlem, New York. When it failed after just six months, he himself headed for Harlem, arriving in September 1925. The younger Thurman became a scathing critic of the bourgeois attitudes that motivated the Harlem Renaissance old guards like Alain *Locke and W. E. B. *Du Bois, charging that they professed their intellectual and artistic freedom while seeking white approval with slanted portrayals of African Americans. Eventually, he was able to articulate clearly, if not achieve completely, the aesthetic principles of the Harlem Renaissance from the late 1920s to the 1930s.

Thurman's *New Republic* essay, "Negro Artists and the Negro" (31 August 1927), decries the popular tendency to reduce African American music, fiction, poetry, and painting to the level of a fad presented in a "conventional manner about the 'best people.'" He claimed that many of the artists receiving praise from white and black critics alike were more interested in sociology and propaganda than art and, with few exceptions such as Langston *Hughes and Eric *Walrond, refused to create forms best suited for candid African American expression. Thurman published the experimental journal *Fire!!* (1926), which "was purely artistic in intent and conception," to address this problem. Contributors such as Langston Hughes, Zora Neale *Hurston, Arna *Bontemps, and Thurman himself were mainly interested in depicting African Americans "who still retained some individual race qualities and who were not totally white American in every respect save skin color." When the magazine folded after only one issue and left him with a thousand dollar debt (that took four years to discharge), he began the longer-running journal *Harlem, A Forum of Negro Life* (1928), which eventually suffered a similar financial fate. Undaunted, Thurman went on to write two novels. *The *Blacker the Berry* (1929) addresses a variety of controversial themes including homosexuality, intraracial prejudice, abortion, and ethnic conflict between African Americans and Caribbean Americans. The satiric *Infants of the Spring* (1932) is the only renaissance novel that evaluates the renaissance itself and the judgment rendered is harsh and unsparing. A third novel, *The Interne* (1932), written in collaboration with white Abraham L. Furman, is an exposé of unethical behavior at City Hospital on Welfare Island (now Roosevelt Island), where Thurman ultimately died. In his short life, Thurman was a prolific author whose works include published essays, screenplays, poetry, and short fiction.

While Thurman had an exceptional mind and was regarded as the spokesman for the younger generation of Harlem artists—especially by Langston Hughes who in *The *Big Sea* (1940) marvels at his voracious reading ability—his bohemian behavior and personality tended to undermine his artistic ability. Many of his literary efforts failed not because they lacked merit but because they lacked funds, which he tended to dissipate in a decadent lifestyle imitative of literary counterparts from Greenwich Village. Even his greatest financial success, *Harlem* (1929), a play produced in collaboration with William Jourdan Rapp, editor of *True Story* magazine, left him in debt. Significantly, whenever Thurman became strapped for money, his high artistic standards quickly evaporated. For example, Thurman ghostwrote stories for the lowbrow *True Story* magazine under such pseudonyms as Ethel Belle Mandrake and Patrick Casey.

Thurman's greatest literary shortcoming was his inability to sustain serious criticism of white America. Indeed, in an essay in the *Independent* (24 September 1927) magazine, Thurman goes so far as to claim that whites could probably write the African American story better than African Americans because the whites could be more objective about it. Thus, even while he sharply castigates African Americans for assimilating into the American mainstream to the point of losing their unique identity, he cannot imagine that the fear of dark skin traditionally exhibited by whites might also render them unobjective in their portrayal of African Americans. Essentially, then, Thurman's works reflect the struggle during the Harlem Renaissance to articulate an African American aesthetic while coping with the self-hatred that always hinders this endeavor. So far there is no biography or full-length critical study of his literary achievements.

• Dorothy West, "Elephant's Dance: A Memoir of Wallace Thurman," *Black World* 20 (Nov. 1970): 77–85. Mae Gwendolyn Henderson, "Portrait of Wallace Thurman," in *The Harlem Renaissance Remembered,* ed. Arna Bontemps, 1972, pp. 147–170. Arthur P. Davis, *From the Dark Tower: Afro-American Writers 1900 to 1960,* 1974. David Levering Lewis, *When Harlem Was in Vogue,* 1979. Daniel Walden, "The Canker Galls . . . , or, the Short Promising Life of Wallace

Thurman," in *The Harlem Renaissance Re-Examined,* ed. Victor A. Kramer, 1988, pp. 201–211.

—SallyAnn H. Ferguson

TILLMAN, KATHERINE DAVIS CHAPMAN (1870–?), poet, novelist, playwright, and essayist of the post-Reconstruction era. Born on 19 February 1870 in Mound City, Illinois, Katherine Tillman began writing as a child. At the age of eighteen she published her first poem, "Memory," in the *Christian Recorder.* Tillman attended the State University of Louisville in Kentucky and Wilberforce University in Ohio. After her marriage to the Reverend G. M. Tillman, she continued writing for the publications of the AME Church, especially the *A.M.E. Church Review,* which serialized her two novellas—*Beryl Weston's Ambition: The Story of an Afro-American Girl's Life* (1893) and *Clancy Street* (1898–1899). The *Review* also published her essays on famous African American women, poetry, Aleksandr Pushkin, and Alexandre Dumas. The A.M.E. Book Concern published *Recitations* (1902), a collection of verse, and three dramas—*Aunt Betsy's Thanksgiving* (n.d.), *Thirty Years of Freedom* (1902), and *Fifty Years of Freedom, or From Cabin to Congress* (1910).

Tillman's career demonstrates that African American women were very much a part of black literary culture during the post-Reconstruction era (1877–1915). Women writers like Frances Ellen Watkins *Harper, Amelia E. *Johnson, and Emma Dunham *Kelley defined roles for black women not only as wives and mothers but also as professionals and community leaders. In doing so these writers used literature to appropriate, critique, and revise the dominant conventions of race, gender, and class. Even more important, African American women writers, like their male counterparts, employed literature to explore the possibilities of self-definition and U.S. citizenship at a time when such prerogatives invited racist violence.

• Claudia Tate, introduction to *The Works of Katherine Davis Chapman Tillman,* 1991. Claudia Tate, *Domestic Allegories of Political Desire: The Black Heroine's Text at the Turn of the Century,* 1992.

—Claudia Tate

Tituba of Salem Village (1964) is a novel for young adults by Ann *Petry. Before this novel, Arthur Miller's *The Crucible* (1953) was the only major work to explore the Salem witch trials and to include an analysis of Tituba Indian, an African Barbadian slave indicted of witchcraft and, in 1692, sentenced to hang. Miller's impressions of Tituba's personality and character, however, are familiar stereotypes.

Unlike Miller, Petry examines Tituba's life history and arrives at more convincing interpretations of her character. In Petry's version, Tituba appears perceptive yet sometimes naive; courageous yet a victim; an outsider yet a survivor; a slave yet a heroine. The novel moves chronologically, emphasizing her servitude in Barbados, Boston, and Salem Village. Petry includes people whose words and actions affected Tituba's life—John Indian, her wise and devoted husband; Susanna Endicott, her uninhibited mistress in Barbados who sells her and John to raise cash to pay a gambling debt; Reverend Samuel Parris, her owner in Salem Village who prays and lectures about a loving God but votes to hang Tituba when people in the community accuse her of witchcraft; and Abigail, Parris's adolescent niece who first instigates the witch scare that ensnarls Tituba. The novel concludes with dramatizations of the arrests and trials of Tituba, Goody Good, and Goody Osborne, and the events that lead to the two women's deaths and Tituba's pardon.

Tituba emerges in this novel as a rounded character whose complexity derives from her words, thoughts, actions, and deeds within a dialogic context of circumstances surrounding her life as a slave and a foreigner. To paraphrase Petry, from her essay "The Common Ground" (*Horn Book Reflections,* 1969), which discusses the juvenile work, Tituba's history is retold across the centuries in her voice and the voices of her husband, owners, and accusers.

Following its publication, criticism of *Tituba* appeared mostly in library journals, newspapers, and popular magazines. Only after the 1970s did critics begin to analyze the work in scholarly journals and books. While critics praise the book for its absorbing story and convincingly human characters, their classifications differ. Throughout the 1960s critics applauded the book as biography for adolescents. In the 1970s critics noted the influence of history and called it a historical novel. In the 1990s critics began to reread *Tituba* as a novel that evolves from historical tidbit, similar to how Toni *Morrison created **Beloved* (1987).

• Lloyd W. Brown, "Tituba of Barbados and the American Conscience: Historical Perspectives in Arthur Miller and Ann Petry," *Carribean Studies* 13.4 (Jan. 1974): 118–126. Robert E. Morsberger, "The Further Transformation of Tituba," *New England Quarterly,* 48.3 (Sept. 1974): 456–458. Hazel Arnett Ervin, *Ann Petry: A Bio-Bibliography,* 1993. Trudier Harris, "Before the Stigma of Race: Authority and Witchcraft in Ann Petry's *Tituba of Salem Village*" in *Recovered Writers, Recovered Texts,* ed. Dolan Hubbard, forthcoming 1997.

—Hazel Arnett Ervin

TODD CLIFTON, more so than any other black male in the Harlem episode of Ralph *Ellison's **Invisible Man* (1952), seems programmed for success in mainstream America. He is personable (*Ras the Destroyer sees in him an ancient prince), intelligent, handsome (the narrator tells us that he had that "velvet-over-stone, granite-over-bone" look), and charismatic (he leads the black youths of Harlem); and he has managed to bridge the gap between his black world, Harlem, and the mainstream by working for the Brotherhood (an organization that represents the

Communist Party in the novel). Yet this progressive Black male is shot down on the street like a common criminal—by a white officer who does not see Todd Clifton, the promising Black youth.

In the novel, Todd Clifton is a foil for the narrator to demonstrate the narrator's lack of vision and insight. From the structure of the novel it is obvious that long before the narrator realizes the duplicity of the Brotherhood, Clifton does, and, as a result, leaves the organization. In a brutal fight with the narrator, Ras is about to cut Clifton's throat, but he is afraid that in killing Clifton he might be killing a future king, so he pleads with Clifton to leave the Brotherhood and join his nationalistic group in its liberation struggle. Immediately after the altercation, Clifton thanks the narrator for saving his life, and the narrator responds: "you didn't have to worry. He [Ras] wouldn't have killed his king." The narrator then says Clifton "turned and looked at me as though he thought I meant it." Although the narrator does not realize it, Ras has affected Clifton profoundly, for Todd's response to the narrator is that they will have to watch Ras because "on the inside . . . [Ras] is strong." The narrator assumes that Todd is referring to Ras's infiltration of the Brotherhood. A more reasonable interpretation is that Clifton means that while outwardly Ras is disorganized and chaotic, internally he is a very strong individual who because of his inner resolve will be an extremely difficult opponent.

Both Clifton and the narrator see Ras as being "outside of history," outside the mainstream, but Clifton admits that in order for Blacks to maintain their sanity they have to "plunge outside of history." That Clifton has come to see the Brotherhood as a negative force is evident in his behavior. In the next brawl with Ras, instead of beating Ras's men he beats up the white boys in the Brotherhood, his own men, pretending it was accidental, and shortly thereafter leaves the party. Clifton's selling the *Sambo dolls is symbolic of his own behavior in particular and Blacks in general. In the same way that he becomes the puppeteer manipulating the doll, the Brotherhood has become the puppeteer and he has been the organization's puppet.

—Ralph Reckley, Sr.

TOLSON, MELVIN B. (1898–1966), poet, novelist, playwright, newspaper columnist, and educator. The son of a Methodist preacher and a seamstress, Melvin Beaunorus Tolson was born in Moberley, Missouri, and grew up in several small midwestern towns. His father had an eighth-grade education and was skeptical of the value of college, but he instilled in his son a strong desire for knowledge. Tolson attended Fisk University from 1918 to 1919 and then transferred as a freshman to Lincoln University in Pennsylvania, where he graduated, receiving a BA with honors in June of 1923.

While at Lincoln University he met Ruth Southall; they married on 29 January 1922 and had four children. After graduating Tolson took a job as an instructor of English and speech at Wiley College in Marshall, Texas, where he remained for seventeen years. In addition to his teaching duties he coached the junior varsity football team, directed the theater club, cofounded the black intercollegiate Southern Association of Dramatic and Speech Arts, and organized the Wiley Forensic Society, a debating club that earned a national reputation by breaking the color barrier throughout the country and meeting with unprecedented success. Tolson also taught at Langston University in Oklahoma.

Working to support his family and becoming passionately involved in his projects, Tolson nevertheless reserved time for the arts. As a boy he enjoyed painting but was forced to give up that endeavor when his mother disapproved of a bohemian artist who expressed interest in taking the child to Paris. Turning to poetry, Tolson found an appropriate outlet for his creativity. In 1912 he published his first poem, "The Wreck of the Titanic," in the local newspaper of Oskaloosa, Iowa, where he was then living with his family. Several years later he was senior class poet at Lincoln High School in Kansas City, Missouri, and published two short stories and two poems in the school yearbook.

Tolson's first significant poem was published in 1939. "Dark Symphony" won the national poetry contest sponsored by the American Negro Exposition and was subsequently published in *Atlantic Monthly*, attracting the attention of an editor who would eventually publish Tolson's first collection of verse, *Rendezvous with America*, in 1944. This work was widely reviewed and generally well received.

During the academic year of 1931 to 1932 Tolson received a fellowship to pursue an MA in comparative literature at Columbia University, where he came into contact with the major figures of the Harlem Renaissance. Taking as the subject of his master's thesis the Harlem writers, Tolson was inspired by the achievements of those around him and resolved to contribute to the legacy black writers were establishing. While at Columbia Tolson was working on another collection of poetry, published posthumously in 1979 as *A Gallery of Harlem Portraits*. Both works reflect the early influence of Walt Whitman, Edgar Lee Masters, and Langston *Hughes and highlight Tolson's proletarian convictions and optimistic spirit; his later interest in the theme of black dignity is already obvious, as is his celebration of multiracial diversity in America.

Between the years 1937 and 1944, Tolson also contributed a weekly newspaper column to the *Washington Tribune*. Entitled "Caviar and Cabbage," the columns contain Tolson's views on race and class and have been collected in *Caviar and Cabbage: Selected Columns by Melvin B. Tolson* (1982), edited by Robert M. Farnsworth.

By the mid-1940s Tolson had written several novels and plays, all of which remain unpublished; several have been lost entirely. He was, however, gaining success as a poet. Named the poet laureate of Liberia, he published *Libretto for the Republic of Liberia* in 1953. The work marks Tolson's increasing poetic ambition. The *Libretto* is long, complex, and allusive, in places a surreal dream-vision. Allen Tate, in the preface, commends Tolson not only for assimilating the modernist tradition but for contributing to it.

As Tolson began to adopt the tenets of modernism, he was compared stylistically with T. S. Eliot, Ezra Pound, and Hart Crane, though he shared little of the fame and popularity they enjoyed in his lifetime. Nor did he share their vision. Instead of looking backward to the decaying civilizations of the European past, Tolson embraced Africa and its rich, vital heritage. He maintained that artists must follow the direction of their imaginations to find freedom, and Tolson finally found poetic freedom in the people of Harlem.

While working on revisions of *Libretto,* Tolson returned to some of the poetry he had written in Harlem. Those poems became the inspiration for an epic of Harlem that Tolson intended to dramatize black life in America. He designed the project to have five books, each representing a stage of the African American diaspora, but he only lived to complete one book, a collection entitled *Harlem Gallery: Book I, The Curator* (1965), told from the point of view of the curator. He shares vignettes, conversations, and philosophy, commenting on daily occurrences in his art gallery and facilitating a discussion of the role of the black artist in white America.

This work demonstrates Tolson's poetic maturity as well as his unique ability to combine the high formality of modernism with the bluesy, oral quality of African American storytelling. The work is linguistically precise and stylistically complex, but the lyrical quality of the poem never suffers, and critics placed it in a category with *The Waste Land, The Bridge* and *Paterson.*

The first volume of *Harlem Gallery* was introduced by Karl Shapiro, whose remark that Tolson "writes and thinks in Negro" contributed to the controversy over Tolson's place in poetry. His work was not well received during the 1960s, largely because members of the Black Aesthetic movement accused Tolson of posturing for a white audience and condemned his verse as too esoteric for the masses. Tolson's poetry indeed shares both the assimilationist tendencies Tate praised in his introduction to the *Libretto* and the distinctly African qualities Shapiro celebrated in his foreword to *Harlem Gallery,* making it difficult to classify him as either a modernist or a writer in the African American folk tradition. The publication of Robert Farnsworth's definitive biography in 1984, however, sparked renewed interest in Tolson; his work is now valued for the ethnic perspective it lends to modernism, and his poetry is now more frequently anthologized.

Melvin B. Tolson died in 1966, several months after being named to the Avalon Chair in humanities at Tuskegee Institute and receiving grants from the National Institute and American Academy of Arts and Letters and the Rockefeller Foundation. These honors indicate that *Harlem Gallery* had secured him public recognition in his lifetime and an established reputation that continues to grow.

• Joy Flasch, *Melvin B. Tolson,* 1972. Robert M. Farnsworth, *Melvin B. Tolson, 1898–1966: Plain Talk and Poetic Prophecy,* 1984. Michael Berube, "Masks, Margins, and African American Modernism: Melvin Tolson's *Harlem Gallery,*" *PMLA* 105 (Jan. 1990): 57–69. Melvin B. Tolson, Jr., "The Poetry of Melvin B. Tolson," *World Literature Today* 64 (Summer 1990): 395–400. Aldon L. Nielsen, "Melvin B. Tolson and the Deterritorialization of Modernism," *African American Review* 26 (Summer 1992): 241–255. Raymond Nelson, ed., *"Harlem Gallery" and Other Poems of Melvin B. Tolson* (1999), with an introduction by Rita Dove.

—Elizabeth Ann Beaulieu

TOOMER, JEAN (1894–1967), poet, dramatist, novelist, essayist, and philosopher. Jean Toomer is the author of **Cane* (1923) and a bridge between two distinct but contemporaneous groups of American writers. The first group consists of authors such as Langston *Hughes and Zora Neale *Hurston whose writings define the scope of the New Negro or Harlem Renaissance. The second group consists of such writers as Waldo Frank and Gorham Munson who dominated the literary scene of Greenwich Village and whose writings are characterized by experimentalism and political liberalism. Toomer was a comrade-in-letters to Frank and Munson, and a distant but influential figure to Hughes and Hurston, who admired the achievement of *Cane* (1923), the three-part collection of sketches, poetry, and drama that established a standard for the writers of the New Negro movement and that conveyed the profound search for meaning at the core of American modernism.

The only child of Nina Pinchback and Nathan Toomer, Nathan Pinchback Toomer was born on 29 March 1894 in Washington, D.C. Five years later Nina Pinchback divorced Nathan Toomer and returned to the home of her parents, Nina Hethorn Pinchback and P. B. S. Pinchback, former lieutenant governor of Louisiana during Reconstruction. After Nina Pinchback's death in 1909, the Pinchbacks assumed full responsibility for the rearing of their grandson. Toomer was encouraged in his literary pursuits by his grandmother, to whom *Cane* is dedicated, and by his uncle Bismarck Pinchback.

Educated in the public but segregated schools of Washington, Toomer graduated from Paul Laurence Dunbar High School in 1914. Between 1914 and 1919 he explored a spectrum of intellectual interests and attended such institutions as the University of Wisconsin, the American College of Physical Training in Chicago, the University of Chicago, and New York

University. In 1919 Toomer returned to Washington with neither a college degree nor an income. However, in the previous year Toomer had completed "Bona and Paul," the first of several stories in *Cane.* Although without firm prospects, Toomer's career as a writer was slowly assuming significance. In 1920 during a sojourn in Greenwich Village where he established friendships with Frank and Munson, Nathan Pinchback Toomer assumed the name of Jean Toomer. In search of a means to solidify his emerging identity as a writer, Toomer adopted the new name shortly after his immersion in the literary life of Greenwich Village and after reading Romain Rolland's *Jean Christophe* (1904) in whose protagonist Toomer had glimpsed his own potentiality as an artist.

More than a change of names, Toomer's acceptance in the summer of 1921 of a two-month appointment as acting principal at the Sparta Agricultural and Industrial Institute in Sparta, Georgia, provided him with the experiences that forged a new identity in art. Visiting the South for the first time, Toomer was captivated by the landscape of Georgia, its complex history of slavery and segregation, and the impact of African Americans upon southern culture. Enthralled by the beauty of African American vernacular culture, Toomer also detected its dissolution in the historic migration of African Americans from the South to the North and in the enlarging reach of industrialization.

Returning to Washington, Toomer began writing the masterpiece that he would later spurn but upon which his reputation as a writer remains secure. By December 1921 he had written "Kabnis," the drama that comprises the third section of *Cane.* One year later he had completed the experimental work that is a record of his discovery of his southern heritage, an homage to a folk culture that he believed was evanescent, and an exploration of the forces that he believed were the foundation for the spiritual fragmentation of his generation. With the assistance of Frank, who wrote the foreword to the first edition, Toomer's first and most important book was published in the spring of 1923 by Horace Liveright. Although it was praised by reviewers, *Cane* sold less than five hundred copies, casting a shadow on Toomer's triumphant literary debut.

After *Cane,* Toomer did not return to the setting that inspired the only book of fiction published during his lifetime. While the search for wholeness remains a central theme in Toomer's large but uneven canon, African American life is never again the subject. The later writings bear the influence of Georgei I. Gurdjieff, the Russian mystic and psychologist whose theories of human development Toomer accepted and promoted as gospel. Beginning in the year of *Cane*'s publication and continuing with few interruptions until his death on 30 March 1967, Toomer's commitment to Gurdjieff's theories had disastrous consequences for his writings. In his unpublished writings, Toomer creates situations that are little more than propaganda for Gurdjieff's theories. In these works one discovers protagonists who bear resemblances to Toomer himself and who function as teachers to characters who possess only a vague awareness of their spiritual potentiality. This regrettable mixture of cant and vanity explains Toomer's growing obscurity after 1923 for publishers foresaw only bankruptcy in such literary ventures. While Toomer continued to write until a few years before his death, he never again produced a work comparable to *Cane.*

Many African American writers claim Toomer as a literary ancestor. The nuanced portrayal of African American women in *Cane* is clearly discernible in Alice *Walker's Meridian (1976) and Gloria *Naylor's *The *Women of Brewster Place* (1980). Toomer's philosophical treatment of identity and race in both *Cane* and *Essentials* (1931), a collection of aphorisms that express his philosophy of life, have influenced the approaches to hybridity in Michael S. *Harper's *Nightmare Begins Responsibility* (1975) and Charles R. *Johnson's *Oxherding Tale* (1982).

Physically white but racially mixed, Toomer did not define himself as an African American but as an American. Toomer's lifelong effort to transcend what he regarded as the narrow divisions of race is fully explored in *Essentials* (1931) and the epic *The Blue Meridian* (1936). Toomer's position on race is the principal reason for the absence of racial themes in the writings produced during and after his discovery of Gurdjieff, as well as for his conscious disassociation from *Cane:* the work that has earned him a central place in the African American literary tradition.

• Nellie Y. McKay, *Jean Toomer, Artist,* 1984. Cynthia Earl Kerman and Richard Eldridge, *The Lives of Jean Toomer, A Hunger for Wholeness,* 1987. Therman B. O'Daniel, ed., *Jean Toomer: A Critical Evaluation,* 1988. Rudolph P. Byrd, *Jean Toomer's Years With Gurdjieff: Portrait of an Artist, 1923–1936,* 1990. Robert B. Jones, *Jean Toomer and the Prison-house of Thought: A Phenomenology of the Spirit,* 1993. Charles R. Larson, *Invisible Darkness: Jean Toomer and Nella Larsen,* 1993. Frederick L. Rusch, ed., *A Jean Toomer Reader: Selected Unpublished Writings,* 1993. Robert B. Jones, ed., *Jean Toomer: An Annotated Checklist of Criticism, 1923–1993 in Resources for American Literary Study* 21 (1995): 68–121. Robert B. Jones, ed., *Jean Toomer: Selected Essays and Literary Criticism,* 1996.

—Rudolph P. Byrd

TOURÉ, ASKIA M. (b. 1938), poet, community activist, lecturer, and educator. Askia M. Touré, in his multifaceted roles as poet, community activist, lecturer, and educator, is recognized as one of the original articulators of the Black Arts movement, an artistic and political movement that exhorted black artists to slough off what Touré termed "the white plaster" of their "negroness" and ultimately bring about the cultural, political, and physical liberation of all black Americans. From the late 1960s through the mid-

1970s, he served in various capacities: as a contributing editor for the magazine *Black Dialogue*, as an editor at large for the *Journal of Black Poetry*, and as a staff writer of *Liberator Magazine* and *Soulbook* with famed activist-playwright Amiri *Baraka and fellow poet-activist-critic Larry *Neal. Effecting a coalescence of poetic vision and social service, Touré has continued to combine his passion for poetry and his zeal for a politics of black sociocultural empowerment in the tradition of Langston *Hughes and Gwendolyn *Brooks and in a way that few "community poets" (griots) have been able to realize as successfully.

Born Rolland Snellings in Raleigh, North Carolina, on 13 October 1938, Touré moved with his father, mother, and younger brother to Dayton, Ohio, in 1944. While a student at Dayton's Roosevelt High School from 1952 to 1956, he poetically expressed himself not as a writer, but as a singer. An accomplished crooner of 1950s doo-wop melodies, Touré, instead of cutting a record deal with King label, opted for a three-year stint in the air force. From 1956 to 1959, Touré, as an air force enlistee, served under what he called "apartheid basic training conditions, defending a country where [he] couldn't even eat in a restaurant."

In 1960 Touré came to New York to study painting at the Arts Students League. A frequenter of Louis Micheaux's Black Nationalist Bookstore on the corner of 125th Street and 7th Avenue, Touré was literally a stone's throw from and within earshot of Black Muslim activist *Malcolm X and his outdoor sermons. "Brother Malcolm" and then-fledgling writers of the pre-Black Arts magazine *Umbra* such as Calvin C. *Hernton, Ishmael *Reed, Lorenzo *Thomas, Tom *Dent, and David Henderson perhaps inspired Touré's pen more than his paintbrush, and in 1963 Touré coauthored with Tom Feelings and Matthew Meade Samory Touré, an illustrated biography of a nineteenth-century African freedom fighter.

In the late 1960s, with the Black Arts movement's political burgeoning into the Black Power movement, Touré continued actively writing and working in Harlem. In 1970, black-run Third World Press published his long poem *Juju: Magic Songs for the Black Nation,* which pays homage to saxophonist John *Coltrane. Three years later, Touré published *Songhai!* A collection of poems and sketches that came out of novelist John O. *Killens's writers workshop at Columbia University, *Songhai!* reflects Touré's Afrocentric vision and his Islamic affiliation as a Sunni Muslim.

In 1974 Touré left a New York of personal, religious, and artistic turbulences for Philadelphia, carrying an intense commitment to community activism. Touré, along with the African People's Party, organized Philadelphia's black and poor communities against the alleged excesses of Mayor Frank Rizzo and the police department's attacks on the radical religious sect MOVE. Touré continued teaching, organizing, and writing into the 1980s, and his work culminated in *From the Pyramid to the Projects: Poems of Genocide and Resistance,* a collection of poems for which he won the American Book Award in 1989. The book, which recounts the horrors of white supremacy and the wonders of black resiliency, was the first American Book Award winner that has as its theme black genocide.

Touré lives and creates in Atlanta, has taught at Clark-Atlanta University, and since 1988 has been a dominant force in shaping and organizing the city's National Black Arts Festival. A tireless champion of his people, since 1985 Touré has spearheaded a campaign to introduce Africana studies in the Atlanta Public Schools System and is educating and organizing the black community against environmental racism throughout the South. Undaunted by such demanding work, Touré still finds time to write, having recently completed *Dawnsong,* which he calls an epic in lyric poetry.

• James A. Page, comp., *Selected Black American Authors,* 1977, pp. 267–268. Joanne V. Gabbin, "Askia Muhammad Touré," in *DLB,* vol. 41, *Afro-American Poets since 1955,* eds. Trudier Harris and Thadious M. Davis, 1985, pp. 327–333.

—James W. Richardson, Jr.

TREMAINE, PAUL. *See* Johnson, Georgia Douglas.

TROUPE, QUINCY THOMAS, JR. (b. 1943), poet, journalist, editor, producer, and educator. Born 23 July 1943 in New York City, Quincy Troupe grew up in St. Louis and later graduated from Grambling College. While playing on the army basketball team from 1962 to 1964, Troupe traveled through Europe and began to write. He met Jean-Paul Sartre who encouraged him to write poetry. He later became influenced by such poets as Pablo Neruda, Aimé Césaire, Jean Joseph Rabearivello, Jean *Toomer, and Sterling A. *Brown.

Troupe's first poem "What Is A Black Man?" was published in *Paris Match* (1964) and examines what it is to be a black man in a racially charged society. In 1972 Troupe published his first collection of poems, *Embryo Poems 1967–1971,* which explores themes of the intense experiences of black people in America. The use of dialect and the influence of jazz found in these poems become characteristic of Troupe's poetic style. *Snake-Back Solos: Selected Poems 1969–1977* (1979) won the American Book Award. Tom *Dent, reviewing Troupe's poetry in *Freedomways,* noted its roots in African oral traditions and found in his work the brilliance of African American music. In the volume of poetry *Skulls Along the River* (1984), Troupe meditates on an array of subjects, including love, family, and the importance of a folkloric past. *Weather Reports* (1991) is a collection of new and previously published poems. Wilfred D. Samuels writes in the introduction to the collection that the poems provide "insights into the hieroglyphics of Black culture deeply encoded in the matrix of its language and the blues dues sounds of its songs." Ishmael *Reed has hailed Troupe as one of few American writers who can authentically embody the jazz aesthetic in poetry, while also noting the power and the strength of Troupe's imagery.

Troupe's poems are also published in various periodicals including *Mundus Artium, Black World, Callaloo, Antioch Review, Umbra, Black Review,* the *Village Voice,* the *Black Scholar, American Music,* and others. His work also has been anthologized in *New Black Poetry, Poetry of Black America, A Rock Against the Wind, Celebrations: A New Anthology of Black American Poetry, The Before Columbus Foundation Anthology,* and *The New Cavalcade: African American Writing from 1760 to the Present,* among others. Troupe has also recorded his poetry with musicians George Lewis, Phil Upchurch, and Donal Fox, and in 1990 released an audio cassette entitled *Shaman Man.*

In 1968 Troupe edited *Watts Poets: A Book of New Poetry and Essays,* a project that arose from his participation in the Watts Writers' Movement. He was also associate editor of *Shrewd* magazine and the founding editor of *Confrontation: A Journal of Third World Literature* and *American Rag.* Troupe coedited with Rainer Schulte *Giant Talk: An Anthology of Third World Writing* (1972), which includes a large sampling of writings by American, African, Caribbean, and Latin American authors. In 1989 he edited *James Baldwin: The Legacy,* a collection of what Malcolm Arthur Whyte, in a review for the *Black Scholar,* calls "touching and revealing." Troupe is currently a contributing editor for *Conjunctions* magazine and senior editor for *River Styx* magazine.

Troupe won the American Book Award for his coauthored book, *Miles: The Autobiography of Miles Davis with Quincy Troupe* (1990). Praised for the frankness, honesty, and sheer depth in which Davis's life and music are discussed, *Miles* is considered by many music critics as a crucial text about the legendary musician. Troupe coproduced the *Miles Davis Radio Project* for PBS (1991–1992), for which he received the Peabody Award and the Ohio State Award.

Troupe coauthored *The Inside Story of T.V.'s "Roots"* (1978) with David L. Wolper. In 1989 Troupe was featured on Bill Moyer's Emmy Award–winning series, *The Power of the Word,* and he was also a writer for the television documentary "Thelonius Monk: An American Composer" (1991).

Quincy Troupe has lectured at many universities and colleges including Richmond College, University of California at Berkeley, Columbia University, University of Ghana at Legon, Lagos University in Nigeria, and others. He is currently a professor of literature at the University of California at San Diego, where he teaches creative writing. Troupe is a member of the board of directors for the Frederick Douglass Creative Arts Center, curator of the reading series held every year at the Museum of Contemporary Art of San Diego, and he is a judge for awards, scholarships, and fellowships offered by organizations such as the National Endowment for the Arts, Poetry Society of America, and the New York Foundation for the Arts.

• Horace Coleman, "Quincy Thomas Troupe, Jr.," in *DLB,* vol. 41, *Afro-American Poets since 1955,* eds. Trudier Harris and Thadious Davis, 1985, pp. 334–338. "Troupe, Quincy (Thomas, Jr.)," in *Black Writers: A Selection of Sketches from Contemporary Authors,* ed. Linda Metzger, 1989, pp. 551–553. *Cavalcade: African American Writing from 1760 to the Present,* vol. 2, eds. Arthur P. Davis et al., 1992, pp. 702–703. Ishmael Reed, "Can Poetry's Big Daddy Deliver San Diego?: Quincy Troupe Goes West," *San Diego Weekly Reader,* 22.5 (16 Dec. 1993).

—Kim Jenice Dillon

TRUEBLOOD. Jim Trueblood has generally been depicted as a Black male who, unable to control his sexual appetites, breaks one of humanity's greatest taboos—incest. He further has the dubious distinction of impregnating both his daughter and his wife. Their swollen bellies attest to both his virility and his shame. In Ralph *Ellison's **Invisible Man* (1952), however, the Trueblood incident involves much more than one Black man's sexuality. First it sheds some light on Mr. *Norton, the founder of the college the narrator attends. In his heart, if not physically, Norton is just as guilty of incest as Trueblood is, but society does not see his behavior as deviant. Secondly, the incident sheds light on the poor living conditions of Blacks in the South. In **Cane* (1923), author Jean *Toomer explores the effects of housing on southern Blacks. In "Karintha," the titular character, while quite young, becomes sexually active; she "had seen or heard, perhaps she had felt her parents loving." Toomer blames the living conditions, the "two room" plan, which force children and adults to sleep in close proximity to one another. In like manner, Ellison attacks the living conditions of the Truebloods. Jim explains that his daughter, Mattie Lou, sleeps with him and his wife because there is no heat and all of them "had to sleep together." The conditions under which the Truebloods survive are evident from Jim's reflections as the family sleeps. He thinks about "how to get some grub [for them] for the next day," because "I tried to get help but wouldn't nobody help us and I couldn't find no work or nothin'." That Mattie Lou is in the bed with Jim or that Jim is awake thinking about providing for his family is more an indictment of the living conditions of southern Blacks than it is about a Black male's sexuality. Finally Trueblood is important in the novel because unlike the narrator who tries to define his selfhood in terms of Westernization, Trueblood identifies with the Black folk tradition and uses this tradition to realize his humanity. At the nadir of his existence, rejected by his family, church, and community, Trueblood turns to the blues. "I sing me some blues that night ain't never been sung before, and while I'm singin' them blues I make up my mind that I ain't nobody but myself. . . ." The blues are cathartic, purging away both pain and guilt and allowing Trueblood to claim his humanity: "I ain't nobody but myself." This epiphany transforms Trueblood from a self-hating reprobate into a confident, self-affirming male, ready to brave family and community. "I'm a man," he affirms, "and a man don't leave his family."

—Ralph Reckley, Sr.

TRUTH, SOJOURNER (c. 1797–1883), itinerant preacher, abolitionist, and feminist. Sojourner Truth, born a slave in Ulster County, New York, a symbol of women's strength and black women's womanliness, is summed up in the phrase "ar'n't I a woman?" Known as Isabella VanWagener until 1843, she changed her name and became an itinerant preacher under the influence of Millerite Second Adventism.

In the 1840s Truth encountered feminist abolitionism during her stay in the Northampton (Mass.) Association of Education and Industry. There she met Olive Gilbert, who recorded *The Narrative of Sojourner Truth: A Bondswoman of Olden Time,* which Truth published in Boston in 1850. During the 1850s and 1860s sales to antislavery and feminist audiences of this narrative provided Truth's main source of income. Truth attended the 1851 Akron, Ohio, convention on women's rights in order to sell her book. The chair of that meeting, Frances Dana Gage, wrote the most popular version of Truth's speech and invented the "ar'n't I a woman?" refrain in 1863, which defined Truth's persona in the twentieth century.

The Narrative of Sojourner Truth went through seven editions, two of which—in 1875 (written) / 1878 (published) and 1884—entailed major additions. In the 1870s Truth's Battle Creek, Michigan, neighbor and manager, Frances Titus, added Truth's "Book of Life" (her scrapbook), which includes letters and clippings from periodicals; after Truth's death, Titus appended obituaries and eulogies. The most commonly reprinted version of Truth's *Narrative* is that of the 1870s, which includes the texts of Harriet Beecher Stowe's 1863 "Sojourner Truth, the Libyan Sibyl," which introduced Truth to a wide audience, and Gage's version of Truth's 1851 speech.

As the story of a religious woman who had been a northern slave, Truth's *Narrative* has not yet found its niche in the literature of former slaves, in which the South figures as the necessary context of slavery. Truth is more widely acknowledged for her speech acts in the 1850s.

• Carleton Mabee, *Sojourner Truth: Slave, Prophet, Legend,* 1993. Nell Irvin Painter, "Representing Truth: Sojourner Truth's Ways of Knowing and Becoming Known," *Journal of American History* 81 (Sept. 1994): 461–492. Nell Irvin Painter, *Sojourner Truth, a Life, a Symbol,* 1996.

—Nell Irvin Painter

TUBMAN, HARRIET (c. 1820–1913), self-emancipated slave, conductor for the Underground Railroad, Union spy, army scout, and nurse. Originally called Araminta, Harriet Ross Tubman was born on the Brodas plantation, Dorchester County, Maryland. She was disabled by narcoleptic seizures throughout her life after sustaining a severe injury to her head during her youth. Despite this frailty, Tubman's considerable strength and endurance were legendary. As a field slave, she mastered the secrets of woodcraft and navigation—skills that ensured her success as a conductor for the Underground Railroad. After her escape in 1849, Tubman returned to the South over fifteen times to rescue more than two hundred slaves. She successfully freed all of her family and never lost a single passenger during any of her escapes. More than forty thousand dollars was offered for her capture.

Tubman was a pivotal character in the war against slavery, first with the Underground Railroad, later with the Union army. She joined forces with the leading abolitionists of the day: William *Still, Thomas Garrett, Frederick *Douglass, Sojourner *Truth, and John *Brown. After emancipation Tubman served in the Union army as a spy, a scout, and a nurse. She was the only woman in American military history to plan and execute an armed expedition against enemy forces.

After the war Tubman recounted the story of her life to Sarah Elizabeth Bradford who wrote her biography, *Scenes in the Life of Harriet Tubman* (1869). Using the small profits from her biography and her military pension, Tubman established a permanent home for aged ex-slaves in Auburn, New York.

Canonized in Robert *Hayden's *"Runagate Runagate," Tubman is a popular icon in African American literature. She has come to symbolize both the Black woman's role in Black liberation and the African American's determination to be free.

—Deborah H. Barnes

TURNER, NAT (1800–1831), slave revolutionary. The leader of the bloodiest and most celebrated slave rebellion in U.S. history, Nat Turner was born the slave of Benjamin Turner on 1 October 1800 in Southampton County, Virginia. In *The *Confessions of Nat Turner* (1831), a portion of which was reputedly taken down from Turner's dictation, the slave rebel portrays himself as a precocious child who was recognized by blacks and whites alike as "intended for some great purpose." He learned to read and write early on and displayed a strong interest in religion. When not employed in field labor, Turner says he dabbled in experiments in making paper and gunpowder.

In 1821, Turner ran away from his master but returned voluntarily after about a month. In the next year he was sold to Thomas Moore, a Southampton farmer. In 1825, Turner received what he called his first heavenly vision, in which he was shown a war between "white spirits and black spirits" and warned of an approaching day of judgment. Communicating this knowledge to a local white man named Etheldred T. Brantley, Turner baptized himself and Brantley in anticipation of the great changes to come. On 12 May 1828, Turner witnessed a second vision, in which he learned of his messianic task: to "fight against the Serpent" in the approaching eschaton. In 1830, Turner was moved to the home of Joseph Travis, a local carriage maker who had married the widow of Thomas Moore. In February 1831, a solar eclipse convinced Turner that the time for an uprising of slaves was at hand. Planned to commence on 4 July 1831, the uprising was postponed until 21 August when Turner and his inner circle met at the home of Joseph Travis and killed Travis, his wife and child, and two apprentices. For the next forty hours, Turner and a varying number of followers (perhaps as many as eighty at the height of the rebellion) attacked a series of farms, executing at least fifty-seven white people, on their way to Jerusalem, the Southampton County seat. Repulsed by white militia on the afternoon of 22 August, Turner's forces became disorganized and scattered. After a final skirmish with whites on the morning of 23 August, Turner escaped, hiding in the general vicinity of the Travis farm until he was captured on 30 October. The next day he was taken to the county jail, where he was interviewed for three days by Thomas R. Gray. At his 5 November trial Turner pleaded not guilty to charges of conspiracy to rebel and making insurrection; he was subsequently found guilty and was executed by hanging on 11 November 1831.

Turner's rebellion traumatized the white South and galvanized the radical antislavery movement in the North. In spite of Gray's attempt in the *Confessions* to portray Turner as a demented religious fanatic, many African Americans in the South and the North regarded "Prophet Nat" as a political hero. Albert E. Stone's *The Return of Nat Turner* (1992) demonstrates that as a symbol of uncompromising militancy in the pursuit of freedom, Turner's example remains as potent and as controversial in the late twentieth century as it was in the antebellum era.

• Henry Irving Tragle, *The Southampton Slave Revolt of 1831*, 1971. Eric J. Sundquist, *To Wake the Nations*, 1993.

—William L. Andrews

TURPIN, WATERS (1910–1968), educator, novelist, playwright, director, television lecturer, and drama critic. Waters Edward Turpin, the only child of Simon and Mary Rebecca (Waters) Turpin, was born 9 April 1910 on the eastern shore of Maryland in Oxford. At the time of his death, 19 November 1968, he had been married to Jean Fisher Turpin for thirty-two years. They had two children—Rosalie Rebecca Turpin Belcher and John Edward Turpin.

Although Turpin's career was multifaceted, he was primarily a teacher. He began his teaching career in 1935 at Storer College in Harpers Ferry, West Virginia, where he taught English and coached football. In June 1938, he left Storer to pursue a doctoral degree at Columbia University, where he had received his master's degree in 1932. (He received the EdD in 1960.) In 1940 Turpin joined the faculty at Lincoln University (Pa.) and stayed there until 1950, when he was invited by Nick Aaron Ford, chair of the English Department, to come to Morgan State College, where his wife Jean was already teaching. Returning to Morgan was returning to his roots. He had received his high school diploma from Morgan Academy and his BA from Morgan State College, where he was editor in chief of the *Morgan Newsletter.*

During his eighteen years at Morgan, Turpin was a teacher of composition and literature, assistant director of drama, chair of the Division of Humanities for two years, television lecturer, coauthor with Nick Aaron Ford of a textbook: *Basic Skills for Better Writing* (1959), and coeditor with Ford of *Extending Horizons: Selected Readings for Cultural Enrichment* (1969). As assistant director of drama, Turpin produced and directed two of his plays: *And Let the Day Perish* (1950) and *St. Michael's Dawn* (1956), a three-act drama of the life of Frederick *Douglass. There are other plays, short stories, and poetry in Turpin's unpublished collection.

However, Turpin's novels are what gained him recognition in African American literary history. Turpin's creative abilities were recognized early, and among those encouraging him to write was novelist Edna Ferber, who was the employer of Turpin's mother. Although Turpin worked on several novels, only three were published. The first, *These Low Grounds* (1937), set on the eastern shore of Maryland, tells the story of four generations of an African American family. The second novel, *O Canaan!* (1939), traces the progress of migratory farmers who left the South for Chicago during the depression. Turpin's third and final published novel, *The Rootless* (1957), is a historical novel that depicts slave practices in eighteenth-century Maryland.

Turpin's eloquent, dramatic, and imaginative writings are accurate portrayals of African American life during the first half of the twentieth century. The literary legacy of Waters Turpin to his students, colleagues, friends, and reading audience is most memorable.

• Nick Aaron Ford, "The Legacy of Waters E. Turpin, Part I and II," *Afro-American Newspaper,* Magazine Section, 14 and 21 Dec. 1968, 1.

—Margaret Ann Reid

"Two Offers, The." Frances Ellen Watkins *Harper's "The Two Offers" was first published in the *Anglo-African Magazine* in 1859 and is considered the first published short story by an African American woman in the United States. Harper provides no racial dimension to the characters, and the thematic purpose of the story is to challenge contradictions inherent in social values regarding women's roles and to offer an alternative to those conventions and traditions. In this regard, the short story suggests strong similarities between black society and white society, as sexism dominates both social spheres. At the same time, it indicates the gender solidarity that existed in the radical abolitionist community and the feminist themes women activists, such as Harper, espoused in their literature.

The story concerns two cousins, Laura and Janette, who consider two offers of marriage extended to Laura. Though cousins, they represent two different classes, one of privilege and the other of poverty. By juxtaposing their class differences, Harper uses economic contrast to suggest that gender perspectives are related to class consciousness.

In particular, Laura feels she must marry or face the fate of becoming an old maid. Janette, on the other hand, is unmarried and has forsaken tradition to keep her independence and to pursue a writing career. In this regard, Janette parallels Harper, who was unmarried when she published the story. Even though Harper married in 1860, she continued to write and to lecture against slavery. Janette, the feminist protagonist, completely rejects the role of woman as wife and mother, and her name, Janette Alston, alludes to Jane Austen, the nineteenth-century English writer.

Janette advises Laura to refuse both proposals because her indecision indicates a deficiency of affection for either of the two men. She also states that for Laura to marry for economic reasons relegates the bond to a business arrangement, which defiles the sanctity of the union. Janette's analysis is a provocative challenge to the economic bondage that many women faced during the nineteenth century, in which marriage offered security and class status, and, conversely, a kind of enslavement.

Ten years later when the cousins reunite, Laura is gazing into death's gaping mouth, having suffered a possessive, repressive marriage to a man who violated their vows and acted as if the marriage contract were a bill of sale. In response, the omniscient narrator reflects the feminist politics of Harper and the women's movement, criticizing society's denial of "the true woman," whose "conscience should be enlightened, her faith in the true and the right established and scope given to her Heaven-endowed and God-given faculties."

Harper's rejection of romantic illusions and her advocacy of women's independent spirit are not a wholesale rejection of marriage, as Janette does commit to an egalitarian union. Harper's intention is to dispel romantic attraction and emotional manipulation as determinants for marriage. Moreover, the theme illustrates how inequitable unions lead to spiritual demise and, in this case, to heartbreak and actual death. But the contrast between the two women represents the real two offers: independence, autonomy, and life, or oppression, depression, and death.

• Jean Fagan Yellin, *Women and Sisters,* 1989. Mary Helen Washington, *Invented Lives: Narratives of Black Women 1860–1960,* 1990.

—Melba Joyce Boyd

U

UNCLE JULIUS McADOO. An aged former slave, Uncle Julius McAdoo serves as the folk narrator in the stories of Charles Waddell *Chesnutt's *The *Conjure Woman* (1889). He connects the frame stories told by his employer, a white midwestern businessman transplanted to the South, with the lives of slaves in eastern North Carolina and the conjuring activities of Aun' Peggy. To a marked degree, Uncle Julius resembles the nineteenth-century stereotype of the loyal family servant found in the nostalgic postbellum fiction of such white writers as Thomas Nelson Page and Joel Chandler Harris, the creator of Uncle Remus. Strongly superstitious, Uncle Julius seems naive and simple, but his remarkable narration reveals that he is imaginative, perceptive, and shrewd. He often uses storytelling as a means to advance his own interests, sometimes at the expense of the white businessman narrator. Julius's stories range widely in mood and effect, from the comic to the tragic. Unlike the "uncles" of Page and Harris, Julius never grows nostalgic for the "good ol' days" before emancipation. Instead his stories emphasize the threats slavery presented to ordinary black people caught in its grip and their ingenuity in resisting slavery's dehumanization. Uncle Julius McAdoo represents one of the earliest adaptations of the slave trickster to literary purposes in the African American tradition.

• Lucinda MacKethan, "Charles Chesnutt's Southern World: Portraits of a Bad Dream," in *The Dream of Arcady,* 1980, pp. 86–104. William L. Andrews, introduction to *The Collected Stories of Charles W. Chesnutt,* 1992.

—Paula Gallant Eckard

UNCLE TOM. Although Harriet Beecher *Stowe's extremely successful 1852 abolitionist novel *Uncle Tom's Cabin* was the original source for the Uncle Tom idiom, its meaning is best understood through an examination of the numerous stage shows loosely based on the best-selling book. Theatrical entrepreneurs who did not share Stowe's antislavery zeal took great liberties with the novel's protagonist. Uncle Toms of the stage were usually depicted as thoroughly subservient individuals who willingly betrayed their black brethren in order to please their white masters. As a result, the Uncle Tom label is assigned to individuals who sabotage other blacks in order to further their own advancement. Known popularly as Tom shows, stage productions of *Uncle Tom's Cabin* were a mainstay of American theater well into the twentieth century. Uncle Tom became a trope, a figure of speech used to refer to fawning, selfish black men. Thus Uncle Tom's ubiquitousness had a definitive impact on mainstream society's assumptions about actual black men.

By the turn of the century, a curious battle developed between the purveyors of popular culture, who continued to promote Uncle Tom, and African American writers and social critics eager to bury the demeaning image. Thus filmmakers made several films similar to the stage shows. Even the Siam-based musical *The King and I* (1951) contains an ode to *Uncle Tom's Cabin.* For a collection of short stories on the black experience in the South, Richard *Wright used the title **Uncle Tom's Children* (1938). Ralph *Ellison noted that a Tom show was one of the original impetuses for his novel **Invisible Man* (1952). Ishmael *Reed manipulated characters' names for his novel **Mumbo Jumbo* (1972), and Robert Alexander wrote a provocative play entitled *I Ain't Yo Uncle: The New Jack Revisionist Uncle Tom's Cabin* (performed in Hartford, 1995). Nonetheless, the negative associations of the name remain consistent. For example, the Uncle Tom label is often applied to staunchly conservative African American Supreme Court Justice Clarence Thomas. It seems likely that this pejorative label will remain in the American vernacular.

—Patricia A. Turner

Uncle Tom's Cabin. *See* Stowe, Harriet Beecher.

Uncle Tom's Children, a collection published in 1938 of four of Richard *Wright's short stories (two of which had appeared previously) and the earliest of Wright's major publications. The book we know as *Uncle Tom's Children* is a somewhat different book from the original because two extraordinarily important additions were made in 1940 in a new edition. These two additions, "The Ethics of Living Jim Crow," a preface to the collection, and "Bright and Morning Star," a new story, changed the shape of the book, giving it a different form and focus. "The Ethics of Living Jim Crow" is an extended essay describing events, largely from Wright's own life, outlining the unspoken rules and regulations governing interaction between blacks and whites in Richard Wright's Mississippi and in the South in general. All of the stories in *Uncle Tom's Children* are about some aspect of racial repression and black response to it.

The first, "Big Boy Leaves Home," is the story of a young, innocent adolescent boy who is forced by circumstances to shoot in self-defense a white man who threatens to take his life. Big Boy, while he hides waiting to escape with his friend on a truck headed north, sees that friend brutally lynched, burned alive, and his body mutilated.

"Down by the Riverside" takes its title from a spiritual of that name. It tells of Mann, who in attempting to save his family during a flood steals a boat and must in self-defense kill the boat's white owner. It is discovered that he killed a white man, and rather than be lynched, he chooses to run for the river knowing he will be killed by soldiers armed with rifles.

"Long Black Song," the third story, tells of a farmer, Silas, and his wife, Sarah. It opens with Sarah tending her baby while Silas has gone to town. A young salesman appears who wants to sell Sarah a clock. Sarah, after a complicated series of events, has sexual relations with him. Silas discovers her infidelity and kills the salesman. A mob forms and Silas is burned to death defending himself with his rifle to the end.

"Fire and Cloud" recounts the experience of Reverend Taylor, a black minister who discovers the necessity of uniting political action with religion as he leads his congregation together with whites on a march to City Hall to obtain the promise of food. The story ends with the assertion, "Freedom belongs to the strong."

The final story in *Uncle Tom's Children,* "Bright and Morning Star," explores the possibility of union between black and white communists in order to achieve common political ends. The story reveals the heroism of an ordinary black Southerner, Johnny-Boy, who fights to organize across racial lines to bring about political and social change. Johnny-Boy's mother, Ant Sue, gives up her life to kill an informer before he is able to impart his information to the sheriff. The story ends with the deaths of both mother and son.

• Donald B. Gibson, *The Politics of Literary Expression: Essays on Major Black Writers,* 1981, pp. 25–35. Edward Margolies, "Wright's Craft: The Short Stories," in *Critical Essays on Richard Wright,* ed. Yoshinobu Hakutani, 1982, pp. 128–138.

—Donald B. Gibson

Up from Slavery. As autobiography, institutional history, and how-to book, *Up from Slavery* (1901) signals the beginnings of African American modernism. Though Booker T. *Washington was born a slave, it would be wrong to categorize *Up from Slavery* as a conventional slave narrative. Indeed Washington makes a conscious effort to avoid an authorial fixation on the evils of slavery. To live as a slave, Washington observes, was to live in "miserable, desolate, and discouraging surroundings," which was the case, he asserts, "not because my owners were especially cruel," but because life as a slave was a life of indigence and want.

Up from Slavery is a compelling literary event because Washington successfully weds his rags-to-riches story with narratives of racial conciliation and uplift. With antiblack sentiment in the South reaching a level where lynching occurred "more than weekly," Washington's task was to assuage the fears of a white citizenry who viewed the relatively new African American labor force as a threat to their economic and political well-being. Washington needed to persuade his largely white readership that African Americans could, in spite of whites' post-Reconstruction enmity with them, make important contributions to the southern economy. Hence the message behind Washington's narrative, from the description of the squalid cabin in which he was born and raised to the triumphant moment when dusting and cleaning a classroom earns him an education at Hampton Institute, is that deprivation is not so much a source of disillusionment as it is an opportunity to prove one's merit. These moments provide signposts that point the reader to Washington's present station, Tuskegee Institute. The reader comes to understand that humility and industry provide entry to the American power elite, not for the purpose of individual gratification but for the improvement of an entire race and, eventually, an entire nation. Tuskegee stands as the physical symbol that blacks in the South have found their way to self-reliance: Washington relates difficulties overcome, remembers the school's humble beginnings in a stable and a hen house, and recounts the students' first attempt to make bricks with which to build the campus.

But it is Tuskegee as symbol that gives Washington space to preach his message of conciliation. The culminating moment of both the book and his life, then, is to be found in his *"Atlanta Exposition Address," delivered in 1895. The speech gave Washington a "reputation that in a sense might be called National." But if Washington allows himself a moment of self-aggrandizement, he quickly tempers it with self-depreciating irony when he states: "What were my feelings when this invitation came to me? I remembered that I had been a slave; that my early years had been spent in the lower depths of poverty and ignorance, and that I had had little opportunity to prepare me for such a responsibility as this."

The speech's startling success, with its claim that the social separation of the races need not impede economic progress in the South, underscores the main theme of *Up from Slavery,* that through cooperation and mutual respect whites and blacks, even in the slavery-scarred South, could move beyond the fears, animosities, and prejudices that had hampered regional development for decades. To accentuate this optimistic view of the South's potential, *Up from Slavery* avoids references to southern racial conflict, denies that racism is pervasive among southern whites, and attempts to inspire its white reader with a sense of moral, if not social obligation, to help lift the formerly enslaved and their children from their disadvantages.

Up from Slavery ends with Tuskegee Institute in a state of financial health and Washington in an exalted position as the confidant of U.S. presidents and the agent of business magnates intent on solving the race problem. The final scene of the autobiography finds

Washington in Richmond, Virginia, the capital of the fallen Confederacy, lionized by whites and blacks alike after delivering a message of "hope and cheer" to a racially mixed audience. Reminded of the fact that as a penniless young man he had "slept night after night under a sidewalk" in Richmond, Washington savors his good fortune, not for himself alone but for the sake of "the state that gave me birth." Although the twentieth century saw many African Americans suffer the indignities of racial discrimination and poverty (both rural and urban), *Up from Slavery* accommodates, on its face, the notion that change was sweeping across the land.

• Booker T. Washington, *Up from Slavery,* ed. William L. Andrews, 1995.

—Herman Beavers

URSA CORREGIDORA. The protagonist and narrator of Gayl *Jones's 1975 novel, **Corregidora,* Ursa is a blues singer and songwriter who descends from a long line of slavery and incest. Her earliest memories revolve around her being told the terrible history of her great-grandmother and grandmother who were enslaved, repeatedly raped, and forced into prostitution by the Brazilian plantation owner Old Corregidora; both Ursa's grandmother and her mother are his daughters. In order that Corregidora's atrocities are never forgotten, Ursa, like her mother, has been charged to "make generations" who will bear witness to this familial narrative of victimization and abuse. But she loses the baby she is carrying and is rendered sterile when Mutt Thomas, her jealous husband, pushes her down a flight of stairs.

Ursa's role as an artist is pivotal to her finding a way to bear witness and simultaneously break free of her foremothers' history; she must learn to identify herself through her voice and her creativity, rather than through her womb. Eventually, by recognizing her own (as well as her foremothers') potential for violence, Ursa also discovers her own capacity for pleasure and desire. Her uneasy acknowledgment of sexual desire alongside her history of racial and sexual abuse entails her understanding and working against the rigid self-identification imposed on her by her foremothers. Through Ursa, Gayl Jones grapples with pernicious stereotypes of black women's sexuality as well as issues of speech, silence, art, history, and self-empowerment, all predominant themes in late-twentieth-century African American women's writing.

• Claudia C. Tate, "*Corregidora:* Ursa's Blues Medley," *Black American Literature Forum* 13 (Fall 1979): 139–141. Missy Dehn Kubitschek, *Claiming the Heritage: African-American Women Novelists and History,* 1991.

—Amy S. Gottfried

V

VAN DYKE, HENRY (b. 1928), editor, journalist, and novelist. Born in Allegan, Michigan, Henry Van Dyke spent his childhood in Montgomery, Alabama, where his father taught at Alabama State Teachers College. He returned to Michigan for high school and remained to receive an MA in journalism from the University of Michigan in 1955. While at Michigan, Van Dyke received the Avery Hopwood Award for Fiction. After graduating he worked as a journalist and editor in Michigan, Pennsylvania, and New York. During his time on the editorial staff at Basic Books in New York he finished his first published novel, *Ladies of the Rachmaninoff Eyes* (1965). His short pieces have appeared in *Transatlantic Review, Generation, Antioch Review,* and *The O. Henry Prize Stories,* 1979.

Van Dyke's work addresses race relations issues prominent in the 1960s and 1970s. He writes about conflict among African Americans, between African Americans and white and Jewish Americans. He is influenced by modernist writers and ideas. The plot of *Ladies of the Rachmaninoff Eyes* revolves around the production of a Gertrude Stein play by self-proclaimed members of her circle. The production serves as the stage for exploring the relations between the young African American protagonist, Oliver, and the Jewish production team. His second novel, *Blood of Stawberries* (1968), is dedicated to the white chronicler of the Harlem Renaissance, Carl Van Vechten. Issues of race relations again arise in *Dead Piano* (1971), his third novel, this time within the African American community. Drawing on current affairs at the time of publication, *Dead Piano* uses an outsider, a militant African American group, to upset the social structure of a light-skinned, middle-class African American family. In the microcosm of a few stressful hours in the family's apartment, the characters address large social issues of assimilation and separatism.

• Granville Hicks, "Literary Horizons," *Saturday Review,* 4 Jan. 1969, 93. Edward G. McGhee, "Henry Van Dyke," in *DLB,* vol. 33, *Afro-American Fiction Writers after 1955,* eds. Thadious M. Davis and Trudier Harris, 1984, pp. 250–255.

—Caroline Senter

VASHON, GEORGE B. (1824–1878), essayist and poet. George Boyer Vashon was the first African American to graduate from Oberlin College and the first to become a lawyer in New York State. Born in Carlisle, Pennsylvania, Vashon attended school in Pittsburgh and served there as secretary of the first Juvenile Anti-Slavery Society in the nation (1838). He earned a BA from Oberlin (1844) and studied law in Pittsburgh but was denied admittance to the bar because of his race. Embarking on a thirty-month exile in Haiti, Vashon stopped in New York, where he was admitted to the bar in 1848. He taught at College Faustin in Port-au-Prince; then from 1850 to 1854 he practiced law in Syracuse, New York, and for the next three years was professor of belles lettres and mathematics at New York Central College in McGrawville. Returning to Pittsburgh, Vashon married Susan Paul Smith (1857), with whom he had seven children. He was a principal and teacher in Pittsburgh schools until 1867 and thereafter held government posts in Washington, D.C., worked for race advancement with the Colored Men of America, and published learned essays, poems, and letters in periodicals. It is commonly thought that he died of yellow fever in Mississippi.

"Vincent Ogé" (1854), Vashon's 391-line epic on the Haitian insurrection (1790–1791), is a signal imaginative achievement in African American poetry of the nineteenth century. The slaves' revolt becomes not only a metaphor for universal racial conflict and mankind's resistance to tyranny, but also a symbol of a world in perpetual chaotic motion. Within a finely structured, dramatic whole Vashon sustains an ambience of instability with image patterns of flickering light, storms, blood, and warfare, and by shifts in diction, in metrical and stanzaic form, voices, and scenes. Measured by the artistry of "Vincent Ogé" and his essays, his labors for racial justice, and his academic achievements, Vashon was a man of extraordinary courage and talent.

• [George B. Vashon obituary notice], *Oberlin Review,* 20 Nov. 1878 (rpt. from People's Advocate, n.d.). Joan R. Sherman, *Invisible Poets: Afro-Americans of the Nineteenth Century,* 2d ed., 1989.

—Joan R. Sherman

VASSA, GUSTAVUS. *See* Equiano, Olaudah.

VELMA HENRY is the main character in Toni Cade *Bambara's *The *Salt Eaters* (1980), whose healing is the connecting thread for the many subplots in the novel. Velma is the kind of woman upon whom others depend and who appears to be perpetually strong. She has, with her husband Obie, founded and managed the now-fragmented and troubled Academy of Seven Arts. She actively participates in a women's political caucus and the Seven Sisters arts collective, as well as maintaining a marriage, raising a son, and working full-time as a computer programmer. The fragmentation and splintering that characterize the community exist also within Velma herself, and she attempts suicide as a means of finally sealing herself off from escalating rage and fear.

Velma's characterization mirrors many of the extraordinarily strong women in much of African American literature, but with a difference. She is one who, by virtue of her inability to remain self-sufficient, is given an alternative: the healing that comes from reconnecting with herself, her past, and the life-giving values she has forsaken in her unremitting struggle for justice. Velma's suicide attempt is the culmination of exhaustion and an alienation from her body and her legacy as an African American and a woman. As the healer *Minnie Ransom says, Velma must release the pain, but that release cannot come until she decides she wants the "weight óf being well," and will return to the community a stronger, more able, but more deeply and spiritually connected human being.

—Ann Folwell Stanford

VESEY, PAUL. *See* Allen, Samuel W.

Voice from the South, A. Published during the period now known as the Woman's Era, Anna Julia *Cooper's *A Voice from the South* (1892) is a landmark feminist text. In this volume of essays and lectures, Cooper argues that just as white people cannot speak for African Americans, so African American men cannot "be wholly expected fully and adequately to reproduce the exact Voice of the Black Woman."

The volume consists of two parts, the first comprised of four essays focused directly on women's issues: "Womanhood, a Vital Element in the Regeneration and Progress of a Race," "The Higher Education of Woman," "Woman vs. the Indian," and "The Status of Woman in America." The second half, also made up of four essays, continues this attention to women's rights while broadening the focus to discuss U.S. history as multicultural from the beginning; representations of African Americans in contemporary American literature, especially fiction by William Dean Howells and Albion W. Tourgée; discrimination against African Americans in housing; and philosophical positivism and skepticism versus Cooper's own articulated belief in Christian optimism.

Cooper's feminism in *A Voice from the South* springs from various sources. It combines Victorian ideologies of true womanhood (the belief that women are by divine design moral, intuitive, spiritual, and nurturing); a radical and uncompromising belief in women's intellectual equality with men; turn-of-the-century class-inflected theories of racial uplift; and Cooper's own deeply felt Christian egalitarianism and hatred of oppression. The result is an impassioned scholarly argument advocating fundamental change in the status and treatment of African American women. While Cooper's main target is white racism, she also criticizes African American men, of whom she observes, "While our men seem thoroughly abreast of the times on almost every other subject, when they strike the woman question they drop back into sixteenth century logic." Also singled out are the hypocrisy and racism of white feminists, including leaders such as Anna Shaw and Susan B. Anthony, whose pitting of white women's goals against the rights of people of color Cooper attacks in "'Woman vs. the Indian.'"

Cooper expresses her core belief in the inseparability of women's issues and the struggle for racial justice in her often-quoted statement, "Only the BLACK WOMAN can say 'when and where I enter, in the quiet, undisputed dignity of my womanhood, without violence and without suing or special patronage, then and there the whole Negro race enters with me.'" She names as basic civil rights issues: protecting African American women from sexual attacks; speaking out against racist female stereotypes; making education available to all African American women; and addressing the economic oppression that consigns the majority of black women and their families to poverty. The African American woman's situation is the race's situation, in her view. Connecting issues of gender and race is mandatory.

Today scholars regard *A Voice from the South* as a pioneering African American feminist text. While it is limited by its class bias, it is nevertheless highly valued for its intellectual and political arguments as well as its literary excellence, including Cooper's satiric wit.

• Hazel V. Carby, *Reconstructing Womanhood: The Emergence of the Afro-American Woman Novelist,* 1987. Claudia Tate, *Domestic Allegories of Political Desire: The Black Heroine's Text at the Turn of the Century,* 1992.

—Elizabeth Ammons

Voice of the Negro, The. *The Voice of the Negro* began publication in Atlanta, Georgia, in January 1904. This journal began by trying to steer a compromise between accommodationists and radicals. The first issues included writing by Booker T. *Washington; however, the magazine soon became the voice for a new generation of writers, including W. E. B. *Du Bois, John Hope, Kelly *Miller, Mary Church *Terrell, and William *Pickens. Confrontations with the city government in Atlanta after the race riots in September 1906 forced J. Max Barber, editor of the *Voice of the Negro,* to move the magazine to Chicago, where it ceased publication the next year.

The Voice of the Negro addressed many social issues, such as African American education, the labor movement, and religion. Although it became mainly associated with activist politics, it also kept the African American in the "New South" abreast of issues in art and culture. *The Voice of the Negro* published a number of respected African American poets, including James D. *Corrothers, Georgia Douglas *Johnson, and Paul Laurence *Dunbar.

• Louis R. Harlan, "Booker T. Washington and the *Voice of the Negro,* 1904–1907," *Journal of Southern History* 45 (Feb.

1979): pp. 45–62. Walter C. Daniel, *Black Journals of the United States,* 1982.

—Daniel J. Royer

VROMAN, MARY ELIZABETH (192?–1967), short fiction writer, novelist, movie script writer, and first African American woman member of the Screen Writers Guild. Born in Buffalo, New York, sometime between 1924 and 1929, Mary Elizabeth Vroman grew up in the West Indies and graduated from Alabama State Teachers College, determined to make a difference in her students' lives. She taught for twenty years in Alabama, Chicago, and New York. Vroman's "See How They Run" focused upon the experiences of an idealistic African American first-year teacher in a third-grade rural Alabama school. Published in the June 1951 *Ladies' Home Journal,* the story elicited five hundred enthusiastic letters from readers.

Praised as the "finest story to come out of the South since Green Pastures," "See How They Run" won the Christopher Award for inspirational magazine writing because of its humanitarian quality. It also appeared in the July 1952 issue of *Ebony.*

The protagonist, Jane Richards, describes her interactions with children in a school with a leaky roof and a potbellied stove. Many youngsters come to class without breakfast and share tattered, outdated textbooks. They help their overworked, underpaid teacher haul water from a well down the road, not far from a foul-smelling outhouse. The story serves as an excellent primary source showing the difficulties and joys of educating African American children in the segregated South.

In 1953, Vroman wrote a movie script of her story for a motion picture entitled *Bright Road,* featuring Harry Belafonte and Dorothy Dandridge. She became the first African American woman member of the Screen Writers Guild.

Vroman's first novel, *Esther* (1963), features a dignified grandmother, Lydia Jones, who saves her money as a midwife to purchase some land and uses her savings to encourage her granddaughter, Esther Kennedy, to pursue a nursing career. *Shaped to Its Purpose* (1965) told the history of the first fifty years of Delta Sigma Theta, a sorority of forty thousand college-trained professional African American women to which the author belonged. Vroman's third book, *Harlem Summer* (1967), was intended for young adult readers and features sixteen-year-old John, from Montgomery, Alabama, who spends the summer living with relatives and working in Harlem.

Mary Elizabeth Vroman honestly depicted African American lifestyles during the decades of the 1950s and 1960s without becoming cynical. In spite of adversities, her characters are proud and resilient. They retain their sense of humanity, finding joy in happy experiences with loving family members and understanding friends. Mary Elizabeth Vroman died in 1967 due to complications following surgery.

• Saul Bachner, "Writing School Marm: Alabama Teacher Finds Literary Movie Success with First Short Story," *Ebony,* July 1952, 23–28. Saul Bachner, "Black Literature: The Junior Novel in the Classroom—Harlem Summer," *Negro American Literature Forum* 7 (Spring 1973): 26–27. Edith Blicksilver, "See How They Run," in *The Ethnic American Woman: Problems, Protests, Lifestyle,* 1978, pp. 125–143.

—Edith Blicksilver

W

WALKER, ALICE (b. 1944), poet, novelist, essayist, biographer, short fiction writer, womanist, publisher, educator, and Pulitzer Prize laureate. Born the eighth child of a southern sharecropper and a part-time maid, Alice Walker has climbed the proverbial ladder of success to become one of America's most gifted and influential writers. She has received notoriety for her taboo-breaking and morally challenging depictions of African American passions and oppressions. Although her work is diverse in subject matter and varied in form, it is clearly centered around the struggles and spiritual development affecting the survival whole of women. Walker's writing exposes the complexities of the ordinary by presenting it within a context of duplicity and change. Within this context, Walker peels back the hard cast cover of African and African American women's lives to reveal the naked edge of truth and hope.

Walker was born in Eatonton, Georgia, where she learned early the value of looking within the hidden spaces of human experience and exploring them creatively. At the age of eight, a BB gun accident blinded and scarred her right eye. The experience of this disfigurement profoundly influenced Walker's life, leading her into a self-imposed isolation that was open only to her thirst for reading and her love of poetry. Her self-imposed alienation, coupled with her fear of becoming totally blind, encouraged the young girl to search people and relationships closely—to discover the inner truths masked by facades of acceptance and equality. Walker used her blinded eye as a filter through which to look beyond the surface of African American women's existence, and discovered that she cared about both the pain and spiritual decay she found hidden there.

Walker graduated from high school as valedictorian of her class and, in 1961, entered Spelman College on a Georgia rehabilitation scholarship. After a two-year stay at Spelman and while a student at Sarah Lawrence College (1963–1965), Walker visited Africa for a summer. There she fell in love and wrote several of the poems that were later included in her first book of poetry, *Once* (1968). Upon her return to Sarah Lawrence, Walker was pregnant and contemplating suicide. She felt trapped by her body and believed that only an abortion could free her. The poems of love, suicide, and civil rights published in *Once* were written during this, her second period of self-imposed isolation. After a serious contemplation of her options, Walker aborted her pregnancy and began her first published short story, "To Hell with Dying." First published in 1967, this story of an old man who is revived from death by the attentive love of two children was later published as a children's book (in 1988) with illustrations by Catherine Deeter.

Walker completed her studies at Sarah Lawrence College and received her bachelor of arts degree in 1965, moved to the lower east side of New York City, and began working for the Welfare Department. On 17 March 1967, she married Melvyn Roseman Leventhal, a Jewish civil rights lawyer, and, later that year, the couple moved to Jackson, Mississippi. While in Mississippi, Walker wrote and supported various civil rights activities. She worked as writer in residence at Jackson State College (1968–1969) and Tougaloo College (1970–1971) and was a black history consultant to the Friends of the Children of Mississippi Head Start program.

Although Walker gained some measure of success as a writer during her marriage to Leventhal, the pressures of racial prejudice prevented many readers from appreciating her creative genius. Her decision to marry outside of her race brought with it criticism and complaints. Existing Mississippi law made it a crime for her to live as Leventhal's legal wife and African American male critics insisted upon focusing on her interracial marriage instead of her writing. The marriage ended in 1977 when the couple divorced amicably. They had one child, Rebecca Grant, born on 17 November 1969.

The ten years of Walker's marriage were the most prolific in her creative career. In addition to the publication of her second book of poetry, titled *Five Poems* (1972), Walker published her first novel, *The *Third Life of Grange Copeland* (1970), joining Toni *Morrison in beginning what was to become known as a renaissance of African American women writers. *The Third Life of Grange Copeland* is a realistic novel that presents three generations of a family whose history is marred by race, class, and gender oppression. The main focus of this novel is not the social conflicts generated by race prejudice that were generally written about during the black nationalist movement. Instead, the novel challenges African Americans to take a scrutinizing look at themselves.

The Third Life of Grange Copeland exposes the abuses and maddening injustices of African American internal familial conflict and oppression. Because of this break with the norm, critics charged Walker with not presenting the "right image" of African American life. Walker refused to let negative criticism stifle her creative spirit, however. She continued to write, challenging the status quo of African American literary decorum at every turn. In 1973, she shared her vision of the victories and tribulations of African American women's lives in a collection of short stories titled *In Love and Trouble: Stories of Black Women.* The collection of thirteen stories won the American Academy and Institute of Arts and Letters Rosenthal Award in 1974. Her third book of poetry, *Revolutionary Petunias and Other Poems* (1973), won the Lillian Smith Award of the Southern Regional Council in 1974 and was nominated for the National Book Award. That same year Walker published two children's books: *Langston Hughes, American Poet* and *The Life of Thomas Hodge.*

Unlike *The Third Life of Grange Copeland,* Walker's second novel, *Meridian* (1976), focuses on the civil rights movement and its fight for social change. However, *Meridian*'s social critique is woman-centered. In many ways, the novel's concern with women, specifically its commentary on African American motherhood, reflects Walker's own conflicts during her first pregnancy and abortion. *Meridian* redefines African American motherhood and reconstructs it as an inner spark that fuels a genuine sense of love and responsibility among people; it does not generate from within the womb, but from within the relationships developed by women that support and build their communities and their world.

In 1979, Walker edited *I Love Myself When I Am Laughing.* The stories this anthology contains were collected by Walker after working incessantly to restore the memory of Zora Neale *Hurston to the annals of history. Walker takes pride in the relationships and continuities developed from within a matrilineal tradition of writing. For Walker, women such as Gwendolyn *Brooks and Hurston are foremothers from whom she and other African American women writers can learn and grow. Although both of these writers are important to Walker and her creative vision, Hurston is an icon for her, representing superb literary achievement and courage. In 1973, Walker journeyed to Florida in search of the writer's past. There she found and marked Hurston's neglected gravesite with a headstone.

Walker is innovative in her attempts to save African American women writers from the dark recesses of oblivion. As co-owner of her own publishing house, Wild Tree Press, Walker promotes and mentors new writers such as J. California *Cooper. In 1977, while teaching at Wellesley College, she introduced academia to one of the first African American women's literature courses. Walker has also taught African American women's studies at Brandeis, the University of Massachusetts, Yale, and the University of California at Berkeley.

Walker's pattern of challenging the minds and morals of her readers continued into the 1980s. In 1982, she stepped across the line of a highly forbidden taboo with her portrayal of *Celie in *The *Color Purple.* This novel examines not only "black-on-black" oppression but also incest, bisexual love, and lesbian love. Written in epistolary form, Walker's third novel exposes the internal turmoil parenting the spiritual decay of African American women who, like the novel's protagonist, silently endure abusive male-dominated relationships. In *The Color Purple,* Celie is raped by a man she believes is her father. Later, she is battered and mentally abused in a loveless marriage. Although this novel ignited controversy (especially from African American men who claimed Walker's novel was creative male-bashing), it was on the *New York Times* bestseller list for twenty-five weeks. Walker achieved the status of a major American writer when the novel won both the Pulitzer Prize for Fiction and the National Book Award in 1983. Two years later, it was adapted as a major motion picture directed by Steven Spielberg.

Walker published a collection of womanist prose entitled **In Search of Our Mothers' Gardens* in 1983. The book is a memoir of Walker's experiences and observations of African American women's culture and continues her exploration of the hidden truths defining female wholeness. In this collection of essays, reviews, and articles, Walker defines her feminist stance as womanism. For her, a womanist is a black feminist who is "committed to survival and wholeness of entire people, male and female." The designation "womanist" and the ideologies it represents has extended Walker's influence beyond literary circles and into the domain of African American religious culture. The term has been adopted by prominent African American theologians such as Katie Cannon (*Black Womanist Ethics,* 1988) and Renita J. Weems (*Just a Sister Away,* 1988), as well as renowned ministers like Prathia Hall Wynn of Philadelphia and Ella Pearson Mitchell of the Interdenominational Theological Center in Atlanta, Georgia.

Walker's concern for spiritual wholeness and cultural connectedness completely ascended the physical in her fourth novel, *The *Temple of My Familiar* (1989), a story that takes the reader into a time before the apparition of physical perfection and ownership began to dominate the mind of humanity. The reception of this novel was mixed and it did not receive the broad popularity of *The Color Purple. The Temple of My Familiar* solidly argues Walker's belief that the roots of African American women's hope for spiritual wholeness lies within the soil of their African origins. But for Walker, even these origins are not above reproach and evaluation.

In her fifth novel, **Possessing the Secret of Joy* (1992), Walker uncovers the mysteries of a ritualist past that has imposed its presence into a changing world—a world that defines clitoridectomy (female circumcision) as sexual blinding, domination, and abuse. *Possessing the Secret of Joy* brings the life and imagination of Tashi, a character who appeared in both *The Color Purple* and *The Temple of My Familiar,* into full view. The chilling reality of oppression and control mandated by the traditions of female circumcision is further explored by Walker in her documentary film (and accompanying book of 1993) *Warrior Marks* (1994), directed by the Indian-British filmmaker Pratibha Parmar.

Walker continued her steady pace of publication in the 1990s with several volumes. Among them are *Alice Walker Banned* (1996), *The Same River Twice: Honoring the Difficult: A Meditation of Life, Spirit, Art, and the Making of the Film, The Color Purple, Ten Years Later* (1996), and *Anything We Love Can Be Saved: A Writer's Activism* (1997). In 1998, she published her sixth novel, *By the Light of My Father's Smile,* which examines Native people's spiritual traditions in Mexico and the impact they have upon a visiting missionary African American family. The novel explores extranatural as well as beyond death experiences.

Alice Walker is one of the first African American women writers to explore the paralyzing effects of being a woman in a world that virtually ignores issues like black-on-black oppression and female circumcision. Her efforts, however, have not always received favorable reception among blacks. In 1996, Walker published *The Same River Twice,* a book in which she addresses the pain of negative criticism. In her attempts to open the blinded eyes of those around her, Walker has written a total of six novels, four children's books, five volumes of poetry (the most recently published volume is *Her Blue Body Everything We Know,* 1991), two collections of short stories, three volumes of essays, one documentary film, and many uncollected articles. Today Walker continues to express creatively her wish for wholeness for those who have been erased from history, torn from their racial heritage, silenced, mutilated, and denied freedom. With incomparable vision and insight, she captures the folklore, language, pain, spirit, and memories of African Americans only to weave them into a quilt of compassion that she spreads before the world—full, rich, and flowing.

[*See also* Brownfield Copeland; Shug Avery.]

• "Alice Walker," in *Black Women Writers at Work,* ed. Claudia Tate, 1983, pp. 175–187. Barbara Christian, "Alice Walker," in *DLB,* vol. 33, *Afro-American Fiction Writers after 1955,* eds. Thadious M. Davis and Trudier Harris, 1984, pp. 258–271. Barbara Christian, "Alice Walker: The Black Woman Artist as Wayward," in *Black Women Writers (1959–1980): A Critical Evaluation,* ed. Mari Evans, 1984, pp. 457–477. Philip Royster, "In Search of Our Father's Arms: Alice Walker's Persona of the Alienated Darling," *Black American Literature Forum* 20.4 (1986): 347–370. Erma Banks and Keith Byerman, *Alice Walker: An Annotated Bibliography, 1967–1986,* 1989. Rudolph P. Byrd, "Spirituality in the Novels of Alice Walker: Models, Healing, and Transformation, or When the Spirit Moves So Do We," in *Wild Women in the Whirlwind: Afra-American Culture and the Contemporary Literary Renaissance,* eds. Joanne M. Braxton and Andrée Nicola McLaughlin, 1990, pp. 363–378. Grace E. Collins, "Alice Walker," in *Notable Black American Women,* ed. Jessie Carney Smith, 1992, pp. 1178–1182. Frank N. Magill, ed., *Masterpieces of African American Literature,* 1992, pp. 107–110, 301–304, 447–450, 573–576. Henry Louis Gates, Jr., and K. A. Appiah, eds., *Alice Walker: Critical Perspectives Past and Present,* 1993.

—Debra Walker King

WALKER, DAVID (1785–1830), abolitionist, orator, and author of *David Walker's Appeal.* Although David Walker's father, who died before his birth, was enslaved, his mother was a free woman; thus, when he was born in Wilmington, North Carolina, in September 1785, David Walker was also free, following the "condition" of his mother as prescribed by southern laws regulating slavery. Little is known about Walker's early life. He traveled widely in the South and probably spent time in Philadelphia. He developed early on an intense and abiding hatred of slavery, the result apparently of his travels and his firsthand knowledge of slavery.

Relocating to Boston in the mid-1820s, he became a clothing retailer and in 1828 married a woman named Eliza. They had one son, Edward (or Edwin) Garrison Walker, born after David Walker's death in 1830. An active figure in Boston's African American community during the late 1820s, David Walker had a reputation as a generous, benevolent person who sheltered fugitives and frequently shared his in-come with the poor. He joined the Methodist Church and in 1827 became a general agent for *Freedom's Journal,* a newly established African American newspaper. During the two years of the newspaper's existence, he regularly supported the New York City–based publication, finding subscribers, distributing copies, and contributing articles. He was also a notable member of the Massachusetts General Colored Association, an antislavery and civil rights organization founded in 1826. In lectures before the association, Walker spoke out against slavery and colonization, while urging African American solidarity.

In September 1829, he published **David Walker's Appeal.* In this pamphlet, which quickly went through three editions, he fiercely denounced slavery, colonization, and the institutional exclusion, oppression, and degradation of African peoples. His *Appeal* was a militant call for united action against the sources of the "wretchedness" of African Americans, enslaved and free. Often reprinted, widely circulated, and highly regarded by a number of African American readers, Walker's *Appeal* generated a vehement response from white Americans, especially in the South. Several southern state legislatures passed laws banning such "seditious" literature and reinforced legislation forbidding the education of slaves in reading and writing. The governors of Georgia and Virginia and the mayor of Savannah wrote letters to the mayor of Boston expressing outrage about the *Appeal* and demanding that Walker be arrested and punished. In Georgia, a bounty was offered on him, ten thousand dollars alive, one thousand dollars dead. In the North, newspapers attacked the pamphlet, as did white abolitionists (and pacifists) Benjamin Lundy and William Lloyd Garrison, who admired Walker's courage and intelligence but condemned the circulation of the *Appeal* as imprudent.

Walker died in the summer of 1830. Although the cause and circumstances of his death are mysterious, many have suspected that he was poisoned. After his death, the *Appeal* continued to circulate in various editions, including Henry Highland *Garnet's 1848 reprinting of the *Appeal* along with his own "Address to the Slaves" in a single volume. As one of the earliest and most compelling printed expressions of African American nationalism, militancy, and solidarity, the *Appeal* has remained a vital and influential text for successive generations of African American activists.

• Herbert Aptheker, *"One Continual Cry": David Walker's Appeal to the Colored Citizens of the World* (1829–30), 1965. Benjamin Quarles, *Black Abolitionists,* 1969. Donald M. Jacobs, "David Walker: Boston Race Leader, 1825–1830," *Essex Institute Historical Collections* 107 (Jan. 1971): 94–107. Jane H. Pease and William H. Pease, *They Who Would Be Free: Blacks' Search for Freedom, 1830–1861,* 1974. Wilson Jeremiah Moses, *Black Messiahs and Uncle Toms: Social and Literary Manipulations of a Religious Myth,* 1982. Sterling Stuckey, *Slave Culture: Nationalist Theory and the Foundations of Black America,* 1987. *David Walker's Appeal,* ed. Sean Wilentz (1995).

—Gregory Eiselein

WALKER, JOSEPH A. (b. 1935), director, choreographer, actor, educator, Tony Award winner, and leading African American playwright of the 1970s. Born in Washington, D.C., in 1935, to working-class parents, Joseph A. Walker began his theatrical career in college with acting roles in several student productions at Howard University. He received his BA in 1956 and went on to begin graduate work in philosophy and serve a term in the U.S. Air Force before deciding to pursue a career in theater.

Like the young protagonist, Jeff, in his most famous play, *The *River Niger,* Walker began military service as a navigation student but found himself too distracted by poetic impulses to continue. Rather than drop out altogether like his fictional creation, however, Walker persevered in the corps, becoming a first lieutenant and second-in-command of his squadron before his discharge in 1960. Evidently he emerged even more determined to write.

With an MFA from Catholic University (1963), Walker embarked on a teaching career—at secondary school in Washington, D.C., at the City College of New York, and finally at Howard University—which proved more amenable to his artistic pursuits. The young Walker had melded his poetic and theatrical abilities and began to show promise as a playwright, and from 1970 to 1971 he was playwright in residence at Yale University. He continued to appear on stage periodically as well during his most productive playwriting years—the late 1960s and early 1970s. He has also had roles in two motion pictures and has various television performances to his credit, including two in Emmy-nominated productions.

Walker's first Off-Broadway production, a coauthored musical, *The Believers,* was given a single performance at New York's Garrick Theatre in May 1968. Then, in 1969, Walker's first professional solo piece was mounted Off-Broadway by the Negro Ensemble Company (NEC), where Walker had been working as an understudy. The play—a series of four one-act works dealing with black men's anger and rebellion in the face of various oppressions—ran a full six weeks to generally positive reviews.

Dorothy Dinroe, who had provided musical collaboration on *The Harangues,* became Walker's second wife and professional partner in 1970 (he had divorced in 1965), when they founded their own musical-dance repertory company, the Demi-Gods. Walker was artistic director, writing and choreographing for the ensemble. The company struggled financially but served as an inspired and inspiring workshop and showcase for Walker's (and Dinroe-Walker's) creativity.

Ododo was the first play to come out of this new venture. Subtitled a "musical epic," the piece was a review of African American history, emphasizing the inevitability of "the black man's" emergence as a revolutionary. Not performed by the Demi-Gods until 1973 (at Howard University), NEC's production of *Ododo* opened to mixed reviews at St. Mark's Playhouse on 24 November 1970. Some critics considered the play too threatening, and others have since viewed it as lacking the sophistication of Walker's later work.

The Demi-Gods mounted the premiere production of Walker's most experimental play, *Yin-Yang,* at the Afro-American Studio in New York in June 1972. This theatrical collage reappeared around New York (including Off-Broadway) and at Howard University over the next two years. Dramatizing ancient and biblical conflicts between good and evil, the piece portrays God as "a hip swinging, fast talking Black mama . . . in conflict with Miss Satan, who is also a Black female swinger" (Walker, "Broadway's Vitality," *New York Times* 5 Aug. 1973). *Yin-Yang* too met with a mixed, if more heated, response from critics and theater-goers.

In 1972, with the smash success of the much more realistic *The River Niger,* Walker became a truly dominant figure in African American theater. First produced Off-Broadway by the NEC, the play was an instant hit and had the longest run on record at that company. Moving on to Broadway, it continued to draw crowds and receive rave reviews. Although critics praised the play partly for its "universality," they also stressed its careful representation of working-class African American life. In fact the play is highly autobiographical, with many of the characters and situations coming directly from the writer's family.

In addition to its popular and financial success, *The River Niger* garnered numerous awards, including a Tony Award for the best play of the 1973 to 1974 season and several Obies. Walker also received the Drama Desk Award for the most promising playwright of 1972 to 1973 and wrote the screenplay adaptation for the 1976 film production of his play. He has also received a Guggenheim Fellowship (1973) and a Rockefeller Foundation grant (1979).

Joseph A. Walker is a full professor of drama at Howard University and continues to be a significant figure in the development of African American theater.

• Maurice Peterson, "Taking Off With Joseph Walker," *Essence,* Apr. 1974, 55, 74, 78, 82. Clark Taylor, "In the Theater of Soul," *Essence,* Apr. 1975, 48–49.

—Sheila Hassell Hughes

WALKER, MARGARET (1915–1998), poet, novelist, essayist, and educator. Margaret Abigail Walker was born on 7 July 1915 in Birmingham, Alabama, the daughter of Sigismond Walker, a Methodist minister, and Marion Dozier Walker, a music teacher. Although she spent her childhood and youth in the racist, segregated South, Walker seems not to have been afflicted by the psychic wound of racism she poignantly describes in *Richard Wright: Daemonic Genius* (1988). The reason is not far to seek. Walker was protected to some extent by having been raised in an educated, middle-class family, surrounded by books and music and imbued with strong Christian values and belief in the innate dignity of humanity. She has drawn special attention to the inspiring character of her family and to the emphasis they placed on education and intellectual life. On the other hand, Walker's childhood was not devoid of exposure to oppression and injustice. The imprint of her formative years is reflected in her creative works, particularly in the poems in **For My People* (1942) that express an ambivalence about the South, and in **Jubilee* (1966), the culmination of her early exposure to stories of slave life from her maternal grandmother, Elvira Ware Dozier.

In 1925 the family moved to New Orleans, Louisiana. There she was educated at Gilbert Academy and finished high school at the age of fourteen. A precocious child, Walker completed two years of college at New Orleans University (Dillard University), where both of her parents taught. She was accustomed during her youth to meeting such famous people as James Weldon *Johnson, Roland Hayes, and W. E. B. *Du Bois.

In 1931 she was introduced to Langston *Hughes, who would have great influence on her career. He read some of her poems and encouraged her to write and to get an education outside the South. The next year she transferred to Northwestern University, from which she received a BA in English in 1935, a few months before her twentieth birthday. Prior to graduation, she had published her first poems in the *Crisis* magazine (1934) and had begun a draft of a Civil War story.

The years Walker lived in Chicago during the Great Depression had a significant impact on her decision to be a writer. Shortly after graduating from Northwestern, she was hired by the Works Project Administration (WPA), first as a social worker and later as a member of the Federal Writers' Project. Assigned to work on the *Illinois Guidebook,* Walker learned much about the urban life of her people and about the craft of writing. In the years between 1936 and 1939, she benefited much from her friendships with the novelists Nelson Algren and Frank *Yerby, poets Arna *Bontemps and Frank Marshall *Davis, the artist Margaret Taylor Goss *Burroughs and the playwright Theodore *Ward. The most significant friendship was that with Richard *Wright, whom she met in February 1936 at a meeting of the South Side Writers Group. She was genuinely impressed with Wright's commitment to social change and his gift for writing. They shared their works, Walker providing technical assistance to Wright, Wright broadening her vision of how literature might be related to political action. It was under Wright's influence that Walker made the decision to be a writer for the people. She continued to help Wright after he moved to New York in 1937, sending him the newspaper clippings and other material pertinent to the Robert Nixon case he was using in writing **Native Son* (1940). During this period Walker also completed an urban novel, "Goose Island," which remains unpublished. Walker's obviously inspiring friendship with Wright ended abruptly in 1939, when she attended the League of American Writers Congress in New York, a rupture that she treats in detail in *Richard Wright: Daemonic Genius.*

Walker's tenure with the Federal Writers' Project ended in 1939, and she enrolled at the University of Iowa to complete studies for the master's degree in creative writing and prepared the poems that would appear in *For My People* as her thesis.

Walker began what would be a long and distinguished teaching career at Livingston College in North Carolina, taught for one year at West Virginia State College, and married Firnist James Alexander in June 1943. The fame she achieved with the publication of her first book was now complemented, and to some degree complicated, by the prospect of trying to write a novel as she handled the responsibilities of motherhood. A Rosenwald Fellowship in 1944 did enable her to resume research for the novel, but the freedom to write was brief. She returned to teaching, moving in 1949 with her husband and three children to Jackson, Mississippi, and a position at Jackson State College, where she taught until her retirement in 1979.

Jackson, Mississippi, became both harbor and site of frustration for Margaret Walker. Teaching duties and domestic responsibilities left little time for sustained writing. She was able to continue her historical research from 1953 to 1954 with the aid of a Ford Fellowship, but with four children to care for she would not be able to do substantial work on the manuscript until she returned to the University of Iowa in 1962 to work on her doctorate in English. She finished both the degree and the dissertation version of *Jubilee* in 1965. The long story of her struggle to bring this novel to life is the subject of her essay "How I Wrote *Jubilee*" (1972).

Walker's output increased dramatically in the years after *Jubilee. Prophets for a New Day* (1970) and *October Journey* (1973) created new audiences for her poetry as did *A Poetic Equation: Conversations between Nikki Giovanni and Margaret Walker.* She completed the long-awaited biography *Richard Wright: Daemonic Genuis* (1988), and published *This Is My Century: New and Collected Poems* (1989) and *How I Wrote Jubilee and Other Essays on Life and Literature* (1990). She is currently writing her autobiography and preparing a second collection of her essays for publication.

Walker's public reception since the 1960s has been enthusiastic, partly because of her status as one of the few surviving members of a transitional generation of African American writers and partly because of her well-earned international reputation. Thus it is surprising that while her works are widely anthologized and taught in African American and women's studies courses, critical attention to her more than fifty years of writing has been less substantial than one might expect. Scholars of African American literature and culture are aware of her impact on such writers as Sonia *Sanchez and Nikki *Giovanni, her place in literary history with the landmark works *For My People* and *Jubilee,* and her special contribution to the academic world in founding the Institute for the Study of the History, Life, and Culture of Black People at Jackson State University (now the Margaret Walker Alexander National Research Center), and in organizing the legendary Phillis Wheatley Festival (1973). Perhaps one must conclude, as Maryemma Graham does in the preface to *How I Wrote* Jubilee *and Other Essays* (1990), that Walker's works have not been canonized because critics tend to be uncomfortable with her complex aesthetic vision. No such discomfort is evidenced by the audiences who respond warmly to Walker's public lectures and readings. It may be that Margaret Walker has the distinction of being canonized by her people.

• John Griffin Jones, "Margaret Walker Alexander," in *Mississippi Writers Talking,* vol. 2, 1983, pp. 1–65. Claudia Tate, "Margaret Walker," in *Black Women Writers at Work,* 1983, pp. 188–204. Joyce Pettis, "Margaret Walker: Black Woman Writer of the South," in *Southern Women Writers,* ed. Tonette Bond Inge, 1990, pp. 9–19. Mary Hughes Brookhart, "Margaret Walker," in *Contemporary Poets, Dramatists, Essayists, and Novelists of the South,* ed. Robert Bain and Joseph M. Flora, 1994, pp. 504–514. Jacqueline Miller Carmichael, *Trumpeting a Fiery Sound: History and Folklore in Margaret Walker's* Jubilee, 1998.

—Jerry W. Ward, Jr.

Walls of Jericho, The. Published in 1928, Rudolph *Fisher's *The Walls of Jericho* presents a rich panorama of social classes in the late 1920s. The novel centers on the evolving relationship between Shine, a piano mover, and Linda, an ambitious maid. Shine's need for his tough-guy exterior, so important for his survival among the "rats," thwarts his feelings for Linda and the confrontation with his own past. An often bemused narrator deftly sketches the choreography of the couple's relationship, movements that summon forth themes of futile vengeance and self-delusion. Shine's conflict is made clear when a minister eloquently shapes the biblical story of Joshua and the walls of Jericho. With the words haunting him afterward, Shine can finally proclaim: "The guy that's really hard is the guy that's hard enough to be soft."

Fisher's comedy is genial here, his satire evenhanded. As comic counterpoint throughout, Jinx and Bubber, coworkers with Shine, voice the irreverent views of the street crowd on a wide range of subjects. The African American bourgeoisie, no less than the white, liberal professional class, comes in for criticism, especially in the longest scene of the novel, the General Improvement Association costume ball. Fisher focuses his judicious satire on the deluded attempts at an easy racial harmony. Society woman Agatha Cramp bears much of the weight of this critique. Pomposity and aloofness are spoofed with quick and telling strokes.

At the novel's end, Shine and Linda have drawn much closer. Merrit, the black-and-blond lawyer who has briefly and mischievously passed for white at the costume ball, will help Shine start his own trucking company. Thus rifts within the African American community, rifts predicated on delusions generated by caste and class, are healed for the moment.

Few other writers employed satire and comedy with much consistency during the Harlem Renaissance. Fisher's shadings are more optimistic than those of Wallace *Thurman (*The Infants of the Spring,* 1932) and less caustic than those of George S. *Schuyler (**Black No More,* 1931). As with his second novel (*The Conjure Man Dies,* 1932) and his body of short fiction, Fisher's achievement was the affection, close criticism, and symmetry he brought to his portraits of the African American encounter with the modern city.

• Leonard J. Deutsch, "Rudolph Fisher's Unpublished Manuscripts: Description and Commentary," *Obsidian* 6 (Spring/Summer 1980): 82–97. John McCluskey, Jr., ed., introduction to *The City of Refuge: The Collected Stories of Rudolph Fisher,* 1987.

—John McCluskey, Jr.

WALROND, ERIC (1898–1966), short fiction writer, journalist, editor, and figure in the Harlem Renaissance. Although his residence in the United States was brief, Eric D. Walrond made lasting contributions to African American literature and culture. Born in

Georgetown, British Guiana, in 1898, Walrond was educated at St. Stephen's Boys' School in Barbados and public schools in Colón, Panama. He left Panama for a ten-year residence in New York (1918–1928), where he continued his education at City College and Columbia University. His experiences with racism in the United States impelled his early fiction and sparked his interest in Marcus *Garvey's Universal Negro Improvement Association (UNIA). After withdrawing his support of the UNIA, Walrond became a protégé of Urban League director Charles S. Johnson. It was during his affiliation with Johnson that Walrond's 1926 collection of short stories, *Tropic Death,* was published in New York by Boni and Liveright.

As the collection's title indicates, Walrond's ten stories set in British Guiana, Barbados, and Panama thematize death and the destruction wrought by natural disasters, colonialism, and modernization. Prominent figures such as W. E. B. *Du Bois and Langston *Hughes praised the collection's impressionistic form and historical content, as did anonymous reviewers from the *New York Times* and the *New York World.* Critics such as Robert Bone and David Levering Lewis note the Gothic strains in "The Yellow One," "The Wharf Rats," and "The White Snake." With the stories "Tropic Death" and "The Black Pin," Walrond explores coerced migration, cultural displacement, and xenophobia, three central concerns of his life as well as his writing.

While impressive thematically and stylistically, the short fiction from *Tropic Death* constituted neither the first nor the last of Walrond's contributions to the Harlem Renaissance. In the early and mid-1920s, eight other stories thematizing race relations in New York and abroad were published in periodicals such as *Smart Set* and the *New Republic.* His fiction also appeared in *Opportunity,* including "Voodoo's Revenge," for which he was awarded third prize in the magazine's 1925 literary contest. He published one more piece in 1927, "City Love," before migrating to Europe, where he died in 1966.

Like Colombian novelist Gabriel García Márquez, Walrond began his writing career as a journalist, producing articles on Harlem and the Great Migration and nuanced critiques of contemporary African American leaders. From 1921 to 1923 he served as editor and co-owner of an African American weekly, the *Brooklyn and Long Island Informer.* His journalistic experience earned the respect of both Garvey and Johnson: Walrond was hired as associate editor of the UNIA's paper, *Negro World* (1923–1925), and business manager of the Urban League's *Opportunity* (1925–1927). An editor, journalist, and one of the first fiction writers to thematize migration and diaspora, Eric D. Walrond is an important, if overlooked, figure from the Harlem Renaissance. His manifold accomplishments during the 1920s ensure him a firm place in African American literary history.

• Jay A. Berry, "Eric Walrond," in *DLB,* vol. 51, *Afro-American Writers from the Harlem Renaissance to 1940,* eds. Trudier Harris and Thadious M. Davis, 1987, pp. 296–300. John E. Bassett, *Harlem in Review: Critical Reactions to Black American Writers, 1917–1939,* 1992. Louis J. Parascandola, ed., "Winds Can Wake Up the Dead": *An Eric Walrond Reader.* 1998.

—Margarita Barceló

WALTER, MILDRED PITTS (b. 1922), author of picture books, novels, and information books for children and young adult readers. Many songs, poems, novels, and plays extol the virtues of home; others lament the heartaches that occur within the confines of home; and a few depict the search for a philosophical home that imparts a sense of meaning, belonging, and identity to an individual's life. Mildred Pitts Walter experienced and writes eloquently about these emotions in her books for youth.

Born in Sweetville, Louisiana, and raised in Gaytine, Louisiana, two small, segregated sawmill towns, Mildred Pitts Walter experienced and developed love of family and community, spiritual rootedness, duty to community uplift, ability to tell stories, and a powerful love of oral and written language. Starting at age seven with a job caring for a white child, she also acquired a strong work ethic.

Walter's teachers encouraged her intellectual growth and inspired her to dream about attending college. She attended Southern University in Louisiana (1940–1944) and graduated with a BA, majoring in English and minoring in social studies. Southern University provided access to intellectuals such as W. E. B. *Du Bois, Mordecai Johnson, and Benjamin E. Mays, who engendered within her a sense of cultural heritage and intellectual curiosity. Walter completed certification requirements in elementary education at California State College; she received a master's degree several years later from Antioch College in Yellow Springs, Ohio.

Walter's sense of adventure took her to Los Angeles, where she worked as a school clerk, eventually earning the credentials to teach in elementary schools. She and her husband, Lloyd Walter, were active members of the Congress of Racial Equality (CORE) and engaged in actions to desegregate schools and public accommodations. Although Walter enjoyed teaching, political activism propelled her career as a writer. Walter wrote a letter to a critic at the *Los Angeles Times* who had disparaged comments made by author James *Baldwin at a CORE fund-raiser. Subsequently, the critic invited Walter to write book reviews for the newspaper. She accepted and her literary career was launched.

Walter questioned an editor about the absence of literature featuring African Americans. The editor responded that she should write the stories because she lived the experience and possessed an insider's perspective. She considered the editor's comments and created *Lillie of Watts* (1969). Lillie is a spunky young girl growing up in gritty circumstances in the Watts section of Los Angeles who must overcome disappointments, make decisions, resolve conflicts, and retain a measure of happiness and hope. The sequel, *Lillie of Watts Takes a Giant Step* (1971), portrays Lillie's coming-of-age during a time of Black Power.

Initial success did not last. Walter submitted manuscripts that were rejected. Rather than becoming discouraged, she honed her creative writing skills through attendance at writer's workshops and discussions with editors and publishers. Soon, publishers' rejections of manuscripts turned into acceptances: in 1975 with *The Liquid Trap,* followed by *Ty's One-Man Band* (1980), *The Girl on the Outside* (1982), *Because We Are* (1983), *My Mama Needs Me* (1983), *Brother to the Wind* (1985), *Trouble's Child* (1985), *Justin and the Best Biscuits in the World* (1986), *Mariah Loves Rock* (1988), *Have a Happy...* (1984), *Two and Two Much* (1990), *Mariah Keeps Cool* (1990), and *The Mississippi Challenge* (1992).

Walter's growth as a writer is evident in such books as *Ty's One-Man Band, Trouble's Child,* and *The Mississippi Challenge.* Themes in these texts include achieving a sense of identity, resolving problems, and understanding one's cultural heritage and history. Walter creates male and female protagonists who usually face a challenge, sometimes as monumental as racism or desegregating a school, and other times less pressing, such as a summer of fun at the pool.

Critical response to Walter's books varies. Some praise her depiction of the cultural milieus in which her characters reside, her ability to capture the nuances of children and childhood, her facility with various dialects, and thematic issues. Other critics cite stock characterization, weak plots, and contrived endings. Nevertheless, Walter's books remain fairly popular and some have garnered children's book awards such as the Coretta Scott King Award for *Justin and the Best Biscuits in the World* and *The Mississippi Challenge.* Walter's lasting contribution to children's and young adult literature is the creation of accessible characters who symbolize the range of experiences found among African Americans.

• "Mildred Pitts Walter," in *Something about the Author Autobiography Series,* vol. 12, ed. Adele Sarkissian, 1992, pp. 283–301.

—Violet J. Harris

WALTER LEE YOUNGER, the complex, fiercely independent, flawed, and angry protagonist of Lorraine *Hansberry's *A *Raisin in the Sun* (1959) is a first for the American stage. More articulate and moral than his 1940s Broadway predecessor, *Bigger Thomas of Richard *Wright's **Native Son* (1940), Hansberry compared him to Willy Loman (*Death of a Salesman*) who is defeated not only by his own shortcomings but also by a social and economic system that has failed him.

Walter Lee represents the dilemma of African American males who inherited the pride and hopes of the civil rights movement but who are thwarted in their achievement of full manhood in the eyes of society. On the one hand, Walter Lee wants and needs for himself and his family the material comfort that will make their lives better; but on the other hand, he risks losing his sense of dignity to rank materialism. His defining moment comes when the white neighborhood offers to buy back his mother's house at a profit, a price that would allow the family to recover its financial loss and Walter Lee regain face. But in a dramatic reversal at the end of the play, Walter rejects the offer, recognizing its demeaning aspects, and moves the family into the new house. The familiarity of *Mama Lena Younger's strong, matriachal figure often competes with Walter Lee for focus, but Hansberry clearly intended *A Raisin in the Sun* to reflect the struggles, potential, and resilience of the working-class African American male in a racist, capitalistic society that devalues human life and aspiration. Walter Lee, a unique protagonist in the history of America's theatrical literature, is the father of more militant characters who strode the boards in the 1960s plays of LeRoi Jones/Amiri *Baraka, Ron *Milner, and others.

• Lorraine Hansberry, "Willy Loman, Walter Lee Younger and He Who Must Live," *Village Voice,* 12 Aug. 1959, 7–8. Douglas Turner Ward, "Lorraine Hansberry and the Passion of Walter Lee," *Freedomways* 19.4 (1979): 223–225.

—Margaret B. Wilkerson

WANIEK, MARILYN NELSON (b. 1946), poet, critic, and educator. A poet who has written for both children and adults, Marilyn Waniek (pronounced Von-yek) was born on 26 April 1946 in Cleveland, Ohio, daughter of Melvin M. (an air force serviceman) and Johnnie (Mitchell) Nelson (a teacher). Her family moved from one military base to another during her childhood. She started writing in elementary school. Waniek's higher education includes a BA from the University of California at Davis (1968), an MA from the University of Pennslyvania (1970), and a PhD from the University of Minnesota (1979). Her doctoral thesis was "The Schizoid Nature of the Implied Author in Twentieth-Century American Ethnic Novels." As a graduate student she argued in an article, "The Space Where Sex Should Be: Toward a Definition of the Black Literary Tradition" (*Studies in Black Literature,* 1975), that the relationships between "Black protagonists and their white friends" portrayed in African American writing substituted for male-female relationships: "[I]n the space where sex should be is instead the awful confrontation of Black self with white self, and the Black self with white society." A seminary-trained Lutheran, Waniek was lay associate in the National Lutheran Campus Ministry program from 1969 to 1970 in Ithaca, New York. She has taught English in Oregon, Denmark, and Minnesota. Her first marriage to Erdmann F. Waniek (1970–1979) ended in divorce; she has two children, Jacob and Dora, through her second marriage to Roger R. Wilkenfield. A 1976 Kent fellow and a 1982 National Endowment for the Arts fellow, Waniek has been a member of the English faculty at the University of Connecticut at Storrs since 1978, and a full professor since 1988.

Waniek's critical articles include "The Schizoid Implied Authors of Two Jewish-American Novels" (1980), "The Power of Language in N. Scott Momaday's *House Made of Dawn*" (1980), "Paltry Things: Immigrants and Marginal Men in Paule Marshall's Short Fiction" (1983), and "A Black Rainbow: Modern Afro-American Poetry" (with Rita *Dove, 1990). Competent in Danish, German, and Spanish, she translated from Danish Phil Dahlerup's *Literary Sex Roles* (1975).

Waniek has published six poetry collections, two for children. In 1982 Waniek and Pamela Espeland published their translation of Danish poet Halfdan Rasmussen's humorous poetry in *Hundreds of Hens and Other Poems for Children* (1982), work that sparked her interest in writing for children and led to *The Cat Walked Through the Casserole and Other Poems for Children* (with Espeland, 1984). In *For the Body* (1978), written predominantly in free verse, Waniek explores childhood memories; in *Mama's Promises* (1985), she experiments with the ballad stanza. In *The Homeplace* (1990), a text interspersed with family trees and photos, Waniek uses dramatic dialogue and a range of ballad, villanelle, and sonnet forms to tell stories about her family, beginning with her great-great-grandmother Diverne and ending with her father and his fellow "Tuskegee Airmen." Her 1994 poetry collection, *Magnificat: Poems* received critical acclaim. In 1997, she published *The Fields of Praise: New and Selected Poems.* Considered to be one of the major young African American poets, Waniek experiments with traditional and free-verse forms.

—Mary Anne Stewart Boelcskevy

WARD, DOUGLAS TURNER (b. 1930), dramatist, actor, director, and producer. Since the 1960s, the African American dramatic literature and aesthetic philosophy of Douglas Turner Ward have been highly influential. Guided by a burning desire to continue the legacy of W. E. B. *Du Bois, Ward was determined to create theater that was primarily written by, performed for, and representative of African American people. In his plays, Ward examines a mixed bag of attitudes and stereotypes that permeate our environment both within and outside the African American community. He uses various comic conventions such as satire, farce, absurdism, and irony to attack widely divergent cultural philosophies, politics, and ethics as well as social, moral, and racial biases.

Douglas Turner Ward was born on 5 May 1930 in Burnside, Louisiana, to Roosevelt Ward and Dorothy Short. Ward spent his formative years on a plantation in this rural town. He was later sent to live with relations in New Orleans in order to attend public school, from which he graduated at the age of fifteen. Dissatisfaction with prevailing racist attitudes among many Southerners influenced Ward's decision to attend college in the North at Wilberforce University in Xenia, Ohio. In 1947 he transferred to the University of Michigan, where he played football on the junior varsity squad. A knee injury at the age of eighteen abruptly ended his career, so he headed for New York City at the end of the school year.

Ward had been involved in left-wing political activities during his undergraduate days, which he continued to practice as a writer for the *Daily Worker* in New York. Interestingly, his association with various political entities provided the desire to write satirical sketches. His newfound avocation was put on hold while he spent three months in jail for draft evasion before being released on appeal; he was then forced to spend two years in Louisiana until the U.S. Supreme Court overturned his conviction. Ward returned to New York City resolved to write plays solely. In order to understand the craft better, he enrolled in acting classes at the prestigious Paul Mann's Actor's Workshop.

Mel Gussow, reviewer for the *New York Times,* wrote that Ward " . . . as actor, playwright, journalist, director, artistic director of the Negro Ensemble Company—is a man of great force, dedication, and verbosity." Ward used these strong character traits to expound his sociocultural and political ideas, which he expressed in perhaps the most influential piece of writing of his career. In an article entitled "American Theatre: For Whites Only?" that appeared in the *New York Times* on 14 August 1966, Ward denounced the racist practices in professional theaters and called for the establishment of a permanent African American theater for playwrights, actors, technicians, and administrators. This article was instrumental in gaining the attention of the Ford Foundation, which ultimately funded the formation of the Negro Ensemble Company (NEC) in 1965 with a $434,000 grant. Ward was cofounder along with actor-director Robert Hooks and Off-Broadway producer Gerald A. Krone.

Throughout his theatrical career, and in the choice of plays and styles of production, Ward has created a repertory that presents world-class drama primarily focused on African American themes. Nonetheless he has never supported the concept of a separatist theater. The NEC has been criticized from the start by some African Americans for selecting plays by nonwhite playwrights, including Peter Weiss, Ray Lawler, and Jean Genet, and for the location of its first theater in lower Manhattan.

As a playwright, Ward is perhaps best known for his controversial one-act plays, *Happy Ending* and **Day of Absence,* both written in 1966. Both comedies examine black-white relations in dramatizing the interdependence between the races. White critics were generally in agreement that although the theme of racial interdependency was topical, the acting style and colloquial language were often exaggerated to the point of being difficult to understand. In spite of such occasional negative reactions and controversial dramatizations of topical subjects, the NEC continued to produce theatrical events of quality and substance with a list of Black artists that represented the elite of contemporary African American theater.

The right-wing shift in the American political climate during the 1980s severely curtailed the availability of government-sponsored arts program funds and private sector fellowships and grants. In order to address a deficit of $500,000, the NEC did not mount any productions during the 1991 and 1992 seasons. In April 1993, the NEC reopened its doors, this time at the La Guardia Performing Arts Center, with a production of Kenneth Franklin-Hoke Witherspoon's *Last Night at Ace High* directed by Ward, who is also president of the company. Although the NEC remains in debt, Susan Watson Turner, producing director, stated in a profile that appeared in *New York Newsday* on 11 May 1993, that it continues to be "a company run by and for African-American artists."

• Fred Beauford, "The Negro Ensemble Company: Five Years Against the Wall," *Black Creation* 3 (Winter 1972): 16–18. Mark Ribowsky, "'Father' of the Black Theatre Boom," *Sepia* 25 (Nov. 1976): 67–78. Trudier Harris, *From Mammies to Militants: Domestics in Black American Literature,* 1982, pp. 143–154. Cheryl McCourtie, "Whatever Happened to the Negro Ensemble?" *Crisis* 99.7 (Oct. 1992): 47–48. Howard J. Faulkner, "A Vanishing Race," in *CLA Journal* 37 (1994): 274–292.

—Floyd Gaffney

WARD, THEODORE (1902–1983), playwright. Although never a real force in American theater, Theodore Ward deserves more critical attention than he currently receives. His two most important plays, *Big White Fog* (1938) and *Our Lan'* (written in 1941) never enjoyed major commercial successes, although they did receive popular and critical notice and managed to generate some controversy. Tackling a myriad of contentious subjects such as Garveyism, anti-Semitism, color prejudice among blacks, the devastating effects of racism, the appeal of Communism, and the failures of the United States Government to live up to its responsibilities to African Americans, Ward never eschews controversy, hoping always to educate and politicize his audience.

Born in Thibodaux, Louisiana, on 15 September 1902, Ward left Louisiana at the age of thirteen, shortly after his mother's death. Earning his living as a bootblack, porter, or bellhop, Ward wandered about the United States during his teens. He began formal literary study at the University of Utah in the late 1920s. In 1931 a scholarship allowed Ward to study creative writing at the University of Wisconsin where he remained until 1935. Moving to Chicago, Ward's ideological life took shape when he joined a John Reed Club and began working for the WPA. His one-act play *Sick and Tiahd* won second prize in a contest sponsored by the labor movement. This success prompted the playwright to join the Federal Theater Project. In 1938 *Big White Fog* was produced by the Theater Project in Chicago. In 1940 the playwright formed the Negro Playwrights Company to produce *Fog* in New York. Over the next thirty-five years other plays followed: *Deliver the Goods* (1942); *Our Lan'* (first produced in 1946); *John Brown* (1950); *Candle in the Wind* (1967); and *The Daubers* (1973). In 1976 Ward received a Rockefeller Foundation grant to produce *Our Lan'* with the Free Southern Theater in New Orleans. He assisted the company again when it produced his *Candle in the Wind* as its final production in 1978. Ward died in Chicago in May 1983.

Fog remains Ward's most significant work. Set in Chicago between 1922 and 1932, the play chronicles the struggles of the Mason family and its patriarch, Victor. Confronting a series of financial and racial crises, Victor tries to keep the family together and instill in its members race pride and a commitment to the struggle for social and economic justice. Before recognizing multiracial Communism as the solution to the economic and racial injustices of America, Victor places his faith and the family's savings in Marcus *Garvey's Black Star Line. With the depression the family's misery increases; finally Victor dies a victim of a gunshot wound inflicted by a sheriff evicting the family from their home. Before dying Victor looks upon his son's comrades who have arrived to aid the family in resisting the eviction. The son tells his father, "I just wanted to show you, they're [the comrades] black and white."

The optimistic conclusion of *Fog* may seem naive in the post-Marxist world, but in 1938 some feared the play's conclusion would prompt riots. Riots never occurred, but then neither did large audiences. Ward, however, never gave up in his attempt to reach large, especially black, audiences, a fact attested to by his commitment to the Free Southern Theater at the end of his career.

• Doris E. Abramson, *Negro Playwrights in the American Theatre, 1925–1959,* 1969.

—Anthony Gerard Barthelemy

WASHINGTON, BOOKER T. (1856–1915), educator, autobiographer, biographer, and race leader. Few public figures in African American life excite as much passion and misunderstanding as Booker Taliaferro Washington. Born a slave on a Virginia plantation in 1856, Washington rose to become the founder and driving force behind Tuskegee Institute in Alabama. Washington is such a compelling subject because he focuses our attention on issues of leadership and public visibility, the nature of work and how it impacts upon the quality of African American life, and the internecine struggles for power within the African American elite. In the late 1980s, many began to view Washington as a man of skewed racial allegiances, a figure for whom white approval was everything. This interpretation of his life, however, relies on Washington's public persona to substantiate its claims. What is very clear is that Booker T. Washington was a man of such complexity that his public guise fails to provide sufficient cause to dismiss his importance.

Though Washington was born a slave, the scope and influence of his public life in the twentieth century rival that of Frederick *Douglass in the nineteenth century. Though his career as racial spokesman was based on the idea that African Americans should eschew political agitation for civil rights in favor of industrial education and agricultural expertise, Washington's secret activities, his attempt to exercise private influence on matters having to do with racial discrimination and segregation, suggest that his was a paradoxical life indeed. For how else are we to account for Washington's "*Atlanta Exposition Address" of 1895 and his attempts to challenge racial discrimination and segregated facilities by covert legal means?

To penetrate the mysteries swirling about the persona of Booker T. Washington, we must understand something of the times in which he lived and why the issues of African American leadership—who would lead and what kinds of political spoils they could garner for the African American community—played such an essential role in the African American's attempt to participate fully in American life. For Washington, participation meant identifying, and being identified with, the status quo, the dominant way of thinking in American life and culture. Thus, as Sheldon Avery has observed, Washington's positions on laissez-faire capitalism, Christian morality, and middle-class values allowed him to channel a large portion of white philanthropic dollars and black patronage through the Tuskegee machine.

If Washington's racial accommodationism is unpalatable, it needs to be understood in light of his beginnings in West Virginia. As the son of Jane Ferguson, a slave, and a white father whom he never knew (though he conjectures in his autobiography that his father was his master), Washington sought to convey that his childhood had been one of poverty, not racial oppression. From working in the coal furnaces and salt mines of West Virginia to doing housework, Washington's insistence is that he achieved his position as racial spokesman through hard physical labor. He goes to great lengths, for example, to describe his admittance into Hampton Institute in Virginia in 1872 as the result of his ability to clean and dust a classroom. It is clear that Hampton would have a profound impact on Washington's views, for it was there he met General Samuel Chapman Armstrong, who would become his mentor and benefactor. Graduating from Hampton in 1875 with honors, Washington returned to Hampton briefly after two years of teaching back in his native West Virginia to implement a program for Native Americans. In 1881 Armstrong recommended Washington to the Alabama legislature, which was seeking to open a normal school for African American students in Tuskegee.

The Booker T. Washington who thus emerges in **Up from Slavery* (1901) is a humble, moral, disciplined man whose life is devoted to the improvement of the Negro. And it is Tuskegee Institute, where he served as principal from 1881 until his death in 1915, that best demonstrates these traits. Culminating with his speech at the Cotton States and International Exposition in Atlanta in 1895, and his honorary degree from Harvard in 1897, Washington's treatment of his life is characterized by his ability to hold the most unassuming exchange up as a shining example of his links to the working man. Though Washington would endear himself to industrialists like Andrew Carnegie and John D. Rockefeller (at least in part because of his antiunion stance), he nonetheless claimed to champion the cause of economic opportunity for all.

Washington's career in the public sphere seems to grow from his success at Tuskegee, but it is just as much a result of the profound link between his life as an educator and fundraiser and his writing, for it is Washington's ability to control his image by recycling the positive assessments of his work into his books that makes him a credible public figure. Between 1896 and 1913 Washington produced nearly twenty works ranging from his two autobiographies, *The Story of My Life and Work* (1900) and the aforementioned *Up from Slavery,* to a biography of Frederick Douglass (1907). Moreover, it could be argued that Washington was one of the first African American writers to connect the "self-help" book to issues of African American citizenship, which explains titles like *Working with the Hands, Putting the Most into Life,* and *Sowing and Reaping.*

Though Washington depicts himself as the primary voice of the African American community, it is important to point out that there were alternatives to Washington's accommodationist philosophy. W. E. B. *Du Bois and newspaper editor Monroe Trotter insisted upon a much more radical and confrontational stance than that put forward by Washington. With his propensity to see himself as the power to whom all other African American leaders should bow, Washington was often highly intolerant of other points of view, especially those that threatened his ability to keep close counsel with white philanthropic and political interests. Indeed, when the Niagara movement began to gain momentum in 1905, Washington used his influence with black newspaper editors, none of whom wished to risk openly repudiating Washington's policies, to get them to either ignore or belittle the movement. And yet, his heavy-handedness notwithstanding, Washington's quest for power was not without its success. He devoted a considerable amount of time, financial resources, and energy to defeating Jim Crow in the courts of the United States. Indeed, he and Du Bois, publicly in disagreement, collaborated as late as 1904 in an attempt to challenge the public statutes upholding separate-but-equal arrangements. In 1907 they coauthored a study entitled *The Negro in the South.* Though the attempt to achieve a judicial remedy for Jim Crow failed, Washington originated a highly secret, well-maintained apparatus by which to affect the legal fortunes of southern blacks, one that other black leaders were forced to acknowledge. Though the Tuskegee machine was well known to whites as a smoothly running, innocuous vehicle, insufficient and, more importantly, ill-suited to mount a serious challenge to white hegemony, Washington's ability to dissemble, to make racial equality his ultimate concern, means he cannot be dismissed.

• August Meier, *Negro Thought in America, 1880–1915,* 1963. Louis R. Harlan, *Booker T. Washington: The Making of a Black Leader, 1856–1901,* 1972. Hugh Hawkins, ed., *Booker T. Washington and His Critics,* 1974. Louis R. Harlan, *Booker T. Washington: The Wizard of Tuskegee, 1901–1915,* 1983. Louis R. Harlan et al., eds., *The Booker T. Washington Papers, 1972–1989.* David L. Dudley, *My Father's Shadow: Intergenerational Conflict in African American Men's Autobiography,* 1991. Booker T. Washington, *Up from Slavery,* ed. William L. Andrews, 1995. Houston A. Baker, *Turning South Again: Re-Thinking Modernism/Re-Reading Booker T.,* 2000.

—Herman Beavers

WATKINS, GLORIA. *See* hooks, bell.

We a BaddDDD People. Sonia *Sanchez's second book of poems (Broadside Press, 1970), similar to *Homecoming* (1969) in experimental form and revolutionary spirit, is dedicated to "blk/wooomen: the only queens of this universe" and exemplifies the poetics of the Black Arts movement and the principles of the black aesthetic. It depicts the experiences of common black folk in courtrooms, slum bars, and on the streets, with pimps and jivers, boogalooing and loving *Malcolm X. It celebrates the majestic beauty of blackness and speaks of revolution in the language of the urban black vernacular. Rhythms deriving from the jazz and blues of John *Coltrane and Billie *Holiday create a poetry of performance in which the audience participates vigorously in meaning-making. Experimental in style, it is antilyrical free verse, using spacing, slash marks, and typography as guides to performance.

Characterizing Sanchez as a genuine revolutionary whose "blackness" is not for sale, Dudley *Randall's introduction leads into the first of three sections, "Survival Poems," which approach survival from political and personal perspectives. Some show how "wite" practices imperil black people's survival, seducing by heroin, marijuana, and wine or by exploding dreams. Others show how blacks undermine their own survival: the "makeshift manhood" underlying sexual neediness in "for/my/ father," the willful blindness of black "puritans," and the hypocrisy of pseudorevolutionaries whose rhetoric masks self-indulgence. Personal poems recording moments of near-hysteria, depression, and longing lead to the revolutionary vision of "indianapolis/summer," proposing communal love as a necessary prelude to real change.

The second section, "Love/Songs/Chants," expresses a bluesy nostalgia for memories of past good times but recognizes that such fantasies are delusive and that we need to face the real world. Poems warn "brothas & sistuhs" to stay clear of "wite highs" spelling death and exhort black men to love "blk wooooomen." The more militant poems of the third section, "TCB-en poems," bristle with outrage, exposing the jive talk of slick black bloods. Taking care of business means taking care of self as well as tradition. Most of all, TCB involves a strident war cry for power, alternating fierce invective and a call to arms with amusement at how "real/bad" we "bees." Sanchez predicts a coming revolution and exhorts her readers to begin the "real work" of building nationhood. The book ends with her explosive "a coltrane/poem," which, to the jazzy rhythms of "Brother John" and "my favorite things," urges setting fire to capitalist millionaires and torturing promise-breaking liberals so that black people may rise and claim their place.

Critics agree that Sonia Sanchez is a revolutionary poet of undisputed integrity whose goal is to better the world, and they praise *We a BaddDDD People* for the originality of its forms and its singing and chanting voice. Some criticize the strident tone of the political poems, calling their message "tiresome," their rhetoric "facile," and find the personal poems, dealing with drug addiction and love relationships, more palatable, even more authentically revolutionary. All, however, seem to concur that Sanchez's most important contribution to African American literature and culture lies in legitimizing urban Black English, in making the language of the streets "sound" throughout the world.

• Haki Madhubuti, "Sonia Sanchez: Bringer of Memories," in *Black Women Writers (1950–1980),* ed. Mari Evans, 1984, pp. 419–432. D. H. Melhem, "Sonia Sanchez: The Will and the Spirit," in *Heroism in the New Black Poetry,* 1990, pp. 132–179.

—Deborah Ayer Sitter

Weary Blues, The. Langston *Hughes's first volume of verse represents a selection of his poetry that had appeared mainly in magazines since the publication of "The *Negro Speaks of Rivers" in the *Crisis* in 1921. The title poem, written in 1923 but held back from publication by Hughes, had won him the first prize in poetry in the 1925 *Opportunity* magazine contest that helped to launch the major phase of the Harlem Renaissance. Indeed, after the awards ceremony the sympathetic white writer Carl Van Vechten approached Hughes about putting together a volume of verse, and within a few days secured for him a contract with his own publisher, Alfred A. Knopf. The volume appeared in January 1926 with an essay, "Introducing Langston Hughes to the Reader," by Van Vechten.

The seven sections of the volume illustrate the variety of Hughes's poetic interests. The first section, also called "The Weary Blues," shows only indirect influence by the blues on Hughes's verse, except in the title poem and a poem such as "Blues Fantasy." Instead the poems explore the urban, jazzy, race-inflected atmosphere of Harlem in the early 1920s, the world of cabarets, singers, dancers, and prostitutes, with an occasional throwback to an earlier age as in "Song for a Banjo Dance."

The second section, "Dream Variations," is touched lightly by race feeling, but dreaming generally takes the poet away from urban and racial themes toward nature, as in "Winter Moon." In the third section, "The Negro Speaks of Rivers," the poems protest against racism in one way or another, either by asserting the beauty and dignity of blacks or by exploring the tragedy of racism in America, as in "Cross," about miscegenation, or "The South." The next section, "Black Pierrot," reflects Hughes's interest in the Pierrot figure, popularized among writers especially by the French symbolist poet Jules Laforgue. Hughes's Pierrot is often but not invariably race-inflected, but speaks mainly to the poet's bohemian desire for freedom and the unconventional.

The poems in the section "Water-Front Streets" have even less to do with race, but capture the sense of loneliness, lyrically expressed, that was a permanent feature of Hughes's psychology and art. "Shadows in the Sun" also emphasizes a fusion of colored exoticism and melancholy, as in "Soledad: A Cuban Portrait" and "To the Dark Mercedes of 'El Palacio de Amor'." The last section, "Our Land," reasserts the racial and political core of the book, with memorable poems such as "Mother to Son" and "Epilogue" ("I, too, sing America"), which powerfully closes the volume.

In general, reviewers praised the book, which established Hughes as the major rival to Countee *Cullen among the younger poets of the renaissance. The volume laid the foundation for Hughes's entire literary career; several poems remained extremely popular with his admirers. While his next volume, *Fine Clothes to the Jew* (1927), would represent a major step forward in his involvement in the blues and his development as a poet, *The Weary Blues* is richly representative of Hughes's sensibility as a poet.

• Langston Hughes, *Collected Poems*, 1994. Arnold Rampersad, *The Life of Langston Hughes*, vol. 1, *1902–1941: I Too Sing America*, 1986.

—Arnold Rampersad

WEBB, FRANK J. (?–?), author of *The Garies and Their Friends* (1857) and two novelettes, "Two Wolves and a Lamb," (1870) and "Marvin Hayle" (1870). The little that is known about Frank J. Webb's life comes from Harriet Beecher *Stowe's brief preface to *The Garies.* According to Stowe, he was born in Philadelphia, probably in the late 1820s or early 1830s. After growing up there, he likely resided in England sometime prior to the London publication of *The Garies* and may have moved in wealthy European social circles. Drawing on these experiences, Webb's novelettes focus on the leisure-time activities of upper-class society in London, Paris, and Cannes. *The Garies*'s prefaces by Stowe and Lord Brougham, both abolitionists, suggest he may have also played a role in the antislavery movement.

Webb's contribution to African American literature is to be found in the number of pioneering themes and subjects addressed in *The Garies.* Published four years after William Wells *Brown's **Clotel, The Garies* is the second of four African American novels published prior to the Civil War. Its contrived plot follows the fortunes of three families with roots in the South: the dark-skinned Ellises, the interracial Garies, and the white Stevenses, headed by the villainous "slippery" George. Drawn together by circumstance in Philadelphia, these families allow Webb to explore the fortunes of the rising African American middle class and the virulence of northern racism, greed, and deceit found among both whites and blacks. The novel argues finally that wealth is the key to African American advancement. *The Garies and Their Friends* was the first novel to describe the lives of free African Americans in the North, to address interracial marriage and the problem of the color line, and the first to make passing a major theme.

• Gregory L. Candela, "Frank J. Webb," *DLB*, vol. 50, *Afro-American Writers before the Harlem Renaissance*, ed. Trudier Harris, 1986, pp. 242–244. Blyden Jackson, *A History of Afro-American Literature*, vol. 1, *The Long Beginning, 1746–1895*, 1989, pp. 323–348. *The Garies and Their Friends*, ed. Robert Reid-Pharr (1997).

—Lawrence R. Rodgers

WELLS-BARNETT, IDA B. (1862–1931), journalist, editor, diarist, autobiographer, lecturer, suffragist, antilynching crusader, and civil rights activist. The essays, pamphlets, and newspaper articles of Ida B. Wells-Barnett shaped the post-Reconstruction discourse on race, while her personal narratives, including two diaries, a travel journal, and an autobiography, recorded the personal struggle of a professional woman to define African American womanhood in a pivotal era of American history. A complex woman of strong character and independent thought, Wells was shaped by firm moral convictions and profound religious beliefs. Her militant ideology of resistance, which found expression through the pen and at the podium, continued the tradition of resistance initiated by earlier African American writers and thinkers such as David *Walker, Maria W. *Stewart, Frederick *Douglass, and Frances Ellen Watkins *Harper.

The eldest of eight children, Ida B. Wells was born to Jim and Elizabeth Warrenton Wells in Holly Springs, Mississippi, on 16 July 1862. Wells attended Shaw University (later Rust College) until the deaths of her parents and youngest brother during the yellow fever epidemic of 1878. Only sixteen years old, she became a county schoolteacher, supporting her brothers and sisters on a salary of just twenty-five dollars a month. In 1882 or 1883 she began teaching in Woodstock, Tennessee, a rural community in Shelby County, but moved to Memphis when she obtained a position in the public schools in 1884.

That same year Wells sued the Chesapeake, Ohio and Southwestern Railroad after she was forcibly removed from the first-class ladies' coach. In December 1884 the circuit court ruled in her favor, but three years later the Tennessee Supreme Court reversed the decision. That experience prompted Wells to write letters to Memphis weeklies and, later, to African American newspapers like the *Detroit Plaindealer, Gate City Press,* and *New York Freeman.* Early articles, such as "Our Women" and "Race Pride," reveal the young journalist's increasing interest in issues of gender and race. In 1886 Wells became "editress" of the *Evening Star* and began writing under the pen name Iola for a religious paper, the *Living Way,* earning the praise of newspapermen such as I. Garland Penn, who called her a militant journalist.

Between 1885 and 1887 Ida B. Wells kept a diary describing her struggle as a single professional woman to forge an independent life committed to work, self-improvement, and racial uplift. She recorded acts of mob violence and the loss of her suit; she wrote about conferences in Kansas and Kentucky, where she was elected secretary of the Negro Press Association and was invited to speak on "Women in Journalism or How I Would Edit." Two years later, she bought an interest in the Memphis *Free Speech and Headlight* and became a full-time journalist in 1891, when she lost her teaching position because of editorials attacking inferior segregated schools.

After three African American grocers were brutally murdered by a white Memphis mob on 9 March 1892, Wells wrote fiery editorials urging citizens to flee the city. She maintained that lynching was a racist strategy to eliminate independent and prosperous Negroes, while the charge of rape, she suggested, often masked consensual relations between white women and African American men. Whites were so incensed by these allegations that they destroyed her newspaper office while Wells was away and dared her to return to Memphis. Unintimidated by threats, Wells kept a gun in her house and advised that "a Winchester rifle should have a place of honor in every black home" (*Southern Horrors,* 1892).

Meanwhile she bought an interest in the *New York Age,* wrote two weekly columns entitled "Iola's Southern Field," and intensified her campaign against lynching through lectures, editorials, and carefully researched, well-documented pamphlets: *Southern Horrors: Lynch Law in All Its Phases* (1892); *A Red Record: Tabulated Statistics and Alleged Causes of Lynching in the United States, 1892, 1893, and 1894* (1895); and *Mob Rule in New Orleans* (1900). A forceful speaker and powerful writer, Wells uses strong, concrete language to examine the economic and political causes of racial oppression. In her writing she analyzes racist sexual ideology, exposes the collusion between terrorists and community leaders, and urges African Americans to resist oppression through boycotts and emigration.

In 1893 Wells cowrote and printed *The Reason Why the Colored American Is Not in the Columbian Exposition—the Afro-American's Contribution to Columbia Literature* to protest the exclusion of African Americans from the World's Columbian Exposition in Chicago. That same year, convinced that international pressure might serve the antilynching cause, she undertook a lecture tour of Great Britain. On the voyage to England she began a short and spirited travel journal, which was later published in her autobiography. When she returned to England in 1894 for a six-month tour, Wells wrote a series of articles entitled "Ida B. Wells Abroad" for the Chicago *Inter-Ocean.*

After her 27 June 1895 marriage to Ferdinand L. Barnett, a Chicago lawyer, newspaperman, and widower with two sons, Wells-Barnett bought the *Chicago Conservator* from her husband. She continued to write following the births of her children, Charles Aked, Herman Kohlsaat, Ida B. Wells, Jr., and Alfreda M. Some of her published essays during this period include "Lynching and the Excuse for It" (1901), "Booker T. Washington and His Critics" (1904), and "Our Country's Lynching Record" (1913).

Wells-Barnett broadened her reformist activities and took up the suffragist cause. She had organized the Ida B. Wells Club in 1893; she later founded the Alpha Suffrage Club and cofounded the Cook County League of Women's Clubs. She was elected secretary of the National Afro-American Council and called for a conference that led to the formation of the NAACP. In 1910 Wells-Barnett formed the Negro Fellowship League to employ southern migrants, using her salary as a probation officer to support the league. Her differences with race leaders became apparent when she challenged the accommodationism of Booker T. *Washington and the integrationist leanings of W. E. B. *Du Bois, while supporting Marcus *Garvey and his Universal Negro Improvement Association.

Wells-Barnett continued her crusade against violence into her fifties. In 1918 she covered the race riot in East St. Louis, Illinois, and wrote a series of articles on the riot for the *Chicago Defender.* Four years later she returned south to investigate the indictment for murder of twelve innocent Arkansas farmers. She then wrote *The Arkansas Race Riot* (1922) and raised money to publish and distribute one thousand copies of her report. Throughout her final years, she continued to write. In 1928 Wells-Barnett began an autobiography, which was edited and published posthumously by her daughter, Alfreda Duster, and she kept a diary in 1930 that depicts an active and vital woman attending meetings and lectures while campaigning for election to the Illinois State Senate. After a sudden illness, she died in Chicago on 25 March 1931.

Ida B. Wells-Barnett was one of the most outstanding women of the late nineteenth century. She was a militant thinker and writer whose essays, pamphlets, and books provide a theoretical analysis of lynching; she was a reformer whose insistence on economic and political resistance to oppression laid the foundation for the modern civil rights movement; and she was an accomplished diarist and autobiographer whose personal narratives offer an insight into the formation of African American female identity in the late nineteenth century.

• Alfreda M. Duster, ed., *Crusade for Justice: The Autobiography of Ida B. Wells,* 1970. Bettina Aptheker, ed., *Lynching and Rape,* 1977. Dorothy Sterling, *Black Foremothers,* 1979. Thomas C. Holt, "The Lonely Warrior: Ida B. Wells Barnett and the Struggle for Black Leadership," in *Black Leaders of the Twentieth Century,* eds. John Hope Franklin and August Meier, 1982, pp. 38–61. Paula Giddings, *When and Where I Enter: The Impact of Black Women on Race and Sex in America,* 1984. Hazel V. Carby, *Reconstructing Womanhood,* 1987. Mildred Thompson, *Ida B. Wells-Barnett,* 1990. Trudier Harris, ed., *Selected Works of Ida B. Wells-Barnett,* 1991. Miriam DeCosta-Willis, *The Memphis Diary of Ida B. Wells,* 1995. Sandra Gunning, *Race, Rape, and Lynching,* 1996.

—Miriam DeCosta-Willis

"We Shall Overcome." The most prominent freedom song of the civil rights movement of the 1960s, "We Shall Overcome" has origins in African American spirituals and has been used in a range of protest movements. The song emerged from multiple sources, including the old spiritual "I Will Overcome" and the church hymn "I'll Overcome Someday" (published in 1901 by Reverend C. A. Tindley). Striking African American tobacco workers in Charleston, South Carolina, used an early version of the song on picket lines in 1945. It achieved wider use as a labor song after two of those union members brought the song to Highlander Folk School, a Tennessee training center for labor and civil rights organizers. In the 1960s student activists in the South used the song at sit-in demonstrations for desegregation. As its use spread, "We Shall Overcome" became the anthem of the civil rights movement, sung at demonstrations, police confrontations, mass meetings, and national events like the 1963 Freedom March in Washington, D.C. In addition to its continued use as a protest song in the United States, it is heard throughout the world in a variety of resistance movements. The adaptability and endurance of this song reveals the continuity of African American folk and spirituals, their ability to be reborn and to reappear in different forms and contexts. While drawing upon the tradition of African American congregational-style singing, various arrangements or styles have marked the song's appearance at different moments (in church, jail, or a mass demonstration; for desegregation, labor, or peace efforts), and new lyrics have been included to suit the occasion (during an armed police raid in Tennessee, for example, teenager Jamila Jones introduced the line "We are not afraid"). "We Shall Overcome" served as a powerful symbol of the civil rights movement and continues to function as a tool of solidarity and resistance.

• Guy Carawan and Candie Carawan, *We Shall Overcome: Songs of the Southern Freedom Movement,* 1963. Bernice Johnson Reagon, *Voices of the Civil Rights Movement: Black American Freedom Songs,* sound recording and accompanying text, Smithsonian Institution, 1980. Jim Brown et al., *We Shall Overcome: The Song that Moved a Nation,* video documentary, California Newsreel, 1989.

—Christina Accomando

WESLEY, DOROTHY PORTER. *See* Porter, Dorothy.

WEST, CORNEL (b. 1953), essayist, public speaker, social activist, and major figure in African American academia. Cornel West was born in Tulsa, Oklahoma, on 2 June 1953. His mother was an elementary school teacher who later became principal; his father, a civilian administrator in the air force. Both of his parents attended Fisk University. The family, including West's brother, Clifton, moved often. They eventually settled in a middle-class African American neighborhood in Sacramento, California. West graduated with a degree in Near Eastern languages and literature from Harvard University. He received his doctorate in philosophy from Princeton University. As director of Princeton's Afro-American Studies Program from 1988 to 1994, and as a professor in Harvard's Department of Afro-American Studies since 1994, West is one of several high-profile scholars who have strengthened African American studies programs. He has taught at America's most prestigious universities and has lectured at many others. The blend of skills and styles employed by West inspires adjectives from his admirers and critics; unadorned nouns seem unable to capture his complexities.

West is a prolific essayist and author. His first book, *Prophesy Deliverance!: An Afro-American Revolutionary Christianity,* appeared in 1982 and attempts to synthesize elements of African American Christianity and thought, Western philosophy, and Marxist thinking. In 1988 West published *Prophetic Fragments,* a collection of essays that discuss similarly disparate elements. *The American Evasion of Philosophy: A Genealogy of Pragmatism* (1989) engages populism and race, class, and gender issues. *The Ethical Dimensions of Marxist Thought* (1991) and *Keeping Faith: Philosophy and Race in America* (1993) continue the discussion of those ideas in the context of modern America. *Prophetic Thought in Postmodern Times* and *Prophetic Reflections: Notes on Race and Power in America* also date from 1993. Throughout his career West has also produced collaborative work: *Post-Analytic Philosophy* (1985), edited with John Rajchman; *Breaking Bread: Insurgent Black Intellectual Life* (1991), cowritten with bell *hooks; *Jews and Blacks: Let the Healing Begin* (1995), authored with Michael Lerner; *The Future of the Race* (1996), with Henry Louis *Gates, Jr., and with Roberto Mangabeira Unger, *The Future of American Progressivism* (1998). West's contributions to journals, popular magazines, and essay collections are myriad. His most influential book is *Race Matters* (1993), a short collection of essays that epitomizes West's careful attention to African American culture.

As a literary figure West is not easily categorized. His strength lies in his interdisciplinary focus. West synthesizes diverse topics in his writing leading to a careful control of language that is often poetic in its precision. He participates in African American oral and musical literary traditions with a spontaneous, performative element in his work that is as much a legacy from his grandfather, a Baptist preacher, as it is a language borrowed from jazz and rap. In his writing he legitimizes all forms of African American speech and bends them to effective use, employing language as a polemical weapon for social activism. This crafting of language and blending of genres mark West's literary style.

Cornel West's contributions to African American literature and thought range across disciplines and worlds to comment upon African American life. His work exemplifies synthesis and innovation.

• Robert S. Boynton, "Princeton's Public Intellectual," *New York Times Magazine,* 15 September 1991, 39+.

—Elizabeth Sanders Delwiche Engelhardt

WEST, DOROTHY (1907–1998), novelist, short story writer, editor, and journalist. Through her various roles as writer, editor, and journalist, Dorothy West has influenced the direction and form of African American literary production. Prior to the publication of her first novel in 1948, West published frequently in the journals of the Harlem Renaissance. As editor and founder of *Challenge* and *New Challenge,* she helped to oversee the transition from the Harlem Renaissance to the naturalistic realism of the 1930s. *The Living Is Easy* appeared about the same time as Ann *Petry's *The *Street* (1946), Gwendolyn *Brooks's *A *Street in Bronzeville* (1945) and **Annie Allen* (1949), and Zora Neale *Hurston's *Seraph on the Sewanee* (1948). It has become an important novel for newer generations of black women writers and critics.

Born into a middle-class black family in Boston, West displayed her literary talent early. As a schoolgirl, her first short story, "Promise and Fulfillment," was published by the *Boston Post.* Another story, "The Typewriter," won second place in an *Opportunity* literary contest. West shared the prize with Zora Neale Hurston. In 1926 West moved to New York to live with her cousin, the poet Helene *Johnson, and shortly thereafter her Harlem Renaissance career began. West became a beloved "little sister" of Harlem Renaissance writers like Zora Neale Hurston, Langston *Hughes, and Wallace *Thurman. Among her many published stories during this period, two—"Funeral" (*Saturday Evening Quill,* Apr. 1928) and "Prologue to a Life" (*Saturday Evening Quill,* Apr. 1929)—rehearse themes that she would explore in greater depth in *The Living Is Easy.*

In addition to her writing, West pursued acting. In 1927 she had a small role in the original stage production of *Porgy* (based on Dubose Heyward's novel) and in 1932 she accompanied Langston Hughes and a group of black intellectuals and artists to the Soviet Union to make a film about race relations in the South. The film was never made and West returned to the United States.

In the 1930s West exerted her influence primarily as an editor and publisher, first of *Challenge* and then of *New Challenge.* She founded and financed both journals. *Challenge* sought to publish "quality" fiction by established writers and to avoid what James Weldon *Johnson called "propaganda." The first two numbers of the journal contained writings by known talents like Hughes, Hurston, and Countee *Cullen. West claimed that younger writers submitted bad fiction. *Challenge* was criticized by members of the Chicago group of writers, including Richard *Wright and Margaret *Walker, who felt it to be too aesthetic and nonpolitical. In 1937 *Challenge* became *New Challenge,* and at West's invitation Richard Wright became associate editor. The new journal leaned toward more political fiction and introduced new writers like Ralph *Ellison and Waters *Turpin. Richard Wright's classic manifesto on black literature, "Blueprint for Negro Writing," appeared in the journal as well. Because of financial difficulty and editorial conflicts between West and Wright, the journal folded after one issue.

Throughout this period West continued to write and publish short stories. From 1926 to 1940 she published several stories in *Opportunity,* the *Messenger,* and *Saturday Evening Quill.* In 1945 she left New York for Martha's Vineyard to work on an autobiographical novel. *The Living Is Easy* was published by Random House in 1948. The story of the fiercely determined and independent Bostonian, Cleo Judson, the novel launches a satirical critique of the class and color politics of the black bourgeoisie. Cleo seeks to acquire a balance between her loving southern upbringing and her aspirations toward material acquisitions and status. In the process she ruins her husband's financial empire and her sisters' marriages. The novel explores marital relations as well as the complex and at times painful relationships between mothers and daughters. West's influence is apparent in the mother-daughter relationship in Paule *Marshall's **Brown Girl, Brownstones* (1959).

When *The Living Is Easy* was republished in 1982, the novel was recognized as an important and influential text in the black woman's literary tradition. While Dorothy West continued to write articles and stories from her Martha's Vineyard home, it was not until 1995 that her second novel, *The Wedding,* appeared. *The Richer, the Poorer,* a collection of stories and reminiscences, was also published in 1995.

• Deborah MacDowell, "Conversations with Dorothy West," in *The Harlem Renaissance Re-Examined,* ed. Victor A. Kramer, 1987, pp. 265–282. Sybil Steinberg, "Dorothy West: Her Own Renaissance," in *Publishers Weekly* 242 (3 July 1995) : 34–35. A. Yemisi Jimoh, "Dorothy West," in *Contemporary African American Novelists,* ed. Emmanuel S. Nelson, 1999, pp. 475–481.

—Farah Jasmine Griffin

WHEATLEY, PHILLIS (c. 1753–1784), the first African American and the second woman to publish a book in the colonies on any subject. Phillis Wheatley was born, by her own testimony, in Gambia, West Africa, about the year 1753. Unlike her African American contemporary, Venture *Smith, who devoted over a third of his 1798 *Narrative* to a detailed recollection of his African homeland, Wheatley, who was seized and taken into slavery when seven or eight years of age, recalled her homeland to her white captors in considerably less detail. While we may never know what memories this remarkable poet and cultivator of the epistolary style shared of her native Africa with her most frequent correspondent and black soulmate, Obour Tanner, we do know that her public memories were at least three.

She did recall the sight of her mother's daily ritual of pouring out water to the sun upon its rising, redolent of hierophantic solar worship, and then immediately prostrating herself in the direction of that rising sun, this practice probably describing the first of five daily prayers of Islam in which the believer kneels or prostrates her or himself toward Mecca, certainly the direction Wheatley's mother assumed. While the other two memories may not be as informative, they are more affecting. In her famous poem "To the Right Honourable William, Earl of Dartmouth," she holds that her "love of Freedom sprung" from the fact that she "Was snatch'd from Afric's fancy'd happy seat." "Steel'd was that soul," the poet continues, "and by no misery mov'd / That from a father seiz'd his babe belov'd." In several rhapsodic and descriptive lines from "Phillis's Reply to the Answer" in which the author to whom she is replying prompts her to respond that "pleasing Gambia on my soul returns," she extols Gambia's "soil spontaneous" which "yields exhaustless stores; / For phoebus revels on her verdant shores."

When the young girl of seven or eight found herself on the slave block in midsummer Boston on 11 July 1761, was she thinking of her fertile, verdant Gambia while she tried to conceal her nakedness in a public place with nothing more than a piece of dirty carpet? The Wheatleys bought her, nevertheless, for a trifle and with diseased imagination named her Phillis after the slave schooner that brought her from Africa to America.

Despite the lamentable disadvantage of her enslavement, only four years later Wheatley had acquired enough skill in the use of English that she could correspond with the Mohegan Indian minister and graduate of Dartmouth College, Samson Occom. As well, she must have begun to experiment with the writing of poetry. Her first published writing, the poem "On Messrs. Hussey and Coffin" (about the remarkable survival of these gentlemen in a hurricane off Cape Cod), appeared on 21 December 1767 in the *Newport Mercury.* At the approximate age of fourteen, then, Wheatley became a published public poet, a capacity in which she continued to function throughout the remainder of her short life.

Probably during this same period Wheatley initiated her classical studies, perhaps being tutored by the Harvard graduate, minister of Old South Church, one-time prolific poet, and encourager of young poets, Mather Byles. Wheatley soon became an excellent student of Latin, as her superb version of Ovid's Niobe episode from Book VI of the *Metamorphoses* ably attests.

On 18 August 1771 Wheatley was baptized by Samuel Cooper, minister and future spiritual and literary advisor to the poet. By 29 February of the following year, Wheatley had composed enough poems to comprise a volume. This volume failed to appear because of a lack of subscribers and, according to William H. Robinson, because of racist reasons. By September 1773, however, Wheatley had found a London publisher with the help of Selina Hastings, philanthropist and Countess of Huntingdon. Prior to the appearance of her **Poems on Various Subjects, Religious and Moral,* Wheatley spent six weeks in London, from June 17 to July 26, during which time she prepared her *Poems* for the press and visited, or was visited by, several London dignitaries, such as Granville Sharp, who escorted the poet on tours of the Horse Armoury, the crown jewels, and the Tower of London; Thomas Gibbons, who Wheatley notes was a professor of rhetoric; the Earl of Dartmouth, who gave the poet five guineas, with which she purchased a set of Alexander Pope's complete *Works;* and Brook Watson, a wealthy merchant who gave Wheatley a folio edition of John Milton's *Paradise Lost.*

While in London Wheatley received Benjamin Franklin, who wrote to his American cousin, Jonathan Williams, that "Upon your recommendation I went to see the black poetess and offered her any services I could do her." Even no less an intellectual lion than Voltaire, who was living in England at the time, wrote in a letter to a French friend in 1774 that Wheatley was the composer of *"très-bons vers anglais"* (very good English verse). Certainly Wheatley earned for herself on this trip an international reputation, the first African American to do so. She had already enjoyed an international reputation of sorts for her elegy on the death of George Whitefield, privy chaplain to the Countess of Huntingdon; appearing first in 1770 in Boston, this elegy was widely reprinted on both sides of the Atlantic and perhaps first brought to the countess's attention the poetic talent of the sixteen- or seventeen-year-old poet.

Soon after the appearance of *Poems,* Wheatley achieved her manumission, as she remarked in a letter of 8 October 1773 to David Wooster, later a general in the Revolutionary War, "at the desire of my friends in England." Not until her pen brought her into the scrutiny of the British public did John Wheatley see fit to "give me my freedom." Wheatley, therefore, is the first African American to free herself by means of her own writing ability. After Susanna Wheatley, the poet's former mistress, died on 3 March 1774, Wheatley continued to live at the Wheatley mansion for a time and to write patriotic verse. She corresponded with George Washington, composing the famous poem "To His Excellency General Washington," on 26 October 1775, and received an invitation from the general to visit him. She did so at Washington's Cambridge headquarters, a few days before the departure of the British under General Howe from Boston, on 17 March 1776. Wheatley married John Peters, a free African American and jack-of-all-trades (grocery keeper, dandy, and advocate for black rights before the Massachusetts courts), on 1 April 1776.

After this time, given the ravages and uncertainties of the American Revolution, Wheatley's fortunes declined rapidly. She tried twice, but unsuccessfully, to solicit subscribers for a second volume of new poems, dedicated to Benjamin Franklin. On 30 October 1779 and in September 1784, just three months before her death, she published proposals for a collection that would have included an "Epithalamium" (perhaps showing the influence of Edmund Spenser), "Niagra," "Chloe to Calliope," "To Musidora or Florello," and several new elegies as well as thirteen letters to such notables as Dartmouth, Benjamin Rush, and the Countess of Huntingdon. During this time, Wheatley served as part-time instructor in a petty school and as a domestic servant while trying to tend to three children. Wheatley died in abject poverty, preceded by her three children, on 5 December 1784, apparently from infection from having just given birth to her last child, unremembered and certainly unappreciated.

This internationally famous and accomplished artist nevertheless experienced an early career similar to that of most fine poets: an apprenticeship during which Wheatley produced a sizable body of juvenilia was followed by a period of maturity marked by poems of apparently aesthetic concerns. Wheatley's apprenticeship is characterized by statements of intense, Christian piety; such poems as "Atheism" and "An Address to the Deist," both from 1767, appear to be the sorts of declarations that a racist white catechist might have exacted from a catechumen of color during this time. "On Friendship" (1769) and "On the Nuptials of Mr. Spence to Miss Hooper" (1768) suggest the aesthetic interests of her mature period, while the poems "America," "On the Death of Mr. Snider Murder'd by Richardson," "On the Affray in King-Street, on the Evening of the 5th of March" (almost certainly written in celebration of Crispus Attucks), and "To the King's Most Excellent Majesty. 1768," predict Wheatley's preoccupation with American patriot politics.

Almost immediately after the publication in late February 1772 of her first proposal for a volume of poems, Wheatley's tone and subject matter shift away from pious testimony toward that of a zealous seeker for her own idea of God and for her own poetic idiom. In such works as "Thoughts on the Works of Providence," which (while naming Jehovah once) makes no mention of Jesus but syncretizes solar worship, animism, and classicism with a broad Judeo-Christianity, and "On Imagination," a complex poem that continues the religious syncretism but which represents a concentrated expression of Wheatley's poetics, Wheatley displays a sophisticated handling of the poetic and intellectual materials available to her. For that matter, this poet suggests by her work that she has recognized full well white duplicity ("Some view our sable race with a scornful eye") and that she has constructed a poetics of subversion.

Several critics of Wheatley have recently recognized a subversive tone within her poetry. In a letter to Samson Occom dated 11 February 1774 and reprinted in colonial newspapers a dozen times during this year, Wheatley defines freedom in the following manner: "in every human Breast, God has implanted a Principle which we call Love of Freedom; it is impatient of Oppression, and pants for Deliverance." Surely any feeling, intelligent soul who can define freedom in these eloquent words can never be satisfied with servility. Lest any suspect Wheatley failed to recognize the implications for her and her black brothers and sisters of the American patriot cry for freedom from the British, observe what she says as she closes her letter to Occom: "How well the cry for Liberty, and the reverse Disposition for the Exercise of oppressive Power over others agree—I humbly think it does not require the Penetration of a Philosopher to determine."

Wheatley assumes her subversive voice in "To Maecenas," the opening poem of the 1773 *Poems.* Here she exploits the potential for subversion present in classical pastoral by donning the mask of an innocuous shepherd and by joining Maecenas, legendary Roman patron of Virgil and Horace, "beneath the myrtle shade," the classic site of pastoral, so that she can profess a burning ambition to achieve the height of expression in the epic mode, descant upon the subject of freedom, and "snatch a laurel," the symbol of poetic maturity, while her white patrons "indulgent smile upon the deed"—hardly the aspirations of an allegedly derivative imitator of the neoclassical manner of composition. This subversive voice is evident in all of her occasional poetry after February of 1772, including "On Being Brought from Africa to America" (written as early as 1768 but doubtless revised for the 1773 *Poems*).

As noted earlier, Wheatley's efforts to articulate her subversive objections to "oppressive Power" went largely unnoticed because of her declining fortunes after her marriage to Peters. This decline came about because of the Revolutionary War, the apparently desultory support of her husband, and the failures of the two proposal attempts to attract subscribers. Her bleak outlook is evident in what is probably one of her last poems, "An Elegy on Leaving _______," for what she is leaving behind is the world of poetry: "No more my hand shall wake the warbling lyre." Despite a despondent conclusion to a remarkably distinguished career, Phillis Wheatley represents a number of firsts in American culture. While she is author of the first book published by an African American, she is also the first woman who published her work largely through the efforts of a community of women: her mistress, Susanna, seems always to have encouraged her to write, and her daughter, Mary, may have served as the poet's first tutor; Obour Tanner, her black soulmate, evidently gave Wheatley encouragement and spiritual counsel, but it was probably through the efforts of Selina Hastings, the Countess of Huntingdon, that she saw one of her volumes come into print. Wheatley also enjoys the distinction of being America's first woman writer who tried to make a living by the use of her pen, and she is certainly one of America's first authors, whether man or woman, to do so. In addition, Wheatley is one of America's first writers to cultivate for publication the epistolary style. According to Henry Louis *Gates, Jr., moreover, she is "the progenitor of the black literary tradition." For all these reasons and more Phillis Wheatley deserves to be recognized as a major American author.

[*See also* Literary History, article on Colonial and Early National Eras.]

• William H. Robinson, *Black New England Letters,* 1977. William H. Robinson, ed., *Critical Essays on Phillis Wheatley,* 1982. William H. Robinson, ed., *Phillis Wheatley and Her Writings,* 1984. Sondra A. O'Neale, "A Slave's Subtle War: Phillis Wheatley's Use of Biblical Myth and Symbol," *Early American Literature* 21.2 (Fall 1986): 144–165. Henry Louis Gates, Jr., *Figures in Black,* 1987. John C. Shields, ed., The *Collected Works of Phillis Wheatley,* 1988. John C. Shields, "Phillis Wheatley," in *African American Writers,* eds. Valerie Smith, Lea Baechler, and A. Walton Litz, 1991, pp. 473–491. Phillip M. Richards, "Phillis Wheatley and Literary Americanization," *American Quarterly* 44.2 (June 1992): 163–191. Frances Smith Foster, *Written by Herself: Literary Production by African American Women 1746–1892,* 1993. John C. Shields, guest ed., *Style: African-American Poetics* 26 (Fall 1993): 172–270. Paula Bennett, "Phillis Wheatley's Vocation and the Paradox of the 'Afric Muse'," *PMLA* 113 (Jan. 1998): 64–76.

—John C. Shields

WHITE, PAULETTE CHILDRESS (b. 1948), short fiction writer, and poet. Paulette Childress White was born in Detroit, Michigan, on 1 December 1948, the third of thirteen children. After one year of art school, financial problems and the birth of the first of five sons interrupted her education. Her first published poem appeared in *Deep Rivers* in 1972, followed by a small collection, *Love Poem to a Black Junkie* (1975). Some of these poems reflect the black nationalism and rediscovery of Africa apparent in current literature while others introduce more original themes that continue into her later work.

One such theme, the impotent anger of many African American men, is demonstrated in the short story "Passing" and recurs in other short stories: in the street-corner argument overheard in "The Bird Cage" (*Redbook,* June 1978), and in the silent protagonist's daily distribution of old newspaper clippings in the neighborhood of a 1967 riot in "Paper Man" (*Michigan Quarterly Review,* Spring 1986).

White also writes of women who eventually bond through reluctant realization of their painful commonality that cuts across artificial lines. The poem "Humbled Rocks" (*Love Poem*) and the short stories "Alice" (*Essence,* Jan. 1977), "Dear Akua" (*Harbor Review,* 1986), and "Getting the Facts of Life" (*Rites of Passage,* ed. Tonya Bolden, 1994) all testify to the spiritual sustenance derived from sisterhood.The recurrence of this theme, encouraged by the rise of feminism, is more directly related to personal experience.

White's writing is highly autobiographical with only minor details changed. "Getting the Facts of Life," in which a girl, sharing with her cohesive family the financial and emotional consequences of her father's employment layoff, makes her first humiliating trip with her mother to the "welfare office" through a racially divided neighborhood, creatively interprets actual events. *The Watermelon Dress: Portrait of a Woman* (1984), a narrative poem, traces the author's development as a closet artist and unfulfilled woman from adolescence through the conflicting demands and needs of a difficult first marriage and child-rearing and a period of emotional unconsciousness to the eventual awareness and challenge of selfhood.

The streets of Detroit are as essential to White's writing as Chicago is to the work of Gwendolyn *Brooks. The memorable and superbly drawn characters who inhabit her world and the hungers that drive them are insightful and authentic. The occasional interplay between the narrator's reflections and the characters' actions and dialogue is effective and original. White's lyricism, sometimes reminiscent of Jean *Toomer's sentence fragments and poetic repetition, and her metaphorical and alliterative use of language make her fiction almost indistinguishable from her poetry.

Paulette White is now remarried, a PhD candidate at Wayne State University, and an instructor at Henry Ford Community College. When her schedule permits her more time for creativity, this unique voice may well encourage other writers to trust the validity of their own experiences as women emerging from the darkness of restriction and concealment into the sunlight of their own personhood and to express those realized selves with sensitivity, insight, and lyrical beauty.

• Mary Helen Washington, introduction to *Midnight Birds: Stories of Contemporary Black Women Writers,* ed. Mary Helen Washington, 1982, pp. 3–7.

—Naomi Long Madgett

WHITE, WALTER (1893–1955), novelist, essayist, civil rights leader, writer and patron of the Harlem Renaissance, and executive secretary of the NAACP. The son of a mail carrier and one of seven children, Walter Francis White grew up in Atlanta on the border between white and African American neighborhoods. During the Atlanta race riots of September 1906, a white mob nearly burned down his family's home. The event was formative for White, then thirteen, inaugurating his awareness of the meaning of racial identity and influencing his subsequent political and literary careers.

A 1916 graduate of Atlanta University, White worked for Atlanta's Standard Life Insurance Company until 1918, when James Weldon *Johnson, then NAACP field secretary, invited him to join the NAACP staff as assistant secretary at its New York City headquarters. Blond-haired and blue-eyed, White was easily able to pass for white and often risked his life to conduct undercover investigations of lynchings. Twelve days into his NAACP job, White was sent to research the circumstances of a lynching in Estill Springs, Tennessee; he himself narrowly escaped being lynched on a trip to Arkansas in 1919. In 1922, the year White married NAACP staff member Leah Gladys Powell, he met writer H. L. Mencken, who encouraged White to try his hand at fiction. White completed the manuscript of *Fire in the Flint,* about a northern-trained African American physician who returns to his native small-town Georgia, in twelve days. Published by Knopf in 1924, the novel, which ends with the doctor's lynching, was praised for its realistic portrayal of southern life, went through several European editions, and became a modest best-seller. *Flight* (1926), White's second, less critically acclaimed novel, centers around a young New Orleans woman who crosses over the color line, then later relinquishes racial passing. White's literary accomplishments earned him a 1926 Guggenheim Fellowship, and he moved to southern France intending to produce a third novel; instead, however, he wrote *Rope and Faggot: The Biography of Judge Lynch* (1929), an important study of the various political, economic, social, and sexual influences of lynching.

White's literary career and his NAACP work were closely intertwined, and throughout the 1920s and 1930s he continued to toil for federal anti-lynching legislation and civil rights while aiding and inspiring Harlem Renaissance artists. Not only did White combine cultural and political leadership, but he also viewed cultural production in a political framework. An advocate of Alain *Locke's New Negro metaphor, White helped start the Negro Fellowship Fund to support young writers and used his NAACP contacts to further their careers. In 1931, he replaced Johnson as the NAACP's second African American executive secretary and oversaw the organization through the crucial years following World War II and the landmark *Brown v. Board of Education* decision of May 1954. In addition to a column for the *Chicago Defender,* White's nonfiction includes *A Rising Wind* (1945), about African American soldiers during World War II, and his 1948 autobiography, *A Man Called White,* which details the history of the NAACP under his direction.

• Edward E. Waldron, "Walter White and the Harlem Renaissance: Letters from 1924–1927," *CLA Journal* 16 (June 1973): 438–457.

—Gayle Wald

WHITFIELD, JAMES MONROE (1822–1871), poet. James Monroe Whitfield worked as a barber all his life, and the bitter militancy of his writings reflects his abortive attempts to secure racial justice and become a man of letters. He was born in New Hampshire, and little is known about his youth or later private life. Whitfield was a barber in Buffalo, New York (1854–1859), and in California (1861–1871), with brief sojourns in his later years in Oregon, Idaho, and Nevada. His public support for colonization began in 1854 when he wrote the call for the National Emigration Convention (Cleveland) and a series of letters to the *North Star;* from 1859 to 1861 he probably traveled in Central America seeking land for an African American colony. From 1849 until his death, Whitfield's forceful protest poetry and letters appeared often in the *North Star, Frederick Douglass's Paper,* the *San Francisco Elevator,* and other African American periodicals, and he read several of his commemorative odes in public. The majority of his writings remain uncollected; his only published volume is *America and Other Poems* (1853). Whitfield died of heart disease and was buried in the Masonic Cemetery of San Francisco.

Whitfield's verse is outstanding for its metrical control, breadth of classical imagery, commanding historical sense, and convincing anger. With biting cynicism, he denounces oppression worldwide and scourges America's morally corrupt church and state in two long antislavery jeremiads, "America" and "How Long?" "America" begins: "America, it is to thee / Thou boasted land of liberty,—/ It is to thee I raise my song, / Thou land of blood, and crime, and wrong." "How Long?" moves from Europe's "princely pomp, and priestly pride" that tramples people's rights, hopes, and spirits to the insidious plague of moral corruption, slavery, infecting America "with foul pestiferous breath." Whitfield's most compelling poems are dark imprecations against a world "disjoint and out of frame" where men, women, religion, love, and nature are tainted and meaningless. With anguished pessimism, particularly in "Yes, Strike Again That Sounding String" and "The Misanthropist," the poet dramatizes the estrangement and defeat of an African American artist. In 1867 Whitfield delivered his robust four-hundred-line *Poem,* which surveys American history, the sowing of freedom in New England and slavery in the South, the Civil War, and now, "Such fiendish murders as of late / Occur in every rebel State." Once again, the nation must be purged of poisonous bigotry; only "equal laws," the poet says, will re-create a "country of the free." No poet of his time combined anger and artistry as forcefully as Whitfield; he was a major propagandist for black separatism and racial retributive justice through his impassioned poetry and prose.

• Doris Lucas Larye, "James Monroe Whitfield" in *DLB,* vol. 50, *Afro-American Writers before the Harlem Renaissance,* ed. Trudier Harris, 1986, pp. 260–263. Joan R. Sherman, *Invisible Poets: Afro-Americans of the Nineteenth Century,* 2d ed., 1989.

—Joan R. Sherman

WHITMAN, ALBERY ALLSON (1851–1901), poet and minister. The "Poet Laureate of the Negro Race" was born to slave parents in Hart County, Kentucky. Although he lived in bondage for twelve years and had only one year of schooling, Albery Allson Whitman published five volumes of poetry, and both his art and his living gave substance to his motto: "Adversity is the school of heroism, endurance the majesty of man, and hope the torch of high aspirations." Orphaned at the age of twelve, Whitman labored on the farm of his birth; then, from 1864 to 1870, in Ohio and Kentucky, he worked in a plough shop, in railroad construction, and as a schoolteacher. He briefly studied under Bishop Daniel A. *Payne at Wilberforce University (1871) and later served as general financial agent of Wilberforce. Although never formally ordained, in 1877 Whitman was pastor of an AME church in Springfield, Ohio, and from 1879 to 1883 he established churches and led congregations in Ohio, Kansas, Texas, and Georgia. During these years, critics and other poets highly praised Whitman's poetry. He died of pneumonia at his Atlanta home.

"Poetry," Whitman wrote, "is the language of universal sentiment. . . . Her voice is the voice of Eternity dwelling in all great souls. Her aims are the inducements of heaven, and her triumphs the survival of the Beautiful, the True, and the Good." Whitman's art is not utilitarian or polemical but rather art for art's sake and for the sake of showing the race's creative talent. He wrote full-blown Romantic poetry, looking back to legendary pastoral worlds (marred by race prejudice); seeing the present as a sphere of unlimited human potentiality; and looking forward to an ideal earth perfected by human love and poetic genius. Whitman tried to emulate the century's great Romantic poets but never had the opportunity to develop their disciplined craftsmanship. Much of his poetry is technically weak and diffuse, marred by careless versification, awkward shifts in diction, overblown rhetoric, and homiletic digressions. Nevertheless, Whitman did supremely well with what he had: a sure dramatic sense; talent for suspenseful narration, romantic description, communication of pathos, irony, and lovers' emotions; a catholic range of subjects; and the courage to employ varied and difficult meters and rhyme schemes in epic-length poems, suiting his music to shifting moods and meanings. To these poetic skills Whitman added a sense of honor, strong race pride, and sensitive perception of universal issues, poignantly personalized. His code of "manliness" challenges the African American man to fight for "place and power!": "The manly voice of freedom bids him rise, / And shake himself before Philistine eyes!" (*The Rape of Florida,* 1884).

The breadth of Whitman's interests are apparent in his long poems. *Leelah Misled* (1873), in 118 stanzas, is a tale of seduction and betrayal; but the poem dwells on man's distortion of nature's laws; the transience of human joy; virtue and sin; the state of Georgia; excellence in women; time; and comparative religions. *Not a Man, and Yet a Man* (1877), in 197 pages contrasts brave Indians, joined by a few rustics and the mulatto hero, Rodney, with treacherous "civilized" white men, as Rodney journeys from slavery to freedom. *The Rape of Florida,* reprinted as *Twasinta's Seminoles* (1885), through 251 Spenserian stanzas rehearses events of the Seminole Wars (1816–1842); but the treacherous "rape" exemplifies the superiority of primeval nature over the world of "Mammon"; of fierce-spirited red and black braves over white men; and of love—of God and among natives—over the hatreds and hypocrisies of the church, state, and army. Whitman's finest lyrics lie within such long poems: "Come now, my love, the moon is on the lake; / Upon the waters is my light canoe;" (*The Rape of Florida*).

Whitman dared to be an innovator and a "fearless manly man" in his poetry. His considerable achievements place him in the first rank of contemporary African American and white poets.

• Albery A. Whitman, prefaces to *Leelah Misled,* 1873; *Not a Man, and Yet a Man,* 1877; *The Rape of Florida,* 1884; *Twas-*

inta's Seminoles, 1885. Carl L. Marshall, "Two Protest Poems by Albery A. Whitman," *CLA Journal* 19 (Sept. 1975): 50–56. Blydon Jackson, "Albery Allson Whitman in *DLB,* vol. 50, *American Writers before the Harlem Renaissance,* ed. Trudier Harris, 1986, pp. 263–267. Blyden Jackson, *A History of Afro-American Literature,* vol. 1, 1989. Joan R. Sherman, *Invisible Poets: Afro-Americans of the Nineteenth Century,* 2d ed., 1989.

—Joan R. Sherman

WIDEMAN, JOHN EDGAR (b. 1941), intellectual, educator, novelist, essayist, biographer, short fiction writer, social critic, and commentator. John Edgar Wideman was born on 14 June 1941 in Washington, D.C., to Edgar and Betty (Lizabeth) French Wideman, but he grew up at the foot of Bruston Hill, in Pittsburgh, Pennsylvania's Homewood community. His maternal great-great-great-grandmother, Sybela Owens, a runaway slave, was among the original founders and settlers of this community. A Phi Beta Kappa graduate of the University of Pennsylvania, which he attended on a Benjamin Franklin Scholarship, he was captain of the university basketball team. Wideman holds the distinction of being the second African American Rhodes scholar. He graduated from Oxford University in 1966. Before doing so, however, he married Judy Ann Goldman of Virginia in 1965. They are the parents of three children.

Wideman began his teaching career in the English department of the University of Pennsylvania, where he also founded and chaired, for one year, its first African American studies program. He continued his career as a teacher at the University of Wyoming in Laramie, where he spent more than a decade. He is a full professor of creative writing and American studies at the University of Massachusetts at Amherst.

From the outset, Wideman, who spent a year as a Kent Fellow in the Creative Writing Workshop at the University of Iowa (1966–1967) and published his first novel at the age of twenty-six, was placed among the most prominent and gifted contemporary African American (male) writers. He has continued to garner lofty accolades, being identified not solely as "our leading black male writer," and as "our most powerful and accomplished artist," but also as "one of this country's brightest literary lights." Critics hurry to compare him to James Joyce, T. S. Eliot, William Faulkner, Virginia Woolf, and even William Shakespeare. Wideman is a two-time recipient ofthe PEN/Faulkner Award and a finalist for both the National Book Critics Circle Award and the National Book Award; he joined the prestigious group of recipients of the MacArthur Prize Fellowship in 1994.

Wideman is the author of eight novels: *A Glance Away* (1967), *Hurry Home* (1970), *The Lynchers* (1973), *Hiding Place* (1981), *Sent for You Yesterday* (1983), *Reuben* (1987), and **Philadelphia Fire* (1990); three collections of short stories: *Damballah* (1981), *Fever* (1989), and *All Stories Are True* (1992). **Brothers and Keepers* (1984), written with his brother Robert (Robby) Wideman, is a collection of autobiographical essays; he continues with more personal vignettes in *Fatheralong; A Meditation on Fathers and Sons* (1994). Wideman contributed an essay to *Behind the Razor Wire: Portrait of a Contemporary American Prison System,* ed., Michael Jacobson-Hardy, 1999.

Accurately identified as a writer-intellectual by critic James Coleman, Wideman has undergone a tremendous personal, ideological, and artistic transformation in the process of overcoming his feelings of alienation from the black community. When he published his first novel, *A Glance Away,* at the apex of the civil rights movement, the African American literary communal voices to which he added his were, for the most part, vociferously championing the validation of a black aesthetic through the Black Arts movement. However, Wideman clearly wanted to distance himself from its most ardent proponents, such as LeRoi Jones (Amiri *Baraka), Larry *Neal, and Addison *Gayle, Jr., whose cardinal goal was to make African American art the "spiritual sister" of the Black Power concept.

The protagonists of *A Glance Away,* Eddie Lawson, a black rehabilitated drug addict, and Robert Thurley, a white English professor, are driven to seek wholeness and meaning by their sense that something is absent in their worlds. The clear existentialist thrust and modernist perspective of Wideman's innovative work do not ignore or totally circumvent issues of race, but they subordinate them to the central theme of this novel. Wideman's second and third novels, *Hurry Home* and *The Lynchers,* confirmed his willingness to continue to glance away from any mandatory validation and fuller exploration of the unique qualities of the African American experience (particularly language and issues of race), which the prophets of the Black Arts movement saw as the serious and legitimate subject matter for art, although *The Lynchers* indicated a minor movement in that general direction.

Wideman peopled the fictional worlds of his first three novels with major white and black characters, establishing a more rudimentary hu(e)man and modernist experience as his principal concern. However, despite this more "universal" target, and despite the continued comparison to Eliot and Joyce made by critics, Wideman could not escape the "black writer" label; nor could he escape being placed in the vanguard of contemporary black literary production and contributions.

From 1975 to 1983 Wideman took an eight-year hiatus during which he tried to learn to use a different voice. He explains: "I was 'woodshedding,' as the musicians would say—catching up. . . . I was learning a new language to talk about my experience." With the publication of his "Homewood Trilogy" (*Damballah, Hiding Place,* and *Sent for You Yesterday*), Wideman emerged from his personal exile to (re)claim with pride his history and heritage as Sybela Owens's great-great-great-grandson. He concluded; "if you've read T. S. Eliot, James Joyce, or William Faulkner . . . those are not the only 'keys to the kingdom.' If you have grown up Black, you also have some 'keys.'" These "keys," Wideman seems to contend in *Fatheralong,* are inextricably intertwined with the "pervasive presence of the paradigm of race." He explains, "The paradigm of race wasn't an illness plaguing society, it was the engine creating and sustaining a particular way of life."

Thus the "Homewood Trilogy" and subsequent work represent a major turning point in the personal life and literary career of John Edgar Wideman. With them he intentionally embarks on a journey back to the historical self which in *Damballah* and *Hiding Place* is inscribed in the signifiers of his family tree, which he instrumentally positions with "beggat charts" at the beginning of these works. Each reconstructs the family history as well as (re)claims and (re)records the central role played by his maternal great-great-great-grandmother in the founding of yet another colonial city upon a hill, located in the space that to Wideman is more than the steel capital of the world. Wideman provides the genesis of yet another pivotal American tale.

For Wideman, Pittsburgh is a city of beginnings. There the Allegheny River, flowing southward from the northeast, converges with the Monongahela, flowing northward from the southeast, to form the beginning of the Ohio River, the line of demarcation between slavery and freedom. However, in his odyssey with his father to Promised Land, South Carolina, recorded in *Fatheralong,* Wideman discovers and claims an equally significant beginning. There, in the South, in the shadows of pine forests, meadows, arable fields, and rich pastures, his paternal grandparents embarked on their quest for freedom. Wideman concludes, "The South is a parent, an engenderer, part of the mind I think with, the mind thinking with me." Paradoxically, Promised Land does not appear on most maps of South Carolina, just as there is no mention of "Africans or slaves or slavery in the closely printed eight page outline of the 'Chronological History of South Carolina (1662–1825).'"

Wideman's inclusion of Africans is crucial, for saliently appurtenant to his remapping and reclamation is the recognition that neither Homewood nor Promised Land can be the sole genesis of his family. History is bound to cultural memory. Wideman writes in *Fatheralong:* "In our minds, our memories beats the pulse of history." Memory and history remain central to the economy of being.

Memory and history bridge the path from America to the African past which Orion, the protagonist of *Damballah,* refuses to relinquish. An African kidnapped and sold into slavery, Orion is lynched for killing the overseer on his plantation. His decapitated body is later found by a slave man/child, who knows that he must throw the murdered slave's head into the river to release his spirit, allowing it to return to Africa. Wideman published *The Cattle Killing* in 1996, and *Two Cities* in 1997.

Since 1981 Wideman has become a "seer/writer" who uses his mediumistic powers as a vehicle through which African American history and culture are accessed, assessed, recorded, and restored. Through them he attempts to "break out, to knock down the walls" of the imprisoning cage(s) known by African Americans, a direct consequence of what he has come to call the "paradigm of race." His major protagonists struggle with memory against forgetting and assiduously work to create spaces to redeem and (re)create their past. Specificity is inscribed and particulars ("who we are and what we are about") are celebrated. Negating the superimposed "American Africanism," as Toni *Morrison calls the construction of African Americans in the literary and historical space assigned them by the Eurocentric mind, Wideman's characters and protagonists work from within the parameters of their marginalized spaces to create, validate, and celebrate alternative realities, such as the rhythm of their language and improvisation of their jazz, providing meaningful insight into the complexity of the African American experience that makes it a unique and distinctive American experience.

• John O'Brien, ed., *Interviews with Black Writers,* 1973, pp. 213–223. Wilfred D. Samuels, "Going Home: An Interview with John Edgar Wideman," *Callaloo* 6.1 (1983): 40–59. Wilfred D. Samuels, "John Edgar Wideman," in *DLB,* vol. 33, *Afro-American Fiction Writers after 1955,* eds. Thadious M. Davis and Trudier Harris, 1984, pp. 271–278. John Bennion, "The Shape of Memory in John Edgar Wideman's Sent for You Yesterday," *Black American Literature Forum* 20.1–2 (Spring–Summer 1986): 143–160. James W. Coleman, *Blackness and Modernism: The Literary Career of John Edgar Wideman,* 1989. Ashraf Rushdy, "Fraternal Blues: John Edgar Wideman's Homewood Trilogy," *Contemporary Literature* 32 (Fall 1991): 312–345. Jan Clausen, "Native Fathers," *The Kenyon Review* 14.2 (Spring 1992): 44–55. Doreatha Drummond Mbalia, *John Edgar Wideman: Reclaiming the African Personality,* 1995. Madhu Dubey, "Literature and Urban Crisis: John Edgar Wideman's *Philadelphia Fire,*" *African American Review* 32:4 (Winter 1998): 579–595. Bonnie TuSmith, ed., *Conversations with John Edgar Wideman,* 1998.

—Wilfred D. Samuels

Wife of His Youth, The. *The Wife of His Youth and Other Stories of the Color Line,* a collection of nine short stories published by Houghton Mifflin in the fall of 1899, was the second major work of fiction by Charles Waddell *Chesnutt. The fundamental social issue, as well as the unifying theme, in most of the stories of *The Wife of His Youth* is miscegenation in the United States. The title story of the volume, as well as "A Matter of Principle" and to a lesser extent "Her Virginia Mammy," analyze with both irony and pathos the racial prejudices of light-skinned, middle-class African Americans in "Groveland" (patterned on

Chesnutt's Cleveland), Ohio. Many of Chesnutt's fictional models in these stories were people he knew from his own membership in the Cleveland Social Circle, an exclusive society of upwardly mobile mixed-race African Americans who were reputed to discriminate against anyone with complexions darker than their own.

"The Wife of His Youth" tells how a leader of one of the Blue Vein Societies triumphs over his class and color prejudices by acknowledging after decades of separation his dark-skinned plantation wife. In a more satirical case, Chesnutt deflates the racial pretensions of Cicero Clayton, the protagonist of "A Matter of Principle," by showing how this mulatto's "principle" of dissociation from dark-skinned Negroes spoils his daughter's chance to marry a congressman. In "Her Virginia Mammy," Chesnutt broke with American social mores and literary tradition in his unhysterical depiction of the betrothal of a Boston Brahmin to a Groveland woman unaware of her black ancestry.

Turning to the South, *The Wife of His Youth* examines social problems that resisted the kinds of individual ethical solutions on which Chesnutt's northern-based stories turn. Although "The Passing of Grandison" allows a tricky slave to hoodwink his complacent master and spirit his entire familyoff to freedom, in "The Web of Circumstance" a former slave who tries to pull himself up by his bootstraps is left broken and degraded by a combination of adverse circumstances, racism, and betrayal. In this story and in "The Sheriff's Children," the tragic tale of a white southern father's post-CivilWar encounter with the mixed-race son he sold away during slavery times, Chesnutt displayed his pessimistic reaction to the rise of white supremacist attitudes and the eclipse of black opportunity in the "New South" of the 1890s. From the sensationalism of "The Sheriff's Children" to the sentimentality of "The Bouquet," the burlesque energy of "The Passing of Grandison," and the urbane satire of "A Matter of Principle," Chesnutt adopted a variety of means in *The Wife of His Youth* to compel his readers to consider contemporary racial realities in the clarifying light of his brand of social realism.

Some critics, such as William Dean Howells, praised the author of *The Wife of His Youth* as a literary realist of the first order. Others were troubled by Chesnutt's concentration on such cheerless topics as segregation, mob violence, and miscegenation. Late twentieth-century critics have proved more hospitable to Chesnutt's color line fiction in general and more appreciative of the prototypical examples of it published in *The Wife of His Youth*.

• Helen M. Chesnutt, *Charles Waddell Chesnutt: Pioneer of the Color Line*, 1952. Sylvia Lyons Render, ed., *The Short Fiction of Charles W. Chesnutt*, 1974. Robert Bone, *Down Home: Pastoral Impulse in Afro-American Short Fiction*, 1975. William L. Andrews, *The Literary Career of Charles W. Chesnutt*, 1980.

—William L. Andrews

WILLIAMS, GEORGE WASHINGTON (1849–1891), Civil War veteran, minister, politician, and historian. Born in Bedford Springs, Pennsylvania, to Thomas and Ellen Rouse Williams on 16 October 1849, George Williams was the oldest son of five siblings. Given the lack of educational opportunities for African Americans in western Pennsylvania, Williams received little formal schooling. In 1863, at the age of fourteen, he enlisted in the Union army. After leaving the army in 1868, Williams applied for admission and was accepted at Howard University in Washington, D.C., in 1869. He dropped out, however, and entered Wayland Seminary, also in Washington. In 1870 Williams entered Newton Theological Institution outside of Boston. Upon graduation from Newton, Williams was ordained and then offered the pastorate of a prominent African American congregation in Boston, the Twelfth Street Baptist Church, in 1875.

While pastor at Twelfth Street Baptist Church, Williams wrote a monograph, *History of the Twelfth Street Baptist Church*. He left the pastorate of Twelfth Street Baptist after a couple of months and returned to Washington to edit a journal, the *Commoner*. By December 1875 the journal was defunct. In 1876 Williams traveled to the Midwest to accept the pastorate of Union Baptist Church in Cincinnati, Ohio. In 1879 he was elected to the Ohio House of Representatives. At this juncture Williams embarked on the distinguishing task of his career—authorship of the first comprehensive history of African Americans, *History of the Negro Race in America from 1619 to 1880* (1883).

Originally published in two volumes by G.P. Putnam's Sons, Williams's *History of the Negro Race in America* offered an ably documented overview of African American history from its inception in Africa to the postbellum years following the Civil War. Favorably reviewed in both the African American and white press, these volumes established Williams as the foremost historian of the race. In 1887 he produced a monograph on African American participation in the Civil War, *History of the Negro Troops in the War of the Rebellion*. Despite these accomplishments Williams was unable to exclusively pursue one career. In 1881 he was admitted to the Ohio bar and to the Boston bar in 1883. In 1885 President Chester Arthur appointed Williams minister to Haiti. However, he was never allowed to officially assume the post by the incoming Democratic administration. Williams devoted the latter portion of his career to influencing Belgian policies in the Congo. While writing a lengthy monograph on Belgian abuses in the Congo, Williams succumbed to tuberculosis and pleurisy and died in Blackpool, England, on 2 August 1891.

Despite his varied careers, Williams's contributions to the field of historical literature were inestimable. He utilized objectivity in constructing his historical narratives and consulted with historians such as Justin Winsor and George Bancroft. A pioneer in the writing of revisionist history and oral history, the utilization of newspapers, and the collection and interpretation of primary material, Williams's work laid the ground, in style, presentation, and methodology for the burgeoning field of historical literature in the late nineteenth century.

• John Hope Franklin, *George Washington Williams*, 1985.
—Stephen Gilroy Hall

WILLIAMS, JOHN A. (b. 1925), novelist, essayist, journalist, editor, and educator. Born in Hinds County, Mississippi, John Alfred Williams grew up in Syracuse, New York. After serving in the navy during World War II, Williams finished high school and enrolled at Syracuse University, graduating in 1950. He started graduate school but soon withdrew for economic reasons. Trying to establish his writing career, Williams contributed to *Ebony, Jet,* and *Holiday* while holding various jobs in the 1950s—foundry worker, grocery clerk, social worker, insurance company employee, and television publicity coordinator. This diversity of experience formed a foundation upon which he has often drawn for inspiration.

The American Academy of Arts and Letters' 1962 failure to deliver the promised Prix de Rome to Williams is also significant. The retraction came after an informal letter of congratulations promised Williams the prize, pending an interview (supposedly a mere formality), which apparently went badly. Williams remains the only candidate to have had the prize retracted; he fictionalized the events in *The *Man Who Cried I Am* (1967) and recounted them in "We Regret to Inform You That," an essay reprinted in his collection *Flashbacks* (1973). How much he has made from this incident indicates how heavily Williams draws on life for his art.

A prolific writer, Williams has produced eleven novels, six nonfiction books, three anthologies, one play, and numerous articles and essays. Throughout his career, Williams has articulated his artist's sense of African Americans' experiences, giving attention to societal power imbalances and exploring political and personal approaches to their resolution. His demands for social justice and frank articulation of its absence in modern society, coupled with his willingness to treat violent themes and suggest force as the means to achieve equality, cause some to label him "angry."

There is anger in his books; however, limiting Williams to that characterization overlooks the richness of his work. His insightful and confrontational nonfiction forces readers to see the realities of African American life in our culture; however, rather than just expressing anger, Williams explains how and why those conditions should be ameliorated. A notable example is *Beyond the Angry Black* (1966), an anthology of essays by black and white writers that describes and comments on American racial politics. In the introduction, Williams talks about reason, the next step beyond anger that he calls on Americans of all colors to make.

Williams also addresses social conditions, raising images of oppression and powerlessness before history in *This Is My Country Too* (1965), the product of an undertaking commissioned by *Holiday* magazine that chronicles Williams's travels across America in 1963. Providing portraits of many strong individuals, the work also reflects much of Williams's experience with the history of racial oppression, experience that he used in writing *The Man Who Cried I Am.*

Often viewed as Williams's major achievement, *The Man Who Cried I Am* marks a significant shift in his fiction. In works such as *One for New York* (1960) and *Sissie* (1963), Williams portrays the struggles of individual African Americans against an oppressive system and offers resolution. Gilbert H. Muller (*John A. Williams,* 1984) notes that the early novels find the characters succeeding within the oppressive system. *In The Man Who Cried I Am,* Williams creates a character who recognizes and fights historical oppression; however, he reaches no understanding with the dominant culture—violence is the only solution. Max Reddick, like Abraham Blackman in *Captain Blackman* (1972), sees himself as waging war on the forces of history that ultimately destroy him—Williams's major concern in the late 1960s and early 1970s.

In addition to sharing this dominant, historically aware, active consciousness, both *The Man* and *Captain Blackman* exhibit one of Williams's most significant stylistic innovations: a flexible chronological movement that starts from a relatively linear plot progression, weaving facts, dates, and experiences around that line and completely problematizing the question of history. For Williams, the concept of a monolithic, accurate, just history appears unacceptable. Many of his works, especially of this era, cite myriad forces shaping events and creating socioeconomic-racial-intellectual tensions that characterize his conception of history. This vision, and his unique creation of a chronological structure to support it, marks Williams as forerunner to and significant influence on other African American writers, such as John Edgar *Wideman and Charles R. *Johnson, attempting to come to grips with and re-form American history.

In certain later works, Williams returns the question of historical, social, and intellectual power relationships to a more personal realm. As Muller notes, in some ways *!Click Song* (1982) is a summation of work begun in *The Man Who Cried I Am. !Click Song*'s narrator, Cato Caldwell Douglass, is in many ways the spiritual descendent of Max Reddick; however, his quest is much more personal, abstracted from Reddick's political struggle by his focus on art. In *The Berhama Account* (1985), Williams fuses the personal approach of *!Click Song* with the more political elements of earlier works, intermingling an examination of love's healing power with a story of effective political struggle.

The Berhama Account treats a faked assassination plot in which the tossing of dummy hand grenades forces positive social action and paves the way for the rectification of a small Caribbean nation's racism. In the midst of this intrigue, a journalist recovering from cancer finds life-affirming love by rekindling an old affair. Several of these plot elements signal a reversal of Williams's earlier ideas. One thinks, for instance, of the King Alfred plot, the murderously real violence, the failure of love, and Max Reddick's deterioration and death in *The Man Who Cried I Am.* Although Williams still has concerns about political and social questions, his later works suggest that his worldview is not so bleak as it once was. In 1999, he published a volume of travel fiction entitled *Clifford's Blues.*

Williams's importance to the development of the African American tradition should not be underestimated. His social, intellectual, and historical innovations mark his work as crucial to our understanding of the development of contemporary African American aesthetics.

• Earl A. Cash, *John A. Williams: The Evolution of a Black Writer,* 1975. Gilbert H. Muller, *John A. Williams,* 1984. Virginia Whatley Smith, "Sorcery, Double-Consciousness, and Warring Souls: An Intertextual Reading of *Middle Passage* and *Captain Blackman,*" *African American Review* 30:4 (Winter 1996): 659–674.

—William R. Nash

WILLIAMS, PAULETTE. *See* Shange, Ntozake.

WILLIAMS, SAMM-ART (b.1946), playwright and actor. Born 20 January 1946 in Burgaw, North Carolina, Samuel Arthur Williams, who from an early age wanted to become a writer, received encouragement from his mother, an English teacher and drama director. He graduated from Morgan State College in Baltimore, Maryland (1968), where he majored in political science in preparation for the legal career many members of his family wanted him to pursue.

One of Williams's plays, *Home,* was selected as a Burns Mantle Yearbook "Best Play of 1979–80"; it also received a Tony nomination and a John Gasner Playwriting Medallion. In addition to *Home,* Williams has written twelve or more representative works and acted in numerous productions with noted theatrical groups including the Freedom Theatre in Philadelphia, an organization he joined soon after arriving there in 1968, and the Negro Ensemble Company of New York. Williams traveled to New York in 1973 and found there the kind of artistic experiences to which he had long aspired. His talent as an actor initially paid greater dividends than did his writing talent.

Williams's range as a playwright encompasses numerous themes, among them crime, shame, pride, confused sexuality, and transcendence. The Negro Ensemble Company, an organization that Williams joined in 1974, produced five of his plays: *Welcome to Black River* (1975), *The Coming* (1976), *A Love Play* (1976), *The Frost of Renaissance* (1978, in workshop and showcase) and *Brass Birds Don't Sing* (1978). *Welcome to Black River* dramatizes the exploitation and racism experienced by a Black sharecropper in the 1950s in North Carolina. *The Coming* depicts the experiences of a New York skid row bum who has the delusion that he is talking to God, who in this drama is an incarnation of several unsavory character types. Conflicting value systems of West Indian Blacks and African Americans receive attention in *Eyes of the American* (1980). The propensity toward capitalism, embodied in the American, becomes his nemesis as his worldview is adopted by his West Indian brother. Both men get what they deserve, learning that each should have been more suspicious of the other. The arrogant American now has a chance to experience the circumstances he once derided.

Another prominent theme in Williams's plays is sexuality. *A Love Play* (1976) dramatizes an exploration by four female characters into lesbianism, a pursuit motivated, in part, by their disappointing relationships with the men in their lives. *Kamilla* (1975) tells the story of a married woman whose dream consciousness forces her to admit to the realities of her sexual preference. *The Last Caravan* explores another dimension of sexuality as an aging protagonist seeks nontraditional cures to restore his fading virility.

Crime and corruption come to the forefront in several of Williams's plays. *Do Unto Others* (1976) dramatizes crime, revenge, and deception in the fury of a woman who escapes a death plot set by her husband, a Chicago numbers racketeer. *The Sixteenth Round* (1980) produced by the Negro Ensemble Company in 1980, tells the story of a desperate fighter who intentionally loses a fight, thereby inviting the wrath of an underworld figure out to kill him. *Eve of the Trial* tells the story of a Russian expatriate stranded in Louisiana. The drama, part of a series of dramas drawn from Chekhov's short fiction, reveals intolerance and the corruption of the legal system.

Home (1979), generally considered Williams's most successful work, returns to the site of *Welcome to Black River,* where both races, bound by circumstances and blood, unite to confront a common challenge. *Home* dramatizes the nostalgia of a young man from North Carolina who migrated north, bearing the heavy responsibility of returning home a winner. In addition to its antiwar emphasis, the play exposes for scrutiny the posturing of African Americans in the North who claim to have reached the promised land while inwardly longing for a return home. *Home* received the Audelco Award and the Outer Critics' Circle Award for Best Play 1980–1981.

Williams's career as a playwright is complemented by his work as an actor of stage, television, and film.

His contribution to the artistic opportunities of African Americans is underscored by his sense of history, vividly portrayed in *Cork* (1986), in which he pays due tribute to the precursors of the modern stage, the black minstrels. He expresses sensitivity for those forerunners who, through shame and humiliation, made possible opportunities for future generations of African American actors. This work and the entire corpus of Samuel Arthur Williams's activities in defining the moral and political contours of our diverse society will no doubt secure his place in American theater and culture.

• Trudier Harris, "Samm-Art Williams," in *DLB*, vol. 38, *Afro-American Writers after 1955: Dramatists and Prose Writers*, eds. Thadious M. Davis and Trudier Harris, 1985, pp. 283–290. Thomas Morgan, "Minstrels: The Myths and the Men," *New York Times*, 27 Dec. 1986, Sec. 1, 11.1. Hal Mays and Susan M. Trosky, eds., *CA*, 1988, pp. 467–469. Bernard L. Peterson, Jr., *Contemporary Black American Playwrights and Their Plays*, 1988, pp. 501–503. Edward Mapp, *Directory of Blacks in the Performing Arts*, 1990, pp. 551–552.

—Robbie Jean Walker

WILLIAMS, SHERLEY ANNE (1944–1999), poet, novelist, critic, professor, and social critic. The life and career of Sherley Anne Williams reveal why she is a major cultural and literary force in the African American and the larger multicultural American community. Williams, who teaches at the University of California at San Diego, La Jolla, was born in Bakersfield, California, on 25 August 1944. She earned a bachelor of arts in English in 1966 and a master's in 1972 from California State University at Fresno and Brown University, respectively. She then went on to teach at several schools and to travel to Ghana under a 1984 Fulbright grant. As scholar, critic, writer, poet, and parent, her range extends from adult to child, and from academia to popular culture. Like Sterling A. *Brown, one of her mentors and role models, she manages to traverse several worlds, and this ability to extend her voice past the literary and into the ever-expanding field of African American cultural forms has been an invaluable contribution to African American literary studies.

As a scholar and critic Williams attributes great worth to exploring African American folk culture, and her literary criticism attests to this fact. The best and perhaps most well-known example is her first endeavor, *Give Birth to Brightness: A Thematic Study in Neo-Black Literature* (1972), a groundbreaking examination of the toast-and-boast traditions. Here she infuses the black aesthetic poetry of the 1960s (e.g., Mari *Evans, Michael S. *Harper, Amiri *Baraka, Etheridge *Knight, David Henderson, and Don L. Lee) into the beginning of each chapter to serve as an intertext and implicit statement that these poets are the next wave of heroes. She reviews how heroism manifests itself along class lines in African American poetry, drama, and prose, in music and performers, and from folklore and history to the urban outlaw. In the process of recording her findings she ensures the position of heroism as a viable element of African American literary studies.

One element of folk culture that informs Williams's writing, both critical and creative, is "call and response." She writes as a response to other things that have been written or spoken and that affect the community, and this is an interesting example of the African American cultural phenomenon call and response performing her. Seen in this light, Williams's dedicating her first work to her son serves as a means of answering questions he may have about his history, and as a way of leaving him a legacy. This gesture represents the larger unspoken thesis of this work, for in investigating the boasts and toasts that come from the urban folk community, Williams affirms that there is an African American cultural legacy that has been passed down for years, that has mutated, and that will continue to mutate into many forms. Her recording and analyzing this work, as well as addressing it to her son, is a step in the process of passing the lore to the next generation. It seems that for Williams to have the scholarly analysis, the critic must converse with and receive affirmation from the folk community.

As a creative writer she invests great pride in African American musical forms and history. While *Give Birth to Brightness* explores primarily male authors and provides an overview of folk heroism, Williams's creative endeavors focus primarily on women. **Dessa Rose* (1986), her critically acclaimed historical novel, or neo–slave narrative, is based on the blues, for it tells of a solitary woman's experience of love thwarted, of bondage, revolt, freedom, and of love regained. This follows the blues's aaba structure, because it repeats and varies a central theme: Dessa's story. Williams, as well, infuses spirituals into *Dessa Rose* and shows how they worked as a means of coded communication, for they help Dessa to escape imprisonment. In keeping with Williams's methodology, this work is also a response to William Styron's flawed historical fiction *The Confessions of Nat Turner* (1967). Through musical form and the assertion of a female slave rebellion, Williams reclaims history, revises the racial memory of slavery, and invests herself with the right to record an African American woman's silenced history.

Another way to record a silenced voice is through poetry, and Williams's first attempt at this is in *The Peacock Poems* (1975) and *Someone Sweet Angel Chile* (1982). She structures these works as well on the blues and spirituals. The poetry incorporates these musical modes in that they talk of an artist's alienation and heroic survival as she struggles to express her feelings and hopes for understanding. The blues also fit perfectly as a means of expressing the lyrical, for their subject matter articulates the historically isolated and silenced African American female voice. Underlying these blues poems is the theme of lost love and misunderstanding among men and women, and again this is Williams responding to a folk community that is at times split by miscommunication. In reaching out and embracing that communication, Williams exhorts the need for spiritual connection, mutual understanding, and respect, for these are the things that give men and women, the folk community, and the individual, life.

Working Cotton (1992) is Williams's latest creation, and it addresses perhaps the most important aspect that gives the folk community life and meaning: the children. It is a gesture that mirrors the dedication of her first work to her son, for this award-winning children's story is dedicated to her grandchildren and to the migrant laborers and their families, whose voices continue to be silenced. *Working Cotton* is a message of hope, pride, and regard for the sheer determination it takes to survive and still see beauty amongst so much harshness. It is written in the blues mode, and Williams, in recording a young girl's (Shelan's) experiences working in the fields with her family, praises the folk community for its endurance. This is her way of embracing one segment of the African American community, and in so doing she again affirms and documents a way of life and a worldview so that future generations will know a part of their history.

Williams's works reveal a bond to folk traditions and history, and a desire to generate, appreciate, and preserve them for future generations. For Williams, this is the role of the academician, and as teacher, writer, social critic, and parent, her efforts responding to the folk community mark her as an integral force in African American letters.

• Shirley M. Jordan, "Sherley Anne Williams," in *Black Women Writers At Work*, ed. Claudia Tate, 1983. pp. 205–213. Mary Kemp Davis, "Everybody Knows Her Name: The Recovery of the Past in Sherley Anne Williams's *Dessa Rose*," *Callaloo* 40.1 (1989): 544–558. Mae G. Henderson, "(W)riting The Work and Working the Rites," *Black American Literature Forum* 23.4 (Winter 1989): 631–660. Anne E. Goldman, "I Made the Ink": (Literary) Production and Reproduction in *Dessa Rose* and *Beloved*," *Feminist Studies* 16.2 (Summer 1990): 313–330. Marta E. Sanchez, "The Estrangement Effect in Sherley Anne Williams' *Dessa Rose*," *Genders* 15 (Winter 1992): 21–36. Sherley Anne Williams, interview by Shirley M. Jordan, in *Broken Silences: Interviews With Black and White Women Writers*, ed. Shirley M. Jordan, 1993, pp. 285–301. Farah Jasmine Griffin, "Textual Healing: Claiming Black Women's Bodies, the Erotic and Resistance in Contemporary Novels of Slavery," *Callaloo* 19:2 (Spring 1996): 519–536. Mae G. Henderson, 'The Stories of O(Dessa): Stories of Complicity and Resistance,'" in *Female Subjects in Black and White: Race, Psychoanalysis, Feminism*, ed. Elizabeth Abel, et al., 1997, pp. 285–304.

—Mildred R. Mickle

WILSON, AUGUST (b. 1945), playwright, poet, essayist, and two-time recipient of the Pulitzer Prize. The winner of Bush, McKnight, Rockefeller, and Guggenheim Foundation fellowships in playwriting, August Wilson also had the distinction in 1988 of having two plays running simultaneously on Broadway: *Joe Turner's Come and Gone* and **Fences*. Clearly, he is one of America's most prominent playwrights, yet his origins offered few indications that he would achieve such dramatic accomplishment.

He was born as Frederick Kittel on "The Hill," a racially mixed area of Pittsburgh, Pensylvania, to Frederick Kittel, a German baker, and Daisy Wilson Kittel, a cleaning woman whose mother walked from North Carolina to Pittsburgh seeking greater opportunity. The fourth of six children, Wilson grew up in a two-room apartment behind a grocery store. His white father was a distant figure whom Wilson seldom saw.

Following his parents' divorce and his mother's subsequent remarriage to David Bedford, Wilson and his family relocated to a white suburb where he encountered increased racism. In 1961—after being falsely accused of plagiarizing a paper he had written about Napoléon—Wilson dropped out of Gladstone High School. Unable to find satisfactory employment, he joined the army in 1963 and one year later was able to wrangle an early discharge.

On 1 April 1965, Wilson bought his first typewriter, having determined that he would become a writer. In the fall of that year, he moved into a rooming house and began a long and varied assortment of menial jobs to support his writing. That same year he helped form the Center Avenue Poets Theatre Workshop and heard Bessie *Smith's records for the first time. The latter had a profound effect upon his determination to capture black cultural and historical experience in his writing. It would also lead directly to one of Wilson's first publications: the poem "Bessie" eventually appeared in *Black Lines* in the summer of 1971.

Throughout the rest of the 1960s, Wilson continued to hone his writing skills and to be active in the community of African American writers, helping Rob Penny found the Black Horizons Theatre Company on the Hill. During this period Wilson was active in the Black Power movement and was also beginning to publish his poetry: his first publication was "For Malcolm X and Others," which appeared in *Negro Digest* in September 1969. He married Brenda Burton, a Muslim, in 1969 as well. Their daughter, Sakina Ansari, was born in 1970.

After the dissolution of this marriage in 1972, Wilson intensified his efforts as a writer. In 1973, he wrote "Morning Statement," a poem that he—borrowing a term from Robert Duncan—often cites as evidence of his achieving "surety" of his craft, and his poem "Theme One: The Variations" was included in the anthology *The Poetry of Black America*. He had also begun writing plays, completing *Rite of Passage* during this period. In 1973, his unpublished play *Recycle* was produced by a community theater in Pittsburgh. In 1976, he saw a production of Athol Fugard's *Sizwe Bansi Is Dead*, which greatly encouraged him about his own ability to write drama, and he wrote *The Homecoming,* which would not be produced until 1989 but whose subject matter foreshadows his first Broadway success, *Ma Rainey's Black Bottom.* A fictitious treatment of episodes in the life of blues singer and guitarist Blind Lemon Jefferson, who froze to death in Chicago in 1930, *Homecoming* illustrates Wilson's growing concern for incorporating traditional black art forms and the lives of African American cultural icons into his work. In 1977, he wrote *Black Bart and the Sacred Hills,* a musical satire based on a group of poems about an outlaw of the Old West. Most critics consider this to be Wilson's serious theatrical debut; the play was produced in St. Paul, Minnesota, in 1981.

In 1978, Wilson moved to St. Paul to write plays for Claude Purdy and to work as a scriptwriter for the Science Museum of Minnesota. The following year he completed *Jitney,* a two-act play about jitney drivers in Pittsburgh, which would serve as his first rejection from the Eugene O'Neill Theatre Center National Playwrights Conference but which would be accepted by the Minneapolis Playwrights' Center in 1980 and produced at the Allegheny Repertory Theatre in Pittsburgh in 1982. In 1980, Wilson received a Jerome fellowship, became associate playwright with Playwrights' Center in Minneapolis, and wrote *Fullerton Street*—his play of the 1940s that looks at urban blacks who have migrated to the North and that remains unpublished and unproduced; this play was also rejected by the O'Neill Center.

In 1981, Wilson married Judy Oliver, a white social worker. The following year he wrote *Ma Rainey's Black Bottom,* which was accepted for workshop production at the O'Neill, and Wilson began the first of many collaborative efforts with Lloyd Richards, the director of the O'Neill and the dean of the Yale Drama School. When this play opened on Broadway at the Cort Theatre in 1984, it brought Wilson critical acclaim and launched his theatrical career. Set in 1920s Chicago, the play looks at the economic exploitation of black musicians by white record companies and at the ways in which victims of racism are forced to direct their rage at each other rather than at their oppressors. Although Clive Barnes criticized the play for its overemphasis on politics and its predictable ending, Frank Rich saw the play as a searing account of white racism's effect upon its victims and gave the play laudatory reviews. The play certainly treats the dangers of misplaced hatred. Because Levee cannot accept the salvation of his heritage, he slays the messenger who reminds him that such possibilities exist: Levee kills Toledo as a substitute for the white men who have raped his mother and those who are now rejecting his music. The play won the New York Drama Critics' Circle Award (1985) and was nominated for a Tony.

Wilson joined New Dramatists in New York in 1983, and *Fences* was produced at the O'Neill. Unfortunately, Wilson's mother died in March before she could witness his Broadway success. Writing at least partly to show his critics that he could follow the traditional European American drama format of focusing on one major character, he gave the play a strong unity. It looks at the struggles of a 1950s working-class family to find economic security. A garbageman, ex-con, and former Negro Baseball League player, Troy Maxson is perhaps Wilson's best-known protagonist, a man who is unable to believe that his son will be allowed to benefit from the football scholarship he is being offered. White critics were quick to point out parallels between Troy and Willy Loman. *Fences* was produced at the Yale Repertory Theatre in 1986, and following its opening at the 46th Street Theatre in New York in 1987, it won the New York Drama Critics' Circle Award, the Drama Desk Award, the Tony, and the Pulitzer; the *Chicago Tribune* selected Wilson as Artist of the Year; and he received the John Gassner Outer Critics' Circle Award for Best American Playwright.

While *Fences* was still enjoying a successful run on Broadway in 1988, *Joe Turner's Come and Gone* opened at the Ethel Barrymore. Written in 1984 and workshopped at the O'Neill that same year, the play had been produced at Yale in 1986. Inspired by the Romare Bearden collage "Millhand's Lunch Bucket," it is Wilson's admitted favorite. It focuses on the personal and cultural aftermath of both slavery and the black northern migration as they are manifested in a Pittsburgh boarding house in 1911. Many critics consider this to be the most Afrocentric of Wilson's plays and his most successful literary effort. It was nominated for a Tony and won the New York Drama Critics' Award. This same year the New York Public Library added Wilson to its list of Literary Lions.

Wilson's fourth play to be produced on Broadway and his second to win a Pulitzer, The **Piano Lesson,* was also inspired by a Bearden collage. It won the Drama Desk, New York Drama Critics' Circle, and the American Theatre Critics Outstanding Play awards. Written in 1986, it was presented at the O'Neill and the Yale Repertory in 1987 and opened after a long tour of regional theaters at the Walter Kerr in 1990. Focusing on the question of who has the right to own a family's heirloom piano, the play is set in 1936 and captures the conflict that arises between African American and mainstream cultural values. During this period, Wilson moved to Seattle.

Wilson was elected to the American Academy of Arts and Sciences in 1991. His play *Two Trains Running,* written in 1989, was produced by the Yale Repertory in 1990, and opened at the Walter Kerr on Broadway in 1992. It was nominated for a Tony and won the American Theatre Critics' Association Award. Returning to the Hill as a setting, Wilson places the action in a coffee shop where regulars converge to discuss their plight in 1960s America. The play stresses the necessity of coming to terms with the past before attempting to move forward. His latest play in the twentieth century cycle is *Seven Guitars,* which was produced in 1996.

At the outset of his career, Wilson envisioned theater as a means to raise the collective community's consciousness about black life in twentieth-century America and committed himself to writing a cycle of ten plays that would rewrite the history of each decade of this century so that black life becomes a more fully acknowledged part of America's theatrical history. His plays are not, however, agitprop. He avoids pat answers; instead, he effects a powerful experience that forces his audience to search for their own political conclusions as an extension of his characters' life situations. A playwright of startling imagination and depth, he is often considered a theatrical spokesperson for the African American experience, and his ability to infuse everyday language with the stuff of poetry is an essential, distinguishing factor of his work. Perhaps he no longer considers himself a poet, but it is his poetic gift that has helped him to become the preeminent playwright in contemporary American drama.

• Chip Brown, "The Light in August," *Esquire,* Apr. 1989, 116–125. Sandra Shannon, "The Good Christian's Come and Gone: The Shifting Role of Religion in August Wilson's Plays," *MELUS: The Journal of the Society for the Study of Multi-ethnic Literature of the United States* 16 (Fall 1989–1990): 127–142. Paul Carter Harrison, "August Wilson's Blues Poetics," in *August Wilson: Three Plays,* 1991, pp. 291–318. Yvonne Shafer, "August Wilson: A New Approach to Black Drama," *ZAA: Zeitschrift fur Anglistik und Amerikanistik,* vol. 39, 1991, pp. 17–27. Mark Rocha, "A Conversation with August Wilson," *Diversity: A Journal of Multicultural Issues* 1 (Fall 1992): 24–42. Alan Nadel, ed., *May All Your Fences Have Gates: Essays on the Drama of August Wilson,* 1993. Marilyn Elkins, ed., *August Wilson: A Casebook,* 1994. Yvonne Shafer, "August Wilson and the Contemporary Theatre," *Journal of Dramatic Theory and Criticism* 12:1 (Fall 1997): 23–38. Sandra G. Shannon, "A Transplant That Did Not Take: August Wilson's Views on the Great Migration," *African American Review* 31:4 (Winter 1997): 659–666. Shafer, *August Wilson: A Research and Production Sourcebook* (1998). Bonnie Lyons, "An Interview with August Wilson," *Contemporary Literature* 40:1 (Spring 1999): 1–21. Mary L. Boqumil, *August Wilson,* 1999.

—Marilyn Elkins

WILSON, HARRIET E. (c. 1827–?), first African American woman novelist. Rarely has an author's identity been so instrumental in the reclamation of her writing. Long thought to be white, Harriet E. Wilson and her one novel, **Our Nig,* had been mere footnotes to nineteenth-century American literary history, and obscure ones at that, until 1981. Henry Louis *Gates, Jr., and David Curtis's research came on the heels of the republication of rediscovered white women writers and the incipient attention paid to early African American women authors. When in 1984 Gates established that Wilson was indeed the first Black person to publish a novel in the United States, there was a developing historical and critical context into which to fit her work. *Our Nig*'s republication is both a reflection of and a key contribution to the vast resurrection of writings by what Toni *Morrison might call disremembered Black women.

Until the 1980s, Frances Ellen Watkins *Harper was widely accepted to be the first Black woman to publish a short story (1859) and a novel (1892). Yet, since *Our Nig* pushed back the conception of Black women's novelistic writing thirty-three years, scores of newly rediscovered writers—Emma Dunham *Kelley and Amelia E. *Johnson, for example—and new novels by authors only established in the last fifteen years (such as Harper's and Pauline E. *Hopkins's) have been republished.

Biographical information on Harriet Adams Wilson remains sketchy, although information on the Bellmonts, whom Barbara White has discovered was the Hayward family of *Our Nig,* has emerged. Nehemiah Hayward, "Mr. Bellmont," married Rebecca Hutchinson, who belonged to a wealthy and established family of Milford, New Hampshire, Harriet Wilson's birthplace. Rebecca, the "she-devil" of *Our Nig,* was a direct descendent of Anne Hutchinson and cousin to the famous abolitionist Hutchinson family singers. Harriet Adams was born between 1825 and 1828 and was left at the Haywards' when she was six. She left when she was eighteen; in 1850, the year the Fugitive Slave Act endangered all Blacks living in the North, she resided with the Boyle family. One year later she married Thomas Wilson, an attractive lecturer who later proved to be a free man passing as a fugitive slave in order to earn his living by speaking of slavery's horrors. Ironically, Thomas Wilson's abandonment of his wife and newborn son proved to be the catalyst for her to write a novel that closely reflected her own experiences; *Our Nig* rivals slave narratives in its description of white violence directed toward the narrators themselves.

The "commands of God" and the demands of poverty were often accepted as proper justifications for a woman's entrance into the public realm of publishing. Harriet Beecher *Stowe claimed to have seen the final scenes of *Uncle Tom's Cabin* in a vision. Because of her confinement to bed, the result of the brutal treatment she received, Wilson was to write *Our Nig* in order to raise money to sustain herself and to reclaim her son; because of her physical and economic situation, he had been placed under others' care. Unfortunately, George Mason Wilson, then seven years old, died five months after the novel's publication; ironically, his death certificate established his mother's racial identity and facilitated her reintroduction to African American letters.

• David Ames Curtis and Henry Louis Gates, Jr., "Establishing the Identity of the Author of *Our Nig,*" in *Wild Women in the Whirlwind: Afra-American Culture and the Contemporary Literary Renaissance,* eds. Joanne Braxton and Andree McLaughlin, 1990, pp. 48–69. Barbara White, "*Our Nig* and the She-Devil: New Information about Harriet Wilson and the Bellmont Family," *American Literature* 65.1 (Mar. 1993): pp. 19–52.

—P. Gabrielle Foreman

WOFFORD, CHLOE ANTHONY. *See* Morrison, Toni.

WOLFE, GEORGE (b. 1954), dramatist, librettist, and innovator in the satirical revue and the black musical. Born in Frankfort, Kentucky, George C. Wolfe took his BA in directing from California's Pomona College in 1976. While attending Pomona, he won the regional festival of the American College Theatre Festival in 1975 with a comedy-satire titled *Up for Grabs* and in 1977 became his region's first repeat winner with *Block Party,* which centered on the difficulties facing a black male attempting to move beyond the block (literal and figurative) that shaped him. Receiving his MFA in playwriting and musical theater from New York University in 1983, he wrote the libretto for Duke Ellington's music in *Queenie Pie,* produced at Washington's Kennedy Center in 1986.

While *Queenie Pie* had a moderate success, Wolfe's main claim to attention and acclaim that year was *The Colored Museum,* a collection of eleven exuberantly inventive exhibits, brief scenes highlighting African American oppression and the culture that evolved with and against it. In the first exhibit, an ever-smiling stewardess addresses the audience as passengers on "Celebrity Slaveship," a device implying the grip of the past and continuing racist exploitation amid apparent progress. Other exhibits, including the upwardly mobile black who temporarily "kills" the raging kid inside him and the Frenchified singer who rewrites her roots, expose the manifold ways in which blacks have striven to evade the pain shaping them. The most noted exhibit, "The Last Mama-on-the-Couch Play," satirizes major black theatrical responses to oppression, from Lorraine *Hansberry's emotive realism and Ntozake *Shange's poetic feminism to race-submerging classicism and the problem-denying black musical. The final exhibit, a party described by the character Topsy Washington, linking opposites like *Aunt Jemima and Angela Davis, proclaims that all the past, pain, complexities, and contradictions are inescapable parts of black identity. While most critics applauded its production at New Brunswick's Crossroads Theatre and the New York Shakespeare Festival, Thulani Davis argued that the play was misogynistic and trivialized black struggle.

In 1989 Wolfe faithfully yet innovatively adapted three short stories by Zora Neale *Hurston for the stage in *Spunk.* Wolfe's device of having the tales introduced by Guitar Man and Blues Speak Woman while interacting with the Folk (a chorus representing black folk) was spiritually akin to Hurston's frame for *Mules and Men* (1935).

In 1990, Wolfe directed an adaptation of Bertolt Brecht's *The Caucasian Chalk Circle.* Apart from the quality and inventiveness of the production, which reset the play in François Duvalier's Haiti, this adaptation was notable for being written by Wolfe's critic Thulani Davis.

Jelly's Last Jam, Wolfe's exhilarating proof that musicals need not sidestep pain and problems to be successful, was produced to wide acclaim in 1991. A tribute to Jelly Roll Morton that shows him denying his black roots as the singer did in *The Colored Museum,* Wolfe's musical emphasizes the role of suffering and community in the creation of jazz. In 1993, he won a Tony as best director for *Angels in America: Millennium Approaches,* and in 1994 he was nominated for the same award for *Angels in America: Perestroika.* A multiple award-winning writer, adaptor, and director, Wolfe is among the most imaginative creators in American theater today.

• "George C. Wolfe," in *Contemporary Literary Criticism,* vol. 49, eds. Daniel G. Morowski et al., 1988, pp. 419–424. Bernard L. Peterson, Jr., "George C. Wolfe," in *Contemporary Black American Playwrights and Their Plays,* 1988, pp. 507–508. Marc Silverstein, "'Any Baggage You Don't Claim, We Trash': Living With(in) History in *The Colored Museum,*" *American Drama* 8:1 (Fall 1998): 95–121.

—Steven R. Carter

Woman Called Fancy, A. Frank *Yerby's 1951 novel, *A Woman Called Fancy,* is his first to have a female protagonist. Set in Augusta, Georgia, the novel covers the period from 1880 to 1894 and races the rise of the heroine, a beautiful South Carolina woman, from poverty to prominence among Augusta's aristocrats. Seeking to escape marriage to an old man to whom her father is indebted, Fancy Williamson leaves South Carolina for Augusta. She begins as a dance girl on a show wagon and eventually marries into a bankrupt aristocratic family of Georgia. Her marriage to Courtland Brantley of the Hiberion Plantation, however, provokes the scorn of aristocrats and begins her downfall.

Three-fourths of *A Woman Called Fancy* chronicles Fancy's efforts to earn respectability in society. Although she cannot escape her sordid past, her background gives her a different set of values. She socializes with African Americans and poor whites, she ignores aristocratic conventions, and she befriends the town's most notorious prostitute. Yerby's characterization of Fancy is, therefore, ironic, emphasizing the ignoble origins of most Southerners. Not only does Fancy contradict southern ideals but in her saintlike manner, she possesses qualities nobler than those of the aristocrats with whom she seeks to identify.

Like all Yerby's novels, *A Woman Called Fancy* presents a protagonist who is an outcast but achieves success in an alien culture, it adheres to his proven formula for historical romance, and it continues his string of best-sellers. *A Woman Called Fancy* is significant, however, in at least one other way: It contains Yerby's most definitive statement about race relations in America before his expatriation. Employing a minor character as a mouthpiece, Yerby declares that African Americans and whites cannot live together in dignity in America. A year later, he quietly left America, and like African American expatriates before him, sought refuge from American racism in Europe.

• Wilbur Watson, "Cloth of Purest Brass," *New York Times,* 6 May 1951, 16. Edward Fitzgerald, "A Woman Called Fancy," *Saturday Review of Literature,* 23 June 1951, 39.

—James L. Hill

Women of Brewster Place, The. The 1982 first novel by Gloria *Naylor, *The Women of Brewster Place* tells the stories of seven African American women who live on a walled-off street in the ghetto of an anonymous northeastern city. While these characters come from varied backgrounds, they all have suffered great hardships, often caused by men.

After a prologue describes the history of the dead-end street, the first section of *The Women of Brewster Place* tells, primarily through flashback, the story of its aging title character, Mattie Michael. Mattie's one sexual experience results in her pregnancy, expulsion from her Tennessee home, and journey northward. As Basil, her son, grows up, Mattie overprotects him, and he becomes irresponsible. Following his accidental murder of another man, Basil skips his bail, causing Mattie to lose her house and sending her to Brewster Place.

The following sketch gives the story of Etta Mae Johnson, a strong-willed, flamboyant woman who stays with Mattie Michael on Brewster Place. After attending a church service, Etta pursues a widowed preacher with whom she dreams of a secure future but only finds a one-night stand. Returning to Mattie's home, Etta realizes that her friendship with Mattie is more valuable than fleeting male attention.

Next Naylor tells of Kiswana Browne, named Melanie by her middle-class mother. Kiswana has changed her name to reflect her new Afrocentrism and has rejected her privileged upbringing to live as an activist on Brewster Place. Yet after Kiswana and her mother undergo a painful interchange, the two women gain a new understanding of each other.

The following chapter relates the story of Lucielia (Ciel) Louise Turner, who has an abortion in order to try to keep her husband. Shortly thereafter, while the couple is arguing about his imminent departure, their toddler daughter is accidentally electrocuted. Ciel's numb response almost results in her own death until Mattie rescues her with loving attention.

Cora Lee is the subject of the next section, which tells of her fixation with having babies, subsequent neglect of them once they mature, and rapid production of seven children. After Kiswana persuades Cora and her children to attend an African American Shakespeare production, Cora begins to realize her irresponsibility, and the chapter ends optimistically.

Next, in "The Two," Naylor tells of a lesbian couple, Theresa and Lorraine, who move into Brewster Place. Disheartened by the community's rejection of them, Lorraine one evening seeks solace with the kind old handyman, Ben. Later that night, delinquent young men in an alley by the Brewster Place wall gang-rape Lorraine. When Ben discovers her, she is so traumatized that she kills him with a brick.

After these tragedies, "The Block Party" relates the grieving community's attempt to go on with life. When it begins to rain during the neighborhood fundraiser, the women perceive the raindrops on the Brewster Place wall as bloodstains, so they destroy the wall. Although these actions appear only to have been in Mattie's dream, the rain and ritual destruction purify the community.

When *The Women of Brewster Place* was first published, Naylor won the 1983 American Book Award for best first novel. The novel was adapted into a television production starring Oprah Winfrey in 1989. Critical interpretations of the novel emphasize its geography, naturalism, and mythical overtones. The novel's emphasis on women's bonding, class, community, and motherhood are also common themes in its criticism, which often takes a feminist approach and compares Naylor to other African American authors, such as Toni *Morrison.

• Barbara Christian, "Gloria Naylor's Geography: Community, Class, and Patriarchy in *The Women of Brewster Place* and *Linden Hills,*" in *Reading Black, Reading Feminist,* ed. Henry Louis Gates, Jr., 1990, pp. 348–373. Henry Louis Gates, Jr., and K. A. Appiah, eds., *Gloria Naylor: Critical Perspectives Past and Present,* 1993.

—Kristine A. Yohe

WOODSON, CARTER G. (1875–1950), historian, educator, and editor. Born in Virginia to former slaves, Carter G. Woodson worked in coal mines until he entered high school at the age of nineteen, finishing in less than two years. Over the next several years, he taught high school and obtained a BL degree at the interracial Berea College (Kentucky). From 1903 to 1906 Woodson worked as supervisor of schools in the Philippines. In 1908 he received both BA and MA degrees from the University of Chicago and began teaching high school in Washington, D.C. He earned a PhD in history from Harvard University in 1912, becoming, after W. E. B. *Du Bois, the second African American to receive a doctorate in history. From 1919 to 1922 he taught at Howard University and West Virginia Collegiate Institute, and served in high administrative posts at both institutions.

In 1915, Woodson, with several other scholars, founded the Association for the Study of Negro Life and History (ASNLH). ASNLH's publishing subsidiary, Associated Publishers, was for many years the leading black-owned press in the United States. The following year he founded the *Journal of Negro History,* the premier professional journal of African American history. He retired from the academy in 1922 to concentrate on the journal and ASNLH, both of which he headed until his death, as well as his own historical writing. He also worked on stimulating popular interest in African American history, initiating Negro History Week (which later became Black History Month) in 1926, and founding the *Negro History Bulletin* (for use in primary and secondary education) in 1937.

Woodson's historical works include *The Education of the Negro Prior to 1861* (1915), *The History of the Negro Church* (1921), and *The African Background Outlined* (1936). He wrote several well-known textbooks, most notably *The Negro in Our History* (1922), popular in both high schools and universities. He was also greatly accomplished as an editor. He collected the speeches of Frederick *Douglass, Booker T. *Washington, and many others in *Negro Orators and Their Orations* (1925). He published a collection of letters, *The Mind of the Negro as Reflected in Letters Written During the Crisis, 1800–1860* (1926), and edited the complete works of the minister and civil rights activist Francis J. Grimké (1942).

Woodson was particularly concerned with social and economic history. His work built on a previous tradition of black historians such as William Wells *Brown and George Washington *Williams, who used history to illustrate the virtues and potential of African Americans, as individuals and as a race. In many cases he pioneered attention to the particular circumstances and contexts of African American history. In *Negro Orators and Their Orations,* for example, he emphasizes the importance of the spoken nature of speeches by black orators, arguing that their performance could never be entirely captured by the printed page. His signficance for the study of African American culture and history, however, derives less from his own work and more from the institutional foundations and personal leadership he provided to the emerging discipline of black history. He inspired (and mentored) an entire generation of historians of African American culture, including Rayford W. Logan, Luther Porter Jackson, James Hugo Johnston, and others. His work, the journal he founded, and the scholarly activity he inspired all contributed to the cultural flowering of the Harlem Renaissance. The ongoing recovery of neglected aspects of African American history, literature, and culture owes much of its impetus to Woodson's founding efforts.

• Rayford W. Logan, "Carter G. Woodson," in *DANB,* eds. Rayford W. Logan and Michael R. Winston, 1982, pp. 665–667. August Meier and Elliott Rudwick, *Black History and the Historical Profession, 1915–1980,* 1986. Jacqueline Goggin, *Carter G. Woodson: A Life in Black History,* 1993.

—Gary Ashwill

WRIGHT, CHARLES S. (1932), novelist, columnist, short fiction writer, and black humorist. Charles Stevenson Wright was born and raised west of Columbia, Missouri, in the small town of New Franklin. Upon his release from the army in 1954, he wrote "No Regrets," an unpublished novel about an affair between a black beatnik from New York City's East Village and an upper-class white girl. Not until the 1960s would Wright begin publishing the blackly humorous, passionately idiosyncratic books that add tragic clarity to the nightmare of contemporary African American existence.

In *The Messenger* (1963), Wright draws so extensively upon his life that fact and fiction often blur. Realistically narrated in the first person by a fair-skinned black Manhattanite named Charles Stevenson, the novel dramatizes the isolation and alienation of persons who fall prey to America's social, economic, and racial caste systems. Stevenson, a New York City messenger, constantly finds himself on the edges of power, yet is utterly devoid of any. A man perceived as neither black nor white, "a minority within a minority," he is cast adrift in the naturalistic city of New York, where victory and defeat are accepted "with the same marvelous indifference."

The Messenger brought Wright recognition and modest commercial success, but initially his 1966 novel *The Wig* was not well-received. Today, however, many people would agree with Ishmael *Reed's 1973 assertion that *The Wig* is "one of the most underrated novels by a black person in this century" (John O'Brien, *Interviews with Black Writers,* 1973).

Wright's use of fantasy and hyperbole distinguishes *The Wig* from most African American fiction of the mid-1960s. Set "in an America of tomorrow," the novel depicts the desperately failed efforts of a twenty-one-year-old black Harlemite named Lester Jefferson to live the American dream. The book ends with his literal (and willed) emasculation, after Jefferson learns that the money he has earned parading around the streets in New York in an electrified chicken suit will prove useless to his successfully courting the black prostitute he has idealized as his "all-American girl."

The years between 1966 and 1973 found Wright in various foreign and domestic locales. But his literary psyche remained firmly planted in New York City, the setting of the nonfictional pieces he began writing for the *Village Voice.* Collected, amended, and supplemented, these columns came to comprise *Absolutely Nothing to Get Alarmed About* (1973), a book filled with the same drug users, male and female prostitutes, abusive policemen, and underinquisitive detectives one finds in his novels. These, plus America's unstinting racism, have rid Wright of his optimism as surely as Mr. Fishback rids Lester Jefferson of his masculinity at the end of *The Wig.*

In 1993, Wright's novels were collected in a publication again titled *Absolutely Nothing to Get Alarmed About: Complete Novels.* Reading this collection makes it clear that Charles Wright is an innovator who in breaking with traditional fictional modes during the 1960s helped to negotiate space for Ishmael Reed, Clarence *Major, and other African American avant-gardists.

• Frances S. Foster, "Charles Wright: Black Black Humorist," *CLA Journal* 15 (1971): 44–53. John O'Brien, "Charles Wright," in *Interviews with Black Writers*, 1973, pp. 245–257. Eberhard Kreutzer, "Dark Ghetto Fantasy and the Great Society: Charles Wright's *The Wig*," in *The Afro-American Novel since 1960*, eds. Peter Bruck and Wolfgang Karrer, 1982, pp. 145–166. Frank Campenni "Charles (Stevenson) Wright" In *Contemporary Novelists*, ed., Susan Windisch Brown, 1996, pp. 1072–73.

—Joe Weixlmann

WRIGHT, JAY (b. c. 1935), poet, playwright, musician, educator, and MacArthur Fellow. Jay Wright's biography is a composite of uncertain and contradictory stories. He was born in either 1934 or 1935 in Albuquerque, New Mexico, to Leona Dailey, a Virginian of African and Native American descent, and George Murphy (also known as Mercer Murphy Wright), a construction worker, jitney driver, and handy man who claimed to be of African American, Cherokee, and Irish ancestry. Wright spent most of his childhood in the care of foster parents in Albuquerque. In his teens, he lived with his father in San Pedro, California. While in high school, Wright began to play minor league baseball and developed what would become a lifelong passion for the bass. From 1954 to 1957, he served in the U.S. Army medical corps. During most of his service, he was stationed in Germany, which gave him the opportunity to travel extensively throughout Europe. After he returned, Wright enrolled in the University of California at Berkeley under the G.I. Bill. He majored in comparative literature and graduated in only three years. Before continuing his literary studies at Rutgers in 1962, Wright spent a semester at Union Theological Seminary in New York. In 1964, Wright interrupted his graduate studies to spend a year teaching English and medieval history at the Butler Institute in Guadalajara, Mexico, one of many extended visits to that country. Back at Rutgers, he completed all but his dissertation in pursuit of a doctoral degree in comparative literature.

While at Rutgers in the 1960s, Wright lived and worked in Harlem, where he encountered several other young African American writers, among them Henry *Dumas, Larry *Neal, and LeRoi Jones/Amiri *Baraka. Unlike the work of these and other poets associated with the Black Arts movement, Jay Wright's poems approach African American spiritual, intellectual, and social history from a cross-cultural perspective. Already in the 1960s and 1970s, Wright's was one of the most original voices in contemporary African American and American poetry, a voice that influenced younger poets such as Nathaniel *Mackey and Cyrus Cassells. But Wright's increasing distance from a budding Black Arts movement that rejected all European-derived literary forms and traditions did not attract a large readership.

Wright's self-declared "passion for what is hidden" (*Elaine's Book*, 1988) frequently takes the shape of a spiritual quest heavily infused with autobiographical elements. From the early collection *The Homecoming Singer* (1971) and the three book-length poems *Dimensions of History* (1976), *The Double Invention of Komo* (1980), and *Explications/Interpretations* (1984)—which, together with *Soothsayers* and *Omens* (1976), make up Wright's first poetic cycle—to *Elaine's Book* and *Boleros* (1991), Wright's poetic persona, which may be both male and female, traverses and connects far-flung geographies: New Hampshire, his home base since 1973; Mexico; the Southwest; California; and, more globally, Western Europe, Africa, the Caribbean, South America, and Asia. Wright's poetry insists on continuities across, as well as within, cultures. The scope and depth of Wright's vision derive from his extensive research in medieval and Renaissance literatures, music, anthropology, the history of religions, and the history of science. An admixture of Italian, German, and Spanish interspersed with Dogon, Bambara, and other African ideograms, Wright's literary English amounts at times almost to a foreign language. African American music, such as the blues, jazz, and a host of Caribbean and Latin American song and dance forms, plays an equally crucial role in his poetic projects.

Wright's poetry exemplifies what the Guyanese novelist Wilson Harris, whose work Wright has often cited as an inspiration, calls a poetics of the cross-cultural imagination (*The Womb of Space: The Cross Cultural Imagination*, 1983). Though his literary vision is firmly rooted in both African American history and African, particularly Akan and Dogon, religions, Wright's poetry seeks to restore to African American literature a sense of all the cultural resources available to it. For him, this very much includes Europe. Starting with his persona's acute consciousness of exile, Wright's poetic journeys retrace and reverse the Middle Passage from Africa to the Americas. His poems offer rites of passage that both remember and try to heal the ruptures and dispersals of traditional cultures, African and Native American alike. Wright provides further insight into his intricate designs in "Desire's Design, Vision's Resonance: Black Poetry's Ritual and Historical Voice" (*Callaloo*, Winter 1987). This programmatic essay shows that his literary and cultural politics have far more in common with those of older poets such as Robert *Hayden and Melvin B. *Tolson than with the cultural nationalism many poets of his own generation espoused.

• Robert B. Stepto, "After Modernism, After Hibernation: Michael Harper, Robert Hayden, and Jay Wright," in *Chant of Saints: A Gathering of Afro-American Literature, Arts, and Scholarship*, eds. Michael S. Harper and Robert B. Stepto, 1979, pp. 470–486. "Jay Wright: A Special Issue," *Callaloo* 6 (Fall 1983). Wilson Harris, *The Womb of Space: The Cross-Cultural Imagination*, 1983. Kimberly W. Benston, "'I Yam What I Am': The Topos of (Un)naming in Afro-American Literature," in *Black Literature and Literary Theory*, ed. Henry Louis Gates, Jr., 1984, pp. 151–172. Vera M. Kutzinski, *Against the American Grain: Myth and History in William Carlos Williams, Jay Wright, and Nicolás Guillén*, 1987. Isidore Okpewho, "From a Goat Path in Africa: An Approach to the Poetry of Jay Wright," *Callaloo* 14 (Fall 1991): 692–726. Vera M. Kutzinski, review of *Boleros, Magill's Literary Annual*, 1992, 56–59.

—Vera M. Kutzinski

WRIGHT, RICHARD (1908–1960), novelist, short story writer, and political commentator. Richard Wright changed the landscape of possibility for African American writers. Wright's defiance, his refusal to give the reading public what it had hitherto demanded of the African American writer, his insistence on the expression of an African American voice, allowed later writers to do the same, allowed Toni *Morrison, for example, to write as she would—without concern for explaining her sometimes obscure meanings (e.g., her references to news events from long ago or words or phrases from African American vernacular speech) to a mainstream reading public. For other African American writers, positioning themselves against Wright allowed them to write about African American culture in a more positive way, to assume a posture not requiring that the subject of the fiction, the African American, be seen as victim.

Richard Wright's influence began primarily with the publication of **Native Son* in 1940. The significance of the novel's publication lay in the new and daringly defiant character of its content and in its adoption by the Book-of-the-Month Club, which signaled for the first time since the nineteenth-century fugitive slave narratives the willingness of a mainstream reading public to give ear to an African American writer, even one who appeared unapologetic in his bald and forthright representation of a large segment of African American culture.

Wright's understanding of African American life is rooted in his southern background. His first book, **Uncle Tom's Children* (1938), a collection of short stories, comes out of his understanding and knowledge of the meaning of being a young black male growing up in the South. Its introduction, "The Ethics of Living Jim Crow" (added along with a fifth short story in 1940), forms the core for his later autobiography, **Black Boy* (1945). The ligature between the two is *Native Son*. It is no happenstance that *Bigger Thomas, the novel's hero, though living in Chicago at the time of the narrative, was born in Mississippi, the birthplace of Richard Wright. Bigger Thomas is conceived in *Uncle Tom's Children* as the character Big Boy, the titular hero of "Big Boy Leaves Home," who by the end of that story flees north to escape a lynch mob. In practically all of Wright's fiction, the hero faces capture and subsequent mutilation or death from some wrongfully avenging agency.

Richard Wright was born on 24 September on a farm near Natchez, Mississippi. His mother, Ella Wilson Wright, was a schoolteacher and his father, Nathan, a tenant farmer. Though *Black Boy* differs in important respects from his life, the general tenor of Wright's narrative is true. The desertion of his father when Wright was only six years old, the constant moves from one house, town, or state to another and back reflect the instability of his life. Poverty and illness were his family's lot; hunger, if we count the number of times the word appears in his autobiographical narrative, a more constant companion than any playmate.

As Wright matured and began to understand his circumstances as a black person in Mississippi in the early twentieth century, he came to know the fear and dread associated with racism and its narrow circumscription of black lives. He is frequently aware of the possibility of being killed or otherwise injured because of anything he might or might not say or do if that might inadvertently violate the "ethics of living Jim Crow." The most frequent mood in his early life is tension, if not the tension arising from direct contact with whites, then tension resulting from the pressures brought to bear on African Americans stemming from the racial climate. Wright makes abundantly clear that the most intimate interactions (involving friends, family members, lovers) among African Americans are largely influenced by the pervasive impact of race. Wright keenly felt, as all his fiction reveals, that in interracial social relations, in both North and South ultimately, race is an omnipresent factor.

His autobiographies *Black Boy* and *American Hunger* give particular attention to his development as a writer. *Black Boy* claims that the author had something of dramatic significance to write about: the career of a black person, a male citizen within the American democratic commonwealth, growing up in the South. It points also to Wright's early sensitivity, to an awarness and predisposition to respond to the forces mediating the relation between self and social environment. It speaks of a youthful early interest in narrative, especially in the gothic children's story "Bluebeard," which prompted his earlier publication, the unrecovered "Voodoo of Hell's Half Acre."

Shortly before he "escapes" from the South (as he in part does because he is afraid to tell the whites who question his motives for moving north why he is leaving), Wright discovered a completely new perspective on American life provided by such national journals as *Atlantic Monthly, Harper's*, and the *American Mercury*. A northern white who managed an optical company where Wright was employed in Memphis, Tennessee, allowed him to use his library card to borrow books (a forbidden act), and he became acquainted with the writers who were most germane to the shaping of his literary career. These include Theodore Dreiser, Sherwood Anderson, Frank Harris, Alexandre Dumas, and O. Henry.

The two major events of Wright's life in Chicago are his employment at the post office and his involvement with the Communist Party. Though employed only intermittently by the post office, he had done extremely well on the competitive civil service examination. At the post office he met others, both black and white, also using the job as a steppingstone to higher status. It was at the post office that he first interacted with whites on a basis of equality, meeting, for example, Abraham Aaron, himself an aspiring writer, who eventually introduced him to the John Reed Club and thence to the Communist Party. In his relations with the Chicago Post Office, Wright finally had the last word. In 1937 he declined a job at $2,000 annually and went to New York to become a writer. The post office and figures he knew there supplied the characters, scenes, and action of his first written (though posthumously published) novel, *Lawd Today* (1963).

His relation to the Communist Party was the subject of most of Wright's fiction and the center around which his life turned even, seemingly, after his break with the party. Though a communist and a marxist, Wright's was never a doctrinaire commitment. He unfailingly challenged the party's interpretation and understanding of marxism, especially as these involved black people. *Uncle Tom's Children* and *Native Son* both instruct the party about its failures in addressing African Americans, thus implying its pathetic lack of knowledge and understanding of black history, culture, and life. *Uncle Tom's Children* shows the depths of blacks' submersion in black history and culture, suggesting that African Americans cannot be politically addressed outside of that context. *Native Son* shows two significant levels of the failure of communication: on one level *Mary Dalton fails to understand her class relation to Bigger Thomas, and Bigger's sense of his class and racial relation to Mary Dalton results in her death. The other more complicated level finds Max, the sophisticated marxist, as unable as Mary Dalton to see and communicate with Bigger Thomas on a totally human level. He understands Bigger's class situation but nothing about how that intersects with race, thus explaining the otherwise enigmatic line at the close of the novel, "Max groped for his hat like a blind man."

"The Man Who Lived Underground" reflects Wright's increasing disaffection with the Communist Party and with marxism. The loneliness and isolation of Fred Daniels, his discovery of the subjectivity of experience, shows Wright looking at the world in a far more psychological and existentially philosophical rather than dialectically materialistic way. Fred discovers the relativity of value, seeing that what he heretofore had seen as the truths and facts of the world are not truths and facts at all but merely arbitrarily assigned values. When the policeman at the conclusion of the novella says of Fred, "You've got to shoot his kind. They'd wreck things," his reference is not to race at all but to any who see behind appearances. With his 1944 article in *Atlantic Monthly,* "I Tried to Be a Communist," extracted from *American Hunger,* Wright made his final break with the party.

In 1947 Richard Wright left the United States for France with his wife, Ellen, and daughter, Julia, in order to further distance himself from Mississippi. Despite his success as the most famous black author ever to have published, Wright still felt beset by tensions arising out of racism. Even in New York it was not possible for him to live freely and easily wherever he chose. Still he was viewed not as a great author but as a great black author. He felt that in Europe, especially France, he could live unhampered by those feelings that harked back to the fear and misery he experienced growing up in the South. Paris had been home to other disillusioned American writers; perhaps it could become home for him, too.

Negative responses to him and to his work were not infrequent after his French exile. Was it because his creative powers did indeed diminish after he left the United States or was the American response to his work related to his politics? Did he indeed "lose touch" with his country when he remained away so long as was often asserted? His work was much better received in France than in the United States, so obviously the French did not see him as an author in decline. His income decreased considerably during the 1950s as the result of his loss of popularity in the United States. It is not clear whether his difficult relations with the State Department might have had something to do with that. (The FBI began a file on Wright in 1943 when an investigation was launched to determine whether his picture essay *12 Million Black Voices* was evidence of sedition. He had difficulty obtaining a passport because of his previous relations with the Communist Party. United States surveillance of his activities while he lived in France was maintained largely because of his political views.) The novels published while he lived in France are *The Outsider* (1953), *Savage Holiday* (1954), and *The Long Dream* (1958). In *The Outsider,* a tale much influenced by Fyodor Dostoyevsky's *Crime and Punishment,* Cross Damon tries to function outside the constraints of law and morality. Its existential orientation derives in part from the influence of European existentialists, especially Jean-Paul Sartre, Simone de Beauvoir, Albert Camus, Martin Heidegger, and Edmund Husserl, and inpart from Wright's understanding of his own experiences in Mississippi. *Savage Holiday,* a novel whose major characters are not African Americans, was published in the United States but only in paperback by Avon. More than any other of his writings it was intended to entertain rather than to effect social change. *The Long Dream,* set in Mississippi, seems an attempt on Wright's part to return to his major theme, social protest against a punishing, unfair racist society.

Nonfiction works published during these years include *Black Power,* Wright's diary written when he visits the Gold Coast (1954); *The Color Curtain: A Report of the Bandung Conference,* an account of the Bandung Conference, in Bandung, Indonesia, in 1955, an international conference of people of color (1956); *Pagan Spain,* a wonderfully written and very readable travelogue (written following an extended motor tour) that reveals much of Wright's intelligence, knowledge, and sensitivity (1956); and *White Man, Listen,* a collection of four lectures delivered between 1950 and 1956 that contains in its author's introduction a sentiment that describes very accurately a sense one gets reading Wright: "I declare unabashedly that I like and even cherish the state of abandonment, of aloneness; . . . it seems the natural, inevitable condition of man, and I welcome it. . . . I've been shaped to this mental stance by the kind of experience I have fallen heir to" (1957).

When Wright died unexpectedly at the age of fifty-two, he was separated from his family, who were in London, where he wanted to live; he was in dire financial straits; and he was in conflict with the black expatriate community for a complex of reasons. The circumstances of his death excited questions of foul play. He was not known to suffer any heart malady; he seemed in better physical condition than he had been of late; he died in a hospital shortly after receiving an injection, his family was not notified of his death; and he was cremated almost immediately afterward without their consent, thus no autopsy was possible. Wright biographer Michel Fabre concludes that if Wright was killed, it was indirectly—through the pressures brought to bear on him at the time by his critics—and probably not by the CIA.

Richard Wright's influence on American literature is nearly inestimable. He demonstrated for the first time that an African American could indeed be a major writer of international fame and stature. He modeled possibilities hitherto not seen or known for African American writers. His influence extended well beyond the writing community, demonstrating that success was possible and that militancy in the face of racism constituted a valuable response. It was not Richard Wright alone who influenced the progressive social changes that occurred in the 1960s, whose effects are yet pervasive, but surely his was a great influence on the time. Because of his place in literary history and because of the widespread influence of his work, many see him as among the greatest writers of the century.

• Richard Abcarian, *Richard Wright's "Native Son": A Critical Handbook,* 1970. Keneth Kinnamon, *The Emergence of Richard Wright: A Study in Literature and Society,* 1972. Michel Fabre, *The Unfinished Quest of Richard Wright,* 1973. Yoshinobu Hakutani, *Critical Essays on Richard Wright,* 1974. Richard Macksey and Frank Moorer, eds., *Richard Wright: A Collection of Critical Essays,* 1984. Joyce Ann Joyce, *Richard Wright's Art of Tragedy,* 1986. James C. Trotman, ed., *Richard Wright: Myths and Realities,* 1988. Margaret Walker, *Richard Wright, Daemonic Genius: A Portrait of the Man, A Critical Look at His Work,* 1988. Eugene Miller, *Voice of a Native Son: The Poetics of Richard Wright,* 1990. Robert J. Butler, *Native Son: The Emergence of a New Black Hero,* 1991. Henry Louis Gates, Jr., and K. A. Appiah, eds., *Richard Wright: Critical Perspectives Past and Present,* 1993. Arnold Rampersad, ed., *Richard Wright,* 1995. Robert J. Butler, ed., *The Critical Response to Richard Wright,* 1995. Robert Felgar, *Understanding Richard Wright's Black Boy,* 1998.

—Donald B. Gibson

WRIGHT, SARAH ELIZABETH (b. 1928), poet, novelist, and lecturer. Sarah Elizabeth Wright was born in Wetipquin, Maryland, began writing in the third grade, and was encouraged to continue. While a student at Howard University, she was inspired by Sterling A. *Brown, Owen *Dodson, and Langston *Hughes. Throughout her career, she has demonstrated a thirst for knowledge and the need to share her craft. As a result, she is a Certified Poetry Therapist, has presented readings, lectured, and taught in a number of forums, including television and radio talk shows, high schools, community centers, libraries, and YMCAs, and spoken at the United Nations International Writers Day celebration of Martin Luther *King, Jr. (1993). Wright has participated in poetry workshops and was a member of the Harlem Writer's Guild. She helped organize the First (1959) and the Second National Conference of Black Writers and the Congress of American Writers (1971). She was president of Pen & Brush, Inc. (1992–1993), the oldest professional organization of women in the United States. Her professional memberships include PEN, the Authors Guild, and the International Women's Writing Guild. Although she has not been a prolific writer, her work has been excellent, honest, and life-affirming. She has received numerous awards, including two MacDowell Colony fellowships for creative writing, the 1975 CAPS Award for Fiction, the 1976 Howard University Novelist-Poet Award, the Middle Atlantic Writers Association Award, and the Zora Neale Hurston Award. Her work has been included in *Freedomways;* the *Amsterdam News* (New York); the *Black Scholar;* the *African American Review; Confrontation; Southern Voices,* edited by John O. *Killens and Jerry Ward; *Court of Appeal,* edited by the staff of the *Black Scholar;* and *Fidel and Malcolm X,* edited by Rosemari Mealy.

Wright's first book, *Give Me a Child* (1955), was coauthored with Lucy Smith. It is a collection of poetry designed to make poetry accessible to the general public through its subject matter and presentation. Her first novel, **This Child's Gonna Live* (1969) was chosen by the *New York Times* as one of 1969's most important books and by the *Baltimore Sun* for the 1969 Readability Award. It is set in Tangierneck, Maryland, and is the story of Mariah Upshur, who struggles against oppressing forces during the depression and refuses to totally succumb to hopelessness. It emphasizes the need for women to be independent and define themselves regardless of race, community, men, or society. Simultaneously, it presents an objective view of Jacob Upshur and points out that men, too, are victims of their definition and the forces that impact them. In 1994, the Feminist Press reissued the novel and Pen & Brush, Inc. celebrated both the novel's silver anniversary and the fact that it had been on sale constantly since 1969. Her third book, A. Philip Randolph, *Integration in the Workplace* (1990), was chosen by the New York Public Library as one of the Best Books for Young Adults published in 1990. In the mid-1990s, Wright was working on the sequel to her first novel, tentatively entitled "Twelve Gates to the City, Halleluh! Halleluh!"

• Virginia B. Guilford, "Sarah Elizabeth Wright," in *DLB,* vol. 33, *Afro-American Fiction Writers after 1955,* eds. Thadious M. Davis and Trudier Harris, 1984, pp. 293–300. Linda M. White, "Sarah Elizabeth Wright," in *Contemporary African American Novelists,* ed. Emmanuel S. Nelson, 1999, pp. 500–504.

—Helen R. Houston

Y

Yellow Back Radio Broke-Down (1969) is Ishmael *Reed's second novel and the first to embody the themes and principles of neohoodooism, Reed's rubric for his African-originated but ultimately pan-cultural aesthetic practice.

Yellow Back Radio is a Western in a double sense, dealing with Wild West themes of lurid yellow-covered dime novels (cowboys, Indians, outlaws) and with Western civilization and its dominational tendencies (us versus them). One of the characters calls it a "horse opera," a colloquial expression for the popular genre of the Western, but also alluding here to Reed's creation of a "hoodoo" Western—hoodoo being the black American derivative of African traditional religious practices in which a state of possession may occur, occasioned by a "spirit" mounting a devotee (its "horse"). In *Yellow Back Radio,* in short, Reed exposes the "other" character of the American West and of Western civilization by recasting their generic myths from a black, "magical" perspective.

Analyzing the title can assist us in understanding Reed's purposes. "Yellow Back Radio" represents the media and their broadcasts of "bad news"—messages of monotheism, monopoly capitalism, and control—that Reed sees as destructive of Nature and a perversion of our fuller human potential. "Broke-Down" indicates an explanation or deconstruction (what Reed would call a "reading") of Yellow Back Radio's functions and meaning, as well as referring to YBR's ultimate defeat by the book's hero, the Loop Garoo Kid—rebel angel, black cowboy, and writer of "circuses"—and the forces of imagination and spiritual pluralism (Reed's "neohoodooism").

The debate in the novel between "neo–social realist" Bo Shmo and the Loop Garoo Kid provides us with one of Reed's most succinct assertions of his aesthetic values (for which Loop is spokesperson and exemplar) and the manner in which these values differ from those of more restrictive "schools" of art. For Reed, a novel can be anything it wants to be, and *Yellow Back Radio Broke-Down* is an excellent demonstration that Reed's novels typically want to be many things at once.

Reed's characters are not intended to be realistic; they are archetypes or stereotypes, embodying aspects of myth that need revamping or exorcising. Thus Loop Garoo, whose name, one of Reed's poems explains, means "change into," represents art as a free, transformative process and the artist as improviser, impresario of the imagination, while his principal adversaries, Drag Gibson and the Pope, epitomize monopolistic practices and rigid orthodoxy.

Neil Schmitz, in an essay on Reed's fiction in *Twentieth Century Literature* (Apr. 1974), judged *Yellow Back Radio* to exhibit a "simplistic" focus and "diffused" energy, although many readers found it to be a comic tour de force. But in apparent reference to some of the harsher assessments of his critics, Reed, in a famous self-interview published in *Shrovetide in Old New Orleans* (1978), asked himself if he was drunk or on dope when he wrote *Yellow Back Radio,* then "defended" himself by stating that it was a "talking book" based on old radio scripts. In fact, much of his style and many of his themes are drawn from folklore and American pop culture, and, to the degree that this has been misunderstood or unappreciated, Reed's fiction has been called cartoonish. But if a work like *Yellow Back Radio Broke-Down* is a cartoon, it is, in the tradition of Krazy Kat (creation of African American artist George Herriman), a cartoon with a brick in its hand, aimed at the head of the status quo.

• Michel Fabre, "Postmodern Rhetoric in Ishmael Reed's *Yellow Back Radio Broke-Down,*" in *The Afro-American Novel Since 1960,* eds. Peter Bruck and Wolfgang Karrer, 1982, pp. 167–188.

—Robert Elliot Fox

YERBY, FRANK (1916–1991), historical novelist, short story writer, poet, and successful popular writer. Frank Garvin Yerby, son of Rufus Garvin and Wilhelmina Yerby, was born 5 September 1916 in Augusta, Georgia. After graduation from Haines Institute, he attended Paine College and there began writing poetry, fiction, and drama. While at Fisk University, Yerby's sister showed his poetry to James Weldon *Johnson who encouraged him, and in 1937, Yerby began graduate studies there.

Yerby's growing up in the South made an indelible impression on him and shaped his life in at least two distinct ways. Favorably, he gained a firsthand knowledge of southern mores and customs—eventually the subject of his fiction. Adversely, the harsh realities of racial segregation and discrimination weighed heavily on him, and like many African Americans before him, he migrated north to escape. After completing his master's degree in 1938, Yerby enrolled in the University of Chicago.

While in Chicago, he worked with the Federal Writers Project of the WPA, through which he met other aspiring writers, including Arna *Bontemps, Richard *Wright, and Margaret *Walker. Yerby taught for brief stints at Florida A & M and Southern Universities (1939–1941), then migrated north again, working first as a technician at the Ford Motor Company at Dearborn, Michigan (1941–1944), and then at Ranger (Fairchild) Aircraft in Jamaica, New York (1944–1945).

During this period, Yerby wrote a protest novel about an African American steelworker who succeeded as a boxer but came to a tragic end. *Redbook* rejected Yerby's novel, but editor Muriel Fuller encouraged him to send her something else. The something else was "Health Card," which Fuller determined was unsuitable for *Redbook* and sent to *Harper's Magazine.* Published by *Harper's* in 1944, "Health Card" won the O. Henry Memorial Award Prize for best first short story. Other stories Yerby published included "White Magnolias," "Homecoming," and "My Brother Went to College."

Following unsuccessful attempts to publish his protest novel, Yerby turned to historical fiction, then in vogue. Believing that he could write more convincingly about African Americans than did Margaret Mitchell in *Gone with the Wind* (1936), he published *The *Foxes of Harrow* in 1946, catapulting himself to immediate financial and popular success unprecedented for an African American writer. In subsequent years, Yerby would publish thirty-two additional novels, which sold more than 55 million copies. Several—*The Foxes of Harrow* (1946), *The Golden Hawk* (1948), and *The Saracen Blade* (1952)—were turned into successful movies.

Yerby's career thrived in the midst of controversy. One of the most maligned of African American writers, Yerby was accused of imperfections in both his craft and his politics. Many reviewers recognized his talents but criticized his uninhibited use of popular fiction conventions. African American writers and intellectuals lauded his achievement as a pioneer in popular fiction but urged him to address racial concerns. Yerby, however, steadfastly refused to comment on contemporary social issues and continued to write best-sellers. By the mid-1950s, serious consideration of his fiction was waning, causing him to have misgivings about his limitations in popular fiction.

He attempted to publish another protest novel, *The Tents of Shem,* in 1963, and several of his novels—*The Serpent and the Staff* (1958), *The Garfield Honor* (1961), and *Griffin's Way* (1962)—focused increasingly on racial issues in the historical South. Another, *Speak Now* (1969), introduced his first black protagonist. Thus, while he continued to write popular fiction, he did explore serious themes, and among his best novels he counted *The Garfield Honor, An Odor of Sanctity* (1965), *Judas, My Brother* (1968), and *The Dahomean* (1971).

Yerby's chosen genre represented a compromise. Abandoning protest fiction in 1946, he proved that an African American could succeed in popular fiction. However, writing about white protagonists forced him outside the African American literary tradition and toward a primarily white audience. But contrary to prevailing critical opinion, he did not totally abandon racial protest. Yerby adapted protest fiction to suit the medium of popular fiction. Enlarging his protest motives and taking aim at inaccuracies in southern history, he became one of America's greatest debunkers of historical myths. Not surprisingly, too, Yerby's protest extended beyond his fiction; it was also personal. In 1952, he expatriated to France because, he said, of racism; and in 1955, he moved to Madrid, Spain, where he spent the last thirty-six years of his life. Little is known about this period of Yerby's life. Except for occasional visits to the States for business or personal reasons, he remained an expatriate. Yerby died on 29 November 1991. His death was as mysterious as his life, for before he died, he exacted a promise from his wife to keep his death a secret for five weeks.

In some ways, Frank Yerby was typical of the cadre of African American writers emerging in the post–World War II era; in other ways, he was their antithesis. Like many African American writers of the 1940s and 1950s, for example, he began his career writing protest literature and served an apprenticeship with the WPA. Like Wright, Chester *Himes, and James *Baldwin, he expatriated early in search of a less racially hostile climate, and like Wright and Himes, he was profoundly influenced by his experiences of living in the South, causing him to make the South the primary focus of his fiction. Unlike his contemporaries, Yerby made a conscious decision to write the more profitable popular fiction. Unlike them, too, he chose to lend neither the prestige of his name nor the power of his pen to the cause of racial justice in America.

The significance of Yerby's novels lies not in the millions of copies he sold nor in his successful manipulation of the conventions of the historical romance novel. His novels present uncompromising criticisms of the romantic view of the South in southern fiction. His fictional recreations of the American South are intended to correct distorted myths and legends about such subjects as slavery, aristocracy, the Civil War, Reconstruction, and the southern gentleman; and beyond America, he targets inaccuracies in the histories of other cultures. Thus, his novels teach more than one usually expects of the costume novelist. Too long discounted as an anomaly in African American literature, Yerby deserves more critical attention.

[*See also* Woman Called Fancy, A.]

• Nick Aaron Ford, "Four Popular Novelists," *Phylon* 15 (Mar. 1954): pp. 29–39. Frank Yerby, "How and Why I Write the Costume Novel," *Harper's,* Oct. 1959, 145–150. William W. Hill "Behind the Magnolia Mask: Frank Yerby as Critic of the South," master's thesis, Auburn University, 1968. Darvin T. Turner, "Frank Yerby as Debunker," *Massachusetts Review* 20 (Summer 1968): 569–577. Maryemma Graham, "Frank Yerby, King of the Costume Novel," *Essence,* Oct. 1975, 70–71, 88–92. James L. Hill, "Anti-Heroic Perspectives: The Life and Works of Frank Yerby," PhD diss., University of Iowa, 1976. James L. Hill, "Between Philosophy and Race: Images of Blacks in the Fiction of Frank Yerby," *Umoja* (Summer 1981): 5–16. Frank

Yerby, "An Interview with Frank Garvin Yerby," interview by James L. Hill, *Resources for American Literary Study* (Fall 1995): 206–239. Louis Hill Pratt, "Frank Garvin Yerby," in *Contemporary African American Novelists,* ed, Emmanuel S. Nelson, 1999, pp. 505–511.

—James L. Hill

YOUNG, AL (b. 1939), poet, novelist, short story writer, screenwriter, editor, essayist, musician, and educator. Born Albert James Young in Ocean Springs, Mississippi, on 31 May 1939, Young later moved to Detroit, Michigan, with his parents. He resides in Palo Alto, California. His parents were Albert James, a professional musician and autoworker, and Mary Campbell Young Simmons. Young married Arline Belck, a freelance artist, on 8 October 1963. They have one son, Michael James. After attending the University of Michigan (1957–1961), Young was a Wallace E. Stegner Fellow in creative writing at Stanford University (1966–1967) and received his BA in Spanish from the University of California at Berkeley (1969). While at Berkeley, he worked as a writing instructor and language consultant for Berkeley Neighborhood Youth Corps and then took the position of the Edward H. Jones Lecturer in Creative Writing at Stanford University (1969–1974). He wrote and collaborated on several screenplays including *Nigger, Sparkle* (1972), and *Bustin Loose* (1981) for Richard Pryor, and edited and founded several multicultural literary magazines such as *Loveletter* (1966–1968), *Quilt* (1981), and, with Ishmael *Reed, *Yardbird* (1972–1976). With Reed, he edited and contributed to *Yardbird Lives!* (1978) and *Calafia: The California Poetry* (1979). He began directing the Associated Writing Programs in 1979 and was writer in residence at the University of Washington, Seattle (1981–1982). In addition, he has been a Mellon Distinguished Professor of Humanities at Rice University. He is the recipient of the San Francisco Foundation's Joseph Henry Jackson Award (1969), National Arts Council awards for editing and poetry (1968–1970), several National Endowment for the Arts fellowships (1968, 1969, 1975), the Pushcart Prize (1980), a Guggenheim Memorial Foundation Fellowship (1974), the California Association of Teachers of English Special Award (1973), the New York Times Outstanding Book of the Year citation (1980), and the Before Columbus Foundation Award (1982).

Young's passion for music permeates all of his writing. His belief in music as a central force in human lives appears in his early work *Snakes* (1970), where the main character MC grows up as he matures in his musical talent. Young's collections of "musical memoirs," *Bodies & Soul* (1966), *Kinds of Blue* (1984), *Things Ain't What They Used to Be* (1987), and *Drowning in the Sea of Love* (1995) all demonstrate the affinity between music and everyday life. As he discusses individual musicians, he illustrates how art intensifies human experiences and how music evokes powerful emotions and memories.

His poetry imitates the improvisational style of jazz music, especially in his first collection of poems, *Dancing* (1969), where Young uses flexible rhythms and juxtaposes long and short lines. His later works, *Geography of the Near Past* (1966) and *The Song Turning Back into Itself* (1971), are tighter and more controlled in both rhythm and structure. The poems in *Geography* narrate specific events such as his wife's pregnancy or a visit to a friend in jail. The rapid, stream-of-consciousness writing and the attention to cultural items show evidence of the Expressionist movement and the Beat poets. Later collections are *The Blues Don't Change: New and Selected Poems* (1982) and *Heaven: Collected Poems 1958–1988* (1989).

Young's novels are realistic and have been compared to those of John Updike because his stories glorify the middle class and focus on the everyday world. He compliments the musician Charles Mingus in the biography *Mingus/Mingus* (1989; cowritten with Janet Coleman) for his ability to incorporate musical traditions and still deliver the "soul and gut and night-and-dayness of being alive." Aware of the tendency on the part of black writers to fulfill popular expectations of African Americans in their writings, Young avoids polemical topics in his works. His much admired poem "Dance for Militant Dilettantes" critiques a white readership demanding a particular black "type" and indicting militant black rights advocates.

Young counteracts stereotypical conceptions of African Americans through his depiction of quirky, offbeat personalities. His characters are endearing not because they are marginal but because they portray those eccentricities that make Americans so fascinating. In *Snakes,* MC's friend Shakes speaks in Shakespearean phrases; the character of Sidney J. Prettymore in *Sitting Pretty* (1976), an aging philosopher of life, becomes a radio talk-show celebrity; and Mamie Franklin's husband in *Seduction by Light* (1988) returns to her as a ghost. Young's characters often search for self-definition and an understanding of how their past fits into their present. Angelina in *Who is Angelina?* (1975) wrestles with this question after a suicide attempt while Durwood Knight, the retired professional basketball player in *Ask Me Now* (1980), struggles to define his role as father and husband. Young's ear for language and music contributes to the success of his books and makes them especially enjoyable when he reads passages aloud in public. His characters' use of dialects grants them a great range of expression. In their mouths, the vernacular discourse provides a more versatile form of expression, much in the same way jazz music offers the musician a personal voice above and beyond the tradition. Most recently, Young turned to editing literature and published *African American Literature: A Brief Introduction and Anthology* (1996).

• Sharon R. Gunton, ed., *Contemporary Literary Criticism,* 1981. Elizabeth Schultz, "Search for 'Soul Space': A Study of Al

Young's 'Who is Angelina?' (1975) and the Dimensions of Freedom," in *The Afro-American Novel Since 1960,* eds. Peter Bruck and Wolfgang Karrer, 1982, pp. 263–287. Al Young, Larry Kart, and Michael S. Harper, "Jazz and Letters: A Colloquy," *Triquarterly* 68 (Winter 1987); 118–158. Irv Broughton, ed., *The Writer's Mind: Interviews with American Authors,* vol. 3, 1990. James P. Draper, ed., *Black Literature Criticism,* vol. 3, 1992. Don Lee, "About Al Young," *Ploughshares* 19.1 (Spring 1993): 219–224.

—Miriam M. Chirico

Z

Zeely, Virginia *Hamilton's first book for children, *Zeely* (1967) tells the story of the summer that a young African American girl, Elizabeth, spends with her brother John at their Uncle Ross's farm. The trip was special because Elizabeth and her brother went alone and because their father had hinted that something was going to happen that Elizabeth must take care of. Elizabeth's unexpected relationship with Zeely, the daughter of Nat Tayber, who rents a small part of Uncle Ross's farm, gives Elizabeth an opportunity to find out what he meant.

On the train, Elizabeth feels that the only way to celebrate the uniqueness of this trip with her brother is for them to change their names; Elizabeth becomes Geeder and John is to answer to Toeboy. This is only the first in a series of stories that Elizabeth creates. Upon arriving at her uncle's farm, Elizabeth renames the nearby town Crystal, and the road leading from the farm to the town Leadback Road. The most significant story that Elizabeth creates, however, surrounds the background of Zeely.

The unique and strikingly regal appearance of Zeely Tayber is enhanced when Elizabeth sees a picture of a Watutsi queen in a magazine and immediately equates Zeely with the woman in the picture. Elizabeth's storytelling increases, and she begins to imagine that she and Zeely are sisters, that she is Zeely's only confidant, and that Zeely eventually makes Elizabeth a queen. Elizabeth's feeling of importance builds as she tells these stories in town to her friends, who take them as the truth. It is only after Zeely meets with Elizabeth and talks about herself through real stories of her own that Elizabeth learns the significance of knowing herself, and of living for herself and not for the stories that she makes up about others.

Zeely originated from an eighteen-page short story that Hamilton had written in college. Only later, after being reminded of its existence by a college friend who was working at a publishing company, did she expand it into a children's book. That the publication of this book coincided with the civil rights and black consciousness movements of the late 1960s further highlights its cultural aspects. Not simply a coming-of-age book, *Zeely* chronicles the development of a young girl into a young women, and her increasing racial awareness as well. Hamilton's weaving of African American folklore and history into the stories of Zeely and other characters encourages readers to learn and to appreciate themselves and their histories.

• Nina Mikkelsen, *Virginia Hamilton,* 1994.

—Saundra Liggins

ZU-BOLTON, AHMOS, II (b. 1935), poet, editor, and journalist. Born 21 October 1935 in Poplarville, Mississippi, and raised in De Ridder, Louisiana, Ahmos Zu-Bolton II is one of the most influential figures in the development of the "new Black poetry" in the South during the 1970s. His career exemplifies the Black Arts movement idea that African American artists should also be "cultural workers" responsive and responsible to their communities, affirming the belief—as Zu-Bolton expresses it in his 1976 poem "Struggle-Road Dance"—that "this place / must be a workshop" for Blacks. Zu-Bolton's role as poet is complemented by his work as a literary editor, small press publisher, teacher, and organizer of cultural events.

Zu-Bolton's free verse poems—collected in *A Niggered Amen* (1975)—employ African American vernacular speech and are sometimes cast in the form of dramatic monologues or modeled on the sermonic tradition. These works reflect the poet's many varied experiences, ranging from cutting sugarcane on Gulf Coast plantations to playing professional baseball for the Shreveport Twins of the American Negro Baseball League in the early 1950s. In 1965 he received a scholarship to Louisiana State University but military service as a medic in Vietnam interrupted his college career, and he eventually graduated from California State Polytechnic University in 1971.

Working at Howard University's Humanities Resource Center between 1973 and 1976 brought him into contact with Stephen E. Henderson, E. Ethelbert *Miller, and other writers who encouraged him to publish the literary magazine *HooDoo.* From 1977 to 1980 he also organized a series of HooDoo Festivals which presented poets and musicians in New Orleans, Galveston, Austin, Houston, and other cities. With Alan Austin and Etheridge *Knight, he coedited *Blackbox,* an innovative poetry magazine issued as tape-recorded cassettes. Throughout the same period Zu-Bolton was also one of the leading figures in the Southern Black Cultural Alliance (SBCA)—a network of writers, musicians, literary journals, and theater groups that promoted the ideas of the Black Arts movement.

For ten years (1982–1992) Zu-Bolton's Copasetic Bookstore and Gallery in New Orleans was one of that city's most active venues for literary events, presenting plays, poetry readings, children's programs, and workshops for young writers. While teaching at Tulane University and Xavier University for various periods, Zu-Bolton was also a journalist contributing articles to the New Orleans *Times-Picayune* and the *Louisiana*

Weekly. His poems are included in anthologies such as *Mississippi Writers: Reflections of Childhood and Youth* (1988), edited by Dorothy Abbott, and *Black Southern Voices* (1992), edited by John O. *Killens and Jerry W. Ward, Jr.

• Lorenzo Thomas, "Ahmos Zu-Bolton II," in *DLB,* vol. 41, *Afro-American Poets since 1955,* eds. Trudier Harris and Thadious M. Davis, 1985, pp. 360–364. "Ahmos Zu-Bolton II," in *Mississippi Writers,* vol. 3, ed. Dorothy Abbott, 1988, p. 423.

—Lorenzo Thomas

Appendix

LITERARY HISTORY. *This entry consists of a five-part discussion of African American literary history from its beginnings to the present. The individual essays deal with the following time periods:*

Colonial and Early National Eras
Antislavery Era
Reconstruction Era
Early Twentieth Century
Late Twentieth Century

These discussions outline major developments in literary genres, cultural values, and the social contexts in which African American literature has evolved. Many of the notable contributors to African American literature are mentioned here. The reader should view these discussions as introductory. The extensive cross-references within and appended to these five articles will lead to more detailed information about the genres, themes, writers, and texts that highlight African American literary history.

COLONIAL AND EARLY NATIONAL ERAS

The writings of the colonial and national eras disclose virtually all the central concerns of African American literature's later periods. Lucy *Terry, Phillis *Wheatley, Jupiter *Hammon, and George Moses *Horton in poetry, Briton *Hammon, John Marrant, Olaudah *Equiano, Venture *Smith (Broteer), and Solomon Bayley in the slave narrative, Jupiter Hammon and Prince Hall in the homiletic address, Johnson Green and John Joyce in confessional narratives, John Browne *Russwurm and an anonymous woman writer in the journalistic essay, and Phillis Wheatley and Benjamin *Banneker in the literary epistle all carry on discourse about freedom for themselves and for their African American brothers and sisters, about equal rights with a perhaps surprising generosity toward all races, and about education, particularly for those African Americans denied the benefits of the fruits of knowledge.

Strongly motivating the drive toward literary production during the formative eras of African American literature was the conviction on the part of figures such as Wheatley, Russwurm, and Banneker that success in a variety of belletristic and practical genres of writing would give the lie to those whites who claimed, with Thomas Jefferson, that the absence of a literature worthy of the name by African Americans provided ample justification for the enslavement of black people.

African American poets composed lyrics, hymns, odes, epyllia (short epics), pastorals, elegies, and pastoral elegies. The poet who wrote in all of these genres was Phillis Wheatley, whose life, work, and example virtually dominate African American literary history until the middle of the nineteenth century. She was not, however, the first African American either to write or to publish. Lucy Terry's "Bars Fight" (written in 1746 but not published until 1855), a ballad commemorating a skirmish between Massachusetts colonists and American Indians, represents the first known writing in English by an African American.

Such poets as Jupiter Hammon and Phillis Wheatley excelled in the subgenre of the hymn. Hammon's "An Evening Thought: Salvation by Christ, with Penitential Cries," the first poem published by an African American, appeared in 1760, on or after 25 December, and is composed in common hymn stanza. This apparently innocuous poem contains two arresting, subversive moments. Calling Jesus "thy captive Slave," Hammon suggests that the central and most acceptable focus of the Christian son of God is Hammon and his African American brothers and sisters, not their white oppressors. The phrase, "To set the Sinner free," especially when read within the context of "thy captive Slave," constructs a subversive "freeing" of Hammon and his fellow slaves. Sondra O'Neale, among others, has recently pointed out the antislavery subtext within "A Dialogue, Entitled, The Kind Master and Dutiful Servant" (1783). After the Master condescendingly commands his Servant to "follow me, / According to thy place," essentially telling him to "follow me" as God, the Servant describes the times as those "of great distress," an oblique reference not to the Revolution, whose fighting ended in 1782, but, according to O'Neale, to the condition of slavery. Finally the Servant rather boldly calls upon the Christian God "To relieve distresses here." Of course, if the "great distress" is slavery, it follows that God has been called upon to give ease to the abominable institution.

The three poems Wheatley labels hymns all depart considerably from the hymn stanza adopted by Hammon. The companion poems "An Hymn to the Morning" and "An Hymn to the Evening" are actually lyrics to nature. They are composed in stanzas of iambic pentameter couplets and offer wholly classical paeans to Aurora and the principle of eventide, each filled with close observation of nature related in largely pastoral rhetoric. The entire Hymn to "Humanity," perhaps more closely resembling an ode, represents an intricate structure indicating the sophisticated mind of a first-rate experimentalist.

Wheatley demonstrates her skills in several other subgenres of poetry. So pervasive is her pastoralism (references to such elements of Vergil's *Eclogues* as shepherds piping "beneath the myrtle shade," where one may discover contemplation's "sacred spring") that the reader may trace a pastoral strain of subversion, especially in her 1773 *Poems.* The poems "To Maecenas" (which introduces the volume), "On Recollection," "On Imagination," "Ode to Neptune," and "A Farewell to America," all odes, Wheatley composed between March 1772 and August 1773; among her very best poems, on the surface they appear to be harmless little ditties treating conventional topics. When Wheatley speaks in "To Maecenas," however, of snatching the laurel or prize of poetic maturity from the "honour'd" heads of her white patrons (or purchasers of her *Poems*) "while you indulgent smile upon the deed," she has seized the moment to proclaim to the world her confidence in her own achievement, despite the fact of her "less happy" circumstance of writing under the yoke of slavery.

In addition to authoring **Poems on Various Subjects, Religious and Moral* (1773), the first book by an African American on any subject, Wheatley enjoyed, however briefly, a career of great distinction, which brought her international fame, prompting Voltaire to write that she was the author of "very good English verse." The poetry of George Moses Horton, though not as accomplished as that of Wheatley, was produced after the United States Constitution's ratification of slavery as a legal institution. Horton's protest against his enslaved state was, consequently, much more daring, passionate, and direct.

Writing more than forty years after Wheatley's death, Horton speaks his protest against slavery in such titles as "Slavery," "The Slave's Complaint," "On Hearing of the Intention of a Gentleman to Purchase the Poet's Freedom," and "On Liberty and Slavery." This last poem appeared in Horton's first collection, *The Hope of Liberty* (1829), and contains the affective stanza: "Say unto foul oppression, Cease: / Ye tyrants rage no more, / And let the joyful trump of peace, / Now bid the vassel soar." In "Slavery," Horton describes a particularly grim moment: "Is it because my skin is black, / That thou should'st be so dull and slack, / And scorn to set me free? / Then let me hasten to the grave. . . ." Significantly this stanza's pattern of a tetrameter couplet followed by four lines of alternating iambic trimeter and iambic tetrameter rhyming *cddc* calls up Wheatley's stanzaic pattern used in the "Humanity" hymn. Horton adopts this stanzaic pattern on several more occasions, and such phrases as "the pensive muse," "the sylvan shade," and the "peaceful grove" whence one may "Survey the flowery plume" resonate with Wheatley's pastoral. When we observe further that in 1838 and again in 1849 Horton's poems were printed in the same volumes with poems by Wheatley (on the latter occasion with letters by Banneker), then we can conclude that Horton's acquaintance with Wheatley was more than casual; as well, we can better learn the veracity of Henry Louis *Gates, Jr.'s pronouncement that Wheatley was "the progenitor of the black literary tradition."

Wheatley's influence may also be traced within the development of the slave narrative, perhaps most strikingly in her woodcut portrait used as a frontispiece to her 1773 *Poems.* Olaudah Equiano, for example, prefaces his 1789 *Interesting Narrative* with his portrait in which he, similar to Wheatley, is holding a book; in this case that book is a Bible. While Wheatley sits musing before a desk on which her hand rests atop a page with her writing visible, a book also rests on this surface in full view. African American women writers of slave narratives and other genres, such as Jarena *Lee, Annie Louise *Burton, Sara Allen (wife of Richard *Allen), L. A. J. Moorer, and others are posed throughout the nineteenth century in varying degrees of likeness to Wheatley, but all have a book in their hand or placed near them. In any event, the point in each case appears to be to make a concrete declaration that African Americans can become just as literate as whites and are, therefore, not likely candidates for slavery.

Equiano makes clear the quest for learning and the difficulty involved in acquiring it in his *Interesting Narrative,* wherein he sets up the trope of the talking book. Having observed his master and others moving their lips and reading out loud when examining a book (a common practice before this century), he, not yet literate, concluded that they were "talking" to the book, appearing to be carrying on a conversation with it. This mysterious circumstance lost its mystery the moment Equiano became literate. The naïveté evident in this episode points directly to Equiano's dual narrator. That is, when telling the events of his early childhood and adolescence, Equiano assumes a naive, childlike persona, but he quickly and often abruptly shifts this persona to that of an experienced, disenchanted adult who has suffered the severe disadvantages of slavery, the exposure of which constitutes the primary commitment of the entire genre of the slave narrative or autobiography. The author of *Interesting Narrative* is particularly poignant in his descriptions of the horrid Middle Passage and of slave beatings, as are the authors of many slave autobiographies. Equiano's *Narrative* enjoyed an immense, international popularity, appearing in Dutch, German, and Russian translations, all published before the end of the eighteenth century.

While not as popular as Equiano's *Narrative,* Briton Hammon's *A Narrative of the Uncommon Sufferings, and Surprizing Deliverance of Briton Hammon, A Negro Man—Servant to General Winslow* enjoys the distinction of being the first published writing by an African American. This first attempt at African Amercian autobiography displays many affinities to later examples of the genre. Apparently written by himself, this tract does not contain the caption "Written by Himself," though it does have the identifying phrase "A Negro Man" and a brief paragraph giving a synopsis of the narrative's action followed by the white Boston printers' names, Green and Russell, all on the title page and serving as a sort of testimony of authentication. Although Hammon says he will "only relate matters of fact as they occur to my mind," he does at several points note that it was "kind Providence" that released him from the clutches of hostile Native Americans or that "the Providence of God" delivered him from confinement in a dungeon. His assertion that he "return'd to my own native land [the American Colonies] to show how great things the Lord hath done for me" aligns his text with such later spiritual slave autobiographies as those by Solomon Bayley, Richard Allen, and Jarena Lee. It should not go without observing that in his *A Narrative of Some Remarkable Incidents in the Life of Solomon Bayley, Formerly a Slave . . . Written by Himself* (2d ed. 1825), the author repeatedly speaks of his "great distress," "my distress," and "the bitterness of distress," echoing J. Hammon's "time of great distress" and J. Hammon's plea that God "relieve distresses here," strengthening the identification of the word "distress" as a code word for the institution of slavery.

A Narrative of the Lord's Wonderful Dealings with John Marrant, A Black (1785) bears obvious parallels in its title to B. Hammon's Narrative, although Marrant's *Narrative* was not written by himself but by a white amanuensis named W. Aldridge. Scattered throughout, such phrases as "his kind providence" and "had a feeling concern for the salvation of my countrymen" clearly fall in line with B. Hammon's stated reason for relating his *Narrative.* Venture Smith's *A Narrative of the Life, and Adventures of Venture, A Native of Africa* (1798) seems self-consciously to be attempting to distance itself from such relations as those of B. Hammon and John Marrant. Although illiterate like Marrant and thus requiring an amanuensis, Smith clearly wants to be known as an African, his displacement notwithstanding. The pride he feels for his native Africa is also self-evident in the detail he gives of his birthplace, Dukandra in Guinea, his fond memories of his mother and father, and of his family's vicissitudes there before he was captured into slavery at the age of eight.

The oral nature of these last two autobiographies by Marrant and Smith points to the homiletic address, products of African American oratory. Perhaps no other genre of African American letters displays a greater affinity with the old traditions of Africa, for with its familiar call-and-response praxis between minister and congregation, this genre most closely duplicates the tribal call and response so prevalent in Africa. While many of these homiletic addresses were delivered by ministers, not all were. For example, the poet Jupiter Hammon presented "An Address to the Negroes in the State of New York" in 1786, which was printed in 1787; it is likely that this delivery was not Hammon's only one. As Hammon made his New York "Address" before a combined audience of whites and African Americans, the temper of this address is somewhat self-conscious in comparison to the later addresses by African American ministers to exclusively African American audiences. After the post-Revolutionary organization of African American congregations, the subject matter of the oratory of such ministers as Prince Hall and Absalom Jones concentratedly focused upon the horrors and injustices of slavery, upon securing equal rights for all Americans, regardless of color, and upon the necessity of education.

Prince Hall, organizer of African American Masonry and early abolitionist, makes reference in "A Charge Delivered to the Brethren of the African Lodge" (25 June 1792) to "our late Reverend Brother *John Marrant.*" Amid a catalog of exemplary ancients, Hall shows familiarity with such church fathers as Tertullian, Cyprian, and even Fulgentius, an early Christian commentator on Vergil's *Aeneid.* Encouraging "love and benevolence to all the whole family of mankind," Hall devoted much time and effort during his career to the setting up of educational facilities for African American youth. In "A Thanksgiving Sermon . . . On Account of the Abolition of the African Slave Trade," delivered on 1 January 1808, the date that the United States Congress effected the end of transatlantic traffic in slaves, Absalom Jones, abolitionist and first African American priest of the Protestant Episcopal church, celebrates the theme of deliverance throughout the history of the world.

The artistry of homiletic oratory is noticeably absent from confessional narratives. Johnson Green's "Life and Confession" (1786) was related to an amanuensis and is remarkable because it was printed as a broadside by Isaiah Thomas, one of America's most famous printers and author of the first history of printing in the American colonies and early republic. The recorder of John Joyce's "Confession" is particularly noteworthy because his name was Richard Allen, founder of the Free African Society and the African Methodist Episcopal church, and an abolitionist. Allen appears to have consciously used the event of Joyce's execution for the murder of a white woman on 14 March 1808 as an occasion to teach African Americans a lesson in morality. Prefacing a description of the trial, the judge's rendering of the sentence, and Joyce's confession is Allen's own "Address to the Public, and People of Colour." The urgency of Allen's admonition to young males, though perhaps a bit stale for today's youth, bespeaks compassion: "The midnight revel, the polluted couch, thy diseased body, and thy affrighted conscience, testify against thee. Perhaps thy Mother's heart is already broken!" If directed toward young African Americans, Allen's exhortation is especially poignant, for his effort here is to assure survival.

Survival with dignity is assuredly a major concern of journalistic essayists' writing during the early republic. John B. Russwurm, a graduate of Bowdoin College who, along with Samuel *Cornish, founded *Freedom's Journal* in 1827, declares in the editorial of 16 March opening the *Journal*'s first issue: "We wish to plead our own course. Too long have others spoken for us. Too long has the publick been deceived by misrepresentations, in things which concern us dearly." In a passage that bears close ties to Richard Allen's "Address to . . . People of Colour," Russwurm continues: "there are others who make it their business to enlarge upon the least trifle, which tends to the discredit of any person of colour." These ill-meaning white folks "pronounce anathemas and denounce our whole body for the misconduct of this guilty one." Russwurm takes great pains to state that one of the central concerns of the *Journal* will be to advance the cause of education among African Americans, for "It is surely time," according to the editor, "that we should awake from this lethargy of years, and make a concentrated effort for the education of our youth." Another central concern of the *Journal* is the "civil rights of a people" which are "of the greatest value," and, so he continues, "it shall ever be our duty to vindicate our brethen, when oppressed."

In an anonymous contribution, a woman writer offered to *Freedom's Journal* an editorial enlisting the public to support women's rights (10 Aug. 1827). Asserting that the "diffusion of knowledge has destroyed" the notion that woman's only office is "to darn a stocking and cook a pudding well . . . men of the present age, allow, that we have minds that are capable and deserving of culture." This progressive author further maintains that it is the duty of "all mothers" to instruct their daughters "to devote their leisure time to reading books, whence they [will] derive valuable information, which [can] never be taken from them." The graceful style, both of Russwurm and the anonymous woman author, doubtless served as models to other writers of the journalistic essay.

Phillis Wheatley cultivated the literary epistle in her proposal for a second volume of poetry, never published, which lists thirteen letters of her authorship to be included, these addressed to such notables as the Earl of Dartmouth, Benjamin Rush, and the Countess of Huntingdon. In her letter of 11 February 1774 to the Native American minister Samson Occom, Wheatley speaks of "the glorious Dispensation of civil and religious Liberty" that "are so inseparately united, that there is little or no Enjoyment of one without the other." With pointed irony toward white American agitators for independence from England she goes on: "How well the Cry for Liberty, and the reverse Disposition for the Exercise of oppressive Power over others agree—I humbly think it does not require the Penetration of a Philosopher to determine."

No examination of the literary epistle in early African American literature can omit Benjamin Banneker's letter to Thomas Jefferson, perhaps the most famous letter by an early African American. Written on 19 August 1791 and published in a pamphlet in 1792, Banneker's letter combined a moral and political protest against slavery aimed at the quintessential representative of America's paradoxical adherence to freedom and human bondage, the slaveholding author of the Declaration of Independence. In his *Notes on the State of Virginia* (1787), Jefferson speculated that blacks lacked analytic intelligence and literary imagination, two qualities basic to any race's claim to civilization, in Jefferson's view. In response Banneker sent Jefferson a copy of *Benjamin Banneker's Almanac* (1792), which contained a completely calculated ephemeris, demonstrating the signal accomplishment of this self-taught African American mathematician and astronomer and, by implication, the capacity of any black person to do intellectual work equal in sophistication to that of whites. Banneker went on to remind Jefferson of his ringing endorsement of human equality in the Declaration of Independence and of the white man's espousal of the ideals of liberty for all mankind when he felt himself under the oppression of the British crown. How then, Banneker asked, could the Virginian continue to own slaves and ignore his own likeness to the once-detested tyrant George III? This challenge to Jefferson's intellectual and moral consistency became one of the central documents of antislavery activism, as well as early African American literature, for the next fifty years.

Writing across a full range of literary forms and activated by a widespread rhetoric of liberation from oppressive power, African Americans participated in the literature of revolution that swept through Europe and the Americas in the late eighteenth and early nineteenth centuries. While the twentieth century has often undervalued Wheatley and her fellow African American writers before Frederick *Douglass, the literature of early black America deserves to be read, studied, and appreciated with the dignity and interest accorded later periods.

• Lorenzo J. Greene, *The Negro in Colonial New England,* 1942. William L. Andrews, *To Tell a Free Story: The First Century of Afro-American Autobiography, 1760–1865,* 1986. William D. Piersen, *Black Yankees: The Development of an Afro-American Subculture in Eighteenth-Century New England,* 1988. Blyden Jackson, *A History of Afro-American Literature: The Long Beginning, 1746–1895,* 1989. Sidney Kaplan and Emma N. Kaplan, *The Black Presence in the Era of the American Revolution,* rev. ed., 1989. Frances Smith Foster, *Written by Herself: Literary Production by African American Women, 1746–1892,* 1993. Sondra A. O'Neale, *Jupiter Hammon and the Biblical Beginnings of African-American Literature,* 1993. Frances Smith Foster, *Witnessing Slavery: The*

Development of Ante-bellum Slave Narratives, 2d ed., 1994. Rose Zimbardo and Benilde Montgomery, guest eds., *African American Culture in the Eighteenth Century,* special issue of *Eighteenth-Century Studies* 27.4 (Summer 1994).

—John C. Shields

ANTISLAVERY ERA

From 1832 through the Civil War, African American writing grew in range, volume, and sophistication. No longer provincial, it took on a national, even international character.

In the earlier period, only one African American newspaper yet existed; by 1860 at least eighteen had been started. Earlier, no abolitionist groups had been active; by the mid-1850s thirty major organizations were at work, with fifty more satellite groups giving support—in New England, New York, across Pennsylvania, Ohio, Indiana, and Illinois, into Canada, the West, and California. Equally telling, they and their British allies usually had presses and periodicals hungry for material. William Lloyd Garrison, driving force of the movement, said that abolitionists venerated the printed word. African American writing thus both entered and helped to extend a climactic phase of American romanticism, one in which the transcendentalist Theodore Parker could exalt the work of Frederick *Douglass and other slave narrators, holding that "all the original romance of America is in them, not in the white man's novel." Yet the spoken antislavery word often preceded the written. Hence it was an age of oratory and journalism, of memorable speeches eagerly recorded by the papers, then reproduced by every significant organ of the movement on two continents.

Much of the work distinctive to the age indeed radiates from the papers. Black and white, they sought to cultivate every possible contributor, every available argument, every possible occasion, and every available form. They printed news, poetry, debate, drama, letters, speeches, histories, biographies, autobiographies, and travel accounts. With less articulate sources, they took the stories by dictation. The gifted they cultivated as agents, writers, lecturers, and correspondents. The assumption that the word would make one not only free but strong had several consequences, important in a nation where one in seven was African American, but only one in seventy was a free black. Language could be assumed to be the nature and expression of self. If expression alone could do much to disprove proslavery arguments, how much more effective would be the personal history of a Harriet A. *Jacobs or the social analyses of a Martin R. *Delany or the eloquence of an Alexander *Crummell.

It was the first great age of autobiographies, the form many take to be the model for all later African American prose narratives. It was likewise the first great age of social and historical studies of black America by black Americans. Personal histories abound, but so too do histories of churches, families, leaders, soldiers, innovators. It was the initial age for the novel, the short story, the drama, and the travel book. It was the earliest age for the large-scale collection of songs and spirituals, proverbs and folktales. The effects of such labor can be seen throughout the period, but in places uncommon for literary study. Opponents did not usually try to answer David *Walker or Henry Highland *Garnet or William Wells *Brown or Harriet Beecher *Stowe. Rather they tried to ban them. In the malevolence of the Fugitive Slave Act of 1850 some Southerners sought to expunge once and for all the entire talented class of free blacks in the North. No small tribute to the power of the pen.

Although not all have survived, African American newspapers were founded throughout the middle of the century, the earliest the work of the indefatigable Samuel *Cornish, who with John Browne *Russwurm established *Freedom's Journal* in New York City in 1827. With its demise, Cornish returned with *Rights of All* in 1829, the *Weekly Advocate* in 1837, and, most influential of all, the *Colored American* 1837–1841, all in New York City. Businessman, skilled essayist, and leader of the Moral Reform Society, William Whipper edited the *National Reformer* in Philadelphia 1838–1839. The *Mirror of Liberty* was the more radical effort of David Ruggles from 1838 to 1840. In Pittsburgh the extremely talented Martin R. Delany published the *Mystery* 1843–1847, then assisted Douglass in Rochester with the *North Star* from 1847 to 1849. With an MD from Harvard, Delany was, in a full life, journalist, physician, lecturer, explorer, ethnologist, army officer, civil servant, trial judge, novelist, and organizer of emigration projects. Only Douglass himself and his three papers (1847–1860) could approach such activity.

The scope of early magazines is suggested by the religious *A.M.E. Magazine* (1841–1842), the political *Douglass's Monthly* (1859–1860), and Thomas Hamilton's literary *Anglo-African Magazine* (1859–1861). Growing in number, the religious magazines were an important outlet for the writing of women, both free and fugitive. On most matters black newspapers worked closely with their white counterparts, especially the *Liberator,* the *Emancipator,* and the *National Anti-Slavery Standard.*

While united against slavery, abolitionists did offer differing strategies to combat it. Open rebellion was the most direct means, with the examples of Toussaint *L'Ouverture, Gabriel Prosser, and Denmark Vesey at hand. Yet no rebel had left a literary testament until *The *Confessions of Nat Turner* was published in 1831. Two years earlier, the most widely circulated work before the 1840s, David Walker's famous *Appeal,* had warned that peace and slavery could not coexist. In the 1830s David Ruggles continued the militant tradition in lectures and articles, as

Henry Highland Garnet did into the succeeding decade. A former slave who ministered to a Presbyterian congregation in Troy, New York, Garnet delivered a fervent "Address to the Slaves of the United States of America" at a convention in 1843, published five years later in a volume with Walker's *Appeal* as a demand for political action. The convention movement, an innovation of the age, was a successful training ground for the education and self-expression of many.

Few promoted rebellion. Many advocated escape. Because the rigors of bondage were growing as rapidly as the spirit of abolition, the rate of flight increased dramatically. So too did tales of flight, making the fugitive slave narrative equally instrument and inscription of the age. Besides being exciting tales of adventure, the narratives were vivid description of the mechanisms of the peculiar institution from across the South, told from within, a point of view unfamiliar to most northern readers. The most popular literary form of the antebellum years, they became the springboards for professional careers. Some two dozen or so fugitives got their starts as agents, lecturers, or writers by recounting their personal histories. Douglass gained his reputation as orator and conscience of the nation by retailing his life story, later turning it into two masterpieces of the genre. The *Narrative* of 1845 is a small gem, surpassed only by **My Bondage and My Freedom* ten years later. As Douglass was launching his independent literary career as editor and publisher (1847–1860), William Wells Brown was developing into a literary pioneer, striking out into fiction, drama, history, biography, and travel writing. After publishing his narrative (1847) and a book of antislavery songs (1848) in Boston, he traveled to England, where, in a season of innovations, he produced *Three Years in Europe*, an important travel book, in 1852, and a year later the earliest African American novel, **Clotel, or The President's Daughter* (later revised with different titles). He followed these with the earliest published play, *The *Escape, or A Leap for Freedom* (1858), a further memoir, more travel writing, and four histories. His method of historical chronicle was to become predominant later in the century. For instance, he contributed a long series of essays on "Celebrated Colored Americans" to newspapers and then combined them into *The Black Man, His Antecedents, His Genius, and His Achievements* (1863). The example of *Clotel* following one year upon *Uncle Tom's Cabin* proved the effect of fiction. Douglass published the short novel "The *Heroic Slave" in the 1853 annual *Autographs for Freedom.* Frances Ellen Watkins *Harper's short story "The *Two Offers" appeared in the *Anglo-African,* which also serialized Delany's unfinished novel, **Blake, or The Huts of America* (1859). The same year saw publication of the initial novel by an African American woman, Harriet E. *Wilson's **Our Nig, or Sketches from the Life of a Free Black.*

Fulfilling the narrative's ambition "to tell a free story," as William L. Andrews happily phrases it, is Harriet Jacobs's **Incidents in the Life of a Slave Girl,* published in 1861 under the pen name Linda Brent. One of very few by a woman and one of the last to be published separately before the Civil War, it attempts the painstaking task of enfolding northern white women readers within the threads of its design as early as its opening sentence, "Reader, be assured this narrative is no fiction." Its subject is taboo, the sexual exploitation of slave women by their owners. Its style is crafted understatement. Its method of release is ingenious: While leaving clues that she has fled north, Jacobs retreats to the tiny garret of her grandmother's house, there for seven years to overlook the growth of her children.

Because of a low rate of escape, heavy responsibility for children once free, and a lack of encouragement from abolitionist sponsors, few fugitive women published their stories as books or pamphlets. Instead they joined free women in the growing women's club movement; their writing is found more readily in the periodicals and antislavery annuals. Important free speakers and writers include Sojourner *Truth, Sarah P. Remond, Maria W. *Stewart, Frances Ellen Watkins Harper, Mary Ann Shadd, and Margretta and Sarah Forten. Narratives by men, on the other hand, appeared with increasing frequency after 1840. Examples are Moses Roper (1839), Lunsford Lane (1842), Moses Grandy (1844), Lewis and Milton Clarke (1845, 1846), Henry *Bibb (1849), James W. C. *Pennington (1849), Josiah *Henson (1849), Henry Box *Brown (1849), Solomon *Northup (1853), Samuel Ringgold Ward (1855), John Brown (1855), William and Ellen *Craft (1860), and J. D. *Green (1864).

While stirring ordinary northerners, the narratives also moved a sizable number of white authors. The gentle poet John Greenleaf Whittier, who had a hand in several, was compelled to tears. Richard Hildreth anonymously offered a novel in 1836 as *The Slave, or Memoirs of Archy Moore.* And the narratives both inspired and created the audience for the single most influential abolition volume of all, *Uncle Tom's Cabin.* Like so many others, it ran first as a serial for nine months in the antislavery press, then appeared in book form in spring 1852, selling three hundred thousand copies in America alone. Equally popular in Europe, it sold more than two million copies in the United States within a decade, making it in relation to population the best-seller of all time. While Harriet Beecher Stowe held that God had inspired the book, the narratives and the fugitive slave law were more immediate instruments. When Abraham *Lincoln was grappling with issues of slavery and emancipation in the summer of 1862, he asked the Library of Congress for a copy of *A Key to Uncle Tom's Cabin,* a later volume citing Stowe's sources in newspapers and narratives.

Included in that work are references to several studies of black American life. Going beyond the information of the periodicals and narratives, volumes were appearing that traced the social, cultural, and historical condition of African Americans. One of the most learned men of the day, James McCune Smith, from 1837 onward contributed dozens of essays to the black press containing what would soon be termed social and political analysis. Smith possessed an MD from the University of Glasgow and brought an international and evolutionary perspective to political questions. Presbyterian minister and holder of a doctorate from the University of Heidelberg, James W. C. Pennington wrote *A Text Book on the Origin and History . . . of the Colored People* (1841) and *The Past and Present Condition, and the Destiny of the Colored Race* (1848). Martin Delany produced in 1852 the most learned account of free blacks before the war, *The Condition, Elevation, Emigration and Destiny of the Colored People of the United States, Politically Considered,* followed by a pamphlet distilling his findings two years later. Within the decade he studied the practicability of various emigration schemes. Others writing political and historical commentary included William C. *Nell, William G. Allen, Lewis H. Putnam, and John B. Meachum.

Quiescent as an issue for nearly a decade, colonization revived on the heels of the Fugitive Slave Act. Most thinkers of the period had rejected emigration, seeing it as at base a proslavery tactic. Theodore S. Wright's impassioned *Address to Three Thousand Colored Citizens of New York* (1846) is a summary of that view. Led by John Russwurm and Alexander Crummell, a small group of intellectuals nevertheless continued to press for colonization. Respected by all for his character and force of mind, Crummell labored for two of his most productive decades in Liberia and Sierra Leone, 1853 to 1873, with schooling and missionary ventures. Probably the most accomplished prose stylist of the century, he offered a nationalist vision of an Africa cleansed of her despoilers in *The Relations and Duties of Free Colored Men in America to Africa* (1861). Some of his finest writing is collected in *The Future of Africa* (1862).

Two poets, George Moses *Horton and James Monroe *Whitfield, were ardent proponents of colonization—a sign that verse had moved away from its nonpolitical position of the late 1820s and early 1830s, when Phillis *Wheatley was the favored figure. As with oratory, poetry too became absorbed in the antislavery cause. A slave at the university in Chapel Hill, Horton pressed his protest in *The Hope of Liberty* (1829, 1837, 1838). Whitfield dedicated his *America, and Other Poems* to Martin Delany. George B. *Vashon, an Oberlin graduate who taught in Port-au-Prince, wrote a long eulogy to a Haitian hero in "Vincent Ogé," (first published 1854). Frances Watkins Harper included "The Slave Mother" and "Bury Me in a Free Land" in *Poems on Miscellaneous Subjects* of 1854 (in its twentieth edition by 1874). Other abolitionist poets were Charles L. Reason, Daniel A. *Payne, and James Madison *Bell.

By its very nature an age of crisis, the antebellum period was catalytic in its interests and intensity. Its accents echo whenever similar conditions recur: the 1890s or 1920s or 1960s. Once asked why the abolitionist press seemed to be thriving, Samuel Ringgold Ward replied, "Any Negro living well is an anti-slavery fighter." An explanation too for the richness and diversity of expression of the age.

• Vernon Loggins, *The Negro Author,* 1931. Jean Fagin Yellin, *The Intricate Knot: Black Figures in American Literature, 1776–1863,* 1972. John Sekora and Darwin T. Turner, eds., *The Art of Slave Narrative,* 1982. William L. Andrews, *To Tell a Free Story: The First Century of Afro-American Autobiography, 1760–1865,* 1986. Shirley Yee, *Black Women Abolitionists: A Study in Activism, 1828–1860,* 1992. Frances Smith Foster, *Written by Herself: Literary Production by African American Women, 1746–1892,* 1993. Frankie Hutton, *The Early Black Press in America, 1827 to 1860,* 1993.

—John Sekora

RECONSTRUCTION ERA

The Reconstruction era (1866–1899) was marked by significant transitions in African American literature. Some of the writers whose careers began before emancipation remained active after. Frances Ellen Watkins *Harper continued to be productive, publishing new poetry and four novels, including her most noted, **Iola Leroy* (1892). William Wells *Brown produced a post-Emancipation edition of **Clotel* (1867), among other, additional works. Frederick *Douglass wrote the final versions of his autobiography, *Life and Times of Frederick Douglass* (1881, 1892) during this time, as well.

But with the end of slavery new forces emerged in African American writing. Education progressed rapidly in African American communities after the Civil War, creating a growing African American middle class with strong literary interests. Literary societies were among the more important community organizations, and literary efforts were encouraged by the explosive growth of an African American press. Newspapers appeared throughout the United States; several prominent journalists whose careers extended into the next century, including T. Thomas *Fortune of the New York *Age* and William Calvin Chase of the Washington *Bee,* began their careers during this period. Among periodicals, the *African Methodist Episcopal Church Review* (founded 1884), initially edited by the scholarly Benjamin T. Tanner and, subsequently, by Levi J. Coppin, played a preeminent role in encouraging African American intellectual and literary activity.

Reconstruction era writing manifested its middle-class roots in its major characteristics. Through the 1890s, African American writers participated in a genteel, sentimental tradition that dominated American middle-class culture generally. Integrationist in orientation, they used literature to emphasize their similarities to other educated Americans and to protest their exclusion from the American mainstream.

Several important writers emerged within this genteel, Victorian framework. The most influential poet to begin his career during the era was Albery Allson *Whitman. Whitman published widely, but his fame rested on two book-length epic poems, *Not a Man, and Yet a Man* (1877) and *The Rape of Florida* (1884; reissued as *Twasinta's Seminoles,* 1885, 1890). Drawing on Victorian models and on verse forms ranging from the strongly rhythmic patterns of Henry Wadsworth Longfellow's "Hiawatha" to Spenserian stanza, Whitman celebrated African American heroism in the face of white racial injustice, his heroes displaying dominant virtues of courage, self-control, and moral virtue.

Other poets, though not attempting the epic, worked within similarly conservative frameworks. Among the more prominent, such poets as Islay Walden, Henrietta Cordelia Ray, and John Willis Menard created paeans to nature, love, and a sentimental piety. They broke with other Victorians only in persistently linking their writing to the demands of protesting prejudice and discrimination.

Writers of fiction also drew on Victorian themes and models. Dramatizing the genteel virtues of their heroes and heroines, they created, at the same time, a fiction of protest, putting their characters into settings of slavery, oppression, and white venality that strongly condemned the injustice of a racist world. Many writers, like James H. W. Howard in his novel *Bond and Free* (1886), also built on the tradition of the "tragic mulatto," the cultured, virtuous young man or woman who grows up as white, and whose subsequent confrontation with racial barriers confirms the arbitrariness as well as the injustice of racial lines.

Their Victorian conservatism should not be taken to mean that writers from this period rejected an African American identity. Encouraged by such figures as Alexander *Crummell, most made racial pride a dominant motif. They took special interest in African American history, details of which they often incorporated into their works. This interest was supported by one of the more ambitious projects in African American letters from the period, that of George Washington *Williams, who published the first scholarly histories of African Americans. One was a two-volume *History of the Negro Race in America from 1619 to 1880* (1883); the other, his *History of the Negro Troops in the War of the Rebellion, 1861–1865* (1888). In Williams's histories and elsewhere, racial pride was central, if expressed less in terms of any distinctive African American characteristics than in terms of African American accomplishments measured within the framework of the larger society.

African American writers began the Reconstruction era on a note of high optimism. Emancipation had raised hopes, as had the relative flexibility of race relations prior to the end of Radical Reconstruction in 1877, including the effective participation of African Americans in the politics of the former slave states. Their writing was inspired by a sense that proof of equality and progress could overcome white prejudice. Williams's histories attempted to document such progress; other writers believed their literary accomplishments would help do so, too.

The last two decades of the century did much to dash that optimism. North and South saw a triumphant racism in Anglo-American thought, culture, and practice; the South was plagued by racial violence, lynching, and increasing segregation, as whites sought to confine African Americans to a subordinate place in social and economic life. The result among middle-class African Americans was, by the 1890s, cultural and ideological turmoil. Many followed Booker T. *Washington, who in his 1895 "*Atlanta Exposition Address" urged postponing integrationist efforts in favor of community building; more continued to hold to integrationist goals, but became increasingly pessimistic about their realization.

In literature, this turmoil was reflected in a reorientation of older motifs and the development of significant new directions. Toward the close of the century, one of the first genuinely nationalistic novels appeared, Sutton E. *Griggs's **Imperium in Imperio* (1899). A few writers began to use the theme of the "tragic mulatto" to say less about the arbitrariness of racial lines than about the virtue of choosing an identity centered in the African American community. Harper moved in this direction with *Iola Leroy;* so did Victoria Earle *Matthews in her short story "Eugenie's Mistake," published in the *A.M.E. Church Review* (1892).

There was also a sense that changing conditions demanded an approach to literature that, in keeping with the increasing isolation of the African American community, would celebrate what was distinctive about African American life. Many people began to think about possibilities for using African American folk traditions to create a distinctively African American literature. Previously, writers had shown little interest in oral traditions. A few, including Harper, William Wells Brown, and Victoria Earle Matthews, sought to use "folk" characters in ways also consistent with their admiration for Victorian ideals, but folk culture as such was seen as part of the past, a legacy to be transcended. New moods, however, led to new orientations toward that legacy.

Outside the middle class, pre-Emancipation oral traditions, with roots in slave culture, had retained their vigor after freedom. The popular trickster tales, celebrating the power of wit in the face of oppression, remained current; so did the spirituals, with their profound understanding of suffering and freedom. Reflecting the abiding force of racism and discrimination, as well as the growing independence of such institutions as the church, these traditions had even come to play a more vital role in folk society in the Reconstruction era, helping to center identity and community ties.

They had also become more widely known. Popular entertainments including minstrelsy, despite a reliance on stereotypes, used genuine African American materials, and, though performed by whites in blackface as well as by African Americans, helped to diffuse those materials. The emergence of a white "plantation tradition" literature, while equally dominated by stereotypes romanticizing the slave society of the Old South, did the same. White Georgia journalist Joel Chandler Harris, through his stories of the obsequious "Uncle Remus," gave traditional African American trickster tales a national audience. Hampton Institute's *Southern Workman,* though a white-edited periodical, became a treasure trove of traditional materials contributed by members of the African American student body, particularly tales, folk beliefs, and songs. Richmond, Virginia, African American preacher John Jasper achieved celebrity status with his much-preached sermon, "De Sun Do Move," providing a popular view of traditional folk religion to white as well as African American audiences.

Interest in the spirituals was particularly strong. Known before the Civil War, they became widely appreciated in the Reconstruction era through their publication by such sympathetic white northern collectors as Thomas Wentworth Higginson and Lucy McKim Garrison. Even more influential were performances of the songs by the Jubilee Singers of Fisk University. The group was founded in 1871 and soon copied by similar organizations from other institutions. Using the songs to raise funds, the Fisk singers and others increased the spirituals' audience in performances given throughout the United States and Europe.

African American writers who hoped to explore the literary possibilities of oral traditions attempted to build on this interest, appealing to an audience that had already shown its receptiveness. Many also wanted to rescue folk society from the kinds of stereotypes that minstrel versions and such plantation writers as Harris employed in their renditions of African American tradition. Such efforts led directly to the success of the first African American writers to achieve a genuine national audience, Charles Waddell *Chesnutt and Paul Laurence *Dunbar.

Chesnutt's work with folk tradition appeared first. Written in a version of African American "dialect," his "*Uncle Julius" stories appeared in such popular journals as the *Atlantic* as early as 1889. Building on the trickster figure, Chesnutt recontextualized the white plantation tradition by deromanticizing the southern setting, dramatizing its violence and exploitation. He created a figure in Uncle Julius who, unlike Harris's Uncle Remus, left no doubt about the stories' aggressive possibilities.

Dunbar, however, had the greater impact, chiefly through his efforts at "dialect poetry," written in the putative voice of the slaves and ex-slaves of the South. When his first major volume, *Lyrics of Lowly Life* (1896), appeared, endorsed by the dean of American letters, William Dean Howells, Dunbar attracted national attention, becoming, perhaps, the most popular poet, white or African American, in the United States. This attention inspired a vogue in dialect poetry, including work by such popular writers as James Edwin *Campbell and James D. *Corrothers. By the end of the century, virtually every African American writer had tried the form.

Neither Dunbar and Chesnutt nor their contemporaries broke entirely with the older plantation tradition. Most, with the possible exception of Campbell, used a dialect based as much on literary models as on folk speech. All used motifs with roots in popular writing as well as in oral tradition. But together, they helped define possibilities for a folk-based literature that few of their predecessors had thought possible.

At the same time, worsening conditions also brought a growing sense of the dilemma of being African American in a racist society, the dilemma of formulating an identity, as earlier writers had, in enthusiastically "American" terms. Here, too, Dunbar and Chesnutt were pioneers, departing from dialect to reorient genteel themes and traditional modes of protest to confront the changing times. Dunbar, who was never entirely comfortable with his success in dialect, expressed his frustration with all received formulations of identity in such works as his novel *The Uncalled* (1898). Chesnutt, in stories published as early as the late 1880s, and appearing most prominently in a collection entitled *The *Wife of His Youth* (1899), used the older motif of racial mixture and the "tragic mulatto" to delineate, pessimistically, relationships between racial structures and questions of identity and moral choice.

The dilemmas Dunbar and Chesnutt identified were to receive increasing attention among African American writers as the Reconstruction era drew to a close, especially as an understanding of those dilemmas was given theoretical shape by W. E. B. *Du Bois in "The Strivings of the Negro People" (1897). There, Du Bois described the "double consciousness" of the African American, a problem of being simultaneously "American" and "African," "American" and "not-American." Du Bois proposed to resolve the problem through the encouragement of distinctive African genius, pointing toward a distinctive African American culture and literature, as well. Although literary attempts to realize Du Bois's vision were not to appear until after 1900, the growing concern about identity he helped delineate was to be a profound legacy from the Reconstruction era to later African American writing.

• J. Saunders Redding, *To Make a Poet Black,* 1939. Lawrence Levine, *Black Culture and Black Consciousness: Afro-American Folk Thought from Slavery to Freedom,* 1977. Arlene Elder, *"The Hindered Hand": Cultural Implications of Early Afro-American Fiction,* 1978. Joel Williamson, *The Crucible of Race: Black-White Relations in the American South since Emancipation,* 1984. Hazel Carby, *Reconstructing Womanhood: The Emergence of the Afro-American Woman Novelist,* 1987. Dickson D. Bruce, Jr., *Black*

American Writing from the Nadir: The Evolution of a Literary Tradition, 1877–1915, 1989. Blyden Jackson, *A History of Afro-American Literature,* vol. 1, *The Long Beginning, 1746–1895,* 1989. Joan Sherman, *Invisible Poets: Afro-Americans of the Nineteenth Century,* 2d ed., 1989. Frances Smith Foster, *Written by Herself: Literary Production by African American Women, 1746–1892,* 1993.

—Dickson D. Bruce, Jr.

EARLY TWENTIETH CENTURY

Between the publication of W. E. B. *Du Bois's *The *Souls of Black Folk* (1903) and Gwendolyn *Brooks's Pulitzer Prize–winning **Annie Allen* (1949), African American culture underwent a series of radical transformations that freed black writers from the reactive postures of the segregation era and encouraged innovative articulations of modernist, American, and diasporic traditions. Sparked by the Great Migration from the rural South to the industrial North, impressive flowerings of cultural activity took place in Washington, Harlem, and Chicago, attracting writers from throughout the hemisphere with the promise of larger inter- and intraracial audiences. Supporting and critiquing the political activity surrounding Du Bois, Marcus *Garvey, and A. Philip Randolph, African American artists investigated the possibilities of nationalism, Marxism, modernist aesthetics, and woman-centered cultural activity that gave rise to a conscious tradition of African American feminism. Like the folk and popular culture forms shaped by those James Weldon *Johnson called the "black and unknown bards," the literary works of Langston *Hughes, Zora Neale *Hurston, and Richard *Wright resound with the burdens and celebrations of individuals and communities adjusting to situations that had been almost unthinkable a generation before.

Toward the Harlem Renaissance. The most influential text of the early twentieth century, Du Bois's *The Souls of Black Folk,* defined crucial issues that have continued to elicit serious intellectual and artistic responses. Identifying the central concern of the new century as "the problem of the color line," Du Bois defined the phenomenon of "double consciousness": the awareness, enforced by oppressive institutions and stereotypes, of one's self as both African and American. For Du Bois and those who responded to his call for the forging of a "better and truer" self, double consciousness required investigations of European, African, and specifically American traditions. Casting his assertive approach in stark relief against Booker T. *Washington's accommodationist philosophy, Du Bois emphasized the responsibility of the "talented tenth" of black professionals to the less privileged members of their communities. Although Du Bois later repudiated the elitism of this position and embraced Marxist perspectives, the ideas of double consciousness and the talented tenth exerted a major influence on African American life prior to and during the Harlem Renaissance.

Inspired by Anna Julia *Cooper, who insisted on the importance of women's contributions to "uplifting the race," and Ida B. *Wells-Barnett, who focused attention on lynching while editing the Memphis *Free Speech,* women working in the club movement combined Du Bois's analytical sophistication with community-based activism. Writers affiliated with the clubs contributed frequently to church publications and journals including *Colored American Magazine* (founded 1900, edited by Pauline E. *Hopkins), the *Crisis* (founded 1910, edited by Du Bois until 1918), *Opportunity* (founded 1923, edited by Charles S. Johnson), and the *Messenger* (founded 1917). Complementing her editorial encouragement of young writers who would mature during the Harlem Renaissance, Hopkins provided a woman-centered perspective on double consciousness in her novel **Contending Forces* (1900), which shares numerous thematic concerns with Paul Laurence *Dunbar's *The *Sport of the Gods* (1902), Charles Waddell *Chesnutt's *The *House Behind the Cedars* (1900), and James Weldon Johnson's *The *Autobiography of an Ex-Colored Man* (1912).

Like their white contemporaries, these novelists usually adhered to conventions of romantic, domestic, and realistic fiction. In addition, they were forced to confront the difficult rhetorical circumstances created by the power of minstrelsy in American culture. In order to publish their work in influential mainstream periodicals, such as *Harper's, Century,* and the *Atlantic,* many African American writers wrote in a dialect derived from the plantation tradition writings of Thomas Nelson Page and Joel Chandler Harris. The dialect poems of Dunbar and James D. *Corrothers often perpetuated stereotypes, thereby intensifying the burden of double consciousness, a situation Dunbar addressed directly in standard English lyrics in "The Poet" and "Sympathy." At times, however, African American writers drew on folk traditions of masking to assert subversive ideas for black audiences while providing white audiences with seemingly innocuous surface meanings. Like the tradition of sacred music Du Bois labeled the "sorrow songs," Chesnutt's "*Uncle Julius" stories employ masking to express the sense of exile and potential for resistance present in the folk tradition.

The tension between minstrelsy, masking, and open expression haunted African American writers throughout the first half of the century. Nowhere was this more evident than in the theater. Prior to the Federal Theatre Project in the 1930s, black playwrights were forced to choose between the lucrative Broadway revues that paid well but catered to white stereotypes and "little theaters" such as Cleveland's Karamu House, Washington's Krigwa

Players, and Harlem's Lafayette Theatre. Although their audiences could not support playwrights financially, these theaters provided authors such as May *Miller, Willis *Richardson, and Georgia Douglas *Johnson with opportunities to focus on significant social problems and explore the theatrical possibilities of folk materials. The most vital forms of African American performance, however, developed on the Theatre Owners Booking Association (TOBA, also known as "tough on black asses") circuit, where comedians such as Pigmeat Markham and blues singers such as Ma *Rainey manipulated minstrel conventions while tapping into the West African–based folk traditions explored at length in Hurston's *Mules and Men* (1935). The lyrics of Rainey, Ida Cox, and Bessie *Smith frequently addressed feminist and lesbian themes with a frankness that would have been impossible for writers such as Nella *Larsen, Marita *Bonner, Jessie Redmon *Fauset, and the diarist Alice Moore *Dunbar-Nelson, who were forced to negotiate genteel literary conventions.

The Harlem Renaissance. The first cultural movement to attain widespread recognition both within and beyond black communities, the flowering that took place in Harlem between the mid-1910s and the mid-1930s occupies a central position in African American cultural history. Also called the "New Negro Movement," the Harlem Renaissance attracted poets, dramatists, writers of fiction, painters, musicians, and intellectuals with its promise of a setting in which black artists could interact relatively freely with one another and with their white contemporaries. Defined by the "Harlem" issue of *Survey Graphic* magazine (Mar. 1925, edited by Alain *Locke and reprinted in expanded form as *The New Negro*), the Renaissance drew energy from the Great Migration, the return of black World War I veterans willing to challenge the Jim Crow system, and the new possibilities for dissenting voices created by the death of Booker T. Washington. Bringing together writers born in the North (Countee *Cullen, Du Bois), South (Hurston, James Weldon Johnson), Midwest (Langston Hughes), West (Wallace *Thurman), and Caribbean (Claude *McKay, Marcus Garvey), the Renaissance drew inspiration and energy from earlier literary scenes centered in Boston (around Hopkins), Washington (around Georgia Douglas Johnson's S Street Salon), and Philadelphia, where Fauset began her career before moving to New York to serve as literary editor of the *Crisis.*

Although Hughes, Hurston, McKay, Larsen, Cullen, and Jean *Toomer (who did not participate directly in the movement) dominate histories of the period, it derived its vitality from a diverse group, including Thurman, Richardson, Rudolph *Fisher, Eric *Walrond, Gwendolyn *Bennett, Eulalie Spence, and Richard Bruce *Nugent, who openly expressed the homosexuality he shared with several of the era's major figures. Most Renaissance writers had direct contact with white patrons and modernist artists (including Eugene O'Neill, William Carlos Williams, and H.D.), many of whom had been inspired by African and African American visual and musical traditions. While the financial support provided by Carl Van Vechten, author of the controversial novel *Nigger Heaven* (1926), and Charlotte Osgood Mason, who supported Hurston and Hughes, helped writers find time for their work, it remains a controversial topic. Many African American intellectuals of the period condemned most white participants for their stereotypical views of black character and the interracial politics of the period received a scathing denuciation in Thurman's *Infants of the Spring* (1932), the dystopian double to the romantic image advanced in McKay's **Home to Harlem* (1928).

In addition to meeting socially at events hosted by Van Vechten and black heiress A'Lelia Walker, Renaissance writers published their work in the *Crisis, Opportunity,* and the short-lived periodicals *Harlem* and *Fire!!* (both edited by Thurman); as well as in anthologies such as Cullen's *Caroling Dust* (1927), Richardson's *Plays and Pageants of Negro Life* (1930), and James Weldon Johnson's *The Book of American Negro Poetry* (1922, expanded 1931). Although it has attracted less recognition, Garvey's *Negro World* newspaper played a unique role in African American literature. The most widely circulated black periodical of the time, *Negro World,* sponsored literary contests and published hundreds of poets and fiction writers from throughout the diaspora while advancing the pan-Africanist agenda of Garvey's Universal Negro Improvement Association.

Both thematically and aesthetically, the Harlem Renaissance introduced issues that dominated African American literary consciousness throughout the century. Locke's "The New Negro," Hughes's "The Negro Artist and the Racial Mountain," and James Weldon Johnson's "Preface" to *The Book of American Negro Poetry* define concerns such as the relationship between African American expression and the American mainstream, the significance of oral and folk traditions, and the impact of modern urban society on literary forms. Similarly, Marita Bonner's essay "On Being Young—A Woman—and Colored" (*Crisis,* 1925) and Elise Johnson McDougald's "The Task of Negro Womanhood" (*The New Negro,* 1925) connect the pioneering work of Wells-Barnett and Cooper with that of later womanists. Anticipating later debates over Afrocentricity, Helene Johnson's "Bottled" and Cullen's "Heritage" raise the question Cullen phrased as, "What is Africa to me?" Like McKay, who expressed his militancy in sonnets such as "If We Must Die," Cullen used highly conventional formal structures to articulate his tormented double consciousness. Conversely, both Hughes and Hurston explored the literary possibilities of the blues, jazz, sermons, and folk tales in experimental forms paralleling those of their white modernist associates. Exploring the ambiguities of its author's position on the margins of both white and black worlds, Toomer's multi-genre epic **Cane* (1923) initiates an African American modernist tradition that includes Hurston's *Moses,*

Man of the Mountain (1939), Hughes's "Montage of a Dream Deferred" (1951), Ralph *Ellison's **Invisible Man* (1952), and Melvin B. *Tolson's *Harlem Gallery* (1965).

The Chicago Renaissance. In contrast to the consensus concerning the importance of Harlem in African American culture of the 1920s, the next two decades have been characterized in a variety of ways. While phrasings emphasizing "proletarian literature," "protest literature," and the "School of Richard Wright" focus on the relationship between African American literature and leftist politics, each represses or distorts important aspects of the tradition. Placing greater emphasis on women's contributions and the lingering influence of the era's sociological premises, the idea of a "Chicago Renaissance" has begun to attract widespread support among cultural historians of the period.

Prior to the 1980s, literary histories of the 1930s and 1940s focused almost obsessively on Richard Wright. By far the most popular novel published by a black writer until that time, **Native Son* (1940) reverberated with a power equivalent to that of John Steinbeck's *Grapes of Wrath* (1939). The first widely read African American novel to express an unequivocal anger over the growing violence of ghetto life, *Native Son* was read—despite Wright's interest in modernist aesthetics—almost entirely as a political "protest" novel. The attention given *Native Son* and **Black Boy* (1945) created a context in which almost every black writer of the 1940s was automatically assigned membership in the "School of Wright." While such an approach seems apt for Willard *Motley's *Knock on Any Door* (1947) or some of the early stories of Frank *Yerby, it seriously distorted the reception of Ann *Petry, Arna *Bontemps, Chester *Himes, and especially Sterling A. *Brown, who was valued more for his protest poems than for his pioneering literary histories or sophisticated modernist lyrics such as "Ma Rainey." Most crucially, Wright's dominance contributed to the invisibility of women writers such as Hurston and Dorothy *West, who did not share his leftist politics or his aggressively masculine perspective. Now recognized almost universally as a classic of African American literature, Hurston's **Their Eyes Were Watching God* (1937) was greeted by critical apathy or hostility and was allowed to fall out of print prior to its rediscovery sparked by literary descendants June *Jordan and Alice *Walker.

Somewhat broader than the "School of Wright," images of the 1930s as a period of proletarian writing acknowledge the links between black writers and white contemporaries such as Theodore Dreiser, Carl Sandburg, and Michael Gold, who, as literary editor of the communist newspaper the *Daily Worker,* played a major role in shaping leftist response to Wright, Hughes, McKay, and William *Attaway. Leftist publications such as *New Masses, Challenge,* and *Anvil* published black writers interested in Marxist approaches to the economic and political problems of the Great Depression. Wright, Ellison, Shirley *Graham (who later married Du Bois), Theodore *Ward, and Margaret *Walker were among the black writers who joined white contemporaries such as Nelson Algren and Saul Bellow in working for the Federal Theatre Project or the Federal Writers' Project of the Works Progress Administration.

Recognizing the gradual shift of cultural activity away from New York, the idea of a black "Chicago Renaissance" (not to be confused with the earlier white-dominated Chicago Renaissance) provides what many critics find the most satisfactory approach to the diverse cultural production of the period and its impact on later developments. Coedited by Wright, Marian Minus, and Dorothy West, who had previously hailed the emergence of "a young Chicago group," *New Challenge* (1937) played a role similar in this new movement to that of the "New Negro" issue of *Survey Graphic* in the Harlem Renaissance. The touchstone of the issue was Wright's "Blueprint for Negro Writing," which highlights the tension between the period's leftist and folk-nationalist tendencies. Literary institutions of the period pursued various approaches to these tensions. Several black writers explored proletarian aesthetics in the communist-sponsored John Reed Clubs. An overlapping group including Wright, Ward, Bontemps, Frank Marshall *Davis, and Margaret *Walker, whose **For My People* (1942) was a touchstone for black poetry of the period, participated in the South Side Writers group. Many South Side poets, including Walker, Davis, Margaret Esse *Danner, and the young Gwendolyn Brooks developed their poetry in workshops such as that sponsored by white socialite Inez Cunningham Stark at the South Side Community Center. Among the Chicago-based publishing outlets available to these writers were *Negro Digest, Negro Story,* published out of the South Side home of Alice Browning, and Harriet Monroe's *Poetry* magazine, where Hughes, Brooks, and other black poets published works alongside those of Ezra Pound, T. S. Eliot, and H.D.

Three other Chicago-based institutions—the *Chicago Defender* newspaper, the Julius Rosenwald Fund, and the sociology department of the University of Chicago—played important roles in shaping the national contours of black culture during the era. Like the *Pittsburgh Courier,* where George *Schuyler developed his black conservative perspective, the New York *Amsterdam News,* and the *Afro-American,* which published editions in several eastern cities, the *Defender* was carried throughout the nation by black railroad workers and porters. Painting a glowing picture of the economic opportunities available in Chicago as part of editor Robert Abbott's crusade to draw blacks away from the South, the *Defender* published literary work including many of Hughes's "*Simple" stories. Despite the disillusionment described in *Native Son,* migrants to the South Side played crucial roles in the transformation of southern folk and musical traditions. Drawing on sources such as the surrealistic blues lyrics of Robert Johnson, transplanted Southerners such as Muddy Waters and Howlin' Wolf established Chicago as a center of the electric blues that would play a crucial role in shaping rock and roll. Similarly, Mahalia Jackson, Sallie Martin, and Thomas A. Dorsey—whose religious songs paralleled blues composer W. C. Handy's polished re-creations of the blues—transformed southern sacred forms into the urban gospel music that formed the basis for the political poetry of the soul music created by Sam Cooke, Aretha *Franklin, and Curtis Mayfield.

If blues and gospel provided the cultural background for Chicago writing, the Rosenwald Foundation offered the patronage provided by individuals during the Harlem Renaissance. Providing an intellectual center for black cultural activity, the foundation funded the work of numerous writers and intellectuals, including Hughes, McKay, Hurston, Du Bois, James Weldon Johnson, Sterling Brown, Marian *Anderson, and Katherine *Dunham, whose research in the Caribbean established the foundation for later scholarship on diaspora culture.

Perhaps even more significant for the long-term development of African American literary culture, however, was the Department of Sociology at the University of Chicago, where black alumni such as Charles S. Johnson and E. Franklin Frazier developed extremely influential approaches to the developing problems of the urban ghetto. Grounded in the theories of Robert Park and articulated most powerfully in Horace Cayton and St. Clair Drake's *Black Metropolis* (1945), the Chicago school established perspectives that had a sometimes unfortunate impact on the understanding of African American culture well into the late twentieth century. Although the Chicago school made real contributions to the political activity culminating in the *Brown v. Board of Education* Supreme Court decision, its assimilationist premises and sociological vocabulary simplified understanding of black writing by focusing obsessively on texts as "representative" expressions of social unrest designed to increase white awareness of the "problems" of black life.

As the 1940s drew to a close, a younger generation of African American writers began to emerge, many of whom openly rejected the idea that political issues should play a central role in literary expression. Ralph Ellison and James *Baldwin published short fiction and essays during the 1940s in which they consciously distanced themselves from the School of Wright. Similarly, most poets who began their careers during the 1940s—Brooks, Melvin B. *Tolson, and Robert *Hayden—rejected the traditions of proletarian poetry and pursued the musical modernism of Langston Hughes. Echoing the intricate suites in which Duke Ellington transformed folk forms into sophisticated modernist compositions, Hughes's "Montage of a Dream Deferred" provided a touchstone both for these emerging major poets and for the poets of Washington's Dasein group, Cleveland's Free Lance group, and New York's Umbra group, whose black experimentalism provides a crucial but largely unrecognized link between the Chicago Renaissance, the universalist modernism of the 1950s, and the Black Arts movement of the 1960s.

• Sterling Brown, *The Negro in American Fiction,* 1937. Sterling Brown, *Negro Poetry and Drama,* 1937. Robert Bone, *The Negro Novel in America,* 1965. Nathan Irvin Huggins, *Harlem Renaissance,* 1971. George Kent, *Blackness and the Adventure of Western Culture,* 1972. Wilson Jeremiah Moses, *The Golden Age of Black Nationalism, 1850–1925,* 1978. Abby Arthur Johnson and Ronald Maberry Johnson, *Propaganda and Aesthetics: The Literary Politics of Afro-American Magazines in the Twentieth Century,* 1979. David Levering Lewis, *When Harlem Was in Vogue,* 1981. Tony Martin, *Literary Garveyism: Garvey, Black Arts, and the Harlem Renaissance,* 1983. Robert Bone, "Richard Wright and the Chicago Renaissance," *Callaloo* 28 (Summer 1986): 446–468; Gloria T. Hull, *Color, Sex, and Poetry: Three Women Writers of the Harlem Renaissance,* 1987. Dickson D. Bruce, *Black American Writing from the Nadir: The Evolution of a Literary Tradition, 1877–1915,* 1989.

—Craig H. Werner

LATE TWENTIETH CENTURY

Writing a survey of post-1951 African American literature, one must take into account the significance of a proliferation of texts by both new and established authors, and even more important, the extraordinary changes in national and global economic, political, and intellectual culture during the second half of the twentieth century. These changes have raised crucial questions about what we mean when we talk about contexts, texts, traditions, and, indeed, what we mean when we talk about African Americans.

For instance, one might ask if contemporary African American literature ought to be read against the backdrop of domestic changes from segregation to affirmative action and threats of its demise, against that of the decolonization of third world countries, or, perhaps more appropriately, against some sense of the interconnections between the two. Moreover, at a time when new social movements have challenged the construction and maintenance of literary canons, one must consider that the category of "literature" includes not only traditional genres such as prose (fiction and nonfiction alike), poetry, and drama, but potentially film and music as well. With the rise of literary and cultural feminism, familiar ideas of African American and other literary traditions have been reformulated in light of whom they include and whom they leave out. And in the context of ongoing debates about the meaning of race as a category (Is it biologically determined or socially constructed? Is there such a thing as an authentic racial subject?), there is not even consensus about what we mean when we talk about African Americans.

The early 1950s ushered in a new, transitional era in U.S. racial politics. An emergent civil rights movement sought to bring about an end to racial segregation of public facilities, modes of transportation, and educational institutions and publicly circulated a rhetoric of racial equality that has dominated ideas of citizenship until the present. At the same time, African American literary figures continued to capture the attention of an ever expanding reading public. It was a time when established writers such as Richard *Wright, Langston *Hughes, Ann *Petry, and Gwendolyn *Brooks developed their craft. Yet it was also a time when a generation of newer writers emerged on the literary scene.

Traditionally, studies of African American literary production identify Wright, Ralph *Ellison, and James *Baldwin as the dominant authors of the period from the early 1950s through the mid-1960s. But recent critiques of canon formation have made it impossible to ignore the significance of a wider range of influential writers of the period.

Wright's most famous work, **Native Son*, was published in 1940, but he continued to loom large as a national and international literary figure throughout the 1950s, publishing three novels—*The Outsider* (1953), *Savage Holiday* (1954), and *The Long Dream* (1958)—and four works of nonfiction—*Black Power* (1954), *The Color Curtain* (1956), *Pagan Spain* (1956), and *White Man, Listen!* (1957). (*Eight Men, Lawd Today,* and *American Hunger* appeared posthumously.) His mentorship of and subsequent breaks with Ellison and Baldwin are often described in critical histories of the period, for their disagreements about the relationship between art and ideology in African American writing prefigure debates that continue to shape ideas about the function of ethnic literatures.

Ellison first met Richard Wright in New York in the mid-1930s; Wright encouraged Ellison's literary aspirations and Ellison enthusiastically admired Wright's achievements. But by 1940 Wright began to feel that Ellison's prose style was derivative from his own and a rift sprang up between the two men. Indeed, by the mid-1960s, Ellison had substantially revised his early praise of Wright's work, considering *Bigger Thomas (the protagonist of *Native Son*) to be a one-dimensional, ideologically driven construction rather than a complex and fully realized character. Ellison published only one novel during his lifetime, **Invisible Man* (1952, which won the 1953 National Book Award), but because of its stylistic and philosophical complexity, as well as its immersion in African American history and folklore, that book was for many years considered to be the premier novel by an African American author. Recently, critics have become less likely to deploy such a formulation for several reasons: first, because it presupposes consensus around the idea of literary quality; second, because it underestimates the significance of other black writers; third, because it obviates the possibility of cross-cultural comparisons; and fourth, because it is complicit with reductive ideas of literary tokenism. These caveats notwithstanding, *Invisible Man, *Shadow and Act* (1964), and *Going to the Territory* (1987)—these last, Ellison's two collections of essays—have contributed substantially to the world of ideas and letters.

Baldwin met Wright for the first time in 1944 (also in New York) and, like Ellison, enjoyed Wright's support for a time. Wright read Baldwin's work and arranged for him to receive a fellowship and a promised reading of his novel. When two presses rejected the novel, Baldwin began to separate himself from Wright. Subsequently, he, like Ellison, published essays that criticized Wright's work on ideological grounds and consolidated the break with his former mentor. Baldwin felt that Wright sacrificed his characters' psychological complexity in order to make political points about racism and injustice. As a result, he argued, Wright's representations confirmed prevalent assumptions about African American inhumanity.

Baldwin was a versatile writer who frequently inspired controversy because of his own homosexuality, the place of homosexual relationships in some of his work, and his unwillingness to adopt easy political positions. The author of major works of fiction including **Go Tell It on the Mountain* (1953), **Giovanni's Room* (1956), **Another Country* (1962), and several plays, including *Blues for Mister Charlie* (1964), he was an especially brilliant essayist. His reputation may rest ultimately on the achievement of collections such as **Notes of a Native Son* (1955), *Nobody Knows My Name: More Notes of a Native Son* (1961), *The *Fire Next Time* (1963), and *The Devil Finds Work* (1976).

Although the significance of Wright, Ellison, and Baldwin to African American and U.S. literary history is indisputable, such a narrow construction of the early contemporary period overlooks many other important figures of the time. To mention but a few, Ann Petry, Chester *Himes, Gwendolyn *Brooks, and Lorraine *Hansberry all experimented with literary forms and explored how rapid demographic and political changes shaped the lives of African Americans.

Ann Petry ranks among the most versatile of African American writers. *The *Street* (1946) addresses the plight of a black mother struggling against race, gender, and class oppression in Harlem during the 1940s. Her second and third novels—*Country Place* (1947) and *The Narrows* (1953)—interrogate with extraordinary subtlety the notion of community in the context of small New England villages. Additionally, Petry has published many short stories, and several books for children and adolescent readers based on black history and folklore.

With more than eighteen books to his credit, Chester Himes was an exceptionally prolific figure whose writing career spanned nearly forty years; he can be said to have expanded the terrain of black literature in at least two ways. First, he is one of the earliest African American writers to consider the impact of the migration west on the lives and expectations of blacks at midcentury. Much fiction by African Americans is set in the urban Northeast or the rural South, but in his first two novels, **If He Hollers Let Him Go* (1945) and *Lonely Crusade* (1947), Himes explores the impact of changes in labor and urbanization in wartime Los Angeles upon the psyches of black men. Second, Himes published eight black detective novels featuring the team of *Coffin Ed Johnson and *Grave Digger Jones, making him (after Rudolph *Fisher) one of the first black writers to work successfully in this popular genre.

Gwendolyn Brooks published her first volume of poetry in 1945 and won the Pulitzer Prize for her second, **Annie Allen,* in 1949. **Maud Martha,* her only novel, appeared in 1953; although at the time it did not receive the attention it merited, it has inspired critical interest in recent decades because of the way in which it situates an exploration of urbanization and labor upon constructions of race, gender, and domesticity in resonant, poetic language. Indeed, her work registers the impact of profound social changes upon the lives and language of African Americans, for her poetry bears the traces of the struggles for civil rights as well as the impact of black nationalism and the Black Arts movement that arose from it.

No history of early contemporary African American literature would be complete without acknowledging the significance of Lorraine Hansberry and especially her ever popular, award-winning play, *A *Raisin in the Sun,* first staged in 1959. (The film version was released in 1961.) The play, Hansberry's first, won her the New York Drama Critics Circle Award, making her the first black, fifth woman, and youngest person ever to receive it. Perhaps because the play is so familiar, it has not received much in the way of sustained critical attention. Nevertheless, it powerfully captures the spirit of the 1950s as it illuminates and brings into tension the changing aspirations of black people at midcentury.

From the mid-1950s through the mid-1960s, the antiracist struggle was defined largely in terms of nonviolent resistance; dominated by established integrated organizations such as Martin Luther *King, Jr.'s Southern Christian Leadership Conference, James Farmer's Congress of Racial Equality, and Whitney Young's Urban League; and inspired by faith in the possibilities of racial integration. In the face of white intransigence and elusive political change, African Americans grew increasingly impatient with the status quo; younger black people especially were compelled by the goals and strategies of nationalist organizations such as the Black Panther Party and the Nation of Islam.

Nationalist platforms presuppose a cultural, political, and spiritual unity among peoples of African descent throughout the African diaspora. For the most part they advocate black economic self-sufficiency, and they seek to separate black people from what they perceive as the destructive power of European culture and ideology. In response to the emergent nationalist movement of the mid- to late 1960s arose its cultural or aesthetic counterpart, the Black Arts movement.

In an effort to consolidate African American economic and cultural power, the Black Arts movement gave rise both to a range of journals such as *Negro Digest* (later known as *Black World*), *The Journal of Black Poetry,* and *Black Expression,* and to presses such as Broadside Press, Jihad Press, Free Black Press, Black Dialogue Press, and Third World Press. The Black Arts movement influenced cultural production in a variety of media: music, theater, art, and dance as well as literature. The leading literary figures were an eclectic mix of poets, fiction writers, playwrights, and essayists, and included LeRoi Jones (Amiri *Baraka), Mari *Evans, Ed *Bullins, Larry *Neal, Addison *Gayle, Jr., Gwendolyn Brooks, Nikki *Giovanni, Etheridge *Knight, Sonia *Sanchez, Ishmael *Reed, and Carolyn M. *Rodgers.

To the extent that the Black Arts movement sought to embrace the range of black cultural and artistic production and to connect aesthetics with the needs of "the black community," it was informed by a spirit of expansiveness. However, it also led to a kind of literary and ideological gatekeeping that judged African American writing on its conformity to a narrowly defined political and aesthetic agenda. By this light, only certain styles, topics, and positions were considered authentically black. Since the 1970s such nationalist policing has been criticized for its monolithic constructions of black art and community, its denial of the interplay between African and non-African cultural traditions, its misogyny, and its homophobia. As a result, the past twenty years have witnessed an expansion of the styles and subjects considered "acceptable" for black literature.

Indeed, the explosion of African American writing since the 1970s has made it increasingly difficult to generalize about the major themes and styles characteristic of the contemporary period. However, some of the most significant trajectories include the rise of African American women's writing, the reclamation of history, the resurgence of autobiography, the rise of black gay literature and lesbian literature, incursions into popular literary forms, and postmodernist experimentations. As we shall see, these areas are not as discrete as they might initially appear; for example, postmodernist experiments often take the topic of slavery as their subject.

The most visible of these newer movements is the rise of black feminist literature. Writers such as Toni *Morrison (Pulitzer and Nobel Prize winner), Alice *Walker (Pulitzer Prize winner), Paule *Marshall (MacArthur Prize winner), Octavia E. *Butler (MacArthur Prize winner), Rita *Dove (Pulitzer Prize winner), Gloria *Naylor, Ntozake *Shange, Toni Cade *Bambara, Gayl *Jones, and a host of others have achieved widespread attention for their powerful achievements in illuminating the interconnections of constructions of race, gender, and class in a range of literary forms.

As this partial list of accolades indicates, these writers have found an enthusiastic reception. However, because they have not shied away from topics that African American writers have often eschewed, such as domestic abuse and sexism, they have met with the disapprobation of some African American male (and indeed female) readers. The controversy surrounding their popularity reflects longstanding anxieties that African Americans often display about the revelation of cultural "dirty laundry."

The contemporary fascination with reclaiming history is nowhere more evident than in the sheer number and variety of novels written about slavery and its aftermath by African Americans since Margaret *Walker's **Jubilee* (1966). Indeed, many of the major black writers of the past twenty years have felt the need to write at least one novel that takes slavery as its subject, although these novels take a variety of forms. From fairly straightforward realist historical accounts such as Alex *Haley's **Roots* (1977), Barbara *Chase-Riboud's *Sally Hemings* (1979), and Louise *Meriwether's *Fragments of the Ark* (1994), to postmodernist experiments such as Gayl Jones's **Corregidora* (1975), Ishmael Reed's **Flight to Canada* (1976), Charles R. *Johnson's *Oxherding Tale* (1982) and *Middle Passage* (1990), and Toni Morrison's **Beloved* (1987), to a science fiction novel such as Octavia Butler's **Kindred* (1979), to impressionist texts such as Sherley Anne *Williams's **Dessa Rose* (1986) or Lorene Cary's *The Price of a Child* (1995), recent black writers have examined how historical distance as well as new literary, intellectual, and political movements have enabled reinterpretations of the meanings that attach to slavery, of inter- and intraracial relationships within the institution, and of the position both of masters and of slaves.

The contemporary authors' engagement with slavery illuminates the space between their reconstructions of a historically distant period and the accounts actually written during the period. Unrestrained by the conventions of an antislavery movement or the expectations of a Victorian reading public, they are free to address areas of experience to which the slave narrators could allude at best. They are freer, for example, to raise issues of sexual abuse and expression, to interrogate the limits of truth telling, indeed to explore the full range of emotions available to slaves. These later texts might be said, then, to reclaim the history of slavery and to liberate the literary ancestors by representing what had previously been deemed unspeakable.

It is perhaps the self-consciousness of these retrospective fictions that made them especially attractive to some of the leading postmodernist writers of the period, such as Charles Johnson and Ishmael Reed. Other writers who have sought to push the boundaries of literary language and black vernacularity include Clarence *Major, Trey *Ellis, Edgar John *Wideman, and Xam Wilson *Cartiér. The more restrained prose of James Alan *McPherson, David *Bradley, and Ernest J. *Gaines, on the other hand, has produced resonant meditations upon the fragmentariness of identity and community in the late twentieth century.

Long a mainstay of African American writing, autobiography continues to flourish in the contemporary period and dovetails with the impulse to reclaim history. Pivotal autobiographical texts of the period include Anne *Moody's *Coming of Age in Mississippi* (1968), Richard Wright's posthumously published *American Hunger* (1977), and the five volumes of Maya *Angelou's life story (especially her acclaimed 1970 book, **I Know Why the Caged Bird Sings*). More recently, African American autobiographers have reflected upon what it meant to come of age before or during the civil rights movement, to be educated in integrated institutions of higher learning, and yet to continue to face veiled forms of racism. Works such as Jill Nelson's *Volunteer Slavery* (1993), Jake Lamar's *Bourgeois Blues* (1991), Itabari Njeri's *Ev'ry Good-bye Ain't Gone* (1990), Henry Louis *Gates, Jr.'s *Colored People* (1994), Gerald *Early's *Daughters* (1994), and Lorene Cary's *Black Ice* (1991) explore how the idea of "authentic" black experience becomes challenged in the context of changing ideas of class and its relation to constructions of race.

Just as black feminist and middle-class narratives challenge notions of the authentic black subject, so too does the growing body of black gay and lesbian literature. The late poet, essayist, activist, and autobiographer Audre *Lorde is, along with Baldwin, perhaps one of the most important figures to theorize the connections among race, gender, and sexuality. However, important figures whose work has continued to explore these issues include Ann Allen *Shockley, the late Steve Corbin, the late Melvin *Dixon, and April Sinclair.

Increasingly, African American writers working in popular literary genres have discovered wide audiences. Terry *McMillan's *Waiting to Exhale* (1992) found an enthusiastic, diverse readership and made hers a household name. African American detective fiction writers such as Walter *Mosley, Gar Anthony Haywood, Barbara *Neely, Eleanor Taylor Bland, and Valerie Wilson Wesley have reached enthusiastic audiences both here and abroad. And speculative fiction writers such as Octavia Butler and Samuel R. *Delany have achieved perhaps the greatest and most sustained notice.

• Addison Gayle, Jr., ed. *The Black Aesthetic,* 1972. Mary Frances Berry and John W. Blassingame, *Long Memory: The Black Experience in America,* 1982. Bernard W. Bell, *The Afro-American Novel and Its Tradition,* 1987. Emory Elliott, ed., *The Columbia History of the American Novel,* 1991. Valerie Smith, ed., *African American Writers,* 1991. Angelyn Mitchell, ed., *Within the Circle: An Anthology of African American Literary Criticism from the Harlem Renaissance to the Present,* 1994.

—Valerie Smith

Editors

William L. Andrews is E. Maynard Adams Professor of English at the University of North Carolina at Chapel Hill. He is the author *of The Literary Career of Charles W. Chesnutt* (1980) and *To Tell a Free Story: The First Century of Afro-American Autobiography, 1760–1865* (1986) and the editor of numerous works on African American literature, including *Sisters of the Spirit* (1986), *Classic Fiction of the Harlem Renaissance* (1994), and *The Oxford Frederick Douglass Reader* (1996). He is a coeditor of the *Norton Anthology of African American Literature* (1997) and general editor of Wisconsin Studies in American Autobiography. His scholarship has received the Norman Foerster Prize from American Literature in 1976 and the William Riley Parker Prize from Publications of the Modern Language Association in 1990.

Frances Smith Foster is Charles Howard Candler Professor of English and Women's Studies at Emory University. She is the author of *Witnessing Slavery: The Development of the Ante-Bellum Slave Narrative* (1979, 2d. ed. 1993), *Written by Herself: Literary Production by African American Women, 1746–1892* and *Minnie's Sacrifice, Sowing and Reaping, Trial and Triumph: Three Rediscovered Novels by Frances Ellen Watkins Harper* (1994), for which she received the College Language Association scholarly Discovery Award in 1995. She is a coeditor of the *Norton Anthology of African American Literature* (1997).

Trudier Harris is J. Carlyle Sitterson Professor of English at the University of North Carolina at Chapel Hill. She is the author of several volumes, including *Exorcising Blackness: Historical and Literary Lynch and Burning Rituals* (1984), *Black Women in the Fiction of James Baldwin* (1985), for which she won the 1987 College Language Association Creative Scholarship Award, *Fiction and Folklore: The Novels of Toni Morrison* (1991), and *The Power of the Porch: The Storyteller's Craft in Zora Neale Hurston, Gloria Naylor, and Randall Kenan* (1996). Among her numerous edited volumes are six in the Dictionary of Literary Biography series, one in the Oxford Schomburg Library of Nineteenth-Century Black Women Writers series, and *New Essays on Baldwin's Go Tell It on the Mountain* (1996). She is also one of the editors of *Call and Response: The Riverside Anthology of the African American Literary Tradition* (1997). Her most recent scholarly study, which she completed during a residency at the National Humanities Center during 1996–1997, focuses on strong black women in African American literature.

Index